The Developing Labor Law

Fourth Edition
2005 Cumulative Supplement

(covering 1999–2004)

BNA Books Authored by the ABA Section of Labor and Employment Law

Covenants Not to Compete: A State-by-State Survey

The Developing Labor Law

Discipline and Discharge in Arbitration

Elkouri & Elkouri: How Arbitration Works

Employee Benefits Law

Employee Duty of Loyalty: A State-by-State Survey

Employment Discrimination Law

Employment Termination: Rights and Remedies, 2003 Supplement

Equal Employment Law Update

The Fair Labor Standards Act

How ADR Works

How to Take a Case Before the NLRB

International Labor and Employment Laws

Labor Arbitration: A Practical Guide for Advocates

Labor Arbitration: Cases and Materials for Advocates

Labor Arbitrator Development: A Handbook

Labor Union Law and Regulation

Occupational Safety and Health Law

The Railway Labor Act

Tortious Interference in the Employment Context: A State-by-State Survey

Trade Secrets: A State-by-State Survey

Wage and Hour Laws: A State-by-State Survey

The Developing Labor Law

The Board, the Courts, and the National Labor Relations Act

Fourth Edition

2005 Cumulative Supplement

(covering 1999–2004)

Editors-in-Chief

Peter A. Janus
Siegel, O'Conner, Zangari, O'Donnell & Beck, P.C.
Hartford, CT

Kenneth L. Wagner
Blitman & King LLP
Syracuse, NY

Barry J. Kearney
National Labor Relations Board
Washington, DC

Committee on the Development of the Law
Under the National Labor Relations Act

Section of Labor & Employment Law
American Bar Association

The Bureau of National Affairs, Inc., Washington, DC

The materials contained herein represent the opinions of the authors and editors and should not be construed to be those of either the American Bar Association or the Section of Labor and Employment Law. Nothing contained herein is to be considered as the rendering of legal advice for specific cases, and readers are responsible for obtaining such advice from their own legal counsel. These materials and any forms and agreements herein are intended for educational and informational purposes only.

Library of Congress Cataloging-in-Publication Data
(Revised for vol. suppl.)

The developing labor law : the board, the courts, and the National Labor Relations Act / editor in chief, Patrick Hardin ... [et al.].–4th ed.
p. cm.
Includes index.
ISBN 1-57018-151-9 (set) –ISBN 1-57018-149-7 (v. 1). –ISBN 1-57018-150-0 (v. 2)
1. Labor laws and legislation–United States. 2. United States. National Labor Relations Act. 3. United States. National Labor Relations Board. I. Hardin, Patrick.

KF3369 .D48 2002
344.7301–dc21

2001052867

Published by BNA Books, 1231 25th St., NW, Washington, DC 20037
http://www.bnabooks.com

ISBN: 1-57018-505-0; 978-1-57018-505-2
Printed in Canada

CHAPTER EDITORS

Gil A. Abramson
Hogan & Hartson L.L.P.
Baltimore, MD

George D. Adams
Greenebaum Doll & McDonald PLLC
Louisville, KY

David S. Adelstein
Geffner & Bush
Burbank, CA

Nelson D. Atkin II
Barran Liebman LLP
Portland OR

Marc J. Bloch
Duvin, Cahn & Hutton
Cleveland, OH

Michael R. Brown
Seyfarth Shaw LLP
Boston, MA

Jerome Buckley
Carney, Buckley & Hays
Portland, OR

Guerino J. (Jody) Calemine III
Committee on Education and the Workforce
U.S. House of Representatives
Washington, DC

Reid Carron
Faegre & Benson LLP
Minneapolis, MN

Robert Clark
United Steelworkers of America
Pittsburgh, PA

George N. Davies
Nakamura, Quinn & Walls, LLP
Birmingham, AL

Gary M. Eby
Manley, Burke, Lipton & Cook
Cincinnati, OH

James M. L. Ferber
Littler Mendelson
Columbus, OH

Laurence Goodman
Willig, Williams & Davidson
Philadelphia, PA

W. Melvin Haas III
Constangy, Brooks & Smith, LLC
Macon, GA

A. John Harper II
Fulbright & Jaworski L.L.P.
Houston, TX

Kevin Harren
New York State United Teachers
Albany, NY

Christopher T. Hexter
Schuchat, Cook & Werner
St. Louis, MO

CONTRIBUTING EDITORS

Jason Aschenbrand
Winston & Strawn LLP
New York, NY

Elliot Stephen Azoff
Baker & Hostetler LLP
Cleveland, OH

John K. Baker
White and Williams LLP
Allentown, PA

Gregory D. Ballew
Fisher & Phillips, LLP
Kansas City, MO

Linda Barge-Miles
Florida Agricultural & Mechanical University
Tallahassee, FL

Denise C. Barton
Littler Mendelson
San Francisco, CA

Ned H. Bassen
Hughes Hubbard & Reed LLP
New York, NY

Thomas J. Bender
Littler Mendelson
Philadelphia, PA

William Bevan III
Reed, Smith, Shaw & McClay LLP
Pittsburgh, PA

Tracy Billows
Seyfarth Shaw LLP
Chicago, IL

Julia Lapis Blakeslee
Winston & Strawn LLP
Los Angeles, CA

Keith R. Bolek
O'Donoghue & O'Donoghue
Washington, DC

Paul Bosanac
National Labor Relations Board
Milwaukee, WI

Jeffrey Bosley
Winston & Strawn LLP
San Francisco, CA

Nathan P. Brenna
Anthony Ostlund & Baer, P.A.
Minneapolis, MN

Mark E. Brennan
Rinehart & Robblee
Seattle, WA

Daniel R. Brice
Blitman & King LLP
Syracuse, NY

Richard S. Brook
Law Offices of Richard S. Brook
Mineola, NY

Lovic A. Brooks III
Brooks Law Firm LLC
Columbia, SC

Lyle B. Brown
Benesch, Friedlander, Coplan & Aranoff, LLP
Columbus, OH

Norman R. Buchsbaum
Law Offices of Norman R. Buchsbaum
Baltimore, MD

Justin Burnard
Allotta, Farley & Widman Co., LPA
Toledo, OH

Robert K. Carrol
Nixon Peabody LLP
San Francisco, CA

Donald C. Carroll
Law Offices of Carroll & Scully, Inc.
San Francisco, CA

Christopher Cassazza
Seyfarth Shaw LLP
Chicago, IL

Ryan J. Cassidy
Reed Smith
Philadelphia, PA

Pamela Chandran
Geffner & Bush
Burbank, CA

Andrea S. Christensen
Kaye Scholer, LLP
New York, NY

William D. Claster
Gibson, Dunn & Crutcher LLP
Irvine, CA

Floyd Clutter
Cohen & Grigsby, P.C.
Pittsburgh, PA

Victoria C. Cohen
Menard, Murphy & Walsh LLP
Boston, MA

Adam Collier
Bullard Smith Jernstedt Harnish
Portland, OR

J. Michael Colloton
Moss & Barnett
Minneapolis, MN

John F. Colwell
National Labor Relations Board
Washington, DC

Richard L. Connors
Stinson Morrison Hecker LLP
Kansas City, MO

Peter Reed Corbin
Ford & Harrison LLP
Jacksonville, FL

Martin Costello
Hughes & Costello
St. Paul, MN

Terrance M. Costello
Schwerin Campbell Barnard LLP
Seattle, WA

Matthew Coyle
Lockheed Martin Corp.
Bethesda, MD

Pamela J. Coyne
Durant, Nichols, Houston, Hodgson & Cortese-Costa, P.C.
Bridgeport, CT

Lauren Richman Crane
Neal, Gerber & Eisenberg
Chicago, IL

Eric J. Cu
Rothner, Segal & Greenstone
Pasadena, CA

John H. Curley
AT&T
Bedminster, NJ

Joshua N. Dalley
Seyfarth Shaw LLP
Chicago, IL

Ellen J. Dannin
Wayne State University Law School
Detroit, MI

Douglas A. Darch
Seyfarth Shaw LLP
Chicago, IL

Lauren J. Darienzo
Bond, Schoeneck & King, PLLC
Garden City, NY

Peggy A. Davis
Winston & Strawn, LLP
Chicago, IL

Francis X. Dee
McElroy, Deutsch, Mulvaney & Carpenter
Newark, NJ

Colleen A. Deep
Jones Day
Columbus, OH

Christopher W. Deering
Ogletree Deakins
Birmingham, AL

Michael F. Delaney
Spencer, Fane, Britt & Browne, LLP
Kansas City, MO

Kristina Detwiler
Rinehart & Robblee
Seattle, WA

Erica Deutsch
Geffner & Bush
Burbank, CA

James R. Dickens
Miller, Nash LLP
Seattle, WA

Nicholas DiGiovanni, Jr.
Morgan, Brown & Joy, LLP
Boston, MA

Michael J. DiMattia
McGuire Woods
New York, NY

Natale V. DiNatale
Durant, Nichols, Houston, Hodgson & Cortese-Costa, P.C.
Bridgeport, CT

Josh Ditelberg
Seyfarth Shaw LLP
Chicago, IL

John R. Doll
Logothetis, Pence & Doll
Dayton, OH

Jeffrey S. Dubin
Huntington, NY

Peter L. Ebb
Ropes & Gray
Boston, MA

Robert Edmund
Porter Wright Morris & Arthur LLP
Columbus, OH

Hollace J. Enoch
National Labor Relations Board
Washington, DC

Henry E. Farber
Davis Wright Tremaine
Bellevue, WA

Gary S. Fealk
Vercruysse Murray & Calzone, P.C.
Bingham Farms, MI

Heidi S. Feldman
Musick, Peeler & Garrett
Los Angeles, CA

Christine M. Fitzgerald
Hughes Hubbard & Reed LLP
New York, NY

Diana Richards Francis
Harrison, Dowell, Fisher & Harris, L.C.
St. Louis, MO

Ross H. Friedman
Jenner & Block, LLC
Chicago, IL

Jonathan C. Fritts
Morgan, Lewis & Bockius LLP
Washington, DC

Amy Moor Gaylord
Katten, Muchin, Zavis Rosenman
Chicago, IL

L. Anthony George
Jackson Kelly PLLC
Denver, CO

Thomas S. Giotto
Klett Rooney Lieber & Schorling
Pittsburgh, PA

Ben Gipson
Kirkland & Ellis
Washington, DC

David M. Glanstein
O'Donnell, Schwartz, Glanstein & Lilly
New York, NY

Joel C. Glanstein
O'Donnell, Schwartz, Glanstein & Lilly
New York, NY

Joseph S. Glynias
Blackwell, Sanders, Peper, Martin LLP
St. Louis, MO

Deborah E. Godwin
Godwin, Morris, Laurenzi & Bloomfield, P.C.
Memphis, TN

Kelly Going
Baker & McKenzie
Palo Alto, CA

Andy Goldberg
Laner Muchin Dombrow Becker Levin and Tominberg, Ltd.
Chicago, IL

N. Victor Goodman
Benesch, Friedlander, Coplan & Aronoff, LLP
Columbus, OH

Katherine Donohue Goudie
Butzel Long
Detroit, MI

Ellen Grachek
Allotta, Farley & Widman Co., LPA
Toledo, OH

Christopher N. Grant
Schuchat, Cook & Werner
St. Louis, MO

Merritt J. Green
General Counsel, P.C.
McLean, VA

Brian S. Greig
Fulbright & Jaworski L.L.P.
Austin, TX

Richard J. Hafets
DLA Piper Marbury Rudnick Gray Cary US LLP
Baltimore, MD

Lewis R. Hagood
Arnett, Draper and Hagood
Knoxville, TN

Rick Hampton
Northwest Food Employers, Inc.
Tigard, OR

David R. Hansen
Hansen & Connolly, P.C.
Denver, CO

Richard Hardick
National Labor Relations Board
Washington DC

Michael C. Harrington
Murtha Cullina LLP
Hartford, CT

Kerry Hastings
Taft Stettinius & Hollister, LLP
Cincinnati, OH

Gerald Hathaway
Little Mendelson
New York, NY

Samuel Heldman
Gardner, Middlebrooks, Fleming, Gibbons & Kittrell, P.C.
Washington, DC

C. John Holmquist, Jr.
Dickinson Wright PLLC
Bloomfield Hills, MI

Edwin S. Hopson
Wyatt, Tarrant & Combs LLP
Louisville, KY

David L. Hoskins
Frost Brown Todd LLC
Louisville, KY

Mark Hudson
Baird, Holm, McEachen, Pedersen, Hamann & Strasheim, L.L.P.
Omaha, NE

Melvin R. Hutson
Greenville, SC

Cynthia Jackson
Baker & McKenzie
Palo Alto, CA

Zachary Jackson
Ogletree Deakins
Chicago, IL

Lynn F. Jacob
Williams Mullen
Richmond, VA

Bernard P. Jeweler
Ogletree Deakins
Washington, D.C.

Keith R. Jewell
Beverly Enterprises
Fort Smith, AR

Jeffrey T. Johnson
Holland & Hart LLP
Denver, CO

Kathleen Jorgenson
Geffner & Bush
Burbank, CA

MARK L. JUSTER
Laner Muchin Dombrow
Becker Levin and
Tominberg, Ltd.
Chicago, IL

WINIFRED KAO
O'Donoghue & O'Donoghue
Washington, DC

HOWARD M. KASTRINSKY
King & Ballow
Nashville, TN

JOEL I. KEILER
Law Offices of Joel I. Keiler
Reston, VA

SIOBHAN KELLY
National Labor Relations
Board
Washington DC

WESLEY G.S. KENNEDY
Allison, Slutsky & Kennedy,
P.C.
Chicago, IL

JAY W. KIESEWETTER
Kiesewetter Wise Kaplan
Prather, PLC
Memphis, TN

DAVID M. KIGHT
Shugart Thomson & Kilroy PC
Kansas City, MO

PAUL J. KINGSTON
Rubin & Rudman LLP
Boston, MA

MICHAEL K. KIRK
Wyatt, Tarrant & Combs LLP
Louisville, KY

RONALD J. KLEPETAR
Jenkens & Gilchrist, LLP
Los Angeles, CA

FRANK L. KOLLMAN
Kollman & Saucier, P.A.
Baltimore, MD

MARK KONKEL
Winston & Strawn LLP
New York, NY

BRIAN KURTZ
Matkov, Slazman, Madoff &
Gunn
Chicago, IL

WILLIAM MORRIS (BILL)
LAMOREAUX
Dallas, TX

RICHARD B. LAPP
Seyfarth Shaw LLP
Chicago, IL

ROBERT H. LAVITT
Schwerin Campbell Barnard
LLP
Seattle, WA

SANG-YUL LEE
DLA Piper Marbury Rudnick
Gray Cary US LLP
Chicago, IL

Thomas A. Lenz
Atkinson, Andelson, Loya,
Rudd & Romo
Cerritos, CA

Alan S. Levins
Littler Mendelson
San Francisco, CA

Jay J. Levit
Levit Mann & Halligan, P.C.
Richmond, VA

Brian E. Lewis
Hinckley, Allen & Snyder, LLP
Boston, MA

D. Michael Linihan
McMahon, Berger, Hanna,
Linihan, Cody & McCarthy
St. Louis, MO

Brian Lipman
McElroy, Deutsch, Mulvaney &
Carpenter
Newark, NJ

Noah Lipschultz
Seyfarth Shaw LLP
Chicago, IL

Lisa Loverdi
Sadler & Sykes LLP
Houston, TX

Thomas M. Lucas
Troutman Sanders LLP
Virginia Beach, VA

Stephen W. Lyman
Hall, Render, Killian, Heath
& Lyman
Indianapolis, IN

Paul V. Lyons
Foley Hoag LLP
Boston, MA

Joseph Mack III
Spilman, Thomas & Battle
PLLC
Pittsburgh, PA

Andrew A. Malahowski
Winston & Strawn LLP
Chicago, IL

Michelle Malloy
Littler Mendelson
Philadelphia, PA

Thomas J. Marcoline
Law Office of Vincent
Toomey
Lake Success, NY

Stefan Jan Marculewicz
Miles & Stockbridge
Baltimore, MD

Barry W. Marr
Marr Hipp Jones & Pepper
Honolulu, HI

Martin P. Marta
Seyfarth Shaw LLP
Chicago, IL

W. Jonathan Martin II
Constangy, Brooks & Smith LLC
Macon, GA

Francis A. Mastro
Apruzzese, McDermott, Mastro & Murphy
Liberty Corner, NJ

Eric Mathis
Butzel Long
Detroit, MI

Mark S. Mathison
Gray Plant Mooty
Minneapolis, MN

Stephen B. Maule
McMahon, Berger, Hanna, Linihan, Cody & McCarthy
St. Louis, MO

John T. McCann
Hancock & Estabrook LLP
Syracuse, NY

James N. McCauley
Law Office of James N. McCauley
Ithaca, NY

J. McCoin
Coca-Cola Enterprises, Inc.
Cincinnati, OH

Terence P. McCourt
Greenberg, Traurig LLP
Boston, MA

Rebecca McGinnis
Lathrop & Gage LC
Kansas City, MO

Kathleen McKinney
National Labor Relations Board
New Orleans, LA

David Miklas
J. David Richeson & Associates, P.A.
Ft. Pierce, FL

Jolynne Miller
National Labor Relations Board
Washington, DC

Frederick C. Miner
Ryley, Carlock & Applewhite
Phoenix, AZ

Allyson C.H. Mitchell
National Labor Relations Board
Washington, DC

Michael J. Moberg
Briggs & Morgan
St. Paul, MN

Scott Moore
Baird, Holm, McEachen, Pedersen, Hamann & Strasheim, L.L.P.
Omaha, NE

Robert W. Morgan
Berry Moormen, PC
Detroit, MI

Rafael E. Morrell
Ogletree Deakins
Washington, DC

Darren Mungerson
Jenner & Block, LLC
Chicago, IL

Bryce G. Murray
McGlinchey Stafford PLLC
New Orleans, LA

Jeffrey E. Myers
Blank Rome Comisky
& McCauley LLP
Philadelphia, PA

Doug Nabhan
Williams Mullen, P.C.
Richmond, VA

Clifford H. Nelson, Jr.
Wimberly Lawson Steckel
Nelson & Schneider, PC
Atlanta, GA

Frank A. Nemia
Coughlin & Gerhart, L.L.P.
Binghamton, NY

Thomas A. Nesbitt
Fulbright & Jaworski L.L.P.
Austin, TX

Raymond D. Neusch
Frost Brown Todd LLC
Cincinnati, OH

Stuart Newman
Jackson Lewis LLP
Atlanta, GA

Ian A. Northon
Butzel Long
Detroit, MI

Jeannine Novak
Jackson Lewis LLP
Atlanta, GA

Dona Nutini
Law Office of Dona Nutini
Scottsdale, AZ

Amanu Nwaomah
Meckler Bulger & Tilson
Chicago, IL

Thomas L.P. O'Donnell
Ropes & Gray
Boston, MA

Paul M. Ostroff
Lane, Powell PC
Portland, OR

Suellen Oswald
Duvin Cahn & Hutton
Cleveland, OH

Jeffrey W. Pagano
King, Pagano & Harrison
New York, NY

Albert W. Palewicz
National Labor Relations Board
Baltimore, MD

PATRICIA E. PALMERI
Law Offices of Richard S. Brook
Mineola, NY

PETER M. PANKEN
Epstein, Becker & Green, P.C.
New York, NY

DANIEL B. PASTERNAK
Greenberg Traurig
Phoenix, AZ

ROBERT E. PAUL
Zwerdling, Paul, Kahn & Wolly P.C.
Washington DC

GERALD L. PAULING II
Seyfarth Shaw LLP
Chicago, IL

W. JUDD PEAK
Ogletree Deakins
Nashville, TN

JESSICA PECORARO
Rider, Bennett, Egan & Arundel, LLP
Minneapolis, MN

D. ("PAT) PATTON PELFREY
Frost Brown Todd LLC
Louisville, KY

LETICIA PEÑA
National Labor Relations Board
Denver, CO

NICOLE CUDA PEREZ
Spivak, Lipton, Watanabe, Spivak & Moss LLP
West Orange, NJ

RUSSELL PERISHO
Perkins Coie LLP
Seattle, WA

D. JAMES PETROFF
Faulkner, Muskovitz & Phillips, LLP
Cleveland, OH

JEFFREY M. PLACE
Spencer, Fane, Britt & Browne, LLP
Kansas City, MO

NATHAN D. PLANTINGA
Miller, Johnson, Snell & Cummiskey, P.L.C.
Grand Rapids, MI

RICHARD D. PORTER
Duvin, Cahn & Hutton
Cleveland, OH

PETER D. POST
Reed, Smith, Shaw & McClay LLP
Pittsburgh, PA

TERRY POTTER
Blackwell, Sanders, Peper, Martin LLP
St. Louis, MO

KRISTA GREEN PRATT
Seyfarth Shaw LLP
Boston, MA

E. FREDERICK PREIS, JR.
McGlinchey Stafford PLLC
New Orleans, LA

BRYAN K. PROCTOR
Butzel Long
Detroit, MI

TRACY S. PYLES
Littler Mendelson
Columbus, OH

JOHN RAUDABAUGH
Butzel Long
Detroit, MI

VINCENT D. REESE
Lewis, Rice & Fingersh, LLC
St. Louis, MO

ELIZABETH D. REHM
Jackson Myrick, LLP
Mobile, AL

CHARLES W. REYNOLDS
Dover Dixon & Horne PLLC
Little Rock, AR

N. ELIZABETH REYNOLDS
Allison, Slutsky & Kennedy, P.C.
Chicago, IL

J. DAVID RICHESON
J. David Richeson & Associates
Fort Pierce, FL

LOUIS ROSNER
Philadelphia, PA

E. MICHAEL ROSSMAN
Jones Day
Columbus, OH

ROSALIND ROWEN-ROSSI
National Labor Relations Board
Brooklyn, NY

CHRISTOPHER J. RUSEK
Wyeth Pharmaceuticals
Collegeville, PA

TIMOTHY F. RYAN
Morrison & Foerster, LLP
Los Angeles, CA

RICHARD C. RYBICKI
Rybecki & Blevans, LLP
Santa Rosa, CA

LISA ANNE SABATINO
Pelino & Lentz
Philadelphia, PA

RICHARD SAMSON
Ogletree Deakins
Chicago, IL

MARK SANDMAN
ABC, Inc.
New York, NY

TODD L. SARVER
Jones Day
Columbus, OH

STANLEY M. SAUNIER, JR.
Lexington, KY

ANN MARIE SCARPINO
National Labor Relations Board
Washington DC

PROFESSOR LORRAINE SCHMALL
Northern Illinois University College of Law
DeKalb, IL

MARK W. SCHNEIDER
Rider, Bennett, Egan & Arundel
Minneapolis, MN

TODD W. SCHNELL
Dorsey & Whitney, LLP
Minneapolis, MN

MARK M. SCHORR
Erickson & Sederstrom, P.C.
Lincoln, NE

ANDREW SCHPAK
Barran Liebman LLP
Portland, OR

JENNIFER SCHUBERT
Davis Wright Tremaine LLP
Seattle, WA

STEPHAN J. SCHULTZ
Merrill, Schultz & Wolds, Limited
San Diego, CA

THEODORE R. SCOTT
Luce Forward Hamilton & Scripps LLP
San Diego, CA

ANNE SENTER
Rinehart & Robblee
Seattle, WA

STEPHEN L. SHEINFELD
Winston & Strawn LLP
New York, NY

ERIN SHIELDS
Mackall, Crounse & Moore, PLC
Minneapolis, MN

HENRY W. SLEDZ, JR.
Schiff Hardin & Waite
Chicago, IL

LAWRENCE J. SONG
Epstein Turner & Song, P.C.
Los Angeles, CA

SONYA SPIELBERG
National Labor Relations Board
Washington, DC

STEPHEN J. STANFORD
Fuller & Henry, Ltd.
Toledo, OH

CRAIG STANLEY
Butzel Long
Detroit, MI

Jefferson M. Starling III
Birmingham, AL

R. Timothy Stephenson
Kirkland & Ellis
Washington, DC

David Streck
Seyfarth Shaw LLP
Chicago, IL

Laurence E. Stuart
Legge, Farrow, Kimmit, McGrath & Brown, LLP
Houston, TX

Jan W. Sturner
Venable LLP
Vienna, VA

Michael L. Sullivan
Goldberg Kohn Bell Black Rosenbloom & Moritz, Ltd.
Chicago, IL

Richard D. Sutton
McGuire Woods
New York, NY

Peter C. Swanson
Cornfield & Feldman
Chicago, IL

Eric A. Taussig
Moultonborough, NH

Michael J. Tedesco
Law Office of M.J. Tedesco
Beaverton, OR

David M. Thomas II
Balch & Bingham LLP
Jackson, MS

Peder Thoreen
Atshuler, Berzon, Nussbaum, Rubin & Demain
San Francisco, CA

George J. Tichy II
Littler Mendelson
San Francisco, CA

William C. Tidwell III
Hand Arendall, L.L.C.
Mobile, AL

Robert P. Tinnin, Jr.
Tinnin Law Firm
Albuquerque, NM

Robert W. Tollen
Seyfarth Shaw LLP
San Francisco, CA

Thomas Trachsel
Felhaber, Larson, Fenlon & Vogt
Minneapolis, MN

Leigh E. Tyson
Wimberly Lawson Steckel Nelson & Schneider, PC
Atlanta, GA

James S. Urban
Jones Day
Pittsburgh, PA

Jason J. Valtos
Osborne Law Offices
Washington, DC

Frederick W. Vogt
Mackall, Crounse & Moore, PLC
Minneapolis, MN

Charles F. Waskevich, Jr.
Herald and Haines, PA
Warren, NJ

J. Roy Weathersby
Weathersby, Howard & Kuck
Atlanta, GA

Annelise (Anna) Wermuth
Meckler Bulger & Tilson
Chicago, IL

Steven D. Wheeless
Steptoe & Johnson LLP
Phoenix, AZ

Norman I. White
McNees, Wallace & Nurick LLC
Harrisburg, PA

Marilyn L. Widman
Allotta, Farley & Widman Co., LPA
Toledo, OH

Thomas J. Wiencek
Brouse McDowell
Akron, OH

Robert A. Wiesen
Clifton Budd & DeMaria, LLP
New York, NY

Paul Wilhelm
Greenebaum Doll & McDonald PLLC
Cincinnati, OH

Brent L. Wilson
Elarbee, Thompson, Sapp & Wilson, LLP
Atlanta, GA

Jeffrey D. Winchester
Jones Day
Columbus, OH

Tiffany Winchester
Gardner, Middlebrooks, Fleming, Gibbons & Kitrell, P.C.
Mobile, AL

Brian N. Woolley
Lathrop & Gage LC
Kansas City, MO

Christy Young
DLA Piper Rudnick Gray Cary US LLP
Chicago, IL

Lawrence T. Zimmerman
Law Offices of Lawrence T. Zimmerman
Washington, DC

Jon Zimring
Duane Morris LLP
Chicago, IL

FOREWORD

Since 1945 the ABA Section of Labor and Employment Law has expanded its stated purposes in response to the evolution of the field. Currently, they include the following: (a) to study and report upon continuing developments in the field of labor and employment law; (b) to provide a forum for members of the Association interested in the field of labor and employment law to meet and confer; (c) to assist the professional growth and development of practitioners in the field of labor and employment law; (d) to establish and maintain working liaison with state, federal, and where applicable, multi-national agencies having jurisdiction over matters affecting labor and employment law toward achieving procedural reform and administrative due process; (e) to study and report upon proposed and necessary legislation and rule making within the field encompassed by the jurisdiction of this Section; (f) to promote justice, human welfare, industrial peace, and the recognition of the supremacy of law in labor-management relations and the employment relationship; and (g) to establish, moderate, and sponsor seminars, workshops, forums, and other programs promoting the advancement of knowledge and practice in the field of labor and employment law.

The Section of Labor and Employment Law is pleased to provide this Supplement to its classic treatise on the National Labor Relations Act as part of its library of books published by BNA Books, a Division of The Bureau of National Affairs, Inc. The combined efforts of many individual authors from the Committee on the Development of the Law under the National Labor Relations Act of the Section are reflected in this Supplement.

The Section wishes to express its appreciation to the committee, and in particular to the editors-in-chief, Peter A. Janus, Kenneth L. Wagner, and Barry J. Kearney, and the associate editors. This group has tried to accomplish two primary objectives: (1) to be equally balanced and nonpartisan in their viewpoints, and (2) to ensure the book is of significant value to the practitioner, student, and sophisticated nonlawyer.

The views expressed herein do not necessarily represent the views of the American Bar Association, or its Section of Labor and Employment Law, or any other organization, but are simply the collective, but not necessarily the individual views of the authors. Information on the affiliation of government employees who contributed to this work is for informational purposes and does not constitute any official endorsement of the information provided herein.

CHARLES A. WERNER
Chair

PATRICIA COSTELLO SLOVAK
Chair-Elect

Section of Labor
and Employment Law
American Bar Association

September 2005

PREFACE

This sixth cumulative Supplement to the fourth edition follows the organization of the fourth edition exactly. It updates the main volume through 2004. This Supplement does not contain headings where there have been no significant developments under that heading since publication of the fourth edition.

The efforts of all the members of the Committee toward publication of this Supplement are deeply appreciated. This is truly a working and producing Committee. In addition, we wish to express our appreciation for the support and assistance of the staff of BNA Books who have spent many hours editing and proofing the manuscript and otherwise working with us on this Supplement. Special thanks are also given to the Section of Labor and Employment Law and its governing Council for their valuable support and encouragement in this endeavor.

We believe that the final product is ample justification for the efforts of all involved.

PETER A. JANUS
KENNETH L. WAGNER
BARRY J. KEARNEY

TABLE OF CONTENTS

PART II

PROTECTED EMPLOYEE ACTIVITY

Part III

THE REPRESENTATION PROCESS AND UNION RECOGNITION

PART IV

THE COLLECTIVE BARGAINING PROCESS

PART V

ARBITRATION AND THE ACT

PART VI

ECONOMIC ACTION

PART VIII

ADMINISTRATION OF THE ACT

Part I

HISTORY OF THE NATIONAL LABOR RELATIONS ACT

BIBLIOGRAPHY

Mark Barenberg, *The Political Economy of the Wagner Act: Power, Symbol and Workplace Cooperation*, 106 HARV. L. REV. 1379 (1993)

Stephen F. Befort, *Labor and Employment Law at the Millennium: A Historical Review and Critical Assessment*, 43 B.C. L. REV. 351 (2002)

Janice R. Bellace, *The Future of Employee Representation in America: Enabling Freedom of Association in the Workplace in Changing Times Through Statutory Reform*, 5 U. PA. J. LAB. & EMP. L. 1 (2002)

William R. Corbett, *Waiting for the Labor Law of the Twenty-First Century: Everything Old is New Again*, 23 BERKELEY J. EMP. & LAB. L. 259 (2002)

Cynthia L. Estlund, *The Ossification of American Labor Law*, 102 COLUM. L. REV. 1527 (2002)

Douglas J. Feeney-Gallagher, *Battle of the Benches: The Wagner Act and the Circuit Courts of Appeals, 1935-1942*, 23 SEATTLE L. REV. 503 (2000)

George Feldman, *Unions, Solidarity, and Class: The Limits of Liberal Labor Law*, 15 BERKELEY J. EMP. & LAB. L. 187 (1994)

Christopher J. Garofalo, *Section 302 of the LMRA: Make Way for the Employer-Paid Union Representative*, 75 N.Y.U. L. REV. 775 (2000)

Julius Getman, *The National Labor Relations Act: What Went Wrong; Can We Fix It?*, 45 B.C. L. REV. 125 (2003)

Michael J. Goldberg, *Derailing Union Democracy: Why Deregulation Would Be a Mistake*, 23 BERKELEY J. EMP. & LAB. L. 137 (2002)

Christopher Grant, *Unions in a Fragmented Society*, 7 CHI.-KENT L. REV. 849 (2002)

Michael C. Harper, *A Framework for the Rejuvenation of the American Labor Movement*, 76 IND. L.J. 103 (2001)

Phillip Harvey, *An Analysis of the Principal Strategies That Have Influenced the Development of American Employment and Social Welfare Law During the 20th Century*, 21 BERKELEY J. EMP. & LAB. L. 677 (2000)

John E. Higgins, Jr., *Labor Czars—Commissars—Keeping Women in the Kitchen—The Purpose and Effects of the Administrative Changes Made by Taft-Hartley*, 47 CATH. U. L. REV. 941 (1998)

Michael H. LeRoy, *Employer Domination of Labor Organizations and the* Electromation *Case: An Empirical Public Policy Analysis*, 61 Geo. Wash. L. Rev. 1812 (1993).

Charles J. Morris, *A Blueprint for Reform of the National Labor Relations Act*, 8 Admin. L.J. Am. U. 517 (1994)

Charles J. Morris, The Blue Eagle at Work: Reclaiming Democratic Rights in the American Workplace (Cornell Univ. Press, 2005)

Michael J. Nelson, *Slowing Union Corruption: Reforming the Landrum-Griffin Act to Better Combat Union Embezzlement*, 8 Geo. Mason L. Rev. 527 (2000)

Theodore J. St. Antoine, *How the Wagner Act Came to Be: A Prospectus*, 96 Mich. L. Rev. 2201 (1998)

Ahmed A. White, *Mutiny, Shipboard Strikes, and the Supreme Court's Subversion of New Deal Labor Law*, 25 Berkeley J. Emp. & Labor L. 275 (2004)

Chapters 1–5

HISTORICAL DEVELOPMENTS

There have been no changes or developments in the law since publication of the Main Edition.

Part II

PROTECTED EMPLOYEE ACTIVITY

BIBLIOGRAPHY

Janice R. Bellace, *The Future of Employee Representation in America: Enabling Freedom of Association in the Workplace in Changing Times Through Statutory Reform,* 5 U. PA. J. LAB. & EMP. L. 1 (2002)

Christopher Brackman, Hoffman v. NLRB, *Creating More Harm Than Good: Why the Supreme Court Should Not Have Denied Illegal Workers a Backpay Remedy Under the National Labor Relations Act,* 71 UMKC L. REV. 717 (2003)

Dennise A. Calderon-Barrera, Hoffman v. NLRB: *Leaving Undocumented Workers Unprotected Under United States Labor Laws?,* 6 HARV. LATINO L. REV. 119 (2003)

Cynthia L. Estlund, *Wrongful Discharge Protections in an At-Will World,* 74 TEX. L. REV. 1665 (1996)

Eric J. Felsberg, *Creating a* Beck *Statute: Recent Congressional Attempts and a Proposal for the Future,* 15 HOFSTRA LAB. & EMP. L.J. 247 (1997)

Matthew W. Finkin, *Employee Representation Outside the Labor Act: Thoughts on Arbitral Representation, Group Representation, and Workplace Committees,* 5 U. PA. J. LAB. & EMP. L. 75 (2002)

Rafael Gely and Leonard Bierman, *Pay Secrecy/Confidentiality Rules and the National Labor Relations Act,* 6 U. PA. J. LAB. & EMP. L. 121 (2003)

Rafael Gely, *Whose Team Are You On? My Team or My Team?: The NLRA's Section 8(A)(2) and the Team Act,* 49 RUTGERS L. REV. 323 (1997)

Jonathan B. Goldin, *Labor-Management Cooperation:* Bath Iron Works'*s Bold New Approach,* 47 ME. L. REV. 415 (1995)

David L. Gregory, *The Supreme Court's Labor and Employment Jurisprudence, 1999-2001,* 36 TULSA L. REV. 515 (2001)

Michael J. Hays, *Has* Wright Line *Gone Wrong? Why Pretext Can Be Sufficient to Prove Discrimination in the National Labor Relations Act,* 65 MO. L. REV. 883 (2000)

H. Victoria Hedian, *The Implications of* Crown Cork & Seal Co. *for Employee Involvement as "Labor Organizations" Under the Wagner Act: What Constitutes "Dealing With" Pursuant to Section 2(5) of the Act Since* Electromation, Inc.*?,* 18 LAB. LAW 35 (2002)

Ann C. Hodges, *Arbitration of Statutory Claims in the Unionized Workplace: Is Bargaining with the Union Required?,* 16 OHIO ST. J. ON DISP. RESOL. 513 (2001)

Michael D. Moberly and Andrea G. Lisenbeer, *Honing Our Kraft? Reconciling Variations in the Remedial Treatment of* Weingarten *Violations*, 21 HOFSTRA LAB. & EMPL L.J. 523 (2004)

Paul More, *Protections Against Retaliatory Employer Lawsuits After* BE&K v. NLRB, 25 BERKELEY J. EMP. & LAB. 205 (2004)

Johanna Oreskovic, *Capturing Volition Itself: Employee Involvement and the Team Act*, 19 BERKELEY J. EMP. & LAB. L. 229 (1998)

Christopher David Ruiz Cameron, *Borderline Decisions:* Hoffman Plastic Compounds, *the New Bracero Program, and the Supreme Court's Role in Making Federal Labor Policy*, 51UCLA L. REV. 1 (2003)

Scott E. Schaffer, Echazabal v. Chevron USA, Inc.: *Conquering the Final Frontier of Paternalistic Employment Practices,* 33 CONN. L. REV. 1441 (2001)

Paul M. Secunda, *Politics Not as Usual: Inherently Destructive Conduct, Institutional Collegiality, and the National Labor Relations Board*, 32 FLA. ST. U. L. REV. 51 (2004)

Katherine E. Seitz, *Enter at Your Own Risk: The Impact of* Hoffman Plastic Compounds v. National Labor Relations Board *on the Undocumented Worker,* 82 N.C. L. REV. 366 (2003)

Calvin William Sharpe, *"By Any Means Necessary"—Unprotected Conduct and Decisional Discretion Under the National Labor Relations Act*, 20 BERKELEY J. EMP. & LAB. L. 203 (1999)

Cathy Shuck, *That's It, I Quit: Returning to the First Principles of the Constructive Discharge Doctrine*, 23 BERKELEY J. EMP. & LAB. L. 401 (2002)

Clyde W. Summers, *Employment At-Will in the United States: The Divine Right of Employers*, 3 U. PA. J. LAB. & EMP. L. 65 (2000)

Thomas J. Walsh, Hoffman Plastic Compounds, Inc. v. NLRB: *How the Supreme Court Eroded Labor Law and Workers Rights in the Name of Immigration Policy*, 21 LAW & INEQ. 313 (2003)

Chapter 6

INTERFERENCE WITH PROTECTED RIGHTS

I. OVERVIEW

B. Section 7—Rights of Employees

2. *To Refrain From Such Activities*

The Section 7 right guaranteeing employees the right to refrain from engaging in concerted activities was not violated by the Virgin

Islands Wrongful Discharge Act.[1] The Act specified nine lawful grounds for dismissal of employees in the Virgin Islands, and allowed those grounds for dismissal to be modified only through a collective bargaining agreement. The court held that the statute set minimum employment standards that did not invade the free play of economic forces envisioned by Congress, and therefore was not preempted by the Act.

3. *Other Concerted Activities*

Section 7 protects concerted employee activity unrelated to union organization.[2] While the scope of Section 7 remains very broad, employee activity still must be "concerted" in order to be protected.[3]

---

[1]24 V.I. CODE ANN. §76. *See* St. Thomas-St. John Hotel & Tourism Ass'n, Inc. v. Government of the U.S. Virgin Islands, 218 F.3d 232, 164 LRRM 2705 (3d Cir. 2000), *overruling* Bell v. Chase Manhattan Bank, 40 F. Supp. 2d 307, 163 LRRM 2370 (D.V.I. 1999), *on remand,* 216 F. Supp. 2d 460 (D.V.I. 2002), *vacated in part and remanded,* 357 F.3d 297 (3d Cir. 2004) (Virgin Islands Wrongful Discharge Act applies to nonexecutive, nonprofessional supervisors without conflicting with Act but is preempted as applied to supervisors).

[2]Mojave Elec. Coop. Inc., 327 NLRB 13, 163 LRRM 1288 (1998), *enforced,* 206 F.3d 1183, 163 LRRM 2917 (D.C. Cir. 2000) (employee and co-workers petitioned for injunctive relief against harassment by two officials of employer's subcontractor). *See also* Odyssey Capital Group, 337 NLRB 1110, 170 LRRM 1387 (2000) (employees engaged in concerted activity when they refused to perform work based upon belief work presented safety hazard).

[3]Mobil Exploration & Producing U.S, Inc., v. NLRB, 200 F.3d 230, 163 LRRM 2387 (5th Cir. 1999) (employee's statements to co-workers in lunchroom that employer was trying to fire him and had security investigator after him for "trying to right a wrong" and about his opposition to union president was concerted activity); International Trans. Serv., 344 NLRB No. 22, 2005 WL 429747 (2005) (recognitional picketing by lone employee was protected); Office Depot, 330 NLRB 640, 163 LRRM 1169 (2000) (employee's telling individual who was picking up order for newspaper whose employees were on strike, "Oh, you work for the scab newspaper," was protected concerted activity, where employee's use of term "scab" was expression of support for striking newspaper employees and amounted to making common cause with protected concerted activity of employees of another employer); Mauka, Inc., 327 NLRB 803, 167 LRRM 1352 (1999) (unfair labor practice strike by one employee was continuation of concerted activity and, therefore, protected); *Mojave, supra* note 2. *But see* Williams v. Watkins Motor Lines, Inc., 310 F.3d 1070, 171 LRRM 2342 (8th Cir. 2002) (team of two married employees who refused to drive a truck that violated Missouri weight restrictions did not engage in protected concerted activity where they operated as a "single individual for the purposes of employment").

Courts, in agreement with the Board, continue to hold that it is not necessary for an employee to be appointed by co-workers to represent their interests for the employee's actions, taken on their behalf, to be concerted.[4] Employees who espouse the cause of other employees are engaged in concerted activity.[5] Similarly, conduct that is maliciously false is not protected.[6]

The Board and the courts continue to hold that an individual employee's action to enforce the terms of a collective bargaining agreement, even though pursued singly, constitutes concerted activity under Section 7.[7]

While activity by a single employee for the individual's own personal benefit is not concerted activity, the fact that self-interest is a factor in an employee's decision to engage in the activity at issue does not deprive otherwise concerted activity of protection under

---

[4]NLRB v. Main St. Terrace Care Ctr., 218 F.3d 531, 164 LRRM 2833 (6th Cir. 2000).

[5]Air Contact Transp., 340 NLRB No. 81, 173 LRRM 1429 (2003) (questions raised by individual at a staff luncheon regarding relationship between employer's evaluation system and pay raises considered concerted activity); Triangle Elec. Co., 335 NLRB 1037, 169 LRRM 1146 (2001) (holding that nonstriking employee who distributed a strike newspaper at site unrelated to strike was engaging in protected concerted activity); Carrier Corp. & Crosby, 336 NLRB 1141, 171 LRRM 1296 (2001) (employee engaged in concerted activity when he solicited signatures for letter to corporate headquarters about direct supervisor); Caval Tool Div., Chromalloy Gas Turbine Corp., 331 NLRB 858, 168 LRRM 1067 (2000), *enforced,* 262 F.3d 184, 168 LRRM 2180 (2d Cir. 2001); Lockheed Martin Astronautics, 330 NLRB 422, 163 LRRM 1049 (2000) (employee who discussed concerns about employer's accommodations for disabled employee with fellow employees and supervisor was engaged in protected concerted action even when such complaints formed basis for disabled employee's hostile work environment claim).

[6]Sprint/United Mgmt. Co., 339 NLRB 1012, 173 LRRM 1445 (2003) (employee e-mail falsely informing co-workers that anthrax was found at employer's facility was not protected because some facts contained therein were not verified, and others were intentionally false or made with reckless disregard for the truth).

[7]New Orleans Cold Storage & Warehouse Co. v. NLRB, 201 F.3d 592, 163 LRRM 2330 (5th Cir. 2000) (employer violated Act by taking adverse employment action against employee because of number of grievances filed by employee under collective bargaining agreement); United States Postal Serv., 332 NLRB 340, 169 LRRM 1127 (2000), *enforced,* 25 Fed. Appx. 41 (2d Cir. 2001) (employees engaged in protected concerted activity when they refused to work overtime after employer failed to provide 1-hour notice required by collective bargaining agreement). *But see* ALCOA, 338 NLRB 20, 170 LRRM 1478 (2002) (employee engaged in protected concerted activity when he threatened to file grievance under collective bargaining agreement, but lost protection of § 7 when he used profane language).

the Act.[8] Likewise, although an individual employee's assertion of a statutory right enjoyed by other employees is not always concerted activity, employees who collectively seek to improve their working conditions through resort to administrative or judicial forums have been found to be engaged in concerted activity.[9]

Once concerted activity is found, however, the Board and courts continue to interpret broadly the protective umbrella of Section 7,[10]

---

[8]Meyers Indus., 268 NLRB 493, 115 LRRM 1025 (1984), *rev'd sub nom.* Prill v. NLRB, 755 F.2d 941, 118 LRRM 2649 (D.C. Cir.), *cert. denied sub nom.* Meyers Indus. v. Prill, 474 U.S. 971, 120 LRRM 3392 (1985), *decision on remand,* 281 NLRB 882, 123 LRRM 1137, *enforced,* 835 F.2d 1481, 127 LRRM 2415 (D.C. Cir. 1987), *cert. denied,* 487 U.S. 1205, 128 LRRM 2664 (1988). *But see* Plumbers Local 412, 328 NLRB 1079 (1999) (union staffer was engaged in pursuit of personal interest, not protected concerted activity, when she discussed ineligibility for pension plan with employees at training school next to union hall, with co-worker, and with union's executive board).

[9]*See* Mojave Elec. Coop., Inc. v. NLRB, 206 F.3d 1183, 163 LRRM 2917 (D.C. Cir. 2000) (co-workers jointly filing, with support of other employees, judicial petition seeking injunction against harassment from contractors hired by employer, engaged in concerted activity); Georgia Farm Bureau Mut. Ins. Co., 333 NLRB 850, 170 LRRM 1041 (2001) (employer violated §8(a)(1) when employer constructively discharged two employees who contacted state insurance commissioner about fellow employee's fraudulent acts); Tri-County Transp., Inc., 331 NLRB 1153, 171 LRRM 1031 (2000) (employer violated §8(a)(1) by terminating employees who acted collectively in filing for unemployment benefits); 127 Restaurant Corp., 331 NLRB 269, 170 LRRM 1447 (2000) (employees joining to file civil action against employer regarding payment of wages engaged in concerted activity). *But see* Tradesmen Int'l, Inc. v. NLRB, 275 F.3d 1137, 169 LRRM 2212 (D.C. Cir. 2002) (denied enforcement of Board's decision that employee engaged in concerted activity when he contacted city administrators about employer's failure to obey city subcontractor bond ordinance because the ordinance did not concern employment-related matters).

[10]*See, e.g.,* Frazier Indus. Co. v. NLRB, 213 F.3d 750, 164 LRRM 2516 (D.C. Cir. 2000) (union supporter who persistently discussed union with co-workers was engaged in protected activity, despite employer's contention that employee was impermissibly harassing co-workers during work time); Mojave Elec. Coop., Inc., 327 NLRB 13, 163 LRRM 1288 (1998), *enforced,* 206 F.3d 1183, 163 LRRM 2917 (D.C. Cir. 2000) (employee and co-worker, pursuant to common concern for workplace safety, petitioned for injunctive relief against harassment by two officials of employer's subcontractor, and employee's actions not found disloyal so as to lose protection); Epilepsy Found. of Northeast Ohio, 331 NLRB 676, 164 LRRM 1233 (2000), *enforcement denied in part,* 268 F.3d 1095, 168 LRRM 2673 (D.C. Cir. 2001), *cert. denied,* 536 U.S. 904, 170 LRRM 2224 (2002) (written memos in which employee, along with co-worker, attempted to convince employer to dismiss their supervisor and also raised other issues related to employees' terms and conditions of employment, were protected; circuit court critical of Board regarding such finding and refused to enforce Board orders on this point); Office Depot, 330 NLRB 640, 163 LRRM 1169 (2000).

though concerted activity that is disloyal, in breach of contract, or is found to be an impermissible strike continues to be unprotected.[11]

Section 7 protections can extend to situations in which employees seek to improve terms and conditions of employment through channels outside the immediate employee–supervisor relationship, such as situations in which an employee raises complaints regarding working conditions in the media,[12] in group meetings called by the employer,[13] or by distributing literature to the public.[14]

---

[11] *See* Abell Eng'g & Mfg., Inc., 338 NLRB 434, 171 LRRM 1051 (2002) (employee considered disloyal and therefore not engaged in protected activity when he attempted to persuade co-worker to quit employer for union position at competitor); St. Luke's Episcopal-Presbyterian Hosp., Inc., 331 NLRB 761, 168 LRRM 1271 (2000), *enforcement denied,* 268 F.3d 575, 168 LRRM 2481 (8th Cir. 2001) (TV interview in which employee disparaged employer's services was not protected); District 17 v. Island Creek Coal Co., 179 F.3d 133, 161 LRRM 2463 (4th Cir. 1999) (employees fired for picketing over grievable disputes in violation of labor contract were not engaged in protected activity).

[12] *See* Allstate Ins. Co., 332 NLRB 759, 165 LRRM 1293 (2000) (employer unlawfully disciplined employee for magazine interview critical of employer where several employees participated and interview was done in part to alert other employees of the complained-of conditions). *But see St. Luke's, supra* note 11 (TV interview in which employee disparaged employer's services was not protected).

[13] *See* CKS Tool & Eng'g, Inc., 332 NLRB 1578, 168 LRRM 1047 (2000) (employee who protested employer's position regarding employee productivity at meeting called by employer was protesting on behalf of co-workers with whom he had previously discussed issue and appealing to his co-workers to support protest, and therefore his actions constituted concerted activity); Caval Tool Div., Chromalloy Gas Turbine Corp., 331 NLRB 858, 168 LRRM 1067 (2000), *enforced,* 262 F.3d 184, 168 LRRM 2180 (2d Cir. 2001) (employee who questioned and commented on employer's proposed change in company's break policy at employer-called meeting was espousing cause of co-workers and was therefore engaged in concerted activity); 127 Restaurant Corp., 331 NLRB 269, 170 LRRM 1447 (2000) (employee expressing concerns about working conditions at meeting called by employer engaged in concerted activity); Bethlehem Temple Learning Ctr., Inc., 330 NLRB 1177, 167 LRRM 1006 (2000) (employees raising concerns about signing noncompetition agreements at employer-called meeting engaged in concerted activity); *cf.* Mobil Exploration & Producing U.S., Inc. v. NLRB, 200 F.3d 230, 163 LRRM 2387 (5th Cir. 1999), *enforcing* 325 NLRB 176, 156 LRRM 1273 (1997) (employee's statements to group of employees during work break qualified as concerted activity).

[14] *See* Arlington Elec. Inc., 332 NLRB 845, 166 LRRM 1049 (2000) (employee who discussed formation of employee association with co-workers was seeking to initiate, induce, or prepare for group activities by distributing flyers critical of employer's insurance coverage and was therefore engaged in protected concerted activity). *But see* New York New York, LLC v. NLRB, 313 F.3d 585, 171 LRRM 2651 (D.C. Cir. 2002) (denied enforcement of Board's decision that employees of employer's contractor working on employer's property engaged in protected concerted activity when they distributed handbills to customers on employer's property).

In *Petrochem Insulation*,[15] the Board held that petitioning state governmental agencies with objections to environmental standards of employer contracts is protected area-standards activity within the meaning of the mutual aid or protection provision of Section 7 of the Act. According to the Board, working conditions may include the safety and health of all employees who may eventually be employed at a particular worksite.

The Board continues to hold that employee conduct on behalf of the employees of another employer who are engaged in protected concerted activity is itself concerted activity under Section 7.[16] Similarly, in some, but not all, circumstances, employee protests regarding nonemployees such as supervisors can constitute concerted activity.[17]

C. Employer Interference With Section 7 Rights: Section 8(a)(1)

3. *Motive Not an Essential Element of Section 8(a)(1) Violations*

The Board continues to adhere to its position that motive is not an essential element of a Section 8(a)(1) violation.[18] The Board con-

---

[15] 330 NLRB 47, 163 LRRM 1276 (1999), *enforced,* 240 F.3d 26, 166 LRRM 2433 (D.C. Cir.), *cert. denied,* 534 U.S. 992 (2001).

[16] *See* Office Depot, 330 NLRB 640, 163 LRRM 1169 (2000) (employee's use of term "scab" to person crossing picket line of employees of another employer was expression of support for striking employees and amounted to making common cause with protected concerted activity of those employees); Electronic Data Sys. Corp., 331 NLRB 343, 164 LRRM 1211 (2000) (employee engaged in protected concerted activity when she solicited fellow employees via e-mail to support striking employees of another employer).

[17] *See* Trompler, Inc., 335 NLRB 478, 172 LRRM 1144 (2001), *enforced,* 338 F.3d 747, 172 LRRM 3201 (7th Cir. 2003) (employee walkout because of supervisor's conduct was protected concerted activity); Southern Pride Catfish, 331 NLRB 618, 171 LRRM 1369 (2000) (employee walkout over discharge of supervisor, who was fired because employees she supervised wore union T-shirts, was concerted activity); Senior Citizens Coordinating Council of Riverbay Cmty. Inc., 330 NLRB 1100, 166 LRRM 1074 (2000), *enforced,* 2001 U.S. App. LEXIS 7809 (2d Cir. 2001) (employee actions in seeking to replace executive director constituted protected concerted activity). For complete treatment of this subject, see Section III.A.3. [Other Concerted Activity; Protected Concerted Activity: In General; Employee Activity for "Other Mutual Aid or Protection"], *infra.*

[18] *See* Pratt Towers, Inc., 338 NLRB 61, 170 LRRM 1533 (2002); Eckert Fire Protection, Inc., 332 NLRB 198 (2000); Multi-Ad Servs., Inc., 331 NLRB 1226, 165 LRRM 1157 (2000), *enforced,* 255 F.3d 363, 167 LRRM 2450 (7th Cir. 2001); SOS Staffing Servs., Inc., 331 NLRB 815, 165 LRRM 1011 (2000); Medic One, Inc., 331 NLRB 464 (2000); Yoshi's Japanese Restaurant, Inc., 330 NLRB 1339 (2000); Westwood Health Care Ctr., 330 NLRB 935, 163 LRRM 1225 (2000).

tinues to apply the principles set forth in *NLRB v. Burnup & Sims.*[19] When an employer discharges an employee for misconduct arising out of a protected activity, the employer has the burden of showing that it held an honest belief that the employee engaged in serious misconduct. Once the employer establishes that it acted based upon such belief, the burden shifts to the general counsel to affirmatively establish that the misconduct did not in fact occur.[20] The courts follow this rule as well.[21]

D. Union Restraint and Coercion—Section 8(b)(1)(A)

2. *Nature of the Violation*

The Board continues to hold that it is not a violation of Section 8(b)(1)(A) for a union to enforce its own valid rules against its members.[22] The Board, however, continues to find that certain attempts by unions to discipline their members violate Section 8(b)(1)(A).[23]

---

[19]379 U.S. 21, 57 LRRM 2385 (1964). *See* Belle of Sioux City, L.P., 333 NLRB 98, 171 LRRM 1432 (2001) (distinguishing discrimination and pretext cases where motive "is the very point of the analytical methodology").

[20]Accurate Tool Mfg., Inc., 335 NLRB 1096 (2001) (employer's good faith belief in misconduct no defense when general counsel proves misconduct did not occur); Pepsi-Cola Co., 330 NLRB 474, 164 LRRM 1013 (2000), *supplemented by* 333 NLRB 87 (2001) (case remanded to judge for explicit determination of whether employer affirmatively established that it had honest belief that employee made statements calling for work stoppage and whether general counsel carried its burden of showing that employee did not engage in misconduct).

[21]*See* Valmont Indus. Inc., 244 F.3d 454, 166 LRRM 2782 (5th Cir. 2001); Webco Indus., Inc., 217 F.3d 1306, 164 LRRM 2845 (10th Cir. 2000), *relying on Burnup & Sims, Inc.*, 379 U.S. at 22–23.

[22]Steelworkers Local 9292, 336 NLRB 52, 168 LRRM 1492 (2001); Teamsters Local 710, 333 NLRB 1303, 171 LRRM 1432 (2001); Service Employees Local 254, 332 NLRB 1118, 165 LRRM 1321 (2000); Office & Professional Employees Local 251, 331 NLRB 1118,1417, 165 LRRM 1089 (2000).

[23]NLRB v. Teamsters Local 439, 175 F.3d 1173, 161 LRRM 2571 (9th Cir. 1999) (Act prohibits union from disciplining member for reporting co-worker misconduct, when member is required to do so by employer); Auto Workers v. NLRB, 168 F.3d 509, 160 LRRM 2955 (D.C. Cir. 1999) (union rule that discriminates between members and nonmembers in processing of grievances violates Act); Denver Newspaper & Graphics Communications Local 22, 338 NLRB 130, 171 LRRM 1069 (2002) (union violated §8(b)(1)(A) by causing denial of overtime opportunities for member who failed to pay union fines and by filing internal disciplinary charges against member in retaliation for member's filing of Board charge against union); Operating Eng'rs Local 3, 331 NLRB 369, 164 LRRM 1217 (2000).

The Board held that a union may not enforce a one calendar month annual window-period limitation on the filing of *Beck* objections against members who resign their union membership later in the calendar year, but rather, must give the resigning member a reasonable time in which to assert a *Beck* objection after resigning.[24]

In *Randell Warehouse of Arizona*,[25] the Board overruled its decision in *Pepsi-Cola Bottling Co.*[26] and held that union photographing or videotaping of employees engaged in protected activities during an election campaign, without more, does not necessarily interfere with employees' Section 7 rights. The D.C. Circuit refused to enforce the Board's order, holding that it failed to explain why it departed not only from its holding in *Pepsi-Cola Bottling Co.*, but also from its holding in *Mike Yurosek & Son, Inc.*,[27] where union representatives' threats toward employees, concurrent with union photography of employee activity, were found to be unlawful.[28]

The Board's decision in *Metropolitan Regional Council of Philadelphia & Vicinity*[29] held that union picketers' provocative statements, concurrent with union videotaping and photography, would reasonably tend to restrain and coerce employees' exercise of their Section 7 rights. The majority of the Board adhered to its decision in *Randell Warehouse of Arizona*,[30] and rejected the dissent's argument that photography or videotaping alone would interfere with employees' Section 7 rights.

The Board does not require evidence of unlawful intent to support a finding of a violation of Section 8(b)(1)(A). Under appropriate circumstances, an implied threat may constitute a violation.[31]

---

[24]Transport Workers of Am., 329 NLRB 543, 169 LRRM 1344 (1999).

[25]328 NLRB 1034, 161 LRRM 1265 (1999), *enforcement denied and remanded,* 252 F.3d 445, 167 LRRM 2340 (D.C. Cir. 2001).

[26]289 NLRB 736, 128 LRRM 1275 (1988).

[27]292 NLRB 1074, 130 LRRM 1308 (1989).

[28]Randell Warehouse of Ariz. v. NLRB, 252 F.3d 445, 167 LRRM 2340 (D.C. Cir. 2001).

[29]335 NLRB 814, 169 LRRM 1498 (2001), *enforced,* 2002 WL 31424666, 171 LRRM 2128 (3d Cir. 2002); *see also* Teamsters Local 890, 335 NLRB 686, 168 LRRM 1347 (2001) (union's videotaping of replacement workers' license plates and calling out license plate numbers with bullhorn was violation of the Act).

[30]*See* Randell Warehouse of Ariz., *supra* note 28.

[31]*See* Teamsters Local 122 (Busch & Co.), 334 NLRB 1190 (2001) (union member violated §8(b)(1)(A) when he impliedly threatened employer's retail service supervisor that another union member might attempt to sleep with supervisor's young daughter); *see also* Healthcare Employees Local 339, 333 NLRB 1399, 171

National Ass'n of Letter Carriers Local 3825[32] involved a charge that the union violated Section 8(b)(1)(A) by implicitly threatening, in a union newsletter, to refuse to represent employees who make complaints against union officers and who cooperate in employer investigations of union officers. The Board concluded, however, that the newsletter, which criticized union-member informants as ungrateful, and contained a statement that "what goes around comes around," did not constitute an implied threat of retaliation in violation of Section 8(b)(1)(A).

E. "Freedom of Speech"—Section 8(c) in General

1. *Threat or Prophecy?*

The Board and courts continue to consider the effect of statements made during a union election campaign from the employee's perspective, taking into account "the economic dependence of the employees on their employers, and the necessary tendency of the former, because of that relationship, to pick up intended implications of the latter that might be more readily dismissed by a more disinterested ear."[33] Statements beyond mere expression of opinion

---

LRRM 1214 (2001) (union representative violated §8(b)(1)(A) when he threatened to have bargaining unit employees outsourced during contract negotiations after they filed decertification petition, given employer's history of attempts to outsource employees).

[32]333 NLRB 343, 166 LRRM 1217 (2001).

[33]NLRB v. St. Francis Healthcare Ctr., 212 F.3d 945, 164 LRRM 2324 (6th Cir. 2000) (employer's chief executive officer unlawfully threatened closure of healthcare facility when he predicted that no entity would affiliate with facility if employees elected union, where only likely affiliate had expressed concerns about possible unionization of facility and where, from employees' perspective, CEO's exaggeration of objective evidence was material); NLRB v. General Fabrications Corp., 222 F.3d 218, 164 LRRM 2974 (6th Cir. 2000) (employer unlawfully threatened changes in work rule enforcement); Multicraft Int'l, 328 NLRB 851, 161 LRRM 1296 (1999) (employer that provides assembly services to company that manufactures dashboards for Mercedes automobile violated §8(a)(1) when its general manager told employee that company had contract with Mercedes that would not let a union happen, and if a union were formed, company would lose its contract with Mercedes, employees would leave, and employees would lose their jobs); ITT Auto. v. NLRB, 188 F.3d 375, 161 LRRM 3132 (6th Cir. 1999) (statements did not merit §8(c) protection because they reasonably tended to coerce employees, where supervisors' economic predictions that after unionization plant might close if it became unprofitable or that strikes might occur as result of employer's refusal to give in to union demands were not supported by objective facts that "did not refer to matters over which [the employer] exercised no control"); Wallace Int'l de Puerto Rico, 328 NLRB 29, 161 LRRM 1123 (1999) (employer unlawfully threatened

continue to be found to be outside Section 8(c) protection,[34] although employers remain entitled to freely express the opinion that the company does not need a union.[35]

An employer violated Section 8(a)(1) when, following the announcement of a union election victory, one manager told his employees "you're going to regret this all year," where the Board viewed the statement in the context of other unlawful statements, and based its decision on the totality of the relevant circumstances.[36]

Similarly, an employer's inquiry to an employee as to how a union-organizing meeting went constituted interrogation and created an impression of surveillance and, under all the circumstances and coupled with other statements by the owner, violated Section 8(a)(1).[37]

---

employees by showing video suggesting that plant closure would result if they voted for union).

[34]*See, e.g.*, Sheridan Manor Nursing Home, Inc. v. NLRB, 225 F.3d 248, 165 LRRM 2132 (2d Cir. 2000) (Board reasonably found employer violated §8(a)(1) when, one week before scheduled vote on ratification of tentative labor contract, it distributed to employees memo that criticized exclusion of nonunion members from ratification process, despite contention that memo was employer speech protected by §8(c). The court reasoned that the memo, which used phrases such as "you should object now and refuse being on membership board if you have not already," constituted conduct beyond mere expression of opinion and beyond §8(c) protection. However, the court also questioned whether protection of §8(c) is limited only to speech that is unrelated to unfair labor practice charge) *See also* Colden Hills, Inc., 337 NLRB 560, 170 LRRM 1057 (2002) (during an interview with a union organizer/applicant, employer's statement that she did not think union members could work for nonunion companies did not constitute violation of §8(a)(1) since she merely stated her opinion).

[35]Pacific Custom Materials, Inc., 327 NLRB 75, 165 LRRM 1132 (1998) (employer lawfully maintained handbook stating that there was no need for union at company, that all its employees were treated fairly, and that "an employee who would want to become a member of union in the future should expect nothing more than an employee who is not a union member").

[36]Ebenezer Rail Car Servs., 333 NLRB 167, 166 LRRM 1204 (2001).

[37]Fred'k Wallace & Son, Inc., 331 NLRB 914, 171 LRRM 1388 (2000); Metfab, Inc., 344 NLRB No. 6 (2005) (employer statement that he knew how the election would turn out, down to the precise number of employees who would vote against the union, would lead an employee to assume that the employer was monitoring the union sympathies of its individual employees; it is irrelevant that the employer reached his conclusion by lawful means rather than through actual surveillance because it is the impression conveyed to the employee that violated the Act). *But see* TVI, Inc., 337 NLRB 1039, 170 LRRM 1366 (2002) (Board affirmed without discussion ALJ's holding that employer did not create impression of surveillance when observing union supporters' unruly behavior in employer's store and commenting on what she had seen within hearing range of employees involved in organizing campaign).

On the other hand, the Board in *Curwood, Inc.*[38] found that the employer did not violate the Act when it conveyed to employees that "[b]eing unionized is also viewed negatively by our customers. They are concerned about potential work stoppages and product interruptions.... That is why we say remaining union-free affects our business and our livelihood."[39] The Board held that these statements were not threatening and merely conveyed concerns maintained by the employer's customers.

2. *The Outer Limit of Employer Speech*

Employers cannot solicit employees individually to participate in an employer campaign video. They can, however, solicit employees to be in a campaign video if the solicitation is in the form of a general announcement that discloses that the employees' pictures will be used in the video, includes assurances that participation is voluntary and will not result in rewards or benefits and that nonparticipation will not result in reprisals, and is undertaken in an atmosphere free from serious or pervasive unfair labor practices.[40]

II. ORGANIZATIONAL AND PREELECTION ACTIVITY

A. In General: Relation of Unfair Labor Practices to "Laboratory Conditions" Required for Elections

The Board addressed an employer grant of wage increases during an organizational effort in *Overnite Transportation Co.*[41] At the height of the union's organizing effort, in what the Board referred to as a "carrot and stick campaign," the employer granted its unrepresented workers an unprecedented wage increase just months after granting their normal annual pay raises. Simultaneously, it announced in the company newsletter that "unfortunately" employees at the four facilities that had elected union representation "will not get these

---

[38]339 NLRB 1137, 173 LRRM 1149 (2003). *See also* Enjo Architectural Millwork, 340 NLRB No. 162, 173 LRRM 1580 (2003) (finding that there is nothing inherently unlawful about asking employees to "think twice" about unionization in light of employer's lack of success in the market).

[39]*Curwood*, 339 NLRB at 1137, 173 LRRM at 1150.

[40]Allegheny Ludlum Corp., 333 NLRB 734, 166 LRRM 1353 (2001), *enforced*, 301 F.3d 167, 170 LRRM 2923 (3d Cir. 2002).

[41]329 NLRB 990, 166 LRRM 1101 (1999).

pay increases," but will "have to wait for negotiations." This, coupled with a variety of other violations, led the Board to find a bargaining order to be appropriate. The Fourth Circuit denied enforcement of the bargaining order and remanded the case for new elections.[42] The court further held that the Board's decision was not supported by sufficient evidence to justify the extraordinary relief of a bargaining order.

The Board continues to apply the policy that conduct violative of Section 8(a)(1) is, a fortiori, conduct that interferes with the exercise of a free and untrammeled choice in an election, except where "the misconduct is de minimis: 'such that it is virtually impossible to conclude' that the election outcome has been affected."[43] In deciding whether misconduct could have affected the results of an election, the Board considers the number of violations, their severity, the extent of dissemination, the size of the unit, closeness of the election, proximity of the conduct to the election date, and the number of unit employees affected. For example, in *Freund Baking Co.,*[44] the Board ruled that the maintenance of an employee handbook, which prohibited employees from discussing confidential information (that employees could reasonably construe as prohibiting them from discussing wages, hours, and other terms and conditions of employment) with anyone outside the company, violates Section 8(a)(1) of the Act, and is objectionable conduct, notwithstanding a substantial margin of victory for the employer.[45]

---

[42]Overnite Transp. Co. v. NLRB, 280 F.3d 417, 169 LRRM 2469 (4th Cir. 2002), *denying enforcement and remanding* 329 NLRB 990, 166 LRRM 1101 (1999).

[43]Bon Appetit Mgmt. Co., 334 NLRB 1042, 169 LRRM 1068 (2001), quoting Sea Breeze Health Care Ctr., 331 NLRB 1131, 1145, 168 LRRM 1418 (2000).

[44]336 NLRB 847, 168 LRRM 1310 (2001).

[45]*See also* IRIS U.S.A., Inc., 336 NLRB 1013, 169 LRRM 1144 (2001) (Board found employer violated §8(a)(1) by maintaining confidentiality provision in its employee handbook and that violation was more egregious than in other cases because language of handbook provision stated "any doubts about the confidentiality of information should be resolved in favor of confidentiality"); *see also* Double Eagle Hotel & Casino, 341 NLRB No. 17, 174 LRRM 1088 (2004) (Board found employer violated §8(a)(1) of the Act by maintaining confidentiality provision that specifically listed "disciplinary information, grievance/complaint information, performance evaluations, salary information, salary grade, types of pay increases and termination date of employees" as confidential information for which any breach would lead to disciplinary action up to and including termination).

In *Safeway, Inc.*,[46] the Board distinguished *Freund Baking Co.*[47] and held that where there has been an incumbent union during the critical period, the employer's maintenance of a confidentiality rule will not be considered objectionable conduct requiring a rerun of a decertification election. In assuming, arguendo, that the confidentiality rule was overbroad, the Board concluded that the maintenance of the rule could not reasonably have affected the results of the election. Further, the Board in *Safeway* noted that the union had been in place for 3 years and had successfully negotiated at least one collective bargaining agreement. Therefore, to the extent that any employee was confused about his or her statutory rights, the "union was ideally placed to advise employees of their rights."[48]

In *Delta Brands, Inc.*,[49] the Board reinforced its decision in *Safeway, Inc.*[50] holding that the employer's rule restricting workplace solicitation was not objectionable conduct requiring the rerun of an election because the union failed to establish that (1) the employer brought the rule to the employees' attention during the critical period; (2) the employer enforced the rule; or (3) employees were actually influenced in voting or deterred by the rule from engaging in Section 7 activity. Citing *Safeway, Inc.*, the Board held that the mere maintenance of an arguably overbroad rule within its policy manual is not a basis to set aside an election.

B. Unlawful Employer Conduct

1. *Employer's Restrictions on Union and Employee Activity on Employer's Property*

a. Basic Presumptions

The Board continues to hold that employer no-distribution rules are presumptively valid only if employees have the right to distribute union literature in nonworking areas on company property when neither they nor the employee recipients are expected to be actively working.[51] The Board also requires that valid no-distribution rules

---

[46]338 NLRB 525, 171 LRRM 1169 (2002).
[47]*Supra* note 44.
[48]*Safeway*, *supra* note 46, 171 LRRM at 1171.
[49]344 NLRB No. 10 (2005).
[50]*Supra* note 46.
[51]Eby-Brown Co. L.P., NLRB 496, 168 LRRM 1165 (1999).

allow for distribution of union literature in nonwork or mixed-use areas during nonwork times.[52]

b. Rights of Employees Over Nonemployees

The Board and courts continue to disagree over the rights of employee versus nonemployee organizers. When a union does not have a reasonably effective means of communicating with employees away from the employees' job sites, Section 7 compels the employer to allow nonemployee union organizers access to its property for organizational purposes.[53]

In *Sandusky Mall Co. v. NLRB*,[54] the Sixth Circuit rejected the Board's finding that union organizers were engaged in protected activity. Union organizers had attempted to handbill mall patrons because one mall tenant had hired a nonunion contractor, and had threatened to handbill another tenant for the same reason. The owner of the mall permitted distribution by a charitable organization, but prohibited union handbilling. The court distinguished between nonorganizational solicitation by "charitable, civic and even commercial organizations to enter a mall for solicitations, displays, and presentations,"[55] and handbilling by nonemployee union organizers, based on the manner in which the mall wished to present itself to the public. In concluding that there was no discrimination, the court reaffirmed its earlier decision in *Cleveland Real Estate Partners v. NLRB*[56] that "alleged 'discriminatory' conduct in allowing solicitation and handbilling required that the 'discrimination be among comparable groups or activities' and that the activities themselves under *consideration* must be *'comparable.'*"[57]

In *Albertson's, Inc. v. NLRB*,[58] the Sixth Circuit held that an employer does not unlawfully discriminate against unions by allowing charities to distribute information and solicit its customers on its

---

[52]UPS, Inc. 331 NLRB 338, 164 LRRM 1200 (2000).

[53]Nabors Alaska Drilling, Inc. v. NLRB, 190 F.3d 1008, 162 LRRM 2197 (9th Cir. 1999).

[54]242 F.3d 682, 166 LRRM 2641 (6th Cir. 2001), *denying enforcement to* 329 NLRB 618, 162 LRRM 1191 (1999).

[55]*Id.* at 690.

[56]95 F.3d 457, 153 LRRM 2338 (6th Cir. 1996), *denying enforcement to* 316 NLRB 158, 149 LRRM 1037 (1995).

[57]*Sandusky Mall, supra* note 54 242 F.3d at 690.

[58]301 F.3d 441, 170 LRRM 2769 (6th Cir. 2002), *denying enforcement to* 332 NLRB 1132, 166 LRRM 1003 (2000).

property while prohibiting unions from doing the same. The general rule, said the court, is that an employer is not required to allow solicitation or distribution by nonemployee union organizers on the employer's property. The court rejected the Board's argument that the general rule is that "an employer . . . [that] denies a union access to its property while regularly allowing other individuals, groups and organizations to use its premises for various activities unlawfully discriminates against the union solicitation."[59] To the contrary, the court held, "discrimination" means "favoring one union over another, or allowing employer-related information while barring similar union-related information."[60] Because there was no evidence that the employer favored one union over another, or that the employer itself engaged in activities that it denied the unions, its actions did not violate the NLRA.

In *Wolgast Corp. v. NLRB*,[61] the Sixth Circuit held that its decisions in *Sandusky Mall* and *Albertson's* did not allow the extension of property rights to prevent union access for representational purposes. In enforcing the Board's decision, the court said that a general contractor with an asserted property interest was obliged to yield its interest to the subcontracted employees' Section 7 right to be represented. The union representative in this case did not seek access to organize employees, handbill patrons, boycott, or other similar activities addressed in *Sandusky Mall* and *Albertson's.* Rather, access was sought as the direct representative of the subcontractor's employees to check on a new employee and investigate the safety of scaffolding. These activities were authorized by the collective bargaining agreement, and the contractor's property rights could not prevail over the employees' representational right.

In *6 West Ltd. Corp. v. NLRB*,[62] the Seventh Circuit held that employee solicitation of other employees at a restaurant was not protected activity, although the restaurant had in the past permitted employees to sell Christmas cookies, hand-made Christmas ornaments, hand-painted water bottles, theater tickets, and raffle tickets.[63] The court extended the distinction drawn by the Sixth Circuit

---

[59] *Id.*, 301 F.3d at 446.

[60] *Id.* at 450.

[61] 349 F.3d 250, 173 LRRM 2416 (6th Cir. 2003), *cert. denied,* 124 S. Ct. 1656, 174 LRRM 2608 (2004).

[62] 237 F.3d 767, 166 LRRM 2221 (7th Cir. 2001), *denying enforcement to* 330 NLRB 527, 163 LRRM 1113 (2000).

[63] *Id.*

in *Sandusky Mall Co.*[64] and *Cleveland Real Estate Partners*[65] to include employees engaging in "an activity as innocent as the sale of Girl Scout cookies or the sale of hand-blown Christmas ornaments during the yuletide season," as opposed to efforts by some employees to organize others.[66]

In *Weis Markets, Inc. v. NLRB*,[67] the Seventh Circuit refused to enforce that portion of a Board order that found it unlawful for an employer to order nonemployee organizers off property (in which the employer held an easement) adjacent to its retail store. The court found that under state law, the employer had the right to evict organizers because they were not members of the public who might benefit the employer's enterprise.

In *NLRB v. Calkins*,[68] the Ninth Circuit enforced a Board order prohibiting a stand-alone grocery store from threatening nonemployee union organizers with arrest for trespassing on its parking lot and walkway. A California statute prohibited owners of shopping malls and general access supermarkets from excluding speech activity on their private adjacent sidewalks and parking lots. The court rejected the employer's assertion that the California law was preempted by the need for uniform application of Section 7 access rights across the country. Because the California statute enhanced Section 7 protection and did not conflict with or frustrate the federal scheme, the court held that the Board's ruling, which granted more union accommodation than federal law requires, was rational and consistent with the Act.[69]

However, in *Waremart Foods v. NLRB*,[70] the D.C. Circuit held that under California law, nonemployee union organizers have no right to distribute literature on a stand-alone grocery store's private property. The court's holding reflects its disagreement with the Ninth

[64]242 F.3d 682, 166 LRRM 2641 (6th Cir. 2001), *rev'g* 392 NLRB 618, 162 LRRM 1191 (1999).

[65]95 F.3d 457, 153 LRRM 2338 (6th Cir. 1996), *denying enforcement to* 316 NLRB 158, 149 LRRM 1037 (1995).

[66]*6 West*, *supra* note 62, 237 F.3d at 780, 166 LRRM at 2229–30.

[67]265 F.3d 239, 168 LRRM 2265 (4th Cir. 2001), *modifying* 325 NLRB 871, 161 LRRM 1215 (1998).

[68]187 F.3d 1080, 161 LRRM 3121 (9th Cir. 1999), *cert. denied*, 529 U.S. 1098, 164 LRRM 2256 (2000).

[69]*Id.*, 187 F.3d at 1095, 161 LRRM at 3131–32.

[70]354 F.3d 870, 174 LRRM 2010 (D.C. Cir. 2004).

Circuit's holding that picketing and handbilling on private property by union organizers are protected activities under California law.[71]

In *Glendale Associates, Ltd.*,[72] the Board allowed the operator of a shopping center to enforce its rule requiring identification of handbillers prior to their engaging in handbilling activities. The Board based its decision on the fact that under California state law the exercise of speech and petitioning rights in private shopping centers is subject to reasonable time, place, and manner regulations. The Board did rule, however, that the mall operator could not regulate the content of the handbills.

In *Equitable Life Assurance Society of the U.S. dba Fashion Valley Shopping Center*,[73] the Board found that a retail shopping mall violated Section 8(a)(1) by adopting and maintaining a rule prohibiting consumer boycott handbilling. The mall adopted rules and regulations applicable to all individuals and organizations seeking to engage in expressive activities at the mall. The rule at issue prohibited speech "urging or encouraging in any manner" customers to boycott any one of the shopping center's stores. The Board held that the rule constituted an unlawful content-based restriction on speech (in violation of California state law) which had the purpose and effect of shielding "the [shopping center's] tenants . . . from otherwise lawful consumer boycott handbilling." Maintaining such a rule violated Section 8(a)(1) of the Act, as did the shopping center's attempt to enforce the rule upon union members and supporters who were engaged in handbilling in front of one of the shopping center's stores.

The Board and circuit courts disagree on how employees of subcontractors, who regularly and exclusively work on a certain property owner's premises, should be treated for the purpose of determining their right to solicit and distribute on the owner's premises. In *New York New York Hotel, LLC*,[74] the Board held that such employ-

---

[71] *See NLRB v. Calkins, supra* note 68.

[72] 335 NLRB 27, 169 LRRM 1328 (2001), *enforcement granted by* 347 F.3d 1145, 173 LRRM 2551 (9th Cir. 2003); *accord* Equitable Life Assurance Soc'y dba Fashion Valley Shopping Center, 343 NLRB No. 57, 176 LRRM 1181 (2004) (following *Glendale Associates*). *See also* Union of Needletrades, Industrial & Textile Employees [UNITE] v. Superior Court of Los Angeles County, 56 Cal. App. 4th 996, 155 LRRM 3047 (1997) (finding it proper for shopping centers to learn in advance identity of participants because this is information that case law had held could be taken into consideration in deciding whether to require insurance).

[73] 343 NLRB No. 57, 176 LRRM 1181 (2004).

[74] 334 NLRB 762, 169 LRRM 1502 (2001), *enforcement denied by* 313 F.3d 585, 171 LRRM 2651 (D.C. Cir. 2002).

ees should be treated as employees of the property owner. The D.C. Circuit disagreed however, and denied enforcement of the Board's order.[75] The court remanded the case and directed the Board to consider whether, in light of *Lechmere, Inc. v. NLRB*,[76] these employees should enjoy the same rights as the owner's employees, by balancing the employees' Section 7 rights with the employer's right to control the use of its premises and run its business.

The Board continues to hold that employers cannot prohibit on-site solicitation by off-duty employees in nonwork areas.[77] In *First Healthcare Corp. dba Hillhaven Highland House*,[78] the Board announced new solicitation rules for off-duty employees from another facility of the same employer. The Board held that employees assigned to one employer site who visit another of the employer's worksites to engage in solicitation and distribution activities have nonderivative Section 7 access rights, for organizational purposes. Although an employer may have heightened private property-right concerns when off-site (as opposed to on-site) employees seek access to its property in order to exercise Section 7 rights, the Board held that, on balance, the Section 7 organizational rights of off-site employees entitle them to access the outside, nonworking areas of an employer's property. The Board did recognize, however, that an employer might be able to establish business reasons to regulate such activity that are different than the justifications necessary to restrict on-site employee access.

c. No-Solicitation and No-Distribution Rules Generally

The Board and the courts continue distinguishing between employee solicitation and distribution of literature. Solicitation by

---

[75]313 F.3d 585, 171 LRRM 2651 (D.C. Cir. 2002). *See also* NLRB v. Pneu Elec. Inc., 309 F.3d 843, 170 LRRM 3249 (5th Cir. 2002) (remanding case to Board under similar circumstances).

[76]502 U.S. 527, 139 LRRM 2225 (1992).

[77]TeleTech Holdings, Inc., 333 NLRB 402, 166 LRRM 1241 (2001).

[78]336 NLRB 646, 168 LRRM 1368 (2001), *enforcement granted by* 344 F.3d 523, 173 LRRM 2296 (6th Cir. 2003); *accord* ITT Indus., Inc., 341 NLRB No. 118, 174 LRRM 1449 (2004) (Board applied *First Healthcare* and found that the employer violated §8(a)(1) of the Act by denying access to off-site employees handbilling in its parking lot); Smithfield Packing Co., 344 NLRB No. 1 (2004). *See also* Section II.B.1.g. [Organizational and Preelection Activity; Unlawful Employer Conduct; Employer's Restriction on Union and Employee Activity on Employer's Property; No-Access Rules], *infra*.

employees can be prohibited only during working time,[79] although employers cannot prohibit employees from discussing unionization during working times if other work time discussions are not prohibited.[80] Employers may lawfully prohibit distribution of literature by employees in work areas at any time.[81] Employers may not prohibit distribution in nonwork areas, or in mixed areas, during nonworking time.[82]

The Board continues treating employee efforts to obtain signatures on authorization cards as solicitation rather than distribution of literature.[83]

(1) Presumptions of Validity

Recent decisions confirm that a presumptively valid rule prohibiting solicitation may still be unlawful if it is promulgated or enforced in a discriminatory manner.[84] An invalid rule violates the Act even if the rule is not enforced.[85]

(2) Facial Validity of Rule

Employers may not draw no-solicitation rules so broadly as to encompass nonworking time; such a rule is presumptively unlawful.[86]

---

[79]Valmont Indus. v. NLRB, 244 F.3d 454, 166 LRRM 2782 (5th Cir. 2001). *But see* NLRB v. Pneu Elec. Inc., 309 F.3d 843, 170 LRRM 3249 (5th Cir. 2002) (presumed validity of prohibition on solicitation during working time evaporates when the rule is applied discriminatorily).

[80]Frazier Indus. Co., 328 NLRB 717, 163 LRRM 1024 (1999), *enforced,* 213 F.3d 750, 164 LRRM 2516 (D.C. Cir. 2000).

[81]UPS, Inc., 327 NLRB 317, 160 LRRM 1148 (1998), *aff'd,* 228 F.3d 772, 165 LRRM 2358 (6th Cir. 2000); RCN Corp., 333 NLRB 295 (2001); *see also* Adtranz, ABB Daimler-Benz Transp., 331 NLRB 291, 167 LRRM 1196 (2000), *vacated on other grounds,* 253 F.3d 19 (D.C. Cir. 2001) (evaluation of whether e-mail rules represent unlawful solicitation or distribution policies is analogous to well-established Board principles involving bulletin boards or telephones).

[82]*Id.*; UPS, Inc., 331 NLRB 338, 164 LRRM 1200 (2000).

[83]Mid-Mountain Foods, Inc., 332 NLRB 229 n.2, 168 LRRM 1450 (2000), *enforcement granted by* 269 F.3d 1075, 169 LRRM 2528 (D.C. Cir. 2001).

[84]Webco Indus. v. NLRB, 217 F.3d 1306, 164 LRRM 2845 (10th Cir. 2000); Wexler Meat Co., 331 NLRB 240, 170 LRRM 1264 (2000).

[85]Beverly Health & Rehab. Svcs., 332 NLRB 347, 170 LRRM 1273 (2000), *enforced,* 297 F.3d 468, 170 LRRM 2577 (6th Cir. 2002).

[86]*Wexler Meat Co., supra* note 84; Waste Mgmt. of Palm Beach, 329 NLRB 198, 167 LRRM 1059 (1999) (rule prohibiting solicitation and distribution of literature during nonworking time in nonworking areas is facially invalid); Eby-Brown Co. L.P., 328 NLRB 496, 168 LRRM 1165 (1999).

In *Flamingo Hilton-Laughlin*,[87] the Board held that the employer's no-solicitation policy was overbroad to the extent that it covered off-duty employees in public areas of the employer's property. The Board refused, however, to find that it was overbroad to the extent that it covered gaming areas, because the retail department store "selling area" exception covers gaming areas.

In *Cooper Health Systems*,[88] the Board held that a hospital's prohibition against solicitation in all work areas was presumptively invalid because it applied to nonworking time in working areas other than immediate patient care areas.[89] Further, the hospital failed to show that solicitation in working areas that are not immediate patient care areas would either disrupt care or disturb patients, a showing that is required to justify the exception for health care institutions.

In *Washington Fruit & Produce Co.*,[90] the Board reversed an administrative law judge's finding that the employer violated its facially valid no-solicitation rule by disciplining employees who talked about the union during worktime but did not engage in conduct amounting to "solicit[ing] or promot[ing] support for any cause or organization" in violation of the employer's no-solicitation rule. Although the Board did not find that the employees engaged in prohibited "solicitation" or "promotion," it held that the employees' conduct "clearly fell within the ambit of the [no-solicitation] rule."

The Board and the courts continue to hold that describing the period in which solicitation and distribution is prohibited as "working hours" is ambiguous and, thus, overly broad and facially invalid.[91]

(3) Unlawful Promulgation or Enforcement

The Board continues holding that evidence of a discriminatory purpose in the adoption or application of a presumptively valid rule

---

[87]330 NLRB 287, 167 LRRM 1203 (1999).

[88]327 NLRB 1159, 167 LRRM 1288 (1999).

[89]*See also* Brockton Hosp., 333 NLRB 1367, 170 LRRM 1167 (2001), *enforced*, 2002 U.S. App. LEXIS 16521 (D.C. Cir. 2002), *cert. denied*, 537 U.S. 1105, 171 LRRM 2768 (2003) (finding policy unlawful that improperly expanded definition of immediate patient care areas that are off limits to solicitation and distribution to include "halls and corridors used by patients"); *accord* Jewish Home for the Elderly, 343 NLRB No. 117 (2004).

[90]343 NLRB No. 125 (2004).

[91]Nations Rent, Inc., 342 NLRB No. 19, 175 LRRM 1416 (2004); St. George Warehouse, Inc., 331 NLRB 454, 171 LRRM 1398 (2000), *enforced*, 261 F.3d 493 (3d Cir. 2001).

will rebut the presumption of validity.[92] In *Pioneer Hotel v. NLRB*,[93] the D.C. Circuit held that the employer's hotel policy prohibiting employees access to the hotel dining room 30 minutes before their shift was valid on its face. However, the policy could not be enforced selectively to block efforts to circulate petitions. Similarly, in *Cooper Health Systems*,[94] when evidence demonstrated that a hospital employer had previously allowed commercial and other nonunion solicitation and distribution in immediate patient care areas, it could not lawfully enforce its no-solicitation/no-distribution policy against union organizing activity by its employees in such areas.

In *Gallup, Inc.*,[95] the Board found unlawful the employer's promulgation and enforcement of a rule prohibiting solicitation and distribution in the workplace, as well as the use of e-mail to solicit for nonbusiness matters, where the rule was promulgated in response to a union organizing campaign. Promulgation of even facially valid rules is unlawful if they are in response to union organizational activities, unless the employer can show that the union's organizing efforts substantially disrupted work.

The Board and certain circuit courts continue to disagree regarding the rights of employees and nonemployees with respect to the enforcement of solicitation and distribution rules.[96] The Board

---

[92]Clinton Elecs., Corp., 332 NLRB 479, 169 LRRM 1314 (2000), *enforced in part and enforcement denied in part*, 284 F.3d 731, 169 LRRM 2934, *en banc reh'g denied*, 2002 U.S. App. LEXIS 12552 (7th Cir. 2002); Waste Mgmt. of Palm Beach, 329 NLRB 198, 167 LRRM 1059 (1999).

[93]182 F.3d 939, 161 LRRM 2785 (D.C. Cir. 1999).

[94]327 NLRB 1159, 167 LRRM 1288 (1999).

[95]334 NLRB 366, 173 LRRM 1485 (2001); Dillon Co., 340 NLRB No. 151, 173 LRRM 1517 (2003) (finding violation of Act where employer promulgated no-solicitation policy in response to union's organizing campaign).

[96]*See* discussion at Section II.B.1.h. [Organizational and Preelection Activity; Unlawful Employer Conduct; Employer's Restriction on Union and Employee Activity on Employer's Property; Prohibiting Protected Activity on Private Property Open to the Public], *infra*; *see also* 6 West Ltd. Corp. v. NLRB, 237 F.3d 767, 166 LRRM 2221 (7th Cir. 2001), *denying enforcement to* 330 NLRB 527, 163 LRRM 1113 (2000); Four B. Corp. v. NLRB, 163 F.3d 1177, 160 LRRM 2015 (10th Cir. 1998), *enforcing* 325 NLRB 186, 157 LRRM 1068 (1997); Lucile Salter Packard Children's Hosp. v. NLRB, 97 F.3d 583, 153 LRRM 2513 (D.C. Cir. 1996), *enforcing* 318 NLRB 433, 152 LRRM 1194 (1995); Guardian Indus. Corp. v. NLRB, 49 F.3d 317, 148 LRRM 2665 (7th Cir. 1995), *denying enforcement in part to* 313 NLRB 1275, 146 LRRM 1159 (1994); Riesbeck Food Mkts. v. NLRB, 91 F.3d 132, 153 LRRM 2320 (4th Cir. 1996) (unpublished decision); Fleming Cos., 336 NLRB 192, 171 LRRM 1527 (2001), *aff'd in part and reversed in part by* 349 F.3d 968, 173 LRRM 2621 (7th Cir. 2003).

takes the position that a violation of the Act occurs when an employer denies union representatives access while regularly allowing nonunion organizations to solicit and distribute literature on its property.[97] The Sixth Circuit disagrees, and held in *Sandusky Mall Co. v. NLRB*[98] that a mall owner's nonsolicitation policy could be applied differently to nonemployee union handbillers than to private, civic, and religious organizations' solicitations.

d. Implementation of Rules: Timing as an Element of Legality

The Board continues to consider the timing of implementation of a no-solicitation or no-distribution rule as an important factor in determining the rule's validity.[99]

e. Union Buttons and Insignia

The Board continues to adhere to its position that an employer may lawfully promulgate and enforce a rule prohibiting the wearing of union buttons and insignia only if "special circumstances" exist.[100]

---

[97]Cleveland Real Estate Partners, 316 NLRB 158, 149 LRRM 1037 (1995), *enforcement denied*, 95 F.3d 457, 153 LRRM 2338 (6th Cir. 1996).

[98]242 F.3d 682, 166 LRRM 2641 (6th Cir. 2001), *rev'g* 329 NLRB 618, 162 LRRM 1191 (1999). *See* factual summary of *Sandusky* and discussion of *Albertson's, Inc.* at Section II.B.1.b. [Organizational and Preelection Activity; Unlawful Employer Conduct; Employer's Restriction on Union and Employee Activity on Employer's Property; Rights of Employees Over Nonemployees], *supra*.

[99]Gallup, Inc., 334 NLRB 366, 173 LRRM 1485 (2001); *In re* Teledyne Advanced Materials, 332 NLRB 539, 166 LRRM 1033 (2000); Waste Mgmt. of Palm Beach, 329 NLRB 198, 167 LRRM 1059 (1999) (solicitation and distribution policy implemented in response to union organizing campaign violated Act).

[100]Mt. Clemens Gen. Hosp. v. NLRB, 328 F.3d 837, 172 LRRM 2513 (6th Cir. 2003) (buttons with inscription "F.O.T.," in a red circle with diagonal slash, held to be silent protest of forced overtime and was considered protected activity for nurses even without contemporaneous negotiations and where employer failed to show special circumstances prohibiting buttons in nonpatient care areas); NLRB v. St. Francis Healthcare Ctr., 212 F.3d 945, 957–60, 164 LRRM 2324 (6th Cir. 2000); Pioneer Hotel, Inc. v. NLRB, 182 F.3d 939, 161 LRRM 2785 (D.C. Cir. 1999); Albis Plastics, 335 NLRB 923, 170 LRRM 1545 (2001) (need to identify employees with safety training justifies prohibition of union stickers on caps); *In re* Eckert Fire Prot., Inc., 332 NLRB 198, 169 LRRM 1098 (2000); Pathmark Stores, Inc., 342 NLRB No. 31, 175 LRRM 1057 (2004) (special circumstance found where insignia bore message, "Local 342-50 says: Don't Cheat About the Meat," to protest employer's sale of prepackaged meat, instead of meat cut fresh in store, as ambiguity could reasonably lead customers to believe that the employer was cheating with regard to the meat it offered for sale); Komatsu Am. Corp., 342 NLRB No. 62, 175 LRRM 1209 (2004) (inflammatory comparison between employer's outsourcing

An employer's attempt to prohibit wearing union insignia will be difficult to justify if it is not based on an announced, generally applicable rule.[101] A rule banning unauthorized decals, including union stickers, from company hardhats has been upheld where there were special circumstances and employees were permitted to wear union insignia on their clothing.[102] An "overly broad" rule prohibiting the wearing of union insignia, however, was invalidated in its entirety where it was promulgated for unlawful retaliatory reasons, even though the employer asserted a "special circumstances" defense.[103] The Board considers the size of union insignia to be a significant factor in determining whether an employer may prohibit displaying the insignia.[104]

In *Lee v. NLRB*,[105] the Fourth Circuit rejected the Board's "special circumstances" analysis and held that a collectively bargained uniform policy that required employees to display both the employer and the union logos on their company uniform violated the Act. The Board had concluded that the uniform policy was lawful based on a balancing test examining whether "special circumstances" outweighed the Section 7 interests of employees.[106] The "special circum-

---

and Japan's "sneak attack" on United States: "December 7, 1941" and "History Repeats Negotiate Not Intimidate," worn on front and back of T-shirts, was a special circumstance justifying prohibition of T-shirts); *see also* Flamingo Hilton-Laughlin, 330 NLRB 287, 167 LRRM 1203 (1999) (customer exposure to union insignia alone is not special circumstance allowing employer to prohibit display of union insignia by employees).

[101]*See* Waterbury Hotel Mgmt. v. NLRB, 314 F.3d 645, 171 LRRM 2781 (D.C. Cir. 2003), *enforcing* 333 NLRB 482, 171 LRRM 1348 (2001) (employer violated §8(a)(1) where, in the face of an across-the-board "no buttons" policy, it allowed employees to wear shamrock buttons, but later discharged same employees for wearing union buttons); NLRB v. Autodie Int'l, Inc., 169 F.3d 378, 160 LRRM 2681 (6th Cir. 1999).

[102]Timken Co., 331 NLRB 744, 171 LRRM 1426 (2000), *enforced*, 171 LRRM 3215 (6th Cir. 2002); Eastern Omni Constructors, Inc. v. NLRB, 170 F.3d 418, 160 LRRM 2669 (4th Cir. 1999). *But see* Eby-Brown Co. L.P., 328 NLRB 496, 168 LRRM 1165 (1999) (employer may not normally prohibit union insignia on company-issued property if its placement does no damage to that property).

[103]Wal-Mart Stores, 340 NLRB No. 76, 173 LRRM 1249 (2003) (T-shirt worn by off-duty employee with the message "Sign a card . . . Ask me how" was not subject to antisolicitation rule as it did not prompt an immediate response from employees); E & L Transp. Co. LLC, 331 NLRB 640, 171 LRRM 1318 (2000).

[104]Produce Warehouse of Coram, Inc., 329 NLRB 915, 169 LRRM 1128 (1999).

[105]393 F.3d 491, 176 LRRM 2321 (4th Cir. 2005), *vacating* BellSouth Telecommunications, Inc., 335 NLRB 1066, 168 LRRM 1049 (2001).

[106]335 NLRB 1066, 168 LRRM 1049 (2001).

stances" in that case included the company's legitimate public image business objectives, as well as the fact that the policy reflected a joint initiative arising from a lengthy and mature collective bargaining relationship.

The Fourth Circuit assumed without deciding that the employer "may require the display of the union insignia if the *absence* of the union logo unreasonably interferes with its established public image."[107] However, it found "no evidence that the display of the union insignia convey[ed] [the employer's] intended message" and thus held there was no basis to impinge on the objecting employees' Section 7 rights.[108]

In *St. Joseph's Hospital*,[109] the Board declined to decide whether the displaying of a union-related message as a computer screen saver should be analyzed under existing law applicable to the wearing of union insignia or postings on employer-provided bulletin boards. The Board found, however, that the employer's discriminatory prohibition of union-related messages was unlawful under either standard.

An employer's offering of antiunion buttons to employees,[110] making negative remarks about employees wearing union buttons,[111] or refusing to consider job applicants because they wore union buttons[112] is also unlawful under Section 7 of the Act.

f. "Captive-Audience" Speeches, Conferences, and Interviews

The Board continues to apply the *Peerless Plywood*[113] standard to permit employers and unions to make campaign speeches on or off company premises during the 24-hour period prior to election, provided employee attendance is voluntary and on the employees' own time. In *NLRB v. Glades Health Care Center*,[114] the union held a rally the day before a representation election on a site 50 yards from the

---

[107]393 F.3d at 495.

[108]*Id.* at 496.

[109]337 NLRB 94, 169 LRRM 1049 (2001).

[110]ITT Auto. v. NLRB, 188 F.3d 375, 161 LRRM 3132 (6th Cir. 1999).

[111]Decca Ltd. P'ship, 327 NLRB 980, 164 LRRM 1040 (1999) (negative comment on performance evaluation about employee's wearing of union button).

[112]NLRB v. Pneu Elec., Inc., 332 NLRB 616, 168 LRRM 1269, *enforced in relevant part*, 309 F.3d 843, 170 LRRM 3249 (5th Cir. 2002).

[113]107 NLRB 427, 33 LRRM 1151 (1953).

[114]257 F.3d 1317, 168 LRRM 2867 (11th Cir. 2001).

employer's facility. There was no violation of the *Peerless Plywood* prohibitions where, although the union used loudspeakers, its message was broadcast to those who voluntarily attended the rally. The Board refused to hold that the union rally, held off premises but close enough to the employees' place of business that some peripheral sounds could be heard in the facility, was an election violation, where such sounds did not rise to the level of coherent election speech.[115]

g. No-Access Rules

In defining the right of off-duty employees to enter or remain on plant premises for the purpose of engaging in union activities, the Board continues to apply the principle of *Tri-County Medical Center.*[116] Where the employer does not have a rule banning employees' off-duty access to its property, and where a rule is promulgated in response to organizing activity,[117] the Board does not apply the principles of *Tri-County.*[118]

In *First Healthcare Corp. dba Hillhaven Highland House,*[119] the Board reiterated that off-site employees of the same employer have access

[115] *Id.*

[116] 222 NLRB 1089, 91 LRRM 1323 (1976). *See* Mediaone of Greater Fla., Inc., 340 NLRB No. 39, 173 LRRM 1201 (2003) (prohibition on "entering company property after hours without authorization," where employer operates around the clock, unlawfully restricted employees' right to come onto exterior of property); Timken Co., 331 NLRB 744, 171 LRRM 1426 (2000), *enforced,* 171 LRRM 3215 (6th Cir. 2002) (application of *Tri-County* test to employee handbillers); Flamingo Hilton-Laughlin, 330 NLRB 287, 167 LRRM 1203 (1999) (holding that employer's policy violated §8(a)(1) because it barred employees from patronizing the employer's property during the 8 hours before their shift but failed to establish a business reason for the rule); R&R Plaster & Drywall Co., 330 NLRB 87, 163 LRRM 1105 (1999) (employer's failure to provide evidence of its property interest precludes it from proving its right to exclude union representation from its site). *Cf.* New York New York, LLC, 313 F.3d 585, 171 LRRM 2651 (D.C. Cir. 2002), *denying enforcement of* 334 NLRB 762, 169 LRRM 1502 (2001) (court reversed Board's decision that off-duty employees may engage in protected solicitation and distribution in nonwork areas of owner's property and remanded for further proceedings); *see supra* notes 72–75 and accompanying text.

[117] Donaldson Bros. Ready Mix, Inc., 341 NLRB No. 124, 175 LRRM 1069 (2004).

[118] Santa Fe Hotel, Inc., 331 NLRB 723, 169 LRRM 1212 (2000) (employer violated §8(a)(1) by enforcing its no-distribution policy so as to prohibit off-duty employees from distributing union-related literature in nonworking area).

[119] 336 NLRB 646, 168 LRRM 1368 (2001), *enforced,* 344 F.3d 523, 173 LRRM 2296 (6th Cir. 2003). *See also* discussion at Section II.B.1.b. [Organizational and Preelection Activity; Unlawful Employer Conduct; Employer's Restriction on Union and Employee Activity on Employer's Property; Rights of Employees Over Nonemployees], *supra,* regarding employer policies toward off-duty employees.

rights to other facilities of the employer.[120] There, employees from one of the employer's facilities attempted to distribute organizational flyers in the parking lot of another of the employer's facilities. Other employees attempted to distribute organizational literature in an outdoor break area at a third facility and to talk to employees about organizing. Managers of both facilities ordered the off-site employees to leave the property. The Board concluded that: (1) off-site employees have a nonderivative access right, for organizational purposes, to their employers' facilities; (2) an employer may have heightened private property-right concerns when off-site employees seek access to its property; and (3) on balance, the Section 7 organizational rights of off-site employees entitle them to access to the outside, nonworking areas of the employer's property, except where restriction is justified by business reasons, which may involve considerations not applicable to access by off-duty, on-site employees.

The Board's application of this rule to the employees of a contractor working on property under another employer's control has not received uniform acceptance from the circuit courts of appeal.[121] The Board continues to find the Section 7 rights of a contractor's employees equivalent to those of the property owner's employees.[122] The Fifth and D.C. Circuits, however, have remanded cases to the Board to explain why, in light of the distinction *Lechmere, Inc. v. NLRB*[123] draws between employees and nonemployees, a contractor's

---

[120]*See* ITT Indus., Inc., 341 NLRB No. 118, 174 LRRM 1449 (2004) (applying *Hillhaven, supra* note 119, Board held employer unlawfully denied access to off-site employees seeking to handbill in parking lot), *on remand from* ITT Indus., Inc. v. NLRB, 251 F.3d 995, 167 LRRM 2557 (D.C. Cir. 2001), *vacating and remanding* 331 NLRB 4, 164 LRRM 1127 (2000).

[121]*See* discussion at Section II.B.1.b. [Organizational and Preelection Activity; Unlawful Employer Conduct; Employer's Restriction on Union and Employee Activity on Employer's Property; Rights of Employees Over Nonemployees], *supra*; *Santa Fe Hotel, supra* note 118 (regarding employer policies toward off-duty employees).

[122]*See* New York New York, LLC, 334 NLRB 762, 169 LRRM 1502 (2001); Pneu Elec., Inc. 332 NLRB 616, 168 LRRM 1269 (2000); *but see* USPS, 339 NLRB 1175 (2003), *review denied*, 370 F.3d 25, 174 LRRM 3343 (D.C. Cir. 2004) (employer lawfully denied access to a nonemployee union organizer and an employee of its subcontractor who sought access to a building to which they did not regularly and exclusively have access).

[123]502 U.S. 527, 139 LRRM 2225 (1992).

employees should enjoy the same Section 7 rights vis-à-vis the property owner as the property owner's own employees.[124]

h. Prohibiting Protected Activity on Private Property Open to the Public

A difference of opinion exists between the Board and certain circuit courts regarding the disparate application of solicitation and distribution policies to union representatives on employers' private property. In *Lechmere, Inc. v. NLRB*,[125] the Supreme Court provided guidance in this area by holding that "[s]o long as nonemployee union organizers have reasonable access to employees outside an employer's property,"[126] an employer may prohibit all access by such individuals to its premises.

The Board continues to hold that *Lechmere* will not shield an employer that discriminates by allowing solicitation or distribution by other persons and groups while denying like access to a union.[127] However, in *6 West Ltd. Corp. v. NLRB*,[128] the Seventh Circuit ruled that prohibiting employee solicitation for union support, while allowing employee solicitation for Girl Scout cookies, Christmas ornaments, and raffle tickets, did not constitute discriminatory application of the employer's no-solicitation policy. The court held that the

[124]NLRB v. Pneu Elec., Inc., 309 F.3d 843, 170 LRRM 3249 (5th Cir. 2002), *enforcing in part, vacating in part* 332 NLRB 616, 160 LRRM 1269 (2000); New York New York, LLC, v. NLRB, 313 F.3d 585, 171 LRRM 2651 (D.C. Cir. 2002), *denying enforcement of* 334 NLRB 762, 169 LRRM 1502 (2001). *But see* Wolgast Corp. v. NLRB, 349 F.3d 250, 173 LRRM 2587 (6th Cir. 2003) *enforcing* 334 NLRB 203, 170 LRRM 1489 (2001) (nonunion general contractor unlawfully denied access to nonemployee union representative of subcontractor's employees whose labor agreement contained union access clause).

[125]*Supra* note 123.

[126]502 U.S. at 538.

[127]*See* discussion in Main Edition; *see also* discussion at Section II.B.1.b. [Organizational and Preelection Activity; Unlawful Employer Conduct; Employers Restriction on Union and Employee Activity on Employer's Property; Rights of Employees Over Nonemployees], *supra*; Albertson's, Inc., 332 NLRB 1132, 166 LRRM 1003 (2000), *enforcement denied*, 301 F.3d 441, 170 LRRM 2769 (6th Cir. 2002).

[128]237 F.3d 767, 166 LRRM 2221 (7th Cir. 2001), *denying enforcement of* 330 NLRB 527, 163 LRRM 1113 (2000); *see also* Wal-Mart Stores, Inc., 340 NLRB No. 144, 173 LRRM 1503 (2003) (where employer maintained a policy of permitting solicitation in areas 15 feet beyond its store entrances and had a practice of informing solicitors of this policy, its failure to allow union solicitation 15 feet beyond the entrance, and failure to inform union solicitors of the policy, was discriminatory).

latter activities were not "similar" to union solicitations and, therefore, allowing them while banning the union solicitations did not violate Section 8(a)(1). The court also found that the union solicitations were disruptive in the workplace because some employees complained to management. The court found, on the other hand, that an "activity as innocent as the sale of Girl Scout cookies" was "beneficial to all employees."[129] Other courts have reached similar conclusions in refusing to enforce Board orders in this area.[130]

The Board's supplemental decision in *Farm Fresh, Inc.*,[131] a case on remand from the D.C. Circuit, provides certain additional guidance in this area. The Board accepted the D.C. Circuit's finding that the employer did not rely solely on its no-solicitation rule when it ejected union organizers from the snack bar. In fact, the employer had no such policy, and had evicted the union organizers because of prior trespass warrants issued against them. The Board ruled that there was no evidence of discrimination against union solicitation and reaffirmed that the employer did not violate Section 8(a)(1). Because the Board found that the employer had met the nondiscrimination requirements, it applied the *Lechmere* analysis and determined that the employer's right to exclude is derived from the relevant state property law. In applying Virginia law, however, the Board

---

[129]*Id.* at 780. *But see* NLRB v. Clinton Elec., 284 F.3d 731, 169 LRRM 2934 (7th Cir. 2002), *enforcing* 332 NLRB 479, 169 LRRM 1314 (2000) (permitting sports and other pools, and school-related events, while prohibiting union solicitation constitutes discriminatory enforcement).

[130]*See* discussion at Section II.B.1.c.(3). [Organizational and Preelection Activity; Unlawful Employer Conduct; Employer's Restriction on Union and Employee Activity on Employer's Property; No-Solicitation and No-Distribution Rules Generally; Unlawful Promulgation or Enforcement], *supra*; Sandusky Mall Co. v. NLRB, 242 F.3d 682, 166 LRRM 2641 (6th Cir. 2001); Cleveland Real Estate Partners v. NLRB, 95 F.3d 457, 153 LRRM 2338 (6th Cir. 1996); Guardian Indus. Corp. v. NLRB, 49 F.3d 317, 148 LRRM 2665 (7th Cir. 1995). *See also* discussion of *Albertson's, Inc.*, at Section II.B.1.b. [Organizational and Preelection Activity; Unlawful Employer Conduct; Employer's Restriction on Union and Employee Activity on Employer's Property; Rights of Employees Over Nonemployees], *supra*.

[131]326 NLRB 997, 159 LRRM 1201 (1998), *petition for review granted*, 222 F.3d 1030, 169 LRRM 2205 (D.C. Cir. 2000), *on remand*, 332 NLRB 1424, 171 LRRM 1380 (2000).

found that the employer lacked a sufficient exclusionary interest to eject union organizers from the sidewalk outside its store.[132]

i. Prohibiting Distribution of Political Materials

Handbilling is protected under *Eastex, Inc. v. NLRB*,[133] where employees, in nonworking areas on nonworking time, distribute "political" material regarding laws that have a significant and direct bearing on a basic concern of employees as employees.

In *Triangle Electric Co.*,[134] the Board ruled that the employer violated the Act by firing an employee for soliciting subscriptions to a newspaper produced by striking newspaper employees, where the newspaper was a means to promote the ultimate success of the strike.

j. Effect of Contractual Waiver of Right to Solicit or Distribute

The Board and the courts continue to apply *NLRB v. Magnavox Co.*[135] in a variety of situations, including holding that a collective

---

[132]*Id. See also* Wild Oats Mkts., Inc., 336 NLRB 179, 168 LRRM 1305 (2001) (employer did not hold property interest that entitled it to exclude nonemployee union representatives from shopping center parking lot in front of its store because lease granted it only an easement and nonexclusive right to use common areas); Indio Grocery Outlet, 323 NLRB 1138, 155 LRRM 1210 (1997), *enforced,* 187 F.3d 1080, 161 LRRM 3121 (9th Cir. 1999), *cert. denied,* 529 U.S. 1098, 164 LRRM 2256 (2000) (holding that, as a threshold matter, employer must show a property right entitling it to exclude individuals engaged in §7 conduct; without such showing, any exclusion or threat of exclusion from the property is a violation of §8(a)(1). *But see* Waremart Foods v. NLRB, 354 F.3d 870, 174 LRRM 2010 (D.C. Cir. 2004) (under California law, union organizers had no right to engage in handbilling on privately owned parking lot of grocery store, which stood alone adjacent to its parking lot on 10-acre parcel, where customers could enter store only through parking lot, and where store prohibited solicitors), *denying enforcement in relevant part to* 337 NLRB 289, 169 LRRM 1244 (2001); Snyder's of Hanover, Inc., 39 Fed. Appx. 730, 170 LRRM 2448 (3d Cir. 2002), *denying enforcement in relevant part to* 334 NLRB 183, 167 LRRM 1211 (2001) (under Pennsylvania law private property owner may exclude union handbillers from adjacent easement if those activities exceed easement's intended purposes; circuit court reversed Board and found no violation of §8(a)(1) because handbilling not included among easement's explicit purposes).

[133]437 U.S. 556, 98 LRRM 2717 (1978); *see, e.g.*, Kenworth Truck Co., 327 NLRB 497, 166 LRRM 1215 (1999) (employee engaged in protected activity when he distributed, during nonwork time and outside the worksite, political material advocating repeal of a new law that reduced benefits available to workers under Ohio's workers' compensation system).

[134]335 NLRB 1037, 169 LRRM 1146 (2001), *enforcement denied,* 78 Fed. Appx. 469, 173 LRRM 2576 (2003).

[135]415 U.S. 322, 85 LRRM 2475, *reh'g denied,* 416 U.S. 952 (1974).

bargaining agreement, absent specific waiver language, cannot be read to restrict employee rights to distribute campaign material in support of the bargaining agent.[136]

In *Awrey Bakeries, Inc.*,[137] the Board ordered the parties to cease giving effect to a provision in the collective bargaining agreement in which the union agreed that its members would not conduct any union activities on company property "during working hours." The Board rejected the employer's contention that the contract clause at issue had, in practice, been read to mean "working time." Rather, the Board emphasized that this provision was in the collective bargaining agreement for every employee to read, which tended to dissuade employees from freely engaging in protected conduct at work and chilled employees' exercise of their Section 7 rights.

In *Hotel & Restaurant Employees Local 5 v. Honolulu Country Club*,[138] *Magnavox* was discussed, but distinguished on the facts. The court ruled that "working hours" included the paid meal breaks given to employees. Therefore, a provision in the parties' collective bargaining agreement that prohibited solicitation "during working hours" was only a partial waiver of the employees' Section 7 rights. *Magnavox*, said the court, focused on the unions' power to consent to the total elimination of either distribution or solicitation. Relying on *NLRB v. United Tech Corp.*,[139] the court upheld this partial limitation on solicitation by the union.

2. *Specific Conduct That Violates Section 8(a)(1)*

a. Threats to Withdraw, and Withdrawals of, Benefits

The Board continues to examine closely the discontinuation of existing benefits in the context of union activity among employees. In *Climatrol, Inc.*,[140] an employer's termination of vacation benefits

---

[136]Summa Health Sys., Inc., 330 NLRB 1379, 170 LRRM 1308 (2000); Mead Corp., 331 NLRB 509, 170 LRRM 1496 (2000); *see also* Belle of Sioux City, 333 NLRB No. 98, 171 LRRM 1432 (2001).

[137]335 NLRB 138, 172 LRRM 1223 (2001), *enforced*, 59 Fed. Appx. 690, 173 LRRM 2128 (6th Cir. 2003). *See also* Titanium Metals Corp., 340 NLRB No. 88, 173 LRRM 1402 (2003), *vacated in part*, 392 F.3d 439, 176 LRRM 2073 (D.C. Cir. 2004), *opinion withdrawn*, 2005 U.S. App. LEXIS 3109 (D.C. Cir. Feb. 22, 2005) (refusing to defer to settlement in which employee's discharge for distributing his own newsletter was upheld).

[138]100 F. Supp. 2d 1254, 164 LRRM 3021 (D. Haw. 1999).

[139]706 F.2d 1254, 113 LRRM 2326 (2d Cir. 1983).

[140]329 NLRB 946, 169 LRRM 1385 (1999).

and holiday pay violated Section 8(a)(1) when the benefit termination followed one of the most successful years in the employer's history and was announced on the heels of recent union activities by the employees.[141]

In *Overnite Transportation Co.*,[142] an employer violated Section 8(a)(1) by implying that employees who voted for the union would forfeit future pay increases when it announced a pay increase that excluded all employees working at a location where the union had recently been certified. In *Eby-Brown Co., L.P.*,[143] an employer violated Section 8(a)(1) when an executive told employees that the only reason they had no retirement plan was because the company had spent so much money fighting employee grievances.

The withdrawal of, or the threat to withdraw, benefits need not entail a significant change. Any threatened or actual change may be found unlawful, even where the change is slight.[144] The Board continues to examine the context of the employer's statements in determining whether the overall effect of the message conveys an unlawful threat.[145]

---

[141] *Id.*

[142] 329 NLRB 990, 166 LRRM 1101 (1999), *enforced*, 240 F.3d 325, 166 LRRM 2577 (4th Cir. 2001).

[143] 328 NLRB 496, 168 LRRM 1165 (1999).

[144] NLRB v. General Fabrications Corp., 222 F.3d 218, 231, 164 LRRM 2974, 2982–83 (6th Cir. 2000) (employer statements that threaten employee working conditions, "however slightly," necessarily affect employee sentiment regarding the union), citing United Artists Theatre Circuit, Inc., 277 NLRB 115, 121, 121 LRRM 1283 (1985). *See also* Aldworth Co. Inc., 338 NLRB 137, 171 LRRM 1033 (2002) (employer statements threatening loss of benefits as a result of unionization and promising better wages and benefits for not unionizing violated §8(a)(1)).

[145] Teletech Holdings, Inc., 342 NLRB No. 92, 175 LRRM 1400 (2004) (employer's asking an employee what he or she thinks of the union might, under the circumstances, reasonably be understood by an employee to indicate that future action might be taken depending on what the employee's answer was); La Gloria Oil & Gas Co., 337 NLRB 1120, 170 LRRM 1337 (2002) (supervisor's statement that employer would fire everyone, including himself, if union succeeded constituted a threat of job loss, and supervisor's inclusion of himself in the statement did not render his remark any less of a threat; however, supervisor's statement that he also would lose his job in response to another employee's opinion that employees would lose their jobs if union succeeded did not constitute a threat of job loss because supervisor's statement merely mirrored the employee's already expressed opinion); *Aldworth Co., supra* note 144 (employer's statement to employees during a meeting about union campaign, "not to grab onto somebody with one foot out the door for lateness and another for stealing company time and sleeping on the job," falsely accused union proponent employees of misconduct and could reasonably be interpreted by other employees as conveying that pursuit of union activities could lead to job loss); Venture Indus., Inc., 330 NLRB 1133,

(1) Permissible Predictions and Prohibited Threats

More than 30 years after *NLRB v. Gissel Packing Co.*,[146] the Board and the courts continue struggling with the distinction between permissible predictions and unlawful threats of reprisal.[147] To avoid violating Section 8(a)(1), an employer must provide an objective factual basis, outside its own control, for predictions of adverse consequences of unionization.[148]

In *Mercy Healthcare Sacramento*,[149] the Board found impermissible statements from supervisors that if employees voted for union representation, they would no longer be able to follow the current practice of granting requests for time off, and accrued vacation benefits would be lost. Where the supervisors failed to disavow or qualify the statements, the statements constituted an objectionable threat of loss of benefits.

In *Penn Tank Lines, Inc.*,[150] the statement, "you guys would have been better off without the Union. You could have formed your driver committee and represented yourself better, and wouldn't have had to pay the dues,"[151] did not unlawfully encourage employees to take future action to abandon the union. Rather, the Board found that the statement merely conveyed the economic reality that if the em-

---

164 LRRM 1173 (2000) (employer statement that "UAW" means "You Ain't Working" held, in context, to be an unlawful threat that employees would lose jobs, and CEO's statement that, as far as he was concerned, the plant would never be a union shop, held, in context, to be a threat that "voting for union representation was futile").

[146]395 U.S. 575, 71 LRRM 2481, *reh'g denied*, 396 U.S. 869 (1969).

[147]Webco Indus., Inc. v. NLRB, 217 F.3d 1306, 1316, 164 LRRM 2845 (10th Cir. 2000), *enforcing* 327 NLRB 172 (1998).

[148]Office Depot, 330 NLRB 640, 163 LRRM 1169 (2000) (employer's statement "was not supported by any objective facts"); *General Fabrications Corp.*, *supra* note 144, at 230, 164 LRRM at 2975 (employer's statement violated §8(a)(1) because it was "not a factual prediction about the likely future"); Aqua Cool, 332 NLRB 95, 171 LRRM 1159 (2000) (statement that employees were unlikely to win anything more and might get less at bargaining table than bulk of the employer's employees independently violated §8(a)(1) by implying that it would be futile for employees to elect union representation).

[149]334 NLRB 100, 168 LRRM 1438 (2001) (citing St. Vincent's Hosp., 244 NLRB 84, 92, 102 LRRM 1196 (1979)), *vacated*, 336 NLRB 1047, 168 LRRM 1450 (2001) (vacated at request of the parties following voluntary settlement agreement). *See also* Wake Elec. Membership Corp., 338 NLRB 298, 173 LRRM 1011 (2002) (manager's statement to employees that other electrical cooperatives would not work with employer if it became unionized violated §8(a)(1) where manager provided no basis for his statement).

[150]336 NLRB 1066, 169 LRRM 1088 (2001).

[151]*Id.* at n.2.

ployees had decided to form their own committee, they would not be subject to the dues that unions typically collect from the employees they represent.[152]

In *TVI Inc.*,[153] the Board found a supervisor's remark that "if the union ever did come in, the store wasn't making enough money to . . . pay off higher wages, and it would be a possibility that everybody would lose their job"[154] was a lawful prediction of potential consequences of unionization where the supervisor knew that the store was losing money at the time. The Board found that the supervisor's statement was both carefully phrased and based on objective fact. The supervisor's statement was based on what the store manager had told her, and the supervisor had shown employees a document depicting the store's daily earnings in support of her statement. Also, the employer's financial records indicated that the store was not profitable at the time. The Board found irrelevant the fact that the supervisor did not know of the employer's overall financial situation, as her prediction was in regards only to that particular store. The Board stated that "the employees would reasonably view [the supervisor's] remark as indicating that any store closure would be economically driven rather than retaliatory."[155]

In evaluating the objective basis offered to support statements made by an employer, courts will closely scrutinize the language used by the employer to determine whether the objective basis offered supports the entire statement. However, it also has been emphasized that, far from recognizing Section 8(c) as codifying "an absolute right" of an employer to convey its view regarding unionization to its employees, the expression of an employer's views or opinion under Section 8(c) is merely "permissible."[156]

---

[152]*Id. See also* President Riverboat Casinos, 329 NLRB 77, 162 LRRM 1081 (1999) (manager's response to employee's question that it was a "possibility" wages would go down found to be coercive and implied reprisal if union was voted in, where manager made no reference to collective bargaining process, economic necessities, or other objective facts).

[153]337 NLRB 1039, 170 LRRM 1366 (2002). *See also* Jewish Home for the Elderly of Fairfield County, 343 NLRB No. 117 (2004) (employer's poster listing 16 nursing homes that were organized by the union and subsequently closed, together with comments from managers about closing the facility, constituted threat of closure if employees voted for union representation).

[154]*Id.*

[155]*Id.*

[156]Auto Workers v. Dana Corp., 278 F.3d 548, 560, 169 LRRM 2193 (6th Cir. 2002).

For example, in *NLRB v. St. Francis Healthcare Center*,[157] the Sixth Circuit held that the employer's prediction that "no company" would affiliate with it if the union won the election was unlawful because it "exaggerated" the facts. Focusing on the employer's precise language, the Sixth Circuit found that although the objective evidence may have supported the prediction that certain companies would not affiliate with the employer, it "hardly support[ed] the prediction that no company would."[158]

(2) Futility of Organizing

The Board continues to hold that conveying to employees the futility of organizing a union violates the Act. In *Keith Miller*,[159] the employer's statement that the employee was "wasting his time," when made in conjunction with an unlawful threat of plant closure, indicated that seeking union representation would be futile because it would result in the employer closing its business, and violated Section 8(a)(1).

In a case on remand from the D.C. Circuit, the Board held that certain language in an employer handbill, stating the extremely divergent positions prior to bargaining, was lawful and served an objective basis for additional statements indicating the potential for "long bitter negotiations" and "a long and ugly strike."[160] The Board found that this language was not distinguishable from language found lawful in prior Board decisions, because the employer was not telling its employees that union representation would be futile. Rather, the employer was explaining to its employees that if the parties are

---

[157]212 F.3d 945, 164 LRRM 2324 (6th Cir. 2000).

[158]*Id.* at 955.

[159]334 NLRB 824, 168 LRRM 1382 (2001). *See also* Kelly Bros. Sheet Metal, Inc., 342 NLRB No. 9, 175 LRRM 1120 (2004) (employer's statement that "he could afford to keep us working year-round right now but if we went union, he couldn't keep us working because there wasn't [sic] that many union jobs around" was found to be unlawful); Wake Elec. Membership Corp., 338 NLRB 298, 173 LRRM 1011 (2002) (manager's statement to employees that they would not receive any benefits if there was a "high vote" for the union was "best described as a threat of futility"); Overnite Transp. Co., 329 NLRB 990, 166 LRRM 1101 (1999) (employer repeatedly cited example of another of its facilities where, despite 13 years of bargaining and a strike, union had not been able to negotiate a collective bargaining agreement, giving message to employees that bargaining would be futile).

[160]General Elec. Co., 332 NLRB 919, 165 LRRM 1335 (2000).

sharply divided, negotiations can indeed become protracted and bitter.[161]

(3) Inevitability of Strikes or Violence

The Board continues to closely scrutinize statements depicting strikes as a possible consequence of unionization. Where statements depict the possibility of a strike after hard bargaining, the Board will not find a violation of Section 8(a)(1).[162] The Board, however, found a violation of Section 8(a)(1) where, two days after threatening to close the doors if the union got in, the employer stated that the union would call a strike and the employees would be replaced by new workers earning less money.[163]

(4) Assessing Recurrent Phrases and Themes

(b) "Bargaining Will Start From Scratch." "Bargaining will start from scratch" statements continue to be the subject of litigation, with the context in which such a statement is made, the timing of the statement, and the opportunity for the union to respond being key factors in determining whether the Act was violated.[164] For example, an employer violated Section 8(a)(1) when one of its representatives told its employees, "if [a union] was voted in, then that means [the employees] would have to start from scratch," referring to the negotiations between the employer and the union.[165] Another employer

---

[161]*Id. See also* Ready Mix Inc., 337 NLRB 1189, 170 LRRM 1401 (2002) (manager's answers to employees' inquiries that company was "not unionized or had no plans to go union or to be union" did not constitute coercive statements of futility regarding unionization where manager did not state or imply that company intended to ensure its nonunion status through discriminatory or coercive means; rather, manager's responses were, in context, noncoercive statements regarding company's nonunion status and would not reasonably cause employees to believe that efforts to obtain union representation would be futile); K.W. Elec., Inc., 342 NLRB No. 126, 157 LRRM 1499 (2004) (employer's statements that the company is a nonunion company and will be a nonunion company was found to be unlawful when made within the context of earlier threats to close).

[162]*General Elec. Co., supra* note 160.

[163]Rankin & Rankin, Inc., 330 NLRB 1026, 165 LRRM 1221, 1222 (2000). *See also* AP Auto. Sys., Inc., 333 NLRB 581, 166 LRRM 1302 (2001) (employer violated Act when it told employees it would rather see plant closed by a strike than slowly die because it agreed to union demands that would place plant in financial trouble).

[164]Automation & Measurement Div. Bendix Corp. v. NLRB, 400 F.2d 141, 146, 69 LRRM 2157 (6th Cir. 1968).

[165]Overnite Transp. Co. (Overnite I), 329 NLRB 990, 166 LRRM 1101 (1999), *enforcement denied and remanded,* 280 F.3d 417, 169 LRRM 2469 (4th Cir. 2002); *see also* Superior Emerald Park Landfill LLC, 340 NLRB No. 54, 174 LRRM 1445 (2003)

violated Section 8(a)(1) when it warned employees that the company would bargain "very hard" and, as a consequence, employees may not "end up with as good a wage benefit package as [they] have now!"[166]

Conversely, an employer in the Sixth Circuit was found not to have engaged in unlawful conduct when it stated bargaining would start "from scratch" or "from zero" if the employees voted for union representation.[167] The Sixth Circuit held that although such statements in isolation may be objectionable, the statements in that case were made to a limited number of employees, the union had ample time to respond, and the employer also distributed literature during the preelection period stating that "employees could expect to remain at their current levels of pay and benefits during negotiations but could ultimately lose or gain benefits as a result of the bargaining process."[168]

(c) Statements Regarding Plant Closings. The Board and courts continue to grapple with statements concerning plant closings. In some instances, the cases involved substantial interplay between Sections 8(c) and 8(a)(1) and were analyzed to determine if there was any objective basis for the prediction of a plant closure.[169] In other in-

---

(statement that bargaining would start from "zero" or "scratch" was unlawful); Overnite Transp. Co. (Overnite II), 334 NLRB 1074, 168 LRRM 1058 (2001); Aqua Cool, 332 NLRB 95, 171 LRRM 1159 (2000) (employer violated the Act when it stated that if employees elected union they would lose all their benefits and would have to "start [negotiations] from zero").

[166]ITT Auto. v. NLRB, 188 F.3d 375, 385, 161 LRRM 3132 (6th Cir. 1999).

[167]NLRB v. St. Francis Healthcare Ctr., 212 F.3d 945, 164 LRRM 2324 (6th Cir. 2000).

[168]*Id.* at 957. *Accord* Pearson Educ., Inc., 336 NLRB 979, 169 LRRM 1012 (2001) (employer violated Act when it stated that negotiations would "start at zero" if employees selected union representation; employer did not dispel effect of threat through additional communications explaining that any reductions in wages or benefits would occur only as a result of normal give and take of collective bargaining); Noah's Bay Area Bagels, LLC, 331 NLRB 188, 166 LRRM 1175 (2000).

[169]*See, e.g.,* Tellepsen Pipeline Servs. Co. v. NLRB, 320 F.3d 554, 171 LRRM 3065 (5th Cir. 2003) (statement that if union won election, employer could lose contract and employees "could possibly lose jobs" was unlawful); *St. Francis Healthcare, supra* note 167 at 954–55; *ITT Auto., supra* note 166; Daikichi Corp., 335 NLRB 622, 169 LRRM 1197 (2001) (statement that employer "might" close plant, instead of "would" close plant, was still unlawful where employer failed to cite any objective facts that it would no longer be able to compete and might have to close for reasons beyond its control).

stances, the statements were naked assertions not coupled with factors outside the employer's control.[170] Indeed, unlike interrogation, which is coercive only if a reasonable person would perceive it as such, a threat of plant closure is a per se violation of Section 8(a)(1).[171]

In *Springs Industries, Inc.*,[172] the Board established a "rebuttable presumption" test regarding dissemination of threats of plant closure, for purposes of evaluating the effect of such threats on a representation election. The Board overruled *Kokomo Tube Co.*,[173] in which a supervisor's threat of plant closure was found to be insufficient to set aside an election absent evidence of dissemination to other employees.[174] The Board held that it would, in future cases, require the employer to demonstrate through record evidence "either that the

---

[170]*See, e.g.*, NLRB v. General Fabrications Corp., 222 F.3d 218, 230, 164 LRRM 2974 (6th Cir. 2000); V&S Pro Galv, Inc. v. NLRB, 168 F.3d 270, 278, 160 LRRM 2518 (6th Cir. 1999) (CEO's response to unionization attempt, that employer would lock its doors and employees could kiss investment fund goodbye, violated Act); Bonham Heating & Air Conditioning, Inc., 328 NLRB 432, 161 LRRM 1113 (1999); *ITT Auto.*, *supra* note 166, 188 F.3d at 385 (employer violated §8(a)(1) when supervisor's speech reflecting economic predictions that, after unionization plants might close if they became unprofitable, was not based on objective facts); Amptech Inc., 342 NLRB No. 117, 175 LRRM 1016 (2004) (employer's statement to employees that it viewed union organizing drive to be a "personal attack," and would "explore all of [its] options for the future," constituted an unlawful implicit threat of plant closure). *See also* Atlantic Veal & Lamb, Inc., 342 NLRB No. 37, 175 LRRM 1456 (2004) (statement that if union was elected the employer would "close the business and move to Indiana" violated the Act); Shearer's Foods, Inc., 340 NLRB No. 132, 173 LRRM 1459 (2003) (employer violated §8(a)(1) when manager told employees that if company president "had his say, the plant would shut down if the Union came in"); L.W.D., Inc., 335 NLRB 241, 168 LRRM 1176 (2001) (employer violated Act when its president told employees to vote in upcoming election "as if their jobs depended on it"); Cogburn Healthcare Ctr., 335 NLRB 1397, 171 LRRM 1021 (2001) (supervisor's statement to employee that company would "sell the place first" before it bargained with union was unlawful).

[171]Fleming Cos. v. NLRB., 349 F.3d 968, 173 LRRM 2621 (7th Cir. 2003); Multi-Ad Servs. v. NLRB, 255 F.3d 363, 167 LRRM 2450 (7th Cir. 2001); NLRB v. St. Francis Healthcare Ctr., 212 F.3d 945, 164 LRRM 2324 (6th Cir. 2000). *See also* Avondale Indus., Inc., 329 NLRB 1064, 165 LRRM 1228 (1999).

[172]332 NLRB 40, 165 LRRM 1161 (2000).

[173]280 NLRB 357, 122 LRRM 1254 (1986).

[174]The Board cited *General Stencils, Inc.*, 195 NLRB 1109, 1110, 79 LRRM 1608, *enforcement denied*, 472 F.2d 170, 82 LRRM 2081 (2d Cir. 1972), and *Coach & Equip. Sales Corp.*, 228 NLRB 440, 94 LRRM 1391 (1977). *But see* Caron Int'l, 246 NLRB 1120, 103 LRRM 1066 (1979) (threats to discharge union proponents are not presumed to be disseminated).

employees threatened did not tell other employees about the threat, or that those employees whom they told did not in turn tell any other employees about the threat."[175]

In *Keith Miller,*[176] an employer that threatened to "shut his doors" if the union "tried to organize him" violated the Act even though the statements were directed to paid union officials who applied for employment as "salts."

b. Promises and Grants of Benefits

The Board continues to apply its presumption that benefits conferred during an organizing campaign are meant to influence employees to relinquish their support for the union.[177] For example, in *Waste Management of Palm Beach,*[178] the employer unlawfully accelerated its announcement of an increase in its matching contribution to the company's 401(k) plan, announcing the increase at a "benefits dinner" three days before the union election.[179] On the other

---

[175]*Springs Indus., supra* note 172. *See Cogburn Healthcare Ctr., supra* note 170 (employer's remarks reported in the *Wall Street Journal* were not unlawful promises where unit employees neither read nor were aware of the article, and where there were no direct quotes in the article attributable to the employer).

[176]334 NLRB 824, 168 LRRM 1382 (2001).

[177]Pacific FM, Inc. dba KOFY TV-20, 332 NLRB 771, 171 LRRM 1098, 1101 (2000) (absent showing of legitimate business reason for timing of grant of benefits during organizing campaign, Board will infer improper motive and interference with employee rights). *See also* Superior Emerald Park Landfill LLC, 340 NLRB No. 54, 174 LRRM 1445 (2003) (employer unlawfully announced and implemented postelection wage increases, within one week after union lost election by a tie vote, for the purpose of eroding union support in the event of a second election).

[178]329 NLRB 198, 167 LRRM 1059 (1999).

[179]*See also* McAllister Towing & Transp. Co., 341 NLRB No. 48, 174 LRRM 1225 (2004) (accelerating the timing of a mid-year wage increase, extending a 401(k) plan to eligible voters, and granting five paid holidays weeks before an election violated Act); K-Mart Corp., 336 NLRB 455, 172 LRRM 1102 (2001) (employer violated Act by announcing a 50-cent-per-hour wage increase two days before election, even though it had past practice of granting wage increase in such month followed by explanation of increase in group meetings with employees, where employer also emphasized increase in meeting shortly before election); DMI Distribution of Del., 334 NLRB 409, 172 LRRM 1080 (2001) (employer unlawfully gave $100 bonuses to two employee for Saturday work five days before union election); Niblock Excavating, Inc., 337 NLRB 53, 169 LRRM 1129 (2001) (employer violated Act by promising employees increased contributions to their 401(k) plan during union organizing without establishing a legitimate reason for the timing of the announcement), *enforced,* 59 Fed. Appx. 882, 2003 U.S. App. LEXIS 3955 (7th Cir. Mar. 5, 2003); *Pacific FM, Inc. dba KOFY TV-20, supra* note 177 (employer unlawfully announced new employee break policy on day of election).

hand, the Board found no violation where, in order to maintain a competitive wage package, an employer granted wage adjustments to its employees before an election.[180] In that case, the employer had conducted a local wage survey and planned to grant wage adjustments before learning of union activity.[181]

(1) Employer Inducements

In *V&S ProGalv, Inc. v. NLRB*,[182] the Sixth Circuit affirmed the Board's finding that the employer's proposal of a plan to match union dues in a savings fund violated Section 8(a)(1) by promising employees an additional benefit if they rejected the union. Similarly, the Eighth Circuit affirmed the Board's finding of a violation where the employer tried to dissuade an employee from joining the union and later tried to encourage the employee to withdraw his membership after he had joined.[183] The president of the company offered the employee $2 per hour above the union pay scale if he would refrain from joining. The president later told the employee that he "would like to do away with the union" and offered him a company-sponsored health plan and reimbursement of his union initiation fee if he withdrew his membership.

In *Atlantic Limousine, Inc.*,[184] the Board reversed its position in *Sony Corp. of America*[185] and adopted a ban on all raffles if "(1) eligibility to participate in the raffle or win prizes is in any way tied to voting in the election or being at the election site on election day or (2) the raffle is conducted at any time during a period beginning 24 hours before the scheduled opening of the polls and ending with

[180]Insight Communications Co., 330 NLRB 431, 170 LRRM 1261 (2000).

[181]*Id.; see also* Sara Lee Bakery Group dba International Baking Co., 342 NLRB No. 12, 175 LRRM 1250 (2004) (announcement "more than 1 month prior to the election" of new or enhanced medical, life insurance, and retirement benefits and new company-provided lockers and uniforms was not unlawful where the employer had decided to provide such benefits as part of its benefits review prior to the onset of the union's organizing campaign); *Cf.* Park Assoc., Inc., 334 NLRB 328, 168 LRRM 1262 (2001) (employer violated Act by posting wage and benefit summary—including merit raise program—applicable only to nonunion employees during critical period prior to decertification election), *vacated*, 337 NLRB 643, 170 LRRM 1120 (2002) (vacated at request of the parties following voluntary settlement agreement).

[182]168 F.3d 270, 277–78, 160 LRRM 2518 (6th Cir. 1999), *enforcing* 323 NLRB 801, 157 LRRM 1255 (1997).

[183]McKenzie Eng'g Co. v. NLRB, 182 F.3d 622, 628, 161 LRRM 2641 (8th Cir. 1999), *enforcing* 326 NLRB 473, 161 LRRM 1175 (1998).

[184]331 NLRB 1025, 165 LRRM 1001 (2000).

[185]313 NLRB 420, 145 LRRM 1242 (1993).

the closing of the polls."[186] The Board explained that the o[illegible]nity to win a prize in a raffle that is tied to the voting could be viewed as "something extra" that could make employees feel obligated to vote against the union.

(2) Soliciting or Remedying Employee Grievances

The Board continues to hold that an employer that solicits grievances or complaints from employees during a period of organizing activity may be considered to have made an implied promise that grievances will be favorably resolved. Such an implied promise, if made for the purpose of influencing employee choice, is unlawful.[187] This includes an employer's use of surveys[188] and "roundtable" meetings,[189] and "employee advocacy" programs.[190] However, an employer that has a past practice of soliciting and resolving employee griev-

---

[186]*Atlantic Limousine, supra* note 184. *See also* Ryder Student Transp. Serv., 332 NLRB 1590, 166 LRRM 1073 (2000); Comcast Cablevision-Taylor v. NLRB, 232 F.3d 490, 497, 165 LRRM 2803 (6th Cir. 2000).

[187]*See* Chartwells Compass Group, 342 NLRB No. 121, 176 LRRM 1081 (2004); MEMC Elec. Materials, Inc., 342 NLRB No. 119, 175 LRRM 1476 (2004); Ryder Transp. Servs., 341 NLRB No. 109, 175 LRRM 1179 (2004); Music Express East, Inc., 340 NLRB No. 129 (2003); Federated Logistics & Operations, 340 NLRB No. 36, 173 LRRM 1210 (2003); Beverly Health & Rehab. Servs., 339 NLRB 1243, 173 LRRM 1137 (2003); D&F Indus., Inc., 339 NLRB 618 (2003); Wake Elec. Membership Corp., 338 NLRB 298, 173 LRRM 1011 (2002); Alamo Rent-a-Car, Inc., 338 NLRB 275, 171 LRRM 1383 (2002); Ishikawa Gasket Am., Inc., 337 NLRB 175, 169 LRRM 1241 (2001), *aff'd,* 354 F.3d 534, 173 LRRM 2993 (6th Cir. 2004); Alamo Rent-a-Car, 336 NLRB 1155, 169 LRRM 1026 (2001), *supplemented,* 338 NLRB No. 14, 172 LRRM 1288 (2002); Clark Distrib. Sys., Inc., 336 NLRB 747, 170 LRRM 1071 (2001); Wal-Mart Stores, Inc., 335 NLRB 1310, 169 LRRM 1229 (2001); Laboratory Corp. of Am. Holdings, 333 NLRB 284, 166 LRRM 1219 (2001); Overnite Transp. Co., 329 NLRB 990, 166 LRRM 1101 (1999), *review granted in part,* 280 F.3d 417, 169 LRRM 2469 (4th Cir. 2002); Traction Wholesale Ctr. Co., 328 NLRB 1058, 164 LRRM 1266 (1999), *enforced,* 216 F.3d 92, 164 LRRM 2769 (D.C. Cir. 2000); National Health Care, L.P., 327 NLRB 1175, 161 LRRM 1152 (1999), *aff'd in part, vacated in part,* 234 F.3d 1269, 166 LRRM 2768 (6th Cir. 2000).

[188]Villa Maria Nursing & Rehab. Ctr., Inc., 335 NLRB 1345, 168 LRRM 1209 (2001), *aff'd without opinion,* 2002 WL 31174103, 172 LRRM 2127 (11th Cir. 2002), *cert. denied,* 538 U.S. 922, 172 LRRM 2128 (2003).

[189]Alamo Rent-a-Car, Inc., 338 NLRB 275, 171 LRRM 1383 (2002) (employer violated §8(a)(1) by supporting employee-led "roundtable" meetings where employer used meetings as part of an unprecedented effort to solicit employee grievances with a promise to remedy them).

[190]Amptech, Inc., 342 NLRB No. 117, 176 LRRM 1016 (2004) (employer's solicitation of employees to serve as "employee advocates" to "help resolve employee issues" violated §8(a)(1)).

ances may continue that practice during organizing activity.[191] Moreover, without a promise to take action on a grievance, an employer's solicitation may be permissible under the Act.[192] Further, it may be permissible for an employer to state that it wished its employees had come to it to address their problems before going to the union, where the employer acknowledged that it was now too late to address the problems in the absence of the union.[193] The Board and the courts have also found that a supervisor's request for information about "problems leading to the Union campaign and employee dissatisfaction with management" do not constitute grievance solicitation under the Act.[194]

The Board has held that the standard to determine whether an employer has violated Section 8(a)(1) of the Act by soliciting employee grievances is objective and does not take into account the subjective perception of individual employees regarding the alleged solicitation.[195]

---

[191]Wal-Mart Stores, Inc., 339 NLRB 1187, 173 LRRM 1075 (2003) (no violation where employer increased use of existing job coaching practice during union campaign); Curwood, Inc., 339 NLRB 1137, 173 LRRM 1149 (2003) (employer's continued practice of allowing employee questions did not violate the Act); Wal-Mart Stores, Inc., 340 NLRB No. 76, 173 LRRM 1249 (2003) (no violation where employer had past practice of soliciting grievances through an "open door" policy); MacDonald Mach. Co., 335 NLRB 319, 170 LRRM 1076 (2001) (applying past-practice rule regarding solicitation of grievances in certifying election results). *But see* Superior Emerald Park Landfill, LLC, 340 NLRB No. 54 (2003) (finding lack of past practice where prior practice had been one of mere passive willingness to address employee problems); *Wake Elec., supra* note 187 (finding violation where employer had no past practice of soliciting employee grievances prior to unionizing effort); DMI Distrib. of Del., Ohio, Inc., 334 NLRB 409, 172 LRRM 1080 (2001) (finding lack of past practice at the particular operation); 6 West Ltd. Corp., 330 NLRB 527, 163 LRRM 1113 (2000), *enforcement denied*, 237 F.3d 767, 166 LRRM 2221 (7th Cir. 2001).

[192]*Curwood, supra* note 191; Wal-Mart Stores, Inc., 340 NLRB No. 76, 173 LRRM 1249 (2003); *6 West, supra* note 191. *But see* Gold Kist, Inc., 341 NLRB No. 135, 175 LRRM 1049 (2004) (agreement to listen to concerns of Hispanic employees, standing alone, represented commitment to become more responsive to employees and violated §8(a)(1) where plant manager had previously taken action, including replacing the human resources manager, in response to complaints expressed in employee meetings held during election campaign).

[193]National Propane Partners, L.P., 337 NLRB 1006, 171 LRRM 1496 (2002).

[194]Health Mgmt., Inc., 326 NLRB 801, 160 LRRM 1059 (1998), *enforced in part*, 210 F.3d 371, 164 LRRM 2128 (6th Cir. 2000) (unpublished).

[195]*Curwood, supra* note 191.

(3) Withholding Benefits During an Election Campaign

It remains the general rule that an employer's legal obligation during a campaign is to proceed with the conferral of benefits that would otherwise have been granted.[196] Thus, it is unlawful for an employer to refuse to implement an increase promised to employees prior to the union campaign.[197] Where the decision to implement an increase would otherwise take place during the pendency of the campaign, the Board has held that an employer may postpone a wage or benefit increase if it makes clear that the increase would occur whether or not the employees select a union and that the sole purpose of the adjustment's postponement is to avoid the appear-

---

[196]NLRB v. Aluminum Casting & Eng'g Co., 230 F.3d 286, 165 LRRM 2513 (7th Cir. 2000) (affirming Board's finding of violation where employer failed to give annual across-the-board wage increase during organizational campaign); First Student, Inc., 341 NLRB No. 19, 174 LRRM 1129 (2004) (employer violated the Act by threatening the loss of wage increases and benefits if the union were elected, but not by stating that benefits would remain frozen during collective bargaining where the employer did not have a past practice of regularly improving employee benefits); Jensen Enter., Inc., 339 NLRB 877, 173 LRRM 1018 (2003) (employer violated §8(a)(1) by informing employees that wages would be frozen where employer had practice of granting predetermined wage increases); Earthgrains Baking Cos., 339 NLRB 24, 173 LRRM 1326 (2003), *enforced,* 116 Fed. Appx. 161, 2004 WL 2931022 (9th Cir. 2004) (employer's claim that its hands were tied in regard to expected pay raises because of the union's organizing campaign violated §8(a)(1)); Ishikawa Gasket Am., Inc., 337 NLRB 175, 169 LRRM 1241 (2001), *aff'd,* 354 F.3d 534, 173 LRRM 2993 (6th Cir. 2004) (employer's decrease of employees' annual bonus in midst of union organizing campaign violated §8(a)(1)); Earthgrains Co., 336 NLRB 1119 (2001), *enforced,* 61 Fed. Appx. 1, 173 LRRM 2608 (4th Cir. 2003) (employer's denial of planned wage increase for maintenance employees during organizational campaign, while production employees not involved in campaign received increase, violated Act); More Truck Lines, Inc., 336 NLRB 772, 168 LRRM 1385 (2001), *enforced,* 324 F.3d 735, 172 LRRM 2214 (D.C. Cir. 2003) (employer violated Act by informing employees that if new union were certified, existing collective bargaining arrangement would be "null and void," thereby freezing employee wages and denying them annual wage increases contained in that agreement); Grouse Mountain Assocs. II, 333 NLRB 1322, 169 LRRM 1039 (2001), *enforced,* 56 Fed. Appx. 811, 2003 WL 683415 (9th Cir. Feb. 25, 2003). *See also* Yellow Ambulance Serv., 342 NLRB No. 77, 175 LRRM 1257 (2004) (employer violated the Act by informing employees that they would receive annual evaluations and raises, then refusing to grant raises following the union's election).

[197]Albany Med. Ctr. 341 NLRB No. 145, 175 LRRM 1087 (2004).

ance of influencing the election's outcome.[198] However, in doing so, an employer must avoid disparaging or undermining the union by placing on it the onus for the withholding of benefits.[199] These legal principles apply even where the benefit increase was unexpected by the employees.[200]

In *Noah's Bay Area Bagels, LLC,*[201] the Board found a violation where the employer restored a particular health benefits plan at the request of its managers for all of its store units except the one in the midst of an organizing campaign. The Board found that the restoration of benefits was mitigated by factors other than the union campaign. The employer notified the employees at the store involved in the election campaign that "no change can be made for you at this time" because it wanted to "avoid any risk of improper influence on any upcoming election" through "buying votes."[202] The Board held that the employer should have either: (1) provided assurances that withholding the more desirable health plan from the unionizing store was only temporary, and that the plan would be restored retroactively following the election, regardless of the outcome; or (2) provided the new plan to the employees and established that there was a persuasive business reason demonstrating that the timing of the grant of benefits was governed by factors other than the union campaign.[203]

c. Interrogation and Polling

In *Allegheny Ludlum Corp.*,[204] the Board, in response to the D.C. Circuit's direction to provide clear guidelines as to how to proceed in regard to company videotaping of employees, articulated principles governing the solicitation of employees to appear in an

---

[198]Ansul Inc., 329 NLRB 935, 162 LRRM 1315 (1999) (no violation where employer told employees that results of job evaluation, which was basis used by employer to grant wage increases, would not be announced until after election in order to avoid appearance of impropriety).

[199]*Earthgrains, supra* note 196; Curwood, Inc., 339 NLRB 1137, 173 LRRM 1149 (2003); Met West Agribusiness, Inc., 334 NLRB 84, 167 LRRM 1273 (2001); *Grouse, supra* note 196.

[200]*Grouse, supra* note 196.

[201]331 NLRB 188, 166 LRRM 1175 (2000).

[202]*Id.* at 197.

[203]*Id.* at 191.

[204]333 NLRB 734, 166 LRRM 1353 (2001), *enforced,* 301 F.3d 167, 170 LRRM 2923 (3d Cir. 2002).

employer's campaign video. The Board held that an employer may lawfully solicit employee participation in a campaign video if certain requirements are satisfied. The solicitation must be in the form of a general announcement that discloses the campaign purpose of the filming and includes assurances that participation is voluntary, that nonparticipation will not result in reprisals, and that participation will not result in rewards or benefits.[205] Employees must not be pressured into making the decision in the presence of a supervisor, and the employer must not have engaged in coercive conduct.[206] Likewise, the Board articulated the standard for using images of employees obtained without their consent: (1) the employees must not have been affirmatively misled about the use of their images at the time of the filming; (2) the video must contain a prominent disclaimer stating that it does not intend to reflect the views of the employees appearing in it; and (3) nothing in the video may contradict the disclaimer.[207]

(1) Systematic Polling

The Board recently reanalyzed its standard for polling employees to ascertain their union sentiments, in light of the Supreme Court's decision in *Allentown Mack Sales & Service v. NLRB.*[208] Prior to *Allentown Mack*, the Board had maintained a unitary "good-faith reasonable doubt" standard for an employer's polling of its employees, withdrawal of recognition of a union, and petitioning for a Board-conducted election. In *Allentown Mack*, the Court held that the good-faith reasonable doubt standard must be interpreted to permit an employer to act where it has a "reasonable uncertainty" of the union's majority status, but indicated that the Board could adopt more stringent and nonunitary standards.

In *Levitz Furniture Co.*,[209] the Board prospectively overruled *Celanese Corp.*[210] and its progeny, and held that an employer that withdraws recognition from an incumbent union acts at its peril and has the burden of proof of establishing actual loss of majority status.

[205] *Id.*

[206] *Id.*, 166 LRRM at 1363 (citations omitted).

[207] *Id.*, 166 LRRM at 1365.

[208] 522 U.S. 359, 157 LRRM 2257 (1998).

[209] 333 NLRB 717, 166 LRRM 1329 (2001).

[210] 95 NLRB 664, 28 LRRM 1362 (1951).

This new standard differs from the *Celanese* rule, which permitted withdrawal of recognition either on the basis of evidence of the union's actual loss of majority status or upon a good faith doubt based on objective considerations. The employer under *Celanese* could, therefore, also test the incumbent union's majority status either by petitioning for a Board-conducted election or by polling its employees to ascertain their union sentiments. Under *Levitz,* an employer may unilaterally withdraw recognition from an incumbent union only if it can establish actual loss of majority status. If the employer has a good faith reasonable uncertainty—rather than disbelief—as to a union's continuing majority status, it may petition for an election. The Board stressed that its election procedures are the "most reliable measure of union support—rather than the more disruptive process of unilateral withdrawal of recognition."[211] The Board continues to apply the procedural safeguards set forth in *Struksnes Construction Co.*[212] to employer polls regarding sympathy for the union.[213] Thus, an employer's systematic interrogation of individual employees regarding their support for the union will violate the Act.[214] The Board may also find a violation where an employer indirectly polls employees to ascertain their union sympathies.[215]

In *Sea Breeze Health Care Center, Inc.*,[216] the Board held that the employer's distribution of a "Union Truth Quiz," consisting of 17 questions with an antiunion bias, was tantamount to polling em-

---

[211] *Levitz Furniture, supra* note 209, 333 NLRB at 719. The Board has continued to apply the "reasonable uncertainty" standard established by the Supreme Court in *Allentown Mack* to cases pending prior to its decision in *Levitz Furniture.* Kentucky Fried Chicken Caribbean Holdings, 341 NLRB No. 13, 174 LRRM 1049 (2004); MSK Corp., 341 NLRB No. 11, 174 LRRM 1143 (2004).

[212] 165 NLRB 1062, 65 LRRM 1385 (1967).

[213] Carroll & Carroll, Inc., 340 NLRB No. 159, 174 LRRM 1189 (2003).

[214] *MSK Corp., supra* note 211.

[215] Wake Elec. Membership Corp., 338 NLRB 298, 173 LRRM 1011 (2002) (employer-conducted vote as to whether employees should withdraw union petition violated Act); Public Serv. Co. of Okla., 334 NLRB 487, 171 LRRM 1059 (2001), *enforced,* 318 F.3d 1173, 171 LRRM 2993 (10th Cir. 2003) (communication requesting employees to respond if they no longer wished to be represented by the union violative of Act); Heritage Hall, E.P.I. Corp., 333 NLRB 458, 166 LRRM 1297 (2001) (employer, conducting its own representation election after official election was blocked, violated Act by unlawfully polling employees); TeleTech Holdings, Inc., 333 NLRB 402, 166 LRRM 1241 (2001) (questioning employees about union sympathies and graphically recording comments violated Act).

[216] 331 NLRB 1131, 168 LRRM 1418 (2000).

ployees about their union sentiments. The prize for completing the quiz by the day before the election was $1,427.60, which, according to the employer, represented the amount of money the union would receive in monthly dues payments. Under the circumstances, the employer's conduct was coercive and violated Section 8(a)(1).

Improper polling was also found where a company leadman found an envelope in his truck bearing the words "National Labor Relations Board."[217] The envelope contained a piece of paper that read "I no longer want [the union] to represent me," with spaces for employees to sign. When the leadman showed the company president the petition, the president denied placing the envelope in his truck, but told the leadman to see if he could get some signatures on it, and later told the leadman to circulate another petition after the first one was lost. The Board concluded this amounted to "instigating and soliciting the employee drafting and circulation of a petition seeking the decertification of the Union"[218] in violation of Section 8(a)(1).

(2) Individual or Isolated Questioning

The Board continues to evaluate whether an interrogation is coercive in light of all the surrounding circumstances. For example, requiring job applicants to disclose their union membership or activities violated Section 8(a)(1).[219] However, asking job applicants general questions relating to a union may not violate Section 8(a)(1),

---

[217]V&S ProGalv, Inc. v. NLRB, 168 F.3d 270, 276–77, 160 LRRM 2518 (6th Cir. 1999), *enforcing* 323 NLRB 801, 157 LRRM 1255 (1997).

[218]*Id.* at 275.

[219]Brandeis Mach. & Supply Co., 342 NLRB No. 46, 172 LRRM 1042 (2004), *enforced*, 118 Fed. Appx. 113, 176 LRRM 2640 (8th Cir. 2005) (employer asked applicant what union he belonged to); Zarcon, Inc., 340 NLRB No. 145, 173 LRRM 1478 (2003) (supervisor violated Act by asking applicant during telephone interview if he was "carrying a union card"); American Alpha Constr., Inc., 340 NLRB No. 48, 173 LRRM 1575 (2003) (company president violated Act by interrogating job applicants about their union membership); Roman, Inc., 338 NLRB 234, 171 LRRM 1353 (2002) (employer violated Act by interrogating applicant as to his union status and his activities as a union organizer where employer also stated, in same conversation, that he would not hire union members); Richard Mellow Elec. Contractor Corp., 327 NLRB 1112, 116 LRRM 1018 (1999) (employer who required prospective employees to disclose their union membership on their application forms violated Act).

depending upon the context of the particular question and the underlying discussion.[220]

Similarly, the Board continues to find violations of Section 8(a)(1) when management directly interrogates employees during union organizing campaigns.[221]

---

[220] *See* Oil Capital Elec., 337 NLRB 947, 170 LRRM 1523 (2002) (company president's general questions regarding union affiliation of an applicant's father and why his father's union was not assisting the applicant in his job search were "little more than idle curiosity" prompted by recognition of the father's name and did not violate the Act); Fantasia Fresh Juice Co., 335 NLRB 754, 172 LRRM 1488 (2001) (general discussion between employer and applicant, which included comparison of employer's existing benefits with those that could be found in union setting, was not coercive and did not violate Act). *But see* Lackawanna Elec. Constr., Inc., 337 NLRB 458, 169 LRRM 1444 (2002) (employer violated the Act when he asked job applicant in an interview how he felt about the union); Demco N.Y. Corp., 337 NLRB 850, 170 LRRM 1292 (2002) (low-level supervisor who posed questions in informal setting violated Act by asking employee if he had previously worked for a union and then stating that he mistrusted union members and would consider union affiliation in assigning work).

[221] *See* Donaldson Bros. Ready Mix, Inc., 341 NLRB No. 124, 175 LRRM 1069 (2004) (company president violated Act by calling employee into an office, locking two glass doors, and asking an employee whether he knew anything about union organizing); Atlantic Veal & Lamb, Inc., 342 NLRB No. 37, 175 LRRM 1456 (2004) (employer violated the Act by asking an employee what he knew about the union); Campbell Elec. Co., 340 NLRB No. 93, 174 LRRM 1284 (2004) (company superintendent violated the Act by asking an employee whether he had discussed wage issues with other employees); Carroll & Carroll, Inc., 340 NLRB No. 159 (2003) (employer violated Act by questioning employees as to whether they had signed authorization cards, then telling those who had that they would be terminated); TKC, 340 NLRB No. 102, 174 LRRM 1068 (2003) (manager's unsolicited approach and questioning of crane operator about his union membership violated Act); United Servs. Auto. Ass'n, 340 NLRB No. 90, 173 LRRM 1331 (2003), *review denied*, 387 F.3d 908, 175 LRRM 3318 (D.C. Cir. 2004) (human resource representative violated Act by interrogating employee about after-hours flier distribution); Bristol Nursing Home, 338 NLRB 737, 175 LRRM 1325 (2002) (employer violated Act when it interrogated employees by asking them why they wanted union, who leader was, what employees wanted, and how many people were planning on voting for the union); Guess?, Inc., 339 NLRB 432, 172 LRRM 1361 (2003) (employer's request for names of employees who attended union meetings in deposition for workers' compensation case violated Act); Association of Cmty. Organizations for Reform Now, 338 NLRB 886, 172 LRRM 1094 (2003) (supervisor unlawfully interrogated employees as to why they needed union and what its benefits would be); Phillips & Sons Masonry & Constr., Inc., 338 NLRB No. 19, 173 LRRM 1272 (2002) (employer violated Act where employees were interrogated about their attendance at union meeting, identity of union activist/organizer, and likelihood that they would vote in favor of union); Shamrock Foods Co., 337 NLRB 915, 172 LRRM 1160 (2002), *enforcement granted*, 346 F.2d 1130, 173 LRRM 2454 (D.C. Cir. 2003) (employer violated Act where employee was questioned about whether

For example, an employer violated Section 8(a)(1) when a supervisor questioned an open and active union supporter about her union activities in the employer's office following the employee's annual performance evaluation.[222] The Board found the employer's actions to be coercive despite the fact that the employee answered truthfully and did not fear reprisal from the employer.[223]

The Board also continues to hold that indirect questioning by employers may, in certain circumstances, constitute interrogation in violation of the Act.[224]

Although inquiries conducted in a joking atmosphere are not generally considered coercive, the Board found a violation where, in a background of tension regarding the union's decertification, a company's CEO addressed an employee by saying in a sarcastic fashion, "Oh, by the way, did you have fun talking with the NLRB yester-

---

he had been asked to sign union card, and employer requested him to notify manager if such request was made in future); Golden Mango Corp., 336 NLRB 128, 173 LRRM 1472 (2001) (employer violated the Act by interrogating employees as to why they signed authorization cards and directing them to tell union that they no longer wanted its representation); C.S. Telecom, Inc., 336 NLRB 1193, 173 LRRM 1472 (2001) (employer violated Act where president interrogated employee at company Christmas party by asking whether employee was giving information to union about company jobsite locations); Fixtures Mfg. Corp., 332 NLRB 565, 169 LRRM 1052 (2000) (vice president coercively interrogated employee who had signed union authorization card and distributed union literature during his break periods, by asking him why he was interested in union and accusing him of distributing literature on company time). *But see* Toma Metals, Inc., 342 NLRB No. 78, 175 LRRM 1367 (2004) (question by a low-level supervisor of "what's up with the rumor of the union I'm hearing?" did not violate the Act where employees prompted the question and the conversation happened on the plant floor); John W. Hancock, Jr., Inc., 337 NLRB 1223, 172 LRRM 1031 (2002) *review denied*, 73 Fed. Appx. 617, 174 LRRM 2928 (4th Cir. 2003) (question of "how many men were at the union meeting last night?" posed by low-level supervisor in ordinary conversation during a short ride while on break time was not impermissibly coercive); MTR Sheet Metal, Inc., 337 NLRB 713, 173 LRRM 1031 (2002) (owner did not violate Act when he asked employee if union organizer had inquired about wages, but did not otherwise threaten or make promises to the employee).

[222]Norton Audubon Hosp., 338 NLRB 320, 173 LRRM 1238 (2002).

[223]*Id.*

[224]*See* Ready Mix, Inc., 337 NLRB 1189, 170 LRRM 1401 (2002) (operations manager's statement to employee that he "heard that you were passing out union cards" was invitation to either confirm or deny truth of statement, and therefore was coercive interrogation); La Gloria Oil & Gas Co., 337 NLRB 1120, 170 LRRM 1337 (2002), *aff'd*, 71 Fed. Appx. 441, 2003 U.S. App. LEXIS 13147 (5th Cir. 2003) (supervisor, while not specifically mentioning union by name, violated Act by asking employees who were not open and active union supporters about "rumors" he was hearing around facility).

day?"[225] In the context of the remark, and in light of employer violations, the remark constituted a coercive interrogation.

(3) Preparation of Defense for Trial of Unfair Labor Practice Case

The Board continues to require employers to adhere strictly to the *Johnnie's Poultry Co.*[226] requirements.[227] The Board applied the *Johnnie's Poultry Co.* principles to employer interrogation of employees in preparation for arbitration hearings. In *Beverly Health & Rehabilitation Services, Inc.*,[228] an employer unilaterally implemented a new policy under which employees would face discipline for, among other things, "[r]efusing to cooperate in the investigation of any . . . alleged violation of company rules, laws, or government regulations."[229] Finding that the rule applies to investigations by an employer of unfair labor practice allegation, the Board concluded that the employer's ability to coerce cooperation under the policy constituted a *Johnnie's Poultry* violation of the Act and the promulgation and maintenance of the rule violated Section 8(a)(1).

d. Surveillance and Photographing

The Board continues to find employer or supervisor conduct unlawful where it is intended to impede or discourage employee organization, such as creating an impression among employees that the employer is engaged in surveillance of their protected activities[230]

---

[225]V&S ProGalv, Inc. v. NLRB, 168 F.3d 270, 280, 160 LRRM 2518 (6th Cir. 1999), *enforcing* 323 NLRB 801, 157 LRRM 1225 (1997).

[226]146 NLRB 770, 55 LRRM 1403 (1964), *enforcement denied*, 344 F.2d 617, 59 LRRM 2117 (8th Cir. 1965).

[227]Observer & Eccentric Newspapers, Inc., 340 NLRB No. 18, 173 LRRM 1404 (2003) (Board found it unnecessary to decide whether *Johnnie's Poultry* applied when interrogation involving civil lawsuit was otherwise unlawful); Freeman Decorating Co., 336 NLRB 1, 168 LRRM 1329 (2001) (employer must give former employees every *Johnnie's Poultry* warning, including explicit assurances against reprisal for failure to cooperate), *enforcement denied on other grounds*, 334 F.3d 27, 172 LRRM 2993 (D.C. Cir. 2003).

[228]332 NLRB 347, 170 LRRM 1273 (2000), *enforced*, 297 F.3d 468, 170 LRRM 2577 (6th Cir. 2002).

[229]*Id.* at 347.

[230]*See* Donaldson Bros. Ready Mix, 341 NLRB No. 124, 175 LRRM 1069 (2004) (employer unlawfully identified to an employee the names of five employees who the employer believed were the leaders of union organizing); Sam's Club, 342 NLRB No. 57, 175 LRRM 1185 (2004) (store manager created impression of surveillance when he told employees he heard the employees were circulating a petition where the petition was not circulated openly); Music Express East Inc., 340

NLRB No. 129, 174 LRRM 1364 (2004) (employer created impression of surveillance when it told employees where the next union meeting would be held); St. Francis Med. Ctr., 340 NLRB No. 168, 174 LRRM 1264 (2004) (employer unlawfully told employee it knew who had attended the union meeting); Golden State Foods Corp., 340 NLRB No. 56, 173 LRRM 1278 (2003) (supervisor's comment that "eyes are on you and you need to watch your step" to pro-union employee created impression of surveillance and violated Act); Bristol Nursing Home, 338 NLRB 737, 175 LRRM 1325 (2002) (administrator created impression of surveillance by stating that she knew identity of leader trying to organize union and that particular employee was ringleader); Wake Elec. Membership Corp., 338 NLRB 298, 173 LRRM 1011 (2002) (foreman's allegations that employee had been to meeting and that he and another individual were leaders of union campaign created impression of surveillance); Control Bldg. Servs., Inc., 337 NLRB 844, 170 LRRM 1294 (2002) (group of supervisors engaged in unlawful surveillance by staring at employees for 10 to 15 minutes through a plate glass window of mall restaurant as they met with union organizers); MTR Sheet Metal, Inc., 337 NLRB 713, 173 LRRM 1031 (2002) (foreman's comments that he suspected newly hired employee of being involved with union, and that other employees should "keep an eye on him" created impression of unlawful surveillance); Daikichi Corp., 335 NLRB 622, 169 LRRM 1197 (2001) (violation where employer told employee that it was "an open secret that you've joined the union" despite fact that comment was made during "friendly" discussion and employee did not perceive comment as giving impression of surveillance); Newlonbro, LLC (Connecticut's Own) Milford, 332 NLRB 1559, 171 LRRM 1215 (2000) (violation where manager told employee, "I understand you went to the Union meeting," which reasonably led employee to believe that his activities were under surveillance); Seton Co., 332 NLRB 979, 172 LRRM 1135 (2000), *review denied*, 276 F.3d 579 (3d Cir. 2001) (employer created impression of surveillance among employees when supervisor told employee to be careful because employer was watching union hall and noting comings and goings of employees). *But see In re* Strack & Van Til Supermkts. dba Town & Country Supermkts. & Ultra Foods, 340 NLRB No. 172, 174 LRRM 1001 (2004) (employer did not create impression of surveillance by writing down names of picketers and messages on picket signs); SKD Jonesville Div. L.P., 340 NLRB No. 11, 174 LRRM 1011 (2003) (manager's statement to open union supporter, "I heard that the employees wanted you to organize a union," did not create impression of surveillance); Heartshare Human Servs. of N.Y., 339 NLRB 842, 172 LRRM 1471 (2003) (supervisor's comment that she had heard named employee "and someone else" had been approached by union did not create impression of surveillance, as spy would know the identity of other person); St. Mary Med. Ctr., 339 NLRB 381, 173 LRRM 1042 (2003) (relief supervisor who attended union meeting after receiving invitation from union and who did not report back to employer did not engage in illegal surveillance); Kathleen's Bakeshop, LLC, 337 NLRB 1081, 171 LRRM 1131 (2002), *enforced*, 2003 U.S. App. LEXIS 22029, 173 LRRM 2576 (2d Cir. 2003) (manager's statement, "You are the guy that started the union and that's why I'm here," as he approached employee was insufficient to create impression of surveillance where employee had been openly identified as union supporter more than one month earlier); Shamrock Foods Co., 337 NLRB 915, 172 LRRM 1160 (2002), *enforced*, 346 F.3d 1130, 173 LRRM 2454 (D.C. Cir. 2003) (manager's request for employee to report any future solicitation efforts by union organizer, while violation of the Act, was not sufficient in itself to support finding that employer was generally engaging in surveillance).

and engaging in unjustified recording, photographing, or videotaping of protected activity.[231]

e. Employer's Responsibility for Third-Party Conduct

The Board continues to apply the doctrine of apparent authority to determine whether rank-and-file employees are agents of the employer for purposes of the Act.[232]

---

[231] *See* Snap-on Tools, Inc., 342 NLRB No. 2, 175 LRRM 1124 (2004) (employer unlawfully changed its practice of panning the parking lot with a security camera to pointing the camera at an area where employees were handbilling); Alle-Kiski Med. Ctr., 339 NLRB 361, 174 LRRM 1127 (2003) (hospital security guards who videotaped and photographed union organizers as they distributed handbills off employer's property violated Act); Sage Prof'l Painting Co., 338 NLRB 1068 (2003) (photographing employees engaging in union activity at job site was violation of the Act); Villa Maria Nursing & Rehab. Ctr., 335 NLRB 1345, 168 LRRM 1209 (2001), *aff'd,* 49 Fed. Appx. 289, 172 LRRM 2128 (11th Cir. 2002), *cert. denied,* 538 U.S. 922, 172 LRRM 2128 (2003) (violation when employer hired additional security guards who were stationed within one to six feet of union leafleting activity, and who recorded names and license tag numbers of employees who spoke to union representatives and accepted leaflets); Timken Co., 331 NLRB 744, 171 LRRM 1426 (2000), *enforced,* 29 Fed. Appx. 266 (6th Cir. 2002) (employer's photographing and videotaping of handbilling activity not justified by desire to protect itself from false accusations of assault and battery; surveillance was continuous and unlimited rather than limited to encounters between management and handbillers); Decca Ltd. P'ship, 327 NLRB 980, 164 LRRM 1040 (1999) (employer failed to establish necessity for taking photographs of handbilling); Climatrol, Inc., 329 NLRB 946, 169 LRRM 1385 (1999) (employer violated §8(a)(1) when its agent took pictures of employee while employee sat in company truck and talked with union organizer during employee's lunch break). *But see In re* Strack & Van Til Supermkts. dbaTown & Country Supermkts. & Ultra Foods, *supra* note 230 (photographing picketers as they blocked entrances and impeded vehicles in order to acquire evidence in support of an injunction did not violate the Act); Saia Motor Freight Line, Inc., 333 NLRB 929, 167 LRRM 1024 (2001) (employer established proper justification for photographing handbilling where traffic was impeded, employer had legitimate safety concern because of potential for accidents, and employer did not photograph handbillers until it was dissatisfied with police efforts to minimize traffic congestion).

[232] *See* Amptech, Inc., 342 NLRB No. 117, 176 LRRM 1016 (2004) (employer violated Act where an outside consultant threatened employees since consultant was in position of apparent authority); Property Mkts. Group, Inc., 339 NLRB 199 (2003) (threats of discharge to doormen by nonsupervisory building superintendent violated Act); Mid-South Drywall Co., Inc., 339 NLRB 480, 172 LRRM 1366 (2003) (nonsupervisory leadman's comments to employees were attributable to employer and therefore violated §8(a)(1) of Act); D&F Indus., Inc., 339 NLRB 618 (2003) (assistants to packaging manager, found to have apparent authority to speak for employer, violated Act by informing employees that others had been fired for signing authorization cards); Ready Mix, Inc., 337 NLRB 1189, 170 LRRM 1401 (2002) (mixer/driver assigned temporarily to perform duties of "field repre-

f. Employer Violence

The Board continues to hold that an employer that threatens or uses violence against employees or union organizers violates Section 8(a)(1).[233] Violent actions by agents of management need not occur during working hours or on employer's premises to be found violative of the Act.[234]

g. Discipline and Discharge of Supervisors

Individuals meeting the Section 2(11) definition of "supervisor" under the Act do not enjoy statutory protection and remain

---

sentative" was not agent or supervisor that employees would reasonably believe was acting for management despite his claims that he had authority to direct work and coordinate job tasks); Central Plumbing Specialties, Inc., 337 NLRB 973, 172 LRRM 1006 (2002) (experienced employee, who directed other employees in the performance of routine work, but had no authority to hire, fire, or recommend such actions, was not a supervisor whose statements could be attributed to employer). *See also* PCC Structurals, Inc., 330 NLRB 868, 164 LRRM 1350 (2000) (former manager, whom employee believed was still member of employer's management, violated Act by interrogating employee regarding his contact with union organizer); Tim Foley Plumbing Servs., Inc., 332 NLRB 1432, 166 LRRM 1061 (2000) (senior employee, described as "extension of [employer] at job site," and to whom other employees were told to report all questions and problems, violated Act by interrogating employees about union sympathies).

[233] *See* Northwest Graphics, Inc., 342 NLRB No. 127, 176 LRRM 1188 (2004) (manager unlawfully hit employee's union button and screamed at him regarding union); Corporate Interiors, Inc., 340 NLRB No. 85, 173 LRRM 1547 (2003) (owner violated Act by giving instructions to foreman over two-way cell phone, which were overheard by employees, to tell union organizer to leave job site or "he was going to blow his head off"); Folsom Ready Mix, Inc., 338 NLRB 1172, 173 LRRM 1399 (2003) (manager's attempt to run over union organizers with pickup truck violated Act); Oceania Towel & Linen Serv., Inc., 338 NLRB No. 10, 172 LRRM 1151 (2002) (supervisors violated Act by kicking door off its hinges in direction of organizers, attempting to assault them with lead pipes, and threatening employees and union organizers with physical harm); Niblock Excavating, Inc., 337 NLRB 53, 169 LRRM 1129 (2001), *enforced*, 59 Fed. Appx. 882, 174 LRRM 3248 (7th Cir. 2003) (violation where employer's secretary-treasurer shook finger at employee, called employee a derogatory name, threatened to "get" employee some day, put his finger in the crease of employee's nose, pushed employee's head back, and drew blood).

[234] *See* Kathleen's Bakeshop, LLC, 337 NLRB 1081, 171 LRRM 1131 (2002), *enforced*, 2003 U.S. App. LEXIS 22029, 173 LRRM 2576 (2d Cir. 2003) (manager's off-duty comment to employee in barroom, "You started the Union, and that's why I'm here. I'm here to kill you," violated §8(a)(1)); Wake Elec. Membership Corp., 338 NLRB 298, 173 LRRM 1011 (2002) (foreman, while intoxicated and off duty, violated Act by barging into employee's home, shaking him by shoulders, and punching hole in wall in order to discourage his union activities).

subject to discipline for engaging in union activity or other concerted activity.[235]

3. *Other Unlawful Employer Interference*

a. Bonuses or Benefits to Nonstrikers and Strike Replacements

The Board continues to apply the burden-shifting analysis set forth in *Texaco, Inc.*,[236] in cases involving alleged unlawful withholding of benefits from strikers. In *Dayton Newspapers, Inc.*,[237] the Board held the employer violated Sections 8(a)(1) and (3) by denying a "stay to the end" bonus to employees who participated in a one-day strike, rejecting the employer's contention that the strikers did not remain "actively at work and in good standing."[238]

In *Allen Storage & Moving Co.*,[239] the Board adopted the administrative law judge's finding that the employer locked out its employees in violation of Section 8(a)(3) and 8(a)(1), relying particularly on the fact that the employer allowed the only unit employee who had not participated in the strike to work during the period of both lockouts. The Board noted that two Board members also relied upon, among other things, the employer's failure to pay recalled unit employees for a full orientation meeting or the Good Friday holiday, while replacement employees were so paid.[240]

An employer was permitted to implement different terms of employment for strike replacements because struck employers have no obligation to bargain about terms and conditions of employment for replacements.[241]

b. Requests for Employee Statements to the NLRB

An employer violated the Act by asking employees whether they had provided statements or affidavits to the Board, even though the employees had signed a voluntary release form.[242]

---

[235]Westwood Health Care Ctr., 330 NLRB 935, 163 LRRM 1225 (2000).

[236]285 NLRB 241, 126 LRRM 1001 (1987).

[237]339 NLRB 650, 172 LRRM 1477 (2003).

[238]*Id.* at 655, 172 LRRM at 1479.

[239]342 NLRB No. 44, 175 LRRM 1388 (2004).

[240]*Id.*, 175 LRRM at 1392 n.3.

[241]Ryan Iron Works, 332 NLRB 506, 167 LRRM 1240 (2000), *enforced in part and denied in part on other grounds*, 257 F.3d 1, 167 LRRM 2653 (1st Cir. 2001).

[242]Wire Prod. Mfg. Corp., 326 NLRB 625, 163 LRRM 1261 (1998), *enforced sub nom.* NLRB v. R.T. Blankenship & Assoc., 210 F.3d 375, 163 LRRM 2896 (7th Cir. 2000).

c. Employer Conduct Relating to Authorization Cards

The Board continues to find that supervisory "taint" will invalidate a signed card if: (1) the supervisor's activity implied that the employer favors the union; or (2) there exists a possibility that employees were coerced into signing authorization cards.[243] An employer violates Section 8(a)(1) when it discovers or attempts to discover the identity of employees who have signed authorization cards.[244]

An employer commits a Section 8(a)(1) violation when, during a contract ratification vote, it distributes a memorandum that characterizes the union's ratification procedure as "unfair" and violative of the employees' "freedom of choice" and advises its employees to "object now and refuse to sign a membership card, if you have not already done so."[245] In doing so, the employer goes beyond merely providing information to its employees or expressing an opinion, and disrupts the union's internal ratification procedures.[246] Further, an employer commits a Section 8(a)(1) violation when it distributes a memorandum claiming to inquire into coercive union actions, but uses such information to solicit names of union adherents.[247]

The Board has held that inviting employees to report instances of "harassment" violates Section 8(a)(1) because "[i]t is well settled

---

[243]Waldinger Corp., 331 NLRB 544, 164 LRRM 1280 (2000), *aff'd*, 262 F.3d 1213, 168 LRRM 2099 (11th Cir. 2001).

[244]Wright Elec. Inc., 327 NLRB 1194, 163 LRRM 1077 (1999), *enforced*, 200 F.3d 1162, 163 LRRM 2353 (8th Cir. 2000), *reh'g en banc denied*, 2000 U.S. App. LEXIS 7528 (8th Cir. Apr. 20, 2000). *See also* Webco Indus., Inc., 327 NLRB 172 (1998), *enforced*, 217 F.3d 1306, 164 LRRM 2845 (10th Cir. 2000) (finding violation where employer suspended employee for soliciting signatures on authorization cards when in fact employee conducted no such solicitation).

[245]Sheridan Manor Nursing Home, Inc., 329 NLRB 476, 165 LRRM 1051 (1999), *aff'd*, 225 F.3d 248, 165 LRRM 2132 (2d Cir. 2000).

[246]*Id.*

[247]Aluminum Casting & Eng'g Co., 328 NLRB 8, 161 LRRM 1135 (1999), *enforcement granted in part and remanded by* 230 F.3d 286, 165 LRRM 2513 (7th Cir. 2000), *on remand*, 334 NLRB 1, 168 LRRM 1268 (2001). *See also* Bloomington-Normal Seating Co. v. NLRB, 357 F.3d 692, 174 LRRM 2236 (7th Cir. 2004), *enforcing* 339 NLRB 191, 173 LRRM 1271 (2003)(speech to employees stating in part, "if you are threatened or harassed about signing a union card, I hope you will let us know about it" was unlawful in absence of any evidence of threats or harassment); Tawas Indus., Inc., 336 NLRB 318, 172 LRRM 1276 (2001) (notice to employees stating, "If you feel that you are being subjected to [threats and coercion regarding your view on union affiliation], please report such incidents to the Company," was unlawful because it encouraged employees to identify union supporters and discouraged pro-union employees from engaging in protected activities).

that the Act allows employees to engage in persistent union solicitation even when it annoys or disturbs the employees who are being solicited."[248] However, the Board also has noted that this right is not unlimited.[249]

An employer's strong statements of opinion opposing the signing of authorization cards is protected by Section 8(c). In *John W. Hancock, Jr., Inc.*,[250] a human resources manager referred to employees who solicited authorization cards as "the enemy within." On another occasion, the company president stated the company would do everything within its power to keep the union out. The Board concluded the "enemy within" comment merely communicated the earnestness of the employer's opposition to unionization, and juxtaposing the comment with the president's comment made on another day did not remove it from the protection of Section 8(c).[251] Standing alone, comments to the effect that an employer will do anything in its power to keep the union out are lawful, as there is no objective basis to construe such comments as a threat.[252]

An employer's request that an employee sign a decertification petition, promising benefits for signing such a petition, or conditioning a promotion on signing such a petition, violates Section 8(a)(1).[253] It is also a violation for an employer to initiate a decertifi-

---

[248]Ryder Transp. Servs., 341 NLRB No. 109, 175 LRRM 1179 (2004) (in response to employees' complaints that they were being harassed, supervisor said, "if you feel you are being harassed then you need to put it in writing and then come see me").

[249]Lutheran Heritage Village-Livonia, 343 NLRB No. 75, 176 LRRM 1044, 1048 n.13 (2004) ("Section 7 does not give employees an unlimited right regardless of the circumstances to repeatedly solicit coworkers who have asked them to desist. Our colleagues cite no case in which such a right has been recognized and we decline to do so here").

[250]337 NLRB 1223, 172 LRRM 1031 (2002), *enforced,* 73 Fed. Appx. 617, 174 LRRM 2928 (4th Cir. 2003).

[251]*Id.*

[252]Ross Stores, Inc., 329 NLRB 573, 163 LRRM 1137 (1999), *enforced in part and denied in part on other grounds,* 235 F.3d 669, 166 LRRM 2207 (D.C. Cir. 2001). *Contrast* JHP & Assocs., 338 NLRB 1059, 172 LRRM 1298 (2003) (owner's statement in mandatory meeting that employer would "do anything legally and by any other means to remain an open shop" was unlawful because it implied employer was willing to take unlawful action to avoid unionization).

[253]Bridgestone/Firestone, Inc., 332 NLRB 575, 167 LRRM 1148 (2000), *enforced in part and denied in part sub nom.* Allied Indus. Employees v. NLRB, 47 Fed. Appx. 449, 2002 U.S. App. LEXIS 19947 (9th Cir. 2002); Fritz Cos., 330 NLRB 1296, 169 LRRM 1158 (2000).

cation effort or plant the idea that employees might not want to remain represented by a union, then solicit support for decertification.[254] However, during a decertification campaign, an employer has the right to compare wages and benefits at its nonunion facilities with those received at its union facilities and state its opinion, based on such a comparison, that the employees would be better off without a union.[255] An employer is guilty of unlawful assistance, in violation of the Act, if it provides the language for a decertification petition and requests that a signed petition be sent to company headquarters.[256] Similarly, it is unlawful for the employer to offer the assistance of a management representative with preparing authorization card revocation letters and to allow employees to leave early to prepare such letters.[257] However, the Board continues to follow the rule that an employer may provide "ministerial aid" to an employee who has decided of his or her own volition to file a decertification petition.[258] Such aid may include providing decertification language upon request as long as "the preparation, circulation and signing of the petition constitutes the free and uncoerced act of the employees concerned."[259] Further, an employer does not violate the Act by merely telling employees that revocation forms are available

---

[254]Kentucky Fried Chicken, 341 NLRB No. 13, 174 LRRM 1049 (2004); Sociedad Española de Auxilio Mutuo y Beneficencia de P.R. dba Hospital Español Auxilio Mutuo de P.R., Inc., 342 NLRB No. 40, 175 LRRM 1161 (2004) (manager explained decertification process, but then told employees they should sign a decertification petition because they had lost benefits and solicited employee to sign petition).

[255]Langdale Forest Prods. Co., 335 NLRB 602, 169 LRRM 1465 (2001). *See also* Suburban Journals of Greater St. Louis, LLC, 343 NLRB No. 24, 175 LRRM 1542 (2004); Wal-Mart Stores, Inc., 339 NLRB 1187, 173 LRRM 1075 (2003) (manager's comment that "employees would find out they wasted their time trying to bring in a union" was lawful).

[256]*Bridgestone/Firestone, Inc., supra* note 253.

[257]*See* Air Flow Equip., Inc., 340 NLRB No. 62, 174 LRRM 1157 (2003).

[258]Bridgestone/Firestone, Inc., 335 NLRB 941, 170 LRRM 1516 (2001).

[259]*Id.*

in the break room,[260] or providing other accurate information unaccompanied by an inducement or threat.[261]

d. Suits and Threats of Suits Against Employees

In *BE&K Construction Co. v. NLRB*,[262] the Supreme Court clarified what does and does not constitute a retaliatory suit in violation of Section 8(a)(1). Specifically, the Court held that the Board may not declare a suit unmeritorious and retaliatory merely because the suit was unsuccessful. The Court held that the Board applied an invalid standard by imposing liability for any unsuccessful suit, even if such suit was reasonably based. Rather, the Court held, a suit is not unlawfully retaliatory if the "plaintiff's *purpose* is to stop conduct he reasonably believes is illegal. . . ."[263] Such a petition "is genuine both objectively and subjectively" and is, therefore, protected as advancing First Amendment interests, even if ultimately unsuccessful. The Board cannot declare such suits unlawful merely because they are unsuccessful, even if brought with a retaliatory purpose. The Court did not decide "whether the Board may declare unlawful any unsuccessful but reasonably based suits that would not have been filed but for a motive to impose the costs of the litigation process, regardless of the outcome, in retaliation for NLRA protected activity. . . ."[264]

BE&K appears not to have altered the Board's view that an employer's refusal to dismiss its preempted state lawsuit violates Section 8(a)(1). In *Can-Am Plumbing, Inc. v. NLRB*,[265] the D.C. Circuit agreed with the Board's analysis that *BE&K*'s holding does not ex-

---

[260]Mid-Mountain Foods, Inc., 332 NLRB 229, 168 LRRM 1450 (2000), *enforced*, 269 F.3d 1075, 169 LRRM 2528 (D.C. Cir. 2001). *But see* Mohawk Indus., Inc., 334 NLRB 1170, 172 LRRM 1272 (2001) (in context of numerous and substantial other unfair labor practices, employer violated Act by informing employees of their right to revoke authorization cards and telling them where to find appropriate forms because employees could feel they were in peril if they refrained from revoking their cards).

[261]*See, e.g.*, NLRB v. Transpersonnel, Inc., 349 F.3d 175, 173 LRRM 2609 (4th Cir. 2003), *enforcing* 336 NLRB 484, 169 LRRM 1169 (2001) (it was lawful for manager to respond to employee's question in meeting, about how to end union's representation, that employees would need to provide documentation of majority of employees' preference not to be represented).

[262]536 U.S. 516, 170 LRRM 2225 (2002).

[263]*Id.* at 534.

[264]*Id.* at 536–37.

[265]321 F.3d 145, 171 LRRM 3225 (D.C. Cir. 2003).

tend to a state lawsuit that is preempted under the Act.[266] Instead, the *Loehmann's Plaza* rule continues to be applied to determine when maintaining federally preempted lawsuits constitutes a Section 8(a)(1) violation.[267]

A threat by a union to resort to civil courts as a tactic calculated to restrain employees in the exercise of Section 7 rights violates Section 8(b)(1)(A).[268] In *Delphi/Delco,* several union members distributed a leaflet opposing the incumbent candidate for president of the local, accusing him of various racially offensive remarks. The president sent the leaflet signatories a letter on union stationery demanding a retraction and threatening a defamation lawsuit. The Board upheld the administrative law judge's finding that, because the threat was on official union stationery, it had no legitimate purpose, but was instead "objectively calculated to restrain dissident members' protected campaign activity, in violation of the Act."[269]

III. OTHER CONCERTED ACTIVITY

A. Protected Concerted Activity: In General

1. *Individual Versus Concerted Activity: Employee Claim of Right Under a Collective Agreement*

The Board continues to hold that disparagement of the employer without reference to a labor dispute is an activity unprotected by the Act.[270] Other unprotected activities include partial strikes, in which

---

[266]*Id.* at 151, citing Associated Builders & Contractors, Inc., 331 NLRB 132, 166 LRRM 1086 (2000).

[267]Loehmann's Plaza (I), 305 NLRB 663, 138 LRRM 1452 (1991); *BE&K Constr. Co., supra* note 262, 321 F.3d at 151, citing Associated Builders & Contractors, Inc., 331 NLRB 132, 166 LRRM 1086 (2000); Manno Elec. Inc., 321 NLRB 278, 152 LRRM 1107 (1996), *enforced per curiam mem.,* 127 F.3d 34, 171 LRRM 3215 (5th Cir. 1997).

[268]Delphi/Delco East Local 651, 331 NLRB 479, 164 LRRM 1260 (2000).

[269]*Id.*

[270]*See, e.g.,* Mountain Shadows Golf Resort, 338 NLRB 581, 171 LRRM 1145 (2002), *review denied,* 86 Fed. Appx. 305, 2004 U.S. App. LEXIS 718 (9th Cir. Jan. 12, 2004).

employees refuse to perform some but not all, of their duties;[271] inducing employees to quit their jobs;[272] and unprotected efforts at interference with employers' business contracts.[273]

An employee engaged in concerted activity may, by "opprobrious, profane, defamatory or malicious conduct," lose the protection of the Act, depending on such circumstances as: (1) the place of the discussion; (2) the subject matter of the discussion; (3) the nature of the employee's outburst; and (4) whether the outburst was in any way provoked by an unfair labor practice of the employer.[274] An

---

[271] *See, e.g.*, Vencare Ancillary Servs., Inc. v. NLRB, 352 F.3d 318, 173 LRRM 2865 (5th Cir. 2003), *denying enforcement to* 334 NLRB 965, 168 LRRM 1029 (2001). *But see* Hahner, Foreman & Harness, Inc., 343 NLRB No. 133 (2004) (employee did not lose protection of the Act when he told supervisor that [due to loss of benefits without additional compensation], he might not be able to work as fast as he normally did; the remark "was nothing more than an impulsive reaction expressive of his frustration with the [employer's] conduct, not a genuine threat," and evidence suggested that employer did not rely upon statement to discharge employee).

[272] *See, e.g.*, NLRB v. Interstate Builders, Inc., 351 F.3d 1020, 173 LRRM 2745 (10th Cir. 2003), *enforcing* 334 NLRB 835, 173 LRRM 1242 (2001).

[273] ATC/Forsythe & Assoc., 341 NLRB No. 66, 174 LRRM 1341 (2004) (employee's admitted attempts to interfere with company's contract with municipality was unprotected and, therefore, employee had no statutory right to refuse to cooperate with company's investigation into his conduct, and his termination for refusing to cooperate was lawful).

[274] Felix Indus., Inc. v. NLRB, 251 F.3d 1051, 167 LRRM 2366 (D.C. Cir. 2001), *on remand*, 339 NLRB 195, 172 LRRM 1249 (2003), *enforced*, 2004 U.S. App. LEXIS 13793 (D.C. Cir. July 2, 2004) (employee conduct did not warrant losing protection of Act where employee cursed at employer, but other factors including subject of outburst and whether employer provoked it, mitigated in favor of protecting employee's outburst); Winston-Salem Journal v. NLRB, 394 F.3d 207, 176 LRRM 2385 (4th Cir. 2005), *denying enforcement of* 341 NLRB No. 18, 174 LRRM 1052 (2004) (offensive comments not protected); NLRB v. Honda of Am. Mfg., Inc., 73 Fed. Appx. 810, 2003 U.S. App. LEXIS 17034 (6th Cir. Aug. 14, 2003), *enforcing* 334 NLRB 751, 167 LRRM 1327 (2001); Adtranz ABB Daimler-Benz Transp., N.A. v. NLRB, 253 F.3d 19, 167 LRRM 2566 (D.C. Cir. 2001), *vacating in part on other grounds* 331 NLRB 291, 167 LRRM 1196 (2000); Overnite Transp. Co., 343 NLRB No. 134, 176 LRRM 1169 (2004) (employee union steward did not lose protection of the Act by suggesting that his supervisor should be investigated for war crimes in connection with his service in Vietnam, where there was no evidence that any employees overheard the comments, the comment was made in the context of the employee union steward's attempts to inquire into the termination of other employees and was provoked by the supervisor's refusal to discuss the matter, the comment was unaccompanied by obscenity or any type of threat, and there was evidence that the employer was looking for an "excuse" to discipline the employee); Media Gen. Operations, Inc., 341 NLRB No. 18, 174 LRRM 1052 (2004) (employee's complaint about employer's favoritism among crew members did not lose protection of Act, as crew member meeting was appropriate place to raise concern, em-

employee exceeds the boundaries of activity protected by the Act by falsely and publicly disparaging his or her employer or its products and services.[275]

To be protected as concerted action under the Act, it is not necessary that an employee be appointed by fellow employees to represent their interests. Rather, the relevant inquiry is whether an individual employee acted with the purpose of furthering group goals.[276]

---

ployee was expressing concern other employees had raised, and conduct was not overly inflammatory), *enforcement denied,* 394 F.3d 207, 176 LRRM 2385 (4th Cir. 2005) (court found no protection under the Act for employee who called his supervisor a "racist" at meeting without any underlying facts justifying use of the word); Trus Joist Macmillan, 341 NLRB No. 45, 174 LRRM 1196 (2004) (Board reversed the administrative law judge and found that employee lost the protection of the Act when, in response to supervisor's termination for refusing to downgrade employee's evaluation because of employee's union activities, the employee requested meeting with supervisor's boss and other managers, and launched a planned personal attack, with foul language, obscene gestures, and the repeated claim that the supervisor's boss was the plant manager's prostitute). UPS, Inc., 340 NLRB No. 89, 173 LRRM 1337 (2003) (finding that employer violated Act when it terminated employee it labeled as "troublemaker" for filing several grievances, despite employee's vulgar remarks toward co-workers; Board noted that profanity was common in this workplace and that no other employees had been disciplined for such conduct); Sprint/United Mgmt. Co., 339 NLRB 1012, 173 LRRM 1445 (2003); Bergensons Property Servs., Inc., 338 NLRB 883, 172 LRRM 1026 (2003) (employee who challenged employer on various issues related to working conditions at group meeting did not lose protection of Act by raising her voice and repeatedly interrupting management speaker); *But see* CKS Tool & Eng'g, 332 NLRB 1578, 168 LRRM 1047 (2000) (use of loud profane language did not cause loss of protections of the Act).

[275]St. Luke's Episcopal-Presbyterian Hosp., Inc. v. NLRB, 268 F.3d 575, 168 LRRM 2481 (8th Cir. 2001), *denying enforcement of* 331 NLRB 761, 168 LRRM 1271 (2000). *Contrast* Titanium Metals Corp., 340 NLRB No. 88, 173 LRRM 1402 (2003), *enforced in part and denied in part,* 392 F.3d 439, 176 LRRM 2073 (D.C. Cir. 2004), *opinion withdrawn,* 2005 U.S. App. LEXIS 3109 (D.C. Cir. Feb. 22, 2005) (no evidence that employee's article complaining about nepotism in company was deliberately false, misleading, or inaccurate or written with reckless disregard for truth).

[276]*See, e.g., Media Gen., supra* note 274 (employee complaining about employer's unfair favoritism among crew members during crew meeting was protected, concerted activity); *Bergensons Property, supra* note 274 (employee who challenged employer on various issues related to working conditions at a group meeting that was called for the express purpose of discussing conditions of employment and countering what the union had promised was engaged in protected, concerted activity); Air Contact Transp., Inc., 340 NLRB No. 81, 173 LRRM 1429 (2003) (concerted nature of activity may be shown by comments involving common concern regarding conditions of employment, framing issue as common concern, and raising issue at group meeting); Phillips Petroleum Co., 339 NLRB 916, 172 LRRM 1433 (2003) (employee who raised issue of using sick leave to address family medi-

The Board continues to find that a single employee seeking to enforce a right he or she "honestly and reasonably" believes is conferred by a collective bargaining agreement is engaging in protected, concerted activity, even if the employee has his or her own interests primarily in mind and is mistaken in his or her belief as to his or her rights.[277]

An employee's repeated inquiries concerning personal entitlements that he or she should receive in accordance with a valid collective bargaining agreement does not lose its status as "concerted activity," protected from retaliation under the Act, where the employee's persistence is not flagrant, egregious, or abusive but is, at most, rude and disrespectful.[278] However, where an employee's complaint about a violation of the collective bargaining agreement that would otherwise be protected is severely profane, could reasonably tend to affect workplace discipline, and is not justified by any opposition to grievances on the part of the employer, the complaint loses the protection of the Act.[279]

---

cal emergencies was engaged in protected, concerted activity where employee had discussed issue with co-workers and found they shared his concerns, and at least one co-worker encouraged employee to "speak up" about the issue); NLRB v. Caval Tool Div., Chromalloy Gas Turbine Corp., 262 F.3d 184, 168 LRRM 2180 (2d Cir. 2001), *enforcing* 331 NLRB 858, 168 LRRM 1067 (2000) (phrase "concerted activity" includes actions of a single employee who intends to initiate group activity or action, and such intent may be inferred in context of group meeting held to discuss the terms and conditions of employment). *But see* Roussel v. St. Joseph Hosp., 257 F. Supp. 2d 280 (D. Me. 2003) (employee did not engage in concerted activity where she alone presented note to management to complain about employees being unable to take breaks and had not discussed note with other employees beforehand); Hahner, Foreman & Harness, Inc., 343 NLRB No. 133 (2004) (employee who complained to supervisor about loss of contractual benefits, and employee who complained about company's failure to provide promised pay increase to compensate for lost benefits were engaged in concerted activity where employees also complained to each other, made complaints in front of co-workers, and one joined the other's conversation with supervisor).

[277] *See, e.g.*, *Phillips Petroleum*, *supra* note 276 (employee inquiring about higher wage rate he believed applied to him); Lance Investigation Serv., 338 NLRB 1109, 174 LRRM 1151 (2003) (employee seeking vacation pay).

[278] Union Carbide Corp., 331 NLRB 356, 171 LRRM 1351 (2000), *enforced*, 25 Fed. Appx. 87, 171 LRRM 3215 (4th Cir. 2001).

[279] Aluminum Co. of Am., 338 NLRB 1, 170 LRRM 1478 (2002) (employee shouted obscenities in employee break room and employer had long history of processing grievances without animosity). *But see* Media Gen. Operations, Inc., 341 NLRB No. 18, 174 LRRM 1052 (2004), *enforcement denied*, 394 F.3d 207, 176 LRRM 2385 (4th Cir. 2005) (employee did not forfeit protection of the Act by calling supervisor "racist" and "bastard").

The actions of a nonemployee representative to enforce a collective bargaining agreement may also constitute protected, concerted activity in response to which an employer may not take adverse action against the employees.[280]

The fact that an employee's petition for judicial relief is later dismissed on the pleadings does not, in itself, make the activity unprotected or establish bad faith, so as to lose protected status under the Act.[281]

2. *Individual Versus Concerted Activity: Employee Claim of Right Under Employment, Safety, and Other Laws*

The Board and courts continue to apply the *Meyers Industries*[282] rule that the activities of a single employee are "concerted," within the meaning of the Act, when undertaken with or on the authority of other employees and not solely by and on behalf of the individual.[283]

---

[280]*See* Brad Snodgrass, Inc., 338 NLRB 538, 174 LRRM 1023 (2003) (employer unlawfully sent letter to union threatening layoff of bargaining unit employees in response to union business agent's filing of grievances to enforce collective bargaining agreement).

[281]Mojave Elec. Coop., Inc. v. NLRB, 206 F.3d 1183, 163 LRRM 2917 (D.C. Cir. 2000), *enforcing* 327 NLRB 13, 163 LRRM 1288 (1998).

[282]268 NLRB 493, 115 LRRM 1025 (1984), *rev'd sub nom.* Prill v. NLRB, 755 F.2d 941, 118 LRRM 2649 (D.C. Cir.), *cert. denied,* 474 U.S. 948, 120 LRRM 3392 (1985), *decision on remand sub nom.* Meyers Indus., 281 NLRB 882, 123 LRRM 1137 (1986), *aff'd sub nom.* Prill. v. NLRB, 835 F.2d 1481, 127 LRRM 2415 (D.C. Cir. 1987), *cert. denied,* 487 U.S. 1205, 128 LRRM 3016 (1988).

[283]*See, e.g.,* Mobil Exploration & Producing U.S., Inc. v. NLRB, 200 F.3d 230, 241–42, 163 LRRM 2387 (5th Cir. 1999) (employee that informed co-workers of his sentiment that employer was "trying to dig something up" on him was engaged in protected concerted activity where statement was made in an attempt to enlist support of others in opposition to current union leadership and was not merely personal complaint); Titanium Metals Corp., 340 NLRB No. 88, 173 LRRM 1402 (2003), *enforced in part and denied in part,* 392 F.3d 439, 176 LRRM 2073 (D.C. Cir. 2004), *opinion withdrawn,* 2005 U.S. App. LEXIS 3109 (D.C. Cir. Feb. 22, 2005) (employee's publication of articles containing complaints about such matters as supervisors, safety, wages, hours, and other working conditions was protected, concerted activity); United Servs. Auto. Ass'n, 340 NLRB No. 90, 173 LRRM 1331 (2003) (employee's distribution of flyers criticizing employer's reorganization leading to numerous layoffs was protected activity, and since employer's interrogation regarding flyers was unlawful, employee was under no duty to answer questions truthfully and thus could not be terminated for lying about her involvement); Air Contact Transp., Inc., 340 NLRB No. 81, 173 LRRM 1429 (2003) (employee who stated at group meeting that he had "questions on behalf of myself and my co-workers," after having discussed performance evaluations and compensation with co-workers, was engaged in protected, concerted activity); Sprint/United Mgmt. Co., 339 NLRB 1012, 173 LRRM 1445 (2003) (employee alerting her co-workers

In *K-Mart Corp.*,[284] the employee raised his voice, cursed at his supervisor and refused to permit his supervisor to review rules regarding breaks with him. The Board found that the employee's conduct was not concerted because there was "no evidence in the record that [the employee] was acting either on the authority of, or with, other employees in protesting the break rules—or that he was seeking to initiate or induce or to prepare for group action."[285] The protected, concerted nature of an employee's actions on behalf of a group does not depend on whether the employer first solicited the employees' grievances.[286] Decisions in this area continue to follow the rule that once the activity is found to be concerted, a prima facie case of a violation of Section 8(a)(1) is established if: (1) the employer knew of the concerted nature of the employee's activity; (2) the concerted

---

by e-mail to possible anthrax danger at workplace was not engaged in protected concerted activity, because some of her concerns were not objectively reasonable and other statements were intentionally false or made with reckless disregard for the truth); JCR Hotel, Inc., 338 NLRB 250, 173 LRRM 1109 (2002), *enforced*, 342 F.3d 837, 173 LRRM 2193 (8th Cir. 2003) (employee's remark during discussion among several employees about dissatisfaction with work conditions, that they should walk out one day when hotel was busy, was protected concerted activity); CKS Tool & Eng'g, Inc., 332 NLRB 1578, 168 LRRM 1047 (2000) (employee's activities were undertaken "with or on the authority of other employees" where he participated in joint employee, premeeting discussions during which a consensus was reached); Allstate Ins. Co., 332 NLRB 759, 165 LRRM 1293 (2000) (employee engaged in protected concerted activity when speaking with a reporter of major publication about terms and conditions of employment where employee was expressing her personal concerns as well as those of similarly situated employees); Labor Ready, Inc., 331 NLRB 1656, 170 LRRM 1448 (2000) (two employees engaged in protected concerted activity when they refused to return to work with purpose of pressuring employer to reverse its decision to discharge a third employee); Halle Enters., Inc., 330 NLRB 1157, 167 LRRM 1029 (2000), *enforced*, 247 F.3d 268, 167 LRRM 2332 (D.C. Cir. 2001) (participation in protected concerted activity was found where 11 employees jointly complained about working conditions, including wage increases, uniforms, safety equipment, and tools).

[284] 341 NLRB No. 102, 174 LRRM 1476 (2004).

[285] *Id.* (citation omitted).

[286] Cibao Meat Prods., 338 NLRB 934, 172 LRRM 1097 (2003), *enforced*, 84 Fed. Appx. 155, 174 LRRM 2224 (2d Cir.), *cert. denied*, 125 S. Ct. 497, 175 LRRM 3312 (2004) (at group meeting, after employer announced factory employees had to help open the gate in the morning, employee protested that this was security guard's job, not the factory workers', in a manner that was not so disruptive, egregious, or offensive as to forfeit the protection of Act).

activity was protected by the Act; and (3) the adverse employment action at issue was motivated by the employee's protected activity.[287]

The Board continues to apply the rule expressed in *Mike Yurosek & Son*[288] that "individual action is concerted where the evidence supports a finding that the concerns expressed by the individual are logical outgrowth[s] of the concerns expressed by the group."[289]

In *TNS, Inc. v. NLRB*,[290] the Sixth Circuit upheld the Board's interpretation that Section 502 of the Act[291] applies to situations both where the parties to a collective bargaining agreement have agreed to a no-strike provision and where they have not. Section 502 provides in relevant part: "nor shall the quitting of labor by an employee or employees in good faith because of abnormally dangerous conditions for work at the place of employment of such employee or employees be deemed a strike under this Act."[292] The Sixth Circuit also

---

[287] *United Servs. Auto. Ass'n*, *supra* note 283; Accel, Inc., 339 NLRB 1052, 174 LRRM 1116 (2003) (finding violation where eight employees were terminated for walking off job to protest denial of scheduled break); Kathleen's Bakeshop, LLC, 337 NLRB 1081, 171 LRRM 1131 (2002), *enforced*, 2003 U.S. App. LEXIS 22029, 173 LRRM 2576 (2d Cir. 2003) (unpublished) (employee's complaint to manager that new schedules were unfair to employees, after discussing matter with co-worker, was protected concerted activity, and employee's raising her voice, cursing, and throwing down schedule, if found to have occurred, would not be egregious enough behavior to lose protection of Act); Tradesmen Int'l, Inc. v. NLRB, 275 F.3d 1137, 169 LRRM 2212 (D.C. Cir. 2002), *denying enforcement to* 332 NLRB 1158, 165 LRRM 1347 (2000) (employee's appearance and testimony at administrative hearing on behalf of union did not constitute protected concerted activity where there was no nexus between activity and legitimate employee concerns about employment-related matters). *But see* Garage Mgmt. Corp., 334 NLRB 940, 168 LRRM 1353 (2001) (although employee's filing of unfair labor practice charges, grievances, and complaints to OSHA were protected concerted activities that were motivating factor in his discharge, employee's repeated discourtesy and abusiveness to customers would have led to his dismissal anyway; thus, his discharge was lawful).

[288] 306 NLRB 1037, 140 LRRM 1001 (1992), *aff'd after remand*, 310 NLRB 831, 142 LRRM 1348 (1993), *enforced*, 53 F.3d 261, 149 LRRM 2094 (9th Cir. 1995).

[289] *See, e.g.*, Golden Stevedoring Co., 335 NLRB 410, 169 LRRM 1173 (2001) (employee's threat to stop working if drinking water had not arrived by certain time constituted protected concerted activity as it was "logical outgrowth" of his and other employees' concerns about having drinking water at worksite).

[290] 296 F.3d 384, 170 LRRM 2474 (6th Cir. 2002), *vacating but aff'g in relevant part* 329 NLRB 602, 166 LRRM 1018 (1999), *cert. denied*, 537 U.S. 1106, 171 LRRM 2768 (2003).

[291] 29 U.S.C. §143 (2002).

[292] *Id.*

upheld the Board's interpretation that to be protected by Section 502, employees need only have a good faith belief, supported by ascertainable, objective evidence, that their working conditions are abnormally dangerous, as opposed to having to prove the actual existence of abnormally dangerous working conditions.[293] This conclusion overrules the Board's prior holding that "Section 502 applies only where it has been objectively established that the working conditions are abnormally dangerous."[294] Consequently, employers may not permanently replace employees who have quit working based on a supportable good faith belief that their working conditions are abnormally dangerous.[295]

3. Employee Activity for "Other Mutual Aid or Protection"

In *Petrochem Insulation, Inc. v. NLRB,*[296] the D.C. Circuit expanded the reach of Section 7 protections to unions when it held unions' objections to zoning and construction permits sought by nonunion developers and contractors were concerted protected activity for purposes of "mutual aid or protection." The unions' objections were in response to California building moratoriums associated with pollution allegedly caused by irresponsible companies. The unions sought regulatory action to "force construction companies to pay their employees a living wage, including health and other benefits, and to meet their responsibilities to the community and the environment."[297] When contractors refused to work with the targeted employer to avoid the unions' protests, the employer filed suit against the 21 unions, alleging that they had delayed contractors' projects until they agreed to boycott the employer.[298]

---

[293] *TNS, Inc., supra* note 290. *But see, e.g.,* Airborne Freight Corp. v. Teamsters Local 705, 216 F. Supp. 2d 712, 171 LRRM 2054 (N.D. Ill. 2002) (alleged battery of union steward by supervisor and employer's denial of water to employees on hot day was not safety strike over "abnormally dangerous conditions for work" under LMRA).

[294] Goodyear Tire & Rubber Co., 269 NLRB 881, 115 LRRM 1333 (1984).

[295] TNS, Inc., 296 F.3d 384, 170 LRRM 2474 (6th Cir. 2002), *vacating but aff'g in relevant part* 329 NLRB 602, 166 LRRM 1018 (1999), *cert. denied,* 537 U.S. 1106, 171 LRRM 2768 (2003).

[296] 240 F.3d 26, 166 LRRM 2433 (D.C. Cir.), *cert. denied,* 534 U.S. 992, 168 LRRM 2672 (2001).

[297] *Id.,* 240 F.3d at 27.

[298] *Id.* at 28.

Although the employer claimed that unions do not enjoy Section 7 rights, the court of appeals, citing the Board, said it would be a "curious and myopic" reading of the Act's core provisions "to hold that, although employees are free to join unions and to work through unions for purposes of 'other mutual aid or protection,' the conduct of the unions they form and join for those purposes is not protected by the Act."[299] The court also rejected the employer's assertion that even if unions enjoy Section 7 protection, the unions' regulatory objections in this case were not protected activity. "[T]he unions engaged in a form of 'area-standards activity'—concerted activity protected by Section 7 because of the 'legitimate interest' unions have in 'protecting the employment standards [they have] successfully negotiated from the unfair competitive advantage that would be enjoyed by an employer whose labor cost package was less than those of employers subjected to the area contract standards.'"[300]

In *Tradesmen International, Inc. v. NLRB*,[301] the employer refused to hire a union organizer after he unsuccessfully lobbied and testified before a city regulatory board to require the employer to pay a surety bond for work performed in the city. The employer argued that its refusal to hire the organizer did not violate the Act because the organizer's testimony was not protected activity. Reversing the Board and relying on *Eastex, Inc. v. NLRB*,[302] the D.C. Circuit agreed. "[T]he 'mutual aid or protection' clause in Section 7 includes employees' efforts 'to improve terms and conditions of employment or otherwise improve their lot as employees through channels outside the immediate employee-employer relationship.'"[303] The D.C. Circuit rejected both the organizer's argument that the bonding ordinance would level the playing field between the union and nonunion entities and the Board's determination that the organizer's activity was similar to "area-standards picketing" and would protect local unionized companies.[304] The court assumed, without deciding, that the organizer's activity was concerted activity but found that the relationship between his lobbying efforts and "employees' interests as

---

[299] *Id.* at 29, quoting BE&K Constr. Co., 329 NLRB 717, 162 LRRM 1217 (1999).

[300] *Id.* at 30, quoting Petrochem Insulation, Inc., 330 NLRB 47, 163 LRRM 1276 (1999).

[301] 275 F.3d 1137, 169 LRRM 2212 (D.C. Cir. 2002).

[302] 437 U.S. 556, 98 LRRM 2717 (1978).

[303] *Tradesmen Int'l, supra* note 301, 275 F.3d at 1141, quoting *Eastex, Inc., supra* note 302.

[304] *Id.* at 1142.

'employees' was so attenuated that [it] cannot fairly be deemed to come within the 'mutual aid or protection' clause of Section 7."[305]

In *Trompler, Inc. v. NLRB,*[306] the Seventh Circuit upheld the Board's decision that six employees were unlawfully discharged for walking off the job without telling the employer in advance in order to protest their supervisor's conduct. The employees alleged that the supervisor failed to stop perceived sexual harassment, that he handled another employee's drug problem inappropriately, and that he did not know how to operate the machines used by the workers.[307] The court found that the walk off was a protected, concerted activity, as it was done to protest a supervisor's conduct that impaired the terms and conditions of their employment.[308]

In *Beta Steel Corp. v. NLRB,*[309] the Seventh Circuit reviewed the Board's decision on the issue of whether an employee's submission of safety suggestions and complaints to management constituted concerted protected activity. The employee was suspended after he submitted a safety suggestion to management on behalf of another employee. Because the employee had filed the complaint on behalf of fellow employees, the Seventh Circuit upheld the Board's finding that the employee was engaged in protected activity.[310]

In *Williams v. Watkins Motor Lines,*[311] a husband-wife trucking team was terminated when the husband refused to deliver a load that exceeded the Missouri weight limit. The employer sought dismissal of the husband's lawsuit against it based upon NLRA preemption, and claimed that the husband's acts had the "implicit approval" of the wife, thus making them concerted activity.[312] The Eighth Circuit dis-

---

[305] *Id.*

[306] 338 F.3d 747, 172 LRRM 3201 (7th Cir. 2003), *enforcing* 335 NLRB 478, 172 LRRM 1144 (2001).

[307] *Id.*

[308] *Id.*

[309] 210 F.3d 374 (7th Cir. 2000) (unpublished disposition), *enforcing* 326 NLRB 1267, 160 LRRM 1176 (1998).

[310] *See also* Phillips Petroleum Co., 339 NLRB 916, 172 LRRM 1433 (2003) (employee engaged in protected activity by pursuing right to use sick leave for family medical emergencies); Skyline Builders, Inc., 340 NLRB No. 13, 173 LRRM 1263 (2003) (employee's safety complaints were concerted and involved mutual aid and protection because he consulted other employees before he spoke to management and supervisors about safety concerns, and further finding that employee was unlawfully discharged because employer failed to demonstrate that he would have been discharged absent his protected concerted activity).

[311] 310 F.3d 1070, 171 LRRM 2342 (8th Cir. 2002).

[312] *Id.* at 1072.

agreed, however, because the husband and wife "operated as a single unit" for purposes of their employment with the trucking company.[313]

In *FiveCAP, Inc. v. NLRB*,[314] the Sixth Circuit upheld the Board's conclusion that an employee engaged in protected concerted activity when she circulated a petition among other employees that called for the removal of two managers because they mishandled funds, terminated needed employees, and used the employer's funds to deter unionization. Notwithstanding the employer's no-solicitation policy, the court found the employee "was engaging in protected activity and thus was unlawfully terminated in violation of Section 8(a)(1) and (3)."[315]

In *NLRB v. Main St. Terrace Care Center*,[316] a member of management overheard an employee's statement to the effect that if the employees had a union they would be treated better. Three days later, the employee was fired. Relying on the Fifth Circuit's decision in *Scooba Manufacturing Co. v. NLRB*,[317] the employer argued that the employee's statement arose out of a personal dispute and therefore was not protected concerted activity. The employee in *Main St.*, however, made the remark "during a conversation with a fellow employee regarding unionization,"[318] under circumstances where no personal dispute was involved, and the same employee "had engaged in other protected activity . . . in the past."[319] These factors led the Sixth Circuit to conclude that the employee's remark constituted protected concerted activity.

In *Senior Citizens Coordinating Council of Riverbay Community, Inc*,[320] employees of a social service organization threatened, by letter, not to report for work unless the acting director was expeditiously replaced with a more qualified, full-time director. One of these em-

---

[313] *Id.*

[314] 294 F.3d 768, 170 LRRM 2401 (6th Cir. 2002).

[315] *Id.* at 784. *See also* Santa Maria El Mirador, 340 NLRB No. 84, 173 LRRM 1301 (2003) (finding that employer's overly broad no-access rule violated §8(a)(1), and that by discharging employee for circulating letters to other employees regarding wages, hours, and other terms and conditions of employment, the employer had violated Act).

[316] 218 F.3d 531, 536, 164 LRRM 2833, 2835 (6th Cir. 2000).

[317] 694 F.2d 82, 112 LRRM 2113 (5th Cir. 1982), *cert. denied*, 466 U.S. 926, 115 LRRM 3416 (1984).

[318] *Main St. Terrace, supra* note 316, 218 F.3d at 540.

[319] *Id.* at 531.

[320] 330 NLRB 1100, 166 LRRM 1074 (2000), *enforced*, 2001 U.S. App. LEXIS 7809 (2d Cir. 2001).

ployees was forced to sign a letter retracting her statements about the organization, and the others were terminated. The Board concluded that writing the letter was protected activity because it asserted that a lack of proper supervision directly affected the employees' terms and working conditions.

In *Ishikawa Gasket America Inc.*,[321] the employer offered an employee a separation agreement under which the employee would receive a monetary settlement for her agreement not to "engage in any conduct which is contrary to the Company's interests in remaining union-free" for one year following her termination.[322] The Board found that the separation agreement was "overly broad in that it forces [the employee] to prospectively waive her lawful Section 7 rights."[323] Accordingly, the Board found the employer had violated the Act.

In *Georgia Farm Bureau Mutual Insurance Cos.*,[324] the Board found that four insurance agents who had reported the fraudulent handling of claims by their manager to the insurer's claims department and the state commissioner had engaged in protected concerted activity. After the agents reported the fraudulent practices, the employer ultimately terminated all four employees. The Board found that "the record clearly demonstrates that the agents acted collectively to address a serious work concern [and thus their] conduct was completely within the umbrella of employees' rights that are protected by Section 7 of the Act."[325]

In *Robert F. Kennedy Medical Center*,[326] the Board found that an employer unlawfully discharged three employees for using hospital letterhead to seek assistance from staff physicians in preventing employee layoffs. Although the employer's handbook prohibited the use of hospital letterhead for nonofficial uses, the employer failed to show that it would have discharged the employees for that reason even if the letter had not contained the protected protest.[327]

---

[321]337 NLRB 175, 169 LRRM 1241 (2001), *enforced*, 354 F.3d 534, 173 LRRM 2993 (6th Cir. 2004).

[322]*Id.*, 169 LRRM at 1242.

[323]*Id.*

[324]333 NLRB 850, 170 LRRM 1041 (2001).

[325]*Id.* at 1043.

[326]332 NLRB 1536, 167 LRRM 1334 (2000).

[327]*Id.*

The Board in *Bowling Transportation. Inc.* found that an employer unlawfully threatened and terminated employees for protesting the employer's allocation of a safety incentive bonus paid by the employer's sole contractor.[328] The Board also rejected the employer's argument that the contractor's insistence on the employees' removal from its premises constituted an independent basis for terminating the employees because the contractor's directive was itself illegal under the Act.[329]

In *Cibao Meat Products*,[330] an employer suspended an employee for insubordination due to his comments at an employee meeting. In response to a supervisor's statement that employees were required to help open the plant gate before starting work, the employee stated that it was not his job to open the gate and that "we are the workers, the employees, after you open the factory."[331] The Board held that the protest was protected activity because the employee's comments were in the presence of other employees, proposed a change in an employment term affecting all employees, and was not so "egregious or offensive to lose the protection of the Act."[332]

4. *Limits on Protection of Concerted Activity [New Topic]*

In *St. Luke's Episcopal-Presbyterian Hospital, Inc. v. NLRB*,[333] the Eighth Circuit reversed the Board and found that an employee's statements were materially false and therefore not protected. The employee, a nurse, appeared on a local television news broadcast and accused the employer hospital of jeopardizing the health of mothers and babies by altering the shift assignments and responsibilities of

---

[328]336 NLRB 393, 170 LRRM 1227 (2001), *enforced*, 352 F.3d 274, 173 LRRM 2807 (6th Cir. 2003).

[329]*Id.* (holding that an employer cannot rely on unlawful actions taken by another employer as its *Wright Line* defense). *See also* Loyalhanna Health Care Assocs., 332 NLRB 933, 170 LRRM 1050 (2000) (nurses who were disciplined, threatened, and terminated for complaining about wages, staffing levels, and working conditions with manager, and for testifying at co-worker's unemployment hearing, were engaged in protected concerted activity).

[330]338 NLRB 934, 172 LRRM 1097 (2003), *enforced*, 84 Fed. Appx. 155, 174 LRRM 2224 (2004), *cert. denied*, 125 S. Ct. 497, 175 LRRM 3312 (2004).

[331]*Id.*

[332]*Id. See also* Air Contact Transp., Inc., 340 NLRB No. 81, 173 LRRM 1429 (2003) (employer unlawfully discharged employee for failing to sign memo that reprimanded him for questions asked at manager's goodbye luncheon).

[333]268 F.3d 575, 168 LRRM 2481 (8th Cir. 2001).

the registered nurse assistants in labor and delivery.[334] Finding that an employee "exceeds the boundaries of protected activity when she falsely and publicly disparages her employer or its products and services[,]" the court held that the employee's statement was not protected concerted activity.[335] "[T]here is a point where [an employee's] methods of engaging in [protected activity] would take them outside the protection of the Act."[336] Therefore, the court found, the employee was not terminated because of her union activity but "because her false and disparaging public statement alienated her from her most important coworkers and made her continued employment untenable."[337]

In *Tellepsen Pipeline Services Co. v. NLRB*,[338] the Fifth Circuit reversed the Board's decision as to one employee and found that the employer did not violate the Act by laying off and failing to promptly recall the employee. The court found that the employer would have delayed recalling the laid-off welder regardless of whether he had angered management by publicly questioning the employer's president about company policy during a safety meeting.[339] The court reasoned that the employer had carried its burden of proof in showing that the welder was regularly laid off and was usually among the last welders to be recalled because he was reluctant to complete nonwelding physical tasks.[340]

In *District 17, Mine Workers v. Island Creek Coal Co.*,[341] the Fourth Circuit affirmed an arbitrator's decision upholding the discharge of two union members who engaged in a workplace protest over un-

---

[334]*Id.* at 577.

[335]*Id.* at 580.

[336]*Id.* at 581, quoting NLRB v. Red Top, Inc., 455 F.2d 721, 726, 79 LRRM 2497 (8th Cir. 1972).

[337]*Id.* at 582. *See also* Alldata Corp. v. NLRB, 245 F.3d 803, 167 LRRM 2010 (D.C. Cir. 2001), *denying enforcement to* 327 NLRB 127, 166 LRRM 1039 (1998) (Board erred in finding employee was unlawfully terminated due to his protected concerted activity rather than employer's superseding explanation of poor work performance).

[338]320 F.3d 554, 171 LRRM 3065 (5th Cir. 2003), *rev'g in part* 335 NLRB 1232, 171 LRRM 1256 (2001).

[339]*Id.*, 320 F.3d at 566.

[340]*Id.* at 566–67. *See also* Custom Cut, Inc., 340 NLRB No. 17, 173 LRRM 1166 (2003) (employer lawfully did not recall two laid-off employees who were known to be union members, where employer had substantial turnover in its workforce from layoffs and there was no evidence that other laid-off individuals were rehired).

[341]179 F.3d 133, 161 LRRM 2463 (4th Cir. 1999).

paid wages, vacation time, and sick leave. The court found that the employees' activities did not constitute protected concerted activity because, under the controlling collective bargaining agreement, such matters were subject to a grievance procedure and picketing over grievable matters was a dischargeable offense. The court also rejected the union's argument that the arbitrator's award did not draw its essence from the contract, noting that the "gravamen of the Union's complaint [was] not with [the arbitrator's] failure to properly construe the contract, but with his findings of fact."[342]

The Eighth Circuit held, in *Carleton College v. NLRB*,[343] that it was irrelevant whether the employee, an adjunct professor and organizer of a committee of adjunct professors, was involved in concerted activity, because his misconduct was unprotected. The employee was asked to meet with the dean of the college to discuss professional expectations. During the meeting, the employee was sarcastic and vulgar, referred to the music department as a "laughingstock" and a "pig," expressed loyalty only toward the students and other adjunct faculty, and avoided the dean's request for a commitment to abide by the school's professional expectations. Because of the employee's actions, the dean decided not to offer him a contract. The administrative law judge found that the employee's involvement with the committee was protected activity, that the college had animus toward the committee, that it acted upon that animus by refusing to extend a contract to the employee, and that the reasons cited by the college for dismissing the employee were pretextual. The Board adopted these findings, and ordered that the professor be reinstated.

On appeal, the Eighth Circuit held that "misconduct that is 'flagrant or render[s] the employee unfit for employment' is unprotected," and factors to be considered in this regard include "the nature of the misconduct, the nature of the workplace, and the effect of the misconduct on the employer's authority."[344] The court found that the Board did not consider the college's interest in fostering and maintaining mutual respect among the faculty, which it described as not only a legitimate concern, but a necessary one.[345] The

[342] *Id.* at 138.

[343] 230 F.3d 1075, 1080–81, 165 LRRM 2670, 2674–75 (8th Cir. 2000).

[344] *Id.* at 1081, 165 LRRM at 2675, quoting Earle Indus., Inc. v. NLRB, 75 F.3d 400, 406–07, 151 LRRM 2300 (8th Cir. 1996).

[345] *Id.*

employee's actions evidenced his disrespect for the music department and his unwillingness to commit to behaving in a professional manner. Accordingly, the court denied enforcement of the Board's order.[346]

In *Beverly Health & Rehabilitation Services v. NLRB*,[347] the D.C. Circuit held that the employer had no duty to rehire striking workers where the union had not complied with Section 8(g) of the Act, which was designed to protect health care institutions. In so holding, the court found that the mandatory language of Section 8(g) "could not be plainer or the Congress's intent in enacting it clearer."[348] The union failed to strictly conform to the requirements of this section when organizing its strike, which thus allowed the employer to avoid any obligation to rehire.[349]

In *Vencare Ancillary Services v. NLRB*,[350] the Sixth Circuit held that an employer lawfully discharged five nurses who engaged in an unprotected partial strike when they refused to see patients until the employer responded to their objections to proposed wage cuts. The court reasoned that "while employees may strike to 'protest and seek to change any term or condition of their employment,' thus assuming the risk of losing their jobs, they may not strike and retain the benefits of working at the same time."[351]

---

[346]*See also* Honda of Am. Mfg., 334 NLRB 746, 167 LRRM 1322 (2001) (employer did not violate Act when it disciplined employee who published union newsletter in which he wrote, in reference to a co-worker, "Quit hiding Lee, Come Out of the Closet," and used term "bone us" in reference to employer's bonus program). *But compare with* Honda of Am. Mfg., 334 NLRB 751, 167 LRRM 1327 (2001), *enforced*, 73 Fed. Appx. 810, 2003 U.S. App. LEXIS 17034 (6th Cir. 2003) (same employee's publication in subsequent union newsletter was protected despite personal criticism of manager over benefit issues).

[347]317 F.3d 316, 171 LRRM 3017 (D.C. Cir. 2003), *enforcing in part* 335 NLRB 635, 171 LRRM 1402 (2001).

[348]*Id.*

[349]*See also* Alexandria Clinic, P.A., 339 NLRB 1262, 173 LRRM 1065 (2003) (employer lawfully discharged multiple nurses for their participation in strike that violated strict provisions of §8(g) by beginning four hours after it was scheduled to start). The Board in *Alexandria Clinic* reversed precedent found in *Greater New Orleans Artificial Kidney Ctr.*, 240 NLRB 432, 100 LRRM 1300 (1979).

[350]352 F.3d 318, 173 LRRM 2865 (6th Cir. 2003), *denying enforcement to* 334 NLRB 965, 168 LRRM 1029 (2001).

[351]*Id.*, 352 F.3d at 322. *But see* Mt. Clemens Gen. Hosp. v. NLRB, 328 F.3d 837, 172 LRRM 2513 (6th Cir. 2003), *enforcing* 335 NLRB 48, 170 LRRM 1559 (2001) (buttons worn by nurses constituted protected activity in that they were silent protest against forced overtime, and there was no evidence suggesting that buttons caused nurses to engage in partial strike, slowdown, or intermittent work stoppage).

In *Winston-Salem Journal v. NLRB*,[352] the Fourth Circuit denied enforcement of a Board order, finding that offensive comments made by an employee at a group meeting, and later after a disciplinary meeting, were not made in his capacity as a union member, and were so offensive and derogatory that they were not protected by the Act.[353] The court found that because the employee's discharge was not motivated by antiunion animus, but rather by the employee's individual egregious behavior, it was within the employer's prerogative to suspend and then terminate the employee.

In contrast, in *CKS Tool & Engineering*,[354] the Board held that an employee's use of loud, profane language at an employee meeting did not remove him from the protections of the Act. In response to the plant manager's statements regarding the high scrap rate and the need for increased teamwork to ensure quality production rates, the employee asked several questions and made several comments to the manager regarding his fellow workers. The employee's language was interspersed with obscenities and he was subsequently asked to leave the meeting. Adhering to the rule enunciated in *Meyers Industries*[355] that "the guarantees of Section 7 . . . extend to concerted activity which in its inception involves only a speaker and a listener," the Board determined that the employee's speech was uttered on behalf of his co-workers and constituted an appeal to them to support his protest of the manager's expressed goals. Thus, the Board held it constituted concerted activity. Because argumentative, vulgar language was commonly tolerated by management at these meetings, the Board rejected the employer's contention that the employee's manner and conduct took his speech outside the protections of the Act.[356]

---

[352] 394 F.3d 207, 176 LRRM 2385 (4th Cir. 2005), *denying enforcement to* 341 NLRB No. 18, 174 LRRM 1052 (2004).

[353] *Compare* Cibao Meat Prods., 338 NLRB 934, 172 LRRM 1097 (2003) (employee's protest was protected activity because his comments were in the presence of other employees, proposed a change in an employment term affecting all employees, and were not so egregious or offensive that they lost protection of Act).

[354] 332 NLRB 1578, 168 LRRM 1047 (2000).

[355] 268 NLRB 493, 494, 115 LRRM 1025 (1984), *cert. denied*, 487 U.S. 1205, 128 LRRM 2664 (1988).

[356] *But see* North Am. Refactories Co., 331 NLRB 1640, 170 LRRM 1560 (2000) (employee's complaints about his working conditions exceeded protections of the Act when he complained to his supervisor using profane and vulgar language); Transit Mgmt. of Southeast La., Inc., 331 NLRB 248, 170 LRRM 1447 (2000) (employer did not violate Act when it discharged employee for cursing in front of

In *Education Minnesota Lakeville v. Independent School District No. 194*,[357] a public sector case, the district court found that school district's policy of not allowing anyone to distribute political material through the intra-school mail system did not violate the Act. The court rejected plaintiff union's argument that distributing a John Kerry brochure was "clearly protected" under Section 7 because it dealt directly with issues related to the conditions of employment of the members and how they could make them better.[358] The court found that this relationship was too attenuated to be covered by Section 7, and instead concluded that the principal thrust of the communication was to induce employees to vote for the presidential candidate, not to educate them on political issues relevant to their employment conditions.

In *International Protective Services, Inc.*,[359] the Board found that a strike by the security guards union at federal buildings was not protected under the Act, and that the employer did not violate the Act by terminating the employees who participated in the unprotected strike. The Board reasoned that the guards were entrusted with critical responsibilities of protecting persons and property, and that the union's strike was held with the reckless intention of placing the federal buildings and their occupants at risk. The Board further noted that the safety of the federal buildings was at a greater risk than normal during the union's strike because of the anniversary of the Oklahoma City Federal Building bombing and "several other ominous anniversaries of infamous individuals."

In *Abell Engineering & Manufacturing, Inc.*,[360] an employee attempted to induce a co-worker to quit and take a job with a unionized employer. While the co-worker refused the invitations, the employee continued to discuss union job opportunities with him. The co-worker eventually told his supervisor, and the employee was terminated for disloyalty. The Board upheld the employee's dismissal,

---

other employees where violation of cursing rule was grounds for termination); Carrier Corp., 331 NLRB 126, 170 LRRM 1423 (2000) (employer lawfully warned and suspended employee for interrupting meeting conducted by employer's manager, even if employee was engaged in protected concerted activity, when topic raised by employee was unrelated to meeting and he refused manager's directions to meet later in day to discuss subject at more appropriate time).

[357]341 F. Supp. 2d 1070, 175 LRRM 3164 (D. Minn. 2004).

[358]*Id.* at 1079–80.

[359]339 NLRB 701, 173 LRRM 1023 (2003).

[360]338 NLRB 434, 171 LRRM 1051 (2002).

finding the employee's activities had exceeded the protections of the Act when he attempted to recruit his co-worker to work for another employer.

In *Summit Logistics Inc.*,[361] the Board upheld the discharge of an employee who had discussed workweek and overtime issues with the state labor commission after it found he could also have been terminated for performance-related issues. The Board concluded that even though the employee's protected concerted activity was a substantial and motivating factor in his termination, the employer established that it would have discharged the employee for inadequate performance regardless of his protected concerted activities.[362] Therefore, his discharge was lawful.

In *Yuker Construction Co.*,[363] two employees, using their employer's monitored phone during work hours, were overheard by the employer discussing their dissatisfaction, refusal to work at the employer's off-season pay rates, and intention to look for alternative employment. The Board found that, although the employees' discussion of the pay rate and their refusal to work for the rate was protected concerted activity, their discussion of seeking alternative employment did not constitute concerted conduct within the meaning of the Act. The Board concluded that their discussion was not for the purpose of initiating, inducing, or preparing for group action, nor did it have any relation to group action in the interest of the employees. As a result, the Board held the employees' "misconduct" rendered their activity unprotected.[364]

In *Holling Press, Inc.*,[365] a female employee was terminated for purportedly attempting to coerce co-workers into corroborating an

---

[361]337 NLRB 927, 170 LRRM 1319 (2002).

[362]*Id. See also* Mountain Shadows Golf Resort., 338 NLRB 581, 171 LRRM 1145 (2002), *review denied sub nom.* Jensen v. NLRB, 86 Fed. Appx 305, 2004 U.S. App. LEXIS 718 (9th Cir. 2004) (employer lawfully discharged employee who had engaged in protected activity when inviting competitors to attend a city council meeting, but who had also engaged in unprotected activity by distributing flyer that disparaged employer's operations, where employer established that employee would have been discharged solely for his unprotected activity); American Steel Erectors, Inc., 339 NLRB 1315, 173 LRRM 1310 (2003) (although applicant initially may have been engaged in protected activity when he opposed employer's application for certification of its apprenticeship program, applicant lost any protection afforded by §7 when, through use of deliberate and outrageous exaggerations, he accused employer of unsafe practices).

[363]335 NLRB 1072, 171 LRRM 1071 (2001).

[364]*Id.*

[365]343 NLRB No. 45, 175 LRRM 1449 (2004).

unsubstantiated charge of sexual harassment against one of her supervisors. The Board, in affirming the administrative law judge, found that while the employee's request for help from others was "concerted activity," it was not for their "mutual aid or protection," but rather was only aimed at aiding or protecting her own interests. Thus, no violation was found.[366] Similarly, when an employee filed a grievance where the purpose was to harass another employee for filing a decertification petition, the conduct was unprotected.[367]

In *Wilshire at Lakewood,*[368] the Board overruled an administrative law judge's determination that a registered nurse's act of circulating a petition protesting a proposed change in working conditions was not a protected act because the nurse was a statutory supervisor as opposed to an employee. The Board determined that the nurse was an employee for purposes of Section 2(11), and thus terminating her for circulating the petition was a violation of Section 8(a)(1).

In *Waters of Orchard Park,*[369] the Board found that employee concerns over the "quality of care" and the "welfare" of their patients, while commendable, are not interests protected by the "mutual aid and protection clause" of Section 7. There, a nurse was terminated after calling the state department of health about the oppressive heat and lack of bottled water at the hospital, and then lying about making the call. The Board found that the discharged nurse may have a remedy under the state's whistleblower statute, but her actions were not protected by Section 7.

a. Employer Property and Business Interests [New Topic]

In *Accel Inc.,*[370] the Board rejected the employer's argument that a work stoppage was unprotected because it was a "disproportionately disruptive response to a trivial grievance," finding that the employer had not established that the work stoppage had immediate consequences to employer of loss of business, customers, or income. The Board further found that the employees' grievance was not trivial,

---

[366]*See also* Reynolds Elec., Inc., 342 NLRB No. 16, 175 LRRM 1173 (2004) (employee's continued questioning of his supervisors about whether job was a prevailing wage job was not concerted activity because employee was not acting in concert with anyone else)

[367]Exxon Mobil, 343 NLRB No. 44 (2004).

[368]343 NLRB No. 23, 175 LRRM 1522 (2004).

[369]341 NLRB No. 93, 174 LRRM 1425 (2004).

[370]339 NLRB 1052, 174 LRRM 1116 (2003)

and the work stoppage was prolonged by the employer's own actions.

In *Tracer Protection Services, Inc.*,[371] the Board found that a guard who overheard an informal management discussion and reported on it to a union member was engaged in protected concerted activity. Because the company discharged the guard, but failed to take action against other employees who violated written company policies, the Board determined that the discharge violated Section 8(a)(1).

Similarly, in *Mobil Exploration & Producing U.S., Inc. v. NLRB*,[372] an employee union member expressed dissatisfaction with the union's president during a work break conversation that was overheard by his supervisor. He was subsequently terminated for interfering with an internal investigation and for insubordination. In light of the principle that Section 7 "encompasses the right of employees to oppose the policies and actions of their incumbent union leadership and to seek to persuade other employees to take steps to align the union with"[373] those opposing views, the Fifth Circuit affirmed the Board's finding that the employee's conduct constituted protected concerted activity.

In *NLRB v. Main St. Terrace Care Center*,[374] the Sixth Circuit upheld the Board's finding that the promulgation of a rule prohibiting the discussion of wages constituted an unfair labor practice. The court noted that the test to determine whether the rights granted by Section 7 are violated is "'whether the employer's conduct tends to be coercive or tends to interfere with the employees' exercise of their rights.'"[375] The court emphasized that two managers had told the employees not to discuss their wages, and one of these managers testified that the owner did not want employees talking with each other about wages. It reasoned, therefore, that a "rule prohibiting employees from communicating with one another regarding wages, a key objective of organizational activity, undoubtedly tends to inter-

---

[371] 328 NLRB 734, 162 LRRM 1079 (1999).

[372] 200 F.3d 230, 163 LRRM 2387 (5th Cir. 1999), *enforcing* 325 NLRB 176, 156 LRRM 1273 (1997).

[373] *Id.*, 200 F.3d at 240.

[374] 218 F.3d 531, 538, 164 LRRM 2833, 2836 (6th Cir. 2000), *enforcing* 327 NLRB 522, 164 LRRM 1287 (1999).

[375] *Id.*, 218 F.3d at 537, citing V&S ProGalv, Inc. v. NLRB, 168 F.3d 270, 275, 160 LRRM 2518 (6th Cir. 1999).

fere with the employees' right to engage in protected concerted activity."[376]

B. Protected Concerted Activity: Specific Conduct

1. Work Stoppages

In *Mine Workers District 17 v. Island Creek Coal Co.*,[377] the Fourth Circuit upheld an arbitrator's determination that picketing aimed at causing a work stoppage, over matters that the collective bargaining agreement explicitly provided would be subject to arbitration, is not a protected concerted activity. The union contended on appeal that the picketing was intended merely to publicize its dispute with management. The court rejected this notion, instead accepting the arbitrator's findings that the workers gathered along strategic points on the only access road to the company, that this action caused the other workers to refuse to work, and that the protesters "knew that their actions would cause a work stoppage."[378] Although the workers were also protesting nongrievable medical benefits, the court accepted the arbitrator's determination that the protest was "over predominantly grievable matters."[379]

In *Children's Hospital v. California Nurses Ass'n*,[380] the collective bargaining agreement between the employer-hospital and nurses' union provided that there "shall be no strikes, lockouts . . . or interruptions of work during the life of this agreement."[381] Despite this no-strike clause, the nurses' union notified the hospital that it intended to conduct a sympathy strike. While the strike never occurred, the hospital sought a declaration that the no-strike clause included sympathy strikes. In its analysis, the Ninth Circuit confirmed that the

---

[376] *Id. See also* Keith Miller, 334 NLRB 824, 168 LRRM 1382 (2001) (employer unlawfully directed employee not to attempt to organize or talk to other employees); Keller Ford, Inc., 336 NLRB 722, 169 LRRM 1423 (2001), *enforced*, 69 Fed. Appx. 672 (6th Cir. 2003) (unpublished) (employer unlawfully threatened employee that speaking with co-workers about his dissatisfaction with insurance co-payments "could be hazardous to his health," regardless of whether employee's conversation was protected concerted activity or undertaken only for himself).

[377] 179 F.3d 133, 140, 161 LRRM 2463, 2468 (4th Cir. 1999).

[378] *Id.* at 140.

[379] *Id.*

[380] 283 F.3d 1188, 169 LRRM 2779 (9th Cir. 2002).

[381] *Id.* at 1191.

waiver to engage in sympathy strikes must be clear and unmistakable.[382] The court adopted the reasoning of the Seventh Circuit in *Indianapolis Power & Light Co. v. NLRB*,[383] which held:

> Since the Union's waiver of the employees' statutory rights must be clear and unmistakable, the extrinsic evidence must manifest a clear mutual intent to include sympathy strikes within the scope of the no-strike clause or else the clause will not be read to waive sympathy strike rights.[384]

In *RGC (USA) Mineral Sands, Inc. v. NLRB*,[385] the Fourth Circuit affirmed the Board and found an employees' strike was motivated by the employer's unfair labor practice even though the strike occurred 10 months after the alleged unfair labor practice occurred. The employer and its mechanics differed on whether seniority should prevail in swing shift assignments. The employer made assignments without regard for seniority, which the court found to be an unfair labor practice. Nearly a year later, during collective bargaining, the union continued to advocate a seniority-based system for shift assignments. When the parties failed to agree, the employees went on strike. The employer claimed the strike was strictly economic because of the 10-month lapse between the unfair labor practice and the strike. Affirming the Board, however, the court found the strike was in protest of the shift assignment system and fear of further retaliatory practices. Therefore, the strike was protected and the employees should have been reinstated when they made an unconditional offer to return to work.[386]

---

[382]*Id.* at 1194.

[383]898 F.2d 524, 133 LRRM 2921 (7th Cir. 1990), *enforcing* 291 NLRB 1039, 130 LRRM 1001 (1988).

[384]*Id.* at 528.

[385]281 F.3d 442, 169 LRRM 2633 (4th Cir. 2002), *enforcing* 332 NLRB 1633, 168 LRRM 1094 (2001).

[386]*Id.* at 451. *See also* JCR Hotel, Inc. v. NLRB, 342 F.3d 837, 173 LRRM 2193 (8th Cir. 2003) (requiring employer to reinstate employee who was discharged for attempting to organize walkout); NLRB v. Midwestern Pers. Servs., Inc., 322 F.3d 969, 171 LRRM 3217 (2003) (requiring employer to reinstate employees with backpay and holding that failure to reinstate employees after unfair labor practice strike is itself unfair labor practice).

In contrast, in *Theatrical & Stage Employees v. NLRB*,[387] the D.C. Circuit held that a union-organized strike was not a protected act, as it was illegal under Section 8(d)(3) due to the union's failure to file a dispute notice. The union argued that the employees involved were hired through a hiring hall and were not "employees of the employer" or on referral to the employer at the time of the strike, thus exempting them from the requirements of Section 8(d)(3). The court, however, held that the hiring hall registrants were "employees who engaged in a strike" within the meaning of Section 8(d), and therefore held that the employer's termination of the union and its registrants was lawful.

In *Americorp*,[388] the janitorial service-employer discharged employees for striking and picketing in front of a building at which the employer provided services. The Board, in affirming the ALJ, found the employer unlawfully discharged the employees for engaging in protected concerted activity. The Board found no merit in the employer's contentions that it did not know the employees were on strike at the time of their discharge because a manager witnessed the employees striking and the employer received written and oral notice of the strike on the day of the employees' discharge.[389]

In *St. Barnabas Hospital*,[390] voluntary on-call physicians were terminated after they wrote a letter to their employer in response to proposed policy changes regarding patient care procedures and threatened no longer to perform on-call work. The Board held that this refusal to perform voluntary work was a protected activity and their discharge was unlawful.[391]

In *Bethany Medical Center*,[392] employees of a cardiac catheterization laboratory walked off the job 15 minutes before the first scheduled procedure of the day. Because the employees were not part of a labor organization, the Board affirmed the ALJ's decision that the

---

[387] 334 F.3d 27, 172 LRRM 2993 (D.C. Cir. 2003).

[388] 337 NLRB 657, 170 LRRM 1158 (2002).

[389] *Id. See also* LaSalle Bus Serv., 331 NLRB 1005, 171 LRRM 1063 (2000) (employees were engaged in concerted protected activity when they went on strike to protest discharge of fellow mechanic); McClendon Elec. Servs., Inc., 340 NLRB No. 73, 173 LRRM 1349 (2003) (employer unlawfully discharged nonunion employee for joining union picket).

[390] 334 NLRB 1000, 168 LRRM 1005 (2001), *enforced*, 46 Fed. Appx. 32, 171 LRRM 2064 (2d Cir. 2002) (unpublished).

[391] *Id.*

[392] 328 NLRB 1094, 162 LRRM 1403 (1999).

strike notice requirement of Section 8(g) was inapplicable. The employer contended that the strike was "indefensible" conduct because it endangered the lives of patients at the laboratory and, therefore, removed the workers' actions from the protection of the Act. The Board held the correct test for whether the workers' walkout was indefensible was "whether [the workers] failed to prevent such imminent damage as foreseeably would result from their sudden cessation of work."[393] The Board noted the routine nature of all the procedures scheduled that day, the lack of emergency patients, that approximately 20 other hospitals in the vicinity were capable of performing the procedure, and that the cardiologists who worked there were often tardy, requiring that procedures be rescheduled. Thus, the Board held that the workers' actions "did not foreseeably create such a risk of harm to patients"[394] so as to justify depriving the employees of the protections of the Act.[395]

In *Iowa Packing Co.*,[396] the Board affirmed the decision of an ALJ, holding that an employer violated Section 8(a)(1) by telling employees that they would be considered as having voluntarily quit if they engaged in work stoppage, telling them that "it might be bad for them" to engage in a work stoppage, and discharging 10 employees who walked off the job.

In *Accel Inc.*,[397] the Board affirmed an ALJ's decision and found the employer violated the Act by discharging eight nonunion employees for engaging in the protected activity of walking off the assembly line to protest employer's decision to deny them scheduled work breaks. The Board rejected the employer's contention that work stoppage was a disproportionately disruptive response to a trivial grievance, finding that even if a "proportionality" requirement were applied, denial of scheduled work break was not trivial. It was not established that the walkout had an immediate consequence on the employer's business, customers, or income, and the loss of several

---

[393] *Id.*

[394] *Id.*

[395] *See also* Vencare Ancillary Serv., 334 NLRB 965, 168 LRRM 1029 (2001) (partial strike was concerted protected activity by nonunionized health care employees who refused to see patients until employer responded to memo objecting to wage cuts; any work done after announcing work stoppage was only in preparation for and in conjunction with work stoppage), *enforcement denied*, 352 F.3d. 318, 173 LRRM 2865 (6th Cir. 2003).

[396] 338 NLRB 1140, 173 LRRM 1246 (2003).

[397] 339 NLRB 1052, 174 LRRM 1116 (2003).

hours of production time was due to the employer ordering protestors to leave the facility, thereby turning a temporary work stoppage into a full-blown walkout.

In *Abbott Northwestern Hospital,*[398] the Board affirmed an ALJ's decision finding the hospital in violation of Sections 8(a)(1) and (3) when it refused to hire nurses who were on strike against another hospital with which Abbott Northwestern was strategically partnered for the purpose of union negotiations. Finding it important that the hospitals involved had chosen to bargain with the union separately, the Board found that Abbott Northwestern's refusal to hire striking nurses because they were on strike was discrimination with regard to hire, which discouraged membership in a labor organization, thus violating Sections 8(a)(1) and (3).

2. *Honoring Picket Lines*

In *GPS Terminal Services,*[399] the Board found that employees were engaged in protected concerted activity when they refused to cross a picket line established and maintained for four days by the union in protest of the employer's failure and refusal to recognize the union.

4. Weingarten: *Employee Request or Demand for Union Representation During Investigation*

a. Covered Interviews and Meetings

In *Southwestern Bell Telephone Co.,*[400] an employee who had a history of mental instability was twice referred by his employer to its employee assistance program (EAP) and had received a warning due to a threat he made to a co-worker. Thereafter, the employee told a supervisor that he was "about to snap" and was showing poor work productivity, causing his employer to warn him that he had six weeks to improve. A month after this warning the employee was told by his supervisor that a senior-level manager requested a meeting with him. The employee requested permission to bring a union representative with him, but his request was denied.

---

[398]343 NLRB No. 67, 175 LRRM 1004 (2004).
[399]333 NLRB 968, 168 LRRM 1201 (2001).
[400]338 NLRB 552, 171 LRRM 1193 (2002).

The employee claimed that the employer's refusal to permit a union representative to join him at the meeting was a violation of his rights under *Weingarten.*[401] The Board, however, found that there was "no basis for concluding that [the employee] could have reasonably believed that the . . . meeting would result in discipline. . . ."[402] There was no evidence to show that the employer disciplined employees for low production performance and, even if the manager had referred the employee to the EAP program, the EAP was a benefit provided for the employees and not a form of discipline.[403]

In *Titanium Metals Corp.*,[404] the Board held that an employer unlawfully denied an employee's request for a union representative at a meeting, even though the purpose of the meeting was simply to inform the employee of a decision regarding discipline that the employer had already made. The Board found that the employee had a right to a union representative's presence because the employer went beyond its stated purpose by interrogating and searching the employee for newsletters in an attempt to support its decision to discipline him.[405]

b. Rights of Unrepresented Employees

In *IBM Corp.*,[406] the Board overruled its decision in *Epilepsy Foundation of Northeast Ohio*,[407] choosing instead to return to the principles of *E. I. DuPont & Co.*,[408] holding that the *Weingarten* right does not extend to a workplace where the employees are not represented by a union. The Board concluded that in light of the changing patterns of industrial life, including increased workplace violence, increased workplace investigations related to discrimination and sexual harass-

---

[401]NLRB v. J. Weingarten, Inc., 420 U.S. 251, 88 LRRM 2689 (1975).

[402]*Southwestern Bell, supra* note 400.

[403]*Id.*

[404]340 NLRB No. 88, 173 LRRM 1402 (2003), *enforcement granted in relevant part, denied in part,* 392 F.3d 439, 176 LRRM 2073 (D.C. Cir. 2004), *opinion withdrawn,* 2005 U.S. App. LEXIS 3109 (D.C. Cir. Feb. 22, 2005).

[405]*See also* Dish Network Serv. Corp. 339 NLRB 1126, 175 LRRM 1154 (2003) (employee entitled to have union shop steward attend disciplinary meeting, where union had been certified, but collective bargaining agreement was not yet in effect).

[406]341 NLRB No. 148, 174 LRRM 1537 (2004).

[407]331 NLRB 676, 164 LRRM 1223 (2000), *enforced in relevant part,* 268 F.3d 1095 (D.C. Cir. 2001), *cert. denied,* 536 U.S. 904 (2002).

[408]289 NLRB 627 (1988).

ment, increased incidents of corporate abuse and fiduciary lapses, and also the events of September 11, 2001, national labor relations policy was best served by overruling the existing precedent and returning to the earlier precedent of *DuPont*.

In reaching this decision, the Board in *IBM Corp.* found that exclusion of the *Weingarten* right from the nonunion workplace was a permissible reading of Section 7. The Board noted, however, that the holding of *Epilepsy Foundation* was also a permissible reading of Section 7, but concluded that the reasoning behind *DuPont* was more forceful. The Board cited the following specific reasons for returning to the precedent of *DuPont*: (1) co-workers do not represent the interests of the entire workforce; (2) co-workers cannot redress the imbalance of power between employers and employees; (3) co-workers do not have the same skills as a union representative; (4) the presence of a co-worker may compromise the confidentiality of information; and (5) allowing a nonunion employer to speak individually with a solitary employee in connection with an employment-related matter of potential discipline is in better harmony with the historic distinction between union and nonunion employers.[409]

The Board was careful to state it was not holding that nonunion employees lack the Section 7 right to seek mutual aid or protection; rather, it was merely recognizing that employers often have legitimate reasons for interviewing nonunion employees privately, and the Board does not consider allowing such interviews to be a threat to the exercise of Section 7 rights.[410]

c. Requesting and Selecting the Union Representative

The Board continues to hold that an employee's request for a specific representative at an investigatory meeting must be granted unless there are extenuating circumstances (i.e., the requested union representative is unavailable).[411] The employer must verify that the

---

[409]341 NLRB No. 148, 174 LRRM 1537 (2004).

[410]*Id.; see also* Wal-Mart Stores, Inc., 343 NLRB No. 127, 176 LRRM 1145 (2004) (a post-*IBM* decision where the Board remanded the case to the ALJ to determine whether the employer discharged an employee for requesting the assistance of a co-worker at an investigatory meeting, which would be protected activity, or for the employee's refusal to participate in the investigatory meeting without the presence of a co-worker, which would not be protected activity).

[411]Anheuser-Busch, Inc., 337 NLRB 3, 170 LRRM 1206 (2001), *enforced*, 338 F.3d 267, 172 LRRM 3214 (4th Cir. 2003), *cert. denied*, 124 S. Ct. 1876, 174 LRRM 2736 (2004).

requested union representative is not available and may not merely assume unavailability.[412] This rule is referred to as the "Representation Rule."[413]

Employees do not, however, have the right to insist on the presence of two union representatives at an investigatory meeting.[414] The Board in *Barnard College* held that "[n]either *Weingarten* nor its progeny provide the right to two representatives particularly where, as here, both proposed representatives were on-duty security guards . . . and Respondent offered a reasonable compromise."[415]

d. Role of Union Representative

In *The Mead Corp.*,[416] a union representative "exceeded the permissible role of a *Weingarten* representative" during a meeting regarding three employees' performance by accusing the supervisor conducting the meeting of having a personality and attitude problem and remarking to the supervisor that "you're the dumbest supervisor I've worked for in my life."[417] The Board held that these remarks had nothing to do with counseling employees or objecting to unreasonable or harassing questions and thus were not protected.[418]

On the other hand, the Board has continued to hold that an employer's demand that the union representative be merely an observer, and not be permitted to speak, "is inconsistent with the Supreme Court's recognition that a union representative is present to *assist* the employee being interviewed."[419]

5. *Safety-Related Protests*

In *TNS, Inc.*,[420] the Board held that a walkout at a plant that manufactured ammunition from depleted uranium was protected

---

[412] *Id.*

[413] *Id.*

[414] Barnard Coll., 340 NLRB No. 106, 173 LRRM 1353 (2003).

[415] *Id.*

[416] 331 NLRB 509, 170 LRRM 1496 (2000).

[417] *Id.*

[418] *Id.*

[419] *Barnard Coll.*, *supra* note 414 (quoting NLRB v. J. Weingarten, Inc., 420 U.S. 251, 88 LRRM 2689 (1975)).

[420] 329 NLRB 602, 166 LRRM 1018 (1999). *See also* Avondale Indus., Inc., 329 NLRB 1064, 165 LRRM 1228 (1999) (employees' circulation of petition raising safety concerns constituted protected concerted activity).

by Section 502 because it was motivated in part by concerns over exposure to radiation and toxic heavy metal. The Board created a new test for determining the applicability of Section 502 in cases involving cumulative, slow-acting dangers to employees' health and safety. The test requires the general counsel to demonstrate by a preponderance of the evidence that the employees believed in good faith that their working conditions were abnormally dangerous; that their belief was a contributing cause of the work stoppage; that the employees' belief is supported by ascertainable, objective evidence; and that the perceived danger posed an immediate threat of harm to employee health or safety. The Board concluded that the general counsel met these requirements, and that the employer violated the Act by hiring permanent replacement workers during such a work stoppage.

However, in *TNS, Inc. v. NLRB*,[421] the Sixth Circuit overturned the Board's decision above, but agreed with many of the Board's findings and its new test. The court agreed that Section 502 applies whether or not the workers are bound by a no-strike provision, and that the workers held a good faith belief that their working conditions were abnormally dangerous. The court also agreed that the workers' good faith belief was a cause of the walkout. What the court did not agree with was the Board's finding that the workers' belief was supported by ascertainable, objective evidence. Because 20 years had passed since the event in question, the court vacated the Board's decision and declined to remand the case.

In *Titanium Metals*,[422] an employee published his own newsletter, which he distributed to employees. While the newsletter was not published by the union, many of the articles concerned, among other things, safety issues. The employer initially suspended and later terminated the employee for his publication of the newsletter. The Board, adopting the ALJ's decision, held that the publication and distribution of the newsletter constituted protected concerted activity.

---

[421] 296 F.3d 384, 170 LRRM 2474 (6th Cir. 2002), *cert. denied sub nom.* Paper, Allied Indus., Chem. & Energy Workers v. TNS, Inc., 537 U.S. 1106, 171 LRRM 2768 (2003).

[422] Titanium Metals Corp., 340 NLRB No. 88, 173 LRRM 1402 (2003), *enforced in part,* 392 F.3d 439, 176 LRRM 2073 (D.C. Cir. 2004), *opinion withdrawn,* 2005 U.S. App. LEXIS 3109 (D.C. Cir. Feb. 22, 2005).

Making safety complaints will not prevent an employer from terminating an employee for engaging in misconduct.[423] In *Transit Management*, a bus driver had previously made numerous complaints regarding the unsafe condition of the buses. On one occasion, she complained that her assigned bus had a flat tire. The tire repairman inspected the tire and found nothing wrong. The driver still refused to drive the bus and swore at the repairman and the maintenance supervisor. During her supervisor's investigation of the incident, she swore at her supervisor as well. The employer terminated her for violating its rule against cursing at other employees, which was grounds for termination. While the Board acknowledged that the bus driver's safety complaints constituted concerted activity, it nonetheless held that the employer had lawfully terminated her for violating the no-cursing rule.

6. *Protests Relating to Employment Discrimination*

An employee who engaged in a discussion with a co-worker, urging her to bring a race discrimination claim against their employer for its refusal to hire the co-worker's daughter, was engaged in protected concerted activity.[424] Similarly, an employer's discharge of two employees who served as the union's grievance committeemen violated the Act because the Board held that their discharge was based on, among other things, the employees' protected concerted activity of assisting two female employees with their claims of sexual harassment against the employer.[425]

However, an employee who solicited a co-worker as a witness in her sexual harassment claim against the company (pending with a state administrative agency) was not engaged in protected activity.[426] The Board reasoned that the employee's sexual harassment claim was individual in nature, and the assistance of her co-worker as a witness only advanced the individual employee's interests, not those of her co-workers generally. Unless the co-worker also experienced sexual harassment, the Board concluded, she would not benefit from the employee's claim.

---

[423]Transit Mgmt. of Southeast La., Inc., 331 NLRB 248, 170 LRRM 1447 (2000).

[424]Dearborn Big Boy No. 3, 328 NLRB 705, 168 LRRM 1118 (1999).

[425]U.S. Steel, 340 NLRB No. 22, 173 LRRM 1505 (2003), *review denied*, 112 Fed. Appx. 64, 2004 U.S. App. LEXIS 22407 (D.C. Cir. 2004).

[426]Holling Press, 343 NLRB No. 45, 175 LRRM 1449 (2004).

7. *Appeals to Agencies and Filing of Court Actions*

Where an appeal to an agency "fails in some manner to relate to 'legitimate employee concerns about employment-related matters,'" it is not protected by Section 7.[427] In *Tradesmen International, Inc.*,[428] a union organizer testified at a city hearing that he believed the employer, a staffing company, was violating a city ordinance by failing to post a surety bond. The organizer then inquired about openings with the employer and was told he would not be hired because of his efforts to get the city "to require Tradesmen to pay a surety bond, thus increasing Tradesmen's cost of doing business in Lorain."[429]

The Board found that the employee was engaged in protected activity under the Act, comparing the organizer's conduct to area-standards picketing, and found that his efforts benefited local unionized companies and employment opportunities for union employees.[430] The D.C. Circuit denied enforcement of the Board's order.[431] The court, relying on the Supreme Court's decision in *Eastex, Inc. v. NLRB*,[432] found that there was "no evidence to support a nexus between the organizer's efforts to impose a bond on the employer and any employee-related matters."[433] Although the court acknowledged that Section 7 protections are broad, it failed "to see in the first instance how a bonding ordinance that applies equally to union and non-union entities can be said to be a means of leveling the playing field between the two."[434] Further, the bonding requirement was "wholly unrelated to employment issues."[435]

The Tenth Circuit enforced the Board's decision in *Mojave Electric Cooperative, Inc. v. NLRB*,[436] finding that the employer unlawfully terminated an employee for filing a petition seeking a civil injunc-

---

[427]Tradesmen Int'l, Inc. v. NLRB, 275 F.3d 1137, 1142, 169 LRRM 2212 (D.C. Cir. 2002), *vacating* 332 NLRB 1158, 165 LRRM 1347 (2000).

[428]*Id.* at 1139–40.

[429]*Id.* at 1140.

[430]*Id.*

[431]*Id.* at 1145.

[432]437 U.S. 556, 98 LRRM 2717 (1978).

[433]Tradesmen Int'l, Inc. v. NLRB, 275 F.3d 1137, 1142, 169 LRRM 2212 (D.C. Cir. 2002), *vacating* 332 NLRB 1158, 165 LRRM 1347 (2000).

[434]*Id.*

[435]*Id.*

[436]206 F.3d 1183, 163 LRRM 2917 (D.C. Cir. 2000), *enforcing* 327 NLRB 13, 163 LRRM 1288 (1998).

tion, with the support of co-workers, to prohibit the employer and a subcontractor's supervisor from contacting him and a co-worker at work and at home. The employee did not act out of malice or bad faith, even though the business relationship between the employer and subcontractor might have been disrupted.

Employers are not only prohibited from retaliating against employees for filing safety complaints with government agencies, but may also violate the Act by interrogating employees about the filing and substance of such complaints.[437]

The Board has found, however, that an employee's appeal to a government agency must be "for mutual aid and protection" of the employee to be protected by the Act. In *Waters of Orchard Park*,[438] two nurses called the New York State Department of Health Patient Care Hotline, complaining that the employer's nursing home was excessively hot, and were subsequently terminated. The Board concluded that the employees were not acting for their own mutual aid and protection but rather were seeking to protect the patients. While the Act may not prohibit this conduct, the Board suggested that the employees may have a cause of action under a state whistleblower statute and/or a public policy exception to the employment-at-will doctrine.

C. Unprotected Concerted Activities

1. *Sit-Down Strikes*

The Board continues to find that an in-plant work stoppage is protected, provided it is peaceful, of a reasonable duration, focuses on a specific job-related complaint, and causes only minimal disruption to those employees who continue working.[439] For example, the Board held that a 15- to 20-minute refusal by nonrepresented members of a customer service team to answer calls in response to a "temporary change in procedure" was a "protected in-plant work stoppage" as opposed to "an unprotected sit-down strike."[440] The Board

---

[437]RGC Mineral Sands, Inc., 332 NLRB 1633, 168 LRRM 1094 (2001), *enforced*, 281 F.3d 442, 169 LRRM 2633 (4th Cir. 2002).

[438]341 NLRB No. 93, 174 LRRM 1425 (2004).

[439]Benesight, Inc., 337 NLRB 282, 173 LRRM 1533 (2001). *See generally* Yale Univ., 330 NLRB 246, 162 LRRM 1393 (1999) (unprotected "grade strike" by teaching fellows was analogized to a sit-down strike).

[440]*Benesight, Inc.*, *supra* note 439. *See also* Chapter 19 "The Primary Strike" for discussion on partial and intermittent strikes.

noted that the work stoppage was peaceful, the employees never refused to leave the premises, the action was in response to a "specific job-related complaint," and the employees "returned to work when they were asked to do so."[441]

2. *Partial and Intermittent Strikes*

The Board continues to hold that employees engaging in a partial or intermittent strike may lose their protected status. In this regard, the Board held, in *Yale University*,[442] that the withholding of grades by teaching fellows in an effort to obtain recognition of their union was a partial strike and, thus, unprotected.[443]

However, the Board also continues to hold that a refusal to perform voluntary work does not constitute an unprotected partial strike. Thus, a concerted threat by physicians not to perform "on-call" work was protected where this work was "entirely voluntary."[444]

Similarly, the Sixth Circuit in *Vencare Ancillary Services v. NLRB*[445] denied enforcement of a Board order finding that a work stoppage was protected even though employees continued to perform some work after announcing the work stoppage. The court ruled that employees must completely stop working or risk being discharged for engaging in unprotected activity.[446]

3. *Other Unprotected Activity*

The Board continues to hold that otherwise protected activity may lose the protection of the Act, where the activity is accompanied by unreasonable extraneous circumstances. In *Nynex Corp.*,[447] the Board found that an employer was justified in summoning the police, refusing to accept grievances, suspending 12 employees, and canceling union representatives' access cards in response to a highly disruptive incident. The union representatives and employees en-

---

[441] *Id.*

[442] 330 NLRB 246, 162 LRRM 1393 (1999).

[443] *See also* Electronic Data Sys. Corp., 331 NLRB 343, 164 LRRM 1211 (2000).

[444] St. Barnabas Hosp., 334 NLRB 1000, 168 LRRM 1005 (2001), *enforced*, 46 Fed. Appx. 32, 171 LRRM 2064 (2d Cir. 2002) (unpublished). *See also* Chapter 19 "The Primary Strike" for discussion on partial and intermittent strikes.

[445] 352 F.3d 318, 173 LRRM 2865 (6th Cir. 2003), *denying enforcement to* 334 NLRB 965, 168 LRRM 1029 (2001).

[446] *Id.* at 325.

[447] 338 NLRB 659, 171 LRRM 1329 (2002).

tered the employer's premises with the intent of filing a grievance against the employer, but this incident led to a two-hour work disruption in which union representatives repeatedly refused to leave the employer's premises. The Board held that although filing the grievance was a protected activity, the manner in which that protected activity was carried out justified the employer's actions, including its refusal to accept the grievance.

The Board has also held that an employer who lawfully called the police to seek the removal and arrest of picketers acted unlawfully.[448] The Fourth Circuit, however, disagreed, holding that the employer did not violate the Act by "merely requesting that local law enforcement officials assess the situation and take appropriate action" since there was a "potentially dangerous traffic condition" created as a result of the otherwise protected picketing.[449]

The Board continues to hold concerted activity "indefensible" only where employees fail to take reasonable precautions to protect the employer's plant, equipment, or products from foreseeable imminent damage due to a sudden cessation of work. This same standard of conduct is applied to employees of health care institutions. Thus, the Board, in *Bethany Medical Center*,[450] held that hospital catheterization laboratory employees who walked out to protest working conditions after giving only 15 minutes' advance notice were engaged in protected, concerted activities and did not lose their protection under the Act for an "indefensible" action. The Board held that the catheterization laboratory employees did not create such a risk of harm as to lose statutory protection for their walkout.

Relying on *Bethany Medical Center*, the Board, in *International Protective Services, Inc.*,[451] held that a strike by security guards designed to compromise the security of the federal buildings to which they were assigned was unprotected. The Board stated the test is neither whether there has been adequate notice nor whether there has been actual injury, but instead is whether the strikers failed to take reasonable precautions to protect the employer's operation from such

[448]The Greenbrier, 340 NLRB No. 92, 173 LRRM 1273 (2003), *enforcement denied, review granted,* 377 F.3d 394, 175 LRRM 2328 (4th Cir. 2003).

[449]*Id.*, 377 F.3d at 399–401.

[450]328 NLRB 1094, 162 LRRM 1403 (1999).

[451]339 NLRB 701, 173 LRRM 1023 (2003).

eminent danger as would foreseeably result from their sudden cessation of work.[452]

The Board in *Winston-Salem Journal* determined that a union officer's cursing and disruptive behavior did not cause his actions to lose its protected status since he was speaking out about unfair treatment at work at a meeting with his employer.[453] The Fourth Circuit, however, denied enforcement of the Board's decision and instead held that speech containing words "such as 'b_ _ _ _ _d,' a 'redneck son-of-a-b_ _ _ _h,' and other words of similar import, are devoid of substantive content and of meaningful value that could convey a message of grievance or concern."[454]

a. Breach of Confidentiality

An employer's rule that prohibited "disrespectful conduct towards others" and "disclosure of confidential information relating to other employees" was deemed overly broad by the Board and thus unlawful because it could reasonably be construed to prohibit employee discussion of terms and conditions of employment.[455] However, the D.C. Circuit disagreed, concluding that the Board's interpretation was unreasonable and indefensible. The provision was contained in handbook rules that the court found were clearly directed toward insubordination and disclosure of confidential patient (or employee) information, and could not be read to encompass an employee's discussion of his own employment terms.

A security guard was engaged in protected concerted activity when he disclosed to the union a plan, by the supervisors at the company to which he had been assigned to work, to discipline certain union officials.[456] The guard had overheard the conversation in which the supervisors discussed their plan. The security company violated the Act when it discharged the guard at the request of the company to which he was assigned.

---

[452]*Id.*

[453]341 NLRB No. 18, 174 LRRM 1052 (2004), *enforcement denied*, 394 F.3d 207, 176 LRRM 2385 (4th Cir. 2005).

[454]394 F.3d 207, 176 LRRM 2385 (4th Cir. 2005).

[455]University Med. Ctr., 335 NLRB 1318, 169 LRRM 1334 (2001), *enforcement granted in part*, 335 F.3d 1079, 172 LRRM 3121 (D.C. Cir. 2003).

[456]Tracer Prot. Servs., Inc., 328 NLRB 734, 162 LRRM 1079 (1999).

In *Beverly California Corp. v. NLRB*,[457] the Seventh Circuit overruled the Board's determination that the employer violated Section 8(a)(3) by discharging a known union organizer for copying co-workers' names and telephone numbers and removing them from the premises. The Board had concluded that the personnel information was not confidential. The court found that the information was confidential, thus the employee had not obtained the information in an open and unobjectionable manner, and that there was no evidence the employer would have tolerated this behavior from committed union opponents.

An employer's rule against speaking about medical restrictions justified by the Americans with Disabilities Act was overly broad because it affected working conditions of other employees and was the subject of a possible grievance.[458]

In *Phoenix Transit System*,[459] the Board determined that a termination based on the violation of a confidentiality rule prohibiting employees from discussing sexual harassment complaints among themselves violated the Act, where that rule did not have legitimate and substantial justification. The Board found that the employer violated Section 8(a)(1) by terminating an employee who wrote articles in a union newsletter about the employer's handling of sexual harassment complaints.

On the other hand, where the employer can provide a legitimate and substantial justification for its confidentiality rule, the employer may discipline an employee who violates that rule, even where the disclosure is otherwise protected by the Act.[460] In *Desert*

[457]227 F.3d 817, 165 LRRM 2257 (7th Cir. 2000), *enforcing in part, vacating in part, and remanding* 326 NLRB 153, 159 LRRM 1049 (1998) *and* 326 NLRB 232, 159 LRRM 1033 (1998). *See also* Cook County Coll. Teachers Union Local 1600, 331 NLRB 118, 170 LRRM 1424 (2000) (employee was not engaged in protected activity where she gave union official internal directory of names, titles, home addresses, and telephone numbers of management officials, where use of directory was restricted to work-related purposes).

[458]Lockheed Martin Astronautics, 330 NLRB 422, 163 LRRM 1049 (2000).

[459]337 NLRB 510, 170 LRRM 1001 (2002), *enforced*, 63 Fed. Appx. 524, 2003 U.S. App. LEXIS 9429 (D.C. Cir. 2003) (unpublished).

[460]Desert Palace, Inc., 336 NLRB 271, 168 LRRM 1287 (2001). *See also* Safeway, Inc., 338 NLRB 525, 171 LRRM 1169 (2002) (employer's confidentiality rule prohibiting exchange of proprietary information or other information that would hurt employer's competitive position was lawful and did not justify setting aside election).

Palace, Inc., the Board determined that an employer had a legitimate and substantial justification for imposing a confidentiality rule on employees during a pending internal drug investigation. There had been allegations of a management cover-up and threats of violence associated with the investigation that provided the employer with a substantial business justification for the rule. Witnesses were interviewed individually and given the confidentiality directive to ensure the witness' safety, as well as the sanctity of the investigation.

A divided Board in *Mediaone of Greater Florida, Inc.*[461] concluded that a handbook provision prohibiting the disclosure of "employee information, including organizational charts and databases" was valid as it would be reasonably understood that the rule was designed to protect proprietary information rather than prohibit discussion of wages and working conditions. The dissenting member would have found unlawful any rule containing any ambiguity as to what constitutes information protected from disclosure.[462]

b. False Allegations or Affidavits Concerning the Employer

The Board continues to hold that false, and even defamatory, statements concerning the employer do not lose protection of the Act unless they are made with knowledge of their falsity or with reckless disregard for the truth.[463]

c. Disparagement of the Employer or Its Business Activities

Employees who falsely and publicly disparage their employers or their employers' products and services continue to be found to have exceeded the boundaries of protected activity. Courts disagree with the Board, however, as to what constitutes "disparagement" and whether the falsity must be "malicious." For example, the Eighth Circuit, in *St. Luke's Episcopal-Presbyterian Hospital v. NLRB*,[464] held that

---

[461]340 NLRB No. 39, 173 LRRM 1201 (2003).

[462]Double Eagle Hotel & Casino, 341 NLRB No. 17, 174 LRRM 1088 (2004) (rule prohibiting communication of any confidential or sensitive information concerning company or any of its employees found to be unlawful).

[463]Asplundh Tree Expert Co., 336 NLRB 1106, 168 LRRM 1465 (2001), *vacated by* 365 F.3d 168, 174 LRRM 2929 (3d Cir. 2004) (without deciding whether the employer violated Act, the court held that the Board lacked jurisdiction because Act does not protect employees temporarily working outside the United States for U.S. employer).

[464]268 F.3d 575, 168 LRRM 2481 (8th Cir. 2001), *denying enforcement of* 331 NLRB 761, 168 LRRM 1271 (2001).

the Board erred in finding that a registered nurse was engaged in protected activity when she made a televised statement to a reporter accusing the hospital by whom she was employed of "jeopardizing the health of mothers and babies" by depleting its staff of labor and delivery registered nurses, reducing effectiveness of the remaining registered nurses by increasing their duties, and providing less qualified replacements. The Board had found this statement protected because it was not "maliciously false." The court, however, held the disparaging statement was unprotected because it adversely affected the hospital's reputation with prospective patients and the public at large and was "materially false."

However, employees who communicate with third parties in circumstances where the communication is related to an ongoing labor dispute, and the communication is not disloyal, reckless, or maliciously untrue, continue to be protected. Thus, the Board found that an employee was engaged in protected activity where he distributed literature to the public urging them not to use the hospital because the employer, a subcontractor of the hospital, did not provide paid family health care to its employees.[465]

Similarly, in *American Golf Corp.*,[466] a maintenance employee was found to have engaged in protected activity when he placed a call to his employer's competitor urging him to attend a city council meeting scheduled for the following day where the call was expressly related to the employees' ongoing dispute with the employer. The employee advised the person who answered the phone that maintenance employees were having "union problems" and were having trouble negotiating with the employer. On the other hand, that employee was found not to have engaged in protected activity when he distributed a flyer that related solely to the impact of his employer's capital investment and other business practices on the quality of the service provided to the customers, where the flyer was not part of the appeal for support in the maintenance employees' ongoing dispute with the employer. The flyer made no reference to the labor controversy.

The Board, in *Allstate Insurance Co.*,[467] held that an insurance agent who criticized employment conditions in an interview with a

---

[465]Arlington Elec., Inc., 332 NLRB 845, 166 LRRM 1049 (2000).
[466]330 NLRB 1238, 164 LRRM 1049 (2000).
[467]332 NLRB 759, 165 LRRM 1293 (2000).

magazine reporter was engaged in protected concerted activity because other agents participated in the article and the agent participated in the interview, in part, to alert other agents of the pitfalls she perceived.

In *Tradesmen International, Inc.*,[468] the Board held that an employer could lawfully promulgate a rule prohibiting "verbal or other statements which are slanderous or detrimental to the company or any of the company's employees."[469] Although the Board reiterated its prior holdings that it is unlawful to prohibit "merely false" statements, the rule at issue did not encompass protected concerted activity. Specifically, the Board found that employees could not reasonably believe that the employer's rule applied to statements protected by the Act.

IV. UNION RESTRAINT AND COERCION

A. Section 8(b)(1)(A): Restraint and Coercion of Employees

Unions may violate Section 8(b)(1)(A) in their treatment of nonmembers; nonmembers cannot be discriminated against in the processing of contract grievances.[470]

In *Lee v. NLRB*,[471] the Fourth Circuit held that a union violated Section 8(b)(1)(A) by proposing and agreeing that the union logo be displayed on uniforms that employees were required to wear.

Enforcing the union-security clause of the contract, to collect dues and fees from nonmember employees who object to paying dues in excess of the amounts spent on representation, violates Section 8(b)(1)(A).[472] However, allocating expenditures for organizing is chargeable to objecting nonmember employees, and expending dues and fees collected from them for such activities does not violate Section 8(b)(1)(A).[473]

[468]338 NLRB 460, 172 LRRM 1074 (2002).

[469]*Id.*

[470]Auto Workers v. NLRB, 168 F.3d 509, 160 LRRM 2955 (D.C. Cir. 1999), *enforcing* 325 NLRB 530, 160 LRRM 1158 (1998).

[471]393 F.3d 491, 176 LRRM 2321 (4th Cir. 2005), *vacating* 335 NLRB 1066, 168 LRRM 1049 (2001) (court also held that the employer violated sections §§8(a)(1), (2), and (3).

[472]Painters, District Councils 8, 16 & 33 (Meiswinkel/RFJ, Inc.), 327 NLRB 1020, 162 LRRM 1173 (1999).

[473]Food & Commercial Workers, 329 NLRB 730, 162 LRRM 1177 (1999), *enforced in part by* 307 F.3d 760, 171 LRRM 2063 (9th Cir.), *cert. denied sub nom.* Mulder v. NLRB, 123 S. Ct. 551, 171 LRRM 2256 (2002).

A union did not violate Section 8(b)(1)(A) when it required employees, who had "withdrawn dishonorably" from the union, to pay a fee equivalent to the dues for the period of nonmembership if they should seek to rejoin the union, while allowing employees who had "honorably withdrawn" to rejoin without having to pay such a fee.[474] According to the union's policy, a resignation is dishonorable when the employee remains in a bargaining unit position, while an honorable withdrawal refers to an employee who took a position outside of the unit. The Board, applying *Scofield v. NLRB*,[475] found the union's policy was not coercive or discriminatory and constituted a legitimate exercise of the union's right to prescribe rules of membership.

2. *Fines and Discipline of Union Members*

Following the test set forth in *Scofield v. NLRB*,[476] the Board continues to find that internal union discipline that affects only an employee's relationship with the union does not violate Section 8(b)(1)(A) of the Act.[477] However, in *Operating Engineers Local 3 (Specialty Crushing, Inc.)*,[478] the union was found to have violated Section 8(b)(1)(A) when it disciplined four members for continuing to work for a nonunion employer after being directed to cease working. Without deciding whether the union had properly adopted a rule prohibiting such employment, the Board held that it had been disparately enforced. The union's defense, that it had taken this action in response to having lost an election and for the lawful purpose of obtaining recognition, was rejected.

A union's punishment of a member for complying with his employer's instructions to report co-workers' misconduct also violated Section 8(b)(1)(A).[479]

---

[474]Auto Workers Local 1853 (Saturn Corp.), 333 NLRB 291, 166 LRRM 1201 (2001), *aff'd*, 325 F.3d 749, 172 LRRM 2129 (6th Cir. 2003).

[475]394 U.S. 423, 70 LRRM 3105 (1969).

[476]*Id.*

[477]Commonwealth Edison Co., 341 NLRB No. 43, 174 LRRM 1414 (2004) (union did not violate the Act when it fined employees and threatened to revoke union cards for violating internal union rule prohibiting participation in employer's voluntary time-off program).

[478]331 NLRB 369, 164 LRRM 1217 (2000).

[479]NLRB v. Teamsters Local 439, 175 F.3d 1173, 161 LRRM 2571 (9th Cir. 1999), *enforcing* 324 NLRB 1096, 157 LRRM 1190 (1997). *See also* Teamsters Local 896 (Anheuser-Busch), 339 NLRB 769, 172 LRRM 1411 (2003) (union violated §8(b)(1)(A) by posting notice at employer's facility threatening employees with internal union discipline if they report problems with fellow union members to management, as such threats constitute restraint and coercion in exercise of §7 rights to complain concertedly to management regarding safety violations).

a. Discipline for Activity Protected by Rights "Embedded" in Section 7 and the Labor Laws, Including the Filing of NLRB Petitions and Charges

A union violated Section (8)(b)(1)(A) of the Act when its president filed internal union charges against a member in retaliation for the member filing an unfair labor practice charge against the union.[480] The Board ruled that the union's prompt withdrawal of the internal charges was insufficient to effectively repudiate its unlawful conduct. The "mere withdrawal of the internal union charge...in the absence of an action specifically repudiating the coercive effect of the conduct is insufficient to remedy the 8(b)(1)(A) violation."[481]

b. Impact of Discipline on Employee Relationship

In *Office & Professional Employees Local 251 (Sandia National Laboratories)*,[482] the Board overruled *Carpenters Local 22 (Graziano Construction Co.)*[483] and its progeny and determined that Section 8(b)(1)(A) does not proscribe wholly intraunion conduct and discipline. The Board determined that a purely intraunion dispute between rival union officers, resulting in impeachment petitions, did not affect the relationship of the participants with their employer or impair the policy of the Act.[484]

---

[480]Graphic Communications Local 22 (Rocky Mountain News), 338 NLRB 130, 171 LRRM 1069 (2002).

[481]*Id.* at 131, 171 LRRM at 1070.

[482]331 NLRB 1417, 165 LRRM 1089 (2000).

[483]195 NLRB 1, 79 LRRM 1194 (1972).

[484]Painters Local 466 (Skidmore Coll.), 332 NLRB 445, 165 LRRM 1195 (2000) (union did not violate Act when it disciplined dissident members who filed internal union charges against union officers, "where disciplinary proceedings arose entirely within confines of internal union affairs, had no impact on relationship of those involved to any employer, and impaired no policy of LMRA"); Textile Processors Local 311, 332 NLRB 1352, 166 LRRM 1041 (2000) (union did not violate Act when it refused to accept dissident member's dues, thereby removing her from union membership status and making her ineligible to run for union office since union's actions had purely intraunion effect on rights). *See also* Teamsters Local 170 (Leaseway Motor Car Transp. Co.), 333 NLRB 1290, 167 LRRM 1108 (2001) (finding purely intraunion dispute resulting in intraunion discipline did not violate Act). *But see Teamsters Local 896 (Anheuser-Busch), supra* note 479 (union violated §8(b)(1)(A) where it threatened internal charges against members who reported co-worker safety violations to employer first, and not through union's internal complaint procedure because threats restrained and coerced employees in exercise of §7 rights); *Graphic Communications Local 22, supra* note 480 (union violated Act where it filed internal charges against employee who filed Board charges against union).

The Board, in *Service Employees Local 254 (Brandeis University)*,[485] consistent with its decision in *Sandia National Laboratories*, determined that there was no Section 8(b)(1)(A) violation where a union removed a member from his position as a shop steward and as the union representative on the labor-management committee. The removal did not impact on the member's relationship with his employer, impair his access to the Board's processes, pertain to unacceptable methods of coercion (such as violence), or otherwise impair policies imbedded in the Act.

Subsequent to its decision in *Sandia National Laboratories*, the Board expressly affirmed the continuing validity of those cases in which a union was found to have violated Section 8(b)(1)(A) by conduct that interferes with an employee's employment relationship. The Board ruled that a union violates Section 8(b)(1)(A) when it causes an employer to discriminate against a union member for reasons other than the member's failure to tender dues.[486] The Board found that unions violated Section 8(b)(1)(A) where they (1) demanded that an employer discharge an employee–member who had unsuccessfully challenged a union incumbent for his office;[487] (2) caused an employer not to hire three drivers because of the union's belief that the individuals had crossed a picket line and worked during a work stoppage;[488] (3) asked an employer to deny an employee–member's earned seniority, so that the union president's son-in-law would have top seniority;[489] or (4) threatened to run an

---

[485]332 NLRB 1118, 165 LRRM 1321 (2000), citing Office Employee Local 251 (Sandia Nat'l Laboratories), 331 NLRB 1417 (2000).

[486]Laborers Local 1184 (Nicholson Rodio West Dam Joint Venture), 332 NLRB 1292, 168 LRRM 1176 (2000), citing Wenner Ford Tractor Rentals, 315 NLRB 964, 148 LRRM 1075 (1994) (union violated Act by causing employer to remove member from his position as master mechanic because he had opposed union's officers in election).

[487]USF Red Star, 330 NLRB 53, 162 LRRM 1409 (1999), *enforced*, 230 F.3d 102, 165 LRRM 2665 (4th Cir. 2000). *See also* Strack & Van Til Supermkts, *In re*, dba Town & Country Supermkts. & Ultra Foods, 340 NLRB No. 172, 174 LRRM 1001 (2004) (union violated Act when it requested that employer suspend and discharge union member who allegedly had threatened union president/co-worker when real reason was member's protected dissident union activity).

[488]Newspaper & Mail Deliverers (City Suburban Delivery Sys.), 332 NLRB 870, 172 LRRM 1263 (2000). *See also* Kvaerner Songer Inc., 343 NLRB No. 130, 176 LRRM 1241 (2004) (union violated the Act by demanding employer refrain from hiring members who were not referred through union's nonexclusive hiring hall).

[489]Nationsway Transp. Serv., 327 NLRB 1033, 164 LRRM 1339 (1999).

employee–member off the job unless he transferred his membership from a sister union to the local.[490]

A union violated Section 8(b)(1)(A) when it prosecuted and fined union members for working mandatory overtime in violation of the union's directive to members to refuse "forced or voluntary" overtime until it obtained a contract with the employer.[491] Such a refusal by employees would subject them to lawful discipline by the employer. Likewise, a union violated Section 8(b)(1)(A) when it threatened to have employees discharged if they did not pay market recovery program dues owing from their employment on Davis-Bacon jobs.[492] The Board found payments to support such programs are not "periodic dues" for purposes of the Act, because requiring such payment is "inimical to public policy."

However, the Board ruled that the mere fact that a union's internal discipline impacts the member's employment relationship is not necessarily sufficient to find a violation of the Act.[493] When the Board finds that internal union discipline impacts the member's employment relationship, it must determine whether the discipline violates the Act by "balancing [the employee's] Section 7 rights against the legitimacy of the union interests at stake, in accord with longstanding precedent."[494]

---

[490]United Refining Co., 327 NLRB 795, 161 LRRM 1292 (1999).

[491]Communications Workers Local 13000, 340 NLRB No. 2, 174 LRRM 1246 (2003), *enforced*, 2004 U.S. App. LEXIS 23334, 176 LRRM 2576 (3d Cir. 2004).

[492]Electrical Workers (IBEW) Local 48 (Kingston Constructors Inc.), 332 NLRB 1492, 166 LRRM 1090 (2000), *modified by* 333 NLRB 963, 172 LRRM 1253 (2001), *enforced*, 345 F.3d 1049, 173 LRRM 2257 (9th Cir. 2003).

[493]Steelworkers Local 9292 (Allied Signal Tech. Servs. Corp.), 336 NLRB 52, 168 LRRM 1492 (2001) ("even assuming the Union's action had impact on [member's] relationship with his employer," union's suspension of member did not violate the Act "where the Union's legitimate in maintaining control over the grievance process and in policing its internal affairs . . . outweighs [member's] arguably impacted Section 7 rights)".

[494]*Id.* at 54, n.5, 168 LRRM at 1495 n.5, citing Office & Professional Employees Local 251 (Sandia Nat'l Labs.), 331 NLRB 1417, 165 LRRM 1089 (2000) and Service Employees Local 254 (Brandeis Univ.), 332 NLRB 1118, 165 LRRM 1321 (2000) (Board "expressly reaffirmed several Board decisions in which the § 8(b)(1)(A) issue was decided by balancing the employees' §7 right to engage in or refrain from concerted activity against the legitimacy of the union interest at stake") (citations omitted). *See also* Operating Eng'rs Local 370, 341 NLRB No. 114, 174 LRRM 1432 (2004) (affirming balancing test between employee rights and legitimate union interests).

c. The Effect of Resignation on Legality of Discipline

Continuing to enforce the rule that a union may not fine employees who are no longer union members, the Board ruled that a union violated Section 8(b)(1)(A) when it fined four employees for working for nonsignatory employers.[495] The four employees had resigned their union membership shortly after beginning work for the nonsignatory employers. However, the union fine covered both preresignation and postresignation periods. The Board ruled that the union must rescind the entire fine because, based upon the record, there was no "reasonable basis . . . to apportion the fines."[496]

d. Discipline for Refusal to Engage in Unlawful or Unprotected Activity

The Board continues to hold that union discipline against employee-members for engaging in conduct that is otherwise required under a collective bargaining agreement is unlawful.[497] In *Communications Workers Local 13000 (Verizon Communications, Inc.)*,[498] the union sought to enforce a rule upon its members requiring them not to work overtime (voluntary or mandatory) for a short period of time before the expiration of a collective bargaining agreement. Because refusing to work mandatory overtime constituted unprotected activity, the Board held that the union's efforts to prosecute and fine union members who worked the mandatory overtime was a violation of Section 8(b)(1)(A) of the Act. However, a union may discipline a member for refusing to follow a union rule against participation in voluntary employer activities.[499]

---

[495]Sheet Metal Workers Local 33 (Daimler-Chrysler Corp.), 338 NLRB 116, 171 LRRM 1114 (2002).

[496]*Id.*, 171 LRRM at 1115. *But see* dissenting opinion of Member Liebman, who would have allowed the union the opportunity, at the compliance stage, to propose a reasonable method for apportioning the fine.

[497]Communications Workers Local 13000 (Verizon Communications, Inc.), 340 NLRB No. 2, 174 LRRM 1246 (2003).

[498]*Id.*

[499]*Communications Workers Local 13000 (Verizon Communications), supra* note 497. *See also* Electrical Workers (IBEW) Local 15 (Commonwealth Edison Co.), 341 NLRB No. 43, 174 LRRM 1414 (2004).

e. Discipline for Intraunion Activity

The Board, in *Office & Professional Employees Local 251 (Sandia National Laboratories)*,[500] expressly overruled a number of cases,[501] holding that Section 8(b)(1)(A) does not proscribe wholly intraunion conduct. The Board ruled that

> Section 8(b)(1)(A)'s proper scope, in union discipline cases, is to proscribe union conduct against union members that impacts on the employment relationship, impairs access to the Board's processes, pertains to unacceptable methods of union coercion (such as physical violence in organizational or strike contexts), or otherwise impairs policies imbedded in the Act.[502]

In *Sandia*, the Board ruled that the union did not violate Section 8(b)(1)(A) when it imposed internal union discipline against its members for opposing the policies of the union's president. In reaching its conclusion, the Board ruled:

> What is of critical significance in our judgment is that the only sanctions visited on the Charging Parties by the victorious intraunion faction were internal union sanctions, such as removal from union office and suspension or expulsion from union membership. The relationship between the Charging Parties and their Employer, Sandia, was wholly unaffected by the discipline. Nor are any policies specific to the National Labor Relations Act implicated by the union discipline at issue.[503]

Consistent with the Board's modified application of Section 8(b)(1)(A), the Board cited, with approval, the Seventh Circuit's decision in *NLRB v. Operating Engineers Local 139 (Associated General Contractors of America, Wisconsin Chapter)*.[504] There, the court refused

[500]331 NLRB 1417, 165 LRRM 1089 (2000). *See also* Teamsters Local 170, 333 NLRB 1290, 167 LRRM 1108 (2001) (finding purely intraunion dispute resulting in intraunion discipline); Textile Processors Local 311, 332 NLRB 1352, 166 LRRM 1041 (2000) (union's refusal to accept dues tender falls outside all categories of conduct that might invoke proscriptions of §8(b)(1)(A)).

[501]*See, e.g.*, Carpenters Local 22 (Graziano Constr. Co.), 195 NLRB 1, 79 LRRM 1194 (1972); Teamsters Local 579 (Janesville Auto Transp.), 310 NLRB 975, 144 LRRM 1054 (1993), *enforcement denied*, 145 LRRM 2200 (7th Cir. 1994); Laborers Local 324 (AGC of Cal.), 318 NLRB 589, 150 LRRM 1118 (1995), *enforcement denied in relevant part*, 123 F.3d 1176, 156 LRRM 2054 (9th Cir. 1997); Laborers Local 652 (Southern Cal. Contractors Ass'n), 319 NLRB 694, 151 LRRM 1088 (1995).

[502]Office & Professional Employees Local 251 (Sandia Nat'l Labs.), 331 NLRB 1417, 165 LRRM 1089 (2000).

[503]*Id.* at 1418.

[504]796 F.2d 985, 123 LRRM 2021 (7th Cir. 1986), *denying enforcement in part to* 273 NLRB 992, 118 LRRM 1396 (1984).

to enforce the Board's finding that a union violated Section 8(b)(1)(A) by bringing charges against and fining a member who circulated a newsletter critical of the local's leadership.

In *Steelworkers Local 9292 (Allied Signal Technical Services Corp.)*,[505] the Board held that the union did not violate Section 8(b)(1)(A) when it suspended for six months and filed internal charges against a member who had filed numerous internal charges accusing the union of mishandling grievances. The Board reasoned that the member's rights were outweighed by the union's "legitimate and substantial interest in policing its internal operations."[506] Furthermore, filing these charges could adversely affect the collective bargaining process, as well as jeopardize and weaken the union's control over the grievance process. The remedy that the union used was narrowly tailored to address the problems created by the member filing numerous internal charges.[507]

In *Graphic Communications Local 22 (Rocky Mountain News)*,[508] the union violated Section 8(b)(1)(A) when it filed internal charges against a member in retaliation for his filing of an unfair labor practice charge against the union. Although the union dropped the charges immediately, the mere act of filing the charges had the coercive effect of discouraging the use of the processes available under the Act.

The Board reaffirmed its position in *Communications Workers of America Local 13000 (Verizon Communications, Inc.)*,[509] when it found that the union did not violate Section 8(b)(1)(A) when it filed internal charges against members that defied its "non-participation policy" by participating in a voluntary remote parking program at Verizon. The Board found that because the program was voluntary, the union members did not have a reasonable basis to fear that they would be

---

[505]336 NLRB 52, 168 LRRM 1492 (2001).

[506]*Id.* at 52.

[507]*Id.* (distinguishing Operating Eng'rs Local 400, 225 NLRB 596, 92 LRRM 1494 (1976), *aff'd mem.*, 561 F.2d 1021, 95 LRRM 3010 (D.C. Cir. 1977)).

[508]338 NLRB 130, 171 LRRM 1069 (2002); *see also* discussion at *supra* notes 500–502. *See also* Mail Handlers Local 307 (USPS), 339 NLRB 93, 172 LRRM 1244 (2003) (union violated § 8(b)(1)(A) by refusing to provide charging party with copies of witness statements after his grievance settled and because another employee received paid time-off during for his misconduct, while charging party did not for same misconduct).

[509]343 NLRB No. 21 (2004).

disciplined by Verizon if they failed to participate in its remote parking program.

The Board also found, in *Teamsters Local 657 (Texia Productions),*[510] that a union violated Section 8(b)(1)(A) when it removed a member from a referral list because he complained about the operation of a hiring hall.

3. *Violence and Threats*

In analyzing threats by unions, the Board uses an objective test to determine whether the comments can reasonably be interpreted as threats, regardless of their actual effect upon the listener.[511]

In *Teamsters, & Local 890 (Basic Vegetable Products),*[512] the union violated Section 8(b)(1)(A) by making abusive remarks to replacement employees while videotaping the employees and their vehicles and license plates as they entered and exited the employer's premises. The Board concluded that this conduct could reasonably instill fear of retaliation in those who might cross the picket line.

In *Service Employees Local 1119 (Staten Island University Hospital),*[513] the Board held that the union's conduct toward managers during a two-week period prior to a strike violated the Act. A union organizer's threats of bodily harm and repeated unprovoked verbal abuse, including profanity, racial, and sexual slurs, toward managers sent a clear message to employees that they would be subjected to the same treatment if they did not support the union's actions.

The Board in *Iron Workers Local 433 (Steel Fabricators Ass'n)*[514] found that a local union violated the Act when it threatened to apply, and later did apply, the monies paid towards a union member's dues to pay a fine that had been levied against the member by the union. The union further violated the Act when it threatened the member with a suspension for failure to pay union dues.

The Board has left open the question of whether two unions can act in a joint venture in making threats or committing violence.[515]

---

[510]342 NLRB No. 59, 175 LRRM 1030 (2004). *See also* Main Edition, Chapter 26, "Union Security," Section V. [Hiring-Hall and Job-Referral Practices].

[511]Battle Creek Health Sys., 341 NLRB No. 119, 175 LRRM 1256 (2004).

[512]335 NLRB 686, 168 LRRM 1347 (2001).

[513]339 NLRB 1059, 173 LRRM 1177 (2003).

[514]341 NLRB No. 68, 174 LRRM 1356 (2004).

[515]Electrical Workers Local 98 (IBEW) (MCF Servs.), 342 NLRB No. 74, 175 LRRM 1235 (2004)

In *Electrical Workers Local (IBEW) 98 (MCF Services),*[516] the Board, declining to consider the administrative law judge's finding of a joint venture between two unions,[517] applied common law agency principles and found that the union organizer making the threat was an agent of both unions and that both were therefore liable. A union steward may also be an agent of the union when making threats.[518]

B. Sections 8(b)(1)(B) and 8(b)(4)(A): Restraint and Coercion in Selection of Employer Representatives

1. *Interference With the Employer's Choice of Representatives*

The Board reaffirmed in *Food & Commercial Workers Local 342-50 (Pathmark Stores)*[519] that a union may violate Section 8(b)(1)(B) if its conduct tends to "adversely affect" an employer representative's performance of his covered duties, even if there is no proof of actual harm to a representative's performance of his duties. In that case, the union threatened not to deal with the employer's representative unless their meetings were tape-recorded. The Board found a violation because the union's conduct tended to inhibit the type of spontaneous, informal discussion essential to the grievance adjustment process. Also, the union's conduct effectively forced the employer to choose between limiting its representative's service in favor of another representative who had not been targeted by the union or accepting its representative's continued, but encumbered representation.

2. *Union Discipline of Supervisor–Members*

In *Elevator Constructors Local 1 (National Elevator Industry),*[520] a supervisor–member was fined because he assigned four employees to move an escalator section even though the union had demanded that additional employees be assigned to safely perform the task.

---

[516]*Id.*

[517]The Third Circuit has rejected the joint venture theory, requiring the use of common law agency principles. *See* Sheet Metal Workers Local 19 (Delcard Assocs.), 316 NLRB 426, 149 LRRM 1270 (1995), *enforcement denied,* 154 F.3d 137, 159 LRRM 2087 (3d Cir. 1998).

[518]Battle Creek Health Sys., 341 NLRB No. 119, 175 LRRM 1256 (2004).

[519]339 NLRB 148, 172 LRRM 1318 (2003).

[520]339 NLRB 977, 173 LRRM 1487 (2003).

The Board held that the union violated Section 8(b)(1)(B) where its imposition of the fine would likely have an inhibiting effect on the member's future conduct as a supervisor, a company representative, and a grievance adjuster. In making future decisions on staffing, he would be motivated not solely by the employer's interests, but by the actions the union may take against him.

In *Elevator Constructors Local 10 (Thyssen General Elevator Co.)*,[521] the Board found that the union violated Section 8(b)(1)(B) when it disciplined a supervisor–member for performing duties for the employer that were related to contract interpretation and not for the dismissal of a union member, as argued by the union. The supervisor was engaged in grievance adjustment and contract interpretation within the meaning of Section 8(b)(1)(B) when he initially denied the employee's wage grievance. When the employee continued to complain about his pay, the supervisor recommended the employee's termination because the complaints slowed and otherwise interfered with his work. Following the supervisor's recommendation, the employee was terminated.

The supervisor's denial of the wage claim was "inextricably intertwined" with the employee's misconduct and discharge, and the resultant union discipline of the supervisor. Thus, the Board concluded that the supervisor "would reasonably fear that denying similar grievances in the future would lead to the same causal chain of events, i.e., misconduct by the employee, punishment therefore, and resultant union discipline."[522] As a result, the supervisor might be induced to forgo adherence to the employer's interpretation of the collective bargaining agreement in response to grievances. Therefore, the employer would be deprived of the uncoerced representation of its interests in dealing with the union in collective bargaining, grievance adjustment, and related activities, in violation of Section 8(b)(1)(B).

In *Elevator Constructors Local 2 (Unitec Elevator Services)*,[523] the Board held that the union did not coerce or restrain the employer in the selection of its representative for adjusting grievances and collective bargaining, where it was shown that the union initiated disciplinary action against the supervisor/member after such employment had ended.

---

[521] 338 NLRB 701, 171 LRRM 1196 (2002).
[522] *Id.*
[523] 339 NLRB 941, 173 LRRM 1040 (2003).

The Board in *Comfort Conditioning Co.*[524] continued to hold that supervisory status alone does not make an employee a Section 8(b)(1)(B) representative of the employer. The union did not violate the Act by bringing intraunion disciplinary charges against a member for working for a nonunion company where, as jobsite supervisor, he resolved only minor work-related complaints on the jobsite but did not participate in any formal grievance procedure.

The Board has also continued to hold that a supervisor is protected under Section 8(b)(1)(B) only where the union has a collective bargaining relationship with the employer or is seeking such a relationship. On remand from the District of Columbia Circuit, the Board rendered a decision in *Electrical Workers Local 494 (Gerald Nell, Inc.),*[525] as the law of the case, consistent with the circuit court's holding[526] that Section 8(b)(1)(B) was violated when a union levied a sizable fine against a supervisor-member after he suggested that his new employer would not likely become unionized. The union organizer's inquiry regarding unionization of the employer was proof that the union was seeking a collective bargaining relationship, although the union did not demand recognition or engage in public organizing efforts. In the earlier proceedings, the Board found that the union-supervisor was a grievance adjuster and that the excessive fine was intended to adversely affect the supervisor-member's performance of his Section 8(b)(1)(B) duties; however, it had rejected the administrative law judge's finding that a collective bargaining relationship existed.[527]

---

[524]340 NLRB No. 149, 173 LRRM 1510 (2003).

[525]341 NLRB No. 71, 175 LRRM 1007 (2004), *supplementing* 332 NLRB 1223, 166 LRRM 1010 (2000).

[526]274 F.3d 536, 169 LRRM 2177 (D.C. Cir. 2001).

[527]332 NLRB 1223, 166 LRRM 1010 (2000).

Chapter 7

DISCRIMINATION IN EMPLOYMENT

II. EMPLOYER DISCRIMINATION

A. Persons Within the Protection of Section 8(a)(3)

The Board continues to hold that a company violates Sections 8(a)(3) and (1) of the Act by failing and refusing to hire a union organizer because of his or her protected activity.[1]

The Board also continues to extend the discrimination protection of Section 8(a)(3) to undocumented aliens.[2] However, the Supreme Court held that federal immigration policy, as expressed in

[1]Exterior Sys., 338 NLRB 677, 171 LRRM 1297 (2002); Aztech Elec. Co., 335 NLRB 260, 168 LRRM 1073 (2001), *enforced in relevant part, enforcement denied on other grounds sub nom.* Contractors' Labor Pool v. NLRB, 323 F.3d 1051, 172 LRRM 2065 (D.C. Cir. 2003); Tradesmen Int'l Inc., 332 NLRB 1158, 165 LRRM 1347 (2000), *enforcement denied on other grounds*, 275 F.3d 1137, 169 LRRM 2212 (D.C. Cir. 2002) (actions of union organizer did not qualify as protected activity); Hartman Bros. Heating & Air Conditioning, 332 NLRB 1343, 166 LRRM 1211 (2000), *enforced*, 280 F.3d 1110, 169 LRRM 2385 (7th Cir. 2002) (employer unlawfully discriminated against union organizer by sending him home, and then discharging him when it found out he had lied on his application about his status as a union organizer). *See also* Main Edition, Chapter 7, Section II.C.7. [Employer Discrimination; Specific Conduct; Discrimination Against Union Organizers and "Salts"].

[2]Nortech Waste, 336 NLRB 912, 168 LRRM 1361 (2001) (investigation and termination of undocumented aliens just after successful union election violated §8(a)(3)).

the Immigration Reform and Control Act,[3] foreclosed the Board from awarding backpay to an undocumented alien who had been discriminatorily discharged but never legally authorized to work in the United States,[4] thereby rejecting Board precedent that provided backpay to such an alien until such time as the employer first learned that the employee was not legally authorized to work in this country.[5]

In *Freeman Decorating Co.*,[6] after the union unlawfully called a strike without filing a Section 8(d)(3) notice, several employers responded by sending "termination" notices to every individual who had ever been referred for work by the union's hiring hall. The Board found that because there was no actual employment relationship between those individuals and the employers at the time the union called the strike, Section 8(d)'s provision concerning loss of protected status did not apply and the individuals who received "termination" notices retained their protected status as employees within the meaning of Section 8(a)(3). The D.C. Circuit denied enforcement, rejecting the Board's determination that hiring hall registrants were not "employees" for purposes of the loss of status provisions of Section 8(d) as unreasonable and ruling that the registrants lost the protection of the Act when the union called a strike without giving a Section 8(d)(3) notice.[7]

B. Purpose of the Discrimination

Courts continue to hold that discrimination generally designed to encourage or discourage union activities or support is unlawful.[8]

---

[3]8 U.S.C. §1324a *et seq.*

[4]Hoffman Plastic Compounds, Inc. v. NLRB, 535 U.S. 137, 169 LRRM 2769 (2002).

[5]*See, e.g.*, County Window Cleaning Co., 328 NLRB 190, 163 LRRM 1221 (1999); Met Food, 337 NLRB 109 (2001).

[6]336 NLRB 1, 168 LRRM 1329 (2001), *enforcement denied sub nom.* Theatrical & Stage Employees Local 39 v. NLRB, 334 F. 3d 27, 172 LRRM 2993 (D.C. Cir. 2003).

[7]*Id.*

[8]E.C. Waste, Inc. v. NLRB, 359 F.3d 36 (1st Cir. 2004)(employer violated §8(a)(3) when it discharged employee, allegedly for absenteeism, after it learned that the employee intended to vote for the union in an upcoming election); JHP & Assocs., LLC v. NLRB, 360 F.3d 904 (8th Cir. 2004)(employer violated §8(a)(3) when it discharged employee that it perceived to be supportive of the union); Ark Las Vegas Restaurant Corp. v. NLRB, 334 F.3d 99, 172 LRRM 3012 (D.C. Cir. 2003)(employer violated §8(a)(3) when it discharged eight employees for union

1. *Conduct Requiring Proof of Union Animus: The* Wright Line *Rule*

The Board has held that, because the motive of the employer is at issue, it is appropriate to use the *Wright Line* analytical framework when considering Section 8(a)(3) allegations arising from alleged Section 8(b)(1)(A) and (2) conduct by a union.[9] The Board has also determined that *Wright Line* applies in evaluating an employer's defense that it disciplined a pro-union employee in an organizing campaign in order to protect a disabled employee from alleged harassment and to comply with the Americans with Disabilities Act (ADA), and that the ADA does not bar the Board from finding that such disciplinary action violates the Act.[10]

The Fifth Circuit recently disagreed with the Board that there was sufficient circumstantial evidence of union animus to support a finding of employer pretext. Thus, in *Valmont Industries, Inc. v. NLRB,*[11] the court ruled that where neither direct nor circumstantial evidence of antiunion animus was demonstrated by the general counsel, a finding that the reasons given by the employer for its action were pretextual, standing alone, will not support a conclusion that the action was improperly motivated. Where union animus is established, the general counsel must also demonstrate that animus was a motivating factor in the employment decision.[12] Under *Wright Line,* once

---

activities); Wright Elec. Co. v. NLRB, 200 F.3d 1162, 163 LRRM 2353 (8th Cir. 2000) (nonunion electric contractor was motivated by antiunion animus, violating §8(a)(3) of Act by refusing to hire union electrician); Ross Stores Inc. v. NLRB, 235 F.3d 669, 166 LRRM 2207 (D.C. Cir. 2000) (employer violated §8(a)(3) when it discharged pro-union employee, allegedly for violating employer's written time-off policies, where employer knew that employee was participating in ongoing union organization campaign); Beverly Cal. Corp. v. NLRB, 227 F.3d 817, 165 LRRM 2257 (7th Cir. 2000), *cert. denied,* 533 U.S. 950, 167 LRRM 2640 (2001) (employer violated §8(a)(3) when its assistant director required active union supporter to obtain formal certification before she returned to work after she experienced one bout of nausea early in her pregnancy, whereas other employees were able to work during their pregnancies); Frazier Indus. Co. v. NLRB, 213 F.3d 750, 164 LRRM 2516 (D.C. Cir. 2000) (employer's discharge of union supporter who persistently discussed union with co-workers violated §8(a)(3)); NLRB v. Hospital San Pablo Inc., 207 F.3d 67, 163 LRRM 2999 (1st Cir. 2000) (hospital violated §8(a)(3) when it discharged known union activist during union-organizing campaign, allegedly for insubordination in leaving work early, as evidence established that employee was discharged because of hospital's antiunion animus).

[9]Nationsway Transp. Serv., 327 NLRB 1033, 164 LRRM 1339 (1999).

[10]PCC Structurals Inc., 330 NLRB 868, 164 LRRM 1350 (2000).

[11]244 F.3d 454, 466, 166 LRRM 2782, 2791 (5th Cir. 2001).

[12]Operating Eng'rs Local 470 v. NLRB, 350 F.3d 105, 173 LRRM 2739 (D.C. Cir. 2003).

the general counsel's burden has been met, it is the respondent's burden to show that in the absence of the union activity it not only *might* have taken the action it did but that it *would* have done so.[13]

In *Swardson Painting Co.*,[14] two employees engaged in a protected concerted walkout in order to protest their wage rate. When negotiating with the employees, the employer refused to give them a raise and told them that if they wanted to quit, they could "go on down the road" in search of another job. The employees never returned to work, and claimed that they were discharged in violation of Section 8(a)(3). The Board, however, found that the employer's actions did not constitute discharge, and that the employees had voluntarily quit. Thus, despite the employees' participation in a protected activity, the employer did not discharge them, and therefore did not violate the Act.

The Board continues its practice of not applying the framework set forth in *Wright Line* in striker misconduct cases,[15] but instead applies the analysis developed in *Clear Pine Mouldings*[16] and *Rubin Bros.*[17] In addition, the *Wright Line* framework is not applied in situations that do not involve a dual motive for employer action.[18]

---

[13] *See* American Armored Car, 339 NLRB 600, 172 LRRM 1385 (2001) (employer met its *Wright Line* burden when it discharged union supporters for refusal to take a polygraph during investigation of a theft); Becker Group, Inc., 329 NLRB 103, 169 LRRM 1434 (1999); Avondale Indus., Inc., 329 NLRB 1064, 165 LRRM 1228 (1999); Coyne Int'l Enters. Corp., 326 NLRB 1187, 163 LRRM 1080 (1998). For cases in which the employers met their burdens of showing that the same adverse actions would have been taken in the absence of union activity, see *Fresno Bee*, 337 NLRB 1161, 170 LRRM 1404 (2002); *American Coal Co.*, 337 NLRB 1044, 170 LRRM 1361 (2002); *Montano Elec.*, 335 NLRB 612, 170 LRRM 1065 (2001).

[14] 340 NLRB No. 24, 173 LRRM 1206 (2003).

[15] Siemens Energy & Automation, Inc., 328 NLRB 1175, 162 LRRM 1083 (1999).

[16] 268 NLRB 1044, 1046, 115 LRRM 1113 (1984), *enforced*, 765 F.2d 148, 120 LRRM 2631 (9th Cir. 1985), *cert. denied*, 474 U.S. 1105, 121 LRRM 2368 (1986); General Tel. Co., 251 NLRB 737, 105 LRRM 1288 (1980); Axelson, Inc., 285 NLRB 862, 129 LRRM 1344 (1987).

[17] 99 NLRB 610, 30 LRRM 1109 (1952).

[18] *See* Shamrock Foods Co. v. NLRB, 346 F.3d 1130, 173 LRRM 2454 (D.C. Cir. 2003) (*Wright Line* analysis improper in case where employer admittedly discharged employee for protected activity; employer's only defense being that employee committed misconduct in the course of such activity, but in fact evidence showed that such misconduct never occurred); *see also* USF Red Star, Inc. v. NLRB, 230 F.3d 102, 108 n.3, 165 LRRM 2665, 2669 n.3 (4th Cir. 2000); Church Homes dba Avery Heights, 343 NLRB No. 128 (2004); Nor-Cal Beverage Co., 330 NLRB 610, 163 LRRM 1268 (2000).

In *Starcon v. NLRB,*[19] the Seventh Circuit agreed with the Sixth Circuit's ruling in *NLRB v. Fluor Daniel, Inc.*,[20] concerning the application of *Wright Line* in cases involving an employer's refusal to hire "salts." Both circuits held that the employer must be allowed at the hearing to show on the merits that it would not have hired the discriminatees even in the absence of their union activity or affiliation. This was contrary to the Board's position that deferred consideration of the employer's defense until the compliance stage of proceedings. The Seventh Circuit disagreed, however, with the Sixth Circuit's holding in *Fluor Daniel* that as part of meeting its burden of proof on the merits in a refusal-to-hire violation, the general counsel must match qualified applicants with job openings. Instead, the court in *Starcon* determined that to meet its *Wright Line* burden on the merits, the general counsel need only show that one applicant was discriminated against to establish a refusal-to-hire violation warranting a cease-and-desist order.

In *FES, a Division of Thermo Power (FES (I))*,[21] the Board revised its approach to applying *Wright Line* in refusal-to-hire and in refusal-to-consider cases. The Board accepted the Seventh Circuit's *Starcon* application of *Wright Line* to refusal-to-hire cases, emphasizing that in the case on the merits the general counsel must show that the employer was hiring or had concrete plans to hire, that the applicants had the training or experience relevant to the openings, and that union animus contributed to the employer's refusal to hire. Once these showings have been made, then the employer would be permitted to show that it would not have hired the applicants in the absence of their union activity.

In refusal-to-consider cases, the Board ruled in *FES (I)* that the general counsel's *Wright Line* burden on the merits is to show that the employer excluded applicants from the hiring process and that antiunion animus contributed to the decision not to consider, and that this burden could be met even when no hiring is occurring. The Board held that once this burden is met by the general counsel, the burden shifts to the employer to show that it would not have considered the applicants even in the absence of union activity. The appropriate remedy for a refusal-to-consider violation, the Board ruled, is

[19]176 F.3d 948, 161 LRRM 2233 (7th Cir. 1999).

[20]161 F.3d 953, 159 LRRM 2794 (6th Cir. 1998).

[21]331 NLRB 9, 164 LRRM 1065 (2000), *supplemented,* 333 NLRB 66, 166 LRRM 1166 (2001), *enforced,* 301 F.3d 83, 170 LRRM 2729 (3d Cir. 2002).

a cease-and-desist order; an order to consider the discriminatees for future openings in accord with nondiscriminatory criteria; and an order to notify the discriminatees, the charging party, and the regional director of future openings for which the discriminatees applied or for substantially equivalent positions.

Finally, in *FES (I)*, the Board also provided direction on the appropriate use of compliance proceedings in connection with job openings arising after the unfair labor practice trial has begun in both refusal-to-hire cases and refusal-to-consider cases.

After a remand to an administrative law judge (ALJ) for a determination of whether a refusal-to-hire violation had been established under the new framework for analysis, the Board in *FES (II)*[22] ruled that the employer had violated Section 8(a)(3) by refusing to hire nine union applicants. In enforcing the Board's order, the Third Circuit did not reach the Board's refusal-to-consider doctrine because the Board had not relied on that doctrine in reaching its decision on the refusal-to-hire claims.[23]

In *Webasto Sunroofs, Inc.*,[24] the Board held that the *FES (I)* test did not apply in cases where the employer refuses to convert temporary employees into permanent employees. In cases of this type, the Board concluded that the relevant inquiry was whether the employer unlawfully refused to convert the status of temporary employees into permanent employee status, not whether the employer had unlawfully refused to hire the temporary employees. The Board went on to apply the analytical framework of *Wright Line* instead of *FES (I)*. An employer that refuses to hire striking employees of another employer due to their status as strikers violates the Act.[25]

The Fifth Circuit, in *NLRB v. Pneu Electric Inc.*,[26] criticized the refusal-to-consider doctrine adopted by the Board in *FES (I)*, reasoning that relieving the general counsel of having to show that applicants are qualified or that job openings are available is not an "equitable balance between the interests of individual applicants and those of the employer."[27] Nevertheless, the court determined that the Board's discrimination findings were supported by substantial evi-

---

[22]333 NLRB 66, 166 LRRM 1166 (2001).
[23]NLRB v. FES, 301 F.3d 83, 96 n.7, 170 LRRM 2729, 2740 n.7 (3d Cir. 2002).
[24]342 NLRB No. 124, 175 LRRM 1502 (2004).
[25]Abbott Northwestern Hosp., 343 NLRB No. 67 (2004).
[26]309 F.3d 843, 170 LRRM 3249 (5th Cir. 2002).
[27]*Id.* at 858, 170 LRRM at 3259.

dence, regardless of whether the court's preferred approach in refusal-to-consider cases (which would have required the general counsel to establish applicant qualifications and available job openings) or the *FES (I)* approach were followed.[28]

In *Fluor Daniel Inc. v. NLRB*,[29] the Sixth Circuit noted its continued disagreement with the Board concerning refusal-to-consider cases, holding that the Board's position that an employer can violate Section 8(a)(3) even if no jobs are actually available at the time union "salts" apply for employment "is in conflict with our case law."[30] The court accordingly remanded to the Board its finding of refusal-to-consider violations for a determination of whether jobs were available at the time of the Board's finding of violations.

2. *Conduct Inherently Destructive of Section 7 Rights*

Additional types of employer conduct have been classified by the Board as "inherently destructive" of important employee rights, such that they violate Section 8(a)(3) even without proof of antiunion motive. In *Aztech Electric Co.*,[31] a "salting" case,[32] the employer's "30-percent rule" (a policy of not hiring or considering any applicant with a recent wage history of earning 30 percent or more than the employer's starting wage) was found to be so inherently discriminatory and destructive of Section 7 rights that no proof of antiunion motivation was necessary. The Board rejected the employer's argument that the 30-percent rule discriminated only on economic grounds rather than on the basis of Section 7, concluding that the hiring standard penalized union supporters by automatically disqualifying those who recently earned union contract wages. The Board also rejected the employer's contention that the 30-percent rule was not inherently discriminatory because it excluded from hiring eligibility applicants whose wage history had no connection with union membership; the Board noted that the rule operated to exclude vir-

---

[28] *Id.* at 859, 170 LRRM at 3260.

[29] 332 F.3d 961, 172 LRRM 2673 (6th Cir. 2003), *cert. denied*, 125 S. Ct. 964, 176 LRRM 2448 (2005).

[30] *Id.* at 975, 172 LRRM at 2684.

[31] 335 NLRB 260, 168 LRRM 1073 (2001), *enforcement denied in part and granted in part sub nom.* Contractors' Labor Pool v. NLRB, 323 F.3d 1051, 172 LRRM 2065 (D.C. Cir. 2003).

[32] For additional discussion, *see* Section II.C.7. [Employer Discrimination; Specific Conduct; Discrimination Against Union Organizers and "Salts"], *infra*.

tually all applicants with a recent union wage history, while excluding only some applicants with a recent nonunion wage history.

This impact on those who had worked in an organized workforce, the Board reasoned, necessarily discouraged union membership. In reaching that conclusion, the Board analogized its inherently destructive theory to the disparate impact analysis applied in Title VII cases, where facially neutral employment policies that are "fair in form" are deemed unlawful if "discriminatory in operation." On appeal, the D.C. Circuit refused to enforce that part of the Board's order premised on the finding that the employer's "30 percent rule" was inherently destructive of important employee rights.[33]

The court found that inasmuch as the Board had expressly held that the "30 percent rule" was not applied for an antiunion purpose but rather for a legitimate business purpose (to lessen the incidence of turnover in the employer's workforce), "it was not possible for the board to rely on the inherently destructive rationale" to condemn the refusal to hire "salts."[34] The court went on to hold that

> indispensable to a determination of a violation of Section 8(a)(3) . . . is a finding that an employer acted out of an anti- (or pro-) union motivation. Whatever legitimate inference that might be drawn from petitioner's adoption of the 30-percent rule, the Board certainly cannot conclude explicitly that petitioner's motivation is benign and then hold that its practice independently violates Section 8(a)(3).[35]

Finally, the court expressed doubt that the Board could legitimately support its inherently destructive finding with respect to the 30-percent rule by relying on the disparate impact theory applied in Title VII cases.[36]

In *Freeman Decorating Co.*,[37] "terminating" or refusing to accept for employment any union members referred from the hiring hall

---

[33]Contractors' Labor Pool v. NLRB, 323 F.3d 1051, 172 LRRM 2065 (D.C. Cir. 2003).

[34]*Id.* at 1058, 172 LRRM at 2069.

[35]*Id.* at 1059, 172 LRRM at 2071. *See also* Ken Maddox Heating & Air Conditioning, Inc., 340 NLRB No. 7, 173 LRRM 1113 (2003) (inherently destructive theory not alleged in complaint; employer's hiring based on uniformly applied neutral hiring practices); Operating Eng'rs Local 150 v. NLRB, 325 F.3d 818, 172 LRRM 2072 (7th Cir. 2003)(inherently destructive theory not part of general counsel's contentions).

[36]*Contractors' Labor Pool, supra* note 33, 323 F.3d at 1059–60, 172 LRRM at 2071.

[37]336 NLRB 1, 168 LRRM 1329 (2001), *enforcement denied sub nom.* Theatrical & Stage Employees Local 39 v NLRB, 334 F.3d 27, 172 LRRM 2993 (D.C. Cir. 2003).

based solely on their union affiliation and without evidence of employee misconduct was deemed inherently destructive of Section 7 rights even though the union had called a strike without notifying the Federal Mediation and Conciliation Service (FMCS) in accordance with the requirements of Section 8(d)(3). The D.C. Circuit refused enforcement, rejecting the Board's finding that refusing to accept hiring hall referrals was inherently destructive conduct, on the ground that the hiring hall referrals were illegal strikers who had lost the Act's protections.[38] In another case, the Board determined that an employer's hiring rule that prohibited applicants from marking application forms to reveal activity protected by the Act (such as status as a voluntary union organizer) was inherently destructive of employee rights, concluding that because an employee's ability to disclose protected activity in the application process is the first step toward exercise of protected rights, prohibition of such disclosure would destroy an integral part of the collective bargaining process.[39]

In *Midwest Generation, EME, LLC,*[40] the Board held that limiting a lockout to strikers while excluding nonstrikers and crossover employees was not inherently destructive of employees' Section 7 rights nor motivated by antiunion considerations, concluding that because the purpose of the lockout was to apply economic pressure in support of a legitimate bargaining proposal, such constituted a legitimate and substantial business justification for the partial lockout.

C. Specific Conduct

1. *Discharge or Discipline for Union Activity*

b. Constructive Discharge

In *Intercon I (Zercon),*[41] the Board articulated two theories of constructive discharge. Under the "traditional" theory, the employee quits

---

[38]*Id.*

[39]Mainline Contracting Corp., 334 NLRB 922 (2001). In so ruling the Board declined to follow the Eleventh Circuit's decision in *Boilermakers v. NLRB,* 127 F.3d 1300, 156 LRRM 2881 (11th Cir. 1997), holding that a similar ban on disclosure of protected activity was not inherently destructive of §7 rights.

[40]343 NLRB No. 12, 175 LRRM 1461 (2004). *See also* Bunting Bearings Corp., 343 NLRB No. 64, 175 LRRM 1513 (2004)(partial lockout of nonprobationary employees while retaining probationary employees who were not union members not "inherently destructive" of employee rights or motivated by antiunion considerations) and Section II.C.2. ["Lockouts"], *infra.*

[41]333 NLRB 223, 168 LRRM 1145 (2001).

because the employer deliberately made working conditions unbearable. It must be shown that the burdens placed upon the employee were intended to cause the employee's resignation and that the reason for these burdens was the employee's union activity.[42] Under the "Hobson's Choice" theory, the employee quits because the employer conditions continued employment on the employee's abandonment of Section 7 rights.

c. Employer's Knowledge of Employee's Union Activity

In the Board's view, a prima facie case may be established without proving that an employer had specific knowledge of an employee's union sympathies or activities where it is reasonable to infer from other circumstances that the employer suspected or had information permitting the probable identification of union supporters. Such circumstances include knowledge of general union activity, antiunion hostility, the timing of the employer's adverse employment action, the assertion of pretextual reasons for the action, and the existence of a close relationship between the employee and a known union supporter.[43] Where sufficient evidence is not present to establish

---

[42]*See also* L.S.F Transp., Inc. v. NLRB, 282 F.3d 972, 169 LRRM 2797 (7th Cir. 2002) (employer's sudden reassignment of employee from short-haul runs to long-haul runs, contemporaneous with antiunion statements and actions by management, creates intolerable working conditions supporting finding of constructive discharge); Kathleen's Bakeshop, LLC, 337 NLRB 1081, 171 LRRM 1131 (2002), *enforced,* 2003 U.S. App. LEXIS 22029, 173 LRRM 2576 (2d Cir. 2003) (threatening employee's life and failing to assure him of his personal safety because of his support for union campaign supports finding of constructive discharge).

[43]SCA Tissue N. Am., LLC v. NLRB, 371 F.3d 983, 174 LLRM 3377 (7th Cir. 2004) (selective policy application by employer evidence of antiunion animus), *granting enforcement to* 338 NLRB 175, 173 LRRM 1327 (2003); NLRB v. Interstate Builders, Inc., 351 F.3d 1020, 173 LRRM 2745 (10th Cir. 2003) (pretextual reasons for discharge); Enjo Architectural Millwork, 340 NLRB No. 162, 173 LRRM 1580 (2003) (unlawful interrogation, knowledge of general union activity, antiunion sentiment, and pretextual reasons for discharge); La Gloria Oil & Gas Co., 337 NLRB 1120, 170 LRRM 1337 (2002) (knowledge of union activity inferred from general knowledge of union activities coupled with the small size of the plant); Pan-Oston Co., 336 NLRB 305, 170 LRRM 1026 (2001); Tubular Corp. of Am., 337 NLRB 99, 169 LRRM 1098 (2001); Martech MDI, 331 NLRB 487, 171 LRRM 1323 (2000), *enforced,* 2001 U.S. App. LEXIS 10963 (D.C. Cir. 2001); Regional Home Care, Inc., 329 NLRB 85, 166 LRRM 1112 (1999).

knowledge, a violation will not be found.[44] Circumstances giving rise to a reasonable inference of union animus can also include events occurring after an employee's termination.[45]

d. Inferential Proof of Employer's Animus

With respect to the evidence of animus necessary to support an inference that the motivation of a discharge was unlawful, the Eighth Circuit has cautioned that, "[w]hile hostility to [a] union is a proper and highly significant factor for the Board to consider when assessing whether the employer's motive was discriminatory . . . general hostility toward the union does not itself supply the element of unlawful motive."[46] The Seventh Circuit rejected the Board's imputation of union animus to an employer based on a supervisor's knowledge of union activity on the ground that the supervisor who recommended the discharges of two employee union supporters for gross misconduct, apparent theft, and insubordination was pro-union.[47] In another, the Eighth Circuit refused to enforce the Board's conclusion that an employer's decision to impose "attendance points" for employee's "no-call, no-show" and to refuse an employee's request for a day off was motivated by union animus.[48]

The Board, moreover, continues to hold that employer statements, which do not themselves violate the Act, may still be used in

[44]*See, e.g.*, Sears, Roebuck & Co. v. NLRB, 349 F.3d 493, 173 LRRM 2626 (7th Cir. 2003) (knowledge of union activity could not be inferred from employee's pro-union statement at antiunion meeting where decisionmaker appeared at meeting after employee had finished speaking), *denying enforcement to* 337 NLRB 443, 169 LRRM 1441 (2002); Tomatek Inc., 333 NLRB 1350, 170 LRRM 1495 (2001); TeleTech Holdings, Inc., 333 NLRB 402, 166 LRRM 1241 (2001) (union activist successfully acted in secrecy from employer).

[45]*SCA Tissue N. Am., LLC, supra* note 43.

[46]GSX Corp. v. NLRB, 918 F.2d 1351, 1356, 135 LRRM 3001 (8th Cir. 1990), cited in Carleton Coll. v. NLRB, 230 F.3d 1075, 165 LRRM 2670 (8th Cir. 2000).

[47]Vulcan Basement Waterproofing of Ill., Inc. v. NLRB, 219 F.3d 677, 164 LRRM 2961 (7th Cir. 2000), *denying enforcement to* Vulcan Waterproofing Co., 327 NLRB 1100, 164 LRRM 1326 (1999).

[48]NLRB v. La-Z-Boy Midwest, 390 F.3d 1054, 1060–61, 176 LLRM 2141 (8th Cir. 2004).

an unfair labor practice proceeding to show an employer's animus.[49] In addition, evidence of suspicious timing, false reasons given for employment action, failure to adequately investigate alleged misconduct, departures from past practices, tolerance of behavior for which the employee was disciplined, disparate treatment of the affected employee, and discriminatory enforcement of facially valid work rules or policies may support inferences of animus and discriminatory motivation.[50] A discharge resulting from the enforcement of a rule that is unlawful under the Act, moreover, will itself be unlawful.[51]

2. *Lockouts*

The D.C. Circuit has reiterated that the motive or purpose underlying an employer's lockout of its employees continues to be the critical factor in determining whether the lockout constitutes a Section 8(a)(3) violation. In *Electrical Workers (IBEW) Local 702 v. NLRB*,[52] the court upheld the Board's finding that the employer did not violate the Act by locking out its employees in response to "inside-game" tactics used by the two unions in lieu of a strike during contract negotiations.

---

[49]NACCO Materials Handling Group, Inc., 331 NLRB 1245, 170 LRRM 1139 (2000). *But see* NLRB v. Lampi, LLC, 240 F.3d 931, 166 LRRM 2321 (11th Cir. 2001), *denying enforcement to* 327 NLRB 222, 160 LRRM 1234 (1998) (§8(c) precludes inference of union animus from employer's statement of opposition to unions and announcement of decision to appeal ALJ's ruling).

[50]SCA Tissue N. Am., LLC v. NLRB, 371 F.3d 983, 174 LRRM 3377 (7th Cir. 2004) (disparate treatment and discriminatory enforcement of facially valid work rules); JHP & Assocs., LLC v. NLRB, 360 F.3d 904, 910–11, 174 LRRM 2558 (8th Cir. 2004) (suspicious timing and pretextual reasons for termination); JCR Hotel, Inc. v. NLRB, 342 F.3d 837, 173 LRRM 2193 (8th Cir. 2003) (suspicious timing); Waterbury Hotel Mgmt., LLC v. NLRB, 314 F.3d 645, 171 LRRM 2781 (D.C. Cir. 2003) (suspicious timing, disparate treatment and discriminatory enforcement of facially valid work rules); Supershuttle of Orange County, Inc., 339 NLRB 1, 172 LRRM 1177 (2003) (disparate treatment); L.S.F. Transp., Inc. v. NLRB, 282 F.3d 972, 169 LRRM 2797 (7th Cir. 2002) (suspicious timing, false reasons for discharge); Tubular Corp. of Am., 337 NLRB 99, 169 LRRM 1098 (2001) (suspicious timing, disparate treatment, departure from past practices, unfair investigation); Bowling Transp., Inc., 336 NLRB 393, 170 LRRM 1227 (2001), *enforced*, 352 F.3d 274, 173 LRRM 2807 (6th Cir. 2003) (reliance on action taken by another employer for an unlawful reason).

[51]Aldworth Co., 338 NLRB 137, 171 LRRM 1033 (2002); Frazier Indus. Co., 328 NLRB 717, 163 LRRM 1024 (1999), *enforced*, 213 F.3d 750, 164 LRRM 2516 (D.C. Cir. 2000).

[52]215 F.3d 11, 164 LRRM 2193 (D.C. Cir. 2000), *cert. denied*, 531 U.S. 1051, 165 LRRM 3056 (2001).

The court first determined that the lockout was not "inherently destructive of employee rights" under *American Ship Building Co. v. NLRB*,[53] and therefore did not fall into the category of cases in which the Board need not inquire into employer motivation. The court found that the Board correctly applied the Supreme Court's decision in *NLRB v. Great Dane Trailers*[54] in concluding that the inquiry is "whether the Respondent possessed a legitimate and substantial business justification for the lockout"[55]—in other words, a legitimate defense against the union's inside-game tactics. The court agreed with the Board's determination that the employer had "substantial and legitimate business objectives"[56] for locking out the employees and that its good faith attempts to reach a contract settlement as well as a long history of a stable bargaining relationship mitigated against a finding of improper motivation. The court also found that letters from the employer to the union on the day the lockout was initiated supported the Board's finding that the motivation for the lockout was to facilitate a successful conclusion to contract negotiations.

That the motivation for a lockout is still the determining factor as to whether the lockout is in violation of the Act is further illustrated by *Midwest Generation, EME, LLC.*[57] There, the only issue before the Board was whether the company violated Sections 8(a)(1) and (3) of the Act by locking out and/or refusing to reinstate economic strikers at the time of the union's unconditional offer to return to work while allowing nonstrikers and crossover employees to continue to work. The general counsel argued that a partial lockout of "full-term" strikers was unlawful under the "comparatively slight" and "inherently destructive" tests set forth in *NLRB v. Great Dane Trailers,* as it also sent a "clear message that supporting the union will result in severe penalties."[58]

The employer argued that the partial lockout was in support of its lawful bargaining proposals. It explained that it was an attempt to pressure the employees who were still participating in the strike to abandon their demands, and that this constituted a business justifi-

[53]380 U.S. 300, 58 LRRM 2672 (1965).

[54]388 U.S. 26, 65 LRRM 2465 (1967).

[55]Central Ill. Pub. Serv. Co., 326 NLRB 928, 931, 159 LRRM 1217, 1220 (1998).

[56]*Electrical Workers, supra* note 52, 215 F.3d at 18, 164 LRRM at 2197.

[57]343 NLRB No. 12, 175 LRRM 1461 (2004).

[58]343 NLRB No.12 at 2, 175 LRRM at 1464 (citing NLRB v. Great Dane Trailers, 388 U.S. 26, 65 LRRM 2465 (1967)).

cation under *American Shipbuilding Co. v. NLRB.* This business justification established that there was no evidence of union animus. Because the nonstriking and crossover employees had previously returned to work, the employer argued that it was not necessary to apply pressure by locking them out. A Board majority (Member Liebman dissenting) determined that the employer had supplied a legitimate and substantial business justification for the partial lockout, stating that "[t]he evidence here clearly establishes that the Respondent's lockout was for the purpose of applying economic pressure in support of its legitimate bargaining proposals."[59] The Board concluded that there had been no showing of antiunion considerations in the implementation of the partial lockout.

The Board adopted the rationale of *Midwest Generation* in *Bunting Bearings Corp.*[60] in concluding that a partial lockout of nonprobationary employees, all of whom were union members, while retaining in probationary employees, none of whom were union members, did not violate the Act because the partial lockout was in support of legitimate bargaining demands and there was no proof that it was motivated by antiunion animus. The Board majority (Member Liebman dissenting) reasoned that treating nonprobationary employees differently than probationary employees was not tantamount to discrimination on the basis of union affiliation. Probationary employees, the Board majority concluded, had a lesser interest than nonprobationary employees in the employer's bargaining proposals because the employer and the union treated probationary employees less favorably under their expired contract than nonprobationary employees were treated. Additionally, they were disenfranchised by the union from voting on whether to accept any of the company's proposals. Thus, the Board majority ruled that it was reasonable for the employer to lock out only the nonprobationary employees, "since they were the ones who had a more vital interest in the proposals for a new contract."[61]

---

[59]343 NLRB No. 12, slip op. at 3, 175 LRRM at 1464.

[60]343 NLRB No. 64, 175 LRRM 1513 (2004).

[61]343 NLRB No. 64, slip op. at 3, 175 LRRM at 1515. *But see* Allen Storage & Moving Co., 342 NLRB No. 44, 175 LRRM 1388 (2004) (lockout found illegal where employer allowed nonstriking employee to work and locked out all former strikers, and lockout not in support of legitimate bargaining objectives).

In *Tidewater Construction Corp.*,[62] an employer locked out 25 bargaining unit employees as well as 40 other individuals whose names had been included on an *Excelsior* voting eligibility list compiled 10 months before the lockout and 16 individuals who were neither strikers nor on the *Excelsior* list, in addition to refusing to consider six former unit employees for temporary replacement jobs during the lockout. The Board concluded that the employer's lockout did not violate Section 8(a)(3) because it was not directed only at union members, but at members of the bargaining unit and any individuals with a "reasonable employment nexus" with the unit. The Board also found the employer's conduct to be lawful because it made acceptance of its bargaining proposals, rather than abandonment of union membership, a condition of returning to work. One Board member dissented, finding that the employer had revealed impermissible antiunion considerations by subjecting former unit employees to the lockout.

The D.C. Circuit remanded the case, finding that the Board did not adequately explain the basis for its ruling that there was no unlawful antiunion motivation with respect to: (1) the employer's inability to explain why, of the 16 individuals who were neither strikers nor on the *Excelsior* list, the employer locked out the 10 individuals whom the employer believed to be union members; (2) the employer's falsely informing the six former unit employees it refused to employ that there was no work for them instead of telling them they had been locked out as it subsequently claimed in the Board proceedings; and (3) the employer's decision to lock out 10 individuals who were not current employees but appeared on an *Excelsior* list compiled 10 months before the lockout.[63] On remand, the Board, contrary to its original decision, determined that the employer's treatment of the six former unit employees who had applied for temporary work during the lockout was motivated by antiunion animus and in violation of Section 8(a)(3)because of the employer's proffer of lawful but false reasons for its refusal to hire the six; its shifting positions on, and failure to offer "credible" reasons for, including on the lockout list the 10 nonstrikers not on the

[62]333 NLRB 1264, 167 LRRM 1051 (2001), *vacated and remanded sub nom.* Operating Eng'rs Local 147 v. NLRB, 294 F.3d 186, 170 LRRM 2497 (D.C. Cir. 2002).

[63]*Operating Eng'rs Local 147 v. NLRB*, *supra* note 62.

Excelsior list, and a supervisor's remark revealing a nonunion hiring policy.[64]

3. *Plant Closings*

b. Partial Closings

A partial closing or a transfer of work may violate Section 8(a)(3). The Board continues to determine the legality of partial closings by focusing on the motive underlying the employer's decision. In *Bonham Heating & Air Conditioning, Inc.*,[65] the Board held that an employer engaged in plumbing, heating, and air conditioning work violated Section 8(a)(3) when it ceased its plumbing business, slowed down bidding, and laid off employees after a majority of them had signed a petition requesting union representation. Similarly, in *Electrical South, Inc.*,[66] the employer's closing of its engineering department shortly after the employees voted in favor of union representation was found to be discriminatorily motivated, where the employer's economic justifications were unsupported by substantial evidence. However, in *Coyne International Enterprises Corp.*,[67] the Board held that the employer lawfully closed its terminal, even though union animus was a factor in its decision, where the employer proved that it would have closed the terminal in any event because of a continuing and escalating loss of sales.

---

[64]Tidewater Constr. Corp., 341 NLRB No. 55, 174 LRRM 1249 (2004).

[65]328 NLRB 432, 161 LRRM 1113 (1999), *enforced*, 230 F.3d 1359, 2000 U.S. App. LEXIS 30389 (6th Cir. 2000).

[66]327 NLRB 270, 160 LRRM 1202 (1998). *See also* Laboratory Corp. of Am. Holdings, 333 NLRB 284, 166 LRRM 1219 (2001) (employer that operated patient service centers unlawfully closed one center and discharged union activist who was sole employee at that center); Delchamps Inc., 330 NLRB 1310, 168 LRRM 1023 (2000) (employer violated §8(a)(3) when it closed its ice plant and discharged 14 employees because of their union activity).

[67]326 NLRB 1187, 163 LRRM 1080 (1998). *See also* Orange County Publications, 334 NLRB 350, 167 LRRM 1300 (2001) (employer lawfully restructured its delivery operations and eliminated full-time driver classification where employer established that it would have taken the same action in absence of employees' union activity).

c. Transfer of Work: The "Runaway Shop"

In *Reno Hilton Resorts v. NLRB*,[68] the court upheld the Board's determination that a hotel unlawfully contracted out its security service and laid off security workers after a union election victory, notwithstanding the evidence of cost savings presented by the employer. In *O'Dovero v. NLRB*,[69] the D.C. Circuit enforced the Board's determination that the diversion of work from a unionized entity to the nonunion entity of a family-owned integrated enterprise violated Section 8(a)(3) because it had been shown that the diversion occurred in response to union efforts to organize the nonunion entity's employees and because the employer failed to show that the diversion would have taken place in the absence of union activity. However, in *Daikichi Corp.*,[70] the Board found that a fast food employer

---

[68]196 F.3d 1275, 162 LRRM 2961 (D.C. Cir. 1999), *enforcing* 326 NLRB 375, 162 LRRM 1405 (1998). *See also* Vico Prods. Co. v. NLRB, 333 F.3d 198, 172 LRRM 2903, (D.C. Cir. 2003), *enforcing* 336 NLRB 583, 170 LRRM 1124 (2001) (employer unlawfully transferred bargaining unit work and laid off 33 employees shortly after union was certified, where employer was unable to prove that work relocation and layoffs would have occurred in absence of union activity); Cold Heading Co., 332 NLRB 956, 172 LRRM 1354 (2000)(employer unlawfully routed equipment to nonunion facility and transferred other equipment from unionized to nonunion facility where employer failed to prove its business justification for relocation); Naperville Ready Mix Inc., 329 NLRB 174, 166 LRRM 1244 (1999), *enforced*, 242 F.3d 744, 166 LRRM 2712 (7th Cir.), *cert. denied*, 534 U.S. 1040, 168 LRRM 2896 (2001) (employer unlawfully devised sham subcontracting transactions, discharged bargaining-unit employees, and transferred their work to nonunit personnel); Westchester Lace Inc., 326 NLRB 1227, 163 LRRM 1181 (1998) (employer unlawfully subcontracted all of its bargaining-unit work in response to employee grievance filings where there was no showing subcontracting would have occurred in absence of grievance activity); G&T Terminal Packaging Co., 326 NLRB 114, 160 LRRM 1169 (1998), *enforced in part and remanded*, 246 F.3d 103, 166 LRRM 2837 (2d Cir. 2001) (employer unlawfully transferred potato-packing operations).

[69]193 F.3d 532, 162 LRRM 2618 (D.C. Cir. 1999). *See also* Douglas Foods Corp. v. NLRB, 251 F.3d 1056, 167 LRRM 2380 (D.C. Cir. 2001) (Board's finding that food caterer's sales of its hot trucks and catering routes were sham transactions motivated by union animus was not supported by substantial evidence).

[70]335 NLRB 622, 169 LRRM 1197 (2001). *See also* St. Vincent Med. Ctr., 338 NLRB 888, 172 LRRM 1025 (2003) (employer lawfully discharged employees in its respiratory care department and subcontracted out their work where general counsel failed to establish that antiunion animus was motivating factor in subcontracting decision).

did not violate Section 8(a)(3) when it contracted out its hot kitchen operation and laid off employees, where the employer established that the contracting out would have occurred notwithstanding the union activity of its employees because it had experienced quality problems for a considerable period of time.

5. *Replacement and Reinstatement of Economic Strikers*

a. Development of the Law

The Board continues to hold that informing economic strikers that they have been permanently replaced when, in fact, the employer has not hired replacements or made any arrangements for hiring them constitutes a discharge of strikers in violation of Section 8(a)(3).[71]

The Board ruled that employees who quit work in circumstances governed by Section 502 of the Act, which protects refusals to work in the face of "abnormally dangerous" working conditions, are not economic strikers for purposes of the rules pertaining to permanent replacement of economic strikers and are, therefore, entitled to immediate reinstatement to employment on making an unconditional offer to return to work.[72]

In *Detroit Newspaper Agency*,[73] the Board declined to overrule *Service Electric Co.*,[74] and adhered to the established doctrine that an employer is not obligated to bargain with a union concerning the terms and conditions of employment for replacements hired during a strike. The Board continues, however, to follow its rule that once the strike has ended, any replacements who remain employed assume the same status as other unit employees. As they are no longer

---

[71]Allied Mech. Servs., Inc., 341 NLRB No. 141, 175 LRRM 1224 (2004); Consolidated Delivery & Logistics Inc., 337 NLRB 524, 170 LRRM 1033 (2002), *enforced*, 63 Fed. Appx. 520 (D.C. Cir. 2003) (citing American Linen Supply Co., 297 NLRB 137, 132 LRRM 1313 (1989)), *enforced*, 945 F.2d 1428, 138 LRRM 2554 (8th Cir. 1991). *See also* Noel Foods v. NLRB, 82 F.3d 1113, 152 LRRM 2174 (D.C. Cir. 1996) (employer's contract with employment agency to prepare roster of replacement candidates made before informing employees that if they struck they would be replaced precluded determination that they had been discharged when strike began).

[72]TNS, Inc., 329 NLRB 602, 166 LRRM 1018 (1999), *vacated on other grounds*, 296 F.3d 384, 170 LRRM 2474 (6th Cir. 2002), *cert. denied*, 537 U.S. 1106, 171 LRRM 2768 (2003).

[73]327 NLRB 871, 161 LRRM 1033 (1999).

[74]281 NLRB 633, 124 LRRM 1318 (1986).

strike replacements, the terms under which the former strike replacements' work will be governed by the newly bargained contract[75] and the union is presumptively entitled to their names.[76]

b. Nature of the Duty to Reinstate

The Board continues to grant preferential reinstatement rights to economic strikers.[77] The Board held that an offer to return to work under the terms of an expired contract, after an employer had lawfully implemented its final offer for a new contract, was not an "unconditional" offer.[78]

The Board continues to impose the duty on a striking employee to advise the employer, personally or through the union, that he or she is ready to return to work.[79] In the absence of an offer to return, the employer could not have known of a striker's desire to return and the employer, therefore, has no duty to reinstate the striker.[80] Once a striking employee has made an unconditional offer to return to work, the employer is obligated to respond by indicating its acceptance of the offer and setting a reasonable starting date.[81]

The Board continues to hold that unreinstated economic strikers are entitled to preferential reinstatement to job vacancies created by the departure of strike replacements.[82] The Ninth Circuit has held that, although an employer may not offer returning strikers only entry-level positions while promoting nonstriking replacements to higher-level vacancies occurring after the strike's conclusion, an employer may reinstate returning strikers in an order determined

[75]*Detroit Newspaper, supra* note 73.

[76]Grinnell Fire Protection, 332 NLRB 1257, 165 LRRM 1345 (2000), *enforced in part,* 272 F.3d 1028, 168 LRRM 2976 (8th Cir. 2001) (union entitled to strike replacements' names but not their addresses because union had other opportunities to communicate with them away from their homes).

[77]Golden Stevedoring Co., 335 NLRB 410, 169 LRRM 1173 (2001).

[78]Taylor Lumber & Treating, Inc., 326 NLRB 1298, 161 LRRM 1031 (1998). *See also* Pan Am. Grain Co., 343 NLRB No. 47, 175 LRRM 1497 (2004) (finding offer to return to work not "unequivocally unconditional" where union stated that employees were "available to work without conditions," but that employer must still abide by allegedly agreed-upon conditions).

[79]Diamond Walnut Growers, Inc., 340 NLRB No. 135, 174 LRRM 1406 (2003) (union's letters on behalf of striking employees to return to work did not have to use word "unconditional" in order to be valid).

[80]Sacramento Theatrical Lighting, 333 NLRB 326, 172 LRRM 1223 (2001).

[81]Jackson County Comm'n on Aging, 339 NLRB 962, 174 LRRM 1519 (2003).

[82]Pirelli Cable Corp., 331 NLRB 1538, 168 LRRM 1273 (2000).

by relative merit, rather than by seniority, where neither past practice nor a collective bargaining agreement establishes a right of recall by seniority order.[83]

c. Defenses and Limitations

The Board continues to recognize that one legitimate and substantial justification for not immediately reinstating former strikers is a "bona fide absence of available work" for the strikers in substantially equivalent or prestrike positions.[84] Where permanent subcontracting is used as a justification for refusing to reinstate economic strikers, the employer must establish a legitimate and substantial business justification for the permanent subcontracting.[85] However, even if the Board finds that the employer was motivated by the requisite business justification, the Board might nevertheless find an unfair labor practice if the employer's conduct is inherently destructive of employee rights.[86] The Board may also find an unfair labor practice if the employer had an independent unlawful motive for hiring permanent replacements.[87]

The Board continues to follow its rule that, to show replacements were hired permanently, the employer is required to show that it had a "mutual understanding" with the replacements that they were permanent.[88] Based on the limited allegations of the complaint,

[83]Sever v. NLRB, 231 F.3d 1156, 165 LRRM 2833 (9th Cir. 2000).

[84]Zimmerman Plumbing & Heating Co., 334 NLRB 586, 170 LRRM 1134 (2001).

[85]Fairfield Tower Condominium Ass'n, 343 NLRB No. 101, 176 LRRM 1280 (2004) (employer failed to establish legitimate motive for subcontracting work of striking employees when it extended beyond the duration of the strike).

[86]*Id.* (Board did not reach "inherently destructive" issue); Abbott Northwestern Hosp., 343 NLRB No. 67, 176 LRRM 1004 (2004) (same); Capehorn Indus. Inc., 336 NLRB 364, 168 LRRM 1400 (2001)(same).

[87]Church Homes dba Avery Heights, 343 NLRB No. 128 (2004) (hiring of permanent replacements was not for independent unlawful purpose, but to gain economic leverage over union in bargaining, and to continue operations during the strike).

[88]Quantum Elec., Inc., 341 NLRB No. 146, 175 LRRM 1134 (2004) (construction industry employer adduced no evidence that replacement journeymen were specifically told they were permanent replacements; however, record was clear that employer hired all electricians to remain on the job until workflow or job completion dictated otherwise); Consolidated Delivery & Logistics Inc., 337 NLRB 524, 170 LRRM 1033 (2002)("mutual understanding" lacking in absence of evidence showing (1) that employment agency engaged to supply replacements understood that it was to supply permanent replacements and (2) that individual replacements

the Board held that an employer did not violate the Act by not displacing crossovers during a three-day period following a 1-day strike, where the employer was operating under a four-day contract for the supply of temporary workers.[89]

The Board's "substantially equivalent position" definition, as set out in *Rose Printing Co.*,[90] was applied to require the employer to reinstate a striker to a newly created position of "polisher" because it was substantially equivalent to the apprentice painter job.[91] On remand from the Fourth Circuit, the Board held that the discharge of economic strikers who had been reinstated to positions that were not substantially equivalent to their prestrike jobs and who were subsequently discharged were still entitled to an offer of reinstatement to a substantially equivalent job. The Board determined that the reinstatement rights had not been extinguished under these circumstances, because there was a "causal nexus" between the failure to reinstate the strikers to their prestrike positions and their subsequent terminations.[92] Strikers are not required to accept reinstatement to a position that is not the same as or substantially equivalent to their former jobs, and refusal to accept such an offer does not eliminate their reinstatement rights.[93] Generally, a vacant position requiring lower skills and providing lower pay than the former striker's prestrike

---

understood that they were permanent replacements); *Capehorn Indus. Inc.*, *supra* note 86 (statement "as long as [she] had work in [her] company, [she] would give them work to do" does not represent "mutual understanding" between employer and replacements that they were hired on a permanent basis); Dino & Sons Realty, 330 NLRB 680, 170 LRRM 1120 (2000), *enforced*, 37 Fed. Appx. 566 (2d Cir. 2002) (unpublished) ("mutual understanding" between employer and replacements is not established by statement that replacements would be permanent if they performed well).

[89]Encino-Tarzana Reg'l Med. Ctr., 332 NLRB 914, 167 LRRM 1135 (2000).

[90]304 NLRB 1076, 138 LRRM 1188 (1991).

[91]Towne Ford, Inc., 327 NLRB 193, 166 LRRM 1392 (1998), *enforced sub nom.* Machinists Peninsula Lodge No. 1414 v. NLRB, 238 F.3d 429 (9th Cir. 2000) (unpublished) (for purposes of determining whether positions are "substantially equivalent," the Board takes into account "changes which the Respondent [has] made in its organization of the work," and considers whether former striker would logically have moved to position in question).

[92]Beltway Transp. Co., 336 NLRB 850, 169 LRRM 1077 (2001), *on remand from* NLRB v. D&D Enters., Inc., 125 F.3d 200, 156 LRRM 2228 (4th Cir. 1997).

[93]Florida Wire & Cable, Inc., 333 NLRB 378, 173 LRRM 1325 (2001). *See also* Diamond Walnut Growers, Inc., 340 NLRB No. 135, 174 LRRM 1406 (2003) (employer is prohibited from treating strikers discriminatorily because they are strikers; however, employer is not obligated to apprise strikers of nonequivalent jobs or to allow them to bid on those jobs).

job is not substantially equivalent.[94] Passage of time is irrelevant to the analysis of whether a poststrike position is substantially equivalent to a prestrike position.[95]

The Board continues to follow its rule that the employer bears the burden of affirmatively demonstrating that strikers have abandoned their reinstatement rights by engaging in strike misconduct.[96]

7. *Discrimination Against Union Organizers and "Salts"*

The Board continues to apply strict standards in evaluating employer defenses attempting to demonstrate that refusal to consider or hire union organizers and "salts" would have occurred even absent knowledge of union-organizing activity, and, in most cases, has rejected the defenses.[97] In those cases in which no violations were

---

[94]Salem Elec. Co., 331 NLRB 1575, 171 LRRM 1498 (2001).

[95]Omahaline Hydraulics Co., 342 NLRB No. 86, 175 LRRM 1484 (2004).

[96]Zimmerman Plumbing & Heating Co., 339 NLRB 1302, 173 LRRM 1118 (2003); Pirelli Cable Corp., 331 NLRB 1538, 168 LRRM 1273 (2000); Detroit Newspapers, 340 NLRB No. 121, 173 LRRM 1455 (2003); Pratt Towers, Inc., 338 NLRB 61, 170 LRRM 1533 (2002) (former strikers entitled to reinstatement despite their participation in unlawful strike as the employer's requirement that they renounce union amounted to unlawful yellow-dog contract).

[97]*See, e.g.*, Tri-County Paving, Inc., 342 NLRB No. 122 (2004) (employer acted unlawfully by purposefully excluding union applicants from consideration based on fear of salting and antiunion animus); C.T. Taylor Co., Inc., 342 NLRB No. 102, 175 LRRM 1359 (2004) (proffered reason for discharge was pretextual due to employer's inconsistent actions when employee's "salt" status was discovered); Commercial Erectors, Inc., 342 NLRB No. 94, 176 LRRM 1386 (2004) (Board found violation where employer made unlawful threat which demonstrated animus, qualifications of salts were as good if not better than applicants, and employer made false statements to salts; also, employer's reasons for failure to hire were shifting and pretextual); Network Dynamics Cabling, Inc., 341 NLRB No. 107, 174 LRRM 1470 (2004) (employer's shifting and unsupportable defenses do not rebut prima facie case of illegal refusal to hire); Solvay Iron Works, Inc., 341 NLRB No. 25 (2004) (union salt's misrepresentation as to his name did not excuse employer's discriminatory change in hiring policies after it learned of deception); Zarcon, Inc., 340 NLRB No. 145, 173 LRRM 1478 (2003), *enforced*, 118 Fed. Appx. 113, 176 LRRM 2640 (8th Cir. 2005) (employer's contention that it did not care whether employees were union or not was completely rebutted by substantial admissions at hearing showing that it operated with antiunion animus); Corporate Interiors, Inc., 340 NLRB No. 85, 173 LRRM 1547 (2003) (employer's proffered defenses of nondiscriminatory hiring practices and other alleged salt misconduct were found to be pretextual); ADS Elec. Co., 339 NLRB 1020, 173 LRRM 1540 (2003) (employer's proffered reason for laying off employees for lack of work after discovering that they were union salts was found pretextual); Jon Bohnenkemper dba South State Builders, Inc., 339 NLRB 465, 173 LRRM 1607 (2003) (arguably legitimate reasons for laying off union salts were found to be discriminatory because employer

found, the employers were successful in either establishing lack of knowledge of union activity or showing an application of valid nondiscriminatory hiring criteria.[98] The Board has also held that an

---

could have laid off two junior nonunion employees instead); Tim Foley Plumbing Serv. Inc., 337 NLRB 598, 170 LRRM 1107 (2002) (employer's use of temporary labor agencies for hiring needs was aimed at avoiding hiring union applicants); Niblock Excavating, Inc., 337 NLRB 53, 169 LRRM 1129 (2001) (facts did not support employer's claim that it only hired inexperienced employees and selection of union salt for "random" drug test further showed antiunion animus); Americlean Restoration & Maint. Corp., 335 NLRB 1052, 169 LRRM 1389 (2001) (employer did not utilize qualification requirements used to disqualify union applicants when hiring other applicants); Hartman Bros. Heating & Air Conditioning, Inc., 332 NLRB 1343 (2000), *enforced,* 280 F.3d 1110, 169 LRRM 2385 (7th Cir. 2002) (lie on employment application about "salt" status, which does not involve falsehood about job qualifications, does not privilege refusal to hire); H.B. Zachry Co., 332 NLRB 1178, 165 LRRM 1351 (2000) (employer claim that phone calls to salt applicants to offer employment went unanswered deemed a sham because evidence revealed that caller hung up as soon as call was answered); Merit Elec. Co., 328 NLRB 212, 163 LRRM 1196 (1999) (employer failed to show hiring would not have occurred in absence of knowledge that applicants were "salts"); Lin R. Rogers Elec. Contractors, Inc., 328 NLRB 1165, 161 LRRM 1297 (1999) (employer failed to prove that it exclusively followed policy of hiring only employees who have worked at its other jobsites); North Bay Plumbing, Inc., 327 NLRB 899, 161 LRRM 1139 (1999) (employer failed to prove that it followed policy of not hiring individuals who had formerly been in competing business, and applicant no longer operated competing business in any event); Custom Top Soil, Inc., 327 NLRB 121, 161 LRRM 1142 (1999) (reasons for not hiring found to be pretextual). *See also* Kentucky Gen., Inc. v. NLRB, 177 F.3d 430, 161 LRRM 2435 (6th Cir. 1999) (enforcing Board order finding failure of employer to prove that it followed policy of hiring only those applicants whose skills were already known to employer).

[98]*See, e.g.*, Quantum Elec., Inc, 341 NLRB No. 146, 175 LRRM 1134 (2004) (salt applicant's satisfactory test score alone was insufficient to infer antiunion motivation in the refusal to hire); Jacobs Heating & Air Conditioning, 341 NLRB No. 128, 174 LRRM 1473 (2004) (policy of requiring certain qualifications upheld as a legitimate reason for not hiring salts); *See also* Operating Eng'rs v. NLRB, 325 F.3d 818 (7th Cir. 2003) (employer's nondiscriminatory hiring policy of giving preference to referred applicants was uniformly applied), *enforcing sub nom.* Brandt Constr. Co., 336 NLRB 733, 169 LRRM 1455 (2001); Quality Mech. Insulation, Inc., 340 NLRB No. 91, 173 LRRM 1486 (2003) (employer successfully demonstrated that its priority hiring system was nondiscriminatory and Board also held that salt's use of alias would have been grounds for termination despite union affiliation); Ken Maddox Heating & Air Conditioning, Inc., 340 NLRB No. 7, 173 LRRM 1113 (2003) (employer established that its policies of first considering referred applicants and other applications on a "top of the pile" basis were nondiscriminatory); Oil Capital Elec., 337 NLRB 947, 170 LRRM 1523 (2002) (general counsel failed to show that 20 of 21 applicants possessed requisite training and experience and employer had hired other qualified applicants whose applications revealed union affiliation); Colburn Elec. Co., 334 NLRB 532, 170 LRRM 1141 (2001) (valid insurance reasons justified refusal to issue or accept applications at job site); B&C Contracting

applicant's disruptive, intimidating, and disrespectful activity can justify an employer's refusal to consider or hire, even though the applicant is also engaging in union activity.[99] Where otherwise valid nondiscriminatory hiring criteria are disparately applied to disqualify only union supporters, however, the Board concludes that a violation has occurred.[100]

In *Aztech Electric Co.*,[101] the Board concluded that the employer's wage comparability policy of not hiring or considering any applicant with a recent wage history of earning 30 percent or more than the employer's starting wage was inherently destructive of employee rights and a violation of Section 8(a)(3).[102] In so ruling, the Board

---

Co., 334 NLRB 218, 167 LRRM 1161 (2001) (applicants' refusal to travel is valid disqualification criterion); TNT Techs., Ltd., 330 NLRB 78, 163 LRRM 1009 (1999) (no showing that refusals to hire were result of union activity); Little Rock Elec. Contractors, Inc., 327 NLRB 932, 164 LRRM 1100 (1999) (employer established that it validly applied its rule against considering or hiring applicants who held simultaneous employment with another entity); J.O. Mory Inc., 326 NLRB 604, 161 LRRM 1109 (1999) (employer lawfully applied its policy of not hiring those who currently earn more than employer's entry-level wage).

[99]Exterior Sys., Inc., 338 NLRB 677, 171 LRRM 1297 (2002); *see also* NLRB v. Wolfe Elec. Co., 314 F.3d 325, 171 LRRM 2586 (8th Cir. 2002) (union applicant's possession of video camera and tape recorder which upset owner's wife who was working as a receptionist in the hiring office was not so offensive, abusive, or obscene as to remove the protections of the Act).

[100]Smucker Co., 341 NLRB No. 10, 174 LRRM 1252 (2004) (violation found where 30-day application expiration policy not uniformly and fairly applied); Masiongale Elec.-Mech., Inc., 337 NLRB 42, 169 LRRM 1105 (2001), *enforced in relevant part,* 323 F.3d 546, 172 LRRM 2086 (7th Cir. 2003) (applications considered stale and invalid if more than 30 days old; policy of not hiring employees with recent high wage histories); Fluor Daniel Inc. (III), 333 NLRB 427, 166 LRRM 1265 (2001), *enforced in relevant part,* 332 F.3d 961, 172 LRRM 2673 (6th Cir. 2003), *cert. denied,* 125 S. Ct. 964, 176 LRRM 2448 (2005) (hiring preference for former employees certified by an in-house craft certification program; 42-month craft work experience; preference to former employees whether certified or not; applications considered stale and invalid if 60 or more days old); Nelson Elec. Contracting Corp., 332 NLRB 179, 168 LRRM 1148 (2000), *enforced,* 51 Fed. Appx. 33, 171 LRRM 2512 (2d Cir. 2002) (unpublished) (policy of hiring only employees transferred from other projects or applicants with positive referrals from other sources).

[101]335 NLRB 260, 168 LRRM 1073 (2001*), enforcement denied in part, enforced in part sub nom.* Contractors' Labor Pool v. NLRB, 323 F.3d 1051, 172 LRRM 2065 (D.C. Cir. 2003).

[102]*See also* Mainline Contracting Corp., 334 NLRB 922, 171 LRRM 1138 (2001), (rule forbidding disclosure of protected activity (such as status as a voluntary union organizer) on employment application was inherently destructive of §7 rights and declining to follow *Boilermakers v. NLRB,* 127 F.3d 1300, 156 LRRM 2881 (11th Cir. 1997)).

emphasized that its conclusion was limited to the facts of the case and that it was not passing on the legality of other wage comparability rules that may have a lesser exclusionary effect or that may be more narrowly drawn and essential to an employer's business operations.[103] The four-member Board split evenly on whether a "disabling conflict" defense can be employed to defeat unfair labor practice charges filed on behalf of "salts." That defense contends that a union's salting campaign that consisted of challenging employer practices in unfair labor practice proceedings, regardless of the merits of the charges, increasing employer operating expenses, and attempting to force the employer into bankruptcy or out of business loses the protection of Section 7.[104]

On appeal, the Court of Appeals for the D.C. Circuit held that because the Board found that the wage comparability rule was not motivated by union animus, the employer's application of that rule

---

[103]*Aztech Elec. Co.*, *supra* note 101 at 263 n.20, 168 LRRM 1073, 1078 n.20. *See, e.g.*, MicroMetl Corp., 333 NLRB 1133, 168 LRRM 1055 (2001) (policy of not hiring applicants who had previously earned more than $10 per hour is valid); Northside Elec. Contractors, Inc., 331 NLRB 1564, 168 LRRM 1108 (2001) (policy of not hiring applicants with wage history of earning $22 per hour, where employer's maximum salary was $12 per hour, is valid); Kelly Constr. of Ind., 333 NLRB 1272, 168 LRRM 1097 (2001) (hiring preference for applicants accustomed to earning wages within range offered by employer is valid, despite evidence that one applicant who did not satisfy policy was hired).

[104]Members Liebman and Walsh rejected the use of "disabling conflict" as a viable defense in a salting case; Members Truesdale and Hurtgen would recognize the defense in an appropriate factual situation; and Member Hurtgen concluded that it should be available to the employer in the case before him to toll backpay liability. Member Truesdale joined Members Liebman and Walsh in concluding that the defense was unavailable to the employer in the case before them because it had not relied on "disabling conflict" as the basis for disqualifying union applicants. *See also* NLRB v. Interstate Builders, Inc., 351 F.3d 1020, 173 LRRM 1242 (10th Cir. 2003) (court of appeals held that employer's defense that the union was engaging in a "disabling conflict" was unsupported by the evidence and at odds with employer's alternate defense that it did not hire the union employees because they applied through a union representative instead of individually); Tri-County Paving, Inc., 342 NLRB No. 122 (2004) (employer's disabling conflict failed because employer's "panic attack" after reviewing information about salting on Internet occurred after unlawful refusal to hire union applicants);); Casino Ready Mix, Inc., 335 NLRB 463, 171 LRRM 1446 (2001), *enforced*, 321 F.3d 1190, 171 LRRM 3289 (D.C. Cir. 2003) (employer's "disabling conflict" defense failed because there was no evidence of any economic strike, subterfuge, bad faith, or sabotage by the union designed to drive employer out of area or business); Little Rock Elec. Contractors Inc., 336 NLRB 146, 170 LRRM 1520 (2001) ("disabling conflict" defense found to be a pretext for not hiring union applicants).

could not be discriminatory.[105] This holding also determined that in order for an employer rule to be "inherently destructive," it must evince *some* union animus.[106]

The Board's rule that a backpay award for a paid union organizer wrongfully denied employment by a nonunion contractor need not be offset by earnings received from the union during the backpay period has been accepted by the Second Circuit[107] and the D.C. Circuit.[108]

9. *Discrimination Based on Terms of Collective Bargaining Agreement*

a. Enforcement of Union-Security Provision

The Board continues to apply its rule that an employer violates Section 8(a)(3) if it discharges or takes similar action against an employee pursuant to a union's demand under a union-security agreement when the employer has reasonable grounds to believe that the demand was for a reason other that the failure to tender dues and fees. Satisfaction of the employer's duty to investigate the circumstances behind the union's demand depends on (i) the facts known to the employer; (ii) the degree of doubt those facts raise; (iii) the burden the inquiry would impose; and (iv) the likelihood that an investigation would lead to a prompt resolution of the employer's

---

[105] *Aztech Elec. Co., supra* note 101.

[106] The court went on to address the "disabling conflict" defense raised by the employer and held that this defense would not be available where the employer was unaware of the employees' union status at the time of its discriminatory conduct. Contractor's Labor Pool v. NLRB, 323 F.3d 1051, 1060–61, 172 LRRM 2065, 2071–72 (D.C. Cir. 2003).

[107] NLRB v. Ferguson Elec. Co., 242 F.3d 426, 166 LRRM 2513 (2d Cir. 2001), *enforcing* 330 NLRB 514, 163 LRRM 1081 (2000).

[108] Tualatin Elec., Inc. v. NLRB, 253 F.3d 714, 167 LRRM 2743 (D.C. Cir. 2001) ("salts" are not required to mitigate backpay liability by accepting nonunion employment that would subject them to union discipline). *See also* Aneco, Inc. v. NLRB, 285 F.3d 326, 169 LRRM 2833 (4th Cir. 2002) (rejecting employer's argument that paid union organizer did not exercise reasonable job search because union rules restricted paid organizer from applying at unionized companies and at companies with too few or too many employees that would be difficult for the union to organize); A.P. Painting & Improvements, Inc., 339 NLRB 1206, 173 LRRM 1367 (2003) (employer's offer of reinstatement was not "specific, unequivocal and unconditional" such that the backpay period should have been tolled when it informed salt that he could return to work as long as he did not try to organize on "company time").

doubts.[109] A union's attempt to require an employer to terminate an employee for a reason other than nonpayment of dues or initiation fees continues to be a Section 8(b)(2) violation.[110]

b. Compliance With Superseniority Provision

The Board continues to hold that contractual provisions granting superseniority to union stewards are lawful only insofar as they are limited to layoff and recall. In *Electrical Workers Local 221 (Kidder, Inc.)*,[111] the collective bargaining agreement's superseniority provision was so limited on its face and therefore lawful, but the union attempted to advance an unlawful interpretation of the clause through arbitration and thus violated the Act. The employer in *Kidder* had prepared a layoff/job elimination list for a particular department on which the local union president's name appeared. Rather than exercise his superseniority right to bump an employee in another department, however, the union president insisted that he had the right under the superseniority provision to remain in his current position (at his current rate) and that he would not bump another employee to avoid layoff. When the employer refused to agree with that position, the union filed a grievance and then a demand for arbitration. The Board held that the union violated Sections 8(b)(1)(A) and (2) of the Act by the union president's demand to remain in his current position and the union's demand for arbitration of the issue. It reasoned that the union was not seeking protection from layoff for its president (or otherwise seeking to further the "effective administration of the collective bargaining agreement"), but instead to guarantee him wage and job classification protection, and concluded that Board law does not permit use of a superseniority provision to lay claim to a particular job, or to secure a certain wage, but only to avoid layoff.

---

[109] *See* L.D. Kichler Co., 335 NLRB 1427, 1431, 168 LRRM 1376 (2001); Yellow Freight Sys. of Ind., 327 NLRB 996, 996 n.2, 1008–09, 167 LRRM 1282 (1999) (employer violated §8(a)(3) by refusing to call employee into work where it knew that union's insistence that employee not be called in was for reason other than employee's failure to pay dues and employee did not object to paying dues).

[110] *See* District Council 9 & Painters Local 18 (Creative Finishes Ltd.), 336 NLRB 674, 676, 173 LRRM 1325 (2001).

[111] 333 NLRB 1149, 172 LRRM 1046 (2001). *See also* Section III.B. [Union Inducement of Employer to Discriminate; Violations Relating to Seniority Provisions], *infra*.

III. UNION INDUCEMENT OF EMPLOYER TO DISCRIMINATE

A. Union Inducements as Unfair Labor Practice Prohibited by Section 8(b)(2)

The Board continues to find that a union violates Section 8(b)(2) by attempting to cause or causing an employer to discharge a member for criticizing the union. Types of protected intraunion activity include filing internal charges against incumbent union officers and running for office against incumbents.[112] Recent cases also continue to hold that a union violates Section 8(b)(2) by attempting to cause or causing an employer to discriminate against those who choose not to support the union, either by being nonmembers or by crossing picket lines,[113] or by expressing their opposition to the union.[114]

The cases also continue to hold that discrimination under Section 8(b)(2) can involve refusals to hire or rehire,[115] to offer overtime opportunities,[116] to honor an employee's seniority,[117] or to refer

---

[112]Bo-Ty Plus, Inc., 334 NLRB 523, 172 LRRM 1239 (2001); Painters Local 466 (Skidmore Coll.), 332 NLRB 445, 165 LRRM 1195 (2000); USF Red Star, Inc., 330 NLRB 53, 162 LRRM 1409, *enforced*, 230 F.3d 102, 165 LRRM 2665 (4th Cir. 2000); Nationsway Transp. Serv., 327 NLRB 1033, 164 LRRM 1339 (1999); *but see* Precoat Metals, 341 NLRB No. 143, 175 LRRM 1110 (2004) (no violation where it was not established that union caused or attempted to cause employer to discipline employee for violating work rules; employer would have disciplined employee regardless of his unsuccessful candidacy against incumbents in union election).

[113]Letter Carriers Branch 3126 (U.S. Postal Serv.), 330 NLRB 587, 163 LRRM 1190 (2000), *enforced*, 281 F.3d 235, 169 LRRM 2581 (D.C. Cir. 2002); Newspaper & Mail Deliverers (City & Suburban Delivery), 332 NLRB 870, 172 LRRM 1263 (2000); *but see* Operating Eng'rs Local 12 (Kiewit Indus.), 337 NLRB 544, 170 LRRM 1037 (2002) (no violation where it was not established that union requested employer to lay off member).

[114]*In re* Strack & Van Til Supermkts. dba Town & Country Supermkts. & Ultra Foods, 340 NLRB No. 172, 174 LRRM 1001 (2004); Graphic Communications Local 1-M (Bang Printing), 337 NLRB 662, 170 LRRM 1123 (2002).

[115]Laborers Local 334 (Kvaerner Sonyer), 335 NLRB 597, 169 LRRM 1220 (2001); Laborers Local 1184 (Nicholson Rodio), 332 NLRB 1292, 168 LRRM 1176 (2000); *Newspaper & Mail Deliverers, supra* note 113; *Painters Local 466, supra* note 112.

[116]*Letter Carriers Branch 3126, supra* note 113.

[117]Letter Carriers Branch 109 (U.S. Postal Serv.), 336 NLRB 1182, 174 LRRM 1158 (2001); *Nationsway Transp., supra* note 112.

individuals for employment where the union is the sole and exclusive source of referrals.[118]

B. Violations Relating to Seniority Provisions

The Board continues to hold that a union violates Section 8(b)(2) when it agrees with an employer to base seniority on whether employees have exercised or refrained from exercising their Section 7 rights. In *Newspaper & Mail Deliverers (City & Suburban Delivery System),*[119] a union unlawfully caused an employer making permanent hiring decisions to refuse to recognize the seniority of certain casual employees because those employees had worked during an earlier strike. The union's actions violated Section 8(b)(2) even though the contract did not provide for seniority to be used as a basis for hiring; the employer's expressed desire was to use seniority as the basis for hire.

In *Letter Carriers Branch 109 (U.S. Postal Service),*[120] the Board found that a union president's attempts to reduce an employee's seniority amounted to two independent Section 8(b)(2) violations. After the president unsuccessfully requested that the employer reduce the employee's seniority by 14 months, he unilaterally withdrew the employee's seniority grievance and filed his own class action grievance. Even though a reduction in the employee's seniority was consistent with past arbitration decisions interpreting the collective bargaining agreement, the Board found that Sections 8(b)(1)(A) and (2) were violated, because the president's actions were motivated by "personal animosity," citing *Miranda Fuel Co.*[121]

---

[118]Freeman Decorating Co., 335 NLRB 103, 171 LRRM 1056 (2001); Brede, Inc., 335 NLRB 71, 169 LRRM 1295 (2001), *enforced on other grounds,* 315 F.3d 906, 171 LRRM 2656 (8th Cir. 2003); Bo-Ty Plus, Inc., 334 NLRB 523, 172 LRRM 1239 (2001). *See* Section III.D. [Union Inducement of Employer to Discriminate; Violations Relating to Hiring and Referral Halls], *infra.*

[119]332 NLRB 870, 172 LRRM 1263 (2000).

[120]*Supra* note 117.

[121]140 NLRB 181, 51 LRRM 1584 (1962), *enforcement denied,* 326 F.2d 172, 54 LRRM 2715 (2d Cir. 1963).

The Board addressed a putative superseniority issue in *Nationsway Transport Service*,[122] in which an employee was denied a top seniority position because the union and employer had entered into an agreement to award the first seniority spot to an employee who would act as the union's "spokesman" or "shop steward." The Board reasoned that the union violated Section 8(b)(2) because the particular agreement between the union and employer did not trump the parties' past practice of placing employees on a seniority list in the order that they arrived at a new trucking terminal. In reaching its ruling, the Board did not discuss its *Dairylea Cooperative*[123] line of cases or its *Gulton* rule[124] relating to superseniority issues.

In *Electrical Workers Local 221 (Kidder, Inc.)*,[125] the union was found to have violated Section 8(b)(2) by submitting to arbitration a grievance that asserted the superseniority provisions of the collective bargaining agreement should be interpreted to exclude the union president from layoff lists, so that he would not need to "bump" other employees and could maintain his rate of pay. Although the union's interpretation of the agreement would not cause a "detriment" to any other employees, it was nonetheless unlawful because it extended superseniority protection to job bidding and bumping, and was not limited to layoff and recall procedures, and was therefore beyond the minimum limit necessary for the union to carry out its representational duties.

C. Violations Relating to Union-Security Provisions

1. *Introduction and Overview*

Subject to state law, Section 8(a)(3) allows an employer and a union to negotiate a union-security clause in a collective bargaining agreement, provided that the union is the majority representative of the employees pursuant to Section 9(a).[126] A union-security clause is

[122] 327 NLRB 1033, 164 LRRM 1339 (1999).

[123] 219 NLRB 656, 89 LRRM 1737 (1975), *enforced sub nom.* NLRB v. Teamsters Local 338, 531 F.2d 1162, 91 LRRM 2929 (2d Cir. 1976).

[124] Gulton Electro-Voice, 266 NLRB 406, 112 LRRM 1361 (1983), *enforced sub nom.* Electrical Workers (IUE) Local 900 v. NLRB, 727 F.2d 1184, 115 LRRM 2760 (D.C. Cir. 1984).

[125] 333 NLRB 1149, 172 LRRM 1046 (2001).

[126] 29 U.S.C. §158(a)(3). *See generally* Main Edition, Chapter 26, "Union Security."

a contractual provision that requires the tendering of periodic dues to a union as a condition of employment on or after the thirtieth day (or eighth day in the construction industry) after the beginning of the employment or the effective date of the collective bargaining agreement. Under Section 8(b)(2), a union may lawfully cause the discharge of an employee under a union-security clause for failure "to tender the periodic dues and the initiation fees uniformly required as a condition of acquiring or retaining membership."[127]

Section 8(b)(2) prohibits, however, a union from negotiating and/or enforcing a union-security clause when the union does not represent a majority of employees in the bargaining unit. For example, a union violated Section 8(b)(2), as well as Section 8(b)(1)(A), when it negotiated and enforced a union-security clause after the employer voluntarily recognized the union based upon a coerced showing of interest. In *Duane Reade, Inc.*[128] and *Clock Electric, Inc.*,[129] the employers' agents and/or supervisors provided unlawful assistance to a union by coercing employees to sign authorization cards. The union used these coerced cards as its showing of majority support to obtain the employer's voluntary recognition. After being recognized as the majority representative, the union and the employer entered into a collective bargaining agreement containing a union-security clause. The Board found that, given the employer's unlawful assistance, which violates Sections 8(a)(2) and (1), the union did not represent an uncoerced majority of employees in the bargaining unit. Accordingly, the union violated Sections 8(b)(1)(A) and (b)(2) when it entered into an agreement containing a union-security clause.[130]

In *Northwest Protective Services*,[131] the Board found a union violated Sections 8(b)(1)(A) and (b)(2) by coercing an employer into voluntarily recognizing the union by threatening to engage in illegal picketing. The employer, which provided security guards, previously withdrew recognition from the union because, after a merger, the union's membership constituted a mixed-guard union. The employer recognized a different, pure-guard union. However, the mixed-

---

[127] *Id.*

[128] 338 NLRB 943, 172 LRRM 1147 (2003), *enforced,* 99 Fed. Appx. 240, 2004 U.S. App. LEXIS 11129 (D.C. Cir. 2004).

[129] 338 NLRB 806, 172 LRRM 1003 (2003).

[130] *See also* Alliant Foodservice, Inc., 335 NLRB 695, 171 LRRM 1075 (2001).

[131] 342 NLRB No. 120 (2004).

guard union threatened to picket the employer. In addition to the threats, a majority of the Board found that the mixed-guard union was a minority union at the time it demanded and obtained the employer's coerced recognition.

Section 8(b)(2) also prohibits a union from attempting to apply a union-security clause in a collective bargaining agreement to employees who are not part of the bargaining unit, or who are part of another bargaining unit.[132] For example, in *Kaiser Foundation Hospital*,[133] the Board found a union violated Sections 8(b)(1)(A) and (b)(2) when it accepted recognition as the majority representative of, and applied the collective bargaining agreement's union-security clause to, research assistants. Historically, the parties had excluded the classification of research assistants from the bargaining unit. In finding a violation, the Board rejected the parties' claims that the addition of research assistants to the unit was a proper accretion or, in the alternative, a proper recapture of work.

In *Allied Trades Council*,[134] a union pursued an arbitration with the goal of obtaining an accretion of employees into the union's bargaining unit, even though those employees were previously found by a regional director to constitute a separate, appropriate unit. The Board found that the union violated Section 8(b)(1)(A) by insisting that its collective bargaining agreement, which contained a union-security clause, apply to the employees at issue. The Board further found the union violated Section 8(b)(2) by causing the employer to discriminate against these employees in violation of Section 8(a)(3).

By contrast, a union does not violate Sections 8(b)(1)(A) and (b)(2) by negotiating the return of bargaining-unit work that was being performed by previously unrepresented employees and by applying the collective bargaining agreement to those employees.[135] In that case, the general counsel did not allege that the employer and the union were attempting to expand the bargaining unit to include employees who were historically excluded from the unit.

---

[132]*Kaiser Found. Hosp.*, 343 NLRB No. 8 (2004); Newspaper & Mail Deliverers (Jalt Corp. dba U.N.D.S.), 337 NLRB 1102 (2002); American Med. Response, Inc., 335 NLRB 1176 (2001); Keystone Shipping Co., 327 NLRB 892, 160 LRRM 1225 (1999).

[133]343 NLRB No. 8 (2004).

[134]342 NLRB No. 103 (2004).

[135]Lockheed Martin Tactical Aircraft Sys., 331 NLRB 1407 (2000).

Rather, the union and the employer negotiated the transfer of 26 employees who were performing bargaining-unit work into the unit.

There are slightly different considerations with respect to the construction industry. In *Incisa, U.S.A., Inc.*,[136] the Board held that a union's acceptance of voluntary recognition under Section 9(a), while a valid election petition was pending, did not implicate Section 8(b)(2); however, the acceptance of that recognition violated Section 8(b)(1)(A). The contract was originally a Section 8(f) prehire agreement in which the union-security clause was permissible without majority status. However, in *Builders, Woodworkers & Millwrights Local 1 (Glen Falls Contractors Ass'n)*,[137] the Board found a union violated Sections 8(b)(1)(A) and (b)(2) by entering into a collective bargaining agreement, with a union-security clause that covered a bargaining unit already represented by another union pursuant to a different collective bargaining agreement. The Board noted that, regardless of whether the respondent union entered into a Section 8(f) or Section 9(a) relationship, the employers could not repudiate the agreement with the second union and recognize the respondent union.

In *Flying Dutchman Park, Inc.*,[138] the Board found that a union violated Section 8(b)(2) when it enforced a union-security clause that contained a requirement that the employee obtain a "referral" from the union before commencing employment. The Board found that the union and the employer, which was not engaged in the construction industry, negotiated a collective bargaining agreement that lacked a hiring-hall provision but contained a union-security clause that required employees to obtain a "referral" from the union. The Board found that the union-security clause was unlawful on its face.

2. *Discriminatory Enforcement Prohibited*

A union violates Section 8(b)(1)(A) by collecting full membership dues from a *Beck* objector, but the union does not thereby vio-

---

[136]327 NLRB 563, 167 LRRM 1228 (1999). *See also* Hovey Elec., Inc., 328 NLRB 273, 165 LRRM 1343 (1999) (union did not violate §§8(b)(1)(A) and 8(b)(2) because parties lawfully converted §8(f) relationship into a §9(a) recognition). *See also* Main Edition, Chapter 13, "The Duty to Bargain," at Section VIII.B. [The Construction Industry: Section 8(f); The *Deklewa* Decision: Binding Section 8(f) Agreements and the Duty to Bargain].

[137]341 NLRB No. 54 (2004).

[138]329 NLRB 414, 162 LRRM 1283 (1999).

late Section 8(b)(2) so long as the union does not attempt to cause the employer to discharge or discriminate against the objector.[139] Also, a union does not violate Section 8(b)(2) by attempting to collect an amount equal to a *Beck* objector's share of representational expenses.[140]

A building and construction trades union will violate Section 8(b)(1)(A) by denying a referral to a job that is not covered by a union-security clause because a union member has a dues arrearage. In *Electrical Workers Local 16 (ACCL Enterprises)*,[141] the member had a dues arrearage and sought employment through the union's exclusive referral hall. The union denied a referral to the member, even though a project labor agreement with a signatory employer, Toyota, did not contain a union-security clause. Moreover, the Toyota agreement provided that it overrode any other collective bargaining agreements and that referrals should not be affected by any obligation of union membership, policies, or requirements. After rejecting the union's claim that the Toyota agreement incorporated referral provisions from a master agreement with an employer association, the ALJ found, and the Board affirmed, that the union violated Section 8(b)(1)(A) when it failed and refused to refer the member because of his dues arrearage.

A building and construction trades union will similarly violate Sections 8(b)(1)(A) and (b)(2) when it denies referrals to a member to jobs covered by a union-security clause after telling the member that any dues payments he made would be applied to the balance of an outstanding disciplinary fine. In *Iron Workers Local 433 (Steel Fabricators)*,[142] the Board found a violation where the union re-

---

[139]Transport Workers (Johnson Controls World Servs., Inc.), 329 NLRB 543, 169 LRRM 1344 (1999); Steelworkers (George E. Failing Co.), 329 NLRB 145, 162 LRRM 1097 (1999); Polymark Corp., 329 NLRB 9, 162 LRRM 1033 (1999), *enforced in part, denied enforcement in part sub nom.* Mohat v. NLRB, 1 Fed. Appx. 258, 166 LRRM 2256 (6th Cir. 2001) (unpublished). *See also* Carlon A. Lamson & Sessions Co., 328 NLRB 983, 161 LRRM 1019 (1999) (noting ALJ found union did not violate §8(b)(2) because there was no evidence union took affirmative action to enforce allegedly unlawful union-security clause).

[140]*Polymark Corp., supra* note 139; Kroger, Inc., 327 NLRB 1237, 167 LRRM 1309 (1999). *But see* Teamsters Local 75 (Schreiber Foods), 329 NLRB 28, 162 LRRM 1057 (1999) (modifying ALJ's decision to find a violation of only §8(b)(1)(A), but not §8(b)(2), based on union's attempt to enforce union-security clause without informing objectors of their *Beck* rights).

[141]341 NLRB No. 8, 174 LRRM 1071 (2004).

[142]341 NLRB No. 68, 174 LRRM 1356 (2004).

peatedly told the member that dues payments were going to be applied to the fine balance and he would not receive a referral without a paid-up dues receipt. Although the member never registered on the out-of-work list for a referral, the Board nevertheless found a violation because, by virtue of the union's statements, any attempt to register would have been futile given the union's position.

A union violates Section 8(b)(2) when it seeks the discharge of an employee whose dues payments were refused by the union. In *Painters District Council 9 (Creative Finishes Ltd.)*,[143] the Board also held that a union violated Section 8(b)(2) when it filed a grievance alleging that the employment of a "non-union man" breached the union-security clause in the collective bargaining agreement. In that case, a former financial secretary-treasurer resigned from office and an audit disclosed that almost $27,000 was allegedly missing. Charges were filed against the former officer and a hearing committee found him guilty of the charges. The hearing committee expelled the officer with the condition that he could be reinstated if he paid a fine and made restitution. The former officer neither paid the fine nor made restitution; however, he sought to continue paying dues. The union rejected the former officer's dues payments. When the union subsequently learned that a signatory contractor employed the officer, the union filed a grievance alleging a breach of the union-security clause. The Board determined that the union was seeking the discharge of the former officer on a ground other than his "failure to tender periodic dues and the initiation fees uniformly required as a condition of retaining membership."[144] In reaching this decision, the Board distinguished *Philadelphia Inquirer*,[145] on the ground that the former officer in that case had been convicted of embezzling union funds and that was the reason the union sought his termination. The union did not act under color of the union-security clause.

3. Dues and Fees That May Be Exacted

In *Electrical Workers Local 48 (Kingston Constructors, Inc.)*,[146] the Board addressed whether market-recovery dues constituted periodic

---

[143]336 NLRB 674 (2001). *See also* Teamsters Local 251 (Ryder Student Transp.), 333 NLRB 1009, 168 LRRM 1007 (2001).

[144]*Id.*, 336 NLRB 674, quoting 29 U.S.C. §158(b)(2).

[145]189 NLRB 829, 76 LRRM 1811 (1971).

[146]332 NLRB 1492, 166 LRRM 1090 (2000), *modified*, 333 NLRB No. 122 (2001), *enforced*, 345 F.3d 1049, 173 LRRM 2257 (9th Cir. 2003).

dues or assessments that may be required as a condition of acquiring or retaining membership. Market-recovery dues are part of job-targeting programs, in which unions subsidize part of employees' wages to allow union contractors to bid competitively on construction projects. In addressing this issue, the Board found that its decision in *Teamsters Local 959 (RCA Service Co.),*[147] which held that the term "periodic dues" referred only to those payments that are for the purpose of supporting the union's role as collective bargaining agent, was implicitly overruled by its later decision in *Detroit Mailers Local 40.*[148] In the latter case, the Board held that "periodic dues" included any payments under a union-security clause "so long as they are periodic and uniformly required and not devoted to a purpose which would make their mandatory extraction otherwise inimical to public policy."[149]

Applying *Detroit Mailers* to market-recovery dues, the Board found that the union could collect market-recovery dues from employees on non–Davis-Bacon projects. However, the Board also found that the union could not enforce a union-security clause to recover market-recovery dues on Davis-Bacon projects. Relying on the Davis-Bacon Act and Wage Appeals Board decisions, the Board found that the extraction of market-recovery dues pursuant to a union-security clause was inimical to public policy under the Davis-Bacon Act, which limits the instances in which employees' wages can be returned to contractors and prohibits the deduction of employees' wages that benefits employers.[150]

The Board also found that under Section 8(b)(2), as well as Section 8(a)(3), a union may require employees to pay initiation fees pursuant to the union-security clause in their collective bargaining agreement.[151] Unions may also notify employees that they are required to pay initiation fees under the union-security clause.[152]

---

[147]167 NLRB 1042, 66 LRRM 1203 (1967).

[148]192 NLRB 951, 78 LRRM 1053 (1971).

[149]*Id.* at 952.

[150]*Id. See also* Can-Am Plumbing, Inc. v. NLRB, 321 F.3d 145, 171 LRRM 3225 (D.C. Cir. 2003) (granting review and denying enforcement of Board order finding job-targeting program was protected activity even though program was supported in part by dues unlawfully withheld on Davis-Bacon projects).

[151]Paperworkers (Sun Chem. Corp. of Mich.), 327 NLRB 1011, 161 LRRM 1028 (1999).

[152]*Id.* The Board noted that any such notice must be consistent with the requirements of *California Saw & Knife Works,* 320 NLRB 224, 151 LRRM 1121 (1995), *enforced sub nom.* Machinists v. NLRB, 133 F.3d 1012, 157 LRRM 2287 (7th Cir.), *cert. denied,* 525 U.S. 813, 160 LRRM 2064 (1998).

4. *Union Must Supply Information to Employees*

The Board continues to hold that a union violates Section 8(b)(2) by seeking the discharge of an employee under a union-security clause without providing notice of the employee's rights under *Beck* and *General Motors*, the amount owed, how that amount was calculated, and a reasonable time to pay the amount owed.[153] In connection with this obligation, the Board has found that a union is entitled to wage information from an employer so that the union can calculate the dues owed by employees.[154] The Board further stated that the union does not need to claim that any employee is in arrears or that it is seeking to discharge employees when making the request for wage information.[155]

In *Auto Workers Local 95 (Various Employers)*,[156] the Board dismissed a complaint alleging that the international union violated Section 8(b)(2) by seeking the discharge of a nonmember after he failed to comply with the union's demand for payment of dues. There was no allegation that the employee ever exercised his right under *Beck* to object to the payment of dues for nonrepresentational activities. The international union had distributed a *Beck* notice to the nonmember; however, the international union had provided a report on the breakdown of its expenditures only to *Beck* objectors. On these facts, the Board found the international union satisfied its duty to provide the *Beck* notice. The Board also found that the nonmember failed to comply with the union's request for the payment of dues and that the union's subsequent attempts to have the nonmember discharged did not violate Section 8(b)(2).

---

[153]L.D. Kirchler Co., 335 NLRB 1427, 168 LRRM 1376 (2001); Teamsters Local 251 (Ryder Student Transp.), 333 NLRB 1009, 168 LRRM 1007 (2001); Yellow Freight Sys. of Ind., 327 NLRB 996, 167 LRRM 1282 (1999); Incisa USA, Inc., 327 NLRB 563, 167 LRRM 1228 (1999). *But see* Electrical Workers (ACCL Enters.), 341 NLRB No. 8, 174 LRRM 1071 (2004) (finding no violation for failing to provide information regarding dues arrearage before refusing to refer employee to job where dues arrearage was small and employee was 30-year member of union and former business manager).

[154]Farmer Bros. Co., 342 NLRB No. 55, 175 LRRM 1232 (2004).

[155]*Id.*

[156]328 NLRB 1215, 164 LRRM 1177 (1999), *enforced in part, remanded in part sub nom.* Thomas v. NLRB, 213 F.3d 651, 164 LRRM 2577 (D.C. Cir. 2000). This case also involved the validity of the "local preemption" for determining "chargeable and nonchargeable expenses." The Board held that it was permissible for an international union to apply the same ratio of its expenses to the fees and dues expended by its local union.

On appeal, however, the D.C. Circuit held that its previous decision in *Penrod v. NLRB*[157] was controlling. In *Penrod*, the court held that potential objectors were entitled to be informed of the amounts that their fees would be reduced if they became *Beck* objectors.[158] Because the international union had not provided information about the breakdown to the nonmember, the D.C. Circuit remanded the case to the Board to determine the remedy.[159]

On remand, the Board accepted as law the D.C. Circuit's decision that the union violated Section 8(b)(1)(A) by not providing the nonmember with a *Beck* notice that contained the amount of the reduction.[160] The Board concluded that the nonmember was provisionally entitled to a make-whole remedy. However, the Board allowed the union to prove at the compliance stage that the nonmember was a "free rider," that is, that he "willfully and deliberately sought to evade his union-security obligations."[161] The Board stated that it would not strictly construe the *Beck* and *General Motors* notice requirements so rigidly "as to permit a recalcitrant employee to profit from his own dereliction in complying with his obligations as a union member."[162] If the union makes this showing, the nonmember would not be entitled to any backpay.

Thereafter in the compliance proceeding, the Board found that the union failed to satisfy the burden of proving that the employee was a "free rider."[163] The Board based its decision upon a record that included evidence of the employer and the union refusing the employee's request for assistance on becoming a *Beck* objector. While the employee could have done more, including responding to the union's letters, the Board adopted the administrative law judge's conclusion that the employee did not willfully and deliberately attempt to evade the union-security option.

---

[157]203 F.3d 41, 163 LRRM 2513 (D.C. Cir. 2000).

[158]*Id.*

[159]*Thomas v. NLRB, supra* note 156.

[160]Auto Workers Local 95 (Various Employers), 337 NLRB 237 (2001).

[161]*Id.* at 240.

[162]*Id.* at 240, quoting Teamsters Local 630 (Ralph's Grocery), 209 NLRB 117, 124, 85 LRRM 1604 (1974). *See also* Food & Commercial Workers Local 368A (Professional Servs.), 317 NLRB 352, 149 LRRM 1344 (1995).

[163]Auto Workers (Colt's Mfg. Co.), 342 NLRB No. 6, 175 LRRM 1056 (2004).

5. *Obligations of Employers*

The Board found in *Polymark Corp.*[164] that an employer does not violate Section 8(a)(3) by collecting an amount equal to the full union dues after the objector perfects a *Beck* objection but before the union informs the employer of the reduced dues owed for chargeable expenses. The Board found the circumstances in *Polymark Corp.* were governed by its decision in *Auto Workers Local 1752 (Schweizer Aircraft Corp.)*.[165] In the latter case, the Board held that an employee's "resignation of membership . . . under a lawful security clause does not privilege the employee to make an untimely revocation of his checkoff authorization, and therefore a union's efforts aimed at continued enforcement of that checkoff after the employee's resignation do not violate the Act."[166] An employee's resignation does not completely void his or her dues obligation. Likewise, an employee's resignation does not revoke his or her checkoff authorization. Employees are required to continue to pay dues until they perfect their *Beck* objection. After that, the union may lawfully seek to enforce the checkoff provision for an amount equal to the employee's share of representational expenses.[167]

An employer may violate Section 8(a)(5) by ceasing to deduct and remit dues from an employee who remained obligated to make dues payments even after resigning from union membership. In *Hearst Corp. Capital Newspaper Division*,[168] the Board found an employer violated the Act by ceasing to deduct dues from an employee's pay after the employee resigned from union membership but specifically stated that she wished to continue having her dues deducted from her pay.

---

[164]329 NLRB 9, 162 LRRM 1033 (1999), *enforced in part, denied in part, sub nom.* Mohat v. NLRB, 1 Fed. Appx. 258, 166 LRRM 2256 (6th Cir. 2001) (enforcing Board's findings of facial validity of union-security clause and finding that employee's claim of inadequate *Beck* notice was nonreviewable, but holding that employer violated Act when it refused to honor employee's revocation of dues checkoff and remanding to Board for further proceedings).

[165]320 NLRB 528, 115 LRRM 1286 (1995), *enforced sub nom.* Williams v. NLRB, 105 F.3d 787, 153 LRRM 2986 (2d Cir. 1996).

[166]*Id.* 320 NLRB at 531.

[167]*Polymark Corp.*, *supra* note 164.

[168]343 NLRB No. 79 (2004).

D. Violations Relating to Hiring and Referral Halls

The Board continues to hold that a union violates Sections 8(b)(1)(A) and 8(b)(2) by refusing to refer individuals from an exclusive hiring hall because they are not union members,[169] are travelers from sister locals,[170] have criticized union leadership,[171] filed internal union charges,[172] or have used other sources of employment.[173]

Recent Board and court decisions have also intensified the debate on the nature of a union's duty of fair representation in an exclusive hiring hall context. While the Board has long held that any departure from established hiring hall procedures violates the duty of fair representation and Sections 8(b)(1)(A) and (2) unless the union can show that the departure was taken pursuant to a valid union-security clause or necessary to the union's effective performance of its representative function,[174] case law developments suggest additional room for departures due to inadvertent mistake or accident.

In *Plumbers Local 342* (*Contra Costa I*),[175] for example, the Board found that the union's negligent failure to refer the charging party for a job through its exclusive hiring hall did not violate its representational duties or Sections 8(b)(1)(A) and (2) of the Act. In so finding, the Board relied on the Supreme Court's decisions in *Steelworkers v. Rawson*[176] and *Air Line Pilots Ass'n v. O'Neill.*[177] In *Rawson,* the

---

[169] *In re* Electrical Workers Local 3 (White Plains), 331 NLRB 1498 (2000).

[170] Electrical Workers Local 357 (Newtron Heat Trace, Inc.), 343 NLRB No. 136 (2004) (union placed travelers from sister local on separate referral list and threatened and forced the travelers to surrender their referrals to the home local's own members).

[171] Teamsters Local 657 (Texia Prods.), 342 NLRB No. 59 (2004) (union failed to refer member for criticizing union officers' failure to enforce exclusive hiring hall agreement); Independent Dock Workers Local 1 (Trans Ocean Maritime Servs.), 330 NLRB 1348 (2000) (union refused to refer complainant for future jobs because of his complaints about the operation of the union's hiring hall).

[172] Freeman Decorating Co., 335 NLRB 103 (2001); Brede, Inc., 335 NLRB 71 (2001); Bo-Ty, Plus, Inc., 333 NLRB No. 54 (2001).

[173] Theatrical Stage Employees Local 39 (Nth Degree, Inc.), 337 NLRB No. 57 (2002). *Cf.* Teamsters Local 391 (U.S. Pipeline, Inc.), 339 NLRB 346 (2003) (citing TK Prods., 332 NLRB 110, 123–124 (2000), for permissible discrimination where hiring-hall arrangement between employer and union is nonexclusive).

[174] Plumbers Local 342 (Contra Costa Elec.), 336 NLRB 549, 550, *enforced sub nom.* Jacoby v. NLRB, 325 F.3d 301 (D.C. Cir. 2003).

[175] *Id.*

[176] 495 U.S. 362, 134 LRRM 2153 (1990).

[177] 499 U.S. 65, 136 LRRM 2721 (1991).

Court applied the "arbitrary, discriminatory, or in bad faith" standard set forth in *Vaca v. Sipes* to hold that a union's mere negligence does not violate its duty of fair representation.[178] The Court in *O'Neill* held that the same "arbitrary, discriminatory, or in bad-faith" standard applies to *all* union activity, including hiring hall operations.[179]

On appeal, however, the D.C. Circuit held that the Board misinterpreted Supreme Court case law and rejected the Board's uniform duty-of-fair-representation standard for all union activity. Citing the Supreme Court's decision in *Breininger v. Sheet Metal Workers Local 96*, the court of appeals found that the union's employer-like function and corresponding potential for abuse in the hiring hall context *increased*, not decreased, the union's responsibility. The court of appeals accordingly held that unions owe a "heightened duty of fair dealing in the context of a hiring hall" and remanded the case.[180]

On remand, while accepting the "heightened duty" standard for purposes of the decision, the Board in *Contra Costa II* nonetheless held that inadvertent mistakes in the operation of an exclusive hiring hall, arising from "mere negligence," do not violate the union's duty of fair representation or Sections 8(b)(1)(A) and (2).[181] The Board reasoned that while volitional departures from established hiring hall procedures necessarily demonstrate the union's power over the workers' livelihoods and thereby impermissibly coerce and restrain workers' Section 7 rights, the same may not be said of inadvertent mistakes by the union which do not signal the same message.[182] The Board cautioned, however, that, while mere negligence may not violate a union's representational duties, gross negligence demonstrating deliberate or reckless indifference clearly would.[183]

---

[178]495 U.S. at 372, citing Vaca v. Sipes, 386 U.S. at 190.

[179]499 U.S. at 67.

[180]Jacoby v. NLRB, 233 F.3d 611, 617, 165 LRRM 2993 (D.C. Cir. 2000) (emphasis added).

[181]Plumbers Local 342 (Contra Costa II), 336 NLRB 549, 168 LRRM 1256 (2001), *aff'd in* Jacoby v. NLRB (Jacoby II), 325 F.3d 301 (D.C. Cir. 2003).

[182]*Contra Costa II*, 336 NLRB at 550.

[183]*Id.* at 552 n.9. *See also Jacoby II*, 325 F.3d at 309 (affirming on second petition for review that "one act of simple negligence does not come close to violating the 'heightened duty' standard"); Electrical Workers Local 48 (Oregon-Columbia Chapter of Nat'l Elec. Contractors Ass'n), 342 NLRB No. 10 (2004) (noting that apart from the number of mistakes, the kind of mistakes committed and the ease with which they might have been avoided must also be considered in assessing negligence in hiring hall operations).

This "heightened duty" standard has since been adopted by the Ninth Circuit as well. Citing the D.C. Circuit *Jacoby* cases, in *Lucas v. NLRB*,[184] the Ninth Circuit reasoned that the union's added role as an employer in the exclusive hiring hall context should be distinguished from the contract negotiation context that was the focus in *O'Neill*. The Ninth Circuit accordingly remanded the Board's decision in *Theatrical Stage Employees Local 720 (AVW Audio Visual)*,[185] finding that the Board had failed to apply the heightened duty standard to the union's refusal to allow an individual to use its exclusive hiring hall because of a history of alleged misconduct toward employers, other employees, and clients. The court also reversed the Board's finding that the refusal was necessary to protect the union's effective representation of its constituency.[186]

Despite these court reversals, in *Teamsters Local 631 (Vosburg Equipment, Inc.)*,[187] a subsequent case involving alleged changes to the union's hiring hall rules, the Board specifically declined to rule on what standard of duty should be applied by the Board in the case. Instead, the Board underscored that unions are accorded "a wide range of discretion in serving the employees whom they represent," cautioned that it had only applied the "heightened duty" standard in *Contra Costa II* as required on remand, and noted that, at any rate, the result in the instant case under either standard would have been the same.[188]

IV. DISCRIMINATION BECAUSE OF INVOLVEMENT WITH NLRB PROCEDURES: SECTION 8(a)(4)

The Board continues to give a broad interpretation to the conduct protected by Section 8(a)(4). In *Belle Knitting Mills, Inc.*,[189] the

---

[184]333 F.3d 927 (9th Cir. 2003).

[185]332 NLRB 1, 165 LRRM 1163 (2000) (finding that union's actions were within acceptable range of reasonableness and not arbitrary, even though it did not act pursuant to explicit written policy).

[186]*See* Theatrical Stage Employees (AVW Audio Visuals II), 341 NLRB No. 147 (2004) (ordering remedy on remand pursuant to the Ninth Circuit's reversal).

[187]340 NLRB No. 96, 173 LRRM 1477 (2003).

[188]*Id.* at n.4 and its accompanying text. *See also* Electrical Workers Local 48 (Oregon-Columbia Ch. of Nat'l Elec. Contractors Ass'n), 342 NLRB No. 10 (2004) (refusing to apply or decide whether the heightened duty standard applies to charging parties' duty of fair representation claim but finding result would have been the same in either case).

[189]331 NLRB 80, 171 LRRM 1294 (2000).

Board found that retaliatory action against an employee who appeared at an NLRB representation hearing with union representatives, but who was not called to testify, violated Section 8(a)(4). The employer in *RGC (USA) Mineral Sands, Inc.*[190] violated Section 8(a)(4) by issuing retaliatory warnings to two employees who had been named as discriminatees in an unfair labor practice charge filed by a coworker, and who the employer believed were assisting the charge.[191] In *Ready Mix, Inc.*,[192] however, the suspension of an employee who had testified at a representation hearing was held not to violate Section 8(a)(4) where the record was unclear as to which side the employee's testimony favored and there was no other showing of unlawful animus.

The Board recently reaffirmed that because Section 8(a)(4) is to be construed liberally, "it protects even false testimony [in a Board proceeding] so long as such testimony was not willingly and knowingly false and uttered with intent to deceive."[193] The employer has the burden of proving that the employee's testimony in the Board proceeding was false, was uttered with intent to deceive, and was related to a substantial issue.[194] The employer's honest but mistaken belief that the employee lied at a Board hearing is not a defense to a Section 8(a)(4) charge.[195]

In *Alamo Rent-a-Car*,[196] the employer questioned an employee about whether he had any knowledge about the allegations in an NLRB complaint; the employee claimed that he knew nothing and signed a declaration to that effect. Subsequently, the employee testified in detail for the general counsel at the unfair labor practice hearing. He was discharged on the ground that he had lied to the employer. The Board found that the employee was discharged for

---

[190]332 NLRB 1633, 168 LRRM 1094 (2001), *enforced*, 281 F.3d 442, 169 LRRM 2633 (4th Cir. 2002).

[191]*Id.* at 1638–39, citing National Surface Cleaning, Inc. v. NLRB, 54 F.3d 35, 149 LRRM 2407 (1st Cir. 1995).

[192]337 NLRB 1189, 170 LRRM 1401 (2002).

[193]Superior Protection, Inc., 339 NLRB 954, 174 LRRM 1222 (2003) (quoting Glover Bottled Gas Co., 275 NLRB 658, 673, 119 LRRM 1177 (1985)), *enforced*, 801 F.2d 391 (2d Cir. 1986), *cert. denied*, 479 U.S. 1085 (1987)), *enforced*, 105 Fed. Appx. 561, 175 LRRM 2512 (5th Cir. 2004).

[194]*Id.*

[195]Cardinal Home Prods., Inc., 338 NLRB 1004, 174 LRRM 1290 (2003).

[196]336 NLRB 1155, 169 LRRM 1026 (2001), *supplemented*, 338 NLRB No. 14, 172 LRRM 1288 (2002).

his testimony, not for lying, and that his discharge violated Section 8(a)(4).

The employer in *Belle of Sioux City, L.P.*[197] discharged, for reasons the Board found to be pretextual, a union activist who was already named as a discriminatee in a pending unfair labor practice charge. The employer also suspended a second employee for the same pretextual reasons. The Board found that the second employee was suspended to create the appearance of evenhandedness in order to shore up the discharge of the discriminatee. The suspension of the second employee thus "was an integral part of the unfair labor practice directed at" the discriminatee, and violated Section 8(a)(4).[198]

Conduct designed to buy an employee's silence will also violate Section 8(a)(4). The Board held in *McKesson Drug Co.*[199] that it was a violation of Section 8(a)(4) to discharge an employee for refusing to sign a "last chance agreement" that contained a release of claims and an agreement not to file unfair labor practice charges against the employer. The Board found in *Metro Networks, Inc.*[200] that the employer violated Section 8(a)(4) when it offered a discharged union activist severance pay, to which he was not otherwise entitled, on the condition that he sign an agreement not to "assist or otherwise participate, except as may be required by law, in any . . . investigation or other proceeding"[201] and not to disclose any information about his employment. No NLRB proceedings were pending when the employer offered the severance agreement, but the discharged employee had openly participated in an ongoing organizing campaign. However, in *EPI Construction*,[202] the Board reversed the ALJ and found that establishing a grievance and arbitration procedure during an organizing campaign did not violate Section 8(a)(4). The Board rejected the ALJ's conclusion that the new grievance procedure had a chilling effect on the employees' right to invoke Board processes, because the procedure was not mandatory and its existence had been announced only to the union, not to employees.

---

[197]333 NLRB 98, 171 LRRM 1432 (2001).

[198]*Id.* By contrast, the activist's discharge was found not to have been motivated by the pending NLRB charge and thus not a §8(a)(4) violation, although it violated §8(a)(3) because it was in retaliation for her union activity.

[199]337 NLRB 935, 171 LRRM 1148 (2002).

[200]336 NLRB 63, 169 LRRM 1191 (2001).

[201]*Id.* at 64.

[202]336 NLRB 234, 170 LRRM 1015 (2001).

General antiunion bias is insufficient to prove a causal connection between an employee's participation in NLRB proceedings and the employer's adverse action. In *NLRB v. Lampi, LLC*,[203] the Eleventh Circuit concluded that there was insufficient evidence linking an employee's termination to her testimony in a Board hearing; the court rejected the Board's reliance on the statement by the employer's president to a television reporter that he did not like unions. In *United Parcel Service*,[204] where the only evidence of hostility based on participation in Board proceedings was that a manager asked the alleged discriminatee, "why are you filing these bull shit charges against us,"[205] the evidence of animus was too ambiguous to establish a Section 8(a)(4) violation, although the Board found that the employee's discharge violated Section 8(a)(3).

The Board reaffirmed its use of the *Wright Line*[206] analysis in Section 8(a)(4) cases in *American Gardens Management Co.*[207] and remanded the Section 8(a)(4) allegations for further consideration because the ALJ concluded that the employees' discharges were not discriminatory without citing *Wright Line* or following its burden-shifting analysis.

An employer's commission of other unfair labor practices may be relied on to establish the motivational link in the *Wright Line* prima facie case.[208] In *St. Mary's Nursing Home*,[209] the Board remanded with instructions to reopen the record because the ALJ improperly excluded evidence relating to a previously settled unfair labor practice charge that tended to show the employer's antiunion animus.

It is sufficient to establish a Section 8(a)(4) violation if a supervisor whose recommendation contributed to the adverse employment decision had an unlawful motivation.[210]

---

[203] 240 F.3d 931, 166 LRRM 2321 (11th Cir. 2001), *denying enforcement to* 327 NLRB 222, 160 LRRM 1234 (1998).

[204] 340 NLRB No. 89, 173 LRRM 1337 (2003).

[205] *Id.*, slip op at 9.

[206] Wright Line, Wright Line Div., 251 NLRB 1083, 105 LRRM 1169 (1980), *enforced*, 662 F.2d 899, 108 LRRM 2513 (1st Cir. 1981), *cert. denied*, 455 U.S. 989, 109 LRRM 2779 (1982). *See generally* Main Edition, Chapter 7, "Discrimination in Employment" at Section II.B.1. [Employer Discrimination; Purpose of the Discrimination; Conduct Requiring Proof of Union Animus: The *Wright Line* Rule].

[207] 338 NLRB 644, 171 LRRM 1265 (2002).

[208] *See* NLRB v. Regional Home Care Servs., Inc. dba North Atl. Med. Servs., 329 NLRB 85, 166 LRRM 1112 (1999), *enforced*, 237 F.3d 62, 166 LRRM 2326 (1st Cir. 2001).

[209] 342 NLRB No. 100, 175 LRRM 1361 (2004).

[210] Dattco, Inc., 338 NLRB 1, 170 LRRM 1497 (2002); Eby-Brown Co. L.P., 328 NLRB 496, 527 n.86, 168 LRRM 1165 (1999).

Proximity in time between the employee's protected conduct and the adverse employment action is evidence of discriminatory motive[211] and may even be sufficient in itself to establish unlawful motivation.[212]

Factors supporting a finding of unlawful motivation under the *Wright Line* analysis in Section 8(a)(4) cases have included an employer's reliance on outdated misconduct as a reason for discipline,[213] reinvestigating past misconduct that was previously resolved,[214] reprimanding the employee for a practice that had gone on for years without objection,[215] involvement of counsel or top-level management in directing the discipline or discharge,[216] attempting to obtain a release of claims or an agreement not to file unfair labor practice charges,[217] failure to investigate the employee's alleged misconduct or allow the employee an opportunity to respond to the allegations,[218] and public humiliation of the employee.[219] The employer's use of false or pretextual reasons to justify an adverse employment action may also give rise to an inference that discriminatory animus was the true reason for the action.[220]

Evidence of disparate treatment may undermine an employer's claim that the adverse employment action would have occurred without regard to the employee's protected activity.[221] The discharge of

---

[211]Superior Prot., Inc., 339 NLRB 954, 174 LRRM 1222 (2003), *enforced*, 105 Fed. Appx. 561, 175 LRRM 2512 (5th Cir. 2004).

[212]Grand Cent. P'ship, 327 NLRB 966, 167 LRRM 1230 (1999) (citing cases); DynCorp, 343 NLRB No. 124 (2004).

[213]Pacific Micronesia Corp. dba Dai-Ichi Hotel Saipan Beach, 337 NLRB 469, 169 LRRM 1473 (2002) (discharge purportedly based on instance of insubordination two and a half years earlier).

[214]Ishikawa Gasket Am., Inc., 337 NLRB 175, 169 LRRM 1241 (2001), *enforced*, 354 F.3d 534, 173 LRRM 2993 (6th Cir. 2004).

[215]Cardinal Home Prods., 338 NLRB 1004, 174 LRRM 1290 (2003).

[216]Robert Orr/Sysco Food Servs., 343 NLRB No. 123, 176 LRRM 1217 (2004); Superior Prot., Inc., 339 NLRB 954, 174 LRRM 1222 (2003), *enforced*, 105 Fed. Appx. 561, 175 LRRM 2512 (5th Cir. 2004); *Ishikawa Gasket, supra* note 214.

[217]McKesson Drug Co., 337 NLRB 935, 171 LRRM 1148 (2002).

[218]*Robert Orr/Sysco, supra* note 216 (citing cases); Grand Cent. P'ship, 327 NLRB 966, 167 LRRM 1230 (1999).

[219]*Superior Protection, supra* note 211. Furthermore, the employer may not use public humiliation to provoke the employee into an inappropriate response and then use that response to justify the adverse employment action. *Id.*

[220]Waterfront Servs. Co., 340 NLRB No. 154, 174 LRRM 1349 (2003); Pacific Micronesia Corp. dba Dai-Ichi Hotel Saipan Beach, 337 NLRB 469, 169 LRRM 1473 (2002).

[221]*Robert Orr/Sysco Food Servs., supra* note 216 (citing cases).

an employee two days after he testified in a Board proceeding was found to violate Section 8(a)(4) notwithstanding the fact that the employee had threatened to stab a co-worker; the ALJ observed that verbal threats were common at the employer's facility and no other employee had ever been terminated for such a threat.[222] It was an abuse of discretion for the ALJ to revoke the general counsel's subpoena duces tecum for documents concerning the employer's enforcement of its attendance policy against other employees where the employer claimed that the alleged discriminatee was terminated for absenteeism.[223] However, the fact that other employees who had not engaged in protected activity were disciplined along with an alleged discriminatee does not necessarily insulate an employer from a finding of retaliatory motive.[224]

Employers have succeeded in rebutting the general counsel's prima facie proof of unlawful motivation by establishing that the alleged discriminatee would have been disciplined for poor performance[225] or disobeying a direct order[226] without regard to his or her protected activity, or that the alleged discriminatee had already been placed on the employer's "not eligible for rehire" list for other reasons before he filed an unfair labor practice charge.[227] Employers were found to have rebutted the general counsel's prima facie case where an employee's layoff was motivated by lack of work[228] or the employee was selected for layoff on the basis of seniority.[229] Conversely, where there was evidence that the employer normally relied on seniority for promotions, the employer's departure from seniority contributed to the Board finding a violation of Section 8(a)(4).[230]

---

[222]*Grand Cent. P'ship, supra* note 218.

[223]PPG Indus., Inc., 339 NLRB 821, 172 LRRM 1451 (2003).

[224]McKesson Drug Co., 337 NLRB 935, 171 LRRM 1148 (2002) (suspension on pretext of unfounded drug use allegations violated §8(a)(4) even though a few other employees who had not filed unfair labor practice charges were similarly disciplined); *see also* Belle of Sioux City, L.P., 333 NLRB 98, 171 LRRM 1432 (2001).

[225]Lamar Advertising of Hartford, 343 NLRB No. 40, 176 LRRM 1156 (2004).

[226]DynCorp, 343 NLRB No. 124 (2004); Las Vegas Limousine, 340 NLRB No. 120, 175 LRRM 1030 (2003).

[227]Sasco Valley Elec., 329 NLRB 60, 169 LRRM 1160 (1999).

[228]American Gardens Mgmt. Co., 343 NLRB No. 104, 176 LRRM 1274 (2004).

[229]Food & Commercial Workers Local 204, 338 NLRB 38, 171 LRRM 1566 (2002).

[230]Audubon Reg'l Med. Ctr., 331 NLRB 374, 169 LRRM 1213 (2000).

In *Dole Fresh Vegetables,*[231] the Board applied a *Great Dane Trailers*[232] analysis, rather than *Wright Line,*[233] where the employer reduced the wage rates of employees who had recently testified at a representation hearing. The ALJ followed *Wright Line* and found that the general counsel had proven the wage cuts were unlawfully motivated by the employees' testimony. The Board affirmed the finding of a Section 8(a)(4) violation, but held that under *Great Dane Trailers* proof of unlawful motive was not required because the employer's conduct had an adverse effect on employees' right to participate in Board proceedings and the employer's stated reason for the wage reduction—to provoke an unfair labor practice charge in which it could test its claim that the affected employees were statutory supervisors—failed to establish a substantial business justification.[234]

The Board continues to apply Section 8(a)(4) to retaliatory acts short of discharge, such as a threat of discipline,[235] a disciplinary warning,[236] a reduction in work hours and overtime,[237] a refusal to recall from layoff,[238] and a refusal to allow an employee to return

---

[231]339 NLRB 785, 173 LRRM 1004 (2003).

[232]NLRB v. Great Dane Trailers, Inc., 388 U.S. 26, 65 LRRM 2465 (1967).

[233]Wright Line, Wright Line Div., 251 NLRB 1083, 105 LRRM 1169 (1980), *enforced,* 662 F.2d 899, 108 LRRM 2513 (1st Cir. 1981), *cert. denied,* 455 U.S. 989, 109 LRRM 2779 (1982).

[234]*Dole Fresh Vegetables, supra* note 231. Under *Great Dane Trailers,* discriminatory conduct that is "inherently destructive" of employee rights violates the Act regardless of motive, while if the conduct has a "comparatively slight" effect on employee rights, the employer may shift the burden of proving motive onto the general counsel by showing a substantial business justification for its conduct. *Great Dane Trailers, supra* note 232. *See* Main Edition, Chapter 7, at Section II.B.7. [Employer Discrimination; Purpose of the Discrimination; Conduct Inherently Destructive of Section 7 Rights.]. The Board applied the latter analysis in *Dole Fresh Vegetables, supra.* The Board also stated that, in the alternative, a §8(a)(4) violation was established because the affected employees had testified in the representation case that they were not supervisors, and the wage cuts were motivated by the employer's desire to prove that they were. *Id.* at n.12.

[235]Cardinal Home Prods., Inc., 338 NLRB 1004, 174 LRRM 1290 (2003).

[236]Avante at Boca Raton, 332 NLRB 1648, 171 LRRM 1214 (2001); RGC (USA) Mineral Sands, Inc., 332 NLRB 1633, 168 LRRM 1094 (2001), *enforced,* 281 F.3d 442, 169 LRRM 2633 (4th Cir. 2002).

[237]U.S.A. Polymer Corp., 328 NLRB 1242, 168 LRRM 1427 (1999), *enforced,* 272 F.3d 289, 168 LRRM 2897 (5th Cir. 2001), *cert. denied,* 122 S. Ct. 2620, 170 LRRM 2288 (2002).

[238]*Cardinal Home Prods., supra* note 235; Belle Knitting Mills, Inc., 331 NLRB 80, 171 LRRM 1294 (2000); Climatrol, Inc., 329 NLRB 946, 169 LRRM 1385 (1999).

from medical leave when released by his doctor.[239] In *Eby-Brown Co., L.P.*,[240] lowering an employee's score on an evaluation, withholding a bonus, denying disability pay, and reneging on a promise to give an employee light duty consistent with his doctor's restrictions were all found to violate Section 8(a)(4) when done in retaliation for the employee's support of unfair labor practice charges. Transferring a witness from light duty to a job she was physically unable to perform was found to be a termination in violation of Section 8(a)(4) in *Cogburn Healthcare Center, Inc.*[241] Post-termination conduct may also violate Section 8(a)(4), as in *Grand Central Partnership*,[242] where the employer reneged on a promise not to contest an employee's application for unemployment benefits because he filed an unfair labor practice charge.

Where a lesser retaliatory act in violation of Section 8(a)(4), such as a warning, is subsequently relied on in discharging the employee under a progressive disciplinary system, the discharge also violates Section 8(a)(4) even though the discharge itself was not directly motivated by the employee's participation in a Board proceeding.[243]

Refusal to hire, where the manager who recommended the refusal was motivated by the applicant's involvement in a prior unfair labor practice charge, violated Section 8(a)(4).[244] However, it was not a Section 8(a)(4) violation to inform union salts who were the subject of a refusal-to-hire charge, and who returned to apply again for employment, that the employer was not hiring because charges were pending, at least where the employer was not in fact hiring at the time.[245]

Harassment and humiliating treatment may also violate Section 8(a)(4). In *Krist Oil Co.*,[246] after an experienced employee who was discharged filed an unfair labor practice charge, the employer violated Section 8(a)(4) by reinstating her into a trainee position and

[239]Tres Estrellas de Oro, 338 NLRB 503 (2002) (summary judgment).

[240]328 NLRB 496, 168 LRRM 1165 (1999).

[241]335 NLRB 1397, 171 LRRM 1021 (2001).

[242]327 NLRB 966, 167 LRRM 1230 (1999).

[243]Avante at Boca Raton, 332 NLRB 1648, 171 LRRM 1214 (2001).

[244]Dattco, Inc., 338 NLRB 1, 170 LRRM 1497 (2002); *see also* Harvest Select Farms, LLC, 340 NLRB No. 100, 173 LRRM 1357 (2003).

[245]Mid-State, Inc., 331 NLRB 1372, 171 LRRM 1525 (2000).

[246]328 NLRB 825, 167 LRRM 1230 (1999).

arranging her schedule in such a way that a manager could constantly "keep an eye on her." In *U.S.A. Polymer Corp.*,[247] it was found to be a Section 8(a)(4) violation for a supervisor to increase a witness's production requirements, refuse to give him a helper, and tell him that the supervisor had been instructed to try to provoke him to quit because of his testimony. The Sixth Circuit affirmed a finding by the Board that an employer violated Section 8(a)(4) by falsely accusing a witness of theft, demanding that she provide documentation for days off where the employer's own written policy did not require it, requiring her to teach with her door open, demoting her to teaching assistant, and causing her constructive discharge.[248]

Telling an employee who was subpoenaed to attend a Board hearing that his absence would be unexcused was a Section 8(a)(4) violation, even though the employer ultimately marked the absence excused, where the employee was never notified of the correction.[249] In *U.S.A. Polymer Corp.*,[250] it was a violation for a supervisor to question employees about what had been said at a hearing where they testified, to ask other employees whether they had been subpoenaed, and to tell them to ignore the subpoenas.[251] The Board found in *Parts Depot, Inc.*[252] that an employer violated Section 8(a)(4) by telling a subpoenaed employee that he could not attend the hearing and by impliedly threatening him with discharge.

Changes in terms and conditions of employment for an entire bargaining unit have been found to violate Section 8(a)(4). Where an employer discontinued a past practice of permitting employees to take unpaid leave for union business and stated that one of its reasons for canceling the leave policy was that the union president had spent his leave time preparing "frivolous complaints with the

---

[247]328 NLRB 1242, 168 LRRM 1427 (1999), *enforced,* 272 F.3d 289, 168 LRRM 2897 (5th Cir. 2001), *cert. denied,* 122 S. Ct. 2620, 170 LRRM 2288 (2002); *see also* Parts Depot, Inc., 332 NLRB 733, 170 LRRM 1014 (2000) (employer imposed onerous workload on witness and placed his work under close scrutiny).

[248]FiveCAP, Inc. v. NLRB, 294 F.3d 768, 170 LRRM 2401 (6th Cir. 2002), *enforcing in relevant part* 332 NLRB 943, 170 LRRM 1190 (2000).

[249]Mid-Mountain Foods, Inc., 332 NLRB 251, 168 LRRM 1482 (2000), *enforced,* 11 Fed. Appx. 372, 169 LRRM 2448 (4th Cir. 2001).

[250]328 NLRB 1242, 168 LRRM 1427 (1999), *enforced,* 272 F.3d 289, 168 LRRM 2897 (5th Cir. 2001), *cert. denied,* 122 S. Ct. 2620, 170 LRRM 2288 (2002).

[251]*Id.*; *but see* Alexis Painting Co., 342 NLRB No. 108 (2004) (declining to pass on whether interrogating employees about Board charges, and threatening to discharge them if they did not answer, violated §8(a)(4)).

[252]332 NLRB 733, 170 LRRM 1014 (2000).

NLRB," the Board found a violation of Section 8(a)(4).[253] In *Gulf Caribe Maritime, Inc.*,[254] where a union filed a petition and unfair labor practice charges challenging the employer's voluntary recognition of and entry into a collective bargaining agreement with a competing union, the employer violated Section 8(a)(4) by announcing that it was rolling back wages and benefits to their pre-recognition levels as a result of the NLRB litigation. The employer violated Section 8(a)(4) in *Wyandanch Engine Rebuilders, Inc.*,[255] by withdrawing recognition from the union and banning union representatives from its property in retaliation for bargaining unit employees' cooperation with the Board in an unfair labor practice proceeding.

In *Garage Management Corp.*,[256] the Board found that bringing an unsuccessful state court action to enjoin an employee's unfair labor practice charges violated Section 8(a)(4).

The Board confirmed in *Wright Electric, Inc.*[257] that the proper procedure under *Bill Johnson's Restaurants v. NLRB*[258] is to hold in abeyance a charge alleging a reasonably based but retaliatory lawsuit until there has been a final adjudication of the employer's state court action. A complaint was issued on a Section 8(a)(1) and (4) charge in *Wright Electric* while the employer's state court lawsuit was still pending, and the ALJ dismissed the charge on the ground that there had been no final adjudication of the state court claims. The Board reversed and remanded with instructions to the ALJ to hold the *Bill Johnson's* allegations in abeyance until the state court case was resolved.

However, when the employer's state court lawsuit is preempted by the NLRA, it will not be held in abeyance. The employer in *Webco*

---

[253]Condea Vista Co., 332 NLRB 1275, 169 LRRM 1047 (2000), *enforcement denied sub nom.* Sasol N. Am., Inc. v. NLRB, 275 F.3d 1106, 169 LRRM 2152 (D.C. Cir. 2002). The D.C. Circuit found that the Board had misunderstood the employer's prior leave policy and had erroneously failed to consider the employer's *Wright Line* defense.

[254]330 NLRB 766, 170 LRRM 1287 (2000).

[255]328 NLRB 866, 168 LRRM 1239 (1999).

[256]334 NLRB 940, 168 LRRM 1353 (2001).

[257]327 NLRB 1194, 163 LRRM 1077 (1999), *enforced,* 200 F.3d 1162, 163 LRRM 2353 (8th Cir. 2000).

[258]461 U.S. 731, 113 LRRM 2647 (1983); *see also* BE&K Constr. Co. v. NLRB, 122 S. Ct. 2390, 170 LRRM 2225 (2002); Chapter 6, "Interference with Protected Rights," *supra,* at Section II.B.3.d. [Organizational and Preelection Activity; Unlawful Employer Conduct; Other Unlawful Employer Interference; Suits and Threats of Suits Against Employees].

Industries, Inc.[259] sued two former employees in state court alleging breach of contract and unjust enrichment, on the ground that they breached their severance agreements by participating as alleged discriminatees in a pending unfair labor practice proceeding. The Board obtained a Section 10(j) injunction halting the employer's suit.[260] The Board agreed that the employer's suit had been preempted under *Garmon*[261]—and thus subject to injunction—at the time it was filed.[262] However, the underlying unfair labor practice charge with respect to one of the two alleged discriminatees was subsequently dismissed. The Board held that the dismissal of that charge rendered the employer's equitable claims against that individual no longer preempted. Accordingly, the Board concluded that the employer could resume litigating its state court claim for equitable relief against the employee whose charge was dismissed, subject to the possibility of later facing a *Bill Johnson's* charge if the state court action were ultimately unsuccessful.

The Board stated in *Webco* that if an employer's suit is preempted, no showing of antiunion motive is necessary to establish a Section 8(a)(4) violation.[263] The Board also held that the express allegations of the employer's state court complaint—that the participation of the two employees in NLRB proceedings was a breach of contract—established a retaliatory motive. The Board noted, but rejected, the D.C. Circuit's view expressed in *Petrochem Insulation, Inc. v. NLRB*[264] that such a rule would reduce the retaliatory motive step of the *Bill Johnson's* analysis to a tautology.

The Board consistently holds that Section 8(a)(4) charges are not deferrable to arbitration.[265]

---

[259]337 NLRB 361, 169 LRRM 1109 (2001).

[260]*See* Sharp v. Webco Indus., Inc., 265 F.3d 1085, 168 LRRM 2385 (10th Cir. 2001) (affirming grant of §10(j) injunction based on federal preemption of employer's suit).

[261]San Diego Bldg. Trades Council v. Garmon, 359 U.S. 236, 43 LRRM 2838 (1959).

[262]*Webco, supra* note 259.

[263]*Id.*, citing Manno Elec., 321 NLRB 278, 152 LRRM 1107 (1996), *enforced,* 127 F.3d 34, 171 LRRM 3280 (5th Cir. 1997); noting contrary indication in American Pac. Concrete Pipe Co., 292 NLRB 1261, 130 LRRM 1501 (1989).

[264]240 F.3d 26, 166 LRRM 2433 (D.C. Cir.), *cert. denied,* 534 U.S. 992 (2001).

[265]United Parcel Serv., Inc., 333 NLRB 1202, 171 LRRM 1431 (2001) (citing cases); Edward S. Quirk Co., 330 NLRB 917, 166 LRRM 1235 (2000), *enforced in part, vacated in part, and remanded on other grounds,* 241 F.3d 41, 166 LRRM 2666 (1st Cir. 2001).

Chapter 8

EMPLOYER DOMINATION OF AND ASSISTANCE TO LABOR ORGANIZATIONS

I. Introduction: Section 8(a)(2)

Section 8(a)(2) of the Act prohibits employer domination of, interference with the formation or administration of, or contribution of financial or other support to any labor organization.[1] Recent decisions have generally followed the cases in the Main Edition.

[1]The additional language of §8(a)(2) reads as follows: "Provided, That subject to the rules and regulations made and published by the Board pursuant to Section 6, an employer shall not be prohibited from permitting employees to confer with him during working hours without loss of time or pay. . . ."

An employer violates Section 8(a)(2) when it recognizes a labor organization that does not represent a majority of the employees, even if the action is taken in good faith, or when it provides assistance to a labor organization or dominates it. In determining whether a violation of Section 8(a)(2) has occurred, the Board engages in a two-pronged inquiry. First, the Board determines whether the employee group at issue is a labor organization, as defined by Section 2(5) of the Act. If the group meets the definition of a labor organization under the Act, the Board next considers whether the employer has dominated, interfered with the formation or administration of, or supported the labor organization.[2]

The Board continues to draw a line between prohibited employer *support* and permitted employer *cooperation*, a line that at times may be difficult to perceive, particularly when good faith intention is not material to a violation.[3] For example, in *NLRB v. Autodie International*,[4] a prospective purchaser of a business violated Section 8(a)(2) when it recognized a shop committee and later a successor organization, because the petition signed by a majority of the seller's employees did not necessarily represent a majority of those who would be employed by the purchaser and because the petition merely indicated that the signers preferred an in-house committee over the United Auto Workers (UAW). Likewise, in *Deferiet Paper Co.*,[5] the Board found that the employer violated Section 8(a)(2) when, despite dismissal of its unit clarification petition that sought accretion of employees represented by one labor organization, it recognized another labor organization as the exclusive bargaining representative of those employees.

II. LABOR ORGANIZATION DEFINED

Section 2(5) of the Act defines a labor organization as any organization of any kind, or any agency or employee representation com-

---

[2]Polaroid Corp., 329 NLRB 424, 162 LRRM 1129, 1129–30 (1999), citing Electromation, Inc., 309 NLRB 990, 996, 142 LRRM 1001 (1992), *enforced*, 35 F.3d 1148, 147 LRRM 2257 (7th Cir. 1994).

[3]Addicts Rehab. Ctr. Fund, Inc., 330 NLRB 733, 742, 170 LRRM 1359 (2000) (it is not necessary to establish union animus or other unlawful motive to find §8(a)(2) violation).

[4]169 F.3d 378, 160 LRRM 2681 (6th Cir. 1999), *enforcing* 321 NLRB 688, 153 LRRM 1242 (1996).

[5]330 NLRB No. 89, 166 LRRM 1040, *enforcement denied on other grounds*, 235 F.3d 581, 166 LRRM 2107 (D.C. Cir. 2000).

mittee or plan, in which employees participate and which exists for the purpose, in whole or in part, of dealing with employers concerning grievances, labor disputes, wages, rates of pay, hours of employment, or conditions of work.

Based on this statutory definition, the Board has ruled that an organization can be considered a labor organization only if "(1) employees participate; and (2) the organization exists, at least in part, for the purpose of 'dealing with' employers; and (3) these dealings concern conditions of work or concern other statutory subjects, such as grievances, labor disputes, wages, rates of pay, or hours of employment."[6] The definition of a labor organization is broad, and includes "very loose, informal, unstructured, and irregular meeting groups."[7] The cases generally focus on two statutory prerequisites: employee participation and having the purpose of dealing with employers.

A. Requirement of Participation by "Employees"

Groups composed of individuals excluded from the definition of employees under Section 2(3), such as public employees, are not labor organizations within the meaning of Section 2(5).[8]

B. Requirement of "Dealing With" Employers

Both the Board and the courts continue to interpret the "dealing with" language broadly.[9] The Board has ruled that "dealing with"

---

[6]*Polaroid, supra* note 2. *See also* Miller Indus. Towing Equip., Inc., 342 NLRB No. 112, 176 LRRM 1103 (2004); Georgia Power Co., 342 NLRB No. 18, 175 LRRM 1130 (2004).

[7]*Id. See also Addicts Rehab. Ctr., supra* note 3 (ALJ noted that "there may also be a requirement that the employees in the committee act in representational capacity"); Coinmach Laundry Corp., 337 NLRB 1286, 170 LRRM 1432 (2002) (fact that organization is ineffective, has substandard contacts, has officers with criminal records, and its funds have been stolen or misused cannot affect Board's conclusion that it is labor organization); New Silver Palace Restaurant, 334 NLRB 290, 171 LRRM 1532 (2001) (Board found "labor organization" status despite fact that no current union members were employed and allegations that union was not "democratic" and was a "criminal enterprise").

[8]Pacific N. Maritime Ass'n v. Longshoremen (ILWU) Local 63, 198 F.3d 1078, 162 LRRM 3037 (9th Cir. 1999), *cert. denied,* 530 U.S. 1213, 164 LRRM 2576 (2000); Ahmed v. Peralta Cmty. Coll. Dist., 2003 WL 1344636 (N.D. Cal. 2003).

[9]V&S ProGalv v. NLRB, 168 F.3d 270, 160 LRRM 2518 (6th Cir. 1999), *enforcing* 323 NLRB 801, 157 LRRM 1255 (1997).

involves a bilateral mechanism that ordinarily entails "a pattern or practice in which a group of employees, over time, make proposals to management, and management responds to those proposals by acceptance or rejection by word or deed."[10] The Board has reaffirmed the principle that ordinarily there is a pattern or practice of a group of employees making proposals, over time, to management, and management responding to such proposals.[11]

Isolated incidents, such as a concerted strike activity, do not constitute a "pattern or practice" sufficient to satisfy the Board's "dealing with" definition.[12] On the other hand, the Board has consistently ruled that employee committees that interact and "deal with" management are labor organizations.[13] In *Polaroid Corp.*,[14] the Board ruled that the employer-created Employee-Owners Influence Council (EOIC) was a labor organization because it functioned as a bilateral

---

[10]Polaroid Corp., 329 NLRB 424, 425, 162 LRRM 1129 (1999), citing E.I. du Pont de Nemours & Co., 311 NLRB 893, 894, 143 LRRM 1268 (1993).

[11]EFCO Corp., 327 NLRB 372, 375, 160 LRRM 1049 (1998), *enforced*, 215 F.3d 1318, 164 LRRM 2632 (4th Cir. 2000).

[12]Vencare Ancillary Serv., Inc., 334 NLRB 965, 168 LRRM 1029 (2001), *enforcement denied on other grounds*, 352 F.3d 318, 173 LRRM 2865 (2003) (isolated action of employee group that coalesced in response to announced wage cuts, presented its memo to management on this single issue, and then began work stoppage did not establish "dealing with" because it did not rise to "pattern or practice"); Music Express E., Inc. 340 NLRB No. 129, 174 LRRM 1364 (2003).

[13]*See, e.g.*, Summa Health Sys., Inc., 330 NLRB 1379, 170 LRRM 1308 (2000) (employer's "process enhancement teams" were labor organizations, dealing with employer, because they were "created, formed, funded, directed, and constituted" by employer, they were designed to represent employees, and there was "interactional exchange of proposals, a discussion, and a reaching of consensus between managerial team participants"); Permanente Med. Group, Inc., 332 NLRB 1143, 171 LRRM 1285 (2000) (employer's use of groups of design employees to refine proposals to be presented to union did not constitute "dealing with" an employee committee for purposes of §8(a)(2)); Beverly Cal. v. NLRB, 227 F.3d 817, 165 LRRM 2257 (7th Cir. 2000), *enforcing in part* 326 NLRB 153, 159 LRRM 1049, *and* 326 NLRB 232, 159 LRRM 1033 (1998), *cert. denied*, 533 U.S. 950, 167 LRRM 2640 (2001) (management-created employee council was labor organization because evidence revealed that (1) unit employees would participate in council; (2) at least part of purpose of council was to deal with employer; and (3) dealings with employer would concern grievances, labor disputes, wages, rates of pay, hours of employment, or conditions of work); Addicts Rehab. Ctr. Fund, Inc., 330 NLRB 733, 170 LRRM 1359 (2000) (employer violated Act by creating and supporting "pro-action committee" that dealt with employer with regard to employee grievances); Naomi Knitting Plant, 328 NLRB 1279, 168 LRRM 1392 (1999) (design team was labor organization under Act, because team went far beyond "brainstorming" and addressed issues of drug testing and job-bidding procedure).

[14]*Polaroid, supra* note 10.

mechanism in which employees, acting in a representational capacity, made group proposals relating to concerns such as conditions of work and employee benefits. The Board emphasized that the EOIC process went beyond mere group proposals and entailed the employer's response to such proposals.[15] In doing so, the Board cautioned that "if there are only isolated instances in which the group makes ad hoc proposals to management followed by a management response of acceptance or rejection by word or deed, the element of dealing is missing."[16]

Similarly, in *V&S ProGalv v. NLRB*,[17] the Sixth Circuit enforced the Board's determination that the employer's "in-house committee" was "dealing with" the employer. The committee was formed at the behest of the company president and presented employment issues and proposals to the company. The company president met with the committee to discuss the proposals. The Sixth Circuit said that "all that is required to satisfy the definition of 'dealing with' is that management respond to the proposal, either by acceptance *or rejection*."[18]

In *EFCO Corp.*,[19] the Board held that the employer's employee benefits and policy review committees were labor organizations. Both committees operated in representational capacities on behalf of the employees, formulating and presenting proposals, which management would either accept or reject.[20] The employer's safety committee was also held to be a labor organization because it involved employees who made proposals to management about safety policies and programs, including proposals about employee compensation.[21]

Although the Board broadly defines the "dealing with" provision, it has set forth a number of safe havens for employee involvement that do not violate Section 8(a)(2). In *Polaroid Corp.*,[22] the Board ruled that when employee proposals are made to the employer and implemented without the give-and-take of negotiations, there is no

---

[15] *Id.*

[16] *Id.*

[17] 168 F.3d 270, 160 LRRM 2518 (6th Cir. 1999), *enforcing* 323 NLRB 801, 157 LRRM 1255 (1997).

[18] *Id.* (emphasis in original).

[19] 327 NLRB 372, 160 LRRM 1049 (1998), *enforced*, 215 F.3d 1318, 164 LRRM 2632 (4th Cir. 2000).

[20] *Id.*

[21] *Id.*

[22] 329 NLRB 424, 162 LRRM 1129, 1130 (1999).

violation of the Act. Thus, "suggestion boxes" and "brainstorming" groups do not violate the Act where the purpose is merely to develop ideas that management may or may not adopt.[23]

The Board also has reiterated the rule of *General Foods Corp.*,[24] which distinguishes committees that exercise managerial authority for the employer from those that "deal with" management. In *Crown Cork & Seal Co.*,[25] the Board upheld an administrative law judge's determination that seven employee committees did not exist for the purpose of dealing with the company and, therefore, did not constitute labor organizations within the meaning of the Act. The seven committees consisted of four production teams, each having 32 production and maintenance employees and one management employee as members, and three administrative oversight committees, also comprising a mix of production and management employees. Each of the seven committees made decisions by consensus, with management members having no greater authority than other members. The four production committees were empowered to "decide and do" with respect to a wide variety of workplace issues, including disciplinary actions short of suspension and discharge.

Also in *Georgia Power Co.*,[26] the Board concluded that the employer did not violate the Act by creating its workplace ethics committee. The Board reasoned that the committee did not exist for the purpose of "dealing with" the employer. Rather, the committee actually made management-level decisions regarding ethics complaints filed by employees. In addition, the Board found the creation of an employee committee to provide input regarding the crew leader selection process was not unlawful direct dealing. The Board concluded that the employer was only seeking employee input into the process because of complaints of unfairness in selecting crew leaders and that the employer would not change the process without negotiating with the union.

---

[23]*Id.*; EFCO Corp., 327 NLRB 372, 160 LRRM 1049 (1998), *enforced*, 215 F.3d 1318, 164 LRRM 2632 (4th Cir. 2000) (employee suggestion screening committee was not labor organization because it "performed clerical or ministerial function that facilitated employer's consideration of suggestions made by the employees").

[24]231 NLRB 1232, 96 LRRM 1204 (1977).

[25]334 NLRB 699, 167 LRRM 1257 (2001).

[26]342 NLRB No. 18, 175 LRRM 1130 (2004).

III. EMPLOYER DOMINATION

Prohibited domination of a labor organization exists when the organization is controlled or directed by the employer, rather than by the employees. The Board and the courts continue to apply the *Electromation, Inc.*[27] standards for determining when a labor organization is "dominated." Recent cases confirm that the Board and courts are in agreement that domination exists where the employer plays a significant role in the creation of the labor organization and the selection of its members. For example, in *Beverly California Corp. v. NLRB*,[28] the Seventh Circuit enforced the Board ruling that the employer dominated an employee council because it was the "creature of the facility's management."[29] In *V&S ProGalv, Inc. v. NLRB*,[30] the Sixth Circuit ruled that substantial evidence supported the Board's finding of employer domination of an employee committee where there was testimony that management decided how many employees should be on the committee, how they should be chosen, and how the committee should function.

The Board continues to hold that a labor organization is unlawfully dominated where an employer exerts control over the organization, such as control of the organization's agenda and involvement in the operation of the organization.[31] In *Summa Health System*,[32] the

---

[27]309 NLRB 990, 142 LRRM 1001 (1992), *enforced*, 35 F.3d 1148, 147 LRRM 2257 (7th Cir. 1994).

[28]227 F.3d 817, 165 LRRM 2257 (7th Cir. 2000), *enforcing in part* 326 NLRB 153, 159 LRRM 1049 *and* 326 NLRB 232, 159 LRRM 1033 (1998), *cert. denied*, 533 U.S. 950, 167 LRRM 2640 (2001).

[29]*Id.* at 836.

[30]168 F.3d 270, 160 LRRM 2518, 2528 (6th Cir. 1999), *enforcing* 323 NLRB 801, 157 LRRM 1255 (1997).

[31]*See, e.g.*, Miller Indus. Towing Equip., Inc., 342 NLRB No. 112, 176 LRRM 1103 (2004) (continuous improvement committee violated §8(a)(2) where employer conceived of and established committee, chose employee representatives, and committee met on employer time, in locations provided by employer, used materials supplied by employer, and had no existence outside the will of employer); Grouse Mountain Lodge, 333 NLRB 1322, 169 LRRM 1039 (2001), *enforced*, 56 Fed. Appx. 811 (9th Cir. 2003) (employer violated §8(a)(2) through its involvement in quality assurance program, but only assisted and did not dominate labor organization); Addicts Rehab. Ctr. Fund, Inc., 330 NLRB 733, 170 LRRM 1359 (2000) (employer violated §8(a)(2) by creating and supporting "pro-action committee"); Naomi Knitting Plant, 328 NLRB 1279, 168 LRRM 1392 (1999) (employer violated §8(a)(2) by creating and organizing design team).

[32]330 NLRB 1379, 170 LRRM 1308 (2000).

Board ruled that the employer dominated its "process enhancement teams" because it created the teams, funded them, played a role in selecting the employee participants, and controlled the teams' operations and agendas. In *Addicts Rehabilitation Center Fund*,[33] the Board found that an employer dominated an employee committee charged with conveying employee grievances to management because the employer "dominated the process of forming the committee."[34] The Board also noted that the employer determined the committee's structure and agenda and provided its space and material needs.[35]

IV. EMPLOYER INTERFERENCE

A. Unlawful Recognition or Other Assistance

Unlawful assistance, rather than domination, is found where the labor organization is deemed capable of functioning as a union in the absence of the unlawful interference or assistance. The difference between unlawful domination and unlawful assistance is one of degree.[36] In determining whether unlawful assistance has taken place, the Board looks to the totality of the circumstances to determine whether the employer's conduct tainted the union's majority status.[37] Such circumstances include improper conduct of the employer both before and after recognition and execution of a collective bargaining agreement.[38]

The Board generally finds the existence of unlawful assistance when the employer has engaged in affirmative acts of tangible benefit to a labor organization that are not sufficiently serious to constitute illegal domination.[39] Unlawful assistance is found most commonly where a labor organization is recognized at a time when it does not

---

[33] *Supra* note 31.

[34] *Id.*

[35] *Id.*

[36] Homemaker Shops, 261 NLRB 441, 442, 110 LRRM 1082 (1982), *enforced in part*, 724 F.2d 535, 115 LRRM 2321 (6th Cir. 1984).

[37] Mar-Jam Supply Co., 337 NLRB 337, 171 LRRM 1203 (2001).

[38] Siro Sec. Serv., Inc., 247 NLRB 1266, 1272, 103 LRRM 1362 (1980).

[39] *Id. See also* Lee v. NLRB, 393 F.3d 491, 176 LRRM 2321 (4th Cir. 2005) (employer violated §8(a)(2) by requiring employees to wear union logos on their uniforms).

have majority status.[40] A violation can occur even where the employer recognizes the minority union because of an unlawful threat to picket.[41]

In *Keystone Shipping Co.*,[42] the Board held that the employer violated Section 8(a)(2) by recognizing a union as representative of employees on two ships as part of a fleetwide bargaining unit when the employer assumed control of the vessels, where another union had previously represented a separate bargaining unit composed of the two vessels, and there was no showing of majority support for the change.[43] In *Lockheed Martin Tactical Aircraft Systems*,[44] however, the Board found that the transfer of unrepresented employees into bargaining unit positions, based on job audits that established that they were performing bargaining unit work, did not constitute an accretion to the bargaining unit or a violation of Section 8(a)(2).

An employer also violates the Act by deducting dues payable to a union that does not represent a majority of the employees in the applicable unit.[45]

The Board has held that an employer who paid the attorneys' fees for a group of employees who opposed their independent union's affiliation with the UAW did not violate the Act.[46] The Board rea-

---

[40]Alliant Foodservice, Inc., 335 NLRB 695, 171 LRRM 1075 (2001); O-J Transp. Co., 333 NLRB 1381, 173 LRRM 1021 (2001) (employer unlawfully recognized union at time when it did not employ substantial and representative complement of employees in unit); *Mar-Jam Supply Co., supra* note 37; Planned Bldg. Servs., Inc., 330 NLRB 791, 170 LRRM 1375 (2000); Gulf Caribe Maritime, Inc., 330 NLRB 766, 170 LRRM 1287 (2000); Ryder Integrated Logistics, Inc., 329 NLRB 1493, 169 LRRM 1285 (1999); Incisa USA, Inc., 327 NLRB 563, 167 LRRM 1228 (1999).

[41]Northwest Protective Serv., 342 NLRB No. 120, 175 LRRM 1405 (2004).

[42]327 NLRB 892, 160 LRRM 1225 (1999).

[43]*See also* Inter-Regional Disposal & Recycling, Inc., 341 NLRB No. 56, 174 LRRM 1333 (2004) (employer violated §8(a)(2) when after acquisition of another employer it recognized an incumbent union as representative of all employees, but failed to establish a consolidation or merger of the two units); North Hills Office Serv., 342 NLRB No. 25 (2004) (employer violated §8(a)(2) by recognizing union after taking over operations without a showing of majority support).

[44]331 NLRB 1407, 165 LRRM 1145 (2000).

[45]Wayne County Neighborhood Legal Servs., Inc., 333 NLRB 146, 166 LRRM 1169 (2001); Ryder Integrated Logistics, Inc., 329 NLRB 1493, 169 LRRM 1285 (1999).

[46]RTP Co., 334 NLRB 466, 167 LRRM 1293 (2001), *enforced*, 315 F.3d 951, 171 LRRM 2717 (8th Cir.), *cert. denied*, 540 U.S. 811, 173 LRRM 2416 (2003).

soned that once the independent union validly affiliated with the UAW, the independent ceased to be a labor organization. Because the independent union was not a labor organization, employer contributions to it did not violate Section 8(a)(2).

B. Employer Preference Among Contending Unions

Actions of an employer that aid one labor organization at the expense of another constitute unlawful "assistance" in violation of Section 8(a)(2).[47] For example, in *Mar-Jam Supply Co.*,[48] the Board found several violations of Section 8(a)(2) where the employer recognized a union that did not have majority support after a rival union filed an election petition.[49] In addition, the employer assisted the preferred union by (1) threatening to discharge employees who supported the rival union; (2) promising increased wages and benefits to employees who supported the preferred union; (3) promising reimbursement of dues paid to the preferred union; (4) soliciting employees to sign authorization cards for the preferred union; and (5) distributing the preferred union's hats and literature to employees.[50] Similarly, in *Ryder Integrated Logistics, Inc.*,[51] the Board held that the employer violated Section 8(a)(2) when it threatened employees with plant closure if they supported a particular union seeking recognition over its rival union.

---

[47]APF Carting, Inc., 336 NLRB 73, 170 LRRM 1454 (2001), *enforced*, 60 Fed. Appx. 832 (2003); Mar-Jam Supply Co., 337 NLRB 337, 171 LRRM 1203 (2001); Regal Recycling, Inc., 329 NLRB 355, 163 LRRM 1245 (1999); King David Ctr., 328 NLRB 1141, 168 LRRM 1458 (1999).

[48]*Supra* note 47.

[49]*See also* AT Sys. W., Inc., 341 NLRB No. 12, 174 LRRM 1203 (2004) (despite document indicating lack of majority support for incumbent union, employer violated §8(a)(2) by recognizing rival union when unfair labor practices were unremedied and settlement agreement required employer to bargain with the incumbent union).

[50]*See also* Niblock Excavating, Inc., 337 NLRB 53, 169 LRRM 1129 (2001), *enforced*, 59 Fed. Appx. 882 (7th Cir. 2003); Dobbs Int'l Servs., Inc., 335 NLRB 972, 170 LRRM 1541 (2001) (finding unlawful assistance by employer who allowed outside union to organize on its premises by conducting meetings in its cafeteria, and simultaneously assisting incumbent union by requiring employees to attend incumbent union's meetings and paying them overtime for attending); McLaren Health Care Corp., 333 NLRB 256, 167 LRRM 1330 (2001) (finding that employer unlawfully granted recognition to union, and union unlawfully accepted such recognition, where rival union had filed valid election petition in same bargaining unit).

[51]329 NLRB 1493, 169 LRRM 1285 (1999).

An employer also violates Section 8(a)(2) when it grants one union access to its facility to campaign and denies such access to another union.[52] In *Duane Reade, Inc.*,[53] the Board found that the employer provided unlawful assistance to a union it preferred by, among other acts, (1) providing meeting space to the union on company time contrary to the employer's own no-solicitation policy; (2) requiring employees to attend organizational meetings conducted by the union during paid work time; and (3) denying equal access to a rival labor organization. Notably in *Detroit Medical Center Corp.*,[54] the Board overruled the hearing officer in a postelection objections context and found that an employer does not have an affirmative duty to notify a union that it has either granted or denied access to a rival union, where one union requested access to the employer's facilities, but its rival did not.[55]

C. Conduct of Supervisors

The Board continues to hold that participation by supervisors or agents of an employer in an organizing campaign is unlawful.[56] Thus, an employer violated Section 8(a)(2) when its agent encouraged employees to sign authorization cards and participated in the selection of union representatives for employees. In addition, the presence of the employer's agent at a union meeting gave the impression that the meeting was endorsed by the employer.[57] Further,

---

[52]*Regal Recycling, Inc., supra* note 47; *King David Ctr., supra* note 47.

[53]338 NLRB 943, 172 LRRM 1147 (2003), *enforced*, 99 Fed. Appx. 240 (D.C. Cir. 2004).

[54]331 NLRB 878, 166 LRRM 1386 (2000).

[55]*Id.*

[56]Planned Bldg. Servs., Inc., 330 NLRB 791, 170 LRRM 1375 (2000); Meyer's Transp. of N.Y., Inc., 338 NLRB 958, 174 LRRM 1423 (2003) (supervisor unlawfully distributed authorization cards and either asked or directed employees to sign those cards).

[57]North Hills Office Serv., 342 NLRB No. 25 (2004) (employer violated §8(a)(2) by arranging and remaining present during a meeting at which union representatives distributed and solicited employees to sign authorization cards); Niblock Excavating, Inc., 337 NLRB 53, 169 LRRM 1129 (2001); Dobbs Int'l Servs., Inc., 335 NLRB 972, 170 LRRM 1541 (2001) (supervisor's presence during rival union's on-site organizational meeting was sufficient basis for finding unlawful assistance by employer); *Planned Bldg. Servs., Inc., supra* note 56.

an employer violates the Act by threatening employees with discharge if they do not agree to sign a union checkoff authorization card or join the union.[58]

In *Harborside Healthcare, Inc.*,[59] the Board overruled *Millsboro Nursing & Rehabilitation Center, Inc.*,[60] which held that the solicitation of authorization cards by supervisors is not objectionable where the supervisor's request could not be viewed as threatening or intimidating. Instead, the Board held that such solicitations are inherently coercive absent mitigating circumstances.

V. THE REQUIREMENT OF EMPLOYER NEUTRALITY

Section 8(a)(2) prohibits an employer from contributing "support" to a labor organization, but, in the absence of unlawful interference, it does not prohibit expressions of preference for one union over another.

A. When a Union Is Incumbent

When presented with rival unions, an employer violates the Act by assisting either an outside union or an incumbent to organize its employees.[61] The employer's motivation or good faith is immaterial.[62] This doctrine can apply in many contexts, such as an employer's acquisition of a company. In *Judge & Dolph Ltd.*,[63] the employer violated Section 8(a)(2) when, in the absence of a lawful accretion, it required employees of the acquired facility to withdraw from their chosen union and join the union that represented employees at the employer's existing plant. However, where an employer allows one union access to its employees without providing access to another

---

[58]Lockheed Martin Tactical Aircraft Sys., 331 NLRB 1407, 165 LRRM 1145 (2000).

[59]343 NLRB No. 100, 176 LRRM 1113 (2004).

[60]327 NLRB 879, 160 LRRM 1209 (1999).

[61]Duane Reade Inc., 338 NLRB 943, 172 LRRM 1147 (2003); Clock Elec. Inc., 338 NLRB 806, 172 LRRM 1003 (2003); Dobbs Int'l Servs. Inc., 335 NLRB 972, 170 LRRM 1541 (2001).

[62]Judge & Dolph Ltd., 333 NLRB 175, 168 LRRM 1205 (2001); Mastronardi Mason Materials Co., 336 NLRB 1296, 174 LRRM 1019 (2001), *enforcement granted*, 64 Fed. Appx. 271 (2d Cir. 2003).

[63]*Supra* note 62.

union, there is no violation if the employer is unaware that the other union is attempting to organize its employees.[64]

B. When No Union Is Incumbent

Following its *Bruckner Nursing Home* decision,[65] the Board continues to hold that an employer violates Section 8(a)(2) of the Act by recognizing a union after a rival union has filed a valid representation petition.[66] In *McLaren Health Care Corp.*,[67] the Board applied the *Bruckner* rule, even though one union had a card check agreement before the rival union filed its petition.

Although an employer may rely on authorization cards to recognize a union, the Board continues to apply its "dual-card" doctrine, which does not allow an employer to count an employee toward majority status if that employee signed cards authorizing two different unions to act as that employee's representative.

A 2003 NLRB Advice Memorandum addressed a case in which an employer was charged with violating Section 8(a)(2) by not offering to enter into an election procedure agreement with one union (CNA) when it had entered into such an agreement with a rival union (SEIU). The advice found that the employer did not violate Section 8(a)(2) because CNA did not offer to enter into the same overall election procedure agreement as SEIU.[68]

Finally, the Board continues to hold that during the period after the lawful recognition of a union but before the parties finalize an initial labor agreement, the "recognition serves as a bar for a reasonable period of time to allow the parties to bargain free from challenge to the union's majority status."[69]

---

[64]Tecumseh Corrugated Box Co., 333 NLRB 1, 172 LRRM 1111 (2001).

[65]262 NLRB 955, 110 LRRM 1374 (1982).

[66]Mar-Jam Supply Co., 337 NLRB 337, 171 LRRM 1203 (2001); Innovative Communications Corp., 333 NLRB 665, 169 LRRM 1260 (2001), *aff'd*, 39 Fed. Appx. 715, 170 LRRM 2448 (3d Cir. 2002); Incisa USA, Inc., 327 NLRB 563, 167 LRRM 1228 (1999).

[67]333 NLRB 256, 167 LRRM 1330 (2001).

[68]Riverside Cmty. Hosp., Case No. 21-CA-35537 (July 8, 2003).

[69]Livent Realty dba Ford Center for the Performing Arts, 328 NLRB 1, 161 LRRM 1037 (1999) (reasonable time had not passed; therefore, recognition of union barred petition by rival union); MGM Grand Hotel, Inc., 329 NLRB 464, 162 LRRM 1202 (1999) (Board barred decertification petition filed before parties had reached tentative agreement). However, in *Dana Corp. Metaldyne Corp.*, 341 NLRB No. 150, 174 LRRM 1521 (2004), the Board granted review to determine whether to process a decertification petition, notwithstanding the voluntary recognition bar, where the voluntary recognition was pursuant to a card check/neutrality agreement.

VI. SUPPORT VERSUS COOPERATION

In *NLRB v. Midwestern Personnel Services, Inc.*,[70] the Seventh Circuit discussed the factors that will be examined to determine whether an employer's lawful cooperation with a union has crossed the line into unlawful "domination or interference with the formation or administration of a union, or contribution of financial or other support to a union, with the effect of interfering with the employees' organizational rights guaranteed by Section 7 of the NLRA."[71] The court explained:

> Whether an employer actually intended to interfere with the employees' selection of a bargaining representative, or whether employees actually felt coerced by their employer's actions does not matter—the gravamen of the violation is whether the employer's assistance reasonably tends to coerce the employees in the exercise of their organizational rights . . . . In determining whether management-labor cooperation has crossed over from permissible cooperation to unlawful coercion, courts consider a confluence of factors, with no one factor being dispositive. This non-exclusive list of factors includes whether the employer solicited contact with the union; the rank and position of the company's solicitor; whether the employer silently acquiesced in the union's drive for membership; whether the employer shepherded its employees to meetings with a prospective union; whether management was present at meetings between its employees and a prospective union; whether the signing of union cards was coerced; and whether the employer quickly recognized the assisted union after the employees signed authorization cards yet exhibited prejudice against another union selected by the employees.[72]

In applying this standard, the court upheld the Board's finding of unlawful assistance where the employer's president had personally solicited and entered into an agreement with the union before determining whether the union had majority support, and managers attended meetings between the union and employees, took attendance, made introductions, and suggested that employees who

[70]322 F.3d 969, 171 LRRM 3217 (7th Cir. 2003), *enforcing* 331 NLRB 348, 171 LRRM 1262 (2000).

[71]*Id.* 322 F.3d at 977.

[72]*Id.* at 977–78.

did not sign authorization cards would lose their jobs.[73] In another case, the Fourth Circuit found that the employer and union violated the Act by requiring employees to wear uniforms with the union logo alongside the employer's logo, despite the fact that the requirement was the product of collective bargaining.[74]

However, arranging for a union representative to meet employees on company property is not per se illegal support under Section 8(a)(2). For example, in *Tecumseh Corrugated Box Co.*,[75] the Board found no violation when, at the close of a mandatory company meeting called to inform the employees that their employer had just changed ownership, an officer of the new owner told the employees that the company liked to work with unions, then introduced a union representative and left the room. The Board affirmed the ALJ's dismissal of the complaint, stating that, even if the employer paid the employees during the time they were meeting with the union representative, this did not constitute a violation of Section 8(a)(2) "under all of the circumstances."[76]

---

[73] *Id.* at 980, 171 LRRM 3217. *See also* Miller Indus. Towing Equip., Inc., 342 NLRB No. 112, 176 LRRM 1103 (2004) (employer violated §8(a)(2) by forming, sponsoring and assisting "Continous Improvement Committee"); Duane Reade Inc., 338 NLRB 943, 172 LRRM 1147 (2003), *enforced*, 99 Fed. Appx. 240 (D.C. Cir. 2004) (employer and union committed unfair labor practices when employer provided, and union accepted, assistance and recognition, by (a) providing meeting space at seven of its pharmacy stores to union, contrary to employer's own no-solicitation policy, (b) requiring employees to attend organizational meetings conducted by union with employer representatives present during paid work time, (c) denying equal access to rival labor organization for purposes of organizing by concealing existence of stores from its representative and ordering them to leave stores under threat of arrest, (d) telling employees they had to sign union's authorization cards and forbidding them from signing with any other labor organization, and (e) instantly recognizing union after cards were signed, based on demand by union made even before it signed up any employees); Grouse Mountain Lodge, 333 NLRB 1322, 169 LRRM 1039 (2001), *enforced*, 56 Fed. Appx. 811 (9th Cir. 2003) (employer unlawfully assisted "quality assurance" program, which was found to be labor organization, where employer's supervisor arranged time, date, and location of meetings); Addicts Rehab. Ctr. Fund, Inc., 330 NLRB 733, 170 LRRM 1359 (2000) (employer violated §8(a)(2) by creating and supporting employee pro-action committee, where committee was labor organization under the Act, and employer dominated process of forming committee and provided committee with time to meet as well as space and materials).

[74] Lee v. NLRB, 393 F.3d 491, 497, 176 LRRM 2321 (4th Cir. 2005), *vacating and remanding* BellSouth Telecomm, Inc., 335 NLRB 1066, 168 LRRM 1049 (2001).

[75] 333 NLRB 1, 172 LRRM 1111 (2001).

[76] *Id.* at n.1.

Finally, the Board continues to hold that an employer provides unlawful assistance to a union where it improperly deducts union dues on behalf of a union that does not represent a majority of the employees in the applicable bargaining unit.[77]

VII. THE UNION AS PARTY TO THE EMPLOYER'S DOMINATION, ASSISTANCE, OR SUPPORT

Employer conduct that violates Section 8(a)(2) often involves a derivative violation of Section 8(b)(1)(A) by the union, as the union is deemed to have restrained or coerced the employees by accepting the employer's unlawful support or assistance.[78] The Board continues to rule that a union that accepts recognition without majority support or executes a collective bargaining agreement when it represents a minority of employees violates Section 8(b)(1)(A).[79] It is a violation of the Act for the union to accept recognition from an employer at a new facility in the absence of a lawful accretion.[80] A union also violates Section 8(b)(1)(A) when it threatens to have employees fired if they refuse to sign union membership applica-

---

[77]Wayne County Legal Servs., Inc., 333 NLRB 146, 166 LRRM 1169 (2001). *See also* North Hills Office Serv., 342 NLRB No. 25 (2004) (employer violated §8(a)(2) by deducting dues for union that did not represent an "uncoerced majority," and union violated §8(b)(1)(A) by accepting recognition).

[78]Duane Reade Inc., 338 NLRB 943, 172 LRRM 1147 (2003), *enforced*, 99 Fed. Appx. 240 (D.C. Cir. 2004) *supra* note 73.

[79]McLaren Health Care Corp., 333 NLRB 256, 167 LRRM 1330 (2001); Gulf Caribe Maritime, Inc., 330 NLRB 766, 170 LRRM 1287 (2000) (union violated §8(b)(1)(A) when it accepted recognition based on tainted authorization cards); Incisa USA, Inc., 327 NLRB 563, 167 LRRM 1228 (1999) (union violated §8(b)(1)(A) by seeking and accepting recognition at time when valid recognition petition was pending before Board).

[80]Keystone Shipping Co., 327 NLRB 892, 160 LRRM 1225 (1999).

tions and dues checkoff authorization cards before it has obtained lawful recognition, or when it causes an employer to terminate an employee because of his or her refusal to join the union prior to lawful recognition.[81]

VIII. Remedies

Where the Board determines that an employer's violations are limited to unlawful interference and support but do not rise to the level of domination, the Board orders the employer to cease and desist from such conduct.[82] If the employer unlawfully recognizes a minority union that is not dominated, the Board generally will issue a cease-and-desist order that prohibits the employer from recognizing the union and from giving any effect to any contract between the parties until the union is properly certified.[83] In *President Container, Inc.*,[84] the Board set aside an election. On the eve of the election the employer's owner announced at a bargaining session with the incumbent union, in front of 25 employees, that he would not deal or negotiate further with the incumbent union. The Board found this conduct discredited the union in the eyes of the employees and affected their ability to choose freely in the election. It remains the

---

[81]Lockheed Martin Tactical Aircraft Sys., 331 NLRB 1407, 165 LRRM 1145 (2000); *Keystone Shipping Co., supra* note 80 (union violated §8(b)(1)(A) by telling employees that it would ask employer to discharge them if they did not pay dues and fees; by requesting that employer discharge employees; and by receiving aid, assistance, and support from employer in form of dues deducted from wages of employees).

[82]Mar-Jam Supply Co., 337 NLRB 337, 171 LRRM 1203 (2001); APF Carting, Inc., 336 NLRB 73, 170 LRRM 1454 (2001); Grouse Mountain Assocs. II, 333 NLRB 1322, 169 LRRM 1039 (2001); Niblock Excavating, Inc., 337 NLRB 53, 169 LRRM 1129 (2001); Wayne County Legal Servs., Inc., 333 NLRB 146, 166 LRRM 1169 (2001).

[83]*Mar-Jam Supply Co., supra* note 82; Innovative Communications Corp., 333 NLRB 665, 169 LRRM 1260 (2001); Temple Sec., Inc., 337 NLRB 372, 169 LRRM 1161 (2001); *McLaren Health, supra* note 79; Deferiet Paper Co., 330 NLRB No. 89, 166 LRRM 1040, *enforcement denied on other grounds*, 235 F.3d 581, 166 LRRM 2107 (D.C. Cir. 2000); Planned Bldg. Servs., Inc., 330 NLRB 791, 170 LRRM 1375 (2000); *Gulf Caribe, supra* note 79; *Keystone Shipping Co., supra* note 81; *Incisa USA, supra* note 79; Ryder Integrated Logistics, Inc., 329 NLRB 1493, 169 LRRM 1285 (1999).

[84]328 NLRB 1277, 162 LRRM 1254 (1999).

Board's policy to order disestablishment where company unions or employee committees are dominated by an employer.[85]

When the Board prohibits an employer from giving effect to any contract with an unlawfully assisted union, the employer is not required to cease giving effect to the wages, benefits, and conditions provided under the agreement.[86] In *Keystone Shipping Co.*,[87] the Board stated that "nothing in the remedial order shall require [the employer] to withdraw or eliminate any wage increases or other benefits, terms or conditions of employment which may have been established pursuant to any such [collective bargaining] agreement." When union dues or initiation fees have been collected pursuant to unlawful recognition of a union, the employer and union will be jointly ordered to reimburse all unit employees for fees and other sums deducted from their pay, with interest.[88] An employer will not be jointly liable for such fees where it recognized and signed a contract with a minority union as the result of the union's unlawful threat of picketing.[89] However, when an employer unlawfully recognizes one union while it has a collective bargaining agreement with another, the employer may be required to make all payments not made under the agreement including trust fund contributions and dues not checked off and to reimburse unit employees for expenses resulting from its failures to make such payments.[90]

The Board continues to impose *Gissel* bargaining orders to remedy serious violations of Section 8(a)(2). In *AT Systems West, Inc.*,[91] an employer unlawfully withdrew recognition from one union and recognized another. The Board ordered the employer to bargain for a

---

[85]Miller Indus. Towing Equip., Inc., 342 NLRB No. 112, 176 LRRM 1103 (2004); Summa Health Sys., 330 NLRB 1379, 170 LRRM 1308 (2000); Addicts Rehab. Ctr. Fund, Inc., 330 NLRB 733, 170 LRRM 1359 (2000); Naomi Knitting Plant, 328 NLRB 1279, 168 LRRM 1392 (1999); Polaroid Corp., 329 NLRB 424, 162 LRRM 1129, 1130 (1999); EFCO Corp., 327 NLRB 372, 160 LRRM 1049 (1999).

[86]*Innovative Communications Corp., supra* note 83; *Temple Sec., Inc., supra* note 83; Gulf Caribe Maritime, Inc., 330 NLRB 766, 170 LRRM 1287 (2000).

[87]327 NLRB 892, 160 LRRM 1275 (1999).

[88]Kaiser Found. Hosp., 343 NLRB No. 8, 176 LRRM 1411 (2004); Newspaper & Mail Deliverers (Jalt Corp. dba U.N.D.S.), 337 NLRB 1102, 174 LRRM 1420 (2002); Alliant Foodservice, Inc., 335 NLRB 695, 171 LRRM 1075 (2001); Planned Bldg. Servs., Inc., 330 NLRB 791, 170 LRRM 1375 (2000); Ryder Integrated Logistics, Inc., 329 NLRB 1493, 169 LRRM 1285 (1999).

[89]Northwest Protective Serv., 342 NLRB No. 120, 175 LRRM 1405 (2004).

[90]Gem Mgmt. Co., 339 NLRB 489, 173 LRRM 1573 (2003).

[91]341 NLRB No. 12, 174 LRRM 1203 (2004).

reasonable period of time, thereby creating a decertification bar, to restore the status quo ante.[92] But where the violations are not serious enough to warrant imposition of a bargaining order, the Board will direct the employer to cease and desist from unlawful assistance and order a new election. For example, in *Regal Recycling*,[93] the employer violated Section 8(a)(2) by denying access to its employees and facility to one labor organization but providing such access to another. The Board refused to impose a *Gissel* bargaining order because of the lengthy delay in processing the case at the Board. Rather, the Board ordered that (1) a second election be held in the event that the disfavored organization did not prevail in the first election, and (2) the employer, on request, provide to the disfavored organization the names and addresses of all current unit employees.

---

[92] *Id.*

[93] 329 NLRB 355, 163 LRRM 1245 (1999).

Part III

THE REPRESENTATION PROCESS AND UNION RECOGNITION

BIBLIOGRAPHY

Craig Becker, *Democracy in the Workplace: Union Representation Elections and Federal Labor Law*, 77 MINN. L. REV. 495 (1993)

James J. Brudley, *Neutrality Agreements and Card Check Recognition: Prospects for Changing Paradigms*, 90 IOWA L. REV. 819 (2005)

R. Wayne Estes and Adam M. Porter, Babcock/Lechmere *Revisited: Derivative Nature of Union Organizers' Right of Access to Employer's Property Should Impact Judicial Evaluation of Alternatives*, 48 SMU L. REV. 349 (1995)

Matthew W. Finkin, *Employee Representation Outside the Labor Act: Thoughts on Arbitral Representation, Group Representation, and Workplace Committees*, 5 U. PA. J. LAB. & EMP. L. 75 (2002)

Rafael Gely and Leonard Bierman, *Labor Law Access Rules and Stare Decisis: Developing a Planned Parenthood-Based Model of Reform*, 20 BERKELEY J. EMP. & LAB. L. 138 (1999)

Christopher Grant, *Unions in a Fragmented Society*, 7 CHI.-KENT L. REV. 849 (2002)

Grant M. Hayden, *"The University Works Because We Do": Collective Bargaining Rights for Graduate Assistants*, 69 FORDHAM L. REV. 1233 (2001)

Michael J. Hayes, *Let Unions Be Unions: Allowing Grants of Benefits During Representation Campaigns*, 5 U. PA. J. LAB. & EMP. L. 259 (2003)

Eve T. Kraszewski, *Overhauling the Good Faith Reasonable Doubt Test: Unions Should Be Obligated to Provide Annual Mandatory Polls to Determine Continuing Union Majority Status*, 36 J. MARSHALL L. REV. 377 (2003)

Peter Levine, *The Debate Over Unionization and Collective Bargaining of Private Physicians*, 18 HOFSTRA LAB. & EMP. L.J. 659 (2001)

Kathleen C. McGowan, *Unequal Opportunity in At-Will Employment: The Search for a Remedy*, 72 ST. JOHN'S L. REV. 141 (1998)

Sarah Pawlicki, Levitz Furniture Co.: *The End of* Celanese *and the Good-Faith Doubt Standard for Withdrawing Recognition of Incumbent Unions*, 78 CHI.-KENT L. REV. 381 (2003)

Joshua Rowland, *"Forecasts of Doom": The Dubious Threat of Graduate Teaching Assistant Collective Bargaining to Academic Freedom*, 42 B.C. L. REV. 941 (2001)

Deborah L. Stein, *Keep off the Grass: Prohibiting Non-Employee Union Access Without Discriminating*, 73 N.Y.U. L. Rev. 2029 (1998)

John W. Teeter, Jr., *Dueling Democracies: Protecting Labor Representation Elections From Governmental Interference*, 106 W. Va. L. Rev. 121 (2003)

Alan L. Zmija, *Union Organizing After* Lechmere, Inc. v. NLRB—*A Time To Reexamine the Rule of Babcock and Wilcox*, 12 Hofstra Lab. L.J. 65 (1994)

CHAPTER 9

RESTRICTIONS ON PREELECTION ACTIVITY: "LABORATORY CONDITIONS"

I. INTRODUCTION

[Editor's Note: The reader is also directed to the Board's publication "An Outline of Law and Procedures in Representation Cases" available on the Board's website: www.nlrb.gov.]

A. The Board's Authority Under Section 9

1. Relation to Unfair Labor Practices

In *Crown Bolt, Inc.*,[1] a divided Board held that dissemination of even serious threats, such as plant closures, would not be presumed. The *Crown Bolt* majority expressly overruled *Spring Industries*[2] and "all other decisions in which the Board presumed dissemination of plant-closure threat or other kinds of coercive statements" and returned to the evidentiary requirement of *Kokomo Tube Co.*[3] that the objecting union has the burden of proving dissemination of a threat. Both the majority and the partial dissent of Members Liebman and Walsh extensively analyzed evidentiary presumptions in general and the Board case law on this particular issue. The decision is prospective,[4] so that all pending cases must be decided under the *Spring Industries* standard.

Some cases reported on earlier would appear to be unaffected by the above change in the Board's position. Thus, in one case, a threat to a single employee that her wages would be decreased if she voted to be represented by a union was deemed sufficiently isolated

[1] 343 NLRB No. 86, 176 LRRM 1065 (2004).
[2] 332 NLRB 40, 165 LRRM 1161 (2000).
[3] 280 NLRB 357, 122 LRRM 1254 (1986).
[4] *Crown Bolt, Inc., supra* note 1.

to not warrant setting aside the election.[5] In another case, an employer's unlawful interrogation of a single employee coupled with its intrusion into a parking lot meeting between four employees and two union representatives resulted in setting aside an election that the employer had won by only four votes.[6]

A threat to terminate an employee for defacing an employer's antiunion literature was found to warrant setting aside the election where the Board found that the threat was effectively disseminated among employees.[7] Similarly, the employer's discriminatory enforcement of its posting policy, by removing union literature during the critical period before the election, which affected the dissemination of information to all employees, warranted setting aside the election.[8]

B. Timing of the "Laboratory Period"

The Board continues to hold that the "laboratory conditions" period begins with the filing of the petition[9] and that unfair labor practices or objectionable conduct occurring before the date of the petition cannot form the basis for setting aside an election, but that

---

[5]Bon Appetit Mgmt. Co., 334 NLRB 1042, 169 LRRM 1068 (2001), *distinguishing Spring Indus. Inc., supra* note 2.

[6]Grass Valley Grocery Outlet, 338 NLRB 877, 173 LRRM 1541 (2003), *enforced sub nom.* NLRB v. Cubitt, 2005 US App LEXIS 419 (9th Cir. 2005).

[7]Waste Mgmt. Inc., 330 NLRB 634, 163 LRRM 1129 (2000).

[8]Allied Mech., Inc., 343 NLRB No. 74 (2004).

[9]DynCorp., 343 NLRB No. 124, 176 LRRM 1341 (2004) (threat to eliminate ESOP benefit that was made during the protected period was objectionable); Sara Lee Bakery Group dba International Baking Co., 342 NLRB No. 12, 175 LRRM 1250 (2004) (announcing new unpaid holiday and gain sharing bonus program during the critical period was objectionable conduct, but announcing new prepetition decisions regarding enhanced medical, life insurance and retirement benefits after the petition was filed but well prior to the election was not found to be objectionable conduct). In *U Save Foods*, 341 NLRB No. 22, 174 LRRM 1073 (2004), the Board found that announcing the selection of the unit employees' store as one of the "lucky five" in the region chosen for remodeling so close to the election was a benefit and objectionable conduct because the employees would get new cash registers to use and the particular store would be more likely to remain open than if it were not selected.

such conduct may be considered when it adds meaning and dimension to related postpetition conduct.[10]

In *Harborside Healthcare Inc.*,[11] a divided Board, on remand from the Sixth Circuit, ruled on the issue of pro-union supervisory conduct, setting a standard for what type of such conduct is objectionable. The majority found that a supervisor's prepetition solicitation of union authorization cards was objectionable, even though the conduct occurred before the critical period, since the impact of the supervisor's solicitation would continue to be felt during the critical period. The dissent suggested that the majority decision eroded the critical period.[12]

Likewise, the Board continues to hold that activity occurring after an election cannot form the basis for objectionable conduct to set aside the election.[13]

C. Procedural Considerations

In *Virginia Concrete Corp., Inc.*,[14] the Board expressly overruled *Ellicott Machine Corp.*,[15] holding that the withdrawal of an unfair labor practice charge does not operate as a waiver of a party's right to file objections based upon the same conduct.

---

[10]BCI Coca-Cola Bottling Co. of Los Angeles, 339 NLRB 67, 172 LRRM 1226 (2003) (employer's prepetition threat that employees would lose 401(k) benefits if union won election added "meaning and dimension" to employer's ambiguous postpetition conduct which failed to disavow or correct the prepetition threat, thus forming basis to set aside an election decided by a single-vote margin); *see also* Cedars-Sinai Med. Ctr., 342 NLRB No. 58, slip op. at 3, 175 LRRM 1221 (2004); Sodexho Marriott Servs., 335 NLRB 538, 172 LRRM 1060 (2001); VJNH, Inc., 328 NLRB 87 n.34, 167 LRRM 1358 (1999).

[11]343 NLRB No. 100, 176 LRRM 1113 (2004).

[12]*Id.* at 1123.

[13]Naomi Knitting Plant, 328 NLRB 1279, 168 LRRM 1392 (1999). However, after an election and pending resolution of any objections thereto, "an employer that chooses unilaterally to change its employees' terms and conditions of employment . . . does so at its own peril if the union is ultimately certified." Overnite Transp. Co., 335 NLRB 372, 169 LRRM 1004 (2001), citing Mike O'Connor Chevrolet-Buick-GMC Co., Inc., 209 NLRB 701, 85 LRRM 1419 (1974).

[14]338 NLRB 1182, 172 LRRM 1169 (2003).

[15]54 NLRB 732, 13 LRRM 194 (1944).

II. GROUNDS FOR SETTING ASIDE ELECTIONS

A. Employer and/or Union Conduct

1. *Misrepresentations*

b. *Hollywood Ceramics* Overruled: Voters Allowed to Assess Misrepresentations

(2) *Return to* Shopping Kart: Hollywood Ceramics *Again Abandoned*

The Board and many courts continue to apply the *Midland National* rule,[16] holding that employees should be left the task of evaluating campaign propaganda by themselves and that the Board will not set aside elections based on campaign misrepresentations absent evidence of the use of forged documents.[17] The Board and courts also continue to treat misrepresentations of Board law in the same manner as other election misrepresentations—under the *Midland National* standard.[18] The Sixth Circuit, however, continues to apply a modified form of the *Midland National* rule, holding that an

[16]Midland Nat'l Life Ins. Co., 263 NLRB 127, 110 LRRM 1489 (1982).

[17]National League of Prof'l Baseball Clubs, 330 NLRB 670, 170 LRRM 1194 (2000) (overruling objections to election based on misrepresentations that were addressed and debated during election and did not involve use of forged documents). *See also In re* Allegheny Ludlum Corp., 333 NLRB 734, 742 n.63, 166 LRRM 1353 (2001), *enforced*, 301 F.3d 167, 170 LRRM 2923 (3d Cir. 2002) (reaffirming holding that regulation of substance of misleading campaign propaganda unnecessary because employees are capable of recognizing it as such); NLRB v. Queensboro Steel Corp., 217 F.3d 839, 164 LRRM 3024 (4th Cir. 2000) (affirming that many courts have adopted the *Midland National* standard).

[18]Virginia Concrete Corp., 338 NLRB 1182, 172 LRRM 1169 (2003) (finding that employer's campaign literature, stating that union filed unfair labor practice charges against the employer as an attempt to take away employees' wage increase, was, at most, a mere misstatement of Board law or possible future Board action, which is not objectionable under *Midland National*); *see also* NLRB v. Sliman's Sales & Servs., Inc., 75 Fed. Appx. 457, 173 LRRM 2416 (6th Cir. 2003) (finding, under the Sixth Circuit standard, that even if union business representative's statement to three voting employees that the union could be voted out "as fast as it was voted in" if employees became dissatisfied misrepresented the certification year bar, statement was not objectionable); United Steel Serv., Inc., 340 NLRB No. 30, 176 LRRM 1064 (2003) (finding, under *Midland National* or the Sixth Circuit's modification thereof, that union's misrepresentation regarding what Board law required as the starting point for bargaining over wages and benefits was not objectionable).

employee's free and fair choice will be affected where the misrepresentation is so persuasive and the deception so artful that employees will be unable to separate truth from untruth, even where no forgery can be proved.[19]

3. *Misuse of the Board's Election Process*

c. Electioneering at the Polls

The Board continues to hold that brief innocuous conversations between election observers and potential voters in the polling area do not constitute objectionable conduct sufficient to overturn the results of an election. In *S.F.D.H. Associates,*[20] the union's observer spoke to 5 or 6 (of approximately 100) voters in the polling area during the election. Each conversation was brief, lasting a few seconds to a minute, and the content of the conversations was innocuous. The Board determined that these "brief remarks to five or six voters could not have affected the results of the election and are not sufficient grounds for setting it aside."[21]

In a similar case, the Sixth Circuit held that an observer's brief exchange with an employee in a cafeteria and a 90-second conversation with another employee in the polling area about a piece of machinery did not constitute objectionable conduct.[22]

---

[19]NLRB v. St. Francis Healthcare Ctr., 212 F.3d 945, 164 LRRM 2324 (6th Cir. 2000) (refusing to enforce Board order certifying election applying five-factor test, including (1) timing of misrepresentation; (2) whether employer had opportunity to respond; (3) nature and extent of misrepresentation; (4) whether source of misrepresentation was identified; and (5) whether there is evidence that employees were affected by misrepresentation); NLRB v. Gormac Custom Mfg. Inc., 190 F.3d 742, 162 LRRM 2156 (6th Cir. 1999) (Board erred in refusing to conduct evidentiary hearing on whether the union unlawfully misrepresented extent of support among employees by distributing handbill two to three hours before election that listed names and purported signatures of 31 of 45 eligible voters allegedly supporting union, where at least three employees whose signatures appeared on handbill did not support union); Maremont Corp. v. NLRB, 177 F.3d 573, 161 LRRM 2338 (6th Cir. 1999) (upholding Board's conclusion that union's "vote yes" handbill containing signatures of 446 of 664 eligible voters did not constitute grounds for setting aside representation hearing); NLRB v. Dave Transp. Servs. Inc., 176 F.3d 484 (9th Cir. 1999) (reiterating the Ninth and most other circuits' adoption of the *Midland National* standard, and recognizing that the Sixth Circuit has established exceptions to that standard even absent forgery of Board documents).

[20]330 NLRB 638, 163 LRRM 1173 (2000).

[21]*Id.* at 638.

[22]Sawyer Lumber Co. v. NLRB, 225 F.3d 659, 165 LRRM 2678 (6th Cir. 2000).

In *Midway Hospital Medical Center, Inc.*,[23] the Board held that a union observer's outbursts against the employer in close proximity to the hallway where approximately 20 employees were waiting to vote did not reasonably tend to interfere with those employees' free choice. Accordingly, the Board refused to set aside the results of the election.

Likewise, nonverbal conduct in the voting area ordinarily does not constitute objectionable conduct provided that the conduct does not involve electioneering. For example, in *Health Care & Retirement Corp. of America v. NLRB*,[24] the Sixth Circuit affirmed the Board's conclusion that a union observer's reading the Bible to himself in the polling area, without communicating with any voter, was not objectionable conduct.[25]

In *NLRB v. V & S Schuler Engineering, Inc.*,[26] the Sixth Circuit held that the Board properly denied, without evidentiary hearing, an employer's objection to the election because an eligible voter revealed his marked ballot to the union election observer. The court reasoned that the eligible voter was not an agent of the union and his conduct did not interfere with the exercise of other voters' free choice in the election. In contrast, the Third Circuit in *Trimm Associates, Inc. v. NLRB*[27] held that the Board improperly denied an evidentiary hearing on an employer's objection to the election because of undisputed, prolonged conversations between two former employees and voters. The court reasoned that if the former employees were agents of the union, as alleged, the election must be set aside.[28]

Courts continue to enforce Board orders that apply a different, more lenient standard to electioneering conduct of third parties than to parties and representatives of parties.[29]

---

[23]330 NLRB 1420, 164 LRRM 1090 (2000).

[24]255 F.3d 276, 165 LRRM 2064 (6th Cir. 2000).

[25]*Id.*

[26]309 F.3d 362, 171 LRRM 2104 (6th Cir. 2002).

[27]351 F.3d 99, 173 LRRM 2801 (3d Cir. 2003).

[28]*Id.* at 106. (proffer of evidence consisted of union's reference to two individuals as their two lead organizers in unfair labor practice charge that union had filed on their behalf, preelection meeting between two individuals and union representatives, and employee affidavits that described two individuals as union organizers).

[29]NLRB v. Sliman's Sales & Servs., Inc., 75 Fed. Appx. 457, 173 LRRM 2416 (6th Cir. 2003) (conduct of nonagent employee who yelled to employees on shop floor to "come in and vote if you haven't voted yet" was not objectionable as it did not substantially impair exercise of free choice so as to require new election).

Electioneering in the voting area can constitute objectionable conduct. In *Brinks, Inc.*,[30] the Board concluded that a union observer's actions constituted improper electioneering and therefore set aside the election results. In that case, the union's observer told four separate employees, as they approached the observer table, to vote for the union. One of the persons standing in line repeated this message to other employees waiting to vote. The union observer also gave the "thumbs up" signal to other employees as they approached the table.[31] The Board recently distinguished *Brinks* from a situation where a union observer only gave the "thumbs up" signal and smiled at certain voters. In *U-Haul Co. of Nevada, Inc.*,[32] the Board found the union observer's conduct not objectionable because, unlike the union observer in *Brinks*, no explicit instructions to vote for the union were given as voters approached the table, and the thumbs up and smiles alone from the union's observer were not viewed by the Board to convey any particular message.

In another electioneering case, the D.C. Circuit vacated and remanded the Board's decision to overrule the employer's objections to electioneering in a no-electioneering zone.[33] In that matter, union agents sat in a car outside the entrance to the building where the election was conducted so that the voters had to pass by them to enter the polling area, and honked and gestured at the employees as they walked in to vote. The court held that the Board failed to explain why the union agents' continued presence at the entrance to the site of the election is any different than the prohibited act of standing outside the room where employees actually vote.[34]

Moreover, the mere presence of electioneering materials in the voting area may constitute objectionable conduct. For example, in

---

[30]331 NLRB 46, 164 LRRM 1140 (2000); *see also* ITT Auto. v. NLRB, 188 F.3d 375, 161 LRRM 3132 (6th Cir. 1999) (employer coerced employees by positioning supervisors in aisle through which employees had to pass to vote).

[31]Brinks Inc., 331 NLRB 46, 164 LRRM 1140 (2000).

[32]341 NLRB No. 26, 174 LRRM 1111 (2004).

[33]Nathan Katz Realty, LLC v. NLRB, 251 F.3d 981, 167 LRRM 2395 (D.C. Cir. 2001). *See also U-Haul Co. of Nev., Inc., supra* note 32 (Board also concluded that union officials presence in parking lot 20 to 100 feet across from polling area and conversation with a few employees after most of unit was already inside polling area was not objectionable, citing *Nathan Katz Realty).*

[34]*Nathan Katz, supra* note 33.

Pearson Education, Inc.,[35] the Board concluded that an employer's posting of an antiunion poster within an area curtained off for the election, which every employee had to pass in order to vote, constituted objectionable conduct.

In *Tyson Fresh Meats, Inc.*,[36] the Board noted that its rule against electioneering near the polls applies to parties to the election.

The Board also continues to recognize limits on the selection of election observers.[37] Although the Board has long recognized that an employer cannot select a supervisor as its election observer, the Board in *Family Service Agency, San Francisco*[38] expanded this rule by prohibiting any party, employer, or union, from using a statutory supervisor as its election observer.

In *Liquid Transporters, Inc.*,[39] the Board held that an employer's objection to the supervisory status of the union's election observer was waived because it was not raised at the preelection conference. In so holding, the Board explained that an employer "must raise the alleged supervisory status of a union's election observer at the time of the pre-election conference; otherwise, any such objection is precluded, and the employer may not raise the issue for the first time in its post-election objections."[40]

A job title alone does not determine whether the employee can lawfully act as an observer in a representation election. In *VJNH, Inc.*,[41] the Board rejected the union's objection to the employer's use of a "dietary supervisor" as an election observer because the employee, despite her title, was not a statutory supervisor and because the bargaining-unit employees should have known that her job was not to supervise but to check on the dietary needs of patients and to ensure their diets were appropriate.[42]

---

[35]336 NLRB 979, 169 LRRM 1012 (2001). *Compare* American Med. Response, 339 NLRB 23 (2003) (pro-union poster affixed to tree approximately 100 feet from polling area but not visible from polling room as well as distribution of pro-union flyers to employees 50 to 80 feet from the polling area was not improper electioneering), *aff'd*, 373 F.3d 127, 131 (D.C. Cir. 2004).

[36]343 NLRB No. 129 (2004).

[37]331 NLRB 850, 164 LRRM 1305 (2000).

[38]*Id.* (union's use of statutory supervisor as its observer in election constituted objectionable conduct and ordering new election be conducted).

[39]336 NLRB 420, 168 LRRM 1387 (2001).

[40]*Id.* at 420.

[41]328 NLRB 87, 167 LRRM 1358 (1999).

[42]*Id.*

The Board has also held that union representatives may in certain situations serve as election observers particularly where the representatives are also employees. For example, in *DLC Corp. dba FleetBoston Pavilion,*[43] the Board concluded that a local union's use of its president as its election observer did not constitute objectionable conduct because the individual was an employee of the employer. The Board noted that, although the local union president was not currently working for the employer, his absence was due to an injury sustained on the job and he intended to return to work for the employer if surgery for the injury was successful.

In *Butera Finer Foods, Inc.,*[44] the Board examined the issue of whether a nonemployee agent of an incumbent union can serve as an observer in a decertification election. In holding that use of a business agent as an election observer was objectionable conduct in a decertification election, the Board reasoned "that the neutrality of the election process in a decertification context is best fostered by a bright-line rule prohibiting incumbent labor organizations from using their non-employee agents as election observers."[45]

d. Other Conduct In and Around the Polls

The Board continues to hold that if observers or others keep a list of employees who have voted (aside from the official Board eligibility list used to check off voters as they receive their ballots), then objectionable conduct has occurred that can be the basis to set aside an election.[46] The Board upheld an employer's objection to an election where the union observer kept a list of those whom he thought were voting "yes" and "no" during the election. Some employee voters saw the observer keeping the list of names. The Board found that because the employee voters witnessed the union observer keeping a list, the voters reasonably could have concluded that the observer was keeping track of how people voted. The Board continues to allow observers to keep a list of voters to be challenged.[47]

In *Elizabethtown Gas Co. v. NLRB,*[48] the Fourth Circuit found no merit to the employer's position that the election should be over-

[43]333 NLRB 655, 166 LRRM 1367 (2001).
[44]334 NLRB 43, 167 LRRM 1081 (2001).
[45]*Id.*
[46]Cross Pointe Paper Corp., 330 NLRB 658, 169 LRRM 1518 (2000).
[47]Mead S. Wood Prods., 337 NLRB 497, 169 LRRM 1497 (2002).
[48]212 F.3d 257, 164 LRRM 2257 (4th Cir. 2000).

turned because its observer kept a piece of paper on his lap during the voting. The Board agent had instructed the observers not to keep any lists of those who had voted. However, at the instruction of the employer's lawyer, the employer's observer kept a duplicate list of the names of all voters and checked off the names of those who had actually voted. The Board agent noticed that the employer's observer was holding a piece of paper, and instructed him to place any paper or list other than the official voter eligibility list on his lap. The employer lost the election but contended that the election should be overturned because its observer was allowed to keep a list of voters on his lap. The court enforced the Board's decision to certify the election. The court agreed that the employer should not be permitted to overturn an election based on its own misconduct. In addition, because there was no evidence that any voter noticed the employer's observer's recording of his or her vote, there was no basis to conclude that maintaining the list affected any voter.[49]

In *Snap-On Tools, Inc.*,[50] the Board reversed the ALJ's finding that the employer's alternate observer engaged in objectionable list keeping. The alternate observer in question was located in a position where he could observe the employees return to work after voting. The evidence showed that the alternate observer stated the names of the employees after they had voted, and appeared to write something down. However, the Board determined that the ALJ erred in inferring that the alternate observer was keeping a list of voting employees. Indeed, the Board found that the ALJ's inference was not supported by the record, as no employees actually testified to having seen a list.[51]

The Board continues to hold that a supervisor's "continued presence" near the polling area where employees are required to pass can constitute objectionable conduct on the part of the employer.[52] However, the mere presence of a supervisor near the polling area,

---

[49] *Id.* at 266–67, 164 LRRM at 2263–64. *See also* Chrill Care, Inc., 340 NLRB No. 123, 174 LRRM 1237 (2003) (while maintaining a separate list of voters is generally prohibited, there was no evidence that employees knew their names were being recorded).

[50] 342 NLRB No. 2, 175 LRRM 1124 (2004).

[51] *Id.*, 175 LRRM at 1127–28.

[52] Mountaineer Park, Inc., 343 NLRB No. 135, 176 LRRM 1378 (2004); *see also* Performance Measurements Co., Inc. 148 NLRB 1657, 57 LRRM 1218 (1964).

without more, is not objectionable.[53] Further, the Board has held that evidence concerning the brief presence of a police officer (hired by the employer to act as a security guard) at the polling area was too ambiguous to warrant an unfair labor practice finding.[54]

The Board also continues to apply the *Anthbro*[55] standard, and sets aside elections where the conduct of a Board agent "tends to destroy confidence in the Board's election process or could reasonably be interpreted as impairing the election standards the Board seeks to maintain."[56] Under this standard, the Board concluded in *Alamo Rent-A-Car* that a Board agent's statements of personal opinion may be sufficiently partisan to necessitate setting aside an election, even if the statements were made to a limited audience, and even if the statements were unaccompanied by procedural irregularities or other actions creating a perception that the election will be administered unfairly.[57] In this case, the Board concluded that while the Board agent's remarks regarding reasons why companies do not like unions were partisan, intemperate, and inappropriate, they were insufficient to overturn the election. The subject comments were only heard by two employees in an election won by a union by a large margin and therefore did not reflect a level of bias or impropriety that they destroyed confidence in Board election procedures.

The Board has also found that officials calling members at home to tell them to bring their mail ballots to the jobsite and later mailing the ballots for the employees was objectionable conduct, even though the ballots were sealed.[58]

---

[53]*Mountaineer Park, supra* note 52, at slip. op. 12 (no objectionable conduct where evidence showed that employer's security supervisor (1) was seen near polling area on only one occasion by only one employee; (2) was unable to observe employees inside the building where polling area was located; and (3) did not speak, or otherwise interfere with, any employees).

[54]Alamo Rent-A-Car, Inc., 338 NLRB 275, 171 LRRM 1383 (2002). *See also* Quest Int'l, 338 NLRB 856, 172 LRRM 1001 (2003) (employer's implementation of security measures which included a security guard and dog along with an armed off-duty police officer dressed in security company's uniform was not objectionable as guards and the dog were not near polling area).

[55]Anthbro Precision Eng'g Corp., 166 NLRB 966, 65 LRRM 1699 (1967), *vacated sub nom.* Electrical, Radio & Mach. Workers v. NLRB, 67 LRRM 2361 (D.D.C.), *acquiesced*, 171 NLRB 21, 68 LRRM 1001 (1968), *enforced*, 423 F.2d 573, 73 LRRM 2355 (1st Cir. 1970).

[56]Sonoma Health Care Ctr., 342 NLRB No. 93, 175 LRRM 1305 (2004).

[57]*Id.* at slip op. 1–2, 175 LRRM at 1305–1306

[58]Fessler & Bowman Inc., 341 NLRB No. 122, 174 LRRM 1455 (2004).

4. *Appeals to Racial Prejudice*

The courts have enforced Board decisions finding that isolated appeals to racial prejudice, or such appeals made by nonagent third parties during the preelection period, do not constitute grounds for setting aside a representation election.[59] These cases were decided on the specific factual situations involved and have not changed the underlying principles set forth by the Board in *Sewell Manufacturing Co.*,[60] which govern such comments.

5. *The 24-Hour Rule Barring Speeches to Massed Employees*

In *NLRB v. Glades Health Care Center*,[61] the Eleventh Circuit affirmed the Board's finding of no *Peerless Plywood*[62] violation, even though the day before an election, the union staged a rally 50 yards from the employer's facility and broadcast pro-union speeches by loudspeaker. The Board found no violation of the *Peerless Plywood* rule because attendance at the rally was voluntary and because employees who were working inside the facility at the time testified that they could not hear the speakers' exact words. In another context in *Virginia Concrete Corp.*,[63] the Board found no *Peerless Plywood* violation

---

[59]*See* NLRB v. Foundry Div. of Alcon Indus., Inc., 260 F.3d 631, 167 LRRM 2834 (6th Cir. 2001), *cert. denied*, 535 U.S. 1057 (2002) (concluding racial epithets used by union supporter in polling area were not an appeal to racial prejudice that warrants setting aside election where there was no evidence that supporter was trying to appeal to alleged racial prejudice held by employee or that language was used to try and garner union votes based on racial animosity—offensive language was used in joking manner); NLRB v. Flambeau Airmold Corp., 178 F.3d 705, 161 LRRM 2385 (4th Cir. 1999) (representation election union won by two votes was not rendered invalid by racially inflammatory rumor, spread day before the election, that white managers had used racial slurs because neither employer nor union was responsible for starting rumor—and rumor did not so inflame and taint atmosphere as to make reasoned choice impossible); Family Serv. Agency of San Francisco v. NLRB, 163 F.3d 1369, 160 LRRM 2288 (D.C. Cir. 1999) (union did not use appeals to racial prejudice to interfere with vote, even assuming union was responsible for turmoil between African American and Latino employees over alleged existence of rule prohibiting employees from speaking Spanish at work—union statements were reasonably accurate description of facts and were not calculated to spark racial prejudice).

[60]138 NLRB 66, 50 LRRM 1532 (1962).

[61]257 F.3d 1317, 168 LRRM 2867 (11th Cir. 2001).

[62]107 NLRB 427, 33 LRRM 1151 (1953).

[63]338 NLRB 1182, 172 LRRM 1169 (2003).

resulting from the employer sending a brief electronic "Vote No" text message to employees' mobile data units, the day before the election, as the message was not audible, could easily be deleted, and was delivered to unit employees (drivers) individually, in their trucks.

a. Paychecks

In *Tinius Olsen Testing Machine Co.*,[64] the Board held that the employer's inclusion of a 3 percent increase to employees' paychecks on election day did not violate the *Kalin Construction*[65] rule. The Board noted that although an election day pay increase would likely be a violation of the rule, the employer had demonstrated that a collective bargaining agreement required the employer to increase employees' pay on the next pay day, which happened to fall on election day. Because the employer demonstrated a legitimate business reason for the increase, the Board held that there was no *Kalin Construction* violation.

B. Employer Conduct

3. Voter Eligibility List

The Board continues to apply its *Excelsior*[66] rule requiring that the employer provide a list of the full names and addresses of the unit employees. Failure to comply with the rule is grounds for setting aside the election and the Board will do so where the union is "prevented from making full use of the *Excelsior* list because of its delayed receipt," even though the delay was not caused by the employer.[67] The Board also continues to make a distinction, however, between inaccurate or incomplete lists of names versus addresses; the Board is much more apt to overturn an election when employee names are left off of a voter list than if addresses are incorrect. Where

---

[64]329 NLRB 351, 163 LRRM 1192 (1999).

[65]Kalin Constr. Co., 321 NLRB 649, 152 LRRM 1226 (1996) (applying 24-hour rule to prohibit any changes in normal paycheck process during this period).

[66]Excelsior Underwear, 156 NLRB 1236, 61 LRRM 1217 (1966).

[67]Special Citizens Futures Unlimited, 331 NLRB 160, 164 LRRM 1195 (2000). *But see* Bon Appetit Mgmt. Co., 334 NLRB 1042, 169 LRRM 1068 (2001) (minimal delay not objectionable).

the list is incomplete or inaccurate, the Board will determine whether the employer has substantially complied with the *Excelsior* rule by examining (1) the number of names omitted in relation to the overall electorate, (2) whether the number of names omitted involves a determinative number of voters, and (3) the employer's reasons for omitting the names.[68] However, where the list is incomplete or inaccurate as to correct and current addresses of its employees, the Board analyzes whether the employer acted in bad faith or in a grossly negligent manner and also reviews the percentage of errors before determining whether to set an election aside.[69] Where an employer substantially complies with its *Excelsior* obligation, but a union does not receive the *Excelsior* information in a timely manner due to the region's failure to provide the complete list of names to the union, the Board will set aside an election if the region's oversight put the union at an "obvious disadvantage" and interfered with "employees' full opportunity to be informed of the arguments concerning representation."[70]

---

[68]Fantasia Fresh Juice Co., 335 NLRB 754, 172 LRRM 1488 (2001) (election set aside where employer deliberately omitted names of seven strike replacements from *Excelsior* list and failed to supply addresses of nine other newly hired employees in a timely manner); Woodman's Food Mkt., Inc., 332 NLRB 503, 165 LRRM 1209 (2000). *See also* Merchants Transfer Co., 330 NLRB 1165, 170 LRRM 1457 (2000) (setting aside election where employer provided union with out-of-date address list). *But see* Villa Maria Nursing Ctr., 335 NLRB 1345, 168 LRRM 1209 (2001) (no *Excelsior* violation where employer submitted list with four incorrect addresses as list contained errors of less than 3% for all eligible voters).

[69]Washington Fruit & Produce Co., 343 NLRB No. 125, 176 LRRM 1362 (2004) (finding that ALJ incorrectly relied on *Woodsman's Food Mkt., Inc.*, 332 NLRB 503, 165 LRRM 1209 (2000) because that case involved the omission of names, not inclusion of inaccurate addresses; Board relied instead on *Women in Crisis Counseling*, 312 NLRB 589, 146 LRRM 1037 (2000) in finding that a 28% inaccuracy rate that was later corrected to a 9% inaccuracy rate was insufficient to set aside an election where there was no evidence or contention that the address inaccuracies on the *Excelsior* list were intentionally or negligently misrepresented). *But see* Merchants Transfer Co., 330 NLRB 1165, 170 LRRM 1457 (2000) (setting aside election where employer was grossly negligent in providing union with out-of-date address list, employer admitted that it knew that a significant number of employee addresses were incorrect, employer no longer mailed W-2 forms to its employees due to problems with its list of their addresses, and employer did not direct anyone to call employees using supervisors' updated telephone lists to verify the accuracy of address list).

[70]J.P. Phillips, Inc., 336 NLRB 1279, 169 LRRM 1293 (2001) (quoting Special Citizens Futures Unlimited, 331 NLRB 160, 164 LRRM 1195 (2000)).

5. *Raffles [New Topic]*

The Board has announced a "bright-line" rule that bans any employer-sponsored (or union-sponsored) raffle conducted within 24 hours prior to the beginning of the polling period of a representation election.[71] In previous cases, the Board conducted a case-by-case analysis to determine if a specific raffle interfered with a representation election given the specific circumstances involved in the case and developed a multifactor test that examined issues such as whether the raffle was used to propagandize about union dues, whether the raffle occurred in conjunction with any electioneering at or near the polls, whether the raffle or prize was contingent on how an employee voted or on the outcome of the election, and whether the value of the prize was so substantial as to induce a vote in favor of the sponsoring party.[72] This analysis, however, led to inconsistency in the Board's raffle decisions.

Recognizing these inconsistencies, the "confusing" nature of the varying cases, that the "elaborate exercise in line drawing" involved in the Board's previous raffle cases created time-consuming litigation, divided Board decisions, confusing and inconsistent results, and unwarranted delays in completion of representation proceedings, the Board overruled its previous line of election-day raffle cases and announced a bright-line test for determining whether a raffle during an election period is objectionable conduct.[73] The Board held that raffles will now be prohibited if "(1) eligibility to participate in the raffle or win prizes is in any way tied to voting in the election or being at the election site on election day or (2) the raffle is conducted at any time during a period beginning 24 hours before the scheduled opening of the polls and ending with the closing of the polls."[74] "Conducting a raffle" was defined by the Board to include "(1) announcing a raffle; (2) distributing raffle tickets; (3) identify-

---

[71]Atlantic Limousine, Inc., 331 NLRB 1025, 165 LRRM 1001 (2000).

[72]*See e.g.*, Sony Corp. of Am., 313 NLRB 420, 145 LRRM 1242 (1993); Hollywood Plastics, Inc., 177 NLRB 678, 71 LRRM 1397 (1969); Buzza-Cardozo, 177 NLRB 589, 71 LRRM 1390 (1969); Sony Corp. of Am., 313 NLRB 420, 145 LRRM 1242 (1993).

[73]*Atlantic Limousine, supra* note 71; Beverly Enterprises-Tenn. dba Allenbrooke Healthcare Ctr., 331 NLRB 1065, 165 LRRM 1370 (2000).

[74]*Atlantic Limousine, supra* note 71, at 1033.

ing the raffle winners; and (4) awarding the raffle prizes."[75] If a raffle is shown to have been conducted during the proscribed period, the election will be set aside.

Even if a raffle does not fall within either of the two prongs expressly identified by the Board in *Atlantic Limousine*, the Board still will scrutinize an objected-to raffle, and set aside an election, if the raffle "involve[s] promises or grants of benefit that would improperly affect employee free choice; or . . . allow[s] the employer to identify employees who might or might not be sympathetic, and thus to learn where to direct additional pressure or campaign efforts."[76]

6. *Videotaping [New Topic]*

The Board also clarified its position regarding employer requests for employees to appear in election campaign video materials. In *Allegheny Ludlum Corp.*,[77] a case on remand from the D.C. Circuit, the Board held that an employer, unlike unions, cannot lawfully solicit employees on an individual basis to appear in campaign video presentations, because such requests would unlawfully pressure employees to make an observable choice for or against union representation. Instead, the Board held that an employer may lawfully solicit employees to appear in a campaign video only if (1) solicitation is in the form of a general announcement that discloses the purpose of the filming; (2) assurances are given that participation is voluntary; (3) participation will not result in rewards and benefits; (4) nonparticipation will not result in reprisals; (5) employees are not pressured into making a decision in the presence of a supervisor; (6) the employer has not engaged in serious or pervasive unfair labor practices connected with the organizing campaign; and (7) the employer's solicitation of consent does not exceed legitimate video participation purposes.

---

[75] *Id. See also* Ryder Student Transp. Serv., 332 NLRB 1590, 166 LRRM 1073 (2000) (employer's announcement shortly before an election that it would raffle off two trips to Disney World or $1,000 in cash if 1,450 employees cast ballots in election violated *Atlantic Limousine* rule); *Beverly Enterprises-Tenn. dba Allenbrooke Healthcare Ctr., supra* note 73 (employer violated both prongs of *Atlantic Limousine* rule).

[76] 331 NLRB 1025, 165 LRRM 1001 (2001). *See also* BFI Waste Sys., 334 NLRB 934, 174 LRRM 1118 (2001).

[77] 333 NLRB 734, 166 LRRM 1353 (2001), *enforced*, 301 F.3d 167, 170 LRRM 2923 (3d Cir. 2002).

The Board concluded by clarifying its holding in *Sony Corp. of America*[78] that an employer does not have to have employees' explicit consent before including their images when (1) the video in question does not represent employee views regarding union representation; (2) employees were not misled about the uses of their images at the time of filming; (3) the video contains a predominant disclaimer stating that it is not intended to reflect the views of the employees appearing in it; and (4) nothing in the video contradicts this disclaimer.[79]

If an employer photographs and/or videotapes employees without justification and while the employees are engaged in protected concerted activity such as handbilling, the employer may be found to have committed unlawful surveillance.[80] For example, in *Robert Orr-Sysco Food Services*,[81] the Board found that the positioning of a surveillance camera in order to videotape employee handbilling activities was objectionable. However, "an employer has the right to

---

[78]313 NLRB 420, 145 LRRM 1242 (1993).

[79]*Allegheny Ludlum Corp.*, *supra* note 77, 333 NLRB at 745, 166 LRRM at 1365, discussing Sony Corp. of Am., 313 NLRB 420, 145 LRRM 1242 (1993).

[80]Community Action Comm'n of Fayette County, Inc., 338 NLRB No. 79, 173 LRRM 1588 (2002); Amber Foods, Inc., 338 NLRB 712 (2002); Cogburn Healthcare Ctr., 335 NLRB 1397, 171 LRRM 1021 (2001). *See also* Timken Co. v. NLRB, 29 Fed. Appx. 266, 171 LRRM 3215 (6th Cir. 2002) (employer committed unlawful surveillance where it did not provide legitimate justification for "indiscriminately" videotaping employees engaged in handbilling); *but see* Alamo Rent-A-Car, Inc., 338 NLRB 275, 171 LRRM 1383 (2002) (employer showed legitimate reason for videotaping employees engaging in handbilling where videotaping was conducted briefly and solely in response to reports that employees were blocking cars).

[81]334 NLRB 977 (2001). *See also* Snap-On Tools, Inc., 342 NLRB No. 2, 175 LRRM 1124 (2004) (employer violated Act by changing its normal practice of panning parking lots with surveillance camera to pointing the camera at the plant gate where employees were handbilling); Timken Co. v. NLRB, 29 Fed. Appx. 266, 171 LRRM 3215 (6th Cir. 2002) (employer committed unlawful surveillance where it did not provide a legitimate justification for "indiscriminately" videotaping employees engaged in handbilling; *but see Alamo Rent-A-Car, supra* note 80 (employer showed legitimate reason for videotaping employees engaging in handbilling where videotaping was conducted briefly and solely in response to reports that employees were blocking cars).

maintain security measures necessary to the furtherance of legitimate business interests during the course of union activity."[82]

7. *Pro-Union Conduct by a Supervisor [New Topic]*

In *Harborside Healthcare, Inc.*,[83] a divided Board, on remand from the Sixth Circuit, set forth the standard for setting aside an election based on a supervisor's pro-union conduct.

The majority disavowed language in *Pacific Physician Services*,[84] which had required supervisory pro-union conduct to involve an explicit threat of reprisal or promise of benefits to invalidate an election, and restated earlier precedent that such conduct warrants a new election if it (1) reasonably tended to coerce or interfere with an employee's free choice in an election, considering the nature and degree of a supervisory authority and the nature, extent, and context of the conduct and (2) materially affected the outcome of the election, based on factors such as margin of victory, whether the conduct was widespread or isolated, timing of the conduct, extent to which the conduct became known, and the lingering effect of the conduct. The majority said the Board may take into account the antiunion statements of higher company officials to the extent to which they may disavow coercive pro-union conduct of supervisors.[85]

The majority found the first prong of the restated legal standard—whether the conduct reasonably tended to coerce or interfere with employee free choice—was satisfied, where the supervisor

---

[82]National Steel & Shipbuilding Co., 324 NLRB 499, 156 LRRM 1146 (1997), *enforced,* 156 F.3d 1268 (D.C. Cir. 1998) (employer violated Act by using video cameras and other image or sound capturing devices to monitor and/or record employees engaged in protected activity). *See also* Washington Fruit & Produce Co., 343 NLRB No. 125, 176 LRRM 1362 (2004) (following the principles set forth in *National Steel & Shipbuilding Co.,* Board found employer's concerns with trespassing and safety to be reasonable and thus lawful); *but see* Trailmobile Trailer, LLC, 343 NLRB No. 17, 176 LRRM 1433 (2004) (vandalism that occurred eight months before the employer installed security cameras was not motivation for their installation; a camera was also installed to view the entrance to the facility and no evidence was submitted that employer had experienced vandalism there).

[83]343 NLRB No. 100, 176 LRRM 1113 (2004).

[84]313 NLRB 1176, 146 LRRM 1049 (1994).

[85]*Pacific Physician, supra* note 83, 176 LRRM at 1118.

(1) had significant authority over unit employees, including the ability to both reward or retaliate against them, and (2) repeatedly threatened employees that they would lose their jobs if the union lost the election, made numerous repeated references to "job security" and her need to "count on" employees to vote for the union, told an employee she "had to" attend union meetings, solicited union cards from a dozen employees, repeatedly pressured at least one employee to wear a union pin, badgered an employee about voting for the union, and solicited signatures on union petition from at least three or four employees.[86]

The majority found the second prong of the Board's restated legal standard—whether the conduct materially affected the election outcome—was satisfied where (1) the union's margin of victory was relatively small and the supervisor's conduct undoubtedly affected a critical number of employees relative to this margin, (2) the supervisor threatened job loss and badgered employees within two weeks before the election, (3) the effect of the supervisor's threats and pro-union solicitation would tend to linger, and (4) the employer's antiunion campaign did not mitigate the coercive impact of the supervisor's conduct.[87]

The majority overruled *Millsboro Nursing*,[88] which had held that supervisory solicitation of union authorization cards is not objectionable conduct unless there is potential reprisal, punishment, or intimidation, and held that, absent mitigating circumstances, solicitation of cards by supervisors has an inherent tendency to interfere with an employee's freedom to choose to sign a card or not, even if an employer or union believed the individual is not a supervisor, even if unions may be deprived of solicitors who might be "natural leaders," and even if the conduct occurs outside of the critical period, since the impact of a supervisor's solicitation would ordinarily continue to be felt during the critical period.[89]

The majority also overruled *B.J. Titan Service Co.*[90] to the extent it held that a pro-union supervisor's statement linking job security to support of a union is never objectionable and held that whether such statements are coercive will depend on the circumstances.[91]

---

[86]*Id.*, 176 LRRM at 1118–121.
[87]*Id.*, 176 LRRM at 1121–122.
[88]327 NLRB 879, 880, 160 LRRM 1209 (1999).
[89]*Id.* at 880, 160 LRRM 1209.
[90]296 NLRB 668, 132 LRRM 1386 (1989).
[91]*Pacific Physician, supra* note 89, 176 LRRM at 1122 n.24.

C. Union Conduct

2. *Specific Promises and Grants of Benefits*

In *DLC Corp. dba FleetBoston Pavilion,*[92] the Board reaffirmed its decision in *Smith Co.,*[93] in which it had held that

> [e]mployees are generally able to understand that a union cannot obtain benefits automatically by winning an election but must seek to achieve them through collective bargaining. Union promises . . . are easily recognized by employees to be dependent on contingencies beyond the Union's control and do not carry with them the same degree of finality as if uttered by an employer who has it within his power to implement promises or benefits.[94]

Because the union in *DLC Corp.* had promised to negotiate a contract that based entitlement to work on the amount of time the employee had worked for the employer, and because it was clear the union did not have exclusive control over hiring, staffing, and referrals, the union's promise did not improperly affect the election.[95] The Board decision in *DLC* noted that there is the "limited exception to this general rule" where the union actually controls the benefits.[96] But, even where the promised benefits are within a union's power to grant, the union's conduct is not objectionable where the benefits are not conditioned on support for the union. In *Allen's Electric Co.,*[97] the Board held that the union's preelection promise to reimburse voters for wages actually lost due to time taken off work to vote did not amount to objectionable conduct where the offer was limited to voters who actually missed work hours because of the election and the offer was not conditioned on support for the union.[98] Additionally, in *NLRB v. Sliman's Sales & Service, Inc.,*[99] the Sixth Circuit found that a union's promise to distribute free hats, T-shirts, and stickers to all eligible voters if it won an election was not objectionable since the items were of only limited value and no gifts were actually distributed prior to the secret ballot election, leaving the union with no way to determine who had voted for it.[100]

---

[92] 333 NLRB 655, 166 LRRM 1367 (2001).
[93] 192 NLRB 1098, 78 LRRM 1266 (1971).
[94] *DLC Corp. dba FleetBoston Pavilion, supra* note 92 at 655.
[95] *Id.*
[96] *See* Alyeska Pipeline Serv. Co., 261 NLRB 125, 110 LRRM 1011 (1982).
[97] 340 NLRB No. 119, 173 LRRM 1425 (2003).
[98] *Id.*, slip op. at 2, 173 LRRM at 1427.
[99] 75 Fed. Appx. 457, 173 LRRM 2416 (6th Cir. 2003).
[100] *Id.* at 461–64.

The Board and the courts continue to disagree in those situations where the union actually grants benefits prior to an election. In *Comcast Cablevision—Taylor v. NLRB*,[101] the Sixth Circuit refused to enforce the Board's bargaining order where the union made a preelection offer to employees of a free weekend trip to Chicago for a meeting with union officials. The court deemed the trip, consisting of transportation and one night's lodging, together with the union meeting, sufficiently valuable to influence voters. A similar result was reached by the D.C. Circuit in *Freund Baking Co. v. NLRB*.[102] In that case, the court held that a union's sponsorship of a lawsuit against an employer on behalf of eligible voters seeking recovery of alleged unpaid overtime violated the Board's rule against providing benefits to voters in the critical period before a representation election.

More recently, the Seventh Circuit refused to enforce a Board decision overruling an employer's election objection in *NLRB v. River City Elevator Co., Inc.*[103] In that case, the court disagreed with the Board's conclusion that a union's preelection offer to furnish mechanic's cards to all employees regardless of whether they had completed the requisite course work or exams to obtain the mechanic's card was not objectionable conduct. The court deemed the mechanic's cards sufficiently valuable to influence voters since a mechanic's card would give the employees access to more lucrative jobs at a far lesser cost.

In *Maremont Corp. v. NLRB*,[104] however, the Sixth Circuit enforced the Board's bargaining order, holding that the union did not unlawfully influence employees to sign a "vote yes" petition by giving out T-shirts. The court relied on the testimony of the employees that they were not obligated to sign the petitions to receive the T-shirts. In so holding, the court followed its earlier precedent that a union may distribute inexpensive campaign propaganda, such as T-shirts, at a union meeting.[105]

---

[101] 232 F.3d 490, 165 LRRM 2803 (6th Cir. 2000).

[102] 165 F.3d 928, 160 LRRM 2299 (D.C. Cir. 1999).

[103] 289 F.3d 1029, 170 LRRM 2001 (7th Cir. 2002).

[104] 177 F.3d 573, 161 LRRM 2338 (6th Cir. 1999).

[105] *Id.*, citing NLRB v. Dickinson Press, Inc., 153 F.3d 282, 158 LRRM 2832 (6th Cir. 1998).

3. *Waiver of Initiation Fees*

In assessing whether a promise by a union during an election campaign to either waive or reduce its initiation fees or dues is permissible under *NLRB v. Savair Manufacturing Co.*,[106] the crucial distinction continues to be whether the waiver offer was made across-the-board to all employees regardless of preelection union support, a permissible promise, or whether the waiver offer was made only to those employees who manifested preelection union support or who voted for the union, an impermissible promise. Thus, an across-the-board waiver offer to all employees is not permissible when the offer is conditioned on all employees signing authorization cards before a certain date.[107] Conversely, preelection offers to waive initiation fees are lawful where they apply to all employees, and "not simply those who signed a union authorization card before the election."[108]

Further, even in cases where the union promises to waive the initiation fee only for those who support it, the employer must still show that the offer was in fact disseminated to enough voters to have affected the outcome of the election. In *Erie Brush & Manufacturing Corp.*,[109] the Board granted summary judgment in favor of the union where the union won an election by a wide margin and the employer failed to show that the union's preelection offer to waive initiation fees for supporters was disseminated to a sufficient number of employees to have affected the outcome of the election.[110] The Board found that, as in cases involving an employer's promise of benefits, "dissemination is relevant and may not be presumed in cases involving a union's promise to waive initiation fees."[111]

Where an impermissible promise to waive initiation fees is later corrected by a permissible one, a substantial material issue of fact is raised, necessitating a hearing.[112] The court found that the Board erred in certifying the union after only conducting interviews with

---

[106]414 U.S. 270, 84 LRRM 2929 (1973).
[107]Gulf Caribe Maritime, Inc., 330 NLRB 766, 170 LRRM 1287 (2000).
[108]U-Haul Co. of Nev., Inc., 341 NLRB No. 26, 174 LRRM 1111(2004).
[109]340 NLRB No. 169, 174 LRRM 1047 (2003).
[110]*Id.*
[111]*Id.*
[112]NLRB v. Superior of Mo., Inc., 233 F.3d 547, 165 LRRM 2785 (8th Cir. 2000).

several employees and concluding that even if the first impermissible statement was made by the union's organizer, it was effectively corrected before the election. Raising the possibility that not all employees who heard the improper offer were present to hear the clarification, the court found that the employer's evidence raised factual issues that required the Board to hold a hearing. After the hearing, the Board found that the union permissibly promised to waive its initiation fees for all employees, and any misperception of an impermissible promise was corrected.[113]

4. *Other Union Conduct*

a. Interrogation

Courts continue to recognize that unions may lawfully poll eligible voters regarding their union sympathies, even though employer polls are generally unlawful.[114] However, an employer may successfully challenge such polling if the employer can demonstrate that the union's polling activities were, in fact, coercive.[115] In *Gormac Custom Manufacturing Inc.*,[116] the Sixth Circuit held that the Board must conduct an evidentiary hearing to determine the propriety of union polling activities where prima facie evidence of coercion is presented.

c. Videotaping [New Topic]

Photographing or videotaping of employees by unions during the preelection period generally will not constitute grounds for set-

---

[113]Superior of Mo., Inc., 338 NLRB 570, 171 LRRM 1354 (2002), *enforced,* 351 F.3d 805 (8th Cir. 2003). *See also* Hollingsworth Mgmt. Servs., 342 NLRB No. 50, 176 LRRM 1059 (2004) (union effectively corrected any objectionable fee waiver offer by stating on campaign flyers and authorization cards that offer was available to all employees regardless of union support).

[114]NLRB v. Media Gen. Operations, Inc., 360 F.3d 434, 174 LRRM 2481 (4th Cir. 2004) (union's distribution and circulation of "vote yes" petitions with encouragement that union wanted "everyone to sign this" did not interfere with employees' free choice in election); Keeler Die Cast v. NLRB, 185 F.3d 535, 162 LRRM 2028 (6th Cir. 1999) (finding preelection polling by union not inherently coercive), *cert. denied,* 529 U.S. 1018 (2000); Maremont Corp. v. NLRB, 177 F.3d 573, 161 LRRM 2338 (6th Cir. 1999) (union's circulation of "vote yes" petition during preelection period not per se objectionable conduct).

[115]NLRB v. Gormac Custom Mfg., Inc., 190 F.3d 742, 162 LRRM 2156 (6th Cir. 1999). *See also Keeler Die Cast, supra* note 114, 185 F.3d at 539, 162 LRRM at 2030.

[116]190 F.3d at 750–51, 162 LRRM at 2161–62.

ting aside the results of a representation election unless accompanied by threats or other coercive conduct. The Board overruled its decision in *Pepsi-Cola Bottling Co.*[117] and held that a union's photographing or videotaping of employees engaging in protected election campaign activities, absent evidence of any express or implied threats or other coercion, does not interfere with employee free choice.[118] The Fourth Circuit has since agreed with the Board's new position.[119]

In order to establish that a union is engaged in objectionable conduct by photographing or videotaping employees who come to the employer's premises to vote in an election, the employer must ordinarily present evidence that an agent of the union took photographs of voters and that unit employees were aware that photos were being taken. For example, in *Chrill Care, Inc.*,[120] the Board overruled the employer's objection that the union had unlawfully photographed voters where the evidence was "vague and contradictory" and there was no credible evidence that either photographs were taken of voters or that unit employees were aware of any photography.[121] For similar reasons, the Board also rejected the employer's objection regarding union "note taking or recording of voter's names," noting that "the Board generally does not find such list making coercive in the absence of evidence that employees knew their names were being recorded."[122]

The Board has found, however, that a union violated Section 8(b)(1)(A) by videotaping replacement employees, their vehicles, and their license plates as they entered and exited the employer's facility.[123] The Board noted that while there may be legitimate reasons for the use of video cameras by unions at picket lines, the union failed to provide any valid reason for recording the license plate of each car entering and exiting the plant at shift change times.[124] Simi-

[117]289 NLRB 736, 128 LRRM 1275 (1988).

[118]Randell Warehouse of Ariz., Inc., 328 NLRB 1034, 161 LRRM 1265 (1999), *enforcement denied*, 252 F.3d 445, 167 LRRM 2340 (D.C. Cir. 2001).

[119]Overnite Transp. Co. v. NLRB, 294 F.3d 615, 170 LRRM 2362 (4th Cir. 2002).

[120]340 NLRB No. 123, 174 LRRM 1237 (2003).

[121]*Id.*

[122]*Id.*

[123]Teamsters Local 890, 335 NLRB 686, 168 LRRM 1347 (2001).

[124]*Id.*

larly, in *Metropolitan Regional Council of Philadelphia & Vicinity*,[125] the Board found that the union violated the Act when the union's pickets patrolled the employer's reserve gate, videotaped employees as they arrived for work and made threatening remarks while doing so. The Board instructed that a finding of a violation turns not on evidence that a particular employee was actually restrained or coerced, but whether the union's conduct would have a reasonable tendency to restrain or coerce employees. Thus, when videotaping of employees by union pickets takes place in conjunction with other actions indicating that a union might react adversely to employees who cross a picket line, the Board will find a violation of Section 8(b)(1)(A).[126]

d. Pro-Union Conduct by a Supervisor [New Topic] (See discussion at §II.B.7.)

D. Third-Party Conduct

The Board continues to hold that the conduct of pro-union employees who are not agents of the union is judged under a third-party standard, namely, that the employer must establish that the conduct "during the election was so aggravated as to create a general atmosphere of fear and reprisal rendering a fair election impossible."[127] In *Accubilt, Inc.*,[128] pro-union employees who were not agents of the union told a co-worker that if he "wanted to keep his new car looking the way it did, he needed to vote yes in the election."[129] Other nonagent employees told the same co-worker "they were 'going to get [him] back'" if he voted against the union. The Board held that because the threats "were directed only to him and were not disseminated,"[130] they did not create a general atmosphere of fear and re-

---

[125]335 NLRB 814, 169 LRRM 1498 (2001), *enforced*, 50 Fed. Appx. 88, 171 LRRM 2320 (3d Cir. 2002).

[126]*Id.*

[127]Cal-West Periodicals, Inc., 330 NLRB 599, 600, 163 LRRM 1155 (2000). *See also* Corner Furniture Discount Ctr., Inc., 339 NLRB No. 146, 173 LRRM 1287 (2003) (finding union supporter statement to co-workers that "they" will know who voted against union is not coercive under third-party conduct standard); Robert Orr-Sysco Food Serv., 338 NLRB 614, 171 LRRM 1457 (2002) (nonagent threats by union supporters to employees and their property were sufficient to set aside close election).

[128]340 NLRB No. 161, 173 LRRM 1545 (2003).

[129]*Id.*

[130]*Id.*, 173 LRRM at 1547.

prisal. Similarly, the Board found no reason to overturn an election in *Lamar Advertising of Janesville*,[131] where nonagent employees told a co-worker they would "kick his ass" if he did not vote for the union. The Board stated that such language, "without more, is mere bravado that is unlikely to intimidate the listener" and concluded, "under all the circumstances," the record did not show that "a reasonable employee in [the coworker's] position would have been put in fear by the threat.[132]

In *Cross Pointe Paper Corp.*,[133] the Board ruled that a rumor concerning an ethnic slur by a high-ranking management official that circulated among the workforce on the day of the election did not create an atmosphere of fear or confusion sufficient to render a fair election impossible. Even though the rumor was used by some employees to urge fellow employees to vote for the union, the source of the rumor was not attributable to the union, the rumored slur did not include a threat of reprisals against the ethnic group at issue if the group voted for the union, and the management official at issue denied making the statement. Moreover, ethnic pride was not a central issue to the election. The Board applied its third-party analysis and concluded that, even if the alleged ethnic slur had been uttered, it was not clear "that the rumor was either widespread enough or believable enough to have made a fair or free election impossible."[134]

In *Corner Furniture Discount Center, Inc.*,[135] the Board refused to overturn an election after a nonagent employee told co-workers that their election votes were not secret. The Board held that "even if we assume . . . that the statements constituted implicit threats of reprisal,"[136] they did not "tend to create a general atmosphere of fear and reprisal rendering a free election impossible."[137]

---

[131]340 NLRB No. 114, 173 LRRM 1377 (2003).

[132]*Id. See also* Lamar Advertising of Janesville, 341 NLRB No. 96, 175 LRRM 1384 (2004) (denying respondent's request for reconsideration of the Board's decision, made in light of comments by two of the four Board members in *Accubilt, Inc.*, that they "would set aside an election in circumstances where the 'critical period' misconduct of the third party affected a determinative number of voters, even if that conduct did not 'create a general atmosphere of fear and reprisal'").

[133]330 NLRB 658, 169 LRRM 1518 (2000).

[134]*Id.*

[135]339 NLRB 1122, 173 LRRM 1287 (2003).

[136]*Id.*, 173 LRRM at 1288.

[137]*Id.* at 1287.

Certain courts have continued to hold that the Board must conduct an evidentiary hearing to resolve material issues of fact regarding the agency status of individuals alleged to have interfered with Board-supervised elections where the employer provides prima facie evidence of coercion in the course of the union's polling activities. For example, in *AOTOP, LLC v. NLRB*,[138] the court noted that

> [i]n view of the factual nature of [determining whether a union (or employer) is responsible for the misconduct of its supporters], an evidentiary hearing ordinarily will be required in order to resolve a dispute about the relationship between a person alleged to have interfered with a Board-supervised election and one of the parties to that election.[139]

Agreeing with the reasoning of the D.C. Circuit, the Third Circuit, in *Trimm Associates, Inc. v. NLRB*,[140] found that the Board abused its discretion by not granting the employer's request for an evidentiary hearing "to resolve material issues of fact regarding the agency status"[141] of the accused individual where the employer made a "nonconclusory proffer of evidence … regarding specific events and specific people."[142] Moreover, the court went on to note that where the agency determination could be dispositive of the case due to either the Board's per se rule against prolonged conversations with voters in the polling area under *Milchem*[143] or due to the closeness of the election results, the Board has "a duty to take particular care in its evaluation of the company's objections."[144]

In *NLRB v. V&S Shuler Engineering, Inc.*,[145] the Sixth Circuit enforced a Board bargaining order even though the Board did not hold an evidentiary hearing concerning the employer's election objections. One of those objections concerned statements by a known union supporter that ballot procedures were not secret. The supporter made the statement to a union election observer in the presence of three other voters. Because the supporter was found not to be a union agent, the Board applied its third-party conduct standard

[138]331 F.3d 100, 172 LRRM 2691 (D.C. Cir. 2003).
[139]*Id* at 104.
[140]351 F.3d 99, 173 LRRM 2801 (3d Cir. 2003).
[141]*Id.* at 106.
[142]*Id.* at 106–07, 173 LRRM at 2806–07
[143]Milchem, Inc., 170 NLRB 362, 67 LRRM 1395 (1968).
[144]*Trimm Assocs., supra* note 140, 351 F.3d at 107.
[145]309 F.3d 362, 171 LRRM 2104 (6th Cir. 2002).

and held that the statement did not create an atmosphere of fear and reprisal rendering a fair election impossible. Finding that the employer failed to raise substantial issues sufficient to warrant a hearing—in part because the union's large margin of victory precluded a showing that the conduct materially affected the election results—the Sixth Circuit found that the Board did not err by denying the employer's objections without an evidentiary hearing.

On the other hand, the Eleventh Circuit denied enforcement of a Board bargaining order because of objectionable third-party conduct in *Associated Rubber Co. v. NLRB.*[146] In that case, a union supporter told an employee who refused to accept union literature that he would "pay for it the next day."[147] A few days later, while both employees were working a dangerous piece of equipment, the union supporter accelerated the equipment's output rate, making the other employee's job more difficult and even dangerous. The Board did not find the risk of injury to be severe, and also noted that other employees laughed off the incident.[148] The Eleventh Circuit disagreed with the Board's assessment, however, and found that the incident—which occurred just three days before the election—was both coercive and sufficiently material to affect the union's narrow three-vote victory margin. Accordingly, it denied enforcement of the Board's bargaining order.

More recently, in *Hollingsworth Management Service,*[149] the Board ordered that an election be set aside due to the electioneering of three nonagent union supporters. In so deciding, the Board stated that the standard for "evaluating electioneering by nonparties . . . is 'whether the conduct at issue so substantially impaired the employees' exercise of free choice as to require that the election be set aside.'"[150] In that case, three nonparty union supporters persistently approached employees in line to vote, asked them how they intended

---

[146]296 F.3d 1055, 170 LRRM 2385 (11th Cir. 2002).

[147]*Id.* at 1058.

[148]*Id.* at 1059.

[149]342 NLRB No. 50, 176 LRRM 1059 (2004).

[150]*Id.*, slip op. at 3 (quoting Rheem Mfg. Co., 309 NLRB 459, 463 (1992)); *see also* Tyson Fresh Meats, Inc., 343 NLRB No. 129, 176 LRRM 1202 (2004) (reversing hearing officer's recommendation and quoting *Hollingsworth Management Service* rule that the proper standard for determining objectionable electioneering by a third party is "'whether the conduct at issue so substantially impaired the employees' exercise of free choice as to require that the election be set aside'").

to vote, exhorted the employees to vote for the union over extended conversations, and physically manhandled at least two employees, one of them in front of as many as 30 voters.[151] Under these circumstances the Board concluded that the nonparty electioneering activities "so substantially impaired the employees' exercise of free choice as to require that the election be set aside."[152]

In *Saint-Gobain Abrasives, Inc.*,[153] the Board found the statements of a congressman urging employees to vote for the union were not objectionable.

E. Violence and Threats

An employee's free and uncoerced choice in an election may be interfered with by actions that create an impression that an employer is not in control of its own facilities and that it is not capable of standing up to the union. Following the rationale of the Board in *Phillips Chrysler Plymouth, Inc.*,[154] the D.C. Circuit in *North of Market Senior Services Inc. v. NLRB*[155] refused to validate an election where there was a direct challenge by the union on the day of the election of the employer's assertion of its property rights, resulting in an impression that it was helpless to control the situation. The union officials walked around the facility and into patient examination rooms without the employer's permission, and repeatedly disagreed with the employer's executive director as to when employees were entitled to vote. The court held that this behavior had the purported imprimatur of the Board because the Board agent conducting the election had delegated to union officials the task of telling employees when to vote. As a result, the court remanded the case to the Board to, at a minimum, conduct a hearing on the employer's objections.

The Board in *Cal-West Periodicals, Inc.*[156] further distinguished between preelection threats by a party to engage in violence and such threats by employees who are not agents of either party, finding that "employees reasonably have a greater concern about threats emanating from the union that may become their exclusive repre-

---

[151]*Hollingsworth Mgmt. Serv., supra* note 149.
[152]*Id.*
[153]337 NLRB 82, 169 LRRM 1116 (2001).
[154]304 NLRB 16, 138 LRRM 1025 (1991)
[155]204 F.3d 1163, 163 LRRM 2711 (D.C. Cir. 2000).
[156]330 NLRB 599, 163 LRRM 1155 (2000).

sentative than they would have from threats uttered by a single nonagent individual." Accordingly, the Board refused to set aside the election. In *Robert Orr-Sysco Food Services,, LLC*,[157] however, a Board majority distinguished *Cal-West* and concluded that where union supporters made multiple threats of picket-line violence, threatened physical retaliation for voting against the union, and threatened deportation for voting against the union, a close election should be set aside and rerun. In another case, the Fourth Circuit in *NLRB v. Kentucky Tennessee Clay Co.*[158] held that pro-union employees were union agents, even though they were never recognized as part of an in-plant committee. The court found that their threats that co-workers who did not vote for the union would lose their jobs warranted reversing the Board and setting aside the election. The court stated that their threats could be imputed to the union because the union organizer took no steps to inform co-workers that the two employees were not union agents. It then found the Board erred in finding no basis to set aside the election where the election was close and the two employees threatened several employees.

The Seventh Circuit held that pro-union lobbying by an employee who later appeared at the election as a union observer did not constitute intimidation in *NLRB v. Americold Logistics*.[159] The court held that even though the employee in question had been "pushy" in lobbying co-workers to vote for the union, and even though some co-workers felt "intimidated and bothered" by his enthusiastic pro-union actions, those actions did not "create such an atmosphere of fear and reprisal that his fellow workers would have been rendered incapable of voting in a rational, uncoerced manner." Therefore, absent any evidence of "bullying" by the co-worker, the court ruled that there were insufficient grounds for invalidating the election or for ordering a hearing into the matter.

In *Accubilt, Inc.*,[160] the Board held that "four alleged threats . . . known to no more than three employees in a unit of over 150, did not create a general atmosphere of fear and reprisal."

---

[157]338 NLRB 614, 171 LRRM 1457 (2002).
[158]295 F.3d 436, 170 LRRM 2522 (4th Cir. 2002).
[159]214 F.3d 935, 164 LRRM 2636 (7th Cir. 2000).
[160]340 NLRB No. 161, 173 LRRM 1545 (2003).

The Board set aside an election in *Cedars-Sinai Medical Center*[161] because two antiunion bargaining unit employees received anonymous telephonic threats placed from a union office and such threats were discussed with a determinative number of employees in the voting unit. The Board held that the threats were no less "threatening" because they were made anonymously as opposed to directly; rather, the anonymous threats were potentially even more disturbing than direct threats because the callers had personal information about the threatened employees, and therefore the target employees could not protect themselves against individuals whose identities they did not know.

III. REMEDIES

A party to an election is generally estopped from profiting from its own misconduct.[162] Where a party to an election causes an employee to miss the opportunity to vote, however, such action will support an objection to the election by the other party "if the employee's vote is determinative . . . and the employee was disenfranchised through no fault of his own."[163] This disenfranchisement test typically applies to situations in which some, but not all, employees are alleged to have been denied the chance to vote.[164]

The Board in *Baker Victory Services, Inc.*[165] changed the standard to be used for determining whether an election should be set aside because of severe weather conditions on the day of the election. The new standard is whether the conditions "reasonably denied eligible voters an adequate opportunity to vote and a determinative number did not vote."[166] The Board's decision abandoned the test used by the plurality in *Glass Depot, Inc.*,[167] namely, whether a "representative

[161]342 NLRB No. 58, 175 LRRM 1221 (2004).

[162]*See* Elizabethtown Gas v. NLRB, 212 F.3d 257, 164 LRRM 2257 (4th Cir. 2000).

[163]Cast N. Am. Trucking, Ltd. v. NLRB, 207 F.3d 994, 163 LRRM 2995 (7th Cir. 2000), citing Sahuaro Petroleum & Asphalt Co., 306 NLRB 586, 139 LRRM 1316 (1992).

[164]NLRB v. City Wide Insulation of Madison, 370 F.3d 654, 658 (7th Cir. 2004).

[165]331 NLRB 1068, 165 LRRM 1057 (2000).

[166]*Id.* at 1068.

[167]318 NLRB 766, 150 LRRM 1055 (1995).

complement" of employees voted, and adopted the position taken by the dissent in *Glass Depot* and by the Board's decision in *V.I.P. Limousine, Inc.*[168]

The Board in *Miller Industries Towing Equipment, Inc.*, denied a request by the union for special notice and access remedies for a rerun election but ordered a *Lufkin Rule* notice.[169]

[168]274 NLRB 641, 118 LRRM 1399 (1985).
[169]342 NLRB No. 112 fn.4, 176 LRRM 1103 (2004).

CHAPTER 10

REPRESENTATION PROCEEDINGS AND ELECTIONS

I. QUESTIONS CONCERNING REPRESENTATION

A. Petitions by Labor Organizations and Employees

1. Showing of Interest

It is the Board's established policy not to require a current showing of interest when an election is set aside because of a meritorious objection. In *Freund Baking Co.,*[1] the Board rejected the argument that the showing of interest was stale when it ordered a second election.

When the unit that is found appropriate differs from that of the petitioned-for unit, the union is to be given reasonable time to procure additional showing of interest.[2]

[1]330 NLRB 17, 167 LRRM 1110 (1999); *see also* River City Elevator Co., 339 NLRB 616, 172 LRRM 1409 (2003) (sustaining employer's objection and ordering second election without requiring new showing of interest).

[2]Alamo Rent-A-Car, 330 NLRB 897, 163 LRRM 1289 (2000). *See also* Brown Transp. Corp., 296 NLRB 1213, 132 LRRM 1219 (1989); Casale Indus., 311 NLRB 951, 143 LRRM 1291 (1993).

In *Perdue Farms,*[3] the Board restated its policy that evidence that a showing of interest was obtained by fraud or duress should be submitted to the regional director.

The Board has indicated that fraud or duress in obtaining the showing of interest may also be considered as objectionable conduct.[4]

In *Dejana Industries,*[5] the Board characterized as a "bright-line rule" its policy of excluding all cards directly solicited by a supervisor.

B. Petitions by Employers

2. *History Under the Taft-Hartley Act*

a. Unrecognized Unions

The Board holds that a mere request for a Section 8(f) agreement does not amount to a present demand for recognition. In *Western Pipeline, Inc.,*[6] the Board further concluded that an unsubstantiated claim that the employer was an alter ego of the signatory contractor and obligated to sign the contract was nothing more than a request to sign a Section 8(f) agreement and therefore did not raise a question concerning representation. Similarly, a union's request for neutrality and a card check did not constitute a demand for recognition.[7]

Informational picketing under the second proviso to Section 8(b)(7)(c) that truthfully advises the public that an employer does not have a contract with the union is not a claim for recognition within the meaning of Section 9(c)(1)(B).[8]

---

[3]328 NLRB 909, 162 LRRM 1010 (1999).

[4]St. Peter More v. NLRB, 327 NLRB 878, 161 LRRM 1174 (1999). *See also* Millsboro Nursing & Rehab. Ctr., Inc., 327 NLRB 879, 160 LRRM 1209 (1999).

[5]336 NLRB 1202, 169 LRRM 1003 (2001).

[6]328 NLRB 925, 163 LRRM 1119 (1999).

[7]Brylane, L.P., 338 NLRB 917, 171 LRRM 1513 (2003).

[8]New Otani Hotel, 331 NLRB 1078, 167 LRRM 1039 (2000).

b. Incumbent Unions

In *Raven Government Services Corp.*,[9] the Board found that an employer fails to meet the *Allentown Mack*[10] test when it commits and fails to remedy serious unfair labor practices and bases its withdrawal of recognition on a hearsay report of a decertification petition and the alleged inactivity of the union.

3. Disclaimer of Interest

A regional director has the discretion to allow a petitioner to withdraw its petition while objections are pending when the petitioner agrees, in writing, that it will not seek a new election within one year after the last election, even when the employer objects to the withdrawal.[11]

In *VFL Technology Corp.*,[12] the Board found a clear and unequivocal disclaimer of interest by the union after it had lost a "no raid" proceeding under Article XX of the AFL-CIO constitution.

II. TIMELINESS OF PETITIONS

A. The One-Election-per-Year Rule

1. The Statutory Bar

A party may not avoid the Section 9(c)(3) one-year bar by requesting withdrawal of an election petition after a valid election is conducted. In *E Center*,[13] the Board noted that, even if a petition is withdrawn after election, no labor organization may file a subsequent election petition within the 12-month period following the otherwise valid election.

2. The Certification Year

An employer cannot withdraw recognition from a union after the expiration of the certification year on the basis of an antiunion

---

[9]331 NLRB 651 (2000), *enforced*, 315 F.3d 499, 171 LRRM 2606 (5th Cir. 2002).

[10]Allentown Mack Sales & Serv., 316 NLRB 1199, 149 LRRM 1051 (1995), *enforced*, 83 F.3d 1483, 152 LRRM 2257 (D.C. Cir. 1996), *rev'd and remanded*, 522 U.S. 359, 157 LRRM 2257 (1998).

[11]Baltimore Gas & Elec. Co., 330 NLRB 3, 162 LRRM 1386 (1999).

[12]332 NLRB 1443, 166 LRRM 1043 (2000).

[13]337 NLRB 983, 170 LRRM 1501 (2002).

petition circulated and presented to the employer during the certification year. The Board expressly affirmed its holding in *United Supermarkets*[14] and overruled its holding in *Rock-Tenn Co.*,[15] to the extent that it "suggests that, based on evidence received during the certification year, an employer may announce that it intends to withdraw recognition from the union at the end of the certification year."[16] However, the Board has approved reliance on a petition signed by some employees on the final day of the certification year, and presented to the employer the next week.[17]

The Board has long held that when an employer informally settles Section 8(a)(5) charges with an agreement to bargain, it is precluded from withdrawing recognition for a reasonable period after the settlement is reached.[18] In *Wyndham Palmas del Mar Resort & Villas*,[19] the Board applied this rationale to a case involving an informal settlement of a Section 8(a)(1) charge that the employer had solicited employees to sign a decertification petition. The D.C. Circuit refused to enforce the Board's decision, concluding that the *Poole Foundry* rationale did not apply in the absence of a bargaining provision in the settlement agreement.[20]

In *Lexus of Concord, Inc.*,[21] the Board rejected a finding of an ALJ that an employer's statement in a letter that it would resume negotiations, and the regional director's dismissal of a refusal to bargain charge based on that letter, met the standards for a settlement bar so as to negate a question concerning representation raised by a majority of employees expressing disaffection from the union.

The Board also has held that the end of the certification year will terminate the one-year bar, and will not convert to a contract bar, when one party hastily accepts a contract offer that is not sufficient to establish the identity or terms of the agreement.[22]

---

[14]287 NLRB 119, 127 LRRM 1210 (1987), *enforced*, 862 F.2d 549, 130 LRRM 2212 (5th Cir. 1989).

[15]315 NLRB 670, 148 LRRM 1148 (1994), *enforced*, 69 F.3d 803, 150 LRRM 2714 (7th Cir. 1995).

[16]Chelsea Indus., 331 NLRB 1648, 165 LRRM 1118 (2000), *enforced*, 285 F.3d 1073, 169 LRRM 2961 (D.C. Cir. 2002).

[17]LTD Ceramics, Inc., 341 NLRB No. 14, 174 LRRM 1105 (2004).

[18]Poole Foundry & Mach. Co., 95 NLRB 34 (1951), *enforced*, 192 F.2d 740 (4th Cir. 1951); AT Sys. W., Inc., 341 NLRB No. 12, 174 LRRM 1203 (2004).

[19]334 NLRB 514, 167 LRRM 1260 (2001).

[20]BHP & Co. v. NLRB, 333 F.3d 213, 172 LRRM 2865 (D.C. Cir. 2003).

[21]343 NLRB No. 94, 176 LRRM 1284 (2004).

[22]Waste Mgmt. of Md., Inc., 338 NLRB 1002, 172 LRRM 1113 (2003).

3. *Voluntary Recognition Bar*

The Board refuses to extend the narrow exception for rival union petitions, announced in *Rollins Transportation Systems,*[23] to the recognition bar rule. In *Triangle Building Products Corp.*,[24] the Board held that if a rival union fails to petition for an appropriate unit, the employer's voluntary recognition of the other union constitutes a bar to the rival petition.

The Board continues to review the effect neutrality/card-check agreements have on the processing of election petitions. In *Baseball Club of Seattle Mariners,*[25] an employer's voluntary recognition of a union after an arbitrator's certification of the union's majority status pursuant to a written neutrality/card-check agreement created a recognition bar to the processing of a decertification petition, notwithstanding that the petition was supported by a 30 percent showing of interest. Similarly, the Board held that a neutrality/card-check recognition agreement barred a union's petition to represent certain employees in locations covered by the agreement.[26]

On December 8, 2004, the Board granted review in *Shaw's Supermarkets.*[27] The regional director had dismissed the RM petition finding that "the Union's demand for recognition based on an alleged contractual 'after-acquired' clause does not entitle the Employer to demand an election under Section 9(c)(1)(B)." The Board granted review on the following:

(1) whether the employer clearly and unmistakably waived the right to a Board election; and
(2) if so, whether public policy reasons outweigh the employer's private agreement not to have an election.

In granting review the Board commented that the *Central Parking* decision is "contrary to the general rule that the Board does not defer representation case issues to arbitration [and that] by grant-

---

[23] 296 NLRB 793, 132 LRRM 1185 (1989).

[24] 338 NLRB 257, 171 LRRM 1539 (2002).

[25] 335 NLRB 563, 168 LRRM 1219 (2001) (distinguishing *Smith's Food & Drug Ctrs.*, 320 NLRB 844, 151 LRRM 1345 (1996), where there is no recognition bar when two or more unions simultaneously are conducting organizing campaigns).

[26] Verizon Info. Sys., 335 NLRB 558, 168 LRRM 1136 (2001).

[27] 343 NLRB No. 105, 176 LRRM 1220 (2004).

ing review here we keep open the possibility that the Board will abide by the general rule rather than *Central Parking.*"

In *Dana Corp. & Metaldyne Corp.*,[28] the Board granted review of the administrative dismissal of three unit decertification petitions filed after recognition based on a card-check agreement entered into when the union had no majority support, as raising substantial issues regarding whether the employers' voluntary recognition barred such petitions. The Board majority stated that the increased usage of recognition agreements, the varying contexts in which a recognition agreement can be reached, the superiority of Board supervised secret-ballot elections, and the importance of Section 7 rights of employees all were factors that warrant a critical look at the extent to which, if any, a voluntary recognition should be given election "bar quality."

4. *Successor Bar*

In *MV Transportation*,[29] the Board returned to its prior position that an incumbent union in a successorship situation receives only a rebuttable presumption of continuing majority status. The Board expressly overruled its 1999 decision in *St. Elizabeth Manor*,[30] holding that the rebuttable presumption will not bar otherwise valid decertification, rival union, or employer petitions or any other valid challenge to the union's majority status. However, the decision was not applied retroactively.[31]

B. Pendency of Unfair Labor Practice Charges

The Board continues to hold that petitions filed during the posting period of a settlement agreement will be dismissed.[32]

---

[28]341 NLRB No. 150 (2004).

[29]337 NLRB 770, 170 LRRM 1233 (2002).

[30]329 NLRB 341, 162 LRRM 1146 (1999); Torch Operating Co., 338 NLRB 941 n.2, 172 LRRM 1073 (2003); Williams Energy Servs., 340 NLRB No. 87, 173 LRRM 1276 (2003) (affirming and reiterating *MV Transportation* doctrine).

[31]Aramark Sch. Servs., Inc., 337 NLRB 1063, 170 LRRM 1494 (2003).

[32]Hertz Equip. Rental Corp., 328 NLRB 28 (1999).

D. Fluctuating Workforce

In *Yellowstone International Mailing, Inc.*,[33] the Board applied an analysis similar to *Gerlach Meat Co.*[34] when considering an employer's plans to relocate and expand its overall workforce at a new but nearby facility. Finding that the current workers comprised approximately 38 percent of the anticipated workforce, and reflected 100 percent of the anticipated job positions, the Board held that the current workers were a "substantial and representative complement" of the anticipated larger workforce.

E. Contract-Bar Doctrine

The Board continues to follow its *Briggs Indiana* rule[35] that a union will be barred from seeking representation of employees if it has agreed with the employer not to seek such recognition during the life of the agreement. In *Lexington House*,[36] the Board held that such an agreement does not have to be part of the collective bargaining agreement.

1. *Requisites of the Contract*

The Board continues to hold that a contract to bar a representation petition must be in writing, must be signed by both parties prior to the filing of the petition, and must contain substantial terms and conditions of employment sufficient to stabilize the parties' bargaining relationship.[37] Although the contract need not be a formal document, its terms must be clearly discernable from the face of the document(s), without resort to extrinsic evidence.[38] However, the absence of an execution date in a contract does not remove it as a bar if the date of execution was before the petition and that date can be established.[39]

---

[33] 332 NLRB 386, 165 LRRM 1193 (2000).
[34] 192 NLRB 559, 77 LRRM 1832 (1971).
[35] 63 NLRB 1270, 161 LRRM 1126 (1945).
[36] 329 NLRB 894, 161 LRRM 1225 (1999).
[37] Waste Mgmt. of Md., Inc., 338 NLRB 1002, 172 LRRM 1113 (2003).
[38] *Id.*
[39] Cooper Tank & Welding Corp., 328 NLRB 759, 161 LRRM 1209 (1999).

3. *Unlawful Clauses*

The Board holds that a finding of an unlawful union security clause, which is sufficient to remove the contract's bar status, must be made solely from the face of the contract and not with the use of extrinsic evidence.[40]

A union-security clause was not illegal on its face and therefore the contract did not lose its bar status. In finding that the clause was not illegal on its face the Board noted that the clause did not require payment of an "assessment." It also noted that an alleged denial of the 30-day grace period did not appear on the face of the agreement and the contract was not effective retroactively so as to preclude a 30-day grace period.[41]

A contract entered into in violation of Section 8(a)(2) of the Act cannot lawfully be given effect, and does not bar a representation petition.[42]

The negotiation of a collective bargaining agreement intended to resolve outstanding unfair labor practice charges operates as a bar to a petition by a rival union, where there was no evidence that the underlying charges were frivolous.[43]

F. Clarification of Units

Explicitly reaffirming the relitigation rule it implicitly established in *I.O.O.F. Home of Ohio*,[44] the Board dismissed an employer's unit-clarification petition and held that the employer was estopped from challenging the nonsupervisory status of certain employees following its stipulation to include them in the bargaining unit and its failure to reserve the issue for postelection determination.[45]

The Board continues to hold that a unit-clarification petition is appropriate for resolving ambiguities concerning the unit placement of individuals who come within a newly created classification.[46] The

---

[40]Four Seasons Solar Prods. Corp., 332 NLRB 67, 165 LRRM 1177 (2000).

[41]*Id.*

[42]Morgan v. LaFarge N. Am., Inc., 286 F. Supp. 2d 1002, 1014 (N.D. Ind. 2003); Dura Art Stone, Inc., 340 NLRB No. 113, 174 LRRM 1041 (2003).

[43]Supershuttle of Orange County, Inc., 330 NLRB 1016, 163 LRRM 1275 (2000).

[44]322 NLRB 921, 154 LRRM 1122 (1997).

[45]Premier Living Ctr., 331 NLRB 123, 164 LRRM 1296 (2000).

[46]E.I. Du Pont de Nemours, Inc., 341 NLRB No. 82 (2004).

Board has a longstanding doctrine of refusing to entertain clarification petitions unless the classifications have undergone recent and substantial changes.[47] The Board did not deviate from its longstanding doctrine that it will not entertain a unit clarification into a unit dispute despite a change in the Board's decisional law.[48]

III. Election Procedures

A. Preelection Matters

1. *Types of Elections*

The Board generally will allow a party to withdraw an election petition without prejudice before completion of a preelection hearing or approval of an election agreement, which then permits the party to file a second petition for representation.[49]

In *Gardon Manor Farms, Inc.*,[50] a divided Board approved withdrawal of a petition that had been pending review by the Board and the union intended to file a new petition.

2. *Details of the Election*

c. Place

The decision to conduct an election on or off the employer's premises or by mail or manual ballot is within the discretion of the regional director.[51]

3. *Voter List and Eligibility*

a. The *Excelsior* List of Eligible Voters' Names and Addresses

An analysis that focuses solely on the percentage of omissions from the *Excelsior*[52] list fails to effectuate the purposes of the *Excelsior* rule. The Board, reexamining its substantial compliance analysis, held

[47]Kaiser Found. Hosps., 337 NLRB 1061, 170 LRRM 1317 (2002).

[48]*Id.*

[49]NLRB v. Davenport Lutheran Home, 244 F.3d 660, 166 LRRM 2943 (8th Cir. 2001); NLRB Casehandling Manual §11112.

[50]341 NLRB No. 24 (2004).

[51]San Diego Gas & Elec., 325 NLRB 1143, 158 LRRM 1257 (1998).

[52]Excelsior Underwear, 156 NLRB 1236, 61 LRRM 1217 (1966).

that although it will continue to consider the percentage of names omitted, it also will consider whether the number of omissions is determinative in the election as well as the employer's reasons for the omissions.[53] The Board continues to distinguish inaccurate addresses from omissions, accepting a higher percentage of inaccurate addresses where bad faith and gross negligence are not factors.[54]

The Board has recently addressed late filings of *Excelsior* lists and reached different conclusions depending on their completeness. Thus, where the list was late and incomplete, the election was set aside.[55] Where it was complete and only one day late, however, the election was not set aside.[56]

b. Eligibility

Bargaining-unit employees who have been selected for a promotion to management that is not effective until after the election still share a community of interest with the bargaining-unit employees and are eligible to vote.[57]

The voting eligibility of union members who obtain employment with an employer for the purpose of organizing its employees, also known as "salts," does not depend on whether the union pays them for their organizing activities, but solely on whether they share a "community of interest" with other unit employees.[58]

c. Construing Stipulations of the Parties in Representation Cases [New Topic]

The Board will accept stipulations of parties unless they are contrary to the record evidence, the Act, or Board policy.[59] The Board has adopted a three-prong analysis for resolving determinative challenged ballots in cases involving stipulated bargaining units. If the

---

[53]Woodman's Food Mkts., 332 NLRB 503, 165 LRRM 1209 (2000).

[54]Washington Fruit & Produce Co., 343 NLRB No. 125 (2004) (28% inaccuracy rate in addresses).

[55]Special Citizens Futures Unlimited, 331 NLRB 160, 164 LRRM 1195 (2000).

[56]Bon Appetit Mgmt. Co., 334 NLRB 1042, 169 LRRM 1068 (2001).

[57]Nichols House Nursing Home, 332 NLRB 1428, 167 LRRM 1180 (2000).

[58]Tradesource, Inc. v. NLRB, 168 LRRM 2799 (4th Cir. 2001) (table).

[59]C.K.E. Enters. dba Carl's Jr., 285 NLRB 975, 129 LRRM 1332 (1987). *Compare* Hollywood Med. Ctr., 275 NLRB 307, 119 LRRM 1118 (1985) (rejection of stipulation would have resulted in postelection challenge as to agreed-upon professional employees) *and* Cabrillo Lanes, 202 NLRB 921, 923 n.12, 82 LRRM 1725 (1973) (stipulation that would have excluded regular part-time employees was rejected prior to election).

objective intent of the parties is expressed in clear and unambiguous terms in the stipulation, the agreement will be enforced. If the stipulation is ambiguous, the Board will seek to determine the parties' intent by reference to extrinsic evidence. If the parties' intent cannot be ascertained using either of these tests, the placement of the disputed classification will be determined using the traditional "community-of-interest" test.[60]

When there is a contention that there is a difference between intent and the language of the stipulation, evidence of subjective intent is permissible only if objective intent cannot be determined from the language of the stipulation.[61] A classification will be deemed to be excluded if it is not mentioned in the inclusions and there is an exclusion for "all other employees."[62] A stipulation, however, cannot override a statutory mandate.[63] For a description of the Board's approach to ascertaining the parties' intent, see *Viacom Television*.[64] For a discussion of policies concerning the effect of stipulated election agreements, see *T&L Leasing*.[65]

4. *Notice of Election*

A notice of election that was posted seven working days before the election was sufficient to meet the Board's rule that notices of

[60]Desert Palace, Inc. dba Caesars Tahoe, 337 NLRB 1096, 170 LRRM 1344 (2002); Kroger Co. , 342 NLRB No. 20, 175 LRRM 1194 (2004); Los Angeles Water & Power Employees Ass'n, 340 NLRB No. 146 (2003).

[61]McFarling Foods, Inc., 336 NLRB 1140, 168 LRRM 1491 (2001); South Coast Hospice, 333 NLRB 198, 166 LRRM 1214 (2000); Royal Laundry, 277 NLRB 820, 821, 121 LRRM 1066 (1985).

[62]Bell Convalescent Hosp., 337 NLRB 191, 169 LRRM 1138 (2001); Peirce-Phelps, Inc., 341 NLRB No. 78, 174 LRRM 1353 (2004).

[63]Pontiac Osteopathic Hosp., 327 NLRB 1172, 161 LRRM 1003 (1999) (stipulation to include medical technologists cannot override mandate that Board conduct *Sonotone* elections).

[64]268 NLRB 633, 115 LRRM 1086 (1984). *See also* Southwest Gas Corp., 305 NLRB 542, 139 LRRM 1116 (1991); Business Records Corp., 300 NLRB 708, 136 LRRM 1085 (1990).

[65]318 NLRB 324, 150 LRRM 1035 (1995) (regional director cannot vary terms of agreement absent special circumstances); Grant's Home Furnishings, 229 NLRB 1305, 95 LRRM 1257 (1977) (alleged breach of agreement by regional director because of Board agent tardiness); Sunnyvale Med. Clinic, 241 NLRB 1156, 101 LRRM 1156 (1979); Dynair Servs., 314 NLRB 161, 146 LRRM 1204 (1994) (changed circumstances caused by intervening labor organization); Consolidated Print Works, 260 NLRB 978, 109 LRRM 1243 (1982) (consequences of failing to object to changed circumstances).

elections be posted at least three full working days before the election, even though the eligible voters were not scheduled to work on six of those days where the parties to the stipulated election agreement were aware of the employees' work schedule.[66] Notices of election posted seven and eight hours late warranted setting aside election results.[67] An election also was set aside where official notices of election were posted only at the employer's main offices and not at its various worksites, allowing no access to the notices by the majority of employees.[68]

B. The Election Proper

1. *Observers*

The Board announced a new rule prohibiting both employers and unions from using statutory supervisors as observers because their use by either party calls into question the integrity of the election process.[69]

The Board set aside an election where a Board agent allowed the voting to proceed with two employer observers present but no union observers, where the stipulated election agreement provided for an equal number of observers from both sides.[70]

The Board has established a "bright-line" rule prohibiting incumbent labor organizations from using their nonemployee agents as election observers in decertification elections.[71]

2. *Balloting*

c. Mail Ballots

The Board, noting that secrecy of balloting is a hallmark of election procedures, announced a new rule that an election may be set aside where mail ballots come into the possession of a party to the election.[72]

---

[66]Cleveland Indians Baseball Co., 333 NLRB 579, 166 LRRM 1346 (2001).

[67]Sara Lee Bakery Group dba International Baking Co., 342 NLRB No. 12, 175 LRRM 1250 (2004).

[68]Systems W. LLC, 342 NLRB No. 82, 175 LRRM 1281 (2004).

[69]Family Serv. Agency, 331 NLRB 850, 164 LRRM 1305 (2000).

[70]Browning-Ferris Indus., 327 NLRB 704, 160 LRRM 1145 (1999).

[71]Butera Finer Foods, Inc., 334 NLRB 43, 167 LRRM 1081 (2001).

[72]Fessler & Bowman, Inc., 341 NLRB No. 122, 174 LRRM 1455 (2004), *overruling in relevant part*, Pacific Gas & Elec. Co., 89 NLRB 938, 26 LRRM 1056 (1950).

It is not an abuse of a regional director's discretion to refuse to allow an employee who will be on vacation to vote by absentee ballot.[73]

The Board permitted a vote cast by a mail ballot on a sample ballot provided with the official election kit rather than on an official ballot to be counted. The ballot clearly indicated the voter's intent and giving effect to that intent avoided unnecessary disenfranchisement.[74]

C. Standards for the Conduct of Elections

1. *The Opportunity to Vote*

When election polls are not opened at the scheduled time, a new election should be ordered if the number of employees possibly disenfranchised by the tardy opening would affect the results of the election.[75]

An election will be set aside where severe weather conditions on election day reasonably denied an adequate opportunity to vote and a determinative number of eligible voters did not vote.[76]

It is not an abuse of a regional director's discretion to refuse to allow an employee who will be on vacation to vote by absentee ballot.[77]

2. *Conduct In and Around the Polling Areas*

The Board continues to hold that elections should be held in an atmosphere free from improper influence. Following this principle, it determined that a union's use of a sound truck, which broadcast pro-union music that could be heard by anyone entering the employer's premises all day on election day, interfered with the election and violated the *Peerless Plywood* rule.[78] However, the posting of a

---

[73]NLRB v. Cedar Tree Press, 169 F.3d 794, 160 LRRM 2685 (3d Cir. 1999).

[74]Aesthetic Designs, LLC, 339 NLRB 395, 173 LRRM 1189 (2003).

[75]Desert Palace, Inc. dba Caesars Tahoe, 337 NLRB 1096, 170 LRRM 1344 (2002) (determinative employee appeared during voting hours when polls were not yet opened, but stated after the fact that he had "decided not to vote").

[76]Baker Victory Servs., 331 NLRB 1068, 165 LRRM 1057 (2000) (rejecting "representative component" test of *Glass Depot, Inc.*, 318 NLRB 766, 150 LRRM 1055 (1995)).

[77]NLRB v. Cedar Tree Press, 169 F.3d 794, 160 LRRM 2685 (3d Cir. 1999).

[78]Bro-Tech Corp., 330 NLRB 37, 162 LRRM 1399 (1999).

pro-union poster on a tree and the distribution of pro-union literature 50 to 80 feet from a polling place was not improper.[79]

However, where an employer customarily text messaged its mobile employees in their company vehicles and sent a brief electronic "vote no" message within 24 hours of the elections, the Board held that the employer's message was more analogous to campaign literature than to a campaign speech or sound truck.[80]

The Board has also adopted a new bright-line rule prohibiting election-day raffles.[81] Rejecting its earlier case-by-case analysis, the Board determined that raffles are unlawful if (1) eligibility to win is tied to voting in the election or presence at the election site on election day, or (2) they are conducted during the time that the polls are open or in the 24-hour period before the beginning of the election.[82] Similarly, in *Comcast Cablevision*,[83] the Board ordered a second election where the union offered employees a free weekend trip to Chicago following the election.

In *Hollingsworth Management Service*,[84] the Board found improper electioneering where employees were manhandled in front of others by individuals who came to the polling area "for the apparent purpose of systematically targeting voters with last minute campaigning."

3. *The Integrity of the Ballots and the Ballot Box*

The Board continues to hold that it will uphold challenges to the integrity of the election process only where there is "a 'reasonable doubt as to the fairness and validity of the election.'"[85] Applying

---

[79]American Med. Response, 339 NLRB 1, 174 LRRM 1440(2003).

[80]Virginia Concrete Corp., Inc., 338 NLRB 1182, 172 LRRM 1169 (2003). *See also* Mountaineer Park, Inc., 343 NLRB No. 135 (2004) (election flyer accompanying pay check within 24 hours of election did not violate rule because employer regularly handed out pamphlets with employees' paychecks). *But see* Tyson Fresh Meats, Inc., 343 NLRB No. 129 (2004) (election set aside where union stewards spoke to employees waiting in excessively long lines to vote).

[81]Atlantic Limousine, Inc., 331 NLRB 1025, 165 LRRM 1001 (2000).

[82]*Id. See also* Beverly Enterprises-Tennessee, Inc. dba Allenbrooke Healthcare Ctr., 331 NLRB 1065, 165 LRRM 1370 (2000) (applying new rule).

[83]338 NLRB 1089, 173 LRRM 1509 (2003).

[84]342 NLRB No. 50 (2004).

[85]Sawyer Lumber Co., 326 NLRB 1331, 160 LRRM 1140 (1998).

this standard, the Board declined to set aside an election where the Board agent took a break during the election and left the ballot box in the voting room "under the watchful eyes" of both election observers.[86]

4. Conduct of Board Agents

An election had been scheduled at the employer's facility beginning at 6:00 a.m. The Board agent assigned to oversee the election overslept and did not arrive at the time the polls were scheduled to open. The employer kept its voters, who were truck drivers, at the facility until 6:45 a.m., when, having heard nothing from the Board agent, the employer released them to begin their routes. The Board unilaterally rescheduled the election for the following week, and the Board agent delivered new election notices that did not explain why he had failed to appear the previous week.[87]

Before the rescheduled election, the employer distributed a letter apologizing to employees for any inconvenience, stated that the employer was not at fault, and urged the employees to vote in the rescheduled election. The employees were never told why the Board agent had failed to show up for the first election. The employer filed objections to the conduct of the election based on sworn affidavits submitted by bargaining-unit and nonbargaining-unit employees that stated that the employees were upset and blamed the employer when they could not start work on time because the Board agent failed to appear for the original election. The sworn affidavits also recounted a rumor that spread among the employees that the employer had paid off the Board agent so that the Board agent would not show up to hold the election. The objections were overruled without an evi-

---

[86]*Id. See also* Elizabethtown Gas Co. v. NLRB, 212 F.3d 257, 164 LRRM 2257 (4th Cir. 2000) (upholding Board decision that election need not be set aside where Board agent required employees to vote with eraserless pencils, Board agent briefly left ballot box unattended except for election observers, and Board agent allowed observers to take unescorted breaks, because acts did not raise reasonable doubt about fairness or validity of election). *See also* Sir Francis Drake Hotel, 330 NLRB 638, 163 LRRM 1173 (2000) (denying employer's objection where union observer ignored Board agent's instructions and spoke to 5 or 6 of the approximately 100 voters in polling area—conversations were brief and lasted from few seconds to 1 minute, and evidence established that conversations were innocuous and in no way suggested to voters that it was union rather than Board that was conducting election).

[87]NLRB v. Superior of Mo., 233 F.3d 547, 165 LRRM 2785 (8th Cir. 2000).

dentiary hearing. The Eighth Circuit denied enforcement of the Board's order, holding that the employer was entitled to a hearing on its objections because it had made a prima facie showing of objectionable conduct that may have affected the outcome of the election.[88]

In a similar case, the Seventh Circuit held that an evidentiary hearing is not obligatory when no facts are set forth showing a real basis for a fear that the employer had somehow subverted the election. A mere postponement of six days for a scheduled election without an appearance that the election was postponed because of favoritism or opposition to the union is insufficient to set aside the election.[89]

Board agents cannot delegate official election tasks to observers, where doing so would compromise the integrity of the election.[90] Applying this rule, the D.C. Circuit held that an employer presented a prima facie case that the integrity of an election was impugned where union agents were allowed to walk through the plant, in union regalia, announcing that the Board had sent them to tell employees when they could vote.[91]

Like Board agents, Board interpreters must not influence employees' wishes.[92] Thus, the Board set aside an election where an interpreter asked employees, "Do you know where to put your yes vote?"[93] For an extensive discussion of the standards for Board agents at election, see *Sonoma Health Care Center.*[94]

D. Resolution of Challenges and Objections to the Election

3. *Resolution of Challenges and Objections*

Parties may request subpoenas from the regional director or the hearing officer.[95] On proper motion, subpoenas may be revoked.[96]

---

[88] *Id.* at 551–52, 165 LRRM at 2787–88.

[89] NLRB v. Citywide Insulation of Madison, Inc. dba Builders' Insulation, Inc., 370 F.3d 654, 174 LRRM 3249 (7th Cir. 2004).

[90] North of Mkt. Senior Servs. v. NLRB, 204 F.3d 1163, 163 LRRM 2711 (D.C. Cir. 2000).

[91] *Id.*

[92] Renco Elecs. Inc., 330 NLRB 368, 163 LRRM 1053 (1999). *But see Citywide Insulation of Madison, Inc., supra* note 89 (declining to extend *Renco*).

[93] *Id.*

[94] 342 NLRB No. 93 (2004).

[95] Rules & Regs. §102.66(c).

[96] *Id.*

Parties are not entitled to subpoenas that result in mere fishing expeditions.[97] For purposes of subpoena-enforcement proceedings, the Board has held that parties need not prove that a subpoena was actually received.[98] Instead, an attorney's affirmation of service of a subpoena by mail "was sufficient to establish service of the subpoena."[99]

Parties seeking the testimony of a Board agent in a representation hearing must request and obtain written approval from the general counsel.[100] Absent "unusual circumstances," Board employees are typically not involved as witnesses in Board litigation.[101]

E. Runoff and Rerun Elections

Rerun elections are not new elections; they are subsequent phases of the first election.[102] Accordingly, the Board has held that a union that was not on the ballot in the original election cannot intervene and appear on the ballot in a rerun election.[103]

---

[97]Millsboro Nursing & Rehab. Ctr., 327 NLRB 879 n.2, 160 LRRM 1209 (1999).

[98]Best W. City View Motor Inn, 327 NLRB 468, 160 LRRM 1221 (1999).

[99]*Id.* at 469.

[100]Rules & Regs. §102.118.

[101]*See Millsboro, supra* note 97, 327 NLRB 879 at n.2, and cases cited therein for discussion of the policy reasons behind such decisions. *See also* Brinks, Inc., 331 NLRB 46 n.2, 164 LRRM 1140 (2000) (regional director did not abuse his discretion in denying request for Board agent testimony where both parties presented witnesses and matter was fully litigated without agent's testimony).

[102]W.M. of New York, 326 NLRB 1126, 161 LRRM 1064 (1998).

[103]*Id.*

Chapter 11

APPROPRIATE BARGAINING UNITS

[**Editor's Note:** The reader is also directed to the Board publication "An Outline of Law and Procedure in Representation Cases" available on the Board's website: www.nlrb.gov.]

I. BACKGROUND

In *Allen Health Care Services,*[1] the Board held that where the petitioned-for unit is not presumptively appropriate, it has an affirmative, statutory obligation to determine the appropriateness of the unit and cannot simply close a hearing because no employer position was presented on the appropriateness of the unit. Because the unit in *Allen* was not presumptively appropriate, the case was remanded to the regional director for hearing.

When the parties disagree as to the inclusion of certain classifications to a stipulated unit, the Board will engage in a three-prong analysis to ascertain the intent of the parties and determine whether the intent is inconsistent with any statutory provision or established Board policy.[2] Under this approach, if the stipulation is clear and unambiguous, the Board enforces the agreement.[3] However, if the stipulation is unclear or ambiguous, the Board determines the intent through normal methods of contract interpretation.[4] If the in-

[1]332 NLRB 1308, 165 LRRM 1378 (2000).

[2]Desert Palace, Inc. dba Caesars Tahoe, 337 NLRB 1096, 170 LRRM 1344 (2002); Los Angeles Water & Power, 340 NLRB No. 146, 173 LRRM 1449 (2003). *See also* Bell Convalescent Hosp., 337 NLRB 191, 169 LRRM 1138 (2001) *and* Chapter 10, "Representation Proceedings and Elections," Section III.A.3.c. [Election Procedures; Preelection Matters; Voter List and Eligibility; Construing Stipulations of the Parties in Representation Cases], *supra.*

[3]*Desert Palace, Inc. dba Caesars Tahoe, supra* note 2.

[4]*Id.*

tent still cannot be discerned, the Board determines the bargaining unit by relying upon community-of-interest principles.[5] To withdraw from an approved election agreement, the Board requires a showing of unusual circumstances.[6] Under this standard, it is not enough to show that the Board would have defined the appropriate bargaining unit differently.[7]

The Board generally attempts to select a unit that is the smallest appropriate unit covering the petitioned-for employees. For example, in *Overnite Transportation Co.*,[8] the Board ordered an election in the smallest appropriate unit containing the employees sought by the petition and rejected the employer's request for a wall-to-wall unit. More than one unit can be appropriate and a union may seek an election in any appropriate unit.[9]

II. GENERAL FACTORS IN UNIT DETERMINATIONS

A. Community of Interest Among Employees

In determining whether one group of employees has a community of interest with another, the Board continues to apply the following traditional factors:

> [W]hether the employees are organized into a separate department; have distinct skills and training; have distinct job functions and perform distinct work, including inquiry into the amount and type of job overlap between classifications; are functionally integrated with the Employer's other employees; have frequent contact with other employees; interchange with other employees; have distinct terms and conditions of employment; and are separately supervised.[10]

---

[5] *Id.*

[6] NLRB v. MEMC Elec. Materials, Inc., 363 F.3d 705, 174 LRRM 2801 (8th Cir. 2004), *enforcing* 338 NLRB 142 (2003).

[7] *Id.*

[8] 331 NLRB 662, 164 LRRM 1257 (2000). *See also* Bartlett Collins Co., 334 NLRB 484, 168 LRRM 1404 (2001).

[9] Publix Supermarkets, 343 NLRB No. 109 (2004).

[10] United Operations, Inc., 338 NLRB 123, 171 LRRM 1004 (2002). *See also* Los Angeles Water & Power Employees Ass'n, 340 NLRB No. 146 (2003).

The Board has rejected the argument that it has a special per se rule for unit determinations in the research-and-development industry. Instead, it used a community-of-interest standard for deciding the unit in that industry.[11]

In *Oakwood Care Center*,[12] the Board overruled *M.B. Sturgis*,[13] and rejected the application of the community-of-interest test when combining temporary workers who are jointly employed by a supplier employer and a user employer and regular workers who are solely employed by the user employer. Instead, the Board held inclusion of these two groups in the same bargaining unit constituted a multiemployer unit, the creation of which is only permissible with the consent of both employers.[14]

D. Bargaining History

In *Red Coats, Inc.*,[15] the Board decided unit issues based in part on bargaining history.

The Board remains reluctant to disturb historical bargaining units that have had long periods of successful bargaining.[16] However, a long history of collective bargaining for two facilities in a single contract has been deemed insufficient to rebut the presumption of the appropriateness of a single-facility unit.[17]

E. Employer's Organizational Structure

The Board continues to apply a multifactor test in deciding between multi- and single-facility unit contentions.[18] The presence of

---

[11]Aerospace Corp., 331 NLRB 561, 166 LRRM 1221 (2000).

[12]343 NLRB No. 76, 176 LRRM 1033 (2004).

[13]331 NLRB 1298, 165 LRRM 1017 (2000).

[14]*See* Section II.E. [General Factors in Unit Determinations; Employer's Organizational Structure], *infra*.

[15]328 NLRB 205, 161 LRRM 1100 (1999).

[16]Canal Carting, Inc., 339 NLRB 969, 173 LRRM 1002 (2003).

[17]U.S. Tsubaki, Inc., 331 NLRB 327, 164 LRRM 1201 (2000).

[18]*See, e.g.*, Stormont-Vail Healthcare, Inc., 340 NLRB No. 143, 173 LRRM 1489 (2003) (RNs at clinics have community of interest with RNs at hospital); Basha's, Inc., 337 NLRB 710, 170 LRRM 1178 (2002) (multi-facility unit is not appropriate where no common supervision, no functional integration or significant interchange of employees, and no geographic coherent unit); Alamo Rent-A-Car, 330 NLRB 897, 163 LRRM 1289 (2000) (transfers, supervisors); Waste Mgmt. Northwest, Inc., 331 NLRB 309, 165 LRRM 1316 (2000) (geographic separation, interchange of employees); New Britain Transp. Co., 330 NLRB 397, 163 LRRM 1087 (1999) (supervision, plant integration, and similarity of skills).

centralized administration and control of some labor relations policies and procedures is not inconsistent with a finding that sufficient local autonomy exists to support a single-location presumption.[19]

Returning to longstanding precedent with *Oakwood Care Center*,[20] the Board will include temporary workers with a user employer's regular workers in the same bargaining unit only when both the user employer and supplier employer consent.

III. TYPES OF UNITS

A. Unit Classifications Required by the Act

1. *Professionals*

Following its decision in *Group Health Ass'n*,[21] the Board uses a rebuttable presumption that medical technologists are professional employees. The Board also held that when it has sufficient notice that there is an issue of professional status in a case, it must conduct an inquiry, and it cannot rely on the failure of the parties to raise the issue.[22]

In *Pratt & Whitney*,[23] the Board explained that the *Sonotone*[24] voting procedures for professional/nonprofessional elections do not alter the unit after the election has taken place.[25] The Board reaffirmed its use of the *Sonotone* procedures and ordered the hearing officer to take evidence on the professional issue to determine whether a *Sonotone* election should have been held.

---

[19]North Hills Office Servs., 342 NLRB No. 25 n. 3, 176 LRRM 1271 (2004); *New Britain Transp. Co., supra* note 18. *Cf. Waste Mgmt. Northwest, supra* note 18.

[20]343 NLRB No. 76, 176 LRRM 1033 (2004), *overruling* M.B. Sturgis, Inc., 331 NLRB 1298, 165 LRRM 1017 (2000).

[21]317 NLRB 238, 149 LRRM 1129 (1995).

[22]Pontiac Osteopathic Hosp. & Serv. Employees Int'l Union, 327 NLRB 1172, 161 LRRM 1003 (1999). The Board also held that when it has sufficient notice that there is an issue of professional status in a case, it must conduct an inquiry, and it cannot rely on the failure of the parties to raise the issue.

[23]327 NLRB 1213, 160 LRRM 1241 (1999).

[24]Sonotone Corp., 90 NLRB 1236, 26 LRRM 1354 (1950).

[25]*Pratt & Whitney, supra* note 23 (distinguishing Hamilton Test Sys. v. NLRB, 743 F.2d 136, 117 LRRM 2248 (2d Cir. 1984)). *See also* NLRB v. Lorimar Prod., 771 F.2d 1294, 120 LRRM 2425 (9th Cir. 1985).

2. *Guards*

Disagreeing with the Board, the Seventh Circuit declared that, under Section 9(b)(3), the only limitation on the Board's power with regard to "mixed" guard/nonguard units is that the Board may not certify unions to represent guard employees if the union also includes nonguards.[26] As a consequence, the duty of collective bargaining imposed by Section 8(a)(5) still applies to an existing unit of guard and nonguard employees.[27]

The Board continues to hold that a union representing police officers in the public sector is not disqualified from representing guards employed in the private sector due to some perceived conflict of interest.[28]

Assigning firefighters to property protection duties during a strike will not result in a finding that the firefighters are guards.[29]

In *Madison Square Garden*,[30] the Board concluded that employees who resolve disputes with patrons seeking to enter civic center events are guards.

In *Corrections Corp. of America*,[31] the Board applied *Monsanto Chemical Co.*,[32] and found that an agreement covering a mixed guard/nonguard unit does not bar a petition for a guard-only unit.

B. Unit Classifications in General

3. *Plant and Employer Units*

In determining whether the single-facility presumption has been rebutted, the Board continues to analyze the traditional factors: (1) employee skills and duties; (2) terms and conditions of employment; (3) employee interchange; (4) functional integration; (5) geographic proximity; (6) centralized control of management and su-

---

[26]General Serv. Employees Local 73 v. NLRB, 230 F.3d 909, 165 LRRM 2580 (7th Cir. 2000), *rev'g* Temple Sec. Inc., 328 NLRB 663, 161 LRRM 1129 (1999).

[27]*Id.* Notably, a contract covering a mixed guard/nonguard bargaining unit does not serve as a bar to a petition for a guard-only unit. Corrections Corp. of Am., 327 NLRB 577, 160 LRRM 1165 (1999), *following* Monsanto Chem. Co., 108 NLRB 870, 34 LRRM 1099 (1954).

[28]Guardian Armored Assets, LLC, 337 NLRB 556, 170 LRRM 1058 (2002).

[29]Boeing Co., 328 NLRB 128, 166 LRRM 1306 (1999).

[30]333 NLRB 643, 168 LRRM 1141 (2001).

[31]327 NLRB 577, 160 LRRM 1165 (1999).

[32]108 NLRB 870, 34 LRRM 1099 (1954).

pervision; and (7) bargaining history.[33] The presence of centralized administration and control of some labor relations policies and procedures is not inconsistent with a finding that sufficient local autonomy exists to support a single-location presumption.[34]

Notwithstanding its tendency to find systemwide units in the oceanic transport industry, the Board found a less-than-fleetwide unit to be appropriate in *Keystone Shipping Co.*[35]

While expressing doubt as to whether a wireless telephone company is a public utility, the Board determined that the presumption of a systemwide unit does not apply to retail employees.[36]

C. Specialized Units

1. *Units in Health Care Institutions*

b. Development of the Law: Application of Community of Interest Standard and the Eight-Unit Result

(1) Physicians, Interns, and Residents [Amended Heading]

In *Boston Medical Center Corp.*,[37] the Board overruled *Cedars-Sinai Medical Center*[38] and held that residents and interns are employees under the Act.

(2) Registered Nurses

In *Crittenton Hospital*,[39] the Board rejected the argument that under its Health Care Rule all registered nurses (RNs) be included in a petitioned-for unit, and held that a nonconforming unit of RNs that excluded certain specialty RNs was appropriate because of the 25-year representation of the unit by another union. In *Salem Hospi-*

---

[33] *See, e.g.*, Basha's, Inc., 337 NLRB 710, 170 LRRM 1178 (2002) (petitioned-for multi-facility unit inappropriate); Budget Rent-A-Car Sys., Inc., 337 NLRB 884, 170 LRRM 1265 (2002) (rebutting single-facility presumption). *See also* Alamo Rent-A-Car, 330 NLRB 897, 163 LRRM 1289 (2000); Waste Mgmt. Northwest, 331 NLRB 309, 165 LRRM 1316 (2000); New Britain Transp. Co., 330 NLRB 397, 163 LRRM 1087 (1999).

[34] *New Britain Transp. Co., supra* note 33. *Cf. Waste Mgmt. Northwest, supra* note 33.

[35] 327 NLRB 892, 160 LRRM 1225 (1999).

[36] Verizon Wireless, 341 NLRB No. 63, 174 LRRM 1273 (2004).

[37] 330 NLRB 152, 162 LRRM 1329 (1999).

[38] 223 NLRB 251, 91 LRRM 1398 (1976).

[39] 328 NLRB 879, 161 LRRM 1022 (1999).

tal,[40] the Board found individuals performing utilization review or discharge planning work were not included in an RN unit where the employer does not require RN licensing for the job.

e. Application of the Rule

In *St. Mary's Duluth Clinic*,[41] the Board held that a nonincumbent union could seek to represent a nonconforming unit consisting of some, but not all, of a hospital's employees who would otherwise constitute an appropriate unit under the Board's Health Care Rule.[42] Under the bargaining rule, where nonconforming units exist, additional units are appropriate only if they conform "insofar as practicable" to an enumerated unit.[43] The Board ruled that to require an incumbent union with a longstanding bargaining relationship to represent additional employees with possible conflicting interests would ignore the importance of labor stability and collective bargaining history.

f. Units in Nonacute Health Care Institutions

Under the *Park Manor Care Center*[44] analysis, the Board does not apply the health care bargaining-unit rule in nonacute health care facilities, and instead uses a "pragmatic or empirical community of interest" analysis to decide bargaining units. The Board has now applied this analysis in connection with RN units at home health care and hospice facilities,[45] and a medical equipment and services facility.[46]

However, in *Kaiser Foundation Health Plan*,[47] the Board relied upon the principles established in *St. Mary's Duluth Clinic*[48] (a decision based on its Health Care Rule), in allowing a nonincumbent union to represent a residual unit of employees. The Board made clear, though, in contrast to an acute-care facility, analysis of the propriety of a residual unit in the nonacute health care institution re-

---

[40] 333 NLRB 560, 170 LRRM 1354 (2001).
[41] 332 NLRB 1419, 166 LRRM 1057 (2000).
[42] 29 C.F.R. §103.30.
[43] *Id.*
[44] 305 NLRB 872, 139 LRRM 1049 (1991).
[45] South Hills Health Sys., 330 NLRB 653, 163 LRRM 1185 (2000); Allen Health Care Servs., 332 NLRB 1308, 165 LRRM 1378 (2000).
[46] CGE Caresystems, Inc., 328 NLRB 748, 161 LRRM 1299 (1999).
[47] 333 NLRB 557, 166 LRRM 1284 (2001).
[48] 332 NLRB 1419, 166 LRRM 1057 (2000).

quires consideration of an additional factor relating to the community of interest among employees.[49]

g. Related Issues

(1) Single-Facility Versus Multi-Facility Units

In the health care industry, the Board continues to adhere to the single-facility unit as presumptively appropriate. To determine whether the single-facility presumption has been rebutted, the Board examines such factors as geographic proximity, employee interchange and transfer, functional integration, administrative centralization, common supervision, and bargaining history.[50]

In *Massachusetts Society for the Prevention of Cruelty to Children v. NLRB*,[51] the First Circuit, while commenting that the absence of history of bargaining does not favor or disfavor a single-facility finding, nonetheless found that the regional director did not abuse her discretion in relying on it for a single-facility finding.

2. *Units in College and Universities*

b. Development of the Law: Basic Structure of Professional Units and the Impact of *Yeshiva*

(3) Yeshiva *Applied to Faculty*

In *LeMoyne-Owen College v. NLRB*,[52] the District of Columbia Circuit Court of Appeals remanded the case to the Board for an explanation of how the case was consistent with previous cases applying the multi-factor test set out in *NLRB v. Yeshiva University*.[53]

(4) Other Specific Inclusions and Exclusions

k. Graduate Students. In *Brown University*,[54] the Board overruled *New York University*,[55] and held teaching assistants, research assistants, and proctors are primarily students and not statutory employees.

---

[49] *Kaiser Found. Health Plan, supra* note 47, at n.7.

[50] St. Luke's Health Sys., Inc., 340 NLRB No. 139, 173 LRRM 1473 (2003).

[51] 297 F.3d 41 (1st Cir. 2002).

[52] 357 F.3d 55, 174 LRRM 2225 (2004), *granting review from* 338 NLRB No. 92 (2003).

[53] 444 U.S. 672, 103 LRRM 2526 (1980).

[54] 342 NLRB No. 42, 175 LRRM 1089 (2004).

[55] 332 NLRB 1205, 165 LRRM 1241 (2000).

D. Multi-Employer Bargaining Units

2. *Establishment of the Multi-Employer Unit: Its Consensual Nature*

The Board continues to require employer consent to form a multi-employer unit.[56] In *Oakwood Care Center*,[57] the Board reversed *M.B. Sturgis*[58] and returned to the prior precedent of *Greenhoot*[59] and *Lee Hospital*[60] to require employer consent when a petitioned-for unit includes both temporary and regular employees of a user employer. In so holding, the Board acknowledged that a unit consisting solely of jointly employed employees may constitute an appropriate unit.[61]

There is a distinction between an employer who is a member of a multi-employer bargaining unit and an employer who, while not a member of that unit, nonetheless agrees to sign the multi-employer agreement with the union.[62]

3. *Dissolution of the Unit*

b. Withdrawal After Bargaining Begins

In *Road Sprinkler Fitters Local 669 v. Simplex Grinnell*,[63] the district court strictly followed *Retail Associates*,[64] requiring written notice prior to the agreed-upon date for the commencement of multi-employer negotiations. In particular, the court found the employer's oral notice ineffective and untimely.[65]

In *D.A. Nolt, Inc.*,[66] the Board held that an employer did not effectively withdraw from a multi-employer bargaining unit, despite the fact that negotiations for the new collective bargaining agreement were kept confidential. The employer contended that the secret negotiations met the *Retail Associates*[67] exception for "unusual

---

[56]Oakwood Care Ctr., 343 NLRB No. 76, 176 LRRM 1033 (2004); Arbor Constr. Personnel, Inc., 343 NLRB No. 38, 176 LRRM 1100 (2004).

[57]*Supra* note 56.

[58]331 NLRB 1298, 165 LRRM 1017 (2000).

[59]205 NLRB 250, 83 LRRM 1656 (1973).

[60]300 NLRB 947, 136 LRRM 1348 (1990).

[61]*Oakwood, supra* note 56, slip op. at 4.

[62]HCL Inc., 343 NLRB No. 95, 176 LRRM 1183 (2004).

[63]251 F. Supp. 2d 1201, 172 LRRM 2160 (W.D.N.Y. 2003).

[64]120 NLRB 388, 41 LRRM 1502 (1958).

[65]*Simplex Grinnell, supra* note 63 at 1205.

[66]340 NLRB No. 152, 173 LRRM 1513 (2003).

[67]*Retail Assocs., supra* note 64.

circumstances" allowing the employer to withdraw. Relying upon *Chel LaCort,*[68] the Board held that notice to member-employers is not required.[69]

On the other hand, despite an untimely attempt to withdraw from a multi-employer association, a union may be found implicitly, through its conduct, to have consented to or acquiesced in the attempted withdrawal.[70] In *CTS, Inc.,*[71] despite the employer's untimely attempt to withdraw, the union accepted the withdrawal through its willingness to engage in individual bargaining.

[68]315 NLRB 1036, 148 LRRM 1051 (1994).

[69]*D.A. Nolt, supra* note 66; *see also* Resort Nursing Home v. NLRB, 389 F.3d 1262, 176 LRRM 2147 (D.C. Cir. 2004), *enforcing* 340 NLRB No. 77, 174 LRRM 1157 (2003).

[70]I.C. Refrigeration Serv., 200 NLRB 687, 81 LRRM 1529 (1972).

[71]340 NLRB No. 99, 173 LRRM 1305 (2003).

Chapter 12

RECOGNITION AND WITHDRAWAL OF RECOGNITION WITHOUT AN ELECTION

III. ELEMENTS OF A BARGAINING OBLIGATION IN THE ABSENCE OF AN ELECTION

A. Majority Representation

The initial inquiry in cases of majority representation is whether a majority of the employees in an appropriate unit have signed authorization cards as of the date of the employer's alleged refusal to bargain. In one case, the Ninth Circuit held that a district court abused its discretion by finding insufficient evidence of majority status to support an interim injunctive bargaining order.[1] Ruling that the district court applied an erroneous legal standard and based its decision on clearly erroneous findings of fact, the Ninth Circuit concluded that the regional director established a sufficient likelihood of success on the issue of majority status. The court found that the employer did not refute the validity of an unambiguous union authorization card on which the majority turned. In this regard, there was no showing that the employee card signer was told that the card would be used for any purpose other than to call for an election. Rather, the employee testified that she was told that the card would be used for the purpose of an election, and could not recall whether she had been told anything more.

The Board continues to hold that an employer has no obligation to forgo an election and accept a card count as proof of majority status, absent a clear agreement to do so.[2] The Board has de-

---

[1]Scott ex rel. NLRB v. Stephen Dunn & Assocs., 241 F.3d 652, 662–64, 166 LRRM 2385 (9th Cir. 2001).

[2]Terracon, Inc., 339 NLRB No. 35, 172 LRRM 1293 (2003), *enforced*, 361 F.3d 395, 174 LRRM 2551 (7th Cir. 2004); Jefferson Smurfit Corp., 331 NLRB 809, 165 LRRM 1219 (2000) (examining and copying cards does not constitute clear agreement by employer to accept card count as proof of majority status).

clined to reconsider its 1984 decision that majority support for a union is a prerequisite for a remedial bargaining order.[3]

1. *Form of Designation*

Even in the face of contrary solicitation, unambiguous single-purpose cards remain valid for purposes of establishing majority support absent affirmative proof that the signer was explicitly told that the card would be used *solely* to obtain an election.[4]

2. *Name of Union*

It remains unchanged that a union designation indicated in general terms, without identifying either a particular local or the international union, is sufficient.

3. *Status of the Solicitor*

The Board applies a "bright-line" rule that all authorization cards directly solicited by a supervisor may not support a showing of interest.[5] In *Waldinger Corp.*,[6] the Board held that cards were not tainted by a supervisor's statements in support of a union or by his presence at a union meeting while cards were distributed and signed. The Board explained that to find supervisory taint, the supervisor's conduct must either imply that the employer favored the union or coercively induce employees to sign the cards because of fear of supervisory retaliation.[7] However, the Board, in finding a supervisor's

---

[3]Nabors Alaska Drilling, 325 NLRB 574, 158 LRRM 1004 (1998) (Board declined to reconsider propriety of its earlier holding in *Gourmet Foods, Inc.*, 270 NLRB 578, 116 LRRM 1105 (1984)), *enforcement granted and remanded*, 190 F.3d 1008, 162 LRRM 2197 (9th Cir. 1999); *accord* First Legal Support Servs. LLC, 342 NLRB No. 29, 175 LRRM 1141 (2004).

[4]Overnite Transp. Co. v. NLRB, 240 F.3d 325, 339–40, 166 LRRM 2577 (4th Cir. 2001), *enforcing* 329 NLRB 1, 166 LRRM 1101 (1999) (union obtained valid authorization cards from majority of employees, even if solicitors told employees that purpose of cards was to have election), *petition for review granted in part on other grounds*, 280 F.3d 417, 169 LRRM 2469 (4th Cir. 2002) (en banc); *Scott ex rel. NLRB*, *supra* note 1.

[5]Dejana Indus., 336 NLRB 1202, 169 LRRM 1003 (2001).

[6]331 NLRB 544, 164 LRRM 1280 (2000), *enforced*, 262 F.3d 1213, 168 LRRM 2099 (11th Cir. 2001).

[7]*Id.* Member Hurtgen dissented, finding that the supervisor's actions tainted the card-signing process.

solicitation of cards to be objectionable conduct, disavowed language in prior Board decisions[8] that required an express threat or promise by a pro–union supervisor in order to find the conduct objectionable.[9]

4. *Time of Execution*

Majority status at a new employer facility can be established by counting union authorization cards signed by employees while working at another employer facility, prior to their transfer to the new facility. The authorization cards remain valid as to the emerging bargaining unit at the new facility, even though the employees signed while not formally employed at the new facility.[10] The Board and Fourth Circuit distinguished the situation of transferring employees, who are invested in a company and its unionized status, from that of job applicants, who have not been hired and whose knowledge of the terms and conditions of employment is extremely limited.[11]

5. *Authentication*

The Board continues to hold that an authorization card can be properly authenticated by a person other than the signer or a witness to the card signing.[12]A judge or handwriting expert may authenticate a signature on a union authorization card by comparing the signature on the card with signatures on subpoenaed employ-

---

[8]Pacific Micronesia, 326 NLRB 458 (1998); Sutter Roseville Med. Ctr., 324 NLRB 218 (1997); Pacific Physicians Servs., 313 NLRB 1176 (1994).

[9]Haborside Healthcare, Inc., 343 NLRB 100, 176 LRRM 1113 (2004).

[10]*Overnite Transp. Co., supra* note 4, 240 F.3d at 340–41, 166 LRRM at 2588–89.

[11]*Id.* at 341 n.10, citing Koons Ford of Annapolis, Inc., 282 NLRB 506, 124 LRRM 1167 (1986).

[12]*See, e.g.*, Douglas Foods Corp., 330 NLRB 821, 163 LRRM 1201 (2000) (card properly authenticated by solicitor who received signed card from signatory but did not witness execution of card), *enforced in relevant part*, 251 F.3d 1056, 167 LRRM 2380 (D.C. Cir. 2001); *but see* First Legal Support Servs. LLC, 342 NLRB No. 29, 175 LRRM 1141 (2004) (signed card not properly authenticated because two witnesses offered conflicting testimony as to how card came into existence).

ment documents.[13] In *Traction Wholesale Center Co.*,[14] the Board entered a bargaining order based on a card majority where a dispositive union authorization card was authenticated by an administrative law judge (ALJ) who compared the card signature with signatures on the employee's employment application and work-rules form. The Board found that the ALJ's conclusion was reinforced by its own independent comparison of the employee's signature on a W-4 form with the other signatures in evidence. The Board rejected the employer's purported lack of knowledge about the authenticity of the signatures on business records that it maintained and relied on in the course of business.[15]

B. Demand for Recognition in an Appropriate Unit

Typically, a union need not demonstrate proof of majority status when it makes a demand for recognition; it is sufficient that the union possesses signed authorization cards from a majority of employees in an appropriate unit. The Board continues to hold that a union is not required to present authorization cards from a majority of the unit to support its demand for recognition under Section 9(a) of the Act if the employer accepts the union's representation.

1. Section 8(f) Agreements (New Topic)

In *Staunton Fuel & Material, Inc. dba Central Illinois Construction*,[16] the Board adopted the requirements stated by the Tenth Circuit in *NLRB v. Triple C Maintenance, Inc.*[17] and *NLRB v. Oklahoma Installation Co.*[18] Thus, a union will be deemed by the Board to be a Section

---

[13]Traction Wholesale Ctr. Co., 328 NLRB 1058, 164 LRRM 1266 (1999), *enforced*, 216 F.3d 92, 164 LRRM 2769 (D.C. Cir. 2000); Parts Depot, Inc., 332 NLRB 670, 170 LRRM 1005 (2000) (judge or handwriting expert may determine genuineness of signatures on authorization cards by comparing them to W-4 forms in employer's records). *See also* Le Marquis Hotel LLC, 340 NLRB No. 64, 174 LRRM 1270 (2003) (ALJ compared signatures on two different authorization cards for competing unions and concluded signatures were identical).

[14]*Traction Wholesale Ctr.*, *supra* note 13.

[15]*Id.*

[16]335 NLRB 717, 168 LRRM 1121 (2001).

[17]219 F.3d 1147, 164 LRRM 2785 (10th Cir. 2000), *enforcing* 327 NLRB 1048, 163 LRRM 1048 (1998).

[18]219 F.3d 1160, 1164–66, 164 LRRM 2841 (10th Cir. 2000), *denying enforcement and remanding* 325 NLRB 741, 158 LRRM 1081 (1998).

9(a) representative of employees in the construction industry where language in a collective bargaining agreement or recognition agreement

> unequivocally indicates that (1) the union requested recognition as the majority or Section 9(a) representative of the unit employees; (2) the employer recognized the union as the majority or Section 9(a) bargaining representative; and (3) the employer's recognition was based on the union's having shown, or having offered to show, evidence of its majority support.[19]

If those requirements are not met, then the presumption that a Section 8(f) rather than a Section 9(a) relationship was formed governs.[20]

In discussing these requirements, the Board also observed that (1) a request for recognition may be fairly implied from the employer grant of recognition; (2) the grant of recognition must be express and unequivocal; and (3) statements that a Section 8(f) representative "represents" the unit or that the majority of unit employees are members (in a union-security context) do not satisfy the test for establishing "majority support."[21]

In *Nova Plumbing v. NLRB*,[22] however, the D.C. Circuit held that while contract language and intent are "perfectly legitimate 'factors'" that the Board may consider in determining whether the *Deklewa* preemption of Section 8(f) status has been overcome, standing alone, contract language and intent cannot be dispositive where record evidence contains "strong indications" that the union lacked majority status.[23]

C. Employer Unfair Labor Practices

1. *Conduct Warranting a* Gissel *Bargaining Order*[24]

b. "Hallmark" Violations: Invasive Employer Conduct

The Board and courts continue to hold that an employer's discharge of union supporters constitutes "hallmark" violations that

---

[19] *Staunton Fuel & Material dba Central Ill. Constr.*, supra note 16.

[20] *Oklahoma Installation Co.*, *supra* note 18, 219 F.3d at 1164–66.

[21] *Staunton Fuel & Material dba Central Ill. Constr.*, *supra* note 16.

[22] 330 F.3d 531, 172 LRRM 2700 (D.C. Cir. 2003), *granting petition for review and denying cross petition for enforcement of* 336 NLRB 633, 169 LRRM 1276 (2001).

[23] *Id.*, 330 F.3d at 537–38, 172 LRRM at 2704–05.

[24] *See generally* General Counsel Memorandum 99-8 (Guidelines Memorandum 99-8, Guideline Memorandum Concerning *Gissel*).

justify bargaining orders. Recent "hallmark" violations cited by the Board have included a combination of improper actions, such as discharges and layoffs, and threats, such as those involving plant closures and pay cuts.[25]

c. Other Specific Employer Unfair Labor Practices

(1) Threats

The Board has issued bargaining orders where, among other unfair labor practices, the employer threatened employees with adverse consequences if they honored Board subpoenas or testified in Board proceedings;[26] threatened discharge, loss of work, or plant closing because of union activity;[27] threatened to refuse to permit

---

[25] *See, e.g.*, M.J. Metal Prods., Inc., 267 F.3d 1059, 168 LRRM 2800 (10th Cir. 2001), *enforcing* 328 NLRB 1184, 163 LRRM 1164 (1999) (employer discharged 4 union supporters out of a unit of 15 and threatened to sell business and shut down operations); Orland Park Motor Cars, Inc., 333 NLRB 1017, 171 LRRM 1081 (2001) *enforced*, 309 F.3d 453, 171 LRRM 2139 (7th Cir. 2002) (employer threatened to discharge employees who started the union's organizing campaign, discharged the leading advocate, and discharged employee for rejoining picket line after previously deciding to cross picket line and work); Douglas Foods Corp., 330 NLRB 821, 163 LRRM 1201 (2000), *enforced in part, vacated in part, and remanded*, 251 F.3d 1056, 167 LRRM 2380 (D.C. Cir. 2001) (employer discharged two union supporters, conducted sham sale of business operation, and threatened to eliminate work and impose pay cuts if employees organized a union); Debbie Reynolds Hotel, Inc., 332 NLRB 466, 170 LRRM 1277 (2000) (employer subcontracted most of unit work, laid off and discharged employees, and threatened job loss and hotel closing); General Fabrications Corp., 328 NLRB 1114, 162 LRRM 1100 (1999) (employer discharged, laid off, and suspended employees who engaged in union activity and made threats of job loss, plant closure, and futility in event of union victory), *enforced*, 222 F.3d 218, 164 LRRM 2974 (6th Cir. 2000). *But see* Hialeah Hosp., 343 NLRB No. 52, 176 LRRM 1254 (2004) (bargaining order not warranted despite unlawful discharge and various 8(a)(1) violations); Desert Aggregates, 340 NLRB No. 170, 174 LRRM 1361 (2003) (employer's layoff of two leading union supporters paired with its unlawful solicitation and promise to remedy employee grievances were found to be "hallmark" violations due to highly coercive nature of actions, but bargaining order was not warranted).

[26] Parts Depot, Inc., 332 NLRB 670, 170 LRRM 1005 (2000); *Douglas Foods Corp., supra* note 25.

[27] *Debbie Reynolds Hotel, Inc., supra* note 25; *Douglas Foods Corp, supra* note 25; L.S.F. Transp., Inc., 330 NLRB 1054, 169 LRRM 1309 (2000), *enforced*, 282 F.3d 972, 169 LRRM 2797 (7th Cir. 2002); Traction Wholesale Ctr., 328 NLRB 1058, 164 LRRM 1266 (1999), *enforced*, 216 F.3d 92, 164 LRRM 2769 (D.C. Cir. 2000).

the union to represent employees;[28] or threatened to deny work uniforms.[29]

(2) Promise or Grant of Benefits

The Board has granted bargaining orders where, among other unfair labor practices, the employer granted an employee a pay raise before an election, while suggesting that the employee vote against the union;[30] promised wage and benefit increases if an employee voted against the union;[31] or offered the union an increase in wages and benefits for unit employees if it promised not to file further unfair labor practice charges or postelection objections.[32]

(3) Unlawful Efforts to Undermine or Discourage Union Support

The Board has issued bargaining orders where, among other unfair labor practices in retaliation for union support or in an effort to undermine or discourage such support, the employer refused to recognize or bargain with the union, or withdrew recognition from the union;[33] solicited employee sentiment about matters that were mandatory subjects of bargaining;[34] solicited employee grievances;[35] refused to reinstate unfair labor practice strikers on their unconditional offers to return to work;[36] unilaterally altered wages, hours, and other terms and conditions of employment, except for the terms and conditions of replacement workers hired during a strike;[37] suggested that it would be futile for employees to select the union as their bargaining representative;[38] changed work assignments or re-

---

[28]*Debbie Reynolds Hotel, Inc., supra* note 25.

[29]*Traction Wholesale Ctr., supra* note 27.

[30]*Douglas Foods Corp., supra* note 25.

[31]*Id.*; Equipment Trucking Co., Inc., 336 NLRB 277 (2001).

[32]Cogburn Healthcare Ctr., Inc., 335 NLRB 1397, 171 LRRM 1021 (2001).

[33]Penn Tank Lines, Inc., 336 NLRB 1066, 169 LRRM 1088 (2001) (among other unfair labor practices); Ryan Iron Works, Inc., 332 NLRB 506, 167 LRRM 1240 (2000); Debbie Reynolds Hotel, 332 NLRB 466, 170 LRRM 1277 (2000); Traction Wholesale Ctr., 328 NLRB 1058, 164 LRRM 1266 (1999), *petition for review denied in part, enforced in relevant part,* 216 F.3d 92, 164 LRRM 2769 (D.C. Cir. 2000); L.S.F. Transp., Inc., 330 NLRB 1054, 169 LRRM 1309 (2000), *enforced,* 282 F.3d 972, 169 LRRM 2797 (7th Cir. 2002).

[34]*Ryan Iron Works, supra* note 33.

[35]*Debbie Reynolds Hotel, supra* note 33.

[36]*Ryan Iron Works, supra* note 33.

[37]*Id.*

[38]Douglas Foods Corp., 330 NLRB 821, 163 LRRM 1201 (2000), *vacated in relevant part,* 251 F.3d 1056, 167 LRRM 2380 (D.C. Cir. 2001).

fused to assign work to union supporters;[39] discontinued a practice of extending cash advances to employees;[40] instituted new work rules;[41] imposed onerous working conditions;[42] prohibited employees from wearing clothing reflecting union membership;[43] decreased overtime;[44] discharged employees;[45] subcontracted bargaining-unit work;[46] or laid off employees.[47]

(4) Interrogation

The Board has issued bargaining orders where, in the context of other unfair labor practices, the employer coercively interrogated employees about their union activities and the union activities of other employees.[48]

(5) Other Unfair Labor Practices [Amended Title]

The Board has issued bargaining orders where, in the context of other unfair labor practices, the employer created the impression of surveillance of employees who supported the union.[49]

Although a bargaining order is more likely in the case of a small-sized bargaining unit, where the effects of employer unfair labor

---

[39]L.S.F. Transp., Inc., 330 NLRB 1054, 169 LRRM 1309 (2000), *enforced*, 282 F.3d 972, 169 LRRM 2797 (7th Cir. 2002).

[40]*Id.*

[41]*Id.*; Michael's Painting Inc., 337 NLRB 860, 171 LRRM 1186 (2002); Cogburn Healthcare Ctr., Inc., 335 NLRB 1397, 171 LRRM 1021 (2001).

[42]Parts Depot, Inc., 332 NLRB 670, 170 LRRM 1005 (2000).

[43]Aldworth Co., Inc., 338 NLRB 137, 171 LRRM 1033 (2002); *Cogburn Healthcare, supra* note 41.

[44]Douglas Foods Corp., 330 NLRB 821, 163 LRRM 1201 (2000), *vacated in relevant part*, 251 F.3d 1056, 167 LRRM 2380 (D.C. Cir. 2001).

[45]Debbie Reynolds Hotel, Inc., 332 NLRB 466, 170 LRRM 1277 (2000); Traction Wholesale Ctr., 328 NLRB 1058, 164 LRRM 1266 (1999), *enforced in relevant part*, 216 F.3d 92, 164 LRRM 2769 (D.C. Cir. 2000); L.S.F. Transp., Inc., 330 NLRB 1054, 169 LRRM 1309 (2000), *enforced*, 282 F.3d 972, 169 LRRM 2797 (7th Cir. 2002).

[46]*Debbie Reynolds Hotel, supra* note 45.

[47]*Id.*; Kajima Eng'g, 331 NLRB 1604, 168 LRRM 1356 (2000); *L.S.F. Transp., Inc., supra* note 45.

[48]*Debbie Reynolds Hotel, Inc., supra* note 45; *Traction Wholesale Ctr., supra* note 45; *Douglas Foods Corp., supra* note 44; Scott Bros. Dairy, 332 NLRB 1542, 169 LRRM 1118 (2000).

[49]*Douglas Foods Corp., supra* note 44; *L.S.F. Transp. Inc., supra* note 45.

practices are less likely to be dissipated, a bargaining order may nonetheless be appropriate in a large unit where the impact of the employer's unfair practices is felt throughout the bargaining unit.[50] The Board continues to be more likely to issue a bargaining order where unfair labor practices are committed by the employer's highest officials.[51]

2. *Conduct Not Warranting a* Gissel *Bargaining Order*

The Board continues to refuse to issue *Gissel* bargaining orders in situations in which traditional Board remedies would lead to a fair election.[52] In addition, bargaining orders continue to be inappropriate in situations in which the unfair labor practices have been extended to only one or a few employees.[53] The Board in *Burlington Times, Inc.*[54] declined to enter a bargaining order recommended by a judge. The Board determined that the non-economic benefits granted by the employer had less direct significance to employees than wage increases, and were therefore unlikely to have such an enduring effect on election conditions.

The Board has also refused to issue *Gissel* orders in more fact-specific situations. For example, the Board recognized that a bargaining order would likely be unenforceable when it had unjustifiably delayed the case for more than four years.[55] In an attempt to avoid further unnecessary litigation, the Board ordered the parties to proceed directly to a second election[56] or have ordered special

---

[50] *See* Scott ex. rel. NLRB v. Stephen Dunn & Assocs., 241 F.3d 652, 166 LRRM 2385 (9th Cir. 2001) (granting interim bargaining order pursuant to §10(j), despite large size of unit, where employer's unfair labor practices affected entire unit).

[51] Aldworth Co., 338 NLRB 137, 171 LRRM 1033 (2002); Rankin & Rankin, Inc., 330 NLRB 1026, 165 LRRM 1221 (2000).

[52] *See generally* Hialeah Hosp., 343 NLRB No. 52, 176 LRRM 1254 (2004); Willamette Indus., Inc., 331 NLRB 523, 167 LRRM 1177, *enforcement denied and remanded*, 253 F.3d 720, 167 LRRM 2573 (D.C. Cir. 2001); Canned Foods, Inc., 332 NLRB 1449 (2000); Aqua Cool, 332 NLRB 95, 171 LRRM 1159 (2000).

[53] Mid-Mountain Foods, Inc., 332 NLRB 229, 168 LRRM 1450 (2000), *enforcement granted*, 269 F.3d 1075, 169 LRRM 2152 (D.C. Cir. 2001) (bargaining order inappropriate where handbill containing threat of plant closure was distributed to only one employee).

[54] 328 NLRB 750, 163 LRRM 1281 (1999).

[55] Wallace Int'l de P.R., 328 NLRB 29, 161 LRRM 1123 (1999); *accord* Jonbil, Inc., 332 NLRB 652 (2000).

[56] *Id.*

remedies.[57] Finally, the Board has in particular circumstances considered employee turnover to determine whether a bargaining order is warranted.[58]

D. The Bargaining Order as an Extraordinary Remedy

The Board has continued to issue *Gissel* bargaining orders where an employer engages in conduct that is seriously coercive even in the absence of a Section 8(a)(5) violation. Where the Board does enter a *Gissel* order, the courts require an explanation as to why traditional remedies are insufficient to remedy the unfair labor practices.[59] In *General Trailer, Inc.*,[60] the Board issued a bargaining order to remedy serious Section 8(a)(1) violations, including the employer's use of armed guards, the locking of its gate on the day of the election, and the prevention of discharged employees from casting challenged ballots.

The Board has continued to issue bargaining orders after finding unlawful withdrawal of recognition based upon an unlawful poll of employees and direct dealing with employees. In addition to the requirement that an employer comply with the standards of *Struksnes Construction Co.*,[61] the Board has ruled that polling concerning union representation without giving the union advance notice violates Section 8(a)(1).[62] In its decision on remand, the Board, in finding no

---

[57]Charlotte Ampitheater Corp. dba Blockbuster Pavilion, 331 NLRB 1274, 169 LRRM 1254 (2000) (order must be justified at time of its issuance).

[58]Research Fed. Credit Union, 327 NLRB 1051, 161 LRRM 1156 (1999) (Board sought and obtained remand from court to analyze propriety of bargaining order); Overnite Transp. Co., 329 NLRB 990, 160 LRRM 1101 (1999), *enforced,* 240 F.3d 325, 166 LRRM 2577 (4th Cir.), *vacated on rehearing en banc, denying enforcement and remanding* 280 F.3d 417, 169 LRRM 2469 (4th Cir. 2002).

[59]Transportation Maint. Servs. v. NLRB, 275 F.3d 112, 169 LRRM 2070 (D.C. Cir. 2002), *vacating and remanding* 328 NLRB 691, 161 LRRM 1145 (1999); Garvey Marine, Inc. v. NLRB, 245 F.3d 819, 167 LRRM 2001 (D.C. Cir. 2001); Traction Wholesale Ctr. Co. v. NLRB, 216 F.3d 92, 164 LRRM 2769 (D.C. Cir. 2000); Vincent Indus. Plastics, Inc. v. NLRB, 209 F.3d 727, 164 LRRM 2039 (D.C. Cir. 2000); *Charlotte Ampitheater Corp. dba Blockbuster Pavilion, supra* note 57.

[60]330 NLRB 1088 (2000); *see also* Orland Park Motor Cars, Inc., 333 NLRB 1017 (2001), *enforced,* 309 F.3d 452, 171 LRRM 2139 (7th Cir. 2002).

[61]165 NLRB 1062, 65 LRRM 1385 (1967); Allegheny Ludlum Corp., 333 NLRB 734, 166 LRRM 1353 (2001), *enforced,* 301 F.3d 167, 170 LRRM 2923 (3d Cir. 2002); Scott Bros. Dairy, 332 NLRB 1542, 169 LRRM 1118 (2000).

[62]*E.g.,* Henry Bierce Co. v. NLRB, 307 NLRB 622, 141 LRRM 1089 (1992), *enforced as modified,* 23 F.3d 1101, 146 LRRM 2419 (6th Cir. 1994), *supplemental order,* 328 NLRB 646, 163 LRRM 1209 (1999).

reasonable good faith doubt, distinguished the Supreme Court's holding in *Allentown Mack Sales & Service, Inc. v. NLRB*,[63] noting that the only employee statement alleged to evidence union disaffection did not meet the *Allentown Mack* test, however phrased. The Board rejected the employer's contention that its violations of the collective bargaining agreement and the union's lack of opposition to the employer's failure to comply with its contractual commitments constituted a good faith doubt of the union's majority status. To do otherwise, according to the Board, would provide employers with an incentive to violate their collective bargaining agreements and would vitiate the Act's objective of industrial peace.

The Board has also imposed a bargaining order on a successor employer for refusing to recognize the union.[64]

V. DEFENSES TO THE REMEDIAL BARGAINING ORDER

B. Change of Circumstances

The Board continues to hold that the validity of a *Gissel* bargaining order depends on "an evaluation of circumstances when the unfair labor practices were committed."[65] In *Audubon*, the Board found that the unfair labor practices were so "serious and substantial in character" that the possibility of correcting these practices by traditional remedies was slight, and therefore a bargaining order was appropriate. The Board recognized, however, that high levels of turnover among employees made it unlikely that the courts would enforce a bargaining order. The Board, therefore, ordered a second election.[66]

---

[63]522 U.S. 359, 157 LRRM 2257 (1998).

[64]C.E.S. Sutton Realty Co., 336 NLRB 405, 169 LRRM 1262 (2001); Park Assocs., Inc., 334 NLRB 328, 168 LRRM 1262 (2001), *vacated and remanded,* 337 NLRB 643, 170 LRRM 1120 (2002); Williams Energy Servs., 336 NLRB 160, 168 LRRM 1289 (2001), *vacated,* 340 NLRB No. 87, 173 LRRM 1276 (2003) (based on Board's ruling in MV Transp., 337 NLRB 770, 170 LRRM 1233 (2002)).

[65]Audubon Reg'l Med. Ctr., 331 NLRB 374 (2000); *see also* Overnite Transp. Co., 329 NLRB 990, 166 LRRM 1101 (1999), *vacated in relevant part,* 280 F.3d 417, 169 LRRM 2469 (4th Cir. 2002) (en banc).

[66]*Cf.* Parts Depot, Inc., 332 NLRB 670, 170 LRRM 1005 (2000), *enforced,* 24 Fed. Appx.1 (D.C. Cir. 2001) (lingering effect of employer misconduct warranted bargaining order despite employee turnover); Garvey Marine, 328 NLRB 991, 996, 163 LRRM 1253, *enforced,* 245 F.3d 819, 167 LRRM 2003 (D.C. Cir. 2001) (bargaining order where Board viewed violations as likely to "live on in the lore of the shop" despite intervening departure of most of perpetrators, ULP violations, and unit employees); Cogburn Healthcare Ctr., Inc., 342 NLRB No. 11, 175 LRRM 1486 (2004) (claim of extensive turnover and passage of time must be raised promptly).

In those circumstances where the Board has not issued a bargaining order because it would likely be unenforceable in the court of appeals, the Board has found that the employees' rights would be better served by proceeding directly to another election and ordering special remedies.[67] For example, the employer is required to have an employer official read the Board notice or permit a Board agent to read the notice in the presence of an employer official, and, on the union's request, the employer must supply the names and addresses of the current unit employees and provide access to employee bulletin boards.[68]

C. Union Discrimination or Misconduct

In *Comcast Cablevision,*[69] the court set aside a union certification where, before the election, the union offered a free weekend trip to Chicago to attend a two-hour union meeting. Applying the test articulated in *NLRB v. Savair Manufacturing Co.*,[70] the court held that the inducement was "sufficiently valuable and desirable in the eyes of the person to whom it was offered to have the potential to influence that person's vote."[71]

In *NLRB v. Sliman's Sales & Services,*[72] the court held that gifts such as T-shirts, hats, and stickers distributed by the union before the election created no inducement to vote a certain way. The court therefore affirmed the Board's conclusion that the gifts constituted mere campaign propaganda.

---

[67]Charlotte Ampitheater Corp. dba Blockbuster Pavilion, 331 NLRB 1274, 169 LRRM 1254 (2000); *Audubon Reg'l Med. Ctr., supra* note 65; Wallace Int'l de P.R., 328 NLRB 29, 161 LRRM 1123 (1999). *But see* Orland Park Motor Cars, Inc., 333 NLRB 1027, 171 LRRM 1081 (2000), *enforced*, 309 F.3d 452, 171 LRRM 2139 (7th Cir. 2002) (*Gissel* bargaining order warranted where employer engaged in unfair labor practices that undermined union's majority status and made holding fair election unlikely); Cardinal Home Prods., Inc., 338 NLRB 1004, 174 LRRM 1290 (2003).

[68]In other cases, the special remedy was limited to supplying names and addresses. *See, e.g.*, Cooper Hand Tools, 328 NLRB 145, 168 LRRM 1479 (1999); Regal Recycling Inc., 329 NLRB 355, 163 LRRM 1245 (1999). *See also* Federated Logistics & Operations, 340 NLRB No. 36, 173 LRRM 1210 (2003); Comcast Cablevision of Phila., 328 NLRB 487, 161 LRRM 1166 (1999); Research Fed. Credit Union, 327 NLRB 1051, 161 LRRM 1156 (1999).

[69]232 F.3d 490, 165 LRRM 2803 (6th Cir. 2000).

[70]414 U.S. 270 (1973).

[71]*Comcast Cablevision, supra* note 68, 232 F.3d at 495.

[72]2003 U.S. App. LEXIS 19471, 173 LRRM 2416 (6th Cir. 2003).

In *Allen's Electric*,[73] the Board found that a union's promise to reimburse employees for wages lost in voting in a representation election was not objectionable. The Board stressed that the offer was made in response to voter inquiry and was limited to voters who would actually lose paid work hours because of the election. The union's election-day carpool was also found not to be objectionable. The Board found that the union's promise was limited to unavoidable financial consequences of voting rather than election-related benefits, and thus did not reasonably tend to interfere with employee voters' free and uncoerced choice. This was true even though, in at least one instance, the money paid to a voter exceeded his out-of-pocket loss for time actually spent voting.

VI. WITHDRAWAL OF RECOGNITION

The Board overruled its long-held view in *Celanese Corp.*[74] that an employer could withdraw recognition from an incumbent union when it had a good faith doubt (uncertainty or disbelief) about the union's continuing majority status. In *Levitz Furniture Co.*,[75] the Board ruled that an employer may unilaterally withdraw recognition from an incumbent union only where the employer can demonstrate that "the union has actually lost the support of the majority of the bargaining unit employees. . . ."[76] According to the Board, this new standard will foster elections that are the preferred method of resolving questions concerning representation. In consideration of this new standard, the Board discontinued its practice of a unitary standard for withdrawal and RM petitions. For RM petitions, the Board adopted the *Allentown Mack Sales & Service v. NLRB*[77] standard of reasonable uncertainty about the union's continued majority status to obtain such an election.

---

[73]340 NLRB No. 119, 173 LRRM 1425 (2003).

[74]95 NLRB 664, 28 LRRM 1362 (1951), *overruled by* Levitz Furniture Co., 333 NLRB 717, 166 LRRM 1329 (2001).

[75]333 NLRB 717, 166 LRRM 1329 (2001); *see also* Scepter, Inc. v. NLRB, 280 F.3d 1053, 169 LRRM 2524 (D.C. Cir. 2002).

[76]*Id.*, 333 NLRB at 717.

[77]522 U.S. 359, 157 LRRM 2257 (1998), *rev'g and remanding* 83 F.3d 1483, 152 LRRM 2257 (D.C. Cir. 1996), *enforcing* 316 NLRB 1199, 149 LRRM 1051 (1995).

The Seventh Circuit set aside the Board's decision in *Temple Security, Inc.*,[78] where the Board found that the employer acted lawfully when it withdrew recognition from the union on the termination of the contract solely on the ground that the unit was a mixed-guard unit.[79] The court declined to create an exception to the application of Section 8(a)(5) for uncertifiable mixed unions and remanded the case "for consideration of the Union's section 8 claims."[80] On remand, the Board ruled that the employer had violated Sections 8(a)(1) and (5) by withdrawing recognition from and refusing to bargain with the union on and after the termination of the contract.[81] However, in *Northwest Pacific Services*,[82] the Board reaffirmed its *Wells Fargo*[83] doctrine which permits withdrawal of recognition upon expiration of the collective bargaining agreement.

An employer is prohibited from withdrawing recognition during the year after certification, and may not withdraw recognition outside the certification year on the basis of evidence of loss of majority status acquired within the certification year.[84]

Where an employer extends voluntary recognition to a union, a presumption of majority status arises and continues for a reasonable period of time.[85] The Board, in seeking to enable bargaining relationships to become productive, does not measure a "reasonable time" by the number of days or months but by what transpired and what was accomplished in the bargaining sessions.[86] The Board examines the factual circumstances to determine if the parties have

---

[78]328 NLRB 663, 161 LRRM 1129 (1999), *set aside, remanded sub nom.* General Serv. Employees Local 73 v. NLRB, 230 F.3d 909, 165 LRRM 2580 (7th Cir. 2000).

[79]General Serv. Employees Local 73 v. NLRB, *supra* note 78.

[80]*Id.*, 230 F.3d at 916.

[81]337 NLRB 372, 169 LRRM 1161 (2001) (Board accepted ruling of court as law of case).

[82]342 NLRB No. 120, 175 LRRM 1405 (2004).

[83]270 NLRB 787, 116 LRRM 1229 (1984).

[84]Chelsea Indus., Inc., 331 NLRB 1648, 165 LRRM 1118 (2000), *enforced*, 285 F.3d 1073, 169 LRRM 2961 (D.C. Cir. 2002) (antiunion petition was circulated and presented to employer during certification year).

[85]*See* Main Edition, Chapter 12, this Section.

[86]Livent Realty dba Ford Center for the Performing Arts, 328 NLRB 1, 161 LRRM 1037 (1999) (reasonable time for bargaining had not elapsed after more than 10 months of voluntary recognition where parties had a draft agreement in place within few months of recognition and parties "essentially agreed" to few remaining matters).

had sufficient time to reach an agreement. In so doing, the Board considers the degree of progress made in negotiations, whether the parties were negotiating for an initial contract, and whether the parties were at an impasse.[87]

In *St. Elizabeth Manor, Inc.*,[88] the Board held that once a successor's obligation to recognize an incumbent union attaches, the union is entitled to bargain for a reasonable period of time without a challenge to its majority status. The Board overruled *Southern Moldings, Inc.*,[89] and held that a "successor bar" will preclude challenges to the incumbent union during this period. However, in *MV Transportation*,[90] the Board overruled *St. Elizabeth Manor*[91] and returned to its *Southern Moldings*[92] standard, under which an incumbent union in a successor situation is entitled only to a rebuttable presumption of continuing majority status that will not operate to bar otherwise valid decertification, rival union, or employer petitions.

Where an employer has unlawfully withdrawn recognition from an incumbent union, the Board continues to require the employer to resume bargaining for a reasonable period of time before the union's majority status can be challenged.[93] In *Lee Lumber & Building Material Corp.*,[94] the Board held that such a reasonable period will be no less than six months, but no more than one year.

B. Activity or Inactivity by the Union

In *Henry Bierce Co.*,[95] the Board held that the employer unlawfully withdrew recognition because it lacked a good faith belief based

---

[87]MGM Grand Hotel Inc., 329 NLRB 464, 162 LRRM 1202 (1999).

[88]329 NLRB 341, 162 LRRM 1146 (1999); Park Assocs., Inc., 334 NLRB 328, 168 LRRM 1262 (2001), *vacated and remanded*, 337 NLRB 643, 170 LRRM 1120 (2002).

[89]219 NLRB 119, 89 LRRM 1623 (1975).

[90]337 NLRB 770, 170 LRRM 1233 (2002); *see also* MSK Corp., 341 NLRB No. 11, 174 LRRM 1143 (2004).

[91]*Supra* note 88.

[92]*Supra* note 89.

[93]Prime Serv., Inc., 330 NLRB 815, 168 LRRM 1302, *enforced*, 266 F.3d 1233, 168 LRRM 2545 (D.C. Cir. 2001).

[94]334 NLRB 399, 167 LRRM 1185 (2001), *enforced*, 310 F.3d 209, 171 LRRM 2269 (D.C. Cir. 2002).

[95]328 NLRB 646, 163 LRRM 1209 (1999), *enforced in part and remanded*, 234 F.3d 1268, 169 LRRM 2640 (6th Cir. 2000).

on objective evidence that the union lacked majority support. The Board rejected the employer's contentions regarding employee and union activity, where the employer had violated its contractual obligations to pay negotiated wages and benefits and to notify the union of job openings and new hires. The fact that the union filed no grievances, did not replace a steward who had retired, or submit a contract to its members for ratification did not support a good faith doubt, because, the Board held, to do so would be antithetical to the Act's purpose of promoting industrial peace by giving employers an incentive to violate their collective bargaining agreements. As stated in *McDonald Partners Inc.*, "[i]nactivity of a union (short of defunctness) or failure to process grievances is ordinarily an insufficient basis on presumption of continuing majority status."[96]

The Board ruled in *Avery Dennison*[97] that the lawfulness of an employer's withdrawal of recognition is not an appropriate subject for deferral to arbitration because the withdrawal involves "the very existence of the collective bargaining relationship between the parties."[98]

C. Filing of Decertification Petition

In *Vincent Industrial Plastics, Inc.*,[99] the Board found that the employer's unremedied unfair labor practices had tainted the filing of a decertification petition, and the employer could not rely on the petition as the basis for its withdrawal of recognition and refusal to

---

[96]336 NLRB 836, 851, 169 LRRM 1139 (2001), *enforcement denied and remanded,* 331 F.3d 1002 (D.C. Cir. 2003), *complaint dismissed on remand,* 342 NLRB No. 63, 175 LRRM 1188 (2004); *see also* Raven Gov't Servs., Inc., 331 NLRB 651 (2000), *enforced,* 315 F.3d 499, 171 LRRM 2606 (5th Cir. 2002) (union's lack of effort to reach agreement, failure to make proposals to break impasse, inactivity for eight months, high turnover, and rumor of decertification petition insufficient to create a reasonable uncertainty of continued majority status).

[97]330 NLRB 389, 163 LRRM 1033 (1999).

[98]*Id.* at 391.

[99]328 NLRB 300, 163 LRRM 1123 (1999), *enforced in part, remanded,* 209 F.3d 727, 164 LRRM 2039 (D.C. Cir. 2000).

bargain.[100] In *Saint-Gobain Abrasives*, [101] the Board ordered a preelection hearing be held on the alleged taint of the decertification petition.

E. Miscellaneous Factors

The employer in *Red Coats, Inc.*[102] voluntarily recognized the union as bargaining representative in three separate single-location units. After the parties bargained to impasse, the employer claimed that the single-location units were inappropriate and withdrew recognition. The Board found that the employer was equitably estopped from challenging the appropriateness of the units it had agreed to through voluntary recognition. Under these circumstances, where the unit had been agreed to by the parties and is not prohibited by the Act, the unit is appropriate regardless of whether the Board would have certified it ab initio.

---

[100] *See also* Jano Graphics, Inc., 339 NLRB 251, 172 LRRM 1292 (2003); Eby-Brown Co. L.P., 328 NLRB 496, 168 LRRM 1165 (1999); Sheridan Manor Nursing Home, Inc., 329 NLRB 476, 165 LRRM 1051 (1999), *enforced*, 225 F.3d 248, 165 LRRM 2132 (2d Cir. 2000); California Portland Cement Co., 330 NLRB 144, 169 LRRM 1287 (1999), *enforced*, 19 Fed. Appx. 683, 2001 WL 1153246 (9th Cir. 2001); V&S ProGalv, Inc. v. NLRB, 168 F.3d 270, 280–82, 160 LRRM 2518 (6th Cir. 1999), *enforcing* 323 NLRB 801, 157 LRRM 1255 (1997). *But see* Americare Pine Lodge Nursing & Rehab. Ctr. v. NLRB, 164 F.3d 867, 160 LRRM 2201 (4th Cir. 1999), *enforcing in part* 325 NLRB 98, 157 LRRM 1142 (1997); Mathews Readymix v. NLRB, 165 F.3d 74, 160 LRRM 2353 (D.C. Cir. 1999), *enforcing in part* 324 NLRB 960, 157 LRRM 1142 (1997) (reversing findings by Board that decertification petitions were tainted and withdrawal of recognition was illegal); Bunting Bearings Corp., 343 NLRB No. 64, 175 LRRM 1513 (2004); Bridgestone/Firestone, Inc., 335 NLRB 941, 170 LRRM 1516 (2001) (decertification petition not "tainted" where employer had merely provided lawful, ministerial aid to employee in preparing it).

[101] 342 NLRB No. 39, 175 LRRM 1107 (2004).

[102] 328 NLRB 205, 161 LRRM 1100 (1999).

Part IV

THE COLLECTIVE BARGAINING PROCESS

BIBLIOGRAPHY

Keith Alan Byers, *No One is Above the Law When it Comes to the ADA and the Rehabilitation Act – Not Even Federal, State, or Local Law Enforcement Agencies,* 30 Loy. L.A. L. Rev. 977 (1997)

Matthew W. Finkin, *Employee Representation Outside the Labor Act: Thoughts on Arbitral Representation, Group Representation, and Workplace Committees,* 5 U. Pa. J. Lab. & Emp. L. 75 (2002)

Jonathan B. Goldin, *Labor-Management Cooperation:* Bath Iron Works'*s Bold New Approach,* 47 Me. L. Rev. 415 (1995)

Christopher Grant, *Unions in a Fragmented Society,* 7 Chi.-Kent L. Rev. 849 (2002)

Michael C. Harper, *Defining the Economic Relationship Appropriate for Collective Bargaining,* 39 B.C. L. Rev 329 (1998)

H. Victoria Hedian, *The Implications of* Crown Cork & Seal Co. *for Employee Involvement as "Labor Organizations" Under the Wagner Act: What Constitutes "Dealing With" Pursuant to Section 2(5) of the Act Since* Electromation, Inc.*?,* 18 Lab. Law 35 (2002)

Ann C. Hodges, *Arbitration of Statutory Claims in the Unionized Workplace: Is Bargaining with the Union Required?,* 16 Ohio St. J. on Disp. Resol. 513 (2001)

Ann C. Hodges, *The Americans With Disabilities Act in the Unionized Workplace,* 48 U. Miami L. Rev. 567 (1994)

Lacie L. Kaiser, *Revisiting the Impact of the Curt Flood Act of 1998 on the Bargaining Relationship Between Players and Management in Major League Baseball,* 2 DePaul J. Sports L. Contemp. Probs. 230 (2004)

Laurie Ann Krepto, *Labor Law—Employer's Duty to Bargain Over a Plant Relocation: D. C. Circuit Court of Appeals Approves NLRB's New Test*—United Food Workers International Union, Local No. 150-A v. NLRB, *1 F.3d 24 (D.C. Cir. 1993), cert. granted, 62 U.S.L.W. 3653 (U.S. Apr. 4, 1994) (No. 93–1103),* 67 Temp. L. Rev. 473 (1994)

Michael H. LeRoy, *Employer Domination of Labor Organizations and the* Electromation *Case: An Empirical Public Policy Analysis,* 61 Geo. Wash. L. Rev. 1812 (1993).

Tracey I. Levy, *Collective Bargaining in the Elite Professions: Doctors' Application of the Labor Law Model to Negotiations with Health Care Providers*, 13 U. FLA. J.L. & PUB. POL'Y 269 (2002)

Condon A. McGlothlen and Gary N. Savine, Eckles v. Consolidated Rail Corp.*: Reconciling the ADA with Collective Bargaining Agreements: Is This the Correct Approach?*, 46 DEPAUL L. REV. 1043 (1997)

Mary K. O'Melvey, *The Americans With Disabilities Act and Collective Bargaining Agreements: Reasonable Accommodations or Irreconcilable Conflicts?*, 82 KY. L.J. 219 (1993)

Maxine Schmitz, Doe v. Boeing: *The Employer's Duty to Reasonably Accommodate the Handicapped Employee*, 29 GONZ. L. REV. 205 (1993)

Theodore J. St. Antoine, Gilmer *in the Collective Bargaining Context*, 16 OHIO ST. J. ON DISP. RESOL. 491 (2001)

Mark L. Stolzenburg, *Blind Faith or Efficiency? The Differences Between the Fifth Circuit and All Others on the Topic of Private Sector Impasse Bargaining*, 80 WASH. U. L.Q. 1341 (2002)

Jacob E. Tyler, *Mandatory Arbitration of Discrimination Claims Under Collective Bargaining Agreements: The Effects of* Wright, 4 HARV. NEGOT. L. REV. 253 (1999)

Chapter 13

THE DUTY TO BARGAIN

I. INTRODUCTION

B. Elements of the Bargaining Obligation

1. *The Duty to Meet, Confer, and Negotiate*

There is still no per se standard to determine whether the parties have satisfied their Section 8(d) obligation to meet at reasonable times and confer in good faith with respect to wages, hours, and other terms and conditions of employment, or the negotiation of an agreement.[1]

2. *The Obligation to Deal in Good Faith*

The Board and the courts continue to take a case-by-case approach in determining whether a party's conduct at the bargaining table constitutes bad faith bargaining.[2]

---

[1]*See, e.g.*, Victoria Packing Corp., 332 NLRB 597, 172 LRRM 1090 (2000) (employer unlawfully refused to meet and bargain with union representative after representative shouted and yelled at company owner because his conduct did not involve physical contact or explicit threat of force); Altorfer Mach. Co., 332 NLRB 130, 171 LRRM 1029 (2000) ("[A]ttention must be paid to the [party's] 'conduct in the totality of the circumstances in which bargaining took place.'").

[2]*See, e.g.*, Pleasantview Nursing Home, Inc. v. NLRB, 351 F.3d 747, 757–58, 173 LRRM 2882 (6th Cir. 2003) (employer engaged in lawful hard bargaining when it refused to change its initial proposal to eliminate three paid holidays and amount of pension contributions); NLRB v. Suffield Acad., 322 F.3d 196, 198–99, 171 LRRM 3164 (2d Cir. 2003) (withdrawal of tentative agreements is not "per se" violation of Act); Public Serv. Co. of Okla. v. NLRB, 318 F.3d 1173, 1177–78, 171 LRRM 2993 (10th Cir. 2003) (employer engaged in bad faith bargaining when it insisted that "as a price" for agreement, employees give up rights to be properly represented by union); TNT USA Inc. v. NLRB, 208 F.3d 362, 163 LRRM 2989 (2d Cir. 2000) (employer that repudiated tentative agreement after union "threw in the towel" to reach agreement did not bargain in good faith); NLRB v. Waymouth Farms Inc., 172 F.3d 598, 160 LRRM 3018 (8th Cir. 1999) (employer engaged in bad faith

3. *The Subjects of Bargaining*

The Board and the courts continue to apply the *Borg-Warner*[3] distinctions between mandatory, permissive, and illegal subjects of bargaining.[4]

II. PER SE VIOLATIONS

A. Unilateral Changes

An employer's material[5] unilateral change to a mandatory subject of bargaining during the term of a collective bargaining agreement, before an impasse is reached on that subject, remains a prima facie violation of the Act.[6]

---

bargaining by misleading union regarding potential relocation sites, thus impeding union's ability to bargain over effects of relocation); Phelps Dodge Specialty Copper Prods. Co., 337 NLRB 455, 455 n.1, 169 LRRM 1469 (2002) (employer did not engage in bad faith bargaining with respect to union security and dues checkoff where employer made other concessions and explained its position regarding the disputed proposals); Bridgestone/Firestone, Inc., 337 NLRB 133, 169 LRRM 1321 (2001) (employer that withdrew contract offer upon receiving decertification petition required to reinstate offer where employer was required to bargain with the union for 6 months pursuant to settlement agreement); Hardesty Co. dba Mid-Continent Concrete, 336 NLRB 258, 171 LRRM 1016 (2001) (totality of employer's conduct at and away from table demonstrated intent to frustrate negotiations); Lois Dev. Corp., 333 NLRB 410, 416, 173 LRRM 1110 (2001) (employer bargained in good faith when it articulated its position on each and every contract proposal during bargaining sessions); Reading Rock Inc., 330 NLRB 856, 164 LRRM 1325 (2000) (repeated proposal to change scope of bargaining unit is evidence of overall bad faith bargaining); Gadsden Tool Inc., 327 NLRB 164, 163 LRRM 1302 (1998) (bad faith bargaining exists when employer enters negotiations with no intention of reaching agreement).

[3]NLRB v. Borg-Warner Corp., Wooster Div., 356 U.S. 342, 42 LRRM 2034 (1958).

[4]*See, e.g.*, Woodland Clinic, 331 NLRB 735, 164 LRRM 1289 (2000) (pay-for-performance wage proposal that confers on employer broad discretionary powers is mandatory subject of bargaining); *Reading Rock Inc., supra* note 2 (proposal to change scope of bargaining unit is permissive subject of bargaining).

[5]Crittenton Hosp., 342 NLRB No. 67, 175 LRRM 1283 (2004) (employer's unilateral change in the dress code policy is not unlawful because general counsel failed to show that change was material, substantial, or significant); Toledo Blade Co., 343 NLRB No. 51, 175 LRRM 1538 (2004) (a unilateral change in mandatory subject of bargaining is unlawful only if it is a material, substantial, and significant change), citing Flambeau Airmold Corp., 334 NLRB 165, 170 LRRM 1379 (2001).

[6]*See, e.g.*, Beverly Health & Rehab. Servs., Inc. v. NLRB, 317 F.3d 316, 171 LRRM 3017 (D.C. Cir. 2003) (nursing home chain committed unfair labor practice by unilaterally during negotiations replacing HMO coverage for employees in place of union health and welfare fund; nursing home unlawfully denied access by

union to facilities including use of bulletin boards), *enforcing in part* 335 NLRB 635, 171 LRRM 1402 (2001); Chelsea Indus. v. NLRB, 285 F.3d 1073, 169 LRRM 2961 (D.C. Cir. 2002), *enforcing* 331 NLRB 1648, 165 LRRM 1118 (2000) (unilateral change in wages); BP Amoco Corp. v. NLRB, 217 F.3d 869, 164 LRRM 2889 (D.C. Cir. 2000), *enforcing* 328 NLRB 1220, 161 LRRM 1017 (1999) (modifications to health plan); Vincent Indus. Plastics, Inc. v. NLRB, 209 F.3d 727, 164 LRRM 2039 (D.C. Cir. 2000), *enforcing* 328 NLRB 300, 163 LRRM 1123 (1999) (changes in attendance policy, working hours, work duties, and time-keeping method); Alwin Mfg. Co. v. NLRB, 192 F.3d 133, 162 LRRM 2385 (D.C. Cir. 1999) (institution of minimum production standards and change in vacation scheduling policy); Loral Defense Sys.-Akron v. NLRB, 200 F.3d 436, 162 LRRM 3025 (6th Cir. 1999) (change in health care plans); Visiting Nurses Servs. of W. Mass. v. NLRB, 177 F.3d 52, 161 LRRM 2326 (1st Cir. 1999) (increase in wage rate and alteration to vacation policy); Kansas AFL-CIO, 341 NLRB No. 131, 174 LRRM 1567 (2004) (unilateral elimination of bargaining unit position); King Soopers, Inc., 340 NLRB No. 75, 173 LRRM 1363 (2004) (employer unlawfully failed to bargain when it unilaterally implemented policy requiring use of scanner in filling prescriptions, where noncompliance could result in discipline including discharge); Anheuser-Busch, Inc., 342 NLRB No. 49, 175 LRRM 1168 (2004) (employer violated §8(a)(5) by failing to notify and bargain with union prior to installation and use of surveillance cameras in workplace); Trailmobile Trailer, LLC, 343 NLRB No. 17, 176 LRRM 1433(2004) (employer unlawfully failed to notify and bargain with the union about the installation of surveillance cameras, one facing the parking lot and one facing the entrance to its facility); Verizon N.Y. Inc., 339 NLRB 30, 172 LRRM 1193 (2003) (employer acted unlawfully by unilaterally rescinding its longstanding practice of allowing employees to participate in blood drives during working hours); Falcon Wheel Div., LLC, 338 NLRB 576, 171 LRRM 1537 (2002) (unilateral layoff of employee); Lafayette Grinding Corp., 337 NLRB 832, 170 LRRM 1355 (2002) (employer ceased contributions to employees' health and welfare fund); Paul Mueller Co., 337 NLRB 764, 174 LRRM 1043 (2002) (unilateral subcontracting); WWOR-TV Inc., 330 NLRB 1265, 164 LRRM 1358 (2000) (new terms and conditions of employment); Grinnell Fire Protect. Sys. Co., 328 NLRB 585, 161 LRRM 1146 (1999), *enforced*, 236 F.3d 187, 166 LRRM 2065 (4th Cir. 2000), *cert. denied*, 534 U.S. 818, 168 LRRM 2472 (2001) (pre-impasse implementation of changes in wages, job classifications, benefits, and pension plan); Traction Wholesale Ctr., 328 NLRB 1058, 164 LRRM 1266 (1999), *enforced*, 216 F.3d 92, 164 LRRM 2769 (D.C. Cir 2000) (change in lunch time "punch in and out" policy and practice of allowing employees to take company vans home); Leisure Knoll Ass'n, 327 NLRB 470, 165 LRRM 1359 (1999) (change in paid vacation days and elimination of double-time pay for Sundays and holidays); Richard Mellow Elec. Contractors Corp., 327 NLRB 1112, 161 LRRM 1018 (1999) (increase in wage rate); Kurdziel Iron of Wauseon Inc., 327 NLRB 155, 163 LRRM 1285 (1998), *enforced*, 208 F.3d 214, 163 LRRM 2960 (6th Cir. 2000) (discontinuance of practice of granting October wage increase); Consec Sec., 328 NLRB 1201, 162 LRRM 1046 (1999) (imposition of a rule requiring employees to obtain approval from main office for all time off); United Ref. Co., 327 NLRB 795, 161 LRRM 1292 (1999) (changes in wage rates, health plans, cafeteria privileges, sick privileges, and seniority system). *Cf.* Graphic Communications Chicago Local 458-3M v. NLRB, 206 F.3d 22, 163 LRRM 2833 (D.C. Cir. 2000) (parties had reached impasse when employer implemented final offer); Midwest Television, Inc., 343 NLRB No. 83 (2004) (because contractual provision permitting employer to negotiate above scale wages directly with selected employees is a permissive subject of bargaining, employer's unilateral reduction

The Board and several circuit courts[7] continue to rule that when negotiating for an initial or replacement collective bargaining agreement, an employer normally violates the Act when it unilaterally implements a mandatory subject of bargaining where impasse is reached only on that issue and not on the negotiations as a whole. In *Duffy Tool & Stamping, L.L.C. v. NLRB*,[8] the Seventh Circuit rejected the Fifth Circuit's view[9] that an employer may unilaterally implement a mandatory subject of bargaining if impasse is reached on that particular issue.[10] Instead, the court adopted the position favored by the Board and the other circuits that have addressed the issue and held that impasse is not reached until the parties are "deadlocked in the negotiation as a whole."[11] However, in *TXU Electric Co.*, the Board found an exception to the general requirement of an overall impasse and held that the employer did not violate Section 8(a)(5) by

---

of wages of employee working under personal service contract to union scale during term of collective bargaining agreement was not unlawful).

[7]*See, e.g.*, Essex Valley, 343 NLRB No. 92, 176 LRRM 1089 (2004) (unilateral transfer of nurses from administrative in-house positions to field nurse positions violated Act); *Vincent Indus. Plastics, Inc.*, *supra* note 6, at 735; *Visiting Nurses Servs.*, *supra* note 6; RBE Elecs., 320 NLRB 80, 81–82, 151 LRRM 1329 (1995); Intermountain Rural Elec. Ass'n, 305 NLRB 783, 786, 139 LRRM 1003 (1991), *enforced*, 984 F.2d 1562, 142 LRRM 2448 (10th Cir. 1993); NLRB v. Central Plumbing Co., 492 F.2d 1252, 1254, 85 LRRM 2779 (6th Cir. 1974). *But see* TXU Elec., 343 NLRB No. 132 (2004) (employer did not violate Section §8(a)(5) by changing its past practice of annual salary adjustments for unit employees while it negotiated with union for initial contract.) *See also* Saint-Gobain Abrasives, Inc., 343 NLRB No. 68, 176 LRRM 1138 (2004) (where employer had annual process of reviewing and adjusting health insurance programs, it could implement unilateral changes regarding health insurance programs absent overall impasse); Courier-Journal, 342 NLRB No. 113, 175 LRM 1410 (2004) (unilateral change after contract expiration to health care insurance benefits of unit employees not unlawful because made pursuant to well established past practice).

[8]233 F.3d 995, 165 LRRM 2929 (7th Cir. 2000), *enforcing* 330 NLRB 298, 165 LRRM 1372 (1999).

[9]*See, e.g.*, NLRB v. Pinkston-Hollar Constr. Servs., Inc., 954 F.2d 306, 311–12, 139 LRRM 2686 (5th Cir. 1992); Nabors Trailers, Inc. v. NLRB, 910 F.2d 268, 273, 135 LRRM 2188 (5th Cir. 1990).

[10]*Duffy Tool*, *supra* note 8, 233 F.3d at 998.

[11]*Id.*, 165 LRRM at 2932. *But see TXU Elec.*, *supra* note 7, *and* Stone Container Corp., 313 NLRB 336, 145 LRRM 1065 (1993) (Board held that employer that had past practice of wage increases each April did not violate Act by not granting wage increase during bargaining for an initial contract, where employer informed union in advance that it would not grant particular wage increase for economic reasons but did not purport to terminate annual wage review practice; employer expressed willingness to discuss subject, and union did not make any specific counterproposal).

refraining from giving unit employees a recurring, regularly scheduled annual wage adjustment following notice to the union and an opportunity to bargain during negotiations for an initial contract.[12] The Board found that, under the circumstances, piecemeal treatment of the wage issue was unavoidable since a contract would not likely be agreed to prior to the regularly scheduled time for the annual wage adjustment.[13] The Board further stated that it continued "to adhere to the governing principles of collective bargaining that disfavor piecemeal bargaining and preclude unilateral implementation of a bargaining proposal unless the parties have bargained to overall impasse for an agreement as a whole."[14]

B. Bargaining Directly With Employees

The Board continues to hold that an employer violates Section 8(a)(5) by circumventing the union and bargaining directly with the employees,[15] while courts of appeal have varied in

---

[12] *TXU Elec.*, *supra* note 7.

[13] *Id.*

[14] *Id.*

[15] *See, e.g.*, HCL, Inc., 343 NLRB No. 95, 176 LRRM 1183 (2004) (employer violated Act when it dealt directly with employees by offering new wages and benefits); M & M Auto. Group, Inc. dba Broadway Volkswagen, 342 NLRB No. 128, 176 LRRM 1231 (2004) (employer unlawfully dealt directly with unit employees when manager communicated an employee's promotion and wage increase directly to employee); Georgia Power Co., 342 NLRB No. 18, 175 LRRM 1130 (2004) (employer unlawfully dealt directly with unit employees regarding the formation of a workplace ethics program); Northwest Graphics, Inc., 343 NLRB No. 16, 176 LRRM 1167 (2004) (employer unlawfully engaged in direct dealing with employees regarding wages and work hours); Dayton Newspapers Inc., 339 NLRB 650, 172 LRRM 1477 (2003) (employer violated Act by meeting with 18 locked-out employees in one-on-one meetings and asking employees to waive right to strike or picket in the future in exchange for reinstatement); Lafayette Grinding Corp., 337 NLRB 832, 170 LRRM 1355 (2002) (unlawful direct dealing where employer unilaterally increased wages and offered its own health plan directly to employees); Outdoor Venture Corp., 336 NLRB 1006, 169 LRRM 1267 (2001) (employer met with striking employees on picket line to discuss wide range of matters that were also subject of negotiations); Morgan Servs., Inc., 336 NLRB 290, 170 LRRM 1116 (2001) (employer violated Act by changing working hours of two employees after individual discussions with them); Leisure Knoll Ass'n, 327 NLRB 470, 165 LRRM 1359 (1999) (employer negotiated wage rate with individual employee whom it wanted to come to work earlier); Grinnell Fire Prot. Sys. Co., 328 NLRB 585 (1999), *enforced*, 236 F.3d 187, 166 LRRM 2065 (4th Cir. 2000) (employer engaged in direct dealing by offering some employees higher wage rate than offered in last contract proposal); O'Dovero, 325 NLRB 998, 160 LRRM 1071 (1998), *enforced*, 193 F.3d 532, 162 LRRM 2618 (D.C. Cir. 1999) (employer violated Act by dealing

the degree to which they have been willing to accept the Board's position.[16]

C. Refusal to Execute Written Contract

The Board and the courts continue to follow the rule that a party's refusal to reduce to writing or sign a written memorandum of the agreement made is a per se refusal to bargain.[17]

---

directly with employees regarding their wages and benefits); ABF Freight Sys. Inc., 325 NLRB 546, 160 LRRM 1027 (1998) (employer acted unlawfully when manager demanded that employee withdraw her grievance). *But see* Kurdziel Iron of Wauseon Inc., 327 NLRB 155, 163 LRRM 1285 (1998) (conversation between member of union negotiating committee and employer, initiated by committee member, about whether employees would receive raise if union was voted out was not employer's attempt to bargain directly with employee since member initiated conversation in his role as member of the union's negotiating committee).

[16]Overnite Transp. Co. v. NLRB, 280 F.3d 417, 169 LRRM 2469 (4th Cir. 2002), *denying enforcement in relevant part of* 329 NLRB 990, 166 LRRM 1101 (1999) (court found employer's publicizing wage increase proposal was not unlawful direct dealing where communication was first presented to union and was not coercive); AT Sys. W. Inc. v. NLRB, 294 F.3d 136, 141, 170 LRRM 2530 (D.C. Cir. 2002) (employer did not unlawfully bypass employee association and affiliated union when employer held mandatory employee meeting and negotiated contract where employer had no other way to meet with employee association other than by meeting with employees); Ryan Iron Works, Inc. v. NLRB, 257 F.3d 1, 167 LRRM 2653 (1st Cir. 2001), *enforcing in relevant part* 332 NLRB 506, 167 LRRM 1240 (2000) (employer took employee on three-hour driving trip and encouraged employee to abandon union); Americare Pine Lodge Nursing & Rehab. Ctr. v. NLRB, 164 F.3d 867, 160 LRRM 2201 (4th Cir. 1999), *denying enforcement in relevant part of* 325 NLRB 98, 157 LRRM 1142 (1997) (employer did not engage in unlawful direct dealing when supervisor had brief conversation with employee about proposal employer had sent to union offering to extend existing contract for one year in return for wage increases, where supervisor did not go beyond reporting employer's proposal in one conversation).

[17]*See, e.g.*, Sanitation Salvage Corp., 342 NLRB No. 41, 175 LRRM 1137 (2004) (employer's refusal to execute agreement that it had previously agreed to execute was unlawful); B & M Linen Corp. dba Miron & Sons Laundry, 338 NLRB 5, 171 LRRM 1032 (2002) (where there was "meeting of the minds," refusal to execute written contract embodying that agreement unlawful); Flying Dutchman Park Inc., 329 NLRB 414, 162 LRRM 1283 (1999) (employer committed unfair labor practice by refusing to sign collective bargaining contract containing unlawful union-security clause after it learned that decertification petition had been filed); Gadsden Tool, 327 NLRB 164, 163 LRRM 1302 (1998) (employer violated Act by refusing to sign collective bargaining agreement after union surprised employer by accepting employer's position on several subjects). *Cf.* Shaw's Supermarkets, Inc., 337 NLRB 499, 171 LRRM 1128 (2002) (no violation where no evidence that agreement reflected a meeting of minds of parties).

D. Refusal to Meet at Reasonable Times

A party who refuses to meet at reasonable times, or causes unreasonable delay, unlawfully refuses to bargain.[18]

F. Insisting on Nonmandatory Subjects of Bargaining

The Board and the courts continue to follow the rule that a party unlawfully refuses to bargain by insisting to impasse on the addition of a permissive subject of bargaining to the contract.[19] The Ninth Circuit added to the ever-growing category of permissive subjects when it held that the negotiation of personal service contracts was not a mandatory subject of bargaining.[20]

---

[18] *See, e.g.*, Teamsters Local 122 (Busch & Co.), 334 NLRB 1190, 174 LRRM 1176 (2001) (union unlawfully refused to bargain where it engaged in delay tactics by insisting on short negotiating sessions and long breaks between negotiating sessions); Health Care Servs. Group Inc., 331 NLRB 333, 336, 171 LRRM 1399 (2000) (employer engaged in bad faith bargaining by failing to appear at and/or canceling bargaining sessions); Richard Mellow Elec. Contractors Corp., 327 NLRB 1112, 161 LRRM 1018 (1999) (employer unlawfully refused to bargain where it rejected union's proposed meeting dates and failed to respond to union's request for meetings on at least three occasions).

[19] *See, e.g.*, ServiceNet, Inc., 340 NLRB No. 148, 173 LRRM 1553 (2003) (employer unlawfully insisted on bargaining over permissive subjects, including clauses that would allow it to deal directly with unit members and require adherence to the contract after its expiration); Grosvenor Orlando Assocs., Ltd., 336 NLRB 613 (2001) (employer that included proposal to change scope of bargaining unit in its "final" proposal unlawfully insisted to impasse on permissive subject); Dunbar ex rel. NLRB v. Carrier Corp., 66 F. Supp. 2d 346, 161 LRRM 2112 (N.D.N.Y. 1999) (employer committed unfair labor practice by insisting to impasse on proposal to deny bumping and bidding between plants). *Cf.* Reading Rock Inc., 330 NLRB 856, 164 LRRM 1325 66 F. Supp. 2d 346, (2000) (employer that repeatedly proposed to change scope of bargaining unit, a permissive subject of bargaining, did not insist on it to impasse or signal it was price union would have to pay for agreement).

[20] Retlaw Broad. Co. v. NLRB, 172 F.3d 660, 160 LRRM 2909 (9th Cir. 1999); *see also* Midwest Television, Inc., 343 NLRB No. 83 (2004).

III. THE GOOD FAITH REQUIREMENT

A. Totality of Conduct Assessed: *General Electric* and the Proper Role of the Parties

The Board continues to evaluate allegations of an employer's bad faith refusal to bargain based on the totality of the employer's conduct, including the employer's conduct at and away from the bargaining table.[21] For example, in *Burrows Paper Corp.*,[22] the Board adopted the administrative law judge's finding that the employer engaged in surface bargaining based on the employer's proposals, as well as its statements, during negotiations. The employer proposed, among other things, (1) that employees would be paid the minimum wage, which was substantially less than their current pay rate;

[21]NLRB v. Suffield Acad., 322 F.3d 196, 198, 171 LRRM 3164 (2d Cir. 2003), *enforcing* 336 NLRB 659, 171 LRRM 1491 (2001) ("Collective bargaining must be conducted in good faith, and, absent specific evidence of bad faith bargaining, the Board must consider the totality of the circumstances in order to determine whether a party has negotiated in good faith."); Pleasantview Nursing Home, Inc. v. NLRB, 351 F.3d 747, 758, 173 LRRM 2882 (6th Cir. 2003) (Board found that employer's "Overall bargaining conduct indicates good faith and willingness to negotiate"); Public Serv. Co. of Okla. v. NLRB, 318 F.3d 1173, 171 LRRM 2993 (10th Cir. 2003), *enforcing* 334 NLRB 487, 171 LRRM 1059 (2001) ("Board should examine the totality of the circumstances"); St. George Warehouse, Inc., 341 NLRB No. 120, 175 LRRM 1316 (2004) ("From the context of a party's total conduct, the Board determines whether the party is 'engaging in hard but lawful bargaining to achieve a contract that it considers desirable or is unlawfully endeavoring to frustrate the possibility of arriving at any agreement.'"); *ServiceNet, Inc.*, *supra* note 19 ("In determining that an employer's conduct crosses over the line, the Board looks at the totality of an employer's conduct"); Matanuska Elec. Ass'n, Inc., 337 NLRB 680, 171 LRRM 1536 (2002) ("good faith or the lack of it depends upon a factual determination based on overall conduct"); Burrows Paper Corp., 332 NLRB 82, 170 LRRM 1350 (2000); Altorfer Mach. Co., Lift Truck Div., 332 NLRB 130, 171 LRRM 1029 (2000); U.S. Ecology Corp., 331 NLRB 223, 165 LRRM 1197 (2000), *enforced*, 26 Fed. Appx. 435, 169 LRRM 2320 (6th Cir. 2001) ("In order to determine whether a party has bargained in good faith, it is necessary to examine its overall conduct, both at the bargaining table and away from it"); Summa Health Sys., Inc., 330 NLRB 1379, 170 LRRM 1308 (2000) ("It is necessary to scrutinize an employer's overall conduct to determine whether it has bargained in good faith").

[22]332 NLRB 82, 170 LRRM 1350 (2000). A §10(j) injunction had previously been issued against Burrows based on substantially similar allegations. Fleischut v. Burrows Paper Corp., 162 LRRM 2719 (S.D. Miss. 1999).

(2) that the contract would remain effective for only one year from the date of the representation election; and (3) that it would retain sole discretion to make annual adjustments to wage rates of unit employees without any role for the union. The employer also refused to agree to include a grievance and arbitration procedure, while at the same time insisting on a no-strike, no-lockout clause and a management-rights clause that gave it complete discretion to hire, fire, and discipline. The Board stated that the bargaining positions of the employer were to be viewed in light of the employer's chief executive officer's disparaging statements about the union. In concluding that the employer had violated Section 8(a)(5), the Board emphasized that its decision was based on the totality of the circumstances.[23]

Likewise, in *Summa Health System, Inc.*,[24] the Board based its holding that the employer had engaged in bad faith bargaining on more than just the substance of the employer's proposals. The Board stated that in addition to the employer's continued insistence on sweeping proposals concerning work transfer, job classifications, and wages, other factors suggested bad faith, including unlawful unilateral conduct and failing to comply with the union's request for information relevant to the negotiations.

The Board continues to hold that a party's intransigence on a particular subject will not in and of itself support a finding of bad faith bargaining. In *Phelps Dodge Specialty Copper Products Co.*,[25] the Board concluded that the employer did not bargain in bad faith despite refusing to agree to union security and dues checkoff proposals tendered by the union. The Board found that the employer bargained in good faith concerning all other proposals, making concessions in a number of areas, and that the totality of the employer's

---

[23] *Burrows Paper Corp.*, *supra* note 22, 332 NLRB at 82–83.
[24] *Summa Health Sys., Inc.*, *supra* note 21.
[25] 337 NLRB 455, 169 LRRM 1469 (2002).

conduct indicated good faith bargaining notwithstanding its refusal to accede to the union's demand in those specific areas.[26]

Similarly, "a stray statement indicating inflexibility will not overcome the general tenor of good faith negotiation," even if the employer's position does not change during negotiations. In *Pleasantview Nursing Home, Inc. v. NLRB*,[27] the court affirmed in part and reversed in part a Board order finding five instances of bad faith bargaining on the part of the employer. One of those instances related to the employer's alleged failure to negotiate with respect to its proposal for a buy-back of pension and paid holiday provisions.[28] The employer had claimed that the issue was "non-negotiable," but it actively bargained over the issue, exploring several alternatives to its proposals over the course of two months of meetings.[29] The court, in reversing the Board's decision on the issue, focused on the employer's conduct, not its rhetoric, in concluding that the employer had bargained in good faith. Although the employer did not change its original bargaining position regarding the buy-backs, the court found that the employer's conduct displayed a "willingness to listen to alternative ways of reaching agreement" and that neither the employer nor the union was able to "come up with a different plan"[30] acceptable to both parties. The court held that the totality of the employer's conduct evidenced impasse, but not bad faith.

In contrast, in *Public Service Co. of Oklahoma v. NLRB*,[31] the Tenth Circuit upheld a Board order that the employer bargained in bad faith based in large part on the substance of the employer's proposals. The court agreed that the employer's "rigid adherence" to its proposals showed that it was not engaged in meaningful bargaining. The employer's proposals included giving it the unilateral right "to change from time to time for business reasons" employee holidays, vacation, medical insurance, leave time, and accident insurance.[32]

---

[26]*Id. See also* St. George Warehouse, Inc., 341 NLRB No. 120, 175 LRRM 1316 (2004) (where there is no evidence that party's conduct at table indicates an intent not to reach agreement, "away from the table misconduct . . . has not been held to provide an independent basis to find bad-faith bargaining.").

[27]Pleasantview Nursing Home, Inc. v. NLRB, 351 F.3d 747, 173 LRRM 2882 (6th Cir. 2003).

[28]*See id.* at 757.

[29]*Id.* at 758.

[30]*Id.*

[31]318 F.3d 1173, 171 LRRM 2993 (10th Cir. 2003), *enforcing* 334 NLRB 487, 171 LRRM 1059 (2001).

[32]*Id.*, 318 F.3d at 1177.

The employer's proposals also included giving it almost "unfettered" control over discipline and discharge decisions, and included what the Board called an "exhaustively broad" management-rights clause.[33] The court looked to the totality of the employer's conduct, including its proposals, its conduct away from the table, and its unlawful unilateral implementation of its proposals, and held that the employer bargained in bad faith.[34]

B. Indicia of Good or Bad Faith

1. Surface Bargaining

There have been no substantial changes in the Board's position on surface bargaining. Nevertheless, the Board's position on the impact of conduct away from the bargaining table was highlighted in its decision in *U.S. Ecology Corp.*[35] In that case, the Board affirmed the ALJ's finding that the employer violated Section 8(a)(5) by engaging in surface bargaining, even though the parties met on more than 60 occasions. Significant to the Board was the credited testimony by the union vice president that a company manager told him that the plant manager had stated that there would be no contract, regardless of what the union did.

In *Hardesty Co. dba Mid-Continent Concrete,*[36] the Board held that the employer engaged in surface bargaining where, among other things, the employer's proposals called for a substantial reduction in wages and benefits, and the employer engaged in regressive bargaining while failing to provide an explanation for its regressive economic proposals. The employer also failed to make concessions or provide an explanation for its noneconomic proposals, particularly its pro-

---

[33]334 NLRB 487, 488–89, 171 LRRM 1059 (2001), *enforced,* 318 F.3d 1173, 171 LRRM 2993 (2003)

[34]*Public Serv. Co. of Okla., supra* note 31.

[35]331 NLRB 223, 165 LRRM 1197 (2000), *enforced,* 26 Fed. Appx. 435, 169 LRRM 2230 (6th Cir. 2001).

[36]336 NLRB 258, 171 LRRM 1016 (2001), *enforced,* 308 F.3d 859, 171 LRRM 2006 (8th Cir. 2002). *See also Richard Mellow Elec. Contractors Corp.*, 327 NLRB 1112, 161 LRRM 1018 (1999) *and Burrows Paper Corp.*, 332 NLRB 82, 170 LRRM 1350 (2000), where the Board found that employer engaged in surface bargaining by advancing "proposals that would have allowed essentially no role for the Union in determining wage rates."

posal to allow it to assign all bargaining-unit work to employees outside the unit.[37]

However, in *St. George Warehouse, Inc.*,[38] the Board concluded that the employer did not engage in surface bargaining where the employer proposed wage increases on two separate occasions and in many instances gave specific reasons for its rejection of certain union proposals. Further, the employer made several concessions and reached agreement with the union on many issues, including a pay differential for second-shift employees, a 30-day leave of absence, and the appointment of shop stewards.

2. *Concessions, Proposals, and Demands*

a. Concessions

The Board and the courts continue to consider whether a party has made concessions in bargaining in analyzing the totality of the party's bargaining conduct.[39] Even where no concessions are made, they will look at a party's willingness to make concessions as evidenced by its conduct, rather than a "stray statement indicating inflexibility" in finding good faith bargaining.[40] However, concessions can sometimes be considered a tactic to disguise a party's strategy of surface bargaining. In *Mid-Continent Concrete*,[41] the employer made several regressive proposals in the midst of negotiations and after agreement had been reached on numerous subjects. The employer later conceded back to the status quo. The Board found that such concessions were actually evidence of bad faith bargaining by the employer, as the concessions were made in an "orchestrated, almost staged, manner."[42]

---

[37] *Compare* ServiceNet, Inc., 340 NLRB No. 148, 173 LRRM 1553 (2003) (no surface bargaining despite unlawful insistence on several subjects during bargaining).

[38] 341 NLRB No. 120, 175 LRM 1316 (2004); *see also ServiceNet, Inc.*, *supra* note 37 (no surface bargaining despite unlawful insistence on several subjects during bargaining).

[39] St. George Warehouse, *supra* note 38; Phelps Dodge Specialty Copper Prods. Co., 337 NLRB 455, 169 LRRM 1469 (2002); *but see U.S. Ecology Corp.*, *supra* note 35 (although employer made limited concessions, its regressive bargaining was found to be unlawfully motivated by desire to avoid agreement in light of other evidence that employer had no intention of reaching agreement with union).

[40] Pleasantview Nursing Home, Inc., 351 F.3d 747, 173 LRRM 2882 (6th Cir. 2003).

[41] *Supra* note 36.

[42] *Id.*

b. Proposals and Demands

Application of the principles set forth in *Reichhold Chemicals II*[43] has continued to be the subject of numerous Board cases.[44]

The Board also continues to apply the rule that making regressive proposals is permissible when based on changed circumstances, particularly if the party provides a reasoned explanation for the modification at the time it is presented to the other side. In *Oklahoma Fixture Co.*,[45] the Board found that the employer's regressive proposals on hiring hall and union security could not be viewed as being offered in an effort to frustrate the negotiating process given that the employer explained the reasons for them. However, regressive proposals will still be considered as evidence of general bad faith bargaining where the employer fails to provide a reasoned explanation.[46]

Bad faith bargaining continues to be found on the basis of employer demands that the union accept proposals in the area of management rights that would leave the employees in a worse position than if there were no contract at all.[47] For example, in *Summa Health*

---

[43]288 NLRB 69, 127 LRRM 1265 (1988), *rev'd on other grounds*, 906 F.2d 719, 134 LRRM 2481 (D.C. Cir. 1990), *cert. denied*, 498 U.S. 1053, 136 LRRM 2152 (1991).

[44]*St. George Warehouse, supra* note 38 (rejection of union-security clause proposal not bad faith bargaining in the circumstances); ServiceNet, Inc., 340 NLRB No. 148, 173 LRRM 1553 (2003); Pratt Towers, 338 NLRB 61, 170 LRRM 1533 (2002), *rev'd on other grounds*, NLRB v. Service Employees Local 32B-32J, 353 F.3d 197, 173 LRRM 3007 (2d Cir. 2003); Quality House of Graphics, Inc., 336 NLRB 497, 169 LRRM 1511 (2001); Teamsters Local 282, 335 NLRB 1253, 168 LRRM 1185 (2001); Ryan Iron Works, 332 NLRB 506, 167 LRRM 1240 (2000), *enforced in part*, 257 F.3d 1, 167 LRRM 2653 (1st Cir. 2001); Oklahoma Fixture Co., 331 NLRB 1116, 165 LRRM 1122 (2000), *enforced*, 332 F.3d 1284, 172 LRRM 2821 (10th Cir. 2003); Summa Health Sys., Inc., 330 NLRB 1379, 170 LRRM 1308 (2000); Grinnell Fire Prot. Sys. Co., 328 NLRB 585, 161 LRRM 1146 (1999), *enforced*, 236 F.3d 187, 166 LRRM 2065 (4th Cir. 2000); Richard Mellow Elec. Contractors Corp., 327 NLRB 1112, 161 LRRM 1018 (1999); People Care Inc., 327 NLRB 814, 167 LRRM 1095 (1999).

[45]*Oklahoma Fixture Co., supra* note 44. *See also* KSM Indus., Inc., 336 NLRB 133, 169 LRRM 1445 (2001), *reconsidered in part on other grounds*, 337 NLRB 987, 170 LRRM 1313 (2002).

[46]U.S. Ecology, 331 NLRB 223, 165 LRRM 1197 (2000), *enforced*, 26 Fed. Appx. 435, 169 LRRM 2230 (6th Cir. 2001); Hardesty Co. dba Mid-Continent Concrete, Inc., 336 NLRB 258, 171 LRRM 1016 (2001), *enforced*, 308 F.3d 859, 171 LRRM 2006 (8th Cir. 2002).

[47]Public Serv. Co. of Okla. v. NLRB, 318 F.3d 1173, 171 LRRM 2993 (10th Cir. 2003), *enforcing* 334 NLRB 487, 171 LRRM 1059 (2001); Burrows Paper Corp., 332 NLRB 82, 170 LRRM 1350 (2000) (employer proposals would have given union no say in wage determinations, no grievance or arbitration process unless employer

Systems,[48] the Board concluded that the employer's insistence on having unilateral discretion to increase wages was evidence of bad faith bargaining.[49]

3. *Dilatory Tactics: Refusing to Confer at Reasonable Times and Intervals*

The Board continues to apply the rule that a party may not engage in dilatory bargaining tactics to frustrate negotiations.[50] As such, both employers and unions continue to be held accountable for engaging in such tactics.[51]

---

had final say over process, and would have given employer broad management rights, including unlimited rights in many areas); *Summa Health Sys., Inc., supra* note 44 (employer proposals included sweeping new rules concerning work transfer, job classification, wages, and creation of "process enhancement teams" designed to circumvent union). In *Summa Health Sys.*, Member Hurtgen dissented in part, reasoning that the majority's finding of overall bad faith bargaining was undermined because the employer offered to submit disputed bargaining issues to binding arbitration. 330 NLRB at 1380. *Cf. St. George Warehouse, supra* note 38 (insistence on broad management rights clause not unlawful).

[48]*Supra* note 47.

[49]*Id.* The Board distinguished *McClatchey Newspapers*, 321 NLRB 1386, 153 LRRM 1137 (1996), *enforced*, 131 F.3d 1026, 157 LRRM 2023 (D.C. Cir. 1997), on the ground that *McClatchey* involved the unilateral implementation, post-impasse, of a proposal that gave the employer unfettered discretion to adjust merit pay increases.

[50]Teamsters Local 122, 334 NLRB 1190 (2001); Health Care Servs. Group, Inc., 331 NLRB 333, 171 LRRM 1399 (2000). *But see* Teamsters Local 705 (ExxonMobil), 30 AMR ¶40083, also available on the Board's web site. This Division of Advice Memorandum, issued on February 12, 2003, addressed allegations of dilatory conduct, concluding that a union did not unlawfully delay negotiations by, inter alia, canceling one session when its negotiator became unavailable, refusing on one occasion to meet on consecutive days (which refusal allegedly caused an increase in the employer's travel expenses), requesting information on work rules and policies and asking to engage in a "detailed review" of each such work rule, and informing the employer that bargaining "could take weeks or months" after the employer filed a §8(a)(5) charge based on the union's conduct. In doing so, the general counsel emphasized that "in those cases where the Board has found delay unlawful, that conduct has been part of an overall pattern of violations not present [in the case under consideration]."

[51]*See, e.g.*, NLRB v. Teamsters Local 662, 368 F.3d 741, 174 LRRM 3060 (7th Cir. 2004) (enforcing Board order finding that union violated §8(b)(3) after union scheduled a ratification vote and instructed members not to vote on certain provisions, it then later sought to avoid the contract by contending that those same provisions were improperly ratified, conduct the court found to be "unfair and dilatory"); Convergence Communications, Inc., 339 NLRB 408, 173 LRRM 1351 (2003) (employer violated §8(a)(5) by failing to respond to written requests and telephone calls from union regarding negotiations).

4. *Representative With Inadequate Authority to Bargain*

The Board and the courts continue to apply the rule that a party must confer adequate authority on its representative to allow meaningful collective bargaining to occur at the table, even if the representative does not have ultimate authority to enter into an agreement on behalf of the principal.[52] The Board and the courts will require the execution of a contract if the party's representative possesses "apparent authority."[53] However, the employer may refuse to sign the contract if the union was clearly and unambiguously told that the company president, who was not at the bargaining table, had to approve the contract and he did not approve.[54]

5. *Imposing Conditions*

The Board has found that a party engages in a general refusal to bargain when it conditions bargaining on an initial agreement to a nonmandatory subject.[55] However, in *Pleasantview Nursing Home, Inc. v. NLRB*,[56] the Sixth Circuit held that an employer did not illegally impose conditions upon bargaining when it insisted to impasse on a proposal that combined mandatory and nonmandatory subjects of bargaining. The court noted that the Board had severed the mandatory and nonmandatory subjects within the proposal and focused on the nonmandatory subject in finding a violation. The court of appeals reversed, noting that, because the employer's proposal would have merely preserved the status quo and because "[t]he linkage arose organically out of the economic relationship between the mandatory and non-mandatory subjects . . . it was permissible."[57]

---

[52] *Health Care Servs. Group, Inc.*, *supra* note 50.

[53] W.R. Mollohan, Inc., 333 NLRB 1339, 167 LRRM 1097 (2001), *enforced*, 309 F.3d 1, 171 LRRM 2065 (D.C. Cir. 2002).

[54] Mid-Wilshire Health Care Ctr., 337 NLRB 72, 69 LRRM 1001 (2001).

[55] NLRB v. Miller Waste Mills, 315 F.3d 951, 171 LRRM 2717 (8th Cir.), *cert. denied*, 540 U.S. 811, 173 LRRM 2416 (2003); Jano Graphics, Inc., 339 NLRB No. 38, 172 LRRM 1292 (2003) (employer demanded ratification vote by unit members); Reading Rock Inc., 330 NLRB 856, 164 LRRM 1325 (2000). *See also* discussion in Section II.F. [Per Se Violations; Insisting on Nonmandatory Subjects of Bargaining], *supra*.

[56] 351 F.3d 747, 759, 173 LRRM 2882 (6th Cir. 2003).

[57] *Id.* at 760–61.

6. *Unilateral Changes*

The Board and the courts continue to regard an employer's unilateral implementation of new terms and conditions of employment without first bargaining to an impasse as evidence of bad faith bargaining.[58] Moreover, impasse on one or more subjects will not excuse piecemeal implementation of the items on which impasse has been reached unless the items are so crucial to the negotiations that they create impasse in the negotiations as a whole.[59] An employer may implement changes if an economic exigency requires an immediate change in the terms and conditions of employment.[60] However, this burden is difficult to meet.[61] Unilateral changes may also be made if the changes were not mandatory subjects of bargain-

[58]Guard Publ'g Co., 339 NLRB 353 (2003); Beverly Health & Rehab. Servs., Inc v. NLRB, 317 F.3d 316, 171 LRRM 3017 (D.C. Cir. 2003); Scepter, Inc. v. NLRB, 280 F.3d 1053, 169 LRRM 2524 (D.C. Cir. 2002); Raven Servs. Corp. v. NLRB, 315 F.3d 499, 171 LRRM 2606 (5th Cir. 2002); Wanex Elec. Servs., 338 NLRB 111 (2002); Lafayette Grinding Corp., 337 NLRB 832, 170 LRRM 1355 (2002); Grosvenor Orlando Assocs., Ltd., 336 NLRB 613, 172 LRRM 1253 (2001); Lexus of Concord, Inc., 330 NLRB 1409, 170 LRRM 1262 (2000); Summa Health Sys., 330 NLRB 1379, 170 LRRM 1308 (2000); Vincent Indus. Plastics, 209 F.3d 727, 164 LRRM 2039 (D.C. Cir. 2000), *enforcing* 328 NLRB 141, 163 LRRM 1123 (2000); Visiting Nurse Servs. of W. Mass. v. NLRB, 177 F.3d 52, 161 LRRM 2326 (1st Cir. 1999); Anderson Enters., 329 NLRB 760, 166 LRRM 1123 (1999); Grinnell Fire Prot. Sys. Co., 328 NLRB 585, 161 LRRM 1146 (1999), *enforced,* 236 F.3d 187, 166 LRRM 2065 (4th Cir. 2000); Richard Mellow Elec. Contractors Corp., 327 NLRB 1112, 161 LRRM 1018 (1999). *See also* discussion in Section II.A. [Per Se Violations; Unilateral Changes], *supra.*

[59]CalMat Co., 331 NLRB 1084, 171 LRRM 1237 (2000) (impasse on single, critical issue justifies party implementing all of its bargaining proposals if it demonstrates (1) actual existence of good faith bargaining impasse; (2) that issue as to which parties are at impasse is critical issue; and (3) that impasse on this critical issue led to breakdown in overall negotiations such that there can be no progress on any aspect of negotiation until impasse relating to critical issue is resolved).

[60]Eagle Transp. Corp., 338 NLRB 489, 171 LRRM 1117 (2002); Vincent Indus. Plastics, 209 F.3d 727, 164 LRRM 2039 (D.C. Cir. 2000), *enforcing* 328 NLRB 141, 163 LRRM 1123 (2000).

[61]*Id. See also* Elf Atochem N. Am., 339 NLRB 796, 174 LRRM 1101 (2003) (refusing to allow employer to unilaterally implement changes, noting that employer must show "extraordinary" unforeseen event to invoke privilege). *Cf.* Pleasantview Nursing Home, Inc., 351 F.3d 747, 755–56, 173 LRRM 2882 (6th Cir. 2003) (employer's unilateral increase in starting wages after expiration of collective bargaining agreement but during negotiations was unfair labor practice despite employer's argument that such increases were compelled by economic exigency of "intense labor market pressures").

ing,[62] if the union waived bargaining over the issue,[63] if the changes were made pursuant to a well-established past practice,[64] or if impasse is impossible because of union tactics.[65]

Although an employer's unilateral implementation of its final offer while a union information request is pending may still violate the principle set forth in *Decker Coal*,[66] whether the information is relevant to the "core issues" about which the parties are bargaining may determine whether the failure to provide the requested information prevents an impasse and results in a Section 8(a)(5) violation.[67]

7. *Bypassing the Representative: Individual Contracts of Employment*

The Board and the courts continue to apply the rule that bypassing the union and negotiating individual agreements with em-

[62]Pall Corp. v. NLRB, 275 F.3d 116, 169 LRRM 2065 (D.C. Cir. 2002) (no unfair labor practice where employer revoked contract obligation to recognize union voluntarily upon showing of majority status, without election), *reversing* Pall Biomedical Prods. Corp, 331 NLRB 1674, 165 LRRM 1137 (2000) (Board found that voluntary recognition agreement *was* mandatory subject of bargaining); Midwest Television, Inc. 343 NLRB No. 83 (2004).

[63]Mississippi Power Co. v. NLRB, 284 F.3d 605, 169 NLRB 2840 (5th Cir. 2002) (no violation where unions waived right to bargain over medical changes).

[64]*See, e.g.*, Courier-Journal, 342 NLRB No. 118, 176 LRRM 1013 (2004) (employer that had for some 10 years been unilaterally implementing cost and benefit changes relating to union employees' health care coverage that mirrored cost and benefit changes for nonunion employees without opposition from the union did not violate §8(a)(5) by doing so without first bargaining with the union); Post-Tribune Co., 337 NLRB 1279, 170 LRRM 1449 (2002) (employer's unilateral increase in health premiums did not violate §8(a)(5) because such increase did not alter the employer's well-established status quo of allocating health care insurance premiums on the same percentage basis used previously).

[65]Matanuska Elec. Ass'n, 337 NLRB 680, 171 LRRM 1536 (2002) (union's stalling and delay tactics made reaching agreement "a virtual impossibility" and thus employer was permitted to declare impasse and implement its final offer).

[66]301 NLRB 729, 137 LRRM 1257 (1991) (no impasse existed because employer had not fully complied with union's information requests that were directly relevant to issues over which parties had been bargaining for months).

[67]Sierra Bullets, LLC, 340 NLRB No. 32, 173 LRRM 1283 (2003) (no §8(a)(5) violation because information requested did not go to the "core issues" separating parties in negotiations and there was "no convincing argument" that information would have changed parties' deadlock over core issues).

ployees is evidence of bad faith bargaining.[68] In *Grinnell Fire Protection Systems Co.*,[69] the Board found evidence of bad faith where the employer directly offered its employees higher wages than contained in its last contract proposal to the union.[70] Similarly, in *Armored Transport, Inc.*,[71] the employer violated Section 8(a)(5) when it, inter alia, distributed directly to employees "Don't Blame Us" letters to which it attached its new bargaining proposal on the same day, but prior to sending the new proposal to the union. An employer that communicates its bargaining proposals directly with employees after providing it to the union, however, may do so without violating Section 8(a)(5).[72]

8. *Commission of Unfair Labor Practices*

The Board continues to consider evidence of commission of other unfair labor practices in assessing whether the party has en-

[68]Midwest Precision Heating & Cooling, Inc., 341 NLRB No. 52, 174 LRRM 1235 (2004) (employer that "engaged in back-and-forth discussions with individual employees over various matters, including wage rates and vacation time," violated §8(a)(5)); Georgia Power Co., 342 NLRB No. 18, 175 LRRM 1130 (2004) (setting up workplace ethics program without bargaining with the union); Northwest Graphics, Inc., 343 NLRB No. 16, 176 LRRM 1167 (2004) (directly dealing with employees regarding issues of shift assignment and differential violates §8(a)(5)); NLRB v. Miller Waste Mills, 315 F.3d 951 (8th Cir. 2003) (improper company letters to employees regarding wage and benefit increases); ServiceNet, Inc., 340 NLRB No. 148, 173 LRRM 1553 (2003) (insistence to impasse on nonmandatory health care proposal); Hardesty Co. dba Mid-Continent Concrete, 336 NLRB 258, 171 LRRM 1016 (2001), *enforced,* 308 F.3d 859, 171 LRRM 2006 (8th Cir. 2002) (soliciting employee grievances); Lexus of Concord, Inc., 330 NLRB 1409, 170 LRRM 1262 (2000) (granting wage increases); Summa Health Sys., 330 NLRB 1379, 170 LRRM 1308 (2000) (creation of "process enhancement teams" designed to circumvent union); Dayton Newspapers, Inc., 339 NLRB 650, 172 LRRM 1477 (2003) (asking lawfully locked out drivers to waive right to strike and picket in exchange for being allowed to return to work).

[69]328 NLRB 585, 161 LRRM 1146 (1999), *enforced,* 236 F.3d 187, 166 LRRM 2065 (4th Cir. 2000).

[70]*See also* Anderson Enters., 329 NLRB 760, 166 LRRM 1123 (1999).

[71]339 NLRB 374, 173 LRRM 1096 (2003).

[72]*See, e.g.,* Pan Am. Grain Co., 343 NLRB No. 47, 175 LRRM 1497 (2004) (employer's distribution of a proposal for new collective bargaining agreement directly to represented employees within a day or two after providing same proposal to union was not done "to the exclusion of the union" and therefore did not cross the line into an unlawful §8(a)(5) violation).

gaged in bad faith bargaining conduct.[73] The Board examines the "totality of the party's conduct, both at and away from the bargaining table," in its analysis of whether the party has violated its statutory duty to bargain in good faith.[74]

IV. The Duty to Furnish Information

A. The Role of Information in the Collective Bargaining Relationship—An Overview

2. *Representation Under an Existing Collective Bargaining Agreement*

The Board continues to follow the *Acme Industrial*[75] doctrine that the employer's duty to furnish information, like its duty to bargain, "extends beyond the period of contract negotiations and applies to labor-management relations during the term of an agreement."[76]

In *Stevens International Inc.*,[77] the Board found that an employer unlawfully refused to respond to the union's request for information about completion of work following a plant closing. The employer's assertion that the contract had expired—and with it the obligation to provide information—was rejected. The employer was held to have a clear duty to bargain with the union about post-closing work.

---

[73]Kentucky Fried Chicken, Caribbean Holdings, Inc. 341 NLRB No. 13, 174 LRRM 1049 (2003); Wanex Elec. Servs., 338 NLRB 111 (2002); Burrows Paper Corp., 332 NLRB 82, 170 LRRM 1350 (2000); U.S. Ecology Corp., 331 NLRB 223, 165 LRRM 1197 (2000). *Contra* Quirk Tire, 330 NLRB 917, 166 LRRM 1235 (2000) (Board refused to conclude that unremedied unfair labor practices prevented parties from reaching impasse), *enforced in relevant part*, 241 F.3d 41 (D.C. Cir. 2001).

[74]St. George Warehouse, Inc., 341 NLRB No. 120, 175 LRRM 1316 (2004) (noting further that "[t]he Board has been reluctant to find bad-faith bargaining exclusively on the basis of a party's conduct away from the bargaining table." (internal citations omitted); *see also* Pleasantview Nursing Home, Inc. v. NLRB, 351 F.3d 747, 173 LRRM 2882 (6th Cir. 2003) ("[w]here the overall bargaining conduct indicates good faith and willingness to negotiate, a stray statement indicating inflexibility will not overcome the general tenor of good faith negotiations").

[75]NLRB v. Acme Indus. Co., 385 U.S. 432, 64 LRRM 2069 (1967).

[76]*Id.* at 568; *see also* Borgess Med. Ctr., 342 NLRB No. 109, 175 LRRM 1549 (2004).

[77]337 NLRB 143, 172 LRRM 1396 (2001).

3. *Refusal to Furnish Information as an Unfair Labor Practice*

The Board continues to hold that an employer's refusal to furnish relevant information upon request violates Section 8(a)(5).[78] Current Board law provides that allegations of failure to provide information, unlike allegations of unilateral changes, are *not* subject to deferral to the grievance-arbitration process.[79] This rule has the effect of allowing parties to "piggyback" other unfair labor practice allegations that would otherwise be deferrable under the Board's *Collyer* doctrine, where a failure to provide information is also alleged. As a result, the Board presently decides these cases in the first instance.

The Board, in *Shaw's Supermarkets, Inc.*,[80] noted that nondeferral of charges involving failure to provide information facilitates arbitration by allowing the parties to analyze the respective merits of their cases *prior* to engaging in arbitration. The Board in that case recently reaffirmed its nondeferral principle in circumstances where the union sought information *after* an arbitration award was rendered, while the parties were disputing the implementation of the award. The Board rejected the employer's argument that the union was attempting to use the Board as a substitute for district court enforcement of the award pursuant to Section 301 of the LMRA, instead finding on the contrary that the union sought the information to properly determine whether an enforcement action was necessary. Dissenting, Chairman Battista sought to distinguish pre- and post-arbitration information requests, explaining his view that the policy of nondeferral inherently applied to pre-arbitration information requests where the desire to avoid multitiered arbitrations was implicated.[81] Although the Board majority refused to recognize such a distinction, Member Acosta appeared to acknowledge that the unique circumstances of a post-award information request militated against deferral.[82]

Other members of the Board previously reiterated their preference for deferral of information request cases, reasoning that such

---

[78] *Borgess Med. Ctr., supra* note 76; Postal Serv., 337 NLRB 820, 173 LRRM 1435 (2002).

[79] *See, e.g.*, U.S. Postal Serv., 302 NLRB 918, 137 LRRM 1352 (1991).

[80] 339 NLRB 871, 173 LRRM 1163 (2003).

[81] *Id.* at 872.

[82] *Id.*, 871 n.1.

requests often involve questions of contract interpretation, to which arbitration is more aptly suited. In *Phoenix Coca-Cola Bottling Co.*[83] and *Baptist Hospital of East Tennessee*,[84] Members Cowen and Bartlett both expressed support for deferral to arbitration of at least some information request allegations, contending that where a union seeks information to determine if the employer has violated the collective bargaining agreement, a dispute arising out of such an information request should be "addressed in the first instance under the dispute resolution procedures that the parties themselves have agreed to, i.e., through the grievance-arbitration procedure, or in the absence of applicable procedures for arbitrable resolution, Section 301 of the Act."[85]

The Board's general counsel had also urged the Board to reconsider its nondeferral policy with respect to charges involving an alleged refusal to furnish information. In the general counsel's view, more deferrals to private dispute resolution mechanisms facilitate case handling and conserve Board resources, and the Board's ruling on an information request does not always end the information dispute, as parties are often ordered to bargain about cost or confidentiality issues.[86]

4. *The Union's Duty to Supply Information*

A union continues to be obligated to furnish relevant information to an employer.[87]

---

[83] 338 NLRB 498, 171 LRRM 1433 (2002).

[84] 338 NLRB 249, 171 LRRM 1129 (2002).

[85] Phoenix Coca-Cola Bottling, 338 NLRB 498, 498–99, 171 LRRM 1433 (2002) (Cowen, dissenting); Baptist Hosp. of E. Tenn., 338 NLRB 249, 171 LRRM 1129 (2002) (Bartlett, concurring). *See also* Ormet Aluminum Mill Prods., 335 NLRB 788, 790–91, 169 LRRM 1514 (2001) (Member Hurtgen, dissenting, found that extensive information requests prior to arbitration amounted to impermissible "pretrial discovery," and that any disputes concerning scope of union's right to such information should be resolved by arbitrator together with merits of underlying claim).

[86] *See* Report of the General Counsel, released November 8, 2002.

[87] *See, e.g.*, Food Drivers Helpers & Warehouse Employees Local 500 (Acme Markets), 340 NLRB No. 35 (2003) (union was required to produce copies of all its current collective bargaining agreements so that employer could determine whether union was living up to "most favored nations" clause in parties' labor contract, recognizing that "a labor organization's duty to furnish information pursuant to Section 8(b)(3) is 'commensurate with and parallel to an employer's obligation to furnish it to a union' pursuant to Section 8(a)(5).").

B. Nature of the Duty to Furnish Information

1. *Request or Demand*

The duty to furnish information does not arise until an unambiguous request for the information is made. However, if a request is ambiguous, an employer may not flatly reject the request, but instead is under a duty to seek clarification from the union.[88] On the other hand, where the request is unambiguous, a union is under no obligation to "reiterate or clarify its request," and an employer commits an unfair labor practice by not responding.[89]

2. *Relevance or Necessity*

In *Saginaw Control & Engineering, Inc.*,[90] the Board reiterated that "the first question in [an information request] case is always one of relevance. If the information requested has no relevance to any legitimate union collective bargaining need, a refusal to furnish could not be an unfair labor practice."[91] The Board in *Saginaw* held that the union's information request was an improper attempt to engage in discovery concerning an unfair labor practice charge.

The Board continues to use a liberal definition of relevance in assessing whether requested information should be provided and continues to hold that a broad range of information is presumptively relevant.[92] However, since the "duty to furnish . . .information stems from the underlying statutory duty imposed on employers and

---

[88]Pepsi Am., Inc., 339 NLRB 986 (2003).

[89]International Protective Servs., Inc., 339 NLRB 701, 173 LRRM 1023 (2003).

[90]339 NLRB 541, 173 LRRM 1222 (2003).

[91]*Id.*, at 4545 n.5, *citing* Emeryville Research Ctr. v. NLRB, 441 F.2d 880, 883, 77 LRRM 2043 (9th Cir. 1971); *see also* Southern Cal. Gas Co., 342 NLRB No. 56, 175 LRRM 1243 (2004) (employer has no duty to provide information concerning safety issues for a union's use in pursuing a complaint before the California Public Utilities Commission, a third party, when the "mere mention of the word 'safety' was insufficient to warrant a conclusion that the requested information is presumptively relevant for the purposes of collective bargaining").

[92]Lakeland Bus Lines, Inc. v. NLRB, 347 F.3d 955, 173 LRRM 2545 (D.C. Cir. 2003) (employers and unions must exchange information when necessary to substantiate assertions in collective bargaining process); National Steel Corp. v. NLRB, 324 F.3d 928, 172 LRRM 2154 (7th Cir. 2003) (court affirms Board's conclusion that employer is required to provide information concerning use of hidden surveillance cameras, subject to employer's confidentiality concerns); Raven Servs. Corp. v. NLRB, 315 F.3d 499, 171 LRRM 2606 (5th Cir. 2002) (employer must provide union with information to aid union in negotiations); NLRB v. Mid-Continent Concrete, 308 F.3d 859, 171 LRRM 2006 (8th Cir. 2002) (employer must

unions to bargain in good faith with respect to mandatory subjects of bargaining . . . there is no duty to furnish information concerning a nonmandatory subject of bargaining."[93] Moreover, that the parties have previously engaged in voluntary bargaining concerning nonmandatory subjects does not change this principle, as "[p]arties do not have the power to alter this result merely by reaching agreement on the terms of a nonmandatory subject."[94]

For example, where the union seeks information concerning "single employer" or "alter ego" status, the burden of establishing

---

provide wage rates of recently promoted driver and applicants for position filled by nonbargaining unit member); Pacific Bell v. NLRB, 259 F.3d 719, 168 LRRM 2032 (D.C. Cir. 2001) (employer must provide payroll records); Beverly Cal. Corp. v. NLRB, 227 F.3d 817, 165 LRRM 2257 (7th Cir. 2000), *cert. denied*, 533 U.S. 950 (2001) (employer unlawfully failed to furnish union with attendance and disciplinary records of nonunion employees at its nursing home, where union, which was concerned that unit employees were being treated differently than nonunion employees, had valid reason to request such records); Supervalu Inc., Pittsburgh Div. v. NLRB, 184 F.3d 949, 161 LRRM 3115 (8th Cir. 1999), *enforcing* 326 NLRB 1069, 161 LRRM 1240 (1998) (employer must provide copy of its sales agreement with buyer that reopened store with nonunion workforce; information was necessary to assess employer's compliance with its WARN obligations); Retlaw Broad. Co. v. NLRB, 172 F.3d 660, 160 LRRM 2909 (9th Cir. 1999) (employer must furnish union with copies of personal service contracts offered to some of its employees); *Acme Markets, supra* note 87(noting that relevance requirement "is satisfied as long as the information has some bearing upon an issue between the parties and is of probable use to the requesting party"); International Protective Servs., Inc., 339 NLRB 702, 173 LRRM 1023 (2003) (information pertaining to 401k plan relevant); Fleming Co., 332 NLRB 1086, 165 LRRM 1309 (2000) (employer unlawfully refused to provide union with complete copy of employee's personnel file, copies of any work rules applicable at time of employee's discharge, and list of names, addresses, and telephone numbers of all bargaining-unit members employed by the predecessor employer from which employee was discharged so that union could process grievance of employee); Washington Beef Inc., 328 NLRB 612, 163 LRRM 1223 (2000) (employer unlawfully failed to provide union with information relating to employee bonus and retirement plans, wage increases, work hours, overtime hours, sick time, and holiday, and vacation hours); Naperville Ready Mix, Inc., 329 NLRB 174 (1999), *enforced*, 242 F.3d 744, 166 LRRM 2712 (7th Cir. 2001) (employer must provide union with information concerning sale of trucks that had been driven by employees); Atlas Concrete Constr. Co., 329 NLRB 5, 162 LRRM 1423 (1999) (names and dates of hire of replacement workers hired during strike were necessary for union to perform its duties as representative). *But see* Conagra, Inc. v. NLRB, 117 F.3d 1435, 155 LRRM 2769 (D.C. Cir. 1997), *denying enforcement of* 321 NLRB 944, 154 LRRM 1195 (1996) (employer not required to provide financial information to union where it did not claim inability to pay, instead saying the union's demands might put it at competitive disadvantage).

[93]Pieper Elec., Inc., 339 NLRB 1232, 1235, 173 LRRM 1079 (2003).

[94]*Id.*

relevance rests with the union.[95] In *Cannelton Industries, Inc.*,[96] the Board recently reaffirmed that this burden is not met by a "mere suspicion" that such a relationship exists. Instead, a union must establish relevance by showing a "reasonable belief supported by objective evidence"[97] that a single employer or alter ego situation exists. Moreover, the union is not required to disclose the specific facts or evidence underlying its suspicion to the employer at the time it makes such a request, but rather must simply demonstrate a "reasonable belief that such a relationship exists."[98]

Similarly, where a union seeks information about employees at an employer's facility not covered by the collective bargaining agreement, for reasons other than single employer or alter ego status, the Board continues to require the union to make a showing of relevance and necessity (i.e., that the information would be of use to the union in carrying out its statutory obligations).[99]

In *Southern California Gas Co.,* the Board held that the employer lawfully refused to provide the union with certain requested safety information.[100] The Board balanced the "liberal, discovery-type standard" against an employer's legitimate refusal to withhold irrelevant information. The union failed to meet its burden when its "sole reason offered" for seeking the information was to pursue a complaint before the California Public Utilities Commission, a state agency unrelated to collective bargaining or the grievance process. The Board held that "when a union requests information which is not ordinarily relevant to its performance as bargaining representative, but which is alleged to have become so because of peculiar circumstances, the union has the burden of proving relevance before the employer must comply."[101]

---

[95]Cannelton Indus., Inc., 339 NLRB 996, 173 LRRM 1087 (2003).

[96]*Id.* at 997.

[97]*Id. See also* CEC, Inc. 337 NLRB 516 (2002); Mercy Hosp. of Buffalo, 336 NLRB 1282, 171 LRRM 1339 (2001); Oklahoma Fixture Co., 333 NLRB 804, 172 LRRM 1453 (2001), *enforcement denied,* 2003 U.S. App. LEXIS 18782 (10th Cir. 2003).

[98]339 NLRB 997, citing Baldwin Shop N' Save, 314 NLRB 114, 121, 146 LRRM 1296 (1994).

[99]Frito-Lay, Inc., 333 NLRB 1296, 167 LRRM 1065 (2001); Postal Serv., 337 NLRB 820, 173 LRRM 1435 (2002) (in context of grievance concerning denial of transfer request, union properly sought information about new hires at another facility since collective bargaining agreement required that one out of four vacancies at the other facility was to be filled by transfer).

[100]342 NLRB No. 56, 175 LRRM 1243 (2004).

[101]*Id., citing* NLRB v. George Koch Sons, Inc., 950 F.2d 1324, 1331 (7th Cir. 1991).

However, the Board continues to hold that the union's burden of demonstrating relevance is "not exceptionally heavy."[102] In *DaimlerChrysler Corp. v. NLRB*,[103] the D.C. Circuit upheld the Board's decision that the employer unlawfully failed to provide information regarding grievances over last chance agreements. The employer contended that the union's request for information on all grievances involving any last chance agreements was irrelevant because the collective bargaining agreement provided that last chance agreements had no precedential value. The Board had found the denial of the information to be an unfair labor practice because the information sought was "at least probably or potentially relevant" to the union in determining whether to process a grievance to arbitration.[104] Recognizing the "liberal, discovery-type standard" applicable to union information requests, the D.C. Circuit likewise enforced the Board order because the information sought could provide "a helpful barometer" for the union in deciding whether to pursue a grievance.[105]

The Board continues to hold that information sought by a union about nonbargaining unit employees is relevant where the employees at issue were performing bargaining unit work.[106] In *Kathleen's Bakeshop, LLC*,[107] the Board held that an employer unlawfully refused to provide the union with information about wages, benefits, and other terms and conditions of employment of a nonunion facility to which bargaining unit work was being relocated.

3. *Availability*

The Board continues to find that an employer's unreasonable delay in furnishing information is as much of a violation of Section 8(a)(5) as a refusal to provide the information at all.[108] In *Allegheny Power & Allegheny Energy Supply Co.*,[109] the Board observed that "in evaluating the promptness of the response," it "will consider the complexity and extent of the information sought, its availability and the

[102]Saginaw Control & Eng'g, Inc., 339 NLRB 541, 173 LRRM 1222 (2003).

[103]288 F.3d 434, 169 LRMM 3217 (D.C. Cir. 2002), *enforcing* 331 NLRB 1324, 169 LRRM 1493 (2000).

[104]*Id.*, 331 NLRB at 1325.

[105]*Id.*, 288 F.3d at 443, 444.

[106]Phoenix Coca-Cola Bottling Co., 337 NLRB 1239, 171 LRRM 1415 (2002).

[107]337 NLRB 1081, 171 LRRM 1131, 1133 (2002).

[108]Amersig Graphics, Inc. dba American Signature, Inc., 334 NLRB 880, 169 LRRM 1458 (2001); Woodland Clinic, 331 NLRB 735, 164 LRRM 1289 (2000).

[109]339 NLRB 585, 173 LRRM 1125 (2003).

difficulty of retrieving the information."[110] Moreover, where relevant information is outside of the direct control of an employer, the employer may satisfy its obligations under the Act by making a good faith effort to obtain the information.[111] There is no "per se" rule; "what is required is a reasonable good faith effort to respond to the request as promptly as circumstances allow."[112] Furthermore, an employer is not required to produce information that does not exist.[113]

4. *Manner and Form*

The Board continues to hold that when a union is entitled to information and an employer legitimately claims that the information is confidential, the parties must bargain toward a reasonable accommodation.[114] This approach balances the union's need for information and the employer's justified interest.[115] For example, in *Allen Storage*,[116] the Board held that an employer did not violate Section 8(a)(5) by failing to provide the union with information when the employer sought to accommodate the union's request for verification by providing detailed "financials" in lieu of confidential customer information. The Board observed that the dispute concerned the employer's inability to accommodate all strikers who offered to return to work because of a lack of work. The union requested verification of the alleged lack of work in the form of "all estimate sheets, local work order invoices, intrastate and interstate bills of lading, and records of work" referred by other companies. The Board held

---

[110]*Id.* at 587.

[111]Pittson Coal Group, Inc., 334 NLRB 690, 173 LRRM 1345 (2001). *Cf.* International Protective Servs. Inc., 339 NLRB 701, 173 LRRM 1023 (2003) (employer had duty to attempt to secure information not directly in its possession, but which was in possession of third party with which employer had business relationship).

[112]*Allegheny Power*, *supra* note 109, 173 LRRM 1128; *see also* Anheuser-Busch, Inc., 342 NLRB No. 49, 175 LRRM 1168 (2004) (employer was unreasonable and contravened the principles of collective bargaining when it forced an eight-month delay in furnishing information regarding grievances and hidden cameras).

[113]Kathleen's Bakeshop, LLC, 337 NLRB 1081, 171 LRRM 1131 (2002), *enforced*, 2003 U.S. App. LEXIS 22029, 173 LRRM 2576 (2d Cir. 2003).

[114]Crittenton Hosp., 342 NLRB No. 67, 175 LRRM 1283 (2004); Allen Storage & Moving Co., 342 NLRB No. 44, 175 LRRM 1388 (2004).

[115]*Id.*

[116]*Allen Storage & Moving Co.*, Inc., *supra* note 114.

that the employer had a legitimate interest in protecting proprietary information concerning its customers and did not have to turn over the information in the manner and form requested. Further, the Board found no violation by the employer when the union refused to bargain over the manner and form that the employer offered the information and admitted that it had "no reason" for simply rejecting the relevant, nonconfidential "financials" that the employer offered as verification.[117]

5. *Employer Defenses*

a. Claims of Confidentiality or Privilege Based on Employer Interests

The Board continues to hold that "substantial claims of confidentiality may justify refusals to furnish otherwise relevant information," however, a claim of confidentiality[118] must be timely raised,[119] and the employer is required to bargain in good faith with the union to seek an accommodation that resolves the conflicting interests of the employer and the union.[120] In *National Steel Corp.*,[121] the Board

---

[117]*Id.*, slip op. at 2–3.

[118]An employer must present evidence to support its claim of confidentiality. *See* Lasher Serv. Corp., 332 NLRB 834, 166 LRRM 1070 (2000); Rosenburg Forest Prods., 331 NLRB 999, 164 LRRM 1044 (2000); Woodland Clinic, 331 NLRB 735, 164 LRRM 1289 (2000); Retlaw Broad. Co. v. NLRB, 172 F.3d 660, 160 LRRM 2909 (9th Cir. 1999), *enforcing* 324 NLRB 138, 158 LRRM 1135 (1997).

[119]West Penn Power Co. dba Allegheny Power & Allegheny Energy Supply Co., 339 NLRB 585, 173 LRRM 1125 (2003), *enforcement granted in part*, 394 F.3d 233, 176 LRRM 2449 (4th Cir. 2005).

[120]Norris Sucker Rods, 340 NLRB No. 28 (2003) (employer violated §8(a)(5) by refusing to disclose bargaining unit members' doctor notes without attempting to bargain with union over confidentiality concerns raised by request); Metropolitan Edison Co., 330 NLRB 107, 163 LRRM 1001 (1999) (employer violated §8(a)(5) by its blanket refusal to provide union with names of informants who provided information related to workplace theft); Green Bay Area Visitor & Convention Bureau, 327 NLRB No. 150, 163 LRRM 1152 (1999), *enforced*, 202 F.3d 272, 163 LRRM 2576 (7th Cir. 1999) (although employee Social Security numbers need not be supplied, employer must furnish union with employee dates of hire, rates of pay, job classifications, addresses, telephone numbers; and company personnel policies, fringe benefits, job descriptions, discipline, and wage and salary plans); GTE Southwest, Inc., 329 NLRB 563, 164 LRRM 1389 (1999) (because testing information may involve trade secrets, bargaining was required about conditions for providing this information).

[121]335 NLRB 747, 172 LRRM 1055 (2001), *enforced*, 324 F.3d 928, 172 LRRM 1055 (7th Cir. 2003). *See also* Michael J. Hayes, *After "Hiding the Ball" Is Over: How the NLRB Must Change Its Approach to Decision-Making*, 33 Rutgers L.J. 523 (2002).

concluded that an employer unlawfully refused to provide the union with requested information about the location of hidden surveillance cameras and by failing to seek an accommodation with the union over its confidentiality concerns.[122]

In *BP Exploration (Alaska), Inc.*,[123] following an OSHA citation the union requested a report on the citation and also a report from an outside engineering consulting group. The Board upheld the employer's objection to producing these reports on the grounds of attorney-client privilege. The Board stated that while the union might well be entitled to the factual information in the reports, the union had asked only for the reports themselves and had "not demonstrated a need for the actual report that outweighs the Respondent's interest in preserving the attorney-client privilege."[124]

C. When the Duty Exists

The Board continues to follow the principle that an employer acts at its peril if it refuses to provide relevant information on request, even when the request is made after the union has won an election but before the union's certification.[125] More generally, an employer may not refuse to produce information based on the employer's belief that it has no duty to bargain with the union, where that belief later proves to be erroneous. Thus, an employer violates the Act by refusing to produce relevant information while it chal-

[122]*Id.*, 335 NLRB at 748. *See also* Borgess Med. Ctr., 342 NLRB No. 109, 175 LRRM 1549 (2004) (employer violated §8(a)(5) where, after demonstrating substantial confidentiality concerns regarding disclosure of hospital incident reports, it failed to bargain over a reasonable accommodation of its concerns); Anheuser-Busch, Inc., 342 NLRB No. 49, 175 LRRM 1168 (2004) (issue of whether employers can refuse to furnish internal investigatory notes on grounds of confidentiality continues to hinge on fact-specific inquiry regarding the notes).

[123]337 NLRB 887, 170 LRRM 1289 (2002).

[124]*Id. at* 888; *see also* Crittenton Hosp., 342 NLRB No. 67, 175 LRRM 1283 (2004) (where Board deemed information about safety committee meetings presumptively relevant, employer failed to show that union's request for information sought information that was either irrelevant or confidential).

[125]Kolkka Tables & Finnish-American Saunas, 335 NLRB 844, 168 LRRM 1155 (2001).

lenges a union's certification,[126] or following a union's valid request for recognition and bargaining.[127] Similarly, an employer may not refuse to produce information based on a withdrawal of recognition that is found to be invalid,[128] based on an unlawful refusal to recognize a union following its merger with another labor organization,[129]or based on its belief that the local or international union is not party to the collective bargaining agreement.[130] Similarly, an employer may not refuse to produce information based on an erroneous belief that the employee who is the subject of the request is not a bargaining unit employee.[131]

---

[126]Libson Cleaning, Inc., 343 NLRB No. 43, 176 LRRM 1304 (2004); United Cerebral Palsy, 343 NLRB No. 1, 176 LRRM 1215 (2004); Manhattan Ctr. Studios, Inc., 342 NLRB No. 131, 176 LRRM 1216 (2004); St. Clair Die Casting, LLC, 341 NLRB No. 144, 175 LRRM 1088 (2004); Superior Prot., Inc., 341 NLRB No. 35, 174 LRRM 1398 (2004); Trimm Assocs., Inc., 338 NLRB No. 52, 172 LRRM 1432 (2002), *enforcement denied on other grounds*, 351 F.3d 99, 173 LRRM 2801 (3d Cir. 2003); Baker Concrete Constr., Inc., 338 NLRB No. 48 (2002); Evergreen New Hope Health & Rehab. Ctr., 337 NLRB No. 71,71 (2002), *enforcement denied on other grounds*, 2003 WL 21259895 (9th Cir. May 27, 2003); Kentucky Tenn. Clay Co., 334 NLRB No. 33, 170 LRRM 1232 (2001), *enforcement denied on other grounds*, 295 F.3d 436, 170 LRRM 2522 (4th Cir. 2002); River City Elevator Co., 333 NLRB No. 67, 166 LRRM 1296 (2001), *enforcement denied on other grounds*, 289 F.3d 1029, 170 LRRM 2001 (7th Cir. 2002), *supplemented*, 339 NLRB 616, 172 LRRM 1409 (2003); National Cargo Bureau, Inc., 333 NLRB 952, 169 LRRM 1263 (2001).

[127]Eldorado, Inc., 335 NLRB 952, 169 LRRM 1035 (2001). Indeed, in *Eldorado*, the Board reiterated that the request for information itself constituted a request for recognition and bargaining. *Id.* at 953.

[128]Horizon House Dev. Servs., Inc., 337 NLRB 22, 169 LRRM 1356 (2001). *Accord* M & M Auto. Group dba Broadway Volkswagen, 342 NLRB No. 128, 176 LRRM 1231 (2004); Freeman Decorating Co., 336 NLRB 1, 168 LRRM 1329 (2001), *enforcement denied in part*, 334 F.3d 27, 172 LRRM 2993 (D.C. Cir. 2003); Ray Black & Sons Constr., Inc., 335 NLRB 457, 170 LRRM 1407 (2001); Miller Waste Mills, Inc., 334 NLRB 466, 167 LRRM 1293 (2001), *enforced*, 315 F.3d 951, 171 LRRM 2717 (8th Cir. 2002), *cert. denied*, 540 U.S. 811 (2003).

[129]Avante at Boca Raton, Inc., 334 NLRB 381, 173 LRRM 1165 (2001), *review denied*, 2002 U.S. App. LEXIS 23068 (D.C. Cir. 2002).

[130]Boden Store Fixtures, Inc., 342 NLRB No. 68, 175 LRRM 1249 (2004).

[131]Tarmac Am., Inc., 342 NLRB No. 107, 175 LRRM 1455 (2004).

By the same token, when an employer's withdrawal of recognition is found to be lawful, the Board has held that the employer's refusal to provide requested information is similarly lawful.[132]

An employer's refusal to provide information is not unlawful where the union's request was based on an erroneous understanding of the scope of its jurisdiction. Thus, in *Commonwealth Communications, Inc.*,[133] the employer refused to produce information regarding jobs other than the single project the employer asserted was within the union's jurisdiction. The Board's majority held that the refusal was unlawful because the collective bargaining agreement unambiguously extended the union's jurisdiction to all work within a given geographic area.[134] The D.C. Circuit reversed the Board, holding that the agreement was ambiguous and that parol evidence demonstrated it covered only a single project.[135]

The Board continues to hold unlawful an employer's refusal, during the term of a collective bargaining agreement, to provide requested information that is relevant to the union's ability to police compliance with the agreement.[136] Such information must be provided, even independent of a specific grievance, particularly where the information is "relevant and necessary to the effective administration of the grievance procedure in general."[137] In addition, the Board continues to hold that an employer must provide informa-

---

[132]Lexus of Concord, Inc., 343 NLRB No. 94 (2004). However, a lawful withdrawal of recognition does not necessarily excuse a refusal to provide information requested prior to such withdrawal. *M & M Auto. Group dba Broadway Volkswagen*, *supra* note 128.

[133]335 NLRB 765, 171 LRRM 1207 (2001), *enforcement denied*, 312 F.3d 465, 171 LRRM 2513 (D.C. Cir. 2002).

[134]*Id.*, 335 NLRB at 768.

[135]*Id.*, 312 F.3d at 468–70.

[136]*See* Overnite Transp. Co., 343 NLRB No. 134, 176 LRRM 1169 (2004) (information relating to disciplinary grievances); Republic Die & Tool Co., 343 NLRB No. 78 (2004) (information regarding facility improvements and new work, where employer claimed inability to pay); Tarmac Am., Inc., 342 NLRB No. 107, 175 LRRM 1455 (2004) (information about newly created forklift operator position); Meeker Coop. Light & Power Ass'n, 341 NLRB No. 89, 174 LRRM 1518 (2004) (information as to whether the employer contracted out bargaining unit work); Scapino Steel Erectors, Inc., 337 NLRB 992, 171 LRRM 1090 (2002) (information regarding jobs, employees, and hours relevant to employer's compliance with obligations to employee benefit funds).

[137]Ormet Aluminum Mill Prods., Inc., 335 NLRB 788, 790, 169 LRRM 1514 (2001). *See* Pioneer Elec. of Monroe, Inc., 333 NLRB 1192, 173 LRRM 1143 (2001).

tion necessary to assist the union in evaluating specific grievances and preparing for arbitration.[138] This requirement also applies to a successor union's right to evaluate a predecessor's processing and disposition of pending grievances.[139] The Board does not evaluate the merits of a particular grievance in determining whether the employer is obligated to produce information relevant to the grievance.[140]

However, in *Pieper Electric, Inc.*,[141] a three-member Board panel, with one member dissenting, held that an employer was not obligated to provide information regarding employee participation in a unilaterally implemented employee stock ownership program, which arguably violated a contract provision prohibiting employee ownership of company stock, because (according to the majority) the employee ownership program and the contract provision related only to a permissive subject of bargaining.[142]

An employer may not refuse to produce relevant information on the ground that the information has been provided previously, where the union requests an update on the employer's information production.[143] Similarly, an employer may not treat a request as having been abandoned simply because the union does not renew the request.[144]

Nor may the employer avoid production by simply asserting that the information is "confidential."[145] It must seek accommodation by working to balance the employer's justified confidentiality interests with the union's needs.[146] The Board is therefore required to bal-

---

[138] *Overnite Transp. Co., supra* note 136; Quality Building Contractors, Inc., 342 NLRB No. 38, KSM Indus., Inc., 336 NLRB 133, 169 LRRM 1445 (2001), *reconsidered in part on other grounds*, 337 NLRB 987, 170 LRRM 1313 (2002); Tom Rice Buick, Pontiac & GMC Truck, Inc., 334 NLRB 785, 167 LRRM 1343 (2001).

[139] Crittenton Hosp., 343 NLRB No. 81, 176 LRRM 1193 (2004).

[140] Contract Carriers Corp., 339 NLRB 851, 173 LRRM 1043 (2003); Schrock Cabinet Co., 339 NLRB 182, 172 LRRM 1347 (2003).

[141] 339 NLRB 1232, 173 LRRM 1079 (2003).

[142] *Id.* at 1236.

[143] Watkins Contracting, Inc., 335 NLRB 222, 171 LRRM 1352 (2001).

[144] *Schrock Cabinet Co., supra* note 140.

[145] National Steel Corp. v. NLRB, 324 F.3d 928, 937, 172 LRRM 2154 (7th Cir. 2003), *enforcing* 335 NLRB 747 (2001).

[146] *Id.* 324 F.3d at 937 (holding that the Board correctly required employer to bargain with union over information about hidden surveillance cameras). *Accord* United States Postal Serv., 341 NLRB No. 94, 174 LRRM 1486 (2004) (employer was required to balance confidentiality interest in employee's medical records with union's interest in records relating to employer's modification of her work assignment).

ance a union's need for relevant but assertedly confidential information against an employer's legitimate and substantial need for confidentiality. This obligation has been found to exist even when the employer does not specifically raise confidentiality as a defense. In *JHP & Associates, LLC v. NLRB*,[147] the Eighth Circuit noted that even though the employer never argued confidentiality, "[t]he confidentiality of strike replacement employees' home addresses and home telephone numbers should always be a factor to weigh against a union's need for such information."[148]

The Board narrowly interprets the right of an employer to refuse to furnish information that involves, in effect, pretrial discovery prior to an arbitration hearing. The type of information encompassed in the exception is limited to information such as names of witnesses the employer intends to call and the evidence on which it intends to rely at the arbitration hearing.[149] Underlying factual information, including information about an employer's decisionmaking process, is not of this nature, and is therefore relevant and necessary to the effective administration of the grievance process, and must be produced to the union.[150]

At the same time, the Board has held that an employer has no obligation to produce information requested by a union, where the union's purpose is solely to provide evidence in support of a pending 8(a)(3) charge[151] or a complaint before another regulatory agency.[152]

When the employer refuses to furnish information that would illuminate its clandestine repudiation of the agreement, it is reasonable for the union to pursue a course of requesting information even

---

[147]360 F.3d 904 (8th Cir. 2004), *enforcing in part* 338 NLRB 1059, 172 LRRM 1298 (2003).

[148]360 F.3d at 912 n.3.

[149]Ormet Aluminum Mill Prods., Inc., 335 NLRB 788, 169 LRRM 1514 (2001).

[150]*Id. But see* Central Tel. Co. of Tex., 343 NLRB No. 99, 176 LRRM 1441 (2004) (employer's investigation notes regarding discharged union officers protected by work product immunity, when prepared at special direction of counsel in anticipation of grievances).

[151]Saginaw Control & Eng'g, Inc., 339 NLRB 541, 173 LRRM 1222 (2003) However, the mere pendency of an unfair labor practice charge does not absolve the employer from producing information relevant to grievance processing, at least so long as there is "no apparent connection to any pending unfair labor practice charge." Overnite Transp. Co., 343 NLRB No. 134, slip op., at 37, 176 LRRM 1169 (2004).

[152]Southern Cal. Gas Co., 342 NLRB No. 56, 175 LRRM 1243 (2004).

if it causes a delay in filing unfair labor practice charges; the delay will not support a defense of untimely filing, as the delay "may fairly be laid at the company's doorstep."[153]

The Board continues to require employers to produce relevant information regarding the effects of plant relocations and similar reassignment of work performed by bargaining unit employees.[154]

D. Information That Must Be Furnished

1. *Financial Information*

The Board and courts of appeal continue to grapple with the standard to determine when an employer professes an "inability" to pay, which triggers a duty to disclose relevant financial information under *NLRB v. Truitt Manufacturing Co.*,[155] as opposed to a mere "unwillingness" to pay. For instance, in *Lakeland Bus Lines, Inc.*,[156] the Board held that an employer's statements in a letter, which included assertions that the employer was "trying to bring the bottom line back into the black" and that acceptance of the employer's final offer would enable the employer to "retain your jobs and get back in the black in the short term," could be construed as claiming an inability to pay.[157]

But the D.C. Circuit reversed the Board's decision, finding that it was "debatable" whether the statements implied an inability to pay even "when viewed in isolation," and that in light of the record as a whole, although the statements may have implied an inability to pay,

---

[153]Bouille Clark Plumbing, Heating, & Elec., Inc., 337 NLRB 743, 173 LRRM 1295 (2002) (quoting Barnard Eng'g Co., 295 NLRB 226, 133 LRRM 1137 (1989)), *enforced*, 81 Fed. Appx. 377, 173 LRRM 3119 (2d Cir. 2003).

[154]Titan Tire Corp., 333 NLRB 1156, 167 LRRM 1067 (2001); *cf.* Stevens Int'l, Inc., 337 NLRB 143, 172 LRRM 1396 (2001) (employer required to furnish information regarding supervisors performing bargaining-unit work in connection with plant relocation); Natomi Hosps. of Cal., Inc. dba Good Samaritan Hosp., 335 NLRB 901, 172 LRRM 1234 (2001) (information regarding new staffing matrix system that impacted work assignment). *But see* Courier-Journal, 342 NLRB No. 118, 175 LRRM 1013 (2004) (employer not required to provide requested information, where previous Board settlement had required employer to produce information regarding "jobs to which composing room employees might reasonably be expected to be transferred," and union subsequently discovered employees had been transferred into additional jobs).

[155]351 U.S. 149, 38 LRRM 2042 (1956).

[156]335 NLRB 322, 168 LRRM 1126 (2001), *enforcement denied*, 347 F.3d 955, 173 LRRM 2545 (D.C. Cir. 2003).

[157]*Id.* at 324–25.

the employer "unequivocally clarified" that it did not intend to plead financial inability.[158] The employer claimed only short-term losses, and a duty to disclose financial information, therefore, did not arise.

The Board continues to hold that even if an employer initially claims an inability to pay, no duty to disclose arises if the employer subsequently makes clear that it is not claiming a present inability to pay. Thus, in *American Polystyrene Corp.*,[159] the Board held that an employer had not claimed an inability to pay where, one day after asserting at the bargaining table, "I'd go broke," the employer disclaimed any assertion of inability to pay, denied telling the union that it could not afford the union's proposals, and claimed it said only that the union needed to take a more cautious approach. In these circumstances, the Board found that the employer had unequivocally retracted any assertion of financial inability. The Board observed that "the Respondent's response was made immediately and in writing, and it unequivocally advised the Union that the Respondent's ability to pay for the Union's bargaining proposals was not in question."[160]

In *AMF Trucking & Warehouse, Inc.*,[161] the Board announced the standard for analyzing when an employer has claimed an "inability to pay": "'Inability to pay' means that the company presently has insufficient assets to pay or that it would have insufficient assets to pay during the life of the contract that is being negotiated."[162] The Board found that the employer's repeated statements that it was "fighting for its life" and that the union's demands were "pie in the sky" did not meet this standard, because the employer "has neither claimed insufficient assets nor stated that acquiescence to the Union's demands would cause it to go out of business."[163]

Once an employer asserts an inability to pay triggering its obligation to produce financial information under *Truitt*, the employer does not satisfy its obligation by producing derivative information such as an accountant's report, where a reasonable person would insist on direct access to the employer's books and records.[164]

[158]347 F.3d at 958.
[159]341 NLRB No. 67, 174 LRRM 1305 (2004).
[160]*Id.*, 174 LRRM at 1306.
[161]342 NLRB No. 116, 176 LRRM 1052 (2004).
[162]*Id.*
[163]*Id.*
[164]Republic Die & Tool Co., 343 NLRB No. 78 (2004).

Other financial information about the employer can be relevant to the bargaining process and remains, therefore, a legitimate subject for disclosure on request.[165]

2. *Safety Information*

The employer must provide information regarding safety incidents involving bargaining unit employees and such information is presumptively relevant.[166] Information is not presumptively relevant, however, merely because the union's request contains the term "safety."[167]

3. *Other Information*

The Board continues to require an employer to produce information regarding relationships with other entities, where the union shows a reasonable basis for believing there may be an alter ego, single employer, or joint employer relationship.[168] Similarly, information on an employer's sale of assets,[169] impending subcontracting,[170] use of temporary agency employees,[171] or the use of nonunion

---

[165]*See* Mt. Clemens Gen. Hosp., 335 NLRB 48, 170 LRRM 1559 (2001) (information about the amount of money the employer spent on the employment of contract and outside agency nurses), *enforced,* 328 F.3d 837, 172 LRRM 2513 (6th Cir. 2003); Amersig Graphics, Inc. dba American Signature, Inc., 334 NLRB 880, 169 LRRM 1458 (2001) (documents relating to the sale of the company's assets to another corporation); Supervalu, Inc. v. NLRB, 184 F.3d 949, 161 LRRM 3115 (8th Cir. 1999), *enforcing* 326 NLRB 1069, 161 LRRM 1240 (1998) (documents relating to sale of store); Earthgrains Baking Cos., 327 NLRB 605, 166 LRRM 1238 (1999) (pricing information).

[166]Allied Mech. Servs., Inc., 332 NLRB 100, 172 LRRM 1219 (2001). *See also* Crittenton Hosp., 342 NLRB No. 67, 175 LRRM 1283 (2004) (minutes of safety committee meeting).

[167]Southern Cal. Gas Co., 342 NLRB No. 56, 175 LRRM 1243 (2004).

[168]Cannelton Indus., Inc., 339 NLRB 996, 173 LRRM 1087 (2003); U.S. Elec., Inc., 339 NLRB No. 52, 174 LRRM 1351 (2003); CEC, Inc., 337 NLRB 516, 170 LRRM 1384 (2002); Mercy Hosp. of Buffalo, 336 NLRB 1282, 171 LRRM 1339 (2001); Fallon-Williams, Inc., 336 NLRB 602, 171 LRRM 1502 (2001); Pioneer Elec. of Monroe, Inc., 333 NLRB 1192, 173 LRRM 1143 (2001); Oklahoma Fixture Co., 333 NLRB 804, 172 LRRM 1453 (2001), *enforcement denied on other grounds,* 2003 WL 22093906 (10th Cir. 2003); Ormet Aluminum Mill Prods., 335 NLRB 788, 169 LRRM 1514 (2001).

[169]*Amersig Graphics, Inc. dba American Signature, Inc., supra* note 165.

[170]Ingham Reg'l Med. Ctr., 342 NLRB No. 129, 175 LRRM 1511 (2004); Garcia Trucking Serv., Inc., 342 NLRB No. 75, 175 LRRM 1206 (2004); West Penn Power Co. dba Allegheny Power & Allegheny Energy Supply Co., 339 NLRB 585, 173 LRRM 1125 (2003), *enforcement granted in part,* 394 F.3d 233, 176 LRRM 2449 (4th Cir. 2005).

[171]St. George Warehouse, Inc., 341 NLRB No. 120, 175 LRRM 1316 (2004).

casual employees[172] must be provided to a union where it is necessary to negotiate a new agreement or to police existing agreements.[173] However, to the extent such information involves matters outside the bargaining unit, the Board continues to require a union to articulate some reason for requesting such information where the "information is not presumptively relevant, and the union did not demonstrate its relevance."[174] Also, where the information requested is not within the control of the contractor, the employer complies with the Act if it makes a good-faith effort to obtain the requested information, even if such effort is ultimately unsuccessful and the information is not provided to the union.[175]

The Board continues to require the employer to produce a wide variety of information relevant to the union's performance of its responsibilities as bargaining representative. Presumptively relevant information includes the names, classifications, hire dates, race, sex, addresses, telephone numbers, and pay rates of bargaining unit employees, including striker replacements;[176] the names, classifica-

---

[172]Postal Serv., 341 NLRB No. 100 (2004).

[173]West Penn Power Co. dba Allegheny Power & Allegheny Energy Supply Co., 339 NLRB 585, 173 LRRM 1125 (2003), *enforcement granted in part*, 394 F.3d 233, 176 LRRM 2449 (4th Cir. 2005); Schrock Cabinet Co., 339 NLRB 182, 172 LRRM 1347 (2003); Naperville Ready Mix, Inc. v. NLRB, 242 F.3d 744, 166 LRRM 2712 (7th Cir. 2001); Marquis-Stevens, Inc., 334 NLRB No. 35, 172 LRRM 1511 (2001); ATC/Vancom of Nev., 326 NLRB 1432, 162 LRRM 1424 (1998).

[174]*See Ingham Reg'l Med. Ctr., supra* note 170 (information about subcontracting neither presumptively nor demonstratively relevant). *See also* Anheuser-Busch, Inc., 342 NLRB No. 49, 175 LRRM 1168 (2004) (employer violated §8(a)(5) by failing to timely provide requested information about surveillance cameras but did not violate the Act when it promptly responded to an oral request for similar information); Pittson Coal Group, Inc., 334 NLRB 690, 173 LRRM 1345 (2001).

[175]*Pittson Coal Group, Inc., supra* note 174.

[176]On July 19, 2004, Associate General Counsel Richard A. Siegal issued a memorandum containing "Casehandling Instructions for Charges that Concern Information Requests about Strike Replacement," OM 04-72. This memorandum sets forth the general counsel's position for determining whether an employer must furnish information pertaining to strike replacements (such as names, home addresses, and telephone numbers). *See also* Pan Am. Grain Co., 343 NLRB No. 47, 175 LRRM 1497 (2004); *But see* JHP Assocs., LLC v. NLRB, 360 F.3d 904, 912 (8th Cir. 2004) (finding no "compelling need" for union to obtain addresses and telephone numbers of striker replacements), *denying enforcement in relevant part*, 338 NLRB 1059 (2003) (finding that employer unlawfully refused to furnish the names, addresses, and telephone numbers of strike replacements where employer had not established a "clear and present danger" that information would be misused by union).

tions, and wage rates of temporary employees performing bargaining unit work;[177] the names, hours, and rates of pay of employees performing bargaining unit work, and contracts between the employer and customers for the performance of such work;[178] the names of laid-off bargaining unit employees;[179] seniority lists;[180] employee evaluations,[181] employee policy manuals;[182] and information regarding employee evaluations used for merit increases.[183] It also includes information regarding COBRA coverage for bargaining unit employees, and information regarding safety incidents involving bargaining unit employees;[184] W-2 gross earnings information;[185] results of the employer's investigation of employees' criminal records;[186] records of bonuses awarded;[187] employee disciplinary records;[188] information regarding possible sexual or other harassment of bargaining unit employees;[189] information regarding the distribution of overtime among bargaining unit employees;[190] information regarding workplace safety;[191] and information regarding the employer's administration of medical leave for bargaining unit employees.[192] Information about an employer-provided health plan, life insurance

[177]Streicher Mobile Fueling, Inc., 340 NLRB No. 116 (2003), 175 LRRM 1184; Contract Carriers Corp., 339 NLRB 851, 173 LRRM 1043 (2003).

[178]Scapino Steel Erectors, Inc., 337 NLRB 992, 171 LRRM 1090 (2002); *Marquis-Stevens, Inc., supra* note 173.

[179]Amersig Graphics, Inc. dba American Signature Inc., 334 NLRB 880, 169 LRRM 1458 (2001).

[180]Falcon Wheel Div., L.L.C., 340 NLRB No. 42, 176 LRRM 1109 (2003).

[181]LBT, Inc., 339 NLRB 504, 174 LRRM 1479 (2003).

[182]CHS Cmty. Health Sys., Inc., 337 NLRB 998, 171 LRRM 1356 (2002). This is true even in the case of a request for an employer policy by a union steward when the union itself may be in possession of the policy. United States Postal Serv., 339 NLRB 93, 174 LRRM 1016 (2003).

[183]Allied Mech. Servs., Inc., 332 NLRB 1600, 172 LRRM 1219 (2001).

[184]*Id.*

[185]Farmer Bros. Co., 342 NLRB No. 55, 175 LRRM 1232 (2004). *See also* M & M Auto. Group dba Broadway Volkswagen, 342 NLRB No. 128, 176 LRRM 1231 (2004) (list of employees and their pay rates and job classifications); Ethan Enters., Inc., 342 NLRB No. 15, 175 LRRM 1421 (2004) (same).

[186]Overnite Transp. Co., 343 NLRB No. 134, 176 LRRM 1169 (2004).

[187]U.S. Info. Servs., Inc., 341 NLRB No. 129, 174 LRRM 1482 (2004).

[188]Dish Network Serv. Corp., 339 NLRB 1126, 175 LRRM 1154 (2003).

[189]United States Postal Serv., 341 NLRB No. 100, 176 LRRM 1302 (2004).

[190]United States Postal Serv., 339 NLRB 93, 174 LRRM 1016 (2003).

[191]Crittenton Hosp., 342 NLRB No. 67, 175 LRRM 1283 (2004).

[192]*United States Postal Service, supra* note 190; Norris Sucker Rods, 340 NLRB No. 28, 174 NLRB 1269 (2003).

plan, employee retirement, pension, savings or 401(k) plan, and any other benefit plan is also presumptively relevant.[193]

The Board also continues to require information that is not considered presumptively relevant to be provided, if the union demonstrates the relevance of such information. In this regard, the Board has required employers to provide information regarding supervisors and other nonunit members performing bargaining unit work,[194] information regarding possible disparate discipline,[195] regarding the duties performed by employees whose inclusion in the unit is disputed,[196] regarding jobs being performed by the employer,[197] and regarding the wage rates and racial makeup of the employer's workforce at other facilities.[198] The Board has also upheld union requests for information pertaining to seasonal and part-time employees,[199] information about the moving of equipment from and reduction of jobs at one of the employer's facilities,[200] information about the employer's efforts to comply with the federal Worker Adjustment and Retraining Notification Act (WARN),[201] information about employees who received safety training,[202] so-called "last chance" data,[203]

---

[193]MEMC Elec. Materials, Inc., 338 NLRB No. 142, 172 LRRM 1264 (2003), *enforced*, 363 F.3d 705, 174 LRRM 2801 (8th Cir. 2004). *See also* Producer's Dairy Foods, Inc., 338 NLRB No. 131, 172 LRRM 1072 (2003).

[194]West Penn Power Co. dba Allegheny Power & Allegheny Energy Supply Co., 339 NLRB 585, 173 LRRM 1125 (2003), *enforcement granted in part*, 394 F.3d 233, 176 LRRM 2449 (4th Cir. 2005); Phoenix Coca-Cola Bottling Co., 337 NLRB 1239, 171 LRRM 1415 (2002); Stevens Int'l, Inc., 337 NLRB 143, 172 LRRM 1396 (2001).

[195]KSM Indus., Inc., 336 NLRB 133, 169 LRRM 1445 (2001), *reconsidered in part on other grounds*, 337 NLRB 987, 170 LRRM 1313 (2002).

[196]Tarmac Am., Inc., 342 NLRB No. 107, 175 LRRM 1455 (2004).

[197]AEi2, LLC, 343 NLB No. 56, 176 LRRM 1098 (2004).

[198]Frito-Lay, Inc., 333 NLRB 1296, 167 LRRM 1065 (2001).

[199]*Phoenix Coca-Cola Bottling Co.*, *supra* note 194.

[200]Kathleen's Bakeshop, LLC, 337 NLRB 1081, 171 LRRM 1131 (2002), *enforced*, 173 LRRM 2576 (2d Cir. 2003); Titan Tire Corp., 333 NLRB 1156, 167 LRRM 1067 (2001).

[201]Supervalu, Inc. v. NLRB, 184 F.3d 949, 161 LRRM 3115 (8th Cir. 1999), *enforcing* 326 NLRB 1069, 161 LRRM 1240 (1998).

[202]WLVI-TV, Inc., 333 NLRB 1079, 172 LRRM 1096 (2001).

[203]DaimlerChrysler Corp. v. NLRB, 288 F.3d 434, 169 LRRM 3217 (D.C. Cir. 2002), *enforcing* 331 NLRB 1324, 169 LRRM 1493 (2000). The court also affirmed the Board's application of its longstanding rule that allegations involving the employer's refusal to furnish information are not deferrable to arbitration. *Id.* at 477. *See* Section IV.A.3. [The Duty to Furnish Information; The Role of Information in the Collective Bargaining Relationship—An Overview; Refusal to Furnish Information as an Unfair Labor Practice, *supra*.

and a copy of an arbitration award involving the employer and another union.[204] Information about other employers' collective bargaining agreements is not presumptively relevant, and the Board has found that an employer has no obligation to produce such information where the union fails to demonstrate the relevance of such information.[205] However, when the union demonstrates the relevance of other contracts by showing, for instance, that the information may help the union assess potential grievances, the employer must provide the information.[206]

In *Metropolitan Edison*,[207] the Board determined that where the union had a specific concern about discrimination against a union steward, it was entitled to informants' names, rejecting the employer's argument that the request triggered the same confidentiality interests as in *Pennsylvania Power*.[208]

In a departure from earlier Board and judicial decisions, the Eighth Circuit held in *Grinnell Fire Protection Systems Co. v. NLRB*[209] that because employees had a privacy interest in their homes, the employer was not obligated to provide employees' home addresses.[210] The Eighth Circuit reiterated this position in *JHP & Associates*.[211]

It is reasonable for the union to request that information be provided in electronic form, if the employer stores it in that manner.[212]

---

[204]Crowley Marine Servs., Inc. v. NLRB, 234 F.3d 1295, 166 LRRM 2001 (D.C. Cir. 2000) (affirming Board's order).

[205]Saginaw Control & Eng'g, Inc., 339 NLRB 541, 173 LRRM 1222 (2003).

[206]Schrock Cabinet Co., 339 NLRB 182, 172 LRRM 1347 (2003). *See also* West Penn Power Co. dba Allegheny Power & Allegheny Energy Supply Co., 339 NLRB 585, 173 LRRM 1125 (2003), *enforcement granted in part*, 394 F.3d 233, 176 LRRM 2449 (4th Cir. 2005).

[207]330 NLRB 107, 163 LRRM 1001 (1999).

[208]301 NLRB 1104, 136 LRRM 1225 (1991).

[209]272 F.3d 1028, 168 LRRM 2976 (8th Cir. 2001).

[210]*Id.* at 1030.

[211]360 F.3d 904 (8th Cir. 2004) (employer committed an unfair labor practice by failing to provide names of strike replacement workers, but did not commit an unfair labor practice by refusing to provide workers' home addresses and home telephone numbers), *rev'g in part* 338 NLRB 1059, 172 LRRM 1298 (2003). *But see* Ethan Enters., Inc., 342 NLRB No. 15, 175 LRRM 1421 (2004) (employer required to provide employee names, addresses, and phone numbers).

[212]Bouille Clark Plumbing, Heating, & Elec., Inc., 337 NLRB 743, 173 LRRM 1295 (2002), *enforced*, 81 Fed. Appx. 377, 173 LRRM 3119 (2d Cir. 2003).

V. ECONOMIC PRESSURE DURING BARGAINING

Economic pressure during bargaining can take many forms. Overt economic activity by employers during bargaining has primarily involved the use of a lockout. An employer's right to lock out employees for the purpose of pressuring the union to accept its proposals continues to be recognized,[213] and employers continue to be able to lawfully hire temporary replacements and subcontract work (temporarily) during a lockout.[214] Additionally, an employer may lock out employees in response to a union's threat to strike[215] or in response to an "inside-game" strategy under which members of the union agreed, among other things, to refuse to work voluntary overtime and to "work to rule."[216] A lockout in response to such an economic weapon is not inherently destructive of employees' rights, where a legitimate and substantial business justification for the lockout exists. Such justification may exist even if the only purpose is to force the union to cease its inside-game tactics. However, lockouts ruled unlawful may subject employers to substantial back-pay awards.[217]

---

[213]Midwest Generation, EME, LLC, 343 NLRB No. 12, 175 LRRM 1461 (2004); Allen Storage & Moving Co., 342 NLRB No. 44, 175 LRRM 1388 (2004); Sociedad Española de Auxilio Mutuo y Beneficencia de P.R., Inc., Hospital Español Auxilio Mutuo de Puerto Rico, Inc., 342 NLRB No. 40, 175 LRRM 1161 (2004); Dayton Newspapers, Inc., 339 NLRB 650, 172 LRRM 1477 (2003); Drew Div. of Ashland Chem. Co., 336 NLRB 477, 174 LRRM 1022 (2001); Tidewater Constr. Corp., 333 NLRB 1264, 167 LRRM 1051 (2001), *enforcement denied,* 294 F.3d 186 (D.C. Cir. 2002) (while acknowledging employer's prerogative to engage in lockout in support of negotiating position, court found that Board failed to consider evidence of union animus).

[214]*See* CII Carbon, LLC, 331 NLRB 1157, 171 LRRM 1216 (2000) (employer could subcontract dock work at its facility during lockout because of its right to use temporary replacements during lockout).

[215]*Hospital Español Auxilio Mutuo de Puerto Rico, Inc., supra* note 213.

[216]Central Ill. Public Serv. Co., 326 NLRB 928, 159 LRRM 1217 (1998), *enforced sub nom.* Electrical Workers Local 702 v. NLRB, 215 F.3d 11, 164 LRRM 2193 (D.C. Cir.), *cert. denied,* 531 U.S. 1051, 165 LRRM 3056 (2000). The court affirmed a Board decision that an employer did not commit an unfair labor practice when it locked out its employees during contract negotiations, because the Board determined that lockout was not motivated by union animus but instead with the legitimate and substantial business justification of countering the effects of an "inside-game strategy." *See also* Public Serv. Co. of Okla., 334 NLRB 487, 171 LRRM 1059 (2001), *enforced,* 318 F.3d 1173, 171 LRRM 2993 (10th Cir. 2003).

[217]*See, e.g.,* Kaiser Aluminum & Chem. Corp., 2002 NLRB LEXIS 183 (ALJ found that employer unlawfully locked out employees, which, if adopted by Board, could reportedly result in back-pay award of up to $180 million). *See* Daily Labor Report, May 15, 2002, available at http://ippubs.bna.com/ip/BNA/dlr.nsf/is/a0a5n7wlj0.

Employers must inform locked-out workers the circumstances that will enable their return. In *Dayton Newspapers, Inc.*,[218] locked-out workers sent a letter to the employer offering to return to work, and assuring the employer that there would be no further work stoppages (the workers had originally struck, then been locked out when they offered to return to work). The employer refused, stating that there were "a number of changed circumstances" that "may impact our position regarding a return to work for the employees locked out."[219] The union responded that none of the "changed circumstances" should affect a return to work by the locked-out employees. About five weeks later, the employer gave the union a memorandum with a list of things the parties would need to work out before the locked-out employees could return, including such issues including whether the union "might be lying," how the employer could be sure the union would not "secretly authorize" a wildcat strike, and whether the union would post a bond to secure its promise against unannounced work stoppages.[220]

The Board affirmed the ALJ's decision that the employer's failure to reinstate the locked-out employees was unlawful. The Board held that locked-out employees "must not only be informed that they are locked out, but they must be clearly and fully informed of the conditions they must meet to be reinstated."[221] In this case, the Board found that the employer denied the union's offer to return to work, claiming that the union had not accepted the employer's conditions. However, the Board found that the employer had not clearly and fully set forth those conditions. Instead, the employer "presented the Union with unclear and changing conditions that . . . became a 'moving target.'"[222] Thus, the Board held that the locked-out employees could not "knowingly evaluate their position" and obtain reinstatement, and that the employer violated the Act by not explicitly setting forth its conditions for reinstatement.[223]

Employers may in some circumstances institute a partial lockout. In *Midwest Generation,*[224] the Board permitted the employer to

---

[218]*Supra* note 213.
[219]*Id.*, 339 NLRB at 651.
[220]*Id.* at 652.
[221]*Id.* at 656.
[222]*Id.* at 656.
[223]*Id.*
[224]343 NLRB No. 12, 175 LRRM 1461 (2004).

lock out full-term strikers while not locking out nonstrikers and those who had crossed the picket line. The union there had struck the employer, but approximately 8 bargaining unit members continued working, and approximately 47 striking workers returned to work during the union's strike. About two months after its strike began, the union made an unconditional offer to return to work on behalf of all strikers, but the employer refused the union's offer, locked out all individuals on strike who had not yet returned to work, but permitted the 8 nonstrikers and 47 crossovers to continue working. The union alleged that the lockout was discriminatory because it targeted only full-term strikers.

The Board held that the partial lockout was lawful because it was for the purpose of applying economic pressure in support of the employer's bargaining position. The Board reasoned that the partial lockout was unrelated to union affiliation, and that the retention of crossover and nonstrikers was a part of the employer's legitimate effort to maintain production. Finding no evidence of union animus, the Board held the partial lockout to be lawful.[225]

VI. BARGAINING IMPASSES

A. Elements of Impasse

The Board and the courts continue to consider numerous factors when determining whether an impasse exists.[226] For example, in

---

[225] *Id.*, slip. op. at 4. *See also* Bunting Bearings Corp., 343 NLRB No. 64, 175 LRRM 1513 (employer lawfully implemented partial lockout of all nonprobationary employees, in the circumstances of the case, while permitting probationary employees to continue working, where following an impasse in bargaining substantial differences between probationary and nonprobationary employees existed).

[226] Ryan Ironworks v. NLRB, 257 F.3d 1, 167 LRRM 2653 (1st Cir. 2001) (no impasse where employer not adamant on all its proposals and where employer never told union that failure to agree on proposal would result in deadlock or impasse or that proposals would be implemented); NLRB v. Beverly Enter., 174 F.3d 13, 160 LRRM 2935 (1st Cir. 1999) (no impasse even though no bargaining had occurred for six months and union indicated it would be difficult to sell employer's offer and made no counter offer, because this is not same as assertion that union will not move from its bottom line); Duane Reade, Inc., 342 NLRB No. 104, 175 LRRM 1440 (2004) (no impasse where employer gave union its last, best, and final offer, but said it would consider "repackaging" offer at later bargaining session); Northwest Graphics, 343 NLRB No. 16, 176 LRRM 1167 (2004) (no impasse, despite employer's declarations to contrary, where parties continued to negotiate, and employer continued to submit proposals); Elf Atochem N. Am., Inc.,

Grosvenor Orlando Associates, Ltd.,[227] where the union continued to display flexibility and willingness to compromise its bargaining positions, the employer violated Section 8(a)(5) by declaring impasse. In *Grinnell Fire Protection Systems Co.*,[228] the Board held that impasse issues are decided on the basis of the totality of the circumstances, and that no impasse existed, notwithstanding that the employer had

---

339 NLRB 796, 174 LRRM 1101 (2003) (no impasse where no showing of what issues parties were deadlocked on, or that further negotiations would have been futile, particularly since employer had given proposal that generated union movement on same day employer declared impasse); Jano Graphics, Inc., 339 NLRB 251, 172 LRRM 1292 (2003); Lafayette Grinding Corp., 337 NLRB 832, 170 LRRM 1355 (2002) (no impasse where unremedied unfair labor practices existed); Liquor Indus. Bargaining Group, 333 NLRB 1219, 171 LRRM 1118 (2001) (no impasse because totality of employer group's bargaining conduct, including its contract proposals, showed intent to avoid agreement; Board also found violation when three of employer group members implemented part of group's final offer by converting accounts that had been serviced by bargaining unit to "house accounts," and employers were not authorized to bargain separately); Matanuska Elec. Ass'n, Inc., 337 NLRB 680, 171 LRRM 1536 (2002) (despite presence of other unresolved issues and tentative agreements and concessions on many subjects, impasse found where parties were deadlocked on two central issues because deadlock on those issues prevented parties from reaching agreement); Pleasantview Nursing Home, 335 NLRB 961, 168 LRRM 1195 (2001) (amount of union-security fee is not mandatory subject to be bargained to impasse and could not be implemented with remaining offer), *enforcement denied in part*, 351 F.3d 747, 173 LRRM 2882 (6th Cir. 2003); Cotter & Co., 331 NLRB 787 (2000), *enforcement denied in relevant part sub nom.* TruServ Corp. v. NLRB, 254 F.3d 1105, 167 LRRM 2577, *modified*, 2001 U.S. App. LEXIS 18759, 168 LRRM 2036, (D.C. Cir. 2001), *cert. denied*, 534 U.S. 1130, 169 LRRM 2576 (2002) (Board found no impasse even though union told employer that it could not recommend employer's last, best, and final offer, because it is commonplace that experienced negotiators make concessions cautiously and that negative initial reactions are later reconsidered to achieve agreement. Court denied enforcement, and found impasse because the employer faced economic exigencies, had bargained in good faith for eight days, and had made substantial concessions); Royal Motor Sales, 329 NLRB 760, 166 LRRM 1123 (1999), *enforced sub nom.* Anderson Enters. v. NLRB, 167 LRRM 2704 (D.C. Cir. 2001) (although union adamantly opposed employer's flat-rate compensation system, union accepted concept of compensating employees based on flat-rate hours and demonstrated required flexibility to avoid impasse). *See also* discussion at Section III.A. [The Good Faith Requirement; Totality of Conduct Assessed: *General Electric* and The Proper Role of the Parties], *supra*, concerning the good faith requirement. The Sixth Circuit reversed the Board's finding on the union-security fee issue, finding that is was part of a "package" proposal that included both mandatory and nonmandatory subjects (the initiation fees), and that the subjects should not be severed for purposes of impasse analysis.

[227]336 NLRB 613, 172 LRRM 1253 (2001).

[228]328 NLRB 585, 161 LRRM 1146 (1999), *enforced*, 236 F.3d 187, 166 LRRM 2065 (4th Cir. 2000), *cert. denied*, 534 U.S. 818, 168 LRRM 2472 (2001).

asserted that it had reached its final position and the union had not yet offered specific concessions. The union had declared its intention to be flexible and had made previous concessions, including seeking another bargaining session and indicating a willingness to involve a federal mediator. However, neither a party's bare assertions of flexibility on open issues nor its generalized statements that it will submit new proposals are sufficient to defeat impasse.[229]

Impasse can be "tainted" if the employer has insisted on a nonmandatory subject of bargaining, e.g., submission of the final offer to a ratification vote.[230] But an otherwise valid impasse is not voided simply because of a failure to respond to a request for information where the information request is not related to the "core" issues separating the parties.[231]

Such a result was also reached in *Pleasantview Nursing Home, Inc. v. NLRB*.[232] There, notwithstanding the commission of unfair labor practices, impasse was reached and the employer held entitled to implement its final offer. The court reasoned:

> [T]here is no "presumption that an employer's unfair labor practice automatically precludes the possibility of meaningful negotiations and prevents the parties from reaching a good faith impasse." *NLRB v. Cauthorne*, 691 F.2d 1023, 1025 (D.C. Cir. 1982) (citing *Rayner v. NLRB*, 665 F.2d 970, 976–78 (9th Cir. 1982)). "To find otherwise would reflect 'an impermissibl[e] punitive justification for continuing liability when good faith negotiations between the parties have exhausted the prospects of concluding an agreement.'" *La Porte Transit Co. v. NLRB*, 888 F.2d 1182, 1186 (7th Cir. 1989) (quoting *Cauthorne*, 691 F.2d at 1025).[233]

The court also found that the existence of an impasse was not vitiated by the employer's linkage of mandatory and nonmandatory subjects of bargaining: "The linkage arose organically out of the economic relationship between the mandatory and nonmandatory sub-

---

[229] *TruServ Corp. v. NLRB*, *supra* note 226.

[230] Jano Graphics, Inc., 339 NLRB 251, 172 LRRM 1292 (2003); Retlaw Broad. Co., 324 NLRB 138, 158 LRRM 1135 (1997), *enforced*, 172 F.3d 660, 160 LRRM 2909 (9th Cir. 1999) (employer unlawfully implemented proposal that allowed direct dealing with employees over mandatory subjects of bargaining, including merit pay system and personal service contracts with newly hired employees).

[231] Sierra Bullets, LLC, 340 NLRB No. 32, 173 LRRM 1283 (2003).

[232] 351 F.3d 747, 173 LRRM 2882 (6th Cir. 2003).

[233] *Id.* at 762.

jects of bargaining. . . ."[234] The linkage was between the collection of initiation fees (nonmandatory subject) and a union security provision (mandatory subject).

An impasse may also be "broken," in which case unilateral implementation of a mandatory subject again becomes unlawful. In *Raven Services Corp. v. NLRB*,[235] the Fifth Circuit enforced the Board's decision that while the employer had a right to unilaterally implement a management-rights clause because of an earlier impasse, once the impasse was broken, further changes pursuant to that management-rights clause were unlawful. The Fifth Circuit upheld the Board's determination that the impasse was broken because the employer refused to subsequently provide relevant and necessary information, the union had enlisted a new union leader and the employer had no genuine good faith doubt of the union's continued majority status.[236]

B. Effect on the Bargaining Obligation

The Board and the courts (with the exception of the Fifth Circuit)[237] continue to adhere to the rule that an employer may not unilaterally change a mandatory bargaining subject as soon as parties reach deadlock on that issue in negotiations. Rather, the parties must reach impasse in negotiations as a whole.[238] An exception to

---

[234] *Id.* at 761.

[235] 315 F.3d 499, 171 LRRM 2606 (5th Cir. 2003), *enforcing* 331 NLRB 651, 167 LRRM 1196 (2000), *motion for clarification of relief granted*, 336 NLRB 991, 169 LRRM 1056 (2001).

[236] *Id.*

[237] *See* discussion at Section II.A. [Per Se Violations; Unilateral Changes], *supra.*

[238] Visiting Nurse Servs. Inc. v. NLRB, 177 F.3d 52, 161 LRRM 2326 (1st Cir. 1999), *enforcing* 325 NLRB 1125, 159 LRRM 1298 (1998), *cert. denied*, 528 U.S. 1074, 163 LRRM 2192 (2000) (it was violation of §8(a)(5) for employer during negotiations to unilaterally implement certain of its proposals where impasse had not been reached on proposals as a whole, even though union had rejected proposals that were implemented; court opined that such implementation would vitiate role of bargaining representative and preclude meaningful effective collective bargaining); Loral Defense Sys.-Akron v. NLRB, 200 F.3d 436, 162 LRRM 3025 (6th Cir. 1999), *enforcing* 320 NLRB 755, 151 LRRM 1233 (1996) (two employers violated §8(a)(5) by unilaterally implementing final contract offers because changes made to employee health insurance plans were not reasonably comprehended within employer's final pre-impasse offers); Courier Journal, 342 NLRB No. 113, 175 LRRM 1410 (2004); Duffy Tool & Stamping, LLC, 330 NLRB 298, 165 LRRM 1372 (1999), *enforced*, 233 F.3d 995, 165 LRRM 2929 (7th Cir. 2000). *But see* CalMat Co., 331 NLRB 1084, 171 LRRM 1237 (2000) (impasse on single, critical issue justifies party implementing all its bargaining proposals if it demonstrates (1) actual existence of

that rule is that unilateral change is not unlawful if economic exigencies compel prompt action, though this exception is narrowly construed.[239]

In *TXU Electric Co.*,[240] the Board found that an employer was privileged to unilaterally implement changes to a past practice of giving annual salary plan adjustments, despite the parties not reaching overall impasse.[241] In *TXU,* the Board relied heavily on the proposed change involving annual salary adjustments, a subject that was based on a discrete event designed to occur during the bargaining process that was fixed as to the time and criteria but discretionary to amount. The Board found that because "the proposed change involved an annually occurring employment term, scheduled to recur in the midst of collective bargaining, it should be analyzed under its decision in *Stone Container Corp.*[242] instead of *Bottom Line Enterprises,*[243] in which the Board generally required an overall impasse prior to implementation of a change regarding a past practice. The Board in *TXU* observed:

> We adhere to the governing principles of collective bargaining that disfavor piecemeal bargaining and preclude unilateral implementation of a bargaining proposal unless the parties have bargained to overall impasse for an agreement as a whole. In the instance of bargaining subjects with fixed terms, the recognized limited ex-

---

a good faith bargaining impasse; (2) that issue as to which parties are at impasse is critical issue; and (3) that impasse on this critical issue led to breakdown in overall negotiations such that there can be no progress on any aspect of negotiation until impasse relating to critical issue is resolved).

[239]Beverly Health & Rehab. Servs., Inc., 335 NLRB 635, 171 LRRM 1402 (2001) ("economic exigencies" is narrow category of exception and is not commensurate with changes simply deemed as "desirable" by the employer), *enforced in part,* 317 F.3d 316, 171 LRRM 3017 (D.C. Cir. 2003); Vincent Indus. Plastics, Inc., 328 NLRB 300, 163 LRRM 1123 (1999), *enforced in relevant part,* 209 F.3d 727, 164 LRRM 2039 (D.C. Cir. 2000) (no economic exigencies were present to privilege employer's unilateral implementation of new attendance policy where absentee problem was strictly internal matter and was not beyond employer's control to correct; problem was also not one of absenteeism unforeseen or not reasonably foreseeable, because it had existed for long period of time).

[240]343 NLRB No. 132 (2004).

[241]*Id.*

[242]313 NLRB 336 (1993).

[243]302 NLRB 373 (1991), *enforced sub nom.* Master Window Cleaning v. NLRB, 15 F.3d 1087 (9th Cir. 1994).

ceptions to the obligation to bargain to overall impasse are those summarized in *Bottom Line Enterprises*.[244]

The Board found that piecemeal treatment was "unavoidable" in *TXU* because the date for annual review and wage adjustments was fast approaching, and the employer had to do "something" on the issue; it could not wait for an overall impasse.[245] Moreover, the Board found in *TXU* that the union, having been advised on multiple occasions by the employer regarding the impending changes, had "ample time in advance" of the changes to bargain over them, yet failed to request any bargaining.[246]

Unremedied unfair labor practices that contribute to the parties' inability to reach an agreement continue to preclude a finding of a valid impasse and will thus preclude unilateral action.[247] However, the mere fact that an information request remains outstanding will not necessarily preclude a valid impasse. In *Sierra Bullets*,[248] the employer declared impasse even though it had not responded to a union information request. The Board held that the information request, made late in the course of bargaining, was unrelated to the core issues separating the parties in negotiations, and thus was insufficient to preclude a valid impasse.[249]

---

[244]343 NLRB No. 132, slip op. at 4.

[245]*Id.*

[246]*Id.*, slip op. at 3.

[247]Duane Reade, Inc., 342 NLRB No. 104, 175 LRRM 1440 (2004) (unremedied unfair labor practices preclude impasse). *Compare* Alwin Mfg. Co., 326 NLRB 646, 162 LRRM 1120 (1998), *enforced*, 192 F.3d 133, 162 LRRM 2385 (D.C. Cir. 1999) (it was unlawful for employer to unilaterally implement its final proposal where it had not yet remedied previous unfair labor practices) *with* Quirk Tire, 330 NLRB 917 (2000) (there was no evidence that previous unfair labor practices adversely affected bargaining and therefore precluded good faith impasse). *See also* Lafayette Grinding Corp., 337 NLRB 832, 170 LRRM 1355 (2002) (employer's unlawful unilateral ceasing of payments to health and welfare fund precluded impasse); Titan Tire Corp., 333 NLRB 1156, 167 LRRM 1067 (2001) (unremedied unfair labor practices prevented impasse); Detroit Typographical Union No. 18 v. NLRB, 216 F.3d 109, 164 LRRM 2797 (D.C. Cir. 2000) (because the unremedied unfair labor practices were not important to the parties, as demonstrated by negotiations, their existence did not bar reaching of impasse).

[248]340 NLRB No. 32, 173 LRRM 1283 (2003).

[249]*Id.*, slip op. at 2.

Additionally, the Board and the courts continue to explore the parameters of the limitations *McClatchy Newspapers*[250] has placed on an employer's right to implement its final proposal following impasse. In *Detroit Typographical Union No. 18 v. NLRB*,[251] the D.C. Circuit (which earlier enforced the Board order in *McClatchy*) refused enforcement of a Board order finding that the employer violated the Act by post-impasse implementation of a merit pay proposal. The court recognized that the Board could proceed on a case-by-case basis to develop the boundaries of the *McClatchy* doctrine. However, that did not mean "that the Board could simply brandish *McClatchy*, without any real explanation, to prevent an employer from ever implementing a merit pay proposal after impasse."[252] The court went on to distinguish the merit pay proposal in this case from the one in *McClatchy* on the basis that this proposal included details about the plan, included average anticipated increases, set dates for increases, and allowed the use of the grievance procedure to contest the merit pay award. The court found that the Board's failure to consider these distinctions resulted in a "blithe extension of *McClathy* [that was] unreasoned and unreasonable."[253]

The Board has continued to follow its application of *McClatchy* even after *Detroit Typographical*. In *Edward S. Quirk Co.*,[254] the Board again addressed a discretionary merit pay clause. A previous Board decision in that case was denied enforcement by the First Circuit.[255] The First Circuit held that "*McClatchy* is based on employer discretion and discretion is a matter of degree."[256] Thus, the court remanded to the Board. On remand, the Board held that the employer's proposal, which stated that employees would "be paid at a base rate of not less than $8.90 an hour, however, the Company may continue its current pay practices," violated the Act.[257] By including the word "may" in its implemented wage proposal, the employer reserved to itself total discretion to make recurring unilateral changes in wage rates.

---

[250]321 NLRB 1386, 153 LRRM 1137 (1996), *enforced*, 131 F.3d 1026, 157 LRRM 2023 (D.C. Cir. 1997).

[251]*Supra* note 247.

[252]*Id.*

[253]*Id.* at 118. *See also* Edward S. Quirk Co. v. NLRB, 241 F.3d 41, 166 LRRM 2666 (1st Cir. 2001) (merit wage increases).

[254]340 NLRB No. 33, 173 LRRM 1260 (2003).

[255]*See Edward S. Quirk Co.*, *supra* note 253.

[256]*Id.* at 45.

[257] 340 NLRB No. 33, slip op. at 2.

In *KSM Industries, Inc.*,[258] the Board extended *McClatchy,* and found an employer's post-impasse implementation of a health care plan unlawful where the proposal gave the employer sole discretion during the term of the agreement to "change the method and/or means for providing for the medical/hospital and dental benefits,"[259] which included the plan design and the level and administration of benefits, provided that the changes were applied on a companywide basis, the changes were first discussed with the union, and any deductibles and coinsurance limits for the medical/hospital benefit did not exceed specified dollar amounts.[260] The Board reasoned that even though the proposal required "discussion" with the union, because it did not require bargaining, it was analogous to the merit pay increase in *McClatchy,* and therefore unlawful.[261]

VII. Defenses and Exceptions: Waiver, Suspension, and Termination of Bargaining Rights

A. Waiver of Bargaining Rights

The Board continues to find a waiver of the statutory right to bargain based on language contained in a collective bargaining agree-

[258]336 NLRB 133, 169 LRRM 1445 (2001), *modified,* 337 NLRB 987, 170 LRRM 1313 (2002).

[259]*Id.* at 137.

[260]*Id.*

[261]In a subsequent motion for reconsideration, Member Cowen expressed disagreement with the decision in *KSM,* because the changes in *KSM* were not presented as a fait accompli and the union did not request bargaining. Member Cowen also implicitly questioned the holding of *McClatchy,* by noting "[i]n light of my rationale for reversing this violation . . . , I find it unnecessary to address the Board's application of *McClatchy Newspapers* . . . to the [employer's] health insurance proposal in [*KSM I*], . . . or the validity of *McClatchy Newspapers.*" 337 NLRB 987 at 989. *See also* M&G Polymers USA, LLC, 32 Advice Memorandum, September 28, 2004, where the NLRB's Division of Advice concluded that the merit-based employee assessment implemented by the employer did not come within the exception to the "implementation after impasse" rule because the employer had not attempted to exercise unfettered discretion in either designing or implementing the employee assessment procedures and criteria.

ment only if that language is specific regarding the particular subject at issue.[262]

The Board continues to apply the "clear and unmistakable" waiver standard in unilateral change cases. In order for a waiver of bargaining rights to exist under this standard, "[e]ither the contract language relied on must be specific or the employer must show that the issue was fully discussed and consciously explored and that the union consciously yielded or clearly and unmistakably waived its interest in the matter."[263] Waiver can occur by operation of specific language in a collective bargaining agreement, or by the conduct of the parties, including the parties' bargaining history, practices, or inaction relating to a particular subject of bargaining.

1. *Waiver by Express Agreement*

The Board continues to find a waiver of the statutory right to bargain based on language contained in a collective bargaining agreement where the language of the agreement demonstrates a clear and unmistakable waiver of the right to bargain regarding the subject at issue.[264] Because waivers of statutory rights are not to be "lightly

---

[262]Mt. Sinai Hosp., 331 NLRB 895, 169 LRRM 1206 (2000), *enforced*, 8 Fed. Appx. 111, 2001 WL 533552 (2d Cir. 2001) (management-rights clause, which permitted employer to "discontinue, reorganize, or combine any operation even if the effect is a reduction in the unit work or in the number of unit employees," did not privilege employer's reclassification of sous chefs as assistant culinary managers, a new supervisory position); Ryder/Ate, Inc., 331 NLRB 889, 170 LRRM 1285 (2000) (union did not clearly and unmistakably waive its right to bargain about new attendance policy, notwithstanding management-rights clause that permitted employer to make reasonable work rules and rules of conduct and make amendments to these rules); Dorsey Trailers, Inc., 327 NLRB 835, 165 LRRM 1392 (1999), *enforced in relevant part*, 233 F.3d 831, 165 LRRM 3003 (4th Cir. 2000) (union did not clearly and unmistakably waive its right to bargain new attendance policy where union agreed that employer had "the exclusive right to manage the plant and its business and to exercise customary functions of management in all respects and to make fair and reasonable rules for the purpose of maintaining order, safety, and effective operation").

[263]Amoco Chem. Co., 328 NLRB 1220, 1221–22, 162 LRRM 1017 (1999), *enforcement denied*, 217 F.3d 869, 164 LRRM 2889 (D.C. Cir. 2000).

[264]Natomi Hosps. of Cal., Inc. dba Good Samaritan Hosp., 335 NLRB 901, 172 LRRM 1234 (2001) (provision in collective bargaining agreement preserving employer's right "to decide the number of employees to any shift or job . . . or to determine appropriate staffing levels" demonstrated a clear and unmistakable waiver of the union's right to bargain over summer staffing level changes).

inferred," contract language must be specific in order to constitute a waiver of bargaining rights.[265]

The Board's adherence to the waiver analysis has resulted in some judicial criticism and the application by certain courts of the alternative, less rigid "contract coverage" analysis.[266] Under this approach, once a matter is "covered by" the labor agreement, "the union *has exercised* its bargaining right and the question of waiver is irrelevant."[267] The leading case is *NLRB v. Postal*

---

[265]*Mt. Sinai Hosp.*, *supra* note 262 (management-rights clause that permitted employer to "discontinue, reorganize, or combine any operation even if the effect is a reduction in the unit work or in the number of unit employees" did not privilege employer's reclassification of sous chefs as assistant culinary managers, a new supervisory position); *Ryder/Ate, Inc.*, *supra* note 262 (union did not clearly and unmistakably waive its right to bargain about new attendance policy, notwithstanding management-rights clause that permitted employer to make reasonable work rules and rules of conduct and make amendments to these rules); *Dorsey Trailers, Inc.*, *supra* note 262 (union did not clearly and unmistakably waive its right to bargain new attendance policy where union agreed that employer had "the exclusive right to manage the plant and its business and to exercise customary functions of management in all respects and to make fair and reasonable rules for the purpose of maintaining order, safety, and effective operation"); *Amoco Chem. Co.*, *supra* note 263, at 1221-22 (labor contracts did not specifically incorporate reservation-of-rights language contained in summary plan description relied upon by employer), *enforcement denied*, 217 F.3d 869, 164 LRRM 2889 (D.C. Cir. 2000) (court found that labor contracts did incorporate reservation-of-rights language, thus preserving employer's right to make unilateral changes). *See also* TransMontaigne Inc., 337 NLRB 262, 169 LRRM 1229 (2001) (recognition clause that relieved successor employers from adopting contractual obligations did not constitute clear and unmistakable waiver of union's statutory right to recognition); King Soopers Inc., 332 NLRB 32, 37, 167 LRRM 1222 (2000), *enforced*, 254 F.3d 738, 167 LRRM 2612 (8th Cir. 2001) (union did not waive its statutory rights where recitation of store's address in recognition clause was a physical description of location, not geographical limitation).

[266]For a two-sided examination of the debate, see Carron & Broughton, *When is "No" Really "No"—The NLRB's Current Position on the Freedom of Contract, Management Rights, and Waiver*, 13 LAB. LAW. 299 (1997) and Wagner, *"No" Means "No" When a Party "Really" Says So: The NLRB's Continued Adherence to the Clear and Unmistakable Waiver Doctrine in Unilateral Change Cases*, 13 LAB. LAW. 325 (1997).

[267]Department of Navy v. FLRA, 962 F.2d 48, 57, 140 LRRM 2206, 2214 (D.C. Cir. 1992) (emphasis in original) (applying contract coverage analysis under federal service labor-management relations statute); *accord* Chicago Tribune Co. v. NLRB, 974 F.2d 933, 937, 141 LRRM 2209 (7th Cir. 1992) ("[o]f course people should not be tripped into forgoing valuable rights, but where as in this case a union agrees to a broadly worded management-rights clause the scope of that clause depends on the usual principles of contract interpretation rather than on a doctrine that tilts decision in the union's favor"); Electrical Workers (IBEW) Local 47 v. NLRB, 927 F.2d 635, 641, 137 LRRM 2723 (D.C. Cir. 1991) (if "contract fully defines the parties' rights as to what would otherwise be a mandatory subject of

Service,[268] where the D.C. Circuit denied enforcement of the Board's finding of a Section 8(a)(5) violation. The Board had found the employer's unilateral reduction in service hours was unlawful, rejecting arguments that a broadly worded management-rights clause was sufficiently specific to constitute a waiver of the union's right to bargain. On review, the court criticized the Board's approach as a "crabbed reading," which "naïve[ly] . . . assume[s] that bargaining parties anticipate every hypothetical grievance and purport to address it in their contract."[269] Finding the service reductions to be within the "clear compass" of the management-rights clause, the court held that "[t]hese rights surely permit an employer unilaterally to rearrange its employees' work schedules, which the Postal Service contends was the sole result of its service reduction."[270] The D.C. Circuit, however, subsequently distinguished its decision and affirmed a Board decision that a management-rights clause did not constitute a "clear and unmistakable waiver of bargaining" regarding the allocation of certain work, finding that the employer advocated for "a more expansive reading of a much narrower management rights clause" than the one existing in *NLRB v. Postal Service*.[271]

Although the Board's decisions often expressly apply the waiver standard,[272] some Board members have advocated applying the contract coverage test.[273] More recently, the Board has acknowledged

---

bargaining, it is incorrect to say the union has 'waived' its statutory right to bargain; rather, the contract will control and the 'clear and unmistakable' intent standard is irrelevant").

[268]8 F.3d 832, 144 LRRM 2691 (D.C. Cir. 1993).

[269]*Id.* at 838, 144 LRRM at 2695.

[270]*Id.*

[271]Regal Cinemas, Inc. v. NLRB, 317 F.3d 300, 312–13 (D.C. Cir. 2003).

[272]*See* cases cited in nn. 262 and 263, *supra.*

[273]*See, e.g.*, Caraustar Mill Group dba Cincinnati Paperboard, 339 NLRB 1079, n.2, 173 LRRM 1161 (2003); California Pac. Med. Ctr., 337 NLRB 910 n.1, 173 LRRM 1326 (2002); AT&T Corp., 337 NLRB 689, 170 LRRM 1153 (2002); Public Serv. Co. of New Mex., 337 NLRB 193, 172 LRRM 1508 (2001); Stevens Int'l, Inc., 337 NLRB 143, 172 LRRM 1396 (2001) (Chairman Hurtgen, concurring and dissenting in part); Dorsey Trailers, Inc., 327 NLRB 835, 165 LRRM 1392 (1999) (Member Hurtgen, dissenting in part); Exxon Research & Eng'g Co., 317 NLRB 675, 676–77, 150 LRRM 1308 (1995) (Member Cohen, dissenting in part), *enforcement denied on other grounds*, 89 F.3d 228, 152 LRRM 2842 (5th Cir. 1996).

the contract coverage test but determined it unnecessary to pass upon which standard is appropriate, finding the result the same under either test.[274] Despite some disagreement over the proper standard to be applied, a number of courts have upheld the Board's application of the clear and unmistakable waiver standard.[275]

Because waivers of statutory rights are not to be "lightly inferred," contract language that is proffered as a waiver must be specific.[276]

a. "Zipper" Clauses

In *Mississippi Power Co.*,[277] the Board held that a zipper clause did not evince the union's waiver of its right to bargain over insurance plan changes because the changes would not occur until a date outside the term of the agreement. The Fifth Circuit disagreed, and

---

[274] *See, e.g.*, Ingham Reg'l Med. Ctr., 342 NLRB No. 129, 175 LRRM 1511 (2004); BHP (USA) Inc., 341 NLRB No. 149, 175 LRRM 1190 (2004); *Caraustar Mill Group, Inc. dba Cincinnati Paperboard, supra* note 273.

[275] *See, e.g.*, King Soopers, Inc. v. NLRB, 254 F.3d 738, 167 LRRM 2612 (8th Cir. 2001); Bonnell/Tredegar Indus. v. NLRB, 46 F.3d 339, 148 LRRM 2392 (4th Cir. 1995); NLRB v. U.S. Postal Serv., 18 F.3d 1089, 145 LRRM 2704 (3d Cir. 1994). *See also Regal Cinemas, Inc., supra* note 271; Dunbar ex rel. NLRB v. Carrier Corp., 66 F. Supp. 2d 346, 351 n.3, 161 LRRM 2119 (N.D.N.Y. 1999), citing Olivetti Office U.S.A. v. NLRB, 926 F.2d 181, 136 LRRM 2601 (2d Cir.), *cert. denied*, 502 U.S. 856, 138 LRRM 2480 (1991). *But see* BP Amoco v. NLRB, 217 F.3d 869, 164 LRRM 2889 (D.C. Cir. 2000) (court found that Board erroneously applied waiver analysis where bargaining subject was "covered by" collective bargaining agreement).

[276] Amoco Chem. Co., 328 NLRB 1220, 1221–22, 162 LRRM 1017 (1999) (labor contracts did not specifically incorporate reservation-of-rights language contained in summary plan description relied upon by employer), *enforcement denied*, 217 F.3d 869, 164 LRRM 2889 (D.C. Cir. 2000) (court found that labor contracts did incorporate reservation-of-rights language, thus preserving employer's right to make unilateral changes). *See also* TransMontaigne Inc., 337 NLRB 262, 169 LRRM 1229 (2001) (recognition clause that relieved successor employers from adopting contractual obligations did not constitute clear and unmistakable waiver of union's statutory right to recognition); King Soopers Inc., 332 NLRB 32, 37, 167 LRRM 1222 (2000), *enforced*, 254 F.3d 738, 167 LRRM 2612 (8th Cir. 2001) (union did not waive its statutory rights where recitation of store's address in recognition clause was a physical description of location, not geographical limitation).

[277] 332 NLRB 530, 165 LRRM 1225 (2000), *enforcement denied in relevant part*, 284 F.3d 605, 169 LRRM 2840 (5th Cir. 2002).

held that the zipper clause constituted a waiver by the union of its right to bargain over the prospective changes affecting health insurance identified by the employer during the term of the agreement.[278]

b. "Management-Rights" Clauses

The Board continues to hold that a broadly worded management-rights clause is insufficiently specific to constitute a clear and unmistakable waiver of the union's right to bargain.[279] However, where a management-rights clause "specifically, precisely, and plainly" granted the employer the right to subcontract without restriction, the Board found that there was no obligation to engage in decision bargaining with the union.[280]

2. *Waiver by Bargaining History*

The Board continues to consider bargaining history in determining whether or not a party has waived its bargaining rights.[281]

---

[278]Mississippi Power Co. v. NLRB, 284 F.3d 605, 619–20, 169 LRRM 2840 (5th Cir. 2002).

[279]Regal Cinemas Inc., 334 NLRB 304, 167 LRRM 1347 (2001), *enforced*, 317 F.3d 300, 171 LRRM 2944 (D.C. Cir. 2003) (employer's contractual right to implement technological developments did not imply waiver of union's right to bargain over allocation of work among different classifications of employees); Mt. Sinai Hosp., 331 NLRB 895, 169 LRRM 1206 (2000), *enforced*, 8 Fed. Appx. 111, 2001 WL 533552 (2d Cir. 2001) (management-rights clause, which permitted employer to "discontinue, reorganize, or combine any operation even if the effect is a reduction in the unit work or in the number of unit employees," did not privilege employer's reclassification of sous chefs out of the unit); Ryder/Ate, Inc., 331 NLRB 889, 170 LRRM 1285 (2000) (union did not clearly and unmistakably waive its right to bargain over new attendance policy, notwithstanding management-rights clause that permitted employer to make or amend reasonable work rules and rules of conduct); Dorsey Trailers, 327 NLRB 835, 165 LRRM 1392 (1999) (union did not clearly and unmistakably waive its right to bargain new attendance policy, notwithstanding employer's "exclusive right to manage the plant and its business and to exercise customary functions of management in all respects and to make fair and reasonable rules for the purpose of maintaining order, safety, and effective operation").

[280]Allison Corp., 330 NLRB 1363, 1365, 166 LRRM 1064, 1067 (2000); *see also* Ingham Reg'l Med. Ctr., 342 NLRB No. 129, 175 LRRM 1511 (2004) (union waived its right to bargain over a decision to subcontract work based upon specific provisions in collective bargaining agreement, including language in management-rights clause pertaining to subcontracting).

[281]King Soopers Inc., v. NLRB, 254 F.3d 738, 167 LRRM 2612 (8th Cir. 2001); *Amoco Chem. Co.*, *supra* note 276.

3. Waiver by Inaction

Although a union's inaction may constitute a waiver of its right to bargain, "acquiescence in past changes to a bargainable subject does not betoken a surrender of the right to bargain the next time the employer might wish to make yet further changes, not even when such further changes arguably are similar to those in which the union may have acquiesced in the past."[282]

The Board continues to require a union to act with "due diligence" when given notice of an employer's intent to change a term or condition of employment, in order for the union to enforce a bargaining obligation. Thus, in *AT&T Corp.*,[283] the employer announced that layoffs would occur in 60 days and the union did not demand bargaining concerning the matter. The Board found that the union's conduct demonstrated a lack of due diligence in pursuing the layoff, and, therefore, concluded that the employer did not fail or refuse to bargain with the union.[284] The Board found that the union's filing of an unfair labor practice charge did not, on the record construed as a whole, renew the union's request for bargaining.[285] Waiver by inaction will not be found, where the employer implements a unilateral change without giving sufficient advance notice to give a union a reasonable opportunity to request bargaining, or when the union is presented with a fait accompli.[286]

[282]*Amoco Chem. Co.*, *supra* note 276, at 1222 n.6, quoting Exxon Research & Eng'g Co., 317 NLRB 675, 685–86, 150 LRRM 1308 (1995).

[283]AT&T Corp., 337 NLRB 689, 170 LRRM 1153 (2002).

[284]*Id.*, citing Clarkwood Corp., 233 NLRB 1172 (1977), *enforced*, 586 F.2d 835 (3d Cir. 1978); Reynolds Metal Co., 310 NLRB 995, 1000, 144 LRRM 1070 (1993); Goodyear Tire & Rubber Co., 312 NLRB 674, 146 LRRM 1055 n.1 (1993); Bell Atl. Corp., 336 NLRB 1076, 170 LRRM 1150 (2001).

[285]*Id.*; *see also* Boeing Co., 337 NLRB 758, 172 LRRM 1463 (2002) (union, which affirmatively refused to meet and bargain with employer over the terms of new compensation and benefit plan and instead filed unfair labor practice charge, waived its statutory bargaining rights).

[286]*See* UAW-Daimler Chrysler Nat'l Training Ctr., 341 NLRB No. 51, 174 LRRM 1271 (2004) (two weeks' notice was sufficient to allow union reasonable opportunity to request bargaining regarding layoff, but union did not waive its right to bargain because layoff decision was presented as fait accompli).

C. Union Loss of Majority

In response to the Supreme Court's decision in *Allentown Mack Sales & Service v. NLRB*,[287] the Board in *Levitz Furniture*[288] set new rules for determining when an employer may lawfully withdraw recognition from a union.[289] Abandoning the good faith doubt standard for withdrawal of recognition,[290] the Board held that an employer may now "unilaterally withdraw recognition only by a showing that the union has, in fact, lost support of a majority of the employees in the bargaining unit."[291] In defense of an unfair labor practice charge, the employer must show that the union had actually lost majority support at the time of withdrawal, or else it will be found to have violated Section 8(a)(5). Recognizing that *Levitz Furniture* represented a change in Board policy, the Board held that this new standard would not be applied to cases pending when *Levitz* was decided.[292] An employer may avoid its duty to bargain on the grounds of loss of majority status only where the employer has committed no unfair labor practices that tend to undermine employees' support for the union.[293]

---

[287]522 U.S. 359, 157 LRRM 2257 (1998).

[288]333 NLRB 717, 166 LRRM 1329 (2001).

[289]*Id.* For a more detailed discussion of the decision and its implications, see Chapter 10, "Representation Proceedings and Elections," and Chapter 12, "Recognition and Withdrawal of Recognition Without an Election."

[290]The Board overruled *Celanese Corp.*, 95 NLRB 664, 28 LRRM 1362 (1951), and its progeny to the extent "they hold an employer may lawfully withdraw recognition on the basis of a good-faith doubt (uncertainty or disbelief) concerning the union's continued majority status." *Id.* at 717.

[291]*Levitz, supra* note 288.

[292]*Id.*, 333 NLRB at 717 n.1; *see also* BPH & Co. v. NLRB, 333 F.3d 213, 217 n.5, 172 LRRM 2865 (D.C. Cir. 2003).

[293]*See* Regency House of Wallingford, Inc., 2003 WL 201326, n.16 (2003) (ALJ applied *Levitz*, finding that employer's unfair labor practices, which undermined employees' support for union, rendered employer's withdrawal of recognition unlawful); Kentucky Fried Chicken, Caribbean Holdings, Inc., 341 NLRB No. 13, 174 LRRM 1049 (2004) (employer's withdrawal of recognition was not based on a good faith uncertainty regarding the union's continued majority status in light of employer's unlawful solicitation of employee disaffection and its unlawful statements which tended to undermine union's support among unit employees).

VIII. THE CONSTRUCTION INDUSTRY: SECTION 8(f)

B. The *Deklewa* Decision: Binding Section 8(f) Agreements and the Duty to Bargain

The Board continues to follow the principles set forth in *John Deklewa & Sons.*[294] Consistent with the first *Deklewa* principle—that Section 8(f) agreements are enforceable through the mechanism of Sections 8(a)(5) or 8(b)(3) and cannot be unilaterally repudiated during their term—in *South Alabama Plumbing,*[295] the Board found the employer's attempted repudiation two days after signing the Section 8(f) agreement unlawful. The employer asserted that the contract contained an illegal union-security provision and was therefore unenforceable. However, the Board found the agreement's savings and separability clause applicable and ruled that the employer could not avoid its obligation to honor other terms of the contract.[296]

In addition, the Board's decision in *E.S.P. Concrete Plumbing*[297] that the rule of "adoption-by-conduct" applies to Section 8(f) agreements was embraced by the Ninth Circuit in *Southern California Painters & Allied Trade District Council No. 36 v. Best Interiors, Inc.*[298] In that case, the Ninth Circuit held that an employer can adopt a Section 8(f) pre-hire agreement by its conduct, abrogating its earlier decision to the contrary in *Hawaii Carpenters' Trust Funds v. Henry.*[299]

Some courts have upheld Board holdings that language in a pre-hire agreement may itself be sufficient to establish voluntary recognition.[300] This occurs where the contract language includes a Section 9(a) demand for recognition (explicit or implied), an unequivocal statement that the employer recognizes the union as the exclusive representative of the bargaining-unit employees, and a recitation that the union submitted satisfactory proof that it represents a majority

---

[294]282 NLRB 1375, 124 LRRM 1185 (1987), *enforced,* 843 F.2d 770, 128 LRRM 2020 (3d Cir.), *cert. denied,* 488 U.S. 889, 129 LRRM 2528 (1988).

[295]333 NLRB 16, 166 LRRM 1089 (2001).

[296]*Cf.* McKenzie Eng'g Co. v. NLRB, 303 F.3d 902, 170 LRRM 3043 (8th Cir. 2002) (applying principles set forth in *John Deklewa & Sons* and finding no repudiation or breach by the employer of pre-hire collective bargaining agreement).

[297]327 NLRB 711, 160 LRRM 1161 (1999).

[298]359 F.3d 1127, 174 LRRM 2422 (9th Cir. 2004).

[299]906 F.2d 1349, 134 LRRM 2777 (9th Cir. 1990).

[300]Sheet Metal Workers Local 19 v. Herre Bros. Inc., 201 F.3d 231, 163 LRRM 2133 (3d Cir. 1999).

of employees.[301] The Board's application of this principle even if the employer has no bargaining-unit employees at the time it executes the agreement (unless the employer contests the union's majority status within six months thereafter) has also been enforced.[302]

In *Staunton Fuel & Material Inc. dba Central Illinois Construction*,[303] the Board set forth the process by which a union may change its status as a bargaining representative governed by Section 8(f) to that of a majority bargaining representative under Section 9(a). Specifically, a written Section 8(f) agreement "will establish a Section 9(a) relationship if its language unequivocally indicates that the union requested recognition as majority representative, the employer recognized the union as majority representative, and the employer's recognition was based on the union's having shown, or having offered to show, an evidentiary basis of its majority support."[304] It is unnecessary for the written agreement to refer explicitly to Section 9(a), provided the agreement conclusively notifies the parties that a Section 9(a) relationship is intended.[305]

In *Nova Plumbing, Inc. v. NLRB*,[306] the D.C. Circuit refused to enforce a Board order holding that the collective bargaining agreement executed between the union and the company was a Section 9(a) agreement instead of an agreement governed by Section 8(f). In reaching its decision, the Board relied upon language in the agreement falsely stating that the parties agreed that the union represented an uncoerced majority of the employees and this majority was independently verified.[307] Thus, while the court noted that contract language and intent are "perfectly legitimate *factors* that the Board may consider in determining whether the *Deklewa* presumption has been overcome," they cannot, standing alone, be dispositive when the record contains strong indications that the parties had only a Section 8(f) relationship.[308]

---

[301]*Id.* at 241, 163 LRRM at 2139.

[302]NLRB v. Triple C Maint., 219 F.3d 1147, 164 LRRM 2785 (10th Cir. 2000).

[303]335 NLRB 717, 168 LRRM 1121 (2001).

[304]*Id.*, 168 LRRM at 1122.

[305]Nova Plumbing, Inc., 336 NLRB 633, 637, 169 LRRM 1276 (2001), *enforcement denied*, 330 F.3d 531 (D.C. Cir. 2003).

[306]330 F.3d 531, 172 LRRM 2700 (D.C. Cir. 2003).

[307]*Id.* at 535.

[308]*Id.*

Determining whether an employer *has* recognized a union under Section 8(f) begins with the question whether it lawfully *can* do so. The facts must establish three conditions before the parties can enter into a Section 8(f) agreement:

1. The employer must be primarily engaged in the building and construction industry;[309]
2. The employees covered by the agreement must, upon their employment, be engaged in the building and construction industry; and
3. The union must be a labor organization of which building and construction employees are members.[310]

In *Expo Group*,[311] the Board found that an employer that set up and fabricated exhibits for the trade-show/convention industry was not engaged primarily in the building and construction industry, and the construction work of its employees was incidental to its mission of producing trade shows. Even if assembling displays and exhibits were construction industry activity, the Board ruled, the employer was only secondarily and not primarily engaged in the construction industry.

IX. Notice to Terminate or Modify the Labor Agreement

A. Notice Requirements Generally

The Board continues to apply and refine the various notice requirements contained in Section 8(d). An employer violates Section 8(d)(4) by locking out its employees fewer than 60 days after the

[309] *See, e.g.*, Coulter's Carpet Serv., Inc., 338 NLRB 732 175 LRRM 1228 (2002) (employer engaged in retail and nonretail sale and installation of floor coverage is primarily engaged in building and construction industry within meaning of §8(f) despite that complaint did not use term "primarily" and merely alleged that employer was engaged in building and construction industry).

[310] *See* 29 U.S.C. §158(f); John Deklewa & Sons, 282 NLRB 1375, 124 LRRM 1185 (1987), *enforced sub nom.* Iron Workers Local 3 v. NLRB, 843 F.2d 770, 128 LRRM 2020 (3d Cir.), *cert. denied*, 488 U.S. 889, 129 LRRM 2528 (1988).

[311] 327 NLRB 413, 166 LRRM 1014 (1999). *See also* Granite Constr. Co., 330 NLRB 205, 168 LRRM 1109 (1999) (three separate rock, sand, and gravel units found not to be within construction industry as the term is used in §8(f)); Spectacor Mgmt. Group v. NLRB, 320 F.3d 385, 171 LRRM 3057 (3d Cir. 2003), *enforcing* 335 NLRB 586, 171 LRRM 1422 (2001) (installation, assembly, and dismantling of temporary trade show exhibits did not fall within definition of "construction industry").

union's notice to terminate, even if the union's notice is untimely under Section 8(d)(1). In *Drew Division of Ashland Chemical Co.*,[312] the union notified the employer of its intent to terminate their agreement fewer than 60 days prior to the agreement's expiration date. The employer locked out the employees when the agreement expired, but prior to the passage of 60 days following the union's untimely notice. The Board ruled that the employer was required to wait a full 60 days prior to taking economic action against the union, despite the union's failure to comply with Section 8(d)'s notice requirement.

The Board continues to hold that a union may not lawfully call a strike until 30 days after notice has been given to the Federal Mediation and Conciliation Service (FMCS), even if such notice was untimely. In *Freeman Decorating Co.*,[313] the union violated Section 8(d) where neither it nor the FMCS could produce evidence that the FMCS had received the required notice at least 30 days prior to the union's strike. However, the Board held that the employers unlawfully "terminated" 2,200 union members by refusing to accept referrals of these employees from a union hiring hall after the union had gone on this unlawful strike. The D.C. Circuit agreed with the Board's holding that the union had engaged in an unlawful strike, but refused to enforce that portion of the Board's order finding that the employers had violated Sections 8(a)(1) and 8(a)(3) of the Act by announcing the terminations of the individuals who had used the union's hiring hall.[314] The court found that the Board's decision that the union members were not "employees" who had engaged in an unlawful strike—because they were not actively employed by the employers at the time the strike was called—was contrary to the Act.[315] Therefore, the court held that the employers were entitled to "terminate" the employees due to the unlawful strike.[316]

In *New England Cleaning Services, Inc. v. Service Employees Local 254*,[317] the First Circuit adopted the Fifth Circuit's view[318] that, al-

---

[312]336 NLRB 477, 174 LRRM 1022 (2001).

[313]336 NLRB 1, 168 LRRM 1329 (2001), *enforcement denied in part*, 334 F.3d 27, 172 LRRM 2993 (D.C. Cir. 2003).

[314]334 F.3d at 31.

[315]*Id.* at 34.

[316]*Id.* at 37.

[317]199 F.3d 537, 163 LRRM 2068 (1st Cir. 1999).

[318]Communications Workers v. Southwestern Bell Tel. Co., 713 F.2d 1118, 1126, 114 LRRM 2302 (5th Cir. 1983). *See also* Procter & Gamble Indep. Union v. Procter & Gamble Mfg. Co., 312 F.2d 181, 189, 51 LRRM 2751 (2d Cir. 1962) (failure to give timely notice to agencies under §8(d)(3) did not extend expired agreement).

though "failure to notify [the FMCS] might have ramifications for an unfair labor practice claim, it does not serve to extend a contract that could be terminated via notice under section 8(d)(1)."[319] The collective bargaining agreement contained a clause providing that it would automatically remain effective after its stated expiration date, unless terminated by either party's written notice at least 60 days prior to the expiration date. The employer provided the requisite notice to the union, but did not notify FMCS. The union argued that the termination was therefore ineffective. The court disagreed, finding that the purposes underlying Section 8(d) would not be furthered by declaring the agreement to be extended under these circumstances.

In *Boghosian Raisin Packing Co.*,[320] the Board held that an employer did not violate Sections 8(a)(1) and (3) when it terminated and refused to reinstate 42 bargaining unit employees who had engaged in a strike against the employer. The union, by error, failed to provide FMCS with the required Section 8(d)(3) notice. Although the employer learned of the union's failure to notify FMCS approximately one week prior to the strike, the employer did not inform the union of this failure until the strike had commenced. Member Liebman, in dissent, argued that the employer's withholding of the information until the strike had begun was bad faith and the employer should be prohibited from relying on Section 8(d) to terminate the union members.[321] However, the majority noted that "the burden to notify the mediation services in this case was on the Union,"[322] and applied a strict interpretation of the notification requirements of Section 8(d), stating that "[i]n this regard, Section 8(d) contains no exceptions and provides no mitigating circumstances justifying a failure to comply. . . . [T]he Union's failure to file with the FMCS was not deliberate but the product of negligence is not exculpatory."[323] Furthermore, although the majority did not agree with the dissent that the employer had acted in bad faith by not informing the union that it had failed to notify FMCS, the majority stated that the employer's motivation was "immaterial"[324] and that

---

[319] *New England Cleaning Servs.*, *supra* note 317, at 540.
[320] 342 NLRB No. 32, 175 LRRM 1286 (2004).
[321] *Id.* at *13.
[322] *Id.* at *4.
[323] *Id.*
[324] *Id.*

"the [employer's] conduct, even had it been undertaken in bad faith, as the dissent speculates, would not justify an exception [to the Section 8(d) notice requirements]."[325]

[Editor's Note: Due to an editing error, the Fourth Edition incorrectly states the notice requirement contained in Section 8(d)(4). At page 967, the first paragraph, last sentence should read: "Section 8(d)(4) provides that the parties to the labor contract are precluded from striking or locking out (1) for a period of 60 days after the Section 8(d)(1) notice is given, or (2) until the expiration date of the contract, whichever is later."]

B. Notice Requirements in the Health Care Industry

The Board continues to hold that Section 8(g)'s notice requirements apply only to strikes by "labor organizations." In *Bethany Medical Center*,[326] the Board found that a group of employees who were not members of any labor organization did not violate Section 8(g) when they notified their employer of their intent to walk out only 15 minutes prior to the day's first scheduled medical procedure. That the employees engaged in concerted activity was insufficient to make them a de facto labor organization. Because no labor organization was involved, the "employees were not legally required to do anything more than they did to preserve their rights pursuant to Section 7 of the Act when they walked off the job. . . ."[327]

In a similar case, *Vencare Ancillary Services, Inc.*,[328] the Board found that a group of five employees did not violate Section 8(g). The Board, citing the elements set forth in *Electromation, Inc.*,[329] found that the employees did not constitute a labor organization because they did

---

[325] *Id.* at *5. Member Liebman noted that this strict adherence by the Board to the precise language of the statute continues a recent trend that also appears in the Board's decision in *Alexandria Clinic*, 339 NLRB 1262, 173 LRRM 1065 (2003).

[326] 328 NLRB 1094, 162 LRRM 1403 (1999).

[327] *Id.* at 1094.

[328] 334 NLRB 965, 168 LRRM 1029 (2001), *enforcement denied on other grounds*, 352 F.3d 318, 173 LRRM 2865 (6th Cir. 2003) (refusing to decide §8(g) issue because employees' underlying conduct constituted unprotected "partial strike," which rendered conduct unprotected in first instance).

[329] 309 NLRB 990, 994, 142 LRRM 1001 (1992), *enforced*, 35 F.3d 1148, 147 LRRM 2257 (7th Cir. 1994).

not engage in a pattern or practice of dealing with management. Consequently, the employees did not violate Section 8(g) by failing to give a 10-day notice prior to engaging in a short-term work stoppage.

In *New York State Nurses Ass'n,*[330] the Board held that, although Section 8(g) does not prevent employees from exercising their rights under a collective bargaining agreement, in the absence of proper notice it does prohibit a union from inducing employees to exercise such rights as part of the union's efforts to pressure an employer to change terms and conditions of employment. At the union's behest, its members (nurses) declined voluntary overtime, contrary to their established practice. The Board found this constituted a strike within the meaning of Section 2(2)[331] and a "concerted refusal to work" within the meaning of Section 8(g) of the Act. Because Section 8(g) "was intended to cover a broad range of union activity . . . and is not limited to traditional walkouts,"[332] the Board found the union violated the Act by failing to give the requisite 10-day notice of the job action.

In *Beverly Health & Rehabilitation Services, Inc.,*[333] the Board concluded that the employer had violated Section 8(a)(5) by overreaching in response to receipt of the union's 10-day Section 8(g) notice of intent to strike. In anticipation of the strike, the employer cancelled vacations, personal and bonus days, and unpaid leaves. The Board found these actions constituted unilateral changes in the employees' terms and conditions of employment, and that the employer could not avoid its duty to bargain with the union regarding such changes. However, the D.C. Circuit held that the union failed to comply with Section 8(g) when it unilaterally extended the notice and that the employer was not required to immediately rehire the striking workers due to the inadequacy of the strike notice. The court

---

[330]334 NLRB 798, 167 LRRM 1313 (2001).

[331]29 U.S.C. §142(2).

[332]*New York State Nurses Ass'n, supra* note 330, 334 NLRB at 800.

[333]335 NLRB 635, 171 LRRM 1402 (2001), *enforced in part,* 317 F.3d 316, 171 LRRM 3017 (D.C. Cir. 2003).

rejected the Board's view that Section 8(g) permits a union to unilaterally extend the strike deadline for up to 72 hours.[334] Nevertheless, the union's faulty notice did not excuse the unfair labor practices committed by the employer.[335] Similarly, a union's failure to strike after serving the requisite Section 8(g) notice does not justify the employer's refusal to bargain.[336]

In *Alexandria Clinic, P.A.*,[337] the Board overruled its previous position in *New Orleans Artificial Kidney Center*[338] that "substantial compliance" with Section 8(g)'s notice requirements was sufficient, and instead held that the literal notice provisions of Section 8(g) must be strictly followed. In *Alexandria Clinic*, the union, which represented nurses at a health clinic, provided the employer with 10 days' notice of the date and time of an impending strike. However, a few days before the strike was to occur, the union moved the time of the strike back four hours without informing the employer. The employer terminated the employees for violating the notice provisions of Section 8(g), and the union filed an unfair labor practice charge. In reviewing whether the union had complied with Section 8(g)'s notice requirement, the Board focused on the last sentence of Section 8(g), which states that the 10-day notice "once given, may be extended by the written agreement of both parties."[339] The Board held that this language is "clear and unambiguous" in its mandate that "a written agreement of both parties" is the sole statutory exception to the 10-day notice required by Section 8(g).[340]

Section 8(g) has been the subject of several General Counsel Memoranda concerning whether the nature of the employees' underlying conduct triggers notice requirements under that section, whether an employer's conduct excuses the notice requirements, and what constitutes a "health care institution" for purposes of Section 8(g). In a September 18, 2001, General Counsel Memorandum,

---

[334] *Id.*

[335] *Id.*

[336] Marion Hosp. Corp., 335 NLRB 1016, 168 LRRM 1213 (2001), *enforced*, 321 F.3d 1178, 171 LRRM 3281 (D.C. Cir. 2003).

[337] 339 NLRB 1262, 173 LRRM 1065 (2003).

[338] 240 NLRB 432 (1979), *supplemented by* 347 NLRB 973, 103 LRRM 1262 (1980).

[339] 29 U.S.C. §158(g).

[340] *Alexandria Clinic, supra* note 337, 339 NLRB at 1265.

the general counsel concluded that certain actions did not constitute "picketing" and, therefore, did not require a Section 8(g) notice.[341] Approximately 10 to 15 union members and supporters had gathered on a public sidewalk approximately 10 to 20 feet from one of the two driveway entrances to the employer's nursing home and retirement facility. Some wore union T-shirts and one attached to himself a 10-foot tall balloon effigy of a maintenance worker. The group chanted union slogans and listened, for 10 to 20 minutes, to two speakers who used a bullhorn. The group did not march or carry picket signs, but did handbill near the driveway entrances. The gathering lasted approximately one hour. The general counsel concluded that these actions did not constitute picketing because "one of the necessary conditions of picketing is a confrontation in some form between union members and employees, customers, or suppliers who are trying to enter the employer's premises."[342] The general counsel also noted the absence of "signs, placards, or patrolling." Thus, the general counsel concluded, this was "merely a demonstration" involving "only handbilling of motorists at driveway entrances without blocking" and, therefore, did not require Section 8(g) notice.

In another Advice Memorandum the issue examined was whether the employer's alleged unfair labor practices excused the union's failure to give timely notice under Section 8(g).[343] After the employer unilaterally implemented its wage proposal in the midst of negotiations, the union advised the employer that it intended on conducting an unfair labor practice strike in 10 days. The union's strike notice did not specify what time the strike would begin and did not inform the employer that the union intended to picket. Additionally, the union failed to notify the FMCS of its intention to strike and picket. The general counsel rejected the union's contention that the employer's unfair labor practice excused its deficient notice. The general counsel stressed that a union is excused from complying with the notice requirements "only when the employer's

[341]Case No. 5-CG-47, 2001 NLRB GCM LEXIS 55.

[342]*Id.*, quoting Chicago Typographical Union No. 16, 151 NLRB 1666, 1669, 59 LRRM 1001 (1965) (internal quotations omitted).

[343]Teamsters Local 246 [Cowlington Episcopal Life Care Community, Inc.] Advice Memorandum, January 9, 2002.

unfair labor practices are so 'serious' and 'flagrant' that they induce or provoke employees to strike and otherwise leave employees with little choice but to act spontaneously."[344] Here, where the union knew that the employer intended to unilaterally implement its wage proposal and went out on strike approximately 23 days after the employer implemented its wage proposal, the employer's unfair labor practice did not provoke a spontaneous strike by the employees.

On October 29, 2002, the general counsel issued a memorandum addressing what constitutes a health care institution for purposes of Section 8(g).[345] The union had picketed, without notice, a hospital's administrative office building. No patient care was provided in the administrative building and the building was separated from the hospital by two major city streets and a public park. In finding no violation of the Act, the general counsel stated that Section 8(g) "does not automatically apply to every facility of an employer that operates a health care institution; there must be some nexus between that particular facility and patient care."[346]

X. COALITION OR COORDINATED BARGAINING

The Board continues to recognize that as coordinated bargaining is not mandatory, an employer does not violate Section 8(a)(5) by refusing a union's request to engage in coordinated bargaining.[347] An employer that declines coordinated bargaining must, however, be prepared to meet at reasonable times with respect to each of the individual bargaining units. An employer ran afoul of this rule when it rejected the union's suggestion of coordinated bargaining for 23 recently purchased units and then designated the same two negotiators to represent the employer in negotiating each of the contracts. While noting the employer had been free to reject coordinated bargaining, and generally free to designate whomever it pleased as bargaining representative, the Board held that the employer violated

---

[344] *Id.*

[345] Case No. 32-CG-49-1, 2002 NLRB GCM LEXIS 34.

[346] *Id.*

[347] *See, e.g.*, Fruehauf Trailer Servs., Inc. 335 NLRB 393, 173 LRRM 1440 (2001).

Section 8(a)(5) by meeting with one of the 23 bargaining units only once during a 7-month period.[348]

XI. Bargaining during the Term of an Existing Agreement

Parties remain obligated to bargain during the term of a collective bargaining agreement with respect to mandatory subjects that are not covered by the agreement, unless there has been a waiver.[349] Furthermore, under Section 8(d) of the Act, neither party can be required to discuss or agree to any modifications of the terms and conditions that are contained in a contract for a fixed period if the modification is to become effective before the contract expires, or before the matter can be reopened under the provisions of the collective bargaining agreement.[350] Accordingly, it is a violation of Section 8(d) to use economic pressure to force the other party to negotiate, during the term of a contract, over a term or condition of employment contained in the agreement.[351]

The parties remain free, however, to voluntarily negotiate changes to terms contained in an existing agreement, and it is not a violation of the Act for a party to ask the other to discuss or agree to a change.[352] A party that proposes a change to the agreement or that seeks or engages in voluntary negotiations does not thereby incur a duty to bargain over such changes.[353] Either party may refuse to dis-

---

[348] *Id.*

[349] Caritas Good Samaritan Med. Ctr., 340 NLRB No. 6, 173 LRRM 1169 (2003); King Soopers, 340 NLRB No. 75, 173 LRRM 1363 (2003); Courier Journal, 342 NLRB No. 113, 175 LRRM 1410 (2004) (under the circumstances, unopposed past practice was the equivalent of a waiver).

[350] Boeing Co., 337 NLRB 758, 172 LRRM 1463 (2002).

[351] Rangaire Co., 309 NLRB 1043, 143 LRRM 1115 (1992), *enforced*, 9 F.3d 104, 156 LRRM 2864 (5th Cir. 1993) (lockout to coerce employees and union to consent to midterm modification of terms in collective bargaining agreement held to violate §§8(a)(5) (1)).

[352] *Boeing Co., supra* note 350

[353] *Id.*; St. Barnabas Med. Ctr., 341 NLRB No. 151, 175 LRRM 1048 (2004).

cuss the matter or may break off negotiations at any time. If the parties do reach agreement on a mid-term modification, however, it is unlawful to refuse to execute a written document memorializing such agreement.[354]

XII. DUAL EMPLOYER OPERATIONS: THE "DOUBLE-BREASTED" ISSUE

The Board continues to recognize two distinct analyses that apply to issues of whether two employers are to be treated as essentially the same employer. The employers can be analyzed under either an "alter ego" or a "single-employer" theory. One employer is the alter ego of another employer if it is a disguised continuation of the other employer.[355] By contrast, the single-employer analysis applies only "where two ongoing businesses are coordinated by a common master."[356]

The Board analyzes several factors in making an alter ego[357] determination: commonality of management, business purpose, operation, equipment, customers, supervision, and ownership; and whether the alleged alter ego was set up to evade responsibilities under the National Labor Relations Act. The Board has repeatedly held, however, that evidence of an intent to evade responsibilities under the Act, while helpful in making an alter ego determination, is not essential to such a finding.[358] The Board recently reiterated that evi-

[354]B&M Linen Corp. dba Miron & Sons Laundry, 338 NLRB 5, 171 LRRM 1032 (2002).

[355]Michael J. Vorkapic, Inc., 337 NLRB 798 (2002); APF Carting, Inc., 336 NLRB 73, 170 LRRM 1454 (2001); NYP Acquisition Corp., 332 NLRB 1041, 165 LRRM 1281 (2000), *aff'd sub nom.* Newspaper Guild Local 3 v. NLRB, 261 F.3d 291, 167 LRRM 2808 (2d Cir. 2001); *see also* J. Vallery Elec. v. NLRB, 337 F.3d 446, 172 LRRM 2929 (5th Cir. 2003).

[356]*NYP Acquisition Corp., supra* note 355.

[357]Where a finding of alter ego status has been made, the Board has found that service of process on one of the companies constitutes service on the other. Sommerville Constr. Co., 338 NLRB 1178, 172 LRRM 1300 (2003).

[358]*APF Carting, Inc., supra* note 353; Fallon-Williams, 336 NLRB 602, 171 LRRM 1502 (2001); Kodiak Elec. Co., 336 NLRB 1038, 172 LRRM 1359 (2001), *enforced,* 2003 U.S. App. LEXIS 13444 (4th Cir. 2003); Oklahoma Fixture Co., 333 NLRB 804, 172 LRRM 1453 (2001), *enforcement denied on other grounds,* 2003 U.S. App. LEXIS 18782 (10th Cir. 2003); *see also* Massachusetts Carpenters Cent. Collection Agency v. A.A. Bldg. Erectors, Inc., 343 F.3d 18 (1st Cir. 2003) (refusing to find

dence of a legitimate business reason for a change in corporate status will not preclude a finding of alter ego status under the Act.[359] Contrary to the Board's stance, some district courts require evidence of an intent to evade responsibilities under the Act in order to find alter ego status under laws other than the Act.[360]

The Board illustrated the importance of the common business purpose element of the alter-ego analysis in a case involving the bankrupt *New York Post.*[361] The parent company involved in that case set up a wholly owned subsidiary to become the debtor-in-possession of the *New York Post* during the bankruptcy proceeding. Later, the same parent company set up a separate wholly owned subsidiary to purchase the assets of the *Post* and operate the paper when it emerged from bankruptcy. The Board held that the companies' different business purposes precluded them from being alter egos. Accordingly, although the second subsidiary was a successor to the first, it was free to set initial terms and conditions of employment different from those established by the first subsidiary.[362]

The Board continues to apply a four-factor analysis in determining whether two or more employers constitute a single employer: (1) interrelation of operations; (2) centralized control of labor rela-

---

alter ego status in ERISA action in situation where union was not receiving "less than that for which it bargained" after creation of second company, even though number of alter ego characteristics were present); *but see* Crossroads Elec., Inc., 343 NLRB No. 112 (2004) (although majority of the Board did not concur, Chairman Battista agreed with former Chairman Hurtgen's view that the general counsel must show, inter alia, an intent to avoid legal obligations under the Act in order to prove alter ego status).

[359]Michaels Painting, Inc., 337 NLRB 860, 171 LRRM 1186 (2002), *enforced,* 2004 U.S. App. LEXIS 514 (9th Cir. 2004); *see also* Gala Bus Lines, Ltd., 2004 NLRB LEXIS 392 (July 16, 2004).

[360]Hansen Bros. Constr. v. Operating Eng'rs Local 150 Assistance Fund, 39 F. Supp. 2d 957, 161 LRRM 2574 (N.D. Ill. 1999); *Massachusetts Carpenters, supra* note 358; Flynn v. Ohio Bldg. Restoration, Inc., 317 F. Supp. 2d 22 (D.D.C. 2004) (union animus, or employer's desire to deny union benefits of bargain struck in collective bargaining agreement, is a factor that may be relevant when assessing alter ego status, although not an essential one).

[361]NYP Acquisition Corp., 332 NLRB 1041, 165 LRRM 1281 (2000), *aff'd sub nom.* Newspaper Guild Local 3 v. NLRB, 261 F.3d 291, 167 LRRM 2808 (2d Cir. 2001)

[362]*Id.*

tions; (3) common management; and (4) common ownership.[363] It is unnecessary that each of the elements be present.[364] "Rather, single-employer status depends on all the circumstances and is characterized by the absence of the arms-length relationship found among unintegrated companies."[365] Centralized control of labor relations, however, is the single most critical factor.[366] Thus, where the evidentiary record established that there was not common control of labor relations at the respondent and a related firm, a single-employer finding was not proper, notwithstanding some degree of common ownership.[367]

There remains a split among appellate courts as to whether the Board has exclusive jurisdiction to determine appropriate bargaining units for the purpose of determining whether a collective bargaining agreement can be enforced against an employer. The Second Circuit recently found that a district court is not precluded from making this determination where neither side has taken the issue before the Board.[368] However, there remains authority to the contrary.[369]

As discussed in Section IV, *supra,* in *Cannelton Industries, Inc.*,[370] the Board recently addressed an employer's duty to provide information to a union concerning an allegedly double-breasted operation. In *Cannelton,* the Board found that, while a union could not establish the relevance of information relating to an employer's "single employer" or "alter ego" status based on mere suspicion alone,

---

[363]Pontiac Ceiling & Partition Co., 337 NLRB 120, 174 LRRM 1063 (2001); Mercy Hosp. of Buffalo, 336 NLRB 1282, 171 LRRM 1339 (2001); *see also* RC Aluminum Indus. v. NLRB, 326 F.3d 235, 172 LRRM 2321 (D.C. Cir. 2003).

[364]*Mercy Hosp., supra* note 363; Reigel Elec./Cent. Elec. & Servs., 342 NLRB No. 83, 176 LRRM 1240 (2004).

[365]Alexander Painting, Inc., 344 NLRB No. 157, 177 LRRM 1321 (2005); Canned Foods, Inc., 332 NLRB 1449, 172 LRRM 1065 (2000), *aff'd in part and modified in part sub nom.,* Grass Valley Grocery Outlet, 338 NLRB 877, 173 LRRM 1541 (2003); Dow Chem. Co., 326 NLRB 288, 160 LRRM 1013 (1998); *see also* Mingo Logan Coal Co. v. NLRB, 2003 U.S. App. LEXIS 11915, 172 LRRM 2746 (4th Cir. 2003) (joint employer analysis).

[366]*Mercy Hosp., supra* note 363; *Canned Foods, Inc., supra* note 365.

[367]*Mercy Hosp., supra* note 363.

[368]Brown v. Sandimo, 250 F.3d 120, 167 LRRM 2176 (2d Cir. 2001).

[369]Journeymen Local 343 v. Nor-Cal Plumbing, Inc., 48 F.3d 1465, 155 LRRM 2282 (9th Cir. 1994).

[370]339 NLRB 996, 173 LRRM 1087 (2003).

the union is entitled to discover such information if it possess an objective, factual basis for the request. The Board in *Cannelton* addressed the issue of when the union must disclose the facts underlying its belief that the employer is a double-breasted entity and acknowledged a tension between its own view that disclosing such underlying facts at a subsequent unfair labor practice proceeding is sufficient, while some courts of appeal have required the union to disclose its factual basis at the time it requests such information.[371]

[**Editor's Note:** In *Viking Industrial Security Inc. v. NLRB*, 225 F.3d 131, 165 LRRM 2129 (2d Cir. 2000), the appellate court refused to enforce the Board's order against one of the two entities found to be a single employer in *Viking Industrial Security Inc.*, 327 NLRB 146, 164 LRRM 1212, which is cited in the Main Edition on page 990, note 1255. Although the appellate court did not question the Board's finding that the two entities were single employers at the time the unfair labor practices at issue in the case were committed, the court found that the entities had ended their single employer status prior to the commencement of the unfair labor practice proceedings and that one of the entities was not represented at the hearings and thus deprived of due process.]

[**Editor's Note:** Due to an editing error, the Fourth Edition incorrectly lists the citation for *Bricklayers Local 6 v. Heminger, Inc.* on page 996, note 1289. The correct citation is 483 F.2d 129, 84 LRRM 2033 (6th Cir. 1973).]

---

[371] *Compare* Hertz Corp. v. NLRB, 105 F.3d 868, 154 LRRM 2276 (3d Cir. 1997) (disclosure of factual basis for information request must be made at same time information is requested) *with* Baldwin Shop N' Save, 314 NLRB 114, 146 LRRM 1296 (1994).

Chapter 14

EFFECT OF CHANGE IN BARGAINING REPRESENTATIVE DURING THE TERM OF A COLLECTIVE BARGAINING AGREEMENT

I. Context in Which the Issue Arises

In *Mulvaney Mechanical, Inc. v. Sheet Metal Workers Local 38,*[1] the Second Circuit held that an illegal strike in violation of a no-strike clause and without proper notice under Section 8(d) of the Act that resulted in loss of employee status for strikers was not a total repudiation of the labor agreement sufficient to terminate the union's status as bargaining representative when the contract had an interest arbitration provision. The court held that the union had not "judicially died" as the employer urged, but instead that its contract was merely voidable. The court emphasized that "*American Seating* simply held that it was an unfair labor practice for an employer to refuse to bargain with the newly certified union upon the ground that it was bound by a prior contract with a former bargaining representative,"[2] not that the "old agreement . . . automatically ceased to ex-

[1]288 F.3d 491, 169 LRRM 3089 (2d Cir. 2002).
[2]*Id.* at 499, citing American Seating Co., 106 NLRB 250, 32 LRRM 1439 (1953).

ist."[3] So reasoning, the court enforced a successor contract awarded through interest arbitration.[4]

The Board reiterated, in *VFL Technical Corp.*,[5] that a union's disclaimer of representational interest and its contractual obligation would be rejected only where collusion between the parties (the incumbent, disclaiming union, and union seeking an election of the employees) to avoid the contract was shown. A disclaimer predicated on an umpire's "no raid" decision[6] was not grounds to reject the disclaimer.

III. MERGERS AND TRANSFERS OF AFFILIATION

Citing *R.P.C. Inc.*,[7] the Board in *Route 22 Auto Sales*[8] again applied the six-month statute of limitations period in Section 10(b) of the Act to an employer attempting to attack the validity of a change in the bargaining representative. The Board held that a respondent cannot defend a refusal-to-bargain allegation by untimely contesting the original recognition it granted following a union "disaffiliation."

In this case, an uncertified, independent local union agreed to affiliate and then merge with a larger AFL-CIO local union, but retained a five-year right to disaffiliate in its agreement with the larger

---

[3]*Id.* at 500. The Board had subsequently addressed the issue in *RCA del Caribe*, 262 NLRB 963, 966 (1982), holding the contract became "null and void" if the challenging union prevailed. It reaffirmed this ruling in *Wayne County Neighborhood Legal Services, Inc.*, 333 NLRB 146, 148 n.10 (2003).

[4]The U.S. Supreme Court granted certiorari and summarily vacated the Second Circuit's order and remanded for further consideration in light of *Howsam v. Dean Witter Reynolds, Inc.*, 537 U.S. 79, (2002). Mulvaney Mech., Inc. v. Sheet Metal Workers Local 38, 538 U.S. 918, 172 LRRM 2128 (2003). On remand, the Second Circuit again directed the district court to vacate its judgment and remanded for proceedings consistent with its prior panel opinion. Mulvaney Mech., Inc. v. Sheet Metal Workers Local 38, 351 F.3d 43, 173 LRRM 2560 (2d Cir. 2003).

[5]332 NLRB 1443, 166 LRRM 1043 (2000) (decision affirming regional director's supplemental decision following remand in 329 NLRB 458, 162 LRRM 1257 (1999)).

[6]Occurring under Article XX of the AFL-CIO's constitution. *See* Garden Manor Farms, Inc., 341 NLRB No. 24 (2004). The Board granted a union's request to withdraw its petition where the matter was pending before the Board on the employer's request for review. Member Schaumber dissented, arguing the *VFL* decision on such disclaimers was incorrect.

[7]311 NLRB 232, 144 LRRM 1310 (1993).

[8]337 NLRB 84, 171 LRRM 1479 (2001).

union. When the larger local union failed to obtain a contract with the employer, the original independent local union held an employee vote to disaffiliate. After the disaffiliation, the employer recognized the original independent local and entered into a bargaining agreement with it. However, bowing to pressure from the larger local, the employer later withdrew recognition from the independent local and entered into another collective bargaining agreement with the larger union during the term of the existing labor agreement. Though the employer tried to raise the propriety of the disaffiliation in defending the unfair labor practice charge against it for withdrawing recognition, the Board held that it could not contest either the process of disaffiliation or the result of the vote as it had not done so within the six-month statute of limitations. Accordingly, the independent union was lawfully recognized, it enjoyed a presumption of majority status, and, therefore, the employer had no privilege to withdraw recognition.

A. Due Process

Without addressing whether due process continues to be an independent requirement,[9] the Board has continued to give limited consideration to due process issues in addressing mergers and affiliations.[10] However, only twice since *Seattle First National*

[9] *See* Main Edition at pages 1010–11 and nn.57–60.

[10] *See, e.g.,* McDonald Partners, Inc., 336 NLRB 836, 169 LRRM 1139 (2001) *enforcement denied on other grounds,* 331 F.3d 1002, 172 LRRM 2815 (D.C. Cir. 2003); Ridgewell's Inc., 334 NLRB 37, 169 LRRM 1397 (2001) (burden of proof of lack of due process is on party asserting same); Avante at Boca Raton, Inc., 334 NLRB 381, 173 LRRM 1165 (2001), *petition for review denied,* 2002 U.S. App. LEXIS 23068, 54 Fed. Appx. 502 (D.C. Cir. 2002); RCN Corp., 333 NLRB 295, 173 LRRM 1351 (2001); King Soopers Inc., 332 NLRB 32, 167 LRRM 1222 (2000), *enforced on other issues,* 254 F.3d 738, 167 LRRM 2612 (8th Cir. 2001); Mike Basil Chevrolet, 331 NLRB 1044, 165 LRRM 1063 (2000) (fact that vote did not comply with bylaw of affiliating independent union not sufficient; secret ballot vote occurred after notice and opportunity to discuss issue); Defiance Hosp., Inc., 330 NLRB 492, 170 LRRM 1097 (2000) (fact that members of union jointly representing bargaining unit with affiliating union not allowed to vote insufficient). Given the limited consideration of due process issues by the Board, possible alternatives for addressing the issue may exist under §301 of the LMRA as many union constitutions contain specific provisions regarding mergers or affiliations and/or under Title I of the LMRDA. *See, e.g.,* Richardson v. Robinson, 164 LRRM 2474 (N.D. Ga. 2000); Gee v. Textile Processors, 164 LRRM 2049 (N.D. Ill. 2000).

Bank[11] has the Board refused to protect the merged union on the ground of a due process violation.[12]

In *Tawas Industries*,[13] the employees voted to affiliate their independent union with the United Autoworkers Union (UAW). Shortly after the affiliation vote, more than two-thirds of the employees presented the employer with a petition stating that they did not wish to be affiliated with the UAW. The employer notified the UAW's international representative that it refused to recognize the affiliation because the election did not meet due process requirements and that a majority of the employees had stated that they did not support the affiliation. The Board found that the affiliation had been accomplished with adequate due process safeguards and that there was substantial continuity between the pre- and post-affiliation union. A majority of the Board further held that the employer could not base its refusal to recognize the affiliation on the subsequent disaffiliation effort by a significant majority of the employees. The Board reasoned that affiliation and/or disaffiliation decisions involve internal union matters that are to be governed by the union's own procedures and are not subject to an employer's veto.

---

[11]475 U.S. 192, 121 LRRM 2741 (1986).

[12]Allied Mech. Servs., Inc., 341 NLRB No. 141, 175 LRRM 1224 (2004). No vote on the merger of two existing locals of the Plumbers and Pipefitters occurred, and, thus, the newly formed union did not succeed to the bargaining rights of its predecessors. At publication, the general counsel's and union's motions for reconsideration were pending and expressly raised the issue of whether any due process requirement exists. Cold Heading Co., 332 NLRB 956, 172 LRRM 1354 (2000). For 20 years, "leaders" were covered by successive collective bargaining agreements. Then, a year before negotiations, the employer reversed its position and declared that leaders were supervisory personnel. It acted consistently with the declaration, and the union acquiesced in the following year. When negotiations stalled and the independent proposed to merge with a national union, the question of the eligibility of leaders to participate in the merger vote arose. The leaders were allowed to vote by a separate ballot. Their votes were determinative of the negative vote total against affiliation. The employer then declared it no longer considered them to be a part of management and their votes against affiliation should be counted. The dissent argued that the employer should be equitably estopped. The majority found it unnecessary to address the issue, but left open for future consideration whether an estoppel doctrine should be applied. The Board applied this due process standard in coming to its decision without addressing the still-unanswered question whether due process continues to be a requirement in merger or affiliation cases.

[13]336 NLRB 318, 172 LRRM 1276 (2001).

B. Continuity of Representation

The Board has continued to apply the *Western Commercial*[14] factors in assessing whether there is continuity between the new representative and the former union.[15] In *Defiance Hospital, Inc.*,[16] the Board found continuity was established where "the maintenance of traces of a preexisting identity and retention of autonomy over the day-to day administration of bargaining agreements"[17] was found.

The Board continues to emphasize the day-to-day administration factor.[18] For example, in *Mike Basil Chevrolet*,[19] the Board overruled a regional director's decision finding that a question concerning representation was raised when the fundamental character of the union would be greatly altered by a change in affiliation. A small independent labor organization affiliated with a local of the UAW and requested a certification amendment from the Board. The Board found adequate continuity of representation because the independent union would continue to be able to participate in basic labor relations decisions at the local level, even though it had lost much of its autonomy as a result of the affiliation.

---

[14]288 NLRB 214, 127 LRRM 1313 (1988).

[15]*See, e.g.*, U.S.A. Polymer Corp., 328 NLRB 1242 n.10, 168 LRRM 1427 (1999) (burden of proof to show discontinuity of representation is on party asserting it), *enforced on other grounds*, 272 F.3d 289, 168 LRRM 2897 (5th Cir. 2001).

[16]330 NLRB 492, 170 LRRM 1097 (2000), quoting News/Sun Sentinel v. NLRB, 890 F.2d 430, 432, 132 LRRM 2988 (D.C. Cir. 1989).

[17]*Id.*, 330 NLRB at 498.

[18]*See* King Soopers, Inc., 332 NLRB 32, 167 LRRM 1222 (2000), *enforced on other issues*, 254 F.3d 738, 167 LRRM 2612 (8th Cir. 2001); Mike Basil Chevrolet, Inc., 331 NLRB 1044, 165 LRRM 1063 (2000).

[19]*Id. See also* Avante at Boca Raton, Inc., 334 NLRB 381, 173 LRRM 1165 (2001), *petition for review denied*, 2002 U.S. App. LEXIS 23068, 54 Fed. Appx. 502 (D.C. Cir. 2002).

Chapter 15

EFFECT OF CHANGE IN THE EMPLOYING UNIT: SUCCESSORSHIP

III. SUCCESSORSHIP AND THE BARGAINING OBLIGATION

A. Continuity of the Work Force: "The Concept of Majority"

In one interesting case, the Board found that a clause in the predecessor's agreement with the union providing that any successor employer would not be bound by the recognition clause of the agreement could not defeat a *Burns* successor's bargaining obligation.[1] The Board reasoned that the union's right to recognition, and the *Burns* successor's corresponding obligations, are statutory obligations that can be waived only by clear and unmistakable contract language. The Board found that the clause at issue did not satisfy that standard.

2. *The Appropriate Time for Measuring Majority Status*

In *Dupont Dow Elastomers v. NLRB*,[2] the court affirmed the Board's underlying order and found that the employer was a "perfectly clear successor" under *Burns* because it had announced its intention to hire the incumbent's employees and did not initially announce an intention to set new terms and conditions of employment beyond the addition of a retention bonus plan. In doing so, the court rejected the employer's contention that it had the right to set initial terms and conditions without first bargaining with the union because it announced changes prior to the actual commencement of operations; the court reasoned that the employer was required to make an announcement of intended changes *prior* to inviting employees of the incumbent to apply for employment.

3. *Presumption of the Union's Continued Majority Status*

In *St. Elizabeth Manor, Inc.*,[3] the Board overruled its decision in *Southern Moldings, Inc.*[4] and established a new "successor bar." Under

---

[1]TransMontaigne, Inc., 337 NLRB 262, 169 LRRM 1229 (2001).
[2]296 F.3d 495, 170 LRRM 2513 (6th Cir. 2002).
[3]329 NLRB 341, 162 LRRM 1146 (1999).
[4]219 NLRB 119, 89 LRRM 1623 (1975).

Southern Moldings, the ability to challenge the majority status of the incumbent union was not impacted by a change in the employing entity; the Board held that the union is not entitled to greater rights with respect to a successor than it had with a predecessor. However, by its decision in *St. Elizabeth Manor*, the Board held that the union was entitled to an irrebuttable presumption of majority status until at least a reasonable period for bargaining between the union and successor employer had passed.

In *MV Transportation*,[5] the Board overruled *St. Elizabeth Manor* and returned to the rule that an incumbent union in a successorship situation is entitled to only a rebuttable presumption of continuing majority status. In *Aramark School Services, Inc.*,[6] the Board clarified that *MV Transportation* should be applied retroactively in all cases pending before the Board, in whatever stage. The Board requested remand of at least one case in which the Board had filed a petition for enforcement of a decision applying *St. Elizabeth Manor* so that the Board could reconsider the case in light of *MV Transportation*,[7] and in another case it advised the court that the case should be analyzed on the basis of *MV Transportation* even though the Board's original decision was based on *St. Elizabeth Manor*.[8] Accordingly, the incumbent union's majority status in a successorship situation currently is subject to attack through an otherwise valid and timely decertification, rival union or employer petition, or other valid challenge to the union's majority status.

Of course, the challenge must be appropriate under extant Board law. Thus, in *Northern Montana Health Care Center v. NLRB*,[9] the Ninth Circuit agreed with the Board that a successor employer could not rely on the union's statements that it was planning an "old-fashioned" organizing campaign, and the union's collecting of authorization cards, as supporting a good faith doubt that the union lacked majority status. The court determined that a union's attempt to strengthen its support following a change in ownership is not necessarily evidence that the union lacks majority support; such activity is consistent with what a prudent union, with majority support, would do under the circumstances.

---

[5]337 NLRB 770, 170 LRRM 1233 (2002).

[6]337 NLRB 1063, 170 LRRM 1494 (2002).

[7]340 NLRB No. 87, 173 LRRM 1276 (2003).

[8]Community Hosp. of Cent. Cal. v. NLRB, 335 F.3d 1079, 172 LRRM 3121 (D.C. Cir. 2003).

[9]178 F.3d 1089, 1097, 161 LRRM 2469 (9th Cir. 1999).

4. Discriminatory Refusals to Hire Predecessor's Employees

The Board continues to hold that where a new owner engages in discriminatory refusals to hire the predecessor's employees, the Board will infer that all of the former employees would have been retained absent the unlawful discrimination. For example, in *Daufuskie Island Club & Resort*,[10] the Board found that the following employment practices were evidence of discriminatory animus toward the predecessor's union represented employees:

> requiring special approval for hiring predecessor employees; hiring new employees instead of predecessor employees, even though the employer told predecessor employees that it was keeping their applications on file, and the employer had a continuous need for workers; and considering supervisory ratings and discipline with respect to predecessor employees, but not with respect to new applicants.[11]

The Board then reviewed the factors within the *Wright Line*[12] framework, in analyzing the lawfulness of the alleged successor's motive: expressions of union animus; absence of a convincing rationale for the failure to hire the predecessor's employees; inconsistent hiring practices or overt acts of conduct demonstrating a discriminatory motive; and evidence supporting a reasonable inference that the new owner conducted its hiring in a manner precluding the predecessor's employees from being hired in a majority of the new owner's overall workforce.[13] The Board determined that the new owner's unlawful motives required the owner to offer employment to the predecessor's employees.

In another case applying *Wright Line* in a successorship context, the Board affirmed the dismissal of allegations that the successor employers had unlawfully discriminated against the predecessor's employees when they did not offer employment to the employees of the predecessor. In *GFS Building Maintenance, Inc.*,[14] although the new owner harbored and demonstrated antiunion animus, the Board rejected the discrimination claim because the new employer had a past practice of not hiring the employees of predecessor employers.

---

[10] 328 NLRB 415, 168 LRRM 1303 (1999), *enforced*, 221 F.3d 196 (D.C. Cir. 2000).

[11] *Id.*

[12] 251 NLRB 1083, 105 LRRM 1169 (1980).

[13] *Daufuskie Island Club & Resort*, *supra* note 10, citing Galloway Sch. Lines, 321 NLRB 1422, 1423–24, 153 LRRM 1105, 1107–08 (1996).

[14] 330 NLRB 747, 165 LRRM 1304 (2000).

B. Continuity of Identity in the Business Enterprise or Employing Industry

The Board and courts continue to hold that an employer is a "successor" if there is "substantial continuity" of the operations after the new employer takes over from the predecessor.[15]

The Board and the courts examine several factors when determining whether there is substantial continuity including:

> whether the business of both employers is essentially the same; whether the employees of the new company are doing the same jobs in the same working conditions under the same supervisors; and whether the new entity has the same production process, produces the same products and has basically the same body of customers.[16]

Although the Board continues to refer to the "totality of circumstances" when determining whether an employer is a successor, the hiring of a majority of the former workforce remains the focus of this analysis.[17] While no single factor is controlling, the ultimate question is whether the employees retained by the successor "view their job situation as essentially unaltered."[18] Thus, the substantial continuity inquiry is still taken from the employees' as opposed to the employer's perspective.

In *Van Lear Equipment, Inc.*,[19] the Board held: "[W]e would not find the employees' job situation has so changed that they would change their attitude about being represented." The employer took over the school bus transportation services that were previously handled by the local public school district. The employer argued that there was no substantial continuity because it only took over the transportation operations of the predecessor employer. The Board,

---

[15]North Hills Office Servs., 342 NLRB No. 25, 176 LRRM 1271 (2004); 3750 Orange Place L.P. v. NLRB, 333 F.3d 646, 172 LRRM 2871 (6th Cir. 2003); N.K. Parker Transp., Inc., 332 NLRB 547, 172 LRRM 1162 (2000); NLRB v. Onyx Precision Servs., Inc., 129 F. Supp. 2d 230 (W.D.N.Y. 2000) (relocation of facility will not defeat finding of "substantial continuity"). *See also* Bloedorn v. Francisco Foods, Inc., 276 F.3d 270, 169 LRRM 2269 (7th Cir. 2001) (§10(j) case); Hoffman v. Inn Credible Caterers, Ltd., 247 F.3d 360, 166 LRRM 3032 (2d Cir. 2001) (§10(j) case); Elf Atochem N. Am., 339 NLRB 796, 174 LRRM 1101 (2003); Van Lear Equip., Inc., 336 NLRB 1059, 169 LRRM 1301 (2001).

[16]*Bloedorn, supra* note 15, 276 F.3d at 289 (citing Fall River Dyeing Corp. v. NLRB, 482 U.S. 27, 43, 125 LRRM 2441 (1987)). *See also* Shares, Inc., 343 NLRB No. 59 (2004).

[17]Pennsylvania Transformer Tech., Inc. v. NLRB, 254 F.3d 217, 167 LRRM 2552 (D.C. Cir. 2001), *enforcing* 331 NLRB 1147, 167 LRRM 1220 (2000).

[18]*Id.*

[19]336 NLRB 1059, 169 LRRM 1301 (2001).

in holding that there was substantial continuity, noted that the business of the employer and the school district were the same to the extent that the predecessor employer engaged in transportation services. Further, the Board held that the employees were performing the same work under generally similar working conditions as existed with the predecessor employer. The Board also reaffirmed that a private employer may be a successor even though the predecessor is a public employer.[20]

In *Pennsylvania Transformer Technology, Inc. v. NLRB*,[21] the court held that the employer was a successor despite differences in size, facilities, workforce, managerial philosophy, and customer base between the employer and its predecessor. In finding that the employer was a successor, the court relied on the fact that the business was the same, the employees performed the same work, the production process and product were similar, and the successor retained many of the same customers.

Reviewing the *Fall River Dyeing* factors for substantial continuity, the D.C. Circuit examined whether a private hospital that acquired a public hospital constituted a successor employer.[22] The private hospital argued that the change from public to private management; new supervisory and management structure; change in duties, compensation, and benefits of the nurses at the hospital; changes in the nurses' shift schedules and in the organization of support functions; and the adoption of a patient care model all indicated the absence of "substantial continuity."[23] The court noted the Board's finding that the hospital continued to operate as an acute health care facility, in the same location, using the same skills and equipment to provide care for the same general population.

The Board continues to recognize that new owners will often bring new ideas, which will result in some changes to the employees' jobs and the organization. Such changes will not affect the continu-

---

[20]*Id. See also* Lincoln Park Zoological Soc'y, 322 NLRB 263, 153 LRRM 1223 (1996), *enforced*, 116 F.3d 216, 155 LRRM 2598 (7th Cir. 1997); Community Hosp. of Cent. Cal., 335 F.3d 1079, 172 LRRM 3121 (D.C. Cir. 2003).

[21]254 F.3d 217, 167 LRRM 2552 (D.C. Cir. 2001), *enforcing* 331 NLRB 1147, 67 LRRM 1220 (2000).

[22]*Community Hosp., supra* note 20.

[23]*Id.*

ity of the enterprise unless the "employees' job situation has so changed that they would change their attitudes about being represented."[24]

C. Continuity of the Appropriate Bargaining Unit

Successorship may depend on the continued appropriateness of the bargaining unit. The Board and the courts continue to examine when and whether changed circumstances that are the result of the shift in proprietary control are sufficient to render a bargaining unit no longer appropriate.

In *Deferiet Paper Co.*,[25] the Board granted the general counsel's motion for summary judgment and found that the new employer had violated Sections 8(a)(2) and (5) of the Act by recognizing only one of two unions that had represented separate units of the predecessor. The new employer contended that, because of its newly implemented working conditions, the unit represented by one union had accreted to the unit represented by another union and that a separate unit was no longer appropriate. In rejecting this argument, the Board found that the redesignation of job classifications and the issuance of an employee handbook that announced that employees might be required to work in areas other than their traditional craft did not constitute significant changes in the structure and operation of the facility. The Board emphasized that the affected employees continued to perform their various duties in essentially the same manner as before the sale. Thus, the two units had not merged and remained separately appropriate.

On review, the D.C. Circuit determined that the Board applied an incomplete test in reaching its determination that the sepa-

---

[24] *Van Lear Equip., Inc., supra* note 19 (despite new buses, modified routes, and decrease in benefits, drivers perform "same work"). *See also* Waterbury Hotel Mgmt., LLC, 333 NLRB 482, 171 LRRM 1348 (2001), *enforced*, 314 F.3d 645, 171 LRRM 2781 (D.C. Cir. 2003) (renovations to hotel, new managers and corporate policies, and minor changes in job duties not "essential changes"); WXGI, Inc., 330 NLRB 695, 166 LRRM 1293 (2000), *enforced*, 243 F.3d 833, 166 LRRM 2797 (4th Cir. 2001) (building improvements, technological changes, and change in music format did not alter the essential nature of employees' jobs); Santiago-Sanchez v. Gate Eng'g Corp., 291 F. Supp. 2d 7 (D.P.R. 2003) (company that assumed maintenance contract is successor employer, even though it did not acquire assets of prior contract holder, because it employed same employees to do same job at same location).

[25] 330 NLRB No. 89, 166 LRRM 1040 (2000), *enforcement denied*, 235 F.3d 581, 166 LRRM 2107 (D.C. Cir. 2000).

rate units remained appropriate.[26] Quoting from *Trident Seafoods*,[27] the court wrote, "Although the Board places a heavy evidentiary burden on a party attempting to show that historical units are no longer appropriate, this burden can be met if historical units no longer conform reasonably well to other standards of appropriateness."[28] The court said the Board could not simply judge whether the changes implemented by the new employer were "so significant, or so major, or so fundamental that the old unit had been replaced by a new and different one."[29] Instead, the Board must go further and determine whether compelling evidence showed that under the new enterprise the old unit no longer conformed to the Board's contemporaneous standards of appropriateness. When the unit is no longer appropriate, there is no obligation to bargain with the union.[30]

Negligible changes in the unit by a new employer, however, will not destroy its continued appropriateness.[31] The Board and the courts have also found consistently that the continued appropriateness of a unit is usually unaffected by a diminution in the unit size, particularly where the successor acquired only a fraction of the workplaces in a multisite bargaining unit, reduced the size of a single homogeneous unit, or took over only a discrete portion of its predecessor's heterogeneous bargaining unit.

In *NLRB v. Simon DeBartelo Group*,[32] the court upheld the Board's order that the new owner of a mall was obligated to bargain with the union, notwithstanding the fact that it contracted out the work previously performed by 35 housekeeping employees and retained only the four maintenance mechanics from the predecessor's unit. The employer contended that, as a consequence, the new unit was dramatically smaller than the old one and was significantly more homogeneous (i.e., only one job classification versus multiple job clas-

---

[26]235 F.3d 581, 166 LRRM 2107 (D.C. Cir. 2000).

[27]101 F.3d 111, 153 LRRM 2833 (D.C. Cir. 1996).

[28]*Deferiet Paper*, *supra* note 25, 235 F.3d at 582.

[29]*Id.* at 583.

[30]University Med. Ctr., 335 NLRB 1318, 169 LRRM 1334 (2001), *enforced in part*, 335 F.3d 1079, 172 LRRM 3121 (D.C. Cir. 2003) (unit not appropriate where consolidation of two units resulted in professionals and nonprofessionals in same unit).

[31]Concrete Co., 336 NLRB 1311, 171 LRRM 1417 (2001); Brown & Root, Inc., 334 NLRB 628, 169 LRRM 1014 (2001), *enforcement denied on other grounds*, 333 F.3d 628 172 LRRM 2801 (5th Cir. 2003); *see also* 3750 Orange Place L.P. v. NLRB, 333 F.3d 646, 172 LRRM 2871 (6th Cir. 2003).

[32]241 F.3d 207, 166 LRRM 2608 (2d Cir. 2001).

sifications); therefore, it argued, continuity of the unit no longer existed. The court, in line with the Board, found that diminution of the unit through subcontracting did not warrant applying a different standard than the one used in those circumstances where the unit was otherwise downsized. According to the court, the change in the size of the bargaining unit would not lead the continuing employees to perceive their job situations as substantially altered, let alone indicate a loss of support for the union.[33]

In *Mayfield Holiday Inn,*[34] the Board held that separate hotel owners were successors where the owners purchased separate hotels, which comprised a multisite bargaining unit, from the predecessor employer. The Board, in holding that the new owners were successors, stated: "[O]ur decision is consistent with a long line of Board decisions finding substantial continuity when the successor employer has taken over only a discrete portion of its predecessor's bargaining unit, e.g. where the successor has acquired only a fraction of the workplaces within a multisite bargaining unit."[35] However, the Board noted that the employees must still constitute a separate appropriate unit and comprise a majority of the unit under the new operation.[36] While the predecessor employer's unit was a multisite bargaining unit, the Board concluded that the former unit was no longer appropriate and that, instead, two single-site units were appropriate for the successor employers. The Board held that the sale of the hotels to separate entities constituted "compelling circumstances" to warrant changing the historic two-location unit into two separate units.

---

[33] *See also* Tree-Free Fiber Co., 328 NLRB 389, 161 LRRM 1081 (1999) (restating Board's position that where new employer's employees constitute appropriate unit—and majority of those unit employees were employees of predecessor—new employer's successor obligation is not defeated simply because new unit is substantially smaller—only 50 employees, compared with predecessor's 500); Northern Mont. Health Care Ctr. v. NLRB, 178 F.3d 1089, 161 LRRM 2469 (9th Cir. 1999) (enforcing Board's ruling that successor bargaining unit made up of both predecessor's employees and employees of new owner constituted only negligible change in bargaining unit, and therefore did not provide successor employer with defense for refusing to bargain with union representing predecessor's employees).

[34] 335 NLRB 38, 170 LRRM 1392 (2001), *enforced sub nom.* 3750 Orange Place L.P. v. NLRB, 333 F.3d 646, 172 LRRM 2871 (6th Cir. 2003).

[35] *Id.*, 335 NLRB at 39 n.4 (citing *NLRB v. Simon DeBartelo Group, supra* note 32).

[36] *Id.* (citing Bronx Health Plan, 326 NLRB 810, 160 LRRM 1086 (1998), *enforced mem.*, 203 F.3d 51, 166 LRRM 2640 (D.C. Cir. 1999)).

In *Ready Mix USA, Inc.*,[37] the employer purchased the predecessor's assets at two block and batch plants. The employer then offered employment to the predecessor's former unit employees at the two plants. The union requested to meet and bargain with the employer but the employer refused, claiming that the predecessor's 39 employees constituted less than 50 percent of the employer's total workforce of 800 employees.[38] Affirming the ALJ's decision that the employer was a successor, the Board held that because the unit employees were doing the same jobs under mainly the same supervision, in the same locations and under the same working conditions, the employer's changes made in the operations of the newly acquired facilities fell "far short of the heavy evidentiary burden of showing that the historical batch and block plant bargaining unit is no longer appropriate."[39] Similarly, an historical single-facility unit was found appropriate in *University Medical Center*,[40] even though the employer argued it had integrated the hospital and its employees into its other operations.

A successor employer cannot choose to recognize only a portion of an acquired unit because it "is not free to sort through a historical bargaining unit, picking and choosing to what extent it will continue recognizing an incumbent bargaining representative."[41]

D. The Effect of Hiatus

In line with the Supreme Court's decision in *Fall River Dyeing Corp. v. NLRB*,[42] the Board and the courts have continued to view hiatus in a successorship scenario as having a limited effect on the bargaining obligation of the new employer. Thus, a hiatus in operations is "relevant only when there are other indicia of discontinuity."[43]

---

[37]340 NLRB No. 107, 173 LRRM 1359 (2003).

[38]*Id.*

[39]*Id.*

[40]335 NLRB 1318, 169 LRRM 1334 (2001), *enforced in part*, 335 F.3d 1079, 172 LRRM 3121 (D.C. Cir. 2003). *See also* Shares, Inc., 343 NLRB No. 59 (2004) (historical unit of manufacturing employees remained appropriate even though other employees at acquiring employer performed related functions where acquired employees worked in only for-profit operation of otherwise nonprofit employer and worked in separate work environment under separate supervision).

[41] SFX Target Ctr. Arena Mgmt., LLC, 342 NLRB No. 71, 175 LRRM 1512 (2004).

[42]482 U.S. 27, 125 LRRM 2441 (1987).

[43]*Id.* at 45. *See also* Pennsylvania Transformer Tech., Inc. v. NLRB, 254 F.3d 217, 167 LRRM 2552 (D.C. Cir. 2001), *enforcing* 331 NLRB 1147, 167 LRRM 1220 (2000).

In *Tree-Free Fiber Co.*,[44] the Board found that a hiatus of 16 months between the cessation of the predecessor's operation and the commencement of the successor's operations lacked significance in the "substantial continuity" analysis. Therefore, such hiatus could not be relied on by a successor as a basis for refusal to recognize the incumbent union.

In *NLRB v. F & A Food Sales, Inc.*,[45] the Tenth Circuit considered the effect of a hiatus as a result of contracting out of unit work rather than of the cessation of that work. The employer contracted out its trucking operations with the union's acquiescence. The union did not seek to continue to represent the trucking employees after they converted to the control of the subcontractor. About two years later, the subcontractor terminated the arrangement, and the trucking operations reverted to the employer. The employer rebuffed the union's bargaining demand on behalf of those returned employees. The employer argued that any bargaining obligation had terminated because it was now a successor employer to a nonrepresented group of employees and that the union had waived its right to represent the employees because it did not seek to represent them during the subcontracting hiatus. The court found, in agreement with the Board, that the successorship doctrine was inapplicable because "F & A simply returned to its status as original employer after a short hiatus, agreed to by the union, with no substantial changes in the original employment relationship."[46] Moreover, the court concluded, because the union had acquiesced to the subcontracting arrangement expressly contemplated by the collective bargaining agreement, it had not waived its right to resume representation of that group of employees once the subcontract was terminated.

In *New Silver Palace Restaurant*,[47] a two-and-a-half month hiatus, during which the predecessor was in bankruptcy and the successor emerged after an asset purchase through a court-directed auction, did not obviate the bargaining obligation where the new business was substantially unchanged.

---

[44]328 NLRB 389, 161 LRRM 1081 (1999); *see also* Northern Mont. Health Care Ctr. v. NLRB, 178 F.3d 1089, 161 LRRM 2469 (9th Cir 1999) (successor bargaining unit made up of both predecessor's employees and employees of new owner constituted only negligible change in bargaining unit and therefore did not provide successor employer with defense for refusing to bargain with union representing predecessor's employees).

[45]202 F.3d 1258, 163 LRRM 2327 (10th Cir. 2000).

[46]*Id.* at 1262.

[47]334 NLRB 290, 171 LRRM 1532 (2001).

Of course, the Board and the courts continue to allude to the *absence* of a hiatus as one of the relevant factors in finding that there is sufficient continuity between the old and new employers to establish a successor relationship.[48]

E. Determining When the Bargaining Obligation Attaches

The basic principle that a successor employer's bargaining obligation attaches upon the union's valid demand for recognition and the employment by the successor employer of a substantial and representative complement of employees, a majority of whom were employed by the predecessor, remains unchanged.[49]

In general, a successor employer may unilaterally set the initial terms of employment, subject to two recognized exceptions: where it is "perfectly clear" that the successor plans to hire all of the employees in the predecessor's unit and where the successor forfeits that right by refusing to hire union employees or informing them that union representation will not be accepted.[50]

With regard to the issue of employee disaffection and the bargaining obligation, the Board in *MV Transportation*[51] discarded the "successor bar" rule enunciated in *St. Elizabeth Manor, Inc.*,[52] and held that a union in the successorship context has only a rebuttable presumption of majority status, thus paving the way for processing an

---

[48]Northern Hills Office Servs, 342 NLRB No. 25, 176 LRRM 1271 (2004); Community Hosp. of Cent. Ca. v. NLRB, 335 F.3d 1079, 172 LRRM 3121 (D.C.Cir. 2003); TransMontaigne, Inc., 337 NLRB 262, 169 LRRM 1229 (2001); Mastronardi Mason Materials Co., 336 NLRB 1296, 174 LRRM 1019 (2001), *enforced*, 64 Fed. Appx. 271 174 LRRM 2927 (2d Cir. 2003); Crown Textile Co., 335 NLRB 201, 171 LRRM 1392 (2001); NLRB v. Simon DeBartelo Group, 241 F.3d 207, 166 LRRM 2608 (2d Cir. 2001).

[49]Dattco, Inc., 338 NLRB 463, 170 LRRM 1497 (2002); Ridgewell's, Inc., 334 NLRB 37, 169 LRRM 1397 (2001); Prime Serv., Inc. v. NLRB, 266 F.3d 1233, 168 LRRM 2545 (D.C. Cir. 2001); *Simon DeBartelo Group, supra* note 48; Pennsylvania Transformer Tech., Inc. v. NLRB, 254 F.3d 217, 167 LRRM 2552 (D.C. Cir. 2001), *enforcing* 331 NLRB 1147, 167 LRRM 1220 (2000).

[50]Waterbury Hotel Mgmt. v. NLRB, 314 F.3d 645, 171 LRRM 2781 (D.C. Cir. 2003); Dupont Dow Elastomers, LLC v. NLRB, 296 F.3d 495, 170 LRRM 2513 (6th Cir. 2002); Solomon Health Servs., 336 NLRB 1050, 169 LRRM 1210 (2002); Eldorado, Inc., 335 NLRB 952, 169 LRRM 1035 (2001); *New Silver Palace Restaurant, supra* note 47; NLRB v. Advance Stretchforming Int'l, Inc., 233 F.3d 1176, 165 LRRM 2870 (9th Cir. 2000), *cert. denied*, 122 S. Ct. 341, 168 LRRM 2472 (2001).

[51]337 NLRB 770, 170 LRRM 1233 (2002).

[52]329 NLRB 341, 162 LRRM 1146 (1999).

otherwise valid decertification, rival union, or employer petition challenging the union's representational status. In overruling *St. Elizabeth Manor*, the Board majority reverted to the position set forth in *Southern Moldings*,[53] that a union in the successorship context is entitled to no greater rights with the successor than it had with the predecessor. Focusing on balancing the competing policies of protecting employee free choice and maintaining stability in bargaining relationships, the Board determined that the successor bar rule promoted stability of bargaining relationships to the exclusion of employees' Section 7 rights. The Board noted that the "reasonable period of time" during which the bar would preclude decertification or other elections could stretch out significantly if the union and the successor reached an agreement, thus delaying an election for up to three years.

The Board concluded that the *Southern Moldings* rule provided the appropriate balance between free choice and stability because it permits challenges to the union's majority status, but also requires the successor to recognize and bargain with the union unless and until such a challenge is successful.[54] In dissent, Member Liebman argued that given the proliferation of corporate mergers and acquisitions, and anxiety among employees as a result of the "throes of the corporate transition," the union's representational status should not be subject to challenge until after a reasonable time for bargaining has elapsed.[55]

Applying the *MV Transportation* rule in *Williams Energy Services*,[56] the Board, on remand from the Fifth Circuit, reversed its prior decision[57] and dismissed the complaint. Shortly after taking over the predecessor's operations, but after the first bargaining session, the employer received a petition signed by all the bargaining unit employees stating that they no longer wished to be represented by the union. The Board noted that *MV Transportation* could be applied retroactively, and held the employer's withdrawal of recognition was lawful under these circumstances because the union's presumption of majority status had been rebutted.

---

[53]219 NLRB 119, 89 LRRM 1623 (1975).

[54]*MV Transp., supra* note 51, 337 NLRB at 775–76.

[55]*Id.* at 776.

[56]340 NLRB No. 87, 173 LRRM 1276 (2003).

[57]336 NLRB 160, 168 LRRM 1289 (2001).

In *TransMontaigne, Inc.*,[58] the Board rejected a successor's argument that a bargaining obligation had not attached because language in the predecessor's collective bargaining agreement constituted a waiver of the union's representational rights. The Board explained that the union's right to recognition and the successor employer's obligation to recognize and bargain is statutory and not contractual and waiver of such must be "clear and unmistakable." The Board determined that the contract language did not satisfy the waiver test because it only released the new employer from the old employer's contractual recognition clause and did not speak specifically to the independent, statutory duty to recognize and bargain with the union.[59]

Addressing the issue of what constituted a valid demand for recognition, the Board in *Eldorado, Inc.*[60] held that a letter from the union to the predecessor, addressed to its president, who also served as president of the successor, constituted a demand for recognition, even though the letter did not specifically mention recognition and bargaining. Rather, the union sought information about what had transpired at the predecessor, the relationship between the predecessor and the successor, which employees were still working, what their rates were, and other information about employees' terms and conditions of employment. The Board majority found that the letter constituted a demand for bargaining because "it clearly indicates that the [u]nion was seeking to fulfill its role as the exclusive bargaining representative of the former Eldorado employees." Chairman Hurtgen dissented, stressing that the union had not sent the letter to the successor and did not demand recognition; rather the union simply sought information to enable it to determine what, if any, claims it might make.[61]

The Board also found a valid demand for recognition in *MSK Corp.*,[62] where the demand predated the successor's hiring of a representative complement of employees. In that case, the successor's officials met with employees to inform them of the change in owner-

---

[58]337 NLRB 262, 169 LRRM 1229 (2001).

[59]The contract language at issue provided: "In the event of a bona fide sale of the assets or change in ownership, or in the event COMPANY ceases operation of the facility, any successor COMPANY which purchases, acquires or becomes the EMPLOYER of EMPLOYEES presently covered by the Recognition clause shall not be bound by this Recognition clause."

[60]335 NLRB 952, 169 LRRM 1035 (2001).

[61]*Id.* at 956–57.

[62]341 NLRB No. 11, 174 LRRM 1143 (2004).

ship and to encourage them to apply for jobs with the successor. At that meeting, the union president met privately with one of the successor's officials and told him the employer was bound to the predecessor's collective-bargaining agreement. The official disagreed. More than two weeks later, the successor hired a representative complement of the predecessor's employees. The Board held that even though the union president did not specifically use the term "recognition," expressly mention bargaining, or offer alternate contract terms, the successor official understood, "or reasonably should have understood," that the union was asking the then-prospective successor to recognize and bargain with the union. The statements constituted a continuing demand for recognition that matured into a bargaining obligation once the successor hired a representative complement of employees.

The Board and the courts have found a successor's duty to bargain is triggered when the prior successor employer voluntarily recognized the union. In *3750 Orange Place Limited Partnership v. NLRB*,[63] the ownership of a hotel was transferred three times within a three-year span. The housekeepers had been represented by the union for many years. The first successor hired a majority of the predecessor's employees, met with the union, provided information about the bargaining unit employees, and promised to develop a contract proposal. Although no such proposal was made before the hotel was sold to another employer, the court adopted the Board's determination that the first successor's conduct was enough to indicate a voluntary recognition of the union. Because the subsequent purchasers each had hired a majority of the first successor's employees, they were obligated to recognize and bargain with the union.

IV. SUCCESSORSHIP AND THE CONTRACTUAL OBLIGATION

A. The "Alter Ego" Employer

The Board and the courts continue to apply the alter ego doctrine, under which the collective bargaining agreements and obligations of one business enterprise are imposed upon another ostensibly different business enterprise where the second business is, in fact, a disguised continuance of, or a conduit for a diversion of work from, the first. In determining whether one business is the alter ego of

[63]333 F.3d 646, 172 LRRM 2871 (6th Cir. 2003).

another, the Board examines whether the alleged alter ego has substantially identical management, business purpose, operation, equipment, customers, supervision, as well as ownership.[64] Another important factor is whether the alter ego was created to evade its predecessor's responsibilities under the Act.[65] Although the Board has held that no single factor alone—including the motive behind creation of the alleged alter ego—is a controlling one,[66] some courts view improper motive as a necessary element,[67] and recent Board cases suggest that the Board might change its rule.[68]

If the Board holds that the employer is an alter ego, then the alter ego employer, in addition to being bound by its predecessor's labor contracts, may be held jointly and severally responsible for remedying the "predecessor's" unfair labor practices.[69] Prospectively, the alter ego employer has a duty to bargain with the union, and an alter ego's refusal to meet and bargain with the union is a violation of Sections 8(a)(1) and (5) of the Act.[70]

---

[64] *See, e.g.,* J. Vallery Elec. v. NLRB, 337 F.3d 446, 451, 172 LRRM 2929 (5th Cir. 2003); District Council No. 9 v. APC Painting, Inc., 272 F. Supp. 2d 229, 237 (S.D.N.Y. 2003); Crossroads Elec., Inc., 343 NLRB No. 112 (2004); Standard Commercial Cartage, Inc., 330 NLRB 11, 13, 170 LRRM 1055 (1999).

[65] *See Vallery Elec., supra* note 64, 337 F.3d at 451; *Crossroads Elec., supra* note 64, 343 NLRB No. 112, slip. op. at 6; *Standard Commercial, supra* note 64, 330 NLRB at 13.

[66] *See Standard Commercial, supra* note 64, 330 NLRB at 13 ("a finding of antiunion animus is not required in order to find an alter ego relationship"); Martin Bush Iron & Metal, 329 NLRB 124, 124 n.3, 169 LRRM 1238 (1999) ("evidence of unlawful antiunion motive in the creation of a corporation is relevant, but not essential, to a finding of alter ego status").

[67] *See* Sheet Metal Workers Local 67 v. Todd-Ford Mgmt. Co., 2005 U.S. Dist. LEXIS 1302, *9–11, (W.D. Tex. Feb. 1, 2005) (Rodriguez, J.) (holding that in the Fifth Circuit a finding of unlawful motive is essential to an alter ego finding) (relying upon language in *Vallery Elec., supra* note 64, 337 F.3d at 451).

[68] Crossroads Elec., *supra* note 64, 343 NLRB No. 112, slip. op. at 2, n.2 (2004) (where Chairman Battista expressed his view that "the General Counsel must show, inter alia, an intent to avoid legal obligations under the Act in order to prove alter ego status"); Fallon-Williams, Inc., 336 NLRB 602, 171 LRRM 1502 (2001) (Hurgten, dissenting) (citing courts that disagree with the Board's approach and "agree[ing] with those courts that hold that . . . an intention [to avoid statutory obligations] is necessary factor").

[69] *See, e.g.,* Jon Bohnenkemper dba South State Builders, Inc., 339 NLRB 465, 173 LRRM 1607 (2003).

[70] *See* Concourse Nursing Home, 328 NLRB 692, 168 LRRM 1499 (1999).

1. *Alter Ego Status Compared With Single-Employer Status*

In *NYP Acquisition Corp.*,[71] the Board clarified the alter ego/single-employer distinction, stating that under the *Johnstown Corp.*[72] line of decisions, the alter ego theory is not a subset of the single-employer concepts.[73] Instead, the alter ego and single-employer theories are separate but related concepts. The single-employer analysis is inapplicable where the case does not involve two ongoing businesses "coordinated by a common master."[74] The Board went on to state that where the two enterprises were running a newspaper, but had "markedly different business purposes"—one to serve as an interim manager of the business for the limited purpose of preserving its assets and the other solely a purchaser with the normal commercial purpose—and lacked antiunion motive, they are not alter egos.[75]

2. *The Defining Factors of the Alter Ego Employer*

a. The Factor of Common Ownership

In *Standard Commercial Cartage, Inc.*,[76] the Board arguably whittled away, to some extent, at the common ownership requirement when it found two enterprises to be alter egos even though their respective owners were neither identical nor all members of the same family. The first company was owned by one family, but the second enterprise was co-owned by one remaining family member and a former manager from the first company.[77] Nevertheless, the Board found the two enterprises to be alter egos.[78]

In *Midwest Precision Heating & Cooling, Inc.*,[79] the Board confirmed that while "ownership by members of the same family does not compel a finding of substantially identical ownership," it "'militates in favor of an alter ego finding' where . . . other relevant factors are shown."[80]

In contrast, in *Reigel Electric*,[81] the Board found no alter ego where a father and son co-owned an electrical construction company that

---

[71] 332 NLRB 1041, 165 LRRM 1281 (2000).
[72] 322 NLRB 818, 154 LRRM 1053 (1997).
[73] *See NYP Acquisition Corp.*, *supra* note 71, 332 NLRB at 1041 n.1.
[74] *Id.*
[75] *Id.*
[76] 330 NLRB 11, 14, 170 LRRM 1055 (1999).
[77] *Id.*
[78] *Id.*
[79] 341 NLRB No. 52, 174 LRRM 1235 (2004).
[80] *Id.* slip op. at 1.
[81] 341 NLRB No. 3, 174 LRRM 1158 (2004).

was dissolved when the father retired from the business and where the son immediately upon dissolution started up his own electrical construction company.[82] According to the administrative law judge, whose opinion was adopted by the Board, the partially common ownership could not support an alter ego finding because "[t]oo many of the factors traditionally relied upon by the Board to support an alter ego finding [were] absent."[83]

b. The Factor of Employer Motive to Evade Labor Obligations

Although the existence of an unlawful motive to avoid the union remains a strong factor in determining whether an alter ego relationship exists, the Board's latest holding is still that it is not essential to prove such a motive to prove an alter ego relationship.[84] Some courts disagree[85], however, and it appears that the Board may change its rule.[86]

Even where an employer has a number of reasons for ceasing operations and starting a new business and some of those reasons are legitimate, if one of the reasons is an effort to escape further dealings with a union, that reason is enough to justify an alter ego finding.[87]

---

[82]*Id.*, slip op. at 3–5.

[83]*Id.* at 5.

[84]*See* Standard Commercial Cartage, Inc., 330 NLRB 11, 13, 170 LRRM 1055 (1999) ("a finding of antiunion animus is not required in order to find an alter ego relationship"); Martin Bush Iron & Metal, 329 NLRB 124, 124 n.3, 169 LRRM 1238 (1999) ("evidence of unlawful antiunion motive in the creation of a corporation is relevant, but not essential, to a finding of alter ego status").

[85]*See* Sheet Metal Workers Local 67 v. Todd-Ford Mgmt. Co., 2005 U.S. Dist. LEXIS 1302, *9–11, 176 LRRM 2662 (W.D. Tex. Feb. 1, 2005) (Rodriguez, J.) (holding that in the Fifth Circuit a finding of unlawful motive is essential to an alter ego finding) (relying upon language in *J. Vallery Elec. v. NLRB*, 337 F.3d 446, 172 LRRM 2929 (5th Cir. 2003)).

[86]Crossroads Elec., Inc., 343 NLRB No. 112, 1 n.2, 176 LRRM 1303 (2004) (where Chairman Battista expressed his view that "the General Counsel must show, inter alia, an intent to avoid legal obligations under the Act in order to prove alter ego status"); Fallon-Williams, Inc., 336 NLRB 602, 606, 171 LRRM 1502 (2001) (Hurgten, dissenting) (citing courts that disagree with the Board's approach and "agree[ing] with those courts that hold that . . . an intention [to avoid statutory obligations] is a necessary factor").

[87]*See Martin Bush*, supra note 84, 329 NLRB at 124–25. The Board reached a similar conclusion in *Michael's Painting, Inc.*, 337 NLRB 860, 171 LRRM 1186 (2002), *enforced on procedural grounds*, 85 Fed. Appx. 614 (9th Cir. 2004), where the presence of a legitimate business reason (a reduction in insurance premiums) for the establishment of a separate corporation did not preclude a finding of alter ego status based on the alter egos' attempts to "rid themselves" of picketing, pro-union employees.

5. *Application of Alter Ego Test in Section 301 Actions and in Arbitration*

Courts continue to apply alter ego principles in the Section 301 context. For example, in *Sheet Metal Workers Local 38 v. A & M Heating, Air Conditioning, Ventilation & Sheet Metal, Inc.*,[88] the union attempted to force A & M Heating to pay a judgment previously entered for violation of a collective bargaining agreement between the union and another company, Hudson Heating.[89] Hudson Heating had filed for bankruptcy shortly after the judgment was entered, and shortly thereafter, the husband of Hudson Heating's owner created A & M Heating, which engaged in the same business as Hudson.[90] Nonetheless, the court found that A & M Hearing was not Hudson's alter ego, concluding that the two businesses did not share substantially identical management and control because one spouse had owned and controlled Hudson while another spouse (who had also been employed by Hudson as its working foreman) owned and controlled A & M.[91] The court further found that the husband did not create A & M out of antiunion animus, but had to find new work because the union "ruined" Hudson (by refusing to send it workers from the hiring hall) and blacklisted him because he reported alleged racketeering by the union to the FBI.[92]

In *Oil, Chemical & Atomic Workers Local 7-517 v. Uno-Ven Co.*,[93] the Seventh Circuit affirmed a grant of summary judgment against the union, which had sought, in a Section 301 suit, to enforce its labor contract against a "successor" employer. There had been a dissolution of the partnership that had initially signed a labor contract covering employees at the partnership's oil refinery. On the eve of dissolution, one partner transferred its interest in the partnership to an affiliate organization (owned by the same parent company). Upon dissolution, the affiliate received the refinery as its share of the partnership assets and proceeded to hire yet another affiliate (another subsidiary of the same parent corporation) to operate the refinery and thereby to become the employer of the refinery employees. The court concluded that the labor agreement between the partnership

---

[88]314 F. Supp. 2d 332, 174 LRRM 3016 (S.D.N.Y. 2004).

[89]*Id.* at 335, 338.

[90]*Id.* at 338.

[91]*Id.* at 347–52.

[92]*Id.* at 337, 350.

[93]170 F.3d 779, 160 LRRM 2788 (7th Cir. 1999).

and the union would not apply to the new employer as long as the various business entities had "complie[d] with the formalities required by corporation law."[94] Among other theories, the court rejected any argument that the new employer was merely the alter ego of the former partnership, noting that the new employer was "a substantial, long-established, asset-rich, bona fide corporation engaged in the oil-refining business."[95]

6. *Application of Alter Ego Test in Bankruptcy Settings*

The Board continues to treat a bankruptcy trustee as an alter ego of the company that existed before the bankruptcy petition was filed.[96]

Rejecting a collective bargaining agreement in bankruptcy does not affect the agreement's continued existence. The alter ego will be bound to the contract made by the other corporation and cannot avoid liability as an alter ego by claiming as an affirmative defense the protection that the other corporation received in the bankruptcy proceeding.[97] It does not matter that the bankrupt entity rejected the labor agreement pursuant to the Bankruptcy Code.[98] Rejection of the labor agreement pursuant to the Bankruptcy Code merely constitutes a breach of the agreement that is approved by the bankruptcy court; therefore, the contract continues to exist and can be applied to the alter ego where the alter ego was not part of any bankruptcy proceedings.[99]

---

[94] *Id.* at 781.

[95] *Id.* at 783.

[96] *See* Ivaco Steel Processing (New York) LLC, 341 NLRB No. 47, 1 n.1, 174 LRRM 1536 (2004); Wheels Transp. Servs., Inc., 340 NLRB No. 130, 1 n.2, 174 LRRM 1448 (2003).

[97] *See* Martin Bush Iron & Metal, 329 NLRB 124, 124–25, 169 LRRM 1238 (1999).

[98] *Id.* at 125.

[99] *Id.*

C. Adoption of Predecessor's Contract

The Board[100] and the courts[101] continue to apply the case-by-case approach in determining whether a successor employer had

---

[100] *See* Cora Realty Co., 340 NLRB No. 55, 174 LRRM 1137 (2003) (successor's conduct, signing authorization agreement that binds it to current collective bargaining agreement and authorizes a multi-employer group to negotiate subsequent agreements on its behalf and telling the union it had joined group, indicated adoption of contract then in effect); Elf Atochem N. Am., Inc., 339 NLRB 796, 174 LRRM 1101 (2003) ("perfectly clear" successorship status found where purchaser announced in advance of sale that it would provide employment to employees, that their seniority would be recognized, that they would receive equivalent salaries and comparable benefits, and that it intended to maintain current terms and conditions of employment pending negotiations"); Brookville Health Care Ctr., 337 NLRB 1064, 172 LRRM 1187 (2002) (successor's adoption of predecessor's contract established by clear and convincing evidence that successor (1) failed to expressly reject contract; (2) complied with all of contract terms; and (3) participated in arbitration proceedings without asserting as defense absence of binding contract between parties).

[101] Dupont Dow Elastomers, LLC v. NLRB, 296 F.3d 495, 170 LRRM 2513 (6th Cir. 2002), *enforcing* 332 NLRB 1071, 166 LRRM 1206 (2000) (informing employees and union prior to sale that purchaser declined to honor labor agreements, but would hire all employees, adopt current benefit plans, recognize prior service, and apply local pay practices made purchaser a "perfectly clear" successor); Ameristeel Corp. v. Teamsters, 267 F.3d 264, 168 LRRM 2353 (3d Cir. 2001) (successor not bound to predecessor's contract where purchase agreement included various provisions expressly stating that purchaser was not to be bound by terms of contract and, in its dealings with union, purchaser consistently and repeatedly maintained that it was not to be bound by the terms of the contract); Chartier v. 3205 Grand Concourse Corp., 202 F.3d 89, 163 LRRM 2149 (2d Cir.), *on remand*, 100 F. Supp. 2d 210, 165 LRRM 2749 (S.D.N.Y. 2000) (no adoption where purchaser rebuffed union's efforts to discuss assumption and demonstrated belief that it was not bound by contract of sale to assume seller's obligations under collective bargaining agreement); Leber v. Universal Music & Video, 225 F. Supp. 2d 928, 170 LRRM 3270 (S.D. Ill. 2002), *aff'd*, 332 F.3d 452, 172 LRRM 2685 (7th Cir.), *cert. denied*, 124 S. Ct. 925, 173 LRRM 3056 (2003) (joint venture documents did not create intent to assume contract where documents referred to "amended" contract and clearly indicated parties' intentions to change working conditions); Gilbert v. Doehler-Jarvis Inc., 87 F. Supp. 2d 788, 164 LRRM 2821 (N.D. Ohio 2000) (successor that expressly agreed to adopt predecessor's contract bound, under circumstances, to continue retiree health care benefits after termination of contract); Balanoff v. 83 Maiden LLC, 163 LRRM 2337 (S.D.N.Y. 2000) (court enforced arbitrator's award that purchaser of building was bound by agreement entered into by its predecessor, because, as part of purchase agreement, purchaser assumed contract between its predecessor and union); Bricklayers Local 21 of Ill. Apprenticeship & Training Program v. Banner Restoration Inc., 385 F.3d 761, 175 LRRM 2833 (7th Cir. 2004) (paying contractual wages, remitting dues to union and fringe benefit contributions to union trust funds, submitting to a trust fund audit, and failing to challenge jurisdiction of a joint arbitration board demonstrated conduct over seven-year period manifesting assent to be bound to multiemployer contract).

adopted or assumed the labor contract of its predecessor, including in the context of a Section 8(f) contract.[102]

V. SUCCESSORSHIP AND THE CONTRACT-BAR DOCTRINE

See the discussion of *MV Transportation* in Section III.A.3. [Successorship in the Bargaining Obligation; Continuity of the Work Force: "The Concept of Majority"; Presumption of the Union's Continued Majority Status] of this chapter.

VI. LIABILITY OF SUCCESSOR FOR PREDECESSOR'S UNFAIR LABOR PRACTICES

Consistent with the Supreme Court's decision in *Golden State Bottling Co. v. NLRB*,[103] the courts and the Board continue to hold that where a successor continues business without interruption or without substantial change in form, the successor is liable for the predecessor's unfair labor practices if circumstances charge the successor with notice of the practices at the time of acquisition.[104]

[102]E.S.P. Concrete Pumping, Inc., 327 NLRB 711, 160 LRRM 1161 (1999) ("adoption by conduct" theory is applicable in the §8(f) context and successor adopted §8(f) contract by completing job applying terms of contract and relying upon contract to obtain successful project bid).

[103]414 U.S. 168, 84 LRRM 2839 (1973).

[104]WXGI, Inc. v. NLRB, 243 F.3d 833, 166 LRRM 2797 (4th Cir. 2001), *enforcing* 330 NLRB 695, 166 LRRM 1293 (2000) (successor employer jointly and severally liable for predecessor's unfair labor practices despite successor's claim that operational changes prevented finding of successor status; no substantial changes made sufficient to meet standard set forth in *Fall River Dyeing & Finishing Corp. v. NLRB*, 482 U.S. 27, 125 LRRM 2441 (1987)). *See also* Amersig Graphics Inc. dba American Signature, Inc., 334 NLRB 880, 169 LRRM 1458 (2001) (purchaser requested to remedy unfair labor practices by offering reinstatement to former strikers and jointly liable with predecessor for reimbursing employees for losses); AC Elec., 333 NLRB 987, 173 LRRM 1391 (2001) (successor required to remedy violations of its predecessor after finding it was successor employer under *Golden State* analysis).

Chapter 16

SUBJECTS OF BARGAINING

III. Development of the Distinction Between "Mandatory" and "Permissive"

A. *Borg-Warner*—The Basic Principles

In *Liquor Industry Bargaining Group,*[1] the Board determined that the employer's bargaining proposals, seeking complete discretion over wages and workload as well as the unrestricted ability to transfer work out of the bargaining unit, evidenced bad faith. The Board, clarifying *Borg-Warner*'s holding that management-rights clauses giv-

[1]333 NLRB 1219, 171 LRRM 1118 (2001), *enforced*, 50 Fed. Appx. 444, 2002 WL 31236400 (D.C. Cir. 2002); *see also* Public Serv. Co. of Okla. v. NLRB, 318 F.3d 1173, 171 LRRM 2993 (10th Cir. 2003), *enforcing* 334 NLRB 487 (2001).

ing the employer exclusive control over certain decisions are not per se violations of Section 8(a)(5), explained that such clauses *may* evidence bad faith if they are so sweeping that the union is left without the ability to conduct its representative function. The Board stated that, "[i]n examining the totality of bargaining conduct, unrealistically harsh or extreme proposals can serve as evidence that the party offering them lacks serious intent to adjust differences and reach an acceptable common ground."[2] Under this standard, the employer's conduct evidenced bad faith because the employer failed to offer the union "proportionate incentives" to accept the sweeping management-rights clause.

B. *Pittsburgh Plate Glass*—The "Vitally Affects" Test

In *Pall Biomedical Products Corp.*,[3] the Board applied the "vitally affects" test[4] to a letter of agreement in which the employer agreed to extend recognition to the union at a newly acquired facility if unit work were performed there by employees and to provide the union with access to the facility and certain information. The union represented employees at the employer's two other locations. When the employer purchased the new facility, the union sought to include it in the contractual unit. After a strike, the matter was resolved by the letter of agreement, which the employer subsequently repudiated. The administrative law judge (ALJ) found that the letter of agreement codified a nonmandatory subject of bargaining and thus the employer was not statutorily obligated to honor it.

The Board reversed the ALJ, finding that the employer's revocation of the letter of agreement, including the recognition clause, violated Section 8(a)(5). Characterizing the recognition clause in the letter of agreement as one specifically directed at the concerns of the employees that had prompted them to strike over the possible transfer of bargaining-unit work to the new facility, the Board found that the clause indeed vitally affected the unit employees under the *Pittsburgh Plate Glass* test. The Board likened the recognition clause at issue to the "after-acquired store" clause at issue in *Kroger Co.*,[5]

---

[2]*Id.*, 330 NLRB at 1220 (citations omitted).

[3]331 NLRB 1674, 165 LRRM 1137 (2000), *enforcement denied*, 275 F.3d 116, 169 LRRM 2065 (D.C. Cir. 2002). See discussion of case in the context of successorship and application of contract clauses in the Main Edition, Chapter 16, Section IV [Mandatory Subjects of Bargaining], at page 1249.

[4]Allied Chem. & Alkali Workers Local 1 v. Pittsburgh Plate Glass Co., 404 U.S. 157, 78 LRRM 2974 (1971).

[5]219 NLRB 388, 89 LRRM 1641 (1975) (providing for voluntary recognition of union in stores acquired after execution of collective bargaining agreement).

which was designated a mandatory subject of bargaining and interpreted to include, as a matter of law, a requirement of majority support. The Board distinguished the recognition clause from a broader "application of contract" clause held to be a permissive subject of bargaining by the Tenth Circuit.[6]

On review, however, the D.C. Circuit denied enforcement of the Board's order, holding that the letter of agreement involved a permissive subject of bargaining.[7] Although the potential transfer of bargaining-unit work to the new location "vitally affected" the existing bargaining unit, the court found that the letter of agreement was not a "direct frontal attack" on that problem.[8] Instead, the letter of agreement merely prescribed the method by which the union could gain recognition at the new facility. As a result, the subject at issue in the letter of agreement did not "vitally affect" the existing bargaining unit.

E. Application of *First National*: From *Otis Elevator* to *Dubuque Packing*

With a split decision in *Eby-Brown Co.*,[9] the Board viewed relocation "labor costs" broadly to include both direct and indirect costs. Thus, even though the employer's decision to relocate to a recently acquired nonunionized facility was based on factors linked solely to geographical considerations (i.e., lower costs because of closer proximity to customers), the Board agreed with the ALJ that the employer's decision was ultimately based on labor costs because labor costs could affect those other costs; concessions by the union might have changed those other costs enough to cause the employer to reconsider the move. As a result, an employer may be required to bargain if negotiating a decrease in current labor costs might make keeping operations in place more economical than moving the operations.

The law in this area continues to remain "unruly," as evidenced by the Fourth Circuit's decision in *Dorsey Trailers, Inc. v. NLRB*.[10] The

---

[6]Mine Workers (Lone Star Steel), 231 NLRB 573, 96 LRRM 1083 (1977), *enforced in part and denied in part*, 639 F.2d 545, 104 LRRM 3144 (10th Cir. 1980).

[7]Pall Biomedical Prods. Corp. v. NLRB, 275 F.3d 116, 169 LRRM 2065 (D.C. Cir. 2002).

[8]*Id.* at 122.

[9]328 NLRB 496, 168 LRRM 1165 (1999).

[10]233 F.3d 831, 165 LRRM 3003 (4th Cir. 2000), *enforcing in part and denying in part* 327 NLRB 835, 165 LRRM 1392 (1999).

court considered an employer's decision during a union strike to close its trailer manufacturing plant and relocate the work to a newly purchased facility without bargaining over the decision. The ALJ had found, inter alia, that the decision to relocate the work was a mandatory subject of bargaining, that the employer had not bargained in good faith, and that no bargaining impasse existed. Concluding that the employer's failure to bargain over the relocation decision was motivated by its desire to retaliate against the union for striking, the ALJ found violations of Sections 8(a)(3) and (5), and ordered the employer to reopen the plant, reinstate employees terminated because of the closing, and repay lost earnings. The Board affirmed the ALJ's decision and adopted his order. The Fourth Circuit disagreed and denied enforcement of a portion of the Board's order.[11]

The Fourth Circuit noted that *First National Maintenance*[12] did not address the issue of whether relocation of work is a term or condition of employment. The court concluded that the decision to relocate, like the decision to partially close a facility, was "not amenable to resolution through the bargaining process."[13] Given the limited benefits of bargaining, balanced against the employer's loss of "freedom to decide where to locate its business and where to invest its finite capital resources," the court determined that the decision to relocate was not a mandatory subject of bargaining.[14]

In *McClain E-Z Pack, Inc.*,[15] the Board held that the employer violated Section 8(a)(5) of the Act by failing to bargain with the union before instituting economic layoffs. The Board reaffirmed "that managerial decisions regarding such issues as the 'order of succession of layoffs and recalls' fall within the second category of managerial decisions that 'are almost exclusively an aspect of the relationship between employer and employees and as to these there is an obligation to bargain.'"[16]

---

[11]*Id.*

[12]First Nat'l Maint. Corp. v. NLRB, 452 U.S. 666, 107 LRRM 2705 (1981).

[13]*Dorsey Trailers, supra* note 10, 233 F.3d at 842.

[14]*Id.*

[15]342 NLRB No. 27, 175 LRRM 1422 (2004).

[16]Dubuque Packing Co., 303 NLRB 386, 137 LRRM 1185 (1991). *See also* Toma Metals, Inc., 342 NLRB No. 78, 175 LRRM 1367 (2004) (employer violated §8(a)(5) by failing to bargain with the union both before it laid off employees and before it began recalling employees).

IV. MANDATORY SUBJECTS OF BARGAINING

A. Wages

1. General

The Board continues to hold that severance pay is a mandatory subject[17] falling under the heading of "wages."[18] In addition, the Board confirmed in *Guard Publishing Co., dba The Register-Guard*[19] that sales commissions constitute wages.

2. Specific Forms of Compensation

An employer violated Section 8(a)(5) by unilaterally terminating merit pay increases, despite the employer's contention that regular merit pay increases were never a condition of employment, having been previously awarded at the employer's "whim." In *NLRB v. Dynatron/Bondo Corp.*,[20] the court upheld the Board and found convincing the fact that the employees had merit reviews and that the majority of employees had received annual merit pay increases in each of the preceding 13 years.[21]

a. Bonuses

The Fourth Circuit, applying reasoning similar to that of the Board in *Mr. Potty, Inc.*,[22] found that a bonus plan unilaterally implemented and then rescinded by the employer was a form of wages and a mandatory subject of bargaining, rather than a gift.[23] In *NLRB v. Mining Specialists,* the court's analysis turned on the fact that the

---

[17]Champion Int'l Corp., 339 NLRB 672, 174 LRRM 1369 (2003) (employer's unilateral change to eligibility conditions for severance pay violated §8(a)(5)).

[18]*See* Main Edition, Chapter 16, Section IV. [Mandatory Subjects of Bargaining], at pages 1171–72.

[19]339 NLRB 353, 172 LRRM 1313 (2003).

[20]176 F.3d 1310, 161 LRRM 2394 (11th Cir. 1999).

[21]*See also* Pleasantview Nursing Home v. NLRB, 351 F.3d 747, 755–56, 173 LRRM 2882 (6th Cir. 2003) (employer's unilateral increase of starting wages during contract negotiation violated the Act), *enforcing in part* 335 NLRB 961, 168 LRRM 1195 (2001).

[22]310 NLRB 724, 145 LRRM 1045 (1993).

[23]NLRB v. Mining Specialists, Inc., 326 F.3d 602, 172 LRRM 2385 (4th Cir. 2003). *See also* U.S. Info. Servs., Inc., 341 NLRB No. 129, 174 LRRM 1482 (2004) (employer required to provide union with information regarding bonuses).

bonuses were tied to the employee's production and not the financial health of the company.[24]

In *Philadelphia Coca-Cola Bottling Co.*,[25] the Board rejected the employer's argument that the union had waived the right to bargain over an incentive bonus program. The fact that the employer had occasionally given various employees bonuses and other gifts in the past did not establish that the union waived bargaining on the subject.[26] In order to show a past practice establishing waiver, the employer must introduce evidence that it occurred with such "regularity and frequency . . . that employees could reasonably view the bonuses as part of their wage structure and that they would reasonably be expected to continue."[27]

c. *Health and Welfare, and Insurance Plans*

In *Maurer v. Joy Technologies*,[28] the Sixth Circuit reaffirmed that although active employee benefits such as a health insurance plan are a mandatory subject of bargaining, benefits for retirees are not.

The employer in *Brook Meade Health Care Acquirors*[29] violated the Act when it unilaterally increased the employees' contribution to health insurance premiums. The Board held that even if the employer had given the union sufficient notice and an opportunity to bargain over the proposal, the employer would not have been able to implement the proposal unilaterally where the union did not engage in delaying tactics simply by insisting on getting legal advice, and increased premiums affecting only about 10 employees were not "economic exigencies" compelling prompt action.[30]

However, the employer in *Post-Tribune Co.*[31] did not violate the Act when it unilaterally increased the amount deducted from employees' paychecks for health insurance premiums. The Board agreed with the employer that it had an established past practice of allocat-

---

[24] *Id.*

[25] 340 NLRB No. 44, 174 LRRM 1346 (2003).

[26] *Id.*

[27] *Id.* (citations omitted).

[28] 212 F.3d 907, 164 LRRM 2344 (6th Cir. 2000).

[29] 330 NLRB 775, 164 LRRM 1020 (2000).

[30] *See also In re* Life Care Ctrs. of Am., Inc., 340 NLRB No. 57, 173 LRRM 1245 (2003) (employer violated the Act when it unilaterally changed amount of contribution to employee 401(k) plan); Palm Court Nursing Home, 341 NLRB No. 113, 175 LRRM 1559 (2004) (same).

[31] 337 NLRB 1279, 170 LRRM 1449 (2002).

ing health insurance premiums on an 80%/20% and 60%/40% basis, and that this allocation was the status quo. Therefore, the Board held that the employer was simply following its past practice by allocating its insurance carrier's premium increase according to the same percentages.

Similarly, in *Saint-Gobain Abrasives, Inc.*,[32] the employer did not violate the Act when it unilaterally implemented an interim health insurance plan during negotiations for the parties' first contract. The Board noted that the employer had an annual process of reviewing and adjusting its health insurance programs, and thus it was not obligated to refrain from implementing its proposed changes until an impasse was reached in bargaining for a collective bargaining agreement as a whole. In *Nabors Alaska Drilling, Inc.*,[33] the employer did not violate the Act when it unilaterally revised a health insurance plan including making changes to copayment contributions. The Board found that the employer had provided notice to the union and invited bargaining over the changes and that because the health insurance review was an annually occurring event, it could not await an impasse in negotiations.

In *The Courier-Journal*,[34] the employer did not violate the Act when it unilaterally raised employee contribution rates to health insurance following expiration of the contract. The parties' collective bargaining agreement specifically authorized the employer to change costs and benefits for unit employees unilaterally on the same basis as nonunit employees. In addition, the Board noted that the employer previously had made numerous unilateral changes during the term of the agreement and during periods of hiatus between agreements without objection from the union, and thus the employer's practice had become an established term and condition of employment.

The employer in *Posadas de Puerto Rico Associates, Inc. v. NLRB*[35] violated the Act by unilaterally discontinuing a 20-year practice of making payroll deductions to cover premiums for group medical and life insurance policies. The employer in that case argued that the longstanding payroll deduction practice did not substantially affect terms and conditions of employment, because the employer itself never contributed to the payment of premiums, but merely deducted the money for transmittal to the insurance company. The court ruled, however, that the practical effect of the employer's ac-

[32]343 NLRB No. 68, 176 LRRM 1138 (2004).
[33]341 NLRB No. 84, 174 LRRM 1396 (2004).
[34]342 NLRB No. 118, 176 LRRM 1013 (2004).
[35]243 F.3d 87, 166 LRRM 2833 (1st Cir. 2001).

tion was to terminate the group insurance policy, and force the employees to obtain individual policies at a greater cost. Under those circumstances, the payroll deduction practice did substantially affect terms and conditions of employment, and the employer could not terminate that practice without bargaining in good faith.

Similarly, in *Allen Storage & Moving Co.*,[36] the employer violated the Act by unilaterally canceling whole life insurance policies that it had maintained for unit employees. Although the employer contended that neither the parties' collective bargaining agreement nor the pension plan promised whole life policies to employees, the Board affirmed the ALJ's holding that the proscription against unilateral changes applies not only to subjects specifically covered in the contract but also to changes in benefits that have been satisfactorily established by practice or custom.

In *BP Amoco Corp. v. NLRB*,[37] the employer did not violate Section 8(a)(5) when it unilaterally implemented its modified medical plan. The plan's reservation-of-rights provision was incorporated into the collective bargaining agreement, and, therefore, the employer's authority to modify the plan without mandatory bargaining was "covered by" the agreement.

However, in *KSM Industries, Inc.*,[38] the employer committed an unfair labor practice by unilaterally implementing its medical and dental plan proposal after the parties bargained to impasse, where the medical plan reserved all discretion about plan design, administration, and benefits to the employer. The Board applied its decision in *McClatchy Newspapers, Inc.*,[39] which arose in the context of merit pay increases, and determined that the employer's medical plan proposal did not leave room for bargaining between the union and the employer about the "manner, method, and means" of providing medical and dental benefits during the term of the contract.[40] Accordingly, because the employer's medical proposal negated the union's ability to negotiate or grieve about changes to this important benefit, the employer could not unilaterally implement the proposal, even after impasse.

---

[36]342 NLRB No. 44, 175 LRRM 1388 (2004).

[37]217 F.3d 869, 164 LRRM 2889 (D.C. Cir. 2000).

[38]336 NLRB 133, 169 LRRM 1445 (2001), *reconsideration granted in part,* 337 NLRB 987, 170 LRRM 1313 (2002).

[39]*In re* McClatchy Newspapers, Inc., 321 NLRB 1386, 153 LRRM 1137 (1996), *enforced,* 131 F.3d 1026, 157 LRRM 2023 (D.C. Cir. 1997). *See also* McClatchy Newspapers, 322 NLRB 812, 154 LRRM 1086 (1996).

[40]*KSM, supra* note 38, 336 NLRB at 136.

In *ServiceNet, Inc.*,[41] the Board found that an employer violated the Act by insisting to impasse on a proposal that allowed it to bargain directly with an employee committee regarding changes to the health insurance plan.[42] The Board held that the employer's proposal would have allowed the employer to circumvent the union and negotiate directly with the employees over a condition of employment (i.e., the company health insurance plan).

In *Beverly Health & Rehabilitation Services v. NLRB*,[43] the D.C. Circuit held that the employer violated the Act by unilaterally implementing HMO coverage for employees at five of its facilities in place of a union health and welfare fund. The union health and welfare plan had been in place under the terms of an expired settlement agreement that resolved an earlier grievance. The court found that although the employer had the right to terminate the union plan pursuant to the terms of the settlement agreement, it was not free to unilaterally implement a replacement plan after the union made a timely request for bargaining on the matter.

In *Mississippi Power Co. v. NLRB*,[44] the Fifth Circuit held that the employer violated the Act by unilaterally changing company-sponsored life insurance coverage for future retirees. In holding that changes in future retirees' life insurance coverage constituted a mandatory subject of bargaining, the court rejected the employer's arguments that: (1) future retirees were not covered "employees" under the Act; (2) the changes were not material, substantial or significant; (3) the changes did not vitally affect a mandatory subject for current employees; and (4) the changes did not have a tangible effect on a mandatory subject.

d. Profit-Sharing Plans

The Board reaffirmed that profit-sharing plans are a mandatory subject of bargaining in *Kankakee Valley Rural Electric Membership Corp.*[45] In *Kankakee Valley*, the Board held that the employer violated the Act by failing to implement a planned increase to its 401(k) matching contributions. The ALJ's decision, affirmed by the Board, rejected

[41] 340 NLRB No. 148, 173 LRRM 1553 (2003).

[42] *Id.*, slip op. at 2.

[43] 317 F.3d 316, 171 LRRM 3017 (D.C. Cir. 2003).

[44] 284 F.3d 605, 169 LRRM 2840 (5th Cir. 2002), *enforcing in part* 332 NLRB 530, 165 LRRM 1225 (2000).

[45] 338 NLRB 906, 173 LRRM 1423 (2003).

the employer's argument that it made the decision to freeze the increase before the union commenced its representation campaign.[46]

Similarly, in *In re Life Care Centers of America, Inc.*,[47] the Board held that an employer violated Section 8(a)(5) by unilaterally discontinuing its practice of matching employee contributions to a 401(k) plan.

e. Stock Purchase Plans

Although stock purchase plans may be a mandatory subject of bargaining, not all such plans are. In *Pieper Electric, Inc.*,[48] the employer refused to furnish the union with the names of employees who were participating in, or had been solicited to participate in, the employer's employee stock purchase plan. The Board held that the plan was a permissive subject of bargaining, reasoning that the plan did not constitute "wages" since employees received no "emolument of value"[49] and the employer did not make matching contributions to the plan. Furthermore, the plan did not come within the scope of "other conditions of employment" because it did not operate as a retirement plan; the shares acquired in the plan could not be bequeathed; and employees were required to sell back their stock to the employer if they quit, were discharged for cause, or were laid off for longer than a specific length of time.

f. Merit Wage Increases

The Board continues to examine a number of factors to determine whether an employer's unilateral grant or discontinuance of a merit wage increase to unit employees is an unfair labor practice. For example, in *News Journal Co.*,[50] the Board held that the employer did not commit an unfair labor practice by discontinuing its practice of granting wage increases to employees after successful completion of their 90-day probationary periods, without first giving the union an opportunity to bargain. The Board held that there was no evi-

---

[46]*Id.* at 910–11; *see also* Highlanders Alloys, LLC, 340 NLRB No. 12, 173 LRRM 1168 (2003) (employer violated the Act by failing to pay various types of contractual compensation, including 401(k) contributions).

[47]340 NLRB No. 57, 173 LRRM 1245 (2003).

[48]339 NLRB 1232, 173 LRRM 1079 (2003).

[49]*Cf.* Richfield Oil Corp., 110 NLRB 356, 359, 34 LRRM 1658 (1954) (stock purchase plan constituted "wages" because employer made matching contributions).

[50]331 NLRB 1331, 164 LRRM 1129 (2000).

dence that the employer had a practice of granting employees automatic wage increases after completion of their probationary period; rather, a wage increase was given at the discretion of the employer.

By contrast, in *Jensen Enterprises, Inc.*,[51] the Board held that an employer may not unilaterally freeze merit wage increases during collective bargaining. The Board rejected the employer's argument that providing these discretionary increases would violate the Act, reasoning that the employer's past practice of providing merit increases upon annual satisfactory performance reviews was sufficiently definite to make the increases a term and condition of employment.[52]

The Board still adheres to the principle, established in *McClatchy Newspapers*,[53] that an employer cannot unilaterally implement a merit wage increase program, even after bargaining to impasse over the issue, because to do so would give the employer complete discretion in determining all aspects of the wage increase.[54] The courts, however, have suggested that the *McClatchy* rule is limited only to situations where an employer implements a merit pay plan but provides no details about the plan.[55]

In *Edward S. Quirk Co., v. NLRB*,[56] the First Circuit vacated and remanded that part of the Board's order finding that the employer had engaged in an unfair labor practice by unilaterally implementing a new merit wage increase plan. The First Circuit questioned whether *McClatchy* applied because the employer provided some standards for merit increases and allowed the employees to grieve deci-

---

[51]339 NLRB 877, 173 LRRM 1018 (2003).

[52]*Id.* at 877–78.

[53]322 NLRB 812, 154 LRRM 1086 (1996).

[54]Quirk Tire, 330 NLRB 917, 166 LRRM 1235 (2000), *enforced in part, vacated in part*, 241 F.3d 41, 166 LRRM 2666 (1st Cir. 2001). The Board also held that an employer's proposal for a merit wage increase that gives the employer complete discretion in determining wage rates is indicative of unlawful "surface bargaining." *But see* Woodland Clinic, 331 NLRB 735, 164 LRRM 1289 (2000) (Board refused to find unfair labor practice where there was no evidence that employer actually granted any merit wage increases to its employees). *See also* Bakersfield Californian, 337 NLRB 296, 173 LRRM 1054 (2001) (applying *Woodland*, Board found no unfair labor practice where complaint did not allege granting merit wage increase was violation).

[55]Detroit Typographical Union No. 18 v. NLRB, 216 F.3d 109, 164 LRRM 2797 (D.C. Cir. 2000) (employer's merit wage increase plan that provided for raises—averaging 4% in first year and 3% in second and third years—based on employee evaluations and subject to grievance procedure did not violate *McClatchy* rule), *vacating* 326 NLRB 700, 159 LRRM 1065 (1998).

[56]241 F.3d 41, 166 LRRM 2666 (1st Cir. 2001), *vacating and remanding* 330 NLRB 917, 166 LRRM 1235 (2000).

sions regarding increases, and remanded to the Board seeking an explanation of its order.

On remand, the Board affirmed its earlier finding that the employer violated Section 8(a)(5) by unilaterally implementing the wage increase proposal at impasse.[57] The Board held that the employer's wage proposal was impermissible under *McClatchy* because it conferred on the employer the ability to make recurring unilateral decisions whether to adjust the employees' wages and precluded any basis for meaningful review of those decisions.

In *Register-Guard Publishing Co.*,[58] the Board held that the employer violated the Act by unilaterally implementing new sales commissions during bargaining negotiations for a renewal contract. The employer argued that it had a past practice of unilaterally implementing other sales incentive plans without complaint from the union, and that this past practice was within the purview of a clause in the expired contract allowing the employer to offer wages in excess of the established rate.[59] The Board rejected this argument, reasoning that "[a] contractual reservation of managerial discretion, like the provision relied on by the Respondent, does not survive expiration of the contract that contains it, absent evidence that the parties intended it to survive."[60] In addition, the fact that the employer unilaterally implemented one other sales incentive program post-contract did not establish that the union acquiesced to future unilateral changes.[61]

g. *Housing, Meals, Services, and Discounts Supplied by Employer*

Both the Board and courts continue to hold that meal monies and other benefits provided by the employer are mandatory subjects of bargaining.[62] Under some circumstances, changes to or relocation of employee parking is a mandatory subject of bargaining. For

---

[57]Edward S. Quirk Co., 340 NLRB No. 33, 173 LRRM 1260 (2003).

[58]339 NLRB 353, 172 LRRM 1313 (2003).

[59]*Id.*

[60]*Id.* (citations omitted).

[61]*Id.*

[62]Traction Wholesale Ctr. Co. v. NLRB, 216 F.3d 92, 164 LRRM 2769 (D.C. Cir. 2000) (employer committed unfair labor practice by unilaterally changing its policy on employees' personal use of company vans); Kurdziel Iron of Wauseon, Inc., 327 NLRB 155, 163 LRRM 1285 (1998), *enforced*, 208 F.3d 214, 163 LRRM 2960 (6th Cir. 2000) (employer violated §8(a)(5) by threatening unilateral reduction in lunch-break time).

example, in *Dynatron/Bondo Corp.*,[63] the Board ruled that the employer violated Section 8(a)(5) by unilaterally assigning spaces to employees in the employee parking lot, where the employer had previously allowed employee parking on a first-come, first-served basis.

On appeal, the employer argued that assigning parking spots is so trivial a change in working conditions that there was no duty to bargain. Noting that there was Board authority for the employer's position and that the Board had not defended its decision on the issue during the appeal, the Eleventh Circuit refused to enforce that portion of the Board's order, accepting that the change in employee parking privileges did not cause a "material" effect upon working conditions.

In *United Parcel Service*,[64] employees parked in a structure owned by a third party that was located close to their place of work. The parking lot owner changed the location of the employee parking, which added more than half an hour to employees' daily commute. Because it had no role in the decision to relocate the parking area, the employer rejected the union's demands to bargain about the relocation of employee parking. The Board ruled, however, that because the employer had the ability to address the effect of the parking change on employees, the employer was obligated to bargain about the effects upon the request of the union, despite having no control over the decision to relocate the employee parking.[65]

In *Pacific Micronesia Corp. dba Dai-Ichi Hotel Saipan Beach*,[66] the employer, which operated a hotel on the island of Saipan, committed an unfair labor practice by unilaterally increasing the cost of housing and meals for nonresident employees. In addition, the employer committed an unfair labor practice by ceasing to provide employees with free laundry detergent. Although this was a fairly minimal benefit (estimated at $10 per month), it was determined to be a regular benefit to employees and an integral part of their compensation. Thus, it was held to be a mandatory subject of bargaining. The employer also violated the Act by ceasing to permit employees to take drinking water from the hotel for their personal use. The

[63]324 NLRB 572, 156 LRRM 1179 (1997), *enforced in part, vacated in part*, 176 F.3d 1310, 161 LRRM 2394 (11th Cir. 1999).

[64]336 NLRB 1134, 168 LRRM 1489 (2001).

[65]*Id.*

[66]337 NLRB 469, 169 LRRM 1473 (2002).

Board affirmed the ALJ's decision that the employer's change in its water policy constituted a unilateral change in a mandatory subject of bargaining.[67]

B. Hours

The Board continues to prohibit employers from making unilateral changes to lunch and break schedules. In *McClatchy Newspapers, Inc.*,[68] the Board held that the employer violated the Act by failing to bargain over its unilateral lengthening of the employees' unpaid lunch period by one-half hour. In so holding, the Board rejected the employer's argument that the changed lunch period was the inevitable consequence of a new production system that was not a mandatory subject of bargaining.[69] The employer failed to show that effects bargaining would be futile.[70]

In *Jackson Hospital Corp.*,[71] the Board upheld the ALJ's finding that the employer violated the Act by unilaterally implementing strict lunch and break schedules in place of a past practice whereby employees had the option to schedule lunches and breaks when convenient.[72] The ALJ rejected the company's argument that the changes were de minimis, finding that the evidence showed that the changes had a significant impact on employees.[73]

In *Verizon New York Inc. v. NLRB*,[74] the Court of Appeals for the District of Columbia Circuit upheld the Board's decision that the employer violated the Act by unilaterally rescinding its 30-year-old past practice of allowing employees to take off work, with pay, to donate blood. The court reasoned that because wages are a mandatory subject of bargaining, so too are employer policies providing pay to employees for nonwork activities.[75]

---

[67]*See also* NLRB v. Brede, Inc., 315 F.3d 906, 171 LRRM 2656 (8th Cir. 2001) (employer did not give sufficient notice and opportunity to bargain over decision to take hiring system back in house, when previously handled by the union), *enforcing* 335 NLRB 71, 169 LRRM 1295 (2001).

[68]339 NLRB 1214, 173 LRRM 1393 (2003).

[69]*Id.*

[70]*Id.*

[71]Jackson Hosp. Corp. dba Kentucky River Med. Ctr., 340 NLRB No. 71, 174 LRRM 1240 (2003).

[72]*Id.*, slip op. at 1, 10.

[73]*Id.*, slip op. at 11.

[74]360 F.3d 206, 174 LRRM 2609 (D.C. Cir. 2004).

[75]*Id.* at 208.

The Board has found violations of Section 8(a)(5) where employers failed to bargain or give notice before: replacing time clocks with the manual recording of time by supervisors and requiring an additional 15 minutes of overtime;[76] moving employees' start time up by 15 minutes; limiting telephone usage to emergency calls; limiting employees' break time to two 15-minute breaks, and altering employee lunch periods;[77] implementing a new attendance policy;[78] and imposing a monetary charge for lost time cards.[79] In *Beverly California v. NLRB*,[80] the Seventh Circuit affirmed the Board's determination that the employer's unilateral reduction in employees' hours, modification of employees' break time, and refusal to provide to the union attendance records of nonunion employees violated Section 8(a)(5). Although the contract gave the employer the right to "schedule its operations work force," the contractual language was general, and the court found that it did not constitute a clear and unmistakable waiver of the employees' statutory rights.[81]

---

[76]Vincent Indus. Plastics, 328 NLRB 300, 163 LRRM 1123 (1999), *enforcement granted in part, denied in part,* 209 F.3d 727, 164 LRRM 2039 (D.C. Cir. 2000).

[77]Pepsi-Cola Bottling of Fayetteville, Inc., 330 NLRB 900, 170 LRRM 1322 (2000), *enforcement granted in relevant part,* 24 Fed. Appx. 104 (4th Cir. 2001). *See also* Mackie Auto. Sys., 336 NLRB 347, 170 LRRM 1327 (2001) (employer's unilateral change in the practice of providing a paid 30-minute lunch break violated §8(a)(5) and the employer's argument that its customers' reduced demand or bona fide scheduling changes did not exempt the employer from its bargaining obligation where these circumstances did not equate with "compelling economic considerations"); FiveCAP, Inc., 332 NLRB 943, 170 LRRM 1190 (2000), *enforced,* 294 F.3d 768, 170 LRRM 2401 (6th Cir. 2002) (employer violated §8(a)(5) by unilaterally prohibiting its bus drivers from continuing to drive their buses home at night, which change affected the bus drivers' compensation). *See also* Indian River Mem'l Hosp., Inc., 340 NLRB No. 58, 173 LRRM 1433 (2003).

[78]*Vincent Indus. Plastics, supra* note 76; Duffy Tool & Stamping, 330 NLRB 298, 165 LRRM 1372 (1999), *enforced,* 233 F.3d 995, 165 LRRM 2929 (7th Cir. 2000); Dorsey Trailers, Inc., 327 NLRB 835, 165 LRRM 1392 (1999), *enforced in part, denied in part, and remanded,* 233 F.3d 831, 165 LRRM 3003 (4th Cir. 2000). *See also* Pepsi Am., Inc., 339 NLRB 986, 174 LRRM 1347 (2003).

[79]NLRB v. Beverly Enters.-Mass., Inc., 174 F.3d 13, 160 LRRM 2935 (1st Cir. 1999).

[80]227 F.3d 817, 165 LRRM 2257 (7th Cir. 2000), *cert. denied,* 533 U.S. 950, 167 LRRM 2640 (2001), *enforcing in relevant part* 326 NLRB 153, 159 LRRM 1049 (1998), *and* 326 NLRB 232, 159 LRRM 1033 (1998).

[81]*See also In re* Indian River Mem'l Hosp., Inc., 340 NLRB No. 58, 173 LRRM 1433 (2003) (employer violated §8(a)(5) of the Act by making work schedule changes without notice/opportunity to bargain). *But see In re* Caraustar Mill Group, Inc., dba Cincinnati Paperboard, 339 NLRB 1079, 173 LRRM 1161 (2003) (no violation where employer unilaterally changed its "trading time" shift policy to eliminate trades of less than a full shift because collective bargaining agreement allowed such changes).

In *Pepsi America, Inc.*,[82] the Board held that the employer violated Section 8(a)(5) by unilaterally eliminating a provision in its attendance policy that permitted employees with good attendance to earn future paid time off. Although the management-rights clause permitted the employer to establish conduct rules, the attendance credit provision was an employee benefit, not a rule.[83]

C. Other Terms and Conditions of Employment

1. In General

In cases such as *Beverly Health & Rehabilitation Services, Inc.*[84] and *Regal Cinemas, Inc.*[85] the Board continued to reaffirm the status of many topics, such as: vacations, personal/bonus days, layoffs,[86] transfers, leave without pay, absenteeism policy, job descriptions and duties, medical leave, required in-service meetings, payments to health and welfare funds,[87] health insurance benefits,[88] paid time off,[89] among others, as clearly recognized mandatory subjects of bargaining.[90]

Additionally, in *McClatchy Newspapers, Inc.*,[91] the Board reiterated the principle that changes to terms and conditions of employment

---

[82] *Supra* note 78.

[83] *Id.*, 339 NLRB at 986.

[84] 335 NLRB 635, 171 LRRM 1402 (2001) (and cases cited therein), *enforced in relevant part,* 317 F.3d 316 (D.C. Cir. 2003).

[85] 334 NLRB 304, 167 LRRM 1347 (2001), *enforced,* 317 F.3d 300, 171 LRRM 2944 (D.C. Cir. 2003). *See also* NLRB v. Mt. Sinai Hosp., 8 Fed. Appx. 111 (2d Cir. 2001) (employer's unilateral reclassification of bargaining unit sous chefs to supervisory status as "assistant culinary managers" violated the Act where the sous chefs did not meet the statutory criteria for supervisors in the first instance and the reclassification effected a transfer of bargaining-unit work out of the service and maintenance unit).

[86] *See* Falcon Wheel Div., LLC, 338 NLRB 576, 171 LRRM 1537 (2002).

[87] *See* Lafayette Grinding Corp., 337 NLRB 832, 170 LRRM 1355 (2002).

[88] *See* Hardesty Co., Inc. dba Mid-Continent Concrete Co., 336 NLRB 157, 171 LRRM 1314 (2001), *enforced,* 308 F.3d 859, 171 LRRM 2006 (8th Cir. 2002) (employer violated §8(a)(5) by unilaterally changing health insurance benefit plan, regardless of the fact that the plan covered both unit and nonunit employees alike).

[89] Verizon N.Y., Inc, 339 NLRB 30, 172 LRRM 1193 (2003) (employer violated §8(a)(5) by "unilaterally rescinding its longstanding practice of allowing employees to participate in blood drive during paid worktime").

[90] *See* Toma Metals, Inc., 342 NLRB No. 78, 175 LRRM 1367 (2004) (recalling employees from layoff is a mandatory subject of bargaining); Crittenton Hosp., 342 NLRB No. 67, 175 LRRM 1283 (2004) (wearing appropriate apparel at work is a mandatory subject of bargaining).

[91] 339 NLRB 1214, 173 LRRM 1393 (2003).

that are either of "de minimis effect" or "the inevitable consequences" of a permissible unilateral managerial decision are permissive subjects of bargaining and may be unilaterally implemented. However, when changes to terms and conditions of employment arising out of permissible unilateral managerial decisions are *discretionary,* i.e., not inevitable consequences, such "effects" are mandatory subjects of bargaining and may not be unilaterally implemented.

2. *Specific Terms and Requirements*

c. Union-Security Provisions and Hiring Halls

Relying on *Bethlehem Steel Co.,*[92] the Board in *Hacienda Resort Hotel & Casino*[93] found the employers did not violate the Act when they unilaterally ceased dues checkoff after the expiration of the collective bargaining agreement. The Board noted that, although a dues checkoff provision is a mandatory subject of bargaining, the employers' obligation to check off dues does not survive contract expiration.[94] Notwithstanding the general rule that an employer must maintain the status quo—as to mandatory subjects—upon the expiration of the contract, *Bethlehem Steel* held that a union's right to checkoffs was "a contractual right which continued to exist so long as the contracts remained in force." According to *Bethlehem Steel,* this result was compelled by Sections 8(a)(3) and 302(c)(4) of the Act.

In *Wilkes Telephone Membership Corp.,*[95] relying on its *Hacienda* decision, the Board reaffirmed that Section 8(a)(5) is not violated by an employer who unilaterally ceases giving effect to a union dues provision in a collective bargaining agreement upon its expiration, because such provisions are, as explained in the Main Edition, a creature of contract. The Board again expressly rejected the argument that ". . . a checkoff clause that does not implement a union-security

---

[92]136 NLRB 1500, 1502, 50 LRRM 1013 (1962), *enforced in pertinent part,* 320 F.3d 615 (3d Cir. 1963).

[93]Hacienda Hotel, Inc. Gaming Corp. dba Hacienda Resort Hotel & Casino, 331 NLRB 665, 164 LRRM 1273 (2003), *vacated and remanded sub nom.* Local Joint Exec. Bd. of Las Vegas, Culinary Workers Local 226 v. NLRB, 309 F.3d 578, 171 LRRM 2146 (9th Cir. 2002).

[94]*But see* Bulkmatic Transp. Co., 340 NLRB No. 74, 173 LRRM 1447 (2003) (Board found violation of Act where employer ceased to deduct and remit dues to the union upon expiration of rider agreement but before expiration of the master agreement). See *infra* note 100.

[95]331 NLRB 823, 164 LRRM 1338 (2000) (finding that dues checkoff expired with contract as a matter of law).

provision . . . is an employment term that survives the expiration of the contract and cannot be changed without bargaining with the union."[96] However, in *Quality House of Graphics, Inc.*,[97] the Board found a violation of the Act where an employer unilaterally discontinued pension contributions and dues checkoff, holding that the parties' checkoff agreement and employees' written authorizations for the payments were not limited to the contract's duration.

In vacating and remanding the Board's decision in *Hacienda Hotel, Inc.*, the Ninth Circuit noted it ultimately might not have a problem with the substance of the Board's decision, but the Board failed to provide a reasoned explanation for its decision.[98] Citing *Motor Vehicle Manufacturers Ass'n of United States, Inc. v. State Farm Mutual Automobile Insurance Co.*,[99] the court explained it could not uphold the Board's decision because the Board failed in its obligation to provide an adequate explanation of the rationale supporting its decision. The Board's referral, without more, to *Bethlehem Steel* as the authority for its decision was too ambiguous an explanation for its finding in *Hacienda* that the employer's failure to maintain the status quo regarding the dues-checkoff clause did not violate Section 8(a)(5).

The court distinguished *Bethlehem Steel* because that case concerned a dues-checkoff clause that was tied to a union-security clause. In the court's view, the holding in *Bethlehem Steel*, excluding the dues-checkoff clause from the "unilateral change doctrine," was premised upon a view that the clause served to implement the union-security clause—which was not subject to the "unilateral change doctrine" in light of the prohibitions of Sections 8(a)(3) and 302(c)(4) of the Act. Given that the collective bargaining agreement in *Hacienda*, unlike the provision at issue in *Bethlehem Steel*, did not have a union-security clause (because Nevada is a "right-to-work" state), the court held that the Board had presented insufficient justification for treating the stand alone dues-checkoff provision in *Hacienda* the same as a checkoff provision coupled with a union-security clause.

In *Bulkmatic Transport Co.*,[100] the Board reiterated the well-established principle that an employer may not unilaterally discontinue

---

[96] *Id.*

[97] 336 NLRB 497, 169 LRRM 1511 (2001).

[98] 331 NLRB 665, 164 LRRM 1273 (2003), *vacated and remanded sub nom.* Local Joint Exec. Bd. of Las Vegas, Culinary Workers Local 226 v. NLRB, 309 F.3d 578, 171 LRRM 2146 (9th Cir. 2002).

[99] 463 U.S. 29 (1983).

[100] 340 NLRB No. 74, 173 LRRM 1447 (2003).

dues checkoff, a mandatory subject of bargaining, before the expiration of the collective bargaining agreement creating it.

d. Management-Rights and Waiver Clauses

Employers are not permitted to rely on broad management-rights clauses waiving the union's right to bargain if the contract containing the clause has expired. In *Kentucky Fried Chicken LLC,*[101] the Board affirmed the ALJ's recommended decision and order requiring the employer to provide the union with notice and an opportunity to bargain before making a unilateral change of the terms and conditions of employment. A broad management-rights clause waiving the union's right to bargain had expired and there was no evidence that the parties intended the clause to outlive the contract.

e. Plant Rules and Discipline

An employer's unilateral implementation of or changes to plant rules without notice to or consultation with the union may constitute a violation of Section 8(a)(5) where such new rules or changes constitute material, significant, and substantial changes to terms and conditions of employment.[102] Conversely, minor changes that do not

---

[101]341 NLRB No. 13, 174 LRRM 1049 (2004).

[102]Northwest Graphics, Inc. & Local 505-M, Graphic Communications Int'l Union, 342 NLRB No. 127, 176 LRRM 1188 (2004) (violation found where adequate notice not given to union before implementation of work schedule changes); Toledo Blade Co., Inc., 343 NLRB No. 51, 175 LRRM 1538 (2004) (unilateral change of disciplinary policy and work rules); Palm Court Nursing Home N.H., LLC, 341 NLRB No. 113, 175 LRRM 1559 (2004) (unilateral implementation of 401(k) plan, increase of employee contributions to benefits plan, reduction of number of paid holidays, jury duty days, and sick days, increase in the time required for advance notification for absences and tardiness, and elimination of overtime hours for hours over 8 required to be worked in a single day); Anheuser Busch, Inc., 342 NLRB No. 49, 175 LRRM 1168 (2004) (unilateral installation and use of surveillance cameras in work and break areas); Community Health Servs., Inc. dba Mimbres Mem. Hosp. & Nursing Home, 342 NLRB No. 33, 175 LRRM 1028 (2004) (unilateral change in work hours and implementation of fingerprint policy providing new grounds for discipline); MEMC Elec. Materials, Inc., 342 NLRB No. 119, 175 LRRM 1476 (2004) (unilateral change in the areas where hourly maintenance employees were permitted to take their breaks, and discontinuance of its practice of allowing employees to bring personal projects into the plant); BHP (USA) Inc. dba BHP Coal New Mex., 341 NLRB No. 149, 175 LRRM 1190 (2004) (unilateral change in levels of discipline for specific combinations of unexcused absences and tardiness, and discharge based on these unlawfully imposed changes); United States Postal Serv., 341 NLRB No. 100, 176 LRRM 1302 (2004) (unilateral imposition of the requirement that chief steward request time to conduct union business in writing); LTD Ceramics, Inc., 341 NLRB No. 14, 174 LRRM 1105 (2004) (unilateral posting, implementation, and enforcement of a new attendance-discipline policy);

constitute a material departure from previous policies do not violate Section 8(a)(5).[103]

In *King Soopers, Inc.*,[104] the Board refused to apply the "core purposes of the enterprise" exception to an employer's bargaining obligation.[105] The Board found that the employer violated Section 8(a)(5) by failing to bargain before implementing a policy requiring the use of new technology by employees. The employer installed in its pharmacies prescription accuracy scanners used to help prevent errors in filling prescriptions.[106] After installing the scanners, the employer unilaterally implemented a policy requiring that pharmacists and technicians use the scanners on all prescriptions.[107] The Board rejected the employer's argument that the decision to introduce new technology "lies at the core of entrepreneurial control" and was, therefore, not subject to bargaining.[108] In so ruling, the Board noted that although the employer may not have been required to bargain over its entrepreneurial decision to install the scanners, it was obliged to bargain over a work rule implementing that decision.[109]

An employer may also violate the Act by unilaterally converting a previous informal and occasional rule into a written policy statement that includes discipline and applies at all times. In *Scepter, Inc. v. NLRB*,[110] for instance, the employer, an aluminum recycling com-

---

George Power Co., 342 NLRB No. 18, 175 LRRM 1130 (2004) (unilateral implementation of workplace ethics rules); Pan Am. Grain Co., 343 NLRB No. 47, 175 LRRM 1497 (2004) (no violation where employer unilaterally implemented requirement that employees sign overtime schedules to acknowledge their receipt because the rule was not a material and significant change).

[103]Crittenton Hosp., 342 NLRB No. 67, 175 LRRM 1283 (2004) (unilateral change to dress code policy did not constitute a material departure from previous policy).

[104]340 NLRB No. 75, 173 LRRM 1363 (2003).

[105]*See* Main Edition, Chapter 16, at page 1212.

[106]King Soopers, *supra* note 104.

[107]*Id.*

[108]*Id.*

[109]*Id. See also* Verizon N.Y., Inc., 339 NLRB 30, 172 LRRM 1193 (2003), *aff'd*, 360 F.3d 206 (D.C. Cir. 2004) (Board rejected employer's "core of entrepreneurial control" argument concerning sponsoring of blood drives where employer unilaterally ended 30-year practice of allowing employees to participate in blood drives during work time). Similarly, an employer may escape liability for certain unilateral changes if it can satisfy the heavy burden of showing the changes were justified by "compelling economic considerations." MEMC Elec. Materials, Inc., 342 NLRB No. 119, 126, 175 LRRM 1476 (2004), citing Brook Meade Health Care Acquirors dba Maple Grove Health Care Ctr., 330 NLRB 775, 779, 164 LRRM 1020 (2000).

[110]280 F.3d 1053, 169 LRRM 2524 (D.C. Cir. 2002).

pany, unilaterally instituted a new work rule prohibiting the insertion of steel banding into its furnaces. It also required its employees to sign an acknowledgment that violations of the rule would result in termination. Enforcing the Board's order, the D.C. Circuit concluded that the new work rule, which converted a previously informal general policy into a hard and fast rule, and summary discharge, had a significant effect on the conditions of employment. It held, therefore, that Scepter violated the Act in failing to bargain over the implementation of the rule.[111]

In *Pacific FM, Inc. dba KOFY TV-20,*[112] the Board held that an employer is not required to bargain over procedural changes to time-keeping policies. The employer issued a memorandum informing employees of a new time clock system and procedures for using it.[113] Relying on *The Bureau of National Affairs, Inc.*,[114] the Board found that the employer had the right to track employees' hours and that employees were not prejudiced by the new system.[115]

An employer cannot unilaterally implement the use of hidden surveillance cameras in the workplace. In *National Steel Corp.*,[116] the employer periodically used hidden cameras to investigate cases of suspected theft or other instances of wrongdoing. A unit employee was terminated after he was caught on camera using a manager's office to make numerous personal long-distance phone calls. The union filed a grievance and thereafter requested information regarding the location of the hidden cameras and demanded bargaining over the installation of additional cameras. The employer refused. Relying on its 1997 decision in *Colgate Palmolive Co.*,[117] the Board con-

---

[111]*Id. See also* Golden Stevedoring Co., 335 NLRB 410, 169 LRRM 1173 (2001).

[112]332 NLRB 771, 171 LRRM 1098 (2000).

[113]*Id.*

[114]235 NLRB 8, 97 LRRM 1447 (1978). *See also* Unified Creative Programs, Inc., 340 NLRB No. 160, 174 LRRM 1071 (2003) (requirement that employees call in and speak to management when not coming in was not significant change in rule).

[115]KOFY TV-20, 332 NLRB 771, 171 LRRM 1098 (2000). If the modification in time-keeping procedures affects a mandatory subject such as hours, then the employer may not unilaterally implement the change. *See* Main Edition, Chapter 16, at page 1197.

[116]335 NLRB 747, 172 LRRM 1055 (2001), *enforced*, 324 F.3d 928 (7th Cir. 2003).

[117]323 NLRB 515, 155 LRRM 1034 (1997). *See also* Nortech Waste, 336 NLRB 554, 168 LRRM 1361 (2001) (employer's failure to bargain over installation of surveillance cameras was violation of §8(a)(5)). *But see* Anheuser-Busch, Inc., 342 NLRB No. 49, 175 LRRM 1168 (2004) (although the employer violated §8(a)(5) by unilaterally installing and using surveillance cameras, the Board upheld disci-

cluded that the employer had violated Section 8(a)(5) in failing to bargain with the union over the use of the surveillance cameras and in refusing to provide it with information pertaining to existing hidden surveillance cameras.

f. Drug and Alcohol Testing

In *Champion International Corp.*,[118] the Board found a Section 8(a)(5) violation where an employer conditioned receipt of severance pay on making application for employment with the company's asset purchaser where the application process included mandatory drug testing not required by the existing collective bargaining agreement. The Board affirmed the ALJ's finding that drug testing is a mandatory subject, and concluded that the employer denied the union "an opportunity to engage in meaningful effects bargaining in light of its unilateral implementation of preconditions for receipt of severance pay."[119]

The implementation of drug and alcohol testing programs for current employees is a mandatory subject of bargaining. In *Intrepid Museum Foundation, Inc.*,[120] the employer had had a drug testing policy in place since 1990. The policy gave the employer the "right to require employees" to undergo drug testing under certain circumstances. However, on at least two occasions, the employer had elected not to test unit employees suspected of using drugs. In 1997, the employer reissued the drug testing policy with only insignificant language changes. When an employee was tested and terminated pursuant to the policy, the union contended that the drug testing policy had never been formally implemented because the employer had not previously tested unit employees. The union argued that the employer was required to bargain over the reissuance of the drug testing policy or, at minimum, the employer's more stringent enforcement of the policy.

The Board rejected these arguments, however, finding that the drug testing policy did not *require* the employer to conduct testing on suspicion of employee drug use. Rather, the policy merely gave

---

pline of employees who engaged in misconduct discovered by the surveillance cameras, reasoning that an employee discharged or disciplined for misconduct is not entitled to reinstatement and backpay even if the misconduct is uncovered in an unlawful way).

[118]339 NLRB 672, 174 LRRM 1369 (2003).

[119]*Id.*

[120]335 NLRB 1 (2001).

the employer the "right" to do so. The Board refused to equate the employer's election not to test employees with a rescission of the policy and ruled that the employer did not have an obligation to bargain over the reissuance of the existing policy.

g. Grievance Procedures and Arbitration

The procedure for handling grievances is a mandatory subject of collective bargaining.[121] In *Contract Carriers Corp.*,[122] the Board ruled that the employer violated the Act when it refused to meet with the union's designated representative for processing grievances and failed to attend contractual grievance hearings.[123]

In *Exxon Chemical Co.*,[124] an employer's refusal to designate an arbitrator pursuant to the arbitration selection procedures set forth in a collective bargaining agreement and its refusal to arbitrate grievances was found to be a Section 8(a)(5) violation. The Board noted that the employer was not refusing to arbitrate a particular grievance, but was engaging in conduct tantamount to a "unilateral modification or wholesale repudiation of the collective bargaining agreement," by refusing to arbitrate three grievances, each concerning a different provision of the collective bargaining agreement, "and together representing the universe of bargaining issues still pending between the parties at the end of their relationship."[125]

In *Wire Products Manufacturing Corp.*,[126] the arbitration provision in the collective bargaining agreement required that the arbitration panel contain "experienced arbitrators." During the selection of the panel, the employer insisted on "special requirements" that the arbitrators be selected from only certain out-of-state regions and that they all be accredited by the American Arbitration Association. The Board found that such insistence unilaterally altered the arbitration provision in the collective bargaining agreement, and thus violated Section 8(a)(5).

---

[121]TruServ Corp. v. NLRB, 254 F.3d 1105, 167 LRRM 2577 (D.C. Cir. 2001).

[122]339 NLRB 851, 173 LRRM 1043 (2003).

[123]*Id. See also* Arvinmeritor, Inc., 340 NLRB No. 124, 174 LRRM 1350 (2003) (employer unilaterally repudiated its past practice of meeting with union committee for the purpose of processing grievances); Barnard Coll., 340 NLRB No. 106, 173 LRRM 1353 (2003) (employer unilaterally changed grievance handling procedures by refusing to meet with union representatives at second step grievance meetings).

[124]340 NLRB No. 51, 173 LRRM 1253 (2003), *aff'd*, 386 F.3d 1160 (D.C. Cir. 2004).

[125]*Id.*

[126]329 NLRB 155, 165 LRRM 1016 (1999).

h. Safety and Health

Although the Board continues to adhere to its position that health and safety issues are mandatory subjects of collective bargaining, the Board held in *Southern California Gas Co.*[127] that an employer had no duty to provide information which the union requested because it might "impact employee safety." Subsequently, the union stated that it sought the information in order to "represent the members of the union before the [California Public Utilities (CPUC)] Commission." The Board concluded the employer's refusal to provide the information was lawful because the union had abandoned the safety reason and instead sought the information solely to assist it with its complaint before the CPUC. In the Board's view, "mere mention of the word 'safety'" was not sufficient to make the information relevant to collective bargaining.

j. Work Assignments

The Board recently confirmed its earlier ruling that an employer does not violate Section 8(a)(5) when, upon the employees' request, it unilaterally transfers them to a unit represented by a different union where the work of the transferred employees does not remain essentially the same as the work they performed while in the former unit.[128]

l. Change in Operations

In *Essex Valley Visiting Nurses Ass'n*,[129] the Board held the unilateral transfer of nurses from in-house utilization management positions to field nurse positions was unlawful. The Board adopted the ALJ's recommended decision that the transfers were illegal because the "extraordinary events" that could justify unilateral action under *RBE Electronics* were not present in this case.[130] A later decision to discharge the same nurses for "poor performance" was held not to be violative of Section 8(a)(5) or 8(a)(3).

---

[127]342 NLRB No. 56, 175 LRRM 1243 (2004).

[128]Hanson Aggregates Pac. Southwest, Inc., dba Hanson SJC Constr., 342 NLRB No. 98, 175 LRRM 1363 (2004). *Compare* McDonnell Douglas Corp., 312 NLRB 373, 377, 144 LRRM 1137 (1993), *rev'd on other grounds*, 59 F.3d 230 (D.C. Cir. 1995) (employer violated §8(a)(5) by unilaterally assigning bargaining-unit employees to another division and removing them from the unit when their job duties and functions and terms and conditions of employment remained essentially the same).

[129]343 NLRB No. 92, 176 LRRM 1089 (2004).

[130]320 NLRB 80, 151 LRRM 1329 (1995).

In *Natomi Hospitals of California, Inc. dba Good Samaritan Hospital*,[131] the Board ruled that the management-rights clause in the parties' collective bargaining agreement allowed the employer to make staffing changes unilaterally. However, the Board found the employer unlawfully refused to bargain over the *effects* of its unilateral changes. Similarly, in *McClatchy Newspapers*,[132] the Board held the employer lawfully and unilaterally implemented a new printing system. The employer, however, violated the Act by unilaterally changing unpaid lunch and break schedules as a consequence of the change. Thus, this employer was also required to bargain over the effects of the decision.

m. Major Business Changes

(1) Subcontracting and Removal of Work From the Bargaining Unit

In *Regal Cinemas, Inc.*,[133] the Board found that the employer violated Section 8(a)(5) by laying off bargaining-unit employees and transferring their work to nonunion managers, emphasizing "that the reclassification or transfer of bargaining-unit work to managers or supervisors is a mandatory subject of bargaining where it has an impact on unit work."[134] However, the Board also found that the employer did not violate the Act by conditioning the employees' receipt of severance pay on signing a release. Distinguishing *Borden, Inc.*,[135] where the Board found that the employer had unlawfully insisted to impasse on a general release, a permissive subject of bargaining, the Board in *Regal Cinemas, Inc.* held that the evidence failed to establish that the employer had insisted to impasse on a general release in exchange for the severance agreement.[136]

The D.C. Circuit enforced the Board's order, and agreed that it properly applied *Torrington* and *Fiberboard* rather than *First National Maintenance* and *Dubuque Packing*. The court found *Torrington* and *Fiberboard* applicable because the case involved a transfer of work from unit employees to nonunit employees, but did not involve a

---

[131] 335 NLRB 901, 172 LRRM 1234 (2001); *see also* California-Pacific Med. Ctr., 337 NLRB 910, 173 LRRM 1326 (2003).

[132] 339 NLRB 1214, 173 LRRM 1393 (2003).

[133] 334 NLRB 304, 167 LRRM 1347 (2001), *enforced*, 317 F.3d 300, 171 LRRM 2994 (D.C. Cir. 2003).

[134] *Id.*

[135] 279 NLRB 396, 123 LRRM 1239 (1986).

[136] 334 NLRB 304, 305, 167 LRRM 1347 (2001).

relocation of the business, to which the *First National Maintenance* and *Dubuque Packing* balancing test would apply.[137]

Likewise, in *FiveCAP, Inc.*,[138] the ALJ, as affirmed by the Board, found *First National Maintenance* inapplicable to the employer's decision to eliminate one position due to technology and another position due to consolidation of work. These actions did not involve a fundamental change in the scope and direction of the employer's business, as there was no change in the services provided but only in employee duties and numbers. In enforcing the Board's decision, the Sixth Circuit agreed that the changes were "not of the magnitude contemplated in *First National*," but involved slight changes to *FiveCAP*'s infrastructure that did not affect *FiveCAP*'s business purpose or capabilities.[139]

(b) Supreme Court Decisions. In *Eagle Transport Corp.*,[140] the employer violated the Act by failing to notify the union of, or to afford it an opportunity to bargain over, a subcontracting decision made during contract negotiations. The employer argued that the subcontracting of work was motivated by economic reasons, and was undertaken to salvage customer relations damaged by the employer's inability to fulfill fuel delivery orders during peak season using its own employees. Thus, according to the employer, the decision fell within the "economic exigency" exception to the rule barring unilateral changes during bargaining absent an overall impasse. The Board rejected the employer's argument, finding that the claimed emergency was not an "extraordinary event" as enumerated by the Board in *Winn-Dixie Stores*[141] and that the employer failed to establish an economic exigency which waived its bargaining obligation. Accordingly, the employer violated the Act by unilaterally subcontracting the delivery of fuel loads.

In *Naperville Ready Mix, Inc. v. NLRB*,[142] the Seventh Circuit enforced the Board's order compelling reinstatement of truck drivers and restoration of bargaining-unit work following an employer's sale

[137]Regal Cinemas, Inc., 334 NLRB 304, 167 LRRM 1347 (2001), *enforced*, 317 F.3d 300, 171 LRRM 2944 (D.C. Cir. 2003). *See* Main Edition, Chapter 16, at page 1239.

[138]332 NLRB 943, 170 LRRM 1190 (2000), *enforced*, 294 F.3d 768, 170 LRRM 2401 (6th Cir. 2002).

[139]294 F.3d at 790.

[140]338 NLRB 489, 171 LRRM 1117 (2002).

[141]243 NLRB 972, 974 n.9, 101 LRRM 1543, 1536 n.9 (1979).

[142]242 F.3d 744, 166 LRRM 2712 (7th Cir.), *cert. denied*, 534 U.S. 1040 (2001).

of its trucks to nonbargaining-unit independent contractors. According to the Board and the court, a company cannot, consistent with the labor laws, shift unit work to subcontractors in order to save on labor costs without first bargaining in good faith to impasse. Neither the Board nor the court was persuaded by the employer's argument that the sale was lawful because the trucks were legally transferred to independent contractors and therefore the sale was not a "sham." Applying *Fibreboard*[143] principles, the court held that the employer violated Section 8(a)(5) by failing to bargain over the decision prior to implementing the sale.

In contrast, however, in *Lenz & Riecker*,[144] the Board held that the employer did not violate Section 8(a)(5) by subcontracting bargaining-unit work and laying off all employees without bargaining with the union, since the employer was in bankruptcy and attempting to liquidate, and the employer had notified the union and explicitly offered to bargain over the effects of the decision to liquidate. The Board found the union had waived its right to bargain by failing to respond to the employer's offer and request bargaining.[145] Therefore, the employer's agreement not to lay off employees as a "primary and direct result of subcontracting" did not excuse the union's inaction.

(d) Effects of the Decision to Subcontract or Transfer Work. In *Komatsu America Corp.*,[146] the Board held that the employer engaged in meaningful effects bargaining with the union over severance benefits for machine shop employees impacted by the decision to outsource work to Japan.

(e) Relocation of Unit Work. In *AT&T Corp.*,[147] the employer did not violate Section 8(a)(5) by failing to bargain in good faith with the union over its decision to close its Tucson facility, lay off the employees and reassign the work elsewhere. Upon notification by the employer of its decision, union officials discussed the matter with the employer during a conference call, at the end of which the union stated its disagreement with the decision, indicating that it planned

---

[143]Fibreboard Paper Prods. Corp. v. NLRB, 379 U.S. 203, 57 LRRM 2609 (1964).

[144]340 NLRB No. 21, 173 LRRM 1321 (2003).

[145]*Id. See also* Ingham Reg'l Med. Ctr., 342 NLRB No. 129, 175 LRRM 1511 (2004) (employer did not violate §8(a)(5) in subcontracting unit work; under either "clear and unmistakable" waiver standard or under "contract coverage" analysis, union had waived its right to bargain about the decision to subcontract).

[146]342 NLRB No. 62, 175 LRRM 1209 (2004).

[147]337 NLRB 689, 170 LRRM 1153 (2002).

to take up the matter at a different management level. However, the union failed to contest the closure further, instead filing unfair labor practice charges.

The Board found that the parties' contract spelled out a procedure (which had often been used by the parties) governing negotiations over reductions in force, and further found that the union failed to pursue its opportunities under the contract by demanding bargaining over the issue. Declining to decide whether the employer's bargaining obligation arose from the contract or from the Act, the Board held that the union did not exercise due diligence in continuing its bargaining demand. The Board decided that under these circumstances, the employer did not violate Section 8(a)(5).

In *Stevens International, Inc.*,[148] the Board held that the employer's assignment of bargaining-unit work to nonunit supervisors without giving the union an opportunity to bargain over the decision violated Section 8(a)(5) of the Act. In so deciding, the Board rejected the employer's reliance upon its right to assign work as set forth in the management-rights clause, concluding that the contractual language provided for the assignment of work to "employees," and supervisors were excluded from the definition of employees elsewhere in the agreement.[149]

In an analogous case, *St. George Warehouse, Inc.*,[150] the Board held that the employer violated Section 8(a)(5) of the Act by its unilateral transfer of bargaining unit work to temporary agency workers. Prior to the union election, the employer had used a fluctuating number of temporary employees to supplement its workforce. After the election, the employer stopped hiring or replacing permanent employees and instead utilized more temporary agency workers, decreasing the bargaining unit from 42 to 8. In its defense, the employer cited its previous temporary hiring practices. The ALJ, however, compared the situation to *Regal Cinemas, Inc.*,[151] wherein the Board held that the transfer of bargaining unit work to supervisors (who were excluded from the unit) is a mandatory subject of bargaining where the transfer has an impact on unit work. Similarly in *St. George Warehouse, Inc.*, the employer's transfer of unit work to

---

[148]337 NLRB 143, 172 LRRM 1396 (2001).

[149]*See also* Regal Cinemas, Inc., 334 NLRB 304, 167 LRRM 1347 (2001), *enforced*, 317 F.3d 300, 171 LRRM 2944 (D.C. Cir. 2003).

[150]341 NLRB No. 120, 175 LRRM 1316 (2004).

[151]*See supra* note 149.

nonunit temporary employees resulted in the removal of work from the bargaining unit, ultimately diluting the strength of and possibly eliminating the unit.[152] Thus, the employer's failure to bargain over the decision to transfer unit work to agency employees violated the Act.

In a different context, the Board, in *Contech Division SPX Corp.*,[153] found that an employer violated Section 8(a)(5) by failing to give the union notice and opportunity to bargain over its decision (and the effects of the decision on unit employees) to suspend operations at one of its plants and to lay off employees. Citing its decision in *Westinghouse Electric Corp.*,[154] the Board held that the employer's decision to consolidate its facilities and to perform the work with fewer employees involved no change in the scope and direction of its core business; accordingly, the employer was not free to implement the decision unilaterally.[155]

Similarly, in *Vico Products Co. v. NLRB*,[156] the District of Columbia Circuit enforced the Board's order compelling relocation of heavy equipment and restoration of bargaining-unit work to the original facility. Shortly after the election and certification of a union, and a request by the union to begin collective bargaining, the employer promptly removed considerable heavy machinery from its existing facility for transport to a newly purchased facility in another state over the July 4 holiday, and informed 33 unit employees that they were being laid off due to a transfer of work to the out-of-state facility. Just weeks earlier, the employer had informed union representatives that there was no such job transfer plan in place, amid discussions of an understanding that if plans to remove unit work were considered in the future, the union had a right to notice and the opportunity to bargain. The timing of the employer's leaving for the out-of-state facility in relation to the union's certification, combined with evidence that a manager had stated prior to the union's certification that people could be "laid off" if the union "gets in here,"

---

[152] *See supra* note 150; *see also* Lexus of Concord, Inc., 343 NLRB No. 94, 176 LRRM 1284 (2004) (transfer of work from higher-paid unit employees to lower-paid unit employees was a mandatory subject of bargaining).

[153] 333 NLRB 875, 169 LRRM 1349 (2001), *vacated and remanded*, 337 NLRB 439, 169 LRRM 1361 (2002).

[154] 313 NLRB 452, 145 LRRM 1033 (1993), *enforced*, 46 F.3d 1126 (4th Cir.), *cert. denied*, 514 U.S. 1037 (1995).

[155] The case was subsequently dismissed following a non-Board resolution by the parties.

[156] 333 F.3d 198, 172 LRRM 2903 (D.C. Cir. 2003).

contributed not only to the finding that the employer violated Section 8(a)(5), but also the justification for the remedial order of restoration of bargaining-unit work, and reinstallation of all machinery removed from the facility.[157]

(2) Partial Closure, Sale, or Merger of Business, or Plant Relocation

The Board found an employer's argument unpersuasive that closure of a facility was motivated by production and scheduling problems exacerbated by the collective bargaining agreement because the employer had failed to seek relief from the union before closing the facility. Earlier threats of closure were sufficient to establish antiunion animus in the decision to subcontract work.[158]

In *Dorsey Trailers v. NLRB,*[159] the Fourth Circuit, citing *First National Maintenance*[160] and *Arrow Automotive Industries v. NLRB,*[161] held that a decision to relocate a plant was a business decision, not a "term or condition of employment," and thus not a mandatory subject of bargaining. As a consequence, the Fourth Circuit held that the Board erred when it ordered the employer, which had transferred work to a new plant following the union's strike, to transfer work back to the original plant. The court also held that a restoration order exceeded the Board's authority, because closure of the employer's facility did not evidence discriminatory animus by the employer. According to the court, the union could protect its members' interests through bargaining over the effects of a decision to relocate work, which is a mandatory subject of bargaining.

The Board held in *Gannett Co.*[162] that an employer's news release announcing an agreement for sale of a radio station subject to

---

[157]*Id. See also* Sociedad Española de Auxilio Mutuo y Beneficencia de P.R., 342 NLRB No. 40, 175 LRRM 1161 (2004) (in post-election setting, employer found to have violated §8(a)(5) by subcontracting bargaining unit work during pendency of election objections, since neither a change in the scope and direction of the enterprise nor any compelling economic reasons existed to justify such unilateral changes).

[158]Westchester Lace, Inc., 326 NLRB 1227, 163 LRRM 1181 (1998). *See also* Phargo, LLC, 340 NLRB No. 80, 174 LRRM 1423 (2003) (where evidence showed that decision to subcontract work was direct result of discriminatory decision to close); Vico Prods. Co., v. NLRB, 333 F.3d 198, 210–11, 172 LRRM 2903 (D.C. Cir. 2003) (decision to move production unit without notice and opportunity to bargain was motivated by animus).

[159]233 F.3d 831, 165 LRRM 3003 (4th Cir. 2000).

[160]452 U.S. 666, 107 LRRM 2705 (1981).

[161]853 F.2d 223, 128 LRRM 3137 (4th Cir. 1988).

[162]333 NLRB 355, 168 LRRM 1418 (2001).

FCC approval was insufficient notice to allow the union a meaningful opportunity to bargain about the effects of the sale. The employer was ordered to bargain with the union, on request, about the effects of the sale. As an additional remedy, the Board ordered that bargaining-unit employees receive limited back pay from their last date of employment, plus interest, until an agreement was reached, a bona fide impasse occurred, the union failed to request bargaining, or the union failed to bargain in good faith, whichever occurred first. The Board also ordered that all employees would receive at least two weeks' back pay in any event.

In *Automatic Sprinkler Corp. of America v. NLRB*, the Sixth Circuit held that the employer's exercise of its contractual right to subcontract did not constitute an unfair labor practice.[163] However, the Board and two courts of appeals have since rejected the Sixth Circuit's holding.[164] Instead of following the *Automatic Sprinkler* rule, these decisions adhere to the general principle that a party cannot exercise its contractual rights to punish employees for protected activity or in any manner that violates the Act.

n. Successorship and "Application of Contract" Clauses

In *Pall Biomedical Products Corp.*,[165] the Board held that a letter of agreement between the union and the employer providing that the employer would recognize the union at a designated new facility if it employed "one or more employees performing bargaining unit work" was valid, and a mandatory subject of bargaining. Relying on *Kroger Co.*,[166] and distinguishing *Lone Star Steel*,[167] the Board found that the clause at issue was more limited in scope than the "application-of-

---

[163]120 F.3d 612, 620, 155 LRRM 2897 (6th Cir. 1997), *cert. denied*, 523 U.S. 1106 (1998).

[164]Reno Hilton Resorts v. NLRB, 196 F.3d 1275, 162 LRRM 2961 (D.C. Cir. 1999) (specifically rejecting *Automatic Sprinkler's* holding and criticizing the Sixth Circuit's failure to take into account the employer's antiunion animus in assessing the lawfulness of the employer's decision to subcontract work); RGC (USA) Mineral Sands, Inc. v. NLRB, 281 F.3d 442, 169 LRRM 2633 (4th Cir. 2002) (same).

[165]331 NLRB 1674, 165 LRRM 1137 (2000), *enforcement denied*, 275 F.3d 116, 169 LRRM 2065 (D.C. Cir. 2002). *See* discussion of this case in the context of the "vitally affects" test for determining whether a subject of bargaining is mandatory, at Section III.B. [Development of the Distinction Between "Mandatory" and "Permissive;" *Pittsburgh Plate Glass*—The "Vitally Affects" Test], *supra*.

[166]219 NLRB 388, 89 LRRM 1641 (1975) (collective bargaining clause that required employer to recognize union in any newly acquired store held valid by Board where application of clause depended on union's majority status).

[167]Mine Workers (Lone Star Steel Co.), 231 NLRB 573, 96 LRRM 1083 (1977), *enforcement granted in part, denied in part, and remanded*, 639 F.2d 545, 104 LRRM 3144 (10th Cir. 1980), *cert. denied*, 450 U.S. 911, 106 LRRM 2513 (1981).

contract" clause at issue in *Lone Star Steel*, because it specifically pertained to bargaining-unit work at only one other facility in the same geographical area. In addition, the agreement was directed at the concerns of the unit employees and "vitally affect[ed]" the terms and conditions of their employment. The record showed that just before the letter of agreement, the union went on strike over the issue of bargaining-unit work being transferred to the other facility, and that strike did not end until the employer executed the letter of agreement.

The Board's holding was rejected, however, in *Pall Corp. v. NLRB*,[168] when the D.C. Circuit denied enforcement of the Board's order. Stating that the Board's decision was inconsistent with Supreme Court authority,[169] the court disagreed with the Board's holding that the letter of agreement "vitally affected" the terms and conditions of existing unit employees because prescribing a manner of recognition at a new facility is not a "direct frontal attack" upon the transfer of work facing employees at already organized facilities. Accordingly, the court held that the letter of agreement did not concern a mandatory subject of bargaining. The court suggested, however, that had the letter of agreement provided for the automatic extension of the existing collective bargaining agreement to employees at the new facility, the Board would have been justified in its holding that the letter of agreement concerned a mandatory subject of bargaining.

A successorship clause providing that the employer will not sell its operations without first securing the successor's agreement to assume the employer's contractual obligations to the union under the collective bargaining agreement has no effect where the employer sells operations that had previously been closed for legitimate economic reasons.[170]

o. Arrangements and Conditions for Negotiations

In *People Care, Inc.*,[171] the Board held that an employer's insistence on bargaining at evening sessions only was not a violation of Sections 8(a)(1) and (5) because the employer had a legitimate claim

[168]275 F.3d 116, 169 LRRM 2065 (D.C. Cir. 2002).

[169]Teamsters Local 24 v. Oliver, 358 U.S. 283, 43 LRRM 2374 (1959); Allied Chem. & Alkali Workers Local 1 v. Pittsburgh Plate Glass Co., 404 U.S. 157, 185–88, 78 LRRM 2974 (1971).

[170]Mine Workers v. Apogee Coal Co., 330 F.3d 740, 172 LRRM 2695 (6th Cir. 2003) (relying upon the clear and unambiguous meaning of "operations" in a successorship clause as connoting "activity" and the complete lack of any evidence of bad faith in closing the mines).

[171]327 NLRB 814, 167 LRRM 1095 (1999).

that health care aide employees needed to remain on case assignments and not be replaced in order to attend bargaining sessions.

V. PERMISSIVE SUBJECTS OF BARGAINING

A. In General

The Board and the courts continue to hold that neither the employer nor the union can bargain to impasse on a permissive subject of bargaining. In *Connecticut State Conference Board,* the Board emphasized that "the insistence to impasse upon the inclusion of a permissive subject violates the Act."[172] The Board rejected the union's position that the employer violated the Act by insisting on the exclusion of a permissive interest arbitration provision that was already in the parties' collective bargaining agreement, reasoning that the union was also insisting on the inclusion of a permissive subject of bargaining. In *Midwest Television, Inc.*,[173] the Board made clear that parties to a collective bargaining agreement can unilaterally rescind permissive terms of the collective bargaining agreement at any time, before or after its expiration, without violating the Act. In *Pleasantview Nursing Home, Inc. v. NLRB,*[174] the Sixth Circuit, citing *Nordstrom, Inc.*,[175] refused to enforce the portion of the Board's order that held the employer violated the Act by linking its acceptance of the union's security clause to the union's agreement that it would not charge employees initiation fees. The court held there was an economic justification for the linkage, as the fee deduction would reduce net wages received and therefore could affect the employer's ability to recruit and hire employees. Where a party links a mandatory and a permissive subject in a proposal, the Board continues to permit the withdrawal or modification of the mandatory subject if the permissive subject is rejected.[176]

---

[172]339 NLRB 760, 173 LRRM 1574 (2003), citing Sheet Metal Workers, Local 38, 231 NLRB 699, 96 LRRM 1190 (1977).

[173]Midwest Television, Inc. dba KFMB Stations, 343 NLRB No. 83 (2004) (no violation where employer reduced employee's wages to contract scale after exercising contract right to set higher wages).

[174]351 F.3d 747, 759–61, 173 LRRM 2882, 2891–93 (6th Cir. 2003).

[175]229 NLRB 601, 96 LRRM 1092 (1977).

[176]Dependable Storage, Inc., 328 NLRB 44, 164 LRRM 1286 (1999).

The Board also continues to follow the rule that a party may not conclude negotiations by agreeing only to the proposals of the other party that constitute mandatory subjects of bargaining.[177] In addition, where the employer was found not to have bargained in good faith because it impermissibly insisted to impasse on a permissive subject, the Board ordered the withdrawal of the permissive proposal and the resumption of bargaining as a remedy.[178]

B. Specific Subjects

1. *Definition of Bargaining Unit*

Once a specific job has been included within the scope of the unit by either Board action or the consent of the parties, the employer cannot remove the position without first securing the consent of the union or the Board.[179] A proposal to transfer bargaining-unit employees outside the bargaining unit remains a permissive subject of bargaining.[180] However, a decision to transfer bargaining-unit work to managers or supervisors is a mandatory subject of bargaining where it has an impact on unit work.[181]

In *Steelworkers Local 7912 (U.S. Tsubaki, Inc.)*,[182] the union violated Section 8(b)(3) by refusing to bargain separately on behalf of employees of a unit that had been relocated to a facility where the parties had an established bargaining relationship. Complicating matters was the fact that the region agreed with the union that there was one bargaining unit at the facility. The employer bargained on that basis until the Board granted its request for review.[183] In *Des Moines Mailers Union v. NLRB*,[184] the court upheld the Board's deci-

---

[177]California Pie Co., 329 NLRB 968, 162 LRRM 1390 (1999).

[178]*Id.*

[179]Public Serv. Co. of New Mex., 337 NLRB 193, 172 LRRM 1508 (2001). See Main Edition, Chapter 16, at page 1257.

[180]California Portland Cement, 330 NLRB 144, 169 LRRM 1287 (1999), *enforced*, 19 Fed. Appx. 683 (9th Cir. 2001); Dunbar *ex rel.* NLRB v. Carrier Corp., 66 F. Supp. 2d 346, 161 LRRM 2119 (N.D.N.Y. 1999).

[181]Regal Cinemas, Inc., 334 NLRB 304, 167 LRRM 1347 (2001), *enforced*, 317 F.3d 300, 171 LRRM 2944 (D.C. Cir. 2003); *see also* St. George Warehouse, Inc., 341 NLRB No. 120, 175 LRRM 1316 (2004).

[182]338 NLRB 29, 170 LRRM 1473 (2002).

[183]Request for review was granted in *U.S. Tsubaki, Inc.*, 331 NLRB 327, 164 LRRM 1201 (2000).

[184]381 F.3d 767 (8th Cir. 2004), *denying review of* Des Moines Register & Tribune Co., 339 NLRB 1035, 173 LRRM 1480 (2003).

sion that the number of full-time journeymen positions was a mandatory subject of bargaining because the number of positions guaranteed after the collective bargaining agreement's expiration was unresolved by that agreement. In doing so the court agreed with the Board that the contractual provision was ambiguous as to whether the parties intended that it survive the contract's expiration.

An employer may not insist to impasse on a clause in the collective bargaining agreement denying employee status to certain bargaining-unit members because it is a permissive subject of bargaining.[185] For like reasons, the Board found that an employer's insistence to impasse on changing the scope of the bargaining unit by expanding the definition of excluded part-time employees evidenced bad faith bargaining.[186] In another decision, the D.C. Circuit enforced the Board's ruling that the implementation after impasse of a proposal to change the union's work jurisdiction was lawful.[187]

3. *Selection of Bargaining Representative*

The Board continues to hold that selection of bargaining representatives is a permissive subject of bargaining.[188] A proposal for a "most favored nations clause," including not only the local union that was the certified bargaining representative but also the local's international union and any affiliated local unions in a four-state area, constituted an unlawful subject of bargaining because it sought to sweep away basic safeguards provided to employees under the Act concerning the selection of their representatives for the purposes of collective bargaining.[189] The Board indicated that this clause was unlawful because it could subject the employees' terms and conditions of employment to the unrelated bargaining result of entities (parent and sister locals) that the employees had not selected as their bargaining representatives.

---

[185]Reading Rock, 330 NLRB 856, 164 LRRM 1325 (2000).

[186]Grosvenor Orlando Assocs., Ltd., 336 NLRB 613, 172 LRRM 1253 (2001).

[187]Detroit Typographical Union v. NLRB, 216 F.3d 109, 164 LRRM 2797 (D.C. Cir.), *enforcing in relevant part* 326 NLRB 700, 159 LRRM 1065 (2000).

[188]Teamsters Local 662, 339 NLRB 893, 173 LRRM 1575 (2003), *enforced*, 368 F.3d 741, 174 LRRM 3060 (7th Cir. 2004) (union violated §8(b)(3) by its refusal to sign a collective bargaining agreement embodying its agreement that, in exchange for the employer's reinstatement of four additional strikers, the union's bargaining committee would resign from the committee and never again run for or hold any bargaining unit positions).

[189]California Pie Co., 329 NLRB 968, 162 LRRM 1390 (1999).

A union's insistence that an employer accept a contract containing the same terms as the union has previously negotiated with a multi-employer association is not tantamount to forcing the employer to make the multi-employer association its bargaining representative.[190] Section 8(b)(1)(B) is not violated unless the union's bargaining is directed at forcing the employer to accept *future* agreements with a multi-employer association.[191]

5. *Performance Bonds, Indemnifications, and Legal Liability Clauses*

In *Regal Cinemas, Inc.*,[192] the Board held that a proposal linking the payment of severance to signing a release of claims relating to termination of employment is a mandatory subject of bargaining. The Board distinguished its earlier holding in *Borden, Inc.*,[193] where the Board found that a proposal for a general release of all claims was permissive. Unlike a proposal for a general release, a proposal making severance a quid pro quo for a release of claims arising from the termination focuses on the effects of the termination, permitting honest and effective bargaining over the terms on which the employment relation will be ended.

7. *Interest Arbitration and Bi-Level Bargaining*

The Board and the courts continue to hold that interest arbitration is a permissive subject of bargaining.[194] Courts continue to hold

---

[190]Teamsters Local 282 (E.G. Clemente Contracting Corp.), 335 NLRB 1253, 168 LRRM 1185 (2001).

[191]Teamsters Local 705 (Kankakee-Iroquois), 274 NLRB 1176, 118 LRRM 1497 (1985), *petition for review denied sub nom.* Kankakee-Iroquois County Employers Ass'n v. NLRB, 825 F.2d 1091, 125 LRRM 2820 (7th Cir. 1987). *See also* Teamsters Local 282, 335 NLRB 1253, 168 LRRM 1185 (2001).

[192]334 NLRB 304, 167 LRRM 1347 (2001), *enforced*, 317 F.3d 300, 171 LRRM 2944 (D.C. Cir. 2003).

[193]279 NLRB 396, 123 LRRM 1239 (1986).

[194]Electrical Workers (IBEW) Local 898 v. XL Elec., Inc., 380 F.3d 868, 871, 175 LRRM 2449 (5th Cir. 2004); Longshoremen (ILA) Local 1575 (Navieras, NPR, Inc.), 332 NLRB 1336, 165 LRRM 1377 (2000); Hope Elec. Corp., 339 NLRB 933, 172 LRRM 1466 (2003); *In re* Connecticut State Conference Bd., 339 NLRB 760, 173 LRRM 1574, 1574–75 (2003) (union violated §8(b)(3) when it insisted to impasse on interest-arbitration clause in collective bargaining agreement); Sheet Metal Workers Local 24 v. Architectural Metal Works, Inc., 259 F.3d 418, 167 LRRM 2641 (6th Cir. 2001) (interest-arbitration clause may not be included over other party's objection); Electrical Workers (IBEW) Local 666 v. Stokes Elec. Serv., Inc., 225 F.3d 415, 422, 164 LRRM 3089 (4th Cir. 2000) ("Because interest arbitration is not a mandatory subject of bargaining, a dispute about the enforceability of an inter-

that a party may not use an existing interest-arbitration clause to perpetuate that clause.[195]

In *ServiceNet, Inc.*,[196] the Board considered the legality of an evergreen clause proposed by the employer that required adherence to the contract, including any no-strike and no-lockout undertakings, after it expired and while negotiations for a new agreement were ongoing. The Board concluded that there was nothing illegal about a clause where the parties voluntarily forego their respective rights to take economic action in support of their bargaining positions.[197] The Board further concluded, however, that the evergreen clause proposed by the employer was a permissive subject of bargaining since the Board analogized the evergreen clause to an interest arbitration clause, which it has determined to be a permissive subject of bargaining.[198]

8. *Internal Union Affairs*

The Board[199] and the courts continue to follow the rule that procedures relating to adoption, ratification, or acceptance of a col-

---

est arbitration clause is 'primarily contractual.'"); Summa Health Sys., Inc. (State, County & Mun. Employees Local 684), 330 NLRB 1379, 170 LRRM 1308 (2000); *see also* ServiceNet, Inc., 340 NLRB No. 148, 173 LRRM 1553, 1556 (2003).

[195]Electrical Workers (IBEW) Local 545 v. Hope Elec. Corp., 380 F.3d 1084, 1089 n.3, 175 LRRM 2641, 2646 ("[T]his [c]ourt has determined that interest arbitration clauses are not enforceable to 'perpetuate the inclusion of the [clause] in successive bargaining agreements.'") (citations omitted), *reh'g denied, en banc* (8th Cir. 2004); *XL Elec., Inc., supra* note 194 (where the collective bargaining agreement only allowed for interest arbitration while the agreement was effective, plaintiff union could not submit issues for interest arbitration once the agreement had expired); Mulvaney Mech., Inc. v. Sheet Metal Workers Local 38, 288 F.3d 491, 169 LRRM 3089 (2d Cir.), *vacated*, 538 U.S. 918, 172 LRRM 2128, *reh'g denied*, 123 S. Ct. 2125, *aff'd on remand*, 351 F.3d 43, 173 LRRM 2560 (2d Cir. 2003).

[196]340 NLRB No. 148, 173 LRRM 1553 (2003).

[197]*Id.*

[198]*Id.*

[199]*ServiceNet, Inc., supra* note 196, 173 LRRM at 1555 (2003) (employer violated §8(a)(5) when it insisted to impasse on health insurance clause that required committee of five bargaining unit members to meet with employer prior to any changes in group plan; the clause was a nonmandatory subject of bargaining because it allowed employer to circumvent union and deal directly with employees over term and condition of employment); Jano Graphics, Inc., 339 NLRB 251, 172 LRRM 1292 (2003) (holding that Board need not decide whether there was impasse where any impasse was tainted by, inter alia, employer's continued insistence on ratification vote by unit members, which is nonmandatory subject of bargaining); Longshoremen (ILA) Local 1575 (Navieras, NPR, Inc.), 332 NLRB 1336, 165 LRRM 1377 (2000) ("Employee ratification is . . . a permissive subject of bargain-

lective bargaining agreement are permissive subjects of bargaining.[200] The Board continues to hold that union dues, even in the context of a union-security clause, is not a mandatory subject.[201]

12. *Settlement of Unfair Labor Practice Charges*

The Board continues to hold that an employer may not condition bargaining on the withdrawal of unfair labor practice charges or other litigation.[202]

13. *Tape Recordings, Stenographers, and Other Technical Preconditions on the Bargaining Process*

The Board continues to hold that a party cannot insist upon the continuation of a past practice of recording grievance sessions.[203]

14. *Miscellaneous*

In a novel decision involving personal service contracts for television personalities, the Board found that an employer may lawfully

---

ing, and an employer may not insist that the collective bargaining agreement be ratified as a condition of signing the agreement."). *But see* 2004 WL 1910034 (N.L.R.B.G.C.), Case No. 6-CA-33919 (June 28, 2004) (noting that ratification agreements, although permissive subjects of bargaining, "are enforceable if agreed upon by both parties"); Hertz Corp., 304 NLRB 469, 138 LRRM 1383 (1991) (Board held that employer is not bound to a collective bargaining agreement where the parties had expressly made employee ratification a condition precedent to the implementation of the agreement).

[200]Pleasantview Nursing Home v. NLRB, 351 F.3d 747, 173 LRRM 2882, 2891–93 (6th Cir. 2003) (holding that employer did not violate §8(a)(5) when it insisted to impasse upon proposal to eliminate requirement that it remit employee initiation fees to union, which was a permissive subject of bargaining, where the employer linked that requirement with a mandatory subject of bargaining); NLRB v. Concordia Elec. Coop., Inc., 163 LRRM 2300, 2320 (5th Cir. 1999) (employer unlawfully insisted that union follow particular ratification process, a permissive subject of bargaining.)

[201]Pleasantview Nursing Home, Inc. & Textile Processors Local 1, 335 NLRB 77, 168 LRRM 1195 (2001), (Board found violation of §8(a)(5) where employer bargained to impasse proposal to eliminate initiation fees in connection to union-security clause), *enforcement denied in relevant part*, 351 F.3d 747, 173 LRRM 2882 (6th Cir. 2003).

[202]Bryant & Stratton Bus. Inst., 327 NLRB 1135, 166 LRRM 1257 (1999).

[203]Food & Commercial Workers Local 342-50, 339 NLRB 148, 172 LRRM 1318 (2003) (union's insistence that employer tape record informational meetings between management and employees was not an unlawful refusal to bargain because the meetings were not for the purpose of collective bargaining).

insist to impasse on a permissive subject of bargaining where the union seeks a permissive clause on the same subject.[204]

An employer's proposal of "personal service contracts" to be negotiated directly with current and prospective employees is permissive rather than mandatory and may not be implemented on impasse.[205] Similarly, in *ServiceNet, Inc.*,[206] the Board held that the employer had illegally bargained to impasse as to a permissive subject, namely, a clause regarding the company's health insurance plan which would allow the employer to negotiate directly with employees rather than the union on a term or condition of employment, thus diminishing the role of the union. The Board found the clause to be permissive and not mandatory because "it affected the right to bargain over the health benefits plan and not the plan itself."[207]

VI. ILLEGAL SUBJECTS OF BARGAINING

B. Specific Illegal Subjects

The Board, consistent with its holding in *Carpenters District Council of Northeast Ohio (Alessio Construction)*,[208] continues to scrutinize contract clauses that fall within the literal proscription of Section 8(e) under a two-step analysis, including: (1) whether the clause is secondary in nature or has the primary objective of preserving bargaining-unit work for the employees of the signatory employer;[209] and (2) whether the clause has a secondary purpose and is saved from illegality by the construction industry proviso.[210] In *Southwestern Materials*, the Board considered two separate contractual provisions and determined that both had secondary objectives.[211] With respect to the first provision—a cease-doing-business clause—the Board found that it was not sheltered by the construction industry proviso be-

---

[204]Midwest Television, Inc., 343 NLRB No. 83 (2004) (employer had insisted on retaining the right to deal directly with unit employees to pay above-scale wages; the union sought to restrict that right as it applied to new employees).

[205]Retlaw Broad Co. v. NLRB, 172 F.3d 660, 160 LRRM 2909 (9th Cir. 1999), *enforcing* 324 NLRB 138, 158 LRRM 1135 (1997).

[206]340 NLRB No. 148, 173 LRRM 1553 (2003).

[207]*Id.*, slip. op. at 2.

[208]310 NLRB 1023, 143 LRRM 1049 (1993).

[209]29 U.S.C. §158(e).

[210]Iron Workers (Southwestern Materials & Supply), 328 NLRB 934, 161 LRRM 1258 (1999).

[211]*Id.* at 936, 161 LRRM at 1261–62.

cause it fell outside the "categories of secondary activity that Congress intended to be tolerated in the construction industry."[212] The second provision was found to be lawful under Section 8(e) pursuant to the construction industry proviso because there was no evidence that the clause was intended to be applied to work other than at a construction site.[213]

The Board continues to find unlawful union-security clauses obligating an employer to hire only union members and to obtain approval from the union even for employees hired without the union's assistance.[214] However, an employer who had orally agreed to the entire contract, including the unlawful provision, may not refuse to execute the contract where the employer's refusal to sign the contract is motivated by reasons other than the presence of the unlawful provision.[215]

In *Oxy USA, Inc.*,[216] the Board found that the employer's proposal that the union replace the employer as sole sponsor and administrator of the health insurance plan covering unit employees did not contemplate payments to the union and therefore did not violate Section 302(a) of the Labor-Management Relations Act.[217] Accordingly, the employer's insistence to impasse on this bargaining proposal was not a violation of Section 8(a)(5).

In *California Pie Co.*,[218] the Board considered the legality of a "most favored nations" clause insisted on by the employer. Not only would the clause have applied to contracts entered into by the local union, but it would have also applied to contracts entered into by the international union and sister locals in four specified states.[219] The Board concluded that such a clause was illegal because it seeks to substantially alter the character of exclusive representation provided for in Section 9 of the Act.

---

[212]*Id. See also* Operating Eng'rs Local 520 (Massman Constr. Co.), 327 NLRB 1257, 161 LRRM 1001 (1999) (Board found no evidence that joint venture clauses, unlike subcontracting agreements of sort previously found lawful by Board, were part of the pattern of bargaining in construction industry at time of proviso's enactment in 1959).

[213]*Southwestern Materials, supra* note 210.

[214]Flying Dutchman Park, Inc., 329 NLRB 414, 162 LRRM 1283 (1999).

[215]*Id.*

[216]329 NLRB 208, 162 LRRM 1113 (1999).

[217]29 U.S.C. §186(a).

[218]329 NLRB 968, 162 LRRM 1390 (1999).

[219]*Id.* at 974, 162 LRRM at 1391.

In *South Jersey Regional Council of Carpenters (Atlantic Exposition Services)*,[220] the Board considered whether the construction industry proviso covered work that was not performed on an actual construction site. The Board found that parties' union signatory subcontracting agreement was unlawful and secondary in nature, and was not saved from illegality by the construction industry proviso because the work involved—installation, assembly and dismantling of temporary exhibits at trade shows—was not performed on a construction site.

In *Central Pennsylvania Regional Council of Carpenters (Novinger's)*,[221] the Board prohibited the union from enforcing an anti-dual shop provision. The Board ruled that the cease-doing-business clause was invalid on its face because it extended beyond the work historically performed by the employees and was not restricted by its terms to apply only to those entities over which the employer had the right of control and instead applied broadly to all subsidiaries or joint ventures.

In *NLRB v. Service Employees Local 32B-32J*,[222] the Second Circuit denied enforcement of the Board's order[223] and determined that a picket-line clause did not constitute an illegal hot cargo provision. The clause in question provided that no employee would be required to pass picket lines established by any SEIU local union in an authorized strike. The court held that the picket-line clause was limited to those strikes "authorized" by law, as opposed to those strikes authorized by the union.[224] Thus, the clause was limited to lawful primary activity and did not extend to unlawful secondary activity.

In *Super Fresh Food Markets v. Food & Commercial Workers Local 1776*,[225] an employer sought to vacate an arbitration award entered against it based on a clause that required the employer to condition

---

[220]335 NLRB 586, 171 LRRM 1422 (2001), *enforced*, 320 F.3d 385, 171 LRRM 3057 (3d Cir. 2003).

[221]337 NLRB 1030, 171 LRRM 1230 (2002), *enforced*, 352 F.3d 831 (3d Cir. 2003). *See also* South Jersey Reg'l Council of Carpenters, 335 NLRB 586, 171 LRRM 1422 (2001), *enforced sub nom.* Spectacor Mgmt. Group v. NLRB, 320 F.3d 385 (3d Cir. 2003) (finding unlawful an agreement which precluded the employer from subcontracting trade show work to employers who did not have collective bargaining agreements with the union because the agreement lacked a work-preservation objective and the work covered was not performed on a construction site).

[222]353 F.3d 197, 173 LRRM 3007 (2d Cir. 2003).

[223]337 NLRB 317, 169 LRRM 1185 (2001).

[224]353 F.3d at 202, 173 LRRM 3007.

[225]249 F. Supp. 2d 546, 171 LRRM 3153 (E.D. Pa. 2003).

the sale of its business on the successor employer's assumption of the obligations of the collective bargaining agreement. The controversy arose after the employer attempted to sell its business in contravention of such provision. The union thereafter obtained an arbitration award in its favor. In federal court, the employer argued that the arbitration award should be vacated because the provision violated Section 8(e). The federal district court concluded that the clause did not violate Section 8(e) because the transfer of the employer's business did not constitute "doing business" within the meaning of Section 8(e) and because the union's objective in negotiating such a clause was to preserve the work of the employer's employees.[226]

In *Machinists Lodge 964 v. BF Goodrich Aerospace*,[227] an employer appealed a district court decision affirming an arbitral award based on a collective bargaining agreement provision requiring the employer to compensate fully a full-time union steward who investigated and filed grievances on behalf of employees and who participated in grievance meetings with management, but who performed no production work. The employer contended that the provision violated Section 302(a)(1) of the Act, which renders it illegal for an employer to "agree to pay, lend, or deliver, any money or other thing of value . . . to any representative of any of his employees who are employed in an industry affecting commerce." The court found that Section 302(a)(1)'s proscription against corporate payments to union representatives unambiguously applied to the provision. Nevertheless, the court went on to hold the provision enforceable. Despite the employer's contention that the union steward works solely for the union's benefit, the court held that the union steward was the employer's "employee" within the meaning of Section 302(c)(1) and, therefore, did not fall within Section 302(a)(1)'s proscription.

In *Food & Commercial Workers Local 464A v. Foodtown, Inc.*,[228] the union sought to compel arbitration regarding a dispute that arose when the employer licensed its name and trademark to three nonunion stores. The parties' collective bargaining agreement recognized the union as the exclusive representative of employees in "all present and future stores of the employer" within the union's jurisdiction. The employer argued that the grievance was illegal because the union sought to have an arbitrator order a cessation of business

[226]*Id.* at 554, 171 LRRM at 3158–61.
[227]387 F.3d 1046, 175 LRRM 3185 (9th Cir. 2004).
[228]317 F. Supp. 2d 522, 174 LRRM 3303 (D.N.J. 2004).

with the nonunion operator, which would violate Section 8(e) of the Act. However, the federal district court concluded that the union only sought to preserve its contractual right to identify all the employer's stores within its jurisdiction as union stores, and it did not seek to prevent all or any business dealings with the nonunion operator.[229] Thus, the grievance was not illegal.

---

[229] *Id.* at 529, 174 LRRM at 3308.

Part V

ARBITRATION AND THE ACT

BIBLIOGRAPHY

R. Bales, *A New Direction for American Labor Law: Individual Autonomy and the Compulsory Arbitration of Individual Employment Rights*, 30 HOUS. L. REV. 1863 (1994)

Sarah Rudolph Cole, *A Funny Thing Happened on the Way to the (Alternative) Forum: Reexamining* Alexander v. Gardner-Denver *in the Wake of* Gilmer v. Interstate/Johnson Lane, 1997 B.Y.U. L. REV. 591 (1997)

Robert N. Covington, *Employment Arbitration After* Gilmer: *Have Labor Courts Come to the United States?*, 15 HOFSTRA LAB. & EMP. L.J. 345 (1998)

John E. Dunsford, *The Case for Retention of Remedial Jurisdiction in Labor Arbitration Awards*, 31 GA. L. REV. 201 (1996)

Matthew W. Finkin, *Employee Representation Outside the Labor Act: Thoughts on Arbitral Representation, Group Representation, and Workplace Committees*, 5 U. PA. J. LAB. & EMP. L. 75 (2002)

Stephen L. Hayford, *Unification of Labor Law Arbitration and Commercial Arbitration: An Idea Whose Time Has Come*, 52 BAYLOR L. REV. 781 (2000)

Ann C. Hodges, *Arbitration of Statutory Claims in the Unionized Workplace: Is Bargaining with the Union Required?*, 16 OHIO ST. J. ON DISP. RESOL. 513 (2001)

Albert Y. Kim, *Arbitrating Statutory Rights in the Union Setting: Breaking the Collective Interest Problem Without Damaging Labor Relations*, 65 U. CHI. L. REV. 225 (1998)

Carla Wong McMillian, *Collective Bargaining Agreements, Mandatory Arbitration and Title VII:* Varner v. National Super Markets, Inc., 32 GA. L. REV. 287 (1997)

Michelle R. Mitchell, *Arbitration Agreements: When Do Employees Waive Their Rights?*, 14 B.Y.U. J. PUB. L. 83 (1999)

Charles J. Morris, *A Blueprint for Reform of the National Labor Relations Act*, 8 ADMIN. L.J. AM. U. 517 (1994)

John-Paul Motley, *Compulsory Arbitration Agreements in Employment Contracts from* Gardner-Denver *to* Austin: *The Legal Uncertainty and Why Employers Should Chose Not to Use Preemployment Arbitration Agreements*, 51 VAND. L. REV. 687 (1998)

Lucille M. Ponte, *In the Shadow of* Gilmer: *How Post-*Gilmer *Legal Challenges to Pre-Dispute Arbitration Agreements Point the Way Towards Greater Fairness in Employment Arbitration*, 12 OHIO ST. J. ON DISP. RESOL. 359 (1997)

Theodore J. St. Antoine, *The Changing Role of Labor Arbitration*, 76 IND. L.J. 83 (2001)

Ronald Turner, *Employment Discrimination, Labor and Employment Arbitration, and the Case Against Union Waiver of the Individual Worker's Right to a Judicial Forum*, 49 EMORY L.J. 135 (2000)

Ronald Turner, *When the Court Makes Law and Policy (With Special Attention to the Employment Arbitration Issue)*, 19 HOFSTRA LAB. & EMP. L.J. 287 (2002)

Jacob E. Tyler, *Mandatory Arbitration of Discrimination Claims Under Collective Bargaining Agreements: The Effects of* Wright, 4 HARV. NEGOT. L. REV. 253 (1999)

Chapter 17

RELATION OF BOARD ACTION TO ENFORCEMENT OF AGREEMENTS UNDER SECTION 301

II. SECTION 10(a) POWER OF THE BOARD

It remains settled that the Board possesses the authority to resolve questions of contract interpretation in some circumstances.[1] The Board may resort to extrinsic evidence to interpret ambiguous terms,[2] and its interpretation of the scope of a contractual agreement is conclusive if supported by substantial evidence.[3]

However, the Act will not preempt claims where the court merely reviews a collective bargaining agreement to determine that it is silent on a particular issue. The Third Circuit, in *Kline v. Security Guards, Inc.*,[4] held that a lawsuit over workplace surveillance is not preempted because issues of privacy expectations did not require the interpretation of the collective bargaining agreement.

The Supreme Court, in *Circuit City Stores, Inc. v. Adams*,[5] held that arbitration agreements in contracts of employment are enforceable except for those that directly involve moving goods in interstate commerce. However, in *EEOC v. Waffle House, Inc.*,[6] the Court held that such an arbitration agreement did not prevent the EEOC from pursuing actions for victim-specific relief. The Division of Advice, in

---

[1] *See, e.g.*, Des Moines Register & Tribune Co., 339 NLRB 1035, 173 LRRM 1480 (2003) (Board applied contractual analysis to decide whether provision survived expiration of the collective bargaining agreement); *see also* United States v. Douglas, 398 F.3d 407, 176 LRRM 2641 (6th Cir. 2005); Blaize v. Phillip Morris, Inc., 120 Fed. Appx. 576 (6th Cir. 2004); Felix v. Lucent Techs., Inc., 387 F.3d 1146, 175 LRRM 3146 (10th Cir. 2004); Chamber of Commerce of the United States v. Lockyer, 364 F.3d 1154, 174 LRRM 2876 (9th Cir. 2004); Baker v. IBP, Inc., 357 F.3d 685, 174 LRRM 2230 (7th Cir. 2004).

[2] Sanitation Salvage Corp., 342 NLRB No. 41, 175 LRRM 1137 (2004); *see also* Electrical Workers (IBEW) Local 15, 341 NLRB No. 43, 174 LRRM 1414 (2004).

[3] Exxon Chem. Co. v. NLRB, 386 F.3d 1160, 175 LRRM 3159 (D.C. Cir. 2004).

[4] 386 F.3d 246, 175 LRRM 3038, 21 IER Cases 1589 (3d Cir. 2004).

[5] 532 U.S. 105, 85 FEP Cases 266 (2001). *See also* Palcko v. Airborne Express, Inc., 372 F.3d 588, 93 FEP Cases 1775 (3d Cir. 2004); Cooper v. MRM Inv. Co., 367 F.3d 493, 93 FEP Cases 1290 (6th Cir. 2004).

[6] 534 U.S. 279, 12 AD Cases 1001 (2002).

O'Charley's, Inc.,[7] reviewed *Gilmer v. Interstate/Johnson Lane Corp.*,[8] *Circuit City Stores*,[9] and *Bentley's Luggage Corp.*[10] It determined that an arbitration agreement was permissible as long as it only restricts the choice of forum and does not interfere with access to the Board or Section 7 rights.[11]

III. SCOPE AND PURPOSE OF SECTION 301

B. A Source of Federal Substantive Law

Courts continue to require an allegation that a collective bargaining agreement was breached in order to invoke jurisdiction pursuant to Section 301. In *Food & Commercial Workers v. Albertson's, Inc.*,[12] the Tenth Circuit addressed a union's attempt to use Section 301 as a basis for declaring a collective bargaining agreement invalid because it violated the Fair Labor Standards Act (FLSA). Citing the Supreme Court's decision in *Textron Lycoming Reciprocating Engine Division, Avco Corp. v. Auto Workers*,[13] the Tenth Circuit held that the mere contention that a collective bargaining agreement violated the FLSA was insufficient to give rise to Section 301 jurisdiction in the absence of a claim that the employer had actually breached the agreement.[14] Similarly, in *Bedrock Servs. v. Electrical Workers (IBEW) Nos. 238*

---

[7]NLRB Advice Memo., Case 26-CA-19974 (Apr. 16, 2001).

[8]500 U.S. 20, 55 FEP Cases 1116 (1991); *see also* McMullen v. Meijer, Inc., 355 F.3d 485, 93 FEP Cases 236 (6th Cir. 2004).

[9]Circuit City Stores v. Adams, 532 U.S. 105, 85 FEP Cases 266 (1002).

[10]NLRB Advice Memo., Case 12-CA-16658 (Aug. 21, 1995).

[11]*See also* NLRB Advice Memo., Capitol Ford, Inc., Case 32-CA-18464-1 (Jan. 30, 2002) (analysis of arbitration provision as a mandatory subject of bargaining); EEOC v. Pemco Acroplex, Inc., 383 F.3d 1280, 94 FEP Cases 848 (11th Cir. 2003); Poteat v. Rich Prods. Corp., 91 Fed. Appx. 832 (4th Cir. 2004); Gold v. Deutsche Aktiengescllschaft, 365 F.3d 144, 93 FEP Cases 1125 (2d Cir. 2004); *but see* Electrical Workers (IBEW) Local 545 v. Hope Elec. Corp., 380 F.3d 1084 (8th Cir. 2004). (*Circuit City* did not involve a collective bargaining agreement and LMRA 301 takes precedence over FAA); Hope Elec. Corp., 339 NLRB 933, 172 LRRM 1466 (2003) (interest arbitration a nonmandatory subject of bargaining); NLRB Advice Memo., Triangle Construction and Maintenance, Inc., Case 24-CA-9921 (Nov. 15, 2004) (allowed an employer to unilaterally implement an arbitration procedure whereby bargaining unit members received a cash incentive to waive statutory employment-related discrimination and personal injury claims in court).

[12]207 F.3d 1193, 163 LRRM 2903 (10th Cir. 2000).

[13]523 U.S. 653, 158 LRRM 2193 (1998).

[14]*Albertson's*, *supra* note 12, 207 F.3d at 1197.

& 495,[15] the District Court for the Western District of North Carolina declined jurisdiction where Bedrock filed suit not "because a contract has been violated, but because Bedrock has determined [the contract] is invalid and seeks a declaration of the same."[16] Quoting *Textron*, the district court held that Section 301 does not confer federal jurisdiction solely where a declaratory judgment is sought.[17]

Other courts have held that jurisdiction to determine the validity of a collective bargaining agreement exists if the invalidity of the contract is raised as a defense to a breach of contract action. In *Trustees of the ALA-Lithographic Pension Plan v. Crestwood Printing Corp.*,[18] the court held that it had jurisdiction to determine whether a collective bargaining agreement was invalid on grounds of fraud in the execution. Citing *Textron*,[19] the court declared that it had jurisdiction to adjudicate the validity of the contract because the issue was raised as an affirmative defense to the union's claim that the employer had failed to make pension contributions in accordance with the contract.[20]

Similarly, in *Bulkmatic Transport Co. v. Teamsters Local 407*,[21] the court exercised jurisdiction to determine whether a collective bargaining agreement between the union and the employer's Cleveland facility automatically extended to the employer's Euclid facility. The court held its exercise of jurisdiction was appropriate because resolution of the validity of the agreement as applied to the Euclid facility was necessary to determine whether the employer had, in fact, violated the contract.[22] However, the mere allegation that an employer violated the collective bargaining agreement by refusing to recognize the agreement is insufficient to confer federal jurisdiction because such a refusal concerns the validity of a contract, not its breach.[23]

---

[15]285 F. Supp. 2d 693 (W.D.N.C. 2003).

[16]*Id.* at 701.

[17]*Id.*

[18]127 F. Supp. 2d 475, 166 LRRM 2457 (S.D.N.Y. 2001).

[19]523 U.S. 653 (1998).

[20]*Trustees of the ALA-Lithographic Pension Plan*, *supra* note 18, 127 F. Supp. 2d at 481.

[21]213 F. Supp. 2d 946, 171 LRRM 2041 (N.D. Ind. 2002).

[22]*Id.* at 951.

[23]Chicago & Northeast Illinois Dist. Council Carpenters v. GDCNI/CAWCC, No. 01-C-6097, 2002 U.S. Dist. LEXIS 2567 (N.D. Ill. Feb. 19, 2002); *see also* J.F. Edwards Constr. Co. v. Operating Engineers Local 150, 2004 U.S. Dist. LEXIS 11803, *9, 176 LRRM 3078 (N.D. Ill. June 24, 2004), citing THE DEVELOPING LABOR LAW.

In addition, courts continue to exercise authority to determine the validity of a contract provided the issue is clearly within the supplemental jurisdiction of the court.[24] The Sixth Circuit has held that an employer sued by a plan administrator for pension payments under a collective bargaining agreement can assert a third-party claim against the union, seeking a declaration that the contract is invalid, if the employer also asserts a claim against the union for indemnification and damages in the event that it is liable under the contract.[25]

Courts continue to use Section 301 jurisdiction to enforce agreements referring to or incorporated in collective bargaining agreements. The Second Circuit issued a permanent injunction barring an employer from transferring work until it made every reasonable effort to preserve the work, as a letter agreement incorporated within a collective bargaining agreement required the employer to make "every effort" to preserve work done by the employees covered by the collective bargaining agreement.[26]

The Tenth Circuit held that Section 301 provides federal courts with jurisdiction over a claim by an employee against his employer and union for the breach of a conciliation agreement resolving a prior employment discrimination claim.[27] The court found that the conciliation agreement did not confer any rights upon the employee; rather, the independent source of the rights the employee sought to enforce was the collective bargaining agreement itself.[28]

The Third Circuit held that Section 301 jurisdiction extends to a closing agreement ending a strike.[29] The court determined that the agreement was negotiated by the employer and unions, and that it served the dual purpose of providing striking union members with employment rights and ending their strike against the employer, thereby distinguishing it from a series of individual employment contracts.[30] Moreover, the court ruled that the unions and employer

---

[24]Northwestern Ohio Adm'rs, Inc. v. Walcher & Fox, Inc., 270 F.3d 1018, 168 LRRM 2843 (6th Cir. 2001), *cert. denied*, 535 U.S. 1017, 169 LRRM 3088 (2002); *see also* Burklow v. Baskin-Robbins USA Co., 274 F. Supp. 2d 899 (W.D. Ky. 2003).

[25]*Northwestern Ohio Adm'rs, supra* note 24.

[26]District Lodge 91, Machinists v. United Techs. Corp., 230 F.3d 569, 579, 165 LRRM 2641 (2d Cir. 2000).

[27]Cisneros v. ABC Rail Corp., 217 F.3d 1299, 164 LRRM 2780 (10th Cir. 2000); *see also* Felix v. Lucent Techs., Inc., 387 F.3d 1146, 1164, 175 LRRM 3146 (10th Cir. 2003) (same).

[28]*Cisneros, supra* note 27, 217 F.3d at 1303.

[29]Beidleman v. Stroh Brewery Co., 182 F.3d 225, 161 LRRM 2656 (3d Cir. 1999).

[30]*Id.* at 231.

entered into the closing agreement to establish labor peace and to resolve a controversy, thus bringing the agreement within Section 301.[31]

In *Rock-Tenn Co. v. Paperworkers*,[32] the Fourth Circuit addressed the issue of whether a corporation, rather than merely one of its divisions, may be bound by a collective bargaining agreement. An employer brought a Section 301 action seeking a declaratory judgment that it was not bound by a collective bargaining agreement because it was between its division and the union. The court held that the employer's voluntary participation in the arbitration process without objection precluded the employer from later arguing that it was not bound by the collective bargaining agreement.[33] Further, the court held that the collective bargaining agreement could be reasonably interpreted to bind the corporation and not merely its division and, therefore, the arbitrator's decision should not be vacated.[34]

The Seventh Circuit confronted the issue of whether jurisdiction exists to enforce an arbitral award where the complaint failed to allege the existence of a statutory employer.[35] The court stated that the absence of a statutory employer did not deprive the court of jurisdiction. Rather, a complaint that does not allege the existence of a statutory employer fails to state a claim and the plaintiff loses on the merits.[36] The Seventh Circuit emphasized that its holding meant that an employer that fails to challenge the authority of an arbitrator to issue an award within the state limitations period waives any defense that the arbitrator lacked jurisdiction over the union's complaints.[37]

---

[31] *Id. See also* Rollie Winter & Assocs., Ltd. v. Fox River Valley Bldg. & Constr. Trades Council, 59 F. Supp. 2d 807, 161 LRRM 3159 (E.D. Wis. 1999) (holding that federal court jurisdiction based upon §301 exists over claim seeking to enforce oral job targeting agreement because agreement was significant to maintenance of labor peace).

[32] 184 F.3d 330, 161 LRRM 2862 (4th Cir. 1999).

[33] *Id.* at 336, 161 LRRM at 2866.

[34] *Id.* at 337, 161 LRRM at 2867.

[35] Operating Eng'rs Local 150 v. Gary Rabine, 161 F.3d 427, 159 LRRM 2713 (7th Cir. 1998).

[36] *Id.* at 430, 159 LRRM at 2716.

[37] *Id.* at 431–32, 159 LRRM at 2717.

C. The *Steelworkers* Trilogy

Judicial review of labor arbitration decisions under collective bargaining agreements continues to be very limited. In *Major League Baseball Players Ass'n v. Garvey*,[38] the Supreme Court reversed a court of appeals decision that not only overturned an arbitrator's decision but, without further proceedings, directed that an award be entered in the amount claimed by the former baseball player. The Court reinstated the arbitrator's decision denying the claim and stated that "[w]hen an arbitrator resolves disputes regarding the application of a contract, and no dishonesty is alleged, the arbitrator's 'improvident, even silly, factfinding' does not provide a basis for a reviewing court to refuse to enforce the award."[39]

Further, the Court reiterated that even when an award is properly vacated, the remedy is to remand for further arbitration proceedings and not for the reviewing court to resolve the merits of the parties' dispute.[40]

While an arbitrator's decision is subject to great deference, a court can vacate the arbitrator's order where the evidence demonstrates that the arbitrator, in reaching a decision, ignored clear and unambiguous contract language and substituted the employer's past practice.[41] Recently, the Sixth Circuit reiterated the four situations where an arbitrator's award may be vacated for departing from the essence of the agreement: (1) an award that conflicts with the express terms of the collective bargaining agreement; (2) an award that imposes additional requirements that are not expressly provided in the agreement; (3) an agreement that is without rational support or that cannot be rationally derived from the terms of the agreement; and (4) an award that is based on general considerations of fairness and equity instead of the precise terms of the agreement.[42] Even where an arbitrator commits a clear error by exceeding his contractual authority by modifying an agreement, however, the Third Circuit recently indicated its willingness to find other bases for the

[38]532 U.S. 504, 167 LRRM 2134 (2001).

[39]*Id.* at 509, 167 LRRM at 2137, quoting Paperworkers v. Misco Inc., 484 U.S. 29, 39, 126 LRRM 3113, 3117 (1987).

[40]*Id.* at 511, 167 LRRM at 2137.

[41]Anheuser-Busch, Inc. v. Local 744, 280 F.3d 1133, 1139, 169 LRRM 2513 (7th Cir. 2002).

[42]DBM Tech., Inc. v. Food & Commercial Workers Local 227, 257 F.3d 651, 167 LRRM 2749 (6th Cir. 2001).

arbitrator's ruling. In *Brentwood Medical Associates v. United Mine Workers of America*,[43] the court stated that "even if we were to kick the 'bum leg' of the arbitrator's award, there are still many others upon which this award can stand."[44]

F. Overlapping Jurisdiction: Conflict or Accommodation?

1. *Federal and State Courts*

a. Concurrent Jurisdiction

The Eighth[45] and Ninth[46] Circuits have found that a state's procedural rules govern Section 301 suits commenced in state court and before removal to federal court, without regard to the effect those procedural rules may have on the federal substantive law concerning the statute of limitations. However, the Fourth Circuit has held to the contrary.[47]

b. Statutes of Limitations

The Ninth Circuit considered a case of first impression that questioned whether state procedural rules apply to a hybrid Section 301 action that is filed in state court even though there is a federal statute of limitations. In *Prazak v. Bricklayers Local 1*,[48] the court held that a district court, on removal of a hybrid Section 301 suit commenced in state court, could not dismiss the suit based on the six-month statute of limitations if the suit was commenced under the state's procedural rules within the 10(b) period. Finding that state procedural rules govern hybrid Section 301 actions brought in state court, the court found that the dismissal of the action by the state court for lack of prosecution, and the subsequent refiling of the action in state court within the time prescribed by state law, prevented the district court, on removal, from applying the limitations period as if the action had been originally commenced in federal court.

---

[43]396 F.3d 237, 176 LRRM 2584 (3d Cir. 2005).
[44]*Id.* at 243.
[45]Winkels v. George A. Hormel & Co., 874 F.2d 567, 131 LRRM 2338 (8th Cir. 1989).
[46]Prazak v. Bricklayers Local 1, 233 F.3d 1149, 165 LRRM 2853 (9th Cir. 2000).
[47]Cannon v. Kroger Co., 832 F.2d 303, 126 LRRM 2968 (4th Cir. 1987).
[48]*Supra* note 46.

The courts continue to find that the limitations period of a Section 301 suit is not tolled by pursuit of a Board action,[49] nor is it tolled by a small claims action for unpaid wages.[50] Further, it is not tolled while an employee informally sought help from successive union stewards,[51] nor is it tolled by letters sent to the union by an employee's attorney threatening suit if a grievance was not reopened.[52] It is also not tolled by an attempt to appeal a union's withdrawal of grievances when such attempt was known to be futile.[53] Likewise, the courts continue to find that the hybrid Section 301 six-month limitations period is not tolled absent evidence of positive misconduct by the union or employer that was deliberately designed to lead employees not to bring their challenges within the limitations period.[54] Finally, in *Bailey v. Boilermakers Local 374*,[55] a nonhybrid Section 301 action by employees against their union-employer, the Seventh Circuit held that the employer's unfulfilled promise to rehire employees did not toll the statute of limitations, absent something more, such as an offer to rehire coupled with a request not to sue.

Based on the six-month limitations period, the Eighth Circuit dismissed a hybrid Section 301 action despite the fact that the union formally denied the subject health and safety grievance one month after the suit had been filed.[56] The court found that the employee knew of the union's breach of its duty at the time he filed intra-union charges, more than six months prior to filing his suit, against several members of the union's executive board for failure to pursue his grievance.

---

[49]Glass & Pottery Workers Local 421 v. A-CMI Mich. Casting Ctr., 191 F.3d 764, 162 LRRM 2290 (6th Cir. 1999).

[50]Martin v. Lake County Sewer Co., 269 F.3d 673, 168 LRRM 2631 (6th Cir. 2001).

[51]Christiansen v. AVP Crepaco, Inc., 178 F.3d 910, 161 LRRM 2333 (7th Cir. 1999) (limitations period began to run when union initially failed to file timely grievance and subsequent union action on same grievance did not restart limitations period).

[52]Coppage v. United States Postal Serv., 281 F.3d 1200, 169 LRRM 2396 (11th Cir. 2002).

[53]Garrish v. Auto Workers Local 594, 284 F. Supp. 2d 782, 173 LRRM 2700 (E.D. Mich. 2003).

[54]Barlow v. American Nat'l Can Co., 173 F.3d 640, 161 LRRM 2222 (8th Cir. 1999).

[55]175 F.3d 526, 161 LRRM 2074 (7th Cir. 1999).

[56]Scott v. Auto Workers Local 879, 242 F.3d 837, 166 LRRM 2615 (8th Cir. 2001).

In *Kavowras v. The New York Times Co.*,[57] the Second Circuit held that the hybrid Section 301's six-month statute of limitation commenced when the parties' tentative settlement of an arbitration was placed "on the record" by the arbitrator. The court found that the employee had no expectation of any award concluding the arbitration because the arbitrator understood the dispute to be settled, and therefore, there was no basis for deferring the running of the statute of limitations pending the arbitrator's ruling.

2. The Board and the Courts

In *Pace v. Honolulu Disposal Services, Inc.*,[58] the Ninth Circuit found that the hybrid Section 301 action brought by a group of employees claiming wrongful denial of pay and benefits provided in a series of collective bargaining agreements was primarily contractual in nature and that the district court had jurisdiction despite the claim of the employer and union that the case involved representational issues within the Board's primary jurisdiction. Citing the Supreme Court's holding in *Textron Lycoming Reciprocating Engine Division Avco Corp. v. Auto Workers*,[59] the Sixth Circuit found the federal district court had no jurisdiction to hear a hybrid Section 301 claim brought by employees alleging the invalidity of a plant closing agreement which superseded the last collective bargaining agreement because the employees had not alleged a breach of the plant closing agreement.[60] In *Service Employees Local 399 v. St. Vincent Medical Center*,[61] the union sought to compel an employer to arbitrate the employer's alleged violations of their written agreement restricting the parties' behavior during an organizational drive before a representational election. The Ninth Circuit found that it had jurisdiction to hear this matter in that the issue could not be characterized as "representational," and therefore within the primary jurisdiction of the Board, merely by having representational overtones.

[57]328 F.3d 50, 172 LRRM 2389 (2d Cir. 2003).

[58]227 F.3d 1150, 165 LRRM 2385 (9th Cir. 2000). *Accord* Journeymen v. Valley Eng'rs, 975 F.2d 611, 141 LRRM 2326 (9th Cir. 1992).

[59]523 U.S. 653, 158 LRRM 2193 (1998).

[60]Bauer v. RBX Indust., Inc., 368 F.3d 569, 579, 174 LRRM 3121 (6th Cir. 2004). *See also* Chicago & Northeast Illinois Dist. Council Carpenters v. GDCNI/CAWCC, No. 01 C 6097, 2002 U.S. Dist. LEXIS 2567 (N.D. Ill. Feb. 19, 2002) (no jurisdiction to hear union's §301 claim which was an action for declaratory judgment as to the validity of a purported collective bargaining agreement and did not allege a breach of contract).

[61]344 F.3d 977, 173 LRRM 2289 (9th Cir. 2003).

In *Advance Cast Stone Co. v. Iron Workers Local 1*,[62] a case involving a union jurisdictional dispute, the Seventh Circuit was presented with conflicting determinations between the Board's decision in a Section 10(k) hearing favoring the Bricklayers and a Joint Arbitration Board's decision in favor of the Iron Workers. Unaware that the same parties were litigating the issue in a Section 10(k) proceeding, and just days after the Board's Section 10(k) decision in favor of the Bricklayers, the district court rejected the employer's motion to vacate the Joint Arbitration Board's decision in favor of the Iron Workers. Upon the employer's motion to alter the judgment in light of the Board's Section 10(k) decision, the district court reversed its earlier affirmance of the Joint Arbitration Board's decision based on longstanding federal precedent that a Board's ruling takes precedence over an arbitrator's decision. In affirming the district court, the Seventh Circuit first found that the district court had concurrent jurisdiction with the Board when this matter involved both the interpretation of a collective bargaining agreement and allegations of violation of the NLRA and that the district court was correct in factoring the conflicting Section 10(k) determination into its decision.[63]

Some courts continue to hold that findings by the Board in unfair labor practice cases may bar subsequent Section 301 suits by application of the doctrine of collateral estoppel.[64]

IV. INJUNCTIONS IN AID OF ARBITRATION: SECTION 301 VERSUS NORRIS-LAGUARDIA

B. The *Boys Markets* Injunction: Halting the Strike Over an Arbitrable Grievance

1. *The Prerequisites for Issuance of Injunctive Relief*

a. In General

A court may issue a *Boys Markets* injunction only when the employer shows clearly and undisputably that the dispute underlying the strike is subject to a no-strike provision. Where the right to strike

---

[62]376 F.3d 734, 175 LRRM 2321 (7th Cir. 2004).

[63]*Id.* at 740–41.

[64]Florian v. Sequa Corp., 2001 U.S. Dist. LEXIS 13176, 168 LRRM 2389 (N.D. Ill. Aug. 27, 2001), citing Frye v. Steelworkers, 767 F.2d 1216, 119 LRRM 3542 (7th Cir. 1985).

is interrelated with an ambiguity in a contract, federal courts are without jurisdiction to issue a *Boys Markets* injunction.[65] Thus, where the contract excepts from its arbitration requirement certain types of contract violations and provides that the union retains the right to strike with respect to such violations, a court may not enjoin a strike where the union presents a colorable claim that such violations have occurred.[66]

According to the Second Circuit, "where a case does not concern either conduct enumerated in §4 or a dispute subject to mandatory arbitration, the proper approach is to allow injunctive relief provided the policies of both §301 and the [Norris-LaGuardia Act (NLA)] are thereby advanced."[67] In that case, the union sued for specific performance of the employer's nonarbitrable, contractual undertaking to make "every effort" to preserve certain bargaining-unit work. The employer resisted, arguing that injunctions may issue only where the underlying dispute is subject to mandatory bargaining and an injunction is essential to prevent undermining of the arbitration process. The court disagreed, asserting that these are merely exceptions to the "general rule" that "an injunction may issue only where the dispute is subject to judicial resolution and the conduct to be enjoined is not included within the letter or spirit of §4 of the NLA."[68] In upholding the injunction, the Second Circuit concluded that "[w]here a grievance is not subject to arbitration or any other final and binding dispute resolution procedure, litigation is presumptively available under §301, and courts may issue injunctions consistent with the provisions of the NLA."[69]

In *AT&T Broadband, LLC v. Electrical Workers (IBEW) Local 21*,[70] the Seventh Circuit joined the First, Third, Ninth, and D.C. Circuits in refusing to extend *Boys Markets* and holding that the Norris-LaGuardia Act prohibited courts from enjoining the arbitration of a labor dispute.

---

[65]Allied Sys. Ltd. v. Teamsters Local 327, 179 F.3d 982, 989, 161 LRRM 2493, 2493 (6th Cir. 1999).

[66]*Id.*

[67]Machinists Dist. Lodge 91 v. United Techs. Corp., Pratt & Whitney, 230 F.3d 569, 580, 165 LRRM 2641, 2648 (2d Cir. 2000).

[68]*Id.* at 580, 165 LRRM at 2648.

[69]*Id.* at 580–81, 165 LRRM at 2648.

[70]317 F.3d 758, 171 LRRM 2988 (7th Cir. 2003).

In *Young Brothers, Ltd. v. Longshoremen (ILWU) Local 142*,[71] the district court dismissed the employer's claim for injunctive relief because the employer failed to satisfy Section 108 of the Norris-LaGuardia Act, which prohibits injunctive relief for complainants that have failed to make every reasonable effort to settle the dispute through negotiation, mediation, or arbitration.

In *Otis Elevator Co. v. International Union of Elevator Constructors Local 91*,[72] the court denied the employer's request for an injunction, but denied the union's motion to dismiss the lawsuit based on mootness and failure to exhaust administrative remedy grounds. Rejecting the union's argument that the case was moot because the union no longer was engaged in a work stoppage, the court found that there was an issue of fact as to whether the union would resume work stoppages. The court held that the case fell within the "capable of repetition yet evading review" exception to the mootness doctrine and emphasized the fact that the parties continued to disagree as to whether the contract permitted work stoppages based on employer contract violations. The court also rejected the union's failure to exhaust claim, holding that an employer is not required to file a demand for arbitration prior to seeking an injunction.

In *Pritchard Electric Co. v. Electrical Workers (IBEW) Local 317*,[73] the court denied the employer's motion seeking to enjoin arbitration of a dispute. The employer argued that it was not seeking to enjoin arbitration, but instead seeking to compel arbitration under the parties' national contract rather than their local contract. Based on the employer's argument, the court distinguished this case from decisions in which courts have refused to enjoin arbitration, but, nonetheless, held that Norris-LaGuardia applied and did not authorize an injunction under the circumstances.

In a "reverse *Boys Markets*" case, *Auto Workers Local 1069 v. Boeing Rotorcraft*,[74] the court denied the union request for an injunction because the employer had not attempted to evade or frustrate the arbitration process. The union argued that an injunction was warranted because, although the employer agreed to arbitrate, it continued to lay off employees, which the union alleged violated the

[71]250 F. Supp. 2d 1244, 172 LRRM 2116 (D. Haw. 2003).

[72]2005 U.S. Dist. LEXIS 113, 176 LRRM 2505 (D. Conn. 2005).

[73]306 F. Supp. 2d 603, 174 LRRM 2519 (S.D.W. Va. 2004).

[74]No. 04-3603, 2004 U.S. Dist. LEXIS 18041 (E.D. Pa. Sept. 1, 2004).

parties' contract. The court held that continued layoffs would merely give rise to more grievances, which could be arbitrated, and would not "render arbitration a hollow formality."

c. Strike Over an Arbitrable Dispute

For there to be a finding that there is an arbitrable dispute, the employer must allege that the dispute is subject to a contractual arbitration clause and that it is ready to proceed with arbitration.[75] The arbitrability of the dispute must be "clear" and "undisputed."[76] In *Airborne Freight Corp. v. Teamsters Local 705*,[77] the court found arbitrable a dispute over an abusive supervisor and the denial of water to an employee. The court noted the presumption of arbitrability when a contract contains an arbitration clause and determined that the dispute was covered by the contract's safety and nondiscrimination provisions.

d. Irreparable Injury and the Balance of Equities

An employer was enjoined from liquidating certain assets because doing so would cause irreparable harm by rendering meaningless the arbitration process and any arbitral award of back pay or other damages.[78] Conversely, the court found that allowing the employer to close the facility in question would not cause irreparable harm. The court reasoned that the relevant market in the local area was "reasonably fluid," and that if the arbitrator ordered the facility reopened and the employees reinstated, the employer could regain its customers "over a reasonable period of time."

Although a dispute was subject to arbitration, the court found it lacked jurisdiction to issue an injunction where failure to do so would not render arbitration "a 'meaningless ritual.'"[79] In that case, the union sought to enjoin an employee's forced transfer. The court found that the union had options other than injunctive relief that

---

[75]Pickens-Kane Moving & Storage Co. v. Teamsters Local 705, 161 LRRM 2159, 2162 (N.D. Ill. 1999); Stuart Dean Co. v. Metal Polishers Local 8A-28A, 121 F. Supp. 2d 399 (S.D.N.Y. 2000).

[76]Allied Sys. Ltd. v. Teamsters Local 327, 179 F.3d 982, 989, 161 LRRM 2493, 2498 (6th Cir. 1999). *Accord* Earthgrains Baking Cos. v. Teamsters Local 78, 35 F. Supp. 2d 1203, 160 LRRM 2638 (E.D. Cal. 1999).

[77]216 F. Supp. 2d 712, 171 LRRM 2054 (N.D. Ill. 2002).

[78]Teamsters Local 299 v. U.S. Truck Co. Holdings, Inc., 87 F. Supp. 2d 726, 163 LRRM 2412 (E.D. Mich. 2000).

[79]Chicago Typographical Union No. 16 v. Daily Racing Form, Inc., 1999 U.S. Dist. LEXIS 3370 (N.D. Ill. Mar. 10, 1999).

would preserve the value of arbitration. Specifically, the employee had the option of refusing the transfer and being disciplined or terminated, which the union could then arbitrate.

Although courts must balance the equities, a court need not find a threat of "unlawful acts" to issue an injunction.[80]

In a number of "reverse *Boys Markets*" cases, courts found that the potential harm to the employees did not render the arbitration process frustrated. In *Electrical Workers (IUE)-Communications Workers Local 628 v. Flowserve Corp. of Pennsylvania,*[81] the court found that, because the employer could comply with a potential arbitral order to cease layoffs and continue operations, the arbitral process was not frustrated. Similarly, in *Communications Workers v. Verizon New York, Inc.,*[82] another court found that the arbitrator could remedy the challenged layoffs by reinstating the laid-off workers with back pay.

Similarly, in *Communications Workers v. Verizon Communications, Inc.,*[83] the court found that the employer had not interfered with or frustrated the arbitral process because the employer and the union were responsible for delay in the arbitrator and hearing date selection process. The court also found irreparable harm lacking because the parties' contract provided for full reimbursement of the laid-off employees. The court further noted that the union had the resources to provide low-interest or no-interest loans or other financial assistance to the employees.

In another reverse *Boys Markets* case, *Steelworkers v. Cooper-Standard Automotive,*[84] the court enjoined the employer from selling its stock or transferring its ownership or control. The union argued that successor memoranda covering four plants prevented the employer from selling them without first ensuring that the buyer recognized and entered into an agreement with the union. The court found that the union would be irreparably harmed absent the injunction because the union would be unable to duplicate its presale bargaining strength in postsale bargaining. In finding that a balance of the equities favored the injunction, the court emphasized the employer's refusal to arbitrate and, again, the union's inability to duplicate its

---

[80]Machinists Dist. Lodge 91 v. United Techs. Corp., Pratt & Whitney, 230 F.3d 569, 582, 165 LRRM 2641, 2649 (2d Cir. 2000).

[81]239 F. Supp. 2d 527 (M.D. Pa. 2003).

[82]2002 U.S. Dist. LEXIS 21556, 171 LRRM 2487 (S.D.N.Y. 2002).

[83]255 F. Supp. 2d 479, 172 LRRM 2217 (E.D. Pa. 2003).

[84]2004 U.S. Dist. LEXIS 24640, 175 LRRM 3249 (N.D. Ind. 2004).

presale bargaining position. The court found that these harms outweighed the harm to the employer of not being able to sell 4 of its 47 plants.

f. Limitations on Prospective Relief; Mootness

In *Pace Mechanical Services v. Plumbers Local 98*,[85] the court granted the employer's motion for injunctive relief where the union's threat to refuse to perform certain work, coupled with its past acts, was indicative of future strike activity. The union had already engaged in work slowdowns, vandalism, and failure to provide adequate numbers of workers.

In *Airborne Freight Corp. v. Teamsters Local 705*,[86] the court denied the employer's motion for a temporary restraining order where a four-hour work stoppage had ceased before the employer sought the order. The employer had argued that the union's history of work stoppages demonstrated that the work stoppages would resume. The court distinguished the prior work stoppages, however, and found that the dispute had been resolved and that the stoppages were unlikely to continue.

4. *Injunctions Against Employers to Preserve the Status Quo*

Injunctions against employers are to be issued only in accordance with traditional principles of equity. This requires, inter alia, a showing of irreparable injury in the absence of an injunction.[87]

---

[85]199 U.S. Dist. LEXIS 7635 (E.D. Mich. May 19, 1999).

[86]216 F. Supp. 2d 712, 718–19, 171 LRRM 2054 (N.D. Ill. 2002).

[87]Electrical Workers (IBEW) Local 15 v. Exelon Corp., 191 F. Supp. 2d 987, 170 LRRM 2570 (N.D. Ill. 2001) (employer's motion to dismiss union's complaint for preliminary injunction was granted where there was no showing of irreparable injury); *see also* Communications Workers of Am. v. Verizon Communications, Inc., 255 F. Supp. 2d 479, 484–86, 172 LRRM 2217 (E.D. Pa. 2003) (loss of health care benefits not irreparable injury); Electrical Workers (IBEW) v. First Energy Corp., 233 F. Supp. 2d 913 (N.D. Ohio 2002) (same); Auto Workers Local 1069 v. Boeing Rotorcraft, 2004 U.S. Dist. Lexis 18041 (E.D. Pa. Sept. 1, 2004) (refusing to enjoin employer from laying off employees during arbitration process where it would not frustrate the arbitral process and where the employer was not attempting to evade the arbitral process); Postal Workers v. United States Postal Serv., 16 Fed. Appx. 589 (9th Cir. 2001) (refusing to enjoin employer from transferring priority mail operations where union failed to prove irreparable harm by arguing that the transfer would jeopardize the health and safety of workers in violation of the collective bargaining agreement during the pending mandatory arbitration); Health Care, Professional, Technical Office, Warehouse, & Mail Order Employees Local 743 v.

In a "reverse *Boys Markets*" case, an employer was enjoined from liquidating certain of its assets to prevent the employer from evading the duty to arbitrate or otherwise undermining the integrity of the arbitral process.[88] Allowing the employer to liquidate the assets would have rendered any arbitral award of back pay or other damages meaningless.

C. Injunction Suits in State Courts

In *Dillon Companies, Inc. v. Teamsters Local* 795,[89] the state court had granted a temporary restraining order brought by the employer to enjoin the union from engaging in actions that encouraged customers to boycott its grocery store. The union sought to remove the district court. While recognizing that many federal courts immediately dissolve state court injunctions once a case is removed, the court decided, instead, not to dissolve the previous state court injunction because no injunctive relief could be awarded by it (a federal court) as the case did not fall within the narrow exception created by *Boys*

Rush Univ. Med. Ctr., 2004 U.S. Dist. LEXIS 25708, 176 LRRM 3022 (N.D. Ill. 2004) (refusing to enjoin employer from implementing change in healthcare coverage for union employees, pending resolution of arbitration concerning coverage dispute; holding that a status quo injunction was not necessary to prevent arbitration from being meaningless and that an award might provide union with less than it wanted was not the same as a "meaningless" award); *but see* Electrical Workers (IUE)-Communications Workers Local 628 v. Flowserve Corp. of Pa., 239 F. Supp. 2d 527 (M.D. Pa. 2003), citing Steelworkers v. Fort Pitt Steel Casting, 598 F.2d 1273, 1280, 101 LRRM 2406 (3d Cir. 1979), for proposition that possible lack of medical care due to insurance loss could constitute irreparable harm, but finding none where employer effectively guaranteed health care coverage for three months after termination of employment.

[88]Teamsters Local 299 v. U.S. Truck Co. Holdings, Inc., 87 F. Supp. 2d 726, 736–37, 163 LRRM 2412 (E.D. Mich. 2000); *see also* Machinists Dist. Lodge 91 v. United Techs. Corp., 230 F.3d 569, 165 LRRM 2641 (2d Cir. 2000) (enjoining employer from implementing a major restructuring that would include permanent transfer of production work to facilities in the Midwest; basing injunction on an obligation in the collective bargaining agreement); Steelworkers v. Cooper-Standard Auto. of Bowling Green, 2004 U.S. Dist. LEXIS 24640, 175 LRRM 3249 (N.D. Ind. 2004) (enjoining employer from selling stock prior to arbitration of successorship clause in the collective bargaining agreement where the unions showed likelihood of success and that it would be irreparably harmed without the injunction and where the arbitrator would have no real authority if the sale occurred before the arbitral award issued).

[89]3 F. Supp. 2d 1193, 158 LRRM 2444 (D. Kan. 1998).

Markets. The court held that although it may not have authority pursuant to Section 301 to grant relief requested, it did have authority to hear the matter. Consequently, the court denied remand to the state court, but also held that the injunctive relief granted by the state court was to remain in effect since the union had not yet moved for relief from the injunction.

V. NLRB INTERPRETATION OF THE COLLECTIVE BARGAINING AGREEMENT

A. Statutory Authority to Interpret Agreements

The authority of the NLRB to interpret collective bargaining agreements between parties may extend to include the Board's interpretation of prehire agreements.[90]

In *McKenzie Engineering Co. v. NLRB*,[91] a union filed an unfair labor practice alleging that the employer refused to honor its prehire agreement with a union when it assigned the construction-phase work of a project to a competing union in violation of its duty to bargain under Section 8(a)(5) of the Act. The Board found that the employer violated the Act by repudiating a prehire agreement. The Eighth Circuit Court of Appeals held that it is reasonable for the Board to interpret a prehire agreement to conclude that a construction industry employer violates its statutory duty to bargain if it unilaterally modifies such an agreement. Nonetheless, the court denied the Board's petition to enforce the order based upon an improper interpretation of the prehire agreement and obligations thereunder.

B. Cases Where the Board Interprets Contract Provisions

The authority of the NLRB to interpret contractual provisions has limits. While the Board may interpret a collective bargaining agreement to determine whether there has been an unfair labor practice, the Board may not inject itself into a contract dispute where a party had a "sound arguable basis" based upon contractual interpretation for an action that has been alleged to have violated NLRA.[92]

---

[90]McKenzie Eng'g Co. v. NLRB, 303 F.3d. 902, 170 LRRM 3043 (8th Cir. 2002).
[91]*Id.*
[92]Honeywell Int'l Inc. v. NLRB, 253 F.3d 119, 167 LRRM 2632 (D.C. Cir. 2001).

In *Honeywell International Inc. v. NLRB*,[93] an employer and union entered into a "Competitiveness Agreement" which provided that the employer could terminate the agreement if specified financial arrangements for the plant in question were not made in the federal budget. Due to lack of appropriation of federal funds, the employer's plant was slated to be closed. The employer advised the union that it intended to terminate the Competitiveness Agreement based upon its interpretation of the contractual language. The union filed a Section 8(a)(5) charge, alleging that the company failed to bargain in good faith by unilaterally withdrawing the Competitiveness Agreement, refusing to provide relevant information, and refusing to bargain the decision and effects of the plant closure.

The administrative law judge determined that the employer had a "sound arguable basis" based upon the contractual language to terminate the agreement, and therefore ruled that the employer had not violated the NLRA. The Board reversed on the basis that the "sound and arguable basis" test did not apply because the employer repudiated the agreement in its entirety. The Board determined that the issue of whether the employer could lawfully terminate the agreement was more than a mere contract dispute but rather was "situated at the threshold of matters going to the heart of the collective bargaining relationship."[94] The employer filed a petition for review and the union filed a cross-application for enforcement of the NLRB's order.

Setting aside the Board's decision, the Court of Appeals for the District of Columbia held that the NLRB exceeded its authority by injecting itself into a contract dispute where the employer had a sound arguable basis for its interpretation of the contract. The court held that an employer cannot be deemed to have refused to bargain collectively over a particular subject when it has bargained over that subject matter and memorialized the results in a contract. The Board's interpretation of a contract ended where it determined that a contract covers a mandatory subject of bargaining. The court determined that the parties could only enforce their contract pursuant to an arbitration clause or by bringing suit under Section 301 of the LMRA.

---

[93] *Id.*

[94] *Id.* at 122.

CHAPTER 18

ACCOMMODATION OF BOARD ACTION TO THE ARBITRATION PROCESS

I. Introduction and Historical Development

A. Arbitration and the Courts

In *Circuit City Stores v. Adams*,[1] the Supreme Court ruled that the exclusion provision of Section 1 of the Federal Arbitration Act (FAA) ("seamen, railroad employees or any other class of workers engaged in foreign or interstate commerce") is limited to transportation workers and that the FAA applies to all other contracts of employment of those employed in commerce.

In *Coca-Cola Bottling Co. v. Soft Drink & Brewery Workers Local 812*,[2] the Second Circuit, relying on *Lincoln Mills*,[3] held that the FAA does not apply in cases brought under Section 301 of the Labor Management Relations Act authorizing suits in federal court for violations of collective bargaining agreements. The court affirmed the district court's order compelling arbitration by the parties pursuant to their collective bargaining agreement.

Courts continue to hold that arbitration is a creature of contract and that there is a presumption of arbitrability when a binding collective bargaining agreement exists between the parties. As a result, contractual clauses excluding certain matters from arbitration must be specific as to which types of complaints are excluded from the grievance procedure.[4]

---

[1]532 U.S. 105, 123 (2001).

[2]242 F.3d 52, 171 LRRM 2390 (2d Cir. 2001).

[3]Textile Workers v. Lincoln Mills, 353 U.S. 448, 40 LRRM 2113 (1957).

[4]City of Galveston v. Galveston Mun. Police Ass'n, 57 S.W.3d 532, 537, 171 LRRM 2297 (Tex. Ct. App. 2001) (clause to remove from grievance process "[a]ny matter covered by the City Charter of Galveston, City Ordinances of Galveston,

B. Jurisdiction of the NLRB Over Arbitral Matters

Litton Financial[5] holds that parties must arbitrate a post-expiration action that infringes upon a right that accrued or vested under the agreement during its term. However, a district court held that *Litton* did not apply where a union's right to arbitrate post-expiration grievances did not arise until a new agreement was enacted.[6] The court reasoned that a grievance cannot be deemed to have arisen until the affected party actually receives notice of an adverse action, and not when the complained-of decision was made. In this instance, the employer notified the employees that they could not return to work until the day after the commencement of the new agreement. However, courts continue to apply *Litton* post-expiration where the substance of the dispute arose before expiration[7] or where the agreement contemplated that dues checkoff would survive expiration.[8] They are cautious to point out that arbitrators and courts, not the Board, are the primary interpreters of contracts.[9]

The court in *Honeywell International, Inc. v. NLRB*,[10] relying upon *Litton*, held that expiration of the collective bargaining agreement did not defeat the unilateral change doctrine. Thus, the court denied the petition to review the Board's Section 8(a)(5) order and rejected the employer's argument that arbitration, not the Board, was the appropriate forum.[11]

---

and the statutes and constitutional provisions of Texas" is not a specific exclusion because instead of expressly referring to any precise subjects, it essentially incorporates by reference the entire ever-changing body of Texas statutory law and most of the laws of Galveston). *See also* Adirondack Transit Lines, Inc. v. Transportation Workers Local 1582, 305 F.3d 82, 170 LRRM 3038 (2d Cir. 2002) (holding that employer suing for attorneys' fees was under no duty to arbitrate its request for fees employer incurred in preparing for grievance that union unilaterally withdrew, where narrowly drawn arbitration provision of collective bargaining agreement applies only "if" employee-initiated grievance procedure has been invoked, and attorneys' fees dispute was initiated by employer).

[5]Litton Fin. Printing Div. v. NLRB, 501 U.S. 190, 137 LRRM 2441 (1991).

[6]Metals USA, Inc., v. Sheet Metal Int'l Ass'n Local 19, 2001 WL1231758, 168 LRRM 2575 (E.D. Pa. Oct. 15, 2001).

[7]Halsey Drug Co. v. Drug, Chem., Cosmetic, Plastics & Affiliated Indus. Warehouse Employees, 192 F. Supp. 2d 192, 169 LRRM 3202 (S.D.N.Y. 2002).

[8]Providence Journal Co. v. Providence Newspaper Guild, 308 F.3d 129, 171 LRRM 2012 (1st Cir. 2002).

[9]NLRB v. Oklahoma Fixture Co., 295 F.3d 1143, 170 LRRM 2501 (10th Cir. 2002).

[10]253 F.3d 125, 167 LRRM 2545 (D.C. Cir. 2001).

[11]*But see* Paper, Allied Indus., Chem. & Energy Workers v. Air Prods. & Chems., Inc., 300 F.3d 667, 170 LRRM 2779 (6th Cir. 2002), where the Sixth Circuit, relying on *Carey v. Westinghouse Elec. Corp.*, 375 U.S. 261, 55 LRRM 2042 (1964), held that

C. From Postarbitration Deferral under *Spielberg* to Prearbitration Deferral Under *Collyer*

3. Collyer *in the Reviewing Courts*

Courts continue to uphold the Board's deferral policies under the *Collyer* doctrine.[12]

II. PREARBITRAL DEFERRAL: APPLYING THE *COLLYER* DOCTRINE

A. The Parties' Relationship

The Board continues to refuse to defer under *Collyer* when an employer's conduct evidences an enmity toward the principle of collective bargaining.[13] Where an employer engages in bad-faith bargaining with an intent to avoid a contract, the Board also continues to refuse to defer.[14] Where there is no claim of animosity by the employer toward the employees exercising their protected rights, the Board continues to hold that deferral may be appropriate.[15]

---

arbitration, and not the NLRB, was the appropriate forum to decide a dispute arising from the employer's refusal to apply an existing contract to a new facility, despite the fact that representation questions may have been involved.

[12]DaimlerChrysler Corp. v. NLRB, 288 F.3d 434, 169 LRRM 3217 (D.C. Cir. 2002). The D.C. Circuit held that it was obliged to uphold the Board's policy on the scope of *Collyer* so long as it is rational and consistent with the Act, and that the Board's policy regarding deferral remains unchanged.

[13]Joseph Chevrolet, 343 NLRB No. 2, 176 LRRM 1262 (2004) (refusing deferral when union was decertified and pending charges alleged antiunion animus and a pattern of violations); Arvinmeritor, Inc., 340 NLRB No. 124, 174 LRRM 1350 (2003) (refusing deferral where employer repudiated its obligation to continue meeting with union); Budrovich Constr. Co., 331 NLRB 1333, 171 LRRM 1079 (2000) (refusing deferral in light of employer animus towards employees that filed grievances and evidence of employer's tendency to disregard contract "when it sees fit and for its own business convenience and[without] worry about the consequences with the union"), *enforced*, 20 Fed. Appx. 596, 171 LRRM 3216 (8th Cir. 2000); Wire Prods. Mfg. Corp., 328 NLRB 855, 165 LRRM 1016 (1999) (refusing deferral when employer conduct indicated rejection of collective bargaining process and employee organizational rights).

[14]United States Ecology Corp., 331 NLRB 223, 165 LRRM 1197 (2000), *enforced*, 26 Fed. Appx. 435, 169 LRRM 2320 (6th Cir. 2001).

[15]Republic Die & Tool Co., 343 NLRB No. 78, 177 LRRM 1021 (2004); Caritas Good Samaritan Med. Ctr., 340 NLRB No. 6, 173 LRRM 1169 (2003).

B. The Parties' Willingness to Arbitrate and Arbitrability

The Board has refused to defer under *Collyer* where an employer has prevailed upon the arbitrator to decide the case on a procedural ground, and not on the merits.[16] The Board has also refused to defer when no arbitration agreement exists.[17] Moreover, the Board found deferral under *Collyer* inappropriate where the charging party had no ability to invoke the grievance procedure to resolve the contract dispute.[18]

C. Whether the Dispute Centers on the Collective Bargaining Agreement

1. *Matters Incidentally Related to the Collective Bargaining Agreement*

The Board has found deferral improper where an employer transferred work previously performed by bargaining-unit employees to employees at a different facility. Subsequent to the transfer of work, the employer laid off the bargaining-unit employees, withdrew its recognition of the union, terminated the contract, and implemented new terms and conditions of employment. The Board found that while the decision to transfer may have been subject to arbitration standing alone, the subsequent issues (withdrawal of recognition, termination of the collective bargaining agreement, and changing terms and conditions of employment) were not. Reiterating its policy against bifurcated proceedings, the Board refused to defer.[19]

---

[16]Jackson County Comm'n on Aging, 339 NLRB 962, 174 LRRM 1519 (2003) (finding arbitrator's decision to dismiss without consideration of merits of unfair labor practice allegations cannot serve as basis for deferral); Pepsi-Cola Co., 330 NLRB 474, 164 LRRM 1013 (2000) (employer initially prevailed on arbitrator to decide case on procedural ground, and not merits, and arbitrator thereafter refused to decide case on merits, even though employer ultimately requested that arbitrator decide case on merits), *supp. dec.*, 333 NLRB 87, 172 LRRM 1192 (2001).

[17]Crittenton Hosp., 343 NLRB No. 81, 176 LRRM 1193 (2004); Quirk Tire, 330 NLRB 917, 166 LRRM 1235 (2000), *enforced in part and vacated in part*, 241 F.3d 41, 166 LRRM 2666 (1st Cir. 2001), *reaff'd*, 340 NLRB No. 33, 173 LRRM 1260 (2003). *Cf.* UPS v. Teamsters Local 385, 2001 U.S. Dist. LEXIS 23597, 169 LRRM 2172 (M.D. Fla. Mar. 8, 2001) (refusing deferral when arbitration was not addressed in collective bargaining agreement and parties had no independent agreement).

[18]Chemical Workers Local 6-0682 (Checker Motors Corp.), 339 NLRB 291, 174 LRRM 1102 (2003).

[19]Avery Dennison, 330 NLRB 389, 163 LRRM 1033 (1999); *see also* Arvinmeritor, Inc., 340 NLRB No. 124, 174 LRRM 1350 (2003) ("When as here, an allegation for which deferral is sought is inextricably related to other complaint allegations that

The Board has also refused to defer resolution of a Section 8(a)(1) charge relating to bulletin boards when the issue was not addressed in the parties' collective bargaining agreement.[20] The Board reasoned that deferral was inappropriate absent an assurance that the Section 7 rights at issue were covered by the parties' contract. On the other hand, the Board continues to hold that prearbitral deferral is appropriate where the underlying dispute before the Board implicates the interpretation or application of the collective bargaining agreement.[21]

3. *Matters Involving the Contract: Unilateral Action*

The Board will defer a charge of a Section 8(a)(5) violation based on a unilateral change in terms and conditions of employment if the employer's action arises from its interpretation of a contractual term covering the issue and the contract can plausibly be interpreted to allow the employer's change.[22] If, however, the contractual language will not necessarily resolve the issue, and there is not a clear and unmistakable waiver by the union of its right to negotiate over that term of employment, the Board will find a violation of Section 8(a)(5) and refuse to defer the issue to arbitration.[23]

4. *Demands for Information*

Current Board law provides that allegations of failure to provide information are not subject to deferral to the grievance-arbitration process.[24] This rule has the effect of allowing parties to "piggy-

---

are either inappropriate for deferral or for which deferral is not sought, a party's request for deferral must be denied."); Convergence Comm., Inc., 339 NLRB 408, 173 LRRM 1351(2003) (finding existence of collective bargaining relationship a poor subject for deferral and noting that rationale for deferral loses force when the employer tries to terminate relationship with union); Wonder Bread, Div. of Interstate Brands Corp., 343 NLRB No. 14 (2004) (*Collyer* prearbitral deferral of unfair labor practice charges challenging unilateral changes is appropriate where grievance arbitration clause is extremely broad).

[20]Stevens Graphics, Inc., 339 NLRB 457, 172 LRRM 1327 (2003).

[21]Caritas Good Samaritan Med. Ctr. 340 NLRB No. 6, 173 LRRM 1169 (2003).

[22]Tri-Clover, Inc., 336 NLRB 1048, 168 LRRM 1433 (2001): *In re* Charles S. Wilson Mem'l Hosp., 331 NLRB 1529, 171 LRRM 1484 (2000).

[23]*Id.*

[24]*See, e.g.*, DaimlerChrysler Corp., 331 NLRB 1324 n.3, 169 LRRM 1493 (2000) (allegations that employer has refused to furnish information requested by exclusive bargaining representative are not deferrable); Mt. Sinai Hosp., 331 NLRB 895, 169 LRRM 1206 (2000), *enforced*, 8 Fed. Appx. 111 (2d Cir. 2001); Western Golf &

back" other unfair labor practice allegations that would otherwise be deferrable under the Board's *Collyer* doctrine, where a failure to provide information is also alleged. As a result, the Board presently decides these cases in the first instance.

The Board, in *Shaw's Supermarkets, Inc.*,[25] noted that nondeferral of charges involving failure to provide information facilitates arbitration by allowing the parties to analyze the respective merits of their cases prior to engaging in arbitration. The Board in that case reaffirmed its nondeferral principle in circumstances where the union sought information after an arbitration award was rendered, while the parties were disputing the implementation of the award. The Board rejected the employer's argument that the union was attempting to use the Board as a substitute for district court enforcement of the award pursuant to Section 301 of the LMRA, instead finding on the contrary that the union sought the information to properly determine whether an enforcement action was necessary. Dissenting, Chairman Battista sought to distinguish pre- and post-arbitration information requests, explaining his view that the policy of nondeferral inherently applied to prearbitration information requests where the desire to avoid multi-tiered arbitrations was implicated.[26] Although the Board majority refused to recognize such a distinction, Member Acosta appeared to acknowledge that the unique circumstances of a post-award information request militated against deferral.[27]

Other former Board members have previously reiterated their preference for deferral of information request cases, reasoning that such requests often involve questions of contract interpretation, and thus are more aptly suited to arbitration. In *Phoenix Coca-Cola Bottling Co.*[28] and *Baptist Hospital of East Tennessee*,[29] Members Cowen and Bartlett both wrote opinions expressing support for deferral to arbitration of at least some information request cases, contending that

---

Country Club, 335 NLRB 1085, 171 LRRM 1153 (2001) (deferral to arbitration award is inappropriate where employer has unlawfully withheld information relevant to arbitration proceeding). *See also* Crittenton Hosp., 342 NLRB No. 67, 175 LRRM 1283 (2004) (disfavoring piecemeal approach to deferral).

[25]339 NLRB 871, 173 LRRM 1163 (2003).

[26]*Id.* at 872.

[27]*Id.* at 871 n.1.

[28]338 NLRB 498, 171 LRRM 1433 (2002).

[29]338 NLRB 249, 171 LRRM 1129 (2002).

where a union seeks information to determine if the employer has violated the collective bargaining agreement, a dispute arising out of such an information request should be "addressed in the first instance under the dispute resolution procedures that the parties themselves have agreed to, i.e., through the grievance-arbitration procedure, or in the absence of applicable procedures for arbitrable resolution, Sections 301 of the Act."[30]

The Board's general counsel has also urged the Board to reconsider its nondeferral policy with respect to charges involving an alleged refusal to furnish information. In the general counsel's view, more deferrals to private dispute resolution mechanisms facilitate case handling and conserve Board resources, and the Board's ruling on an information request does not always end the information dispute, as parties are often ordered to bargain about cost or confidentiality issues.[31]

III. Post-Arbitral Deferral: Applying the *Spielberg* Standards

A. The Issue Under the Act Was Presented and Considered in Arbitration

The Board has adhered to precedent and continues to hold that deferral is improper where the arbitrator failed to address or adequately consider the unfair labor practice issue.[32]

---

[30] *Id.* at 498 (Member Bartlett, concurring). *See also* Ormet Aluminum Mill Prods., 335 NLRB 788, 790–91, 169 LRRM 1514 (2001) (Member Hurtgen, dissenting, found that extensive information requests prior to arbitration amounted to impermissible "pretrial discovery," and that any disputes concerning scope of union's right to such information should be resolved by arbitrator together with merits of underlying claim).

[31] See report of the General Counsel, released November 8, 2002, available at http://www.nlrb.gov/nlrb/press/releases/r2464.asp. *See also* Elizabeth Garfield, *Deferral of Information Disputes: A Game of Blind Man's Bluff*, and Marc J. Bloch, Frederick J. Englehart, and Meridith A. Lobitz, *Arbitration Versus the NLRB: Deferral of Charges Involving Union Requests for Information in the Collective Bargaining Context*, presented at the 32nd Annual Midwinter Meeting of the Committee on the Development of the Law Under the NLRA (Feb. 29–Mar. 3, 2004), available at http://www.bna.com/bnabooks/ababna/nlra/2004/Garfield.pdf and http://www.bna.com/bnabooks/ababna/nlra/2004/bloch.doc.

[32] *See* Airborne Freight Corp., 343 NLRB No. 72, 176 LRRM 1529 (2004) (noting that the Board continues to hold that the General Counsel can meet his burden by demonstrating that the arbitrator did not "adequately consider issues rel-

B. Fair and Regular Proceedings

1. *The Arbitral Procedure*

The Board in *Laborers Local 294*[33] adhered to precedent and deferred to two arbitration decisions when it found that the arbitrator had been given all relevant records and all of the affected grievants were represented by independent counsel.[34]

---

evant to the Act"); United Parcel Serv., 340 NLRB No. 89, 173 LRRM 1337 (2003) (refusing deferral where joint committee failed to consider grievant's protected activity); Turner Constr. Co., 339 NLRB 451, 174 LRRM 1102 (2003) (deferral appropriate where general counsel did not prove, inter alia, that contract issues and unfair labor practice issues were not parallel); Yellow Freight Sys., Inc., 337 NLRB 568, 170 LRRM 1218 (2002) (permitting deferral to arbitrators' decision where employee was discharged for leaving worksite following chemical spill and transcript established that arbitrators considered facts relevant to resolving unfair labor practice issue); *see also* Phoenix Transit Sys., 337 NLRB 510, 170 LRRM 1001 (2002) (refusing deferral where arbitrator failed to consider whether employees have right protected by Act to complain about perceived sexual harassment, and whether employee's actions in writing and publishing information about harassment were protected by Act); Pepsi-Cola Co., 330 NLRB 474, 164 LRRM 1013 (2000) (Board refused to defer to arbitrator's award where the arbitrator refused to address merits of dispute, and based decision only on procedural elements of claim), *supplemented*, 333 NLRB 87, 172 LRRM 1192 (2001). *See also In re* Kohler Mix Specialties, Inc., 332 NLRB 630, 172 LRRM 1035 (2000); Western Golf & Country Club, 335 NLRB 1085, 171 LRRM 1153 (2001) (deferral to arbitration award is inappropriate where employer has unlawfully withheld information relevant to arbitration proceeding); New Orleans Cold Storage Warehouse, 326 NLRB 1471, 163 LRRM 1095 (1998), *enforced*, 201 F.3d 592, 163 LRRM 2330 (5th Cir. 2000); Nationsway Transp., 327 NLRB 1033, 164 LRRM 1339 (1999).

[33]331 NLRB 259, 164 LRRM 1169 (2000).

[34]*See also* Airborne Freight Corp., 343 NLRB No. 72, 176 LRRM 1529 (2004) (relying on *Laborers Local 294* for proposition that deferral is appropriate where arbitration proceedings are fair and regular, all parties have agreed to be bound, the decision is not repugnant to the Act, "the contractual issue before the arbitrator is factually parallel to the unfair labor practice issue; and the arbitrator has been presented generally with the facts relevant to resolve any unfair labor practice").

2. *Hostility of the Tribunal or Union Representative Toward the Grievant*

The Board continues to follow the rule that it will not defer to a grievance settlement when the union has shown hostility to the charging party.[35]

C. Agreement of All Parties to Be Bound

The Board continues to adhere to precedent, and requires an agreement that all parties be bound before deferring to an arbitral award.[36]

D. The Award Is Not Repugnant to the Policies of the Act

The Board continues to refuse to defer to an arbitration award when the result would be repugnant to the Act. For example, in *Titanium Metals Corp*,[37] the Board refused to defer where a grievance settlement was reached without the grievant's participation or his agreement to be bound. Indeed, the grievant became aware of the settlement only during preparation for the unfair labor practice hearing. Moreover, the reasons cited for the grievant's discharge in the settlement agreement were not the reasons given him when he was discharged. In the absence of any explanation from the employer or the union for this deviation, the Board found that the settlement agreement "appear[ed] to be an attempt to disguise the real reason for his discharge: [the grievant's] protected concerted activity." Under these circumstances, the Board found the settlement agreement did not satisfy the *Spielberg* standard of fairness and regularity. However, on review, the D.C. Circuit reversed the Board's findings in *Titanium Metals Corp.*, holding that the Board had abused its discretion in determining that the settlement agreement was not fair and regular.[38] Though the Board offered two justifications for the deci-

---

[35]U.S. Postal Serv., 336 NLRB 1182, 174 LRRM 1158 (2001) (no deferral to grievance settlement when interests of charging party discriminatee is in obvious conflict with interests of union).

[36]*See* Laborers Local 271, 341 NLRB No. 70, 174 LRRM 1317 (2004) (holding that, where union repeatedly refused to be bound by arbitrator's decision, and employer's testimony supported this fact, there is no voluntary agreement that would bind the parties).

[37]340 NLRB No. 88, 173 LRRM 1402 (2003).

[38]392 F.3d 439, 176 LRRM 2073 (D.C. Cir. 2004).

sion—the agreement was not disclosed to the affected employee, and the reason given to the employee upon his discharge differed from the reasons contained in the settlement agreement—the court found that neither explanation justified the Board's conclusion, because nothing in the record indicated that the statements contained in the discharge were factually unsupportable. The court concluded that what is "fair and regular" must be measured by reference to the parties' collective bargaining agreement, and not by reference to the "Board's abstract sense of what is right."[39]

Similarly, in *United States Postal Service*,[40] the Board refused to defer when employees engaged in protected activity and the arbitrator ignored Board precedent.[41] In *Mt. Sinai Hospital*,[42] the Board refused deferral where the arbitrator's opinion stated that no statutory provision prevented an employer from unilaterally changing the scope of the bargaining unit. The Board held that the arbitrator's decision contradicted the well-established principle that once a position has been included in a bargaining unit, the employer may not remove the position without the consent of the union.[43]

The Board continues to defer to arbitration awards that are not repugnant to the policies of the Act.[44]

---

[39]*Id.* at 449.

[40]332 NLRB 340, 169 LRRM 1127 (2000), *enforced*, 25 Fed. Appx. 41 (2d Cir. 2001).

[41]*See also* Mobil Exploration & Producing U.S. v. NLRB, 200 F.3d 230, 163 LRRM 2387 (5th Cir. 1999), *enforcing* 325 NLRB 176, 156 LRRM 1273 (1997) (Board properly found that arbitration award—upholding employee's discharge and finding that his remarks to co-worker in lunchroom that employer was trying to fire him and had security guard after him for trying to "right a wrong" and assert his opposition to union president were delivered in insubordinate manner, stripping him of protection—was "clearly repugnant" to purposes and policies of Act).

[42]331 NLRB 895, 169 LRRM 1206 (2000), *enforced*, 8 Fed. Appx. 111, 2001 WL 533552 (2d Cir. 2001).

[43]*Id.*; *see also* U.S. Steel, 340 NLRB No. 22, 173 LRRM 1505 (2003) (no deferral to prearbitration settlement where, inter alia, putative grievance settlement was "clearly repugnant" to principles and policies of Act); *U.S. Postal Serv.*, *supra* note 40.

[44]Bell-Atlantic-Pennsylvania, 339 NLRB 1084, 173 LRRM 1340 (2003) (deferral appropriate notwithstanding that wearing "Road Kill" shirt by customer contract employees was protected activity because arbitrator's decision that §7 rights must give way to employer's legitimate interest in protecting its public image is not repugnant to Act).

IV. OTHER FACTORS AFFECTING THE BOARD'S POST-ARBITRAL DEFERRAL POLICY

A. Representation Cases

The Board continues to adhere to its position that representation case issues, including appropriateness of unit and eligibility to vote, are for the Board to decide and should not be deferred.[45]

B. Certain Unfair Labor Practices: Sections 8(a)(2) and 8(a)(4)

In *Nationsway Transport Service*,[46] the Board affirmed the administrative law judge's refusal to defer to the parties' settlement of a grievance where the "contractual issue resolved by the grievance settlement [was] not factually parallel to the unfair labor practice issues raised by the complaint and . . . therefore, deferral to the settlement [was] not warranted under *Postal Service*."[47]

C. Work-Assignment Disputes, Deferral by Statute

In determining the amount of evidentiary weight to attribute to an arbitration award in a work-assignment dispute under Section 10(k), the Board has given little or no weight to awards when one of the parties did not participate in or agree to be bound by the proceeding.[48] In *Advance Cast Stone Co. v. Iron Workers*, the Seventh Circuit vacated an arbitration award that conflicted with the Board's Section 10(k) determination and endorsed the Board's position that the Board may proceed with a determination of a dispute under Section 10(k) where there is no agreed-upon voluntary mechanism for resolving the dispute.[49]

---

[45]Shaw's Supermarkets & Food & Commercial Workers Local 791, 343 NLRB No. 105, 176 LRRM 1220 (2004).

[46]327 NLRB 1033, 164 LRRM 1339 (1999).

[47]300 NLRB 196, 135 LRRM 1209 (1990).

[48]Operating Eng'rs Local 3 (Westar Marine Servs.), 340 NLRB No. 131, 173 LRRM 1556 (2003); Teamsters Local 179, 334 NLRB 362, 169 LRRM 1250 (2001).

[49]376 F.3d 734, 175 LRRM 2321 (2004).

D. Settlement or Other Disposition Under a Grievance Procedure Short of an Arbitral Award

1. *Deferral to Joint Committee Awards*

The Board continues to hold that deferral is not proper where the arbitration proceedings were not deemed fair and regular, thus failing the *Spielberg* standards.[50]

2. *Deferral to Voluntary Grievance Settlements*

In *Titanium Metals Corp. v. NLRB*,[51] the D.C. Circuit held that the Board abused its discretion when it refused to defer to a grievance settlement on the belief that the "fair and regular" proceedings element of the deferral standard was not met. Rejecting the Board's position that the proceeding was not "fair and regular" where the discharged employee had no knowledge that his union and the employer entered into a settlement agreement, the court found that it was legally irrelevant that the discharged employee had not participated in and was not notified of the settlement agreement.[52] In finding that the grievance settlement was "fair and regular" under the first prong of the deferral standard outlined in *Spielberg*[53] and *Alpha Beta*,[54] the D.C. Circuit clarified that "[w]hat is 'fair and regular' under the first prong of *Alpha Beta* must be measured by reference to the parties' collective bargaining agreement, not by reference to the Board's abstract sense of what is right."[55]

3. *Deferral to Grievances Dropped by the Union*

Where a grievance was withdrawn without the discharged employee's participation in or even knowledge of the settlement

---

[50]U.S. Postal Serv., 336 NLRB 1182, 174 LRRM 1158 (2001).

[51]392 F.3d 439, 176 LRRM 2073 (D.C. Cir. 2004), *denying enforcement to* 340 NLRB No. 88, 173 LRRM 1402 (2001).

[52]*Id.*, 392 F.3d at 448.

[53]112 NLRB 1080, 36 LRRM 1152 (1955).

[54]Alpha Beta Co., 273 NLRB 1546, 118 LRRM 1202 (1985), *aff'd sub nom.* Mahon v. NLRB, 808 F.2d 1342, 124 LRRM 2762 (9th Cir. 1987).

[55]392 F.3d 439, 449, 176 LRRM 2073 (D.C. Cir. 2004).

agreement between the union and the employer, the "fair and regular" proceedings element of the deferral standard was not met.[56]

V. Response of the Reviewing Court to the Board's Deferral Standards

The courts continue to uphold the Board's refusal to defer to an arbitration award in cases where the Board is found to have properly applied the applicable standards to the facts of the particular case.[57]

---

[56] *See Titanium Metals Corp., supra* note 51; U.S. Steel, 340 NLRB No. 22, 173 LRRM 1505 (2003).

[57] *See, e.g.*, Phoenix Transit Sys. v. NLRB, 63 Fed. Appx. 524, 2003 WL 21186045 (D.C. Cir. 2003) (Board properly refused to defer to arbitrator's award where arbitrator limited his decision to whether violation of employer's directive warranted discharge under collective bargaining agreement and arbitrator failed to consider whether the directive, that employees not discuss sexual harassment by a supervisor, violated the Act); DaimlerChrysler Corp. v. NLRB, 288 F.3d 434, 169 LRRM 3217 (D.C. Cir. 2002) (stating that "this court has no authority on this record to second-guess the Board's application of well established precedent" and holding that Board, under *Collyer* doctrine, properly refused to defer to arbitrator regarding dispute over alleged refusal by employer to provide information requested by union for use in grievance process); NLRB v. U.S. Postal Serv., 25 Fed. Appx. 41 (2d Cir. 2001), *enforcing* 332 NLRB 340, 169 LRRM 1127 (2000) (Board properly applied *Spielberg* factors when it refused to defer to arbitration award, where it reasonably determined that employees at issue were wrongfully discharged; upheld findings that arbitrator ignored precedent and parties' collective bargaining agreement and that arbitrator's decision was wrong and repugnant to Act); New Orleans Cold Storage & Warehouse Co. v. NLRB, 201 F.3d 592, 163 LRRM 2330 (5th Cir. 2000), *enforcing* 325 NLRB 176, 156 LRRM 1273 (1997) (Board properly applied *Spielberg* factors in refusing to defer to award, where arbitrator limited decision to question of whether employer was obligated to assign employee to specific job he previously held, and did not consider employee's claim before Board that he had been discriminatorily assigned to different job upon reinstatement and later discharged for engaging in protected activity); Mobil Exploration & Producing U.S. v. NLRB, 200 F.3d 230, 163 LRRM 2387 (5th Cir. 1999), *enforcing* 325 NLRB 176, 156 LRRM 1273 (1997) (Board's refusal to defer to arbitration decision upholding employees' discharge for allegedly breaching duty of confidentiality had sound basis in precedent; Board applied well-established balancing test to determine award was "clearly repugnant" to the Act and found that employees' substantial §7 right to engage in the activity in question was not outweighed by employer's "superficial claim of a confidentiality interest").

Part VI

ECONOMIC ACTION

BIBLIOGRAPHY

Gerald E. Berendt, David Moberg, and Stephen Franklin, *The Labor Strike: Is It Still a Useful Economic Weapon for Unions?*, 35 J. MARSHALL L. REV. 255 (2002)

James K. Bradley and Daniel R. Schuckers, *Toward a Unified Theory of Unemployed Compensation Eligibility for Replaced Striking Employees*, 61 U. PITT. L. REV. 499 (2000)

Alexandra E. Burns, *Eroding "Mutual Aid or Protection": Subjective Motivation and Employee Refusal to Cross Picket Lines*, 48 EMORY L.J. 267 (1999)

Kenneth N. Dickens, Town & Country Electric, Inc. v. The National Labor Relations Board: *Salts: We're Employees—What Happens Now?*, 99 W. VA. L. REV. 561 (1997)

George Feldman, *Unions, Solidarity, and Class: The Limits of Liberal Labor Law*, 15 BERKELEY J. EMP. & LAB. L. 187 (1994)

Julius G. Getman and F. Ray Marshall, *The Continuing Assault on the Right to Strike*, 79 TEX. L. REV. 703 (2001)

Seth D. Harris, *Coase's Paradox and the Inefficiency of Permanent Strike Replacements*, 80 WASH. U. L.Q. 1185 (2002)

Raymond Hogler and Steven Shulman, *The Law, Economics, and Politics of Right to Work: Colorado's Labor Peace Act and Its Implications for Public Policy*, 70 U. COLO. L. REV. 871 (1999)

Michael H. LeRoy, *Employer Treatment of Permanently Replaced Strikers, 1935-1991: Public Policy Implications*, 13 YALE L. & POL'Y REV. 1 (1995)

Michael H. LeRoy and John H. Johnson, IV, *Death By Lethal Injection: Emergency Strikes Under the Taft-Hartley Act and the Moribund Right to Strike*, 43 ARIZ. L. REV. 63 (2001)

Michael D. Moberly, *Striking a Happy Medium: The Conversion of Unfair Labor Practice Strikes to Economic Strikes*, 22 BERKELEY J. EMP. & LAB. L. 131 (2001)

Mindy Schwartz, *The American Federation of Musicians: The Unearned Encore for Featherbedding*, 47 WAYNE L. REV. 1339 (2001)

Chapter 19

THE PRIMARY STRIKE

I. INTRODUCTION: THE RIGHT TO STRIKE

A. Constitutional Protection

The First Amendment to the Constitution of the United States, as well as the constitutions of most states, contains express prohibitions against the enactment of laws that would abridge the freedom of speech. Expression associated with labor strikes, including rallies, picketing, and leafleting are generally forms of constitutionally protected free speech.[1] Consequently, these activities may not be abridged by states,[2] without meeting the requisite constitutional scrutiny.[3]

For example, in *CF&I Steel v. Steelworkers*,[4] the Colorado Supreme Court ruled that a provision of the Colorado Labor Peace Act prohibiting residential labor picketing violated the First and Fourteenth Amendments of the U.S. Constitution. Noting that the law "prohibits all labor picketing regardless of its peacefulness, but does not prohibit any non-labor picketing, whether it be peaceful or not," the court found that "[t]he regulation's categorical prohibition of picketing arising from labor disputes is not narrowly tailored to advance

---

[1]Frisby v. Schultz, 487 U.S. 474, 479 (1988). *See* Dean v. Byerley, 354 F.3d 540, 549–50 (6th Cir. 2004) ("Over sixty years ago, the Supreme Court declared that use of the streets for assembly and communication is a right held by U.S. citizens pursuant to the First Amendment. The Supreme Court has also declared that 'as a general matter peaceful picketing and leafleting are expressive activities involving "speech" protected by the First Amendment.'"). *See also* Hague v. Committee for Indus. Org., 307 U.S. 496, 515–16 (1939); United States v. Grace, 461 U.S. 171, 176 (1983).

[2]*See* New York Times Co. v. Sullivan, 376 U.S. 254 (1964) (acknowledging that although the First Amendment, as originally drafted, does not technically apply to states, it was made applicable to states by virtue of the Fourteenth Amendment).

[3]*See generally* New England Reg'l Council of Carpenters v. Kinton, 284 F.3d 9 (1st Cir. 2002) (in context of union leafleting, court observed that constitutional standard by which validity of restriction on speech will be tested depends on nature of forum in which restriction applies and type of restriction). *See also* Make the Road by Walking, Inc., v. Turner, 378 F.3d 133, 142–44 (2d Cir. 2004) (The Supreme Court has recognized three types of forums across a spectrum of constitutional protection for expressive activity. Restrictions on activity in traditionally public forums must be content-neutral and narrowly tailored to serve a compelling state interest. Designated public forum restrictions are subject to the same restrictions as traditional public forums. Restrictions on expressive activity in limited public forums, a subset of the designated public forum, must be reasonable and viewpoint neutral. Finally, nonpublic forum restrictions need only be reasonable and not designed to suppress expression of selected viewpoints.).

[4]23 P.3d 1197, 167 LRRM 2370 (Colo. 2001).

the state's interest in residential privacy, and therefore violates the First Amendment."[5] In addition, because "any valid interest the state may have in preserving residential privacy and tranquility is not furthered by [the statute's] selective prohibition of labor picketing . . .[,] the Act may not stand under the Equal Protection Clause" of the Fourteenth Amendment.[6]

The particular level of scrutiny that the courts will apply in affording constitutional free speech protection to expressive activities incident to labor strikes may depend on the nature of the location in which unions express their views. In *Hotel & Restaurant Employees Local 100 v. New York City Department of Parks & Recreation (HEAREU)*,[7] for example, the Second Circuit considered whether union picketing in the central plaza of Lincoln Center, a performing arts complex, was a constitutionally protected activity. Lincoln Center had a policy of restricting the public's organized use of the plaza to events "having a performance, entertainment or other artistic component."[8] The court rejected the union's argument that the plaza was a "hybrid of a park, sidewalk and public thoroughfare and therefore [deserved] traditional public forum status."[9] Had the plaza been deemed a public forum, any content-based restriction would have been subject to strict scrutiny.

Further, the court declined to decide, on the facts presented, whether the plaza was a limited public forum or a nonpublic forum, holding that even if it were a limited public forum, "the union's proposed activities fall outside the class of expressive uses for which the Plaza has been opened."[10] The court reasoned that Lincoln Center's policy, though content-based, was viewpoint-neutral and thus permissible, even in a limited public forum.[11]

In addition, the court found Lincoln Center's enforcement of its policy of prohibiting political and labor-related demonstrations to be reasonable in light of Lincoln Center's purpose and function.

---

[5] *Id.* at 1204, 167 LRRM at 2376.

[6] *Id.*

[7] 311 F.3d 534, 171 LRRM 2321 (2d Cir. 2002).

[8] *Id.* at 553, 171 LRRM at 2323.

[9] *Id.* at 549, 552, 171 LRRM at 2330, 2332.

[10] In *Lincoln Center for the Performing Arts, Inc.*, 340 NLRB No. 134, 174 LRRM 1486 (2003), the Board distinguished the adjacent Columbus Avenue sidewalk from the plaza as a public forum, and prevented Lincoln Center from interfering with the union's free speech activity on the sidewalk.

[11] *Hotel & Restaurant Employees Local 100, supra* note 7, 311 F.3d at 553.

"The reasonableness of the Government's restriction . . . must be assessed in light of the purpose of the forum and all the surrounding circumstances, and must be consistent with the government's legitimate interest in preserving the property for the use to which it is lawfully dedicated."[12]

B. Preemption

Courts have applied the preemption doctrine to cases in which state action was taken to aid the target of union activity. In *New England Healthcare Employees District 1199 v. Rowland*,[13] the court considered whether anticipatory subsidies provided to nursing homes in advance of a massive strike of nurses and aides were preempted. The subsidies, calculated to cover the costs associated with obtaining strike replacement workers, were made available under the umbrella of the state's Medicaid program and pursuant to a state statute authorizing expenditures for the payment of "extraordinary and unanticipated costs."[14] The state defended the subsidies by citing its obligations under the Social Security Act and state law to safeguard the health and welfare of its indigent elderly. The court held that such anticipatory subsidies could be valid (i.e., not preempted) if it were shown that they were "necessary to avoid the immediate negative impact to residents' health"[15] caused by a nursing home's financial inability to prepare for a strike. However, in that case, prior to making the subsidy payments, the state undertook only a cursory, aggregate analysis of the nursing homes' ability to cope with the strike.[16] Thus the subsidies were preempted. In order not to have been preempted, a case-by-case analysis would have been required, utilizing a "minimally reliable process for determining that a nursing home could not avoid the threat to resident health and safety."[17]

---

[12] *Compare* American Civil Liberties Union of Nev. v. Las Vegas, 333 F.3d 1092, 1104 (9th Cir. 2003) ("Where the Court held that government intent is a factor in evaluating traditional public forum status, [*HEAREU*] attempts to distinguish the myriad of cases to the contrary by stating that they should stand only for the proposition that 'government may not alter by fiat what is indisputably a traditional public forum.' . . . We respectfully disagree with this reading of the cases, as well as with the practical implications of this holding.")

[13] 221 F. Supp. 2d 297, 171 LRRM 2070 (D. Conn. 2002).

[14] *Id.* at 306, 171 LRRM at 2075 (citing CONN. GEN. STAT. §17b-340).

[15] *Id.* at 333, 171 LRRM at 2079.

[16] *Id.* at 335, 171 LRRM at 2079.

[17] *Id.*

Courts have continued to hold that state statutes infringing on an employer's right to replace strikers are preempted by the Act. For example, in *State v. Labor Ready, Inc.*,[18] the Washington State Court of Appeals held that a strikebreaker statute providing that employers could not use services of third parties in securing replacement personnel was preempted. Courts have been much less willing, however, to conclude that common law claims brought by individuals hired as strike replacements are preempted,[19] relying on the Supreme Court's decision in *Belknap, Inc. v. Hale*.[20]

Similarly, in *Road Sprinkler Fitters Local 669 v. Herman*,[21] the D.C. Circuit rejected a union's claim that the Department of Labor's (DOL) certification of an apprenticeship program to train strike replacement workers was preempted. The union argued that the DOL had invaded the province of the Board, as the certification turned on the DOL's determination that the union was not the "collective bargaining representative" of the replacement workers. The court found that the agency had "done nothing more than resolve the [union's] representation status under agency regulations, not under the NLRA,"[22] and that "the phrase 'collective bargaining agent' need not mean the same to each" agency and did not affect the union's authority to bargain about the provisions of the training program.

---

[18]103 Wash. App. 775, 14 P.3d 828, 169 LRRM 2052 (Wash. Ct. App. 2001).

[19]*See* Baldwin v. Pirelli Armstrong Tire Corp., 3 S.W.3d 1, 160 LRRM 2541 (Tenn. Ct. App. 1999) (holding that NLRA did not preempt breach of contract claim of replacement workers who were allegedly promised permanent employment but then discharged at conclusion of strike).

[20]463 U.S. 491, 113 LRRM 3057 (1983). *But see* Law v. Operating Eng'rs Local 37, 818 A.2d 1136, 171 LRRM 3299 (Md. Ct. App. 2003) (distinguishing *Belknap*, and holding that LMRA preempts negligent misrepresentation action brought against the union in state court by employees who were discharged for engaging in recognitional strike and picketing of healthcare facility where they worked without first giving the 10-day notice required by Act).

[21]234 F.3d 1316, 166 LRRM 2008 (D.C. Cir. 2000).

[22]*Id.* at 1320, 166 LRRM at 2011.

C. Statutory Protections and Restrictions

2. *Restrictions on the Right to Strike*

The Board continues to hold that "the special strike notice requirements of Section 8(g) of the Act apply only to labor organizations, not to groups of employees."[23]

In *Beverly Health & Rehabilitation Services, Inc. v. NLRB*,[24] the D.C. Circuit rejected the Board's construction of Section 8(g) as permitting unions "to unilaterally extend a strike deadline for up to 72 hours."[25] The court held that such an interpretation of Section 8(g) was contrary to the plain meaning of the statute.

Pursuant to the emergency provisions of the Taft-Hartley Act, upon request of the President, a district court may enjoin a strike or lockout if the court determines that a threatened or actual strike or lockout will imperil national health or safety.[26] In *United States v. Pacific Maritime Ass'n*,[27] the court granted the United States' motion for a temporary restraining order enjoining longshore and warehouse unions and their members from engaging in strikes or lockouts. The court subsequently approved a joint request by the United States and the union that the temporary restraining order be converted to a preliminary injunction.[28]

The Board and courts continue to struggle with the proper standard for applying Section 502 of the Taft-Hartley Act in situations in which employees engage in work stoppages over inherently danger-

---

[23]Bethany Med. Ctr., 328 NLRB 1094, 162 LRRM 1403 (1999); Vencare Ancillary Servs., 334 NLRB 965, 168 LRRM 1029 (2001), *enforcement denied on other grounds*, 352 F.3d 318 173 LRRM 2865 (6th Cir. 2003) (enforcement denied on grounds that discharged employees were engaged in partial strike by refusing to see patients while performing other duties); Alexandria Clinic, P.A., 2003 NLRB LEXIS 509, 173 LRRM 1065 (2003) (noting that §8(g) notice is only required when a union, not individual employees, is involved in a strike). *But see* New York State Nurses Ass'n, 334 NLRB 798, 167 LRRM 1313 (2001) (nurses who refused to volunteer for overtime and those who refused assigned overtime upon recommendation of union for purpose of pressuring employer to change staffing practices engaged in concerted refusal to work within meaning of §8(g)); *see also* nn. 86–88, and accompanying text, *infra*, for a discussion of the §8(g) 10-day notice.

[24]317 F.3d 316, 171 LRRM 3017 (D.C. Cir. 2003).

[25]*Id.* at 320, 171 LRRM at 3021.

[26]29 U.S.C. §178(a).

[27]United States v. Pacific Maritime Ass'n, 2002 WL 31301033 (N.D. Cal. 2002).

[28]United States v. Pacific Maritime Ass'n, 229 F. Supp. 2d 1008, 171 LRRM 2121 (N.D. Cal. 2002).

ous conditions created by toxic hazards. In *TNS, Inc. v. NLRB*,[29] the Sixth Circuit considered the Board's interpretation of Section 502 and approved under a *Chevron*[30] analysis the Board's conclusions that: (1) Section 502 covers situations where the relevant employees are not bound by a no-strike provision; (2) to fall within the protections of Section 502, employees must have a good-faith belief in the existence of abnormally dangerous working conditions and the belief must be supported by ascertainable, objective evidence; and (3) Section 502 precludes employers from permanently replacing workers engaged in a Section 502 work stoppage. However, the court vacated the Board's order of reinstatement and back pay, finding that such a remedy was unrealistic 18 years after the events at issue.[31]

II. STRIKES PROTECTED UNDER THE ACT

B. Economic and Unfair Labor Practice Strikes

1. *Unfair Labor Practice Strikes*

In reaffirming the principle that unfair labor practice strikers cannot be permanently replaced, the Board and the courts have grappled with the issue of whether an economic dispute or an unfair labor practice actually caused a work stoppage. For example, in *Alwin Manufacturing Co. v. NLRB*,[32] the court agreed with the Board that the employer's unfair labor practices, which included the unilateral implementation of new production standards, contributed to the breakdown of negotiations over a new collective bargaining agreement and to the employees' resulting decision to strike.[33] The court

---

[29]296 F.3d 384, 170 LRRM 2474 (6th Cir. 2002), *cert. denied*, 537 U.S. 1106 (2003). This decision from the Sixth Circuit originated from a Board ruling from which the union sought review in the D.C. Circuit in *Oil, Chemical & Atomic Workers v. NLRB*, 46 F.3d 82 148 LRRM 2461 (D.C. Cir. 1995). The case was subsequently remanded to the Board because it had failed to "articulate an appropriate majority-supported statement of the rule that [it] will be applying . . . ." *TNS, Inc.*, 296 F.3d at 389, 170 LRRM at 2479. After the Board ruled on remand, however, the employer petitioned for review in the Sixth Circuit, which resulted in this opinion.

[30]Chevron v. National Resources Defense Council, Inc., 467 U.S. 837, 842–43 (1984).

[31]*TNS, Inc.*, 296 F.3d at 389–94, 170 LRRM at 2490–91.

[32]192 F.3d 133, 162 LRRM 2385 (D.C. Cir. 1999), *enforcing* 326 NLRB 646, 162 LRRM 1120 (1998).

[33]*Id.* at 141, 162 LRRM 2390–91.

held, therefore, that the Board had properly classified the strike as an unfair labor practice strike requiring the reinstatement of strikers who had been replaced.[34] The Board has reached similar results, even when there was a substantial delay between the occurrence of unfair labor practices and the commencement of a strike[35] or when the unfair labor practices were just one of the reasons for the work stoppage.[36] In *Precision Concrete v. NLRB*,[37] however, the D. C. Circuit denied enforcement of a Board reinstatement order on the ground that the Board lacked jurisdiction to consider the single alleged unfair labor practice that the Board found was a cause of the strike because no charge was brought on the alleged unfair labor practice within six months of its occurrence, as required by Section 10(b). The court held that, as a result, the strike could not be characterized as an unfair labor practice strike and that strikers had no greater reinstatement rights than economic strikers.

---

[34]*Id.* at 141–42, 162 LRRM at 2391–92. *See also* Citizens Publ'g & Printing Co., 331 NLRB 1622, 168 LRRM 1103, 1105 (2000), *enforced*, 263 F.3d 224, 235–36, 168 LRRM 2303, 2309–10 (3d Cir. 2001) (substantial evidence supported Board finding of unfair labor practice strike where employer's unilateral decision to subcontract work without collective bargaining led to strike).

[35]NLRB v. Midwestern Personnel Servs., Inc., 322 F.3d 969, 980, 171 LRRM 3217, 3225 (7th Cir. 2003), *enforcing* 331 NLRB 348, 171 LRRM 1262 (2000) (finding unfair labor practice strike where unfair labor practices were "fairly remote in time" but "by no means 'dead issues'"); RGC (USC) Mineral Sands, Inc., 332 NLRB 1633, 168 LRRM 1094, 1096 (2001), *enforced*, 281 F.3d 442, 451, 169 LRRM 2633, 2639 (4th Cir. 2002) (strike motivated, at least in part, by unfair labor practice that had occurred 10 months earlier). *But cf.* California Acrylic Indus., Inc. v. NLRB, 150 F.3d 1095, 1101, 158 LRRM 2901, 2906 (9th Cir. 1998) (fact that strike began two weeks after unfair labor practice, but only one day after Board regional director postponed hearing on union's petition for representation election, "strongly suggest[ed]" that strike was a representation or economic strike, not an unfair labor practice strike), *denying enforcement in relevant part to* 322 NLRB 41, 155 LRRM 1054.

[36]Insta-Print, Inc., 343 NLRB No. 49, 176 LRRM 1334 (2004) (finding that economic strike was converted into unfair labor practice strike once strike was motivated, in part, by unfair labor practices); Ryan Iron Works, Inc., 332 NLRB 506, 167 LRRM 1240 (2000) (employer's unfair labor practices may convert economic strike into unfair labor practice strike), *enforcement denied in relevant part*, 257 F.3d 1, 167 LRRM 2653 (1st Cir. 2001) (unfair labor practices did not prolong strike); Boydston Elec., Inc., 331 NLRB 1450, 1452, 168 LRRM 1226, 1229–30 (2000) (unfair labor practice strike was found where employer's unlawful conduct at least partially caused employees' decision to strike, regardless of whether unfair labor practices were flagrant, serious, or pervasive).

[37]334 F.3d 88, 172 LRRM 3113 (D.C. Cir. 2003), *denying enforcement to* 337 NLRB 211, 172 LRRM 1370 (2001).

The Board continues to hold that unfair labor practice strikers who make unconditional offers to return to work are entitled to immediate reinstatement, even if the employer purported to hire permanent replacements.[38] An employer may avoid its reinstatement obligation if it establishes that a striker abandoned his or her reinstatement rights by accepting other "regular and substantially equivalent employment" within the meaning of Section 2(3), although the Board maintains that acceptance of interim employment does not constitute abandonment.[39]

Applying the established rule that one joint employer can be liable for the unfair labor practices of another,[40] the Board held a joint employer liable for the unlawful refusal by another joint employer to reinstate unfair labor practice strikers.[41]

2. *Economic Strikes*

The *Mackay*[42] doctrine allowing an employer to replace permanent economic strikers retains its vitality, but the Board has contin-

---

[38]Dorsey Trailers, Inc., 327 NLRB 835, 856, 165 LRRM 1392 (1999), *enforced in relevant part*, 233 F.3d 831, 839, 165 LRRM 3003, 3007 (4th Cir. 2000). *Cf.* Sierra Bullets LLC, 340 NLRB No. 32, 173 LRRM 1283, 1285 (2003) (finding that, because the strikers were economic and not unfair labor practice strikers, the employer did not violate the law by informing employees that they could be permanently replaced while on strike).

[39]Zimmerman Plumbing & Heating Co., 339 NLRB 1302, 173 LRRM 1118 (2003).

[40]Capitol EMI Music, Inc., 311 NLRB 997, 1000, 143 LRRM 1331, 1335–36 (1993), *enforced*, 23 F.3d 399, 146 LRRM 2448 (4th Cir. 1994) (unpublished) (setting forth test for joint employer liability in the context of a supplier of employees where the nonacting joint employer (1) "knew or should have known that the other employer acted against the employee for unlawful reasons and (2) acquiesced in the unlawful action").

[41]Action Temp. Employment dba Action Multi-Craft, 337 NLRB 268, 270, 169 LRRM 1232, 1234 (2001) (joint employer had duty to investigate reason for which unfair labor practice strikers were no longer employed by other joint employers considering that refusal to reinstate unfair labor practice strikers would be unlawful regardless of employer's motive). *See also* Le Rendezvous Rest., 332 NLRB 336, 337, 165 LRRM 1341, 1342–43 (2000) (applying *Capitol-EMI* test to conclude that joint employer is liable for other employer's unlawful refusal to hire employees).

[42]NLRB v. Mackay Radio & Tel. Co., 304 U.S. 333, 2 LRRM 610 (1938); *see also* Church Homes dba Avery Heights, 343 NLRB No. 128 (2004) (employer who hired permanent replacements "in secret" did not violate the Act in the absence of a showing of independent unlawful motive); *Sierra Bullets, LLC, supra* note 38 (no violation to reinstate strikers immediately upon offers to return to work where Board found strike was economic strike).

ued placing the burden on the employer to demonstrate that it is justified to refuse reinstatement to strikers who seek to return to work.[43] An employer may not refuse to reinstate economic strikers on the ground that their work has been permanently subcontracted, in the absence of a legitimate and substantial business reason for implementing the permanent subcontract during the strike.[44] An employer also may not excuse its refusal to reinstate an employee at the conclusion of an economic strike on the ground that other employees came back to work immediately without waiting for a formal offer of reinstatement.[45]

In *Diamond Walnut Growers, Inc.*,[46] the Board held that the employer did not violate the Act when it failed to notify former economic strikers, who had made unconditional offers to return to work, that it was posting openings for jobs that were not equivalent to the strikers' prestrike jobs. The Board affirmed that an employer has no legal obligation either to apprise strikers of nonequivalent jobs, or to allow strikers to bid on them. The employer's only legal requirement is not to treat strikers discriminatorily because they are strikers.[47] Also, an employer does not violate the Act by refusing to rein-

---

[43]Omahaline Hydraulics Co., 340 NLRB No. 104, 173 LRRM 1297 (2003) (rejecting employer's contention that elimination of strikers' jobs precluded them from being eligible to vote in representation election); Pirelli Cable Corp., 331 NLRB 1538, 168 LRRM 1273 (2000) (unlawful for employer to condition reinstatement of economic strikers on submission of letters expressing desire and availability for reinstatement); Erman Corp., 330 NLRB 95, 163 LRRM 1042 (1999) (to disenfranchise striking employee, employer cannot rely on temporary economic downturn; rather it must show that employee's job was permanently eliminated).

[44]Fairfield Tower Condominium, 343 NLRB No. 101 (2004) (violation for refusal to reinstate strikers where employer lacked legitimate business justification for "permanent subcontract"); Capehorn Indus., Inc., 336 NLRB 364, 168 LRRM 1400 (2001) (failure to reinstate economic strikers upon their unconditional offers to return to work unlawful where employer failed to demonstrate permanent subcontract was supported by legitimate and substantial business justification); *see also* Consolidated Delivery & Logistics, Inc., 337 NLRB 524, 170 LRRM 1033 (2002) (employer failed to demonstrate that workers from Labor Ready, a temporary employment agency, were permanent replacements for striking workers).

[45]Jackson County Comm'n on Aging, 339 NLRB 962 (2003) (ordering reinstatement of striker who reported to work five days after strike ended, instead of next day like his co-workers).

[46]340 NLRB No. 135, 174 LRRM 1406 (2003) (that an employee is qualified to perform an available job does not establish that the job is substantially equivalent to the employee's prestrike job).

[47]*Id.*, slip op. at *2; *see also* Dayton Newspapers, Inc., 339 NLRB 962, 172 LRRM 1477 (2003) (employer's stated justifications for refusing to reinstate economic strikers who had made unconditional offers to return to work were not true for all

state economic strikers who have lost their protected status by reason of their union's failure to provide notice as required under Section 8(d).[48]

An employer may permanently replace economic strikers, but it may not discharge them prior to their being permanently replaced.[49] Thus, an employer's false declaration that economic strikers have been permanently replaced constitutes an unlawful discharge because it withholds from the strikers their rights to return to their unoccupied jobs.[50] The Board has continued to apply the "reasonable employee" standard to determine whether an employer has in fact discharged striking employees.[51] In *Kolkka Tables & Finnish-American Saunas,*[52] the Board overruled *Kerrigan Iron Works, Inc.*,[53] in which the Board had recognized that, in certain circumstances, discharge threats to strikers may constitute a lawful management tactic. The Board in *Kolkka* held that an employer violates Section 8(a)(1) of the Act if threats of discharge based on employees' strike activity lead to the employees' reasonable belief that they have been discharged.[54]

---

strikers, thus §8(a)(3) violation); *Cf.* Zimmerman Plumbing & Heating Co., 339 NLRB 1302, 173 LRRM 1118 (2003) (after unfair labor practice strike, employer should have considered striker for employment after he inquired about "the availability of work").

[48]Boghosian Raisin Packing Co., 342 NLRB No. 32 (2004).

[49]NLRB v. International Van Lines, 409 U.S. 48, 52, 81 LRRM 2595 (1972).

[50]Citizens Publ'g & Printing Co. v. NLRB, 263 F.3d 224, 168 LRRM 2303 (3d Cir. 2001).

[51]*See, e.g.*, North Am. Dismantling Corp., 331 NLRB 1557, 166 LRRM 1370 (2000) (discharge of striking employees occurs when employer's words and conduct would reasonably lead employees to believe they had been discharged).

[52]335 NLRB 844, 168 LRRM 1155 (2001).

[53]108 NLRB 933, 34 LRRM 1118 (1954), *aff'd sub nom.* Shopmen's Local 733 v. NLRB, 219 F.2d 874, 35 LRRM 2559 (6th Cir.), *cert. denied,* 350 U.S. 835, 36 LRRM 2716 (1955).

[54]*See also* Insta-Print, 343 NLRB No. 49 (2004) (applying *Kolkka* and determining that strikers were unlawfully terminated based on prestrike management statements); Dayton Newspapers, Inc., 339 NLRB 962, 172 LRRM 1477 (2003) (violation of §8(a)(1) for supervisor to tell employees on picket line that union "just cost you guys all—cost all you guys your jobs").

III. Unprotected and Prohibited Strikes

A. Unlawful or Wrongful Means

2. *Minority Strikes*

In *Engelhard Corp.*,[55] a minority of the workforce picketed the company's shareholders meeting at an off-site location. The company discharged these workers for engaging in an unauthorized strike because they violated the collective bargaining agreement's no-strike provision. The Board ruled that such discharges were unlawful, as the local union had in fact authorized the workers' conduct, and such conduct had as its objective the furtherance of the goals of the union and workforce as a whole.[56]

3. *Partial and Intermittent Strikes*

The Board continues to hold that employees who engage in partial or intermittent strikes lose the protection of the Act. For example, the Board found no violation of the Act where an employer discharged a customer service representative who asked co-workers not to interact with a vendor whose employees were striking. The Board reasoned this was solicitation to participate in an intermittent, partial work stoppage, which was an unprotected activity.[57] Similarly, the Board approved an administrative law judge's (ALJ) recommendation that a "grade strike" by teaching fellows at Yale University was an unprotected activity because it was a partial strike and the strikers had effectively misappropriated property of the university as a result of this activity.[58]

The Board found that five employees at a nursing facility who refused to see patients while at the same time continuing to perform

---

[55]342 NLRB No. 5, 175 LRRM 1001 (2004).

[56]The Board also held that the picketing did not contravene the proscriptions of the bargaining agreement, as it did not serve to disrupt or suspend any work performed at the plaint.

[57]Electronic Data Sys. Corp., 331 NLRB 343, 164 LRRM 1211 (2000).

[58]Yale Univ. & Graduate Employees & Students Orgs., 330 NLRB 246, 162 LRRM 1393 (1999). *But see* Mt. Clemens Gen. Hosp. v. NLRB, 328 F.3d 837, 172 LRRM 2513 (6th Cir. 2003) (nurses' wearing of button with cryptic union message was not an attempt to conduct a series of intermittent strikes, thus wearing the button was a protected activity); Iowa Packing Co. & Joseph L. Walsh, 338 NLRB 1140, 173 LRRM 1246 (2003) (finding that employees did not engage in an unprotected partial or intermittent strike when they engaged in a total work stoppage).

other tasks associated with patient care were not engaged in an unprotected partial strike.[59] The Board found that any work done after the employees announced that they were refusing to see patients was done in preparation for, and in conjunction with, the work stoppage. Prior to engaging in a work stoppage and while waiting for the employer's response to their complaints about a proposed wage cut, most of the employees used that short period of time to make sure that patient records were up to date. They did not expect to be compensated and they left immediately when directed to do so by the employer. In these circumstances, the Board found that the employees were not attempting to set their own terms and conditions of employment because they were not defiantly performing only some of their duties while insisting on being paid for such tactics.

However, the Sixth Circuit denied enforcement of the Board's order, finding that the employees' actions constituted an unprotected partial strike and that their discharge was lawful.[60] The court, unlike the Board, found it significant that the employees did some work after making their demands known. Although the Board implied that they were doing work necessary for the protection of patients, the Sixth Circuit found no evidence that any of the performed work fell into that category. The court reiterated that employees must completely stop working or risk being discharged for engaging in an unprotected activity.[61]

The Board continues to hold that refusal to perform voluntary work is not an unprotected partial strike. For example, in *St. Barnabas Hospital*,[62] the Board held that a hospital violated Section 8(a)(1) by terminating four physicians for threatening to cease voluntary work. The Board reasoned that threatening to cease voluntary work—in that case voluntary on-call work—was a protected concerted activity and the employer could not use the threats as a substantial factor in its decision to fire the employees.

The Board also continues to hold that concerted intentionally inefficient work performance constitutes an unlawful partial strike

[59]Vencare Ancillary Servs., Inc., 334 NLRB 965, 168 LRRM 1029 (2001), *enforcement denied*, 352 F.3d 318, 173 LRRM 2865 (6th Cir. 2003).

[60]352 F.3d 318, 173 LRRM 2865 (6th Cir. 2003).

[61]*Id.* at 323, 173 LRRM at 2869.

[62]St. Barnabas Hosp., 334 NLRB 1000, 168 LRRM 1005 (2001), *enforced*, 46 Fed. Appx. 32, 171 LRRM 2064 (2d Cir. 2002). *See also* Main Edition, Chapter 6, "Interference with Protected Rights," at Section III.C.2. [Other Concerted Activity; Unprotected Concerted Activities; Partial and Intermittent Strikes].

that an employer may legally discipline. The Board found that construction employees intentionally installed utility boxes improperly, resulting in a work slowdown.[63] Although the evidence showed that the employer's discipline was the result of an unlawful discriminatory motive, the Board held that under *Wright Line*, the employer would have otherwise been justified in disciplining the employees for the intentional slowdown. As a result, the Board maintained its rule that work slowdowns or partial stoppages are unprotected conduct.[64]

4. *Picket Line Misconduct; Strike Violence*

The Board has continued to recognize that an employer may discharge employees who engage in picket line misconduct during the course of a strike. For example, in *Siemens Energy & Automation, Inc.*,[65] the Board held that the discharge of a striker who kicked cars and threw roofing tacks onto the roadway at the vehicular entrance to the employer's plant did not violate the Act. The Board found that such conduct may reasonably tend to coerce or intimidate employees in the exercise of their right to refrain from participating in the strike. In another case, *CalMat Co.*,[66] the Board found no Section 8(a)(1) violation where an employer told a striker—who was retired—that he was not eligible for rehire. In that case, the striker had threatened a security guard with physical harm and carried a collapsible nightstick on the picket line. In the same case, another striker was lawfully discharged for stepping in front of a slow-moving truck as it attempted to cross the picket line, and then trying to assault the truck driver.[67] In *Electrical Workers (IBEW) Local 98*,[68] the Board ruled that an organizer's conduct was unlawful and unprotected where he blocked a nonunion state employee from using his forklift at a jobsite, threatened him with physical harm, and videotaped and photographed him and other nonunion workers in a coercive, menacing manner. The Board further ruled that an organizer was acting as an agent of two locals, which were both, therefore, vicariously liable for

---

[63]Framan Mech., Inc., 343 NLRB No. 53 (2004).

[64]*Id.*, slip op. at *42.

[65]328 NLRB 1175, 162 LRRM 1083 (1999).

[66]326 NLRB 130, 161 LRRM 1016 (1998).

[67]*Id. See also* KSM Indus., Inc., 336 NLRB 133, 169 LRRM 1445 (2001) (employer lawfully discharged striker who assaulted supervisor on picket line), *aff'd on reconsideration*, 337 NLRB 987, 170 LRRM 1313 (2002).

[68]342 NLRB No. 74, 175 LRRM 1235 (2004).

his conduct.[69] Even though Local 380 had not authorized or ratified the organizer's particular acts, it had empowered him to represent it within the general area in which he acted, and the organizer acted with apparent authority on Local 380's behalf.

In *Detroit News, Inc.*,[70] the Board ruled that an employer properly discharged a union member for engaging in harassing and intimidating behavior that interfered with the employer's attempt to interview applicants off site for summer internship positions. An editor of the *Detroit News* was at the University of Michigan's Ann Arbor campus interviewing students. A reporter for the newspaper was at the university attending a solidarity rally against the *Detroit News* with members of other unions. During the rally, a speaker announced that the *Detroit News* was in the process of conducting interviews on campus at that very moment. The rally then made its way to the academic building where the editor was meeting with students. The demonstrators entered the building and made so much noise that the interviews ended, and the students grew fearful. Fifty demonstrators then burst into the interview room and formed a horseshoe around the editor and students, who had tried to contact security but were not audible over the demonstrators' shouts. In the wake of the incident, the newspaper terminated the reporter for his participation. The administrative law judge found, and the Board affirmed, that the reporter's conduct was not protected because he had no right to directly interfere with the *Detroit News*' effort to hire employees—even student interns—in the manner he did.

In *Patrick Media Group*,[71] however, the Board concluded that the employer's discharge of a striker for provoking and engaging in a fight with the employer's security guard violated Section 8(a)(1) because the evidence did not establish that anything more than a verbal altercation had taken place. Likewise, in *Detroit Newspaper Agency*,[72] the Board ruled that the conduct of a striker was not sufficiently egregious to bar his reinstatement where the employer terminated the striker because it believed that while he was on the picket line, he had squirted a liquid into the eyes of a security guard, causing a burning sensation. As it turned out, the striker had a water pistol, which he was using to squirt various people on the picket line

---

[69] *Id.*

[70] 341 NLRB No. 125, 175 LRRM 1399 (2004).

[71] 326 NLRB 1287, 163 LRRM 1064 (1998), *enforced*, 203 F.3d 53 (D.C. Cir. 1999).

[72] 342 NLRB No. 24, 175 LRRM 1200 (2004).

(including fellow strikers), and to drink from. In response to the security guard's following the striker around with a video camera, the striker squirted his water pistol at the camera's lens, accidentally spraying the security guard in the eye with water. The Board ruled that it had been unreasonable for the employer to conclude that any person who witnessed the occurrence would have felt coerced or intimidated by the striker's use of the water pistol.

The Board also rejected in *Overnite Transportation Co.* an employer's attempt to use alleged strike misconduct on the part of an international union as a defense to a refusal to bargain with a newly certified local union, as there was no evidence that the international union was acting as the agent of the local unions.[73] Under principles of agency law, the local unions could not be held responsible for the actions of their international union. In contrast, in *Detroit News, Inc.*,[74] although a protesting union member was not accountable for the activities of other demonstrators from other unions, the group activity was itself unprotected and the union member's being an active participant in it (he was far more than a passive observer) sufficed to sustain his discharge.

In *Sodexho Marriott Services, Inc.*,[75] the Board held that when the evidence establishes that the reason for an employee's discharge was unlawful, it is unnecessary to determine whether the employee's misconduct during a group meeting was sufficient to deprive the employee of protection of the Act because the evidence establishes such a reason is pretextual.[76]

Union officials can be held liable for strike misconduct if they purposefully choose not to prevent such misconduct. In a decision by the First Circuit, union officials verbally told strikers to not engage in misconduct, but did nothing to prevent such misconduct at the picket line.[77] The court of appeals issued an injunction against union officials after finding that they waited until after an important

---

[73]333 NLRB 472, 166 LRRM 1280 (2001), *enforced*, 294 F.3d 615, 170 LRRM 2362 (4th Cir. 2002).

[74]341 NLRB No. 125, 175 LRRM 1399 (2004).

[75]335 NLRB 538, 172 LRRM 1060 (2001).

[76]*See also* Pratt Towers, Inc., 338 NLRB 61, 170 LRRM 1533 (2002) (although strikers engaged in misconduct, employer wrongfully refused to rehire them because it conditioned rehire on striker renouncement of union, condition Board characterized as "a yellow dog contract").

[77]Univar, U.S.A. v. Teamsters Local 251, 98 Fed. Appx. 21 (1st Cir. 2004).

delivery to the employer was delayed. It held that such intentional inaction by union officials effectively "authorized" the misconduct.[78]

In *Church Homes, Inc. dba Avery Heights,*[79] the Board, in overruling the decision of the administrative law judge, found that verbal insults by a striking worker directed at the relative of a customer sufficiently constituted strike misconduct such that discharge of the employee was justified.

B. Unlawful or Wrongful Ends

1. *Strikes in Violation of the Act*

The Board has continued to hold that a strike or other economic action in support of a proposal on a nonmandatory bargaining subject is unlawful.[80] The Board held that a union does not violate Section 8(b)(1)(B) by pressuring an independent employer to sign a contract containing the same provisions as those in an agreement the union has already negotiated with a multi-employer association.[81] This action by the union does not coerce employers to select the multi-employer association as their collective bargaining representative where there is no evidence the union insisted that the independent employer make the multi-employer association its representative for future collective bargaining.

The Act also limits the actions unions can take with respect to work jurisdiction issues. The Board found reasonable cause to believe that a carpenters union violated Section 8(b) by engaging in a strike with the object of obtaining exclusively work that was being distributed to employees represented by a roofers union.[82]

---

[78] *Id.* at 23.

[79] 343 NLRB No. 128 (2004).

[80] Detroit Newspaper Agency, 327 NLRB 799, 160 LRRM 1193 (1999), *rev'd on other grounds*, 216 F.3d 109, 164 LRRM 2797 (D.C. Cir. 2000).

[81] Teamsters Local 282 (E.G. Clemente Contracting Corp.), 335 NLRB 1253, 168 LRRM 1185 (2001), *overruling* Commercial Workers Local 1439 (Food City W.), 262 NLRB 309, 110 LRRM 1285 (1982), *and* Laborers Local 652 (Thoner & Birmingham Constr. Corp.), 238 NLRB 1456, 99 LRRM 1683 (1978) (to extent that those cases are inconsistent with general rule that while union violates §8(b)(1)(B) by insisting that employer make multi-employer association its representative for purpose of future collective bargaining, there is no violation where union pressures independent employer to sign contract containing same provisions as those in multi-employer association agreement). *See* Teamsters Local 705 (Kankakee-Iroquois), 274 NLRB 1176, 118 LRRM 1497 (1985), *petition for review denied sub nom.* Kankakee-Iroquois County Employers' Ass'n v. NLRB, 825 F.2d 1091, 125 LRRM 2820 (7th Cir. 1987).

[82] Chicago & Northeast Illinois Dist. Council of Carpenters, 341 NLRB 73, 175 LRRM 1150 (2004).

Failing to provide notice of a strike violates the Act. The Board held that a worker did not lose protected status as an employee when the worker's union failed to give proper notice under Section 8(d) of its refusal to refer workers from a hiring hall.[83] In reversing the Board, the D.C. Circuit ruled that a union's failure to provide all Section 8(d) notices prior to striking made all of the hiring-hall's registrants unlawful strikers.[84] As a result, registrants were no longer protected by the NLRA, and the employers could legally refuse to hire union members from the union hiring hall, even if they were not actually employed at the time of the strike.

In another case, the Board held that an employer was not required to reinstate strikers because they had lost their protected status under the Act by failing to file a notice with the Federal Mediation and Conciliation Service prior to striking as required by the Section 8(d).[85]

In *Alexandria Clinic*,[86] a divided Board held nurses who began a strike four hours after the time designated in their union notice to a health clinic were legally discharged for failing to comply with notice provisions of Section 8(g) of the Act, which require unions representing employees at a health care facility to provide at least 10 days' notice "before engaging in any strike, picketing, or other concerted refusal to work" and to notify the employer of the "date and time that such action will commence."[87] Although the notice requirements do allow for an extension "by written agreement of both parties,"[88] the union did not inform the clinic the strike would be postponed by four hours, nor seek an extension.

2. *Strikes in Breach of Contract*

The Eighth Circuit recently affirmed an award of damages to an employer for breach of contract where there was evidence that picketing was a disguise for grievances subject to arbitration under the parties' agreement and was effectively a work stoppage and where

---

[83]Freeman Decorating Co., 336 NLRB 1, 168 LRRM 1329 (2001).

[84]Theatrical & Stage Employees v. NLRB, 334 F.3d 27, 172 LRRM 2993 (D.C. Cir. 2003).

[85]Boghosian Raisin Packing Co., 342 NLRB 32, 175 LRRM 1286 (2004).

[86]Alexandria Clinic P.A., 339 NLRB 1262, 173 LRRM 1065 (2003).

[87]*Id.*, 173 LRRM at 1066 n. 3.

[88]*Id.*, 173 LRRM at 1066 (quoting Greater New Orleans Artificial Kidney Ctr., 240 NLRB 432, 100 LRRM 1300 (1979)).

the union failed to provide contractually required notices in advance of striking.[89]

The Fourth Circuit has held that where picketing regarding grievable matters is intended to cause a work stoppage, it is not informational picketing, no matter how few workers participate.[90] Therefore, such picketing is not protected by Section 7 of the Act.

By contrast, a Board panel majority held that picketing the company's shareholders meeting at a hotel more than 70 miles away from the employer's facility did not violate a no-strike provision in the collective bargaining agreement between the employer and the union.[91]

The Eighth Circuit, in *Teamsters Local 682 v. KCI Construction Co.*, remanded to the district court the issue of whether a union violated a project agreement by striking.[92] In order to make that determination, the Eighth Circuit instructed the district court to decide whether the provision at issue was a no-strike clause or an impermissible "hot cargo agreement" which requires the employer to cease its business relationships with another employer.[93]

IV. Rights of Employees Respecting Picket Lines: Sympathy Strikes

B. Effect of Contractual Waiver of Rights

In reaffirming earlier holdings that waiver of the right to engage in sympathy strikes must be clear and unmistakable, the Ninth Circuit in *Children's Hospital Medical Center of Northern California v. California Nurses Ass'n*[94] adopted the reasoning of the *Indianapolis Power*[95] cases and examined extrinsic evidence to determine if a no-

---

[89]Allied Systems, Ltd. v. Teamsters Local 604, 304 F.3d 785, 170 LRRM 3033 (8th Cir. 2002), *cert. denied*, 538 U.S. 924, 172 LRRM 2128 (2003).

[90]Mine Workers v. Island Creek Coal Co., 179 F.3d 133, 161 LRRM 2463 (4th Cir. 1999).

[91]Engelhard Corp., 342 NLRB No. 5 (2004).

[92]384 F.3d 532, 175 LRRM 2848 (8th Cir. 2004).

[93]*Id.* at 541.

[94]283 F.3d 1188, 169 LRRM 2779 (9th Cir. 2002).

[95]Indianapolis Power & Light Co., 273 NLRB 1715, 118 LRRM 1201 (1985), *rev'd and remanded sub nom.* Electrical Workers (IBEW) Local 1395 v. NLRB, 797 F.2d 1027, 122 LRRM 3265 (D.C. Cir. 1986), *decision on remand*, 291 NLRB 1039, 130 LRRM 1001 (1988), *enforced*, 898 F.2d 524, 133 LRRM 2921 (7th Cir. 1990).

strike clause, which was general in scope, was intended to include sympathy strikes. In that case, extrinsic evidence including the parties' bargaining history, the context in which the contract was negotiated, the interpretation of the contract by the parties, and the parties' past practice demonstrated that there was no mutual intent to waive the employees' right to engage in sympathy strikes.[96]

The Ninth Circuit followed *Children's Hospital*[97] in *Standard Concrete Products, Inc. v. Teamsters Local 952*[98] to find no waiver. The court held that a contract provision prohibiting reprisals against employees who refused to cross picket lines approved by the union demonstrated that the parties did not intend the contract's no-strike clause to encompass a ban on sympathy strikes. The court observed that the employer, which had long maintained separate agreements covering separate bargaining units, had negotiated the no-reprisal provision recognizing that employees in one unit were free to participate in a sympathy strike in support of fellow employees in the other unit.

The Sixth Circuit has held that a union could not be enjoined from striking over an employer's decision that one facility's pay rate would govern when it was merged with another, despite the presence of a no-strike clause in the collective bargaining agreement, because the issue of whether the strike was covered by the provision of the agreement was itself arbitrable.[99] Meanwhile, the Seventh Circuit held that a collective bargaining agreement's no-strike clause was meant to apply to sympathy strikes for the signatory union's own picket lines, where the agreement's sympathy-strike exception explicitly referred only to the picket lines of other unions and not to those of the signatory union.[100]

---

[96]*Supra* note 94, 283 F.3d at 1195–96, 169 LRRM 2786.

[97]*Supra* note 94.

[98]353 F.3d 668, 173 LRRM 2897 (9th Cir. 2003).

[99]Allied Sys. Ltd. v. Teamsters Local 327, 179 F.3d 982, 161 LRRM 2493 (6th Cir.), *cert. denied*, 528 U.S. 965, 162 LRRM 2704 (1999). *See also* Earthgrains Baking Cos. v. Teamsters Local 78, 35 F. Supp. 2d 1203, 160 LRRM 2638 (E.D. Cal. 1999) (court denied employer's request for preliminary injunction where court found that issue of whether no-strike clause of collective bargaining agreement was applicable would have to be addressed before any ruling on injunctive relief).

[100]R.L. Coolsaet Constr. Co. v. Operating Eng'rs Local 150, 177 F.3d 648, 161 LRRM 2195 (7th Cir.), *cert. denied*, 528 U.S. 1004, 162 LRRM 2832 (1999).

CHAPTER 20

THE LOCKOUT

I. INTRODUCTION: HISTORICAL PERSPECTIVE

C. Evolution of Justifiable Lockouts: The Defensive Lockout

1. The Single-Employer Defensive Lockout

The Board and the courts continue to adhere to the principle that defensive lockouts are permissible where an employer's actions are not motivated by a purpose to interfere with and defeat its employees' union activities,[1] and where such actions are intended to avoid severe economic hardships caused by a union's use of economic weapons.[2]

---

[1]Pepsi Cola Bottling Co. of Montgomery, 72 NLRB 601, 19 LRRM 1208 (1947).

[2]*See, e.g.*, Tomco Communications, 220 NLRB 636, 90 LRRM 1321 (1975), *enforcement denied*, 567 F.2d 871, 97 LRRM 2660 (9th Cir. 1978), and other cases cited in the Main Edition, Chapter 20, Section I.C.1., at page 1518, nn. 40–42.

In *Electrical Workers (IBEW) Local 702 v. NLRB*,[3] the D.C. Circuit denied a request for review of the Board's decision in *Central Illinois Public Service Co.*[4] The court affirmed the Board's conclusion that the employer did not act unlawfully when it locked out its employees in response to the union's "inside game" tactics such as working to rule and refusing voluntary overtime, as well as to pressure from the union to reach agreement. The court agreed with the Board that because the lockout was not inherently destructive of employee rights, it was necessary to establish that the employer's motivation for the lockout was improper to find the lockout to be unlawful. The court held that the employer had the right to engage in the lockout as a defensive measure to counteract the union's "inside game" tactics, even assuming that such tactics were protected activity.

In *CII Carbon*,[5] the employer locked out only those employees who worked at a location where an act of sabotage occurred. The Board held that the employer had a legitimate and substantial business justification for the lockout because sabotage was an unprotected activity, the employer acted out of a concern for safety, and the employer's preliminary investigation revealed that the sabotage could have occurred only with the complicity or knowledge of the unit employees at that particular location. Moreover, the Board found no probative evidence that the employer had an antiunion motivation in locking out the employees.

In *Techno Construction Corp.*,[6] the Board held that a temporary layoff of four employee drivers in response to their expressions of union support violated Section 8(a)(3) and was not a lawful defensive lockout as contended by the employer.

Sociedad Española de Auxilio Mutuo y Beneficencia de P.R. dba Hospital Español Auxilio Mutuo de P.R., Inc.,[7] involved a lockout by a health care institution in response to the union's announcement of two 48-hour strikes spaced approximately one week apart during the Christmas and New Year's holidays. When the union notified the employer that the first strike would be cancelled, the employer moved the lockout forward to coincide with the time the first strike had been scheduled to begin. The Board held that the employer had a substantial and legitimate business justification for locking out the employees

---

[3]215 F.3d 11, 164 LRRM 2193 (D.C. Cir.), *cert. denied*, 121 S. Ct. 654, 165 LRRM 3056 (2000).

[4]326 NLRB 928, 159 LRRM 1217 (1998).

[5]331 NLRB 1157, 171 LRRM 1216 (2000).

[6]333 NLRB 75, 166 LRRM 1121 (2001).

[7]342 NLRB No. 40, 175 LRRM 1161 (2004).

because it had a reasonable concern that it would not be able to find replacements during the holidays. The Board also viewed the employer's comments that the lockout was caused by the union as "truthful" statements rather than evidence of a discriminatory motive.

II. CONTEMPORARY LAW OF LOCKOUTS

A. The Offensive Economic Lockout—In General

The Board continues to apply the standards set forth in *American Ship Building v. NLRB*[8] and *NLRB v. Brown Food Store*[9] in evaluating whether the use of the lockout as an offensive weapon in the collective bargaining process is lawful.

1. *Lockouts Occurring in Conjunction With Employer Unfair Labor Practices*

In *Eddy Potash, Inc.*,[10] the employer bargained to impasse and insisted, as a condition of reaching any final collective bargaining agreement, that the unions agree to 12-hour shifts for employees working in underground mines. The employer locked out its employees to pressure the unions to agree to this proposal. The Board concluded that the 12-hour-shift proposal was an illegal subject of bargaining because it violated the Mineral Lands and Mining Act of 1920, and, therefore, that it was unlawful for the employer to insist to impasse on that proposal. As a consequence, the employer's offensive lockout to force agreement to that proposal was also found to be unlawful.

In *Graphic Communications Local 458-3M (Chicago) v. NLRB*,[11] the D.C. Circuit affirmed the Board's conclusion that the employer's offensive lockout was lawful because its purpose was to apply economic pressure on the employees to support its legitimate bargaining position. The court agreed with the Board that although the employer's bargaining position may have been regressive, it did not

---

[8]380 U.S. 300, 58 LRRM 2672 (1965).

[9]380 U.S. 278, 58 LRRM 2663 (1965).

[10]331 NLRB 552, 170 LRRM 1406 (2000).

[11]206 F.3d 22, 163 LRRM 2833 (D.C. Cir. 2000), *denying petition for review*, 325 NLRB 1166, 158 LRRM 1241 (1998).

amount to bad faith bargaining. Therefore, the lockout in support of the position was not unlawful.[12]

Royal Motor Sales[13] involved two offensive lockouts that were found illegal under *American Ship Building.*[14] Regarding the first lockout, the employer claimed it had a substantial business justification because the lockout was necessitated by contractual provisions as a prerequisite to lawful implementation of its final proposal. The Board rejected this argument and held that the lockout was unlawful because the union had waived any such contractual requirements, and the lockout merely served as a preliminary step to an unlawful implementation because the parties were not at impasse, given the context of serious unremedied unfair labor practices.

Regarding the second lockout, the employer implemented its final offer at a time when it had neither reached a lawful impasse nor asserted the existence of economic exigencies. The Board found that the employer locked out its employees with the intent of retaliating against them because their bargaining representative insisted on good faith collective bargaining. Moreover, the Board found that the employer locked out its employees with the intent of coercing the union to accept its unilaterally implemented final offer. Because the employer's unilateral, pre-impasse implementation of its final offer constituted an unfair labor practice, the final offer was held to be an illegitimate bargaining position that the employer was not free to pursue through the use of a lockout.[15]

In *Operating Engineers v. NLRB,*[16] the employer created a "lockout list" that included striking employees, prior employees who were on a nearly 10-month old *Excelsior* list, and other individuals who were neither strikers nor on the *Excelsior* list. The employer, in hiring replacements during the lockout, falsely informed six applicants on the lockout list that no work was available. The D.C. Circuit con-

---

[12]*See also* Electrical Workers (IBEW) Local 702 v. NLRB, 215 F.3d 11, 164 LRRM 2193 (D.C. Cir.), *cert. denied,* 121 S. Ct. 654, 165 LRRM 3056 (2000), in which the court affirmed the Board's findings that the lockout was lawful under both defensive and offensive criteria.

[13]329 NLRB 760, 166 LRRM 1123 (1999), *enforced,* 2 Fed. Appx. 1, 167 LRRM 2704 (D.C. Cir. 2001).

[14]American Ship Bldg. v. NLRB, 380 U.S. 300, 58 LRRM 2672 (1965).

[15]*Royal Motor Sales, supra* note 13, 329 NLRB at 764, 166 LRRM at 1142.

[16]294 F.3d 186, 170 LRRM 2497 (D.C. Cir. 2002), *granting review and remanding* 333 NLRB 1264, 167 LRRM 1051 (2001).

cluded that the false statement to the six applicants who were union members but not strikers precluded them from being able to "re-evaluate their positions."[17] The court, applying the Board's refusal-to-hire burden shifting analysis set forth in *FES, a Division of Thermo Power*,[18] held that the Board failed to consider evidence of the employer's union animus from the employer's inclusion on the lockout list of individuals who were neither strikers nor on the *Excelsior* list, from the employer's false statement, and from the employer's use of the outdated *Excelsior* list. The matter was remanded to the Board for further proceedings. On remand, the Board found that the employer's failure to consider for hire the six applicants on the lockout list was unlawfully motivated by animus toward union members.[19]

3. *The Pre-Impasse Lockout*

Although the existence of an impasse is still not a prerequisite for a finding of a lawful offensive lockout,[20] the impasse and lockout doctrine continue to intersect in cases arising under Sections 8(a)(1), (3), and (5).[21]

5. *The Partial Lockout*

In *Allen Storage & Moving Co.*,[22] the Board found unlawful an employer lockout during which the employer allowed the sole non-striker in the unit to work. The Board found that allowing the non-striker to work during the lockout was evidence of discriminatory motivation sufficient to invalidate the employer's lockout. The Board also found the lockout unlawful as it was designed to force the employees to accept unlawful unilateral change in connection with an insurance benefit.

---

[17] *Id.*, 294 F.3d at 191, 170 LRRM at 2500.

[18] 331 NLRB 9, 164 LRRM 1065 (2000), *enforced*, 301 F.3d 83, 170 LRRM 2729 (3d Cir. 2002). For a discussion of this decision, see Chapter 7, "Discrimination in Employment," Section II.B.1. [Employer Discrimination; Purpose of the Discrimination; Conduct Requiring Proof of Union Animus: The *Wright Line* Rule].

[19] Tidewater Constr. Corp., 341 NLRB No. 55, 174 LRRM 1249 (2004).

[20] Darling & Co., 171 NLRB 801, 68 LRRM 1133 (1968), *enforced sub nom.* Lane v. NLRB, 418 F.2d 1208, 72 LRRM 2439 (D.C. Cir. 1969).

[21] *See, e.g.*, Royal Motor Sales, 329 NLRB 760, 166 LRRM 1123 (1999), *enforced*, 2 Fed. Appx. 1, 167 LRRM 2704 (D.C. Cir. 2001).

[22] 342 NLRB No. 44, 175 LRRM 1388 (2004).

By contrast, in *Midwest Generation, EME, LLC*,[23] the Board found lawful a lockout of strikers during which crossovers and nonstrikers were allowed to work. The Board held that while the employer could have locked out all the employees, "it was no longer necessary for [the employer] to place additional pressure upon [the crossovers] in order for the [the employer] to achieve its bargaining goals, for these employees had already eschewed the strike weapon during the strike." Moreover, the Board concluded that nothing in the Act requires an employer to use the "maximum economic pressure" available.

In *Bunting Bearings Corp.*,[24] the Board held that the employer lawfully distinguished between probationary and nonprobationary employees when it locked out only nonprobationary employees following an impasse in negotiations. The Board concluded that the partial lockout was legally justified on the basis that the probationary employees had a lesser interest in the employer's bargaining proposals and had not been included in the union vote on the employer's final contract offer. The Board determined that the employer was motivated by legitimate business justifications in its decision to exert economic pressure on the nonprobationary employees, as it was the group that controlled whether its bargaining proposals would be accepted. Although all nonprobationary employees were union members and all probationary employees were not union members, the Board found that the employer drew its distinction between the two groups on the basis of probationary status and not union membership.

8. *Notification of Purpose of Lockout [New Topic]*

A fundamental principle underlying economic lockouts is that the union may end the lockout and return the employees to work by agreeing to the employer's demands. In *Dayton Newspapers, Inc.*,[25] the employer failed to give the union a clear set of conditions for the return of the employees, instead demanding acceptance of undefined "operational changes." Expanding upon *Eads Transfer*,[26] the

[23]343 NLRB No. 12, 175 LRRM 1461 (2004).

[24]343 NLRB No. 64, 175 LRRM 1513 (2004).

[25]339 NLRB 650, 172 LRRM 1477 (2003).

[26]304 NLRB 711, 138 LRRM 1168 (1991), *enforced*, 989 F.2d 373, 142 LRRM 2967 (9th Cir. 1993).

Board emphasized "employees must not only be informed that they are locked out, but they must be clearly and fully informed of the conditions they must meet to be reinstated."[27] Calling the employer's demands a "moving target," the Board found that the employer's refusal to reinstate the employees following their agreement not to call further work stoppages and to return to work violated Sections 8(a)(5) and (1).

Where an employer and union began contract negotiations despite a late 60-day notice by the union, the employer could not lock out employees fewer than 60 days after the union's late termination notice.[28]

---

[27]*Dayton Newspapers, supra* note 25, 172 LRRM at 1484.

[28]Drew Div. of Ashland Chem. Co., 336 NLRB 477, 174 LRRM 1022 (2001).

CHAPTER 21

PICKETING FOR ORGANIZATION AND RECOGNITION

III. PROSCRIBED ORGANIZATIONAL OR RECOGNITIONAL OBJECTIVE

A. Evidence of Proscribed Object

The Board continues to determine whether or not picketing is for organizational or recognitional purposes based on an analysis of the union's overall conduct, including events preceding the picketing, as well as those that accompany the picketing.[1]

[1]Electrical Workers (IBEW) Local 3 (Genmar Elec. Contracting, Inc.), 332 NLRB 1288, 171 LRRM 1064 (2000); Roofers, Waterproofers & Allied Workers Local 11 (Funderburk Roofing, Inc.), 331 NLRB 164, 171 LRRM 1127 (2000) (signs

In a series of cases pending before the Board at the time of publication, the general counsel has alleged that the display of large banners at neutral sites is picketing and thus within the proscriptions of Section 8(b)(4). On November 29, 2004, the general counsel directed the regions to consult with the Division of Advice as to whether or not to hold in abeyance proceedings in bannering cases that may otherwise warrant further proceedings until the Board resolves the bannering issues in pending cases.[2] The resolution of this issue in these pending cases may also have implications for Section 8(b)(7) cases where bannering is alleged to be picketing.

C. Area-Standards Picketing

1. *Area-Standards Object Not Proscribed*

The Board continues to examine carefully a union's claim of area-standards picketing for evidence of an unlawful objective.[3]

In *Petrochem Insulation*,[4] the Board held that petitioning state governmental agencies with objections to environmental standards of employer contracts is protected area-standards activity within the meaning of the mutual aid or protection provision of Section 7 of the Act. According to the Board, working conditions may include the safety and health of all employees who may eventually be employed at a particular worksite.

2. *Picketing on Private Property*

In determining whether an employer's exclusion of area-standards picketers violates Section 8(a)(1), the Board continues to con-

---

that say employer "does not employ members of" may impart an organizational objective); Operating Eng'rs Local 150 (R.J. Corman Derailment Serv.), Gen. Couns. Adv. Mem., Case Nos. 8-CP-383 & 17-CP-363 (2003).

[2]Regional Office Procedures for Handling Pending Section 8(b)(4)(ii)(B) Charges Involving Union "Bannering" of Neutral Persons, Operations Management Memo 05-14 (Nov. 29, 2004) is available at www.nlrb.gov.

[3]Electrical Workers (IBEW) Local 134 (Pepper Constr. Co.), 339 NLRB 123, 172 LRRM 1289 (2003); Operating Eng'rs Local 542 (Caldwell Tanks, Inc.), 338 NLRB 507, 171 LRRM 1335 (2002); Electrical Workers (IBEW) Local 98 (Swartley Bros. Eng'rs, Inc.), 337 NLRB 1270, 170 LRRM 1467 (2002); Electrical Workers (IBEW) Local 98 (The Fairfield Co.), 337 NLRB 793, 170 LRRM 1267 (2002). *See also* Kasper Trucking, Inc. v. General Chauffeurs, 2002 U.S. Dist. LEXIS 10678, 2002 WL 1315612 (N.D. Ill. 2002) (prerequisite to area-standards picketing is an investigation by the union revealing wages below area standards).

[4]330 NLRB 47, 163 LRRM 1276 (1999), *enforced*, 240 F.3d 26, 166 LRRM 2433 (D.C. Cir.), *cert. denied*, 534 U.S. 992, 168 LRRM 2672 (2001).

sider, as a threshold matter, whether the employer truly has a protectable private property interest that entitles it to exclude trespassers from the property in question. In *Best Yet Market*,[5] the employer operated a supermarket in leased space that was part of a larger shopping center. The Board concluded that neither the employer's lease nor New York law gave it the right to remove individuals from the shopping center's common areas and parking lot. At most, the Board found the employer had "parking privileges," or a "nonexclusive easement interest for limited business purposes," with respect to such areas.[6] Accordingly, the Board held the employer violated Section 8(a)(1) when it acted to exclude area-standards picketers from the center's parking lot.

The Board has found that where an employer has an insufficient property interest to exclude individuals from private property, the employer violates Section 8(a)(1) by notifying the property owner of lawful picketing and handbilling activity where it is foreseeable that such notice will interfere with the protected activity by causing the owner to take actions to remove the individuals from its private property.[7]

If an employer possesses a protectable private property interest, the Board continues to find that the *Babcock & Wilcox* discrimination exception bars an employer from prohibiting union picketing on its property when the employer allows other organizations to solicit and distribute literature, such as the Salvation Army, Boy Scouts and Girl Scouts, public schools, Veterans of Foreign Wars, and so forth.[8] The Fourth and Sixth Circuits have rejected the Board's position, find-

---

[5]339 NLRB 860, 173 LRRM 1511 (2003).

[6]*Id.* at 863–64.

[7]*Id.*; Wild Oats Mkts., Inc., 336 NLRB 179, 168 LRRM 1305 (2001).

[8]Albertson's, Inc., 332 NLRB 1132, 166 LRRM 1003 (2000), *enforcement denied*, 301 F.3d 441, 170 LRRM 2769 (6th Cir. 2002). On September 28, 2001, the Board's general counsel issued a Guidance Memorandum in response to the September 11, 2001, terrorist attacks, confirming that "an employer may lawfully permit a small number of isolated beneficent acts as exceptions to a valid non-solicitating/no-distribution rule" and explained that "in determining whether certain beneficent acts fall within this exception, the Board evaluates the 'quantum of . . . incidents' involved." Gen. Couns. Memorandum GC 01-06. For instance, in *Alle-Kiski Med. Ctr.*, 339 NLRB 361, 174 LRRM 1127 (2003), the Board rejected the employer's reliance on its no-solicitation/no-distribution policy to justify a challenged disciplinary action because it found the policy was overbroad and had been applied in a discriminatory manner. Specifically, the Board found the employer permitted numerous instances of charitable and noncharitable solicitation for extended periods of time on an annual basis.

ing that the conduct of union handbillers or organizers is not similar to that of civic and charitable organizations who obtain permission to use the property in a limited way deemed beneficial to the owner or the tenants.[9]

In contrast to cases involving charitable solicitations, the Board has held that an employer does not open its private property to nonemployee union solicitation by virtue of allowing other nonemployee solicitation that is deemed "work-related," or "an integral part" of the employer's functions and responsibilities. For example, in *Teletech Holdings, Inc.*,[10] the union challenged the employer's exclusion of handbillers on grounds that it regularly permitted a food vendor to access its parking lot for the purpose of selling lunches to its employees. The Board concluded the employer had not engaged in unlawful disparate treatment. As explained by the ALJ, the on-site access of the lunch vendor as a convenient food source to employees was beneficial to the employer and employees, and could therefore be considered work related in the sense that it assisted the employer in carrying out its functions.

In *Golden Gateway Center v. Golden Gateway Tenants Ass'n*,[11] the California Supreme Court severely limited the protection it had previously afforded for access to private property. The court held that the actions of a private property owner would constitute state action for purposes of California's constitutional free speech clause only if the property is freely and openly accessible to the public. A residential complex was found not sufficiently accessible to the public. The Board subsequently concluded, however, that *Golden Gateway* does not represent a change in the right of access to private property allowed under California law for concerted activities in support of col-

---

[9]Albertson's, Inc. v. NLRB, 301 F.3d 441, 170 LRRM 2769 (6th Cir. 2002); Sandusky Mall Co. v. NLRB, 242 F.3d 682, 692, 166 LRRM 2614 (6th Cir. 2001); Bi-Lo Stores v. NLRB, 126 F.3d 268, 156 LRRM 2261 (4th Cir. 1997); Cleveland Real Estate Partners v. NLRB, 95 F.3d 457, 153 LRRM 2285 (6th Cir. 1996). In addition to the circuit courts, the Board's discrimination analysis has received attention from members of Congress. In May, 2001, Senator Tim Hutchinson (R-AR) introduced the Preserve Charitable Giving Act to amend the Act to allow employers to permit charitable solicitations without risk that doing so would undermine the validity of their no-solicitation policies as applied to unions. 147 CONG. REC. §5438. A corresponding bill was introduced in the House of Representatives by Representative William Asa Hutchinson (R-AR). Both bills were referred to committees.

[10]342 NLRB No. 92, 175 LRRM 1400 (2004).

[11]29 P.3d 797 (Cal. 2001).

lective bargaining.[12] The Board concluded that California cases arising in the context of such political expressive activities have little if any relevance to cases arising in the context of labor-based expressive activities.[13] The D.C. Circuit disagreed and denied enforcement.[14] Applying California law, the court held that labor organizing activities may be conducted on private property only to the extent that California permits other expressive activity to be conducted on private property. Relying on several California intermediate appellate court decisions,[15] and rejecting precedent from the Ninth Circuit,[16] the court held that union organizers had no right to engage in handbilling on the privately owned parking lot of a stand-alone grocery store.

3. *Picketing on Public Property*

Contrary to picketing activity occurring on an employer's private property, the Board has held that "'an employer's exclusion of union representatives from public property violates Section 8(a)(1), so long as the union representatives are engaged in activity protected by Section 7 of the Act.'"[17] However, it is also established that an employer may lawfully seek to have police take action against picketing activity on public property where the employer is motivated by some reasonable concern, such as public safety or interference with legally protectable interests.[18]

---

[12]Winco Foods, Inc., 337 NLRB 289 n.1, 169 LRRM 1244 (2001), *enforcement denied*, 354 F.3d 870, 174 LRRM 2010 (D.C. Cir. 2004).

[13]*Id.*, 337 NLRB at 289 n.1.

[14]Waremart Foods v. NLRB, 354 F.3d 870, 174 LRRM 2010 (D.C. Cir. 2004).

[15]Albertson's, Inc. v. Young, 107 Cal. App. 4th 106, 131 Cal. Rptr. 2d 721 (Ct. App. 2003); Trader Joe's Co. v. Progressive Campaigns, Inc., 73 Cal. App. 4th 425, 86 Cal. Rptr. 2d 442 (Ct. App. 1999). The court also cited *Waremart, Inc. v. Progressive Campaigns*, 85 Cal. App. 4th 679, 102 Cal. Rptr. 2d 392 (2000), *review granted*, 105 Cal. Rptr. 2d 386 (2001), *review dismissed and cause remanded*, 119 Cal. Rptr. 2d 697 (2002), but did not rely on that opinion because it has been depublished.

[16]NLRB v. Calkins, 187 F.3d 1080, 161 LRRM 3121 (9th Cir. 1999), *cert. denied*, 529 U.S. 1098, 164 LRRM 2256 (2000).

[17]Greenbriar, 340 NLRB No. 92, 173 LRRM 1273 (2003) *enforcement denied sub nom.* CSX Hotels v. NLRB, 377 F.3d 394, 175 LRRM 2328 (4th Cir. 2004) (quoting Bristol Farms, 311 NLRB 437, 143 LRRM 1217 (1993)).

[18]Nations Rent, Inc., 342 NLRB No. 19, 175 LRRM 1416 (2004) (employer did not violate the Act when it called police regarding public property picketing because it was concerned that pickets were trespassing on its property, monitoring a police scanner and following employees home); *see also CSX Hotels v. NLRB, supra* note 17 (denying enforcement to Board decision concerning employer's actions in calling police regarding public property picketing near highway because employer was motivated by reasonable concern for public safety).

IV. Picketing When Another Union Is Currently Recognized

The Board continues to hold that a Section 8(b)(7)(A) violation will be found only when the incumbent union is lawfully recognized.[19] Thus, the Board has held that a union did not violate Section 8(b)(7)(A) when it threatened to picket an employer for recognition two days before the employer's agreement to recognize another union was to become effective.[20] Moreover, the Board held that there was also no violation once the agreement was supposed to have become effective because, although the threat remained, the employer reneged on its agreement and did not recognize the other union.[21]

The Board also continues to hold that a Section 8(b)(7)(A) violation will be found even if only one of the objectives of picketing is recognitional or organizational.[22] Whether picketing is for organizational or recognitional purposes is a question of fact to be determined from the union's overall conduct.[23] The informational nature of a picket is not a defense to a Section 8(b)(7)(A) charge in a case where the picket also has an organizational or recognitional objective.[24]

VI. Picketing of an Unreasonable Duration Absent a Petition

The Board continues to hold that Section 8(b)(7)(C) prohibits a labor organization from threatening to picket any employer with a recognitional object where such picketing has been conducted without a petition under Section 9(c) being filed within a reasonable period of time not to exceed 30 days from the commencement of such picketing.[25]

---

[19] *See* Northwest Protective Servs., 342 NLRB No. 120, 175 LRRM 1405 (2004).

[20] *Id.*, slip op. at 3.

[21] *Id.*

[22] *See* Roofers, Waterproofers & Allied-Workers Local 11 (Funderburk Roofing, Inc.), 331 NLRB 164, 171 LRRM 1127 (2000).

[23] *See* Electrical Workers (IBEW) Local 3, 332 NLRB 1288, 171 LRRM 1064 (2000) (citing Teamsters Local 618 (S&R Auto Parts), 193 NLRB 714 (1971)).

[24] *See Roofers, supra* note 22 (finding that recognition was "at the least, an objective" of picketing despite union's claim that picketing was solely informational and union's use of disclaimers of any recognitional objective).

[25] Northwest Protective Servs, Inc., 342 NLRB No. 120, 175 LRRM 1405 (2004) (citing General Serv. Employees Local 73, 239 NLRB 1233 (1979)).

The Board continues to hold that picketing for recognition in a stable one-person unit does not come within the proscriptions of Section 8(b)(7)(c) because the Board will not hold an election in a one-person unit.[26] However, Chairman Battista and Member Schaumber have declined to pass on the correctness of *Villa-Barr,* stating that they will continue to apply that precedent "in the absence of a three-member Board majority to overrule *Villa-Barr.*"[27]

The Board continues to hold that threats to or picketing for recognition by an uncertifiable mixed guard union (a union that admits both guards and nonguards) violates Section 8(b)(7)(c).[28]

A. Reasonable Period of Time

The Board continues to adhere to its position that, in certain circumstances, recognitional picketing of any duration violates Section 8(b)(7)(C).[29] For example, recognitional picketing by a union that represents guards and admits nonguards into membership violates Section 8(b)(7)(C) because under Section 9(b)(3) such a union may not be certified by the Board.[30]

VII. THE INFORMATIONAL PICKETING PROVISO

The Board and courts continue to hold that truthful picketing to inform customers that an employer does not employ members of a labor organization is protected Section 7 conduct.[31]

---

[26]*See* Teamsters Local 115 (Villa-Barr Co.), 157 NLRB 588, 61 LRRM 13, 86 (1966).

[27]International Transp. Servs., Inc., 344 NLRB No. 22 n.2 (2005).

[28]*Northwest Protective Servs., supra* note 25.

[29]*Id.* (where mixed-guard union threatens to and does picket an employer for recognition, union has violated §8(b)(7)(C) because it had not been and could not be certified as representative of employees).

[30]*Id.*

[31]*See, e.g.*, Indio Grocery Outlet, 323 NLRB 1138 n.12, 155 LRRM 1210 (1997), *enforced*, 187 F.3d 1080, 161 LRRM 3121 (9th Cir. 1999), *cert. denied*, 529 U.S. 1098, 164 LRRM 2256 (2000) (because California state law does not protect shopping mall or supermarket owners' interest in excluding speech activity from their adjacent sidewalks and parking lots, nonemployees may lawfully inform customers that employer did not employ members of labor organization; under §8(b)(7)(C)'s second proviso).

A. Scope of the Proviso: Dual-Purpose Picketing

The Board continues to permit picketing with an object of recognition or organization when the statements made on signs are limited to language that is expressly sanctioned by the second proviso to Section 8(b)(7)(C). Picketing to advise the public that an employer does not employ members of, or have a contract with, a union does not, without more, establish that the union has made a present demand for recognition as required by Section 9(c)(1)(B).[32]

The Board has found, however, that a union's dual-purpose picketing constituted a "present demand for recognition," thereby supporting the processing of a petition under Section 9(c)(1)(B), where the union contemporaneously submitted a court affidavit that it had achieved majority support through signed authorization cards.[33] The Board distinguished *New Otani Hotel*[34] as the claim by the union of majority status was not mere campaign "puffery," but rather was contained in a formal court statement under penalty of perjury.

---

[32]*See* New Otani Hotel & Garden, 331 NLRB 1078, 167 LRRM 1039 (2000) ("statements made on the Union's placards, advising the public that the Employer does not have a contract with the Union and requesting a boycott, were limited to language that is expressly sanctioned under that proviso . . . [and] such picketing does not constitute evidence of a present demand for recognition that would support the processing of a petition under Section 9(c)(1)(B)").

[33]Rapera, Inc., 333 NLRB 1287, 167 LRRM 1033 (2001).

[34]*New Otani Hotel & Garden*, *supra* note 32.

CHAPTER 22

SECONDARY ACTIVITY: HANDBILLS, PICKETS, AND STRIKES

II. SECTION 8(b)(4)(B): PROHIBITED SECONDARY ACTIVITY DEFINED

A. Definitions of Terms

In *Food & Commercial Workers Local 1996 (Visiting Nurse Health System, Inc.)*,[1] the Board held that a union may lawfully engage in secondary boycott activity against a neutral (nonprimary) employer for the purpose of enforcing its certification as a representative of the primary employer's employees, even when the primary employer is contesting that certification in court. As a consequence, the union's picketing and handbilling of a United Way office, to protest that the primary employer, which received funds from United Way, had refused to bargain with the union as the certified agent, did not constitute illegal secondary activity. The threatened picketing, the picketing itself, and the accompanying handbilling all sought to have the United Way withdraw its funding of the primary employer and encouraged the public to withhold contributions to the United Way until it took such steps.

The Board held that, although Section 8(b)(4) prohibits certain "cease doing business" and "recognition" boycotts, the plain language of the Act permits recognition boycotts, including those seeking a cessation of business with the neutral employer if the union is

---

[1]336 NLRB 421, 168 LRRM 1241 (2001), *reconsideration denied*, 338 NLRB 1074, 172 LRRM 1155 (2003).

the certified bargaining agent of the primary employer's employees and the purpose of its secondary activity is to compel the primary employer to honor the certification.[2] The majority rejected the dissent's argument that the "cease doing business" objective was illegal regardless of whether the picketing also had a recognitional objective.[3] The majority also stated that the union's right to picket did not illegally dilute the employer's right to seek court review of a certification.[4]

Courts continue to closely examine picketing[5] and handbilling activities to determine whether the activities "induce or encourage" neutral employees within the meaning of Section 8(b)(4)(i). In *Warshawsky & Co. v. NLRB*,[6] the D.C. Circuit reversed the Board's holding and found that the totality of the circumstances established that the union's handbilling was intended to "induce" neutral employees to cease work: The handbilling occurred only at times when neutral employees would be arriving at the jobsite; the handbillers engaged the neutral employees in conversation as they approached the site; and none of the neutral employees proceeded to work on the days the handbilling occurred.[7]

Courts also continue to interpret the terms "threaten, coerce or restrain" under Section 8(b)(4)(ii).[8] In *George v. National Ass'n of Letter Carriers*,[9] the Fifth Circuit stated that "the possibility of economic ramifications" does not transform otherwise lawful conduct into "threats, coercion, or restraint" under the statute. The court concluded that a union's dispatch of letters to another union

---

[2]*Id.*, 336 NLRB at 421, 168 LRRM at 1245.

[3]*Id.* at 426, 168 LRRM at 1248.

[4]*Id.* at 428, 168 LRRM at 1250.

[5]The Board has adhered to the proposition that "picketing" within the meaning of the statute does not require "patrolling." Painters District Council 9 (We're Assocs., Inc.), 329 NLRB 140, 169 LRRM 1224 (1999) ("milling around," carrying signs, and mounting sign on automobile to confront vehicles constituted "picketing").

[6]182 F.3d 948, 161 LRRM 2772 (D.C. Cir. 1999), *cert. denied sub nom.* Ironworkers Local 386 v. Warshawsky & Co., 529 U.S. 1003, 163 LRRM 2704 (2000).

[7]*Cf.* Electrical Workers (IBEW) Local 98 (Telephone Man), 327 NLRB 593, 167 LRRM 1178 (1999) (violation of §8(b)(4)(i)(B) based on harsh comments by union to neutral employees: "The words 'induce or encourage' are broad enough to include in them every form of influence and persuasion.").

[8]*See generally* Pettibone, *Bannering Neutral—Coercive Secondary Boycott or Free Speech?*, 18 LAB. L. 349 (2003).

[9]185 F.3d 380, 162 LRRM 2137 (5th Cir. 1999), *cert. denied*, 528 U.S. 1156, 163 LRRM 2576 (2000).

to persuade the latter union's members to join the union's boycott did not violate Section 8(b)(4)(ii)(B). The court noted that letter writing had even fewer potentially coercive, threatening, or restraining characteristics than lawful handbilling or other in-person communication.[10]

The term "doing business" under Section 8(b)(4) has been interpreted to include "continuing long-term negotiation over the purchase of a new asset from a neutral party."[11]

B. The Elusive Distinction Between Primary and Secondary Conduct

Distinguishing primary conduct from secondary conduct remains an issue requiring precise analysis. In *Service Employees Local 525 (General Maintenance Service Co.)*,[12] a divided Board held that membership in a trade organization that included both primary and neutral employer-members and that actively assisted the primary employers to lessen the impact of primary activity by unions did not, standing alone, cause the neutral employer-members to lose their neutrality in primary labor disputes involving other members of the trade organization. An otherwise neutral employer remains neutral even if it has an economic interest in the outcome of the primary dispute. The Board explained that a loss of neutrality will be found

[10]*Id.* at 391, 162 LRRM at 2145. To apply the Act, courts examine the means and tone of the communication. CalMat Co. v. Local 12, 165 LRRM 2628 (C.D. Cal.), *aff'd*, 211 F.3d 1272, 165 LRRM 2639 (9th Cir. 1998) (union unlawfully threatened and coerced customers of primary employer), *cert. denied*, 531 U.S. 943, 165 LRRM 2640 (2000); Moore-Duncan v. Metropolitan Reg'l Council of Philadelphia & Vicinity, 162 LRRM 2615 (E.D. Pa. 1999) (creating vastly excessive noise levels by broadcasting protest message over loudspeaker constituted coercion), *aff'd*, 225 F.3d 649, 164 LRRM 3024 (3d Cir. 2000); Printpack, Inc. v. Graphic Communications Local 761S, 988 F. Supp. 1201, 161 LRRM 2154 (S.D. Ind. 1997) (refusing motion to dismiss employer's action brought under §303 where language of letter sent by union to employer's customers could be considered threatening).

[11]Taylor Milk Co. v. Teamsters, 248 F.3d 239, 167 LRRM 2087 (3d Cir.), *cert. denied*, 534 U.S. 1055, 168 LRRM 2960 (2001) (union interfered with primary employer's attempts to purchase business from secondary person; primary intended to transfer work to purchased business and close its existing facility at which union represented employees; rejecting union's argument that it was "within its rights" to engage in secondary conduct, court noted that "we look to the intention of the parties in coercing neutral parties, not to the general rights of parties to take particular actions"), *appeal after remand*, 69 Fed. Appx. 71 (3d Cir. 2003).

[12]329 NLRB 638, 169 LRRM 1362 (1999), *enforced*, 52 Fed. Appx. 357, 173 LRRM 2256 (9th Cir. 2002).

where the employer has an "ally"[13] relationship or exercises "substantial, actual and active control" over the working conditions of the primary employees.[14]

In *Kim's Trucking Inc. v. Teamsters Local 179*,[15] Kim's Trucking, a secondary employer, alleged a violation of Section 8(b)(4)(B) because a union "threatened" Kim's Trucking that it would picket the primary contractor that subcontracted work to Kim's if the subcontracting continued. The court found that the alleged conduct did not violate the Act and also found that the union's single-person picket at the primary employer's worksite was a "textbook example" of a proper picket of a primary employer.[16]

But an employer is not a primary employer simply because it engaged a nonunion employer to provide the services that a unionized employer had been providing.[17]

When a union threatened to picket a secondary employer at the secondary employer's premises "whether . . . it's illegal or not," it violated Section 8(b)(4)(B). Thus in *Intercity Maintenance Co. v. Service Employees Local 254*,[18] where a union's representatives threatened to picket at a neutral business's headquarters to pressure it to stop doing business with the primary employer with whom the union was seeking a contract, a jury was entitled to decide whether the neutral's decision to stop doing business with the primary was caused by the union's actions or for other reasons.[19]

In *Electrical Workers (IBEW) Local 98 (Telephone Man)*,[20] the Board held that an "observer" at a neutral gate engaged in "signal picketing" undertaken for an impermissible secondary object where the observer engaged in conduct going beyond mere observation, such as flashing the reverse side of the sign containing the primary picket-

---

[13] *See* Main Edition, Chapter 22, Section II.E, at pages 1670–81, for a discussion of the ally doctrine.

[14] In this case, the Board also held that a law firm that represents a primary employer in its dispute with a union is not, by virtue of its representation, a primary employer, *supra* note 12.

[15] 13 F. Supp. 2d 715, 162 LRRM 2179 (N.D. Ill. 1998).

[16] *Id.* at 718, 162 LRRM at 2181. *Cf.* Intercity Maint. Co. v. Service Employees Local 254, 241 F.3d 82, 166 LRRM 2656 (1st Cir.), *cert. denied*, 534 U.S. 818, 168 LRRM 2472 (2001) (threatening to picket secondary employer at secondary employer's premises violated §8(b)(4)[B]).

[17] Teamsters Local 557 (General Motors), 338 NLRB 896, 172 LRRM 1050 (2003).

[18] *Supra* note 16.

[19] *Intercity Maintenance Co.*, *supra* note 16, at 87–88, 166 LRRM at 2659.

[20] 327 NLRB 593, 167 LRRM 1178 (1999).

ing language, talking to employees of neutrals as they used the gate, and entertaining visits from pickets from the primary gate. The Board also affirmed that conduct that has the foreseeable effect of causing neutral employees to strike, such as a union agent's telling employees of a neutral to "get out of my building" because primary employees were also working there and calling the attention of neutral employees to a primary picket line at a gate not used by them, constitutes Section 8(b)(4)(i)(B) inducement. Finally, the Board held that a strike by employees of a neutral resulting from Section 8(b)(4)(i)(B) conduct also constitutes coercion of the neutral employer within the meaning of Section 8(b)(4)(ii)(B).

C. The Situs of the Dispute

2. *Common and Ambulatory Situs*

The Board continues to analyze the lawfulness of secondary picketing under the *Moore Dry Dock* standards.[21] For example, in *Painters District Council 9 (We're Associates, Inc.)*,[22] the Board found that the union failed to comply with the *Moore Dry Dock* standards because it picketed an office building at which the primary employer had not engaged in activities or work for more than one month.[23] *Moore Dry Dock* standards apply, however, only if there is a common situs at which the primary and neutral employers are both engaged in normal business operations. Where the primary employer is not performing business operations at a situs, the situs is purely secondary. Thus, although a piece of property (the situs) was owned by the primary employer and the primary employer employed an employee at the property for security reasons, picketing the primary employer at this situs was secondary activity in violation of Section 8(b)(4)(B).[24] Similarly, when the primary employer had sold a situs to a secondary employer, but still owned nearby property that it was not using for any purpose, the existence of the primary employer's unused property did not create a common situs with the secondary employer, and picketing at the primary employer's unused property, 50 feet

[21] 92 NLRB 547, 27 LRRM 1108 (1950).

[22] 329 NLRB 140, 169 LRRM 1224 (1999).

[23] *See also* Electrical Workers (IBEW) Local 98 (Telephone Man), *supra* note 20 (union violated *Moore Dry Dock* by continuing to picket after having received fax notification that primary was not working at site).

[24] Mine Workers Dist. 2 (Jeddo Coal Co.), 334 NLRB 677, 174 LRRM 1045 (2001).

from the secondary employer's location, was found to violate Sections 8(b)(4)(i) and (ii)(B).[25]

A common situs does exist, however, when an employer is in the business of selling raw materials it owns, even if the extraction of these materials is done by a secondary employer, when the employer is paid for the material extracted and not for lease of the land.[26]

Santiago v. Teamsters Local 705[27] involved a union's strike against the operator of a multibuilding complex. The union had picketed at the complex's gate reserved for employees and customers of a movie production company that had leased part of the complex from the operator. Notwithstanding the union's claim that leasing space at the facilities to film and television production companies was one of the regular ongoing aspects of the operator's business, the court held that the operator's regular lease of parts of the complex to others did not transform the lessees' employees into persons whose work contributes to the day-to-day operation of the employer's business.

Where the union admitted that all of its actions were part of one strike, the proof of an unlawful motive regarding the picketing at any one site tainted the picketing at all of the sites.[28]

D. The Reserved Gate and the Related-Work Test

3. *Application in the Construction Industry*

In *Warshawsky & Co. v. NLRB*,[29] the D.C. Circuit held that a union representing a subcontractor's employees engaged in an unlawful secondary boycott by directing handbills at neutral employees of the general contractor and other subcontractors. The handbills' language; the time, place, and manner of their distribution; and the simultaneous conversations between the union agents and the neutral employees established that the union sought to induce the neutral employees to cease work.

The Seventh Circuit, applying the Board's "totality of the circumstances" test to determine the motive for the union's conduct,

---

[25] *Id.* at 687.

[26] *Id.* at 688.

[27] 2000 U.S. Dist. LEXIS 17063, 166 LRRM 2142 (N.D. Ill. 2000), *rulings on motion in limine*, 2001 U.S. Dist. LEXIS 44, 166 LRRM 2147 (2001).

[28] Engineering Consulting Servs. Ltd. v. Operating Eng'rs Local 150, 173 LRRM 2695 (N.D. Ill. 2003).

[29] 182 F.3d 948, 161 LRRM 2772 (D.C. Cir. 1999), *cert. denied sub nom.* Ironworkers Local 386 v. Warshawsky & Co., 529 U.S. 1003, 163 LRRM 2704 (2000).

found that the union engaged in unlawful secondary activity when it picketed a gate to a public utility's storage facility reserved for a unionized independent contractor and picketed a main gate that was occasionally used by a nonunion primary employer to retrieve supplies.[30] One of the union's objectives was to pressure the contractor and public utility to cease doing business with the primary employer.

4. *Application Generally: The Totality of Conduct Test*

Electrical Workers (IBEW) Local 98 (Telephone Man)[31] involved "signal picketing" undertaken for an impermissibly secondary objective—activity short of true picketing that acts as a signal to neutrals that sympathetic action on their part is desired by the union. The observer carried a sign that read "observer" on one side, but had the primary message on the reverse that "conveniently" flipped over from time to time whenever anyone entered the area. The observer stationed himself at the gate and spoke with the neutral's employees, who then did not report to work. The union also unlawfully picketed in violation of the *Moore Dry Dock*[32] standards by maintaining pickets at a neutral gate for five hours after being notified of the reserved gate. Also, the union agent stated to the neutral employer that he should "pay the men what they're worth," thereby evidencing a secondary objective.

In another case, the Board held that the union did not violate Section 8(b)(4) at secondary sites by holding gatherings or rallies that did not rise to the level of picketing.[33] Further, the Board held that comments by a union organizer that employees were being treated "shabbily" were too ambiguous to violate Section 8(b)(4) and that the organizer's attempts to bait a security guard into a fight similarly did not violate Section 8(b)(4), because it was not an appeal to an employee to withhold services or to disrupt business relations.

Moore Dry Dock is an evidentiary test and "it is unnecessary to apply [the *Moore Dry Dock*] . . . criteria and presumptions" where "it is

---

[30]R.L. Coolsaet Constr. Co. v. Operating Eng'rs Local 150, 177 F.3d 648, 161 LRRM 2195 (7th Cir. 1999), *cert. denied*, 528 U.S. 1004, 162 LRRM 2832 (1999).

[31]327 NLRB 593, 167 LRRM 1178 (1999).

[32]92 NLRB 547, 27 LRRM 1108 (1950).

[33]Service Employees Local 525 (General Maint. Serv. Co.), 329 NLRB 638, 169 LRRM 1362 (1999), *enforced*, 52 Fed. Appx. 357, 173 LRRM 2256 (9th Cir. 2002).

clear from the credited [testimony] evidence that the picketing had no unlawful object."[34]

In *Painters Distinct Council 9 (We're Associates, Inc.)*,[35] the Board applied *Moore Dry Dock* and found that the union unlawfully picketed secondary buildings by failing to identify the primary employer on its signs and picketing when the primary's employees were not on site after the union had received notice that they would not be there. The Board rejected the union's argument that limiting it to picketing late at night when the primary's employees were at the site would deprive the union of the opportunity to appeal to the public. The Board did not find the limitation analogous to the problems of a reserved gate at a remote site, which effectively would eliminate the union's ability to bring the labor dispute to the public's attention. The union also unlawfully picketed private homes of employees of the secondary employers because the object of the picketing was to exert improper influence on a neutral party. Appearing at night with candles was inherently intimidating, despite the fact that the union obtained a parade permit. A divided Board held that the delivery of a sealed envelope to a secondary employer's manager did not have the "reasonably foreseeable effect" of threatening, coercing, or restraining the manager within the meaning of Section 8(b)(4)(ii)(B).

In *Warshawsky & Co. v. NLRB*,[36] the D.C. Circuit refused to enforce the Board's ruling that handbilling a neutral employer's employees did not have secondary effects. The court held that the union's conduct had the foreseeable effect of inducing the neutral's employees to walk off the jobsite; the handbills themselves did not have a sufficiently large disclaimer; the handbilling took place at a time and place when only the neutral employees were present; and there were simultaneous conversations between the union agents and the neutral employees.

In another decision, the Seventh Circuit held that the union violated Section 303 and was liable for damages because the union

[34]Pacific Northwest Carpenters, 339 NLRB 1027, 174 LRRM 1097 (2003) (union signs clearly disclosed that dispute was only with primary employer because signs used word "attention" and did not refer to neutrals ["Attention Dental Show: DWA [the primary] does not pay area standard wages and benefits; Pacific Northwest Regional Council of Carpenters"]).

[35]329 NLRB 140, 169 LRRM 1224 (1999) (union picketed at common situs when primary employer was not at site, failed to follow valid reserved gate, and failed to identify primary employer on its picket signs).

[36]182 F.3d 948, 161 LRRM 2772 (D.C. Cir. 1999), *cert. denied sub nom.* Ironworkers Local 386 v. Warshawsky & Co., 529 U.S. 1003, 163 LRRM 2704 (2000).

engaged in secondary picketing in violation of Section 8(b)(4) by the following activities:[37] picketing a gate reserved for another unionized contractor's employees and a main gate occasionally used by the nonunion primary employer; using employees of the unionized secondary employer on the picket line; maintaining a picket regardless of whether the primary employer was on site; failing to target the primary employer but focusing instead on areas where the unionized secondary employer worked; and telling the secondary employers that it would remove the pickets only if the primary nonunion employer ceased work at the jobsite.[38]

In *NLRB v. Ironworkers Local 433*,[39] the union was found to be in contempt of a seven-year-old consent decree when it engaged in secondary picketing. The court found unpersuasive that the current union officers were unaware of the existence of the consent decree because they were not in office at the time the decree was issued and that the union's attorney simply forgot about the decree.

E. The Ally Doctrine

2. *The Straight-Line Operation/Single-Employer Status*

In *Service Employees Local 525 v. NLRB*,[40] the Ninth Circuit rejected the union's argument that landlords, tenant, and their attorneys made themselves "allies" of the employers. The landlords, tenants, and their attorneys did not perform struck work and did not have common ownership, control, or integration of operations with the primary employers. The court concluded that the ally doctrine "does not permit secondary action against non-employers merely because some of them have a preference or economic interest disserved by the prospective union."[41]

---

[37]R.L. Coolsaet Constr. Co. v. Operating Eng'rs Local 150, 177 F.3d 648, 161 LRRM 2195 (7th Cir.), *cert. denied*, 528 U.S. 1004, 162 LRRM 2832 (1999).

[38]*See also* Kennedy & Co. v. Teamsters Local 90, 315 F. Supp. 2d 992, 176 LRRM 2682 (S.D. Iowa 2004) (genuine issue of material fact as to the intent of the union's use of picket signs and American flags where there were no reserve gates; Board had ordered the union to cease using the flags).

[39]169 F.3d 1217, 160 LRRM 2736 (9th Cir. 1999) (fines for violations of consent decree did not trigger need for criminal procedural safeguards).

[40]52 Fed. Appx. 357, 173 LRRM 2256 (9th Cir. 2002), *enforcing* 329 NLRB 638, 169 LRRM 1362 (1999).

[41]*Id.* at 360.

F. Applying the Primary-Secondary Tests

1. *Conduct Other Than Picketing*

A Section 10(l) injunction was issued against a union that deliberately used vastly excessive noise volumes in broadcasting its protest that a contracting firm working at an apartment complex was compensating its carpenters at wage rates below those prevailing in the area.[42] The extreme noise levels could constitute coercive action, constituting a violation of Section 8(b)(4)(B). In the subsequent unfair labor practice proceeding, the Board held that, in broadcasting its protest against a construction firm working at an apartment complex with amplified bullhorns, the union had engaged in coercive activity in violation of Section 8(b)(4)(B).[43]

The Board found that a grocery store union violated the Act by filing a grievance and demanding arbitration about the store's Cinnabon bakery operation.[44] The union claimed that its members should have performed the work of preparing and selling Cinnabon's products, which was being done by Cinnabon employees at leased premises within the store. The Board concluded that the union's grievance and demand for arbitration had an unlawful secondary objective of forcing the store to cease doing business with Cinnabon. It held that the union had "failed to present a colorable contractual claim to the work in controversy."[45] The work was not "fairly claimable" by the union, because union members had never performed baking duties similar to those done by Cinnabon employees. Finally, the Board concluded that the grocery store did not have the "right to control" the work of handling and selling Cinnabon's products.[46]

In *Taylor Milk Co. v. Teamsters*,[47] the union violated the Act by interfering with the primary employer's attempts to purchase a business from a secondary person; the primary employer intended to

---

[42]Moore-Duncan v. Metropolitan Reg'l Council of Philadelphia & Vicinity, 1999 WL 96099, 162 LRRM 2615 (E.D. Pa. 1999), *aff'd*, 225 F.3d 649, 164 LRRM 3024 (3d Cir. 2000).

[43]Metropolitan Reg'l Council of Philadelphia & Vicinity (Society Hill Towers Owner's Ass'n), 335 NLRB 814, 169 LRRM 1498 (3d Cir. 2001), *enforced mem.*, 50 Fed. Appx. 88, 171 LRRM 2320 (3d Cir. 2002).

[44]Food & Commercial Workers Local 367 (Quality Food Ctrs., Inc.), 333 NLRB 771, 166 LRRM 1377 (2001).

[45]*Id.*, 166 LRRM at 1378.

[46]*Id.* at 1379.

[47]248 F.3d 239, 167 LRRM 2087 (3d Cir.), *cert. denied*, 534 U.S. 1055, 168 LRRM 2960 (2001), *aff'd on remand*, 69 Fed. Appx. 71 (3d Cir. 2003).

transfer work to the new business and close its existing facility at which the union represented the employees. On the other hand, a court held that a union did not violate Section 8(b)(4)(ii)(B) where it threatened to write to other affiliated locals asking them to boycott a company that sold uniforms.[48] The court found the proposed letter-writing campaign did not constitute coercive, threatening, or restraining behavior under the Act.[49] But at a construction site where the secondary employer had established primary and other reserved gates, a union's "direct solicitation" of support on the picket line from the secondary employer's employees, which it represented, before any picket line had been established, demonstrated that the union's "likely objective was to keep [the secondary employer's] employees off the job."[50]

In *Petrochem Insulation, Inc.*,[51] the Board followed *DeBartolo II*[52] and held that the unions' petitioning of state governmental agencies to seek denial of environmental permits to nonunion construction companies did not constitute "coercion" under Section 8(b)(4)(ii)(B). The Board stated that governmental lobbying by a union, like handbilling, is activity protected by the First Amendment.

3. *Location of the Picketing*

Where a union's picketing satisfies the *Moore Dry Dock*[53] standards about the location of the picketing, the union does not violate the Act's prohibition against secondary activity.[54]

Unlawful secondary activity occurs when a union pickets a gate reserved for a neutral contractor whose employees are unionized and also pickets a main gate that the nonunion primary contractor used only occasionally and does so without regard to the time and

---

[48]George v. National Ass'n of Letter Carriers, 185 F.3d 380, 162 LRRM 2137 (5th Cir. 1999), *cert. denied*, 528 U.S. 1156, 163 LRRM 2576 (2000).

[49]*Cf.* Electrical Workers Local 98 (MCF Servs., Inc.), 342 NLRB No. 74, 175 LRRM 1235 (2004) (violation where organizer stated that he "could throw up [a] picket line in 30 days" and that "no one would come in or out and this would cause a lot of delays.").

[50]F.A. Wilhelm Constr. Co. v. Carpenters, 293 F.3d 935, 170 LRRM 2243 (6th Cir. 2002).

[51]330 NLRB 47, 163 LRRM 1276 (1999), *enforced*, 240 F.3d 26, 166 LRRM 2433 (D.C. Cir.), *cert. denied*, 594 U.S. 992 (2001).

[52]Edward J. DeBartolo Corp. v. Building & Constr. Trades Council (Florida Gulf Coast), 485 U.S. 568, 128 LRRM 2001 (1988).

[53]Sailors' Union (Moore Dry Dock), 92 NLRB 547, 27 LRRM 1108 (1950).

[54]Kim's Trucking v. Teamsters Local 179, 13 F. Supp. 2d 715, 162 LRRM 2179 (N.D. Ill. 1998) (union picketed only at times primary asphalt contractor's trucks

location of the primary nonunion employer's work activities, where the union's object is to force the primary employer off the site by putting pressure on both the secondary employer and the site owner.[55]

In *Kobell v. African American Workers*,[56] the court entered a Section 10(l) injunction against a union that had a primary dispute with a city, county, and public auditorium authority. The injunction barred picketing at a stadium construction site. The union claimed that the picketing was informational, but the signs did not identify with whom the union had the dispute. Some of the signs read: "Picket Line Crossing Is Union Busting AAWU." The court found that the government agencies were not engaged in their normal business at the site. The union's objective was to enmesh the contractors in the dispute between the government agencies and the union.

The Board continues to apply its well-established definition of "picketing," which does not require patrolling or carrying picket signs. Thus, in *Mine Workers District 2 (Jeddo Coal Co.)*, [57] the Board held that individuals standing across the street, and who were not patrolling, were nonetheless engaged in conduct that was the equivalent of picketing, even though picket signs were not carried, but instead, were propped on a lawn chair, taped to a car, draped on a reflector pole, and leaned on a car windshield. This conduct violated Section 8(b)(4). The Board dismissed the Section 8(b)(4) charge as to one site, however, because the picketing occurred at a common situs where the primary employer was actively engaged in mine-related work and there were no reserved gates.

III. HANDBILLING

A. *DeBartolo II*: Consumer Handbilling Not Prohibited by Section 8(b)(4)(B)

As discussed in the Main Edition, in *DeBartolo II*,[58] the Supreme Court held that Section 8(b)(4)(ii)(B) does not prohibit peaceful

---

were on site and engaged in contractor's regular business, picketed only in immediate vicinity of asphalt contractor's trucks, and clearly disclosed on its signs that dispute was with asphalt contractor).

[55]R.L. Coolsaet Constr. Co. v. Operating Eng'rs Local 150, 177 F.3d 648, 161 LRRM 2195 (7th Cir.), *cert. denied,* 528 U.S. 1004, 162 LRRM 2832 (1999).

[56]1999 WL 734129, 162 LRRM 2235 (W.D. Pa. 1999).

[57]334 NLRB 677, 174 LRRM 1045 (2001).

[58]Edward J. DeBartolo Corp. v. Building & Constr. Trades Council (Florida Gulf Coast) (DeBartolo II), 485 U.S. 568, 128 LRRM 2001 (1988).

handbilling, unaccompanied by picketing, that urges customers and consumers not to patronize a neutral employer. In *George v. National Ass'n of Letter Carriers,*[59] the Fifth Circuit held that publicity, such as letter writing—unconnected with picketing, patrolling, or violence—is not "coercion, threats or restraint," even if it effectively persuaded consumers not to patronize a secondary employer. Handbilling that is accompanied by coercive high-volume broadcasting of the message in the handbill violates the Act.[60]

On the other hand, the D.C. Circuit distinguished *DeBartolo II* in *Warshawsky & Co. v. NLRB,*[61] finding the evidence to "fairly demand" an inference that the union sought to induce neutral employees to refuse to work through the distribution of handbills unconnected with picketing or patrolling. The court concluded that *DeBartolo II* was fundamentally different because it involved Section 8(b)(4)(ii)(B) and not conduct that sought to directly induce or encourage a secondary strike under Section 8(b)(4)(i)(B).

B. Standards for Lawful Handbilling

1. *The Conduct of Handbilling*

Handbilling activity directed at the employees of a neutral employer, rather than consumers, may violate Section 8(b)(4). In *Warshawsky & Co. v. NLRB,*[62] the union had a labor dispute with a subcontractor on a construction site. The union distributed area-standards handbills in proximity to a road used primarily by persons going to and from the construction site. The site was not open to members of the general public. The D.C. Circuit held that the protections afforded by *DeBartolo II* do not extend to area-standards handbilling directed at neutral employees.

---

[59]185 F.3d 380, 162 LRRM 2137, *reh'g en banc denied,* 194 F.3d 1310 (5th Cir. 1999), *cert. denied,* 528 U.S. 1156, 163 LRRM 2576 (2000); Galveston Linehandlers, Inc. v. Longshoremen (ILA), Local 20, 140 F. Supp. 2d 741, 167 LRRM 2231 (S.D. Tex. 2001).

[60]Metropolitan Reg'l Council of Philadelphia Carpenters, 335 NLRB 814, 169 LRRM 1498 (2001), *enforced,* 50 Fed. Appx. 88, 171 LRRM 2320 (3d Cir. 2002).

[61]182 F.3d 948, 161 LRRM 2772 (D.C. Cir. 1999), *denying enforcement to* Iron Workers Local 386, 325 NLRB 748, 158 LRRM 1180 (1998), *cert. denied,* 529 U.S. 1003, 163 LRRM 2704 (2000).

[62]*Id.*

2. *Location of Handbilling*

a. *Lechmere*: Nonemployee Access to Employer Property Curtailed

The Board and the courts continue to examine state law to determine whether an employer has sufficient property rights to exclude union representatives from private property.[63] In *Farm Fresh, Inc.*,[64] the Board held that under Virginia law a lease that did not specifically include sidewalks among the leased areas but did impose an obligation on the lessee to clean and maintain the sidewalks created a sufficient property interest to permit the lessee to exclude union representatives.[65] The D.C. Circuit found that the Board had misinterpreted Virginia law and remanded the case to the Board for further proceedings.[66] On remand, the Board concluded that the maintenance provisions in the lease agreements did not create a sufficient property interest to permit exclusion of union representatives.[67]

However, an employer's employee who works at a different facility than the handbilled facility is not subject to the limitations that are applicable to nonemployees; the employee may engage in handbilling outside of the employer's buildings for purposes of organizing.[68]

b. Limitations on Nonemployee Handbilling on Employer Property After *Lechmere*

The Board maintains the position that where an employer allows nonemployee solicitation but does not allow union solicitation, the fact that the allowed solicitation is charitable or not controversial does not preclude a finding of discrimination. In *Albertson's, Inc. v. NLRB*,[69] however, the court refused to enforce the Board's hold-

---

[63]Waremart Foods v. NLRB, 354 F.3d 870, 174 LRRM 2010 (D.C. Cir. 2004) (circuit court construed California property law to prohibit handbilling on privately owned parking lot of grocery store after requesting and not receiving an opinion from the California Supreme Court).

[64]326 NLRB 997, 159 LRRM 1201 (1998), *enforcement denied in part*, 222 F.3d 1030, 169 LRRM 2205 (D.C. Cir.), *on remand*, 332 NLRB 1424, 171 LRRM 1380 (2000).

[65]*Id.*, 326 NLRB at 1001–02, 159 LRRM at 1206.

[66]*Id.*, 222 F.3d at 1036, 169 LRRM at 2212.

[67]*Farm Fresh*, *supra* note 64, 332 NLRB at 1426, 171 LRRM at 1382–83.

[68]First Healthcare Corp. v. NLRB, 344 F.3d 523, 173 LRRM 2296 (6th Cir. 2003).

[69]301 F.3d 441, 170 LRRM 2769 (6th Cir. 2002). *See also* Sandusky Mall Co., 329 NLRB 618, 162 LRRM 1191 (1999) (violation of §8(a)(1) where employer allowed

ing that the employer violated Section 8(a)(1) by allowing the Salvation Army, youth and student groups, and veterans groups to solicit on the employer property and not allowing union handbilling for the purpose of soliciting support for the union among the employer's employees. The court applied its principle that an employer does not violate the Act where the employer "allows charities to disseminate information on the employer's property while it bars unions from doing the same."[70]

In *New York New York, LLC v. NLRB*,[71] the court refused to enforce a Board order[72] that a contractor's employees who worked on the employer's premises have the same rights as the employer's employees.

In light of California property law principles, the Board found that a mall owner violated the Act by requiring the handbilling union to remove the name of the employer at whom the union directed the handbilling; however, the mall owner could require the union to provide, in advance of the handbilling, the names of the handbillers.[73]

One court has rejected a union's argument that the government's support of the construction of a private mall transformed the private property into public property on which the union should have been allowed to picket.[74]

---

other groups to solicit in mall concourse but did not allow union handbillers), *enforcement denied*, 242 F.3d 682, 166 LRRM 2614 (6th Cir. 2001). *Compare with* 6 West Ltd. Corp. v. NLRB, 237 F.3d 767, 780, 166 LRRM 2221 (7th Cir. 2001), *denying enforcement to* 330 NLRB 527, 163 LRRM 1113 (2000) (finding no violation where employer allowed solicitations for Girl Scout cookies, Christmas ornaments, and raffle tickets but did not allow union solicitations, stating: "A restaurant in the United States of America should be free to prohibit solicitations on the premises that interfere with or bother employees or customers, and allow those solicitations which neither interfere with nor bother employees or customers.").

[70]*Albertson*'s, Inc., *supra* note 69, 301 F.3d at 450–51, 170 LRRM at 2775–77.

[71]313 F.3d 585, 171 LRRM 2651 (D.C. Cir. 2002) (The court noted: "No Supreme Court case decides whether a contractor's employees have rights equivalent to the property owner's employees—that is, *Republic Aviation* rights to engage in organizational activities in non-work areas during non-working time so long as they do not unduly disrupt the business of the property owner—because their work site, although on the premises of another employer, is their sole place of employment.").

[72]334 NLRB 762, 772, 169 LRRM 1502 (2001).

[73]Glendale Assocs. Ltd., 335 NLRB 27, 169 LRRM 1328 (2001), *enforced*, 347 F.3d 1145, 173 LRRM 2551 (9th Cir. 2003); Equitable Life Assurance Soc'y of the U.S. dba Fashion Valley Shopping Center, 343 NLRB No. 57, 176 LRRM 1181 (2004) (applying *Glendale* and holding that the shopping mall's restrictions on handbilling were improperly broad content-based restrictions).

[74]Food & Commercial Workers Local 919 v. Crystal Mall Assoc. LP., 270 Conn. 261, 852 A.2d 659, 175 LRRM 2347 (2004).

IV. CONSUMER PICKETING

B. Development of the Law After *Tree Fruits*

1. "Merged Products" and Other Problems of the Economic Setting

The Fifth Circuit set forth a detailed analysis and explanation of the *Tree Fruits,*[75] *Safeco,*[76] and *DeBartolo I*[77] and *II*[78] decisions in concluding that a union official's threats to write letters to other union locals urging a consumer boycott were not prohibited by Section 8(b)(4)(B), because such conduct alone did not constitute coercion within the meaning of subsection (ii).[79] In so doing, the court noted that the *Safeco* principle prohibits only consumer *picketing* or similar coercive conduct that has the effect of urging a total boycott of a business,[80] and that letter writing has even fewer potentially coercive characteristics than does handbilling.[81]

If the neutral employees of a business are also consumers and the consumer picketing, accompanied by handbilling, is directed at them as consumers and not as employees, then such picketing and handbilling "cannot be said" to be "designed to induce or encourage" them "in their status as employees of a secondary employer to withdraw their services," and therefore such picketing does not violate Section 8(b)(4)(i)(B).[82]

Applying *DeBartolo II* in a Section 10(l) proceeding, the court held that a union's display of a 4-foot tall and 20-foot long banner,

---

[75]Fruit & Vegetable Packers Local 760 (Tree Fruits Labor Relations Comm.), 132 NLRB 1172, 48 LRRM 1496 (1961), *remanded,* 308 F.2d 311, 50 LRRM 2392 (D.C. Cir. 1962), *vacated and remanded,* 377 U.S. 58, 55 LRRM 2961 (1964).

[76]Retail Clerks Local 1001 (Land Title Ins. Co. of Pierce County & Safeco Title Ins. Co.), 226 NLRB 754, 93 LRRM 1338 (1976), *enforcement initially granted in* 99 LRRM 3330 (D.C. Cir. 1978), *enforcement denied,* 627 F.2d 1133, 101 LRRM 3084 (D.C. Cir. 1979), *rev'd and remanded,* 447 U.S. 607, 104 LRRM 2567 (1980).

[77]Building Trades Council (Florida Gulf Coast) (Edward J. DeBartolo), 252 NLRB 702, 105 LRRM 1273 (1980), *aff'd,* 662 F.2d 264, 108 LRRM 2729 (4th Cir. 1981), *rev'd,* 463 U.S. 147, 113 LRRM 2593 (1983).

[78]Edward J. DeBartolo Corp. v. Building & Constr. Trades Council (Florida Gulf Coast) v. NLRB, 796 F.2d 1328, 123 LRRM 2001 (11th Cir. 1986), *aff'd,* 485 U.S. 568, 128 LRRM 2001 (1988).

[79]George v. National Ass'n of Letter Carriers, 185 F.3d 380, 162 LRRM 2137 (5th Cir. 1999), *cert. denied,* 528 U.S. 1156, 163 LRRM 2576 (2000) (and also citing PATRICK HARDIN, ed., DEVELOPING LABOR LAW (3d. ed.)).

[80]*Id.* at 389, 162 LRRM at 2141.

[81]*Id.* at 391–92, 162 LRRM at 2145.

[82]Teamsters Local 122 (Busch & Co.), 334 NLRB 1190, 1191–92, 174 LRRM 1176 (2001), *enforced,* 2003 WL 880990 (D.C. Cir. 2003) (picketing and handbilling

on a public sidewalk, with "Shame on Cadillac/SAAB" in large red letters flanked by "Labor Dispute" in smaller black font did not constitute secondary picketing in violation of Section 8(b)(4)(ii)(B). The court found that, since the union's bannering activity was nonthreatening, the conduct did not override the union's free speech rights.[83]

3. *Specificity of the Union's Appeal: Location and Timing*

The Ninth Circuit enforced a Board decision that a supermarket committed an unfair labor practice by threatening to have union representatives arrested for handbilling and picketing on a privately owned walkway and parking lot in furtherance of a consumer boycott.[84] Initially, the court rejected the supermarket's assertion that because the union representatives' conduct was improperly located on its private property, such conduct was not protected by Section 7. The court indicated that whether conduct is protected by Section 7 and where it may be exercised are distinct inquiries.[85] The court determined that the union representatives' handbilling and picketing, which was designed to truthfully inform customers that the supermarket did not employ members of a labor organization, was clearly protected by Section 7.[86] The court also found that inasmuch as California law prohibited owners of shopping malls and general-access supermarkets from excluding speech on their private sidewalks and parking lots, the union representatives were legally entitled to engage in protected activity on the supermarket's privately owned sidewalk and parking lot.[87]

---

by union in front of restaurant, where radio station was broadcasting as part of promotion by primary employer, a beer distributor, where pickets encouraged persons entering restaurant to boycott both it and radio station, is not made illegal by fact that unbeknown to union some of the persons entering restaurant were its employees and employees of radio station; however, the consumer picketing directed at obtaining total boycott of restaurant and radio station rather than product that was being promoted and sold violated §8(b)(4)(ii)(B) of Act.).

[83]Kohn v. Southwest Reg'l Council of Carpenters, 289 F. Supp. 2d 1155 (C.D. Cal. 2003); Benson v. Carpenters, Local 184 & 1498, 337 F. Supp. 2d 1275, 175 LRRM 2988 (D. Utah 2004); Overstreet v. Carpenters Local 1506, 2003 WL 23845186 (S.D. Cal. 2003); Ryan & Davis, *Banners, Rats, and Other Inflatable Toys: Do They Constitute Picket Activity? Do They Violate Section 8(B)(4)?*, 20 LAB. L 137 (2004).

[84]NLRB v. Calkins dba Indio Grocery Outlet, 187 F.3d 1080, 161 LRRM 3121 (9th Cir. 1999), *cert. denied*, 529 U.S. 1098, 164 LRRM 2256 (2000).

[85]*Id.*, 187 F.3d at 1088–89, 161 LRRM at 3126.

[86]*Id.*

[87]*Id.* at 1089–93. The court distinguished its holding from *Sparks Nugget, Inc. v. NLRB*, 968 F.2d 991, 140 LRRM 2747 (9th Cir. 1992), in which it found that a

V. ACTIONS FOR DAMAGES UNDER SECTION 303

A. Nature of the Action

1. *Relationship to Section 8(b)(4)*

Regardless of the application of the *Moore Dry Dock*[88] standards, the ultimate inquiry to determine whether unlawful secondary activity has occurred is the union's state of mind.[89] Intent can be "inferred from the nature of the conduct, evaluated in light of the practical realities of a given situation."[90]

A trial court will apply Federal Rule of Evidence 403 to determine whether an NLRB regional office's conclusions regarding a related secondary boycott charge may be admitted into evidence in a Section 303 case.[91]

2. *Who Can Sue and Be Sued?*

Because the Act does not apply to unions representing public employees, an employer cannot sue a union representing public employees for conduct that violates Section 8(b)(4)(B).[92]

---

casino owner *could* prohibit conduct similar to that in the instant case from its private sidewalk and parking lot, on the grounds that Nevada law, unlike California law, does not extend special protection to free-speech interests at the expense of a store owner's property interests. 187 F.3d at 1093–94. In *Wild Oats Markets, Inc.*, 336 NLRB 179, 168 LRRM 1305 (2001), the employer violated the Act by calling the mall owner about the union's activity against the employer's store where the employer knew or should have known that the mall owner (who called the police) could not lawfully stop the handbilling solely because of its location. *See* CSX Hotels, Inc. v. NLRB, 377 F.3d 394, 175 LRRM 2328 (4th Cir. 2004) (resort did not violate Act by contacting police regarding safety issues involving picketers outside entrance); Nations Rent, Inc. 342 NLRB No. 19, 175 LRRM 1416 (2004) (employer did not violate Act by contacting police regarding picketers acting in violation of law).

[88]92 NLRB 547, 27 LRRM 1108 (1950).

[89]R.L. Coolsaet Constr. Co. v. Operating Eng'rs Local 150, 177 F.3d 648, 161 LRRM 2195 (7th Cir.), *cert. denied*, 528 U.S. 1004, 162 LRRM 2832 (1999).

[90]Intercity Maint. Co. v. Service Employees Local 254, 62 F. Supp. 2d 483, 494, 162 LRRM 2099 (D.R.I. 1999), *remanded on other grounds*, 241 F.3d 82, 166 LRRM 2656 (1st Cir.), *cert. denied*, 534 U.S. 818, 168 LRRM 2472 (2001) (trial court should have submitted claim to jury regarding loss of business because sufficient evidence existed to raise issue of causal relationship between union's conduct and loss).

[91]North Am. Roofing & Sheet Metal Co. v. Building & Constructions Trades Council of Philadelphia, 2005 WL 44520, 176 LRRM 2527 (E.D. Pa. 2005).

[92]Pacific N. Maritime Ass'n v. Longshoremen (ILWU) Local 63, 198 F.3d 1078, 162 LRRM 3037 (9th Cir. 1999), *cert. denied*, 530 U.S. 1213 (2000).

A union is liable under Section 303 for its agent's threats that, unless the neutral ceased doing business with the primary employer, the neutral would experience strike action, property damage, and assaults against the neutral's employees.[93] Section 303 does not create a claim against union officers in their individual capacity.[94] An international union is not liable for the conduct of its local union unless the international instigated, supported, ratified, or encouraged the local union's conduct.[95]

An employer may be required to arbitrate its Section 303 damage claim if an applicable collective bargaining agreement provides for an arbitration procedure with an extremely broad scope.[96]

C. The Measure of Damages

In *Taylor Milk Co. v. Teamsters*,[97] the employer claimed that its damage was the lost opportunity to purchase another facility in which it expected to save its failing business. The union contended that the labor agreement did not permit the employer to move the work from the existing business to the new facility. The employer responded that, even if the labor agreement prohibited the transfer of the work, it would have still purchased the new facility. The district court stated that it could not award damages because it would have to interpret the labor agreement, which only an arbitrator could do. The court of appeals held that the district court must interpret the labor agreement as part of the process of determining damages. The court of appeals outlined what damages would be awarded if the district court concluded that the labor agreement either permitted the work transfer or prohibited the work transfer.[98]

---

[93]American Dev., Inc. v. Operating Eng'rs Local 150, 1999 WL 543207 (N.D. Ill. 1999).

[94]*Intercity Maintenance Co., supra* note 90.

[95]*Id. See also* Mine Workers Dist. 2 (Jeddo Coal Co.), 334 NLRB 677, 174 LRRM 1045 (2001) (district union office liable for local's conduct where it is shown that there is sharing of collective bargaining responsibility between district and local).

[96]Interstate Brands Corp. v. Bakery Drivers & Bakery Goods Vending Machs. Local 550, 167 F.3d 764, 160 LRRM 2404 (2d Cir.), *cert. denied*, 528 U.S. 822, 162 LRRM 2448 (1999); NYP Holdings, Inc. v. Newspaper & Mail Deliverers' Union, 170 LRRM 3056 (S.D.N.Y. 2002).

[97]248 F.3d 239, 167 LRRM 2087 (3d Cir.), *cert. denied*, 534 U.S. 1055 (2001).

[98]*Id.* at 249, 167 LRRM at 2093–94. If the labor agreement did not permit the work transfer, there would not be damages because the employer admitted that

Prejudgment interest may be ordered in a Section 303 action even though the damages award could not be calculated with absolute precision.[99]

D. Limitations, Federal Preemption, and Supplemental Jurisdiction

1. *Statutes of Limitations*

In Rhode Island, the 10-year statute of limitations for tortious interference with business relationships is applicable to Section 303 claims.[100]

2. *Federal Preemption*

Section 303 generally preempts state law tortious interference claims based on secondary activity unless the claims concern the union's actual or threatened violence. However, to avoid preemption, the claim must be based on actual or threatened violence that occurred during the period of the alleged tortious interference.[101]

---

the purchase of the new facility alone would not generate a profit. If the labor agreement permitted the work transfer and it would have led to a profit, the employer could recover future profits. However, the payment for a purchase option and the out-of-pocket expenses in connection with the purchase would be offset against the recoverable future profits.

[99]R.L. Coolsaet Constr. Co. v. Operating Eng'rs Local 150, 177 F.3d 648, 161 LRRM 2195 (7th Cir.), *cert. denied*, 528 U.S. 1004, 162 LRRM 2832 (1999) (interest allowed on equipment expenses for employer-owned equipment).

[100]Intercity Maint. Co. v. Service Employees Local 254, 62 F. Supp. 2d 483, 162 LRRM 2099 (D.R.I. 1999), *remanded on other grounds*, 241 F.3d 82, 166 LRRM 2656 (1st Cir.), *cert. denied*, 534 U.S. 818, 168 LRRM 2472 (2001).

[101]Pickens-Kane Moving & Storage Co. v. Teamsters Local 705, 1999 WL 89649, 161 LRRM 2159 (N.D. Ill. 1999).

Chapter 23

SECTION 8(e): THE "HOT CARGO" AGREEMENT

III. Interpretation and Application

A. Definitions and Coverage

In *Teamsters Local 166 (Shank/Balfour Beatty)*,[1] the Board affirmed the administrative law judge's (ALJ) uncontested finding that the parties entered into an agreement within the meaning of Section 8(e) based on a letter written by the employer in response to repeated statements by union officials that the union would file a grievance under its project labor agreement (PLA) if the employer hired certain owner-operators to haul concrete. The ALJ noted that the employer's letter, in which it agreed to use haulers according to the terms of the PLA, was never disavowed by the union.[2]

---

[1]327 NLRB 449, 160 LRRM 1147 (1999).
[2]*Id.* at 454.

A clause prohibiting an employer from applying its trade name to stores operated nonunion does not violate Section 8(e). In *Food & Commercial Workers Local 464A v. Foodtown, Inc.*,[3] the court ordered the employer to submit to arbitration the union's grievance asserting a violation of this provision.

An unusual use of Section 8(e) as a defense to an employer's grievance alleging the union breached the no-strike clause was urged in *Teamsters Local 682 v. KCI Construction Co.*[4] The union asked the court to deny enforcement of an arbitration award finding the union had breached the no-strike provision in a project construction agreement because its members, working for a subcontractor, had gone on strike to secure a successor agreement and were therefore refusing to deliver concrete to the construction site. The union argued that the arbitration award in favor of the employer could not be enforced because application of the no-strike clause implicated application of a separate contract provision requiring that "local onsite deliveries of construction material and equipment [would] utilize employees who are represented by Unions affiliated with the AFL-CIO Building Trades."[5] The court held that enforcement of the no-strike clause necessarily involved application of the separate contract provision, and if that provision was improper under Section 8(e), the court could not enforce the no-strike clause in that context.[6]

B. Picket Line Clause

A union risks violating Section 8(b)(4)(ii)(A) even if its strike is not motivated by the employer's rejection of an unlawful "picket line clause." In *Service Employees Local 32B-32J (Pratt Towers)*,[7] the Board held that a union violated Section 8(b)(4)(ii)(A) of the Act when it struck an employer in support of a proposed contract that included a picket line clause illegal under Section 8(e) even though the par-

---

[3]317 F. Supp. 2d 522, 528 (D.N.J. 2004).

[4]384 F.2d 532 (8th Cir. 2004).

[5]*Id.* at 534.

[6]*Id.* at 539. The court remanded for the trial court to either determine whether the disputed clause fell within the construction industry proviso to §8(e) or the work preservation exception, or stay the proceeding pending the outcome of the unfair labor practice proceeding.

[7]337 NLRB 317, 169 LRRM 1185 (2001).

ties did not devote negotiating time to the clause. During the parties' initial meeting, the union proposed a contract that included the following clause:

> No employee covered by this agreement should be required by the Employer to pass picket lines established by any Local of the Service Employees International Union in an authorized strike.[8]

The Board determined that the clause was unlawful because it was not limited to lawful primary activity. The Board found that the union violated Section (8)(b)(4)(ii)(A) because an object of the strike was to force or require the employer to enter into a contract that contained an illegal "picket line clause." In the Board's view, it was irrelevant that the parties did not negotiate over the terms of the clause and that its inclusion in the union's last proposal may not have been the reason that the employer refused to sign the contract. The union's use of a strike to compel the employer to sign a contract that included the unlawful clause was sufficient for the Board to find that the strike had an unlawful object and thus violated Section 8(b)(4)(ii)(A).[9]

The Second Circuit denied enforcement of the Board's order in *Pratt Towers*,[10] holding that the picket line clause was limited to strikes that were "authorized" by law (as opposed to strikes authorized by the union); therefore, the clause was limited to lawful primary activity. The court determined that the phrase "authorized strike" was ambiguous and that "ambiguously worded contracts should not be interpreted to render them illegal and unenforceable where the wording lends itself to a logically acceptable construction that renders them legal and enforceable."[11] Having found that the clause at issue did not violate Section 8(e), the Second Circuit did not reach the question whether the union struck with an unlawful object in violation of Section 8(b)(4)(ii)(A).

---

[8] *Id.* at 317.

[9] *Id.*

[10] 353 F.3d 197, 173 LRRM 3007 (2d Cir. 2003), *denying enforcement to* 337 NLRB 317, 169 LRRM 1185 (2001).

[11] *Id.* at 202.

D. Subcontracting and Work-Allocation Clauses

3. Application of *National Woodwork*

a. Work-Preservation Clauses Generally

The Second Circuit held in *Bermuda Container Line Ltd. v. Longshoremen (ILA)*[12] that Section 8(e) was not violated by a provision prohibiting the employer from relocating to a port that did not employ longshoremen represented by the union. The employer was a member of a multi-employer association, which had negotiated the collective bargaining agreement with a union representing longshoremen on the Atlantic and Gulf coasts. The court found that the agreement defined both the bargaining unit and the primary employment relationship on a coastwide basis, and thus the provision was a valid work-preservation agreement.

In *Sun Ridge LLC*,[13] the Division of Advice authorized the issuance of complaint alleging a violation of Section 8(e) where a developer of residential and commercial property required buyers of its property to utilize union contractors for any on-site construction work in the development of that property. The Division of Advice concluded that the sale of land to builders was not a one-time sale of capital assets but instead was part of the "normal course" of the employer's business. Thus, because this was not the permanent sale of capital assets, the "cease doing business" language of Section 8(e) was applicable. It was further concluded that the employer was not "in the construction industry" because it did not itself do construction work and was directly involved in any contracting for construction work.

b. Union-Standards Clauses

In *Painters & Allied Trades v. NLRB*,[14] the D.C. Circuit overruled the Board and held that a successorship clause in a collective bargaining agreement, which explicitly provided that it was to take effect only when the employer's business was "in whole or in part, sold, leased, transferred or taken over" by another entity, and stated that its purpose was only to prevent the employer from evading the agreement, was not unlawful. The Board had interpreted the clause to

[12] 192 F.3d 250, 162 LRRM 2257 (2d Cir. 1998).

[13] NLRB Advice Memorandum, Case 32-CE-77-1, 78-1, 79-1 (Apr. 5, 2004).

[14] 309 F.3d 1, 171 LLRM 2065 (D.C. Cir. 2002), *enforcing in part* 333 NLRB 1339, 167 LRRM 1097 (2001).

violate Section 8(e) insofar as it applied to "leases." The reasoning was that a lease could apply regardless of whether the unit employees were retained, and, therefore, the clause exceeded the legitimate primary purpose of protecting unit work. The D.C. Circuit disagreed, emphasizing, first, that the clause applied only in the successorship context (that is, where the employer's business was transferred to another entity) and, second, that by its express terms the clause was intended only to prevent efforts to use a lease transfer to evade the agreement. Thus, it was designed to protect employees' legitimate and primary interests in retaining the benefits of the contract in the event of a transfer, and did not violate Section 8(e).

E. Construction Industry Proviso Allowing Agreements Concerning Job-Site Work

2. *Job-Site Work*

The Board continues to apply its long standing rule when interpreting contract clauses under the Section 8(e) construction industry proviso. In *Iron Workers (Southwestern Materials & Supply Inc.)*,[15] the Board considered the lawfulness of two contract clauses against the charge that both violated Section 8(e). The Board concluded that the first—an anti-dual shop clause—violated Section 8(e) because it bound neutral employers, related to the signatory employer but not a signatory to the labor contract, in the circumstance where the signatory employer had no control over the work assignments of these related neutral employers. The Board held that anti-dual shop clauses fall outside of the "categories of secondary activity that Congress intended to be tolerated in the construction industry."[16]

The second clause prohibited the signatory employer "from subcontracting work within the union's jurisdiction to any person or entity that does not have a contract with the union."[17] The Board found that this clause had a secondary, rather than a primary, work-preservation objective, in violation of Section 8(e). Although the clause was not limited to the particular job sites at which both union and nonunion workers are employed, the Board held that it fell within the construction industry proviso of Section 8(e) because there was no showing that the clause had been or was intended to be applied to off-site work.

---

[15]328 NLRB 934, 161 LRRM 1258 (1999).
[16]*Id.* at 937, 161 LRRM at 1262.
[17]*Id.* at 936, 161 LRRM at 1262.

3. *Obtaining and Enforcing Subcontracting Agreements*

In *Operating Engineers Local 520 (Massman Construction Co.)*,[18] the Board found that a joint-venture clause violated Section 8(e) because the clause attempted to control the signatory employer's business relations even where the signatory employer had no control over the labor relations of the joint venture. In addition, the clause was not protected by the construction industry proviso because the clause went beyond the specific exemptions envisaged by Congress when it passed the proviso in 1959.

Where a union entered into an agreement with an employer prohibiting the employer from employing owner-operators to deliver materials to one of two entrances to a construction site, the Board ordered the union to cease and desist from enforcing the prohibition at both entrances because in either case the transportation and delivery of materials was not job-site work.[19]

Enforcing the Board's order in *Spectacor Management Group v. NLRB*,[20] the Third Circuit held that the union and a convention center managing company (SMG) violated Section 8(e) by attempting to enforce a provision prohibiting the convention center managing company from subcontracting the installation, assembly, and dismantling of temporary tradeshow exhibits to employers who did not have a labor agreement with the union. The court observed that the provision had an unlawful secondary purpose. By subcontracting the work, the convention center managing company had removed itself from the role of employer. In addition, the union insisted that the neutral subcontractor enter into a labor agreement covering work beyond the convention center managed by SMG.

The Third Circuit upheld the Board's finding that the "construction industry proviso" did not save the invalid provision because the tradeshow floor at issue was not a "site of construction." Deciding an issue of first impression, the court held that although the phrase "site of construction" is ambiguous, the Board's construction of the phrase so as to limit its reach to traditional construction sites was entitled to deference.

---

[18] 327 NLRB 1257, 161 LRRM 1001 (1999).

[19] Teamsters Local 166 (Shank/Balfour Beatty), 327 NLRB 449, 160 LRRM 1147 (1999).

[20] 320 F.3d 385, 171 LRRM 3057 (3d Cir. 2003).

4. *Clauses Prohibiting Double-Breasting*

The Board continues to apply the two part test articulated in *NLRB v. Longshoremen (ILA)*[21] for determining whether an anti-double-breasting clause is a lawful work preservation clause. If the clause does not meet this test, and thus falls within the general proscription of Section 8(e), the Board will determine whether the clause is saved by the construction industry proviso.[22] In this regard, the Board continues to construe strictly the construction industry proviso to shelter only those clauses common to the construction industry when the proviso was adopted in 1959.[23]

In *NLRB v. Central Pennsylvania Regional Counsel of Carpenters,*[24] the Third Circuit enforced a Board order holding that the union violated Section 8(e) by attempting to enforce an invalid "anti-dual-shop" clause. The provision read: "The employers stipulated that any of their subsidiaries or joint venture to which they may be parties when such subsidiaries or joint venture engage in multiple dwelling, commercial, industrial, or institutional building construction work shall be covered by the terms of this agreement."[25] The court held that the provision had an unlawful secondary object because it extended beyond work traditionally done by the employees and was not restricted to entities over which the signatory employer had the right of control. The court did not address the union's contention that the provision did not violate the Act as applied, because it concluded the provision was facially invalid.

---

[21]447 U.S 490, 104 LRRM 2552 (1980).

[22]Iron Workers (Southwestern Materials & Supply, Inc.), 328 NLRB 934, 161 LRRM 1258 (1999) (subcontracting clause was lawful absent evidence that it was intended to be applied off site).

[23]*Id.*; *see also* Operating Engineers Local 520 (Massman Constr. Co.), 327 NLRB 1257, 161 LRRM 1001 (1999) (finding that anti-dual-shop clause covering joint ventures was not part of pattern of bargaining in construction industry at time of construction proviso's enactment).

[24]352 F.3d 831, 174 LRRM 2928 (3d Cir. 2003).

[25]*Id.* at 831, 174 LRRM at 2928.

CHAPTER 24

JURISDICTIONAL DISPUTES AND "FEATHERBEDDING"

II. JURISDICTIONAL DISPUTES

B. Enactment of Sections 8(b)(4)(D) and 10(k)

3. Scope of Section 8(b)(4)(D)

The basic principles stated in the Main Edition regarding the scope of Section 8(b)(4)(D) of the Act remain the same. Unions often defend against a Section 8(b)(4) allegation by claiming that they have engaged in picketing for recognition or work-preservation purposes. However, such claims fail where at least one of the objectives of the picketing is for the purpose of forcing the target employer to assign the work to the picketing union.[1]

The Board continues to find that a jurisdictional dispute cannot exist unless there are two competing claims to a particular work assignment.[2] Competing claims for disputed work exist even if the claims are made by separate groups of workers who are represented by the same union local.[3] In addition, the Board has found that active competing claims to work exist when union workers employed by a subcontractor have a collective bargaining agreement assigning work to them and employees of the principal employer at issue also claim the work in question.[4]

The Board continues to hold that an active competing claim to a work assignment does not exist when the dispute merely involves a question about which union will represent a group of employees performing the work at issue and no objection has been made about the employees performing the work:[5]

---

[1]Carpenters Local 13 (First Chicago NBD Corp.), 331 NLRB 281, 164 LRRM 1263 (2000) (union's claim that picketing was for recognition purposes failed where only one truck driver was asked to sign recognition card and union never approached company about recognition); Operating Eng'rs Local 150 (Diamond Coring Co.), 331 NLRB 1349, 166 LRRM 1084 (2000) (union not engaging in recognitional picketing when previously it threatened work stoppage); Carpenters Local 13 (Millenium Constr.), 336 NLRB 1002, 169 LRRM 1419 (2001) (work assignment was "an object" of area-standards picketing). *See also* Betal Envtl. Corp. v. Asbestos Laborers Local 78, 162 F. Supp. 2d 246, 255–58 (S.D.N.Y. 2001).

[2]*See* Main Edition, Chapter 24, this section.

[3]Teamsters Local 174 (Airborne Express, Inc.), 340 NLRB No. 20, 173 LRRM 1217 (2003) (competing claim by employees in separate bargaining units but represented by same local union); Electrical Workers (IBEW) Local 98 (Honeywell, Inc.), 332 NLRB 526, 165 LRRM 1338 (2000) (competing claims for work by installers and electricians where local union attempted to force employer to reassign system installation work from installers to electricians, even though both employee groups represented by same union).

[4]*Carpenters Local 13 (First Chicago NBD Corp.), supra* note 1, 331 NLRB at 283, 164 LRRM at 1265; Carpenters Local 275 (Lymo Constr. Co.), 334 NLRB 422, 167 LRRM 1209 (2001) (question concerning representation does not qualify as jurisdictional dispute).

[5]*Teamsters Local 174 (Airborne Express, Inc.), supra* note 3 (where there is conduct inconsistent with the disclaimer, and the disclaimer itself is not clear and unambiguous, there is no valid disclaimer); Carpenters Local 1307 (Dearborn Village, LLC), 331 NLRB 245, 164 LRRM 1283 (2000); *Carpenters & Joiners Local 275 (Lymo Constr. Co.), supra* note 4. *But see* Graphic Communications Workers Local 508M (Joseph Berning Printing Co.), 331 NLRB 846, 168 LRRM 1388 (2000) (dispute not merely over which union would represent employees currently performing work because union sought to have work reassigned to employees whom it represented).

> There must, in short, be either an attempt to take a work assignment away from another group, or to obtain the assignment rather than have it given to the other group.
>
> . . .
>
> A demand for recognition as bargaining representative for employees doing a particular job, or in a particular department, does not to the slightest degree connote a demand for the assignment of work to particular employees rather than to others.[6]

A bona fide disclaimer of jurisdiction of disputed work by a labor organization that originally claimed the work will eliminate an active competing claim to the work. As a result, the Board will not find reasonable cause to believe that a jurisdictional dispute exists in such circumstances. The party asserting that a disclaimer has occurred that negates the existence of a jurisdictional dispute has the burden of proving "a clear, unequivocal, and unqualified disclaimer of all interest in the dispute."[7]

C. Procedure in Jurisdictional Dispute Cases

1. *Generally*

The Board's authority to decide jurisdictional disputes under Section 10(k) requires it to consider whether there is reasonable cause to believe that a Section 8(b)(4)(D) violation has occurred. The Board has used this same analysis to determine the appropriateness of its subpoena power. In *Plumbers Local 562 (C&R Heating & Service Co.)*,[8] the Board quashed a union subpoena seeking employer-association testimony to prove that a rival union's threats were collusive and not genuine. According to the Board, the union failed to meet the threshold requirements for Section 10(k) proceedings that there was reasonable cause to believe that Section 8(b)(4)(D) had

---

[6]*Carpenters Local 1307 (Dearborn Village, LLC)*, *supra* note 5, 164 LRRM at 1285, citing Laborers Local 1 (DEL Constr.), 285 NLRB 593, 595, 127 LRRM 1099, 1101 (1987) (quoting Food & Commercial Workers Local 1222 (FedMart Stores), 262 NLRB 817, 819, 110 LRRM 1383, 1385 (1982)).

[7]Plumbers Local 562 (Grossman Contracting Co.), 329 NLRB 516, 164 LRRM 1313, 1317 (1999), quoting Machinists (Hudson Gen. Hosp.), 326 NLRB 62, 65, 159 LRRM 1017, 1020 (1981); Carpenters Local 13 (First Chicago NBD Corp.), 331 NLRB 281, 164 LRRM 1263 (2000); Laborers Local 113. (Super Excavators, Inc.), 338 NLRB 472, 171 LRRM 1173 (2002). *See* Main Edition, this Section.

[8]328 NLRB 1235, 162 LRRM 1300 (1999).

been violated. In the absence of evidence that threats were not genuine or were made in collusion with the employer, the Board declined to permit the union "to engage in a fishing expedition."[9]

2. *Voluntary Adjustment*

The Board continues to find that an agreement that constitutes "an agreed method of voluntary adjustment," and thus deprives the Board of Section 10(k) jurisdiction to hear and determine the underlying dispute, must be one to which all parties to the dispute, including the employer, are bound.[10]

3. *Disclaimer*

The Board continues to rule that the party asserting that a disclaimer negates the existence of a jurisdictional dispute has the burden to prove a clear, unequivocal, and unqualified disclaimer of all interest in the work in dispute.[11] Moreover, the Board continues to hold that a disclaimer is insufficient where the union engages in behavior that is inconsistent with its professed intent to disclaim the disputed work.[12]

---

[9]*Id.* at 1237, 162 LRRM at 1301; Stage Employees Local 6 (Savvis Ctr.), 334 NLRB 214, 168 LRRM 1496 (2001) (existence of no-strike clause did not render strike threat "sham"); Laborers Local 860 (Anthony Allega Cement Contractor, Inc.), 336 NLRB 358, 170 LRRM 1089 (2001) (threat characterized as use of "legal means" is still threat); Iron Workers Local 1 (Goebel Forming, Inc.), 340 NLRB No. 136, 173 LRRM 1524 (2003) (sufficient that union claimed it "might have to" pull its employees off job site if work was not assigned to it).

[10]*See* Laborers Int'l (E&B Paving, Inc.), 340 NLRB No. 150, 174 LRRM 1034 (2003); Operating Eng'rs Local 150 (Diamond Coring Co.), 331 NLRB 1349, 166 LRRM 1084 (2000); Bricklayers (W.R. Weis Co.), 336 NLRB 699, 171 LRRM 1164 (2001) (union must have authority to resolve work assignment dispute).

[11]*See* Teamsters Local 295 (Emery Freight Corp.), 332 NLRB 1140, 168 LRRM 1044 (2000); Carpenters Local 558 (Joyce Bros. Storage & Van Co.), 331 NLRB 1022 (2000).

[12]Carpenters Local 13 (Millenium Constr.), 336 NLRB 1002, 169 LRRM 1419 (2001); Teamsters Local 259 (Globe Newspaper Co.), 327 NLRB 619, 160 LRRM 1195 (1999) (union's pursuit of contract grievance and arbitration procedures was inconsistent with its asserted disclaimer).

D. Factors Determining Jurisdictional Disputes

The Board continues to follow the factors announced in *Jones Construction*[13] in determining which employees should be assigned disputed work.[14] Although it is unable to establish the weight to be given the various factors, the Board continues to assert that "[e]very decision will have to be an act of judgment based on experience and common sense rather than on precedent."[15] In a majority of the cases, the Board's analysis of the facts and application of the factors continue to lead to awards that support the employer's assignment of the work.[16]

When making a determination, one of the factors the Board continues to consider is the certification and collective bargaining agreements between employers and unions. Where two collective bargaining agreements both arguably cover disputed work, the Board will favor the agreement currently in effect over an expired agree-

---

[13]Machinists Lodge 1743 (J.A. Jones Constr. Co.), 135 NLRB 1402, 49 LRRM 1684 (1962). For the list of *Jones Construction* factors, see Main Edition, Chapter 24.

[14]*See, e.g.*, Craftworkers Local 1 (Cretex Constr. Servs., Inc.), 343 NLRB No. 110, 176 LRRM 1198 (2004); Carpenters Local 624 (T. Equip. Corp.), 322 NLRB 428, 154 LRRM 1057 (1996); Iron Workers Local 1 (Fabcon, Inc.), 311 NLRB 87, 144 LRRM 1047 (1993); Elevator Constructors Local 5 (Stuart-Dean Co.), 310 NLRB 1189, 143 LRRM 1283 (1993).

[15]*Machinists Lodge 1743, supra* note 13; Electrical Workers (IBEW) Local 98 (NFF Constr., Inc.), 332 NLRB 1262 (2000); Carpenters Local 1006 (J.P. Patti Co.), 332 NLRB 830, 166 LRRM 1194 (2000); Electrical Workers (IBEW) Local 98 (Honeywell, Inc.), 332 NLRB 526, 165 LRRM 1338 (2000); Operating Eng'rs Local 12, (Winegardner Masonry, Inc.), 331 NLRB 1669, 166 LRRM 1286 (2000); Operating Eng'rs Local 150 (Diamond Coring Co.), 331 NLRB 1349, 166 LRRM 1084 (2000); Electrical Workers (IBEW) Local 98 (AIMM, Inc.), 331 NLRB 1075, 165 LRRM 1155 (2000); Graphic Communications Local 508M (Joseph Berning Printing Co.), 331 NLRB 846, 168 LRRM 1388 (2000); Electrical Workers (IBEW) Local 1049 (Asplundh Constr. Corp.), 331 NLRB 779, 166 LRRM 1036 (2000); Carpenters Local 13 (First Chicago NBD Corp.), 331 NLRB 281, 164 LRRM 1263 (2000); Laborers Local 320 (N.W. Natural Gas Co.), 330 NLRB 594, 163 LRRM 1133 (2000); Laborers (E & B Paving Co.), 340 NLRB No. 150, 174 LRRM 1034 (2003).

[16]*See* Electrical Workers (IBEW) Local 3 (Slatterky Skanska, Inc.), 342 NLRB No. 21, 175 LRRM 1216 (2004); *Electrical Workers (IBEW) Local 1049 (Asplundh Constr. Corp.), supra* note 15; Bakery Workers Local 334 (Interstate Brands Corp.), 334 NLRB 1161, 169 LRRM 1272 (2001) (assigning employer's past practice is considered or, if none, practice of predecessor employer); Construction & General Laborers' District Council of Chicago (Henkels & McCoy, Inc.), 336 NLRB 1044, 169 LRRM 1123 (2001) (area and industry practice also factors); Operating Eng'rs Local 150 (United Drilling), 337 NLRB 651, 170 LRRM 1250 (2002).

ment.[17] Furthermore, the Board has ruled that where two extant collective bargaining agreements cover the disputed work, neither will be considered in a Section 10(k) proceeding because the agreements do not favor either group of employees.[18] In the same case, the Board ruled that an interunion agreement does not favor an award of the disputed work to either group of employees where there is no conclusive evidence about whether the interunion agreement applies to the disputed work whether the area and industry practice conforms to the terms of the agreement.[19]

In considering the factor of economy and efficiency of operations, the Board typically favors those employees who perform multiple functions or who can perform the job in question with fewer employees.[20] While the Board continues to favor awards that do not result in any loss of jobs,[21] it has recently found this factor outweighed by countervailing factors.[22]

E. Post-Hearing Procedure

In jurisdictional dispute cases, the Board also declines to issue broad prospective awards in the absence of evidence that similar work disputes are likely to arise in the future or that the offending union has a proclivity to engage in unlawful conduct to obtain work similar to that in the dispute.[23]

---

[17]*See* Laborers Local 210 (Concrete Cutting & Breaking), 328 NLRB 1314, 162 LRRM 1117 (1999).

[18]*See* Plumbers Local 562 (Charles E. Jarrell Contracting), 329 NLRB 529, 163 LRRM 1056 (1999).

[19]*Id.*

[20]*See, e.g.*, Laborers Local 113 (Super Excavators, Inc.), 338 NLRB 480, 171 LRRM 1173 (2002); Electrical Workers (IBEW) Local 702 (F.W. Elec.), 337 NLRB 594, 170 LRRM 1062 (2002).

[21]*See,* e.g., Iron Workers Local 1 (Advance Cast Stone), 338 NLRB 43 (2002); Plumbers Local 123 (Florida Maint.), 338 NLRB 429, 171 LRRM 1065 (2002).

[22]Bakery Workers Local 6 (Bachman Co.), 337 NLRB 407, 169 LRRM 1289 (2002) (factors of employee preference, area industry practices, and economy and efficiency of operations outweigh countervailing factor of loss of jobs).

[23]*See* Operating Eng'rs Local 12 (Winegardner Masonry, Inc.), 331 NLRB 1669, 166 LRRM 1286 (2000) (finding that evidence failed to show that union had proclivity to engage in unlawful conduct to obtain similar work); Operating Eng'rs Local 150 (Diamond Coring Co.), 331 NLRB 1349, 166 LRRM 1084 (2000) (concluding that requisite showing that similar disputes are likely to arise in future or that respondent union has proclivity to engage in unlawful conduct to obtain similar work had not been made); Electrical Workers (IBEW) Local 98 (AIMM, Inc.), 331 NLRB 1075, 165 LRRM 1155 (2000) (holding employer's request for award covering all installation work exceeded defined work in dispute, and therefore was

F. Relationship of Section 8(b)(4)(D) Proceedings to Other Actions and Unfair Labor Practice Proceedings

Joining other circuits, the Eighth Circuit ruled it was appropriate to stay a Section 301 action to enforce an arbitration award pending the Board's determination in a Section 10(k) or Section 8(b)(4)(D) proceeding.[24] The Board's decision overrides that of an arbitrator in the event of a conflict.[25]

III. "FEATHERBEDDING"

C. Application of the Law

The Board continues to adhere to *American Newspaper*,[26] which interpreted Section 8(b)(6) narrowly. In *Teamsters Local 282 (TDX Construction Corp.)*,[27] the Board reversed the administrative law judge's finding that the union had violated Section 8(b)(6) by picketing the employer's job site in an effort to force the employer to hire an on-

---

overly broad); Electrical Workers (IBEW) Local 1049 (Asplundh Constr. Corp.), 331 NLRB 779, 166 LRRM 1036 (2000) (finding broad award inappropriate); Carpenters Local 13 (First Chicago NBD Corp.), 331 NLRB 281, 164 LRRM 1263 (2000) (concluding that broad order was inappropriate where evidence fell short of establishing proclivity); Plumbers Local 562 (C&R Heating & Serv. Co.), 328 NLRB 1235, 162 LRRM 1300 (1999) (declining to grant broad prospective award even though work-jurisdiction dispute between two unions was ongoing, where each of disputes involved distinct type of work and thus work likely to be disputed in future could be anticipated); Laborers Local 210 (Concrete Cutting & Breaking), 328 NLRB 1314, 162 LRRM 1117 (1999) (declining to issue areawide award without evidence that offending union had proclivity to engage in unlawful conduct to obtain similar work); Electrical Workers (IBEW) Local 103 (Lucent Techs.), 333 NLRB 828, 167 LRRM 1103 (2001) (likelihood of recurrent disputes and union's proclivity warranted broad order). *Cf.* Laborers Local 860 (Anthony Allega Cement Contractor, Inc.), 336 NLRB 358, 170 LRRM 1089 (2001) (no broad order where union sought only to maintain assignment of disputed work); Elevator Contructors Local 91 (Otis Elevator Co.), 340 NLRB No. 14, 173 LRRM 1173 (2003) (award limited to job site where unlawful activity occurred when there was no evidence of proclivity to engage in unlawful conduct to obtain disputed work).

[24]Sheet Metal Workers Local 36 v. Murphy Constr. Co., 191 F.3d 909, 910–11, 162 LRRM 2334 (8th Cir. 1999).

[25]*Id.*; T. Equip. Corp. v. Massachusetts Laborers' Dist. Council, 166 F.3d 11, 160 LRRM 2257 (1st Cir. 1999).

[26]American Newspaper Publishers Ass'n v. NLRB, 345 U.S. 100, 31 LRRM 2422 (1953).

[27]332 NLRB 922, 165 LRRM 1305 (2000).

site steward that it did not need or want. The Board held that there was no violation of the Act because the union "did not seek payment for an employee to stand idly by" or for work that was "not relevant" to the employer's general activities on the work project.[28]

---

[28] *Id.* at 925.

Part VII

RELATIONS BETWEEN EMPLOYEE AND UNION

BIBLIOGRAPHY

David M. Burns, *Requiring Unions to Notify Covered Employees of Their Right to be an Agency Fee Payer in the Post* Beck *Era*, 48 CATH. U. L. REV. 475 (1999)

Jeff Canfield, *What a Sham(e): The Broken* Beck *Rights System in the Real World Workplace*, 47 WAYNE L. REV. 1049 (2001)

Eric J. Felsberg, *Creating a* Beck *Statute: Recent Congressional Attempts and a Proposal for the Future*, 15 HOFSTRA LAB. & EMP. L.J. 247 (1997)

Christopher J. Garofalo, *Section 302 of the LMRA: Make Way for the Employer-Paid Union Representative*, 75 N.Y.U. L. REV. 775 (2000)

Michael J. Goldberg, *Derailing Union Democracy: Why Deregulation Would Be a Mistake*, 23 BERKELEY J. EMP. & LAB. L. 137 (2002)

Christopher Grant, *Unions in a Fragmented Society*, 7 CHI.-KENT L. REV. 849 (2002)

Aaron Gregg, *The Constitutionality of Requiring Annual Renewal of Union Fee Objections in an Agency Shop*, 78 TEX. L. REV. 1159 (2000)

Harry G. Hutchison, *Reclaiming the Labor Movement Through Union Dues? A Postmodern Perspective in the Mirror of Public Choice Theory*, 33 U. MICH. J.L. REFORM 447 (2000)

CHAPTER 25

THE DUTY OF FAIR REPRESENTATION

II. JURISDICTION AND PROCEDURES TO ENFORCE THE DUTY

A. The Courts

In *Lucas v. NLRB*,[1] the Ninth Circuit held that the Board's reliance on the very deferential standard for union action in *Air Line Pilots Ass'n v. O'Neill*[2] was inappropriate when the issue arose in the context of an exclusive hiring hall. The court found that when a union has control over workers' livelihood, it has an added responsibility. The case was remanded "so that the Board may enter the appropriate remedial order in favor of Lucas." The Board accepted the court's decision as the law of the case and ordered the standard remedies.

1. Exhaustion of Contractual Remedies

Before an individual employee may bring an action alleging breach of a labor agreement, the employee must exhaust the available grievance procedure.[3] However, if the employee can fully demonstrate the futility of completing the grievance process, either because of the employer's repudiation of contractual procedures or because the employee's union, which has exclusive authority to invoke higher levels of the procedure, wrongfully refuses to process the grievance, then the employee may be permitted to proceed with a Section 301 claim against the employer and/or the union.[4] Although there have been no changes in the law underlying exhaustion of contractual remedies, two cases have applied these principles to different situations, arriving at different results.

In *Duerr v. Minnesota Mining & Manufacturing Co.*,[5] a former employee commenced an action for breach of contract and violation of the Illinois Wage Payment Act. The employee made no claim that the employer had repudiated the contract's grievance process

---

[1]333 F.3d 927, 172 LRRM 2206 (9th Cir. 2003), *rev'g and remanding* 332 NLRB 1, 165 LRRM 1163 (2000).

[2]499 U.S. 65, 136 LRRM 2721 (1991).

[3]Republic Steel Corp. v. Maddox, 379 U.S. 650, 652–53, 58 LRRM 2193 (1965).

[4]Vaca v. Sipes, 386 U.S. 171, 185, 64 LRRM 2369 (1967).

[5]101 F. Supp. 2d 1057 (N.D. Ill. 2000). *See also* Bennefield v. Hoechst Celanese Corp., 230 F.3d 1351 (4th Cir. 2000) (where court, in per curiam decision, dismissed employee's age discrimination and retaliation claims against employer, because employee had not filed her lawsuit within 90 days after receiving right-to-sue letter, and dismissed her duty of fair representation claim against union because she failed to exhaust contractual grievance and arbitration procedure).

or that the union had wrongfully refused to process his grievance. Instead, he claimed, in part, that at the time he pursued his lawsuit against the employer, he was no longer employed and was no longer a member of the union, and the union, therefore, could not invoke the grievance process on his behalf.[6]

The court rejected the employee's excuse for not exhausting the grievance process because he *had* been employed at the time that the union's president informed him that he would not receive additional overtime payments following his resignation.[7] The court cited a case with analogous facts to support its decision, and distinguished another case where the employees could not pursue the grievance procedure because the change in their employment status and subsequent inability even to file a grievance was beyond their control.[8]

The court in *Meredith v. Louisiana Federation of Teachers*[9] reached the opposite result where the employer repudiated the grievance-arbitration process, and the employee was not in a position to pursue her contractual rights effectively. The employee was employed as a field representative with the Louisiana Federation of Teachers when she negotiated an individual contract to work for the local St. Tamany Federation under the same terms of employment she enjoyed with the Louisiana Federation. The St. Tamany Federation subsequently terminated the plaintiff's employment; the state federation took the position that the plaintiff no longer worked for it, making her ineligible to use the grievance procedure, and her union, the United Professional Staff Association, ignored the plaintiff's requests for assistance.

Citing *Vaca v. Sipes*,[10] the court overruled the Louisiana Federation's motion to dismiss for lack of subject-matter jurisdiction, because the federation had taken the position that the employee was not covered by its collective bargaining agreement with the Pro-

---

[6]*Duerr, supra* note 5, 101 F. Supp. 2d at 1059–60, 1062–63.

[7]*Id.* at 1063.

[8]*Id.* at 1063–64, citing Roman v. United States Postal Serv., 821 F.2d 382, 125 LRRM 2623 (7th Cir. 1987) (where court dismissed employee's lawsuit for back pay allegedly owed him because employee had resigned his job without first filing grievance seeking back pay) and distinguishing Anderson v. AT&T Corp., 147 F.3d 467 (6th Cir. 1998) (where employees were permitted to sue employer without exhausting contractual procedures after being transferred to another plant at same company whose employees were in another bargaining unit).

[9]209 F.3d 398, 164 LRRM 2099 (5th Cir. 2000).

[10]386 U.S. 171, 64 LRRM 2369 (1967).

fessional Staff Association and would not consider the employee's grievance.[11]

2. *Exhaustion of Internal Union Remedies*

In *Clayton v. Auto Workers,*[12] the Supreme Court identified three factors that must be considered in determining whether the plaintiff-employee is excused from exhausting internal union procedures: (1) whether the union's officers are so hostile to the employee as to eliminate any hope for a fair hearing on the employee's claim; (2) whether the internal union procedures would have been inadequate to restore the employee's grievance or to award the employee full relief under Section 301; and (3) whether exhausting the internal union remedies would have unreasonably delayed the employee's opportunity for a judicial hearing on the merits of his or her claim.[13]

Other courts have found that the inquiry as to whether exhaustion of internal union remedies can be excused is fact specific and not limited to the guiding factors identified by the Supreme Court.[14] Key to the inquiry is whether it is reasonable to impose exhaustion under the circumstances.[15] In that regard, the absence of evidence of hostility toward the member on the part of the union, evidence that the review procedures are fair, the possibility of reactivation of a grievance through the grievance procedure, and the fact that exhaustion would not have unduly delayed the member's access to judicial proceedings have all been found to render exhaustion reasonable under the circumstances.[16] By contrast, ignorance of the available internal appeals procedures continues to be viewed as an inexcusable basis for failing to exhaust those procedures.[17]

---

[11]*Meredith, supra* note 9, 209 F.3d at 402–03.

[12]451 U.S. 679, 107 LRRM 2385 (1981).

[13]*Id.* at 689.

[14]Akers v. AM Gen. Sales Corp., 167 LRRM 2439, 2000 WL 3309435 (S.D. Ind. 2000); *but see* Casumpang v. Longshore & Warehouse Union Local 142, 297 F. Supp. 2d 1238, 174 LRRM 2085 (D. Haw. 2003).

[15]McClimon v. Auto Workers, 168 LRRM 2891, 2001 WL 1537373 (C.D. Ill. 2001).

[16]*See, e.g.,* Arnold v. Mine Workers, 293 F.3d 977, 170 LRRM 2213 (7th Cir. 2002) (hostility by one union executive does not excuse exhaustion of internal procedures); Moore v. Auto Workers Local 598, 165 LRRM 3016, 2000 WL 33374410 (E.D. Mich. 2000); Cottor v. Daimler-Chrysler, 87 F. Supp. 2d 746, 164 LRRM 2111 (E.D. Mich. 2000).

[17]Edwards v. Ford Motor Co., 179 F. Supp. 2d 714, 168 LRRM 2599 (W.D. Ky. 2001).

The duty to exhaust internal union appeal procedures has also been discussed in the context of procedures provided by collective bargaining agreements.[18]

3. *Parties to Fair Representation Actions*

Courts continue to recognize that individual union officers are not proper defendants in fair representation actions.[19]

B. The Labor Board

1. *Unfair Labor Practice Cases*

The Board and courts continue to hold that "mere negligence" in the operation of an exclusive hiring hall does not breach the duty of fair representation. In *Jacoby v. NLRB*,[20] however, the D.C. Circuit found that "gross negligence" or reckless business practices in the operation of an exclusive hiring hall would violate the duty of fair representation. Relying on *Jacoby*, the Board, in *Electrical Workers (IBEW) Local 48 (Oregon-Columbia Chapter, NECA)*,[21] found that the union had violated its duty of fair representation by granting preferential referrals to "salt and peppers" in violation of its established referral procedures constituted gross negligence in the operation of its hiring hall.

3. *Preemption and Accommodation*

The courts continue to hold that contract, tort, or other claims and theories nominally derived from state law are preempted when in fact they are premised on the duty of fair representation or a related breach of contract. The preemption rule has blocked actions by employees based on state law claims of: (1) fraudulent misrepresentation, tortious interference, and civil conspiracy;[22] (2) breach of a settlement agreement, covenant of good faith and fair dealing, promissory estoppel, breach of fiduciary duties, and retaliation and gender discrimination;[23] and (3) religious discrimination, state wrongful discharge, and civil conspiracy claims.[24]

---

[18]Duerr v. Minnesota Mining & Mfg. Co., 101 F. Supp. 2d 1057 (N.D. Ill. 2000).

[19]Capozza Tile Co. v. Joy, 223 F. Supp. 2d 307 (D. Me. 2002).

[20]325 F.3d 301, 172 LRRM 2199 (D.C. Cir. 2003).

[21]342 NLRB No. 10 (2004).

[22]Beidleman v. Stroh Brewery Co., 182 F.3d 225, 161 LRRM 2656 (3d Cir. 1999).

[23]Audette v. Longshoremen Local 24, 195 F.3d 1107, 162 LRRM 2705 (9th Cir. 1999). *See also* Lemerich v. Operating Eng'rs, 2002 WL 655333, 171 LRRM 2560 (D. Me. 2002).

[24]Thomas v. Letter Carriers, 225 F.3d 1149, 1158 (10th Cir. 2000).

In these cases, the courts found that the claims were based on, centered around, or importantly affected by labor contracts, labor-based settlement agreements, or a local labor memorandum of understanding. As a consequence, these claims entwined the union in employees' disputes with the employer and turned the issue into what duty the unions owed to the employees. As one court observed, "[w]here a plaintiff's allegations fall within the scope of the duty of fair representation, federal labor law governs and ordinarily preempts any state law claims based on those allegations."[25] In *Bergeron v. Henderson*,[26] the court found a state law claim of sex discrimination against a union to be wholly preempted and entered judgment for the union on the pleadings.

III. NATURE OF THE DUTY

B. The Nature of the Duty in Grievance Handling and Contract Administration

There has been no change in the showing that an employee must make when claiming a breach of the duty of fair representation to establish a "hybrid" claim. The union, with its exclusive statutory authority to represent all members of the designated unit, has the "statutory obligation to serve the interests of all members without hostility or discrimination toward any, to exercise its discretion with complete good faith and honesty, and to avoid arbitrary conduct."[27] Thus, to prove a breach of the duty of fair representation, the plaintiff-employee must show that the union's conduct was "arbitrary, discriminatory, or in bad faith."[28] To prevail against an employer, an employee must show not only that the discharge or other action against the employee violated the collective bargaining agreement but also that the union breached its duty of fair representation.[29] Proof that the union breached the duty of fair representation is necessary even to raise the question of whether the employer violated the collective bargaining agreement.[30]

---

[25] *Id.* at 1158.

[26] 52 F. Supp. 2d 149, 161 LRRM 2761, 2763–65 (D. Me. 1999).

[27] Vaca v. Sipes, 386 U.S. 171, 177, 64 LRRM 2369 (1967).

[28] *Id.* at 190.

[29] United Parcel Serv. v. Mitchell, 451 U.S. 56, 62, 107 LRRM 2001 (1981).

[30] *Id.*; Mulvihill v. Top-Flite Golf Co., 335 F.3d 15, 27, 172 LRRM 3041, 3049 (1st Cir. 2003) (because employee failed to carry his burden to prove that employer breached contract, his breach of duty of fair representation claim against

This standard continues to be applied to situations where the employee's challenge relates to the union's processing of a grievance under the governing labor agreement. In such cases, the Board adheres to the view that mere negligence on the part of the union in handling a grievance does not breach the duty of fair representation.[31] Rather, the Board applies the test of *Air Line Pilots v. O'Neill*[32] and asks whether the union's conduct in processing and evaluating the grievance was "so far outside a wide range of reasonableness as to be irrational."[33] This standard is applied at all stages of the grievance and arbitration process.[34]

Cases demonstrate the wide latitude accorded to unions in grievance handling. In *Postal Workers Local 551*,[35] the employee filed a grievance after he was excluded from an overtime list. At the first step meeting, the employer offered to settle the grievance by placing the employee on the overtime list and compensating him for lost overtime. The union rejected the settlement on the basis of its policy against late additions to the overtime list. The union then dropped the grievance. The Board found that the union had not violated its duty of fair representation because there was no evidence that the union had acted with a discriminatory motive or that the union had applied its policy against late additions to the overtime list in an arbitrary fashion.

Although the standard is high, a union can be found to have acted "irrationally" where its decision making on matters of contract administration is based on the employee's status as a member or

---

union necessarily fails); Hodges v. Philip Morris USA, Inc., 281 F. Supp. 2d 807, 812–13 (E.D. Va. 2003), *aff'd*, 88 Fed. Appx. 584, 2004 WL 326963 (4th Cir. 2004) (employee's claims against union and employer are "'interlocked: neither claim is viable if the other fails'") (quoting Crider v. Spectrulite Consortium, Inc., 130 F.3d 1238, 1241, 156 LRRM 2993, 2995 (7th Cir. 1997)).

[31]Letter Carriers Local 3825, 333 NLRB 343, 166 LRRM 1217 (2001). *See also* Baird v. Burlington N. & Santa Fe Ry. Co., 24 Fed. Appx. 629, 2001 WL 1512540, 2001 U.S. App. LEXIS 25355 (8th Cir. 2001) (union's action developing considered opinion that employee was ineligible to receive benefits only constituted mere negligence and did not breach duty of fair representation); Buford v. Runyon, 160 F.3d 1199, 159 LRRM 2848 (8th Cir. 1998) (union's actions were only mere negligence when union pursued employee's grievance through proper procedure but excluded one medical report).

[32]499 U.S. 65, 67, 136 LRRM 2721 (1991).

[33]*Letter Carriers Local 3825*, *supra* note 31.

[34]American Fed'n of Musicians & Atlanta Fed'n of Musicians, 333 NLRB 1108 (2001).

[35]337 NLRB 550, 170 LRRM 1085 (2002).

nonmember of the union. Thus, in *Letter Carriers Local 3825*,[36] the ALJ found the union's denial of an employee's request for documents pertaining to a pending grievance "discriminatory . . . arbitrary and irrational"[37] because the denial was based on his status as a nonmember of the union. Similarly, where a union asked about the membership status of an employee who wanted to initiate a grievance, thereby giving the message that membership in the union was a precondition to obtaining union assistance in the grievance process, the union breached its duty of fair representation and violated Section 8(b)(1)(A) of the Act by restraining or coercing the employee in the exercise of rights guaranteed by Section 7.[38]

A breach can also be found where the union discriminates on an arbitrary basis among its members. For example, in *Electrical Workers (IBEW) Local 724 (Albany Electrical Contractors Ass'n)*,[39] the Board held that the union violated its duty of fair representation by routinely failing to operate a referral hall in conformity with the requirements of its collective bargaining agreement and by arbitrarily requiring only one of many registrants to comply fully with the application requirements of the collective bargaining agreement to the detriment of that individual. Similarly, a union violated its duty of fair representation by refusing to process a grievance for an employee because the employee had opposed the incumbent union officers in internal union matters.[40]

In contrast, proof of thoughtful analysis regarding the merits of a grievance will defeat a fair representation claim. Thus, where a union accepted the strict terms of an employer's "zero tolerance" drug policy, it did not act irrationally or unreasonably in its handling of an employee's grievance based on its opinion that it was unlikely that it would prevail in an arbitration of the employee's claims.[41]

---

[36]*Letter Carriers Local 3825*, *supra* note 31. *See also* Letter Carriers Branch 758 (Postal Serv.), 328 NLRB 952, 162 LRRM 1091 (1999) (breach by denying employees access to their grievance files and refusing to provide employees with copies of their grievance files at reasonable copying cost); National Postal Mail Handlers Local 308, 2002 NLRB LEXIS 108, at *27 (2002) (breach by denying employees access to information on first grievance settlement).

[37]*Id.*, *Letter Carriers Local 3825*, *supra* note 31, slip op. at 15.

[38]American Postal Workers, 328 NLRB 281, 161 LRRM 1237 (1999).

[39]327 NLRB 730, 160 LRRM 1177 (1999).

[40]Communications Workers Local 3410 (BellSouth Tel.), 328 NLRB 920, 168 LRRM 1358 (1999).

[41]Wilder v. GL Bus Lines, 164 LRRM 2906 (2000), *aff'd in relevant part*, 258 F.3d 126, 168 LRRM 2203 (2d Cir. 2001). *See also* Martin v. American Airlines, Inc., 390 F.3d 601, 606, 176 LRRM 2065 (8th Cir. 2004) (union officials' conduct, in-

Before rejecting the employee's request to take his grievance to arbitration, the union consulted two experts to test the employee's claims that various over-the-counter medicines he had been taking produced a false positive result in the urine sample collected by the employer's testing laboratory. Once the union learned that the over-the-counter medicines were not likely to produce false positive results, the court concluded that having "accepted the terms of [the employer's] 'zero tolerance' drug policy,"[42] the union would have had little likelihood of success in arbitration. Similarly, a union's decision not to have an employee testify on his own behalf at an arbitration hearing of a grievance over the employee's termination was held not to be arbitrary where the record contained a statement by the employee denying the charges for which he was terminated, and the union made a reasoned judgment that the employee would not be a credible witness.[43]

In a significant decision, *Steamfitters Local 342*,[44] the Board overruled *Iron Workers Local 118 (California Erectors)*,[45] which had imposed liability on unions for ordinary errors in operating referral halls. Relying on the Supreme Court's holding in *Steelworkers v. Rawson*[46] that "mere negligence" by a union in the exercise of its obligations does not breach the duty of fair representation applies in the context of an exclusive referral hall, the Board held the union did not breach its duty to a member who lost an employment opportunity as a result of the union's honest, inadvertent mistake in failing to refer him to a job in the proper order. The Ninth Circuit, however, has cited the union's "heightened duty of fair dealing" in the management of a hiring hall, holding that a union breached its duty of fair representation by permanently barring an employee from the hiring hall, where it was unable to show that the expulsion was necessary to "promote the efficiency and integrity of its hiring hall operations.[47]

---

cluding reviewing relevant documentation, discussing grievant's case with various management representatives, discussing strategy, and attempting to have grievant reinstated, demonstrated nothing less than "concern" and "solicitude" for grievant).

[42]*Id.*, 164 LRRM at 2914.

[43]Connell v. Merck & Co., 76 Fed. Appx. 438 (3d Cir. 2003).

[44]329 NLRB 688 (1999), *decision on remand*, 336 NLRB 549, 168 LRRM 1256 (2001) (reaffirming that inadvertent mistakes arising from mere negligence do not violate the duty). *See also* Plumbers Local 375 (H.C. Price Constr.), 330 NLRB 383, 163 LRRM 1041 (1999).

[45]309 NLRB 808, 142 LRRM 1168 (1992).

[46]495 U.S. 362, 134 LRRM 2153 (1990).

[47]Lucas v. NLRB, 333 F.3d 927, 172 LRRM 2206 (9th Cir. 2003).

The union's duty of fair representation in grievance handling does not require union members on joint grievance panels to vote automatically to sustain an employee's grievance. Rather, courts have generally found that union panel members should act as arbitrators, and that the panel members satisfy their duty of fair representation by acting impartially.[48]

C. The Duty in Collective Bargaining

Since the Supreme Court's decision in *Air Line Pilots v. O'Neill*,[49] there have been no changes in the legal standards governing unions' obligations to the employees they represent in their handling of the basic obligations of collective bargaining, including negotiating and settling of agreements. A union is entitled to a "wide range of reasonableness" in its actions, which allows the union to make discretionary decisions, even if those decisions are ultimately wrong. As a consequence, "a settlement is not irrational (and thus arbitrary) simply because it turns out in retrospect to have been a bad settlement."[50]

Thus, in *Fay v. Teamsters Local 553*,[51] a Section 301 hybrid action arising from the merger of bargaining units of combined companies, the district court held that the union did not breach its duty of fair representation by deciding to dovetail rather than endtail the seniority lists. Similarly, in *White v. White Rose Food*,[52] the court held that a union was not required under the Act or its own constitution or bylaws to submit an amendment to the collective bargaining agreement to its membership for ratification, even though the original agreement had been so ratified.[53]

In *Longshoremen (ILA) Local 1575*,[54] employees charged that their union denied them the right to vote on whether to ratify a contract. In a membership meeting held to ratify the new contract, 80 percent of the membership stood in protest to a new contract provision. The union president then requested that all those in favor of the new

---

[48]*E.g.*, Early v. Eastern Transfer, 699 F.2d 552, 112 LRRM 3381 (1st Cir. 1983).

[49]499 U.S. 65, 67, 136 LRRM 2721 (1991).

[50]*Id.* at 79 (quoting Ford Motor Co. v. Huffman, 345 U.S. 330, 338, 31 LRRM 2548 (1953)). *See, e.g.*, Clarett v. National Football League, 369 F.3d 124 (2d Cir. 2004) (negotiation that favors one group of employees over another not breach of duty).

[51]67 F. Supp. 2d 86 (E.D.N.Y. 1999).

[52]237 F.3d 174, 166 LRRM 2281 (2d Cir. 2001).

[53]*See, e.g.*, Schwarz v. Brotherhood of Maint. of Way Employees (Burlington Sys.), 264 F.3d 1181, 168 LRRM 2233 (10th Cir. 2001).

[54]332 NLRB 1336, 165 LRRM 1377 (2000).

contract stand up, then announced that the contract had been ratified by those who were actually standing in protest. The Board found that the union had not breached its duty of fair representation on the ground that the union was not required to request a vote of its membership to ratify the contract. Membership ratification is a permissive subject of bargaining, and the parties had not agreed that such a vote was required to make the contract effective.[55]

In *Williams v. Molphus*,[56] the Sixth Circuit reversed the grant of summary judgment and, applying the *Air Line Pilots v. O'Neill*[57] standard, remanded for further proceedings to determine whether a union acted in bad faith or with discriminatory intent when it endtailed seniority pursuant to a negotiated rider to a national agreement.

The union's duty in negotiating a collective bargaining agreement is not breached by failing to negotiate every possible term. In *Conrad v. Machinists*,[58] the Eighth Circuit held that a union did not breach its duty of fair representation when it did not bargain for a checkoff provision for employees who paid reduced union dues.

IV. Statutes of Limitations

There is continuing discussion in the courts about the application of the Section 10(b) 6-month statute of limitations adopted for hybrid actions in *DelCostello v. Teamsters*.[59] On the question of whether an employee can sue only the employer for breach of a collective bargaining agreement, and not the union for breach of the duty of fair representation more than 6 months after the act giving rise to the claim, several courts have held that the employee could not avoid the 6-month statute of limitations by bringing only the breach of contract action against the employer.[60] In *Scott v. Auto Workers Local*

---

[55]*Id.*, 165 LRRM at 1378.

[56]171 F.3d 360, 160 LRRM 2803 (6th Cir. 1999). *See also* Ramey v. Machinists District 141, 378 F.3d 269, 175 LRRM 2467 (2d Cir. 2004) (evidence of retaliatory animus in determining seniority dates constitutes bad faith and breach of duty.).

[57]499 U.S. 65, 136 LRRM 2721 (1991).

[58]338 F.3d 908, 172 LRRM 3262 (8th Cir. 2003).

[59]462 U.S. 151, 169–70, 172, 113 LRRM 2737 (1983).

[60]Smith v. Masters, Mates & Pilots, 296 F.3d 380, 170 LRRM 2534 (5th Cir. 2002), *cert. denied*, 123 S. Ct. 691, 171 LRRM 2576 (2002); Carrion v. Enterprise Ass'n, 227 F.3d 29, 165 LRRM 2280 (2d Cir. 2000); Scott v. Auto Workers Local 879, 242 F.3d 837, 166 LRRM 2615 (8th Cir. 2001). *Cf.* Van Court v. Postal Workers, New Orleans Local #83, 99 Fed. Appx. 562, 563 (5th Cir. 2004) (the fact that plain-

879,[61] the court reasoned that, because the class was time barred from bringing suit against the union for breach of the duty of fair representation, summary judgment for the employer with respect to the Section 301 claim was also appropriate. These decisions follow the admonition of *DelCostello*, which stated that "the employee may, if he chooses, sue one defendant and not the other; but the case he must prove is the same whether he sues one, the other, or both."[62]

In *White v. White Rose Food*,[63] the court held that the fact that the employees were barred by the statute of limitations from bringing a suit against the union did not mean that they were precluded from bringing suit against the employer in a separate Section 301 action. However, the court ruled that, although the union's joinder in the suit was time barred, the employees nevertheless had to prove both that the employer breached a collective bargaining agreement and that the union breached its duty of fair representation.[64]

In *Prazak v. Bricklayers Local 1*,[65] the Ninth Circuit held that an employee who initially filed a hybrid Section 301/fair representa-

---

tiff sued only his union and "chose not to sue his employer does not preclude application of the six-month statute of limitations").

[61] *Supra* note 60, 242 F.3d at 840, 166 LRRM at 2617.

[62] *DelCostello, supra* note 59, 462 U.S. at 165. *See also* Bartholomew v. AGL Res., Inc., 361 F.3d 1333, 1342, 174 LRRM 2545, 2550 (11th Cir. 2004) (plaintiffs' hybrid suit was time barred because they did not timely sue after learning that "union would not submit their grievances to arbitration"); *Scott, supra* note 60, 242 F.3d at 840 (hybrid suit was time barred by virtue of employee's failure to timely sue the union upon constructive notice of a violation); Spaulding v. Transportation Workers, 279 F.3d 901, 912, 169 LRRM 2530, 2538 (10th Cir. 2002) (dismissal of plaintiffs' breach of duty of fair representation claim against union as time barred required dismissal of plaintiffs' breach of contract claim against employer because viable duty of fair representation claim is predicate for correlative claim against employer).

[63] 128 F.3d 110, 156 LRRM 2680 (2d Cir. 1997).

[64] *Accord* Waldron v. Boeing Co., 388 F.3d 591, 594, 175 LRRM 3211, 3212 (8th Cir. 2004) ("in order to bring an individual suit directly against the employer for breach of the CBA, [the employee] must allege and prove the union breached its duty of fair representation"); DeGuzman v. New Jersey, 113 Fed. Appx. 438, 441–42 (3d Cir. 2004) ("[t]o succeed on [Section 301] claim, plaintiff 'must prove the same two facts to recover money damages: that the employer's action violated the terms of the collective bargaining agreement and that the union breached its duty of fair representation'") (quoting Teamsters Local 391 v. Terry, 494 U.S. 558, 564 (1990)); *Bartholomew, supra* note 62, 361 F.3d at 1342, 174 LRRM at 2550 (same); White v. White Rose Food, 237 F.3d 174, 178, 166 LRRM 2281, 2283 (2d Cir. 2001).

[65] 233 F.3d 1149, 165 LRRM 2853 (9th Cir. 2000); *see also* Bryan v. Fireman's Fund Ins. Co., 35 Fed. Appx. 591, (9th Cir. 2002) (hybrid suit in state court filed within 6-month statute of limitations is not time barred if subsequently removed to federal court).

tion claim in state court within the 6-month statute of limitations period was not barred by the statute of limitations rule set forth in *DelCostello* and *West v. Conrail*[66] when the case was subsequently removed to federal court. The court stated that *DelCostello* and *West* did not seek to create strict uniformity in federal court responses to application of state versus federal jurisdictional rules, but rather both decisions may be viewed as "crafting limited rules in order to facilitate the filing of hybrid actions."[67] *Prazak* directly conflicts with the Fourth Circuit's decision in *Cannon v. Kroger*,[68] where the court found that "the statute of limitations applicable to 'hybrid' actions runs until the action is properly commenced under the dictates of the Federal Rules of Civil Procedure."[69]

Fundamental to determining whether an action has been commenced within the limitations period is the issue of when the claim accrued.[70] The courts continue to use varying terminology in stating the rule governing accrual.[71] However, the courts appear to be in

[66]481 U.S. 35, 124 LRRM 3137 (1987).

[67]*Prazak, supra* note 65, 233 F.3d at 1152.

[68]832 F.2d 303, 126 LRRM 2968 (4th Cir. 1987).

[69]*Id.* at 305–06. *But see* Winkels v. George A. Hormel & Co., 874 F.2d 567, 131 LRRM 2338 (8th Cir. 1989).

[70]See Main Edition, Chapter 25, Section IV, at page 1937.

[71]*See*, e.g., Kavowras v. New York Times Co., 328 F.3d 50, 55–56, 172 LRRM 2389, 2392 (2d Cir. 2003) (claim accrued at conclusion of arbitration hearing where tentative settlement was reached and no participant had any expectation that award would be rendered, at which time employee "'knew or reasonably should have known that [a breach of the duty of fair representation] had occurred'") (quoting Santos v. District Council, 619 F.2d 963, 969, 103 LRRM 3082 (2d Cir. 1980)); Coppage v. United States Postal Serv., 281 F.3d 1200, 1204, 169 LRRM 2396, 2399 (11th Cir. 2002) (claim accrues when plaintiff knew or should have known of union's or employer's "final action"); Albright v. Virtue, 273 F.3d 564, 572–73, 169 LRRM 2001, 2007 (3d Cir. 2001) (claim accrues when plaintiff received "notice that the union will proceed no further with a grievance," a standard that has been characterized as "court-inspired vagueness"); Hazard v. Southern Union Co., 275 F. Supp. 2d 214, 224, 173 LRRM 2027 (D.R.I. 2003) (claim accrued when employee knew that union would not pursue his grievance); Marrero v. City of New York, 172 LRRM 2253, 2256, 2003 WL 1621921 (S.D.N.Y. 2003) (same); Balderas v. Cessna Aircraft Co., 172 LRRM 2347, 2352 (D. Kan. 2003) ("[w]hen a union represents an employee throughout a grievance procedure, and takes the grievance to arbitration, the statute of limitations does not begin running until 'the dispute resolution process has been completely exhausted.'") (quoting Lucas v. Mountain States Tel., 909 F.2d 419, 421, 134 LRRM 3065 (10th Cir. 1990)); Ramey v. Machinists District 141, 378 F.3d 269, 278–79, 175 LRRM 2467 (2d Cir. 2004) (claim did not accrue when union informed employees of intent to breach, but only when employees knew breach had actually occurred).

agreement that the "continuing violation" theory cannot be utilized to create a new accrual date once an action has ripened in the first instance.[72]

V. REMEDIES

A. The Board

1. Unfair Labor Practice Cases

The Board ordered a make-whole back-pay remedy, to be determined at the compliance stage of the proceedings, for a class of unidentified applicants subjected to a union's hiring-hall referral practices in contravention of contractual referral rules. The Board also ordered the union to refer the one identified discriminatee in conformity with the hiring-hall rules and to make him whole for any losses from its previous failure to treat him in the same manner as other applicants.[73]

In *Communications Workers Local 3410 (BellSouth Telecommunications)*,[74] the Board applied the evidentiary burdens as reallocated in *Iron Workers Local 377 (Alamillo Steel Corp.)*.[75] The reallocation requires the general counsel, in a case alleging a union's mishandling of a grievance, to demand make-whole relief in the complaint and to show not only that the union breached its duty of fair representation but also that the grievant would have prevailed in the grievance-arbitration procedure had the union not breached its duty. The showing that the grievant would have prevailed, however, is postponed to the compliance stage of the proceeding, thus affording the union an opportunity to resolve the grievance through the contractual machinery. If the union is unable to secure resolution, the general counsel then must establish in the compliance proceeding that the grievance was meritorious. The principal effect of the change is to avoid

---

[72]Strassberg v. New York Hotel & Motel Trades Council Local 6, 31 Fed. Appx. 15, 17 (2d Cir.), *cert. denied*, 123 S. Ct. 193 (2002); Tapia v. Hotel Employees & Rest. Employees Local 11, 11 Fed. Appx. 941, 942 (9th Cir. 2001); Devitt v. Potter, 234 F. Supp. 2d 1034, 171 LRRM 2395 (D.N.D. 2002).

[73]Electrical Workers (IBEW) Local 724 (Albany Elec.), 327 NLRB 730, 160 LRRM 1177 (1999). The make-whole remedy may include allowing the grievant to be represented by an attorney of his or her own choosing at the subsequent arbitration with the union bearing that expense. *See, e.g.*, Warehousemen Local 6, 336 NLRB No. 104 (2001).

[74]328 NLRB 920 (1999).

[75]326 NLRB 375, 159 LRRM 1097 (1998).

litigation of the merits of the grievance in the initial unfair labor practice proceeding.

In *Letter Carriers v. NLRB*,[76] the court enforced a Board order that a union, which breached its duty of fair representation by refusing to file a nonmember's nonfrivolous overtime grievance, pay for independent legal representation. The court held that this was a standard remedy imposed by the Board in these circumstances and that an explanation as to its rationale did not have to be given anew by the Board in every case.

In *Denver Newspaper & Graphic Communications Local 22 (Rocky Mountain News)*,[77] the union retaliated against a member, who had filed an unfair labor practice charge against the union, by filing an internal union charge against him under the international union's constitution. Shortly thereafter, on the advice of counsel, the union withdrew the internal charge, but maintained the charge in the union's file along with a notation that it had been withdrawn. The Board held that the filing of the internal union charge itself constituted a Section 8(b)(1)(A) violation, and that withdrawal of the internal charge alone was not a repudiation of the violation. The Board ordered the union to remove from its files any reference to the internal charge previously filed against the member. The Board further ordered the union to assure the member and its other members of their rights, and to guarantee that it would not engage in such conduct in the future.

In *Food & Commercial Workers Locals 951, 7 & 1036 & Meijer, Inc.*,[78] on remand from the Ninth Circuit, the Board modified an "overbroad remedy" that had required the union to notify all bargaining unit members that, contrary to the union's welcoming letter to new bargaining unit members, new members were not required to become union members. The Board found that only those employees who had received the letter and had objected to it would be entitled to relief, including reimbursement for reduction in dues and fees that they had incurred. The Board held that the union's welcoming letter violated Section 8(b)(1)(A) of the Act, as the letter failed to state the right of new employees to remain nonunion members, their right as nonmembers to object to paying for nonrepresentational activities, and their right to obtain a reduction in union fees for these activities.

---

[76]281 F.3d 235, 169 LRRM 2581 (D.C. Cir. 2002).
[77]338 NLRB 130, 171 LRRM 1069 (2002).
[78]341 NLRB No. 133, 174 LRRM 1531 (2004).

2. *Representation Proceedings*

The Board decided in *Handy Andy, Inc.*[79] that it will not consider a union's breach of the duty of fair representation as a bar to certification in a proceeding prior to certification.

B. The Courts

1. *Damages*

In *Higdon v. Entenmann's Sales Co.*,[80] a former employee brought a hybrid claim for wrongful termination against the employer and breach of the duty of fair representation against the union. Following a jury verdict in favor of the employee, the employee moved to alter the judgment to include an award of reinstatement or front pay, additional back pay, injunctive relief, prejudgment and postjudgment interest, and attorneys' fees and costs. In recognizing the Supreme Court's holding that "'the fundamental purpose of unfair representation suits is to compensate for injuries caused by violations of employee rights,'"[81] the court granted the employee's requests and awarded reinstatement in lieu of front pay.[82]

2. *Attorneys' Fees*

In *Higdon*,[83] the court awarded a former employee attorneys' fees, recognizing the right of successful plaintiffs in hybrid 301 suits to recover such fees as compensatory damages. The court made clear, however, that "unlike fee-shifting statutes," the employee's recovery is "limited to the amount he actually expended in prosecuting his case."[84]

3. *Injunctions and Other Equitable Remedies*

In *Executive Board of Transport Workers of Philadelphia v. Transport Workers*,[85] members of the executive board of a local union brought

---

[79] 228 NLRB 447, 94 LRRM 1354 (1977).
[80] 2002 WL 1821666, 170 LRRM 3234 (N.D. Ill. 2002).
[81] *Id.* at *3 (quoting Electrical Workers (IBEW) v. Foust, 442 U.S. 42 (1979)).
[82] *Id.* at *5–6.
[83] *Id.* at *6.
[84] *Id.*
[85] 236 F. Supp. 2d 480, 171 LRRM 2968 (E.D. Pa. 2002).

an action against the local union president and the international union pursuant to Section 301 of the LMRA. The lawsuit challenged the union leadership, which had interpreted the union constitution as giving the president the exclusive right to initiate topics on which the board could make its decisions. While recognizing the reluctance of courts "to substitute their judgment for that of union officials in the interpretation of the union's constitution,"[86] the court explained that "such deference yields to a determination that an interpretation is patently unreasonable [where there is] no arguable authority in the constitution itself to substantiate that interpretation."[87] Upon review of the relevant provisions of the constitution, the court granted the plaintiff's request for a preliminary injunction, concluding that "giving deference to Defendants' interpretation would condone verbal violence against the plain meaning of the union's Constitution."[88]

The Third Circuit dissolved the preliminary injunction on appeal, finding that "courts typically defer to a union's interpretation of its own constitution and will not override that interpretation unless it is 'patently unreasonable.'"[89] The court cited an earlier case explaining that "'[c]ourts are reluctant to substitute their judgment for that of union officials in the interpretation of the union's constitution, and will interfere only where the official's interpretation is not fair or reasonable.'"[90] Based upon a review of the record, the court found that "a reading of all of the applicable provisions [of the Constitution] shows that there is no unambiguous grant of power to either party," and accordingly, the court "was constrained to accept the Union's interpretation, not because it is compelled by the language but only because of the considerable deference we owe to it."[91]

---

[86] *Id.* at 487.

[87] *Id.* at 488.

[88] *Id.* at 493–94.

[89] Executive Bd. of Transp. Workers of Phila. v. Transport Workers, 338 F.3d 166, 170, 172 LRRM 3185 (3d Cir. 2003) (citing Local 334, Journeymen v. Journeymen, 669 F.2d 129, 131, 109 LRRM 2506 (3d Cir. 1982)).

[90] *Id.*

[91] *Id.* at 175.

In *Higdon v. Entenmann's Sale Co.*,[92] an employee requested, among other forms of relief, an injunction prohibiting further violations of the collective bargaining agreement by the employer and union. The court noted that the same individuals who had discharged the employee remained in positions of power at the employer and the union and issued the requested injunction "to provide [the employee] with the legal protection he won at trial."[93]

4. *Apportionment of Liability*

In *Kinslow v. American Postal Workers Union*,[94] the Postal Service denied an employee overtime, and the union did not file a grievance despite the employee's request that it do so. The employee claimed, and the court found, that the union's decision not to file the grievance was based on the employee member's request to examine the union's financial records after the local president was indicted for embezzling union funds.[95] The court held that the union was liable only for the loss of overtime pay that it caused by failing to file the grievance that would have rectified the employer's withholding of overtime in violation of the agreement.[96] In dictum, the court stated that if the employee had sued the Postal Service, it could have been held liable for lost overtime wages resulting from its violation of the collective bargaining agreement up to the time when the union should have processed the employee's complaint by filing the grievance.[97]

---

[92] 2002 WL 1821666, 170 LRRM 3234 (N.D. Ill. 2002).
[93] *Id.* at *6.
[94] 222 F.3d 269, 164 LRRM 3025 (7th Cir. 2000).
[95] *Id.* at 272.
[96] *Id.* at 278.
[97] *Id.* at 275–76.

Chapter 26

UNION SECURITY

II. REQUIRED MEMBERSHIP—THE UNION SHOP

A. In General

In three cases[1] involving union conduct undertaken before the Board's *California Saw*[2] decision, the Board held that the union violated the Act by continuing to charge nonmember employees for nonrepresentational activities after the nonmember employees had filed a *Beck* objection. However, in *Meiswinkel*[3] and *Carlon A. Lamson,*[4] the Board held that the union was still entitled to collect dues related to representational activities even if notice of *General Motors* and *Beck* rights had not been given employees as required by *California Saw.*

Regarding notice requirements, the D.C. Circuit held that a union violated its duty of fair representation by providing *Beck* objectors with only general categories of expenditures; failing to disclose payments to affiliates and how those affiliates used those funds; and not informing employees who had not yet exercised their *Beck* rights of what percentage of dues was spent on nonrepresentational activities.[5] On remand, the Board ordered the union to provide audited expense reports, a list of its major activities and the percentages of each activity that it considered to be chargeable and nonchargeable, as well as a detailed explanation of expense calculations.[6]

When notice is proper, a nonmember who fails to exercise his or her *Beck* rights and is terminated under a union-security clause may be considered a "free rider" (i.e., someone who willfully and deliberately seeks to evade a union-security obligation, and not entitled to back pay).[7]

---

[1]Painters District Council Nos. 8, 16, & 33 (Meiswinkel/RFJ, Inc.), 327 NLRB 1020, 162 LRRM 1173 (1999); Teamsters Local 435 (Mercury Warehouse & Delivery Serv.), 327 NLRB 458, 160 LRRM 1130 (1999); Carlon A. Lamson & Sessions Co., 328 NLRB 983, 161 LRRM 1019 (1999).

[2]California Saw & Knife Works, 320 NLRB 224, 151 LRRM 1121 (1995), *enforced sub nom.* Machinists v. NLRB, 133 F.3d 1012, 157 LRRM 2287 (7th Cir.), *cert. denied sub nom.* Strang v. NLRB, 525 U.S. 813, 160 LRRM 2064 (1998).

[3]*Meiswinkel, supra* note 1, 327 NLRB at 1021, 162 LRRM at 1175.

[4]*Carlon A. Lamson & Sessions Co., supra* note 1.

[5]Penrod v. NLRB, 203 F.3d 41, 163 LRRM 2513 (D.C. Cir. 2000).

[6]Teamsters Local 166, 333 NLRB 1145, 167 LRRM 1049 (2001).

[7]Auto Workers Local Lodges 95 (Unit #9), 148, 376, 509, 699, 723, 887, 1609, and 172, 337 NLRB 237 (2001).

Expenditures for organizing within the same competitive market in which the bargaining-unit employees are employed may be charged to objecting nonmember employees, and dues and fees collected from nonmember employees may be expended for such activities.[8]

3. *Miscellaneous Requirements*

The Board has held that a union unlawfully charged an employee a service fee equal to full union dues when it spent a portion of the fee for purposes unrelated to collective bargaining after the employee resigned his membership in the union and filed a *Beck* objection.[9]

The Board has also held that a union violates its duty of fair representation by failing to grant employees who resign their union memberships a separate window period following resignation in which to file a *Beck* objection.[10]

B. Enforcement Procedures

In *Yellow Freight Systems of Indiana,*[11] the Board held that the union violated its duty of fair representation by failing to inform employees, covered by a collective bargaining agreement containing a union-security clause, of their *General Motors* and *Beck* rights.

Likewise, in *Incisa, USA, Inc.*,[12] the Board concluded that a union violated the Act by failing to notify an employee of his *Beck* rights when it first sought to obligate him to pay dues, and by causing the employer to terminate the employee for not joining the union.

An employer committed an unfair labor practice by refusing to execute an agreed-on contract, that included an unlawful union-security clause, because the employer was in fact motivated by a decertification petition filed by some of its employees after the parties had agreed to final terms of a collective bargaining agreement. The clause

---

[8]Food & Commercial Workers Locals 951, 7, & 1036 (Meijer, Inc.), 329 NLRB 730, 162 LRRM 1177 (1999), *enforced in part, remanded in part,* 284 F.3d 1099, 169 LRRM 2786 (9th Cir.) (en banc), *cert. denied sub nom.* Mulder v. NLRB, 123 S. Ct. 551, 171 LRRM 2256 (2002).

[9]Paperworkers Local 987 (Sun Chem. Corp. of Mich.), 327 NLRB 1011, 161 LRRM 1028 (1999).

[10]Polymark Corp., 329 NLRB 9, 162 LRRM 1033 (1999), *rev'd in part on other grounds sub nom.* Mohat v. NLRB, 1 Fed. Appx. 258, 166 LRRM 2256 (6th Cir. 2001).

[11]327 NLRB 996, 167 LRRM 1282 (1999).

[12]327 NLRB 563, 167 LRRM 1228 (1999).

at issue required an employee to obtain a "referral from the union before starting to work," but the collective bargaining agreement in question did not contain an exclusive hiring-hall clause.[13]

E. The Belated Tender

Unions are expected to provide members with a reasonable period, of not fewer than 30 days after their resignation, to make an objection to paying for nonrepresentational expenses.[14]

In *Thomas v. NLRB*,[15] an employee failed to tender any part of his union dues, because his notice from the union informing him that he was not required to pay nonrepresentational expenses did not include the amount by which his fees would be reduced were he to become a *Beck* objector. The employee was discharged for failure to pay union dues. The Board dismissed the complaint holding that the duty of fair representation does not require that potential objectors be apprised in the initial *Beck* notice of the percentage of funds spent by the union on nonrepresentational activities.[16] The D.C. Circuit granted the employee's petition for review, and held that employees are entitled to know the amount by which their fees would be reduced if they were to become *Beck* objectors.[17] At the same time, the D.C. Circuit approved the union's use of the "local presumption" that the local union could rely on international union's allocation of mergeable expenditures.[18] The D.C. Circuit remanded the case to the Board for a determination of the appropriate remedy.[19]

---

[13]Flying Dutchman Park, Inc., 329 NLRB 414, 162 LRRM 1283 (1999).

[14]Polymark Corp., 329 NLRB 9, 162 LRRM 1033 (1999), *rev'd in part on other grounds sub nom.* Mohat v. NLRB, 1 Fed. Appx. 258, 166 LRRM 2256 (6th Cir. 2001).

[15]213 F.3d 651, 164 LRRM 2577 (D.C. Cir. 2000).

[16]Auto Workers Local Lodges 95 (Unit #9), 148, 376, 509, 699, 723, 887, 1609, and 172, 328 NLRB 1215, 164 LRRM 1176 (1999).

[17]*Thomas, supra* note 15, 213 F.3d at 656, 164 LRRM at 2580.

[18]*Id.* at 660, 164 LRRM at 2584.

[19]*Id.* at 662–63, 164 LRRM at 2585. *See also* Auto Workers Local Lodge No. 376 (Colt's Mfg. Co.), 2003 NLRB LEXIS 811 (NLRB Dec. 24, 2003) (ALJ held that where union and employer refuse to assist objector to determine how to become *Beck* objector that objector could not be terminated because he did not willfully and deliberately attempt to evade his union-security obligation).

F. The Contract Bar

1. *Representation Elections*

In *Four Seasons Solar Products Corp.*,[20] the regional director decided the contract did not bar a representation petition due to an unlawful union-security provision that appeared to require, as a condition of employment, the payment of assessments. The Board disagreed, reasoning that the contract language regarding certain payments to the union did not operate to remove the contract bar to the petition.[21] The contract contained no express requirement that an employee pay assessments as a condition of employment. The Board observed that *Paragon Products Corp.*[22] delineates three instances where a contract will not bar the processing of a petition because of an unlawful union-security provision: (1) those provisions that expressly and unambiguously require the employer to give preference to union members (a) in hiring, (b) in laying off, or (c) for purpose of seniority; (2) those that specifically withhold from incumbent nonmembers or new employees the statutory 30-day grace period; and (3) those that expressly require, as a condition of continued employment, the payment of sums of money other than "periodic dues and initiation fees uniformly required."[23]

In *Four Seasons,* the dues-checkoff clause contained no statement that payment of "uniform assessments" was a condition of employment or even required. Moreover, the union-security clauses that did contain "condition of employment" language mentioned only dues and initiation fees and required only that employees "be and remain members of the Union in good standing."[24] Under those circumstances, the Board concluded that the contract did not expressly require the payment of assessments as a condition of employment and thus did not fall within the ban set forth in *Paragon Products.*[25]

[20]332 NLRB 67, 165 LRRM 1177 (2000).
[21]*Id.* at 67, 165 LRRM at 1179.
[22]134 NLRB 662, 49 LRRM 1160 (1961).
[23]*Four Seasons, supra* note 20, 332 NLRB at 68, 165 LRRM at 1179.
[24]*Id.* at 67, 165 LRRM at 1178.
[25]*Id.* at 69, 165 LRRM at 1179.

G. The 8(f) Exception: The Construction Industry

Once an 8(f) agreement expires, an employer can be deemed to have adopted the successor 8(f) agreement by its conduct without actually executing the successor 8(f) agreement.[26]

IV. SECTION 14(b) AND STATE "RIGHT-TO-WORK" LAWS

At least one circuit has recognized that federal labor law does not prohibit other sovereigns from creating right-to-work laws.[27] The San Juan Pueblo Tribal Council adopted a right-to-work ordinance and a lease containing similar restrictions. The Board filed suit for injunctive and declaratory relief, arguing that the NLRA preempted the Pueblo's right to enact these provisions.[28] The district court's summary judgment in favor of the Pueblo was affirmed en banc by the Tenth Circuit.[29] The Tenth Circuit concluded that the Pueblo had the sovereign authority to regulate labor relations, specifically right-to-work provisions, even though Section 14(b) makes no mention of its applicability to Indian tribes, and Congress did not intend for the NLRA to divest the Pueblo of its rights.[30]

Since 1962, the Board has held that an employer's checkoff obligation, and union-security clauses in general, terminate with the contract's expiration.[31]

In *Wilkes Telephone Membership Corp.*,[32] the general counsel argued that this line of cases establishing that dues-checkoff clauses expire with the contract[33] should not be considered controlling where state

---

[26]Southern Cal. Painters & Allied Trade Dist. Council No. 36 v. Best Interiors, Inc., 359 F.3d 1127, 174 LRRM 2422 (9th Cir. 2004) (citing E.S. P. Concrete Pumping, Inc., 327 NLRB 711, 160 LRRM 1161 (1999)).

[27]NLRB v. Pueblo of San Juan, 276 F.3d 1186, 169 LRRM 2129 (10th Cir. 2002).

[28]*Id.* at 1188, 169 LRRM at 2130.

[29]*Id.* at 1200, 169 LRRM at 2139.

[30]*Id.* at 1198, 169 LRRM at 2137. *Cf.* Dawavendewa v. Salt River Project Agric. Improvement & Power Dist., 276 F.3d 1150, 87 FEP Cases 1106 (9th Cir.), *cert. denied,* 123 S. Ct. 98, 89 FEP Cases 1888 (2002) (court recognized that, as a sovereign, Navajo Nation can negotiate land leases that mandate preferential hiring of Navajos, because Title VII's proscriptions under 42 U.S.C. §2000e-2 do not apply).

[31]Bethlehem Steel, 136 NLRB 1500, 50 LRRM 1013 (1962), *remanded on other grounds sub nom.* Marine & Shipbuilding Workers v. NLRB, 320 F.2d 615, 53 LRRM 2878 (3d Cir. 1963), *cert. denied,* 375 U.S. 984, 55 LRRM 2134 (1964).

[32]331 NLRB 823, 164 LRRM 1338 (2000).

[33]*See, e.g., Bulkmatic Transp. Co.*, 340 NLRB No. 74, 173 LRRM 1447 (2003), in which the Board affirmed the ALJ's finding of a §8(a)(5) violation where an employer stopped deducting and remitting dues to the union upon expiration of a rider agreement, but before expiration of the master agreement, which contained the union-security provisions.

law prohibits union-security provisions. The Board rejected that argument and held that, even in right-to-work states, such provisions are ordinary creatures of contract.[34]

The Board decided *Hacienda Hotel, Inc.*,[35] in the same month as *Wilkes Telephone Membership Co.*,[36] and reached the same conclusion. However, in *Local Joint Executive Board of Las Vegas v. NLRB*,[37] the Ninth Circuit held that it was unable to discern the Board's rationale for excluding dues checkoff from the unilateral change doctrine in the absence of a union-security provision, and, therefore, vacated the Board's decision in *Hacienda Hotel*, and remanded it to the Board either to articulate a reasoned explanation for its rule or to adopt a new rule with a reasoned explanation.

A union policy, which establishes a fee schedule for all nonmembers for grievance representation, does not violate a state's right-to-work law.[38] This is so because payment of a service fee for representation is not a condition of employment. Rather, individuals affected by the provision may opt to hire their own counsel, instead of paying the union the representation fee, and may do so without fear of losing their jobs. Accordingly, the union's charge of nonmembers for representation in individual grievance procedures did not violate Nevada right-to-work laws.[39]

Section 14(b) gives states only the right to make laws that are more restrictive than federal law of union-security agreements. Accordingly, Colorado's union-security law, which allows deauthorization petitions to be filed during a 15-day window only 4 months before the end of a contract or its 3-year anniversary, was preempted by the NLRA, which allows deauthorization petitions at any time.[40]

---

[34] *Wilkes Tel. Membership Corp.*, *supra* note 32, 331 NLRB at 824, 164 LRRM at 1339. Because the Board's decision was based on the *Hacienda Hotel, Inc.* decision that was vacated by the Ninth Circuit, 331 NLRB 665, 164 LRRM 1273 (2000), *vacated and remanded sub nom.* Local Joint Exec. Bd. of Las Vegas, Culinary Workers Local 226 v. NLRB, 309 F.3d 578, 171 LRRM 2146 (9th Cir. 2002), the vitality of the *Wilkes* decision is in some doubt. Subsequent cases have cited to *Wilkes* and its holding, while limiting its application. *See, e.g.*, Tribune Publ'g Co., 2003 NLRB LEXIS 45 (NLRB Feb. 5, 2003) (although dues checkoff provisions do expire with contract under *Wilkes*, employee authorization for direct deposit for union dues' fund does not, and employer who cancelled them violated §8(a)(5)).

[35] 331 NLRB 665, 164 LRRM 1273 (2000).

[36] 331 NLRB 823, 164 LRRM 1338 (2000).

[37] 309 F.3d 578, 171 LRRM 2146 (9th Cir. 2002).

[38] Cone v. Nevada Serv. Employees Union, 998 P.2d 1178, 164 LRRM 2202 (Nev. 2000) (per curiam).

[39] *Id.* at 1182, 164 LRRM at 2205.

[40] Albertson's/Max Food Warehouse, 329 NLRB 410, 162 LRRM 1169 (1999).

In *Teamsters Local 435 (Mercury Warehouse)*,[41] the Board also held that Colorado could not authorize union-security clauses that allow unions to charge nonmembers for nonrepresentational activities, contrary to the Supreme Court's interpretation of the NLRA in *Beck*. Although Section 14(b) of the Act allows states to regulate union security, they are free only to pursue more *restrictive* policies in matters of union-security agreements, and state law cannot sanction a more expansive union-security arrangement than that permitted by federal law.[42] The Board rejected the union's argument that under Section 14(b), Colorado law controlled all union-security clauses and, therefore, if a contract ratified in Colorado did not adopt federal protections for dues objectors, *Beck* would not apply.[43]

In September 2001, Oklahoma amended its constitution to include a right-to-work provision.[44] The amendment specifically prohibits requiring any person, "as a condition of employment or continuation of employment," to "[p]ay any dues, fees, assessments, or other charges of any kind or amount to a labor organization."[45] There are now right-to-work laws in 23 states.[46]

V. HIRING-HALL AND JOB-REFERRAL PRACTICES

A. General Rules

A union's negligence in handling referrals from an exclusive hiring hall, even without discriminatory intent, may violate the union's duty of fair representation.

In *Jacoby v. NLRB*,[47] the employee, a member of the union, registered for employment through the union's hiring hall and was placed on the highest priority list.[48] However, because of negligence, the union mistakenly dispatched lower-priority employees before the employee with higher priority.[49] The Board had held that the union's

---

[41]327 NLRB 458, 160 LRRM 1130 (1999).

[42]*Id.* at 459, 160 LRRM 1131.

[43]*Id.* at 460, 160 LRRM 1132–33. *Cf.* Byrd v. State, County & Mun. Employees, 781 N.E.2d 713, 171 LRRM 3000 (Ind. Ct. App. 2003) (right-to-work laws do not prohibit "fair share" fees in the public sector).

[44]OKLA. CONST. art. XXXIII, §1A .

[45]*Id.*, art. XXIII, §1A(B)(3).

[46]Indiana's right-to-work law is only applicable to school employees.

[47]233 F.3d 611, 165 LRRM 2993 (D.C. Cir. 2000).

[48]*Id.* at 613, 165 LRRM at 2995.

[49]*Id.*

negligence did not violate the duty of fair representation or the Act.[50] The D.C. Circuit disagreed, holding that the fact that the union's action was merely negligent did not mandate a finding that it did not breach its duty of fair representation.[51] The Board was directed to consider on remand "whether, given the union's heightened duty of fair dealing in the context of a hiring hall, the union's negligent failure to adhere to its referral standards was an unfair labor practice."[52]

On remand, the Board found that, even assuming that a union has a "heightened duty of fair dealing" in the operation of an exclusive hiring hall, inadvertent mistakes in the operation of an exclusive hiring hall do not violate the union's duty of fair representation or Sections 8(b)(1)(A) and (2) of the Act.[53]

However, a union's arbitrary actions may violate its duty of fair representation owed to those individuals who seek to use the union's hiring hall.[54] In addition, in hiring-hall cases where a union prevents an employee from being hired or causes an employee's discharge, the Board still holds that the union may rebut the presumption that it has "encouraged union membership" by showing that its action "was necessary to the effective performance of its function of repre-

---

[50]Plumbers Local 342 (Contra Costa Elec., Inc.), 329 NLRB 688, 162 LRRM 1156 (1999).

[51]*Jacoby*, 233 F.3d at 617, 165 LRRM at 2997.

[52]*Id.* at 611, 617, 165 LRRM at 2997.

[53]Plumbers Local 342, 336 NLRB 549, 168 LRRM 1256 (2001), *petition for review denied sub nom.* Jacoby v. NLRB, 325 F.3d 101, 172 LRRM 2199 (D.C. Cir 2003). *Compare* Electrical Workers (IBEW), Local 48, 342 NLRB No. 10, 175 LRRM 1033 (2004) (union's numerous departures from objective hiring criteria went beyond simple inadvertence and constituted gross negligence in violation of the Act) *with* Pipefitters & Steamfitters Local 247, 332 NLRB 1029, 171 LRRM 1236 (2000) (Board acknowledged that "union does not violate the Act when its actions in regard to an exclusive hiring hall are a result of mere negligence").

[54]*Compare* Lucas v. NLRB, 333 F.3d 927, 172 LRRM 2206 (9th Cir. 2003) (reversing Theatrical Stage Employees Local 720, 332 NLRB 1, 165 LRRM 1163 (2000)) (union violated heightened duty of fair dealing that applies in hiring-hall context by arbitrarily denying former members reapplication to its hiring hall) *with* Electrical Workers (IBEW) Local 3 (White Plains), 331 NLRB 1498, 170 LRRM 1560 (2000) (union's actions not arbitrary or discriminatory). *See also* Denver Theatrical Stage Employees Union No. 7, 339 NLRB 214, 2003 NLRB LEXIS 295 (2003) (union's undisclosed scheme for ranking workers, based on its subjective perception of who sought to earn a living as a stage hand, violated §§8(b)(1)(A) and (2) of Act).

senting its constituency."[55] The Board has also reiterated its prohibition of discrimination based on an employee's engagement in protected activity or lack of union membership or local membership.[56]

In *Carpenters Local 370*,[57] a case involving a nonexclusive hiring hall, the Board held that

> [a]bsent either a finding that the Union owed the [employee] a duty of fair representation in these circumstances, or a finding that the Union was retaliating against the [employee] because he engaged in Section 7 activity, there is no basis to conclude that the Union violated the Act by failing to provide [the employee] with the requested information [regarding the Union's operation of the nonexclusive hiring hall].[58]

Courts continue to recognize that an employee may sue a union for violation of Title I of the LMRDA in hiring-hall situations.[59]

In *Laborers Local 294 (Associated General Contractors of California, Inc.)*,[60] a case involving the union's alleged violation of Sections 8(b)(1)(A) and (2) by dispatching individuals out of order to job

---

[55] *Compare* Electrial Workers (IBEW), Local 48, 342 NLRB No. 10 175 LRRM 1033 (2004) (union failed to show that its deliberate, preferential dispatching of workers, which included the referral of "salts" and "peppers" to nonunion employers to assist in organizational campaigns was necessary to the effective performance of its representative function) *with* Theatrical Stage Employees Local 720, 332 NLRB 1, 165 LRRM 1163, 1166 (2000)) (union demonstrated that its denial of former member's reapplication to its hiring hall was based on former member's history of misconduct and was necessary to protect representative role that union performs in administering exclusive hiring hall).

[56] Teamsters Local 657 (Texia Prods., Inc.), 342 NLRB No. 59, 175 LRRM 1030 (2004) (union discriminatorily removed employee from referral list after he criticized the union's referral system); Newspaper & Mail Deliverers (City & Suburban Delivery Sys.), 332 NLRB 870, 172 LRRM 1263 (2000) (union discriminated in refusing to refer employees who engaged in protected activity); Electrical Workers (IBEW) Local 3 (White Plains), 331 NLRB 1498, 170 LRRM 1560 (2000) (union violated Act when it required employees who use its exclusive hiring hall to comply with its constitution and bylaws and refused to register nonmember on its out-of-work list and refer him for employment because of his nonmember status); Pipefitters & Steamfitters Local 247, 332 NLRB 1029, 171 LRRM 1236 (2000) (union discriminatorily failed to place employee who was not member of local on out-of-work list, although union did not unlawfully fail to refer employee to work).

[57] 332 NLRB 174, 165 LRRM 1211 (2000).

[58] *Id.* at 1212.

[59] Kaufman v. Electrical Workers (IBEW) Local 461, 124 F. Supp. 2d 1127, 166 LRRM 2025 (N.D. Ill. 2000) (court denied union's motion for summary judgment on employees' claim that union brought charges against them in retaliation for their support of changes to union's job-referral system).

[60] 331 NLRB 259, 164 LRRM 1169 (2000).

sites, the Board deferred to arbitrators' rulings that sustained a grievance by two employees that they were improperly denied referrals under the contract and hiring-hall rules and a separate ruling that denied a similar grievance by another employee. The Board held that the standards for deferral set forth in *Spielberg Manufacturing Co.*[61] and *Olin Corp.*[62] had been met.[63]

In a case brought pursuant to Title VII and Section 1981, and not alleging unfair labor practices under Section 8(b) of the Act, the Sixth Circuit, in *Alexander v. Laborers Local 496*,[64] affirmed a district court's ruling that a union hiring hall's referral practice was unlawful because of its discriminatory disparate treatment of African Americans. The plaintiffs established a prima facie case of racially based disparate treatment by demonstrating that they were African American, that they were available for referral by the union, that job opportunities were available, that they were not referred by the union to such job opportunities, and that white nonunion members were referred for work at a power plant.[65] The union's proffered legitimate nondiscriminatory reason for its selection of individuals for referral was that the employer requested only those persons "working-in-the-calling." Finding this to be a pretext for disparate-treatment race discrimination, the Sixth Circuit held that the "working-in-the-calling" policy had been routinely waived for white applicants, but not for African-American applicants.[66]

B. Remedies

The Board continues to provide orders to cease and desist from further discrimination and back pay for discriminatees as its basic relief.[67] Where the identities of the adversely affected workers are not known at the time of the unfair labor practice hearing, the Board will only order backpay relief where those unidentified workers are part of a defined and easily identified class.[68]

---

[61]112 NLRB 1080, 36 LRRM 1152 (1955).

[62]268 NLRB 573, 115 LRRM 1056 (1984).

[63]*Laborers Local 294*, *supra* note 60, 331 NLRB at 261, 14 LRRM at 1173.

[64]177 F.3d 394, 79 FEP Cases 1057 (6th Cir. 1999), *cert. denied*, 528 U.S. 1154, 86 FEP Cases 736 (2000).

[65]*Id.*, 177 F.3d at 403, 79 FEP Cases at 1061.

[66]*Id.* at 405, 79 FEP Cases at 1062.

[67]*See, e.g*, Teamsters Local 657 (Texia Prods., Inc.), 342 NLRB No. 59, 175 LRRM 1030 (2004); Electrical Workers (IBEW) Local 3 (White Plains), 331 NLRB 1498, 170 LRRM 1560 (2000).

[68]Electrical Workers (IBEW) Local 357, 343 NLRB No. 136, 176 LRRM 1244 (2004).

VI. THE DUES CHECKOFF

A. The LMRA and the Courts

A checkoff authorization form with a portability clause may allow deductions when the employee leaves employment and returns to the same employer. In *Food & Commercial Workers District Local 540 v. Pilgrim's Pride Corp.*,[69] several employees who had signed checkoff authorization forms and subsequently left employment were later rehired. The union requested the company to deduct union dues from the employees' paychecks, and the company complied. The company later stopped withholding the dues after some of the employees objected. An arbitrator ruled that the employer was obligated to honor the earlier authorization forms when the employees returned to work with the same employer.[70] The district court enforced the ruling, and the Fifth Circuit affirmed, reasoning that the arbitrator's decision was in conformity with the collective bargaining agreement and national labor policy.[71]

C. The NLRB

The Board has found that a union violated Section 8(b)(1)(A) of the Act by threatening employees with discharge for failing to pay dues under the union's "market recovery program," owing from their employment on Davis-Bacon projects.[72] At the same time, attempts to collect market recovery programs dues based on earnings on non–Davis-Bacon projects did not violate the Act.[73]

The Board found an unfair labor practice where the union accepted and retained dues deducted from the wages of an employee who resigned from the union in the absence of a union-security provision requiring payment of such dues, and when the union sued to collect such dues.[74]

The Board continues to hold that an employer does not violate Sections 8(a)(5) and (1) by unilaterally ceasing a checkoff arrange-

---

[69]193 F.3d 328, 162 LRRM 2513 (5th Cir. 1999).

[70]*Id.* at 330–31, 162 LRRM at 2514.

[71]*Id.* at 332–33, 162 LRRM at 2515–16.

[72]Electrical Workers (IBEW) Local 48 (Kingston Constructors, Inc.), 332 NLRB 1482, 166 LRRM 1090 (2000), *modified*, 333 NLRB 963 (2001).

[73]*Id.*, 166 LRRM at 1101.

[74]Graphic Communications Local 735-S (Quebecor Printing Hazelton, Inc.), 330 NLRB 32, 166 LRRM 1349 (1999), *enforced sub nom.* Quick v. NLRB, 245 F.3d 231, 166 LRRM 2897 (3d Cir. 2001).

ment after the expiration of the collective bargaining agreement, regardless of whether the contract also contains a union-security clause, because the employert's duty to maintain a checkoff arrangement ends when the contract creating the checkoff expires.[75] However, in *Local Joint Executive Board of Las Vegas v. NLRB*,[76] the Ninth Circuit recognized that the Board's initial determination to exclude dues checkoff from the unilateral change doctrine was based on its finding that the dues checkoff clause served to implement union-security provisions that could not stand after the expiration of a collective bargaining agreement under Section 8(a)(3). Accordingly, the Ninth Circuit held that it was unable to discern the Board's rationale for excluding dues checkoff from the unilateral change doctrine in the absence of a union-security provision, and, therefore, vacated the Board's decision in *Hacienda Hotel, Inc.*,[77] and remanded it to the Board either to articulate a reasoned explanation for its rule or to adopt a new rule with a reasoned explanation.[78]

VII. Constitutional Dimensions and Other Statutory Requirements

A. Constitutionality of the Union Shop

In 2004, the Court of Appeals for the Third Circuit reaffirmed that a private sector union's implementation of an opt-out procedure for *Beck* objectors did not constitute state action.[79]

B. Effect of Political Expenditures

As prescribed in *Lehnert*,[80] courts continue to determine which expenses may be charged to nonmembers on a case-by-case basis.[81]

---

[75] *See, e.g.,* Hacienda Hotel, Inc., 331 NLRB 665, 164 LRRM 1273 (2000), *vacated sub nom.* Local Joint Exec. Bd. of Las Vegas v. NLRB, 309 F.3d 578, 171 LRRM 2146 (9th Cir. 2002); Wilkes Tel. Membership Corp., 331 NLRB 823, 164 LRRM 1338 (2000).

[76] 309 F.3d 578, 171 LRRM 2146 (9th Cir. 2002).

[77] 331 NLRB 665, 164 LRRM 1273 (2000).

[78] *Local Joint Executive Bd. of Las Vegas, supra* note 76, 309 F.3d at 586, 171 LRRM at 2151.

[79] White v. Communications Workers of Am., Local 13000, 370 F.3d 346, 174 LRRM 3337 (3d Cir. 2004).

[80] Lehnert v. Ferris Faculty Ass'n, 500 U.S. 507, 137 LRRM 2321 (1991).

[81] *See* Wagner v. Professional Eng'rs, 169 LRRM 3167, 3171 (E.D. Cal. 2002) (costs of legislative activity, initiatives, and legislative political action not shown to

Courts continue to apply the principles set forth in *Chicago Teachers Union v. Hudson*[82] and *Ellis v. Brotherhood of Railway, Airline & Steamship Clerks*,[83] when determining whether proper notice of the right to object to the imposition of fees used for purposes other than collective bargaining, in both substance and form, was provided to employees, and identifying which union activities properly may be charged to dissenters.[84]

In *Lutz v. Machinists*,[85] the court addressed the issue of whether a union operating under the Railway Labor Act[86] could, consistent with the First Amendment, prohibit nonmember employees from filing a "continuing objection" to the payment of union dues unrelated to the costs associated with collective bargaining and contract administration.[87] Under the union's procedure, objectors were required to submit such objections on an annual basis, and failure to

---

be germane to collective bargaining activity), *aff'd in part, rev'd in part, and remanded*, 354 F.3d 1036, 174 LRRM 2015 (9th Cir. 2004); Cummings v. Connell, 177 F. Supp. 2d 1060, 1071–72, 170 LRRM 2798, 2804–05 (E.D. Cal. 2001) (costs of union board meetings held chargeable; "organizing campaign" chargeable when it constituted campaign among existing bargaining-unit members to discuss contract proposals and to generate support among union members for union's bargaining positions), *aff'd in part, rev'd in part, and remanded*, 316 F.3d 886, 171 LRRM 2707 (9th Cir.), *cert. denied*, 123 S. Ct. 2577, 174 LRRM 2096 (2003); Otto v. Pennsylvania State Educ. Ass'n, 107 F. Supp. 2d 615, 623, 165 LRRM 2466, 2472 (M.D. Pa. 2000) (holding that union's extra-unit litigation expenses were not related to collective bargaining or contract administration and could not constitutionally be charged to objectors), *aff'd in part, rev'd in part*, 330 F.3d 125, 172 LRRM 2452 (3d Cir.), *cert. denied*, 124 S. Ct. 466, 173 LRRM 2576 (2003); Belhumeur v. Labor Relations Comm'n, 432 Mass. 458, 471, 165 LRRM 2458, 2465 (2000) (expenses incurred by teachers' union in advocating public education funding held to be political speech and therefore nonchargeable to dissenting employees, whereas article published in union publication characterized as "informational support services" did not constitute political speech and was chargeable), *cert. denied*, 532 U.S. 904, 166 LRRM 2768 (2001).

[82]475 U.S. 292, 121 LRRM 2793 (1986).

[83]466 U.S. 435, 116 LRRM 2001 (1984).

[84]*See, e.g.*, Tavernor v. Illinois Fed'n of Teachers & Univ. Prof'ls Local 4100, 226 F.3d 842, 846–47, 165 LRRM 2193, 2195–96 (7th Cir. 2000) (analyzing whether union's "fair share fees" collection procedure violated First Amendment rights of objectors); Wessel v. City of Albuquerque, 327 F. Supp. 2d 1332, 1342, 175 LRRM 2663, 2667 (D.N.M. 2004) (refunding fair share fees because the union could not show what portion of fees collected actually went to chargeable expenses); Harrington v. City of Albuquerque, 329 F. Supp. 2d 1237, 1243, 175 LRRM 2739, 2741 (D.N.M. 2004) (same); Swanson v. University of Haw. Prof'l Assembly, 269 F. Supp. 2d 1252, 1258, 172 LRRM 2740, 2743 (D. Haw. 2003) (the *Hudson* notice in question was legally insufficient).

[85]121 F. Supp. 2d 498, 166 LRRM 2032 (E.D. Va. 2000).

[86]46 U.S.C. §§151–188.

[87]*Lutz*, *supra* note 85, 121 F. Supp. 2d at 499–500, 166 LRRM at 2033.

do so resulted in waiver of any earlier objection for the forthcoming year and precluded fee reduction.[88] The court held that the procedure contravened *Chicago Teachers Union v. Hudson*,[89] and that mandating an annual objection to dues was not "carefully tailored to minimize the infringement" on nonmembers' constitutional rights.[90] The court observed that the D.C. Circuit, the Sixth Circuit, and the District Court of Maryland upheld union procedures requiring annual objections of private-sector employees under the more deferential duty-of-fair-representation standard.[91]

Rejecting the contrary position of the NLRB, the Court of Appeals for the District of Columbia ruled, in *Penrod v. NLRB*,[92] that unions have an affirmative obligation pursuant to their duty of fair representation to inform all "potential objectors," including new employees and financial core payers, as well as those who had not objected to the payment of certain union dues as permitted under *Beck*,[93] of the percentage of dues spent on nonrepresentational union activities.[94] Specifically, the court concluded that unions must "give employees 'sufficient information to gauge the propriety of the union's fee'—i.e., the percentage reduction."[95]

In a rehearing en banc, the Ninth Circuit enforced a NLRB decision holding that certain organizing costs are chargeable to nonmembers as agency fees.[96] Citing "extensive economic research" and other data, the court agreed with the NLRB's finding that the costs of organizing in the "competitive market" of the represented employees are germane to collective bargaining.[97] Thus, nonmembers

---

[88] *Id.* at 500, 166 LRRM at 2034.

[89] 475 U.S. 292, 121 LRRM 2793 (1986).

[90] *Lutz, supra* note 85, 121 F. Supp. 2d at 506, 166 LRRM at 2038.

[91] *Id.* at 502, 166 LRRM at 2035, citing Abrams v. Communications Workers, 59 F.3d 1373, 1381, 149 LRRM 2928, 2935 (D.C. Cir. 1995); Tierney v. City of Toledo, 824 F.2d 1497, 1506, 125 LRRM 3217, 3222 (6th Cir. 1987); Kidwell v. Transportation Communications Int'l Union, 731 F. Supp. 192, 205, 133 LRRM 2692, 2702 (D. Md. 1990), *aff'd in part, rev'd in part*, 946 F.2d 283, 138 LRRM 2537 (4th Cir. 1991).

[92] 203 F.3d 41, 163 LRRM 2513 (D.C. Cir. 2000).

[93] Communications Workers v. Beck, 487 U.S. 735, 128 LRRM 2729 (1988).

[94] *Penrod, supra* note 92, 203 F.3d at 47–48, 163 LRRM at 2517. *Accord* Thomas v. NLRB, 213 F.3d 651, 653, 655–56, 164 LRRM 2577, 2578, 2580 (D.C. Cir. 2000).

[95] *Penrod, supra* note 92, 203 F.3d at 48, 163 LRRM at 2517, quoting Chicago Teachers Union v. Hudson, 475 U.S. 292, 121 LRRM 2793 (1986).

[96] Food & Commercial Workers Local 1036 v. NLRB, 284 F.3d 1099, 169 LRRM 2786 (9th Cir.), *cert. denied sub nom.* Mulder v. NLRB, 123 S. Ct. 551, 171 LRRM 2256 (2002).

[97] *Id.*, 284 F.3d at 1108, 169 LRRM at 2793.

may be compelled to pay for organizing by their bargaining representative within the same "competitive market," such as among their employer's competitors. The court left to the NLRB to decide in subsequent cases what expenses relate to such organizing.

Several class actions have been approved in California concerning union collection and retention of fair-share payments under public employee collective bargaining agreements. The California state government code was amended, effective January 1, 2000, to require fair-share payments by all employees in represented bargaining units in the California state university and University of California systems.[98] In each of the cases, employees claimed their bargaining representative did not provide proper *Hudson* procedural safeguards.[99]

In *Cummings v. Connell*,[100] the court held that the fair-share fee notices failed to adequately explain the basis for the fair-share fee and, thus, infringed on the employees' First Amendment rights. The notices failed to contain sufficient financial disclosures so that the employees could gauge the propriety of the fee; it did not suffice for the union to offer to send the employees, upon request, a copy of an independent audit of the union's finances.[101]

In *Wagner v. Professional Engineers*,[102] the federal district court held, and the Ninth Circuit affirmed in relevant part, that fair-share fee notices were unconstitutional under *Hudson*, because they were not independently audited. It did not matter that income/expense statements were audited, and the union used those audited numbers to

---

[98]CAL. GOV'T. CODE §3583(5)(a)(1) (Deering 2000).

[99]Murray v. State, County & Mun. Employees Local 2620, 192 F.R.D. 629, 164 LRRM 2359 (N.D. Cal. 2000); Friedman v. California State Employees Ass'n (CSEA), 163 LRRM 2924 (E.D. Cal. 2000); Cummings v. Connell, 163 LRRM 2086 (E.D. Cal. 1999); Wagner v. Professional Eng'rs, 163 LRRM 2715 (E.D. Cal. 1999).

[100]177 F. Supp. 2d 1060, 170 LRRM 2798 (E.D. Cal. 2001), *aff'd in part, rev'd in part, remanded*, 316 F.3d 886, 171 LRRM 2707 (9th Cir.), *cert. denied*, 123 S. Ct. 2577, 174 LRRM 2096 (2003)).

[101]*Id.*, 177 F. Supp. 2d at 1067–68; 170 LRRM at 2801 (representation that figures have been audited is insufficient under *Hudson*, but a full copy of audit is not always required to be included in notice under *Hudson*, if there is a statement from independent auditor that summarized figures have been audited and have been correctly reproduced from audited report; an allocation audit is *not* required under *Hudson*).

[102]169 LRRM 3167 (E.D. Cal. 2002), *aff'd in part, rev'd in part, and remanded*, 354 F.3d 1036, 174 LRRM 2015 (9th Cir. 2004) (stating that the remedy for a defective *Hudson* notice is a new proper notice with a renewed opportunity to object and a refund of any amount to which objection is lodged, with interest, and it does not require the immediate refund of all nonchargeable amounts).

establish the expenditures detailed in the notice, because the union must have an independent auditor verify the expenditures detailed in the *Hudson* notice.[103]

Two decisions have further refined the independent audit requirement for *Hudson* notices. In *Harik v. California Teachers Ass'n,*[104] the Ninth Circuit explained that the required independent review of expenditures on the *Hudson* notice does not need to consist of a full-blown audit; rather, a threshold level of independent verification that fees are not being used for nonchargeable expenditures is all that is required. In *Wessel v. City of Albuquerque,*[105] the Tenth Circuit ruled that although the union's notice contained the schedule of expenses and a statement that it was independently audited information, the notice was defective, because *Hudson* required that the notice contain the auditor's explanation of why fees to be deducted are permissible.

Currently, there is a split among the circuit courts regarding whether Hudson's independent audit verification requirement applies to small unions. In *Harik v. California Teachers Ass'n,*[106] the Ninth Circuit determined that a local union with under $50,000 in estimated annual revenues was not required to obtain independent auditor verification of its expenditures. The court held that small unions could either disclose the full financial material necessary to verify its expenditures, or an independently sanctioned verification of the local union's chargeable and nonchargeable expenditures.[107] To the contrary, in *Otto v. Pennsylvania State Education Ass'n,*[108] the Third Circuit held that local unions, regardless of their size, are required to obtain independent audits of their financial expenditures.

---

[103]*Id.*, 169 LRRM at 3171.

[104]326 F.3d 1042, 172 LRRM 2193 (9th Cir.), *cert. denied sub nom.* Sheffield v. Aceves, 124 S. Ct. 429, 173 LRRM 2512 (2003).

[105]299 F.3d 1186, 170 LRRM 2718 (10th Cir. 2002). In 2004, on remand, the district court held that the union had corrected its original defective notice, but that the union had failed to satisfy its burden of proof with regard to the chargeable allocation of fees and required that the fair share fees be refunded in their entirety. Wessel v. City of Albuquerque, 327 F. Supp. 2d 1332, 175 LRRM 2603 (D.N.M. 2004).

[106]326 F.3d 1042, 172 LRRM 2193 (9th Cir.), *cert. denied sub nom.* Sheffield v. Aceves, 124 S. Ct. 429, 173 LRRM 2512 (2003).

[107]*Id.*, 326 F.3d at 1047, 172 LRRM at 2196–97.

[108]330 F.3d 125, 134, 172 LRRM 2452, 2459 (3d Cir.) (declining to find a "small local union" exception to *Hudson* safeguards), *cert. denied*, 540 U.S. 982, 173 LRRM 2576 (2003).

The Seventh Circuit struck down the system used to collect fair-share fees from certain university clerical employees in Illinois.[109] Under that system, the union denoted more than 80 percent of full union dues as the estimated fair-share fee. However, the union collected and escrowed an amount equal to 100 percent of union dues. In addition, nonmember objections to the proposed fair share were not processed until 6 months after the initial deduction was made, and a determination was not made until at least one year after the deduction was first made.

In *Whitley County Teachers Ass'n v. Bauer,*[110] the court examined a collective bargaining agreement's fair-share provision. Teachers were given three options at the start of the school year: pay a fair-share fee equivalent to full dues; pay an estimated amount for only those expenses germane to the collective bargaining function; or pay nothing pending an arbitrator's determination. In light of the third option, which was imposed if the two payment options were not chosen, the fair-share provision was held constitutional.[111] Furthermore, even though *Hudson* safeguards were not set out in the collective bargaining agreement, their existence protected the fair-share provision.[112]

Another variation of the *Hudson* principles arose in *Robinson v. Pennsylvania State Corrections Officers Ass'n.*[113] Nonunion employees sued the union alleging that it had violated their First Amendment rights by collecting a fair-share fee without prior notice. The union argued that it was excused from providing a notice, because it was a new organization that had no history upon which to base a fee. Thus, any notice that it provided would be based on insufficient information and thus constitutionally deficient. The court rejected this argument and held that the union could not collect any fair-share fee. "A union that cannot satisfactorily explain the method used to compute a fair share fee cannot impose the fee."[114]

Several states have enacted legislation aimed at limiting the ability of unions to use revenue generated by dues and fees collected through payroll deductions from its members and nonmembers to make political contributions.[115] In *State ex rel Washington State Public Disclosure*

---

[109]Tavernor v. Illinois Fed'n of Teachers & Univ. Prof'ls Local 4100, 226 F.3d 842, 165 LRRM 2193 (7th Cir. 2000).

[110]718 N.E.2d 1181, 163 LRRM 2875 (Ind. Ct. App. 1999).

[111]*Id.* at 1188, 163 LRRM at 2879.

[112]*Id.*

[113]299 F. Supp. 2d 425, 174 LRRM 2261 (M.D. Pa. 2004).

[114]*Id.* at 430, 174 LRRM at 2266.

[115]*See* IDAHO CODE §44-2603 (2003); UTAH CODE ANN. §34-32-1.1 (2003); REV. CODE WASH. §42.17.760 (2004).

Commission v. Washington Education Ass'n,[116] a Washington appellate court held the Washington act unconstitutionally creates a presumption that all nonunion employees object to the use of their agency fees for union's political expenditures and unduly requires unions to protect nonmembers through use of an "opt-in" procedure, which restriction would upset the balance between nonmembers' rights and rights of the union and majority to use nonobjectors' agency fees on political expenditures.

C. Religious Objectors

Section 19 of the NLRA permits an individual who holds sincere religious beliefs that preclude him or her from holding membership in a union or from financially supporting a union to pay the equivalent of dues to a charity rather than to a union.[117] In *Bushouse v. Auto Workers Local 2209,*[118] a union asked an employee claiming such beliefs to identify the religious body or sect to which he belonged and to submit a certificate signed by a pastor or church elder attesting to that fact. The union subsequently changed its procedure also to require an independent corroboration from the employee of his religious beliefs. The employee filed a Title VII lawsuit, claiming that the union's requirement that he be a member of a religious body and provide corroboration of his beliefs constituted religious discrimination in failing to accommodate his religious beliefs. The court rejected the claim, holding that it was appropriate for the union to inquire into the sincerity of the employee's belief and whether the belief was, in fact, religious, before permitting the employee accommodations based on that belief.[119]

In January 2000, the California government code was amended to require union-security payments by represented employees in the California state university and University of California systems. Section 3584 of the code provides an exception to payment of the fair-share fee by members "of a bona fide religion, body, or sect that has historically held conscientious objections to joining or financially

[116]71 P.3d 244, 173 LRRM 2232 (Wash. Ct. App. 2003), *review granted,* 150 Wash. 2d 1032, 84 P.3d 1229 (2004) (2004).

[117]29 U.S.C. §169.

[118]164 F. Supp. 2d 1066, 87 FEP Cases 150 (N.D. Ind. 2001).

[119]*Id.* at 1078, 87 FEP Cases at 158–59. *See also* EEOC v. Union Independiente de la Autoridad de Acueductors y Alcantarillados de Puerto Rico, 279 F.3d 49, 87 FEP Cases 1722 (1st Cir. 2001) (summary judgment in favor of EEOC reversed, because there was issue of material fact as to whether employee held bona fide religious belief that prevented him from joining union to keep his job).

supporting public employee organizations."[120] In lieu of dues, the employee may pay a sum "equal to the amount of the fair share fee . . . to a religious, nonlabor charitable fund. . . ."[121]

In *Baird v. California Faculty Ass'n*,[122] the Ninth Circuit explained that it is a reasonable accommodation of religious observance required by Title VII to allow a person who sincerely holds beliefs antithetical to unions to substitute a charitable contribution for required union dues, which accommodation does not violate First Amendment rights. Because Title VII does not contain the "bona fide religion" requirement of Section 3584, it would have been unlawful for the union to consider this factor in reviewing applications for religious exemption to agency fee requirements. However, because the union's denial of the plaintiffs' applications was based on whether their asserted beliefs were "religious" and "sincerely held," and not on the "bona fide religion" factor, the union's implementation of Section 3584 did not result in legal injury to the plaintiffs.

The "bona fide religion" factor was addressed in *Madsen v. Associated Chino Teachers*.[123] A religious objector claimed that the requirement that she pay a "service fee" to a charitable organization, rather than a fair-share fee constituted religious discrimination under federal and state law. The court reasoned that the religious objector was not similarly situated to the agency fee payers and to allow her to pay a reduced fee to charity would constitute preferential treatment that is not required under Title VII or the California Fair Employment and Housing Act.[124] Further, the religious objector argued that the California statute which required religious objectors to pay the full service fee to charitable organizations violated the Establishment Clause of the United States and California Constitutions. The court held that the statute had a secular legislative purpose to accommodate the free exercise of religion, did not have a primary effect of either advancing or inhibiting religion, and avoided excessive government entanglement with religion. Finally, the statute had a rational basis to improve personnel management and employer-employee relations and there was a rational relationship between this goal and the union security laws that facilitate effective representation of employees. [125]

---

[120]CAL. GOV'T CODE §3584 (Deering 2000).

[121]*Id.*, §3584(a).

[122]34 Fed. Appx. 303 (9th Cir. 2002).

[123]317 F. Supp. 2d 1175, 174 LRRM 2997 (C.D. Cal. 2004)

[124]*Id.* at 1184, 174 LRRM at 3003.

[125]*Id.* at 1187, 174 LRRM at 3005.

Part VIII

ADMINISTRATION OF THE ACT

BIBLIOGRAPHY

James J. Brudney, Sara Schiovani, and Deborah J. Merritt, *Judicial Hostility Toward Labor Unions? Applying the Social Background Model to a Celebrated Concern*, 60 OHIO ST. L.J. 1675 (1999)

Dennise A. Calderon-Barrera, Hoffman v. NLRB: *Leaving Undocumented Workers Unprotected Under United States Labor Laws?*, 6 HARV. LATINO L. REV. 119 (2003)

Christopher David Ruiz Cameron, *Borderline Decisions:* Hoffman Plastic Compounds, *the New Bracero Program, and the Supreme Court's Role in Making Federal Labor Policy*, 51 UCLA L. REV. 1 (2003)

Kenneth N. Dickens, Town & Country Electric, Inc. v. The National Labor Relations Board: *Salts: We're Employees—What Happens Now?*, 99 W. VA. L. REV. 561 (1997)

R. Wayne Estes and Andrea Josephs, *Missing Analytical Link in Supreme Court's "Salting" Decision Disturbs Balance of Union-Management Rights: A Critical Analysis of* NLRB v. Town and Country Electric, 30 IND. L. REV. 445 (1997)

Douglas J. Feeney-Gallagher, *Battle of the Benches: The Wagner Act and the Circuit Courts of Appeals, 1935-1942*, 23 SEATTLE L. Rev. 503 (2000)

Christopher J. Garofalo, *Section 302 of the LMRA: Make Way for the Employer-Paid Union Representative*, 75 N.Y.U. L. REV. 775 (2000)

Grant M. Hayden, "*The University Works Because We Do*": *Collective Bargaining Rights for Graduate Assistants*, 69 FORDHAM L. REV. 1233 (2001)

Michael J. Hely, *Impact of* Sturgis *on Bargaining Power For Contingent Workers in the U.S. Labor Market*, 11 WASH. U. J.L. & POL'Y 295 (2003)

Neil Hutchens and Melissa B. Hutchens, *Catching the Union Bug: Graduate Student Employees and Unionization*, 105 GONZ. L. REV. 105 (2003-2004)

Daniel B. Klaff and Ronald G. Ehrenberg, *Collective Bargaining and Staff Salaries in American Colleges and Universities*, 57 INDUS. & LAB. REL. REV. 92 (2003)

Patrick M. Kuhlmann, *The Enigma of NLRA Section 2(11): The Supervisory Exclusion and the Case of the Charge Nurse*, 2000 WIS. L. REV. 157 (2000)

Richard Lapp, *A Call for a Simpler Approach: Examining the NLRA's Section 10(j) Standard*, 3 U. PA. J. LAB. & EMP. L. 251 (2001)

Michael H. Leroy and Wallace Hendricks, *Should "Agricultural Labors" Continue to be Excluded From the National Labor Relations Act?*, 48 EMORY L.J. 489 (1999)

Nathan Newman, *The Conflict of the Courts: RICO, Labor, and Legal Preemption in Union Comprehensive Campaigns*, 51 DRAKE L. REV. 307 (2003)

Jonathan L.H. Nygren, *Forcing the NCAA to Listen: Using Labor Law to Force the NCAA to Bargain Collectively With Student-Athletes*, 2 VA. SPORTS & ENT. L.J. 359 (2003)

Judy Prutzman Osgood, NLRB v. Health Care & Retirement Corporation of America: *A Setback for Nurses' Unions?*, 46 SYRACUSE L. REV. 135 (1995)

Joshua Rowland, *"Forecasts of Doom": The Dubious Threat of Graduate Teaching Assistant Collective Bargaining to Academic Freedom*, 42 B.C. L. REV. 941 (2001)

Paul M. Secunda, *Politics Not as Usual: Inherently Destructive Conduct, Institutional Collegiality, and the National Labor Relations Board*, 32 FLA. ST. U. L. REV. 51 (2004)

Katherine E. Seitz, *Enter at Your Own Risk: The Impact of* Hoffman Plastic Compounds v. National Labor Relations Board *on the Undocumented Worker*, 82 N.C. L. REV. 366 (2003)

Theodore J. St. Antoine, Gilmer *in the Collective Bargaining Context*, 16 OHIO ST. J. ON DISP. RESOL. 491 (2001)

Thomas J. Walsh, Hoffman Plastic Compounds, Inc. v. NLRB: *How the Supreme Court Eroded Labor Law and Workers Rights in the Name of Immigration Policy*, 21 LAW & INEQ. 313 (2003)

Chapter 27

JURISDICTION: COVERAGE OF THE ACT

I. CONSTITUTIONALITY

B. The Shadow of the First Amendment: Jurisdiction Over Religious Organizations

In *Ukiah Adventist Hospital dba Ukiah Valley Medical Center & California Nurses Ass'n,*[1] citing earlier decisions[2] and assuming that the Religious Freedom Restoration Act of 1993 (RFRA)[3] was constitutional, the Board asserted jurisdiction over a hospital operated by the Seventh Day Adventist Church. The Board held that its assertion of jurisdiction did not violate the First Amendment or the RFRA because assertion of such jurisdiction is in furtherance of a compelling interest in preventing labor strife and protecting employees' rights to organize and bargain and is the "least restrictive means of accomplishing the goals of the Act."[4]

The D.C. Circuit, however, vacated one of the decisions the Board relied upon in *Ukiah Adventist Hospital.* In *University of Great Falls v. NLRB,*[5] the court stated that, in determining whether it possessed jurisdiction over a university, "it was inappropriate for the NLRB to inquire into the university's 'substantial religious character,'" otherwise known as the *Catholic Bishop*[6] test. Rather, the court ruled that the appropriate test to be used to determine whether the Board's exertion of jurisdiction over the university was appropriate was whether the university held itself out to the public as a religious institution, was nonprofit, and was religiously affiliated.[7] This test was first used by the First Circuit in *Universidad Central de Bayamon v. NLRB.*[8] In applying the *Bayamon* test to *University of Great Falls,* the

---

[1]332 NLRB 602, 165 LRRM 1258 (2000).

[2]University of Great Falls & Mont. Fed'n of Teachers, 331 NLRB 1663, 165 LRRM 1150 (2000).

[3]42 U.S.C. §2000bb-1.

[4]*University of Great Falls, supra* note 2.

[5]278 F.3d 1335, 169 LRRM 2449 (D.C. Cir. 2002).

[6]NLRB v. Catholic Bishop of Chicago, 440 U.S. 490, 100 LRRM 2913 (1979).

[7]*University of Great Falls, supra* note 2.

[8]793 F.2d 383, 120 LRRM 3457 (1st Cir. 1985) (en banc).

D.C. Circuit held that the university was exempt from the jurisdiction of the Board. It held itself out in its course catalogue, mission statement, student bulletin, and other public documents as providing an education that, although primarily secular, was presented in an overtly religious, Catholic environment. Also, it was a not-for-profit educational institution, sponsored by, owned by, and with control ultimately reserved to, a recognized religious organization. Finally, the university's employment of non-Catholic faculty, admission of non-Catholic students, and its "secular" board of trustees did not disqualify it from its claimed religious character.

The Board concluded it did not have jurisdiction over a Roman Catholic Church and related elementary and high schools in *St. Edmund's Roman Catholic Church.*[9] In that case, the Board dismissed a representation petition filed on behalf of custodians working at the church and both of its schools, finding that the church and schools constituted a single employer and that the schools were part of the religious mission of the church.

II. STATUTORY JURISDICTION

A. Basic Coverage: "Commerce" and "Affecting Commerce"

Federal courts have continued to decide NLRA questions that arise as collateral issues in cases brought under other federal statutes. In *Albany Specialties v. Board of Education,*[10] the court held that because the plaintiff raised antitrust claims in addition to labor claims relating to enforcement of a project labor agreement, the plaintiff was entitled to seek injunctive and declaratory relief in federal court rather than before the Board.

B. Foreign Operations

The Board asserted jurisdiction over an American company performing work in Canada.[11] The employees were Americans who were employed by an American employer and who performed their regular work in the United States. Their assignment in Canada was

---

[9]337 NLRB 1260, 170 LRRM 1425 (2002).

[10]162 LRRM 3071 (N.D.N.Y. 1999).

[11]Asplundh Tree Expert Co., 336 NLRB 1106, 168 LRRM 1465 (2001), *enforcement denied,* 365 F.3d 168, 174 LRRM 2929 (3d Cir. 2004).

both brief and temporary and they were supervised by an American supervisor. The Board agreed with the administrative law judge (ALJ) that the respondent did not simply replace the employees on their Canadian assignment, but instead effectively fired them from their jobs back in the United States. Moreover, the Board agreed that the respondent's actions were not extraterritorial, that its assertion of jurisdiction would not interfere with Canadian law or affect the employment conditions of Canadian employees, lead to a conflict between the laws of the United States and Canada, or otherwise interfere with foreign relations, and that a remedial order would have no demonstrable extraterritorial effect.

E. Nonprofit Organizations

The Board and the courts continue to find NLRA jurisdiction over nonprofit community service organizations in some, but not all, cases. For example, in *NLRB v. Young Women's Christian Ass'n*,[12] the court enforced a Board decision asserting jurisdiction over a private, not-for-profit corporation engaged in administering a federal Head Start program, despite the fact that the program was subject to extensive governmental control. Similarly, in *MCAR, Inc.*,[13] the Board asserted jurisdiction over a not-for-profit corporation operating community residential and rehabilitation services for mentally retarded and developmentally disabled persons, notwithstanding previous refusals to assert jurisdiction and assertion of jurisdiction by a state labor relations board. In *Brevard Achievement Center, Inc.*,[14] however, the Board applied its rule that it will not assert jurisdiction over relationships that are "primarily rehabilitative," and declined to assert jurisdiction over a nonprofit corporation that assisted adults with severe disabilities by providing them with training, education, and rehabilitative services. In *FiveCAP, Inc.*,[15] the Board asserted jurisdiction over a nonprofit community action agency that administers various state and federal antipoverty programs and that received annual gross revenues in excess of $1 million and received federal

---

[12]192 F.3d 1111, 162 LRRM 2268 (8th Cir. 1999); *see also* Jacksonville Urban League, Inc., 340 NLRB No. 156, 174 LRRM 1125 (2003) (asserting jurisdiction over nonprofit operator of Head Start program).

[13]333 NLRB 1098, 172 LRRM 1431 (2001).

[14]342 NLRB No. 101, 175 LRRM 1329 (2004).

[15]332 NLRB 943, 170 LRRM 1190 (2000), *enforced*, 294 F.3d 768, 170 LRRM 2401 (6th Cir. 2002). *See also* FiveCAP, Inc., 331 NLRB 1165, 170 LRRM 1181 (2000).

funds in excess of $50,000. In doing so, it rejected the employer's contention that it was a political subdivision.

F. Relation to Jurisdictions of Other Agencies

1. *Railway Labor Act*

The Board has continued to focus on whether an employer meets the definition of "carrier" under the Railway Labor Act when assessing if the employer is exempt from coverage under the NLRA. For example, in *Globe Aviation Services*,[16] the Board, after submitting the jurisdiction issue to the National Mediation Board (NMB), declined jurisdiction over a company that provided skycap, wheelchair, preboard screening, and cleaning services to four airlines, finding that the employees were within the jurisdiction of the NMB because they performed work traditionally done by carriers covered by the Railway Labor Act and because the carriers exercised substantial control over the employees.[17]

A different result had been reached in *D & T Limousine Service Inc.*,[18] where the employer had contracted with a railroad to provide transportation services to railroad employees. The Board, noting two prior decisions finding NLRA jurisdiction, adopted the ALJ's finding that the employer's retention of a wide range of control in operating the business (i.e., hiring, firing, setting wages, and setting policies) established that it was not "controlled" by the railroad and was, therefore, subject to the NLRA.[19]

---

[16]334 NLRB 278, 167 LRRM 1138 (2001). *See also* Foreign & Domestic Car Serv., Inc., 333 NLRB 96, 166 LRRM 1173 (2001) (declining jurisdiction over company that provided rail loading services to common carrier).

[17]*See* also Ogden Ground Servs., Inc., 340 NLRB No. 137, 173 LRRM 1454 (2003) (declining jurisdiction over employer that provided baggage handling, maintenance of aircraft service equipment, and cleaning and restocking of aircraft cabins because various carriers exerted substantial control over company's operations); Aviation Safeguards, 338 NLRB 770, 171 LRRM 1379 (2003) (declining jurisdiction over company that provided skycap, wheelchair, and baggage handling services to air carriers because carriers exercised significant control over company's business and its employees); Aircraft Serv. Int'l Group, 342 NLRB No. 99, 175 LRRM 1395 (2004) (relying on NMB decision and declining jurisdiction over company that provided fueling services, maintenance of related machinery, and quality control services).

[18]328 NLRB 769 (1999).

[19]*See also* DHL Worldwide Express, Inc., 340 NLRB No. 122, 173 LRRM 1425 (2003) (after referral to NMB, Board held employer that provided package delivery by air and ground was not "carrier" subject to RLA and was therefore subject to NLRA). *Cf.* Evergreen Aviation Ground Logistics, 327 NLRB 869, 162 LRRM 1014

In *Spartan Aviation Industries, Inc.*,[20] the Board asserted jurisdiction over a flight training school for airline employees, which provided initial pilot training. In doing so, the Board rejected the argument that the school was subject to coverage under the RLA because employees of the school were performing tasks traditionally undertaken by airline employees. Instead, the Board found that the airlines did not conduct initial flight training, but only advanced training.

III. DEFINITIONS AND LIMITATIONS ON COVERAGE

B. Employer

1. *Single-Employer Status*

In *Beverly California*,[21] the Seventh Circuit affirmed a Board finding of single-employer status. The same court subsequently affirmed another single-employer finding, where evidence showed that three business entities were owned primarily by a single individual and his wife, and that few others exercised any management responsibility over the businesses.[22]

Where two corporations were a single employer at the time of termination but not during the unfair labor practice proceeding, due process requires notice of those proceedings to both companies.[23]

The D.C. Circuit has rejected an employer's argument that a union was estopped from asserting single-employer status against unionized and nonunion construction companies operated by the

(1999) (after referral to NMB, Board held employer that provided ground services and ground equipment maintenance for airlines was "carrier" and not subject to NLRA).

[20]337 NLRB 708, 170 LRRM 1177 (2002).

[21]227 F.3d 817, 165 LRRM 2257 (7th Cir. 2000).

[22]Naperville Ready Mix, Inc. v. NLRB, 242 F.3d 744, 166 LRRM 2712 (7th Cir.), *cert. denied*, 534 U.S. 1040, 168 LRRM 2896 (2001). *Compare* Newspaper Guild of N.Y. v. NLRB, 261 F.3d 291, 167 LRRM 2808 (2d Cir. 2001) (court affirmed Board and found single-employer analysis inapplicable to case involving subsidiary of parent corporation formed to manage bankrupt newspaper, and second subsidiary incorporated by parent to purchase newspaper, reasoning that two subsidiaries were not ongoing businesses coordinated by single parent); Reigel Elec. & Cent. Elec. Servs. (Alter Ego and/or Successor) & Electrical Workers (IBEW) Local 577, 341 NLRB No. 3, 174 LRRM 1158 (2003) (refusing to find single-employer or alter ego status).

[23]Viking Indus. Sec. v. NLRB, 225 F.3d 131, 165 LRRM 2129 (2d Cir. 2000).

same family, despite a contention that the union had been aware of the relationship for 20 years.[24]

The Board continues to hold that to establish that two or more employers are joint employers, the two entities "must share or codetermine matters governing essential terms and conditions of employment."[25] In applying this analysis, the Board has continued to look to a number of critical factors, including common ownership and management, common supervision, employee interchange, sharing of offices and equipment, and centralized control of labor relations.[26] Moreover, although the Board considers common control of labor relations to be a "critical factor" in finding two or more employers to be joint employers,[27] the Seventh Circuit, in *Naperville Ready Mix*,[28] rejected an argument that the Board erred by failing to give primacy to that factor. The court noted that the Board has consistently stated that no one factor is determinative. Thus, although centralized control of labor relations was the one factor that did not support the Board's conclusion, the court enforced the Board's decision to treat two businesses as a single employer.[29]

In *RC Aluminum Industries v. NLRB*,[30] the D.C. Circuit affirmed the Board's ruling in which it found that two separate corporations constituted a "single employer" where both companies shared the same officers, the president of both companies was in charge of dealing the with union on behalf of both companies, one company manufactured products for the second company, and one company paid fringe benefits on behalf of the second company.

The issue of single-employer or joint-employer status has become particularly relevant in the context of the contingent workforce. In *M.B. Sturgis Inc.*,[31] the Board found that a shipbuilder (user em-

---

[24]O'Dovero v. NLRB, 193 F.3d 532, 162 LRRM 2618 (D.C. Cir. 1999).

[25]Le Rendezvous Restaurant, 332 NLRB 336, 165 LRRM 1341 (2000); J.E. Higgins Lumber Co., 332 NLRB 1172, 166 LRRM 1188 (2000).

[26]Francis Bldg. Corp., 327 NLRB 485, 166 LRRM 1199 (1999); Techno Constr. Corp., 333 NLRB 75, 166 LRRM 1121 (2001); Wyandanch Engine Rebuilders, Inc., 328 NLRB 866, 168 LRRM 1239 (1999).

[27]*See* Main Edition, Chapter 27, Section III, at page 2094 n.166. The Fourth Circuit focuses on common control, holding that "the test for joint-employer status turns upon indicia of control." Mingo Logan Coal Co. v. NLRB, 172 LRRM 2746, 2753 (4th Cir. 2003) (unpublished).

[28]242 F.3d 744, 166 LRRM 2712 (7th Cir. 2001).

[29]*Id.* at 753.

[30]326 F.3d 235, 172 LRRM 2321 (D.C. Cir. 2003).

[31]331 NLRB 1298, 165 LRRM 1017 (2000). *See also* J.E. Higgins Lumber Co., 332 NLRB 1172, 166 LRRM 1188 (2000).

ployer) and a second employer that supplied it with employees (supplier employer) were joint employers of the supplied or contingent employees, where the two employers meaningfully affected and codetermined numerous conditions of employment, including supervision, assignment, direction, and discipline. In *Oakwood Care Center*,[32] the Board overruled *Sturgis*. It held that jointly employed contingent employees could not be combined with solely employed workers of the user employer to form a multi-employer unit, absent the consent of both employers. In its ruling, the Board returned to precedent established in *Greenhoot Inc.*[33] and *Lee Hospital*.[34] The Board now holds that the requirement of employer consent for bargaining does apply to units that combine jointly employed and solely employed employees of a single-user employer.

2. *Agents*

The Seventh Circuit has held that where a known antiunion employee expressed antiunion views at captive-audience meetings and where such employee could be construed as having actual or apparent authority to speak as the employer's agent, the employer is properly held to have violated Section 8(a)(1) of the Act by the employee's statements.[35] The Sixth Circuit reversed a Board finding that an assistant bookkeeper was an "agent" of the employer because employees reasonably believed the bookkeeper was speaking to employer policies in four antiunion meetings held by the employees.[36] The court found insufficient evidence that employees could reasonably believe the bookkeeper was acting for management where the meetings were not on the employer's premises and she was off the clock. The Fifth Circuit imposed agency status on an employer's leadperson and junior foreman, reasoning that they had apparent authority to act on behalf of management with regard to union matters.[37] The court noted that these individuals were generally responsible for making job assignments, directing work, relaying messages

---

[32]343 NLRB No. 76, 176 LRRM 1033 (2004).

[33]205 NLRB 250, 83 LRRM 1656 (1973).

[34]300 NLRB 947, 136 LRRM 1348 (1990).

[35]Beverly Cal. v. NLRB, 227 F.3d 817, 165 LRRM 2257 (7th Cir. 2000), *cert. denied*, 533 U.S. 950, 167 LRRM 2640 (2001).

[36]National Health Care, L.P. v. NLRB, 234 F.3d 1269, 166 LRRM 2768 (6th Cir. 2000) (unpublished), *enforcing in part and denying enforcement in part* 327 NLRB 1175, 161 LRRM 1152 (1999).

[37]Poly-America v. NLRB, 260 F.3d 465, 168 LRRM 2010 (5th Cir. 2001).

to management, training new employees, and holding weekly meetings. The court also found the employer's security guards were agents.

The Board continues to find apparent authority as a basis for determining agency status. Whether an individual possesses apparent authority depends on whether, under all the circumstances, employees would reasonably believe that the alleged agent's actions reflected company policy and that he was speaking and acting for management.[38] A finding of apparent authority does not turn on whether the alleged agent was acting pursuant to specific instructions, but on whether the employer placed the alleged agent in a position where employees could reasonably believe that he was speaking on behalf of management.[39] In *Nelson Electrical Contracting Corp.*,[40] the Board found a foreman to be the agent of his employer where he was the highest ranking management representative on the employer's worksite, the local union organizer dealt with him in efforts to refer union employees, and he specifically told the organizer that he did not need any additional job applicants. Consequently, the Board imputed the foreman's knowledge concerning the union affiliation of certain applicants to his employer.[41] Moreover, where an employer openly aligns itself with an employee's statements and actions, the Board may find agency status.[42] In *Overnite Transportation Co.*,[43] the Board found employees from other service centers to be

---

[38]Facchina Construction Co., 343 NLRB No. 98, 176 LRRM 1407 (2004).

[39]*Id.*

[40]332 NLRB 179, 168 LRRM 1148 (2000), *enforced*, 171 LRRM 2512 (2d Cir. 2002) (unpublished).

[41]*Id. See also* James Heavy Equip. Specialists, 327 NLRB 910, 167 LRRM 1307 (1999) (Board imposed agency status on office manager who had unlawfully questioned unit employee concerning benefit plan participation, reasoning that her job included responsibility for coordinating employer's participation in various benefit plans); Transportation Repair & Serv., 328 NLRB 107, 168 LRRM 1183 (1999) (office clerk acted as agent of employer in questioning employees where employees believed he spoke for management, and employer's owner had asked clerk to scrutinize employees' work, and to tell them when their work was deficient). *Cf.* Eagle-Picher Indus., 331 NLRB 169, 167 LRRM 1131 (2000) (Board declined to impose agency status on employer's facilitator, who was responsible for training employees on how to work as team, in absence of evidence that facilitator conveyed job-related information to employees when he trained them).

[42]National Health Care, L.P., 327 NLRB 1175, 161 LRRM 1152, *enforcement denied in pertinent part*, 234 F.3d 1269, 166 LRRM 2768 (6th Cir. 2000) (unpublished). *Cf.* Monastra v. NYNEX Corp., 165 LRRM 2500 (S.D.N.Y. 2000) (union business agent could not be sued as discharged employee's employer under Act, despite contention that business agent had so aligned himself with management as to become employer).

[43]334 NLRB 1074, 1113, 168 LRRM 1058 (2001).

agents of the employer, where the employer had encouraged them to visit their sister facility on the day prior to a representation election in order to show their support for the employer. The Board reasoned in part that the employer had reimbursed them for associated hotel and rental car costs.[44]

Conversely, in *Ready Mix Inc.*,[45] the Board found that the employer's driver/mixer who was temporarily assigned the duties of "field representative" or coordinator was not an agent of the employer. Although the alleged supervisor made various representations to employees that he had the authority to direct work and to coordinate job tasks, there was no evidence that the employer conferred this authority on him or "cloaked him with apparent authority to act as its agent."[46] Moreover, employees did not perceive the performance of field representative duties as a managerial function because all employees were expected to perform such field duties if they were the first to arrive at a job site. Accordingly, the Board did not find any evidence that led employees to "reasonably believe that the alleged agent was reflecting company policy and speaking and acting for management."[47]

3. *Exclusions From Coverage of the Act*

In *NLRB v. Chapa-De Indian Health Program*,[48] the court held that the LMRA is a statute of general applicability, and therefore may be applicable to the activities of Indian tribes. The court noted that there was no evidence introduced that Congress intended to exclude Indian tribes from coverage under the LMRA, and reasoned that application of the statute would not interfere with the tribe's right to self-governance.

---

[44]*Id. See also* Saia Motor Freight Line, 333 NLRB 784, 167 LRRM 1024 (2001) (security investigator employed by employer's parent corporation was acting as employer's agent when he set up cameras in employer's guard shack and took photographs of union handbillers); Tres Estrellas de Oro, 329 NLRB 50, 168 LRRM 1234 (1999) (brother of employer's president, who was co-owner of second company owned by same family, spoke with apparent authority and was therefore acting as agent of employer when he made statement to organizer regarding employer's knowledge of his union activities); *In re* Property Markets Group, Inc., 339 NLRB 199, 174 LRRM 1535 (2003) (employer's nonsupervisory building superintendents had real and perceived authority that made them employer's agents).

[45]337 NLRB 1189, 170 LRRM 1401 (2002).

[46]*Id.*, 170 LRRM at 1402.

[47]*Id.*

[48]316 F.3d 995, 171 LRRM 2769 (9th Cir. 2003).

In *San Manuel Indian Bingo & Casino*,[49] the Board overruled its prior precedent and established a new standard for determining the circumstances under which it will assert jurisdiction over Indian-owned and -operated enterprises. Under the Board's prior precedents, *Sac & Fox Industries, Ltd.*[50] and *Yukon Kuskokwim Health Care Corp.*,[51] the location—not the nature—of the enterprise was the determinative factor in assessing whether a tribal enterprise was excluded from the Act's jurisidiction. If the enterprise was located on a reservation, jurisdiction was not asserted. In *San Manuel*, the Board modified *Sac & Fox*, and overruled *Fort Apache Timber Co.*[52] and *Southern Indian Health Council.*[53] According to the Board, a statute of general applicability, such as the Act, should be applied to the conduct of Indian tribes, regardless of location, unless the law touches exclusive rights of self-government in purely intramural matters, the application of the law would abrogate treaty rights, or there is proof in the statute or legislative history that Congress did not intend the law to apply to Indian tribes. Applying this standard, the Board asserted jurisdiction over the casino in *San Manuel Indian Bingo & Casino*, but in a companion case declined to assert jurisdiction over a health service corporation in *Yukon Kuskokwim Health Corp.*[54]

The Board continues to apply the two-part standard for determining whether an organization is exempt as a "political subdivision." In *Hinds County Human Resources Agency*,[55] the Board noted that an employer is a political subdivision if it is either (1) created directly by the state to constitute a department or an administrative arm of government, or (2) administered by persons who are responsible to public officials or the general public. In that case, the Board found the agency was exempt because it was created by the county pursuant to state statute, the state statute specifically provided for local government control of the agency, and the agency received all funds from state and federal government sources. In *Regional Medical Center at Memphis*,[56] the Board found that a hospital and associ-

[49]341 NLRB No. 138, 174 LRRM 1489 (2004).
[50]307 NLRB 241, 140 LRRM 1054 (1992).
[51]328 NLRB 761, 161 LRRM 1161 (1999).
[52]226 NLRB 503, 93 LRRM 1296 (1976).
[53]290 NLRB 436, 129 LRRM 1013 (1988).
[54]341 NLRB No. 139, 174 LRRM 1510 (2004).
[55]331 NLRB 1404, 165 LRRM 1172 (2000).
[56]343 NLRB No. 48, 176 LRRM 1303 (2004).

ated clinics administered by board members responsible to the mayor and county commissioners were a political subdivision exempt from the Board's jurisdiction.

In *Kentucky River Community Care, Inc. v. NLRB,*[57] the Sixth Circuit rejected an argument for political subdivision status by a private, nonprofit organization operating as a regional mental health board because the organization was established by an individual person in his capacity as a citizen of Kentucky.[58]

In *FiveCAP Inc. v. NLRB,*[59] the court enforced the Board's ruling that a nonprofit corporation that administered various welfare programs was not a political subdivision exempt from the coverage of the Act. The Board reached this conclusion even though one-third of the corporation's board of directors were elected public officials or their representatives, it received funding from the Community Services Block Grant Act, it was exempt from certain taxes, and it was established through a petition filed with a county board.

In *NLRB v. Young Women's Christian Ass'n,*[60] the Eighth Circuit joined the Fourth, Sixth, Seventh, and Tenth Circuits in upholding the Board's *Management Training Corp.*[61] standard on the ground that it was a valid exercise of the Board's discretion in exercising its statutory jurisdiction. The Board rejected arguments that it lacked jurisdiction over a daycare center, because the federal government maintained pervasive control over its employees' terms and conditions of employment and it was therefore prevented from engaging in meaningful collective bargaining.

The court upheld the Board's decision to extend and decline comity to certain representation elections conducted by the Michigan Employment Relations Commission (MERC) in *Michigan Com-*

---

[57]193 F.3d 444, 162 LRRM 2449 (6th Cir. 1999), *aff'd,* 532 U.S. 706, 167 LRRM 2164 (2001).

[58]*See also* FiveCAP, Inc., 331 NLRB 1165, 170 LRRM 1181 (2000) (Head Start program not political subdivision where not created directly by state and its board not directly responsible to electorate).

[59]294 F.3d 768, 170 LRRM 2401 (6th Cir. 2002); Connecticut State Conference Bd., 339 NLRB 760, 173 LRRM 1574 (2003) (asserting jurisdiction over management company that operates public bus transit system and determining that entity did not meet political subdivision exemption even though it received financial support from state and state owned its assets).

[60]192 F.3d 1111, 162 LRRM 2268 (8th Cir. 1999).

[61]317 NLRB 1355, 149 LRRM 1313 (1995). *See also* Jacksonville Urban League, Inc., 340 NLRB No. 156, 174 LRRM 1125 (2003) (asserting jurisdiction over nonprofit operator of Head Start program).

munity Services Inc. v. NLRB.[62] In that case, MERC had conducted representation elections for employees of nonprofit corporations operating group homes for people with disabilities. The corporations had close ties, through funding, to the Michigan Department of Mental Health, and became subject to the Board's jurisdiction pursuant to *Management Training Corp.* The Board extended comity to representation elections conducted by MERC prior to the Board's *Management Training Corp.* decision, but not to MERC elections conducted after that decision.

C. Employee

1. *In General*

Several recent Board decisions on the question of "employee" status have depended on whether the relationship is (in the Board's view) primarily an economic one or is of some other nature. For instance, the Board held in *Brevard Achievement Center*[63] that certain disabled workers were not employees, where their relationship with the center was "primarily rehabilitative in nature" rather than "primarily an economic one." In reaching this conclusion, the Board noted that the disabled workers were assigned a trainer who instructed them on performing janitorial and custodial jobs and provided them with counseling and problem-resolution services. The Board also noted that the facility applied different performance and disciplinary standards to the disabled employees; i.e., the disabled workers worked at their own pace and received additional training rather than discipline for substandard performance.

Using a similar analysis and overruling its decision in *New York University,*[64] the Board held in *Brown University*[65] that graduate students working in teaching positions were not employees within the meaning of the Act. The Board found that graduate student assistants, who perform services at a university in connection with their studies, have a predominantly academic, rather than economic, relationship with the school. By contrast, the Board has held that medical residents are employees.[66]

---

[62]309 F.3d 348, 171 LRRM 2129 (6th Cir. 2002), *cert. denied,* 538 U.S. 1012, 172 LRRM 2448 (2003).

[63]342 NLRB No. 101, 175 LRRM 1329 (2004)

[64]332 NLRB 1205, 165 LRRM 1241 (2000).

[65]342 NLRB No. 42, 175 LRRM 1089 (2004).

[66]Boston Med. Ctr. Corp., 330 NLRB 152, 162 LRRM 1329 (1999).

The Board found that there was an economic relationship in *Seattle Opera Ass'n*,[67] holding that auxiliary choristers were employees rather than volunteers. The auxiliary choristers were subject to the employer's rules and expectations, and could progress to alternate or regular chorister positions as well as perform alongside those employees. The remuneration of $214 that auxiliary choristers received at the end of a production was compensation for their work, and the Board therefore found that an economic relationship existed, as well as an employer-employee relationship, even though the payment was less than a minimum or living wage.

Following the Supreme Court's decision in *Sure-Tan*,[68] the Board has continued to treat undocumented aliens as employees within the meaning of the Act.[69] However, the Supreme Court, in *Hoffman Plastic Compounds, Inc. v. NLRB*,[70] has held that the Board may not order an employer to pay back pay to workers who are illegally in the United States even when their firing constitutes an unfair labor practice. An employee who is an illegal alien may still be able to collect damages under certain state labor statutes. For example, in *Madeira v. Affordable Housing Foundation, Inc.*,[71] the court held that an illegal alien who suffered injuries at the worksite was still eligible to receive compensatory damages for an employer's violation of New York labor law. Citing an Opinion Letter from the Attorney General of New York, the court stated *Hoffman* does not prevent the New York Department of Labor from enforcing the state's wage payment laws on behalf of illegal immigrants as long as no federal constitutional or statutory right is implicated.[72]

Following the Supreme Court's decision in *Town & Country Electric*,[73] the Board has continued to hold that "salts" are employees within the meaning of the Act, even where the employer contends that the salts' goal is to destroy the employer rather than to organize

---

[67]331 NLRB 1072, 165 LRRM 1273, *aff'd*, 333 NLRB No. 37 (2001), *enforced*, 292 F.3d 757 (D.C. Cir. 2002). *See also* WBAI Pacifica Found., 328 NLRB 1273, 162 LRRM 1070 (1999) (holding that unpaid volunteer staff of radio station were not employees).

[68]Sure-Tan v. NLRB, 467 U.S. 883, 116 LRRM 2857 (1984).

[69]*See, e.g.*, Nortech Waste, 336 NLRB 554, 168 LRRM 1361 (2001); County Window Cleaning Co., 328 NLRB 190, 163 LRRM 1221 (1999).

[70]535 U.S. 137, 169 LRRM 2769 (2002).

[71]315 F. Supp. 2d 504, 506–07 (S.D.N.Y. 2004).

[72]*Id.* at 507.

[73]NLRB v. Town & Country Elec., 516 U.S. 85, 150 LRRM 2897 (1995).

its employees.[74] An employee does not lose the protections of the Act merely by being a salt, but an employee salt can lose the protection of the Act by engaging in unprotected activity that emanates from disabling conflicts arising in connection with the salting.[75]

In *Wright Electric v. Ouellette*,[76] the court was faced with a suit against a "salt" and his union on several tort theories such as fraudulent concealment and breach of duty and loyalty. There, the Board had previously refused to issue a complaint against the employer for terminating the salt for falsifying his employment application. Nevertheless, the court dismissed the state law action on the basis that the union had made an arguable case that the salt's activity may have been protected, and therefore the claims were preempted by the National Labor Relations Act.

In *Contractors' Labor Pool, Inc. v. NLRB*,[77] the D.C. Circuit affirmed the Board's decision that the employer could not rely on the disabling conflict defense, because it could not demonstrate that at the time it took discriminatory action against two employees who expressed union sympathies that it knew the two employees were salts or that they had engaged in disabling conduct. The court likened the disabling defense to a *Wright Line* defense, and held that the employer must demonstrate that it took action based on the salts' unprotected activities.

The Board noted in *Freeman Decorating*[78] that, as a general matter, employees who are referred through hiring halls are protected employees for the purpose of Section 2(3) of the Act. The decision in *Freeman Decorating* primarily involved the loss-of-employee-status provision of Section 8(d) of the Act, regarding persons who engage in strikes commenced without required notice.[79]

---

[74]Aztech Elec., 335 NLRB 260, 168 LRRM 1073 (2001), *enforced in part*, 323 F.3d 1051, 172 LRRM 2065 (D.C. Cir. 2003).

[75]Casino Ready Mix v. NLRB, 321 F.3d 1190 (D.C. Cir. 2003).

[76]686 N.W.2d 313, 318 (Minn Ct. App. 2004).

[77]323 F.3d 1051, 172 LRRM 2065 (D.C. Cir. 2003).

[78]336 NLRB 1, 168 LRRM 1329 (2001), *enforcement denied sub nom.* Theatrical Stage Employees Local 39 v. NLRB, 334 F.3d 27, 172 LRRM 2993 (D.C. Cir. 2003).

[79]*See also* Main Edition, Chapter 19, "The Primary Strike," Section III.B.1. [Unprotected and Prohibited Strikes; Unlawful or Wrongful Ends; Strikes in Violation of the Act] at pages 1497–98.

2. *Excluded Categories of Employees*

a. Supervisors

In determining whether a person is a "supervisor" within the meaning of Section 2(11) and therefore excluded from the definition of "employee" in Section 2(3), the principles discussed in the Main Edition remain controlling.[80] Specifically, the Board continues to hold that the authority to use independent judgment in effecting any one of the statutorily identified supervisory tasks is sufficient to establish that an individual is a supervisor.[81] However, in certain respects the decision of the Supreme Court in *NLRB v. Kentucky River Community Care*[82] has altered the Board's governing standard.

Kentucky River, like *NLRB v. Health Care & Retirement Corp. of America*[83] a few years earlier, involved the much-litigated topic of supervisory authority among nurses. In *Kentucky River*, the dispositive portion of Section 2(11) was the phrase "independent judgment." The Board, in a series of cases involving nurses (as well as cases involving other categories of employees), had held that employees do not use "independent judgment" in directing others (and therefore are not supervisors) when they exercise "ordinary professional or technical judgment in directing less-skilled employees to deliver services in accordance with employer-specified standards."[84] The Supreme Court rejected the Board's categorical determination that

---

[80]*See* Main Edition, Chapter 27, Section III.C.2.a., at pages 2110–20. Additional discussion of the law on supervisory status, and citation to relevant Board decisions, are included in Chapter 17 of the Board's "Outline of Law and Procedure in Representation Cases," currently available at www.nlrb.gov/outline.html.

[81]Westwood Health Care Ctr., 330 NLRB 935, 163 LRRM 1225 (2000).

[82]532 U.S. 706, 167 LRRM 2164 (2001).

[83]511 U.S. 571, 146 LRRM 2321 (1994), discussed in the Main Edition, Chapter 27, Section III.C.2.a., at page 2118. *Health Care & Retirement* dealt with the "in the interest of the employer" portion of §2(11). Although the Supreme Court rejected the Board's interpretation of that phrase, it bears noting that the phrase still remains relevant as a limitation on the definition of "supervisor" in certain cases. For instance, in *Allstate Ins. Co.*, 332 NLRB 759, 165 LRRM 1293 (2000), an insurance agent was held not to be a supervisor even though she responsibly directed her office assistants; the critical point was that, because whether to hire such assistants was completely her own decision based on her own business and economic interests, the Board concluded that her direction of them was 'in the interest' not of the employer but of herself.

[84]*Kentucky River*, *supra* note 82, 532 U.S. at 713.

decisions made through "ordinary professional or technical judgment" do not constitute the exercise of supervisory authority.[85]

The Supreme Court in *Kentucky River* did, however, endorse the Board's rule that the burden of proof on the issue of supervisory authority rests with the party that asserts the existence of such authority.[86] The Court also affirmed that the Board does have the discretion to interpret Section 2(11), by (among other things) determining the *degree* of independent judgment that an employee must utilize in order to be deemed a supervisor. The Court further recognized that the existence of employer-specified standards, rules, and regulations may constrain the employee's judgment to such a degree that the direction of others does not rise to the level of supervisory authority.[87]

In *Hospital General Menonita v. NLRB*,[88] the First Circuit affirmed the Board's application of the *Kentucky River* test and held that the registered nurses did not exercise sufficient judgment to rise to the level of supervisory authority. The nurses assigned work by consensus among those who would be affected by the assignments. The court found that assignment of work through this cooperative process did not meet the criteria of "independent judgment" required to be a supervisor under the Act. The court upheld the Board's finding that the staff registered nurses' direction of the patient care tasks of the licensed practical nurses and technicians was constrained by physician's orders and detailed protocols which set forth in detail the diagnostic and treatment standards, thereby negating the potential for any meaningful supervisory discretion.

In *Dynamic Science Inc.*,[89] the Board applied a *Kentucky River* analysis, finding that test leaders of a military facility are not supervisors. In addition to nurses, other job categories have likewise given rise to substantial bodies of recent case law on supervisory issues, including employees of electrical utilities, who monitor and oversee electrical distribution systems,[90] and employees on barges, tugboats, and other

[85] *Id.* at 714–21.

[86] *Id.* at 711–12.

[87] *Id.* at 713–14.

[88] 393 F.3d 263, 268, 176 LRRM 2257 (1st Cir. 2004).

[89] 334 NLRB 391, 167 LRRM 1237 (2001). *See* note 93, *infra*.

[90] *See, e.g.*, Public Serv. Co. of Colo. v. NLRB, 271 F.3d 1213, 168 LRRM 2833 (10th Cir. 2001) (denying enforcement of Board decision, concluding that Board's decision was based on same view that Supreme Court had rejected in *Kentucky River*); Entergy Gulf States v. NLRB, 253 F.3d 203, 167 LRRM 2445 (5th Cir. 2001) (denying enforcement of Board decision, and finding electrical transmission employees to be supervisors).

vessels.[91] After *Kentucky River*, the courts of appeals continue to be willing to overturn the Board on questions of supervisory status as to these and other job categories.[92]

Since *Kentucky River*, the Board has reaffirmed some of the limitations on supervisory authority that were not disturbed by, or were in some cases reaffirmed by, *Kentucky River*. For instance, the Board has focused on the degree of independent judgment involved in the direction of others, finding in some cases that the degree was too slight to constitute supervisory authority.[93] The actual use of independent judgment in assigning work is considered by the Board to be a primary indicia of supervisory authority.[94]

The Board has reaffirmed that the fact that a person is called a supervisor, by himself or herself, the employer, or other employees,

---

[91]*See, e.g.*, Brusco Tug & Barge Co. v. NLRB, 247 F.3d 273, 167 LRRM 2148 (D.C. Cir. 2001) (denying enforcement of Board decision and remanding for further consideration by Board in light of *Kentucky River* and other factors); Alter Barge Lines, 336 NLRB 1266, 169 LRRM 1440 (2001) (finding that barge pilots were supervisors, following supplemental briefing in light of *Kentucky River*); Ingram Barge Co., 336 NLRB 1259, 169 LRRM 1239 (2001) (same).

[92]*See also* Beverly Enters.–Minn. v. NLRB, 266 F.3d 785, 168 LRRM 2417 (8th Cir. 2001) (denying enforcement, and remanding for further consideration in light of *Kentucky River*, where Board had found nurses not to be supervisors); NLRB v. Quinnipiac Coll., 256 F.3d 68, 167 LRRM 2487 (2d Cir. 2001) (denying enforcement, where Board had found security employees not to be supervisors).

[93]Dynamic Science, Inc., 334 NLRB 391, 167 LRRM 1237 (2001) (finding that artillery test leaders were not supervisors where authority is circumscribed by detailed orders); Williamette Indus., 336 NLRB 743, 169 LRRM 1480 (2001) ("routine direction of simple tasks or the issuance of low-level orders" is not supervisory); Los Angeles Water & Power Employees' Ass'n, 340 NLRB No. 146, 173 LRRM 1449 (2003) (employee was not supervisor even where she filled in for office manager in his absence; employee's authority with regard to instructing other employees to fill in for one another during breaks, and the like, did not involve exercise of independent judgment); Armstrong Mach. Co., 343 NLRB No. 122 (2004) (employee was not supervisor where his assignment of tasks to other employees, based on his knowledge as to their respective skills and as to which ones worked well together, did not amount to sufficient "independent judgment"); Volair Contractors, 341 NLRB No. 98, 175 LRRM 1297 (2004) (where employee's authority to assign and direct was circumscribed by others' orders, and where the employee's statement that he used independent judgment was conclusory, employee was not supervisor); Wilshire at Lakewood, 343 NLRB No. 23, 175 LRRM 1522 (2004) (individual was not a supervisor by virtue of her permitting employees to leave work early in medical emergencies, where no independent judgment was involved); *see also* NLRB v. Dole Fresh Vegetables, 334 F.3d 478, 172 LRRM 2935 (6th Cir. 2003) (lead employees were not supervisors where they did not assign or prioritize tasks, only followed instructions of their supervisor in filling out employee warning notices, and could interview but not hire new employees).

[94]Arlington Masonry Supply, 339 NLRB 817, 172 LRRM 1437 (2003).

does not make him or her a supervisor within the meaning of Section 2(11).[95] With regard to the power to discipline other employees or to effectively recommend such discipline—one of the enumerated supervisory powers under Section 2(11)—the Board has held that a program manager's limited role in the disciplinary process was nothing more than a mere "reportorial" function and, therefore, does not constitute supervisory authority,[96] and that the issuance of warnings to other employees does not constitute supervisory authority without proof that such warnings concretely impact the warned employee's status or that they are a step in a progressive discipline system.[97] Similarly, the power to evaluate another employee does not make one a supervisor, in the absence of evidence as to whether such evaluations lead directly to changes in the evaluated employee's status or tenure.[98] And as to the adjustment of grievances—another of the enumerated supervisory powers under the statute—the Board has held that a limited authority to resolve minor disputes or personal conflicts does not constitute supervisory power.[99] Finally, isolated, sporadic, or minor exercises of supervisory authority are generally insufficient to establish supervisory status.[100]

Recent Board decisions have explored the meaning of the phrase "effectively recommend," in the definition of supervisory status. For instance, in *Donaldson Bros. Ready Mix*,[101] the Board held that the

---

[95]Pan-Oston Co., 336 NLRB 305, 170 LRRM 1026 (2001).

[96]Ken-Crest Servs., 335 NLRB 777, 168 LRRM 1189 (2001); *see also* Progressive Transp. Servs., 340 NLRB No. 126, 174 LRRM 1183 (2003) (distinguishing and explaining *Ken-Crest,* and finding employee to be supervisor based on her authority to effectively recommend disciplinary actions that affected employees' status).

[97]*Williamette Indus., supra* note 93; *Wilshire at Lakewood, supra* note 93.

[98]*Williamette Indus., supra* note 93.

[99]*Ken-Crest Servs., supra* note 96.

[100]Kaznowha Stone Co., 334 NLRB 235, 169 LRRM 1246 (2001). In *Webco Indus. v. NLRB,* 173 LRRM 3056, 2003 WL22954295 (10th Cir. 2003), the court affirmed the Board's decision that an employee only had "minor supervisory duties" insufficient to establish supervisory status, even though the employee (1) trained veteran employees on how to use equipment; (2) initialed time cards; (3) critiqued employees on how well they were doing their jobs and offered input on whether an employee would advance from one pay level to another; (4) offered recommendations on whether to keep a probationary employee; (5) assisted in the employee evaluation process; (6) signed reprimands of other employees at the instruction of his supervisor; and (7) attended management meetings. *See also* Volair Contractors, 341 NLRB No. 98, 175 LRRM 1297 (2004) (authority that is sporadically or infrequently exercised will not be sufficient to demonstrate supervisory status, where there is no evidence that the individual in question was actually instructed by higher-ups that he or she had that authority).

[101]341 NLRB No. 124, 175 LRRM 1069 (2004).

individual in question was a supervisor, where he performed the hiring interviews and his hiring recommendations had been followed by higher official after a cursory review of employment applications. To similar effect is *Mountaineer Park*,[102] concerning the power to effectively recommend discipline.

As noted in the Main Edition, the Board in the past has looked to nonstatutory indicia as background evidence on the question of supervisor status. They are not themselves dispositive of the issue in the absence of evidence indicating the existence of one of the primary or statutory indications of supervisor status.[103] A court has noted the Board's reluctance to find so-called secondary indicia determinative of supervisory status.[104] Two such secondary indicia are the ratio of alleged supervisors to employees[105] and differences in terms and conditions of employment.[106]

In 2003, the Board called for amicus briefs on various questions relating to supervisory authority, in cases styled *Oakwood Healthcare, Beverly Enterprises-Minnesota*, and *Croft Metals*.[107] Those cases are pending as of this writing; readers are advised to ascertain whether decisions have been rendered in those cases and (if so) whether those decisions work any change in the law.

b. Managerial Employees

In *Allstate Insurance Co.*,[108] the Board found that although an employee insurance agent exercised considerable discretionary authority, it was not the type of authority that involved formulating or effectuating company policies on behalf of her employer because the risks assumed by such actions ran to the employee. Thus, there was no risk of divided loyalty and no basis for finding the employee functioned in a managerial role. In *Boston Medical Center Corp.*,[109] the Board affirmed the regional director's conclusion that chief residents are not statutory supervisors or managerial employees.

---

[102]343 NLRB No. 135, 176 LRRM 1278 (2004).

[103]*See* Training Sch. at Vineland, 332 NLRB 1412, 167 LRRM 1274 (2000); Chrome Deposit Corp., 323 NLRB 961, 963 n.9, 156 LRRM 1217 (1997).

[104]NLRB v. Dole Fresh Vegetables, 334 F.3d 478, 172 LRRM 2935 (6th Cir. 2003).

[105]Harborside Healthcare Inc., 330 NLRB 1334, 164 LRRM 1160 (2000).

[106]Ken-Crest Servs., 335 NLRB 777, 168 LRRM 1189 (2001).

[107]Order not reported in bound volumes, available at http://www.nlrb.gov/nlrb/press/releases/kyriver.pdf.

[108]332 NLRB 759, 165 LRRM 1293 (2000).

[109]330 NLRB 152, 162 LRRM 1329 (1999).

In *LeMoyne-Owen College*,[110] the NLRB had certified a bargaining unit consisting of full-time faculty members finding that the faculty members were not managerial because (1) they did not possess absolute control over any facet of the school's operations; (2) they did not effectively recommend policies affecting the school's administration; and (3) their recommendations were subject to change by higher levels of authority in the school. The college had argued that its faculty performed a similar role to the faculty in *NLRB v. Yeshiva University*,[111] where faculty members were held to be managerial employees. The court vacated the NLRB's order and remanded the case back to the NLRB, holding that the NLRB had failed to articulate how the faculty at LeMoyne-Owen was not like the Yeshiva faculty.[112]

In *Evergreen America Corp. v. NLRB*,[113] the D.C. Circuit upheld the Board's determination that port captains, assistant port captains, and port engineers for a shipping company were not managerial employees. The court held that those employees "exercise professional discretion in a few matters affecting the ships, but their decisions are closely monitored by and subject to the direction of the section manager,"[114] and so they were not managerial employees under the *Yeshiva University* test.

Current law on managerial status seems to exclude employees from the protections of the Act when they are also shareholders of the employer and can, together with other employee-shareholders, have an effective voice in the formulation and determination of corporate policy.[115]

c. Confidential Employees

On remand from the Seventh Circuit decision in *E & L Transport Co. v. NLRB*,[116] which is discussed in the Main Edition,[117] the Board accepted as "the law of the case" that a confidential secretary to the terminal manager was a "confidential" employee under the

[110] 338 NLRB No. 92, 171 LRRM 1376 (2003).

[111] 444 U.S. 672, 103 LRRM 2526 (1980).

[112] LeMoyne-Owen Coll. v. NLRB, 357 F.3d 55, 174 LRRM 2225 (D.C. Cir. 2004).

[113] 362 F.3d 827, 174 LRRM 2737 (D.C. Cir. 2004).

[114] *Id.* at 839–40.

[115] Citywide Corporate Transp., Inc., 338 NLRB 444, 171 LRRM 1308 (2002). Member Liebman, concurring in *Citywide*, suggested that this issue was ripe for reconsideration.

[116] 85 F.3d 1258, 152 LRRM 2449 (7th Cir. 1996).

[117] *See* Main Edition, Chapter 27, Section III.C.2.c., at page 2125.

Act because the manager for whom the secretary worked was responsible for formulating the company's labor relations policies, and the secretary prepared confidential documents and had regular access to confidential information relating to labor relations policies.[118]

Reaching a different result, the Board declined to find confidential status of an employee in *Ryder Student Transportation Services, Inc.*[119] The Board found that an employee was not in a confidential position even though he attended a management meeting where the attendees were told they were on the "front line" of the company's campaign against the union. The company could not confer confidential status on the employee simply by declaring him an antiunion leader. Moreover, although the employee possessed the expertise to break into the company's computer system containing confidential labor relations information, this was insufficient to make him a confidential employee.

In *Waste Management de Puerto Rico,*[120] the Board reaffirmed the existing test for "confidential employee" status, and (among other things) held an employee not to have such status "because she does not work on labor relations issues on a regular basis."[121]

d. Agricultural Laborers

The Board continues to recognize the existence of both a primary and secondary component to the application of the agricultural exception to NLRB jurisdiction, as set forth in *Farmers Reservoir & Irrigation Co. v. McComb.*[122]

e. Independent Contractors

(3) Owner-Operators in the Trucking Industry

In *Corporate Express Delivery Systems,*[123] the Board found that owner-operators were not independent contractors where owner-operators

---

[118]E & L Transp. Co., 327 NLRB 408, 160 LRRM 1115 (1998).

[119]336 NLRB 882, 173 LRRM 1510 (2001).

[120]339 NLRB 262, 174 LRRM 1155 (2003), *enforced,* 359 F.3d 36, 174 LRRM 2417 (1st Cir. 2004).

[121]*Id.* at 262 n.2.

[122]337 U.S. 755 (1949). *See also* Pictsweet Mushroom Farm, 329 NLRB 852, 162 LRRM 1278 (1999) (where Board held that employees involved in employer's mushroom-slicing operation are agricultural employees engaged in secondary agricultural activity).

[123]332 NLRB 1522, 166 LRRM 1017 (2000), *enforced,* 292 F.3d 777, 170 LRRM 2193 (D.C. Cir. 2002).

and company drivers performed similar functions for the company. These functions were an integral part of the company's operation and the owner-operators worked for the company on a full-time basis. They were not free to add or delete customers, were required to use insurance recommended by the company, and could not independently negotiate compensation rates with the company. In *Douglas Foods Corp.*,[124] the Board found that lease-route operators were employees despite factors suggesting an independent contractor relationship, including a significant degree of control over their compensation, ownership of the product on their trucks from which they kept their daily profit, and assumption of risk of waste or theft. The Board concluded that these factors were outweighed by various indications of employee status. However, on appeal, although the D.C. Circuit upheld the bulk of the Board's unfair labor practice findings, it found that the Board's findings relating to alleged "sham" sales of catering trucks and routes to their operators were inadequate and vacated the Board's order.[125]

In *Slay Transportation Co.*,[126] the Board reversed the regional director's finding of independent contractor status for owner-operators who leased their trucks to the employer. The Board disagreed with the regional director's finding that limited entrepreneurial opportunities, including the ability to hire other drivers to operate their vehicles and to control their costs and income, warranted the conclusion that the owner-operators were independent contractors. Instead, the Board focused on the fact that the owner-operators, like company drivers, drove tractors leased by the employer, were trained and tested by the employer, used the company's dispatchers, and were subject to a compensation system established and controlled by the employer.

In *Time Auto Transportation, Inc.*,[127] a divided Board affirmed the ALJ finding that the drivers were statutory employees under the "right-of-control" test. The employer selected and controlled the equipment used by the drivers in its car hauling operation, and engaged in strict oversight of the manner and means by which the drivers performed their work. The employer had a direct financial stake in

---

[124] 330 NLRB 821, 163 LRRM 1201 (2000), *review granted in part, denied in part*, 251 F.3d 1056, 167 LRRM 2380 (D.C. Cir. 2001).

[125] 251 F.3d 1056, 167 LRRM 2380 (D.C. Cir. 2001).

[126] 331 NLRB 1292, 165 LRRM 1213 (2000).

[127] 338 NLRB 626, 171 LRRM 1519 (2002), *aff'd*, 377 F.3d 496, 175 LRRM 2334 (6th Cir. 2004).

the amount of cargo hauled by its drivers because it received a percentage of the gross for their loads, and it engaged in extensive review of their productivity. The fact that drivers were able to hire extra drivers and set their pay was insufficient to establish that the drivers were independent contractors. The employer was still involved in the hiring process, could prevent the hiring of an extra driver, and effectively controlled the extra drivers' compensation, since their wages were set within the overall compensation rate established by the employer.

(6) Taxicab Owner-Operators and Lessees

The Board continues to assess the level of control an employer asserts over taxi drivers in determining whether they are independent contractors or employees. In *Stamford Taxi, Inc.*,[128] the Board applied the right-of-control test and concluded that the drivers were employees rather than independent contractors because the employer retained title to vehicles, assigned work hours, required the use of its dispatchers, enforced work rules, and linked the employee's income directly to the drivers' fares.

(9) Miscellaneous Classifications

In *AmeriHealth Inc./AmeriHealth HMO,*[129] the Board adopted a regional director's conclusion that primary care and specialty physicians who participated in a health maintenance organization (HMO) were independent contractors and not employees within the meaning of Section 2(3) of the Act. Applying the right-of-control test, the Board acknowledged that the HMO had the right to control many details of the services that the physicians delivered to HMO members, but found that other factors, including the physicians' ability to contract with other insurance companies and to provide services not covered by the HMO to HMO members if the members were willing to pay for them, evidenced that the physicians were independent contractors rather than employees of the HMO.

---

[128]332 NLRB 1372, 170 LRRM 1483 (2000). *See also* Metro Cab Co., 341 NLRB No. 103, 175 LRRM 1275 (2004) (finding that taxi drivers were employees.) *But see* Citywide Corporate Transp., Inc., 338 NLRB 444, 171 LRRM 1308 (2002) (considering cases involving independent contractors and finding that limousine drivers who were shareholder-employees were not employees within meaning of Act because they could, as group, effectively formulate and determine corporate policy, including labor relations policy); AAA Cab Servs., 341 NLRB No. 57, 175 LRRM 1021 (2004) (finding taxi drivers to be independent contractors).

[129]329 NLRB 870, 165 LRRM 1069 (1999).

In *Ridgewell's, Inc.*,[130] the Board determined that caterers working in the U.S. House of Representatives cafeterias, coffee shops, and snack bars are statutory employees, rather than independent contractors. The Board found that the wait staff possessed most of the well-established indicia of employee status. They worked scheduled hours, were supervised by on-site managers with the power to terminate their employment, performed very little outside work, and drew unemployment compensation when Congress was in recess.

In *BKN Inc.*,[131] the Board found freelance writers, designers, and artists to be employees, not independent contractors, because of extensive supervision by the employer. In *Pennsylvania Academy of Fine Arts*,[132] a divided Board found artists' models to be independent contractors because they were paid by the class and received 1099 forms instead of W-2s, supplied their own costumes and equipment, could take outside employment and work the number of hours they wished, were engaged in a different occupation (modeling) than the school, and were not subject to evaluations or discipline.

f. Family Members and Relationships

The Board continues to exclude relatives of a manager who are not owners or shareholders from the definition of "employee" under Section 2(3) of the Act if the relative enjoys a "special status" on the job because of the relationship that aligns the interests of the relative more closely with management than with the bargaining unit employees.[133]

---

[130] 334 NLRB 37, 169 LRRM 1397 (2001).

[131] 333 NLRB 143, 166 LRRM 1185 (2001).

[132] 343 NLRB No. 93, 176 LRRM 1249 (2004).

[133] R & D Trucking, Inc., 327 NLRB 531, 160 LRRM 1113 (1999) (son-in-law of employer's president excluded from unit because his familial relationship afforded him job-related privileges not available to unit members and greater access to management). *See also* Regional Home Care, Inc., 329 NLRB 85, 166 LRRM 1112 (1999) (sustaining challenges to three ballots because of "special status" resulting from familial relationship), *enforced*, 237 F.3d 62, 166 LRRM 2326 (1st Cir. 2001); Peirce-Phelps, Inc., 341 NLRB No. 78, 174 LRRM 1353 (2004) (high school student supervised by nonowner father not excluded from the bargaining unit where he did not enjoy any special privileges or benefits by virtue of the familial relationship). *Cf.* New Silver Palace Rest., 334 NLRB 290, 171 LRRM 1532 (2001) (brother-in-law of owner was employee under §2(3) of Act where there was no evidence that he enjoyed special status or enjoyed special privilege because of his familial relationship).

h. Medical Residents and Interns

In *Boston Medical Center*,[134] the Board held that medical interns and residents (house staff) are statutory employees, and not just students. In *New York University*,[135] the Board, applying the principles from its decision in *Boston Medical*, concluded that graduate student assistants are employees under the Act. More recently, in *Brown University*,[136] the Board expressly overruled *New York University* and held that graduate student assistants are not statutory employees. In so holding, the Board specifically refused to express an opinion regarding its decision in *Boston Medical Center*.[137] The Board's failure to reaffirm *Boston Medical Center* while overruling *New York University* suggests that the Board may review the analysis and outcome in *Boston Medical Center* when the opportunity arises.

In one case decided after *Boston Medical Center*, the Board adopted the view of an ALJ that certain physicians were not the statutory supervisors of house staff and other medical professionals.[138]

IV. DISCRETIONARY ADMINISTRATIVE JURISDICTIONAL STANDARDS

B. Specific Assertions or Denials of Coverage

1. **Nonretail Enterprises**—In *Electrical Contractors, Inc. v. NLRB*,[139] the Second Circuit upheld the Board's exercise of jurisdiction over an electrical contracting business based on the employer's admission that it was engaged in commerce within the meaning of the Act. The employer argued that the Board had failed to prove that the unfair labor practices had "affected commerce." The court denied this claim on the basis that any unfair labor practice committed by the employer necessarily "affected commerce" within the meaning of Sections 2(7) and 10(a) of the Act.

---

[134] 330 NLRB 152, 162 LRRM 1329 (1999).

[135] 332 NLRB 1205, 165 LRRM 1241 (2000).

[136] 342 NLRB No. 42, 175 LRRM 1089 (2004).

[137] *Id.*

[138] *See* St. Barnabas Hosp., 334 NLRB 1000, 168 LRRM 1005 (2001), *enforced*, 171 LRRM 2064, 2002 WL 31060408 (2d Cir. 2002) (unpublished). *See also* FHCS Physician Servs., 2003 NLRB GCM LEXIS 34 (Mar. 27, 2003) (general counsel opined that attending physician in teaching hospital supervised house staff).

[139] 245 F.3d 109, 166 LRRM 2913 (2d Cir. 2001).

In *Hobart Crane Rental, Inc.*,[140] the Board declined to assert jurisdiction over two companies that were alleged to have constituted a single employer, where the two companies had a total of $487.07 in direct inflow in 1997 and $42,640.29 in direct and indirect inflow in 1998.

2. **Retail Enterprises**—The Board declined to exercise jurisdiction over an exotic dance club in *Jonbruni Inc. dba Temptations.*[141] The club did not meet the Board's threshold of $500,000 in discretionary sales, excluding compensation directly paid by the customers to the dancers.

8. **National Defense/Federal Funds**—A significant amount of revenue from federal funds warrants a finding of Board jurisdiction.[142]

18. **Nonprofit, Private Educational, and Religious Institutions**—The Board continues to decide jurisdiction over religiously affiliated organizations by closely examining the underlying facts.

The Board asserted jurisdiction over a hospital operated by the Seventh Day Adventist Church whose teachings prohibit its members from participating in labor unions, paying dues to labor unions, or operating with the presence of a labor union.[143] The Board agreed with the regional director that applying the Act to this workplace was the least restrictive means of furthering the government's compelling interest of preventing labor strife and protecting the employees' ability to exercise their rights under Section 7 of the Act. This case also is consistent with the Board's general view that health care facilities are within the Board's jurisdiction even when they may be sponsored and administered by religious organizations.[144]

In contrast, the Board declined to assert jurisdiction over a unit of custodial employees employed by a Roman Catholic church.[145] A union had sought to represent these

---

[140]337 NLRB 506, 170 LRRM 1055 (2002).

[141]337 NLRB 376, 169 LRRM 1073 (2001).

[142]Electrical Workers Local 48 (Kingston Constructors), 332 NLRB 1492, 166 LRRM 1090 (2000), *modified*, 333 NLRB 963, 172 LRRM 1253 (2001), *enforced*, 345 F.3d 1049, 173 LRRM 2257 (9th Cir. 2003).

[143]Ukiah Valley Med. Ctr., 332 NLRB 602, 165 LRRM 1258 (2000).

[144]*See* Mid Am. Health Servs., Inc., 247 NLRB 752, 103 LRRM 1234 (1980).

[145]St. Edmund's Roman Catholic Church, 337 NLRB 1260, 170 LRRM 1425 (2002).

custodial employees. The primary responsibility of the employees was the cleaning and maintenance of an elementary school located in the same building as the church and a detached high school operated by the church. In addition to their duties in the schools, the employees occasionally worked in the church, the church's rectory, and a church-affiliated convent.

29. Activities Intimately Connected to Operations of Exempt Employer—Both the Tenth and Eighth Circuits joined the Fourth and Sixth Circuits in upholding the Board's *Management Training Corp.*[146] standard. In *Aramark Corp. v. NLRB*,[147] the court affirmed the Board's exercise of jurisdiction over a contractor that was substantially controlled by an exempt governmental entity. The court expressly overruled a contrary line of precedent in finding that the control test is not a prerequisite to the Board's exercise of jurisdiction over a government contractor. Similarly, in *NLRB v. Young Women's Christian Ass'n*,[148] the court found that the Board properly asserted jurisdiction over a government contractor without determining whether the contractor could engage in meaningful collective bargaining.

C. Advisory Opinions and Declaratory Orders

Section 102.98 of the Board's Rules and Regulations provides that a state agency or court may file a petition with the Board for an advisory opinion on whether the Board would decline to assert jurisdiction over the parties before the agency or court.[149]

In *Townley Service, Inc.*,[150] two plaintiffs filed a wrongful termination suit against their former employer in state court, claiming that they were discharged in retaliation for attempting to unionize the workplace and for communicating with a union organizer. Presumably in response to the employer's argument that the suit was pre-

---

[146]317 NLRB 1355, 149 LRRM 1313 (1995).

[147]179 F.3d 872, 161 LRRM 2441 (10th Cir. 1999).

[148]192 F.3d 1111, 162 LRRM 2268 (8th Cir. 1999).

[149]The parties to pending state proceedings are no longer permitted to petition the Board for advisory opinions on whether the Board would assert jurisdiction under its commerce standards. *See* 61 Fed. Reg. 65,180 (Dec. 11, 1996).

[150]339 NLRB 301, 173 LRRM 1587 (2003).

empted by the Act, the court dismissed the suit without prejudice, allowing the plaintiffs to file a request for an advisory opinion with the Board. The Board denied the petition for an advisory opinion. The petition did not dispute the commerce data supplied by the employer, which confirmed that the employer met the Board's jurisdictional standard. Instead, the petition sought the Board's opinion on whether the parties' dispute was cognizable under the Act, and/or whether the court lacked jurisdiction under principles of NLRA preemption. The Board held that such questions are not properly addressed by the Board in an advisory opinion. The Board declined to reach the issue of whether, in light of the court's order, it was proper for the plaintiffs, rather than the court, to file the petition.

Chapter 28

FEDERAL PREEMPTION OF STATE REGULATION

II. Evolution of Preemption Doctrine

D. Federalism: Recognizing Important Matters of Particular Local Concern

The courts continue to hold that in enacting the NLRA, Congress did not intend to prevent states from establishing minimum employment standards.[1]

For example, under *San Diego Building Trades Council v. Garmon*,[2] the Act does not preempt a state law requiring payment of prevailing wages to employees in apprenticeship programs on public work projects.[3] The Ninth Circuit determined that the California law does not disrupt collective bargaining rights because it establishes minimum labor standards, and does not attempt to regulate conduct that is arguably protected or prohibited by the Act.[4] Nor does the Act preempt California's apprentice wage requirement as it applies to apprentices working on private projects.[5] On the other hand, a state labor department's refusal to process an employer group's apprenticeship program application was upheld where processing the application would have required the agency to make determinations that arguably fell within the Board's unfair labor practice jurisdiction.[6]

---

[1]*See* St. Thomas-St. John Hotel & Tourism Ass'n Inc. v. Virgin Islands, 218 F.3d 232, 164 LRRM 2705 (3d Cir. 2000) (statute that limits lawful bases for discharging employees to those enumerated in statute, or provided for in collective bargaining agreement, is not preempted by Act). But see St. Thomas-St. John Hotel & Tourism Ass'n, Inc. v. Virgin Islands, 357 F.3d 297, 174 LRRM 2312 (3d Cir. 2004) (holding that same statute is preempted as applied to supervisors).

[2]359 U.S. 236, 43 LRRM 2838 (1959).

[3]Dillingham Constr., Inc. v. County of Sonoma, 190 F.3d 1034, 162 LRRM 2193 (9th Cir. 1999).

[4]*Id.* at 1040.

[5]Associated Builders & Contractors v. Nunn, 356 F.3d 979, 174 LRRM 2001 (9th Cir. 2004).

[6]Building Trades Employers' Educ. Ass'n v. McGowan, 2001 U.S. Dist. LEXIS 8056, 169 LRRM 2439 (S.D.N.Y. 2001).

G. A Foundation: *Garmon* Preempts State Regulation of Conduct Arguably Protected or Prohibited by the Act

The courts continue to refine and apply the core principle that matters involving conduct arguably prohibited or protected by the Act are preempted under *San Diego Building Trades Council v. Garmon.*[7]

Executive Order 13,201, signed into law by President George W. Bush effective April 18, 2001, requires employers with federal contracts to post notices informing employees of their right not to join a union or pay certain union fees. The D.C. Circuit upheld the executive order against a preemption challenge on the basis that the posting requirements are neither arguably protected by Section 7 nor arguably prohibited or protected by Section 8.[8]

In contrast, the Tenth Circuit invalidated the so-called right-to-work provisions in the Oklahoma constitution making it a misdemeanor for an employer to require an individual to resign from or disassociate with a labor organization.[9] According to the court, the Act preempts this supplementary remedy to Section 8.[10]

A supervisor's claims of breach of contract and wrongful discharge in retaliation for his providing testimony unfavorable to the employer during a contractual grievance arbitration were held preempted under *Garmon.*[11] Because the evidence in the state court implicated Sections 7 and 8 of the Act and "would *not be distinctly* different" from that presented in an unfair labor practice proceeding, primary jurisdiction over the matter was vested exclusively in

---

[7]359 U.S. 236, 43 LRRM 2838 (1959).

[8]UAW-Labor Employment. & Training Corp. v. Chao, 325 F.3d 360, 172 LRRM 2287 (D.C. Cir. 2003), *cert. denied,* 124 S. Ct. 2014, 174 LRRM 2928 (2004) (reversing district court's ruling that executive order was preempted under *Garmon* because posting requirements conflicted with Act by imposing duty on employers that Act did not require). *See also* Trollinger v. Tyson Foods, Inc., 370 F.3d 602, 174 LRRM 3313 (6th Cir. 2004) (rejecting employer's contention that, under *Garmon,* Act preempts employees' RICO claim predicated on allegations that employer knowingly employed illegal immigrants to suppress employee wages); Baker v. IBP, Inc., 357 F.3d 685, 174 LRRM 2230 (7th Cir. 2004) (same).

[9]Transport Workers Union Local 514 v. Keating, 358 F.3d 743, 174 LRRM 2318 (10th Cir. 2004).

[10]*Id.*

[11]Ruscigno v. American Nat'l Can Co., 84 Cal. App. 4th 112, 166 LRRM 3002 (Cal. Ct. App. 2000).

the Board.[12] Similarly, the Maine Human Relations Act was held preempted where a female union member's gender discrimination claim presented the same allegations that would be presented in an unfair labor practice case; none of the exceptions to the *Garmon* preemption applied to the plaintiff's allegations that her union had improperly opposed a wage increase to her by the employer.[13]

The Ninth Circuit, however, held that state law claims of false arrest, false imprisonment, and malicious prosecution were not preempted by the Act even though the state court likely would have to determine whether the persons asserting the claims were engaged in "lawful union activity."[14] The state claims grew out of an inspection of a nonunion contractor's worksite by union officials who asserted they were looking for unsafe conditions or violations of prevailing wage obligations. The contractor caused the union officials to be arrested and charged under California's trespass law. Following their acquittal of the trespass offense, the union officials brought the state tort claims against the contractor, who then argued that the claims were preempted by the Act. Pointing out that California trespass law contains an exception for "persons engaged in lawful labor union activities which are permitted to be carried out on the property by the . . . National Labor Relations Act,"[15] the contractor argued that the validity of the false arrest, false imprisonment, and malicious prosecution claims depended on a finding that the union officials were engaged in activities on the property protected by Section 7 of the Act, a matter within the exclusive jurisdiction of the Board. Although conceding that the contractor's actions could form the basis of an unfair labor practice complaint before the Board, the court of appeals found that the issues in the Board proceeding would not be identical to the state tort claim issues.[16] In holding that preemption was inappropriate, the court also noted the state's "substantial interest in protecting its citizens from false arrest, false imprison-

---

[12]*Id.* at 128, 166 LRRM at 3011 (emphasis in original); *see also* McCormack v. Keohokalole, 170 LRRM 3155, 2002 Haw. LEXIS 515 (Haw. 2002) (state law claim by employee of union, who alleged his termination was in retaliation for filing unfair labor practice charges and testifying in Board proceeding, was preempted where allegations were presented to Board).

[13]Lemerich v. Operating Eng'rs, 2002 U.S. Dist. LEXIS 7102, 171 LRRM 2560 (D. Me. 2002).

[14]Radcliffe v. Rainbow Constr. Co., 254 F.3d 772, 167 LRRM 2525 (9th Cir.), *cert. denied*, 534 U.S. 1020, 168 LRRM 2800 (2001).

[15]*Id.*, 254 F.3d at 785, 167 LRRM at 2533.

[16]*Id.* at 786, 167 LRRM at 2534.

ment and malicious prosecution" and the Board's inability to award substantial compensatory or punitive damages to injured parties.[17]

Where an employer terminated an employee who had lied about his prior work history on his employment application to conceal that he was a union "salt," an Indiana statute that criminalizes such conduct was held preempted, as applied.[18]

H. *Briggs & Stratton* Overruled: States May Not Regulate Economic Weapons Furnished by Congress

The Ninth Circuit analyzed California's prevailing wage law of employees in apprenticeship programs under the *Machinists* doctrine,[19] which proscribes state regulation of activity intended by Congress to be unregulated.[20] "[B]ecause federal law unequivocally permits regulation of apprenticeship standards" and the California law established nothing more than minimum labor standards for apprentices, the court held *Machinists* preemption inapplicable.[21]

Efforts to criminalize the hiring of strike replacements run afoul of *Machinists'* protection of economic weapons of self-help left unregulated by the Act.[22] However, a state regulation is not automatically preempted simply because it has some impact on the ability of employers to hire strike replacements.[23] Consequently, regulations having no impact on the availability and/or use of economic weapons of self-help do not implicate *Machinists* preemption.[24]

---

[17] *Id.* at 786–87, 167 LRRM at 2534.

[18] Hartman Bros. Heating & Air Conditioning v. NLRB, 280 F.3d 1110, 169 LRRM 2385 (7th Cir. 2002).

[19] Machinists Lodge 76 v. Wisconsin Employment Relations Comm'n, 427 U.S. 132, 141, 92 LRRM 2881, 2887 88 (1976).

[20] Dillingham Constr. v. County of Sonoma, 190 F.3d 1034, 162 LRRM 2193 (9th Cir. 1999); *see also* Rondout Elec., Inc. v. New York State Dep't of Labor, 335 F.3d 162, 172 LRRM 3255 (2d Cir. 2003), *cert. denied*, 540 U.S. 1105, 173 LRRM 3120 (2004) (state's benefits annualization regulation, which implements prevailing wage rate on public works projects, is not preempted by *Machinists* doctrine).

[21] *Id.* at 1038–40, 162 LRRM at 2195 97.

[22] *See, e.g.*, Caterpillar, Inc. v. Lyons, 318 F. Supp. 2d 703, 174 LRRM 3200 (C.D. Ill. 2004) (Illinois statute's imposition of criminal penalties against employers who replace striking employees by knowingly hiring a professional strikebreaker or knowingly contracting with a temporary labor service agency is preempted by Act).

[23] *See, e.g.*, Southern Union Gas Co. v. Rhode Island Div. of Pub. Utils. & Carriers, 306 F. Supp. 2d 129, 174 LRRM 2601 (D.R.I. 2004) (denying cross-motions for summary judgment as to whether statute prescribing experience and accreditation standards impermissibly restricted employer's ability to hire strike replacements).

[24] *See, e.g.*, Alcantara v. Allied Props., LLC, 334 F. Supp. 2d 336, 345 (E.D.N.Y. 2004) (requiring purchasers of large buildings to retain the selling party's service

Courts continue to refine the distinction between permissible proprietary conduct under *Boston Harbor*[25] and regulatory conduct that is preempted under *Machinists*. One court explained:

> The law has traditionally recognized a distinction between . . . actions taken to serve the government's own needs rather than those of society as a whole . . . . [W]hen a state or municipality acts as a participant in the market and does so in a narrow and focused manner consistent with the behavior of other market participants, such action does not constitute regulation subject to preemption.[26]

The court also provided guidelines for determining when government action is sufficiently "narrow and focused" so as to rule out a regulatory purpose. First, the action should be compared to the conduct of similarly situated private parties to determine if the action advances "the entity's own interest in its efficient procurement of needed goods and services."[27] Second, the court must determine if the narrowness of the action overcomes the inference that the entity's "primary goal was to encourage a general policy rather than address a specific proprietary problem."[28] Recent arguments relying on the "proprietary" exception have been largely unsuccessful,[29] though not always.[30]

---

employees for at least 90 days "does not regulate economic self help activities" as prohibited by *Machinists*).

[25]Building & Constr. Trades Council (Metropolitan Dist.) v. Associated Builders & Contractors of Mass./R.I., 507 U.S. 218, 142 LRRM 2649 (1993).

[26]Cardinal Towing & Auto Repair, Inc. v. City of Bedford, 180 F.3d 686, 691 (5th Cir. 1999).

[27]*Id.* at 693.

[28]*Id.*

[29]*See,* e.g., Chamber of Commerce of U.S. v. Lockyer, 364 F.3d 1154, 174 LRRM 2876 (9th Cir. 2004) (rejecting contention that state statutes forbidding employers who receive state funds in excess of $10,000 from acting to "assist, promote or deter union organizing" are proprietary and holding that statutes are preempted); New England Health Care Employees Dist. 1199 v. Rowland, 221 F. Supp. 2d 297, 171 LRRM 2070 (D. Conn. 2002) (state was preempted from providing "extraordinary and unanticipated cost" subsidies to nursing homes under Medicaid program during strike because the subsidies constituted regulatory conduct unlike any proprietary conduct engaged in by private entities); Ohio State Bldg. & Constr. Trades Council v. Cuyahoga County Bd. of Comm'rs, 98 Ohio St. 3d 214, 781 N.E.2d 951 (Ohio 2002) (state statutes prohibiting project work agreements were regulatory and preempted under *Machinists*).

[30]*See, e.g.,* Building & Constr. Trades Dep't, AFL CIO v. Allbaugh, 295 F.3d 28, 170 LRRM 2449 (D.C. Cir. 2002), *cert. denied,* 537 U.S. 1171, 171 LRRM 2896 (2003) (upholding executive order providing that project labor agreements will not be preempted or required in federally funded construction contracts on ground that government is acting in a proprietary capacity).

Thus, the Third Circuit held that the Act does not preempt a city from conditioning a grant of tax increment financing (TIF) on the developer's acceptance of a labor neutrality agreement.[31] The city's conduct fell within the *Boston Harbor* exception because (1) it was "specifically tailored" to the city's proprietary interest in the transaction, and (2) the condition was limited to projects receiving TIF funds.[32]

III. *GARMON* PREEMPTION IN SPECIFIC SITUATIONS

B. Trespass

In *NLRB v. Calkins*,[33] the court rejected the employer's argument that the need for a uniform national body of law precludes Section 7 rights from being defined by individual state trespass laws. The court enforced the Board's determination that a supermarket committed an unfair labor practice by threatening to have, and by having, nonemployee union representatives arrested for handbilling and picketing in furtherance of a consumer boycott on a privately owned walkway and parking lot, because the union's actions constituted protected activity under Section 7, and California law did not give the employer the right to exclude union organizers from its property. In enforcing the Board's order, the court rejected the employer's argument that *Lechmere, Inc. v. NLRB*[34] created a federal law doctrine that nonemployee union organizers can, with certain limited exceptions, be excluded from an employer's private property, and that this federal doctrine preempts state trespass laws that are at variance with the federal doctrine.[35]

C. Violence, Threats of Violence, and Intimidation

A state law injunction barring picketing at the homes of company employees, including peaceful residential picketing, was not preempted by the Act, on the ground that "regulation of public safety, including preclusion of residential picketing is a matter of local con-

---

[31]Hotel Employees Local 57 v. Sage Hospitality Res., LLC, 390 F.3d 206, 175 LRRM 3328 (3d Cir. 2004).

[32]*Id.* at 216–18.

[33]187 F.3d 1080, 161 LRRM 3121 (9th Cir. 1999), *cert. denied*, 529 U.S. 1098, 164 LRRM 2256 (2000).

[34]502 U.S. 527, 139 LRRM 2225 (1992).

[35]*Calkins, supra* note 33, 187 F.3d at 1094–95, 161 LRRM at 3131–32.

cern," such that it could not be inferred that Congress deprived the state of the power to act.[36]

In *Terzi Productions, Inc. v. Theatrical Protective Union Local 1*,[37] the court found that the plaintiff's state law claim was not preempted under *Garmon*, where there was ample evidence of violence in the record for the jury to have properly found that violence or threats of violence against the plaintiff and neutral parties were a direct cause of the plaintiff's damaged business relations with its clients. Such conduct avoids preemption, because it "touches concerns deeply rooted in local feelings or responsibilities."[38] Conversely, where an employer's claims of tortious interference with contractual and business relations and expectancies lacked any allegations of violence or imminent threat to public order, the Board's motion to dismiss pursuant to *Garmon* was granted.[39]

D. Other Intentional Torts

1. *Defamation:* Linn v. Plant Guard Workers

The courts continue to hold that under *Linn*,[40] a state law defamation claim based on utterances made during an organizing campaign is preempted unless the complainant can plead and prove that the statements were made with "actual malice" and caused actual damages.[41]

---

[36]CF&I Steel, L.P. v. Steelworkers, 990 P.2d 1124, 164 LRRM 2604 (Colo. Ct. App. 1999), *aff'd*, 23 P.3d 1197, 167 LRRM 2370 (Colo. 2001), *appeal on remand*, 74 P.3d 513 (Colo. Ct. App. 2003) (injunction against union vacated because evidence did not show that union participated in, authorized, or ratified tortious conduct).

[37]2000 U.S. Dist. LEXIS 12601, 166 LRRM 2485 (S.D.N.Y. 2000).

[38]*Id.*, 166 LRRM at 2489. *Cf.* Intercity Maint. Co. v. Service Employees Local 254, 62 F. Supp. 2d 483, 162 LRRM 2099 (D.R.I. 1999), *aff'd in part, rev'd in part, and remanded on other grounds*, 241 F.3d 82, 166 LRRM 2656 (1st Cir.), *cert. denied*, 168 LRRM 2472 (2001) (employer's state law tortious interference claims held preempted under *Garmon*, notwithstanding allegations of union threats of violence, because alleged threats were unrelated to tortious interference claims).

[39]Labor Ready Mid-Atlantic, Inc. v. Tri-State Bldg. & Constr. Trades Council, 2001 WL 1358708, 168 LRRM 2642 (S.D.W. Va. 2001).

[40]Linn v. Plant Guard Workers Local 114, 383 U.S. 53, 61 LRRM 2345 (1966).

[41]*Intercity Maintenance Co.*, *supra* note 38 ("plaintiffs who endure even malicious libels during a labor dispute must present evidence of harm from defamation in order to recover, notwithstanding the law of states such as Rhode Island in which damages would otherwise be presumed"). *Accord* Duane Reade, Inc. v. Local 338, Retail, Wholesale, Dep't Store Union, 2004 N.Y. Misc. LEXIS 2567, 176 LRRM 2125 (Sup. Ct. N.Y. Cty. 2004) (because union's Web site did not contain "mali-

Of course, in addition to malice, the plaintiff must show there was a false statement of purported fact. Whether the allegedly defamatory statement asserted or implied a verifiable fact is determined under a totality of circumstances standard. Thus, during a bargaining dispute, statements by a union president to assembled members that the company president was "making money" and "hiding" the money in a holding company were found to be fiery rhetoric of a call to arms and unlikely to be regarded by the audience as provable assertions of objective fact.[42] And where the evidence showed the plaintiff had in fact crossed picket lines during a lawful sympathy strike so that use of the commonplace epithet "scab" was "literally and factually true," the claim was dismissed.[43]

The *Linn* standard does not apply where the defamation occurred outside the context of a labor dispute.[44]

Issuance of a complaint by the general counsel alleging that a pending state court defamation lawsuit is baseless and retaliatory[45] does not preempt the lawsuit while the unfair labor practice case is pending before the Board.[46] Thus, "the defamation suit cannot be enjoined as soon as the complaint issues, because no determination has yet been made, by the Board, on the baselessness issue."[47]

---

cious" statements, employer's defamation claim was preempted); Duane Reade, Inc. v. Local 338, Retail Wholesale Dep't Store Union, 2003 N.Y. Misc. LEXIS 1651, 174 LRRM 2144 (Sup. Ct. N.Y. Cty. 2003) (employer's defamation claim preempted where union president's accusation that employer had interfered with employees' right to cast free and uncoerced vote did not meet *Linn* standard); Fiori v. Truck Drivers Local 170, 130 F. Supp. 2d 150, 2001 U.S. Dist. LEXIS 4212 (D. Mass. 2001) (claim for libel arising out of internal union dispute not preempted where plaintiff alleged malice and lost wages), *later proceeding*, 354 F.3d 84, 173 LRRM 3057 (1st Cir. 2004) (affirming $150,000 jury verdict on libel claim); Shepard v. Courtoise, 115 F. Supp. 2d 1142 (E.D. Mo. 2000).

[42]Steam Press Holdings v. Hawaii Teamsters Local 996, 302 F.3d 998, 170 LRRM 2833 (9th Cir. 2002), *cert. denied*, 537 U.S. 1232, 171 LRRM 3216 (2003).

[43]Dunn v. Air Line Pilots Ass'n, 193 F.3d 1185, 162 LRRM 2577 (11th Cir. 1999), *cert. denied*, 530 U.S. 1204, 164 LRRM 2448 (2000).

[44]J&J Constr. Co. v. Bricklayers Local 1, 245 Mich. App. 722, 168 LRRM 2110 (Mich. Ct. App. 2001) (union official's alleged misrepresentations concerning quality of nonunion employer's work, made in testimony before city council, were not entitled to *Linn* privilege where they could not "properly be characterized as statements made in the course of a labor dispute"), *rev'd on other grounds*, 468 Mich. 722, 664 N.W.2d 728 (Mich. 2003), *cert. denied*, 540 U.S. 1142 (2004). *Cf.* Delaney v. Auto Workers Local 94, 675 N.W.2d 832, 174 LRRM 2661 (Iowa 2004) (*Linn* standard applies to defamation claims by former union members against union for derogatory statements made in its newsletter).

[45]Bill Johnson's Rest., Inc. v. NLRB, 461 U.S. 731, 113 LRRM 2647 (1983).

[46]Beverly Health & Rehab. Servs., 336 NLRB 332, 170 LRRM 1046 (2001).

[47]*Id.* at 333.

2. *Inflicting Emotional Distress:* Farmer v. Carpenters

The courts continue to apply the narrow exception to federal preemption of intentional infliction of emotional distress claims established in *Farmer v. Carpenters Local 25.*[48]

In *Simo v. UNITE,*[49] the Ninth Circuit ruled that threatening and intimidating visits by union officers to employees' residences could form the basis of a claim for intentional infliction of emotional distress, notwithstanding that such conduct could also constitute an unfair labor practice. At the homes of employees who had signed a decertification petition, the union allegedly engaged in screaming and name-calling, threatened employees with loss of their jobs and health insurance, and stated that undocumented aliens would be reported to immigration authorities. On the merits of the tort claims, however, the Ninth Circuit held that the conduct alleged was exactly the type described in *Farmer* as commonplace in labor disputes, and that therefore it failed to satisfy the elevated standard of outrageousness required to establish the tort of intentional infliction of emotional distress.[50]

3. *Fraud, Misrepresentation, and Other Intentional Torts [New Topic]*

Where an employer made material misrepresentations on which the union assertedly relied in negotiating a plant closing agreement, the union's state law fraud claim was subject to *Garmon* preemption. Because the claim was essentially that the employer did not bargain in good faith, it was subject to the Board's primary jurisdiction over unfair labor practices.[51] There was no *Garmon* preemption, however, of a state law claim that the employer had fraudulently induced former employees into accepting an early retirement package, because no bargaining obligation existed with respect to the employer's closure decision, and the employees' claim was solely that the employer committed fraud in a direct communication to them.[52] Where a physi-

---

[48]430 U.S. 290, 94 LRRM 2579 (1977). *See, e.g.*, EEOC v. Electrical Workers (IBEW) Local 998, 343 F. Supp. 2d 655, 176 LRRM 2008 (N.D. Ohio 2004); North Am. Roofing & Sheet Metal Co. v. Building & Constr. Trades Council, 164 LRRM 2367 (E.D. Pa. 2000).

[49]316 F.3d 974, 171 LRRM 2844 (9th Cir.), *cert. denied,* 540 U.S. 873, 173 LRRM 2416 (2003).

[50]*Id.* at 992.

[51]Lopresti v. Merson, 168 LRRM 2427 (S.D.N.Y. 2001).

[52]Voilas v. General Motors Corp., 170 F.3d 367, 160 LRRM 2641 (3d Cir. 1999). *See also* Alongi v. Ford Motor Co., 386 F.3d 716, 174 LRRM 3025 (6th Cir. 2004); Burklow v. Baskin-Robbins USA, Co., 274 F. Supp. 2d 899 (W.D. Ky.), *aff'd,* 2003 U.S. App. LEXIS 27928 (6th Cir. 2003) (employees' fraud claim based upon mis-

cian sued her former employer for wrongful discharge and its executives for tortious interference, her claims were not preempted because, as a supervisor, her conduct was not protected by the Act.[53]

An employer's third-party claim that a union had fraudulently misrepresented the scope of project labor agreements to induce their execution was not preempted under *Garmon*. Because the union was not the certified or recognized representative of the employees, its allegedly fraudulent conduct was not arguably governed by the Act.[54] In an unusual fact pattern, an employer's state law action against the union for making misrepresentations during collective bargaining and interfering with the company's third-party contractual relations was not preempted, where the entire negotiation was allegedly a sham to protect a competing business owned by the union.[55] The court reasoned that although such bad faith bargaining was clearly an unfair labor practice, the union's alleged conduct was sufficiently dissimilar from most labor disputes as to be merely a peripheral concern of the Act and was instead more akin to the type of business disputes traditionally regulated by state law.

Conversely, an employer's state law claims of tortious interference against the union were preempted under *Garmon* because the alleged threats of violence by the union were found unrelated to the employer's claims of tortious interference.[56] Applying the *Garmon* doctrine in the Railway Labor Act context, the Fifth Circuit held preempted a class action by displaced airline passengers who claimed that the pilots' union tortiously interfered with contract negotiations by engaging in an unlawful sick out.[57]

---

representation that plant would remain viable for duration of collective bargaining agreement not preempted under *Garmon*, because statements were made outside of negotiations to deter employees from seeking other employment).

[53]Smith v. CIGNA HealthPlan of Ariz., 52 P.3d 205, 170 LRRM 2884 (Ariz. Ct. App. 2002), *review denied*, 2003 Ariz. LEXIS 48 (Ariz. 2003).

[54]Northwestern Ohio Adm'rs Inc. v. Walcher & Fox, Inc., 270 F.3d 1018, 168 LRRM 2843 (6th Cir. 2001), *cert. denied*, 535 U.S. 1017, 169 LRRM 3088 (2002); *see also* Capozza Tile Co. v. Joy, 223 F. Supp. 2d 307, 170 LRRM 2202 (D. Me. 2002) (absent statutory duty to bargain with union, employer's misrepresentation claim was not preempted).

[55]Galveston Linehandlers, Inc. v. Longshoremen (ILA) Local 20, 140 F. Supp. 2d 741, 167 LRRM 2231 (S.D. Tex. 2001).

[56]Intercity Maint. Co. v. Service Employees Local 254, 62 F. Supp. 2d 483, 162 LRRM 2099 (D.R.I. 1999), *aff'd in part, rev'd in part, and remanded on other grounds*, 241 F.3d 82, 166 LRRM 2656 (1st Cir.), *cert. denied*, 534 U.S. 818, 168 LRRM 2472 (2001).

[57]Kaufman v. Allied Pilots Ass'n, 274 F.3d 197, 168 LRRM 2838 (5th Cir. 2001), *cert. denied*, 535 U.S. 1034, 169 LRRM 3152 (2002).

In an unusual case, the Ninth Circuit ruled that union representatives' claims against an employer for false arrest, false imprisonment, and malicious prosecution following their alleged trespass on company property to investigate prevailing wage and safety law violations by the company were not subject to *Garmon* preemption even though the company's effort to remove the representatives was arguably subject to the Board's jurisdiction. The court found the lack of complete identity between the unfair labor practice and state law claims and the state's substantial interests in defining property rights and in protecting its citizens from such torts outweighed the potential for interference with the federal scheme.[58]

E. Internal Union Matters

In *Mitchell-Carr v. McLendon*,[59] the New Mexico Supreme Court held that, because Section 8(a)(3) arguably protected the union's causing the discharge of employees for nonpayment of dues, their state law claim was preempted by *Garmon*. On the other hand, a prima facie tort claim was held not to be preempted where the employees' removal from union office and suspension from membership was not an unfair labor practice under Section 8; rather, the allegation was found to concern internal union matters governed by the Labor-Management Reporting and Disclosure Act,[60] which expressly provides that state law claims are not preempted.[61]

IV. Preemption Under Section 301

B. The Preemptive Effect of Section 301

Federal and state courts continue to rule that Section 301[62] preempts a variety of state law claims. The five Supreme Court decisions

---

[58]Radcliffe v. Rainbow Constr. Co., 254 F.3d 772, 167 LRRM 2525 (9th Cir.), *cert. denied*, 534 U.S. 1020, 168 LRRM 2800 (2001). *See also* Russell v. Kinney Contractors, Inc., 342 Ill. App. 3d 666, 795 N.E.2d 340 (Ill. App. Ct.), *appeal denied*, 206 Ill. 644, 806 N.E.2d 1073 (2003) (false imprisonment claim not preempted), *appeal denied*, 342 Ill. App. 3d 666, 795 N.E.2d 340 (Ill. App. Ct. 2003)

[59]980 P.2d 65, 161 LRRM 2479 (N.M. 1999).

[60]29 U.S.C. §§401–531

[61]*Mitchell-Carr*, *supra* note 59, 980 P.2d at 74–75, 161 LRRM at 2486–87, citing 29 U.S.C. §413. *See also* Casumpang v. Longshoremen (ILU) Local 142, 13 P.3d 1235, 168 LRRM 3073 (Haw. 2000) (former union officer's state law claim for unpaid vacation not preempted under LMRDA).

[62]29 U.S.C. §185.

issued in the 1985 to 1990 period[63] and the Court's 1994 *Lividas v. Bradshaw*[64] decision, which are discussed in the Main Edition, remain the governing law in shaping judicial resolution of Section 301 preemption issues.

In general, Section 301 is preemptive if the claim is "founded directly on rights created by collective bargaining agreements,"[65] if resolution of the claim is "substantially dependent on analysis of [a collective bargaining agreement],"[66] or if it is "inextricably intertwined" with the terms of the labor agreement.[67] But when the meaning of contract terms is not in dispute, the mere fact that a collective bargaining agreement will be consulted in the course of state law litigation does not invoke the doctrine of federal preemption.[68] Moreover, that the state law analysis involves attention to the same factual considerations as a determination under the labor agreement does not mandate preemption so long as the state law claim can be resolved without interpreting the agreement itself.[69]

These principles have been applied in cases involving state law claims for breach of contract,[70] breach of a covenant of fair deal-

---

[63]Allis Chalmers Corp. v. Lueck, 471 U.S. 202, 118 LRRM 3345 (1985); Caterpillar Inc. v. Williams, 482 U.S. 386, 125 LRRM 2521 (1987); Electrical Workers (IBEW) v. Hechler, 481 U.S. 851, 125 LRRM 2353 (1987); Lingle v. Magic Chef, Norge Div., 486 U.S. 399, 128 LRRM 2521 (1988); Steelworkers v. Rawson, 495 U.S. 362, 134 LRRM 2153 (1990).

[64]512 U.S. 107, 146 LRRM 2513 (1994).

[65]*Lingle, supra* note 63, 486 U.S. at 410, 128 LRRM at 2525 n.10, quoting *Caterpillar Inc., supra* note 63, 482 U.S. at 394, 125 LRRM at 2524.

[66]*Id.*, quoting *Hechler, supra* note 63, 481 U.S. at 859, 125 LRRM at 2356 n.3.

[67]*Allis-Chalmers, supra* note 63, 471 U.S. at 213, 118 LRRM at 3350.

[68]*Lividas, supra* note 64, 512 U.S. at 123–26, 146 LRRM at 2520.

[69]*Lingle, supra* note 63, 416 U.S. at 409–10, 128 LRRM at 2525.

[70]Bartholomew v. AGL Res., Inc., 361 F.3d 1333, 174 LRRM 2545 (11th Cir. 2004) (§301 preempted employees' state law breach of contract claim because it was premised upon collective bargaining agreement); Steinbach v. Dillon Cos., 253 F.3d 538, 167 LRRM 2538 (10th Cir. 2001) (labor agreement was only contract on which interference claim could be based); Garley v. Sandia Corp., 236 F.3d 1200, 17 IER Cases 224 (10th Cir. 2001) (claims for breach of implied contract preempted because policies cited by employee were intended to be read in harmony with collective bargaining agreement); Aguilera v. Pirelli Armstrong Tire Corp., 223 F.3d 1010, 165 LRRM 2203 (9th Cir. 2000) (§301 preempted state law claims of breach of individual contracts made by permanent strike replacements who asserted employer promise, on hiring, that they would not be replaced by returning strikers); Robinson v. Fred Meyers Stores, Inc., 184 F. Supp. 2d 968, 170 LRRM 2310 (D. Ariz. 2002); Birch v. Pepsi Bottling Group, Inc., 207 F. Supp. 2d 376, 170 LRRM 2004 (D. Md. 2002) (claims for breach of implied contract to provide safe workplace and of oral contract preempted by §301 because collective bargaining agreement created employment relationship and was sole employment contract); Sokos v. Hilton Hotels Corp., 283 F. Supp. 2d 42, 173 LRRM 2712 (D.D.C.

ing,[71] tortious interference with contract,[72] fraud and misrepresentation,[73] defamation,[74] civil conspiracy,[75] invasion of privacy,[76] mechan-

---

2003) (former employee's wrongful discharge claim based on employment handbook required interpretation of collective bargaining agreement). *But see* Alexander v. UDV N. Am., Inc., 78 F. Supp. 2d 614, 163 LRRM 2606 (E.D. Mich. 1999) (claim for breach of predecessor employer's promise of continued employment to individual employees who were subsequently laid off under terms of labor agreement negotiated by successor was not preempted).

[71] *Garley, supra* note 70; *Robinson, supra* note 70; Ortiz v. Prudential Ins. Co., 94 F. Supp. 2d 225, 164 LRRM 2400 (D. Conn. 2000).

[72] *Bartholomew, supra* note 70 (§301 preempted employees' state law tortious interference with business relations claims to extent they were based upon statements made prior to employees' termination or during grievance process because determination of whether defendants' alleged statements were "improper" and "without privilege" required consideration of collective bargaining agreement); Mine Workers v. Rag Am. Coal Co., 392 F.3d 1233, 176 LRRM 2325 (10th Cir. 2004) ("[t]here is no doubt here that resolution of the [] tortious interference claim requires interpretation or application of the CBA"); Mattis v. Massman, 355 F.3d 902, 173 LRRM 2997 (6th Cir. 2004) (question of whether supervisor "interfered" with employee's business relationship required delving into rights and responsibilities of plant supervisors under collective bargaining agreement); Sprewell v. Golden State Warriors, 266 F.3d 979, 168 LRRM 2225 (9th Cir. 2001) (claims for intentional interference with contract and business relations not preempted to extent they are based on alleged violations of California law and not violations of the collective bargaining agreement); Kimbro v. Pepsico, Inc., 215 F.3d 723, 164 LRRM 2449 (7th Cir. 2000); *Sokos, supra* note 70, 283 F. Supp. 2d 42, 173 LRRM 2712 (D.D.C. 2003) (former employee's tortious interference with contractual relations claim required interpretation of collective bargaining agreement); Beidleman v. Stroh Brewery Co., 182 F.3d 225, 161 LRRM 2656 (3d Cir. 1999).

[73] Felix v. Lucent Techs., Inc., 387 F.3d 1146, 175 LRRM 3146 (10th Cir. 2004) (state law claim that employer fraudulently induced employees to accept early retirement benefits package by making misrepresentations was not preempted by §301); Wynn v. AC Rochester, 273 F.3d 153, 168 LRRM 2853 (2d Cir. 2001) (state law claim of fraudulent misrepresentation regarding what benefits were available under labor contract not preempted); Northwestern Ohio Admin'rs Inc. v. Walcher & Fox, Inc., 270 F.3d 1018, 168 LRRM 2843 (6th Cir. 2001) (third-party claim of fraudulent inducement not preempted by §301); *Aguilera, supra* note 70; Voilas v. General Motors Corp., 170 F.3d 367, 160 LRRM 2641 (3d Cir. 1999); *Beidleman, supra* note 72.

[74] Fitzgerald v. Roadway Express, Inc., 262 F. Supp. 2d 849 (W.D. Ohio 2003) (employee's claim for defamation preempted because determination whether statements were privileged required interpreting parties' collective bargaining agreement); *Garley, supra* note 70; Caci v. Laborers Int'l Union, 2000 U.S. Dist. LEXIS 4876, 166 LRRM 2232 (W.D.N.Y. 2000) (local union officer's defamation claims preempted where assessing veracity of statements by general executive board's attorney charging organized crime influence could not be assessed without interpreting international union's constitution); Carpenter v. Communications Workers, 163 LRRM 3023 (N.D. Ga. 2000).

[75] *Garley, supra* note 70.

[76] Kline v. Security Guards, Inc., 386 F.3d 246, 174 LRRM 3038 (3d Cir. 2004) (invasion of privacy claim against employer for installing surveillance cameras that

ics' liens,[77] intentional infliction of emotional distress,[78] tortious drug testing,[79] retaliation under state workers' compensation and other

---

monitored work area and hallways not completely preempted by §301 because employer's duties were independent of collective bargaining agreement); Cramer v. Consolidated Freightways, Inc., 255 F.3d 683, 167 LRRM 2353 (9th Cir. 2001) (en banc) (claim for invasion of privacy based on surreptitious videotaping by employer of employee restrooms through two-way mirrors not preempted because labor contract did not purport to allow such conduct and in any event employer's use of mirrors was per se unlawful under California penal law), *vacating* 209 F.3d 1122, 164 LRRM 2129 (9th Cir. 2000); Robinson v. Fred Meyers Stores, Inc., 184 F. Supp. 2d 968, 170 LRRM 2310 (D. Ariz. 2002) (claim based on requirement to give urine sample and lengthy interview covering inappropriate topics preempted because interpretation of collective bargaining agreement was fundamental to determination).

[77]*In re* Bentz Metal Prods. Co., 253 F.3d 283, 167 LRRM 2344 (7th Cir. 2001) (en banc) (state law mechanic's lien not preempted by §301); Swift Elec. Supply Co. v. Township of Lakewood, 168 LRRM 2826, 2832 (D.N.J. 2001) (no preemption because collective bargaining agreement was only "tangentially involved" in claim under New Jersey mechanic's lien law).

[78]Bartholomew v. AGL Res., Inc., 361 F.3d 1333, 174 LRRM 2545 (11th Cir. 2004) (§301 preempted employees' state law intentional infliction of emotional distress claim because determination as to whether defendants' conduct was "extreme and outrageous" required consideration of labor contract); Harless v. CSX Hotels, Inc., 389 F.3d 444, 174 LRRM 3338 (4th Cir. 2004) (§301 did not preempt intentional infliction of emotional distress claims that allege distress caused by discriminatory conduct that could not be condoned by a collective bargaining agreement); Mattis v. Massman, 355 F.3d 902, 173 LRRM 2997 (6th Cir. 2004) (determining whether alleged harassment constituted "outrageous conduct" would require review of collective bargaining agreement); *Fitzgerald, supra* note 74 (employee's claim for intentional infliction of emotional distress was preempted because determination whether statements were outrageous required interpreting parties' collective bargaining agreement); Foy v. Giant Food, Inc., 298 F.3d 284, 170 LRRM 2655 (4th Cir. 2002) (preempted because determination of whether employer's actions in dealing with and terminating employee were outrageous required interpretation of collective bargaining agreement); Steinbach v. Dillon Cos., 253 F.3d 538, 167 LRRM 2538 (10th Cir. 2001) (emotional distress claim that supervisor abused plaintiff by cutting short her vacation and charging her with unwarranted absence required interpretation of labor contract); Garley v. Sandia Corp., 236 F.3d 1200, 17 IER Cases 224 (10th Cir. 2001) (preempted with respect to employee's discharge but not with respect to those emotional distress claims arising from retaliatory actions allegedly taken after arbitrator's ruling); *Robinson, supra* note 76; Ortiz v. Prudential Ins. Co., 94 F. Supp. 2d 225, 164 LRRM 2400 (D. Conn. 2000).

[79]Karnes v. Boeing Co., 335 F.3d 1189, 20 IER Cases 305 (10th Cir. 2003) (employee's claim for violation of state's drug testing law was independent of collective bargaining agreement); *Robinson, supra* note 76 (under *Cramer* standard, claim that employer's drug policy failed to comply with state law held preempted); Hanson v. DrugScan, Inc., 95 F. Supp. 2d 868, 165 LRRM 2317 (N.D. Ill. 2000) (no preemption under §301 of employee's claim that negligent drug testing caused misidentification of drug sample).

laws,[80] violation of state wage and hour laws,[81] and attorneys' fees.[82] Employment discrimination claims meet with mixed results depending on their connection to a collective bargaining agreement.[83]

---

[80]Harper v. AutoAlliance Int'l, Inc., 392 F.3d 195, 176 LRRM 2266 (6th Cir. 2004) (employee's retaliation claim was not preempted notwithstanding that labor agreement governed employee's discharge for alleged theft and his grievance rights); Sullivan v. Raytheon Co., 262 F.3d 41, 168 LRRM 2129 (1st Cir. 2001), *cert. denied*, 534 U.S. 1118, 169 LRRM 2256 (2002) (retaliation claim under Massachusetts law preempted because it required interpretation of collective bargaining agreement); Trevino v. Levi Strauss & Co., 197 F.3d 777, 163 LRRM 2096 (5th Cir. 1999), *cert. denied*, 531 U.S. 1036, 165 LRRM 2992 (2000) (retaliation claim under Texas workers' compensation law not preempted because it involved only factual issues concerning employee's conduct and employer's motivation); Naples v. New Jersey Sports & Exposition Auth., 102 F. Supp. 2d 550, 165 LRRM 2476 (D.N.J. 2000) (no preemption of state law claims of disability discrimination and retaliation for filing workers' compensation claim). *But see* Audette v. Longshoremen Local 24, 195 F.3d 1107, 162 LRRM 2705 (9th Cir. 1999) (employees' claim of gender discrimination and retaliation were preempted where premised on alleged breach of settlement agreement by employer association and union).

[81]Vera v. Saks & Co., 335 F.3d 109, 172 LRRM 3050 (2d Cir. 2003) (claim that retail employer's purchase returns policy and its actions thereunder violated wage deduction provisions of New York state law was preempted because claim necessarily required substantial analysis of labor agreement); Firestone v. Southern Cal. Gas Co., 219 F.3d 1063, 164 LRRM 2897 (9th Cir. 2000) (distinguishing *Lividas*, court held claim for overtime compensation under California wage payment law was preempted by §301 because resolution of statutory claim hinged on interpretation of disputed contractual provision); Balcorta v. Twentieth Century-Fox Film Corp., 208 F.3d 1102, 164 LRRM 2071 (9th Cir. 2000) (claim under California wage payment law for waiting time penalties not preempted where all that was required to determine whether employer had violated state law was "a clock or a calculator," not interpretation of labor agreement); Harrison v. Superior Carpet Installers, Inc., 2002 U.S. Dist. LEXIS 2844, 171 LRRM 2425 (S.D. Ind. 2002) (state-law wage claim preempted); Arnold v. Cabot Corp., 165 LRRM 2179 (N.D.W. Va. 2000) (claim under state's wage act held preempted because threshold issue of whether employee was entitled to pay could be resolved only by interpretation of parties' labor agreement and practices).

[82]Slurry Seal v. Laborers Local 1184, 241 F.3d 1142, 166 LRRM 2662 (9th Cir. 2001) (where agreement permitted union to recover attorneys' fees in certain disputes, prevailing nonunion subcontractor's attempted application of California statute making reciprocal an otherwise unilateral contract provision for attorneys' fees was preempted).

[83]Fant v. New England Power Serv. Co., 239 F.3d 8, 166 LRRM 2129 (1st Cir. 2001) (state-law disability discrimination claim preempted); Frazier v. Ford Motor Co., 2001 U.S. Dist. LEXIS 18253, 168 LRRM 2516 (W.D. Ky. 2001) (§301 preempts race bias claim of black employee that union did not pursue grievance, as essence of claim involves violation by union of duty to represent employees fairly); Moreno v. STP Nuclear Operating Co., 172 F. Supp. 2d 857, 168 LRRM 2795 (S.D. Tex. 2001) (employee's claim that he was not promoted to temporary supervisor because of his Mexican ancestry preempted, as promotion procedure was set forth in agreement). *But see* Humble v. Boeing Co., 305 F.3d 1004, 170 LRRM 3025 (9th

Although a claim that an employer discriminatorily denied an employee his or her seniority rights would normally be preempted under Section 301, in *Lydon v. Boston Sand & Gravel Co.*[84] the court held that where the parties had previously agreed before an arbitrator that the collective bargaining agreement did not address the issue and that state law provided the employee's exclusive remedy, the employer was estopped from later interposing a federal preemption defense.

In *Voilas v. General Motors Corp.*,[85] the Third Circuit found no Section 301 preemption where employees alleged that the company had fraudulently induced them to accept an early retirement severance package by representing to them that the plant was scheduled for closure. The court rejected the employer's contention that resolution of the issue required interpretation of the collectively bargained severance pay plan, noting that the employees were not claiming that the employer misrepresented the plan. Instead, they were claiming that the employer had lied to them about the plant closing to induce them to end their employment and take the severance plan. Accordingly, because the fraud claim was not based on the collective bargaining agreement or the terms of the severance pay plan—nor would its resolution require an interpretation of those agreements—the claim was not preempted under Section 301.[86]

In *Northwestern Ohio Administrators, Inc. v. Walcher & Fox, Inc.*,[87] the Sixth Circuit applied similar reasoning to a third-party claim by an employer against a union for fraudulent misrepresentation; it held that claims that the union fraudulently induced the employer to sign certain project agreements did not require a resort to the terms of the agreements, but rather should focus upon the representations made by the union to the employer.

Cir. 2002) (disability claim under Washington's Law Against Discrimination not preempted because interpretation of collective bargaining agreement was only potential and limited); Bredesen v. Detroit Fed'n of Musicians Local 5, 165 F. Supp. 2d 647, 168 LRRM 2530 (E.D. Mich. 2001) (§301 did not preempt female opera house employee's sex discrimination claim based on union's negotiation of pay scale that was half what male employees were paid); LaResca v. AT&T, 161 F. Supp. 2d 323 (D.N.J. 2001) (disability accommodation claim was not preempted because it required only reference to agreement, not interpretation).

[84]175 F.3d 6, 160 LRRM 2981 (1st Cir. 1999).

[85]170 F.3d 367, 160 LRRM 2641 (3d Cir. 1999).

[86]The *Garmon* preemption argument made by the employer is addressed in Section III.D.3. [*Garmon* Preemption in Specific Situations; Other Intentional Torts; Fraud, Misrepresentation, and Other Intentional Torts].

[87]270 F.3d 1018, 168 LRRM 2843 (6th Cir. 2001).

Suits for defamation under state law have received mixed results. In *Graham v. Contract Transportation, Inc.*,[88] the Eighth Circuit held that a defamation claim was not preempted under Section 301, where an employee, who was required to take a random drug test by his employer, tested positive, was fired, and later learned that the drug test had not been conducted in accordance with regulations of the federal Department of Transportation. The employer made allegedly defamatory statements about the employee to prospective employers and the agency that processed the employee's unemployment benefits application. Rejecting the employer's preemption argument, the court held that the case turned solely on the factual question of whether the employer lied to others about the employee's use of drugs, a matter that required no analysis of the meaning of the labor contract.

In cases where the defamatory statement was more thoroughly intertwined with the employer's actions taken under the contract, however, courts have found defamation claims to be preempted. For example, in *Garley v. Sandia Corp.*,[89] the Tenth Circuit concluded that an employee's defamation claim alleging that his termination for time-card fraud "publicly branded him as dishonest" would require a determination of whether or not the employer had acted properly under the collective bargaining agreement. Such a defamation claim is therefore preempted. Similarly, in *Reynolds v. Ferguson*,[90] a school counselor's defamation claim was held preempted by Section 301 where the alleged defamatory statements were made in a memorandum prepared by the employer regarding his termination. Because the memorandum was intertwined with the termination provisions of the labor contract, the plaintiff could not demonstrate that the memorandum was an unprivileged communication to a third party without resort to an analysis of the contract.

In *Panayi v. Northern Indiana Public Service Co.*,[91] Section 301 preemption was found in an employee's invasion-of-privacy suit where his employer had obtained records from a third-party Internet pro-

[88]220 F.3d 910, 164 LRRM 3096 (8th Cir. 2000). *See also* Phillips v. Selig, 157 F. Supp. 2d 419, 167 LRRM 2182 (E.D. Pa. 2001) (assessment of disparaging statements forming basis of defamation claim did not require contract interpretation).

[89]236 F.3d 1200 (10th Cir. 2001).

[90]73 F. Supp. 2d 841, 163 LRRM 2813 (W.D. Mich. 1999). *See also* Jones v. Auto Workers, 2002 U.S. Dist. LEXIS 12553, 170 LRRM 3147 (E.D. Mich. 2002) (determination of whether defendant had privilege to publish statement turned on interpretation of collective bargaining agreement).

[91]109 F. Supp. 2d 1012, 165 LRRM 2125 (N.D. Ind. 2000).

vider of all activity on the employee's account arising from a company telephone number in his work area. The employer obtained those records in the course of an investigation that led to the employee's termination. The court ruled that resolution of the privacy claim depended on whether the management-rights clause of the contract permitted the employer to enforce rules against accessing the Internet through company telephone lines and its right to obtain pertinent records reflecting such use. The determination of whether a person in the plaintiff's position would have any reasonable expectation of privacy thus depended on construing the labor contract and the rules promulgated under it.

Section 301(b),[92] which immunizes union officials from individual liability for actions taken on behalf of their union in the collective bargaining process,[93] preempts legal malpractice claims against counsel who perform services in the collective bargaining process in lieu of union officials.[94]

C. Relationship to NLRB

1. *Introduction: Exclusive Jurisdiction of Board Versus Concurrent Jurisdiction*

The courts continue to apply the principle, enunciated in *Smith v. Evening News*,[95] that courts and the Board share concurrent jurisdiction over suits involving conduct that may involve both a contract violation under Section 301 and an unfair labor practice or representation question falling within the Board's exclusive jurisdiction.[96]

---

[92]29 U.S.C. §185(b).

[93]Atkinson v. Sinclair Ref. Co., 370 U.S. 238, 50 LRRM 2433 (1960).

[94]Carino v. Stefan, 376 F.3d 156, 175 LRRM 2257 (3d Cir. 2004); Waterman v. Transport Workers Local 100, 176 F.3d 150 (2d Cir. 1999); Arnold v. Air Midwest, Inc., 100 F.3d 857, 153 LRRM 2809 (10th Cir. 1996); Breda v. Scott, 1 F.3d 908, 143 LRRM 3011 (9th Cir. 1993).

[95]371 U.S. 195, 51 LRRM 2646 (1962).

[96]*See, e.g.*, New York Health & Human Servs. Union v. NYU Hosp. Ctr., 343 F.3d 117, 173 LRRM 2211 (2d Cir. 2003) (court compelled arbitration of employer's alleged violations of parties' agreement regarding conduct during organizing campaign, even though dispute implicated representation issues, Board had supervised election, and agreement provided that postelection procedures would be governed by Board's Rules and Regulations); Service Employees v. St. Vincent Med. Ctr., 344 F.3d 977, 173 LRRM 2289 (9th Cir. 2003) (doctrine of primary jurisdiction does not prevent court from compelling arbitration of alleged violations of an agreement governing parties' conduct during an organizing drive, notwithstanding "representational overtones" of dispute and involvement of Board in conducting election); Paper, Allied Indus., Chem. & Energy Workers, Local 5-0550 v. Air

In *Brown v. Sandimo Materials, Inc.*,[97] the Second Circuit held that a district court has jurisdiction under Section 301 to resolve a bargaining-unit dispute when that issue is "related to a contract interpretation question." In reaching this conclusion, the court rejected the Ninth Circuit's view, stated in *Journeymen Local 343 v. Nor-Cal Plumbing*,[98] that appropriate bargaining-unit determinations are within the Board's exclusive jurisdiction. The court instead adopted the Fifth Circuit's approach in *Carpenters Local 1846 v. Pratt-Farnsworth, Inc.*,[99] which held that where "no application had been made to the NLRB on the issue, and where the determination of the single bargaining unit issue was central to a question of contract interpretation, the bargaining unit issue was appropriate for resolution by the district court."[100]

The courts continue to apply the Supreme Court's holding in *Textron Lycoming Reciprocating Engine Division v. Auto Workers*[101] that Section 301 does not bestow subject-matter jurisdiction over direct

---

Prods. & Chems., Inc., 300 F.3d 667, 170 LRRM 2779 (6th Cir. 2002) (court has jurisdiction to enforce arbitration clause where dispute primarily involves matter of contract interpretation, even though dispute potentially implicates representation issue); Sheet Metal Workers v. Lozier Corp., 255 F.3d 549, 167 LRRM 2700 (8th Cir. 2001) (notwithstanding union's earlier pursuit of unfair labor practice charge before Board, district court had jurisdiction over union's action to enforce arbitration provisions of collective bargaining agreement because dispute involved contractual interpretation rather than representational question); Pace v. Honolulu Disposal Serv., Inc., 227 F.3d 1150, 165 LRRM 2385 (9th Cir. 2000) (dispute over whether certain employees were covered by labor agreement was "primarily contractual" and therefore properly before district court and not Board); Mulvihill v. Spaulding Sports Worldwide, Inc., 184 F. Supp. 2d 99, 169 LRRM 2505 (D. Mass. 2002) (court has jurisdiction under §301 even though plaintiff alleged "wrongful discharge and breach of employment contract, thereby committing an unfair labor practice" because legitimate breach of contract claim had been asserted). *But see* Cable Car Advertisers, Inc. v. Teamsters Local 856, 168 LRRM 2945 (N.D. Cal. 2001) (court lacked jurisdiction under §301 where termination of contract was undisputed, and without any contract to interpret court must defer resolution of representation questions to the Board's primary jurisdiction).

[97]250 F.3d 120, 129, 167 LRRM 2176, 2182 (2d Cir. 2001).

[98]48 F.3d 1465, 155 LRRM 2282 (9th Cir. 1994).

[99]690 F.2d 489, 111 LRRM 2787, *amended*, 112 LRRM 2525 (5th Cir. 1982), *cert. denied*, 464 U.S. 932, 114 LRRM 2976 (1983). See Main Edition, Chapter 28, "Federal Preemption of State Regulation," Section IV.C.2. [Preemption Under Section 301; Relationship to NLRB; Jurisdiction in Representation Matters], at page 2245.

[100]*Brown v. Sandimo*, *supra* note 97, 250 F.3d at 129.

[101]523 U.S. 653, 158 LRRM 2193 (1998).

claims of contract invalidity.[102] Thus, the Tenth Circuit dismissed a union's declaratory judgment action, where the union asserted that the parties' collective bargaining agreement was invalid to the extent its terms ran afoul of the Fair Labor Standards Act.[103] Jurisdiction did not lie under Section 301 because the union's lawsuit alleged the invalidity—but not the employer's violation—of the collective bargaining agreement. Similarly, in *Hanley v. Lobster Box Restaurant, Inc.*,[104] the court lacked Section 301 jurisdiction over the employer's third-party action, which sought invalidation of the labor agreement based on the union's alleged fraud during negotiations. The court explained that the employer could not use the underlying action by trustees of employee benefit funds for the collection of unpaid contributions to "bootstrap" its claim of contract invalidity against the union. Conversely, in *Bulkmatic Transport Co. v. Teamsters Local 407*,[105] the court held that an employer may invoke the court's jurisdiction under Section 301 to obtain a declaration that its conduct *does not* violate its collective bargaining agreement, even though, by definition, no violation of the contract had been alleged.

In an action to enforce an arbitration subpoena against a nonsignatory to the underlying collective bargaining agreement, a distinction was drawn between Section 301 jurisdiction and federal question jurisdiction that is premised on federal common law created pursuant to Section 301.[106] Characterizing the grant of jurisdiction by Section 301 as "extremely limited," the Seventh Circuit held Section 301 could not directly provide subject-matter jurisdiction because nonparties are incapable of violating a collective bargaining agreement.[107] Nonetheless, because Section 301 "authorizes federal courts to fashion a body of common law,"[108] and enforcement of the subpoenas against the nonparties was necessary to enforcement of the agreement to arbitrate, federal question jurisdiction existed pursuant to 28 U.S.C. §1331.

---

[102]Burklow v. Baskin-Robbins USA, Co., 274 F. Supp. 2d 899 (W.D. Ky. 2003) (court lacked §301 jurisdiction over breach of contract claim where its adjudication would require court to determine validity of superseding plant closing agreement).

[103]Food & Commercial Workers Local 1564 v. Albertson's, Inc., 207 F.3d 1193, 163 LRRM 2903 (10th Cir. 2000).

[104]35 F. Supp. 2d 366, 161 LRRM 2049 (S.D.N.Y. 1999).

[105]213 F. Supp. 2d 946, 171 LRRM 2041 (N.D. Ind. 2002).

[106]Teamsters Nat'l Auto. Transporters Indus. Negotiating Comm. v. Troha, 328 F.3d 325, 172 LRRM 2326 (7th Cir. 2003).

[107]*Id.* at 329.

[108]*Id.* at 330 (citing Textile Workers v. Lincoln Mills, 353 U.S. 448, 40 LRRM 2113 (1957)).

D. Relationship to the Norris-LaGuardia Act

Courts continue to respect the narrowness of the *Boys Market* exception to the Norris-LaGuardia Act's limitations on issuing injunctions in labor disputes.[109] The Sixth Circuit, in *Allied Systems Ltd. v. Teamsters Local 327*,[110] found that the district court properly denied the employer's request for a preliminary injunction to enjoin the union from striking in response to the employer's decision that one facility's wage rate would govern when two facilities merged. The court limited its holding to a finding that the employer had not demonstrated that its interpretation of the agreement was "so clearly and indisputably correct" to warrant the issuance of a *Boys Market* injunction.[111]

Joining other circuit courts,[112] the Seventh Circuit held that the Norris-LaGuardia Act precludes injunctive relief prohibiting the arbitration of a labor dispute.[113] The court rejected the employer's argument that a dispute over arbitrability is not a "labor dispute" within the meaning of Norris-LaGuardia, and found that the district court properly denied the employer's request to enjoin the arbitration of a dispute concerning its alleged failure to bargain in good faith with the union.[114]

Courts have continued to interpret what it means to safeguard the arbitration process through the grant of a "reverse *Boys Market*" injunction. In *Teamsters Local 299 v. U.S. Truck Co. Holdings Inc.*,[115] a union sought to enjoin the defendant trucking company and its par-

---

[109] 29 U.S.C. §104.

[110] 179 F.3d 982, 161 LRRM 2493 (6th Cir.), *cert. denied*, 528 U.S. 965, 162 LRRM 2704 (1999). *But see* Chicago Dist. Council of Carpenters Pension Fund v. K & I Constr., Inc., 270 F.3d 1060 (7th Cir. 2001) (rejecting Sixth Circuit's "colorable claim" test enunciated in *Allied Systems Ltd.* in favor of stricter standard, whether "arbitration clause is susceptible to more than one reasonable interpretation").

[111] *Allied Sys.*, *supra* note 110, 179 F.3d at 990, 161 LRRM at 2499.

[112] *See* Tejidos de Coamo, Inc. v. Ladies' Garment Workers, 22 F.3d 8, 146 LRRM 2141 (1st Cir. 1994); Lukens Steel Co. v. Steelworkers, 989 F.2d 668, 142 LRRM 2870 (3d Cir. 1993); Camping Constr. Co. v. Iron Workers, 915 F.2d 1333, 135 LRRM 2645 (9th Cir. 1990); *In re* Marine Engineers Beneficial Ass'n, 723 F.2d 70, 114 LRRM 3431 (D.C. Cir. 1983).

[113] AT&T Broadband v. Electrical Workers (IBEW), 317 F.3d 758, 171 LRRM 2988 (7th Cir. 2003).

[114] *See also* Pritchard Elec. Co. v. IBEW, Local 317, 306 F. Supp. 2d 603, 174 LRRM 2519 (S.D.W. Va. 2004) (where parties were signatories to two different agreements containing differing arbitration procedures, court denied employer's application to enjoin union from choosing which arbitration forum it would use).

[115] 87 F. Supp. 2d 726, 163 LRRM 2412 (E.D. Mich. 2000).

ent from closing a freight facility pending arbitration of several grievances regarding the closing. The court enjoined the defendants from liquidating the assets of the trucking company because such an action would compromise the arbitration process by rendering a later award meaningless. However, the court declined to enjoin them from closing operations at the facility, because the mere economic injury to the workers was not sufficient to demonstrate irreparable harm.[116]

In *Machinists District Lodge 91 v. United Technologies Corp.*,[117] the Second Circuit held that an injunction could properly issue requiring an employer to cease and desist from implementing a plan to transfer bargaining-unit work out of state unless and until the employer made contractually required efforts to preserve the work within the bargaining unit. The labor contract contained an article providing that the company would "make every effort" to preserve the work performed by employees in the bargaining unit, and that the company did not intend to use subcontractors or to transfer work elsewhere. This article, the court found, was explicitly not subject to arbitration under the contract. The employer argued that the district court thus erred in issuing an injunction, because the facts did not fit within the *Boys Market* exception.

Rejecting this approach, the Second Circuit observed that the Norris-LaGuardia Act prohibits issuance of injunctions only in certain targeted arenas. Therefore, it reasoned, federal courts may enforce a collective bargaining agreement via an injunction so long as the dispute is not the type governed by Norris-LaGuardia and so long as judicial relief is otherwise appropriate. Because the contractual provision that the employer make every effort to retain work within the bargaining unit was not among the types of subjects addressed by the Norris-LaGuardia Act, the district court did not err in issuing an injunction requiring the employer to comply with this obligation.

---

[116]*See also* IUE-CWA Local 628 v. Flowserve Corp., 239 F. Supp. 2d 527 (M.D. Pa. 2003) ("reverse *Boys Market*" injunction seeking to stop employer's layoffs and transfer of equipment to different facility denied, where union failed to show that arbitration was "hollow formality" because arbitrator could award damages and could not order employer to continue operations); Communications Workers v. Verizon, Inc., 2002 U.S. Dist. LEXIS 21556, 171 LRRM 2487 (S.D.N.Y. 2002) ("reverse *Boys Market*" injunction denied because allegations that threatened layoffs would cause public havoc and economic harm to workers did not establish that arbitration would become "hollow futility" unless layoffs were enjoined pending arbitration).

[117]230 F.3d 569, 165 LRRM 2641 (2d Cir. 2000).

V. Preemptive Effect of Other Statutory Provisions

A. Section 303 Actions

Claims against a union and its officials for tortious interference with business relations and expectancies, arising in connection with alleged secondary boycott activities, are preempted by Section 303.[118]

A district court held that Section 303 "does not have preemptive force so extraordinary that it converts a complaint alleging only a state-law cause of action into one stating a federal claim for purposes of the well-pleaded complaint rule."[119] The court's remand of the plaintiff's state-law claims did not prejudice the defendants' ability to raise preemption defenses in state court.[120]

B. State Power Under Section 14(b) to Regulate Union-Security Agreements

Iowa's right-to-work law does not proscribe the use of project labor agreements, because any broader reading would take it outside the protection of Section 14(b), resulting in federal preemption of the statute.[121]

A Colorado state law involving union-security authorization procedures that placed greater limitations than federal law on the ability of employees to seek deauthorization was preempted by the Act.[122] The Board concluded that the clear purpose of Section 14(b) was to permit the states the power to restrict union-security agreements. However, any state law that would require employees to wait longer than the period established by the Act to rescind a union-security agreement would violate federal statutory rights given to employees, and therefore must yield to federal law.[123]

Provisions of Oklahoma's new right-to-work law that prohibit the use of exclusive union hiring halls and payroll check-off arrangements for the deduction of union dues go beyond the scope of Sec-

---

[118]Labor Ready Mid-Atlantic, Inc. v. Tri-State Bldg. & Constr. Trades Council, 168 LRRM 2642, 2648–50 (S.D.W. Va. 2001).

[119]Brawn v. Coleman, 167 F. Supp. 2d 145, 153, 168 LRRM 2166, 2172 (D. Mass. 2001).

[120]*Id.*, 168 LRRM at 2173.

[121]Master Builders of Iowa, Inc. v. Polk County, 653 N.W.2d 382, 391–92 (Iowa 2002).

[122]Albertson's/Max Food Warehouse, 329 NLRB 410, 162 LRRM 1169 (1999), *overruling* City Mkts., Inc., 266 NLRB 1020, 113 LRRM 1105 (1983).

[123]*Id.*

tion 14(b) and thus are preempted by Section 8(a)(3) and LMRA Section 302(c)(4).[124]

The Act does not preempt an Indian tribal nation from adopting a right-to-work ordinance applicable to employees of a nontribal company engaged in business activities on a reservation.[125] In a case of first impression, the Tenth Circuit rejected the Board's position that because Section 14(b) contains no reference to Indian tribes, parties may enter into a union-security agreement under Section 8(a)(3) in derogation of the ordinance. Rather, the court held that Section 8(a)(3) merely disclaims any federal prohibition against union-security agreements, but has no preemptive effect. Thus, Section 14(b) is not an affirmative grant of power to states and territories, but only a recognition of their preexisting power. Under this reading of the statute, Congress's failure to mention Indian tribes in Section 14(b) is irrelevant, and the preexisting tribal authority to prohibit union-security agreements remains unaltered.[126]

E. Fair Representation

1. *Concurrent Jurisdiction of Board and Courts*

The courts continue to adhere to the general principle that jurisdiction over duty of fair representation claims is concurrent in the Board and the courts.[127] When the Board interprets the duty of fair representation as part of its unfair labor practice jurisdiction, its decision making is entitled to deference under the *Chevron* doctrine,[128] notwithstanding that the duty is judge-made and court-enforced.[129]

---

[124]Transport Workers Local 514 v. Keating, 212 F. Supp. 2d 1319, 1326–27, 170 LRRM 2808, 2813–14 (E.D. Okla. 2002), *aff'd,* 358 F.3d 743, 174 LRRM 2318 (10th Cir. 2004).

[125]NLRB v. Pueblo of San Juan, 276 F.3d 1186, 169 LRRM 2129 (10th Cir. 2002) (en banc).

[126]*Id.* at 1197–98, 169 LRRM at 2136–37.

[127]Marquez v. Screen Actors Guild, 525 U.S. 33, 49, 159 LRRM 2641, 2647 (1998); Communications Workers v. Beck, 487 U.S. 735, 128 LRRM 2729 (1988). *Cf.* Dykstra v. Teamsters Local 406, 2000 U.S. Dist. LEXIS 7011, 164 LRRM 2563 (W.D. Mich. 2000) (employee's duty of fair representation claim within exclusive jurisdiction of Board because crux of putative claim was union's alleged refusal to bargain with his employer).

[128]Chevron, USA, Inc. v. NRDC, 467 U.S. 837 (1984).

[129]Jacoby v. NLRB, 233 F.3d 611, 165 LRRM 2993 (D.C. Cir. 2000).

2. *Federal Law Governs*

Courts continue to hold that state-law fair representation claims against unions, or union agents acting within the scope of their agency, are preempted by the federal duty of fair representation so long as the state-law claim is based on rights or obligations analytically indistinguishable from those created by the federal duty of fair representation.[130]

Much of the judicial activity in this area has been in the context of preemption of state antidiscrimination law claims.[131] For example, in *Jackson v. T&N Van Service*,[132] an African-American employee contended that the union violated the New Jersey Law Against Discrimination (NJLAD) by grieving the employer's decision to discharge

---

[130]*See, e.g.*, Thomas v. Letter Carriers, 225 F.3d 1149, 87 FEP Cases 325 (10th Cir. 2000) (duty of fair representation preempts state law wrongful discharge and civil conspiracy claims); Carr v. Electrical Workers (IBEW) Local 1593, 326 F. Supp. 2d 999, 175 LRRM 2619 (D.N.D. 2004) (state-law claim of misrepresentation and reliance against union preempted by federal duty of fair representation); Burklow v. Baskin-Robbins USA, Co., 274 F. Supp. 2d 899 (W.D. Ky. 2003) (state-law fraud claim arising out of union's handling of plant closing amounted to claim for breach of fair representation duty); Flathau v. Machinists, Dist. 141, 2003 U.S. Dist. LEXIS 8827, 172 LRRM 2526 (W.D. Wash. 2003) (state-law claims of union misconduct are preempted where conduct at issue involves statutory duties of union as exclusive representative); Vancourt v. American Postal Workers Union, 2003 WL 21999348, 173 LRRM 2428 (E.D. La. 2003) (employee's state-law claims that union was negligent in the handling of his grievance were preempted). *See also* Cahoon v. Electrical Workers (IBEW) Local 261, 175 F. Supp. 2d 220, 223 (D. Conn. 2001) (duty of fair representation doctrine preempts plaintiff's state-law negligence claims based upon union's representational activities); Mamorella v. Derkasch, 276 A.D.2d 152, 716 N.Y.S.2d 211 (4th Dep't 2000) (federal law preempts legal malpractice claim against union attorney for work related to collective bargaining process).

[131]*See* EEOC v. Electrical Workers (IBEW) Local 998, 343 F. Supp. 2d 655, 176 LRRM 2008 (N.D. Ohio 2004) (state law claim of intentional infliction of emotional distress against union fell within narrow exception to duty of fair representation preemption where claim was function of particularly abusive manner in which alleged discrimination was accomplished); Lemerich v. Operating Eng'rs, Local 877, 2002 U.S. Dist. LEXIS 7102, 171 LRRM 2560 (D. Me. 2002) (federal law preempted gender discrimination claim against union under state law since it was essentially claim for breach of duty of fair representation); Agosto v. Correctional Officers Benevolent Ass'n, 107 F. Supp. 2d 294, 304, 83 FEP Cases 1042 (S.D.N.Y. 2000) (determining that state human rights law claim against union was preempted by duty of fair representation and noting that "[t]he duty of fair representation and Title VII plainly overlap in that they both prohibit discrimination; indeed, some courts essentially equate the two"). *Contra* Bredesen v. Detroit Fed'n of Musicians, 165 F. Supp. 2d 647, 168 LRRM 2530 (E.D. Mich. 2001) (rejecting preemption defense premised on duty of fair representation).

[132]117 F. Supp. 2d 457, 165 LRRM 2402 (E.D. Pa. 2000).

three co-workers who allegedly subjected the plaintiff-employee to racial harassment. The court agreed with the union that the NJLAD claim was preempted by the duty of fair representation. The court first observed that "if the state claim creates no new rights for an employee and imposes no duty on a union not already present under the federal duty of fair representation, the state claim is preempted."[133] In applying this standard, courts focus "not on the legal label affixed to the cause of action under state law, but to the conduct that is at the root of the controversy."[134] The plaintiff-employee's NJLAD claim against the union was preempted under this standard because the claim essentially involved the union's role in investigating complaints or grievances of alleged harassers and harassees, activities implicating the duty of fair representation.

Courts also frequently analyze preemption of state-law claims against unions under Section 301 preemption principles rather than under the duty of fair representation.[135]

F. Disputes Not Within the Coverage of the NLRA

Because supervisors are excluded from the Act's coverage, state law is typically not preempted where supervisors are concerned.[136]

---

[133]*Id.* at 463, 165 LRRM at 2405, quoting Bergeron v. Henderson, 52 F. Supp. 2d 149, 153, 161 LRRM 2761 (D. Me. 1999).

[134]*Id.*, quoting *Bergeron, supra* note 133, 52 F. Supp. 2d at 154, 161 LRRM at 2764.

[135]*See, e.g.*, Dahl v. Rosenfeld, 316 F.3d 1074, 171 LRRM 2841 (9th Cir. 2003) (employee's state-law claim that law firm representing union committed legal malpractice by not adequately enforcing contract provision is preempted by §301); Marrero v. Modern Maint. Bldg. Servs., Inc., 318 F. Supp. 2d 721, 174 LRRM 3358 (E.D. Wis. 2004) (state-law claim is preempted if it alleges conduct within scope of union's duty of fair representation regardless of whether claim requires interpretation of collective bargaining agreement); Frazier v. Ford Motor Co., 168 LRRM 2516 (W.D. Ky. 2001) (employees' state-law racial discrimination claims against union and its representatives were preempted by §301 because essence of claims was premised on duty of fair representation); Johnson v. Olin Corp., 2000 U.S. Dist. LEXIS 14469, 6 WH Cases 2d 941 (S.D. Ind. 2000) (former employee's state-law breach of contract claim, based on allegation of union's breach of its duty of fair representation, held preempted by §301); Black v. NFL Players Ass'n, 87 F. Supp. 2d 1, 164 LRRM 2566 (D.D.C. 2000) (tortious interference and defamation claims against union preempted by §301); Roach v. Auto Workers, 165 LRRM 2428 (N.D. Okla. 2000) (§301 preempted state law breach of contract and negligence claims against union).

[136]*See* Hanna Mining Co. v. Marine Eng'rs, Dist. 2, 382 U.S. 181, 60 LRRM 2473 (1965).

However, applying the conflict preemption doctrine,[137] the Third Circuit, in *St. Thomas-St. John Hotel & Tourism Ass'n, Inc. v. U.S. Virgin Islands,*[138] found a territorial wrongful discharge statute to be preempted by the Act when applied to supervisors. The statute set forth grounds on which employees could be terminated, and applied to all employees "unless modified by union contract." The court concluded that the statute was preempted when applied to supervisors because it indirectly compelled employers to bargain with supervisors in order to alter or expand the grounds for termination and such action violates Section 14(a).[139]

[137]Conflict preemption arises when a state law makes it impossible to comply with both state and federal law or when state law stands as an obstacle to the accomplishment and execution of the full purpose and objectives of Congress. Hines v. Davidowitz, 312 U.S. 52 (1941).

[138]357 F.3d 297, 174 LRRM 2312 (3d Cir. 2004).

[139]*Id.* at 302–04, 174 LRRM at 2315-17.

CHAPTER 29

ACCOMMODATIONS TO OTHER FEDERAL ENACTMENTS

I. THE NLRA AND THE ANTITRUST LAWS

A. Historical Development of the Antitrust Laws

The Main Edition notes that "union conduct . . . not enjoinable under the Norris-LaGuardia and Clayton Acts [is] . . . immune from criminal prosecution under the Sherman Act."[1] Similarly, union conduct that qualifies as "a labor dispute" is not enjoinable under the Norris-LaGuardia Act even though (1) that conduct violates the antitrust law and (2) the union does not represent or seek to represent the employees involved.[2]

B. Loss of the Exemption Through Combination With Nonlabor Groups

The courts continue to distinguish between valid "work-preservation" clauses and illegal combinations with nonlabor groups intended to create monopolies.[3] In *Sheet Metal Division v. Sheet Metal Workers Local 38*,[4] there was evidence that although fabrication (fab) of duct work previously had been done mostly on site, technological changes had shifted much of this fab work to off-site shops (many of which were lower-wage shops) outside Local 38's jurisdiction. In response, Local 38 negotiated a collective bargaining agreement with

---

[1]Main Edition, Chapter 29, Section I, at page 2275.

[2]Burlington N. Santa Fe Ry. v. Teamsters Local 174, 203 F.3d 703, 711 n.10, 712 n.12, 163 LRRM 2519 (9th Cir. 2000) (en banc). *Burlington Northern* reversed the panel opinion that had enjoined union picketing to compel the railroad to subcontract solely with employers that had collective bargaining agreements with the union because, according to the panel, it did not constitute a labor dispute within the meaning of the Norris-LaGuardia Act.

[3]*See* Sheet Metal Div. v. Sheet Metal Workers Local 38, 208 F.3d 18, 26, 163 LRRM 2910 (2d Cir. 2000).

[4]*Id.*

the local multi-employer bargaining association, which provided that all sheet metal fabrication work would be performed by union members, either on site or in fab shops. Suit was brought by an employer group that did not have a contract with Local 38, alleging that it would be shut out of supplying prefabricated duct work to the Local 38 market by this provision.

The court found that because Local 38 had traditionally performed a substantial portion of this fab work, either on site or in local shops, this was a valid work-preservation clause, not an illegal Section 8(e) hot-cargo clause or an antitrust violation. It was viewed as irrelevant that Local 38 had not historically performed all of this work because it had made no effort to apply the clause to nonsignatories to its collective bargaining agreement.

In *Nevada Independent Service Contractors Ass'n v. Pack Expo West*,[5] the court denied the motion for summary judgment of the defendant union and employers, concluding that the record showed triable issues of fact that the union had conspired with two employers to exclude other employers, members of a trade association, which did not have a contract with the union, from performing set-up work for exhibitors at trade shows. The court noted that summary judgment would be denied in an antitrust case when the evidence is plausibly consistent with both inferences of conspiracy and inferences of innocent conduct. That evidence included: (1) the union and defendant employers held meetings, from which certain association members were excluded and decided to enforce a "labor peace" clause requiring exhibitors to show that they had a current labor contract; (2) a defendant employer participated in preparation of a memorandum that show promoters sent to exhibitors advising them of the labor peace clause and of which contractors were authorized contractors and those who were not; and (3) representatives of the union and defendant employers forced association members off the show floor.

In *Clarett v. National Football League*,[6] the Second Circuit held that the NFL's rule limiting eligibility for the NFL entry draft to players at least three full college football seasons removed from high school graduation fell within the scope of the nonstatutory exemption to antitrust review. The court rejected the reasoning of the district court which held in favor of Clarett based on its application of

[5]170 LRRM 3107 (D. Nev. 2002).

[6]369 F.3d 124 (2d Cir. 2004).

the Eighth Circuit's test in *Mackey v. National Football League.*[7] The district court reasoned that the NFL's eligibility rules (1) are not related to a mandatory subject of bargaining; (2) affect only nonemployees; and (3) are not clearly the product of arm's length negotiations between the NFL and its players union.[8]

The Second Circuit began by noting that it never has regarded *Mackey* as defining the appropriate limits of the nonstatutory exemption. Besides, the court held, the NFL's eligibility rules clearly are a mandatory subject of bargaining related to the conditions under which a prospective player will be considered for employment with the league. These rules, the court noted, "are not dissimilar to union demands for hiring hall arrangements that have long been recognized as mandatory subjects of bargaining."[9] The court concluded that if permitted to go forward, Clarettt's suit would disrupt federal labor policy and "would not vindicate any of the antitrust policies that the Supreme Court has said may warrant the withholding of the non-statutory exemption."[10]

C. The Requirement of a "Labor Dispute"

In *Burlington Northern Santa Fe Railway Co. v. Teamsters Local 174,*[11] the court en banc engaged in a detailed review of the definition of a labor dispute. In that case, Burlington Northern Santa Fe Railroad (BNSF), an interstate railway common carrier, terminated a subcontracting agreement with Eagle Systems, Inc. (Eagle), for loading and unloading services at a Seattle hub and transferred the work to another subcontractor, Parsec, Inc. (Parsec). Defendant Local 174 represented the Eagle employees who lost their jobs when BNSF transferred the work to Parsec. Local 174 also represented employees of other subcontractors who continued to perform work under subcontracts with BNSF. Local 174 did not represent the employees of BNSF or Parsec. A union not affiliated with the Teamsters represented the Parsec employees who performed the work formerly done by Eagle employees.[12]

---

[7]543 F.2d 606 (8th Cir. 1976).
[8]*Clarett, supra* note 6, 369 F.3d at 129, 133.
[9]*Id.* at 140–41.
[10]*Id.* at 143.
[11]203 F.3d 703, 163 LRRM 2519 (9th Cir. 2000).
[12]*Id.* at 705.

After BNSF refused various demands by Local 174, the union threatened to picket in support of its demand that BNSF not subcontract any loading or unloading services to any subcontractor that did not have a current collective bargaining agreement with Local 174. The union limited the demand to future subcontracting agreements and disclaimed any intent to force BNSF to terminate any existing subcontracting agreements. Local 174 never commenced any picketing because BNSF filed an action in federal district court. The district court ruled that the Norris-LaGuardia Act did not bar it from issuing an injunction. A divided three-judge panel of the Ninth Circuit affirmed.[13]

The court en banc vacated the district court's grant of a preliminary injunction and remanded the case to the district court with instructions to dismiss for lack of subject-matter jurisdiction on the grounds that the Norris-LaGuardia Act deprived the federal courts of jurisdiction to issue an injunction to restrain peaceful picketing in "any case involving or growing out of any labor dispute."[14] Specifically, the court stated: "We hold that a dispute between a union and a client company (here, Burlington Northern) over whether the client company's subcontractors must employ that union's members is a Norris-LaGuardia labor dispute. Thus, the dispute between Local 174 and Burlington Northern falls squarely behind Norris-LaGuardia's jurisdictional bar, and the district court had no power to enjoin Local 174 from picketing Burlington Northern."[15]

The court reviewed the history of Norris-LaGuardia Act citing this treatise,[16] for the proposition that the "extraordinary problem" that Congress remedied with the Norris-LaGuardia Act dated back to the final decades of the nineteenth century when federal courts routinely enjoined labor picketing at the behest of employers.[17] The court further held that the only issue before it was whether the district court had jurisdiction to enjoin the threatened picketing. It did not reach the question whether the antitrust laws were implicated.[18]

---

[13] *See* Burlington N. Santa Fe Ry. Co. v. Teamsters Local 174, 170 F.3d 897, 160 LRRM 2769 (9th Cir. 1999). The Ninth Circuit en banc vacated the panel's decision and agreed to rehear the appeal. *Burlington, supra* note 11, 203 F.3d at 706.

[14] 29 U.S.C. §104.

[15] *Burlington, supra* note 11, 203 F.3d at 707.

[16] PATRICK HARDIN, THE DEVELOPING LABOR LAW 7 (3d ed. 1992).

[17] *Burlington, supra* note 11, 203 F.3d at 707.

[18] *Id.*

It noted that for a "labor dispute" to exist "the employer-employee relationship [must be at] the matrix of the controversy."[19]

In *White v. National Football League*,[20] the court applied the definition of a labor group that the Supreme Court utilized in *H.A. Artists & Associates v. Actors' Equity Ass'n.*[21]

F. Application of the Statutory and Nonstatutory Exemption After *Connell*

In *Albany Specialties, Inc. v. Board of Education*,[22] the district court denied the plaintiff's motion for a preliminary injunction, holding that a Project Labor Agreement (PLA) for a school district renovation project was protected by the construction industry proviso of Section 8(f).[23] Adhering to *Laborers Local 210 v. Labor Relations Division of Associated General Contractors*,[24] the court found that because the PLA was the product of collective bargaining, furthered national labor policy goals, and fell within the ambit of the construction-industry proviso of Section 8(f), it was protected from antitrust challenges by the nonstatutory exemption.[25]

At issue in *Sheet Metal Division of Capital District Sheet Metal v. Sheet Metal Workers Local 38*[26] was a clause in an agreement between the defendants Local 38 and Sheet Metal & Roofing Employers Association of Southeastern New York (SENY). This clause provided that all fabrication work performed within Local 38's geographic region would be performed by Local 38 members, but did not forbid contractors from outside Local 38's region from contracting to do work inside the region.[27] The plaintiffs asserted that even though they were not signatories to the agreement between defendants, they were nonetheless bound by the clause because they had their own collective bargaining agreements with other area unions (other than Local 38), which required them to comply with Local 38's work rules

[19]*Burlington, supra* note 11, 203 F.3d at 709, quoting Jacksonville Bulk Terminals v. Longshoremen (ILA), 457 U.S. 702, 712 (1982) (quoting Columbia River Packers Ass'n v. Hinton, 315 U.S. 143, 147 (1942)).

[20]92 F. Supp. 2d 918, 164 LRRM 2913 (D. Minn. 2000).

[21]451 U.S. 704, 107 LRRM 2394 (1981).

[22]162 LRRM 3071 (N.D.N.Y. 1999).

[23]*Id.* at 3077.

[24]844 F.2d 69, 79, 128 LRRM 2060 (2d Cir. 1987).

[25]*Albany Specialties, supra* note 22, 162 LRRM at 3079.

[26]208 F.3d 18, 163 LRRM 2910 (2d Cir. 2000).

[27]*Id.* at 20, 163 LRRM at 2912.

while working in Local 38's region.[28] Thus, according to the plaintiffs, the clause in the defendants' agreement imposed on them "an unlawful boycott of sheet metal products fabricated outside Local 38's jurisdiction."[29]

The defendant SENY filed an unfair labor practice charge to verify the validity of the clause with respect to Local 38 and itself.[30] The Board's investigation did not reveal a Section 8(e) violation with respect to the agreement, and it declined to issue a complaint in the matter.[31] Therefore, the plaintiffs' motion for a preliminary injunction to prevent enforcement of the clause was moot. However, the district court found that the clause violated Section 8(e) and, because it did not fall within any exceptions to the Sherman Act, constituted an unlawful restraint on trade.[32]

On appeal, the Second Circuit determined the record was insufficient for the district court to have found either Section 8(e) or antitrust violations and thus reversed the district court's declaratory judgment in favor of the plaintiffs.[33] Although the court agreed with Local 38 and SENY that the clause was never intended to be enforced against nonsignatories, it nevertheless determined that it was "hard to see how the likelihood that the clause would be directly enforced against [plaintiffs] was sufficiently concrete to warrant a declaratory judgment."[34]

Courts continue to apply *Connell Construction Co. v. Plumbers & Pipe Fitters Local 100*[35] where an allegedly violative agreement is not made in the context of a labor contract.[36]

---

[28]*Id.* at 24–25, 163 LRRM at 2915.

[29]*Id.* at 21, 163 LRRM at 2912.

[30]*Id.*, 163 LRRM at 2913.

[31]Sheet Metal Div. of Capital Dist. Sheet Metal v. Sheet Metal Workers Local 38, 208 F.3d 18, 21, 163 LRRM 2910, 2913 (2d Cir. 2000).

[32]*Id.* at 22, 163 LRRM at 2913.

[33]*Id.* at 25–26, 163 LRRM at 2917.

[34]*Id.* at 25, 163 LRRM at 2915.

[35]421 U.S. 616, 89 LRRM 2401 (1975).

[36]U.S. Info. Sys., Inc. v. Electrical Workers Local 3, 169 LRRM 2676, 2002 WL 91625 (S.D.N.Y. 2002) (refusing to dismiss complaint alleging electrical workers union conspired in violation of Sherman Act because conspiracy alleged was not "explicit or implicit outgrowth of collective bargaining" between defendant contractors and Local 3, was not necessary "to make the collective bargaining process work"); Cool Wind Ventilation Corp. v. Sheet Metal Workers, 139 F. Supp. 2d 319, 169 LRRM 2540 (E.D.N.Y. 2001) (plaintiff stated claim for per se violation of antitrust laws when alleged that competitor threatened to pull its union employees from projects for which contractor was hired).

In *Operating Engineers (Massman Construction Co.) Local 520*,[37] the Board considered a clause that was designed to protect unions from the "potentially detrimental effect" of a joint venture business arrangement. The union insisted on a provision that a condition for entering into any joint venture would be for all parties to the undertaking to accept the terms of the collective bargaining agreement that existed between the union and the employer, a construction company.[38] The Board held that the provision was an attempt to control the signatory employer's business relationships, and as such was outside the scope of the statutory and nonstatutory exemptions.[39] The Board, therefore, found that the clause violated the basic prohibitions of Section 8(e) of the Act. As was noted in the administrative law judge's (ALJ's) order, adopted with modification by the Board, the provision did not fall within the nonstatutory exemption because, under the wording of the clause, it could require entities not controlled by the employer to conform, and therefore would fail the "control" test.[40]

The Board recently considered whether either the statutory or nonstatutory exemptions would apply in the context of a union signatory clause aimed at protecting a union's work installing an assembly of trade show exhibits. In *South Jersey Regional Council of Carpenters Local 623 (Atlantic Exposition Services, Inc.)*,[41] the collective bargaining agreement between the union and the employer contained a provision under which the employer would not subcontract work to other employers without collective bargaining agreements with the union. This union signatory clause was held to be a violation of Section 8(e) because its purpose was not primarily work preservation.[42] The Board held that the geographic scope of the provision, which encompassed seven counties, as well as its requirement that the employer was required to cease doing business with the trade show exhibitor or the subcontractor altogether, was clear evidence that the provision was not aimed primarily at work preservation, but rather to influence the subcontractor's labor relations policies.[43]

---

[37]327 NLRB 1257, 161 LRRM 1001 (1999).

[38]*Id.* at 1258.

[39]*Id.*

[40]*Id.* at 1263.

[41]335 NLRB 586 (2001), *enforced sub nom.* Spectacor Mgmt. Group v. NLRB, 320 F.3d 385 (3d Cir. 2003).

[42]*Id.*

[43]*Id.*

In *Mathiowetz Construction Co. v. Minnesota Department of Transportation*,[44] the court held that the nonstatutory exemption did not apply to a union's "Market Recovery Program" to the extent the program violated the Davis-Bacon Act and/or the Minnesota Prevailing Wage Act, and thus was not a proper subject of collective bargaining.[45]

The issue of union standing to bring antitrust claims has arisen most recently in the context of litigation against tobacco companies. For example, in *Steamfitters Local 420 Welfare Fund v. Philip Morris, Inc.*,[46] union health and welfare funds brought a putative class action against tobacco companies under antitrust laws, the Racketeer Influenced and Corrupt Organizations Act (RICO), and state common law. The funds had paid for tobacco-related health care for their members, and thus claimed injury.[47] The Third Circuit acknowledged that union health and welfare funds could suffer legally cognizable injury from the tobacco companies' alleged fraud, even when they were not the ultimate source of the money used to pay for smoking-related injuries.[48] The court also warned against applying bright-line rules to determine antitrust standing and advocated a case-by-case approach. The court listed several factors to be assessed in an analysis of antitrust standing, including (1) the causal connection between the defendant's wrongdoing and the plaintiff's harm; (2) the defendant's specific intent to harm; (3) the nature of the injury and whether it related to the purpose of the antitrust laws; (4) the directness of the asserted injury; (5) whether the damages claim is highly speculative; and (6) keeping the scope of complex antitrust trials within judicially manageable limits.[49]

The court ultimately ruled that the funds did not show proximate cause sufficient to support standing to sue the companies.[50] The court explained that the tobacco companies could have achieved their alleged aims without the existence of the funds or the relationship between the funds and the smokers. Further, even if the tobacco companies had not prevented health care payers from discov-

---

[44]137 F. Supp. 2d 1144 (D. Minn. 2001).
[45]*Id.* at 1148–49.
[46]171 F.3d 912 (3d Cir. 1999).
[47]*Id.* at 917.
[48]*Id.* at 921.
[49]*Id.* at 923.
[50]*Id.* at 930.

ering the dangers of smoking, there was no claim that the funds would have chosen to not insure smokers.[51]

Several other circuits that have examined similar claims have also found that the union funds lacked standing.[52] Thus, this new attempt at achieving standing for union funds in antitrust actions has to date proved unsuccessful.

In the Main Edition, Chapter 29 at p. 2292, *Sheet Metal Division of Capitol District Sheet Metal v. Sheet Metal Workers Local 38*[53] is discussed, wherein the district court concluded that a clause effectively requiring that all sheet metal fabricating and sketching (including off-site work) only be performed by employees covered under the agreement violated Section 8(e) of the NLRA and was unprotected by the nonstatutory exemption. On appeal, the court remanded the case after concluding that the challenged clause may have had a permissible primary work preservation objective, and therefore, would not be proscribed by Section 8(e), and would be exempt from antitrust scrutiny under the nonstatutory exemption to the Sherman Act.[54]

G. Employer Antitrust Suits as Illegal Retaliation for Protected Activity [New Topic]

Cases which had concluded that an employer violates the Act by filing a nonmeritorious antitrust claim were brought into question, if not abrogated by the Supreme Court's decision in *BE&K Construction Co. v. NLRB.*[55]

In *BE&K Construction Co.,*[56] the employer filed an antitrust lawsuit against the union. The employer withdrew some of the claims, and the remaining claims were ultimately dismissed by the court. The Board applied the "concluded suit" standard of *Bill Johnson's*

---

[51] *Id.*

[52] *See* Laborers Local 17 v. Philip Morris, Inc., 191 F.3d 229 (2d Cir. 1999) (holding, in suit by labor health and welfare funds, that economic injuries were too remote for funds to have standing to sue tobacco companies); Texas Carpenters Health Benefit Fund v. Philip Morris, Inc., 199 F.3d 788 (5th Cir. 2000) (no standing); Teamsters v. Philip Morris, Inc., 196 F.3d 818 (7th Cir. 1999) (no standing); Oregon Laborers-Employers Health & Welfare Trust Fund v. Philip Morris, Inc., 185 F.3d 957 (9th Cir. 1999) (injury too remote); Food & Comm. Workers v. Philip Morris, Inc., 223 F.3d 1271 (11th Cir. 2000) (no standing).

[53] 45 F. Supp. 2d 195, 160 LRRM 2925 (N.D.N.Y. 1999).

[54] 208 F.3d 18, 163 LRRM 2910 (2d Cir. 2000).

[55] 122 S. Ct. 2390, 170 LRRM 2225 (2002).

[56] 329 NLRB 717, 162 LRRM 1217 (1999).

Restaurants v. NLRB,[57] and found the suit was "unmeritorious." The Board held that a retaliatory motive could be inferred from the following factors: (1) the employer's federal suit was "by its terms" directed at conduct that the Board had found was protected under Section 7; (2) the suit "necessarily tended to discourage similar protected activity"; (3) the lawsuit's attempt to have the court impose liability on unions that had not engaged in the conduct at issue indicated that the employer "was interested only in harassing the Unions, not in obtaining justice"; and (4) certain of the employer's claims suffered from an "utter absence of merit."[58]

The Supreme Court reversed the Board.[59] The Court viewed the Board as having adopted a standard centered on whether the plaintiff acted with a subjective motive to interfere with activity protected under the Act. The Court unanimously rejected this standard for application in nonmeritorious, but reasonably based, cases. It explained that a nonmeritorious lawsuit may be reasonably based even though it is ultimately unsuccessful. Even though the suit may attack activity that is ultimately determined to be protected, the suit nevertheless enjoys First Amendment protection if the plaintiff reasonably believes the conduct is unprotected and illegal. Similarly, the Court reasoned that inferring a retaliatory motive from evidence of animus would condemn genuine petitioning in circumstances where the plaintiff's "purpose is to stop conduct he reasonably believes is illegal."[60]

BE&K Construction Co. leaves open several issues that await clarification from the Board.[61] These are:

> (1) whether the Board should adopt the standard articulated in *Professional Real Estate Investors v. Columbia Pictures Industries Inc.*,[62] and discussed in *BE&K*, in determining whether a lawsuit is reasonably based;
>
> (2) if a lawsuit is reasonably based, what standard the Board should apply in determining retaliatory motive;

---

[57]461 U.S. 731, 113 LRRM 2647 (1983).

[58]*BE&K Constr.*, *supra* note 56, 162 LRRM at 1228.

[59]536 U.S. 516, 170 LRRM 2225 (2002).

[60]*Id.* at 534.

[61]*See* Report of the General Counsel on Recent Case Developments (R-2488), May 2, 2003; Memorandum GC 02-09 "Case Handling Instructions for Cases Concerning *Bill Johnson's Restaurants, Inc.* and *BE&K Construction Co.*" (Sept. 20, 2002).

[62]508 U.S. 49 (1993).

(3) whether the filing and maintenance of a reasonably based lawsuit can nevertheless be an unfair labor practice if the evidence of the retaliatory motive is strong enough; and

(4) whether the Board should continue to apply footnote 5 of *Bill Johnson's Restaurants v. NLRB*[63] in preemption and illegal object cases.[64]

The Board addressed the last of these issues in *Allied Trades Council (Duane Reade, Inc.)*.[65] There, the Board applied the "illegal objective" exception in footnote 5 of *Bill Johnson's Restaurants* to a union's demands for arbitration when, without demonstrating majority status, the union sought to apply the collective bargaining agreement to employees outside the unit previously found to be appropriate by the Board. The Board agreed with the D.C. Circuit in *Can-Am Plumbing v. NLRB*[66] that the decision in *BE&K* "did not affect the footnote 5 exemption in *Bill Johnson's*."[67]

II. THE NLRA AND THE BANKRUPTCY CODE

A. Power of Bankruptcy Court to Reject Collective Bargaining Agreement

1. *Requirements for Rejection of a Collective Bargaining Agreement*

Most courts continue to hold that the nine-step analysis set forth in *American Provision Co.*[68] provides the prerequisites for determining whether a collective bargaining agreement should be rejected.[69] Moreover, the majority of courts continue to hold that the debtor

---

[63]461 U.S. 731, 113 LRRM 2647 (1983).

[64]*See* Report of the General Counsel on Recent Case Developments, *supra* note 61.

[65]342 NLRB No. 103, 171 LRRM 1101 (2004)

[66]321 F.3d 145, 151, 171 LRRM 3225 (D.C. Cir. 2003)

[67]*Allied Trades Council, supra* note 65, at n.4

[68]44 B.R. 907, 118 LRRM 2059 (Bankr. D. Minn. 1984).

[69]*See In re* National Forge Co., 279 B.R. 493 (Bankr. W.D. Pa. 2002), *subsequent decision*, 289 B.R. 803 (Bankr. W.D. Pa. 2003); *In re* U.S. Truck Co. Holdings, Inc., 2000 Bankr. LEXIS 1376, 165 LRRM 2521 (E.D. Mich. 2000). *Cf. In re* Horsehead Indus., 300 B.R. 573 (S.D.N.Y. 2003); *In re* Horizon Natural Res. Co., 316 B.R.268, 175 LRRM 3256 (Bankr. E.D. Ky. 2004); *In re* Oremet Corp., 316 B.R. 665 (Bankr. S.D. Ohio 2004).

bears the burden of persuasion by the preponderance of the evidence on all nine elements.[70]

With respect to altering obligations under a collective bargaining agreement, the Third Circuit held that "when . . . a debtor in possession . . . binds itself contractually to obtain a change in the legal relations created by a CBA as a condition precedent to closing a sale of substantially all of the debtor's assets, that constitutes an attempt to effect an alteration of the CBA" under Section 1113, and the debtor is obligated to follow the requirements set forth in Section 1113.[71]

In a case of first impression, in *Family Snacks, Inc.*,[72] the Eighth Circuit held that Section 1113 permits a debtor to reject a collective bargaining agreement even after the debtor has sold virtually all its assets. The court analyzed the "reorganization of the debtor" clause of the "necessary to permit the reorganization of the debtor" test set forth in Section 1113(b)(1)(A), and held that "reorganization" should not be equated with the more narrow concept of "rehabilitation" of the debtor.[73] Accordingly, the court concluded that "necessary to permit the reorganization of the debtor" means "necessary to accommodate confirmation of a Chapter 11 plan."[74] Thus, there is "no principled reason to limit a debtor's right to reject a CBA to a case where the application to reject comes before an asset sale."[75]

Deciding another matter of first impression, the Eighth Circuit in *Family Snacks* also held that the assumption of a collective bargaining agreement does not automatically occur on the bankruptcy court's denial of a debtor's motion to reject.[76] The court emphasized that the assumption of a collective bargaining agreement may not be

---

[70] *See In re* Family Snacks, Inc., 257 B.R. 884, 892, 166 LRRM 2400 (8th Cir. 2001). *But see In re* U.S. Truck Co. Holdings, Inc., *supra* note 69, 165 LRRM at 2531 (debtor has burden of proving ninth factor by higher standard than preponderance of evidence).

[71] American Flint Glass Workers Union v. Anchor Resolution Corp., 197 F.3d 76, 162 LRRM 2897 (3d Cir. 1999). *See also In re* Allegheny Health, Educ. & Research Found., 265 B.R. 88 (2001) (accepting Third Circuit's decision as correct).

[72] 257 B.R. 884, 166 LRRM 2400 (8th Cir. 2001).

[73] *In re Family Snacks, supra* note 70, 257 B.R. at 895. *See also In re U.S. Truck Co. Holdings, supra* note 69, 165 LRRM at 2529, where the court stated that "[s]ection 1113 contains no words of limitation or exclusion, and fails to distinguish between liquidating Chapter 11 cases and Chapter 11 cases where the debtor seeks to rehabilitate a failing business."

[74] *In re Family Snacks, supra* note 70, 257 B.R. at 897.

[75] *Id.*

[76] *Id.* at 906.

implied and, instead, the assumption of an agreement by a debtor requires affirmative action by way of a motion seeking assumption.[77]

The courts have not settled the question of whether a bankruptcy court's power to reject a collective bargaining agreement includes the power to order a modification of a specific provision of the agreement.[78]

2. *Modification of Post-Retirement Health Benefits*

Section 1114(e) commands that the trustee of debtor-in-possession pay "any" retiree benefits as an administrative expense of the bankruptcy estate.[79] The Fourth Circuit held that under Section 1114(e), the term "retiree benefits" is limited to health care, accident, disability, and death benefits, and does not apply to give priority to claims by trust funds that administer only pension benefits for retired coal miners.[80]

In *LTV Steel Co., Inc.*,[81] the court held that premium payments for retiree health benefits that were due under the Coal Industry Retiree Health Benefits Act[82] were entitled to priority status as an administrative expense. The court also concluded that because premiums under the Coal Industry Retiree Health Benefits Act were due annually, the employer was required to pay a full year of premiums, even though it had ceased doing business shortly after the annual premium became due.

In *Horizon Natural Resources Co.*,[83] the bankruptcy court approved, over the union's objections, the debtor's proposed changes in retiree health benefits that were provided under the Coal Industry Retiree Health Benefits Act. The court rejected the union's arguments that retiree health benefits under the Coal Act could not be changed without the consent of the retirees or the union.

---

[77] *Id.* at 905–06.

[78] *See* Direct Press Modern Litho, Inc., 328 NLRB 860, 161 LRRM 1193 n.2 (1999) (recognizing "split of judicial opinion with respect to a bankruptcy court's authority to modify a collective bargaining agreement under Sec. 1113(c) of the Bankruptcy Code in lieu of a rejection determination"). Note that the decision in *In re Alabama Symphony Ass'n*, 155 B.R. 556 (Bankr. N.D. Ala. 1993), cited in the Main Edition, was reversed and vacated in part by *In re Alabama Symphony Ass'n*, 211 B.R. 65 (Bankr. N.D. Ala. 1996).

[79] 11 U.S.C. §1114(e).

[80] Adventure Res., Inc. v. Holland, 137 F.3d 786, 795 (4th Cir.), *cert. denied*, 525 U.S. 962 (1998).

[81] 299 B.R. 863 (N.D. Ohio 2003).

[82] 26 U.S.C. §9701 et seq.

[83] 316 B.R. 268, 175 LRRM 3256 (Bankr. E.D. Ky. 2004).

In *Certified Air Technologies, Inc.*,[84] the court held that delinquent contributions payable to a multi-employer Taft-Hartley Trust Fund that provided health benefits to active and retired employees were "retiree benefits" within the meaning of Section 1114(e), and were allowed as an administrative expense. Even though the employer had no current retired employees receiving benefits from the fund, because the fund provided for health benefits to retirees, all of the contributions had to be covered by Section 1114(a).

In *Hourly Employees/Retirees of Debtor v. Eire Forge & Steel, Inc.*,[85] the district court rejected, on procedural grounds, an appeal from the bankruptcy court's order approving modification of retiree health benefits that had been negotiated with the union. The appellants, who had been active employees when the petition was filed and were subsequently laid off after retiree benefits were terminated, claimed that they were "constructive retirees" entitled to object under 11 U.S.C. §1114. The district court concluded that they lacked standing because (1) they were not retirees when the petition was filed and had not been receiving retiree benefits; and (2) assuming that they were retirees, they had never previously sought appointment of a different representative under Section 1114(c)(1) and were therefore bound by the acts of the union as their authorized representatives.

In evaluating whether the requirements for termination or modification of retiree health benefits have been met, the courts have continued to look to the same standards that apply to rejection of a collective bargaining agreement.[86]

4. Post-Petition Collective Bargaining Agreements

Pursuant to Section 363(c), the debtor may finalize post-petition contracts, including collective bargaining agreements, without court approval only if the contracts are routine and entered into "in the ordinary course of business."[87] When making a determination whether a particular post-petition contract meets this standard, courts

[84]300 B.R. 355 (C.D. Cal. 2003).

[85]2004 U.S. Dist LEXIS 5690 (W.D. Pa. 2004).

[86]*In re* Horsehead Indus., 300 B.R. 573, 582 (S.D.N.Y. 2003); *Horizon Natural Resources Co, supra* note 83, 316 B.R. at 281.

[87]11 U.S.C. §363(c).

continue to analyze the challenged post-petition contract from both a horizontal and vertical perspective.[88]

The court in *North American Royalties, Inc.*[89] held that a termination agreement negotiated by a debtor and a union required court approval because it was not an agreement entered into in the ordinary course of business. Rather, the agreement was negotiated when the debtor decided to shut down its business, and it provided for a pension plan enhancement which used excess funds to make certain "actively employed" employees eligible to receive pension benefits. The court approved the agreement over the objection of disabled employees who were not eligible to receive a pension benefit because they were not "actively employed" within the terms of the agreement.[90]

In *Hillard Development Corp.*,[91] the court approved a post-petition collective bargaining agreement that the parties agreed would become effective upon the bankruptcy court's approval. The court then exercised its discretion to issue an award with retroactive effect, explaining that the agreement did not affect the rights of creditors in the property of the debtor's estate and that equity necessitated retroactive application.[92]

B. Priority of Wage and Employee Benefit Plan Contributions

Section 507(a) and subparts of Title 11, U.S. Code were amended in 2004 and provide as follows:

> (a) The following expenses and claims have priority in the following order;
>
> . . .
>
> (3) Third, allowed unsecured claims, but only to the extent of $4,925 for each individual or corporation, as the case may be, earned within 90 days before the date of the filing of the petition or the date of the cessation of the debtor's business, whichever occurs first, for—

---

[88] *Cf. In re* Lodge Am., Inc., 259 B.R. 728 (D. Kan. 2001) (post-petition short-term loan and subsequent repayment held not in ordinary course of business); *In re* Crystal Apparel, Inc., 220 B.R. 816 (Bankr. S.D.N.Y. 1998) (post-petition employment contracts held in ordinary course of business except to extent contracts incorporated prepetition golden parachute provisions).

[89] 276 B.R. 587 (Bankr. E.D. Tenn. 2002).

[90] *Id.* at 593–94.

[91] 2004 WL 1347049 (Bankr. S.D. Fla. 2004).

[92] *Id.* at *2.

(A) wages, salaries or commissions, including vacation, severance and sick leave pay earned by an individual; or

(B) sales commissions earned by an individual or by a corporation with only one employee, acting as an independent contractor in the sale of goods or services for the debtor in the ordinary course of the debtor's business if, and only if, during the 12 months preceding that date, at least 75 percent of the amount that the individual or corporation earned by acting as an independent contractor in the sale of goods or services was earned from the debtor;

(4) Fourth, allowed unsecured claims for contributions to an employee benefit plan—

. . .

(B) for each such plan, to the extent of—

(i) the number of employees covered by each such plan multiplied by $4,925; less

(ii) the aggregate amount paid to such employees under paragraph (3) of this subsection, plus the aggregate amount paid by the estate on behalf of such employees to any other employee benefit plan.

The Ninth Circuit's Bankruptcy Panel, in *In re San Rafael Baking Co.*,[93] held that Section 1113 did not give the bankruptcy court the authority to order a Chapter 11 debtor-in-possession to continue making employee health benefit contributions after expiration of the collective bargaining agreement where no proceedings were initiated before the expiration.

1. *Prepetition Claims*

The split among the circuits continues with regard to whether unpaid prepetition workers' compensation insurance premiums are considered contributions to an employee benefit plan (i.e., affording the claim priority status under Section 507(a)(4)). Agreeing with the Eighth and Tenth Circuits on this matter, the Sixth Circuit in *Birmingham-Nashville Express, Inc.*[94] held that a claim for unpaid prepetition workers' compensation insurance premiums is *not* a contribution to an employee benefit plan entitled to priority status un-

[93]219 B.R. 860 (9th Cir. 1998).
[94]224 F.3d 511 (6th Cir. 2000).

der Section 507(a)(4). The Bankruptcy Court in *Integrated Health Services, Inc.*[95] disagreed, holding that workers' compensation insurance premiums constitute contributions to an employee benefit plan entitled to priority under Section 507(a)(4).

The courts also disagree as to whether an insurance company or insurance broker is entitled to priority under Section 507(a)(4) in a claim for unpaid premiums. The court in *Ivey v. Great W. Life & Annuity Insurance*[96] held that insurers are among the class of persons intended to receive priority for contributions to employee benefit plans. However, the court in *Edward W. Minte Co.*[97] held that, even if workers' compensation insurance is part of an employee benefit plan, an insurer or insurance broker is not entitled to priority under Section 507(a)(4) for a claim for unpaid premiums. The court held that claims under Section 507(a)(4) are limited to claims by employees or administrators of employee benefit plans representing their interests.[98]

With regard to the treatment of claims for vacation pay, the court in *Crafts Precision Industries*[99] reiterated the limitations period under Section 507 and found that vacation pay earned more than 90 days before the debtor filed its petition for bankruptcy is not given priority under Section 507(a)(4). Furthermore, vacation pay is considered a "wage" and not a fringe benefit or a contribution to an employee benefit plan for purposes of determining priority status under Section 507.

In *Greater Southeast Community Hospital Foundation, Inc.*,[100] the court held that pension contributions due prior to the Chapter 11 filing were entitled to a priority under Section 507(a)(4) and pension contributions due after the filing were entitled to an administrative priority. Employees were held to have continued as employees of the bankrupt employer until they were hired by a purchaser of assets.

[95]291 B.R. 611 (Bankr. D. Del. 2003).
[96]308 B.R. 752 (D.N.C. 2004).
[97]286 B.R. 1 (Bankr. D.C. 2002).
[98]*Id.* at 13.
[99]244 B.R. 178 (1st Cir. 2000).
[100]267 B.R. 7 (Bankr. D.C. 2001).

2. *Post-Petition Claims for Wages and Benefits Due Under an Unrejected Agreement*

The courts continue to struggle with how to reconcile the language in Section 1113(f) with the provisions of Section 507.[101] In *Kitty Hawk, Inc.*,[102] the union claimed that because the debtor failed to modify or reject its collective bargaining agreement with the union in accordance with Section 1113, it was bound by the collective bargaining agreement, and all amounts due under the agreement had to be paid in full—irrespective of the priority status of the claims under Section 507. The bankruptcy court rejected the union's argument, holding that Section 1113 does not establish a super priority for claims under a collective bargaining agreement. Rather, the debtor's obligations under the collective bargaining agreement would be respected, but the financial obligations issuing from the agreement would be accorded priority consistent with Section 507 of the Code.[103]

In *Certified Air Technologies, Inc.*,[104] the court likewise held that Section 1113 does not create a super priority for claims for prepetition employee benefit plan contributions due under an unrejected collective bargaining agreement. However, the court held that a claim for delinquent contributions to a multi-employer health plan that provides medical benefits to retirees is an allowed administrative expense under Section 1114(e)(2).[105] Other courts similarly have followed the Second, Third, and Fourth Circuits in holding that Section 1113 does not alter the payment priority scheme established by Sections 503 and 507.[106]

---

[101]*Compare In re* Typocraft Co., 229 B.R. 685 (Bankr. E.D. Mich. 1999) (cited in Main Edition) (regardless of whether debtor's failure to reject collective bargaining agreement in accordance with §1113(f) is treated as assumption of collective bargaining agreement, debtor was obligated to continue paying pre- and post-petition claims arising under agreement—thereby affording claims super priority), *with* Adventure Res., Inc. v. Holland, 137 F.3d 786 (4th Cir. 1998) (bankruptcy claim arising from breach of collective bargaining agreement may be accorded priority status only to extent it fits one of the exceptions set forth in §507).

[102]*In re* Kitty Hawk, Inc., 255 B.R. 428 (Bankr. N.D. Tex. 2000).

[103]*Id.* at 436. *See also In re* Fleming Packaging Corp., 2004 WL 2106579 (Bankr. C.D. Ill. 2004).

[104]300 B.R. 355 (Bankr. C.D. Cal. 2003).

[105]*Id.* at 371–72.

[106]*In re Fleming Packaging Corp.*, *supra* note 103 (holding that administrative priority status is afforded only to those unpaid obligations under a collective bargaining agreement that arise out of post-petition services); Colorado Springs Symphony Orchestra Ass'n, 308 B.R. 508 (D. Colo. 2004) (giving claims for wages dur-

In *Metro Fulfillment, Inc.*,[107] the Bankruptcy Panel of the Ninth Circuit distinguished the Ninth Circuit's decision in *Palau Corp.*[108] and held that claims for penalty wages due under California law were entitled to administrative priority because they arose out of the debtor's payment of post-petition wages on checks drawn on insufficient funds.

3. *Priority of Claims for Wages and Benefits Due Under Rejected Agreement*

The court in *Typocraft Co.*[109] held that regardless of whether a debtor's failure to reject a collective bargaining agreement in accordance with Section 1113(f) had to be treated as an assumption thereof, the debtor was obligated to continue paying pre- and post-petition claims arising under the agreement. Therefore, these claims were entitled to super-priority administrative expense status.

However, the court in *Certified Air Technologies, Inc.*,[110] surveying a split in circuit court authority, held that nothing in the language or legislative history of Section 1113(f) indicated that Congress intended that section to trump the priorities established under Section 507 of the Bankruptcy Code. The court thus sustained a Chapter 11 debtor-employer's objections to administrative expense claims filed by multi-employer employee benefit plans.

The Fourth Circuit distinguished *Unimet Corp.*[111] and concluded that a bankruptcy claim arising from a breach of a collective bargaining agreement may be accorded priority status only to the extent that it fits into one of the exceptions set forth in Section 507.[112]

---

ing post-petition period administrative priority, even though no work actually performed, because payments were contractually mandated and the employer had the benefit of employees being available to work). *But see* WCI Steel, Inc., 313 B.R. 414 (N.D. Ohio 2004) (following Unimet Corp., 842 F.2d 879 (6th Cir. 1988) (cited in the Main Edition) and holding that §1113 requires pension payments under a collective bargaining agreement regardless of Section 503's requirements).

[107]294 B.R. 306 (B.A.P. 9th Cir. 2003).

[108]18 F.3d 746 (9th Cir. 1994) (cited in the Main Edition).

[109]229 B.R. 685 (E.D. Mich. 1999).

[110]300 B.R. 355 (C.D. Cal. 2003).

[111]842 F.2d 879 (6th Cir. 1988).

[112]Adventure Res., Inc. v. Holland, 137 F.3d 786 (4th Cir.), *cert. denied*, 525 U.S. 962 (1998).

The court in *Continental Airlines, Inc.*[113] held that collectively bargained Labor Protective Provisions constituted an employment contract subject to the limitations of Section 502(b)(7) of the Code.

The district court in *First Alliance Mortgage Co.*[114] reaffirmed that class action claims are not disfavored in bankruptcy cases. The court went on to hold that *private parties* bringing suit under state law on behalf of the general public can qualify as creditors under the Bankruptcy Code.[115] The decision in *First Alliance* extends the majority rule that a government entity, acting on behalf of the public, is a creditor for purposes of the Bankruptcy Code and can collect payment obligations.[116]

4. *Enforcement of an Unrejected Collective Bargaining Agreement*

The courts continue to find that the terms of a collective bargaining agreement should be enforced absent a rejection under Section 1113.[117]

C. Severance Pay and Withdrawal Liability

Courts continue to struggle to determine when severance pay obligations constitute administrative expenses entitled to priority. The Tenth Circuit held that lump-sum severance payments are not administrative expenses unless the *liability* of the debtor-in-possession arose post-petition.[118] In this case, it was not enough that the *right* to the termination payments arose after the debtor-in-possession assumed control since the liability arose when the contracts providing for severance pay were executed (i.e., prepetition).[119] The court also rejected the employees' claim that three weeks of post-petition work was consideration for the lump-sum severance payments. That work, the court held, was consideration for the payment of salaries that the employees received in full.[120]

---

[113]257 B.R. 658 (Bankr. D. Del. 2000).

[114]269 B.R. 428 (C.D. Cal. 2001).

[115]*Id.* at 436–37.

[116]*Id.* at 436. *See also In re* McClung, 304 B.R. 419, 423 (D. Idaho 2004).

[117]Colorado Springs Symphony Orchestra Ass'n, 308 B.R. 508, 521 (D. Colo. 2004); *In re* Family Snacks, Inc., 257 B.R. 884, 166 LRRM 2400 (8th Cir. 2001). *See also In re* U.S. Truck Co. Holdings, Inc., 2000 Bankr. LEXIS 1376, 165 LRRM 2521 (E.D. Mich. 2000).

[118]*In re* Commercial Fin. Serv., Inc., 246 F.3d 1291 (10th Cir. 2001).

[119]*Id.* at 1295.

[120]*Id.*

With regard to the priority of severance pay claims under Section 507, the court in *In re Russell Cave Co.*[121] held that (1) such claims are given administrative priority only to the extent that they are earned *after* the bankruptcy petition was filed, (2) severance pay based on seniority is an administrative expense only to the extent it is earned by service during the bankruptcy case, and (3) prepetition claims for severance pay are given priority only to the extent earned within 90 days of the date of filing of the bankruptcy petition and only up to a limit of $4,300.

In *In re Redco, Inc.*,[122] the court was presented with a situation where a collective bargaining agreement granted employees a severance benefit for up to 10 years of service. After 10 years employees stopped earning additional severance benefits. The trustee argued that the severance benefit had not been earned during the 90-day prefiling period for employees who had greater than 10 years of service. The court held that the debtor's obligation for severance pay vested on the day the collective bargaining agreement became effective even though no new debt for separation pay accrued during the 90-day prefiling period. It still qualified as a Section 507(a)(3)(A) priority debt.

The treatment of severance pay provided for in a contract of employment was addressed by the court in *In re Phones For All.*[123] The court found that the agreement to pay severance constituted a conditional right to payment. The creditor, the debtor's former president and CEO, had a contractual right entitling him to a claim against the debtor's estate to receive his severance. However, the court held that the creditor was not entitled to receive his severance benefits as an administrative expense under Section 503. Under the terms of his employment contract, the severance pay was earned before the debtor filed bankruptcy and thus was not entitled to treatment as an administrative expense.

---

[121]248 B.R. 301 (E.D. Ky. 2000). *See also In re* Acoustiseal, Inc., 290 B.R. 354 (Bankr. W.D. Mo. 2003); *In re* Gateway Apparel, Inc. 238 B.R. 162 (Bankr. E.D. Mo. 1999) (recognizing severance pay claims as administrative expense to extent employees' services were benefit to estate and using formula pro-rating benefit based upon prepetition and post-petition services of employees).

[122]2003 Bankr. LEXIS 259 (Bankr. C.D. Ill. 2003).

[123]262 B.R. 914 (N.D. Tex. 2000).

A Sixth Circuit bankruptcy judge held, in *In re Cincinnati Cordage & Paper Co.*,[124] that where claims asserted by a Chapter 11 debtor's key employees for contractual severance benefits arose from their prepetition executive employment agreements, the claims did not qualify as an administrative expense entitled to priority payment even though the employees' termination occurred post-petition. Although the Chapter 11 debtor's key employees, in continuing to work for the debtor post-petition, may have relied upon an expectation of receiving generous severance benefits pursuant to terms of their prepetition employment agreements with the debtor, the employees were not entitled to recover such benefits, on a priority basis, given the complete lack of evidence that they had been damaged by their continued employment with the debtor.[125]

Similarly, in *In re M Group, Inc.*,[126] it was held that a proof of claim for severance benefits filed by a former employee was not entitled to payment as a prepetition priority claim inasmuch as it was fully earned when she signed a letter agreement with the debtors' predecessor some 6 years prior to filing a petition. There, the claim filed by the Chapter 11 debtors' former employee, which was based on a "termination without cause" type of severance provision, rather than a "length of service" or "termination in lieu of notice" provision, was determined to be a prepetition unsecured claim and not an administrative priority claim.[127] The claimant became eligible for severance pay prepetition when she signed a letter agreement with the debtors' predecessor. The debtors, therefore, assumed that contract when they purchased the predecessor's assets. The claim was held not to be the result of a post-petition transaction with the debtors, nor was it beneficial to the operation of the business.[128]

In *Harnischfeger Industries, Inc.*,[129] a Third Circuit bankruptcy court held that a debtor-employer could unilaterally amend its severance

---

[124]271 B.R. 264 (Bankr. S.D. Ohio 2001). *Cf. In re* Phones For All, Inc., *supra* note 123 (holding that when employment agreement provides for severance in lieu of notice, full claim for severance pay is accorded administrative priority if employee was terminated post-petition).

[125]*Id.*

[126]268 B.R. 896 (Bankr. D. Del. 2001). *See also In re* Worldwide Direct, Inc., 268 B.R. 69 (Bankr. D. Del. 2001) (holding that former employee's claim against Chapter 11 debtor-employer, based on debtor's alleged breach of severance agreement that called for debtor to issue stock, should be subordinated and given nonpriority status).

[127]*Id.*

[128]*Id.*

[129]270 B.R. 188 (D. Del. 2001).

pay policy prior to the termination of its workers' employment and prior to the vesting of their right to benefits. After doing so, the workers could not then assert a proof of claim against the Chapter 11 estate for severance benefits that were allegedly owed under a prior version of the policy.[130]

In *Hechinger Investment Co. of Delaware*,[131] the Third Circuit agreed that claims for "stay-on benefits" owed to former employees of a Chapter 11 debtor's retail stores, which were attributable to the employees' post-petition services, were entitled to administrative expense priority. However, the court rejected the workers' claim that the stay-on benefits attributable to their prepetition services also were entitled to priority. The workers argued that because they did not qualify for the benefits unless they remained with the company until their store closed or they were released, both post-petition events, the benefits actually were earned after the filing of the petition.[132] The employees' reliance on that date when the stay-on benefits were to be paid—at the end of the employees' term—was misplaced, the court held. Instead, Section 503 looks to the time when the services actually were "rendered," not when they were scheduled for payment. Since the consideration furnished by the former employees was the work they performed every day from the time they agreed to the stay-on benefits program until the closing of their stores or their release by the company, some of their services were rendered prepetition and some post-petition.[133]

In *Beverage Enterprises, Inc.*,[134] the bankruptcy court held that a claim asserted under the Worker Adjustment and Retraining Notification Act (WARN Act), based on a debtor's post-petition acts in failing to provide the requisite notice to the workers of the closing of the plant, is entitled to administrative expense priority status. According to the court, a WARN Act claim is analogous to a claim for severance pay required under an employment contract where an employee is laid off without being given a predetermined amount of notification. This type of severance, the court noted, is fully earned at the time of the employee's termination and, if the employer is in

---

[130] *Id.*

[131] 298 F.3d 219 (3d Cir. 2002).

[132] *Id.* at 224–25.

[133] *Id.* at 225. *See also In re* Waste Sys. Int'l, Inc., 280 B.R. 824, 828 (Bankr. D. Del. 2002) (holding that mere fact that prepetition obligation is dependent upon occurrence of post-petition event does not make that obligation a priority administrative expense).

[134] 225 B.R. 111 (Bankr. E.D. Pa. 1998).

bankruptcy at the time of the layoff, the full amount of the severance is deemed an administrative expense of the debtor.[135] Because the WARN Act claim at issue was earned as a result of events that unquestionably took place post-petition, the court determined that under Third Circuit precedent, the claims were entitled to administrative claim status.[136]

Courts continue to hold that an employer-debtor's liability under the Multi-Employer Pension Plan Amendments Act[137] for withdrawing from a multi-employer pension plan is not entitled to first priority status as an administrative expense.[138]

D. Limitations on Jurisdiction of the Bankruptcy Courts

In *San Rafael Baking Co.*,[139] the Ninth Circuit's Bankruptcy Appellate Panel held that Section 1113 did not give the bankruptcy court the authority to order a Chapter 11 debtor-in-possession to continue making employee health benefit contributions *after* expiration of the collective bargaining agreement where no proceedings were initiated before the expiration of the collective bargaining agreement.[140] According to the court, because the Board had exclusive subject matter jurisdiction over the controversy, only the Board could remedy an unfair labor practice based on a failure to bargain.[141]

---

[135]*Id.* at 115. *Cf. In re* Jamesway Corp., 235 B.R. 329, 348 (Bankr. S.D.N.Y. 1999) (holding that where employer made decision to terminate employees 6 days before company filed for Chapter 11 protection, employees' WARN Act claims were not entitled to administrative priority).

[136]*Beverage Enterprises, supra* note 134, 225 B.R. at 115–16. In response to the debtor's argument that WARN Act benefits are not "wages" and therefore not entitled to priority status, the court noted that "once the conclusion is reached that a claim does not fall within the explicitly listed category of wages for services rendered after the commencement of the case, it is still necessary to consider whether the claim would fit within the broader class of actual and necessary costs of preserving the estate." *Id.* at 116.

[137]29 U.S.C. §1381 et seq. (2002).

[138]*See, e.g.*, Bayly Corp., 163 F.3d 1205, 1209 (10th Cir. 1998) (noting that courts have uniformly "denied priority as a post-petition administrative expense to withdrawal liability claims predicated on pre-petition benefit liabilities, despite the fact that the withdrawal occurred post-petition").

[139]219 B.R. 860 (B.A.P. 9th Cir. 1998).

[140]*Id.* at 866. The court also noted that §1113 does not apply to expired collective bargaining agreements. *Id.* at 866–67.

[141]*Id.* at 865.

1. Bankruptcy Code Automatic Stay Provision

The automatic stay provision of the Bankruptcy Code was held to prevent a federal district court from enjoining the sale of the employer's operation pending arbitration of a union grievance over the sale. An earlier decision by a bankruptcy court denying relief to the union but suggesting that there could be remedies outside of bankruptcy law did not constitute the lifting of the automatic stay.[142]

In *Chao v. Hospital Staffing Services, Inc.*,[143] a Sixth Circuit court panel stayed a Fair Labor Standards Act (FLSA) action brought by the Secretary of Labor to prevent a Chapter 7 trustee from transporting records that an employer's staff had produced without compensation. The court recognized that a governmental enforcement action may fall outside Section 302 if it furthers both public and private interests, and the private interests do not significantly outweigh the public benefit from the enforcement.[144] The court, however, found that the Secretary's suit, brought outside the bankruptcy proceedings, should be stayed because it would promote the private rights of unpaid workers vis-à-vis other creditors of the debtor's estate.[145]

---

[142]Steelworkers v. LTV Steel Mining Co., 168 LRRM 2818 (D. Minn. 2001).

[143]270 F.3d 374 (6th Cir. 2001), *reh'g and suggestion for reh'g en banc denied* (Jan. 25, 2002).

[144]*Id.*

[145]*Id. See also* NLRB v. McDermott, 300 B.R. 40 n.8 (D. Colo. 2003) (noting that it cannot be argued that "the Board is not a governmental unit for purposes of section 362(b)(4)" and holding that automatic stay provision of Bankruptcy Code, Section 324(a), did not apply to Board's application for enforcement of subpoenas against wife of party who was found to have engaged in unfair labor practices); *In re* Midway Airlines Corp., 283 B.R. 846, 851 (E.D.N.C. 2002) (holding that actions of North Carolina Department of Labor in seeking to hold debtor-employer liable with respect to prepetition vacation wage claims of its employees were undertaken principally to adjudicate private claims of debtor's employees, and did not come within "police or regulatory power" exception to automatic stay). *But see* Chao v. BDK Indus., L.L.C., 296 B.R. 165 (C.D. Ill. 2003) (holding that, while a FLSA action brought by the Secretary advances the private rights of employees, it serves the public interest as the primary purpose of the action was to protect workers and to discourage unfair competition by employers who would pay substandard wages, particularly since the employees would not receive extra priority as their claims would be pursued in the pending bankruptcy action); *In re* Mohawk Greenfield Motel Corp., 239 B.R. 1 (Bankr. D. Mass. 1999) (holding that monetary award issued by Massachusetts Commission Against Discrimination fell within "police or regulatory power" exception to automatic stay).

2. *Jurisdiction of Bankruptcy Court to Enjoin NLRB Proceedings*

A Third Circuit bankruptcy panel determined in *Allegheny Health, Education & Research Foundation*[146] that it could exercise at least "related to" jurisdiction both over a complaint filed by a purchaser of a debtor's assets to set aside an arbitration award and over a union's counterclaim to enforce the award. The court based its jurisdiction on the fact that these matters potentially affected the Chapter 11 estate.[147] To the extent that the purchaser had not assumed the debtor's "sick leave" obligations, the bankruptcy court's determination on whether to enforce or set aside the arbitrator's award could result in a claim by the union against the estate for sick leave benefits or by the purchaser seeking indemnification from the estate.[148]

E. Bankruptcy of a Labor Organization

In *In re Teamsters Local 890*,[149] the local union sought bankruptcy protection after losing a $1.3 million judgment to an employer group. In response to a challenge by the union's creditors, the court ruled that the local union's collective bargaining agreement and its right to collect future member dues could not be liquidated to pay off the creditors. Accordingly, the proposed reorganization plan was confirmed because it satisfied the "best interests of creditor" test in accordance with Section 1129(a)(7)(A)(ii) of the Bankruptcy Code.[150]

III. THE NLRA AND IMMIGRATION LAW [NEW TOPIC]

In recent years the Supreme Court has twice considered the relationship between the Act and federal immigration statutes. In *Sure-Tan v. NLRB*,[151] the Supreme Court found that undocumented aliens are employees within the meaning of the Act and entitled to the Act's protections. The Court agreed with the Board that the employer constructively discharged its alien employees by reporting them to the Immigration and Naturalization Service, with the result that they were deported. The Court tailored the remedy to the im-

---

[146] 265 B.R. 88 (Bankr. W.D. Pa. 2001).

[147] *Id.*

[148] *Id.*

[149] 265 F.3d 869, 168 LRRM 2161 (9th Cir. 2001).

[150] *Id.*

[151] 467 U.S. 883, 116 LRRM 2857 (1984).

migration status of the employees, with offers of reinstatement conditioned on legal reentry to the United States and no back pay for those periods in which they were not entitled to be present and employed in the United States.

In 2002, the Supreme Court again addressed the relationships between the Act and federal immigration law. In *Hoffman Plastic Compounds, Inc. v. NLRB*,[152] the Court held that an award of back pay under the Act to employees who were undocumented workers under the Immigration Reform and Control Act (IRCA) was in conflict with the prohibitions expressed in IRCA. The Court ruled that the NLRB could not award back pay to undocumented employees for time not worked.

Since *Hoffman Plastic* was decided, the NLRB general counsel issued a "Memorandum on Discriminatees Who May Be Undocumented Aliens."[153] In the memorandum, the general counsel concluded that the *Hoffman* decision foreclosed the Board from awarding back pay to an individual who was not legally authorized to work in the United States during the back-pay period since the award conflicted with federal statutes and policies unrelated to the Act. Prior law was unaffected by *Hoffman* insofar as undocumented aliens are employees entitled to the protections of the Act, and have the right to vote in NLRB elections.[154] The general counsel also noted that an individual's work authorization status is irrelevant to a respondent's liability under the Act, and questions concerning that status should be left for the compliance stage of proceedings. On this basis, regions were advised to continue to object to a charged party's attempt to elicit evidence concerning an employee's asserted undocumented status in order to escape unfair labor practice liability.[155]

Further, the general counsel's memorandum noted that conditional reinstatement is an appropriate remedy for the unlawful discharge of undocumented employees knowingly hired by an employer. In order to be reinstated, however, the former employee must first

---

[152]535 U.S. 137, 169 LRRM 2769 (2002).

[153]BNA Labor Relations Expediter, LRX 43419. Also available on NLRB Web site, www.nlrb.gov.

[154]Citing *County Window Cleaning Co.*, 328 NLRB 190 n.2 (1999).

[155]*See also* Tuv Taam Corp., 340 NLRB No. 86, *6 (2003) (holding in cases where immigration status has no bearing on whether employer has committed unfair labor practice, questions regarding employee status must be litigated at compliance stage and cannot insulate employer from decision on merits of complaint or consequences of its unlawful conduct).

satisfy IRCA's verification procedures. The regions were directed to refrain from seeking conditional reinstatement in cases where an employer establishes that it would not have hired or retained the employee had it known of the employee's undocumented status during the employment period. Back pay is not available for the period a discharged discriminatee is legally unavailable for work. According to the memorandum, regions should not seek back pay in discharge cases concerning undocumented discriminatees at all, even though *Hoffman* did not directly address the activities of an employer who knowingly employed undocumented persons.

In addition, as noted by the general counsel, *Hoffman* does not expressly preclude an award of back pay in nondischarge cases, as it focused on work "not performed." In nondischarge cases, the goal is to make the employees whole for work already performed. The Department of Labor uses this approach in FLSA cases where undocumented workers claim substandard payments.[156]

Back pay for employees unlawfully demoted into lower-paying jobs also remains an open question. The analysis could involve "work not performed," thus, precluding back pay or, alternatively, continued employment with different duties and no further duty to mitigate. In either case, the regions were directed to seek advice on this issue. The traditional Board remedies of cease-and-desist orders and contempt violations still remain available under *Sure-Tan* and *Hoffman.* Moreover, the Board may seek formal settlements for employers that knowingly hire undocumented workers and use work authorization status to threaten and discharge them in retaliation for Section 7 activities.

In light of the limits on back pay, the general counsel deemed posting notices and reading such notices particularly appropriate remedies. The general counsel's memorandum also stated that the Board may seek to compel employers to continue to assist undocumented workers in efforts to become regular employees, and, in an extreme situation, the regions may seek advice on giving union access to employees or to employee rosters to remedy violations during union organizing campaigns.

In cases under the FLSA, courts have manifested the same reluctance to permit discovery of immigration status as the Board in

---

[156]*See* U.S. Department of Labor, Employment Standards Division, Wage & Hour Division, "Application of U.S. Labor Laws to Immigrant Workers: Effect of *Hoffman Plastics* Decision on the Laws Enforced by the Wage and Hour Division" (Fact Sheet No. 48) (Aug. 14, 2002), available on the DOL Web site, www.dol.gov.

resisting attempts to elicit evidence of the undocumented status of employees. In *Zeng Liu v. Donna Karan International, Inc.*,[157] the plaintiffs were Chinese immigrants who brought a class action under the FLSA. Defendant Donna Karan sought discovery of documents pertaining to plaintiffs' immigration status, citing *Hoffman* as a basis for the request. The court denied the request as not relevant. The court noted that even if a confidential agreement were entered, the danger of intimidation existed, possibly destroying the cause of action.[158]

In *Rodriguez v. The Texan, Inc.*,[159] the plaintiffs filed a motion in limine to preclude the defendant employer from arguing that the plaintiffs' status as illegal aliens precluded them from recovering damages under the FLSA. The court held that failure to mitigate damages is an affirmative defense under Rule 8(c) of the Federal Rules of Civil Procedure, the defendant failed to plead it, and the motion in limine was granted based upon the defendant's waiver of the mitigation issue. Similarly, in *De La Rosa v. Northern Harvest Furniture*,[160] the court denied an employer's request for documents confirming that employees were legally authorized to work in the United States. Under *Hoffman* the appropriate period for consideration was post-termination back pay, covering the period after an employee is terminated and before the employer offers reinstatement. Since the employer requested documents for a different period of time, the court did not have to directly address the issue, but it also noted that *Hoffman* was not dispositive of the issues raised in the motion to compel.

In *Flores v. Albertsons, Inc.*,[161] the court again denied a request for documents concerning immigration status because of the in terrorem effect that producing the documents would cause. The court noted it was entirely likely that any undocumented class member forced to produce documents related to his or her immigration status would withdraw from the class action suit rather than produce such documents and face deportation. The court also noted that federal courts are clear that the protections of FLSA are available to citizens and undocumented workers alike. It distinguished *Hoffman* because there the court dealt with work "not performed" rather than a claim under the FLSA to recover unpaid wages to which the plaintiffs claimed

---

[157]207 F. Supp. 2d 191 (S.D.N.Y. 2002).
[158]*Id.* at 193.
[159]No. 01 C 1478, 2002 U.S. Dist. LEXIS 17379 (N.D. Ill. Sept. 13, 2002).
[160]210 F.R.D. 237 (C.D. Ill. 2002).
[161]No. CV 01-00515, 2002 U.S. Dist. LEXIS 6171 (C.D. Cal. Apr. 9, 2002).

they were entitled. The court noted that *Hoffman* did not hold that an undocumented employee was barred from recovering unpaid wages for work actually performed.

In *Singh v. Jutla,*[162] the court held that an illegal alien employee's allegations that his employer reported him to the Immigration and Naturalization Service with retaliatory intent after the employee filed a wage claim against the employer with a state labor commissioner was sufficient to state a claim for retaliation in violation of the FLSA. In that case, the defendants contended that *Hoffman* precluded a cause of action by the plaintiff. The court analyzed *Sure-Tan* and *Hoffman* and noted that in *Patel v. Quality Inn South*[163] the Eleventh Circuit held that the FLSA applies to illegal aliens. The court also said that *Hoffman* did not hold that an undocumented employee is barred from recovering unpaid wages for work actually performed.[164] In *Cortez v. Medina's Landscaping,*[165] the court reached the same conclusion. As in *Singh,* the court distinguished *Hoffman,* stating that it dealt with back pay for work not performed. The court then denied a motion to compel discovery concerning the plaintiff's citizenship status on the grounds that the information was not pertinent.

---

[162] 214 F. Supp. 2d 1056 (N.D. Cal. 2002).

[163] 846 F.2d 700 (11th Cir. 1998).

[164] *Singh, supra* note 162, 214 F. Supp. 2d at 1060.

[165] No. 00 C 6320, 2002 U.S. Dist. LEXIS 18831 (N.D. Ill. Sept. 30, 2002).

CHAPTER 30

RICO AND LABOR LAW

II. HISTORICAL BACKGROUND OF RICO AND ITS APPLICABILITY TO LABOR DISPUTES

B. Subsequent Amendments and Proposals to Limit RICO

As noted in the Main Edition, the decision in *National Organization for Women v. Scheidler*[1] prompted an effort to amend the RICO statute to remove extortion as a predicate act for civil RICO actions. After subsequent proceedings in the lower courts, the Supreme Court granted certiorari again in *Scheidler*.[2] The Supreme Court's holding that a predicate act of extortion will lie only where the RICO defendant pursues or receives "something of value" from the RICO plaintiffs that the defendants could "exercise, transfer, or sell"[3] will affect

[1]510 U.S. 249 (1994).

[2]National Org. for Women v. Scheidler, 267 F.3d 687 (7th Cir. 2001), *cert. granted*, 535 U.S. 1016 (2002).

[3]National Org. for Women v. Scheidler, 537 U.S. 393, 404 (2003).

the use of extortion predicate acts in future RICO suits and possibly prompt additional efforts to amend the RICO statute.[4]

The court in *In re Enron Corporation Securities, Derivative & ERISA Litigation*[5] held that the RICO amendment of the Private Securities Litigation Reform Act of 1995 (PSLRA) that eliminated securities fraud as a predicate act under Section 1961(1) for a private cause of action under RICO, bars claims that could be actionable under the securities laws even when the plaintiff cannot bring an action under the securities laws.

III. Overview of the Statute

A. Key Elements

1. Racketeering Activity

Many of the predicate acts enumerated in the statute have been the basis of RICO allegations in the labor arena. Recent cases include allegations of immigration violations,[6] peonage,[7] involuntary servitude,[8] and embezzlement[9] as well as state law felonies for extortion[10] and attempted murder.[11]

In *Overnite Transportation Co. v. Teamsters*,[12] the district court dismissed predicate acts based on allegations of various state criminal laws. The court found that "assault, attempted assault, felonious as-

---

[4]*See* Section IV.E.3.b. [Predicate Acts Commonly Alleged in Labor Cases; 18 U.S.C. §1951: "Racketeering" Prohibited by the Hobbs Act; Application of the Hobbs Act to RICO Cases After *Enmons*; Property], *infra.*

[5]284 F. Supp. 2d 511, 620 (S.D. Tex. 2003).

[6]Commercial Cleaning Servs. v. Colin Serv. Sys., Inc., 2000 WL 545126 (D. Conn. Mar. 21, 2000), *vacated and remanded*, 271 F.3d 374 (2d Cir. 2001); Mendoza v. Zirkle Fruit Co., 2000 WL 33225470 (E.D. Wash. Sept. 27, 2000), *rev'd*, 301 F.3d 1163 (9th Cir. 2002); Zavala v. Wal-Mart Stores, Inc., Civil Action No. 03-CIV-5309 (JAG) (D.N.J.).

[7]Does v. The Gap, Inc., 2002 WL 1000068 (D. N. Mar. I. May 10, 2002); Does v. The Gap, Inc., 2001 WL 1842389 (D. N. Mar. I. Nov. 26, 2001).

[8]*Id.*

[9]Teamsters v. Carey, 163 F. Supp. 2d 271, 168 LRRM 2439 (S.D.N.Y. 2001), *complaint dismissed on other grounds*, 297 F. Supp. 2d 706 (S.D.N.Y. 2004), *aff'd*, 124 Fed. Appx. 41 (2d Cir. 2005).

[10]Titan Int'l, Inc. v. Becker, 189 F. Supp. 2d 817 (C.D. Ill. 2001).

[11]Overnite Transp. Co. v. Teamsters, 168 F. Supp. 2d 826, 844–46, 167 LRRM 2111 (W.D. Tenn. 2001).

[12]*Id.*

sault, aggravated assault, aggravated vehicular assault, aggravated menacing, battery, felony with a deadly weapon, criminal recklessness, and reckless endangerment are neither an enumerated racketeering activity in Section 1961(1)(A) nor fall within the generic category of any enumerated racketeering activities."[13]

A RICO plaintiff must plead and prove all the elements of each predicate act, or else that allegation will be dismissed (as will be the RICO claim itself, if all such allegations of predicate acts are dismissed). For example, in *Thornton v. United States Department of Labor*,[14] a former official of the Transportation Communications Union alleged that he was wrongfully accused of mismanagement and misappropriation of union funds. His RICO claims were dismissed on the defendants' motion for summary judgment because he failed to allege any acts of "racketeering activity" against other union officials or the government.

In *AK Steel Corp. v. Steelworkers*,[15] the district court dismissed a RICO claim, concluding that allegations that the defendants committed hundreds of violent acts were legal conclusions that needed to be supported by "specific facts" such as the identity of the individuals who committed the violence and their relationship to the union defendants.[16]

Furthermore, a complaint "contain[ing] only general and conclusory allegations with regard to predicate acts" of fraud is insufficient to state a RICO claim.[17]

In *Miller v. Yokohama Tire Corp.*,[18] the plaintiff claimed that the defendants committed predicate acts of mail and wire fraud by falsely informing him he was not entitled to overtime because he was a salaried employee.[19] The court found that the plaintiff failed to state a fraud claim (and therefore failed to state a RICO claim) because of the general rule that fraud cannot be predicated on misrepresentations of law.[20] As none of the exceptions to this general rule applied, the court upheld the dismissal of the RICO claim.[21]

---

[13] *Id.* at 843.

[14] 2000 WL 1923501 (E.D. Mich. Nov. 17, 2000), *aff'd*, 2001 WL 700805 (6th Cir. June 15, 2001).

[15] 2002 U.S. Dist. LEXIS 19676, *1 (S.D. Ohio Mar. 30, 2002).

[16] *Id.* at *17–19.

[17] Walls v. Longshoremen (ILWU) Local 23, 10 Fed. Appx. 485, 488 (9th Cir. 2001).

[18] 358 F.3d 616, 9 Wage & Hour Cases 2d 355 (9th Cir. 2004).

[19] 358 F.3d 616.

[20] *Id.* at 621.

[21] *Id.* at 622.

In *Does v. The Gap, Inc.*,[22] a RICO suit alleging a conspiracy by manufacturers and retailers to exploit garment workers on Saipan, Commonwealth of the Northern Mariana Islands, the plaintiffs' first amended complaint alleged predicate acts of peonage, involuntary servitude, the Hobbs Act, and certain Commonwealth crimes. The district court found that the plaintiffs adequately pleaded all but the involuntary servitude predicates.[23] After amendment, the plaintiffs still failed to plead involuntary servitude.[24]

As noted in the Main Edition, in *National Organization for Women v. Scheidler*,[25] the Supreme Court established that a plaintiff need not assert that the racketeering activity was accompanied by an underlying economic motive. After subsequent proceedings in the lower courts, the Supreme Court granted certiorari again in *Scheidler*[26] to address (1) whether injunctive relief is available in a private civil action under RICO,[27] and (2) whether political protesters' intentional interference with the public's access to a business's premises and with the freedom of its putative customers to obtain services there violates the Hobbs Act.[28]

In reversing a jury verdict for the plaintiffs, the Supreme Court concluded that it would be an unwarranted expansion to characterize the defendants' actions as having "obtained" property because the defendants neither pursued nor received something of value from the plaintiffs, despite the fact that the defendants effectively deprived the plaintiffs of their ability to exercise their property rights by shutting down their clinics. According to the Court, to hold that the defendants' actions were extortionate for purposes of the Hobbs Act would eliminate the distinction between extortion and coercion and conflict with the express language of the Act.[29]

---

[22] 2001 WL 1842389 (D. N. Mar. I. Nov. 26, 2001).

[23] *Id.* at *6–8.

[24] Does v. The Gap, Inc., 2002 WL 1000068, *14–15 (D. N. Mar. I. May 10, 2002).

[25] 510 U.S. 249, 257 (1994).

[26] National Org. for Women v. Scheidler, 267 F.3d 687 (7th Cir. 2001), *cert. granted*, 535 U.S. 1016 (2002).

[27] *See* Section VI.C. [Remedies; Trusteeships and Other Injunctive Relief], *infra*.

[28] *See* Section IV.E.2. [Predicate Acts Commonly Alleged in Labor Cases; 18 U.S.C. §1951: "Racketeering" Prohibited by the Hobbs Act; *Enmons*], and Section IV.E.3.b. [Predicate Acts Commonly Alleged in Labor Cases; 18 U.S.C. §1951: "Racketeering" Prohibited by the Hobbs Act; Application of the Hobbs Act to RICO Cases After *Enmons*; Property], *infra*.

[29] *Scheidler*, 537 U.S. at 405–06.

In its decision in *Scheidler*,[30] the Supreme Court found that there was no dispute that the political protesters "interfered with, disrupted, and in some instances completely deprived the [RICO plaintiffs] of their ability to exercise their property rights."[31] Nevertheless, the Supreme Court held that, because the protestors "did not obtain or attempt to obtain property" from the RICO plaintiffs, there was no basis upon to which to find that the protestors committed extortion under the Hobbs Act.[32]

Although *Scheidler* held that the Hobbs Act requires that property be obtained or that there be an attempt to obtain property, the Court did not alter the definition of property or imply that property be tangible for purposes of the Act. Indeed, the majority explicitly rejected the dissent's suggestion that the Court overruled *United States v. Tropiano*,[33] which held that the intangible right to solicit refuse collection accounts constituted property for purposes of the Hobbs Act.[34]

The court in *Dooley v. Crab Boat Owners Ass'n*,[35] rendering a decision expressly based on *Scheidler*, held that intangible property, such as the right to solicit business, is property for purposes of the Hobbs Act, and that such property can be the object of extortion for purposes of the Act. In *Dooley*, the plaintiffs were in the business of harvesting crab and the defendants were competing associations. The plaintiff alleged that the defendants threatened the plaintiffs' customers with loss of business, threatened violence, and damaged the plaintiffs' property in an attempt by the defendants to obtain a higher price for crab.[36] The *Dooley* court concluded that the plaintiffs had sufficiently alleged predicate acts supporting a claim of attempted Hobbs Act extortion. Analogizing to *Tropiano*,[37] the court held that the defendants did not merely restrict the plaintiffs' activities as petitioners did in *Scheidler*, but rather, wrongfully attempted to acquire something of value through threats, warnings, and property dam-

[30]National Org. for Women v. Scheidler, 537 U.S. 393 (2003).

[31]*Id.* at 404.

[32]*Id.* at 409. The Court also found that state law extortion offenses for purposes of RICO must also contain an "obtaining" requirement, and because the protestors had not obtained or attempted to obtain property, the state law extortion statutes could not support the RICO verdict. *Id.* at 410.

[33]418 F.2d 1069 (2d Cir. 1969).

[34]*Scheidler, supra* note 30, 537 U.S. at 403 n.6.

[35]271 F. Supp. 2d 1207 (N.D. Cal. 2003).

[36]*Id.* at 1209, 1214.

[37]418 F.2d 1069 (2d Cir. 1969).

age, as the defendants did in *Tropiano*. According to the *Dooley* court, the property at issue was the plaintiffs' right to harvest crab and the defendants' attempts to obtain that property were wrongful because the defendants had no legal interest in the property.[38]

Similarly, the court in *Titan International, Inc. v. Becker*[39] denied the union defendant's motion to dismiss Titan's extortion allegations based on *Scheidler*, concluding that the allegations were legally sufficient because the union's alleged use of bomb threats, violence, and other illegal acts to obtain money or other property from Titan may constitute extortion for purposes of the Hobbs Act.[40]

In contrast, the court in *United States v. Bellomo*[41] held that the union members' right to democratic participation in the union's affairs and responsible union representation was not "obtainable" by the defendants because of a statutory prohibition against voting by proxy. In light of *Scheidler*, the district court found itself "constrained to ask how can that union member's right be exercised, transferred, or sold" when the relevant federal statutes prohibit vot-

---

[38]271 F. Supp. 2d at 1214 n.8.

[39]No. 00-3257 (C.D. Ill. July 31, 2003).

[40]In *Titan International, Inc. v. Becker, et al.*, 189 F. Supp.2d 817 (C.D. Ill. 2001), Titan brought a RICO claim that included, inter alia, allegations that the defendants: (1) filed and prosecuted frivolous and objectively baseless workers' compensation claims; and (2) filed a frivolous shareholder derivative lawsuit. The shareholder derivative lawsuit was filed in Illinois state court with the plaintiffs represented by Milberg Weiss. (Beck, et al., v. Taylor, et al., Case No. 00-L-30, Circuit Court of the Eighth Judicial Circuit, County of Adams.) Published reports indicate that Titan's attorneys brought a motion for sanctions accusing Milberg Weiss attorneys of misrepresenting the involvement (or rather, the non-involvement) of the United Steelworkers of America in the derivative suit. *See* The National Law Journal, *Firm Drops Suit Amidst Controversy* (June 23, 2003). The derivative lawsuit was voluntarily dismissed in May 2003 by stipulation of the parties. The Stipulation of Dismissal contains two provisions of note. First, the three law firms representing the plaintiffs (including Milberg Weiss):

> Represent and warrant to Titan and the Defendants that they presently represent no person other than Plaintiffs and Intervenor who has an intent to assert or file any claims against Titan or the Defendants. *These firms further represent and warrant that they will not seek out or take any affirmative steps to seek the representation of any person against Titan or any Defendant involving matters related to Titan.*

Further, Milberg Weiss specifically agreed not to represent any stockholder, person, or party in litigation against Titan in the future. For its part, Titan released and waived all potential claims against the law firms in Titan's RICO suit.

[41]263 F. Supp. 2d 561 (E.D.N.Y. 2003).

ing by proxy.[42] In its attempt to "'divine, as best it can, what would be the result of an appeal,'"[43] the court directed that the relevant counts be stricken "in the belief that *Scheidler* requires it" and further stated, "[b]ecause reasonable minds might conclude that the issue is not entirely free from doubt, the government is encouraged to exercise its right to appeal this determination as it may."[44]

In August 2003, the District Court for the District of Connecticut relied on *Scheidler* in granting the defendants' motions to dismiss certain RICO claims in *Interstate Flagging v. Town of Darien.*[45] In *Interstate Flagging*, the plaintiff provided traffic control services for construction and utility maintenance contractors. Interstate Flagging brought suit against certain municipalities and the presidents of the police officers unions in those municipalities alleging, inter alia, that the union presidents "committed predicate acts that would constitute a pattern of 'racketeering activity'—namely extortion,"[46] by enforcing and encouraging policies, regulations, ordinances, and customs that required that police officers have the exclusive right, or the right of first refusal, to provide traffic control services for construction or utility maintenance contractors within specified areas through the use of extortion and physical threats that affected commerce in violation of RICO and the Hobbs Act.[47] Although the plaintiff alleged that police officers harassed and threatened its employees at work sites, forced its employees off of the work sites, and led companies to cancel their contracts with the plaintiff,[48] the court concluded that the plaintiff did not allege that the defendants obtained any property from the plaintiff.[49] Analogizing to *Scheidler*, the district court dismissed the complaint, stating that the plaintiff failed to allege that the union presidents obtained any property from the plaintiff as a result of the police officers' alleged wrongful actions.[50]

---

[42]*Id.* (citing 29 U.S.C. §§ 402(k) & 481(b)).

[43]*Id.* at 576 (quoting Spector Motor Serv. v. Walsh, 139 F.2d 809, 823 (2d Cir. 1944) (dissenting opinion)).

[44]*Id. Cf.* United States v. Genova, 333 F.3d 750, 758 (7th Cir. 2003) (citing *Scheidler* as the basis for its refusal to adopt an expansive interpretation of RICO, and stating that *Scheidler* "reject[ed] an expansive interpretation of extortion designed to bring noxious activity within RICO").

[45]283 F. Supp. 2d 641 (D. Conn. 2003).

[46]*Id.* at 646.

[47]*Id.* at 646–47.

[48]*Id.* at 644.

[49]*Id.* at 647.

[50]*Id.*

In *Doe v. Unocal Corp.*,[51] the court dismissed RICO claims brought by residents of Myanmar based on Hobbs Act extortion of their labor because RICO did not apply extraterritorally to the defendant American company under the particular facts.[52]

In *Aldana v. Fresh Del Monte Produce*,[53] the plaintiffs asserted RICO claims tied to their leadership in trade union activities.[54] The court dismissed the RICO claims because the allegations essentially concerned prepatory activities for foreign conduct that did not have a substantial effect within the United States.[55]

In *Cobbs v. Sheahan*,[56] the court held that a complaint alleging extortion based on the "alleged demand for a political contribution in return for a patronage job" and satisfied the pleading burden placed on the plaintiff.[57]

3. Enterprise

In *Cedric Kushner Promotions, Ltd. v. King*,[58] the Supreme Court approved the requirement of "nonidentity" of the person and the enterprise for claims under Section 1962(c). The Court held that the distinctiveness requirement is satisfied "when a corporate employee unlawfully conducts the affairs of the corporation of which he is the sole owner—whether he conducts those affairs within the scope, or beyond the scope, of corporate authority."[59] Basing its decision, in part, on the plain language of Section 1962(c), the Court reasoned that "[t]he corporate owner/employee, a natural person, is distinct from the corporation itself, a legally different entity with different rights and responsibilities due to its different legal status. And we can find nothing in the statute that requires more 'separateness' than that."[60]

[51]395 F.3d 932 (9th Cir. 2002), *aff'd by* 248 F.3d 915 (9th Cir. 2002), *reh'g en banc granted,* 395 F.3d 978 (2003).

[52]395 F.3d at 961–62.

[53]305 F. Supp. 2d 1285 (S.D. Fla. 2003).

[54]*Id.* at 1288

[55]*Id.* at 1306. *See also* Sinaltrainal v. Coca-Cola Co., 256 F. Supp. 2d 1345, 1359 (S.D. Fla. 2003).

[56] 319 F. Supp. 2d 865 (N.D. Ill. 2004).

[57] *Id.* at 870.

[58]533 U.S. 158 (2001).

[59]*Id.* at 158.

[60]*Id.* at 163.

Relying on *Kushner,* the court in *Bonavitacola Electrical Contractors, Inc. v. Boro Developers, Inc.*[61] held that an enterprise was adequately pled where the defendant corporation was alleged to constitute the enterprise, and the defendant corporation and two of its employees/officers were alleged to have conducted its affairs through a pattern of racketeering activity.[62]

In *Bucklew v. Hawkins, Ash, Baptie & Co., LLP,*[63] judgment in favor of the defendant was affirmed in a RICO claim involving a parent corporation and its wholly owned subsidiaries on the basis that the parent company and its wholly owned subsidiaries were not distinct.[64] The Seventh Circuit, however, also noted the outcome could be different if the parent's decision to operate through its subsidiaries somehow facilitated unlawful activity.[65]

The plaintiff in *Chen v. Mayflower Transit, Inc.*[66] alleged an enterprise comprised of Mayflower and the local moving companies with which Mayflower did business. Mayflower asserted that the distinctiveness requirement was not met because the alleged enterprise consisted only of Mayflower and its agents acting within the scope of their authority as agents.[67] The district court found that the distinctiveness requirement had been met because: (1) the enterprise was not simply Mayflower by another name, and Mayflower's relationship with the local moving companies was not employer–employee or parent–subsidiary; (2) the local moving companies did substantial business apart from their relationship with Mayflower; (3) Mayflower and the enterprise had distinct roles; (4) the enterprise did not constitute Mayflower's regular business; and (5) the person–enterprise relationship may have empowered Mayflower to perpetrate the alleged fraud.[68]

In *Miller v. Yokohama Tire Corp.,*[69] the court upheld dismissal of the plaintiff's RICO claim against the defendant employer because the employer was not distinct from the enterprise when the plaintiff

---

[61]2003 U.S. Dist. LEXIS 2190 (E.D. Pa. Feb. 12, 2003), *aff'd,* 87 Fed. Appx. 227 (3rd Cir. 2003), *cert. denied,* 125 S. Ct. 57 (2004).

[62]*Id.* at *13–14. The court dismissed the complaint on other grounds.

[63]329 F.3d 923 (7th Cir. 2003).

[64]*Id.* at 934.

[65]*Id.*

[66]315 F. Supp. 2d 886 (N.D. Ill. 2004).

[67]*Id.* at 901.

[68]*Id.* at 903–08.

[69]358 F.3d 616, 9 Wage & Hour Cases 2d 355 (9th Cir. 2004).

alleged the employer should be liable for racketeering committed by its employees based on respondeat superior.[70]

In *Dooley v. Crab Boat Owners Ass'n*,[71] the court found that three fishing associations that cooperated to determine an appropriate price, abided by the decisions of each other as to the agreed price, and voted by majority vote sufficient to set forth an enterprise.[72] Likewise, individual members of the associations who served in executive positions could be found to have participated in the operation of the enterprise.[73] The defendant company and its principal, who were not members of the association, could reasonably be found to have participated in the operation of the enterprise because they abided by the fishing associations' decisions, they picketed, and they were assessed a tax remitted to the associations.[74] Finally, three individual defendants who were not members of the association, but who abided by prices set by the associations, participated in a strike, and otherwise supported the associations could be found to have participated in the enterprise.[75]

In *Williams v. Mohawk Industries, Inc.*,[76] the plaintiffs, a group of current and former employees eligible to be employed in the United States, alleged that the defendant, a large carpet manufacturer with extensive operations in Georgia, violated RICO by knowingly hiring and harboring illegal aliens in order to keep the costs of labor as low as possible. According to the plaintiffs, the defendant's widespread employment and harboring of illegal workers substantially increased the supply of workers from which the defendant hired its hourly workers. The plaintiffs further contended that because of the increased size of the labor pool, the defendant had depressed the wages of its hourly employees, including the plaintiffs.[77] The district court found that the plaintiffs had properly pled an association-in-fact enterprise consisting of the defendant, third-party employment agencies, and other recruiters who supplied the defendant with illegal workers that was sufficiently distinct from the defendant.[78] The court

[70] *Id.* at 620.
[71] 2004 U.S. LEXIS 7117 (N.D. Cal. 2004).
[72] *Id.* at *17–18.
[73] *Id.*
[74] *Id.* at *18.
[75] *Id.* at *20.
[76] 314 F. Supp. 2d 1333 (N.D. Ga. 2004).
[77] *Id.* at 1339.
[78] *Id.* at 1348.

reasoned that whether the third-party recruiters were in fact agents of the defendant was a factual issue that could not be resolved on a motion to dismiss.[79] On this issue the court declined the defendant's invitation to follow the Seventh Circuit's decision in *Baker v. IBP, Inc.*[80] In *Baker*, a case with similar allegations, the Seventh Circuit found among other problems with the plaintiffs' complaint, that the plaintiffs had alleged an enterprise that came "perilously close to alleging that [defendant] plus its agents and employees is an 'enterprise,' a theory that won't fly."[81]

In *Baisch v. Gallina*,[82] the Second Circuit, in reversing the dismissal of the plaintiff's complaint, held that the plaintiff had demonstrated the defendants' discretionary authority and direction of the enterprise by recruiting financing for the enterprise, obtaining bonds and insurance certificates, concealing the enterprise's deceptive payroll practices, and in representing other participants in the enterprise in meetings with the plaintiff.

In *In re Managed Care Litigation*,[83] the court found that the plaintiffs had adequately alleged an association-in-act enterprise consisting of the managed care company defendants, their trade associations, vendors, unidentified health insurance companies not named as defendants, and other third-party entities. The court held that the plaintiffs had alleged sufficient factual detail of the enterprise and its function and purpose and associational links to survive a motion to dismiss.[84]

In *Lockheed Martin Corp. v. Boeing Co.*,[85] a case involving the alleged theft of trade secrets, the court found that an enterprise consisting of Boeing, several former employees and its in-house counsel as well as others known and unknown to the plaintiff was not sufficiently distinct from the defendant person, Boeing, to survive a motion to dismiss.[86]

---

[79] *Id.*

[80] 357 F.3d 685, 691 (7th Cir. 2004), *reh'g en banc denied*, 2004 U.S. App. LEXIS 8689 (7th Cir. 2004), *cert. denied*, 125 S. Ct. 412 (2004).

[81] *Id.* (citing Bucklew v. Hawkins, Ash, Baptie & Co., 329 F.3d 923, 934 (7th Cir. 2003)).

[82] 346 F.3d 366, 376 (2d Cir. 2003).

[83] 298 F. Supp. 2d 1259 (S.D. Fla. 2003).

[84] *Id.* at 1275–76.

[85] 314 F. Supp. 2d 1198 (S.D. Fla. 2004).

[86] *Id.* at *1217.

In *Doe v. Reddy*,[87] the district court stated that there must be some sort of decision-making mechanism within a RICO enterprise and concluded that the plaintiffs adequately plead this requirement by identifying one of the defendants as a "godfather" and the "patriarch" of the family who determined the amount of pay and where the plaintiffs worked when they arrived in the United States.[88]

In *Moses v. Deborah Martin & Deborah Martin Agency, Inc.*,[89] the Court found, consistent with the majority of courts, that a corporation could not be held vicariously liable under Section 1962(c) for the acts of its employees if the corporation is also named as the RICO enterprise.[90]

In *Schwarz v. National Van Lines, Inc.*,[91] the district court, in dicta, seemed to suggest that vicarious liability under Section 1962(c) is appropriate if the enterprise is distinct from the corporation defendant upon whom vicarious liability is sought.[92] The court nevertheless dismissed the plaintiff's Section 1962(c) claim finding that the plaintiff had failed to allege that the defendant was involved in or knew of the other defendant's scheme to steal household goods.[93]

4. Pattern

In *Teamsters v. Carey*,[94] the district court dismissed an international union's RICO complaint for the failure to adequately plead a pattern of racketeering activity. The case arose out of an alleged illegal fund-raising scheme during the 1996 Teamsters' presidential election. In dismissing the case, the court held that predicate acts occurring over a two-month period were insufficient to find closed-end continuity.[95] Moreover, the plaintiff failed to establish open-ended continuity because even though the alleged predicate acts included acts of embezzlement, the alleged enterprise's goal—to re-elect Team-

---

[87] 2003 U.S. Dist. LEXIS 26120 (N.D. Cal. Aug. 4, 2003).

[88] *Id.* at *22-23.

[89] 2004 U.S. Dist. Lexis 24568 (S.D.N.Y. 2004).

[90] *Id.* at *41.

[91] 2004 WL 1497804 (N.D. Ill. 2004).

[92] *Id.* at *3.

[93] *Id.* at *4.

[94] 163 F. Supp. 2d 271, 168 LRRM 2439 (S.D.N.Y. 2001), *aff'd*, 2005 U.S. App. LEXIS 2267, 176 LRRM 2832 (2nd Cir. 2005), *corrected by* 2005 U.S. App. LEXIS 3723. *See also* Teamsters v. Carey, 297 F. Supp. 2d 706, 718 (S.D.N.Y. 2004).

[95] *Id.*,163 F. Supp. 2d at 280–82; *Id.*, 297 F. Supp. 2d at 714, n.3.

sters' president Ronald Carey—had a natural ending point and the plaintiff did not plead any racketeering activity occurring either before or after the 1996 election.[96] "Rather, the complaint describes an effort to achieve a lawful purpose (Carey's re-election) through unlawful means" and "none of the facts alleged in the complaint supports an inference that the crimes alleged would have been continued after the election"[97] sufficient to establish the requisite specific threat of repetition in the future. In dismissing the case with prejudice, the court held that neither the election-related allegations nor the defendants' long-term lucrative relationships with the Teamsters indicated a continuing threat of criminal activity.[98] The Second Circuit, in an unpublished decision, [99] affirmed the district court's dismissal.[100] The Second Circuit agreed with the district court that the union's allegations that suggested a risk of recurrence of criminal activity in some future election was "purely speculative as they depend on, among other things, the same confluence of political and economic factors."[101]

In *Overnite Transportation Co. v. Teamsters,*[102] the district court refused to find closed-ended continuity for activity occurring over a five-month period, but found the plaintiff's allegations of multiple predicate acts of attempted murder that threatened to continue in the future until the plaintiff conceded to the union defendants' demands or went out of business established open-ended continuity.[103]

In *Lopresti v. Merson,*[104] the district court dismissed a union's RICO complaint against employer defendants for allegedly defrauding the union into signing a plant closing agreement that terminated a collective bargaining agreement in connection with a sale of the company. The court found that the alleged predicate acts occurring, at most, over a 20-month period, were insufficient to establish closed-

[96] *Id.* at 282–85; 297 F. Supp. 2d at 715–16.

[97] *Id.* at 284. *See also* 297 F. Supp. 2d at 716–17.

[98] 297 F. Supp. 2d at 716. *See also* Breslin v. Brainard, 2003 WL 22351297 *9–10 (E.D. Pa. 2003) (in case stemming from union trusteeship, court rejected closed-ended continuity claim since period over which acts were alleged amounted to only six months; and rejected open-ended claim since no threat of continuing racketeering activity given validity of trusteeship was no longer in question).

[99] 2005 WL 481573 (2d Cir. Mar. 1, 2005).

[100] 297 F. Supp. 2d 706, 174 LRRM 2189 (S.D.N.Y. 2004).

[101] 2005 WL 481573 at *1.

[102] 168 F. Supp. 2d 826, 167 LRRM 2111 (W.D. Tenn. 2001).

[103] *Id.* at 846–47.

[104] 2001 U.S. Dist. LEXIS 16062, 168 LRRM 2427 (S.D.N.Y. 2001).

ended continuity and the nature of the allegations were essentially that of "[a] single act with no chance of repetition" in the future, which precluded a finding of open-ended continuity.[105]

Likewise, in *Steam Press Holdings, Inc. v. Hawaii Teamsters & Allied Workers Union*,[106] the Ninth Circuit affirmed the dismissal of an employer's RICO claim against a dry-cleaning union for conduct during a strike. The court found that the alleged predicate acts, which occurred during a single strike, did not "'by nature' project into the future or constitute 'a regular way of doing business,'" thus precluding a finding of open-ended continuity to support a RICO claim.

In *Barnes v. Duffy*,[107] the trustee of a health and welfare fund brought suit alleging that the defendants had engaged in a scheme whereby one defendant paid another an amount equal to the union's membership dues and the fund's contributions so that he would be entitled to benefits from the fund. The court refused to find open-ended continuity where the plaintiff made no allegations supporting such a finding and where there was only one underlying scheme, one victim, one injury, and no variety in the predicate acts.[108]

In *Andrea Doreen Ltd. v. Building Material Local 282*,[109] the plaintiff alleged that the union defendant and its trust funds had conspired to put it out of business and to set up a regime to force the company and others in the construction industry in New York City to pay bribes or suffer injury. The court dismissed the claims against the benefit funds' trustees and most of the predicate acts alleged to be committed by the union on various grounds. The court, however, ruled that the company had satisfied the continuity requirement even though the alleged scheme included only four predicate acts, lasted only seven months before the union entered into a consent decree with the government that removed the union officials responsible for the alleged conduct, and the "potential threat of continued activ-

---

[105] *Id.*

[106] 302 F.3d 998, 1011, 170 LRRM 2833 (9th Cir. 2002), *cert. denied*, 537 U.S. 1232 (2003).

[107] 2002 U.S. Dist. LEXIS 24925 (N.D. Ill. Dec. 30, 2002).

[108] *Id.* at *8–12.

[109] 299 F. Supp. 2d 129 (E.D.N.Y. 2004).

ity was stymied."[110] The court rejected the defendants' argument that there was no threat of long-term continuing conduct because the officers were removed and there had been no allegations of similar type behavior after the consent decree was entered into, since the "'fortuitous interruption of that activity' cannot be used to show a lack of threat of continuity."[111] The court, in reaching this conclusion, held that the conduct alleged did not have an "inherently terminable" goal and that a reasonable jury could find that "'there was nothing to stop [the local officials] from continuing' to threaten and intimidate [plaintiff] had they not been removed for corruption."[112]

In *Jackson v. Bellsouth Telecommunications*,[113] the Eleventh Circuit held that the plaintiffs failed to establish either closed- or open-ended continuity. The plaintiffs' RICO allegations against the defendant-employer and law firm centered on the settlement of an employment discrimination lawsuit. The court stated that "where the RICO allegations concern only a single scheme with a discrete goal, the courts have refused to find a closed-ended pattern of racketeering even when the scheme took place over longer periods of time."[114] With respect to open-ended continuity, the court stated that the defendants' "attempts to conceal an initial fraudulent act are not sufficient to establish open-ended continuity."[115]

In *Dooley v. Crab Boat Owners Ass'n*,[116] the court dismissed some of the defendants, finding that the plaintiffs had failed to establish that those defendants committed at least two predicate acts.[117] Moreover, the plaintiffs' conclusory allegations that the "defendants" committed certain predicate acts, unsupported by any evidence affirmatively showing that any of the defendants committed the acts, were found insufficient to establish that each defendant committed at least two predicate acts.[118]

Similarly, in *Troyer v. Boomtown, LLC*,[119] the district court dismissed a RICO claim when the plaintiffs alleged that the defendant employ-

---

[110] *Id.* at 157.
[111] *Id.* at 158.
[112] *Id.*
[113] 2004 U.S. App. LEXIS 11578 (11th Cir. June 14, 2004).
[114] *Id.* at *34-35.
[115] *Id.* at *39.
[116] 2004 U.S. LEXIS 7117 (N.D. Cal. 2004).
[117] *Id.* at *28.
[118] *Id.* at *24 n.13.
[119] 2004 U.S. Dist. LEXIS 25618 (E.D. La. Dec. 16, 2004).

ees used acts of police officers to establish a "continuous threat." The plaintiffs, an employee of a casino and his wife, alleged that other employees had police officers run an illegal background check on him and then provided information to the casino that the plaintiff was once indicted, resulting in the plaintiff's constructive discharge.[120] The plaintiffs alleged that the defendant-employees also had police officers search records for his successor; however, the court concluded that the plaintiffs presented sparse evidence of a continuous threat because performing a search on two separate persons "only show[ed] a limited number of 'predicate acts.'"[121]

In *Maddaloni Jewelers, Inc. v. Rolex Watch USA, Inc.*,[122] the district court, in dismissing the complaint on several grounds, found that the plaintiff had failed to allege two or more predicate acts within ten years. The court held that under the Hobbs Act, "a completed act of extortion along with intermediate steps toward completion of that act constitute one predicate act, not multiple distinct attempts."[123]

5. *Causation*

Two recent cases demonstrate that individualized determinations of causation can preclude class action treatment for RICO claims. In *Patterson v. Mobil Oil Corp.*,[124] the plaintiffs brought a RICO class action alleging that their employer misrepresented its compliance with Texas law requiring procurement of workers' compensation insurance in an attempt to avoid liability for employee injuries caused by negligent acts. The Fifth Circuit reversed class certification because the case required individualized determinations of reliance to prove the underlying predicate acts of fraud that would provide the basis for the RICO claims of each member of the putative class.

Similarly, in *Moore v. Television & Radio Artists*,[125] the Eleventh Circuit affirmed the district court's refusal to certify a class of recording artists attempting to establish that record companies improperly interpreted the provision of the union's collective bargaining agreement that determined the amount of contributions to health

---

[120] *Id.* at *3.

[121] *Id.* at *22-23.

[122] 2004 WL 3015287 (S.D.N.Y. 2004).

[123] *Id.* at *8.

[124] 241 F.3d 417 (5th Cir. 2001).

[125] 216 F.3d 1236 (11th Cir. 2000), *reh'g en banc denied,* 247 F.3d 251 (11th Cir. 2001), *cert. denied,* 533 U.S. 950 (2001).

and retirement funds. The appeals court held that the RICO claims, which were predicated on alleged mail fraud, were inappropriate for class treatment because the claims of the individual plaintiffs did not raise common questions of fact that predominated over individual issues. Although the collective bargaining agreement was common to the RICO claims of the named plaintiffs and putative class members, each singer had one or more different contracts with the record companies that affected the amounts owed. Further, whether each singer relied on the alleged misrepresentations was not susceptible to class treatment.

The district court in *Does v. The Gap, Inc.*[126] certified a class of "All persons other than Saipan resident citizens who, at any time since January 13, 1989, have been employed on Saipan as factory garment workers for one or more of the Contractor Defendants."[127] Their RICO claim, based on among others, alleged predicate acts of peonage and involuntary servitude, challenged "the garment production system on Saipan, Commonwealth of the Northern Mariana Islands" alleging a massive conspiracy "to perpetuate [that] garment production system and to exploit the plaintiff class for defendants' own profit."[128] In certifying the class, the court rejected the defendants' argument that each proposed class member had individual injuries and circumstances. The court reasoned that, despite the "disparate alleged factual circumstances and injuries among the plaintiffs, these differences do not defeat the court's certification of the plaintiff class at this time."[129] Instead, the court analogized to civil rights cases and agreed with the plaintiffs that the injuries "all stem from the same alleged conspiracy amongst the defendants to dominate and control the garment workforce of the Commonwealth."[130]

---

[126] 2002 WL 1000073 (D. N. Mar. I. May 10, 2002).
[127] *Id.* at *1.
[128] *Id.* at *2.
[129] *Id.*
[130] *Id.*

B. Three Substantive Violations

3. *18 U.S.C. §1962(c) (Conducting an Enterprise's Affairs Through Racketeering)*

In *National Organization for Women v. Scheidler,*[131] in further proceedings after remand from the Supreme Court, both individual and corporate defendants that were "organizers of the Pro-Life Action Network (PLAN), which is a loose national organization of groups" engaging in a variety of anti-abortion protests violated Section 1962(c). The jury found that "PLAN was an 'organization or enterprise' for purposes of RICO liability."[132]

a. Person/Enterprise Distinction

The Supreme Court has now ruled on whether the RICO "person" (i.e., the defendant) must be distinct from the "enterprise" to state a claim under Section 1962(c). In *Cedric Kushner Promotions, Ltd. v. King,*[133] the Court agreed with all the circuits, which previously had determined that Section 1962(c) requires some distinctness between the defendant and the RICO enterprise.

In *Miller v. Norfolk Southern Railway Co.,*[134] after the district court held that it lacked subject matter jurisdiction over the union members' RICO claim against their employer arising out of a decertification vote because it fell within the primary jurisdiction of the National Mediation Board pursuant to the Railway Labor Act sufficient to be "arguably representational," the court nonetheless reached the merits of the RICO claim. In so doing, the court alternatively dismissed the RICO claim, finding that the employer could not be both the enterprise and the RICO defendant. The court also dismissed

[131]National Org. for Women v. Scheidler, 267 F.3d 687 (7th Cir. 2001), *reversed on other grounds,* 537 U.S. 393, 409 (2003). *See infra* Sections IV.E.2.

[132]*Id.,* 267 F.3d at 694.

[133]533 U.S. 158 (2001).

[134]183 F. Supp. 2d 996, 1002, 169 LRRM 2343 (N.D. Ohio 2002).

the RICO claim against the individual defendants on the same ground without discussing how the individual defendants failed to satisfy the distinctiveness requirement.[135]

In *Baker v. IBP, Inc.*,[136] the court rejected the plaintiffs' argument that the employer's hiring of aliens who could not lawfully work in the United States violated RICO. The plaintiffs alleged that the illegal aliens were paid a reduced wage, which reduced the wages of all employees.[137] The court found that the "nub of the complaint is that IBP operates itself unlawfully"[138] and therefore dismissed the RICO claim because there was no distinction between the defendant and the enterprise.[139]

(1) Application to Corporate Relationships

In *Kushner*,[140] the Court endorsed the legal principle that Section 1962(c) "requires no more than [a] formal legal distinction between [the] 'person' and 'enterprise'. . . ."[141] The Court found such a distinction between a corporation and its sole shareholder/employee, reasoning that "[a]fter all, incorporation's basic purpose is to create a distinct legal entity, with legal rights, obligations, powers, and privileges different from those of the natural individuals who created it, who own it, or whom it employs."[142] *Kushner* declined to address, among other things, situations involving parent and subsidiary relationships. Even so, the Court's reasoning seems persuasive in such cases. In other words, if Section 1962(c) merely requires a *legal* distinction between the person and the enterprise, then a parent's incorporation of a subsidiary should satisfy that requirement. In such a case, of course, Section 1962(c)'s other requirements still must be met, including the operation or management requirement.[143]

---

[135] *Id.* at 1001–02.
[136] 357 F.3d 685 (7th Cir. 2004).
[137] *Id.* at 692.
[138] *Id.* at 691.
[139] *Id.* at 692.
[140] Cedric Kushner Promotions, Ltd. v. King, 533 U.S. 158 (2001).
[141] *Id.* at 165.
[142] *Id.* at 163.
[143] *See* Section III.B.3.b., in Main Edition.

(2) Application to Association-in-Fact Enterprises

A separate issue is raised where there is partial overlap between the RICO person and the alleged association-in-fact enterprise, such as where the defendant is only one member of several, sufficiently distinct, members constituting the enterprise. Most courts have allowed such claims under Section 1962(c), whether or not all of those members have been named as defendants, reasoning that a collective entity is more than the members of which it is comprised.[144] As discussed in the prior section, the Supreme Court's recent decision in *Cedric Kushner Promotions* would seem to support such a result where each member of an association-in-fact enterprise is legally distinct from the other members.

For example, in *Tran v. Tran*,[145] the plaintiff was a former hotel employee who alleged that his employer had paid bribes to union representatives, who ignored the employer's violations of a collective bargaining agreement by failing to pay union wages, violating union work rules concerning duties and maximum hours of employment, failing to provide safe working conditions, failing to enroll employees in the union, and failing to pay for and provide union benefits. After a bench trial, the court held that the plaintiff had established a pattern of racketeering activity, presumably, but without stating, based on multiple violations of 29 U.S.C. §186(b)(1). The court found a proper RICO enterprise comprised of, among others, the individual defendant, certain hotels operated by the defendant, and the union representatives receiving the bribes.

In *Does v. The Gap, Inc.*,[146] a RICO suit alleging a conspiracy by manufacturers and retailers to exploit garment workers on Saipan, Commonwealth of the Northern Mariana Islands, the plaintiffs' first

---

[144]Titan Int'l, Inc. v. Becker, 189 F. Supp. 2d 817, 824 (C.D. Ill. 2001) (finding that plaintiffs pleaded two different association-in-fact enterprises comprised of union groups and affiliates, which included both defendants themselves and others unaware of the unlawful activity alleged); Overnite Transp. Co. v. Teamsters, 168 F. Supp. 2d 826, 847, 167 LRRM 2111 (W.D. Tenn. 2001) (allegations of association-in-fact enterprise "comprised of individuals who are otherwise employed by or retired from unionized competitors of Overnite and activists and allied groups aiding and abetting them, who have been recruited by IBT officials and agents" were sufficient to survive motion to dismiss).

[145]165 LRRM 2142 (S.D.N.Y. 2000), *reconsideration denied*, 166 F. Supp. 2d 793 (S.D.N.Y. 2001), *rev'd in part on other grounds sub nom.* Tran v. Alphonse Hotel Corp., 281 F.3d 23 (2d Cir. 2002) (RICO claim barred by statute of limitations).

[146]2001 WL 1842389 (D. N. Mar. I. Nov. 26, 2001).

amended complaint alleged two types of RICO enterprises: "(1) many separate enterprises consisting of a single retailer defendant associated in fact with a single manufacturer defendant, and (2) one enterprise consisting of all retailer defendants associated in fact with all manufacturer defendants."[147] As for the first type, the court found them to be pleaded properly. The court reasoned that,

> The relatedness of the individual retailer's and the individual manufacturer's businesses, the allegations of collusion between individual retailers and individual manufacturers to conceal factory conditions thereby permitting the garments to be promoted as "sweat" free", and the alleged longevity of the relationships support the existence of the alleged enterprises and are sufficient to allege that the individual retailers and individual manufacturers functioned as continuing units.[148]

As for the second type of enterprise, despite allegations of various common business purposes and interconnections, the court refused to find a properly pleaded enterprise because there were "no allegations showing an overarching structure and a mechanism for making decisions and directing or controlling the affairs of all retailer defendants and manufacturer defendants as a group on an ongoing basis."[149]

Thereafter, the *Does'* plaintiffs filed a second amended complaint asserting the same two types of enterprises in addition to five new categories of RICO enterprises, which included:

> (1) an association-in-fact enterprise of all manufacturer defendants; (2) an association-in-fact enterprise among all retailer defendants; (3) an association-in-fact enterprise between each retailer and the various manufacturers who manufacture the retailers' garments in the Commonwealth of the Northern Mariana Islands (hereinafter "CNMI"); (4) an association-in-fact enterprise between each retailer and all manufacturers that are members of the Saipan Garment Manufacturers Association (hereinafter "SGMA"); and (5) an association-in-fact enterprise comprising each group of commonly-owned and -operated manufacturers.[150]

---

[147] *Id.* at *1.
[148] *Id.* at *3.
[149] *Id.*
[150] 2002 WL 1000068 (D. N. Mar. I. May 10, 2002).

In deciding the defendants' motion to dismiss, the district court reaffirmed its decision with regard to the original two types of enterprises. As for the five new categories of RICO enterprises, the court, based on a factual discussion of each, upheld the pleading of the first, third, and fifth enterprises, while it rejected the pleading of the second and fourth types of enterprise.[151]

An association-in-fact enterprise must exist separate and apart from the pattern of racketeering. In *Troyer v. Boomtown, LLC,*[152] the district court determined that the plaintiffs failed to provide evidence that the enterprise existed when the plaintiffs alleged that certain employees at a casino and police officers comprised the RICO enterprise when the employees allegedly had certain police officers perform illegal background checks on two of the casino's employees.[153]

Conversely, in *Doe v. Reddy,*[154] the district court concluded that the plaintiffs properly pled an association-in-fact enterprise when the plaintiffs stated that defendants conspired through their family owned business and business connections for legitimate and illegitimate purposes involving peonage, involuntary servitude, and common law torts committed against Indian citizens who were allegedly induced to come the United States and work for the defendants.[155]

b. Operation or Management Requirement

In *Titan International, Inc. v. Becker,*[156] tire and wheel manufacturers filed suit against union groups and their affiliates alleging that the defendants "engaged in strikes against Plaintiffs and implemented a massive conspiracy to extort money."[157] The plaintiffs pleaded two different association-in-fact enterprises comprised of union groups and affiliates, which included both defendants themselves and others unaware of the unlawful activity alleged. The court held the that plaintiffs properly pleaded the *Reves'* operation or management requirement by alleging that "predicate acts of racketeering were knowingly undertaken at the direction of the management of the enterprise" and that "each Defendant knowingly implemented the

---

[151] *Id.* at *1–8.
[152] 2004 U.S. Dist. LEXIS 25618 (E.D. La. Dec. 16, 2004).
[153] *Id.* at *25-26.
[154] 2003 U.S. Dist. LEXIS 26120 (N.D. Cal. Aug. 4, 2003).
[155] *Id.* at *20-21.
[156] 189 F. Supp. 2d 817 (C.D. Ill. 2001).
[157] *Id.* at 821.

decisions of upper management."[158] The court further recognized that "Plaintiffs do not need to allege that each Defendant was a manager or high level employee" to satisfy *Reves.*[159]

As discussed in Section III.B.3.a(2) above, *Does v. The Gap, Inc.*[160] is a RICO suit alleging a conspiracy by manufacturers and retailers to exploit garment workers on Saipan, Commonwealth of the Northern Mariana Islands. Initially, the plaintiffs failed to satisfy the *Reves'* operation or management requirement as to the retailer defendants. In finding the allegations inadequate, the court distinguished between the opportunity to participate in the enterprise and actual participation. The court noted that such things as acquiescence, "[a]lleged economic pressure generated under the terms" of a contract, and "[a] failure to act" do not rise to the level of "participation in the conduct of an enterprise."[161] Thereafter, however, the plaintiffs filed a second amended complaint[162] curing the deficiencies the court identified in its earlier opinion. The court held as to this pleading that "the plaintiffs have adequately alleged affirmative action and participation by the [retailer] defendants in the control and direction of the alleged enterprises."[163] Indeed, "[t]he allegations show that the retailer defendants are involved in the day-to-day operations and have direction and control in the affairs of the alleged enterprises."[164]

4. *18 U.S.C. §1962(d) (Conspiracy to Violate the Substantive Provisions)*

In *Lopresti v. Merson,*[165] a union alleged a RICO conspiracy by employer defendants for allegedly defrauding the union into signing a plant closing agreement that terminated a collective bargaining agreement in connection with a sale of the company. The court held that "conclusory allegations are insufficient to support a claim of RICO conspiracy."

---

[158] *Id.* at 823.
[159] *Id.*
[160] 2001 WL 1842389 (D. N. Mar. I. Nov. 26, 2001).
[161] *Id.* at *9.
[162] 2002 WL 1000068 (D. N. Mar. I. May 10, 2002).
[163] *Id.* at *13.
[164] *Id.*
[165] 2001 U.S. Dist. LEXIS 16062, 168 LRRM 2427 (S.D.N.Y. 2001).

a. Relationship to Substantive RICO Violations

Recent cases in the labor context continue to follow the courts in other RICO cases that routinely dismiss Section 1962(d) conspiracy allegations for failure to state a claim where a plaintiff does not state a claim under Sections 1962(a), (b), or (c).[166] For example, the failure to establish the requirements for an enterprise or a pattern of racketeering will also result in dismissal of a conspiracy claim based on the same elements.[167]

In *Titan International, Inc. v. Becker*,[168] however, the plaintiffs pleaded, in addition to a Section 1962(c) claim, three conspiracy claims under Section 1962(d)—one each to conspire to violate Sections 1962(a), (b), and (c). In denying the defendants' motion to dismiss, the district court found that the plaintiffs had sufficiently pleaded the conspiracy claims despite the defendants' argument that the claims were conclusory.[169]

b. Agreement by the Defendant to the Commission of Predicate Acts

In *Does v. The Gap, Inc.*,[170] a RICO suit alleging a conspiracy by manufacturers and retailers to exploit garment workers on Saipan, Commonwealth of the Northern Mariana Islands, the plaintiffs properly alleged a RICO conspiracy to violate Sections 1962(a) and (c). Applying the teaching of *Salinas* and *Beck* as discussed in the Main Edition, and recognizing that the conspiracy defendant "need not agree to commit or facilitate every part of the substantive offense" or even violate "the substantive RICO provision in order to be liable," the district court held that it could be inferred from the pleadings that "the retailer defendants knew or were aware of the conditions at the garment factories, and knew of the essential nature and scope of the enterprise and agreed to participate in it."[171]

---

[166]Does v. The Gap, Inc., 2001 WL 1842389, at *10 (D. N. Mar. I. Nov. 26, 2001) (dismissing claim for conspiracy to violate §1962(a) because of the failure to adequately allege an investment injury). *But see* Does v. The Gap, Inc., 2002 WL 1000068, *10–11 (D. N. Mar. I. May 10, 2002) (correcting deficiency by amendment). AK Steel Corp. v. Steelworkers, 170 LRRM 2491 (S.D. Ohio 2002) (dismissing RICO conspiracy claim based on dismissal of substantive RICO claim).

[167]Miller v. Norfolk S. Ry. Co., 183 F. Supp. 2d 996, 1003, 169 LRRM 2343 (N.D. Ohio 2002); Teamsters v. Carey, 163 F. Supp. 2d 271, 285, 168 LRRM 2439 (S.D.N.Y. 2001).

[168]189 F. Supp. 2d 817 (C.D. Ill. 2001).

[169]*Id.*

[170]2002 WL 1000068 (D. N. Mar. I. May 10, 2002).

[171]*Id.* at *9–10.

IV. PREDICATE ACTS COMMONLY ALLEGED IN LABOR CASES

A. 18 U.S.C. §664: Embezzlement From Pension and Welfare Funds

In *Board of Trustees of Ironworkers Local 498 Pension Fund v. Nationwide Life Insurance Co.*,[172] the court held that the plaintiffs, a group of union pension and benefits plans, had adequately alleged predicate acts of embezzlement from pension and welfare funds,[173] and unlawful pension fund payments.[174] The plaintiffs alleged a scheme in which the defendants, who were to invest the fund assets, deducted money from fund assets and paid fees, kickbacks and commissions to third party pension administrators.[175] The court also held that the allegations of predicate acts of embezzlement and unlawful pension fund payments did not involve allegations of fraud within the meaning of Federal Rule of Civil Procedure 9, which imposes a heightened pleading standard.[176]

C. 29 U.S.C. §186: Restrictions on Payments and Loans to Labor Organizations

Section 186 by its plain language is exceptionally sweeping in its coverage to protect employers from extortion and to ensure honest, uninfluenced representations of employees by stamping out all forms of bribery between management and labor officials. In *United States v. Wilson*,[177] the Second Circuit affirmed the RICO conviction of a former local union officer and business manager based on multiple violations of, among other things, 29 U.S.C. §186(b)(1), for accepting payments in exchange for concessions to management over a period of about 20 years.

In *United States v. Douglas and Campbell*,[178] the Sixth Circuit reversed the dismissal of an indictment that alleged that the defendants, two UAW local union officials, had among other things, violated 18 U.S.C. §371, which makes it a crime to conspire to commit

---

[172] 2005 WL 711977 (N.D. Ill. March 28, 2005).

[173] 18 U.S.C. §664.

[174] 18 U.S.C. §1954.

[175] 2005 WL 711977 at *6-7.

[176] *Id.* at *3.

[177] 216 F.3d 1074 (2d Cir. 2000) (Table), 2000 WL 778021 (June 15, 2000), *cert. denied*, 531 U.S. 945 (2000).

[178] 398 F.3d 407 (6th Cir. 2005).

an offense or to defraud the United States, in this case, a conspiracy to violate 29 U.S.C. §186, when they allegedly demanded that Pontiac Truck hire non-employee relatives of the defendants for certain highly coveted tradesmen positions, even though the relatives were not qualified for the positions and that the hiring of them would violate the National Agreement between the UAW and GM. The UAW and GM refused the request. The government alleged that all issues of the strike over a local agreement had been settled except for the hiring of the defendants' relatives. The government contended that GM agreed to hire the two relatives into the skilled tradesmen positions to avoid continuation of the strike. The government further alleged that the hiring of the two relatives was concealed from the local union membership during the ratification process and that the two defendants dismissed grievances by Local 594 members over the hiring of the relatives even though the grievances had merit. The indictment alleged that the object of the conspiracy was to amend the National Agreement and the hiring of the two relatives. The defendants moved to dismiss this count of the indictment on the grounds that the defendants could not exercise the authority to amend the National Agreement because such an amendment by them was prohibited by the UAW International Union constitution, therefore any grant of authority to the defendants by GM to amend the National Agreement was invalid and unenforceable, and therefore, this purported grant of authority was not a "thing of value" under the statute. The defendants also argued that Section 302's prohibition against the "payment, loan and delivery of money and things of value" did not prohibit Pontiac Truck from hiring the two relatives because: (1) the statute does not prevent an employer from delivering or agreeing to deliver a thing of value to third parties, and (2) that Section 302 provides an exception that allows employers to provide compensation, *i.e.*, wages, for actual services rendered. The district court agreed with the defendants. The district court held that the government had alleged in essence that GM had paid a thing of value (wages) to the relatives and not the defendants. In dismissing this count of the indictment the district court held that the "[d]efendants may not be liable for a violation of [§302] for the delivery of things of value to third parties when the statute only prohibits an employer from delivering a thing of value to a representative of his employees."[179] The district court, in rejecting the

[179] 291 F. Supp. 2d 547, 552 (E.D. Mich. 2003).

government's argument that the arrangement was akin to payment for "ghost" employees, held that the relatives "were actual employees paid for their services by General Motors, not merely persons to whom General Motors made personal payoff payments instead of to Defendants."[180] The district court rejected the government's contention that additional positions negotiated for the relatives were not a legitimate bargaining objective because they violated the National Agreement. The district court found that this contention could not properly serve as a basis for a criminal charge of extortion, but was "an issue to be resolved between the UAW, Local 594, General Motors and Pontiac Truck through the established labor relations' dispute framework."[181]

The court of appeals reversed and found that the allegations in the indictment did not need to include reference to a "thing of value" under 29 U.S.C. §186 to charge a conspiracy to defraud under 18 U.S.C. §371.[182] The court of appeals also reversed the dismissal of the Hobbs Act count of the indictment. The Sixth Circuit held that the government had sufficiently alleged Hobbs Act extortion in that the defendants' demands were illegitimate because they were in contradiction of the collective bargaining agreement and the union's constitution and that the defendants had forcefully coerced the company negotiators to "exact wage payments in return for the imposed and unwanted services of unqualified, ineligible non-employees."[183] Finally, the Sixth Circuit found that the union members' right to compete for these skilled jobs was property within the meaning of the mail fraud statute and that the indictment had adequately alleged that a scheme to defraud the union members of the honest services of the defendants pursuant to the union's constitution and 29 U.S.C. §501(a) of the Labor Management Reporting and Disclosure Act.[184]

---

[180] *Id.* The district court also dismissed the Hobbs Act count of the indictment, relying on *Enmons,* and finding that the indictment did not allege an "illegitimate objective." The court held "Defendants' bargaining demand for additional skilled trades positions, even if otherwise unwanted by [GM], is not an illegitimate bargaining objective and falls within the *Enmons* exception." *Id.* at 553–54.

[181] *Id.* at 554.

[182] 398 F.3d 407, 412 (6th Cir. 2005).

[183] *Id.* at 415.

[184] *Id.* at 417-419.

D. 29 U.S.C. §501(c): Embezzlement From Union Funds

In *United States v. Boyd*,[185] an indictment alleged that a union official engaged in a scheme to defraud the union and its membership of his honest services under 29 U.S.C. §501(a) of the LMRDA, by securing secret cash payments from attorneys who hoped to acquire or maintain a place on the union's list of "Designated Legal Counsel" to whom members would be referred to with injury claims.[186] The indictment alleged that the defendant took the secret cash payments and used them to fund his internal union election campaigns and for personal use. The defendant moved to dismiss the indictment on various grounds including the argument that the facts alleged in the indictment that purportedly made out a claim of honest services fraud did not amount to a crime as a matter of law because the alleged scheme did not include any allegation of actual or intended harm to the union or its membership.[187] The court denied the motion and found on the honest services claim that "an indictment alleging honest services fraud need not explicitly allege actual or material harm to the victims."[188] The court went further and held that the government need "only prove that the defendant's false representations were material."[189]

E. 18 U.S.C. §1951: "Racketeering" Prohibited by the Hobbs Act

2. *Enmons*

The Supreme Court was asked to consider its *Enmons*[190] decision in a case involving application of civil RICO to abortion protests, in *National Organization for Women v. Scheidler*.[191] One of the issues on which certiorari was granted in *Scheidler* is as follows:

> Whether the Hobbs Act, which makes it a crime to obstruct, delay, or affect interstate commerce by "robbery or extortion"—and which defines "extortion" as "the *obtaining* of *property* from another, with [the owner's] consent," where such consent is "induced by the wrongful use of actual or threatened force, violence or fear" (18

[185] 2004 WL 609301 (S.D. Tex. 2004).
[186] *Id.* at *1.
[187] *Id.* at *2.
[188] *Id.* at *4.
[189] *Id.*
[190] United States v. Enmons, 410 U.S. 396, 82 LRRM 2625 (1973).
[191] 267 F.3d 687 (7th Cir. 2001), *cert. granted*, 535 U.S. 1016 (2002).

U.S.C. § 1951(b)(2) (emphasis added))—criminalizes the activities of political protesters who engage in sit-ins and demonstrations that obstruct the public's access to a business's premises and interfere with the freedom of putative customers to obtain services offered there.[192]

The Supreme Court decision, however, discussed *Enmons* only in passing. Indeed, the Court's decision to remand 117 extortion-based predicate acts under RICO rested on the defendants' failure to obtain or attempt to obtain property from the plaintiffs, not on the statutory the definition of the Hobbs Act found in *Enmons*. However, the Seventh Circuit's subsequent remand based on the four remaining predicate acts under the Hobbs Act would require the district court to interpret the Hobbs Act in order to properly decide the issues presented.[193]

One such interpretation, the so-called "three-way" interpretation, would expand the definition of the Hobbs Act to read the "physical violence" clause independently from underlying acts of robbery, extortion, or conspiracy.[194] As such, this interpretation could, practically speaking, overrule *Enmons*. As the majority of the panel notes, the alternative "two-way" interpretation, (though apparently consistent with *Enmons*) is arguably inconsistent with the legislative history of the Act.[195] In either case, as the dissent noted, any determination made by the district court would almost certainly be appealed and thus, presumably, force either the Seventh Circuit or the Supreme Court to settle the statutory construction issue, including the application of *Enmons*, as a matter of law.[196]

3. *Application of the Hobbs Act to RICO Cases After* Enmons

a. Legitimate Objectives

In *Monterey Plaza Hotel Ltd. Partnership v. Hotel Employees Local 483*,[197] the Ninth Circuit affirmed dismissal of a hotel owner's RICO

---

[192]Petition for a Writ of Certiorari at p. (i), 535 U.S. 1016 (Apr. 22, 2002) (No. 01-1118).

[193]National Org. for Women v. Scheidler, 396 F.3d 807 (7th Cir. 2005), *cert. granted*, 125 S. Ct. 2991 (June 28, 2005), No. 04-1244.

[194]*See* Section VI.C., *infra*.

[195]*Scheidler*, *supra* note 193, 396 F.3d 807, 812-813 (7th Cir. 2005) *citing* Craig M. Bradley, NOW v. Scheidler: *RICO Meets the First Amendment*, 1994 SUP. CT. REV. 129, 142-43 (1994).

[196]*Id.*, 396 F.3d 807, 818 (7th Cir. 2005).

[197]215 F.3d 923 (9th Cir. 2000).

claim against a union for violent picketing, extortion, and intimidation of employees and customers, on, among other grounds, res judicata based on prior state law actions arising out of the same alleged scheme. Thus, the court of appeals declined to address "the district court's statement that the Hotel's claims were sufficient to allege extortion under the Hobbs Act, 18 U.S.C. §1951."[198]

In *Dooley v. Crab Boat Owners Ass'n*,[199] the court rejected the defendants' argument that their strike was "lawful" and that, based on *Enmons*, their violence was not extortion within the Hobbs Act because it was not "wrongful."[200] The plaintiffs in *Dooley* were in the business of harvesting crab;[201] the defendants were several competing fishing associations which refused to harvest crab during the relevant harvesting seasons in an attempt to obtain a higher price for the crab.[202] The plaintiffs alleged that, during the relevant period, the defendants, inter alia, threatened the plaintiffs' customers with loss of business if they purchased crab from the plaintiffs, threatened the plaintiffs and the plaintiffs' crew members with violence if they continued to harvest crab, and damaged the plaintiffs' boat and fishing equipment.[203] In rejecting the defendants' argument that *Enmons* applied, the court stated that Congress intended the Hobbs Act to apply to situations in which the obtaining of property would itself be wrongful because the alleged extortionist had no lawful right to the property.[204] Accordingly, because the property at issue was not the price of crab, but rather, the plaintiffs' right to harvest crab, the defendants' attempts to obtain that property were wrongful because they had no legal interest in the property.[205]

In July 2003, in *Titan International, Inc. v. Becker*,[206] the District Court for the Central District of Illinois Springfield Division denied the union defendants' motion to dismiss the plaintiffs' amended complaint on the basis of the Supreme Court's decision in *Scheidler*.[207] The district court also ruled that the unions' reliance on *Enmons* was misplaced because an activity undertaken to achieve wages in ex-

[198] *Id.* at 924–25, 928.
[199] 271 F. Supp. 2d 1207, 1208 (N.D. Cal. 2003).
[200] *Id.* at 1214 n.8.
[201] *Id.* at 1208.
[202] *Id.* at 1208–09.
[203] *Id.* at 1212.
[204] *Id.*
[205] *Id.*
[206] No. 00-3257 (C.D. Ill. 2003)
[207] *Id.*, at 11.

change for unneeded or unwanted services, or for no services at all, may constitute extortionate conduct under the Hobbs Act.[208] Thus, it was "not clear that Plaintiffs could prove no set of facts entitling them to recover, consistent with the Supreme Court's decision in *Enmons.*"[209]

In *United States v. Douglas,*[210] the Sixth Circuit overruled the lower court, which held two union officials' demand that General Motors hire their relatives for coveted skilled trade positions in exchange for the union agreeing to terms with General Motors were seeking a legitimate purpose as defined under *Enmons* because the creation of jobs was a lawful, legitimate purpose. In reversing, the Sixth Circuit noted that the negotiations were against the policy and constitution of the union and thus were not legitimate and if true constituted extortion.

b. Property

The Seventh Circuit in *National Organization for Women v. Scheidler*[211] affirmed the long-understood interpretations of the Hobbs Act that "property" under the Act includes intangible property "such as the right to conduct a business"[212] and that the alleged extortionist need not actually "obtain" the plaintiff's property to violate the Act.[213] The Supreme Court granted certiorari on the application of the Act and reversed the Seventh Circuit, but not on the issue of whether property under the Hobbs Act includes intangible property.[214]

In its decision in *Scheidler,*[215] the Supreme Court found that the protestors "did not obtain or attempt to obtain property" from the RICO plaintiffs (a necessary requirement for a finding of extortion), and there was no basis upon on which to find that the protestors committed extortion under the Hobbs Act.[216] The Supreme Court

[208] *Id.* at 15–16 (citing *Enmons,* 410 U.S. at 404, 409).
[209] *Id.*
[210] 398 F.3d 407 (6th Cir. 2005).
[211] 267 F.3d 687 (7th Cir. 2001), *cert. granted,* 535 U.S. 1016 (2002).
[212] *Id.* at 709.
[213] *Id.*
[214] National Org. for Women v. Scheidler, 537 U.S. 393 (2003).
[215] *Id.* at 409.
[216] *Id.* The Court also found that state law extortion offenses for purposes of RICO must also contain an "obtaining" requirement, and because the protestors had not obtained or attempted to obtain property, the state law extortion statutes could not support the RICO verdict. *Id.* at 410.

also expressly noted that the dissent was mistaken in its suggestion that the Court's "decision reaches, much less rejects" lower court decisions concluding that intangible rights constitute property under the Hobbs Act.[217] Regardless, the Court's decision may affect application of the Act in the labor arena, where parties often argue that violations of the Hobbs Act occur through the obtaining of intangible property.[218]

c. Nonapplicability of *Enmons* to Other Statutes

In a recent case against union groups and their affiliates, *Titan International, Inc. v. Becker*,[219] tire and wheel manufacturers alleged that the defendants "used bomb threats, violence, threats, and other illegal acts" to force the plaintiffs to give additional medical benefits, unfreeze or make substantial contributions to pension plans, increase wages, and agree to neutrality. Without any discussion of *Enmons*, the district court denied the defendants' motion to dismiss, finding that the plaintiffs had properly pleaded multiple acts of extortion under the laws of three different states and thus stated a RICO pattern of racketeering activity.[220] In a subsequent decision in July 2003, the district court denied the union defendants' motion to dismiss the plaintiffs' amended complaint on the basis of the Supreme Court's decision in *Scheidler*.[221] The district court also ruled that the unions' reliance on *Enmons* was misplaced because an activity undertaken to achieve wages in exchange for unneeded or unwanted services, or for no services at all, may constitute extortionate conduct under the Hobbs Act.[222] Thus, it was "not clear that Plaintiffs could prove no set of facts entitling them to recover, consistent with the Supreme Court's decision in *Enmons*."[223]

---

[217]*Id.* at 402.

[218]*See, e.g.*, G-I Holdings, Inc. v. Baron & Budd, 179 F. Supp. 2d 233, 256–57 (S.D.N.Y. 2001) (discussing the Second Circuit's "'admittedly expansive' view of the concept of property under the Hobbs Act," but distinguishing cases involving union members' intangible property interests in free speech and democratic participation in union affairs from the right to petition the government generally).

[219]189 F. Supp. 2d 817 (C.D. Ill. 2001).

[220]*Id.* at 825–27.

[221]No. 00-3257 at 11 (C.D. Ill. 2003)

[222]*Id.* at 15–16 (citing *Enmons*, 410 U.S. at 404, 409).

[223]*Id.* at 16.

F. Immigration Violations

In *Trollinger, v. Tyson Foods, Inc.*,[224] the Sixth Circuit reversed the district court's dismissal of a RICO claim which alleged that Tyson, with several employment agencies, had at its poultry plants "engaged in a scheme to depress the wages paid to its hourly employees by knowingly hiring undocumented illegal immigrants who were willing to work for wages well below those paid in labor markets composed of only United States Citizens."[225] The plaintiffs alleged that Tyson caused illegal aliens to be brought into the country, transported them, provided them with illegal documents and conspired to violate the immigration laws.[226] The district court dismissed the complaint finding that the plaintiffs could not establish "a 'direct relation between the injury asserted and the injurious conduct alleged.'"[227] The district court also held that since the plaintiffs' wages could have been affected by many different factors "the conclusion that Tyson's hiring of alleged illegal aliens depressed the plaintiffs' wages would require sheer speculation."[228] The district court declined to rule on Tyson's motion to dismiss the complaint for lack of subject matter jurisdiction pursuant to the Supreme Court's decision in *San Diego Building Trades Council v. Garmon*,[229] that the National Labor Relations Act "preempts" the employees' RICO claims. In *Garmon*, the Supreme Court established the general rule that federal courts do not have jurisdiction over activity which is "arguably subject to §7 and §8" of the National Labor Relations Act and that the courts must defer in such instances "to the exclusive competence of the National Labor Relations Board."[230]

The Sixth Circuit, in reaching Tyson's *Garmon* argument, and finding that it did not reach the RICO claims in this case, held that since the plaintiffs did not rely on any state law predicate acts, Tyson had no basis for invoking *Garmon* on that ground and that since the plaintiffs did not need to prove a violation of the NLRA to establish violations of the predicate under which they were proceeding, the

---

[224]370 F.3d 602 (6th Cir. 2004).
[225]*Id.* at 606.
[226]*Id.*
[227]214 F. Supp. 2d 840 (E.D. Tenn. 2003).
[228]*Id.* at 843.
[229]359 U.S. 236 (1959).
[230]*Id.* at 245.

Immigration and Nationality Act.[231] The court held that "[i]n the absence of a federal cause of action that requires the district court in the first instance to interpret the NLRA, it is difficult to see how *Garmon* is implicated in general or how the primary-jurisdiction concern that amplifies this aspect of the *Garmon* doctrine is implicated in particular."[232]

Turning to the standing issue, the Sixth Circuit rejected Tyson's claim that the plaintiffs claims were derivative, and that the union that represented the workers at the plant in question was the party that suffered the direct injury, if any.[233] The court held that the plaintiffs did properly plead an injury that was not exclusively derivative because Tyson employed and paid them directly, notwithstanding the fact that the union served as the plaintiffs' agent for collective bargaining purposes and that it negotiated the wage package under which the plaintiffs were paid.[234] With respect to the proximate cause issue, the Sixth Circuit held that it was premature to dismiss the claim without the benefit of discovery on this basis since it was possible that the plaintiffs could prove their theory of proximate cause.[235]

In *Vega v. Contract Cleaning Maintenance, Inc.*,[236] the plaintiffs, who were recent immigrants and had limited knowledge of employment practices and the English language, were employed at one time by the defendants.[237] The plaintiffs alleged that the defendants, several corporations, partnerships, and individuals in a large and diverse family–run operation, had schemed to "misclassify non-managerial janitors and maintenance workers as independent contractors rather than as employees, and falsified employee records to indicate that individuals classified as employees never worked more than forty hours a week," in order to evade their obligations under the Fair Labor Standards Act and other federal and state employment and tax laws.[238] The district court held that the plaintiffs had sufficiently pled an enterprise in their Section 1962(c) claim that consisted of an association-in-fact enterprise that consisted of all the various corporations, partnerships, and other entities through which the family

---

[231] 8 U.S.C. §1324.

[232] Trollinger v. Tyson Foods, Inc., 370 F.3d 602, 611 (6th Cir. 2004).

[233] *Id.* at 615.

[234] *Id.* at 616.

[235] *Id.*

[236] 2004 WL 2358274 (N.D.Ill. 2004).

[237] 2004 WL 2358274 at *1.

[238] *Id.*

that owned and controlled the businesses provided janitorial and maintenance services.[239] The court also held that the plaintiffs had adequately alleged that the association-in-fact enterprise was an ongoing organization functioning as a continuing unit with a common purpose.

In *Jane Doe I v. Reddy*,[240] the defendants, "a web of extended family members and their related business entities," were alleged to have engaged in a broad conspiracy to fraudulently induce the plaintiffs, a class of young Indian citizens, including many young women, to enter the United States from India and forced them to work long hours under arduous conditions for pay below the minimum wage and in violation of overtime laws and sexually abused and assaulted them. Among claims of peonage, involuntary servitude, slave labor, Alien Tort Claims Act claims and state law claims, the plaintiffs asserted RICO claims alleging predicate acts of immigration fraud occurring over an eight-year period. The court denied the defendants' motions to dismiss on several grounds including rejecting the defendants' assertion of the in pari delicto (in equal fault) and unclean hands doctrine as a bar to recovering under RICO claiming that the plaintiffs were barred from recovery since they were complicit in the immigration violations. The court held that the allegations of the complaint that included among other things, the allegations that the plaintiffs "were vulnerable and powerless" and that the defendants knew that coming into the country would be a violation of the immigration laws, were enough to deny the application of the in pari delicto and unclean hands doctrine. The court held that it could not at this point in the litigation "say as a matter of law that the plaintiffs were 'equally' at fault for the alleged immigration fraud."[241]

V. ISSUES IN CIVIL LITIGATION

A. Standing

2. *Business or Property*

As mentioned in the Main Edition, in *National Organization for Women v. Scheidler*,[242] the Supreme Court noted that "'[a]t the plead-

[239] *Id.* at *13-14.
[240] 2003 WL 23893010 (N.D.Cal. 2003).
[241] *Id.*
[242] 510 U.S. 249 (1994).

ing stage, general factual allegations of injury resulting from the defendant's conduct may suffice, for on a motion to dismiss we presume that general allegations embrace those specific facts that are necessary to support the claim.'"[243] The Court accepted review of the case again to address, inter alia, whether political protesters' intentional interference with the public's access to a business's premises and with the freedom of its putative customers to obtain services there violates the Hobbs Act.[244]

In its decision in *Scheidler,*[245] the Supreme Court found that there was no dispute that the political protesters "interfered with, disrupted, and in some instances completely deprived the [RICO plaintiffs] of their ability to exercise their property rights."[246] Nevertheless, the Court held that because the protestors "did not obtain or attempt to obtain property" from the RICO plaintiffs (a necessary requirement for a finding of extortion), there was no basis upon which to find that the protestors committed extortion under the Hobbs Act.[247] The Court also expressly noted that the dissent was mistaken in its suggestion that the Court's "decision reaches, much less rejects" lower court decisions concluding that intangible rights constitute property under the Hobbs Act.[248]

In *Does v. The Gap, Inc.*,[249] the plaintiff–employees adequately pleaded injury to their "business or property" through "allegations of lost wages caused by the predicate acts of involuntary servitude and peonage" and "allegations of excessive payments for employer-provided food and housing."[250] The district court, however, found that "the deposits plaintiffs allegedly made to the recruiters to ensure completion of their contracts with defendants do not constitute

---

[243]*Id.* at 256, quoting Lujan v. Defenders of Wildlife, 504 U.S. 555, 561 (1992).

[244]*See* Section IV.E.2. *and* Section IV.E.3.b., *supra.*

[245]National Org. for Women v. Scheidler, 537 U.S. 393 (2003).

[246]*Id.* at 404.

[247]*Id.* at 409. The Court also found that state law extortion offenses for purposes of RICO must also contain an "obtaining" requirement, and because the protestors had not obtained or attempted to obtain property, the state law extortion statutes could not support the RICO verdict. *Id.* at 410.

[248]*Id.* at 402.

[249]2001 WL 1842389 (D. N. Mar. I. Nov. 26, 2001).

[250]*Id.* at *4–5.

a concrete financial loss because plaintiffs acknowledge that the deposits will be returned to them upon completion of their contracts and only speculate that the deposits may be lost."[251]

In *Bonavitacola Electrical Contractors, Inc. v. Boro Developers, Inc.*,[252] the court rejected one plaintiff's argument that it met RICO's proximate cause requirement by alleging that, as the second lowest bidder, it would have been awarded the contract awarded to the defendant. The court noted that because other factors can affect the award of a contract, this was insufficient to establish proximate cause.[253] As to the two labor union plaintiffs, the court held that their assertion that they would have received additional contributions to their multiemployer benefit plans if the plaintiff–employer had been awarded the contract constituted an indirect injury and that the unions themselves had failed to allege that they had standing to sue for these damages, which are presumably for the benefit of union members.[254] The Third Circuit[255] affirmed the dismissal of the plaintiffs' RICO claim on several grounds. In doing so, the Third Circuit held that the union's purported RICO injury—their multi-employer benefit plans would have received additional contributions if Bonavitacola had received the contracts—was even more remote than Bonavitacola's claim that it was injured when it was denied the opportunity to compete with Boro on a "fair and honest basis" and consequently lost income and profits it would have earned had it been awarded the contracts.[256]

The court in *Dooley v. Crab Boat Owners Ass'n*,[257] rendering a decision expressly based on *Scheidler*, held that intangible property, such as the right to solicit business, is property for purposes of the Hobbs Act, and that such property can be the object of extortion for purposes of the Act. In *Dooley*, the plaintiffs were a company in the business of harvesting crab and the defendants were competing associations. The plaintiffs alleged that the defendants threatened the plaintiffs' customers with loss of business, threatened violence, and

---

[251]*Id.* at *5.

[252]2003 U.S. Dist. LEXIS 2190 (E.D. Pa. Feb. 12, 2003), *aff'd*, 87 Fed. Appx. 227 (3rd Cir. 2003), *cert. denied*, 125 S. Ct. 57 (2004).

[253]*Id.* at *34–36.

[254]*Id.* at *36–37.

[255]2003 WL 23155074 (3d Cir. 2003), *cert. denied*, 125 S. Ct. 57, 160 L. Ed. 2d 26 (2004).

[256]*Bonavitacola, supra* note 252, 2003 U.S. Dist. LEXIS 2190 at *6, 87 Fed. Appx. at 234.

[257]271 F. Supp. 2d 1207 (N.D. Cal. 2003).

damaged the plaintiffs' property in an attempt by the defendants to obtain a higher price for crab.[258] The *Dooley* court concluded that the plaintiffs had sufficiently alleged predicate acts supporting a claim of attempted Hobbs Act extortion. Analogizing to *Tropiano*,[259] the court held that the defendants did not merely restrict the plaintiffs' activities as petitioners did in *Scheidler*, but rather, wrongfully attempted to acquire something of value through threats, warnings, and property damage, as the defendants did in *Tropiano*. According to the *Dooley* court, the property at issue was the plaintiff's right to harvest crab and the defendants' attempts to obtain that property were wrongful because the defendants had no legal interest in the property.[260]

Similarly, the court in *Titan International, Inc. v. Becker*[261] denied the union defendant's motion to dismiss Titan's extortion allegations based on *Scheidler*, concluding that the allegations were legally sufficient because the union's alleged use of bomb threats, violence, and other illegal acts to obtain money or other property from Titan may constitute extortion for purposes of the Hobbs Act.

In August 2003, the District Court for the District of Connecticut relied on *Scheidler* in granting the defendants' motions to dismiss certain RICO claims in *Interstate Flagging v. Town of Darien*.[262] In *Interstate Flagging*, the plaintiff provided traffic control services for construction and utility maintenance contractors. Interstate Flagging brought suit against certain municipalities and the presidents of the police officers unions in those municipalities alleging, inter alia, that the union presidents "committed predicate acts that would constitute a pattern of 'racketeering activity'—namely extortion,"[263] by enforcing and encouraging policies, regulations, ordinances, and customs that required that police officers have the exclusive right, or the right of first refusal, to provide traffic control services for construction or utility maintenance contractors within specified areas through the use of extortion and physical threats that affected commerce in violation of RICO and the Hobbs Act.[264] Although the plain-

[258] *Id.* at 1209, 1214.
[259] 418 F.2d 1069 (2d Cir. 1969).
[260] *Dooley, supra* note 257, 271 F. Supp. 2d at 1214 n.8.
[261] No. 00-3257 (N.D. Ill. July 31, 2003).
[262] 283 F. Supp. 2d 641 (D. Conn. 2003).
[263] *Id.* at 646.
[264] *Id.* at 646–47.

tiff alleged that police officers harassed and threatened its employees at work sites, forced its employees off of the work sites, and led companies to cancel their contracts with the plaintiffs,[265] the court concluded that the plaintiffs did not allege that the defendants obtained any property from the plaintiffs.[266] Analogizing to *Scheidler*, the district court dismissed the complaint, stating that the plaintiff failed to allege that the union presidents obtained any property from the plaintiff as a result of the police officers' alleged wrongful actions.[267]

3. *"By Reason of"*

Two recent cases addressed Section 1964(c)'s "by reason of" language in the context of hiring illegal immigrants. In *Commercial Cleaning Services v. Colin Service Systems, Inc.*,[268] the plaintiff, a direct competitor of the defendant, alleged that the defendant's "illegal hiring practices enabled it to lower its variable costs and thereby underbid competing firms, which consequently lost contracts and customers to" the defendant.[269] The district court dismissed the case, reasoning that the plaintiff-competitor did not allege facts sufficient to establish that the defendant's alleged RICO violation of hiring illegal immigrants at low wages proximately caused the plaintiff to lose revenue. The Second Circuit, however, vacated the district court's decision holding, among other things, that the defendant's alleged pattern of hiring undocumented aliens satisfied RICO's proximate cause requirement. In short, *Commercial Cleaning Services* stands for the proposition that a direct competitor, upon the showing of proper proof, may state a RICO claim against a company that outbid it on a contract as a result of lowering its costs through immigration violations.

In *Mendoza v. Zirkle Fruit Co.*,[270] lawful employees of the defendant-employer filed a RICO claim based on the employer's alleged illegal hiring of undocumented immigrants. The district court held that the plaintiffs were direct victims of the alleged scheme, but their

[265] *Id.* at 644.

[266] *Id.* at 647.

[267] *Id.*

[268] 2000 WL 545126 (D. Conn. Mar. 21, 2000), *vacated and remanded*, 271 F.3d 374 (2d Cir. 2001).

[269] *Id.*, 271 F.3d at 378.

[270] 301 F.3d 1163 (9th Cir. 2002).

alleged injury of depressed wages was too speculative. The Ninth Circuit, however, reversed the district court's dismissal of the complaint, holding that it was inappropriate for the court to substitute its views on causation for the allegations in the complaint, and that the plaintiffs must be allowed to make their case through presentation of evidence.[271]

Wal-Mart, the nation's largest retailer, was sued under RICO by a group of workers who worked for contractors who cleaned its stores.[272] The nine named class representatives are identified in the complaint as individuals whose "immigration status is that of an undocumented alien who may be subject to deportation from the United States at the initiative of the U.S. Citizenship and Immigration Bureau of the Department of Homeland Security (USCIS)." The plaintiffs allege that Wal-Mart and certain cleaning contractors violated immigration, labor, and other laws by a scheme in which illegal aliens were denied overtime pay despite working at least 56 hours a week, and contractors failed to withhold taxes and make required workers' compensation contributions.

The plaintiffs claimed that Wal-Mart and the contractors engaged in and profited from a nationwide fraudulent scheme designed to defraud the United States government through the nonpayment of taxes and injure and exploit the plaintiffs and those similarly situated through wide-scale violations of protective federal and state labor and employment laws. At the heart of the RICO claims was the allegation that Wal-Mart and the contractor defendants engaged in a criminal enterprise, the purpose of which was systematically to violate immigration and protective federal and state labor and employment laws for their own profit and benefit at the expense of the janitors.

---

[271] *See also* System Mgmt., Inc. v. Loiselle, 303 F.3d 100 (1st Cir. 2002) (reversing district court's judgment in favor of plaintiffs (two former employees) for lack of pattern of racketeering activity, where company's fraudulent effort to maintain its cleaning contract without disclosing violations of state prevailing-wage statute was single narrow episode that did not constitute "closed ended" continuity, and there was no evidence of any plan to bid on contracts on other jobs that would have demonstrated "open ended" continuity).

[272] Zavala v. Wal-Mart Stores, Inc., Civil Action No. 03-CIV-5309 (JAG) (D.N.J. 2003).

In *Mayes v. Operating Engineers Local 106*,[273] an individual union member alleged a variety of improprieties by union officials, including unauthorized pension overpayments and receipt of unauthorized pension contributions, improper hiring of retired union members, facilitating an illegal work stoppage, granting union membership to persons not qualified to be in the union, undertaking an improper ballot initiative to create a new union defense fund, and filing inaccurate reports required by the LMRDA. The district court granted summary judgment on the plaintiff's RICO claims because, among other reasons, "the injuries he alleges, rather than being unique to him, would be the type suffered by Local 106 as a whole"[274] and because "[u]nquantifiable harm to union membership, as he alleges, is not actionable under civil RICO."[275]

In *Anderson v. Ayling*,[276] two employees alleged they were terminated from their jobs after a union official made phone calls in which he alleged the plaintiffs were involved in a beating death and drug ring. The calls were allegedly made in order to punish them for their opposition to the international union's emergency trusteeship of their local union. The court found that the plaintiffs lacked standing since their complaint only alleged that they lost their jobs because of their opposition to the trusteeship. The court reasoned that this allegation was insufficient to provide the plaintiffs with standing to bring a Section 1962(c) claim "because the terminations did not occur 'by reason of' of the RICO violations."[277] The court also rejected the plaintiffs' attempt to claim injury to their "'membership in a racketeer free local of the [IBT].'"[278] The plaintiffs had alleged that all of the members of the local were injured by the corruption of their local by the defendants. The court found that because the plaintiffs had not alleged what injuries they suffered from being denied a "racketeer-free" membership, they had not alleged a concrete financial loss resulting from the alleged racketeering activity to have standing.[279] The Third Circuit[280] affirmed the district court's dismissal,

---

[273]1999 WL 60135, 165 LRRM 2689 (N.D.N.Y. Feb. 5, 1999), *aff'd*, 201 F.3d 431, 1999 WL 1070062, 165 LRRM 2704 (2d Cir. 1999), *cert. denied*, 121 S. Ct. 51 (2000).

[274]*Id.*, 1999 WL 60135 at *3.

[275]*Id.* at *4.

[276]297 F. Supp. 2d 805, 174 LRRM 2205 (E.D. Pa. 2003).

[277]*Id.* at 811-12.

[278]*Id.* at 812.

[279]*Id.* at 813.

[280]396 F.3d 265 (3d Cir. 2005).

holding that the chain of causation between the alleged acts of racketeering (wire fraud) and the plaintiffs' termination of employment was too attenuated as there were several independent causes that intervened between the alleged fraud and the terminations.[281] The court also rejected the plaintiffs' claims that they were not only injured in losing their jobs but were injured by corruption of their local union. The court held that "this corruption is not a cognizable injury that can create RICO standing," because an injury under RICO "requires proof of a concrete financial loss and not a mere injury to a valuable intangible property interest."[282]

In *Bona v. Barasch*,[283] the plaintiffs, current and former union members, alleged that the defendants had engaged in wholesale looting of union benefit funds through the manipulation of investment services contracts and the failure to prudently manage the funds. The court found that the plaintiffs lacked standing to bring a RICO claim because the alleged RICO violations damaged the union and the benefit funds and did not directly injure the plaintiffs.[284]

The Ninth Circuit in *Diaz v. Gates*[285] found that the plaintiff, who alleged wrongful conviction and incarceration stemming from alleged misconduct of various Los Angeles Police Department Officials in the Rampart scandal, lacked standing to bring RICO claims because he failed to sufficiently plead injury to "business or property" as required under Section 1964(c). In *Diaz*, the plaintiff alleged that he was deprived of his ability to earn a living and suffered economic harm because he lost employment, employment opportunities, and wages and compensation he would have otherwise earned but was unable to while defending himself against false charges and

---

[281] *Id.* at 270.

[282] *Id.* at 271 (citing Maio v. Aetna Inc., 221 F.3d 472, 483 (3d Cir. 2000)); *see also* Breslin v. Brainard, 2005 WL 775846 *2(3d Cir., April 7, 2005, unpublished) (affirming district court's dismissal of RICO claims based on loss of job and rejecting plaintiff's alternative claim that he suffered damage to his property interest in a corruption-free union finding that such a claim is not a cognizable injury sufficient to create standing under RICO).

[283] 174 LRRM 2051 (S.D.N.Y. 2003).

[284] *See also* Commer v. State, County, & Municipal Employees, 173 LRRM 2023 (S.D.N.Y. 2003), *aff'd*, 390 F.3d 203 (2nd Cir. 2004) (former president of AFSCME local union lacked standing to bring RICO action since injury he alleged from looting and diversion of benefit funds was incurred by entire union membership).

[285] 354 F.3d 1169 (9th Cir.), *reprinted as amended*, 380 F.3d 480 (9th Cir.), *reh'g en banc denied*, 389 F.3d 869 (9th Cir. 2004).

while he was unjustly incarcerated.[286] The court found the plaintiff failed to demonstrate "proof of concrete financial loss."[287] The court reasoned that the plaintiff's claim was distinguishable from the Ninth Circuit's holding in *Mendoza v. Zirkle Fruit Co.*,[288] not because he "allege[d] loss of wages, but because he has not alleged that the wrongdoing was in any way *tied to or directed at* his business or property."[289] In rejecting the plaintiff's claim, the court held that he had not alleged a "sufficient nexus between the RICO act and his 'business or property.'"[290] The court held that "[a]t most [plaintiff's] alleged injuries could be characterized as 'mere injury to a valuable intangible property interest' in his right to pursue employment."[291]

In contrast, in *Gintowt v. TL Ventures*,[292] the district court held that the plaintiff lacked standing to bring a RICO claim against the defendants for damages incurred incident to his status as a shareholder. The court reasoned that the plaintiff could only bring a claim under the PLSA, and not RICO, for damages arising out of the purchase or sale of stock.[293] The court, however, stated that the plaintiff had standing to sue for damages incurred incident to his termination of employment and resignation of director.[294]

In *Herrick v. South Bay Labor Council*,[295] the plaintiff, an office worker, claimed she was terminated for among other things, reporting the alleged embezzlement of union funds and unspecified fraudulent accounting activities. The plaintiff sought to amend her complaint to add a RICO claim. The district court denied the motion finding that her alleged injury did not stem from any purported racketeering activity, but from the termination of her employment.[296]

---

[286] *Id.*, 354 F.3d at 1170; 380 F.3d at 482.

[287] *Id.*, 354 F.3d at 1171; 380 F.3d at 485-86.

[288] 301 F.3d 1163, 1166 (9th Cir. 2002) (holding that plaintiffs' allegations that fruit growers conspired to hire undocumented workers in order to depress wages sufficiently alleged injury to business or property).

[289] *Diaz, supra* note 285, 354 F.3d at 1172; 380 F.3d at 485-86.

[290] *Id.*, 354 F.3d at 1173; 380 F.3d at 484.

[291] *Id.*, 354 F.3d at 1173; 380 F.3d at 484.

[292] *Id.*, 2004 U.S. Dist. LEXIS 14305 (E.D. Penn. July 22, 2004).

[293] *Id.* at *35-36.

[294] *Id.* at *38.

[295] 2004 WL 2645980 (N.D. Cal. 2004).

[296] *Id.* at *3.

B. Accommodations to the Labor Laws

In *Miller v. Norfolk Southern Railway Co.*,[297] the district court held that a RICO claim by union members against their employer arising out of a decertification vote fell within the primary jurisdiction of the National Mediation Board pursuant to the Railway Labor Act because the dispute was "arguably representational." Accordingly, the case was dismissed for lack of subject matter jurisdiction.[298]

2. *The Emerging Majority Rule*

a. Cases Recognizing Limited Labor Law "Preemption"

In *Overnite Transportation Co. v. Teamsters*,[299] the district court held that the NLRA preempted all of the plaintiff-employer's allegations that the union defendants had committed predicate acts in violation of the Hobbs Act, state extortion statutes, and the Travel Act. In so doing, the court reasoned that the nature of the allegations required an interpretation of the NLRA to determine whether the strike activity at issue was "lawful."[300] The court further refused to permit the plaintiff to rely upon state extortion laws in the labor context, claiming that the Supreme Court has impliedly recognized "the reality that extortion is an integral part of the labor landscape."[301] Moreover, the court noted that the crime of coercion is not a RICO predicate act and that coercive conduct in the labor context is more appropriately within the exclusive jurisdiction of the NLRA. However, the court declined to dismiss allegations of multiple predicate acts of attempted murder.[302]

In *Capozza Tile Co., Inc. v. Joy*,[303] a case about an allegedly fraudulently induced collective bargaining agreement, the court declined to hold that the company's RICO claim against union defendants was preempted. The court found that "[b]ased solely on the allegations in the amended complaint, it is possible that the conduct alleged as the basis of the RICO claim is illegal" without reference to the NLRA.[304]

---

[297] 183 F. Supp. 2d 996, 169 LRRM 2343 (N.D. Ohio 2002).
[298] *Id.* at 998–1000.
[299] 168 F. Supp. 2d 826, 167 LRRM 2111 (W.D. Tenn. 2001).
[300] *Id.* at 840–43.
[301] *Id.* at 842.
[302] *Id.* at 844–46.
[303] 2001 WL 1057682 (D. Me. Sept. 13, 2001).
[304] *Id.* at *5.

In *Baker v. IBP*,[305] the plaintiff union members brought a class action on behalf of hourly wage earners at the defendant's meat processing plant, alleging that the defendant knowingly employed undocumented, illegal immigrants to reduce labor costs by driving down employee wages. The trial court found that "[i]n order for Plaintiffs to prove damages in the form of depressed wages, they must first allege that Defendant bargained in bad faith. Without this allegation, Plaintiffs cannot show that they suffered depressed wages, since there is no allegation that Defendant did not pay the wages agreed to in the collective bargaining agreement. Once this necessary allegation is made, preemption is inevitable, because failing to exercise good faith in collective bargaining is wrongful '*only by virtue of the labor laws.*'"[306] On appeal, the Seventh Circuit found that the labor laws did not preempt the plaintiffs' RICO claim.[307] The plaintiffs alleged that the employer committed predicate acts by employing illegal aliens in violation of the immigration laws in order to depress wages.[308] The court noted that federal statutes do not preempt other federal statutes; the preemption doctrine applies to state laws.[309] The court found the alleged violations of immigration laws were insufficient to warrant preemption.[310]

b. Cases Rejecting Labor Law "Preemption"

In *Lopresti v. Merson*,[311] the plaintiff-union alleged that the employer-defendants had defrauded the union into signing a plant closing agreement that terminated a collective bargaining agreement in connection with a sale of the company. The district court dismissed the plaintiff's RICO claims for failure to state a claim before reaching the preemption issue. The court reasoned that no claim existed

[305]2002 U.S. Dist. LEXIS 24669 *9, 171 LRRM 2355 (C.D. Ill. Oct. 21, 2002), *modified and affirmed on other grounds*, 357 F.3d 685 (7th Cir.), *reh'g en banc denied*, 2004 U.S. App. LEXIS 8689 (7th Cir.), *cert. denied*, 125 S. Ct. 412 (2004) (judgment was modified from dismissal for lack of jurisdiction to dismissal for failure to state claim on which relief may be granted. The Seventh Circuit held that plaintiff did not establish a pattern of racketeering activity because there was no allegation that the employer operated an enterprise and RICO's distinctiveness requirement was not met.).

[306]*Id.*, 171 LRRM at 2357.

[307]357 F.3d 685, 2004 U.S. App. LEXIS 1659 (7th Cir. 2004).

[308]*Id.* at 686.

[309]*Id.* at 688-90.

[310]*Id.* at 691-92.

[311]168 LRRM 2427 (S.D.N.Y. 2001).

for the NLRA to preempt because no claim was stated, and that the issue of "preemption should be decided in the context of specific RICO claims that are sufficient to withstand a motion to dismiss."[312]

E. Statute of Limitations

In *Forbes v. Eagleson*,[313] a post-*Rotella* case, the Third Circuit affirmed summary judgment on former professional hockey league players' class action against their employers and the former executive director of their union on statute of limitations grounds, holding that a civil RICO claim accrues under the "injury discovery" rule.

In *Tran v. Alphonse Hotel Corp.*,[314] the Second Circuit held that the district court abused its discretion in finding that the plaintiff's amendment to the complaint, adding a RICO claim six years after it accrued, "related back" to the filing of the original complaint. The court refused to allow the RICO claim based upon the alleged bribery of union officials to relate back because the "amendment introduced a significant new factual allegation that fundamentally changed the nature of the allegations, both factual and legal, that plaintiff was asserting against defendants."[315] The court further held that the plaintiff could not establish any fraudulent concealment or "due diligence" sufficient to toll the statute of limitations.[316] Accordingly, the plaintiff's RICO claim was dismissed as untimely.

In *John Doe v. Archdiocese of Cincinnati*,[317] an Ohio appeals court, in applying the state RICO act's five-year statute of limitations, found that the RICO claims of the plaintiffs, former students at a Catholic school and parish in Cincinnati, were time barred. The plaintiffs alleged that the Archdiocese's concealment of the sexual misconduct of the offending priest from other victims and parishioners constituted a pattern of corrupt activity under the Ohio RICO statute. Relying in part on *Rotella v. Wood*,[318] the court held that the sexual

---

[312]*Id.* at n.8.

[313]228 F.3d 471, 165 LRRM 2584 (3d Cir. 2000), *cert. denied*, 533 U.S. 929 (2001).

[314]281 F.3d 23 (2d Cir. 2002), *motion for costs and fees granted*, 2002 U.S. Dist. LEXIS 17811 (S.D.N.Y. Sept. 20, 2002), *aff'd*, 2003 U.S. App. LEXIS 11201 (2d Cir. 2003).

[315]*Id.*, 281 F.3d at 36.

[316]*Id.* at 36–37.

[317]2004 WL 2973979 (Ohio App. 1 Dist. 2004).

[318]528 U.S. 549 (2000).

abuse was the injury and that while the Archdiocese's actions of concealment exacerbated the injury, the statute of limitations period for a state RICO claim was "not tolled while the injured person remains unaware that his injury was a part of a larger pattern of injurious conduct."[319] Under the Ohio RICO act, a person had five years from the date the unlawful conduct terminates or the cause of action accrues to commence a RICO action. Because the plaintiffs were minors when the injuries occurred, their claims did not accrue until they reached the age of majority. The court found that at the time the plaintiffs reached majority they were aware of the injury (the sexual abuse), the perpetrator of the injury and that he was employed by the Archdiocese. The court held that since none of the plaintiffs had filed their action within 5 years of reaching majority, their claims were time barred.[320]

VI. REMEDIES

B. Criminal Forfeiture

Co-conspirators are jointly and severally liable for forfeiture, including amounts extorted by one member in exchange for his assistance in maintaining labor peace, even if all the defendants did not receive or share in the improper payments.[321]

In *United States v. Cacace,*[322] indictments charged 42 defendants with various offenses, including RICO, for allegedly extorting union locals, and, with the aid of members of the locals, engaging in fraud schemes at various job sites. The schemes included no-show arrangements and falsely representing hours worked at the sites. The government sought criminal forfeiture and obtained a restraining order freezing union benefits of some of the defendants.[323]

---

[319] *Archdiocese of Cincinnati, supra* note 317, 2004 WL 297379 at *4.

[320] *Id.*

[321] United States v. Corrado, 227 F.3d 543 (6th Cir. 2000), *appeal after remand,* 286 F.3d 934 (6th Cir. 2002).

[322] E.D.N.Y., No. 03-CR-191, indictments unsealed Feb. 26, 2003.

[323] *Id.*

C. Trusteeships and Other Injunctive Relief

In private civil actions under RICO, most circuits that have addressed the issue have either expressly rejected[324] or cast doubt on the availability of equitable relief under RICO, although it may be available on independent grounds. The Seventh Circuit, however, recently held that injunctive relief is available to a private RICO plaintiff pursuant to 18 U.S.C. § 1964(a). In *National Organization for Women v. Scheidler,*[325] the appellate court affirmed the district court's granting of a nationwide injunction after a jury found defendants liable under RICO. The Supreme Court granted certiorari on two issues, including:

> Whether the Seventh Circuit correctly held, in acknowledged conflict with the Ninth Circuit, that injunctive relief is available in a private civil action for treble damages brought under the Racketeer Influenced and Corrupt Organizations Act (RICO), 18 U.S.C. § 1964(c).[326]

In its decision in *Scheidler,*[327] the Court held that because the protestors "did not obtain or attempt to obtain property" from the RICO plaintiffs (a necessary requirement for a finding of extortion), there was no basis upon to which to find that the protestors committed extortion under the Hobbs Act.[328] Because the Court held that its determination with respect to extortion rendered insufficient the bases for the jury's conclusion that the protestors violated RICO, it declined to reach the question of the availability of private injunctive relief.[329] On remand to the Seventh Circuit, the plaintiffs argued that, while the Supreme Court in *Scheidler* disposed of 117 extortion-based predicate acts under RICO, the defendants did not petition

---

[324]*See, e.g.*, Does v. The Gap, Inc., 2001 WL 1842389, at *5 (D. N. Mar. I. Nov. 26, 2001) (following the Ninth Circuit's decision in *Religious Tech. Ctr. v. Wollersheim,* 796 F.2d 1076 (9th Cir. 1986), *cert. denied,* 279 U.S. 1103 (1987), holding that injunctive relief is not available to civil RICO plaintiffs).

[325]267 F.3d 687, 695–700 (7th Cir. 2001), *cert. granted,* 535 U.S. 1016 (Apr. 22, 2002) (No. 01-1118).

[326]Petition for a Writ of Certiorari at p. (i), 535 U.S. 1016 (Apr. 22, 2002) (No. 01-1118).

[327]National Org. for Women v. Scheidler, 537 U.S. 393 (2003).

[328]*Id.* at 409. The Court also found that state law extortion offenses for purposes of RICO must also contain an "obtaining" requirement, and because the protestors had not obtained or attempted to obtain property, the state law extortion statutes could not support the RICO verdict. *Id.* at 410.

[329]*Id.* at 397.

for certiorari on four predicate acts involving "acts or threats of physical violence to any person or property" and thus, the Supreme Court did not decide whether these acts alone supported the district court's injunction.[330] In response, the defendants argued that the Hobbs Act does not outlaw physical violence apart from extortion and robbery and, as a result, the Supreme Court's holding that the defendants did not commit extortion precludes a finding that the acts or threats of violence independently support the injunction.[331] The Seventh Circuit remanded to the district court for consideration of this issue, which was never before the subject of full briefing or judicial consideration.[332] The defendants petitioned for rehearing and rehearing en banc of the February 2004 remand order and the petition was denied in *National Organization for Woman v. Scheidler*.[333]

In its published opinion, a majority of the panel highlighted the questions for the district court to determine on remand in light of the Supreme Court's "general refusal" to decide whether mere acts or threats of physical violence apart from extortion and robbery were a violation of the Hobbs Act, and consequently, a sufficient basis for the district court's nationwide injunction under RICO.[334]

> Specifically, the court may need to determine whether the phrase "commits or threatens physical violence to any person or property" constitutes an independent ground for violating the Hobbs Act or, rather, relates back to the grounds of robbery or extortion. In the alternative, the court may conclude that the proper interpretation of § 1951(a) is immaterial, if it decides that the four acts or threats of physical violence found by the jury are not sufficient standing alone to support the nationwide injunction.[335]
>
> ***
>
> If and only if the district court concludes that some form of injunctive relief would be justified based on the four remaining predicate acts found by the jury, that court will have to confront a more complex legal issue, namely, whether the acts or threats of

---

[330]National Org. for Women v. Scheidler, 2004 U.S. App. LEXIS 4020, at *6–7. (7th Cir. 2004).

[331]*Id.* at *7.

[332]*Id.*

[333]NOW, Inc. v. Scheidler, 396 F.3d 807 (7th Cir. 2005).

[334]*Id.* at 811.

[335]*Id.*, citing 18 U.S.C. § 1951(a).

violence language in the Hobbs Act may serve as an independent predicate act under RICO.[336]

The majority also highlighted competing bookends of the Hobbs Act debate noting that the statute's application will turn on either a "two-way" or "three-way" interpretation. The relevant part of the Hobbs Act reads as follows:

> Whoever in any way or degree obstructs, delays, or affects commerce or the movement of any article or commodity in commerce, by robbery or extortion or attempts or conspires so to do, or commits or threatens physical violence to any person or property in furtherance of a plan or purpose to do anything in violation of this section shall be fined under this title or imprisoned not more than twenty years, or both.[337]

A vigorous dissent by Circuit Judges Manion and Kanne characterized both the majority's decision to remand and its debate over the Hobbs Act without deciding the issue as unnecessary in light of the Supreme Court's clear language and case's two-decade long procedural history.[338]

On March 16, 2005, Scheidler and the other defendants filed petitions to the Supreme Court for the third time seeking a grant writ of certiorari, or in the alternative, a writ of mandamus seeking to vacate the Seventh Circuit's decision to remand to the district court.[339]

In *United States v. Sasso,*[340] the Second Circuit held that RICO's Section 1964(a) authorized the district court to order a retired local union officer to contribute monies for a monitorship that was created to eradicate the possibility of future labor racketeering by local officials.

In *Laborers v. Caruso,*[341] the international union reached an agreement with the U.S. Department of Justice, which included a reform program, to avoid a civil RICO action seeking a receivership. Pursuant to these reforms, the international later brought a trusteeship

[336] *Id.* at 812.
[337] 18 U.S.C. § 1951(a).
[338] *Scheidler, supra* note 333, 396 F.3d at 817-818.
[339] *Cert. granted,* 125 S. Ct. 2991 (June 28, 2005) No. 04-1244.
[340] 215 F.3d 283, 164 LRRM 2613 (2d Cir. 2000).
[341] 197 F.3d 1195, 163 LRRM 2204 (7th Cir. 1999).

complaint against the Chicago District Council. The Seventh Circuit affirmed the district court's finding that the international did not act in bad faith or with unclean hands in its efforts to establish the trusteeship.

Three recent cases demonstrate the vitality of the government's consent decrees in the RICO cases against the Teamsters and the Mason Tenders. First, in *United States v. Teamsters,*[342] the Second Circuit affirmed the Independent Review Board's permanent membership and associational bans against former Teamsters president Ronald Carey and long-time union official William Hamilton.[343] The proceedings arose out of findings of corruption related to fundraising during the 1996 Teamsters election. Next, in *United States v Teamsters*[344] and *United States v. Mason Tenders District Council of Greater New York,*[345] the Second Circuit and the Southern District of New York, respectively, held that the consent decrees entered by the Teamsters and the Mason Tenders prevented the Production and Maintenance Employees Union, Local 116, its President and Treasurer, both expelled members of the Teamsters, from contacting union members subject to the decrees. Both courts, in rejecting the argument that the court lacked the authority to issue injunctive relief over the defendants, held that they could issue relief pursuant to the All Writs Act[346] even though the defendants were not actual parties to the respective consent decrees.[347]

In a case involving the RICO consent decree in *United States v. Teamsters,* the Second Circuit held that the scope of the authority given to the Independent Review Board (IRB) pursuant to that decree was not limited to violations of federal labor or criminal law.[348] The court held that the IRB's investigative and decisional authority,

---

[342]247 F.3d 370, 167 LRRM 2665 (2d Cir. 2001).

[343]*See also* United States v. Carberry, 2002 WL 243247 (2d Cir. Feb. 15, 2002) (affirming disciplinary sanction imposed by the International Review Board on a candidate for Teamsters Vice-President at Large on "Hoffa Slate" arising out of 1996 election).

[344]266 F.3d 45, 168 LRRM 2863 (2d Cir. 2001).

[345]205 F. Supp. 2d 183, 170 LRRM 2097 (S.D.N.Y. 2002).

[346]28 U.S.C. §1651(a).

[347]In August 2003, the media reported that the IBT and federal authorities were discussing an end to federal oversight and the specific steps the IBT must take to end government oversight.

[348]315 F.3d 97, 99, 171 LRRM 2788 (2d Cir. 2002), *cert. denied,* 538 U.S. 998 (2003).

which under the consent decree is coextensive with that of the IBT General President and General Secretary-Treasurer, encompassed conduct that "brought reproach upon the union" under the IBT's Constitution.[349] The conduct at issue was a union officer's and his assistant's scheme to cause appointed business agents to make dues payments untimely in order to make them ineligible to run for local union office. The sanctioned officer and his assistant argued that because their conduct would not state a claim under the LMRDA, it did not bring reproach upon the union.[350] The court rejected this argument and held that the issue was "not whether the business agents have an actionable claim for their membership right to stand for election, but whether the conditioning of union employment on relinquishment of a membership right brought reproach upon the union."[351] The court found that the IRB's findings that the officer and his assistant secretly affected the rights of members was sufficient to support exercise of the IRB's jurisdiction.[352]

D. Damages in Private Actions

Former union officers who failed to demonstrate that their union made RICO allegations against them in bad faith cannot recover attorneys' fees incurred in successfully defending against the claims.[353]

In the past, where an employer filed an unmeritorious RICO claim against unions, the employer's request for treble damages has been held to be evidence, in part, of retaliatory purpose to establish an unfair labor practice, thus supporting a Board order to reimburse the unions for all legal and other expenses incurred in defending against the lawsuit.[354] However, the Supreme Court's recent decision in *BE&K Construction Co. v. NLRB*[355] rejected the Board's standard for finding employers' lawsuits unlawful under the NLRA. Although

---

[349] *Id.*, 315 F.3d at 99.

[350] *Id.*

[351] *Id.* at 100.

[352] *Id.*

[353] Doyle v. Turner, 90 F. Supp. 2d 311, 165 LRRM 2968 (S.D.N.Y.), *aff'd sub nom.* Hughley v. Local 1199, Hosp. & Health Care Employees, 231 F.3d 889, 165 LRRM 2987 (2d Cir. 2000).

[354] Petrochem Insulation, Inc. v. NLRB, 240 F.3d 26, 166 LRRM 2433 (D.C. Cir.), *enforcing* 330 NLRB No. 10, 163 LRRM 1276 (1999), *cert. denied*, 534 U.S. 992 (2001).

[355] 536 U.S. 516, 170 LRRM 2225 (2002).

there are three opinions, all nine Justices agreed that the Board cannot punish an employer for having filed an objectively reasonable lawsuit that failed, where the sole evidence of "retaliatory motive" is based on the loss and the employer's dislike for the union. In light of *BE&K*, the Board will be required to develop a new standard for determining whether losing suits against unions or employees constitute an unfair labor practice.

In its first treatment of suits in retaliation for protected activity, the NLRB, in a divided opinion by a panel of three members, ruled that an employer violated the Act by calling police to remove several union pickets from "public property."[356] The opinion, by Members Liebman and Walsh, concluded that the picketing was protected activity and the fact that the employer summoned local police was retaliatory. The Board concluded that such picketing was a lawful expression of Section 7 rights. In treating the issue, the Board relied primarily upon *Bill Johnson's Restaurants v. NLRB*,[357] and did not discuss the more recent decision of the U.S. Supreme Court in *BE&K Construction v. NLRB*,[358] in which the Court rejected the NLRB's application of *Bill Johnson's* in determining whether an employer's lawsuit was retaliatory and thus constituted an unfair labor practice.

Chairman Battista dissented from the Panel decision. The Chairman concluded that all citizens have a First Amendment right to contact law enforcement for the redress of grievances. However, by footnote, the Chairman expressly distinguished *BE&K* as he "found that Respondent acted within a reasonable basis."

The exact contours of the Supreme Court's decision in *BE&K*[359] have not yet been revealed. Since the Supreme Court's decision in *BE&K*, there has been one reported court of appeals decision in the field of traditional labor law that has cited *BE&K*. In *Can-Am Plumbing, Inc. v. NLRB*,[360] the D.C. Circuit rejected an employer's attempt to "read" *BE&K* as transferring to preempted lawsuits *Bill Johnson's* 'baseless and retaliatory' standard."[361]

[356]CSX Hotels dba The Greenbrier and Operating Eng'rs Local 132, 340 NLRB No. 92, 173 LRRM 1273 (2003), *revised by* 377 F.3d 394 (4th Cir. 2004).

[357]461 US 731, 113 LRRM 2647 (1983).

[358]536 US 516, 170 LRRM 2225 (2002).

[359]*Id.*

[360]321 F.3d 145 (D.C. Cir. 2003).

[361]*Id.* at 151.

In *Can-Am*, a non-union plumbing contractor filed a lawsuit in California state court against a competitor alleging that the Plumbers' Union Job Targeting Program (JTP), in which a competitor received funds from the program to assist it in bidding for a project against a non-union competitor, was illegal under California law. The union, which was not a party to the lawsuit, filed an unfair labor practice charge with the Board. The general counsel issued a complaint and an ALJ determined that the employer's state law suit was preempted under the Board's decision in *Manno Electric,*[362] which held such programs to be protected by Section 7 of the Act. The Board affirmed, and Can-Am argued on appeal that under *BE&K* and *Bill Johnson's*, its state court lawsuit did not violate Section 8(a)(1) because it had a reasonable basis to believe that the JTP program violated California law. Thus, Can-Am argued, the same First Amendment concerns that were applicable in *BE&K* were at stake and applied to preempted lawsuits.

In *Bill Johnson's*,[363] the Supreme Court carved out an exception to its "retaliatory and baseless" analysis for suits that are beyond the reach of state court because they are preempted by federal labor law or that have an illegal objective under federal law. Such suits would not be subject to the First Amendment analysis developed in *Bill Johnson's* and the Board could enjoin these types of suits.[364]

The Court rejected Can-Am's theory, holding that the exception for preempted lawsuits carved out by the Court in footnote 5 of *Bill Johnson's* was undisturbed by *BE&K*:

> Thus, while Can-Am invokes the language of prior restraint in challenging the Board's conclusion that it violated section 8(a)(1), the jurisdictional question of preemption is, as *Bill Johnson's* acknowledged in footnote 5 (and *BE&K* did not disturb), a different matter.[365]

Two recent cases awarding attorneys' fees to the prevailing plaintiffs in civil RICO actions, *System Management, Inc. v. Loiselle*[366] and

---

[362] 321 NLRB 278, 298 (1996), *enforced mem.*, 127 F.3d 34 (5th Cir. 1997).

[363] Bill Johnson's Restaurants v. NLRB, 461 U.S. 731, 113 LRRM 2647 (1983).

[364] *Id.* at 737 n.5.

[365] *Can-Am, supra* note 360, 321 F.3d at 152.

[366] 154 F. Supp. 2d 195 (D. Mass. 2001), *rev'd*, 303 F.3d 100 (1st Cir. 2002) (reversing judgment for plaintiffs on grounds that mooted attorneys' fees issue).

Tran v. Tran,[367] rejected the defendants' attempt to reduce the awards by parsing out time spent on the "successful" claims versus the unsuccessful ones. In *Loiselle* the district court concluded that "a court may, but need not, diminish an award on the basis of unsuccessful claims that are interconnected with successful RICO claims."[368] The court will, however, "discount for time spent on unsuccessful claims that are unrelated to the successful RICO claims and can easily be severed."[369]

E. Arbitration of RICO Claims [New Topic]

In *PacifiCare Health Systems, Inc. v. Book*,[370] the Supreme Court held that physicians who brought a RICO suit against managed health care organizations could be compelled to arbitrate RICO claims, even though the parties' arbitration agreements could be construed to limit the arbitrator's authority to award treble damages.

The district court granted in part and denied in part the defendants' motions to compel arbitration of the RICO and state law claims asserted by the plaintiff-physicians. The court held that where the plaintiffs and the defendants are both signatories to contracts containing enforceable arbitration clauses, the plaintiffs' claims are due to be arbitrated. However, the district court held unenforceable those arbitration clauses that excluded punitive damages on the basis that the plaintiffs would be precluded from recovering treble damages under RICO. The district court also held that managed care companies could not invoke the arbitration clause in a contract to which the company was not a signatory in order to compel arbitration of the plaintiffs' RICO conspiracy and aiding and abetting claims.[371]

The Eleventh Circuit affirmed the district court's order in its entirety, rejecting the defendants' argument that the equitable es-

[367] 166 F. Supp. 2d 793 (S.D.N.Y. 2001), *rev'd in part on other grounds sub nom.* Tran v. Alphonse Hotel Corp., 281 F.3d 23 (2d Cir. 2002) (RICO claim barred by statute of limitations).

[368] *System Mgmt., supra* note 366, 154 F. Supp. 2d at 208.

[369] *Id.*

[370] 538 U.S. 401 (2003).

[371] *In re* Managed Care Litigation, 132 F. Supp. 2d 989 (S.D. Fla. 2000).

toppel principles of *MS Dealer Corp. v. Franklin*[372] were applicable because the plaintiffs alleged a RICO conspiracy between signatory and nonsignatory companies.[373] The Eleventh Circuit explained, "The plaintiff's actual dependence on the underlying contract in making out the claim against the nonsignatory defendant is . . . always the sine qua non of an appropriate situation for applying equitable estoppel."[374]

The Supreme Court granted certiorari to address whether a court or an arbitrator should determine the enforceability of the arbitration provisions that precluded an award of punitive damages. Because the Supreme Court found that it was unclear whether the arbitrator would construe the limitation on punitive damages as a limitation on treble damages, the Court held that the "proper course is to compel arbitration" in order to allow the arbitrator to determine the enforceability of the provision in the first instance.[375]

---

[372]177 F.3d 942 (11th Cir. 1999).

[373]In re Humana Inc. Managed Care Litigation, 285 F.3d 971 (11th Cir. 2002), *on remand*, 333 F.3d 1247 (11th Cir. 2003).

[374]*Id.* at 976.

[375]PacifiCare Health Systems, Inc. v. Book, 538 U.S. 401, 4007 (2003).

CHAPTER 31

NLRB PROCEDURES

I. ORGANIZATION OF BOARD AND OFFICE OF GENERAL COUNSEL

A. Background

The organization of the Board and the office of the General Counsel has not changed since the publication of the Fourth Edition.[1]

B. The Board

As of February 2005, the Board consisted of Chairman Robert J. Battista[2] and members Wilma B. Liebman[3] and Peter C. Schaumber.[4]

---

[1]For a detailed account of the operation of these functions, see NLRB RULES AND REGULATIONS AND STATEMENTS OF PROCEDURE, SERIES 8 (1959), as last amended, January 12, 2003; NLRB CASEHANDLING MANUAL, re-issued by the general counsel, September 2003; GARREN, FOX & TRUESDALE, HOW TO TAKE A CASE BEFORE THE NLRB (7th ed. BNA Books 2000) and 2003 CUMULATIVE SUPPLEMENT.

[2]President George W. Bush appointed, and the Senate confirmed, Battista to serve as chairman for a term expiring December 16, 2007.

[3]President George W. Bush appointed, and the Senate confirmed, Liebman to serve as a member for a term expiring August 27, 2006.

[4]President George W. Bush appointed, and the Senate confirmed, Schaumber to serve as a member for a term expiring August 27, 2005.

Member Ronald E. Meisburg's recess appointment expired on December 8, 2004, and Member Dennis P. Walsh's term expired December 16, 2004. On January 24, 2005, President Bush nominated Meisburg to fill one of the two vacancies and subsequently President Bush nominated Meisburg to be general counsel. Also in April 2005, Dennis Walsh was nominated to fill the other vacancy.

The Board traditionally is comprised of two Democrats, two Republicans, and a fifth member who belongs to the same party as the serving President. To serve a regular term, a nominee must receive Senate confirmation.[5] When a member's 5-year term expires, the next term begins running immediately, regardless of whether a replacement has been confirmed.[6] After the replacement is confirmed, he or she serves out the remainder of the term.[7]

C. The General Counsel

On May 26, 2001, Arthur F. Rosenfeld was confirmed as general counsel to serve a 4-year term. Prior to his confirmation, Mr. Rosenfeld was Senior Labor Counsel to the Senate Committee on Health, Education, Labor and Pensions On July 1, 2005, President Bush appointed Rosenfeld as acting general counsel.

E. The Regional Offices

As of February 2005, there were 32 regional offices, 3 subregional offices, and 16 resident offices.[8]

F. Personnel and Budget

For fiscal year 2005, the Board is operating under a budget of approximately $251,875,000.[9]

---

[5]165 LAB. REL. REP. (BNA) 563 (Aug. 28, 2000).

[6]*Id.*

[7]*Id.*

[8] General Counsel Memorandum GC 05-01, "Summary of Operations (Fiscal Year 2004)."

[9]Consolidated Appropriations Act, 2005, 108 Pub. L. No. 447, 118 Stat. 2809 (Dec. 8, 2004); 2004 Enacted H.R. 4818; 108 Enacted H.R. 4818 for fiscal year ending September 30, 2005.

II. PROCEDURES IN REPRESENTATION CASES

A. The Petition

Because Section 2(2) of the Act provides that the term "employer" shall not include "any person subject to the Railway Labor Act," the Board will not entertain petitions filed by labor organizations seeking to represent workers who may be deemed employees of an air carrier or other such employer subject to the Railway Labor Act.[10] In determining whether the employer is subject to the Railway Labor Act, the Board will solicit the opinion of the National Mediation Board on the subject.[11]

The Board reiterated, in *River City Elevator Co.,*[12] that the 30 percent showing-of-interest requirement is merely an example of an administrative procedure used by the Board within the context of its wide degree of discretion. The issue arose in the context of a second election made necessary by union conduct. Despite the employer's assertion that objectionable union conduct had tainted the original showing of interest and that the passage of time and employee turnover had made the initial showing stale, the Board did not require a new showing. The Board noted the showing is not statutorily required and is not "intended to create a right in any party to protest the conduct of an election."

B. Timeliness of Petitions

In *Suffolk Banana,*[13] the Board found that a contract containing two conflicting termination dates barred a representation petition because at the time the petition was filed it was untimely under either date. The Board concluded that the situation was unlike that in *Bob's Big Boy Family Restaurant,*[14] where the union filed its petition within an ambiguous time period and the petition was, therefore, not barred.

---

[10]Aviation Safeguards, 338 NLRB 770, 171 LRRM 1379 (2003); Ogden Ground Servs., Inc., 340 NLRB No. 137, 173 LRRM 1454 (2003).

[11]*Id.*

[12]339 NLRB 616, 172 LRRM 1409, 1410 (2003) ("It is an intraagency administrative determination, and, as such, is not litigable by the parties.").

[13]328 NLRB 1086, 162 LRRM 1029 (1999).

[14]259 NLRB 153, 108 LRRM 1296 (1981), *enforcement denied*, 693 F.2d 904, 111 LRRM 3132 (9th Cir. 1982).

A decertification petition will be dismissed if it is filed during the posting period of a settlement agreement that provides for bargaining with employees in the involved petition.[15]

In *MGM Grand Hotel, Inc.*,[16] where an employer had voluntarily recognized a union, the Board required dismissal of three decertification petitions, despite the collective bargaining process taking more than 11 months. The Board found reasonable time to bargain had not yet passed when the petitions were filed. In *Lee Lumber,*[17] an unfair labor practice case, the Board held that a reasonable period for bargaining, after a finding of a refusal to bargain in a settlement agreement, is at least 6 months but no more than 1 year, depending on the circumstances of the case.

In *Livent Realty dba Ford Center for the Performing Arts,*[18] a petition by a rival union was barred by the employer's prior voluntary recognition of another union because the employer and the first union had not yet had a reasonable time to bargain. The employer had voluntarily recognized the first union and, over the course of 9 months, had bargained in good faith to establish an initial contract with that union. Under the circumstances, the Board found that the rival union's petition, filed just 2 weeks before the employer and the first union executed their first contract, was barred.

In *St. Elizabeth Manor, Inc.,*[19] the Board held that once a successor employer's obligation to recognize and bargain with an incumbent union attaches, the union is entitled to a reasonable period of time for bargaining without challenge to its majority status. The case, in effect, created a *successor bar* to the filing of a petition, and to the withdrawal of recognition by the employer. The "successor bar" rule established in *St. Elizabeth Manor* was, however, short lived. In July 2002, the Board issued its decision in *MV Transportation,*[20] overruling *St. Elizabeth Manor* and declaring it "an unwarranted departure from well-established Board precedent." After rejecting the "successor bar" rule, the Board declared that it would resume adhering to the rule, established in *Southern Moldings,*[21] that "an incumbent union in a

---

[15]Hertz Equip. Rental Corp., 328 NLRB 28, 161 LRRM 1126 (1999).
[16]329 NLRB 464, 162 LRRM 1202 (1999).
[17]334 NLRB 399, 167 LRRM 1185 (2001).
[18]328 NLRB 1, 161 LRRM 1037 (1999).
[19]329 NLRB 341, 162 LRRM 1146 (1999).
[20]337 NLRB 770, 170 LRRM 1233 (2002).
[21]219 NLRB 119, 89 LRRM 1623 (1975).

successor employer situation is entitled only to a rebuttable presumption of continuing majority status, which will not operate to bar an otherwise valid decertification, rival union, or employer petition."[22]

In *Baltimore Gas & Electric Co.*,[23] the Board upheld a regional director's decision to allow the withdrawal of a petition during the pendency of objections and challenges proceedings. The Board's Case Handling Manual, at Section 11116.1, provides: "A request to withdraw the petition, submitted while objections are pending, should normally not be approved. However, the Regional Director has the discretion to approve a request to withdraw the petition while objections are pending when no party objects or if the petitioner agrees, in writing, that it will not file a petition seeking an election to be held less than a year after the first election." The Board found no abuse of discretion, as the election had been held more than 12 months earlier and any new election based on a new petition would, therefore, not be held within 12 months of the prior election.

In *Waste Management of Maryland, Inc.*,[24] the Board allowed a decertification petition where the employer and union had no prior agreement and the parties, although in final stages of negotiation, had not executed any contract. The Board noted that a formal collective-bargaining agreement was not necessary for the contract-bar rule to apply, but in this case the parties had not yet culminated their negotiations and the exact terms accepted by the union could not be ascertained.

In order for a contract to bar an election, the contract's bargaining unit must fully encompass the petitioned-for unit. In *G.L. Milliken Plastering*,[25] where the petitioned-for unit was larger in geographic scope than the contractual bargaining unit, the Board ordered that an election be held after the regional office determined the proper residual unit.

Due to the "increased usage of recognition agreements" and other factors, the Board has agreed to take a "critical look" at the recognition bar doctrine—preventing decertification petitions for a "reasonable period of time"—where the voluntary recognition has occurred pursuant to a neutrality or card-check agreement reached between the union and the employer "*before* authorization cards, evi-

[22] *MV Transp., supra* note 20.
[23] 330 NLRB 3, 162 LRRM 1386 (1999).
[24] 338 NLRB 1002, 172 LRRM 1113, 1114–15 (2003).
[25] 340 NLRB No. 138, 174 LRRM 1529 (2003).

dencing the majority status, were obtained."[26] Members Liebman and Walsh dissented, noting that voluntary recognition is a "favored element of national labor policy" and that petitioners had presented no compelling reasons to grant review.

C. Investigation of Petitions

In a case involving allegations of forged authorization cards in support of a representation petition, the Board remanded the case to the regional director for further inquiry.[27] The regional director had followed the Board's Case Handling Manual in making signature comparisons, but felt constrained from conducting a full investigation because of a concurrent criminal investigation of the same allegations being conducted by the U.S. Attorney. Upon completion of the criminal investigation, the Board remanded the case to the regional director to conduct a full inquiry into the allegations of fraud.

In *Supershuttle of Orange County*,[28] the Board applied its *Douglas Randall*[29] and *Liberty Fabrics*[30] policies, and dismissed a rival union's petition where the parties had agreed to a collective bargaining agreement to resolve a pending Section 8(a)(5) charge filed by the incumbent union. These cases present a significant bar to the filing of representation petitions where unfair labor practice charges filed in relation to the conduct of bargaining result in a settlement or adjustment. In *Douglas-Randall,* the Board found that only three circumstances exist where the resolution of pending charges similar to those at issue in *Supershuttle* would not result in dismissal of a representation petition. These are where the blocking charges have been (1) unconditionally withdrawn without Board settlement; (2) dismissed as lacking merit; or (3) litigated and found to be without merit.[31] On August 17, 2004, the Board granted review in *Tru Serv*

---

[26]Dana Corp./Metaldyne Corp., 341 NLRB No. 150, 174 LRRM 1521 (2004). *See also* Main Edition, Chapter 10, "Representation Proceedings and Elections," Section II.A.3 [Timeliness of Petitions; The One Election-per-Year Rule; Voluntary Recognition Bar], at pages 516–18.

[27]Perdue Farms, Inc., 328 NLRB 909, 162 LRRM 1010 (1999).

[28]330 NLRB 1016, 163 LRRM 1273 (2000).

[29]320 NLRB 431, 151 LRRM 1281 (1995).

[30]327 NLRB 38, 159 LRRM 1330 (1998).

[31]*Id. See also* Main Edition, Chapter 10, "Representation Proceedings and Elections," Section II.B [Timeliness of Petitions; Pendency of Unfair Labor Practice Charges], at pages 518-20.

Corp.[32] This grant of review suggests that the Board is or may be reconsidering *Douglas Randall, Liberty Fabrics,* and *Supershuttle of Orange County.*

D. Consent Elections

In *Hampton Inn & Suites,*[33] the Board refused to allow an employer to withdraw from a stipulated election agreement where, after entering into the stipulation, the union filed a second petition seeking to represent certain other of the employer's employees. The Board rejected the employer's argument that employees in the stipulated unit shared a community of interest with employees sought in the second petition.

The rule in *Hampton Inn* was followed by the Eighth Circuit in *NLRB v. MEMC Electrical Materials, Inc.,*[34] where the court explained that: "a party may withdraw from an approved election agreement only upon a showing of 'unusual circumstances.' . . . [I]t is not enough to show that, absent the election agreement, the Board would have defined the appropriate bargaining unit differently." In *MEMC,* the consent agreement defined the unit as consisting only of the employer's maintenance employees. Less than one week before the election, the union filed a second petition to represent MEMC's production employees. Arguing that the only proper unit included both categories of employees, the employer moved to withdraw from the agreement and postpone the scheduled election. The motion to withdraw was denied. In enforcing the Board's bargaining order, the Eighth Circuit applied contract law rescission principles, reasoning: "A motion to withdraw from an approved election agreement is analogous to a lawsuit seeking to rescind an executory contract."[35] The court found, therefore, that the union's second petition did not modify the original agreement. Thus, the employer did not establish sufficient grounds for withdrawal.

On January 25, 2005, the Board published final revisions to new Section 102.62(c) allowing for "full" consent elections. Parties now have the opportunity to enter into a voluntary agreement to have

---

[32] 1-RD 1987.
[33] 331 NLRB 238, 164 LRRM 1158 (2000).
[34] 363 F.3d 705, 708 (8th Cir. 2004).
[35] *Id.* at 709.

the regional director conduct a hearing and resolve with finality all preelection factual and legal disputes.[36]

E. Representation Hearings

In June 2003, the Board implemented a pilot "e-filing" project, allowing parties to file certain documents in representation and unfair labor practice cases.[37] The pilot project limited e-filings to such items as requests for time extensions, amicus briefs, and requests for permission to exceed page limits. On March 2, 2004, the Board expanded the e-filing provisions with respect to representation cases.[38] Parties to representation cases pending before the Board may now electronically file all documents. Details of the e-filing program may be found at http://www.nlrb.gov. The Board plans to expand the program to allow e-filing of all documents in unfair labor practice cases at some time in the future.

Evidence at representation hearings is received either in the form of sworn oral testimony or stipulations.[39] Examination and cross-examination of witnesses is permitted and parties are expected to take positions on the matters raised at the hearing. In *Bennett Industries,*[40] the Board held that a party who fails to take a position regarding an issue may be prohibited from presenting evidence regarding such issue. Likewise, "to permit a party to take no position at the hearing when the subject is raised, leading to an uncontested [] finding by the regional director, and then to permit the same party to litigate—or, in effect, relitigate—the same question in a challenged ballot proceeding would be an unwise administrative practice because it would amount to condoning duplicative procedures, unjustified delays, and unnecessary expenses for all parties, including the Board."[41]

In *Allen Health Care Services,*[42] the Board distinguished *Bennett Industries*[43] on a unit issue where there was no legal presumption

---

[36]General Counsel Memorandum OM 05-40, "New 'Full' Consent Election Agreement Procedure."

[37]*See* Press Release R-2494, June 11, 2003, at www. nlrb.gov.

[38]*See* Press Release R-2524, March 2, 2004, at www.nlrb.gov.

[39]Seattle Opera Ass'n, 323 NLRB 641, 155 LRRM 1144 (1997); Mariah, Inc., 322 NLRB 586 n.1, 155 LRRM 1185 (1996).

[40]313 NLRB 1363, 146 LRRM 1145 (1994).

[41]*Id.*

[42]332 NLRB 1308, 165 LRRM 1378 (2000).

[43]*Bennett Indus., supra* note 40.

with respect to the unit in question. In those circumstances, the Board directed the hearing officer to take testimony so that the Board could make a unit determination. In so doing, the Board noted its obligation under Section 9(b) to "decide in each case . . . the unit appropriate. . . ."[44]

On April 10, 2002, Associate General Counsel Richard A. Siegel issued a memorandum directing the Board's regional offices to avoid delays in providing subpoenas to parties in preelection representation cases.[45] The memorandum clarified that "[r]egions are expected to provide subpoenas sufficiently in advance of the start of the 5-day period before the hearing, in order to provide the full time period to file a petition to revoke." Accordingly, the memorandum authorized the regions "to provide requested subpoenas immediately after informing the parties of the proposed hearing date, even if the formal Notice of Hearing has not yet issued, and/or the designated place of the hearing has not been established." To avoid the necessity of providing new subpoenas if a hearing is rescheduled, the regions may include on subpoenas the words "or any adjourned or rescheduled date."

In *Croft Metals, Inc.*,[46] the Board held that parties to a representation case must receive at least 5 working days' notice of the hearing date, absent unusual circumstances or a clear waiver by the parties. Associate General Counsel Richard A. Siegel concluded that letters and informal notices from the regional offices, notifying parties of the regional director's intent to issue a notice of hearing at a later date, do not satisfy the requirements of *Croft Metals*, and that formal notice is required.[47]

In *Marian Manor for the Aged and Infirm, Inc.*,[48] the Board affirmed the decision of a hearing officer who refused to seek enforcement of a subpoena in a preelection hearing. In so doing the Board found that the evidence sought was relevant and necessary, but noted that there was no showing that the information could not be obtained from the employer's own employees and that preelection hearings are investigatory, do not permit credibility resolutions, and require expeditious handling.

---

[44]*Id.*, at 332 NLRB at 1309.

[45]General Counsel Memorandum OM 02-56, "Timely Issuance of Subpoenas in Representation Cases."

[46]337 NLRB 688, 170 LRRM 1121 (2002).

[47]General Counsel Memorandum OM 02-87, "Croft Metals, Inc."

[48]333 NLRB 1084, 172 LLRM 1493 (2001).

In *North Manchester Foundry*,[49] the Board found that a hearing officer failed to comply with the requirements of the Act and the Board's Rules and Regulations when, because of the small size of the group, the hearing officer prevented the employer from presenting evidence that a group of employees should be excluded from the bargaining unit.

F. Representation Decisions

2. *By the Board*

The Board accords finality to a regional director's decision where the Board members are equally divided and there is no majority to grant review.[50]

The practice of the full Board not considering a motion for reconsideration of a panel decision unless the motion is referred to the full Board by the panel has changed.[51] Now any member of the panel may poll the full Board on whether to grant reconsideration.

In *Brevard Achievement Center, Inc.*,[52] the union's motion to reopen the record to present alleged newly discovered evidence was denied, where the union failed to demonstrate why evidence that predated the hearing was not previously presented or that such evidence would produce a different result.

Parties often request leave to file supplemental briefs in pending cases in order to address recent decisions by U.S. courts of appeal. The Board, therefore, has adopted a procedure by which parties may call to its attention pertinent and significant authorities that come into existence after the party's brief has been filed.[53] The letter should not exceed 350 words.

Where the Board refuses review of the regional director's representation decision, employers sometimes refuse to recognize and bargain with the union. Upon an action for enforcement of the Board's order, a federal court must ask only whether the Board's

---

[49]328 NLRB 372, 161 LRRM 1065 (1999).

[50]United Health Care Servs., Inc., 326 NLRB 1379, 163 LRRM 1061 (1998); Rapera, Inc., 333 NLRB 1287, 167 LRRM 1033 (2001).

[51]*See* Main Edition, Section II.F.2 [Procedures in Representation Cases; Representation Decisions; By the Board] at page 2457 n. 79. *Also see* Section III.B.8, *infra.*

[52]342 NLRB No. 101, 175 LRRM 1329 (2004).

[53]Reliant Energy aka Etiwanda, LLC, 339 NLRB 66, 173 LRRM 1053 (2003).

determination as to the unit has warrant in the record and a reasonable basis in law.[54] The court reviews the underlying record of the representation decision and "reverses for lack of substantial evidence only when the record is so compelling that no reasonable factfinder could fail to find to the contrary."[55]

G. The Election

1. *Date and Place*

In those instances when an election is rescheduled for administrative reasons beyond the control of the employer or the union, regional offices will include in the notice of rescheduled election a statement indicating that rescheduling was necessary for administrative reasons. The inclusion of this language is intended to dispel any erroneous impression among employees that either the employer or the union is responsible for the election's rescheduling.[56]

The Board will not overturn a mail-ballot election based solely on testimony that a determinative number of employees did not receive their mail ballots, provided the employees had an adequate opportunity to vote by requesting replacement ballots. Additionally, the Board is not required to send ballots by certified or registered mail where employees received notice that they could request replacement ballots.[57]

A reasonable rescheduling will be allowed for Board agent misconduct or mistake where neither party has been prejudiced and the laboratory conditions have not been destroyed. In *NLRB v. Superior of Missouri, Inc.*,[58] the Board representative overslept on the morning of a scheduled election due to a power outage. The election was rescheduled for the next week. The union won the election and the Board certified the union. The Eighth Circuit first held that the employees were not disenfranchised, as they were given ample notice of the rescheduled election and the vast majority of eligible

---

[54]Evergreen Am. Corp. v. NLRB, 362 F.3d 827, 837, 174 LRRM 2737 (D.C. Cir. 2004).

[55]*Id.* (citations omitted).

[56]*See* General Counsel Memorandum OM 03-54, "Notice to Voters in Rescheduled Elections"; Builders Insulation Inc., 338 NLRB 793, 71 LRRM 1489 (2003).

[57]Antelope Valley Bus Co. v. NLRB, 275 F.3d 1089, 1095–96, 169 LRRM 2089 (D.C. Cir. 2002), *enforcing* 331 NLRB No. 171, 169 LRRM 1048 (2000).

[58]351 F.3d 805, 173 LRRM 2870 (8th Cir. 2003).

employees voted. Second, in upholding the Board's decision and recognizing that both sides were equally affected, the court held that the agent's conduct and rescheduling of the election did not constitute actions of unfairness or impartiality by the Board.

2. *Eligibility of Voters*

The Board continues holding that temporary employees are eligible to vote where there is no date certain for their termination as of the payroll eligibility date. In *New World Communications*,[59] the Board held that a temporary employee, whose tenure the employer had already extended, was eligible to vote. The employer had also told the employee that she was being considered for permanent positions, given her training, and indicated that she should not fear termination. By demonstrating that its "date certain" for termination was not immutable, and by its other actions, the employer rendered the temporary employee an eligible voter. However, where a student is hired for the summer vacation, and there is no evidence that at the time of hire, the student's employment was to continue beyond summer vacation, the student will be deemed a temporary summer employee who is not eligible to vote.[60]

In *Kolkka Tables*,[61] the Board held that undocumented workers are eligible to vote if they are employed in the bargaining unit during the eligibility period. Likewise, individuals scheduled to become supervisors after the date of the election are eligible to vote because they are employees during the eligibility period.[62] An employee is eligible to vote despite the employer's contention that he intended to discharge the employee for absenteeism before the election.[63]

The Board continues to apply its longstanding test for determining whether laid-off employees are eligible to vote; specifically, whether, based on objective factors, they have a reasonable expectancy of reemployment in the near future.[64] The determination of eligibility is based on circumstances extant at the time of the payroll

[59]328 NLRB 3, 161 LRRM 1049 (1999), *enforced*, 232 F.3d 943, 165 LRRM 2890 (8th Cir. 2000).

[60]J.K. Pulley Co., 338 NLRB 1152, 172 LRRM 1153 (2003).

[61]323 NLRB 958, 155 LRRM 1170 (1997), *enforced*, 170 F.3d 937, 160 LRRM 2810 (9th Cir. 1999).

[62]Nichols House Nursing Home, 332 NLRB 1428, 167 LRRM 1180 (2000).

[63]Leisure Centers, Inc., 326 NLRB 1215, 163 LRRM 1183 (1998).

[64]MJM Studios of N.Y., Inc., 338 NLRB 980, 172 LRRM 1486 (2003).

eligibility date and the date of the election.[65] The burden of proof rests on the party seeking to exclude the challenged individuals from voting.[66] An employee is eligible to vote despite the employer's contention that it intended to discharge the employee for absenteeism before the election.[67]

The Fourth Circuit has upheld the Board's application of the "actual work" rule to exclude from voting in an election employees who had accepted job offers, been entered into the payroll system, and received identification cards, but who had not actually worked at the time of the cutoff period.[68]

An employee is eligible to vote even if he or she intends to quit after the election, and does so. In *Saint Gobian Industrial Ceramics v. NLRB*,[69] the court upheld the Board's rejection of an employer's objection to an election that it had lost 18–17. The employer objected to the union withholding knowledge that an employee who was on vacation had already started working for another employer. The Board rejected the employer's objection, noting that the employee's ballot had not been challenged and the union had made no effort to induce or encourage the employee to conceal his new employment.

A 2002 Board decision raised questions about the scope of the Board's decision in *Red Arrow Freight Lines, Inc.*,[70] regarding the eligibility of employees on sick leave. In *Agar Supply Co.*,[71] the Board directed the regional director to conduct a hearing to determine whether an employee, who was on workers' compensation leave at the time of the election, was nonetheless eligible to vote. The Board

[65] *Id.*

[66] *Id. See also* Laneco Constr. Sys., Inc., 339 NLRB 1048 (2003) (holding that employer failed to satisfy its burden of proving that employees who had allegedly been permanently laid off prior to election, and whose ballots employer challenged, actually had no reasonable expectation of recall); Omahaline Hydraulics Co., 340 NLRB No. 104, 173 LRRM 1297 (2003) (holding that, in absence of any affirmative action to effectuate strikers' termination, employer failed to establish that strikers were ineligible to vote in election).

[67] Leisure Centers, Inc., 326 NLRB 1215, 163 LRRM 1183 (1998).

[68] NLRB v. Maryland Ambulance Servs., 192 F.3d 430, 162 LRRM 2405 (4th Cir. 1999), *enforcing* 325 NLRB 1072, 160 LRRM 1128 (1998).

[69] 310 F.3d 778, 781–82, 171 LRRM 2385 (D.C. Cir. 2002), *enforcing* 334 NLRB No. 60, 171 LRRM 1168 (2001).

[70] 278 NLRB 965, 121 LRRM 1257 (1986).

[71] 338 NLRB 506, 171 LRRM 1130 (2002).

reversed its earlier ruling in the case, based upon subsequent evidence suggesting that the employee would never return to the bargaining unit. The Board did not address the effect of this decision on the continued validity of the rule set forth in *Red Arrow,* that an employee on sick leave is presumed eligible to vote absent an affirmative showing that the employee has resigned or been discharged.

An employee may be eligible to vote even though discharged, where an unfair labor practice charge has been filed regarding the employee's discharge and is pending.[72] A disposition of the unfair labor practice charge resolves the eligibility of such voters.[73] Once a ballot is cast, it is no longer in the voter's control, and the Board will not permit a voter to withdraw a ballot.[74]

Because the Board was reconsidering its holding in *New York University*[75] that graduate assistants are employees entitled to representation through the Board's processes, it decided in *Pratt Institute*[76] to grant an employer's request to stay the commencement of a representation hearing. Noting the rarity with which stays are granted, due to the Board's "strong belief in the expeditious handling of representation cases," the Board stated that there are some circumstances "where other policy considerations outweigh the desire for expedition."[77] The Board thereafter overruled *New York University* with its decision in *Brown University.*[78]

The Board has restated its principle that the parties to the election, not the Board, bear the primary responsibility for challenging voter eligibility. In *Lakewood Engineering & Manufacturing Co.,*[79] the union sought review of the eligibility of a total of eight new hires, seven of whom voted in the election which the union had lost by three votes. The union had failed to challenge four of the seven who voted. The Board determined that, while the voter eligibility of all eight may have been in dispute, the Board agent in each instance

---

[72]Trimm Assocs. v. NLRB, 351 F.3d 99 n.1, 173 LRRM 2801 (3d Cir. 2003) (where one discharged employee was ineligible to vote because no unfair labor practice charge was ever filed regarding his discharge).

[73]City Stationery, Inc., 340 NLRB No. 70, 173 LRRM 1500 (2003).

[74]*Id.*

[75]332 NLRB 1205, 165 LRRM 1241 (2000).

[76]339 NLRB 971, 173 LRRM 1001 (2003).

[77]*Id.*

[78]342 NLRB No. 42, 175 LRRM 1089 (2004).

[79]341 NLRB No. 101, 175 LRRM 1355 (2004).

had no "actual knowledge of the voter's ineligibility," and thus could not have been required to challenge the ballots. The Board also restated its principle that challenges to eligibility must be made before the ballots are cast. Absent evidence that the employer attempted to suppress the facts surrounding the eight new hires, the union failed in its post–election eligibility challenges.

3. *Voting Procedure*

The Board announced a new rule in *Fessler & Bowman Inc.*,[80] concerning the handling of mail ballots by parties. In this case, union officers solicited several ballots and then collected two ballots directly from voters for delivery. The Board acknowledged that mail ballots may be susceptible to interference: "[M]ail ballots are accompanied by election kits that clearly specify the precise procedure for casting and returning the ballot. Where such procedures are not followed, and the mail ballots come into the possession of a party to the election, the secrecy of the ballot and the integrity of the election process are called into question."[81] The Board held that "where a party collects or otherwise handles voters' mail ballots, that conduct is objectionable and may be a basis for setting aside the election."[82] The Board remanded the matter to the regional director to determine whether the objectionable conduct could have affected the election result. The Board stopped short of holding that the solicitation of ballots was necessarily objectionable conduct, stating that, while "a party's noncoercive solicitation of mail ballots does not constitute objectionable conduct, we express our disapproval of this practice."[83] Two members dissented, in part, to express that they would have held that solicitation of ballots is itself objectionable.[84] The Board

[80] 341 NLRB No. 122, 174 LRRM 1455 (2004).

[81] *Id.* at 1457.

[82] *Id.*

[83] *Id.* at 1458.

[84] *Id.* at 1459–60 ("In our view, the integrity of the electoral process demands that the employee control his ballot at all times. Any effort to interfere with that process, whether successful or not, undermines the integrity of the process, and is therefore objectionable. . . a party who asks an employee to turn over his cast ballot interferes with the Board's role in conducting secret ballot elections. We find that this attempt to interfere with the Board's role impugns the secrecy and integrity of the election process and renders the solicitation objectionable.") (Battista, Schaumber, concurring in part and dissenting in part). Member Meisburg recused himself and took no part in the consideration of this case. *See id.* at 1456 & n.1.

expressly overruled *Pacific Gas & Electric Co.*,[85] in which the Board had overruled objections to an election where union and employer agents had collected mail ballots from employees and forwarded them to the regional office.[86]

H. Objections to the Election and Challenged Ballots

The Board abandoned long ago its practice of applying a "rule of estoppel" in instances where a party knew of objectionable conduct prior to an election and failed to file an unfair labor practice regarding the conduct, then filed objections after losing the election.[87] The Board has since extended this analysis, and held that the withdrawal of an unfair labor practice charge does not operate as a waiver of a party's right to file objections based on the same conduct.[88]

In *Morgan Services, Inc.*,[89] the Board held a union's objections in abeyance where the employer conduct out of which they arose was also the subject of a grievance arbitration between the parties. "[E]xercising our discretion to hold the objections in abeyance here is consistent with cases in which the Board has held resolution of challenged ballots in abeyance pending determination of voter eligibility through contractual grievance/arbitration machinery."[90]

In cases where the Board sustains an objection to an election and orders that a new election be conducted, it will not require that a union make a new showing of interest.[91] This is so even where the employer argues that the objectionable conduct tainted the original showing of interest.[92]

In *Daimler-Chrysler Corp.*,[93] the Board considered a challenged ballot containing an "X" in the "YES" square, but also including a handwritten question mark (?) immediately adjacent to the "YES" square. The Board held that the question mark did not negate the

---

[85]89 NLRB 938, 26 LRRM 1056 (1950).

[86]174 LRRM at 1457 & n.6 ("We overrule *Pacific Gas & Electric* to the extent it is inconsistent with our decision today.").

[87]Great Atl. & Pac. Tea Co., 101 NLRB 1118, 1119–20, 31 LRRM 1189 (1952).

[88]Virginia Concrete Corp., Inc., 338 NLRB 1182, 172 LRRM 1169 (2003).

[89]339 NLRB 463, 172 LRRM 1393 (2003).

[90]*Id.*

[91]River City Elevator Co., 339 NLRB 616, 172 LRRM 1409 (2003).

[92]*Id.* (involving preelection promises of benefits held objectionable under *NLRB v. Savair Mfg. Co.*, 414 U.S. 270, 84 LRRM 2929 (1973)).

[93]338 NLRB 982, 172 LRRM 1115 (2003).

clear expression of preference for union representation signified by the marking of the "YES" square. It, therefore, counted the challenged ballot. In a subsequent case, the Board applied the *DaimlerChrysler* principles and held that a vote for a union submitted on a sample ballot provided with the official election kit, rather than on an official ballot, should be counted.[94]

In representation cases involving stipulated bargaining units, the Board has adopted a three-part test to resolve disputes over ballots challenged on the ground that the employees are not eligible to vote because they are not within the stipulated unit.[95] First, if the intent of the parties is expressed in clear and unambiguous terms, the Board will enforce that stated intent. If the stipulation is ambiguous, the Board will attempt to determine the parties' intent through traditional rules of contract interpretation, including examining extrinsic evidence.[96] Evidence of the subjective intent of the union and employer is not a proper consideration when examining extrinsic evidence. Finally, if the parties' intent still cannot be determined, the Board will determine the bargaining unit using its traditional community-of-interest test.[97]

In *Los Angeles Water & Power Employees Ass'n*,[98] the Board found that, as to one employee whose ballot was challenged, the unit description set forth in the parties' stipulated election agreement was ambiguous. Finding extrinsic evidence of modifications to that description inconclusive, the Board applied a community-of-interest test and found the employee eligible to vote.

When election polls are not opened at the scheduled time, a new election should be ordered if the number of employees possibly disenfranchised by the tardy opening would affect the results of the election.[99] The Board so ruled, despite objective evidence suggesting that voters were not actually disenfranchised (the determinative employee appeared during voting hours when polls were not yet opened, but stated after the fact that he had "decided not to vote").

---

[94]Aesthetic Designs, LLC, 339 NLRB 395, 173 LRRM 1189 (2003).

[95]Desert Palace, Inc. dba Caesars Tahoe, 337 NLRB 1096, 170 LRRM 1344 (2002); *see also* Los Angeles Water & Power Employees' Ass'n, 340 NLRB No. 146, 173 LRRM 1449 (2003) (following this test).

[96]*Los Angeles Water & Power Employees' Ass'n, supra* note 95.

[97]*Desert Palace, Inc. dba Caesars Tahoe, supra* note 95; *see also* Associated Milk Producers, Inc. v. NLRB, 193 F.3d 539, 541, 162 LRRM 2628, 2629 (D.C. Cir. 1999).

[98]340 NLRB No. 146, 173 LRRM 1449 (2003).

[99]Pea Ridge Iron Ore Co., 335 NLRB 161, 171 LRRM 1190 (2001).

In *Woods Quality Cabinetry Co.*,[100] the Board held that where a faulty notice and sample ballot causes unfairness and may affect the outcome, a new election may be ordered. In this case, an inaccurate notice of election and sample ballot had incorrectly designated the Carpenters as being affiliated with the AFL-CIO. The union had actually withdrawn from the AFL-CIO in March 2000. The parties had made a point of this in the campaign. The Board found "the error in the notice of election and ballots here was not insignificant, and confused the employees regarding the important issue of whether or not the Petitioner was affiliated with the AFL-CIO." Finding that "the issue concerns the very identity of the union," the Board concluded that the inaccurate statement in the notice and sample ballot reasonably could tend to confuse employees and, thus, "reasonably tended to interfere with the election process so that the election should be set aside."[101]

In *Trimm Associates, Inc. v. NLRB*,[102] the Third Circuit declined to enforce a certification-based bargaining order because the Board had resolved substantial and material factual issues in a post-election objections case without an evidentiary hearing. The court noted that, where the election is close, greater scrutiny of the Board's decision, and in particular the Board's decision not to hold a hearing, is warranted.[103]

In *NLRB v. Palmer Donavin Manufacturing Co.*,[104] the Sixth Circuit enforced the Board's order where the only evidence that the employer offered regarding an alleged misrepresentation during the election was a self-serving affidavit from the employer's counsel, attesting that unidentified union officials spread a rumor that employer's counsel had bribed the employer's election observer. The court found that this evidence not only failed to constitute an egregious example of a pervasive deceitful misrepresentation, it also failed to demonstrate that the alleged misrepresentation interfered with any voter's exercise of free choice.

---

[100] 340 NLRB No. 163, 173 LRRM 1577 (2003).

[101] *Id.*

[102] 351 F.3d 99, 173 LRRM 2801 (3d Cir. 2003).

[103] *Id.* at 103. *See also* General Counsel Memorandum OM 04-26, "Administrative Investigations vis-à-vis Hearings in Post-Election Proceedings."

[104] 369 F.3d 954, 174 LRRM 3057 (6th Cir. 2004).

In *NLRB v. MEMC Electronic Materials,*[105] the Eighth Circuit enforced the Board's bargaining order dismissing the employer's objection regarding the regional director's premature counting of ballots, before ruling on the employer's objection regarding the scope of the bargaining unit. The court found that the regional director's error did not disenfranchise any voters, did not destroy the "laboratory conditions" essential for a fair election, and did not reflect improper bias or compromise the neutrality of the election procedures. The court agreed with the Board's observation that it would have been preferable for the regional director to have held the ballot count in abeyance pending consideration of the employer's objection.

In *Majestic Star Casino v. NLRB,*[106] the Court of Appeals for the District of Columbia Circuit followed established Board precedent holding that it is insufficient to object to misleading campaign statements based on the truth or falsity of the parties' campaign statements. Rather, the Board should intervene and set aside an election only in cases where a party has used forged documents which render the voters unable to recognize propaganda for what it is.[107] The court also held that the Board properly found that union's promises to waive dues and initiation fees did not constitute objectionable conduct.

I. Amendment, Clarification, and Revocation

Even if timely filed, the Board will dismiss a unit clarification (UC) petition dealing with positions that have historically been excluded from the bargaining unit and have not been shown to have undergone recent substantial changes.[108]

In *Premier Living Center,*[109] the Board reiterated its longstanding rule that, in the absence of newly discovered and previously unavailable evidence or special circumstances, an employer may not challenge the validity of a union's certification, by a unit clarification petition, on the basis of a belief that unit members are statutory supervisors, if the employer failed to raise that issue during the repre-

---

[105] 363 F.3d 705, 174 LRRM 2801 (8th Cir. 2004).
[106] 373 F.3d 1345, 175 LRRM 2193 (D.C. Cir. 2004).
[107] Midland Nat'l Life Ins. Co., 263 NLRB 127, 110 LRRM 1489 (1982).
[108] Bethlehem Steel Corp., 329 NLRB 243, 163 LRRM 1093 (1999).
[109] 331 NLRB 123, 164 LRRM 1296 (2000).

sentation proceeding. In this case, the employer actually had entered into a preelection stipulation that licensed practical nurses (LPNs) would be included in the unit. After losing the election, the employer filed a post-certification unit clarification petition seeking to exclude the LPNs from the unit, arguing that they were statutory supervisors. The Board rejected the employer's argument that, because the Act statutorily excludes supervisors from the definition of "employee," the regional director should have directed a hearing regarding the LPNs' status notwithstanding the stipulation.

The Board will not defer to contractual arbitration a UC petition filed to clarify whether employees hired at a new facility should be accreted to the existing bargaining unit. The Board is charged with making determinations of questions concerning representation, accretion, and the appropriateness of a bargaining unit, and may interpret provisions of a collective bargaining agreement for that purpose. In *Tweddle Litho, Inc.*,[110] the union's grievance alleged that the employer had violated the contract by assigning unit work to the new employees without incorporating them into the unit. The Board distinguished the facts in *Tweddle* from a case in which the union and employer had specifically agreed that accretion issues would be determined by an arbitrator.[111]

A unit clarification petition is untimely and improper where a current collective bargaining agreement clearly defines the composition of the unit, as noted in *Stanford Hospital & Clinics v. NLRB.*[112] The D.C. Circuit held that the Board improperly granted the union's petition for unit clarification and improperly added employees to the bargaining unit. Applying the rule that the Act would not be served by using "the unit clarification petition to modify a unit which is clearly defined in the current bargaining agreement," the court denied enforcement of the Board's order.

In *Saint-Gobian Adhesives, Inc.*,[113] the Board overruled recent precedent, *Priority One Services*,[114] and held that the regional director cannot simply presume unlawful employer conduct caused employees to file a decertification petition. Instead, the regional director

---

[110]337 NLRB 686, 170 LRRM 1122 (2002).

[111]Verizon Info. Sys., 335 NLRB 558, 168 LRRM 1136 (2001).

[112]370 F.3d 1210, 174 LRRM 3389 (D.C. Cir. 2004) (applying the rule of *Wallace-Murray Corp.*, 192 NLRB 1090, 78 LRRM 1046 (1971)).

[113]342 NLRB No. 39 (2004).

[114]331 NLRB 1527 (2000).

must hold an evidentiary hearing to determine whether a "causal nexus" exists between the unlawful conduct and employee disaffection.

J. Deauthorization and Decertification Elections

The Board has held that state laws regarding union-security authorization procedures that place greater limits on the ability of employees to seek deauthorization are preempted by the Act.[115]

In *H.Y. Floors & Gameline Painting, Inc.*,[116] however, the Board held that an individual is not estopped from timely challenging a construction industry employer's voluntary Section 9(a) recognition of a union, and thus may file a decertification petition. In so holding, the Board stated that the filing of an unfair labor practice charge is not the only means of challenging majority status in circumstances in which a former Section 8(f) union has been voluntarily granted Section 9(a) recognition. The Board found that a union's majority status may also be challenged by filing a timely representation petition.

III. Procedures in Unfair Labor Practice Cases

B. The Unfair Labor Practice Charge

1. *Time for Filing*

The Board continues holding that the Section 10(b) period does not begin running until the aggrieved party receives notice of the conduct that constitutes the alleged unfair labor practice.[117] The requisite notice may be actual or constructive; a party will be charged with constructive notice if it should have become aware of a viola-

[115]Albertson's/Max Food Warehouse, 329 NLRB 410, 162 LRRM 1169 (1999), *overruling* City Mkt., Inc., 266 NLRB 1020, 113 LRRM 1105 (1983).

[116]331 NLRB 304, 164 LRRM 1185 (2000).

[117]CAB Assocs., 340 NLRB No. 171, 174 LRRM 1058 (2003); Flambeau Airmold Corp. 337 NLRB 1025, 171 LRRM 1450 (2002); Amalgamated Transit Union, 335 NLRB 1263, 172 LRRM 1462 (2001); Vallow Floor Coverings, Inc., 335 NLRB 20, 169 LRRM 1306 (2001); Allied Prod. Workers Local 12, 337 NLRB 16, 173 LRRM 1600 (2001) (concluding that §10(b) barred charge by employee who waited 7 months after receiving actual notice of unfair labor practice by letter from union); Concourse Nursing Home, 328 NLRB 692, 168 LRRM 1499 (1999).

tion in the exercise of "reasonable diligence."[118] Because Section 10(b) is an affirmative defense, the Board adheres to the view that it is waived if not timely raised.[119] The burden of proving that the charging party was on notice of the conduct that constitutes the alleged unfair labor practice more than six months prior to the charge being filed "rests squarely" on the party asserting a Section 10(b) defense.[120] The Board has, however, allowed the general counsel to litigate situations in which the "time barred" allegations were found to be "closely related" to the allegations in the original, timely filed charge.[121]

In *Dayton Newspapers, Inc*,[122] the employer argued that a failure to recall allegation was barred by the 6-month time limitation of Section 10(b), because the allegation was not included in the charge and was not added to the complaint until almost a year later. The Board held that the employer had waived an affirmative defense with respect to this issue because it had failed to raise the Section 10(b) defense until its post-hearing brief.

The Board will refuse to limit a remedy to the Section 10(b) period where the charging party union had neither actual nor constructive knowledge of the conduct constituting the unfair labor prac-

---

[118]*CAB Assocs., supra* note 117 (finding no constructive notice where the conduct alleged to have initiated the §10(b) period was ambiguous); *Amalgamated Transit Union, supra* note 117.

[119]Convergence Communications, Inc., 339 NLRB 408, 173 LRRM 1351 (2003) (§10(b) defense is not timely if first asserted in party's post-hearing brief); Malik Roofing Corp., 338 NLRB 930, 175 LRRM 1032 (2003) (finding waiver of §10(b) defense where respondent failed to answer complaint and issuing remedy covering events beyond 6-month limitations period); Dutchess Overhead Doors, Inc., 337 NLRB 162, 172 LRRM 1509 (2001) (§10(b) defense is waived if it is not raised in party's answer or litigated at hearing).

[120]R.G. Burns Elec., 326 NLRB 440, 446, 159 LRRM 1325 (1998).

[121]Ross Stores, Inc., 329 NLRB 573, 163 LRRM 1137 (1999) (*overruling* Nippondenso Mfg. U.S.A., 299 NLRB 545, 135 LRRM 1100 (1990), to the extent it conflicts with *Nickles Bakery of Indiana*, 296 NLRB 927, 132 LRRM 1249 (1989), and other precedent on the ground that *Nippondenso* is an unreasonably restrictive view of the factual-relatedness requirement of the *Nickles Bakery* test). *See also* Vicky Lynn Kaseta, 338 NLRB 1154, 172 LRRM 1195 (2003); Seton Co., 332 NLRB 979 (2000); Bridgestone/Firestone, Inc., 332 NLRB 575, 167 LRRM 1148 (2000); Office Depot, 330 NLRB 640, 163 LRRM 1169 (2000) ("closely related" charges barred by §10(b)); Precision Concrete, 337 NLRB 211, 172 LRRM 1370 (2001) (highlighting disagreement between Board and D.C. Circuit regarding proper method for analyzing "closely related" issue).

[122]339 NLRB 650 n.10, 172 LRRM 1477 (2003).

tice.[123] For example, in *Palm Court Nursing Home N.H., L.L.C.*,[124] the union was not required to determine whether there was a hidden message in the employer's communication which would have put it on notice of a change in benefits and, therefore, the union had not received either actual or constructive notice of the alleged unfair labor practice for purposes of calculating the Section 10(b) date.

The Board continues holding that an amended allegation will not be dismissed as untimely, even though outside the 6-month limitation period, where (1) the untimely allegation involves the same legal theory as the allegation contained in the timely filed charge; (2) both allegations arise from the same factual situation or sequence of events; and (3) both allegations require similar defenses from the respondent.[125]

In *Outdoor Venture Corp.*,[126] the Board held that certain allegations in the complaint were not barred by Section 10(b), even though some of the conduct alleged in the complaint occurred more than 6 months prior to the filing of the charge. The general counsel was not seeking a remedy for those allegations and litigating them was required only to establish that the strike at issue was an unfair labor practice strike.

In *Arrow Line, Inc.*,[127] the Board dismissed a complaint pursuant to Section 10(b), despite the fact that the employer's vacation pay practices within the Section 10(b) period did not comply with the collective bargaining agreement. The Board held that the employer had established its vacation pay practice prior to the Section 10(b) period without challenge from the union, and it did not violate the Act by adhering to that practice thereafter.

In *Neiman dba Concourse Nursing Home*,[128] the Board held that Section 10(b) did not bar a finding that the employer owed union

---

[123]St. George Warehouse, Inc., 341 NLRB No. 120, 175 LRRM 1316 (2004); Vallow Floor Coverings, Inc., 335 NLRB 20, 169 LRRM 1306 (2001). *See also Malik Roofing, supra* note 119 (refusing to limit remedy to the §10(b) period due to respondent's waiver of affirmative defense).

[124]341 NLRB No. 113, 175 LRRM 1559 (2004).

[125]Engelhard Corp., 342 NLRB No. 5, 175 LRRM 1001 (2004), citing Nickles Bakery of Indiana, 296 NLRB 927, 132 LRRM 1249 (1989); Air Contact Transp., Inc., 340 NLRB No. 81, 173 LRRM 1429 (2003), citing Redd-I, Inc., 290 NLRB 1115, 129 LRRM 1229 (1988); Adam's Mark Hotel, 325 NLRB 534, 160 LRRM 1206 (1999).

[126]327 NLRB 706, 160 LRRM 1178 (1999).

[127]340 NLRB No. 5, 173 LRRM 1145 (2003).

[128]328 NLRB 692, 168 LRRM 1499 (1999).

pension fund contributions for licensed practical nurses from the date that the moratorium on such contributions ended, where the situation was at least sufficiently ambiguous as to whether the union had clear and unequivocal notice more than 6 months before the charge was filed that the employer had ceased making pension fund contributions for LPNs. In *St. Barnabas Medical Center*,[129] the Board overruled the ALJ and found that the union's charge, that the employer had failed to recognize the union and apply the collective bargaining agreement with respect to certain classifications, was time-barred under Section 10(b) because the union had clear and unequivocal notice, outside the 6-month limitations period, that the employer had repudiated the contract. The Board held that repudiation is a one-time action which starts the 10(b) period at the moment it occurs, and that each subsequent failure to abide by the collective bargaining agreement is simply a consequence of the repudiation, not a new or independent violation. The Board distinguished repudiation, which it labeled a "completed violation," from a series of contract breaches, which may properly be considered "continuing violations" for purposes of applying the 6-month statute of limitations.

The Eleventh Circuit has held, contrary to the Board, that fraudulent concealment will not toll the statute of limitations where "operative facts" have not been concealed.[130] In *Morgan's Holiday Markets, Inc.*,[131] the Board clarified its fraudulent concealment test, initially specified in *Brown & Sharpe Manufacturing Co.*[132] The D.C. Circuit had criticized the *Brown & Sharpe* test as being internally inconsistent.[133] In *Morgan's Holiday Markets*,[134] the Board agreed that the *Brown & Sharpe* test was internally inconsistent, and adopted a revised test. To obtain reinstatement of a charge based on fraudulent concealment of evidence by the charged party more than 6 months after the occurrence of the activities alleged in the charge,

[129]343 NLRB No. 119 (2004).

[130]NLRB v. Dynatron/Bondo Corp., 176 F.3d 1310, 161 LRRM 2395 (11th Cir. 1999), *denying enforcement in relevant part*, 323 NLRB 1263, 155 LRRM 1225 (1997).

[131]333 NLRB 837, 167 LRRM 1141 (2001).

[132]312 NLRB 444, 144 LRRM 1123 (1993). *See* Main Edition, Chapter 32, "NLRB Orders and Remedies," Section III.B.2. [Orders and Remedies in Complaint Cases (Section 10); Final Orders and Remedies; Special Remedial Problems Involving Employers], at page 2467 n.137.

[133]District Lodge 64, Machinists v. NLRB, 949 F.2d 441, 449–50, 138 LRRM 2928 (D.C. Cir. 1991).

[134]*Supra* note 131.

the general counsel must show that (1) deliberate concealment has occurred; (2) material facts were the object of the concealment; and (3) the injured party was ignorant of those facts without any fault or want of due diligence on its part.

In articulating the second prong of its revised test, the Board redefined what facts it considers material in determining whether fraudulent concealment warrants reinstatement of a charge. Information is material if "the addition of evidence previously fraudulently concealed would, as an objective matter, make the critical difference in determining whether or not there was reasonable cause to believe the act was violated."[135] Reasonable cause is a two-fold inquiry. First, the Board asks whether, based on the evidence before the general counsel at the time of the dismissal, there was no reasonable cause to believe the Act had been violated. Second, the Board asks whether, based on the evidence before the general counsel at the time of the reinstatement of the charge and issuance of the complaint (including the fraudulently concealed evidence), there is reasonable cause to believe that the Act has been violated. If the Board finds that there was "reasonable cause to believe" at the time of dismissal, then the concealed evidence—even if it strengthens the case—is merely incremental and "does not significantly alter the total mix of information available" to the general counsel.[136] The Board will not treat such evidence as "material," and Section 10(b) will bar the complaint.[137]

The Board has allowed the general counsel to pursue charges based on activity that occurred within the Section 10(b) period, where such activity stemmed from activity that occurred more than 6 months before the charge was filed. In *Steel Fabricators Ass'n*,[138] for example, the union first informed the charging party in August 1999, more than 6 months before he filed his charge, that any dues payments he made would be applied to his outstanding fine balance. While a violation based on that statement would have been time-barred, the union engaged in other unlawful conduct (i.e., reiterating that it would apply any dues payments to his fine balance and threatening to suspend him and refuse to allow him to work if he did not pay his dues) within the 10(b) period.

---

[135] *Id.*

[136] *Id.*

[137] *Id.*

[138] 341 NLRB No. 68, 174 LRRM 1356 (2004).

2. *Investigation of Charge*

The general counsel has issued guidelines for its regional offices to assist investigators in avoiding ethical dilemmas involving interviews conducted during investigations of unfair labor practice charges.[139] The guidelines reaffirm longstanding policy that all parties, management, agents, and witnesses involved in unfair labor practice proceedings are entitled to be represented by an individual of their choice. Special guidelines apply if the interviewee is represented by a lawyer. The general counsel has issued separate guidelines for situations where a third-party witness is represented individually by, or otherwise insists on the presence of, the representative of a party.[140]

The Board continues to expand its services to address increasingly diversified and technologically evolving workforces. On November 7, 2003, the Board introduced its redesigned Web site on the Internet at www.nlrb.gov. The site has been made more user friendly, incorporating, inter alia, improved search tools and a regional office locator.[141] The Board has also issued policy guidance on services for non-English speaking individuals[142] and on use of e-mail to communicate with and submit documentation to the Board and its regional offices.[143] On January 12, 2005, the Board expanded its "E-Filing Project" to include virtually all documents in unfair labor practice cases.[144] Briefs, motions, exceptions, and other documents may now be filed electronically with the Office of the Executive Secretary through the Board's Web site. E-filed documents must include a statement of service, must comport with all applicable time requirements, including those found in Section 102.111(b) of the Board's

---

[139]General Counsel Memorandum OM 02-36, "Guidelines Concerning Appropriate Contacts with Represented Persons."

[140]General Counsel Memorandum OM 03-43, "Revision to Informal ULP Casehandling Manual Section 10058.4(c)."

[141]See announcement in General Counsel Memorandum OM 04-10, "Agency's Web Site on the Internet."

[142]General Counsel Memorandum OM 03-69, "Executive Order 13166—'Improving Access to Services for Persons with Limited English Proficiency.'"

[143]General Counsel Memorandum OM 03-74, "Use of Internet E-Mail by Outside Parties to Communicate with Board Agents and Submit Documents to Regional Offices"; General Counsel Memorandum OM 03-83, "The Board's E-Filing Project."

[144]General Counsel Memorandum OM 05-30, "Expansion of the Board's E-Filing Project To Include Selected Documents in Unfair Labor Practice and Representation Cases And Revision of the General Counsel's Internet E-mail Policy."

Rules and Regulations, and are subject to certain size restrictions, including a prohibition against e-filing any document that is more than 10 MB in size.

The Board has reinstated, on a pilot basis, the requirement that regional directors submit an electronic copy of each complaint issued, and the corresponding "decisional document," to the Office of the general counsel.[145] The general counsel took this action in response to lowered litigation success rates and a decreased number of Section 10(j) cases, in an effort to increase the quality of casehandling.

On April 11, 2005, the general counsel issued answers to questions posed by the Practice and Procedure Committee of the Labor and Employment Relations Section of the American Bar Association, addressing such issues as investigatory subpoenas, settlement policy, standards for resetting hearings, and regional office staffing.[146] The general counsel's responses can be found on the Board's Web site.

3. *Disposition of Charge*

The general counsel's decision not to pursue a charge under one section of the Act does not preclude the prosecution of an unfair labor practice allegation under another section of the Act.[147] The general counsel has historically found a basis to issue complaint in less than half of all unfair labor practice cases.[148] A substantial number of cases continue to be closed each year by withdrawals.[149] The courts of appeal continue holding that the general counsel's refusal to issue a complaint based on an unfair labor practice charge is beyond the scope of their review.[150]

---

[145]General Counsel Memorandum OM 05-18, "Pilot Program Re: Electronic Submission of Complaints and Decisional Documents to the Division of Operations-Management."

[146]General Counsel Memorandum GC 05-02, "General Counsel Responses to Questions Propounded by the Practice and Procedure Committee (P&P Committee) of the Labor and Employment Relations Section of the American Bar Association."

[147]Reno Hilton Resorts, 326 NLRB 1421, 162 LRRM 1405 (1998), *enforced*, 196 F.3d 1275, 162 LRRM 2961 (D.C. Cir. 1999).

[148]General Counsel Memorandum GC 05-01, "Summary of Operations (Fiscal Year 2004)" (placing the "merit factor" for charges filed in fiscal year 2004 at 37.7% and the merit factor range since 1980 at between 32 and 40%).

[149]In fiscal year 2000, the most recent year for which a report is available, 30.1% of all cases closed were withdrawals. NLRB 2000 Annual Report, Table 7.

[150]Quick v. NLRB, 245 F.3d 231, 166 LRRM 2897 (3d Cir. 2001).

The general counsel recently developed a new procedure for dismissing charges that are meritorious, but which the general counsel believes are isolated, minor in impact, and unlikely to recur.[151] In cases in which the general counsel feels that a merit dismissal is appropriate, the policy now is to issue a letter to the charging party stating that the charge will be held in abeyance for 6 months from the date of the letter. Absent any additional meritorious charges during that 6-month period, the general counsel will dismiss the charge. In the event of additional meritorious charges within the 6-month period, the merit dismissal will be rescinded. The charging party retains the right to appeal both a decision to hold its charge(s) in abeyance and any subsequent decision to dismiss the charge(s).

4. *Settlement of Unfair Labor Practice Charges*

In a March 11, 2002, memorandum, Associate General Counsel Richard A. Siegel issued a revised Standard Form 4775, for immediate use in settlement agreements.[152] The memorandum encouraged the use of "plain laypersons' language" in the drafting of informal settlement agreements and notices, "consistent with the Board's discussion in *Ishikawa Gasket America*."[153] Attached to the memorandum was a collection of optional paragraphs for use in adapting the standard form to particular circumstances. The memorandum noted that formal settlement agreements should continue tracking "standard language in Board orders." The new form is available online at the Board's Web site: www.nlrb.gov.

During fiscal year 2004, the Board achieved a settlement rate of 96.1 percent in unfair labor practice cases.[154]

a. Informal Settlements

The Board is not statutorily obligated to honor settlement agreements that are at odds with the Board's policies or that do not effectuate the purposes of the Act. In *Beverly California Corp. v. NLRB*,[155]

[151]General Counsel Memorandum GC 02-08, "Revised Procedure for Merit Dismissals."

[152]General Counsel Memorandum OM 02-44, "Revision of Settlement Agreement, Standard Form 4775."

[153]337 NLRB 175, 169 LRRM 1241 (2001).

[154]General Counsel Memorandum GC 05-01, "Summary of Operations (Fiscal Year 2004)."

[155]253 F.3d 291, 295, 167 LRRM 2409 (7th Cir. 2001).

the Seventh Circuit enforced the Board's decision to disregard a settlement agreement between an employer and two employees in a civil rights proceeding, which specifically precluded the award of additional back pay in a Board proceeding. The court found that the settlement agreement "completely circumvented" the Board and the charging party, and was unreasonable.

Where a party withdraws unfair labor practice charges pursuant to a non-Board settlement, the Board is not estopped from proceeding on new charges, filed by an individual who was not a party to the settlement, alleging violations of the Act based on the same underlying conduct as the withdrawn charges.[156]

The Board continues to set aside settlement agreements and reinstate complaints where a party fails to comply with a settlement agreement or where a party commits post-settlement unfair labor practices.[157] Where the settlement agreement so provides, the Board will respect the defaulting party's answers to the underlying complaint allegations, with the result that all complaint allegations are deemed admitted.[158]

In *American Postal Workers Local 735*,[159] the Board set aside a private settlement agreement between a union and one of its members because the union subsequently published statements in its newsletter that undermined the settlement. The settlement agreement also contained a notice provision, which required the union to post assurances that it would observe the rights of all employees in the bargaining unit. The union posted the required notice but in its later newsletter "applauded . . . the conduct alleged to be discriminatory and unlawful."

In *Weldun International, Inc.*,[160] the Board found that private settlement agreements with certain laid-off employees that purported to provide the employer with a complete release of all claims did not preclude a reinstatement order or a back-pay remedy in a subsequent unfair labor practice proceeding. Because the employees signed the agreements before the Board had reached a decision re-

---

[156]KFMB Stations, 343 NLRB No. 83 (2004).

[157]Nations Rent, Inc., 339 NLRB 830, 172 LRRM 1467 (2003).

[158]Bartlett Heating & Air Conditioning, Inc., 339 NLRB 1044 (2003); L.J. Logistics, Inc., 339 NLRB 729 (2003).

[159]340 NLRB No. 166, 173 LRRM 1549 (2003).

[160]340 NLRB No. 79, 174 LRRM 1020 (2003); *see also* Weldon Int'l, Inc., 321 NLRB 733 n.6, 153 LRRM 1021 (1996), *enforced in part*, 165 F.3d 28, 159 LRRM 2576 (6th Cir. 1998).

garding the legality of the layoffs, the Board refused to consider the agreements a bar to a make-whole remedy. Instead, the Board limited its inquiry to how the amounts paid in conjunction with the settlement agreements would affect the back-pay computation.

The Board continues to recognize the importance of finality in settled cases. In *Courier-Journal*,[161] the Board held that the union could not revive a settled charge after the region closed the case. Overruling the ALJ, the Board found that the union's failure to object to the extent of the employer's compliance with the settlement agreement prior to the closure of the case barred it from resurrecting the original dispute.

The Board continues to adhere to the general policy that conduct that has been the subject of a settlement agreement may not be relitigated in a subsequent proceeding, absent an express "reservation of evidence" clause in the settlement agreement.[162] For example, in *Outdoor Venture Corp.*,[163] the Board held that a settlement agreement did not bar the general counsel from using evidence of presettlement conduct to establish an unfair labor practice in subsequent litigation, where the agreement provided that the general counsel reserved the right to use such evidence for any relevant purpose in current or subsequent litigation. The Board continues to hold, however, that evidence acquired in the investigation of a case which ultimately settles may be used in a separate litigation proceeding as background evidence of a respondent's motivation in activities occurring before or after the settlement, regardless of whether or not the relevant settlement agreement contains specific reservation language.[164] In *St. Mary's Nursing Home*,[165] the Board overruled the ALJ's grant of summary judgment to the employer at the hearing, finding that the ALJ improperly refused to allow the general counsel to introduce evidence from a prior settled case to establish the employer's hostility toward a discharged employee. This evidentiary ruling, the Board found, led directly to the ALJ's conclusion that the general counsel had not established the requisite showing

[161]342 NLRB No. 118, 176 LRRM 1013 (2004).
[162]Midwestern Personnel Servs., Inc., 331 NLRB 348, 171 LRRM 1262 (2000).
[163]327 NLRB 706, 160 LRRM 1178 (1999).
[164]Overnite Transp. Co., 335 NLRB 372, 376 n.18, 169 LRRM 1004 (2001).
[165]342 NLRB No. 100, 175 LRRM 1361 (2004).

of union animus. Informal settlements continue to be used with much greater frequency than formal settlements.[166]

b. Formal Settlements

In deciding whether to accept a post-hearing formal settlement agreement, the Board, in *K & W Electric*,[167] reaffirmed the settlement standards set out in *Independent Stave Co.*[168] A settlement agreement bar is an affirmative defense and is waived unless timely asserted.[169] As with informal settlement agreements, the Board will set aside settlement agreements where a party fails to comply with a settlement agreement or where a party commits post-settlement unfair labor practices.[170]

In *Guess?, Inc.*,[171] the Board affirmed the decision of the administrative law judge (ALJ) to refuse to take judicial notice of a judgment entered against the respondent in federal court with respect to certain unfair labor practices. The ALJ found that the entry of the consent judgment was part of a formal settlement agreement that contained a nonadmissions clause and was therefore not admissible evidence that the respondent in fact committed any of the underlying unfair labor practices.

5. The Complaint and the Answer

An ALJ cannot amend a complaint over the general counsel's objections.[172] Such an amendment is possible only when sought or consented to by the general counsel, or when evidence is received into the record on the specific issue without objection.

The Board continues applying the three-part test of *Redd-I, Inc.*,[173] which it adopted in *Nickles Bakery of Indiana, Inc.*,[174] to determine

---

[166]In fiscal year 2000, the most recent year for which a report is available, 35.1% of all cases were closed as a result of informal settlement; only 0.1% were closed by formal settlement. NLRB 2000 Annual Report, Table 7.

[167]327 NLRB 70, 160 LRRM 1174 (1999).

[168]287 NLRB 740, 127 LRRM 1204 (1987).

[169]Richard Mellow Elec. Contractors, 327 NLRB 1112, 161 LRRM 1018 (1999).

[170]Windward Roofing & Constr. Co., 342 NLRB No. 70, 175 LRRM 1266 (2004).

[171]339 NLRB 432, 172 LRRM 1361 (2003).

[172]GPS Terminal Servs., 333 NLRB 968, 168 LRRM 1201 (2001) (ALJ improperly amended complaint to allege that former employees and union formed picket line).

[173]290 NLRB 1115, 129 LRRM 1229 (1988).

[174]296 NLRB 927, 132 LRRM 1249 (1989).

whether the allegations contained in a complaint are "closely related" to the underlying charge.[175] Some courts, however, reject this test.[176]

In *Bridgestone/Firestone, Inc.*,[177] the Board held that allegations in an amended complaint, that an employer engaged in direct dealing by telling employees that it would not release their addresses to the union without the employees' authorization and that the employer unlawfully solicited employees to initiate or sign a decertification petition, were "closely related" to the timely allegations in the initial complaint and, thus, were not time-barred. All the conduct alleged in the amended complaint occurred within a period of several months and was alleged to be part of an overall plan for the employer to rid itself of the union.

In *Air Contact Transport, Inc.*,[178] however, the Board held that an amended complaint, alleging that an employer unlawfully told an employee that a co-worker was fired because he was a union instigator, was untimely and not closely related to a timely filed charge alleging that the employer had violated the Act by reprimanding the co-worker for his protected concerted activity and then terminating him for that activity. In *KFMB Stations*,[179] the Board held that a portion of the complaint, alleging that the employer solicited an individual to initiate a decertification effort in violation of Section 8(a)(1), was not closely related to the charges filed by the individual, which failed to allege any independent Section 8(a)(1) violations. As a result, the Board found that the two allegations necessarily comprised distinct legal theories and required different employer defenses.

In *Cooper Health Systems*,[180] the Board held that a complaint that was amended to allege unlawful maintenance and enforcement of a no-solicitation/no-distribution rule, and unlawful discipline for distributing union literature, is not barred by the 6-month limitations period where new allegations arise from factual circumstances and a sequence of events set out in a timely unfair labor practice charge.

---

[175]Air Contact Transp., Inc., 340 NLRB No. 81, 173 LRRM 1429 (2003); Adams Mark Hotel, 325 NLRB 534, 160 LRRM 1206 (1999).

[176]New Orleans Cold Storage & Warehouse Co. v. NLRB, 201 F.3d 592, 599 n.6, 163 LRRM 2330 (5th Cir. 2000) (declining to apply *Redd-I* test, stating it is "a more rigorous enquiry than the law of this Circuit demands"), quoting Texas World Serv. Co. v. NLRB, 928 F.2d 1426, 1437 n.10, 137 LRRM 2412 (5th Cir. 1991)).

[177]332 NLRB 575, 167 LRRM 1148 (2000).

[178]340 NLRB No. 81, 173 LRRM 1429 (2003).

[179]343 NLRB No. 83 (2004); *see also* Smithfield Packing Co., Inc., 344 NLRB No. 1 (2004).

[180]327 NLRB 1159, 167 LRRM 1288 (1999).

In *Letter Carriers Branch 47*,[181] the Board held that allegations in an amended charge and complaint are sufficiently related to allegations in the original, timely filed charge to satisfy Section 10(b), where the allegations involve the same section of the Act and the same legal theory, and the charge, amended charge, and complaint allegations all involve the same sequence of events and the union was given sufficient notice to prepare and present evidence to defend against the complaint allegations, which were fully litigated at the hearing. In *Garage Management Corp.*,[182] the Board found and remedied a Section 8(a)(4) violation that was inadvertently omitted from the complaint, but that was included in the employee's charge, where, among other things, the issue of the Section 8(a)(4) allegation was closely connected to the subject matter of the complaint and was fully litigated. In *Freeman Decorating Co.*,[183] however, the Board denied the general counsel's motions to consolidate additional charges and to amend the complaint where, among other things, the union and employers were not confronted with the allegations, and proposed amendments did not "flow from the same sequence of events" and did not relate back to litigated issues.

In *Office Depot*,[184] the Board held that, "to the extent that *Lovejoy Industries* . . . departs from precedent holding that the requisite *Nickles Bakery* factual relationship may be based solely on acts that arise out of the same antiunion campaign, *Lovejoy Industries* has not survived *Ross Stores.*"[185] The courts do not necessarily agree with this rule.

In *Ross Stores, Inc. v. NLRB*,[186] the D.C. Circuit declined to enforce the Board's determination that, simply because they arise from the same antiunion campaign, time-barred allegations meet the "closely related" requirement of *Nickles Bakery*.[187] The court found that a pro-union employee's charge alleging an improper no-solicitation admonition was not "closely related" to an earlier timely filed charge relating to the employee's discharge, and that the Board had

---

[181]330 NLRB 667, 168 LRRM 1206 (2000).

[182]334 NLRB 940, 168 LRRM 1353 (2001).

[183]336 NLRB 1, 168 LRRM 1329 (2001).

[184]330 NLRB 640, 163 LRRM 1169 (2000).

[185]*Id.*, citing Lovejoy Indus., 309 NLRB 1085, 143 LRRM 1133 (1992); Ross Stores, 329 NLRB 573, 163 LRRM 1137 (1999), *enforcement denied*, 235 F.3d 669, 166 LRRM 2207 (D.C. Cir. 2001).

[186]235 F.3d 669, 672–73, 166 LRRM 2207 (D.C. Cir. 2001), *denying enforcement in relevant part*, 329 NLRB 573, 163 LRRM 1137 (1999).

[187]296 NLRB 927, 132 LRRM 1249 (1989).

improperly construed Section 10(b) of the Act to allow for prosecution of the no-solicitation charge. The court further found that the mere fact that the comment was made during the same organizing campaign did not itself create a close enough factual relationship to meet the second prong of the *Nickles Bakery* test, particularly where the supervisor who made the no-solicitation admonition was not involved in the employee's discharge.

In *Aldworth Co.*,[188] the Board found it unnecessary to consider the substance of amended complaint allegations that the respondent argued were time-barred under Section 10(b), but noted that "the courts have not universally embraced" the Board's "closely related" standard (which the ALJ had applied).[189] The Board avoided the issue of the courts' disagreement with its application of the "closely related" standard by finding that the disputed allegations of the amended complaint were "cumulative" and, therefore, would not give rise to additional remedial action.

In *Casino Ready Mix, Inc. v. NLRB*,[190] the D.C. Circuit enforced the Board's determination that, although the general counsel's complaint did not specifically allege that the employer's statement violated the Act, the employer had clear notice of the charge and, in addition, did not object to the testimony implicating the employer's agent or pursue an opportunity for cross-examination to contest it. Similarly, in *Steel Fabricators Ass'n*,[191] the Board reiterated its position that it may find and remedy a violation even in the absence of a specific allegation in the complaint, if the issue is closely connected to the subject matter of the complaint and has been fully litigated.

In *McKenzie Engineering Co.*,[192] the Board found that the general counsel's failure to allege an unlawful withdrawal of recognition is not adequately cured by a motion to amend the complaint, made for the first time in an answering brief to the Board in response to the employer's exceptions to the ALJ's findings.

---

[188]338 NLRB 137, 171 LRRM 1033 (2002).

[189]*Id.*, citing *Ross Stores, supra* note 186.

[190]321 F.3d 1190, 171 LRRM 3289 (D.C. Cir. 2003), *enforcing* 335 NLRB 463, 171 LRRM 1447 (2001).

[191]341 NLRB No. 68, 174 LRRM 1356 (2004), citing Pergament United Sales, 296 NLRB 333 (1989), *enforced*, 920 F.2d 130 (2d. Cir. 1990); *see also* Yellow Ambulance Serv., 342 NLRB No. 77, 175 LRRM 1257 (2004); Atlantic Veal & Lamb, Inc., 342 NLRB No. 37, 175 LRRM 1456 (2004); MEMC Elec. Materials, Inc., 342 NLRB No. 119, 175 LRRM 1476. *Cf.* Allina Health Sys. dba Abbott Northwestern Hosp., 343 NLRB No. 67, 176 LRRM 1004 (2004).

[192]326 NLRB 473, 161 LRRM 1175 (1998).

The Board continues to find that a party that files an answer that does not meet the requirements of the Board's Rules and Regulations may be deemed to have admitted the complaint allegations.[193] Nonetheless, the Board has ordered a hearing on an unfair labor practice complaint despite deficiencies in an employer's answer.[194] Specifically, the Board considered that the respondent was pro se, that the answer and amended answer clearly and specifically denied the unfair labor practice allegations, and that the employer tried to cure the deficiencies. The Board also reiterated the policy that its rules permit an answer to be amended any time before trial. In *Eckert Fire Protection*,[195] however, the Board found that an employer's one-page faxed memorandum did not constitute a proper answer to the complaint, even under the more lenient standard applicable to pro se respondents. The memorandum failed to address any of the factual or legal allegations of the complaint and to specifically deny any of the complaint allegations.

In *Precision Concrete v. NLRB*,[196] the D.C. Circuit refused to enforce a Board reinstatement order because the Board failed to identify the necessary factual relationship between alleged misconduct and the allegations contained in the complaint.

The Board revised its rule to clarify its procedure for default judgment where the respondent fails to file a timely answer to the complaint.[197] A party who fails to file an answer within the allotted time may file a motion for leave to file an answer, but must show good cause therein for the failure to answer in a timely manner.[198]

In *Robert W. Lockhart dba Lockhart Concrete*,[199] the Board denied the respondent's motion for leave to file an answer and granted the general counsel's motion for summary judgment. The pro se respondent had filed its motion after the Board issued a Notice to Show Cause why the general counsel's motion for summary judgment should not be granted. The respondent claimed that, because of financial constraints, he had attempted to handle the case without counsel, but that he would retain legal representation if given leave

---

[193]Yonkers Assocs., 94 L.P., 340 NLRB No. 147 (2003).

[194]A.P.S. Prods., 326 NLRB 1296, 161 LRRM 1015 (1998).

[195]329 NLRB 920, 162 LRRM 1281 (1999).

[196]334 F.3d 88, 172 LRRM 3113 (D.C. Cir. 2003), *denying enforcement in relevant part*, 337 NLRB 211, 172 LRRM 1370 (2001).

[197]69 Fed. Reg. 1675–77 (Jan. 12, 2004).

[198]29 C.F.R. §102.20.

[199]336 NLRB 956, 174 LRRM 1160 (2001).

to file an answer. The Board held that "[w]here a *pro se* respondent fails to respond to the complaint until after the Notice to Show Cause had issued, despite having been reminded in writing to do so, and has provided no good cause explanation for its failure to do so, subsequent attempts to answer the complaint will be denied as untimely."[200]

In *Hewlett Packard Co.*,[201] the ALJ granted the general counsel's motion to amended the case caption by substituting "Hewlett Packard Company" for "HP/Compaq Direct" as the respondent. Over the respondent's objections, the Board upheld the amendment, given that Hewlett Packard had defended the case, its managers represented the respondent at the facility at the time of the alleged unlawful discharge and participated in the discharge and it admitted liability for any remedies that might result from the discharge.

6. *The Unfair Labor Practice Hearing*

The Ninth Circuit, in *NLRB v. Kolkka*,[202] addressed the issue of consolidating unfair labor practice proceedings involving the same respondent. The court held that the Board's refusal to consolidate separate proceedings involving distinct legal and factual issues is not an abuse of its discretion.

The First Circuit held that the Board did not violate Section 10(c) by promulgating Rule 102.42, which altered procedure by giving an ALJ discretion to decide whether written briefs or oral argument would be utilized in a particular case.[203] Likewise, the ALJ did not abuse this discretion by waiting until the bulk of the evidence was presented before notifying the parties that, despite the employer's

---

[200]*See also* CCY New Worktech, Inc., 329 NLRB 194, 169 LRRM 1023 (1999) (employer's exceptions asserting that neither president nor employees read English, that president did not receive any notice or letter informing him that employer was subject of complaint made by employees of predecessors and/or alter egos, and that none of its employees recalled receiving any mail from Board are without merit and, therefore, general counsel's motion for summary judgment is granted based on employer's failure to file answer to complaint and appear at hearing).

[201]341 NLRB No. 62, 175 LRRM 1086 (2004).

[202]170 F.3d 937, 160 LRRM 2810 (9th Cir. 1999), *enforcing* 323 NLRB 165, 155 LRRM 1170 (1997).

[203]NLRB v. Beverly Enterprises-Mass., Inc., 174 F.3d 13, 160 LRRM 2935 (1st Cir. 1999), *enforcing* 325 NLRB 598, 160 LRRM 1239 (1998).

objection, they would be required to present oral arguments, rather than written briefs.

In *Oden Mechanical Contractors, Inc.*,[204] the Board rejected the respondent's contention that the ALJ erred by refusing to permit it to file a post-hearing brief prior to the issuance of the bench decision. The Board said that the respondent was relying on a long-outdated version of the Board's Rules and Regulations. In its decision, the Board quoted the current version of Section 102.42 of the Rules and Regulations, which provides that "[i]n the discretion of the administrative law judge, any party may, upon request made before the close of the hearing, file a brief or proposed findings and conclusions, or both . . . ." The Board held that the ALJ's decision not to allow post-hearing briefs was, therefore, within her discretion.

A post-hearing motion to reopen a record to receive certain evidence will be denied absent a showing that the evidence is newly discovered, became available only after the close of the hearing, or otherwise satisfies the "extraordinary circumstances" requirements of Section 102.48(d)(1) of the Board's Rules and Regulations.[205] An ALJ does not abuse his discretion by refusing to reopen the administrative record to admit new evidence, where such evidence would not compel or persuade him to contrary results,[206] or where the parties had an opportunity to, and did, introduce evidence in an objections hearing based on substantially identical conduct and the parties were not prejudiced by the ALJ's rulings.[207]

With regard to the issue of whether a respondent was afforded a full and fair opportunity to defend the charges filed against it, a respondent will be deemed to have been accorded due process if the record shows that it understood the issues and was afforded a full opportunity to meet the charges.[208] Parties participating in an un-

---

[204]336 NLRB 920, 172 LRRM 1149 (2001).

[205]USF Red Star, Inc., 339 NLRB 389, 172 LRRM 1344 (2003); Goski Trucking Corp., 325 NLRB 1032, 160 LRRM 1078 (1998).

[206]E & B Paving, Inc., 340 NLRB No. 150, 174 LRRM 1034 (2003); Reno Hilton Resorts, 326 NLRB 1421, 162 LRRM 1405 (1998), *enforced*, 196 F.3d 1275, 162 LRRM 2961 (D.C. Cir. 1999).

[207]Teamsters Local 299, 328 NLRB 1231, 162 LRRM 1327 (1999).

[208]Casino Ready Mix, Inc. v. NLRB, 321 F.3d 1190, 171 LRRM 3289 (D.C. Cir. 2003), *enforcing* 335 NLRB 463, 171 LRRM 1447 (2001); McKenzie Eng'g Co., 326 NLRB 473, 161 LRRM 1175 (1998), *enforced*, 182 F.3d 622, 161 LRRM 2641 (8th Cir. 1999).

fair labor practice hearing are entitled to procedural due process. In *Lamar Advertising of Hartford*,[209] the Board refused to consider whether an employee's threat to retain counsel and presumably file an unfair labor practice charge was a motivating factor in the employee's discharge. In the complaint and at the hearing, the general counsel's theory of the violation was based on other alleged protected activity. The Board found that this theory was improperly expanded in the general counsel's exceptions to include the employee's threat to hire an attorney. The Board held that recognition of this theory would violate fundamental principles of procedural due process, which require "meaningful notice of a charge and a full and fair opportunity to litigate it." Due process, the Board held, requires an administrative agency to provide "a clear statement of the theory on which the agency will proceed with the case" and prohibits "midstream" changes in legal theories without reasonable notice.

The Board's rules regarding examination of witnesses in unfair labor practice hearings require that "[w]itnesses shall be examined orally under oath."[210] The Board applied a strict interpretation of this rule in *Westside Painting, Inc.*,[211] holding that it required the physical presence of the witness in the hearing room and that testimony taken telephonically during a hearing was inadmissible under the rule. The Board ruled that the only exception to the physical presence requirement is the taking of testimony by deposition upon a showing of good cause.[212]

In another decision involving the use of testimony taken outside of a hearing, the Board held that witnesses' deposition testimony, obtained pursuant to a pre-complaint subpoena issued during the investigation of an unfair labor practice charge, was admissible in the subsequent unfair labor practice hearing.[213] The Board did *not,* however, say that such deposition testimony may simply be admitted in lieu of live testimony. Rather, the Board noted that the

---

[209]343 NLRB No. 40, 176 LRRM 1156 (2004); *see also* Jack In The Box Distrib. Ctr. Sys., 339 NLRB 40, 172 LRRM 1352 (2003) (denying the general counsel's exceptions to the ALJ's failure to find an alleged statement by the employer unlawful for the reason that the general counsel offered the statement at the hearing as background evidence of animus, not as an independent violation of the Act).

[210]29 C.F.R. §102.30.

[211]328 NLRB 796, 797, 161 LRRM 1177 (1999).

[212]*Id.*; 29 C.F.R. §102.30.

[213]North Bay Plumbing, Inc., 327 NLRB 899 n.1, 161 LRRM 1139 (1999).

respondent had stipulated that all the witnesses whose depositions were offered would testify as they had in their depositions, and that all but one did testify during the hearing.[214]

It is still the position of the Board that, so far as practicable, the Board is bound to follow the Federal Rules of Evidence applicable in federal district courts.[215] The Board may take judicial notice of the determination of a state unemployment compensation referee's denial of benefits to an employee, but it is not binding where the issues being tried at the unfair labor practice proceeding differ.[216] Cross-examination of a witness on matters from an unrelated proceeding will not, however, be permitted under Federal Rule of Evidence 103.[217] Further, an individual's false statement in the course of applying for unemployment benefits will not, on that basis alone, discredit the individual as a witness in a Board proceeding if his testimony is otherwise judged to be reliable.[218]

Determinations in previous Board representation hearings will not have a binding effect on subsequent unfair labor practice proceedings, but the prior decision will be given "persuasive relevance" or "administrative comity."[219] Issues to be addressed by the ALJ must, however, have been raised either in the pleadings or at the hearing, and may not be raised for the first time in the post-hearing brief.[220] The Board continues considering the admission of tape-recordings into evidence on a case-by-case basis.[221]

---

[214]*Id.*

[215]29 U.S.C. §160(b); Rogers & McDonald Graphics v. NLRB, 331 F.3d 1002, 172 LRRM 2815 (D.C. Cir. 2003), *denying enforcement and remanding* 336 NLRB 836, 169 LRRM 1139 (2001).

[216]Iron Griddle Rest., 327 NLRB 1234, 167 LRRM 1253 (1999).

[217]Fluor Daniel, Inc., 333 NLRB 427, 166 LRRM 1265 (2001).

[218]Double D Constr. Group, 339 NLRB 303, 172 LRRM 1329 (2003).

[219]Brusco Tugs & Barge Co., 330 NLRB 1188, 167 LRRM 1047 (2000), *enforcement denied,* 247 F.3d 273, 167 LRRM 2148 (D.C. Cir. 2001).

[220]Vencare Ancillary Servs., Inc., 334 NLRB 965, 168 LRRM 1029 (2001).

[221]Quality Mech. Insulation, Inc., 340 NLRB No. 91, 173 LRRM 1486 (2003); Dutchess Res. Mgmt., 327 NLRB 508, 165 LRRM 1359 (1999) (general counsel did not have to produce tape-recording of supervisor/steward conversation that formed basis for allegation of unlawful threat where such tape was not a "statement" under the Rules and Regulations); Senior Citizens Coordinating Council, 330 NLRB 1100, 166 LRRM 1074 (2000) (ALJ properly refused to admit transcript of secretly taped conversation into evidence where tape was partially inaudible and transcript contained language not on the tape).

In *Tasty Baking Co. v. NLRB,*[222] the D.C. Circuit concluded that an ALJ did not abuse his discretion when he applied the witness-sequestration rule to exclude four of the employer's managers from the hearing room while others testified. The employer argued that the witnesses fell under the "essential person" exception to the *Greyhound Lines*[223] witness sequestration standard. In *Greyhound Lines,* the Board had stated that an exception existed for the party's designated representative and to persons "essential to the presentation of the party's case."[224] The court concluded that the ALJ has broad discretion in determining who is "essential" to the party's case.[225] The Board has held that it is not error for an ALJ to deny a motion to sequester, absent a showing of prejudice.[226]

An ALJ has no discretion to permit a charged party's counsel to retain *Jencks*[227] statements after the close of the hearing.[228] An ALJ's finding that the employer's need for such statements in any appeal outweighed the potential misuse of them does not change this, where the Board's rule requiring the general counsel to produce pretrial statement of a witness upon motion after the witness has testified permits use of such statements for the limited purpose of cross-examination, and no persuasive reason for expanding that purpose has been shown. The Board made this ruling in light of no party's attempting during the hearing to enter the statements into evidence or otherwise make them part of the official record.

In *Community Health Services, Inc. dba Mimbres Memorial Hospital & Nursing Home,*[229] the Board found that the employer was not prejudiced by the ALJ's denial of access to witness statements made in preparation for an earlier case involving the same parties and related facts, as the employer had reviewed the statements during the prior hearing and failed to show specific relevance to the later proceeding.

---

[222]254 F.3d 114, 167 LRRM 2496 (D.C. Cir. 2001), *enforcing* 330 NLRB 560, 167 LRRM 1172 (2000).

[223]319 NLRB 554, 153 LRRM 1081 (1995).

[224]*Id.*

[225]*Tasty Baking Co., supra* note 222.

[226]AEI2, LLC, 343 NLRB No. 56, 176 LRRM 1098 (2004).

[227]Jencks Act, 18 U.S.C. §3500 (1957). *See also* Jencks v. United States, 353 U.S. 657, 40 LRRM 2147 (1957).

[228]Wal-Mart Stores Inc., 339 NLRB 64, 172 LRRM 1271 (2003).

[229]342 NLRB No. 33, 176 LRRM 1028 (2004).

In *Ethan Enterprises, Inc.*,[230] the Board upheld the ALJ's decision to proceed with the unfair labor practice hearing after the employer's attorney left in the middle of the hearing when the ALJ sustained an objection to one of his questions on cross-examination.

7. *The Administrative Law Judge's Decision*

The Board continues holding that an ALJ may find and remedy a violation, even in the absence of a specific allegation in the complaint, if the issue is closely connected to the subject matter of the complaint and the matter has been fully litigated.[231] The general counsel need not formally amend the complaint to allege the violation.[232]

In *Diamond Detective Agency, Inc.*,[233] the Board refused to adopt the ALJ's finding that, under *Golden State Bottling Co. v. NLRB*,[234] the employer was bound to remedy its predecessor's unlawful discharge of an employee. The complaint did not allege that the employer was a *Golden State* successor and there was no indication that the general counsel ever advanced that theory of liability.[235] Similarly, in *Cibao Meat Products*,[236] the Board reversed an ALJ's finding of constructive discharge where the contention that an unlawfully suspended employee was constructively discharged was neither alleged in the complaint nor fully and fairly litigated.[237]

---

[230] 342 NLRB No. 15, 175 LRRM 1421 (2004), *citing* Beta Steel Corp., 326 NLRB 1267 n.3, 1268 (1998) *and* Bristol Manor Health Care Ctr., 295 NLRB 1106 n.1 (1989), *enforced mem.*, 915 F.2d 1561 (3d Cir. 1991).

[231] Golden State Foods Corp., 340 NLRB No. 56, 173 LRRM 1278 (2003); Steel Fabricators Ass'n, 341 NLRB No. 68, 174 LRRM 1356 (2004). *But see* Lamar Adver. of Hartford, 343 NLRB No. 40, 176 LRRM 1156 (2004) (Board dismissed an alleged violation for the reason that the general counsel had expanded his theory of the violation beyond what was alleged in the complaint and had failed either to amend the complaint or to litigate the expanded theory at the hearing).

[232] National Ass'n of Letter Carriers Local 3825, 333 NLRB 343, 166 LRRM 1217 (2001) (ALJ found statements of shop steward illegal and closely related to allegation stated in complaint).

[233] 339 NLRB 443, 172 LRRM 1418 (2003).

[234] 414 U.S. 168, 84 LRRM 2839 (1973).

[235] *See also* Sierra Bullets LLC, 340 NLRB No. 32, 173 LRRM 1283 (2003) (ALJ deprived employer of due process by finding, based on broad theory, that parties were not at impasse, where general counsel expressly litigated only a narrow theory of violation).

[236] 338 NLRB 934, 172 LRRM 1097 (2003).

[237] *See also* Pepsi Bottling Group, Inc., 338 NLRB 1123, 172 LRRM 1130 (2003); Ken Maddox Heating & Air Conditioning, Inc., 340 NLRB No. 7, 173 LRRM 1113 (2003); Golden State Foods Corp., 340 NLRB No. 56, 173 LRRM 1278 (2003).

ALJs continue to enjoy wide latitude in making credibility determinations. In *Daikichi Sushi*,[238] the Board upheld the ALJ's determination to credit the testimony of three employees, even though he did not believe all of their testimony and despite their poor English, and also upheld the ALJ's decision to draw an adverse inference against the employer for failing to call its president to controvert the employees' testimony.[239] In *D & F Industries, Inc.*,[240] the Board upheld the credibility determinations of an ALJ who, despite finding no evidence of a meaningful sequestration violation, nonetheless stated that, in assessing the credibility of certain witnesses, he had taken into account the "potential violation" of his sequestration order. In *Church Homes dba Avery Heights*,[241] the Board held that an ALJ was entitled to consider employees' length of service and employment history as one factor in making his credibility determinations. The fact that persons act well in one context "is more than marginally probative of how they would behave" in another.

An ALJ's findings must, however, be supported by the record.[242] In *American Gardens Management Co.*,[243] the Board found that the ALJ failed to clearly apply the proper legal analysis and did not address all the relevant record evidence. The Board, therefore, remanded the case to the ALJ for further consideration. In *Harvest Select Farms,*

---

[238]335 NLRB 622, 169 LRRM 1197 (2001).

[239]*See also* Fluor Daniel, Inc. v. NLRB, 332 F.3d 961, 172 LRRM 2673 (6th Cir. 2003), *enforcing in part and remanding* 333 NLRB 427, 166 LRRM 1265 (2001) (ALJ was free to disregard adverse credibility determination concerning witness by second ALJ in different proceeding); Overnite Transp. Co., 336 NLRB 387, 174 LRRM 1266 (2001) (upholding ALJ's credibility findings despite respondent's contention that ALJ made credibility determinations based on respondent's prior unfair labor practices and thereby violated Rule 404 of the Federal Rules of Evidence, where ALJ's decision included reference to prior ULP decision and stated that "I have taken into account the history of this Respondent in assessing the various issues of this case, giving this history significant weight").

[240]339 NLRB 618, 174 LRRM 1254 (2003) (ALJ Decision, n.4).

[241]343 NLRB No. 128 (2004).

[242]E.S. Sutton Realty Co., 336 NLRB 405, 169 LRRM 1063 (2001) (reversing ALJ's credibility findings where ALJ did not fully address all inconsistencies in record, and relied instead on witnesses whose testimony ALJ described as inaccurate and incomplete and which was contradicted by documentary evidence); PVMI Assocs., Inc. dba King David Ctr., 328 NLRB 1141, 168 LRRM 1458 (1999) (remanding to ALJ complaint allegations that employer violated §8(a)(3), where ALJ did not make credibility determinations or rule on specific allegations); Snap-on Tools, Inc., 342 NLRB No. 2, 175 LRRM 1124 (2004) (reversing the ALJ's factual finding that the employer kept a list of persons who voted, holding that the finding was an impermissible inference that was not supported by the record as a whole).

[243]338 NLRB 644, 171 LRRM 1265 (2002).

LLC,[244] the Board remanded the case to the ALJ for the reason that his bench decision failed to "indicate whether he considered certain undisputed facts that arguably are inconsistent with his credibility determinations." In *Lee Builders, Inc.*,[245] the Board remanded the case where the ALJ failed to set out the bases for his credibility determinations and failed to provide sufficient detail regarding the specific evidence upon which he had relied in resolving the factual issues in dispute.

In *Vico Products Co.*,[246] the Board refused to rely upon an ALJ's fact finding, because it rested upon "simple assumption," rather than on a thorough analysis of the record. The Board reiterated its position that, when "credibility resolutions are not based primarily upon demeanor . . . the Board itself may proceed to an independent evaluation of credibility."[247]

In *Double D Construction Group, Inc.*,[248] the Board found that the ALJ made an "erroneous decision" to discredit a witness "based solely on his use of a false Social Security number to obtain employment." According to the Board, the ALJ "effectively disqualified" the witness for his false statement instead of making a true credibility determination that would have considered the false statement as one factor among many. Stating that the ALJ's error "threatens harm to the effective administration of the Act," the Board remanded the case to the ALJ, instructing him to base his findings on "appropriate considerations in determining credibility."

The failure of a witness to appear and testify to a particular matter or incident may give rise to an adverse inference that said witness' testimony would be unfavorable.[249] While such an adverse inference

---

[244]340 NLRB No. 100, 173 LRRM 1357 (2003).

[245]341 NLRB No. 104, 175 LRRM 1414 (2004).

[246]336 NLRB 583, 170 LRRM 1124 (2001).

[247]*Id.* at 590 n.19, citing J.N. Ceazan Co., 246 NLRB 637, 638 n.6, 102 LRRM 1651 (1979); *see also* RC Aluminum Indus., Inc., 343 NLRB No. 103 (2004) (holding that an independent examination of the record was necessary where the presiding ALJ at the hearing died before issuing a decision, and the ALJ assigned to the case necessarily made his credibility determinations on bases other than demeanor).

[248]339 NLRB 303, 172 LRRM 1329 (2003).

[249]Ferguson Elec. Co., 335 NLRB 142, 168 LRRM 1025 (2001) (upholding adverse inference drawn from employer's failure to call supervisor who saw §8(a)(3) discriminatee giving co-workers directions to union meeting and who terminated employee later that same day); Villa Maria Nursing & Rehab. Ctr., Inc., 335 NLRB 1345, 168 LRRM 1209 (2001) (upholding adverse inference drawn from labor consultant's failure to testify regarding alleged threat to employee in one-on-one conversation, where employee testified to threat).

is not required,[250] failure to rule on a request that an adverse inference be drawn can provide grounds for a Board remand for further consideration.[251]

In *American Armored Car, Ltd.*,[252] the Board disagreed with the ALJ's decision to draw an adverse inference from the respondent's failure to introduce certain records into evidence. The Board found that the general counsel failed to "put the Respondent on notice" that he was challenging witness testimony supported by the records. The Board further noted that the general counsel did not subpoena the records or otherwise request their production.

In the exercise of discretion and in the discharge of duties and responsibilities, an ALJ must remain wholly impartial and must avoid creating even the appearance of partiality.[253] In *Victor's Café 52, Inc.*,[254] the Board found that the ALJ's criticisms of counsel for the general counsel and of one of her witnesses were improper. The ALJ had referred to a witness as a "liar and scum" and as "the stuff that runs through the bottom of sewers," and had strongly criticized counsel for the general counsel for arguing the witness's credibility in her post-hearing brief. The Board declined to conclude that the ALJ was prejudiced or that his conduct invalidated his opinion. The Board, however, emphasized that an ALJ must "scrupulously avoid any conduct that could possibly lead to an appearance of partiality." The Board observed that, even in the absence of prejudice, the ALJ's "intemperate language" and "attacks against fundamental personal integrity" could potentially undermine the confidence of parties and the public in the Board's ability to establish an unbiased record and render fair judgments. In *C. Politis & Co., Inc.*,[255] the Board, in response to the employer's motion to strike, redacted from the ALJ's

---

[250]Tom Rice Buick, Pontiac & GMC Truck, Inc., 334 NLRB 785, 167 LRRM 1343 (2001) (holding that failure of employer's president to testify at ULP hearing on employee's discharge does not require drawing of adverse inference, where, among other things, president acted as employer's nonattorney representative at hearing, and there is no factual dispute that employee's early departure was employer's asserted reason for employee's discharge); *see also* AEI2, LLC, 343 NLRB No. 56, 176 LRRM 1098 (2004) (ALJ did not err in failing to draw an adverse inference where such decisions lie "within the sound discretion of the trier of fact").

[251]PPG Indus., Inc., 338 NLRB 1247, 171 LRRM 1311 (2002).

[252]339 NLRB 600, 172 LRRM 1385 (2003).

[253]St. Mary's Nursing Home, 342 NLRB No. 100, 175 LRRM 1361 (2004).

[254]338 NLRB 753, 171 LRRM 1217 (2002).

[255]343 NLRB No. 28, 176 LRRM 1166 (2004).

decision certain "gratuitous remarks" that reflected "a judgment regarding the Respondent's employment practices and the character of the Respondent's owner." In doing so, the Board emphasized that parties appearing before an ALJ "must be treated with respect." The Board distinguished *Victor's Café 52, Inc.*,[256] stating that the inappropriate remarks were not redacted in that case because they related directly to the ALJ's legal conclusions.

An ALJ's impartiality is not called into question merely because his or her decision incorporates substantial portions of the general counsel's brief.[257] Where this occurs, however, the ALJ's decision must be closely scrutinized.[258]

8. *The Board's Decision*

On September 4, 2002, Associate General Counsel Richard A. Siegel issued a memorandum regarding certain changes to the Board's Rules and Regulations pertaining to the procedure for filing stipulations of fact with the Board.[259] Specifically, the Board has revised Section 102.35(9), which now provides that parties may agree to waive a hearing and decision by an ALJ and submit a stipulation of facts directly to the executive secretary, which, if approved, provides for a decision by the Board.[260] The regulations further provide that "a statement of the issues presented should be set forth in the stipulation of facts and each party should also submit a short statement (no more than three pages) of its position on the issues."

Parties may file exceptions to an ALJ's decision, although those exceptions must comply with the requirements of Section 102.46 of the Board's Rules and Regulations in order to receive consideration. For example, in *Sommerville Construction Co.*,[261] the Board granted the general counsel's motion to strike the employer's untimely response to exceptions, despite the employer's contention that it was not served with a copy of the ALJ's decision, where (1) the employer's alter ego was served with a copy of the decision (such service being

---

[256]*Supra*, note 254.

[257]Casino Ready Mix, Inc. v. NLRB, 321 F.3d 1190, 171 LRRM 3289 (D.C. Cir. 2003), *enforcing* 335 NLRB 463, 171 LRRM 1447 (2001).

[258]Waterbury Hotel, 333 NLRB 482, 171 LRRM 1348 (2001), *enforced*, 314 F.3d 645, 171 LRRM 2781 (D.C. Cir. 2003).

[259]General Counsel Memorandum OM 02-89, "Revised Procedure for Filing Stipulation of Facts with the Board."

[260]*Id.*, citing 29 C.F.R. §102.35(9).

[261]338 NLRB 1178 n.2, 172 LRRM 1300 (2003).

sufficient to constitute service on the employer), and (2) the employer never notified the Board that it had not received a copy and never requested a copy or inquired as to the deadline for filing a response. In *Pratt Towers, Inc.*,[262] certain of the respondent's exceptions were disregarded for failure to allege with particularity the grounds on which the ALJ's allegedly erroneous findings should be overturned. In *Valentine Painting & Wallcovering, Inc.*,[263] the Board refused to rule on an employer's exception to the ALJ's conclusion that the employer unlawfully failed to hire a union organizer, where the employer did not allege the error that it contended the ALJ committed in his conclusion, or the grounds for its contention that the ALJ's decision as to this violation should be overturned. In *NationalExpress Corp. d/b/a ATC/Forsythe & Associates*,[264] the Board granted the employer's motion to strike the charging parties' exceptions with respect to portions thereof that were not supported by record evidence, duplicated arguments made in brief and went beyond the general counsel's theory of the case.

The Board's procedural rules permit a respondent to file a motion to reopen the record after the ALJ has issued a decision but before the Board has ruled.[265] The Board has wide discretion in deciding whether to grant such motions and update the record prior

---

[262]338 NLRB 317, 170 LRRM 1533 (2002).

[263]331 NLRB 883, 167 LRRM 1046 (2000); *see also* Aero Ambulance Serv., Inc., 327 NLRB 639, 167 LRRM 1286 (1999) (refusing to rule on exception to ALJ's finding that employer unlawfully interrogated employee, where employer did not except to this finding in ALJ's original decision, but raised issue in its exceptions brief regarding ALJ's supplemental decision that was issued 10 months later); Hospital del Maestro v. NLRB, 263 F.3d 173, 168 LRRM 2808 (1st Cir. 2001) (holding that Board properly ruled that employer failed to prove "excusable neglect" under §102.111(c) of Board's Rules and Regulations for failing to file timely exceptions to ALJ's decision). *But see* Wyandanch Engine Rebuilders, Inc., 328 NLRB 866, 168 LRRM 1239 (1999) (holding that employer's exceptions are sufficient to warrant consideration, even though they do not comply fully with §102.46 of Rules and Regulations); Dimarco Paving & Constr., Inc., 341 NLRB No. 42, 174 LRRM 1283 (2004) (finding that employer's exceptions failed to conform with the Board's Rules and Regulations in all respects but were nonetheless "not so deficient as to warrant striking"); Hempstead Park Nursing Home, 341 NLRB No. 41, 174 LRRM 1460 (2004) (a letter filed in lieu of formal exceptions found to substantially comply with §102.46).

[264]341 NLRB No. 66, 174 LRRM 1341 (2004).

[265]29 C.F.R. §102.48(b).

to making its decision.[266] Evidence that post-dates the hearing does not provide a basis for reopening the record.[267]

The D.C. Circuit upheld the Board's ruling in *U.S.A. Polymer Corp.*[268] that the employer's motion to reopen the record in a *Gissel* bargaining order case one month after the Board rendered its decision was untimely under the 28-day rule,[269] as the employer could have submitted the motion any time before the Board's decision.[270] The court noted that the Board had taken an extraordinary amount of time in issuing the decision, but that it was not the Board's responsibility to update the facts provided.[271] The Board continues to hold that a motion to reopen the record must be filed "promptly" and that such a motion will not lie to allow a party to attack an ALJ's credibility determinations.[272]

The Board continues to grant motions for reconsideration pursuant to Section 102.48 of the Board's Rules and Regulations upon a showing of "extraordinary circumstances" and "material error."[273] An untimely motion for reconsideration will not be granted, absent a showing of "excusable neglect and lack of prejudice."[274] In *Superior Protection, Inc.*,[275] the Board denied the employer's motion for reconsideration of the decision granting summary judgment against the employer and requiring it to recognize and bargain with the union. The employer failed to establish that it had inadequate time to investigate the status of employees and that new evidence had been unavailable prior the granting of summary judgment.

---

[266]NLRB v. U.S.A. Polymer Corp., 272 F.3d 289, 168 LRRM 2897 (5th Cir. 2001), *enforcing* 328 NLRB 1242, 168 LRRM 1427 (1999).

[267]29 C.F.R. §102.65(e)(1); *see also* Brevard Achievement Ctr., Inc., 342 NLRB No. 101, 175 LRRM 1329 (2004).

[268]U.S.A. Polymer, 328 NLRB 1242, 168 LRRM 1427 (1999).

[269]29 C.F.R. §102.48(d)(2) (party has 28 days from date of Board's decision to file motion for reconsideration, rehearing, or reopening of record).

[270]*U.S.A. Polymer, supra* note 268; *see also* Cogburn Healthcare Center, Inc., 342 NLRB No. 11, 175 LRRM 1486 (2004) (denying the employer's motion to reopen the record and for reconsideration because it failed to state, as required by §102.48(d)(1) of the Board's Rules and Regulations, why the evidence submitted in support of the motion was not presented previously, i.e., before the Board rendered its original decision, despite being available to the employer).

[271]*Id.*

[272]Precoat Metals, 341 NLRB No. 143, 175 LRRM 1110 (2004).

[273]Desert Aggregates, 340 NLRB No. 170, 174 LRRM 1361 (2003).

[274]Visiting Nurse Health Sys., Inc., 338 NLRB 1074, 172 LRRM 1155 (2003).

[275]341 NLRB No. 86, 174 LRRM 1561 (2004).

Section 3(b) of the Act allows the Board to delegate its authority to three-member panels.[276] The full Board will not consider a motion for reconsideration of a panel decision unless the motion is referred to the full Board by the panel.[277] This practice has changed so that now any member of the panel may poll the full Board on whether to grant reconsideration.

The Board has increased its vigilance in enforcing the deadlines set forth in its Rules and Regulations for filing briefs in unfair labor practice cases. In *Elevator Constructors Local 2 (Unitec Elevator Services Co.)*,[278] the Board unanimously adopted a rule that untimely documents filed in cases before the Board will not be accepted if the only reason for lateness is miscalculation of the filing date. In doing so, the Board expressly overruled its decision in *Postal Service*,[279] where it stated that "many parties" had cited as authority for allowing the filing of a brief one day late. Stating that Section 102.111 of the Board's Rules and Regulations "describes in specific detail how to count or compute the days in establishing the due date," the Board held that "[h]enceforth, a late document will not be excused when the reason for the tardiness is solely a miscalculation of the filing date." The Board also announced that it "will strictly adhere" to the requirement in Section 102.222(c) of the Rules and Regulations that a party seeking to file an untimely brief on grounds of excusable neglect must submit a sworn affidavit setting forth the specific facts signed by someone with personal knowledge of those facts.[280]

9. *Compliance Procedures*

The regional offices continue to determine the amount of back pay owed in compliance matters. It is not improper, however, for an ALJ to calculate the amount of back pay owed in tip income where the amounts differ between the employer's claim and the employ-

---

[276]29 U.S.C. §153(b).

[277]Enterprise Indus. Piping Co., 118 NLRB 1, 40 LRRM 1114 (1957).

[278]337 NLRB 426, 169 LRRM 1265 (2002).

[279]309 NLRB 305, 141 LRRM 1161 (1992).

[280]*See also* Metropolitan Regional Council of Phila., Carpenters (R.M. Shoemaker Co.) 332 NLRB 1340, 166 LRRM 1001 (2000) (holding that charging party's answering brief that was delivered to delivery service at airport at approximately 11:45 a.m. on day that it was due, but that did not make it on intended flight and arrived at Board's office following morning was not timely under "postmark rule," nor did its failure to arrive at Board's office in timely manner constitute "excusable neglect").

ees' claims on their tax forms, and the award is merely an approximation within the middle range of the two claimed amounts.[281] Although the method may be imprecise, it is not invalid.[282]

In *Ferguson Electric Co.*,[283] the Board amended its "make records available" remedial order to require respondents in back-pay cases to provide the records at a reasonable place (which may include the Board's regional office, the respondent's facility, or another designated location) designated by the Board within 14 days. The regional director has discretion to expand the 14-day time period upon a showing of good cause.

In *International Business Machines Corp.*,[284] the Board rejected the union's request that the remedial notice be posted electronically. The Board found that a traditional notice posting order does not require electronic posting. If the union wanted this, it should have requested it of the ALJ or the Board in the underlying proceeding. The union did not make the request until the compliance stage.

The Board continues exercising its discretion to fashion remedies different from those announced by ALJs, even in the absence of any exceptions filed by the parties.[285] In *Toll Manufacturing Co.*,[286] the Board agreed with the ALJ's determination that the employer had unlawfully discharged a union activist, but overruled the ALJ's recommendation of reinstatement and full back pay. In the absence of exceptions to the ALJ's decision, the Board, nonetheless determined that the employee had lied under oath during Board proceedings and that his back pay should be tolled as of the date that he first perjured himself. In its subsequent decision in *Precoat Metals*,[287] the Board went one step further and denied both reinstatement and backpay to an employee who was unlawfully discharged but who had "deliberately lied" during Board proceedings.

In *Anheuser-Busch, Inc.*,[288] the Board agreed with the ALJ's finding that the respondent violated the Act by failing to notify and bar-

---

[281]Atlantic Limousine v. NLRB, 243 F.3d 711, 166 LRRM 2864 (3d Cir. 2001), *enforcing* 328 NLRB 257, 166 LRRM 1291 (1999).

[282]*Id.*

[283]335 NLRB 142, 168 LRRM 1025 (2001).

[284]339 NLRB 966, 173 LRRM 1037 (2003).

[285]Miramar Sheraton Hotel, 336 NLRB 1203, 171 LRRM 1346 (2001).

[286]341 NLRB No. 115, 175 LRRM 1009 (2004).

[287]341 NLRB No. 143, 175 LRRM 1110 (2004).

[288]342 NLRB No. 49, 175 LRRM 1168 (2004)

gain with the union prior to installing video cameras, and affirmed the ALJ's proposed remedy refusing to reinstate 16 employees whose misconduct was observed by the cameras. The Board found the general counsel's request for make-whole relief contrary to Section 10(c) of the Act, even though the respondent would not have known of the misconduct if it had not installed the cameras.

10. Applicability of the Equal Access to Justice Act

In *Kinney v. Federal Security, Inc.*,[289] the district court set forth a four-part test for a recovery of attorneys' fees and costs under the Equal Access to Justice Act (EAJA).[290] Under this test, a private party may recover its reasonable attorneys' fees and costs from the government if it satisfies the following requirements: (1) it is a "prevailing party"; (2) the government's position or decision to proceed with litigation was not substantially justified; (3) the prevailing party submits an itemization of its fees and costs; and (4) its net worth does not exceed the statutory maximum. The burden of establishing eligibility for fees is "squarely on the applicant." However, the court noted that the government's conclusory assertion, "that the court would certainly find its position in the underlying actions was substantially justified," was insufficient because "[t]he burden of establishing substantial justification fails squarely on the government."

In *E.W. Grobbel Sons, Inc. v. NLRB*,[291] the Sixth Circuit decided it would determine the appropriate fees and costs to the prevailing employer, even though it ordinarily would remand the case to the Board for such determination. This was to avoid placing the Board, which had rejected the employer's fee application as untimely, in an awkward situation.

The Board will not award attorneys' fees and expenses pursuant to the EAJA where the general counsel's overall position in a case was substantially justified, even though evidence supporting particu-

[289]2002 WL 31017644, 2002 U.S. Dist. LEXIS 16914 (N.D. Ill. 2002).
[290]28 U.S.C. § 2412.
[291]176 F.3d 875, 161 LRRM 2229 (6th Cir. 1999).

lar allegations in the complaint was lacking.[292] In *Meaden Screw Products Co.*,[293] the Board reversed the ALJ's decision granting the respondent's application for attorneys' fees and expenses, where the ALJ had ruled that the general counsel was precluded from "relitigat[ing] the issue of substantial justification in an answer where the General Counsel ha[d] already chosen to litigate that issue by filing a motion to dismiss [the EAJA application]." The Board found that, "[e]ven accepting the judge's credibility resolutions, the General Counsel reasonably argued that the judge should have drawn other inferences from the record that would have supported the General Counsel's position."

An EAJA applicant must have prevailed in a portion of the underlying adversary proceeding that is both "discrete" and "significant." In *Golden Stevedoring Co.*,[294] the employer successfully moved at trial to dismiss a paragraph in the complaint alleging a threat of discharge, after the general counsel admitted that he had no evidence to support the allegation and no defense to the motion. The employer subsequently applied to the Board for attorneys' fees and expenses incurred in defending against the dismissed allegation. The Board found that there was no substantial justification for the inclusion of the alleged threat in the complaint but nonetheless dismissed the employer's application, holding that even assuming the allegation was a discrete portion of the case, it was not, when viewed in the context of 19 other equally serious or more serious charges, a significant one. As a result, the Board found that the general counsel's position, viewed as an "inclusive whole," was substantially justified.

In *Fantasia Fresh Juice Co.*,[295] the Board upheld the ALJ's award of attorneys' fees expended by the employer in responding to the gen-

---

[292]C. Factotum, Inc., 337 NLRB 1, 169 LRRM 1259 (2001) (holding that even though evidence of threats during time frame alleged in one paragraph of complaint was lacking, there was evidence supporting allegations in another paragraph of threats made at different time); Glesby Wholesale, Inc., 340 NLRB No. 128, 173 LRRM 1595 (2003) (determining that complaint allegations "as an inclusive whole" were substantially justified). *But see* Kinney v. Federal Sec., 272 F.3d 924, 168 LRRM 2913 (7th Cir. 2001) (mootness of appeal and vacatur of district court's judgment does not preclude district court's consideration of a party's request for fees under EAJA).

[293]336 NLRB 298, 170 LRRM 1394 (2001).

[294]343 NLRB No. 18, 176 LRRM 1211 (2004).

[295]339 NLRB 928, 173 LRRM 1009 (2003).

eral counsel's exceptions to the ALJ's decision. While the general counsel's prosecution of the case prior to the ALJ's decision was substantially justified, the Board agreed with the ALJ that the general counsel's decision to file exceptions to the ALJ's decision was not. The Board reasoned that the exceptions amounted to an attempt to reverse the ALJ's credibility determinations, an effort that was not justified by the record.

In *Precision Concrete v. NLRB*,[296] the D.C. Circuit awarded attorneys' fees and costs to the employer, on the ground that the Board had pursued litigation based on an allegation that was never included in an unfair labor practice charge. The court found that the Board's failure to limit itself to matters "sharing a significant factual affiliation with the activity alleged in the charge" deprived it of jurisdiction over the matter, and it was therefore not substantially justified in proceeding on the complaint.

The EAJA requires a petitioner to file an application for attorneys' fees within 30 days after a final judgment, and to include in that application a number of substantive declarations, including an allegation that the position of the United States was not substantially justified.[297] In *Scarborough v. Principi*,[298] the Supreme Court held that a timely filed application may be amended after the expiration of the 30-day deadline to include the "not substantially justified" allegation. Such an amendment, the Court held, "relates back" to the timely filed fee application. The Court specifically declined to decide whether the EAJA's other content specifications could likewise be amended or included after the expiration of the 30-day deadline.

IV. PROCEDURES APPLICABLE TO ALL CASES

A. In General

In February 2002, Associate General Counsel Richard A. Siegel issued guidelines to the regional offices regarding ethical issues associated with witness interviews conducted during unfair labor practice proceedings.[299] The memorandum acknowledges the right of

---

[296]362 F.3d 847, 174 LRRM 2820 (D.C. Cir. 2004).

[297]28 U.S.C. § 2412(d)(1)(B).

[298]541 U.S. 401 (2004).

[299]General Counsel Memorandum OM 02-36, "Guidelines Concerning Appropriate Contacts with Represented Persons."

every party and witness to a Board proceeding to be represented by an individual of his or her choice, but provides different guidance depending on whether the representative is an attorney. In February 2003, Associate General Counsel Siegel revised the Unfair Labor Practice Casehandling Manual to provide further guidelines for situations where a third-party witness is represented individually by, or otherwise insists on the presence or assistance of, the representative of a party.[300] In October 2003, Associate General Counsel Siegel issued a memorandum detailing the final revisions to the updated Unfair Labor Practice Casehandling Manual.[301]

In April 2004, General Counsel Arthur Rosenfeld issued a report on case handling developments in the Office of General Counsel, with which he began "a practice of reporting on some of the ethical issues that confront" the Board in the administration of the Act.[302] The issues discussed in the April 2004 report relate to state bar applications[303] of ABA Model Rule 4.2 (communications with represented persons) to agency investigations.[304]

In *Pioneer Hotel, Inc. v. NLRB,*[305] the D.C. Circuit held that an ALJ did not engage in an improper ex parte communication under any applicable rule, including the Board's own rules,[306] by consulting with a colleague on the correct manner for handling a procedural issue in the matter before him. The court noted that the Board's rules prohibit only communications with interested parties outside the agency, and that the consultation was over a procedural, not a factual, issue.

As of January 2005, the Board has expanded its pilot E-Filing Project, which permits online filing of documents, to encompass "all documents in representation and unfair labor practice cases."[307]

[300]General Counsel Memorandum OM 03-43, "Revision to Informal ULP Casehandling Manual Section 10058.4(c)."

[301]General Counsel Memorandum OM 04-01, "Revised Unfair Labor Practice Casehandling Manual."

[302]General Counsel Memorandum GC R-2525, "NLRB General Counsel Arthur Rosenfeld Issues Report on Recent Case Developments."

[303]The state bar rules addressed in the report are Arizona, California, Hawaii, Maryland, Minnesota, and Nevada.

[304]General Counsel Memorandum GC R-2544, "NLRB General Counsel Arthur Rosenfeld Issues Report on Recent Case Developments."

[305]182 F.3d 939, 161 LRRM 2785 (D.C. Cir. 1999).

[306]29 C.F.R. §§102.126–102.133.

[307]General Counsel Memorandum OM 05-30, "Labor Board Expands E-Filing Project To Include All Documents In All Cases."

Despite its characterization of the project as all encompassing, however, the Board does prohibit electronically filing certain documents.[308]

While the Board's Rules and Regulations still allow parties to file post-hearing briefs, in February 2004 Associate General Counsel Siegel issued cost savings instructions to the Regional Offices that encouraged measures to reduce the number of post-hearing briefs and written decisions.[309] Specifically, Associate General Counsel Siegel instructed the Regional Offices to, "*[i]n appropriate cases*, have trial attorneys use oral argument at the end of the hearing in lieu of filing post-trial briefs and encourage administrative law judges to issue bench decisions."[310]

In *Metropolitan Regional Counsel of Philadelphia (R.M. Shoemaker),*[311] the Board held that the use of a same-day delivery service to file an answering brief with the Board on the date it was due, but which arrived too late to be received that day, did not satisfy the requirements of the Board's "postmark" or "excusable neglect" rules. The postmark rule provides that, for a document that is received by the Board after the due date to be considered timely filed, the document must be postmarked no later than the day before the due date and, if a delivery service is used, it must be shown that the document was tendered to the delivery service with sufficient time for it to be delivered by the due date, but no later than the day before the due date.[312] Upon good cause shown based on excusable neglect, the filing of a document within a reasonable period of time after the date due may be considered timely.[313] The Board rejected the argument that the delivery service's failure to deliver as promised satisfied the excusable neglect rule, which applies only to the party filing; it further noted that the filing party did not argue, or present any reason to conclude, that its failure to comply with the rule by depositing its brief with the delivery service the day before it was due was based on any excusable neglect. Therefore, in light of the ex-

[308]Excluded documents include: those filed with the Office of the General Counsel, Division of Judges, or a regional director; those not permitted by the Board's Rules to be filed with the Office of the Executive Secretary; petitions for advisory opinions; and documents that are more than 10 MB in size.

[309]General Counsel Memorandum OM 04-30, "Casehandling Cost Savings Instructions."

[310]*Id.* (emphasis in original).

[311]332 NLRB 1340, 166 LRRM 1001 (2000).

[312]29 C.F.R. §102.111(b).

[313]*Id.* §102.111(c).

plicit language of the rule regarding the use of a delivery service, the party acted at its own risk by using same-day service.

In *Wal-Mart Stores, Inc.*,[314] the Board held that each party seeking to exceed the 50-page limit on briefs must individually request permission from the Board, regardless of whether the opposing party has already sought and received permission. In *Wal-Mart,* the charging party had requested and received permission to exceed the 50-page limit for its brief in support of exceptions. The respondent then filed an 82-page answering brief, and the charging party successfully moved to strike pages 51 through 82. The respondent claimed that it had telephoned an employee in the executive secretary's office who allegedly verified that, like extensions of time to file documents, page enlargements granted at one party's request are shared by all parties. The Board noted that Section 102.46(j) of its Rules and Regulations provides that any party desiring additional pages beyond the 50-page limit must request permission from the Board, and that any advice to the contrary was erroneous. The Board did, however, allow the respondent permission to file a responsive brief that conformed to the page limit.

Associate General Counsel Richard A. Siegel, in an August 9, 2002, memorandum, directed the regional offices to consider the propriety of Section 10(j) interim injunctive relief in every case.[315] In cases where the charged party has refused to cooperate in the investigation and the region believes that it will raise a substantial defense at the administrative hearing, the region is encouraged to reevaluate the propriety of Section 10(j) relief immediately after the close of the hearing. The regions are encouraged to seek such relief at that stage, if it still is warranted. The regions also are encouraged to reassess whether to seek Section 10(j) authority in close Section 10(j) cases where the ALJ issues a favorable decision promptly after the close of the hearing, and the passage of time has not defeated the need for interim relief or the ability to restore the status quo.

---

[314] 343 NLRB No. 71, 176 LRRM 1139 (2004).

[315] General Counsel Memorandum GC 02-07, "Utilization of Section 10(j) Proceedings."

B. Discovery

In *Offshore Mariners United*,[316] the Board reiterated that "pretrial discovery in Board proceedings is neither constitutionally nor statutorily required." Member Cowen, dissenting, opposed this longstanding Board policy and advocated full pretrial discovery. Equating the absence of discovery rights with "trial by ambush," and crediting the general counsel with an "inherent advantage in discovery," Member Cowen stated that it was "incumbent upon the Board to address the unfairness and inefficiency embodied in its current discovery procedures." The Board, instead, specifically reaffirmed its policy against pretrial discovery, citing in particular the potential "chilling effect" that pretrial discovery may have on the Board's investigative sources, including employee and nonemployee statements to the Board.[317]

In *Wright Electric, Inc.*,[318] the Board addressed the extent to which a party may use state court discovery procedures to obtain information from the Board, which it would be unable to obtain in a Board proceeding. The Board held that an employer committed an unfair labor practice by seeking, through discovery in a state court lawsuit against a union, to obtain the authorization cards submitted to the union by its employees. Citing *National Telephone Directory*,[319] the Board reinforced its policy of protecting the confidentiality of the identity of employees engaged in organizing activity.

In *Guess?, Inc.*,[320] the Board reversed the ALJ's finding that the respondent did not violate the Act by asking, during a workers' compensation deposition, for the names of employees who attended union meetings. The ALJ found that the respondent's questions were relevant to its workers' compensation defense and were not discriminatorily motivated. The Board held that further analysis was required, and that having found the respondent's inquiries relevant and lawfully motivated, the ALJ should have proceeded to balance the respondent's need for the information against the employees'

---

[316]338 NLRB 745, 171 LRRM 1225 (2002).

[317]*Id.*, citing NLRB v. Robbins Tire & Rubber Co., 437 U.S. 214, 98 LRRM 2617 (1978).

[318]327 NLRB 1194, 163 LRRM 1077 (1999), *enforced*, 200 F.3d 1162, 163 LRRM 2353 (8th Cir. 2000).

[319]319 NLRB 420, 150 LRRM 1290 (1995).

[320]339 NLRB 432, 172 LRRM 1361 (2003).

rights under the Act. Applying this last factor, the Board found that the respondent's need for the information did not outweigh the employees' Section 7 rights, and that the questions were therefore unlawful.

C. Subpoenas

Board policy continues allowing the issuance of pre–complaint subpoenas during the investigative stages of unfair labor practice proceedings.[321] In furtherance of this policy, the general counsel in 2000 granted regional offices increased freedom to issue investigative subpoenas without first obtaining approval from headquarters.[322]

The Board will revoke a subpoena that is not related to any matter under investigation, fails to describe with sufficient particularity the evidence sought, or is invalid for any other reason sufficient in law.[323] The Board recently denied a petition to revoke a subpoena, despite the fact that the witness would be required to travel more than 1,000 miles to appear and present testimony.[324] The Board found that any burden imposed on the witness was outweighed by the fact that both his attorney and the Board agent to whom the case was assigned maintained offices in the area where the evidence was to be taken.

In *Projections, Inc.*,[325] the Board denied a petition to revoke a Board subpoena to a video production company, which had produced an organizational campaign videotape, for documents related to an employer's purchase of the videotape. The Board rejected the argument that the subpoenaed documents were protected from disclosure by Section 8(c) of the Act regarding the right of an employer to freely express its views on unionism during a campaign. The Board held that the subpoena inquiry was narrowly limited to whether the production company and the employer had an agency relationship and did not seek to determine the legality of its content.

---

[321] *Offshore Mariners United, supra* note 316.
[322] General Counsel Memorandum GC 00-02, "Investigative Subpoenas."
[323] *Offshore Mariners United, supra* note 316, citing 29 C.F.R. §102.31(b).
[324] *Id.*
[325] 331 NLRB 1067, 165 LRRM 1135 (2000).

In *Kaiser Aluminum & Chemical Corp.*,[326] the Board granted the charging party's "Request for Special Permission to Appeal" the ALJ's refusal to revoke a subpoena duces tecum issued by the respondent that requested, in part, copies of position statements submitted by the charging party to the general counsel. The Board held that the charging party's position statements constituted "work product" within the meaning of Rule 26(b)(3) of the Federal Rules of Civil Procedure and that the charging party did not waive its privilege by submitting the position statement to the general counsel. Accordingly, and in the absence of any demonstration of substantial need, the Board quashed that portion of the respondent's subpoena that sought the position statements.

In *Equipment Trucking Co.*,[327] the Board held that an ALJ did not abuse his discretion in striking portions of a respondent's answer to complaint allegations involving two employees alleged to be agents of the respondent, in part because the respondent sent the employees out of town on work assignments after the employees said that they would not appear at a Board hearing at which they had been subpoenaed to testify. The Board found the respondent to be an ally of the employees in their evasion of the Board's subpoenas, justifying striking the answer regarding their conduct.

In *PPG Industries, Inc.*,[328] the Board held that the ALJ abused his discretion by granting the employer's petition to revoke the general counsel's subpoena for documents concerning the employer's administration of its attendance policy. Among other things, the Board found that requiring production of reports showing the entire history of discipline and electronic records was not unnecessarily cumulative or duplicative.

In *NLRB v. Interstate Builders, Inc.*,[329] the Tenth Circuit agreed with the Board that the employer, who was accused of improperly terminating a union "salt," was not harmed by the ALJ's inconsistent reasons for refusing to grant a broad subpoena request. Because the court was not "convinced that the requests were so overbroad so as to constitute a wholesale 'fishing expedition' meriting revocation in almost every particular," it found "that the ALJ abused his discretion in summarily rejecting the bulk of the subpoena." The court, never-

[326]339 NLRB 829, 173 LRRM 1508 (2003).

[327]336 NLRB 277 n.1, 171 LRRM 1561 (2001).

[328]339 NLRB 821, 172 LRRM 1451 (2003).

[329]351 F.3d 1020, 173 LRRM 1020 (10th Cir. 2003), *enforcing* 334 NLRB 835, 173 LRRM 1242 (2001).

theless, held that the employer was not prejudiced by the ALJ's abuse of discretion.

In *United States Postal Service*,[330] the Board adopted the ALJ's decision to strike all of the respondent's defenses because it refused to comply with a subpoena after the ALJ denied respondent's petition to revoke.

In *McAllister Towing & Transportation Co.*,[331] the Board adopted the ALJ's imposition of *Bannon Mills*[332] sanctions against a respondent that failed to produce documents subpoenaed by the general counsel. The respondent had filed timely petitions to revoke the subpoenas, which petitions the ALJ granted in part and denied in part on the morning that the hearing commenced. When the respondent thereafter failed to produce the majority of the subpoenaed documents (which included employees' W-4 forms and job applications), the ALJ imposed sanctions on the grounds that the date of service of the subpoenas, not the date of the order regarding the petitions to revoke, was the date on which respondent was required to begin its attempts to comply with the subpoenas.

In 2001, the Board reaffirmed its policy that "in questions regarding the enforcement or revocation of subpoenas, the Federal Rules of Civil Procedure, although not binding on this Agency, provide useful guidance and should be consulted by Regional Directors and hearing officers when ruling on motions."[333]

The Sixth Circuit has held that a district court in a subpoena enforcement proceeding lacked discretion to delegate to the ALJ the function of conducting an in camera review of the employer's documents subpoenaed by the Board during unfair labor practice proceedings.[334] In an enforcement proceeding in which a party asserts that the subpoenaed documents are privileged, the court, not the ALJ, must determine whether the privilege applies.

Under Section 102.113(e) of the Board's Rules and Regulations, an attorney's unsworn affirmation of service of a subpoena constitutes sufficient proof of service. As a result, in *Best Western City View Motor Inn*,[335] the Board directed the regional director to institute proceedings to enforce the subpoena.

---

[330]339 NLRB 400 n.3, 175 LRRM 1086 (2003).

[331]341 NLRB No. 48, 174 LRRM 1225 (2004).

[332]146 NLRB 611, 633–34, 55 LRRM 1370 (1964).

[333]Marian Manor for the Aged & Infirm, Inc., 333 NLRB 1084, 172 LRRM 1493 (2001).

[334]NLRB v. Detroit Newspapers, 185 F.3d 602, 161 LRRM 3051 (6th Cir. 1999).

[335]327 NLRB 468, 160 LRRM 1221 (1999).

In *Millsboro Nursing & Rehabilitation Center,*[336] the Board reaffirmed the principle that, upon a motion to quash, the Board will quash a broad subpoena for production of records that constitutes a mere "fishing expedition"; there must be some basis in the hearing record that establishes that the records may contain relevant evidence. During an investigation by the general counsel to determine whether evidence would support a *Gissel* bargaining order, the general counsel secured questionnaires from employees who signed authorization cards, but did not testify at the hearing. The Board reaffirmed that such documents in the possession of the general counsel may not be disclosed, even pursuant to a subpoena, without the general counsel's consent,[337] unless they are statements by the witnesses of the general counsel or the charging party, produced after the witnesses have testified.

In an unfair labor practice hearing, the Board affirmed the taking and introduction into the record of pretrial, investigatory depositions that had been obtained pursuant to subpoenas issued by the regional director.[338]

D. Request for Information Under the Freedom of Information Act

The Board added a Freedom of Information Act (FOIA) page to its Web site (www.nlrb.gov) in February 1999. This page includes a number of features, including a detailed FOIA reference guide that explains the right to obtain records under FOIA and instructions for making a FOIA request, a sample FOIA letter, and guidance on where to file a request. It also provides links to an electronic reading room, which provides direct links to the Board's records on the Internet. It is located at www.nlrb.gov, where the FOIA page may be accessed from the Board's home page. The FOIA page was updated in 2001 to allow online "E-FOIA" requests for records from the Board's headquarters.

In November 1999, the Board published a comprehensive FOIA Manual for guiding agency employees in making determinations concerning the public release of agency records under FOIA and in litigating FOIA-based lawsuits. The Manual supersedes all previous general counsel guideline memoranda concerning the processing and litigation of FOIA matters.

---

[336]327 NLRB 879, 160 LRRM 1209 (1999).

[337]Smithfield Packing Co., 334 NLRB 34, 167 LRRM 1085 (2001).

[338]North Bay Plumbing, 327 NLRB 899, 161 LRRM 1639 (1999).

CHAPTER 32

NLRB ORDERS AND REMEDIES

I. GENERAL PRINCIPLES

The Board continues to adhere to the view that it does not have the authority to compel a party to make a bargaining concession or agree to a proposal. Good faith bargaining does not require the parties to agree to a proposal.[1] However, the Board held in *TNT Skypak, Inc.*[2] that the employer committed an unfair labor practice when it

---

[1]Dependable Storage, Inc., 328 NLRB 44, 164 LRRM 1286 (1999). *Accord* Naomi Knitting Plant, 328 NLRB 1279, 168 LRRM 1392 (1999).

[2]328 NLRB 468, 163 LRRM 1299 (1999), *enforced,* 208 F.3d 362, 163 LRRM 2989 (2d Cir. 2000). *See also* Suffield Academy, 336 NLRB 659, 171 LRRM 1491 (2001) (where respondent unlawfully withdrew its tentative bargaining agreement, Board ordered reinstatement of agreement), *enforced,* 322 F.3d 196, 171 LRRM 3164 (2d Cir. 2003); Hardesty Co. dba Mid-Continent Concrete, 336 NLRB 258,

reneged on tentative agreements with the union after it became apparent that the union was going to accept virtually all of the company's positions, making a contract inevitable.

The Supreme Court and the Board have each issued significant decisions regarding back-pay awards. In *Hoffman Plastic Compounds Inc. v. NLRB*,[3] the Supreme Court held that federal immigration policy foreclosed the Board's authority to issue back-pay awards to undocumented workers notwithstanding the fact that their firings constituted unfair labor practices. In *Ferguson Electric Co.*,[4] the Board modified its standard back-pay order to include a paragraph ordering the employer to provide, at a place designated by the Board or its agents, the documents necessary to determine the amount of back pay due.

In *Ishikawa Gasket America, Inc.*,[5] the Board decided that its standard notice language needed to be changed in order to be more clearly and easily understood by employees. The Board modified the standard format to be used in Board notices to include, in simple, straightforward language, a statement of employees' rights; a description of the location, function, and hours of operation of the relevant Board regional office; and the Board's Web site address. The Board

---

171 LRRM 1016 (2001) (issuing order requiring employer to cease and desist from engaging in surface bargaining after concluding that employer had withdrawn initial proposals and introduced regressive proposals), *enforced*, 308 F.3d 859, 171 LRRM 2006 (8th Cir. 2002).

[3]535 U.S. 137, 169 LRRM 2769 (2002). Subsequent to the *Hoffman* decision, the general counsel issued a memorandum to regional offices, which set forth guidance as to how the Supreme Court decision would affect Board procedures and remedies concerning employees who may be undocumented. Memorandum GC 02-06, "NLRB General Counsel Memorandum On Discriminatees Who May Be Undocumented Aliens" (July 19, 2002). *See also* Section III.B.1.c. [Orders and Remedies in Complaint Cases (Section 10); Final Orders and Remedies; Final Orders and Remedies for Employer Misconduct; Sections 8(a)(3) and (4) Violations], *infra*.

[4]335 NLRB 142, 168 LRRM 1025 (2001). The new paragraph reads:

> Preserve and, within 14 days of a request or such additional time as the Regional Director may allow for good cause shown, provide at a reasonable place designated by the Board or its agents, all payroll records, social security payment records, time cards, personnel records and reports, and all other records, including an electronic copy of such records if stored in electronic form, necessary to analyze the amount of backpay due under the terms of this Order.

[5]337 NLRB 175, 169 LRRM 1241 (2001), *aff'd*, 354 F.3d 534, 173 LRRM 2993 (6th Cir. 2004).

"embrace[d] the principle that notices will most effectively apprise employees of their rights, and of the unlawful acts of respondent employers or unions, when they are written in clear laypersons' language."[6] The Board also invited the General Counsel and other parties in future cases to propose simplified notice language describing the specific violations found. In light of *Ishikawa,* the Office of the General Counsel has provided guidelines to regional directors regarding language to include and language to avoid in proposed notices.[7]

II. ORDERS IN REPRESENTATION CASES (SECTION 9)

Extension of the "certification year" rule is within the Board's administrative authority and is reviewed only for an abuse of discretion.[8] In *Chelsea Industries, Inc. v. NLRB,*[9] the D.C. Circuit enforced a Board order that an employer may not withdraw recognition from a union outside the certification year based on evidence received within the certification year.

In representation cases, Board determinations are reviewed under an abuse of discretion standard of judicial review. The courts continue to provide the Board with broad discretion to determine whether the circumstances of a representation election have allowed the employees to exercise free choice in deciding whether to be represented by a union.[10]

---

[6] *Id.* at 176.

[7] Memorandum OM 02-43, "Plain Language in Board Remedial Notices" (Mar. 11, 2002).

[8] NLRB v. Beverly Health & Rehab. Servs. Inc., 187 F.3d 769, 161 LRRM 3066 (8th Cir. 1999) (Board did not abuse its discretion when it extended certification year by 6 months because of employer's bad faith withdrawal from negotiations).

[9] 285 F.3d 1073, 169 LRRM 2961 (D.C. Cir. 2002).

[10] NLRB v. Regional Home Care Servs., Inc., 237 F.3d 62, 166 LRRM 2326 (1st Cir. 2001). *See also* Allen's Elec. Co., 340 NLRB No. 119, 173 LRRM 1425 (2003) (Board refused to set aside election because offer to reimburse some voters for wages actually lost as a result of participation in the election was not a promise of election-related benefits); Quest Int'l, 338 NLRB No. 123, 172 LRRM 1001 (2003) (use of security guards immediately before election did not interfere with employee's free and uncoerced choice in election); NLRB v. Media Gen. Operations, Inc., 360 F.3d 434, 174 LRRM 2481 (4th Cir. 2004) (finding the use of "vote yes" petition was not per se coercive and the regional director's determination that a reasonable employee would not have felt coerced by such conduct was amply supported).

However, the discretion is not unlimited. In *Associated Rubber Co. v. NLRB*,[11] the Eleventh Circuit concluded that the Board erred in certifying a union as the collective bargaining representative where a pro-union employee carried out a threat to punish a co-worker who had opposed the union. Specifically, the pro-union employee punished a co-worker by dropping 450-pound batches of rubber, measuring over 250 degrees Fahrenheit, at faster than normal rates, despite the fact that the co-worker had repeatedly requested a slower pace.

In *Lemoyne-Owen College v. NLRB*,[12] the D.C. Circuit granted a petition for review and remanded the matter to the Board for "an adequate explanation" of its findings. At issue was the regional director's determination to certify a bargaining unit of all full-time faculty employees, while declining to recognize such faculty as managerial employees. In challenging this ruling, the college cited factually similar Board precedent that had been disregarded by the Board when it had denied review. The court of appeals concluded the Board's limited discretion did not allow it to avoid a discussion of the relevant precedent. More specifically, the court concluded that "where, as here, a party makes a significant showing that analogous cases have been decided differently, the agency must do more than simply ignore that argument." While acknowledging the Board could have an appropriate explanation for departing for its precedent, the court noted such an explanation could not be assumed without seeing it and remanded the matter accordingly.

III. ORDERS AND REMEDIES IN COMPLAINT CASES (SECTION 10)

A. Provisional Remedies

1. *General Principles*

a. Discretionary Injunctions Under Section 10(j)

(3) Judicial Standards

In *Pye ex rel. NLRB v. Excel Case Ready*,[13] the First Circuit found that the district court correctly stated the standard for injunctive re-

---

[11]296 F.3d 1055, 170 LRRM 2385 (11th Cir. 2002).
[12]357 F.3d 55, 174 LRRM 2225 (D.C. Cir. 2004).
[13]238 F.3d 69, 166 LRRM 2333 (1st Cir. 2001).

lief in the Section 10(j) context.[14] Although the court considered whether to use a "sliding scale" test to determine whether equitable relief is "just and proper," which would allow a lower threshold for irreparable injury when the likelihood of success on the merits is strong, it did not decide the issue.[15]

In *Willms ex rel. NLRB v. Guard Publishing Co.*,[16] the Ninth Circuit held that in order to secure relief under Section 10(j), the regional director must show either (1) a combination of probable success on the merits and the possibility of irreparable harm, or (2) the existence of serious questions going to the merits, the balance of hardships tipping sharply in its favor, and at least a fair chance of success on the merits. The court also found that a district court, when ruling on the propriety of Section 10(j) relief, must balance the Board's ability to meaningfully adjudicate disputes arising within its jurisdiction against the respondent's showing of hardship.[17]

In *Wells ex rel. NLRB v. Brown & Root, Inc.*,[18] the court found that in the absence of a clear statement of legislative intent or Eleventh Circuit precedent, the court would use traditional equitable principles in interpreting and applying the "just and proper" standards.

In *Schaub v. West Michigan Plumbing & Heating, Inc.*,[19] the Sixth Circuit affirmed the district court's decision that there was reasonable cause to believe that the employer had committed unfair labor practices, and that the regional director's petition for interim injunctive relief was just and proper. The court found interim relief

[14]*Id.* at 76, 166 LRRM at 2338.

[15]*Id.* at 76, 166 LRRM at 2337. Several other circuits have utilized such a test. *See, e.g.*, NLRB v. Electro-Voice, Inc., 83 F.3d 1559, 1568, 152 LRRM 2145, 2152 (7th Cir. 1996); Miller ex rel. NLRB v. California Pac. Med. Ctr., 19 F.3d 449, 460–61, 145 LRRM 2769, 2777–78 (9th Cir. 1994).

[16]25 Fed. Appx. 620, 171 LRRM 2064 (9th Cir.), *cert. denied*, 537 U.S. 826, 171 LRRM 2064 (2002).

[17]*Id.* at 622.

[18]65 F. Supp. 2d 1264 (S.D. Ala. 1999). *Accord* Blyer ex rel. NLRB v. Pratt Towers, Inc., 124 F. Supp. 2d 136 (E.D.N.Y. 2000) (applying "reasonable cause" and "just and proper" standards); Silverman ex rel. NLRB v. J.R.L. Food Corp., 196 F.3d 334, 162 LRRM 2771 (2d Cir. 1999) (district court erred in denying NLRB regional director's petition for temporary injunction where court did not accord ALJ's decision appropriate deference and thus district court's finding of no reasonable cause was not supported by record); Sharp ex rel. NLRB v. Webco, 225 F.3d 1130, 165 LRRM 2353 (10th Cir. 2000) (district court affirmed in granting regional director's petition for temporary injunction where court found that Board produced sufficient evidence to establish reasonable cause for injunction and reinstatement of terminated workers was just and proper relief).

[19]250 F.3d 962 (6th Cir. 2001).

just and proper because it was based on the reasonable conclusion that the effects of the employer's unfair labor practices would "'linger' . . . without such an order and that the employees' ability to exercise their rights to join a union will be chilled if such an order is not issued."[20]

In *Ahearn ex rel. NLRB v. Jackson Hospital Corp.*,[21] the Sixth Circuit affirmed the district court's decision that there was reasonable cause to believe that the hospital's discharge of three strikers violated Sections 8(a)(3) and (5) of the LMRA where hospital "professed a strong anti-union animus, given evidence of supervisors' threats to fire strikers, the Hospital's generally hostile attitude toward the Union, its refusal to engage in collective bargaining, and its display of anti-union signs and use of surveillance during the strike."[22] The court found that multiple terminations of striking employees after the strike ended "would have an inherently chilling effect on other employees."[23] Because of the hospital's actions, the court held that the district court properly found Section 10(j) relief was just and proper.[24]

(4) Temporary Restraining Orders

The district courts continue to issue temporary restraining orders, pending a hearing on the preliminary injunction, pursuant to Section 10(j) of the Act.[25]

(5) Delay in Filing Petition

The effect of a delay in filing the petition for injunctive relief continues to be litigated.[26] In *Blyer ex rel. NLRB v. P&W Electric, Inc.*,[27]

---

[20] *Id.* at 971.

[21] 351 F.3d 226, 173 LRRM 2816 (6th Cir. 2003).

[22] *Id.* at 238, 173 LRRM at 2825.

[23] *Id.* at 239, 173 LRRM at 2825.

[24] *Id.* at 240, 173 LRRM at 2826.

[25] *See, e.g.*, Blyer ex rel. NLRB v. P&W Elec., Inc., 141 F. Supp. 2d 326, 143 Lab. Cas. (CCH) ¶11,063 (E.D.N.Y. 2001); Blyer ex. rel. NLRB v. Platt Towers, Inc., 124 F. Supp. 2d 136 (S.D.N.Y. 2000); Aguayo ex rel. NLRB v. Quadrtech Corp., 129 F. Supp. 2d 1273, 166 LRRM 2293 (C.D. Cal. 2000).

[26] Mattina ex rel. NLRB v. Chinatown Carting Corp., 290 F. Supp. 2d 386, 173 LRRM 2660 (S.D.N.Y. 2003); Moore-Duncan v. Laneko Eng'g, Inc., 2003 WL 23139070, 174 LRRM 2395 (E.D. Pa. 2003).

[27] *P&W Elec.*, *supra* note 25, 141 F. Supp. 2d at 326.

although the Board did not file its petition until 8 months after the employees were discharged, the court found that the Board's delay was not excessive given the amount of time necessary to investigate the charges. Further, the court held that delay by itself is not a determinative factor in whether the grant of interim relief is just and proper.[28]

In *Sharp ex rel. NLRB v. Webco Industries Inc.*,[29] the court found a seven-month delay in the filing of a petition was not unreasonable, although it recognized that the reasonableness of the Board's delay is largely determined on a fact-specific basis. The more time that passes, however, the more difficult it will become to prove the "just and proper" prong of the test.[30]

In *Blyer ex rel. NLRB v. Platt Towers, Inc.*,[31] the employer questioned whether injunctive relief was just and proper given the regional director's delay in filing the petition. In granting the regional director's request for injunctive relief, the court stated that delay should not be considered unless, between the time of the alleged unfair labor practices and the filing of the petition, changes in circumstances occur that affect the appropriateness of such relief.

In *Kentov ex rel. NLRB v. Point Blank Body Armor, Inc.*,[32] the court found that "irreparable harm will be suffered if injunctive relief is not granted."[33] Although a four-month delay occurred between the last firing and the filing of the Section 10(j) petition, the court stated that "it is clear that the delay has not completely weakened the Union, since former employees continue to picket the facility."[34] The employer, citing *Boire ex rel. NLRB v. Pilot Freight Carriers, Inc.*,[35] argued that the delay of four months showed that the granting of an injunction could not be "just and proper."[36] The court, relying on *Arlook ex rel. NLRB v. S. Lichtenberg & Co.*,[37] found that the delay did not de-

[28] *Id.* at 332.

[29] 225 F.3d 1130, 165 LRRM 2353 (10th Cir. 2000).

[30] *Id.* at 1135, 165 LRRM at 2357.

[31] 124 F. Supp. 2d 136 (E.D.N.Y. 2000) (quoting Dunbar ex rel. NLRB v. Carrier Corp., 66 F. Supp. 2d 346, 161 LRRM 2119 (N.D.N.Y. 1999)).

[32] 2003 WL 253063 (S.D. Fla. 2003).

[33] *Id.* at *13.

[34] *Id.*

[35] 515 F.2d 1185, 89 LRRM 2908 (5th Cir. 1975).

[36] *Kentov, supra* note 32, 2003 WL 253063 at *13.

[37] 952 F.2d 367, 139 LRRM 2297 (11th Cir. 1992).

stroy union support and that "relief pursuant to Section 10(j) [would] be much more effective than waiting for a final Board order."[38]

(6) Injunctions Against Employers

In *Aguayo ex rel. NLRB v. Quadrtech Corp.*,[39] the district court issued a temporary restraining order followed by an interim injunction to prevent an employer from laying off employees and relocating operations to Mexico to avoid unionization. The injunctive order required the employer to restore work and equipment that had already been moved, and to bargain in good faith with the recently certified union. *Aguayo* is the first case in which the Board obtained an injunction to prevent an employer from moving its operations to another country.

In *Dunbar ex rel. NLRB v. Carrier Corp.*,[40] on a motion for reconsideration of its order for interim bargaining regarding relocation of bargaining-unit work, pending the outcome of an unfair labor practice proceeding, the court refused both to vacate and to stay its order.[41]

b. Mandatory Injunctions Under Section 10(*l*)

(1) Standards for Issuance

In *Kobell v. African American Workers Union*,[42] the court granted injunctive relief against a labor organization whose picketing at a job site was directed toward municipal and county authorities, as opposed to the contractors working at the site. The court recited several standards involved in reviewing a petition for Section 10(*l*) relief: (1) "the Board faces a relatively insubstantial burden of proof" in Section 10(*l*) proceedings because they are ancillary to the Board's exclusive jurisdiction over unfair labor practices; (2) "[t]he Director's burden is to demonstrate that reasonable cause exists to believe that the elements of an unfair labor practice are present, and that the Director's theory is substantial and not frivolous"; (3) the Board must

---

[38] *Kentov, supra* note 32.

[39] 129 F. Supp. 2d 1273, 166 LRRM 2293 (C.D. Cal. 2000).

[40] 66 F. Supp. 2d 346, 161 LRRM 2119 (N.D.N.Y. 1999).

[41] *See also* Moore-Duncan ex rel. NLRB v. Aldworth Co., 124 F. Supp. 2d 268, 166 LRRM 2338 (D.N.H. 2000) (interim injunction, including reinstatements and bargaining order, approved in light of array of violations asserted).

[42] 162 LRRM 2235 (W.D. Pa. 1999). *Accord* Johnson ex rel. NLRB v. Sunshine Piping, Inc., 238 F. Supp. 2d 1297 (N.D. Fla. 2002).

demonstrate an evidentiary basis for its Section 8(b)(4) violation claim; and (4) the "reasonable cause" standard applies to all legal, factual, and jurisdictional elements as to the violation.[43]

In *Moore-Duncan v. Metropolitan Regional Council of Philadelphia*,[44] the court issued a temporary injunction, pursuant to Section 10(*l*), prohibiting a labor organization from broadcasting protest messages over a sound system outside specified time periods and above acceptable noise levels.

In *Roth ex rel. NLRB v. Electrical Workers Local 15*,[45] the court denied motions filed by third-party businesses to quash the union's subpoenas for depositions and production of documents. The union sought the information in order to establish a defense to the petition for injunctive relief under Section 10(*l*). The court stated that the information sought by the union—the business relationship between the third parties, including the picketed business—was relevant to the issues raised in the petition as well as the union's defense to the allegation of reasonable cause. The court then addressed the scope of discovery in relation to the standard for issuance of injunctive relief. Although inferences from facts are viewed in favor of the petitioner in evaluating whether reasonable cause exists, the question of whether the requested injunctive relief is "just and proper" necessitates an inquiry into the likelihood of the petitioner's success on the merits. Accordingly, union's discovery from third parties would provide additional relevant information as to the merits of the petitioner's case.

In *Kohn ex rel. NLRB v. Southwest Regional Council of Carpenters*,[46] the court refused to issue an injunction to prohibit a union from displaying a banner at a job site because the Board's regional director could not establish a violation of the applicable statutory prohibitions. The court discussed at length the standard that a district court applies in determining whether injunctive relief should issue. The regional director argued that the court, when deciding whether to issue an injunction, should apply the "reasonable cause" analysis that governs the regional director's decision to seek an injunction. Rejecting the regional director's argument, the court noted that it

---

[43] *Id.* at 2238.

[44] 162 LRRM 2615 (E.D. Pa. 1999), *aff'd*, 225 F. 3d 649, 164 LRRM 3024 (3d Cir. 2000).

[45] 2001 WL 1607713 (N.D. Ill. 2001).

[46] 289 F. Supp. 2d 1155 (C.D. Cal. 2003).

"applies traditional equitable criteria in determining whether the requested temporary injunction should issue."[47]

In *Benson v. Carpenters Local 184 & 1498*,[48] the district court also refused to issue injunctions to prohibit unions from displaying banners at or near secondary businesses not directly involved in the unions' labor disputes. The petitioners failed to satisfy the "reasonable cause" prong of the standard for injunctive relief because the unions' conduct did not constitute violations of the prohibition against secondary boycotts. Having denied the requests for injunctive relief due to lack of reasonable cause, the courts declined to address the "just and proper" prong of the analysis.[49]

(2) Injunctions Against Unions

In *Blyer v. Staten Island Cable LLC*,[50] the court enjoined enforcement of collective bargaining agreement provisions that prohibited a contractor from subcontracting work to others not under contract with the union. The court found the injunction necessary to return the situation to the status quo ante because it found the agreement was not a proper work-preservation clause. The case did not involve the Section 8(e) construction-industry proviso as it did not apply to an employer "in the construction industry." In discussing the standard for injunctive relief under Section 10(*l*), the court stated that "where the court finds that the regional director has reasonable cause to find that an unfair labor practice has been committed, 'the district court shall grant injunctive relief as it deems just and proper, notwithstanding any other provision of law.' The propriety of an award of injunctive relief under Section 10 turns upon traditional equity criteria."[51]

B. Final Orders and Remedies

1. *Final Orders and Remedies for Employer Misconduct*

a. Section 8(a)(1) Violations

In *Beverly Health & Rehabilitation Services, Inc.*,[52] the Board disagreed with the ALJ's recommendation of a corporatewide order

---

[47] *Id.* at 1164.
[48] 337 F. Supp. 2d 1275, 175 LRRM 2988 (D. Utah 2004).
[49] *See* Overstreet v. Carpenters Local 1506, 2003 WL 23845186 (S.D. Cal. 2003).
[50] 261 F. Supp. 2d 168 (E.D.N.Y. 2003).
[51] *Id.* at 174.
[52] 339 NLRB 1243, 173 LRRM 1137 (2003).

and notice posting. Although the Board had previously issued corporatewide remedies in other cases involving the respondent, the Board held that this case was distinguishable:

> In those cases, the Respondent committed multiple violations at multiple locations with high-ranking corporate and regional officials either visiting the facilities at issue and playing a role in the unlawful conduct, or taking prominent roles in directing, approving, or knowingly failing to prevent unlawful actions. Here, the Respondent committed three types of unfair labor practices at one facility with a state manager being the perpetrator in two instances. As such, this case involves discrete violations at an individual facility, and, as in other similar cases involving this Respondent, traditional remedies are warranted.[53]

Accordingly, the Board held that a corporate-wide remedy was not warranted.

In *International Business Machines Corp.*,[54] at the compliance stage of the proceeding, the union requested that the Board require the respondent to post the Board's remedial notice on its electronic mail system and intranet, as well as on its traditional paper bulletin boards. The Board declined the union's request, noting that if the union wanted such a provision in the order, it should have sought such from the ALJ and the Board. The Board did not pass on the issue of whether electronic posting should be required by the Board's standard remedial notice posting language where the respondent customarily posts notices to employees in that manner.

Where appropriate, the Board will order special remedies. In *High Point Construction Group, LLC,* the Board issued a broad cease-and-desist order to "cleanse the atmosphere of the effects of the Respondent's unlawful conduct," finding that the imposition of a bargaining order was unnecessary. The Board also ordered that the notice be read aloud to employees by a management official or, alternatively, by a Board agent in the presence of a management official.[55]

---

[53] *Id.*, 173 LRRM at 1139.
[54] 339 NLRB 966, 173 LRRM 1037 (2003).
[55] 342 NLRB No. 36, 175 LRRM 1352 (2004).

Where appropriate, the Board continues to order that notice be mailed to employees.[56]

The Board may also order that a respondent pay reasonable expenses, including legal expenses, that have been incurred in connection with the unlawful conduct.[57]

c. Section 8(a)(3) and (4) Violations

(1) In General

The Board continues to order expungement in disciplinary cases.[58]

The Board will base a back-pay award on an employee's proven income from tips, despite the fact that a lower amount was reported to the Internal Revenue Service by the employee.[59]

In a case that highlighted the problem of lump-sum back-pay payments resulting in extra taxes for employees,[60] the general counsel requested that the employer reimburse the employee for that payment. The Board decided that because the issue was not fully briefed by the parties, it was not appropriate to order the employer to reimburse an employee for additional taxes, because it would involve a change in Board law. The case suggests that the Board may examine this issue if fully briefed by the parties.[61]

When determining a back-pay remedy, the Board continues to consider an employer's "after-acquired evidence" of nondiscrimina-

---

[56]NLRB v. Communications Workers Local 13000, 114 Fed. Appx. 493 (3rd Cir. 2004) (Board order enforced directing respondent union to mail a copy of remedial notice to all 7,500 bargaining unit members); Systems W. LLC, 342 NLRB No. 82, 175 LRRM 1281 (2004) (remedial notice sent to former employees); Reigel Elec. & Cent. Elec. Servs., 341 NLRB No. 3, 174 LRRM 1158 (2004) (respondent closed its facility).

[57]341 NLRB No. 20, 174 LRRM 1088 (2004).

[58]Detroit Newspapers, 340 NLRB No. 121, 173 LRRM 1455 (2003).

[59]Atlantic Limousine, Inc., 328 NLRB 257, 258, 166 LRRM 1291, 1292 (1999), *enforced*, 243 F.3d 711, 166 LRRM 2864 (3d Cir. 2001).

[60]Colden Hills, Inc., 337 NLRB 560, 170 LRRM 1057 (2002).

[61]Smucker Co., 341 NLRB No. 10 (2004) (back pay limited because employee cheated on respondent's pre-employment skills test, despite fact that there was no evidence that respondent had express policy or past practice prohibiting cheating on preemployment exam); ADS Elec. Co., 339 NLRB 1020, 173 LRRM 1540 (2003) (evidence that employees misrepresented their work experience).

tory reasons that the employer would have terminated the employee.[62] However, an employer may not be relieved of the back-pay obligation for an unlawful refusal to recall a laid-off employee, even if the employer contends it would be futile to do so. In *Mining Specialists, Inc.*,[63] the employer was required to pay subsequent back pay to an employee it unlawfully refused to recall despite the employer's contention that it would have been futile to make such a recall offer because the employee was incarcerated at the time.

A union "salt" will be awarded back pay for the term of the construction project, notwithstanding that the "salt" might have resigned after the union organizing efforts were successful or that the "salt" received income from the union for organizing services.[64] Wages paid by the union to the "salt" are earnings from secondary employment and are not offset against gross back pay.[65] A union "salt" is not ineligible for back pay because he follows his usual practice of seeking work through the union's hiring hall.[66] Nor is a union "salt" penalized if he terminates his employment with a nonunion employer because the union withdraws its work authorization, exposing the "salt" to internal union discipline.[67]

In *Diamond Walnut Growers, Inc.*,[68] the Board limited an employee's back-pay award because the employee quit after he was reinstated. In its opinion, the Board discussed its approach to back-pay awards. First, the Board observed that "although there is presumption whenever there is an unlawful deprivation of employment that backpay is owed for the entire period between the discrimination and a valid offer of reinstatement, the presumption is rebuttable."[69] Second, the Board reaffirmed that it has "broad discretion-

---

[62]North Am. Dismantling Corp., 341 NLRB No. 95, 174 LRRM 1525 (2004) (back pay cut off where employee would have been denied reemployment because he attempted to steal company business); Berkshire Farm Ctr., 333 NLRB 367, 166 LRRM 1243, 1244 (2001) (back-pay obligation ceases as of the date the employer discovers nondiscriminatory evidence that would have resulted in termination).

[63]335 NLRB 1275, 172 LRRM 1123 (2001), *enforced*, 326 F.3d 602, 172 LRRM 2385 (4th Cir. 2003).

[64]Ferguson Elec. Co., 330 NLRB 514, 516 n.10, 163 LRRM 1081, 1083–85 (2000), *enforced*, 242 F.3d 426, 432, 166 LRRM 2513, 2516 (2d Cir. 2001).

[65]*Id.*

[66]Tualatin Elec. Inc., 331 NLRB 36, 167 LRRM 1247, 1248–49 (2000), *enforced*, 253 F.3d 714, 167 LRRM 2743 (D.C. Cir. 2001).

[67]*Id.*, 331 NLRB at 37, 167 LRRM at 1248–49.

[68]340 NLRB No. 135 (2003).

[69]*Id.*, slip op. at 4.

ary" authority to tailor its remedies on a case-specific basis to ensure that the remedy is appropriate to the case. Third, the Board also held that the remedial order should not place the employee in a better position than he would have been in had the unfair labor practice not occurred. [70]

In *Hoffman Plastic Compounds, Inc. v. NLRB*,[71] the Supreme Court revisited its 1984 decision in *Sure-Tan, Inc. v. NLRB*,[72] reviewing whether it was appropriate to award back pay to an undocumented worker hired without the employer's knowledge of his immigration status and then unlawfully terminated for his union activities. The Court found that the 1986 Immigration Reform and Control Act, adopted after *Sure-Tan*, is a clear expression of congressional policy prohibiting the employment of undocumented workers. The Supreme Court acknowledged that terminating an undocumented worker for union activities was an unfair labor practice, but held that federal immigration policy precluded the Board from awarding back pay to an undocumented worker who was never authorized to work in the United States.

Because the employer in *Hoffman* was unaware of the employee's undocumented status, the case did not explicitly address the propriety of awarding back pay to unlawfully terminated undocumented employees hired by an employer with knowledge of their undocumented status.[73] Although acknowledging that the *Hoffman* arguably does not affect the Board's remedy for a knowing employer, the general counsel has interpreted *Hoffman* as precluding the award of back pay under either circumstance, because of the Supreme Court's focus on the employee's wrongdoing.[74] Accordingly, regions currently are instructed that back pay should not be sought for any undocu-

---

[70]*Id. See also* Webco Indus., Inc., 340 NLRB No. 1 (2003) (reimbursement for various bonuses was uniquely crafted in light of employee's experience).

[71]535 U.S.137, 169 LRRM 2769 (2002).

[72]467 U.S. 883, 116 LRRM 2857 (1984).

[73]Justice Breyer in his dissent specifically states that the question of a knowing employer is "a circumstance not before us today. . . . ." 535 U.S. at 155, 169 LRRM at 2777. The majority did not question Justice Breyer's assertion. Thus, it is not clear whether the back-pay prohibition in *Hoffman* applies to just unknowing employers or knowing employers as well. *See also* Singh v. Jutla, 2002 WL 1808589, at *4 (N.D. Cal. Aug. 5, 2002) (whether *Hoffman* applies to knowing employer is open question).

[74]Memorandum GC 02-06, "Procedures and Remedies for Discriminatees Who May Be Undocumented Aliens after *Hoffman Plastic Compounds, Inc.*"

mented employees in discharge situations. Back pay may, however, be sought in nondischarge cases,[75] e.g., unilateral changes of pay or benefits.[76]

The Board changed the language in its back-pay specifications, requiring that the respondent make records available at a "reasonable place to be designated by the Board or its agent,"[77] noting that production will not always be appropriate at the region's offices. The Board also gave the regional director discretion to extend the 14-day period for production for good cause. A respondent must produce electronic copies of documents relating to back pay where the documents already exist in that format.[78]

In discriminatory refusal-to-hire cases, where the number of applicants exceeds the number of jobs available, the compliance proceeding will determine which of the applicants would have been hired and the amount of back pay to which they are entitled.[79] In refusal-to-consider cases, the appropriate remedy is a cease-and-desist order; an order requiring the employer to consider the discriminatees for job openings based upon nondiscriminatory criteria; and an order requiring the employer to notify the region, the discriminatees, and the charging party of future openings in the same or substantially equivalent positions.[80] If positions become available after the beginning of the case on the merits of the charge, the general counsel must initiate compliance proceedings to determine whether the employer would have hired the applicants but for illegal discrimination.[81]

The Board continues to deny back pay to discriminatees found to have willfully concealed their interim employment.[82] Similarly, an employee who engages in misconduct or provides false testimony in

---

[75] *Id.* at Section C-2.

[76] *Id.* Thus, the Board will be in a position to make a determination on whether *Hoffman* affects the remedy in the case of a knowing employer only if a charging party, with full participatory rights in a compliance proceeding, argues that *Hoffman* does not affect an undocumented employee's right to back pay in the case of a knowing employer in discharge situations.

[77] Ferguson Elec. Co., 335 NLRB 142, 168 LRRM 1025, 1028 (2001).

[78] Merit Elec. Co., 328 NLRB 212, 214 n.7, 163 LRRM 1196, 1198 n.7 (1999).

[79] FES, 331 NLRB 9, 14, 164 LRRM 1065, 1073 (2000).

[80] *Id.* at 15, 164 LRRM at 1075.

[81] *Id.*

[82] Performance Friction Corp., 338 NLRB 986, 174 LRRM 1104, *enforced*, 118 Fed. Appx. 721, 176 LRRM 2576 (4th Cir. 2004).

a pretrial affidavit or at a hearing may be denied back pay and/or reinstatement.[83]

d. Section 8(a)(5) Violations

(1) In General

The D.C. Circuit has required the Board to justify in each case where a bargaining order is issued why such an order is warranted as a remedy.[84] Specifically, the court has held that the Board must "balance three considerations: (1) the employees' §7 rights; (2) whether other purposes of the Act override the rights of the employees to choose their bargaining representatives; and (3) whether alternative remedies are adequate to remedy the violations of the Act."[85] Despite the court's holding, the Board has yet to abandon its holding in *Caterair International*[86] that an affirmative bargaining order is "the traditional, appropriate remedy for an 8(a)(5) violation."[87]

(2) Duration of Bargaining Order

In *Lee Lumber & Building Material Corp.*,[88] the Board modified its rule governing the presumed insulated period when an employer is ordered to bargain with an incumbent union (not newly certified) and adopted a rule granting the union a minimum period of six months during which the union's majority status may not be challenged. The Board may extend the insulated period a maximum of an additional six months depending on five factors: (1) whether the parties are bargaining for a first contract; (2) the complexity of the issues being negotiated and the bargaining processes; (3) the time

---

[83]Precoat Metals, 341 NLRB No. 143, 175 LRRM 1110 (2004); Toll Mfg. Co., 341 NLRB No. 115, 175 LRRM 1009 (2004) (employee denied back pay after date he lied to NLRB).

[84]*See, e.g.*, Vincent Indus. Plastics v. NLRB, 209 F.3d 727, 164 LRRM 2039 (D.C. Cir. 2000).

[85]*Id.* at 734, 164 LRRM at 2047–48.

[86]322 NLRB 64, 153 LRRM 1153 (1996).

[87]MSK Corp., 341 NLRB No. 11, 174 LRRM 1143 (2004) (affirmative bargaining order ordered); Kentucky Fried Chicken, 341 NLRB No. 13, 174 LRRM 1049 (2004) (Member Schaumber stated that he disagreed with the Board's view expressed in *Caterair International*, and agreed with the D.C. Circuit that an affirmative bargaining order is an "extreme remedy"); Community Health Servs., Inc. dba Mimbres Mem. Hosp. & Nursing Home, 342 NLRB No. 33, 175 LRRM 1028 (2004).

[88]334 NLRB 399, 402, 167 LRRM 1185, 1190–91 (2001), *enforced*, 310 F.3d 309, 171 LRRM 2269 (D.C. Cir. 2002).

since bargaining commenced and the number of bargaining sessions; (4) progress in negotiations and how close the parties are to agreement; and (5) whether the parties are at impasse.

In instances where an employer refuses to bargain with a newly certified union, the Board will issue a bargaining order and a one-year extension of initial certification to begin on the date that the employer begins to bargain in good faith with the union.[89]

(5) Remedies for Particular Kinds of Section 8(a)(5) Violations

(a) *Unilateral Changes.* In instances of unilateral changes, the Board will not necessarily dictate that the changes be reversed. In a recent case, where the employer made unilateral changes that could benefit employees, the Board ordered the employer to rescind the changes only at the union's request.[90] The Board will not necessarily require an employer to rescind the negative consequences that a unilateral action has on employees. In *Anheuser-Busch,* the Board held that an employer was not required to rescind 16 instances of discipline that resulted from the use of a surveillance camera, although the employer unilaterally installed and used the surveillance cameras without giving notice to the union.[91]

(b) Supplying Information. Where the employer has refused to provide the union with information because of a legitimate and substantial confidentiality interest, but the confidentiality is not so great as to preclude all disclosure, the Board may order the employer to bargain with the union over safeguards for the disclosure of the confidential information to remedy the violation of Section 8(a)(5).[92]

(c) *Bargaining Orders Without Certification.* (i) *Where the union can show a majority.* Where a union can establish majority status, the Board continues to issue *Gissel* bargaining orders to remedy employer unfair labor practices that are serious enough to interfere with the Board's election process or preclude a fair Board election. The D.C. Circuit continues to remand a number of these cases to the Board, demanding that it weigh the rights of employees to choose their bar-

---

[89]Kankalee Valley Elec. Corp., 338 NLRB 906, 173 LRRM 1423 (2003).

[90]Fresno Bee, 339 NLRB 1214, 173 LRRM 1393 (2003).

[91]342 NLRB No. 49, 175 LRRM 1168 (2004), *enforced in part,* 2005 WL 1560399 (D.C. Cir. 2005).

[92]Metropolitan Edison Co., 330 NLRB 107, 163 LRRM 1001, 1003 (1999); Garcia Trucking Serv., Inc., 342 NLRB No. 75, 175 LRRM 1206 (2004) (employer ordered to provide explanation as to why outstanding requested information was not available, in addition to providing the information and making reasonable attempts to procure any unavailable information).

gaining representative against whether alternatives methods of enforcement are adequate to remedy violations of the Act.[93] The D.C. Circuit also requires that the Board consider whether changes in the bargaining unit since the commission of the unfair labor practices, including employee turnover, preclude imposition of a bargaining order. Despite significant changes in the bargaining unit, the Board continues to issue bargaining orders.[94] The Board did not issue a *Gissel* bargaining order where there were significant changes in management and the managers who committed the unfair labor practices were no longer employed and where the case had had a "long delay" at the Board. The Board concluded that in these circumstances it "would likely be unenforceable in the courts."[95]

In cases where the union loses the rerun election and the Board does not issue a *Gissel* bargaining order because of the passage of time since the employer's unfair labor practices, the Board may order the employer to provide the union with the names and addresses of all current employees for a period of 12 months so that the union may engage in further organizational efforts free of further coercion.[96]

(d) Execution of Contractual Provisions Where There Is an Agreement. An employer may be required to sign a Section 8(f) collective bargaining agreement, notwithstanding the presence of an illegal clause in the agreement, if a "saving clause" can be used to excise the illegal clause.[97] When the employer has reneged on tentative agreements that would have resulted in a collective bargaining agreement but for the employer's unlawful conduct, the Board's remedy will require that any collective bargaining agreement that results from the union's acceptance of the employer's reinstated offer shall apply retroactively to the date of the employer's unfair labor practice.[98]

---

[93]*See, e.g.*, Douglas Foods Corp. v. NLRB, 251 F.3d 1056, 167 LRRM 2380 (D.C. Cir. 2001).

[94]Garvey Marine, Inc., 328 NLRB 991, 163 LRRM 1253 (1999), *enforced*, 245 F.3d 819, 167 LRRM 2001 (D.C. Cir. 2001) (imposing bargaining order despite change in ownership and substantial turnover).

[95]Audubon Reg'l Med. Ctr., 331 NLRB 374 (2000).

[96]Regal Recycling Inc., 329 NLRB 355, 357, 163 LRRM 1245, 1249 (1999).

[97]W. R. Mollohan, Inc., 333 NLRB 1339, 1340, 167 LRRM 1097, 1099 (2001), *enforced*, 309 F.3d 1, 171 LRRM 2065 (D.C. Cir. 2002).

[98]TNT Skypak, Inc., 328 NLRB 468, 470, 163 LRRM 1299, 1301 (1999) (overruling Driftwood Convalescent Hosp., 312 NLRB 247, 146 LRRM 1009 (1993), to the extent inconsistent), *enforced sub nom.* TNT USA, Inc. v. NLRB, 208 F.3d 362, 163 LRRM 2989 (2d Cir. 2000).

(h) Remedies Against Successor to Bargaining Obligation. Not only is a successor required to recognize and bargain with the collective bargaining representative of its predecessor's employees, it may also be liable to remedy the unfair labor practices of the predecessor.[99] Thus, in *Amersig Graphics, Inc. dba American Signature, Inc.*,[100] a *Golden State* successor employer was ordered to offer reinstatement to former strikers, notwithstanding the policy that a *Burns* successor is generally free to make its own hiring choices.

(i) Withdrawal of Recognition. Where an employer is found to have unlawfully withdrawn recognition, in addition to ordering the employer to recognize and bargain with the union, the Board may order the employer to pay the union the dues that should have been remitted during the contract period, with interest.[101]

2. *Special Remedial Problems Involving Employers*

a. Flagrant Violations

The Board continues to order "extraordinary" remedies in cases in which the employer commits pervasive or outrageous unfair labor practices. In *NLRB v. Beverly California Corp.*,[102] the Board found that the employer had committed over 100 unfair labor practices in a significant number of its facilities across the nation and issued a broad cease-and-desist order to all the employer's facilities nationwide which was enforced by the Seventh Circuit. In response to the Seventh Circuit's enforcement of the order, the Office of the General Counsel issued a memorandum regarding compliance with the nationwide order.[103] The memorandum advised regional offices to review new charges against *Beverly* for contempt of the order.

The Board recently reversed an ALJ recommendation to issue special remedies to a different Beverly location where the unfair labor practices involved discrete violations at an individual facility. In

[99]Golden State Bottling Co. v. NLRB, 414 U.S. 168, 84 LRRM 2839 (1973).

[100]334 NLRB 880, 169 LRRM 1458 (2001).

[101]Heartland Health Care Ctr., 341 NLRB No. 49, 174 LRRM 1263 (2004).

[102]334 NLRB 713, 167 LRRM 1155 (2001), *enforced*, 25 Fed. Appx. 427, 171 LRRM 3215 (7th Cir. 2001).

[103]Memorandum OM 02-38, "Compliance and Possible Violations by Beverly California Corporation f/k/a Beverly Enterprises with Corporate Wide Order in *Beverly II* and *Beverly III*" (Feb. 22, 2002).

Beverly Health & Rehabilitation Services, Inc.,[104] the ALJ found that the corporatewide remedies were warranted because of the company's propensity to violate the Act and its sustained, corporate-level union animus. While the Board agreed that a second election was warranted, it declined to adopt the special corporatewide remedies even though two of the unfair labor practices were committed by a high-level employee.

In *Federated Logistics & Operations*,[105] the Board found that extraordinary remedies were warranted where the company engaged in serious unfair labor practices that pervaded the bargaining unit, were made by high-level management officials in close temporal proximity to the election, and had a long-term coercive impact on the unit. Among the remedies ordered were (1) a broad cease-and-desist order; (2) a public reading of the notice by a Board agent or responsible management official; (3) the furnishing of periodic, updated lists of employee names and addresses to the union; (4) the holding of a second election off site; (5) union access to the facility; and (6) notice and equal time for the union for captive audience meetings.

Yet in *Northwest Graphics, Inc.*, the Board affirmed the ALJ's finding that there was no basis to order the "extraordinary" remedy of requiring the employer's highest-ranking official to read the notice to its employees given the limited nature of the unfair labor practices committed.[106]

In *Avondale Industries, Inc. (Avondale I)*,[107] the Board ordered the employer to comply with the special remedies imposed in *Fieldcrest Cannon, Inc.*[108] The Board concluded that the quantity and severity of the unfair labor practices warranted the imposition of special mailing and published-notice remedies. The Board modified the ALJ's order to provide that the notice could be read to employees by

---

[104] 339 NLRB 1243, 173 LRRM 1137 (2003); *see also* U.S. Postal Serv. Letter Carriers Branch 28, 341 NLRB No. 100, 176 LRRM 1302 (2004) (in light of three districtwide Board orders enforced by the Fifth Circuit in the same vicinty, the Board modified the ALJ's recommendations to issue the special remedy of a districtwide posting to only the postal facilities subject to the unfair labor practice charges).

[105] 340 NLRB No. 36, 173 LRRM 1210 (2003).

[106] 343 NLRB No. 16, 176 LRRM 1167 (2004)

[107] 329 NLRB 1064, 165 LRRM 1228 (1999).

[108] 318 NLRB 470, 473–74, 152 LRRM 1173, 1177–78 (1995).

either a responsible supervisory official of the employer above the departmental level or, at the employer's option, by a Board agent, with the responsible supervisory official present while the notice was read.

The Board also concluded that, in light of the Fifth Circuit's direction of a second election, special access remedies were necessary to eliminate the effects of the employer's widespread, serious, and pervasive unfair labor practices and to ensure a fair and free election. These special remedies required the employer to (1) supply the union, on request made within one year of the date of the decision and order, the full names and addresses of its current employees; (2) on request, grant the union and its representatives reasonable access to the employer's bulletin boards and all places where notices to employees were customarily posted; (3) on request, grant the union reasonable access to its facilities in nonwork areas during employees' nonwork time; (4) give notice of, and equal time and facilities for the union to respond to, any address made by the employer to its employees on the question of union representation; and (5) afford the union the right to deliver a 30-minute speech to employees, on working time, prior to any Board election that may be scheduled in which the union is a participant. Subsequent to that order, however, the parties sought and secured the Board's approval of a settlement agreement providing for the elimination of the special remedies provided by the Board in *Avondale I.*[109]

Exceptional notice requirements were also found appropriate in *Audubon Regional Medical Center*[110] and *Excel Case Ready,*[111] based upon the nature and range of the employers' violations of the Act.[112]

---

[109]Avondale Indus., Inc. (Avondale II), 337 NLRB 33, 171 LRRM 1015 (2001); *but cf. Miller Indus. Towing Equip.*, 342 NLRB No. 112, 176 LRRM 1103 (2004) (Board adopted the ALJ's recommendation to deny the union's request for special notice and access remedies under statute because the violations committed by the employer were not "so numerous, pervasive and outrageous" as to warrant despite a second election being ordered).

[110]331 NLRB 374, 169 LRRM 1213 (2000). *See* discussion at note 102, *supra.*

[111]334 NLRB 4, 169 LRRM 1407 (2001) (adopting ALJ's additional notice and access remedies, including orders to provide union with names and addresses of bargaining-unit employees, to grant reasonable access to employer's bulletin boards, and to have management official or Board agent read notice to employees during work time).

[112]Miramar Sheraton Hotel, 336 NLRB 1203, 171 LRRM 1346 (2001) (rejecting ALJ's recommended affirmative record-keeping remedy).

In *Ishikawa Gasket America, Inc.*,[113] however, the Board in the absence of "full briefing by the affected parties," declined to reverse established Board law to reimburse discriminatees entitled to monetary awards for any extra state income taxes that would result from a lump-sum payment award.[114] The Board also held that the employer's conduct was not so egregious to warrant a requirement that the employer read the notice directly to the employees during working time.

In *International Business Machines Corp.*,[115] following a 2001 ruling that the company had committed unfair labor practices, the Board ordered the company to post copies of the accompanying notice "in conspicuous places including all places where notices to employees are customarily posted."[116] The union argued that the company should have to post the notice on its intranet or distribute it through its e-mail system. The majority of the Board rejected that proposed remedy. Without addressing the policy issue of electronic posting, the majority noted that there was no Board precedent for an order to be electronically posted and that the union should have requested electronic posting during the liability stage of the case instead of during the remedial stage so that both parties could have adequately addressed the issue. Dissenting Member Walsh agreed with the union, noting that the company customarily and almost exclusively used its intranet to communicate with employees and the company lacked physical bulletin boards.

In *Overnite Transportation Co. (Overnite I)*,[117] the Board adopted the ALJ's decision and order issuing *Gissel* bargaining orders at four of Overnite's service centers where the local union lost elections, after finding that the employer engaged in extensive unfair labor practices that involved "hallmark" violations. These "hallmark" violations included the granting of unprecedented wage increases; threats of job loss and closing of business; assertions that bargaining would be futile; promises of better benefits, overtime policies, and vacation; and threats of stricter discipline and more onerous working conditions.[118] On appeal, a divided Fourth Circuit enforced the

---

[113] 337 NLRB 175, 169 LRRM 1241 (2001).

[114] Superior Prot., Inc., 339 NLRB 954, 2003 WL 21802944 (2003) (given that such relief would be change in Board law, Board again deferred to address issue until there is full briefing by affected parties).

[115] 339 NLRB 966, 173 LRRM 1037 (2003).

[116] *Id.*, 173 LRRM at 1037.

[117] 329 NLRB 990, 166 NLRB 1101 (1999).

[118] *See also* General Fabrications Corp., 328 NLRB 1114, 162 LRRM 1100 (1999), *enforced*, 222 F.3d 218, 164 LRRM 2974 (6th Cir. 2000).

Board's order.[119] On rehearing en banc, however, the court vacated its earlier decision, finding that *Gissel* orders were not warranted, remanded the case, and ordered new elections.[120] Specifically, the court held that the Board failed to "direct us to evidence that a new, fair election could not be conducted in the circumstances presented."[121]

The Board has issued bargaining orders in several other cases. Notably, in *Aldworth Co.*,[122] the Board held that the employer engaged in a severe and pervasive campaign to eradicate pro-union sentiment, beginning immediately upon the commencement of the organizational campaign and extending well beyond the election. The unlawful conduct included the solicitation of grievances, threats of unlawful bargaining tactics, threats of job and benefit loss, interrogation, threats of plant closure, the implementation of a new performance standard, the suspensions and terminations of union sympathizers and the reassignments of union sympathizers to less desirable jobs. According to the Board, even though a significant number of employees had since departed, the employer's rampant anti-union conduct created "a legacy of hostility that will pervade the atmosphere for sometime to come,"[123] thus making a bargaining order appropriate.

---

[119]Overnite Transp. Co. v. NLRB, 240 F.3d 325, 166 LRRM 2577 (4th Cir. 2001).

[120]Overnite Transp. Co., 280 F.3d 417, 169 LRRM 2469 (4th Cir. 2002). *See also* MJ Metal Prods., Inc. v NLRB, 267 F.3d 1059, 168 LRRM 2800 (10th Cir. 2001) (court found that discharge of 4 out of 15 employees heightened effect and coupled with other unfair labor practices supported issuance of remedial bargaining order); Parts Depot, Inc. v. NLRB, 24 Fed. Appx. 1, 2001 WL 1610068 (D.C. Cir. 2001) (Category II bargaining order justified on finding that employer's pervasive unfair labor practices undermined election process).

[121]*Overnite Transp. Co.*, *supra* note 120, 280 F.3d at 436, 169 LRRM at 2482. In a separate decision, the Fourth Circuit upheld the Board's order in *Overnite Transp. Co. (Overnite II)*, 334 NLRB 1074, 168 (2001), requiring the employer to bargain with unions who won representation elections at four other sites operated by the employer. Overnite Transp. Co. v. NLRB, 294 F.3d 615, 170 LRRM 2362 (4th Cir. 2002). In *Overnite II*, local unions had won elections at four of Overnite's terminals. Overnite refused to bargain with the local unions because of alleged post-election union violence during a nationwide strike of the international union against Overnite. The Fourth Circuit affirmed the Board's bargaining order requiring Overnite to negotiate with the four local unions.

[122]338 NLRB 137, 171 LRRM 1033 (2002), *enforced sub nom.* Dunkin Donuts Mid-Atlantic Distrib. Ctr. v. NLRB, 363 F.3d 437, 174 LRRM 2746 (D.C. Cir.), *supplemented by* 343 NLRB No. 97, 2004 WL 2899844 (2004).

[123]*Id.*, 171 LRRM at 1050.

In *U.S.A. Polymer Corp.*,[124] the Board issued a *Gissel* bargaining order, despite the passage of several years, because the employer committed numerous, egregious violations that constituted Category I conduct within the meaning of *Gissel*, such as laying off nearly one-half of the bargaining unit, coupled with statements that the layoffs were due to the employees' support of the union. In *State Materials, Inc.*,[125] the Board held that a bargaining order was justified, despite the passage of time, because of the employer's *Gissel* Category II violations. In addition, there was evidence that the employer remained committed to an antiunion position and that a substantial number of unit employees remained employed.

In *Allied General Services, Inc.*,[126] the Board ordered reinstatement, the reestablishment of closed operations, and a *Gissel* order based upon a finding of Category I violations. In *Dorsey Trailers, Inc.*,[127] the Board ordered the employer to reestablish the operations of a closed facility and to bargain with the union. On petition for review, the Fourth Circuit upheld the Board's findings that the employer committed many unfair labor practices, but concluded that these unfair labor practices did not warrant an order requiring the employer to reopen the closed plant.[128] In *Climatrol, Inc.*,[129] the Board held that the employer engaged in conduct that justified imposition of a *Gissel* order under Category I. In *Cogburn Healthcare Center*,[130] the Board

[124] 328 NLRB 1242, 168 LRRM 1427 (1999), *enforced*, 272 F.3d 289, 168 LRRM 2897 (5th Cir. 2001), *cert. denied*, 536 U.S. 939, 170 LRRM 2288 (2002).

[125] 328 NLRB 1317, 168 LRRM 1114 (1999).

[126] 329 NLRB 568, 167 LRRM 1072 (1999).

[127] 327 NLRB 835, 165 LRRM 1392 (1999).

[128] Dorsey Trailers, Inc. v. NLRB, 233 F.3d 831, 165 LRRM 3003 (4th Cir. 2000).

[129] 329 NLRB 946, 169 LRRM 1385 (1999). *See also* Bonham Heating & Air Conditioning Inc., 328 NLRB 432, 161 LRRM 1113 (1999), *enforced*, 230 F.3d 1359 (6th Cir. 2000) (unpublished); Regional Home Care, Inc., 329 NLRB 85, 166 LRRM 1112 (1999), *enforced*, 237 F.3d 62, 166 LRRM 2326 (1st Cir. 2001); Wire Prods. Mfg. Corp., 329 NLRB 155, 165 LRRM 1014 (1999).

[130] 335 NLRB 1397, 171 LRRM 1021(2001). *See also* Michael's Painting, Inc., 337 NLRB 860, 171 LRRM 1186 (2002) (issuing *Gissel* order in Category II case where employer's actions of threatening to close company, discharging five union supporters, demanding documentation of immigration status, interfering with lawful pickets, and interrogating employees prevented the conduct of a fair election), *enforced*, 85 Fed. Appx. 614, 2004 WL 68660 (9th Cir. 2004); Mercedes Benz of Orland Park, 333 NLRB 1017, 171 LRRM 1081 (2001) (bargaining order warranted where employer discharged or threatened to discharge pro-union workers, conducted surveillance of striking workers, abandoned commitment to improve employee benefits, and refused to allow striking workers to return to work in spite of unconditional offers), *enforced sub nom.* NLRB v. Orland Park Motor Cars, 309 F.3d 452, 171 LRRM 2139 (7th Cir. 2002); Joseph Stallone Elec. Contractors, 337 NLRB

adopted the ALJ's recommendation that a *Gissel* bargaining order issue where the employer's misconduct, including coercive interrogations, threats of discharge, actual discharge, establishment of discriminatory rules, and surveillance of union activities, directly affected a substantial percentage of employees and thereby precluded the holding of a fair election. In *Servco Automatic Machine Products Co.*,[131] the Board ordered the employer to bargain with the union concerning the effect on its employees of the closing of its facility and to pay limited back pay. The Board required the employer to mail a copy of the notice to the union and to the last known address of its former employees to inform them of the outcome of the proceeding.[132] In *Traction Wholesale Center Co. v. NLRB*,[133] the court upheld a *Gissel* bargaining order imposed on the employer because of the magnitude of its unfair labor practices, the small size of the unit, the involvement of the employer's owners, and the finding by the Board that the unfair labor practices were so pervasive that a rerun election would not fairly reflect the views of a majority of the unit.

On the other hand, the Board declined to issue *Gissel* orders when there was a long delay between the alleged unfair labor practices and the Board's decision. In *Comcast Cablevision*,[134] for example, the Board directed a second election rather than imposing the *Gissel* bargaining order due to a 9-year delay from the date of the election to the Board's decision in processing the case and to avoid further litigation. The Board did, however, order the employer to supply the union with the names and addresses of all current unit employees,

1139, 171 LRRM 1135 (2002) (adopting ALJ's recommendation that *Gissel* order in Category II case issue where unit was small and employer threatened to and discharged employees engaged in lawful strike, interrogated employees, and laid off pro-union employees).

[131]332 NLRB No. 119, 165 LRRM 1344 (2000) (summary judgment, unpublished NLRB Rep.).

[132]*See also* K & C Supply, Inc., 332 NLRB No. 141, 166 LRRM 1056 (2000) (summary judgment, unpublished NLRB Rep.).

[133]216 F.3d 92, 164 LRRM 2769 (D.C. Cir. 2000). *See also* National Propane Partners, L.P., 337 NLRB 1006, 171 LRRM 1496 (2002) (adopting ALJ's imposition of remedial bargaining order where employer unlawfully terminated 50% of small unit and threatened to close plant during organizing campaign).

[134]328 NLRB 487, 161 LRRM 1166 (1999).

if requested to do so within 1 year of the date of the decision and order.[135]

The Board also refused to issue a *Gissel* order in several other cases, including a case involving only nine employees out of a bargaining unit of approximately 60 employees. In *Cardinal Home Products, Inc.,*[136] the Board reversed the ALJ's finding that a bargaining order was warranted because traditional remedies would adequately ensure a fair rerun election where the company's unfair labor practices did not affect a substantial percentage of the bargaining unit members.

In *Made in France, Inc.*,[137] the Board agreed with the ALJ that an unlawful discharge and the unlawful locking of an employee access gate were not such extensive and pervasive violations as to warrant a bargaining order. In *Masterform Tool Co.*,[138] the Board disagreed with the ALJ's finding that a fair election could not be held. Instead, it found that because the laid-off employees were reinstated approximately three months after their unlawful terminations, and because the alleged Section 8(a)(1) statements were not made by supervisors, a fair election was possible. In *Eby-Brown Co.*,[139] a *Gissel* order

[135]*See also* Cooper Hand Tools, 328 NLRB 145, 168 LRRM 1479 (1999); Wallace Int'l de Puerto Rico, Inc., 328 NLRB 29, 161 LRRM 1123 (1999) (where there were 5-year delays between the elections and the Board's decisions); Research Fed. Credit Union, 327 NLRB 1051, 161 LRRM 1156 (1999) (almost a nine-year delay between election and Board's decision); Regal Recycling, Inc., 329 NLRB 355, 163 LRRM 1245 (1999) (seven-year delay between date of election and Board's decision).

[136]338 NLRB 1004, 174 LRM 1290 (2003); *see also* First Legal Support Serv., LLC, 342 NLRB No. 29, 175 LRRM 1141 (2004) (no showing that traditional remedies were not sufficient to ameliorate unfair labor practices found to have been committed by employer); High Point Constr. Group, LLC, 342 NLRB No. 36, 175 LRRM 1352 (2004).

[137]336 NLRB 937, 174 LRRM 1103 (2001).

[138]327 NLRB 1071, 167 LRRM 1165, 1078(1999). *See also* Tim Foley Plumbing Serv., 337 NLRB 548, 170 LRRM 1107 (2002); Wake Elec. Membership Corp., 338 NLRB 298, 173 LRRM 1011 (2002) (employer's violations did not include "hallmark" violations such as discharge or plant closures, and therefore did not preclude possibility of fair rerun election); Hialeah Hosp., 343 NLRB No. 52, 176 LRRM 1254 (2004) (Board reversed ALJ's recommendation that a *Gissell* bargaining order be issued, and instead ordered a second election).

[139]328 NLRB 496, 168 LRRM 1165 (1999).

was not warranted because the district court had addressed several remedial issues through a consent decree that required recognition and bargaining, thereby sufficiently addressing the effects of the unfair labor practice. In *Hospital Shared Services, Inc.*,[140] violations did not rise to the level of "hallmark violations" and, thus, traditional remedies were sufficient to correct any violations. In *Menlo Food Corp.*,[141] the Board adopted the ALJ finding that violations were minor and not a significant impact on the election process. Similarly, in *Desert Aggregates*,[142] the Board held that a *Gissel* bargaining order was not warranted. Although the company's conduct fell within a Category II classification, it was not so frequent or severe as to warrant a bargaining order. The Board found that the effect of the company's improper layoff of employees was mitigated by the fact that a decline in business was at least a colorable explanation for the layoffs and that the company attempted to recall the employees as soon as business improved.

In *Douglas Foods Corp v. NLRB*,[143] the D.C. Circuit reconfirmed its disapproval of the Board's rationale for issuing *Gissel* orders and remanded to the Board its decision to issue such an order. Despite upholding the Board's findings that the employer committed numerous unfair labor practices, the court held that the Board did not adequately explain its reasoning for issuing the "extreme remedy." In addition, the court held that the Board failed to account for the changes in the employer's operations and the turnover of the employer's workforce.

In *McDonald Partners, Inc. v. NLRB*,[144] the D.C. Circuit vacated the Board's decision to issue an affirmative bargaining order where the employer refused to bargain with the union after the expiration of a collective bargaining agreement. The employer based its refusal to bargain on its reasonable doubt of the union's majority status. Because the case was pending at the time of the Board's decision in *Levitz Furniture Co. of the Pacific*,[145] the court held that the pre-*Levitz* reasonable good faith doubt of union's majority support analysis, rather than actual lack of majority support analysis, applied. The

---

[140] 330 NLRB 317, 166 LRRM 1051 (1999).
[141] 330 NLRB 337, 170 LRRM 1424 (1999).
[142] 340 NLRB No. 38, 174 LRRM 1027 (2003).
[143] 251 F.3d 1056, 1067, 167 LRRM 2380, 2389–90 (D.C. Cir. 2001).
[144] 331 F.3d 1002, 172 LRRM 2815 (D.C. Cir. 2003).
[145] 333 NLRB 717 (2001).

court, in declining to defer to the Board's interpretation of the Supreme Court's decision in *Auciello Iron Works v. NLRB*,[146] found that the Board improperly disregarded evidence of the union's lack of majority support that arose during the term of the original agreement. The court stated that under *Auciello*, once a collective bargaining agreement expires, all evidence, not just evidence that arose after the expiration, can be used to prove the employer's reasonable, good faith belief that the union lacked majority support.

b. Litigation Costs, Attorneys' Fees, and Union Expenses

In addition to imposing remedies for unfair labor practices, the Board continues to apply the rule that so long as the defenses raised by the employer are debatable rather than frivolous, an award of litigation costs to the union is unwarranted.[147]

The Supreme Court reversed a decision by the Board to award attorneys' fees to a group of unions after concluding that the employer's suit filed against the unions in federal district court lacked merit and was filed in retaliation for the unions having engaged in activities protected by Section 7.[148] The Supreme Court concluded that the Board applied an invalid standard in finding that the employer had committed an unfair labor practice by filing an unsuccessful law suit in federal district court against a group of unions for

[146]517 U.S. 781 (1996).

[147]Pratt Towers, Inc., 338 NLRB 61, 170 LRRM 1533 (2002) (ALJ rejected charging party request for fees); Sea-Jet Trucking Corp., 327 NLRB 540, 163 LRRM 1303 (1999) (holding that employer's defenses were not frivolous), *enforced in an unpublished disposition*, 221 F.3d 196 (D.C. Cir. 2000). *Cf.* Halle Enters., Inc., 330 NLRB 1157, 167 LRRM 1029 (2000) (denying fees where there was absence of repeated displays of bad faith or capricious conduct), *enforced*, 247 F.3d 268, 167 LRRM 2332 (D.C. Cir. 2001); *see also* Miller Indus. Towing Equip., Inc., 342 NLRB No. 112, 176 LRRM 1103 (2004). In *Miller*, the union sought an award for the organizing expenses it would have to incur for engaging in a second campaign after the results of an election had been set aside because of the employer's unlawful conduct. In her decision, the administrative law judge noted that generally a union's organizing expenses, like attorneys' fees, are awarded when an employer has engaged in frivolous conduct. *Id.*, slip op. at 18 (citing Wellman Indus., 248 NLRB 325, 103 LRRM 1483 (1980)). The judge further noted that the Board has recognized an exception to this general principle when an employer has exhibited "a long history of flagrant disregard of prior Board and court Orders." *Id.*, slip op. at 18–19 (citing J.P. Stevens, Inc., 244 NLRB 407, 102 LRRM 1039 (1979)).

[148]BE&K Constr. Co., 329 NLRB 717, 162 LRRM 1217 (1999), *rev'd*, 536 U.S. 516, 170 LRRM 2225 (2002).

a retaliatory purpose.[149] Despite the employer's request that the Supreme Court consider the Board's authority to award the unions attorneys' fees, the Court explicitly declined to do so.[150]

The Board ordered the payment of attorneys' fees and other litigation costs where union representatives were unlawfully arrested at the behest of the employer. In *Sandusky Mall Co.*,[151] the Board found that the employer unlawfully prohibited handbilling and distribution and unlawfully called the police to have the nonemployee union representatives arrested. As a remedy, the Board required the employer to reimburse the union and its representatives for "all reasonable legal fees and costs incurred as a result of the arrest [of union representatives]."[152] Although the Sixth Circuit reversed the Board's decision as to the permissibility of the handbill distribution, it did not address the Board's award of attorneys' fees and costs.[153]

The Board also ordered an employer to reimburse an employee for legal and other expenses after finding that the employer filed a "baseless and retaliatory state court lawsuit" against the employee for engaging in protected concerted activities, including filing charges with the Board.[154] The Board found that the lawsuit independently violated Sections 8(a)(1) and (4). It rejected the employer's contention that such a remedy was "extraordinary" and must be specifically pled in the complaint or at the hearing, noting that reimbursement for legal expenses incurred as a result of a frivolous lawsuit is a standard remedy.

c. Imposing Remedial Order on Successor to Wrongdoer

Successor employers remain liable, under certain circumstances, for their predecessors' violations of the Act.[155] In *Tellem v. The New*

---

[149]BE&K Constr. Co. v. NLRB, 536 U.S. 516, 170 LRRM 2225 (2002). *See also* Section III.B.1.a., *supra.*

[150]536 U.S. at 513–14.

[151]329 NLRB 618, 162 LRRM 1191 (1999), *rev'd on other grounds*, 242 F.3d 682, 166 LRRM 2614 (6th Cir. 2001).

[152]329 NLRB at 622, 162 LRRM at 1196.

[153]*Sandusky Mall Co., supra* note 151.

[154]Garage Mgmt. Corp., 334 NLRB 940, 168 LRRM 1353 (2001).

[155]WXGI, Inc. v. NLRB, 243 F.3d 833, 166 LRRM 2797 (4th Cir. 2001) (successor liable for predecessor's unfair labor practices where successor did not alter essential nature of employees' jobs, continued to operate country music radio station with same call numbers, under same FCC license, from same facility, and continued to broadcast country music to same radio market with many of same on-air personalities); Met Food, 337 NLRB 109, 173 LRRM 1483 (2001); Amersig

Silver Palace Restaurant,[156] the court issued a 10(j) injunction requiring that a successor restaurant that had engaged in discrimination against union employees restore the status quo ante.

d. Imposing Remedial Order on Joint Employer

The Board continues to hold one employer responsible for the unfair labor practices of a joint employer when the employer knew or should have known of the joint employer's unlawful conduct but either acquiesced in the conduct or failed to protest the conduct.[157] In *Aldworth Co.*,[158] the Board held that an employer's distribution center and its labor supplier were joint employers; accordingly, both employers were liable for committing numerous unfair labor practices during an organizing campaign. With regard to the Section 8(a)(5) allegations, however, the Board concluded that the union had waived its bargaining rights with respect to the distribution center employer because the union named only the labor supplier employer in its representation petition and had previously demanded recognition only from that employer. The Board reasoned that the union's actions demonstrated "a conscious and deliberate pursuit of a bargaining relationship limited to [the labor supplier employer] alone."[159] Accordingly, the Board limited its findings and order with respect to the Section 8(a)(5) violations to the labor supplier employer.[160]

Graphics, Inc. dba American Signature, Inc., 334 NLRB 880, 169 LRRM 1458 (2001) (holding that predecessor's simple expression that its unfair labor practices had been remedied was legally insufficient to negate successor's liability where successor was aware of pendency of unfair labor practice charge that had not been dismissed or withdrawn); AC Elec., 333 NLRB 987, 173 LRRM 1391 (2001) (rejecting ALJ's rationale that "special and somewhat novel circumstances" warranted imposition of limited back-pay obligation on *Golden State* successor); Wyandanch Engine Rebuilders, Inc. 328 NLRB 866, 168 LRRM 1239 (1999), relying on Golden State Bottling Co. v. NLRB, 414 U.S. 168, 84 LRRM 2839 (1973). *See also* Section III.B.1.d.(5)(h), *supra*.

[156]2000 WL 1152247, 164 LRRM 3062 (S.D.N.Y. 2000).

[157]Action Temp. Employment dba Action Multi-Craft, 337 NLRB 268, 169 LRRM 1232 (2001) (employer liable for joint employer's action where it knew that employees who had engaged in unfair labor strike against it had been terminated but did not attempt to learn reason for their termination).

[158]338 NLRB 137, 171 LRRM 1033 (2002).

[159]*Id.* at 141.

[160]*Id.*

3. *Final Orders and Remedies for Union Misconduct*

a. Sections 8(b)(1)(A) and (B) Violations

In a Section 8(b)(1)(A) case in which a union agent and another person vandalized an employer's vehicle, the Board adopted the ALJ's order requiring the union to cease and desist from damaging property owned by the employer or any other employer.[161] In line with prior Board cases, the Board noted that when misconduct takes place in the presence of a union agent who does nothing to disavow it or to discipline the offenders, the union assumes responsibility for the conduct. However, the Board did not award damages.

The Board reaffirmed the holding of *California Saw & Knife Works*[162] that a union violates its duty of fair representation by failing to grant employees who resign their union membership a separate window period following resignation in which to file a *Beck* objection.[163] The Board found that the union's imposition of a window period limitation on the filing of *Beck* objections on employees who have recently resigned their union memberships violates the union's duty of fair representation[164] because the limitation operates as an arbitrary restriction on the right to resign from the union.

The Board ordered the union to accept the employee's objection, and to provide him with post-objection financial information and assurances, including (1) the assurance that the union would refrain from charging him for nonrepresentational functions; (2) the percentage by which his dues and fees would be reduced; (3) the basis for the union's calculations, including the percentage of expenditures that were representational and nonrepresentational; and (4) the assurance that he would have the opportunity to challenge the union's determination. The Board required the union to make the employee whole for any excess dues and fees paid to the union for nonchargeable expenditures, through a refund of excess amounts, with interest, commencing with the filing of the employee's

---

[161]Electrical Workers Local 98 (Telephone Man), 327 NLRB 593, 167 LRRM 1178 (1999).

[162]320 NLRB 224, 151 LRRM 1121 (1995).

[163]*See* Polymark Corp., 329 NLRB 9, 162 LRRM 1033 (1999); Steelworkers Local 4800 (George E. Failing Co.), 329 NLRB 145, 162 LRRM 1097 (1999); American Nat'l Can Co., 329 NLRB 389, 162 LRRM 1289 (1999); Office Employees Local 29 (Dameron Hosp. Ass'n), 331 NLRB 48, 164 LRRM 1105 (2000).

[164]Transport Workers Local 525 (Johnson Controls World Servs.), 329 NLRB 543, 169 LRRM 1344 (1999).

objection. The Board also ordered the union to amend its policy "concerning the processing of the objections to make clear that they will accept objections from recently resigned perfected *Beck* objectors that are filed within a reasonable time following their resignations."[165]

The Board continues to tailor its remedial orders in *Beck* cases to the specific allegations of the complaint. In one case,[166] the Board declined to order the union to provide a *Beck* notice and related information to the entire bargaining unit when the complaint alleged a lack of notice to only the two complaining employees. In another decision, when the complaint alleged that a union failed to provide notice to the entire bargaining unit, the Board ordered the union to reimburse those objecting employees who should have received notice within the Section 10(b) period.[167]

In a Section 8(b)(1)(B) case involving fines, the Board continues to order rescinding the fine and refunding any monies paid as a result of unlawfully imposed fines.[168]

b. Section 8(b)(2) Violations

(1) General Principles

The Board's remedial orders against unions for Section 8(b)(2) violations continue to extend beyond back wages. In situations where the union causes the employer to unlawfully discharge an employee, the Board continues to require that the union notify the employer in writing, copied to the employee, that it not only has no objection to the employee's reinstatement, but affirmatively requests reinstatement. In addition, the Board continues to order the union to make the employee whole for lost benefits and expenses incurred as well as for lost wages (less interim earnings) from the date of termination until the employee is reinstated to the same or a substantially equiva-

---

[165] *Id.* at 547.

[166] Teamsters Local 166 (Dyncorp Support Servs.), 333 NLRB 1145, 1146, 167 LRRM 1049, 1051 (2001).

[167] Yellow Freight Sys. of Ind., 327 NLRB 996, 997, 167 LRRM 1282, 1284 (1999).

[168] *In re* Local One, 339 NLRB 977, 173 LRRM 1487 (2003).

lent position with his or her former employer or finds substantially equivalent employment elsewhere.[169]

(2) Scope of Order

The Board continues to follow its holding in *Hickmott Foods*[170] to determine whether a broad cease-and-desist order is warranted or whether a narrower "in any like or related manner" order is more appropriate.[171]

(3) Hiring-Hall Cases

The Board found the production of hiring-hall records to compute back pay appropriate in *In re Electrical Workers Local 3 (White Plains)*.[172]

c. Fair Representation Cases

The Board continues to follow its rule requiring the union to produce information improperly withheld from employees.[173] In a duty of fair representation case where a union unlawfully fails to process a grievance, the Board continues to apply the remedy announced in *Iron Workers Local 377 (Alamillo Steel Corp.)*.[174] The Board continues to hold that the union must make employees whole for the increase in damages suffered as a consequence of the union's refusal to process the grievance, with interest.[175] If the grievance can be reinstated, the union must pay the reasonable cost of the em-

---

[169]Incisa, U.S.A., Inc., Int'l Union of Elevator Constructors, 327 NLRB 563, 167 LRRM 1228 (1999); Newspaper & Mail Deliverers (City & Suburban Delivery), 332 NLRB 870, 172 LRRM 1263 (2000); Laborers Local 1184 (Nicholson Radio), 332 NLRB 1292, 168 LRRM 1176 (2000); Teamsters Local 251 (Ryder Student Transp.), 333 NLRB 1009, 168 LRRM 1007 (2001); *In re* Strack & Van Til Supermkts. dba Town & County Supermkts. & Ultra Foods, 340 NLRB No. 172, 174 LRRM 1001 (2004).

[170]242 NLRB 1357 (1979).

[171]Amptech Inc., 342 NLRB No. 117, 176 LRRM 101 (2004); Double Eagle Hotel & Casino, 341 NLRB No. 17, 174 LRRM 1088 (2004).

[172]331 NLRB 1498, 170 LRRM 1560 (2000); *see also* Electrical Workers (IBEW) Local 357 (Newtron Heat Trace, Inc.), 343 NLRB No. 136 (2004).

[173]Laborers Local 294 (AGC of Cal.), 331 NLRB 259, 164 LRRM 1169 (2000); Electrical Workers (IBEW) Local 48, 342 NLRB No. 10, 175 LRRM 1033 (2004).

[174]326 NLRB 375, 159 LRRM 1097 (1998).

[175]Communications Workers Local 3410 (BellSouth Telecommunications), 328 NLRB 920 (1999); Letter Carriers Branch 3126 (Postal Serv.), 330 NLRB 587, 163 LRRM 1190 (2000), *enforced*, 281 F.3d 235, 169 LRRM 2581 (D.C. Cir. 2002).

ployee's attorney of choice to represent the employee at any grievance proceeding, including arbitration.[176]

e. Section 8(b)(4) Violations

The Board continues to issue a broad cease-and-desist order where a union has demonstrated a proclivity to engage in unlawful secondary activities in furtherance of its disputes with primary employers. In *Electrical Workers (IBEW) Local 3 (Teknion, Inc.)*,[177] the Board adopted the judge's recommended broad remedial order, specifically noting that the union had recently consented to entry of an order by the Second Circuit requiring compliance with its obligations under prior outstanding court judgments and that it not further violate Section 8(b)(4) of the Act. The Board noted that the union's violation of Section 8(b)(4)(ii)(B) in the instant case, just a little more than 2 years later, sufficiently demonstrated that the union has a proclivity for violating the Act, and thus warranted a broad order.[178] Having found that the union violated Sections 8(b)(4)(A)(i) and (ii)(B), by coercing employees in the exercise of their Section 7 rights and by enmeshing neutrals in the primary labor dispute, the Board ordered a broad cease-and-desist order.[179]

Similarly, in *Electrical Workers (IBEW) Local 98*,[180] the Board agreed that a broad cease-and-desist order was warranted against a union based on Section 8(b)(4) violations and based on its conduct in prior cases.

---

[176] *Letter Carriers Branch 3126, supra* note 175.

[177] 329 NLRB 337, 169 LRRM 1260 (1999).

[178] *Accord* Electrical Workers Local 98 (Telephone Man), 327 NLRB 593, 167 LRRM 1178 (1999).

[179] Service Employees Local 525 (General Maint. Co.), 329 NLRB 638, 169 LRRM 1362 (1999), *enforced*, 52 Fed. Appx. 357, 173 LRRM 2256 (9th Cir. 2002). *Contra* Teamsters Local 122, 334 NLRB 1190, 174 LRRM 1176 (2001), *enforced*, 2003 WL 880990 (D.C. Cir. 2003).

[180] 339 NLRB 470, 173 LRRM 1447 (2003).

CHAPTER 33

JUDICIAL REVIEW AND ENFORCEMENT

I. INTRODUCTION

Courts continue to hold that the Board's direction of an election in a representation case is not an appealable final order under Sections 10(e) and (f). In *Mid-Mountain Foods, Inc. v. NLRB,*[1] the

[1]269 F.3d 1075, 169 LRRM 2528 (D.C. Cir. 2001).

court noted that it had "repeatedly held that the Board's decision to hold another election is not a 'final order.' Therefore, judicial review is not yet available under the [Act]."[2]

In *NLRB v. Kentucky River Community Care, Inc.*,[3] the employer, consistent with long-established practice, sought review by refusing to bargain with the union, thus prompting the general counsel to file an unfair labor practice complaint under Sections 8(a)(1) and 8(a)(5). The D.C. Circuit acknowledged the viability of the practice of "testing cert" in *Adtranz ABB Daimler-Benz Transportation, N.A., Inc. v. NLRB*:

> This Court has jurisdiction to review a "final order" of the NLRB pursuant to Sections 10(e) and (f) of the NLRA. 29 U.S.C. §§160(e) and (f). An NLRB decision affirming an ALJ's findings of unfair labor practices by an employer is such an order. However, "the Board's direction of a new election is not a final order reviewable under either Section 10(e) or Section 10(f) of the NLRA." *Gold Coast Restaurant v. NLRB*, 995 F.2d 257, 267 (D.C. Cir. 1993) (citing *American Fed'n of Labor v. NLRB*, 308 U.S. 401, 409, 60 S. Ct. 300, 84 L. Ed. 347 (1940)). Should an employer seek "to challenge the new election, it can precipitate an unfair labor practice charge by refusing to recognize the union representation that could result from the election."[4]

The courts continue to follow the rule of *Leedom v. Kyne*,[5] that district courts lack jurisdiction to review Board action in representation cases, except in extraordinary circumstances. In *Titan International, Inc. v. Wells*,[6] the court found that "a dispute over whether an agency charged with a statute's implementation has interpreted it correctly . . . is not the sort of 'egregious' error envisioned [in *Kyne*]." Similarly, in *Detroit Newspaper Agency v. Schaub*,[7] the Sixth Circuit, in

[2]*See also* Sara Lee Bakery Group, Inc. v. NLRB, 61 Fed. Appx. 1 n.4, 173 LRRM 2608 (4th Cir. 2003).

[3]532 U.S. 706, 709, 167 LRRM 2164 (2001).

[4]253 F.3d 19, 24–25, 167 LRRM 2566 (D.C. Cir. 2001). *See also* Trimm Assocs., Inc. v. NLRB, 351 F.3d 99, 102 n.2, 173 LRRM 2801 (3d Cir. 2003), NLRB v. City Wide Insulation of Madison, Inc., 370 F.3d 654, 657 n. 1, 174 LRRM 3249 (7th Cir. 2004).

[5]358 U.S. 184, 43 LRRM 2222 (1994).

[6]168 LRRM 2283 (S.D. Miss. 2001), citing American Airlines, Inc. v. Herman, 176 F.3d 283, 293 (5th Cir. 1999).

[7]286 F.3d 391, 398, 169 LRRM 2965 (6th Cir. 2002). *See also* American Fed'n of Government Employees Local 1617 v. Federal Labor Relations Auth., 103 Fed. Appx. 802, 804-05, 2004 WL 1567106 (5th Cir. 2004).

reversing the district court, held that *Leedom* does not confer jurisdiction where the Board has made "mere errors" of law; rather, the Board must have acted without statutory authority in order for a district court to have subject matter jurisdiction, and "the Board's action must 'wholly deprive' the aggrieved party of a meaningful and inadequate means of vindicating its statutory rights."[8]

In *Contractor Services, Inc. v. NLRB*,[9] an employer tried to access the district court through a different approach. Shortly after the Board found Contractor Services, Inc. (CSI) guilty of unfair labor practices and issued a remedial order, the regional supervisory compliance officer sent a letter to CSI's counsel, accompanied by a document captioned "Compliance Requirements of Settlement Agreements, Administrative Law Judge Decisions, Board Orders and Court Decrees in CA Cases." CSI construed the document as a settlement offer, and "accepted" by complying with its provisions. The Board, thereafter, determined that CSI had not complied with its order, and sought enforcement in the Eleventh Circuit. Alleging breach of the "settlement agreement," CSI sued in district court to enjoin the Board from pursuing further enforcement actions, and to recover attorneys' fees.

According to CSI, this was strictly an action for breach of contract and, therefore, the court had jurisdiction under the Little Tucker Act.[10] The Board countered that, despite CSI's characterization, the underlying basis of the case arose out of the National Labor Relations Act and, therefore, the court of appeals had exclusive jurisdiction. The district court agreed with the Board, finding that, because CSI's primary interest was in equitable relief, which was beyond the scope of the Little Tucker Act, the district court lacked subject matter jurisdiction. The court further found that, even if jurisdiction were otherwise proper, CSI could not prove the existence of a contract. For these reasons, the court dismissed the case.[11]

The Board and courts continue to hold that, under the Act, neither the Board nor the federal courts are empowered to review a decision by the general counsel not to issue an unfair labor practice

---

[8]*Detroit Newspaper, supra* note 7, at 398.

[9]165 LRRM 2902 (S.D. Iowa 2000).

[10]28 U.S.C. §1346(a)(2) (giving district courts original, concurrent jurisdiction in civil actions against United States for damages not exceeding $10,000 based on an express or implied contract).

[11]Prior to the district court dismissing the case, the Eleventh Circuit issued its judgment, enforcing the Board's order.

complaint.[12] When a complaint is issued, the general counsel "exercises exclusive control over the issues" contained in the complaint.[13]

II. APPELLATE REVIEW AND ENFORCEMENT

A. Board's Rulings Subject to Review

1. *Parties Entitled to Enforcement and Review*

In *Quick v. NLRB,*[14] the Third Circuit determined that a charging party who was forced to defend himself in a unlawful lawsuit filed by a union was not an "aggrieved party" for purposes of standing to challenge the Board's refusal to award him attorneys' fees. Patrick Quick filed a claim alleging that the union's lawsuit to collect dues from him following his resignation from the union constituted an unfair labor practice. The ALJ and the Board agreed with Quick, and ordered the union to reimburse him for any expenses incurred in defending the lawsuit, but refused to order the union to pay his attorneys' fees.[15]

On review, the Third Circuit found that Quick was not an aggrieved party under Section 10(f) because he suffered no "adverse effect in fact" from the Board's ruling.[16] The court reasoned that, in order to be an aggrieved party, one must have received less than requested and allowed by law. The Act did not expressly allow or require an award of attorneys' fees.[17] Moreover, Quick admitted at the Board hearing that he incurred no expenses in defending the lawsuit because the National Right to Work Legal Defense Foundation, Inc. had defended him free of charge. Quick, therefore, lacked standing as an aggrieved party.

---

[12]Morgan's Holiday Mkts., Inc., 333 NLRB 837, 167 LRRM 1141 (2001); Quick v. NLRB, 245 F.3d 231, 251, 166 LRRM 2897 (3d Cir. 2001); Operating Engineers Local 150 v. NLRB, 325 F.3d 818, 830, 172 LRRM 2072 (7th Cir. 2003).

[13]Des Moines Mailers Union v NLRB, 381 F.3d 767, 769, 175 LRRM 2660 (8th Cir. 2004); *Operating Eng'rs Local 150 v. NLRB, supra* note 12; *Quick v. NLRB, supra,* note 12.

[14]*Supra* note 12.

[15]*Id.*, 245 F.3d at 240.

[16]*Id.* at 251–52.

[17]*Id.* at 256–57.

3. *Place for Filing Petition for Enforcement and Review*

The Board continues to adhere to its nonacquiescence policy. In *Tim Foley Plumbing Service, Inc.*,[18] the Board, in an Equal Access to Justice Act proceeding, found that "the General Counsel properly applied well-established Board precedent"[19] in relying on an employer's lawful, antiunion comments as background evidence of antiunion animus, despite the Seventh Circuit's rule[20] that such comments cannot be relied upon for such purpose. "The Board's duty to apply uniform policies under the Act, and the Act's venue provisions for review of Board decisions, make it, as a practical matter, impossible for the Board to acquiesce in every contrary decision by the courts of appeals."[21]

4. *Procedure*

Courts continue to hold that compliance with a Board order does not necessarily bar its enforcement. In *NLRB v. King Soopers, Inc.*,[22] the employer argued that its compliance with the Board's order rendered enforcement unnecessary and inequitable. Conceding that mootness is not ground for denying enforcement of a Board order, the employer nonetheless asserted an equitable argument that it claimed was separate and distinct from a mootness argument. Specifically, the employer argued that, although the violations in question were isolated, minor mistakes, and there was no evidence they were likely to be repeated, the Board viewed the employer as an habitual offender and sought enforcement of its order as a broad sanction in an "attempt to achieve ends other than those which can fairly be said to effectuate the policies of the Act." The Tenth Circuit, however, was unpersuaded and "unable to distinguish [the employer's] argument from a mootness argument."[23]

---

[18]337 NLRB 328 (2001).

[19]*Id.* at 330 n.5.

[20]Carry Cos. of Ill. v. NLRB, 30 F.3d 922, 146 LRRM 3069 (7th Cir. 1994).

[21]*Tim Foley Plumbing Serv., supra* note 18. *See also* Sandusky Mall, 329 NLRB 618 n.10, 162 LRRM 1191 (1999), *rev'd,* 242 F.3d 682, 166 LRRM 2614 (6th Cir. 2001); Pathmark Stores, Inc., 342 NLRB No. 31 n.1, 175 LRRM 1075 (2004).

[22]275 F.3d 978, 981, 169 LRRM 2119 (10th Cir. 2001).

[23]*Id.* at 981. *See also* Bolivar Tec's Mfg. Co. v. NLRB, 61 Fed. Appx. 711, 2003 WL 21000933 (D.C. Cir. 2003); NLRB v. MBV Tech., Inc., 2001 WL 128330 *1, 166 LRRM 2512 (6th Cir. 2001) (it is well settled that "the fact a respondent has complied with a Board decision and order does not foreclose enforcement").

It remains the rule that administrative delay does not necessarily render a Board order moot. In *NLRB v. Monson Trucking, Inc.*,[24] the Eighth Circuit rejected the employer's argument that "the five years it took for the Board to issue its Order precludes enforcement of the Order," saying that the issue was "not properly before us because Monson neglected to urge this point to the Board in a motion for reconsideration."[25] Additionally, the court found that there were "no extraordinary circumstances here that would permit us to look past Monson's failure nor does the delay render the Order patently outside the orbit of the Board's authority."[26]

Similarly, in *NLRB v. U.S.A. Polymer Corp.*,[27] the Fifth Circuit concluded that changed conditions that arose during a 3-year delay between an ALJ's decision and the Board's *Gissel*[28] bargaining order did not bar enforcement. As in *Monson Trucking*, the employer failed to take timely action to protect its interests. In its motion for reconsideration, U.S.A. Polymer Corp. argued that conditions had changed during the four and one half-years between the issuance of the complaint and the Board's order such that the Board's order should be reconsidered. The employer's motion, however, was filed shortly after the close of the 28-day period allowed by 29 C.F.R. §102.48(d)(2). The Board refused to reconsider its order and sought enforcement in the Third Circuit.

The employer opposed enforcement, arguing that the Board's regulations give it discretion to accept information that becomes available after the close of the ALJ's hearing, and to accept late motions for reconsideration "upon good cause shown based on excusable neglect and when no undue prejudice would result."[29] The Third Circuit enforced the Board's order, finding that, because U.S.A. Polymer Corp. did not notify the Board of the changed conditions until after the Board issued its order (and not within the 28-day period), its motion for reconsideration was untimely and the Board's refusal to reconsider its order was not an abuse of discretion.[30] "The party

[24] 204 F.3d 822, 163 LRRM 2592 (8th Cir. 2000).

[25] *Id.* at 827–28.

[26] *Id.*

[27] 272 F.3d 289, 168 LRRM 2897 (5th Cir. 2001), *cert. denied*, 536 U.S. 939, 170 LRRM 2288 (2002).

[28] NLRB v. Gissel Packing Co., 395 U.S. 575, 71 LRRM 2481 (1969).

[29] *U.S.A. Polymer*, *supra* note 27, 272 F.3d at 296, citing 29 C.F.R. §§102.48(d) & 102.111(c).

[30] *Id.* at 297.

that seeks to benefit from demonstrating a change of circumstances bears the burden of timely providing the Board with evidence of those changes. . . . The Board's delay does not excuse Polymer's failure to timely provide the evidence it seeks to introduce."[31]

Delay, in and of itself, is not enough to warrant a new election. In *NLRB v. City Wide Insulation of Madison, Inc.*,[32] the election was delayed 6 days due to the Board agent's failure to appear to conduct the election. On appeal, the employer argued that the election was invalid because employees improperly blamed the employer for the delay and could not have made an uncoerced decision in light of the delay. The Court rejected this argument and deferred to the Board's finding that the delay did not deny employees a rational, uncoerced choice.

B. Scope of Review

1. *Questions of Fact*

Courts continue to give deference to the Board's factual determinations, upholding the Board's decisions so long as they are reasonable and supported by substantial evidence on the record as a whole.[33] Although the courts continue to hold that direct evidence is not necessary in order to meet the substantial evidence standard, the Fifth Circuit recently refused to uphold the Board's finding that an employer was unlawfully motivated in discharging an employee where there was no direct evidence and no strong circumstantial evidence of antiunion animus.[34] The court ruled that a finding of pretext alone is not enough to support a finding of antiunion animus.

---

[31] *Id.* at 296–97.

[32] 370 F.3d 654, 657 n. 1, 174 LRRM 3249 (7th Cir. 2004).

[33] *See, e.g.*, Resort Nursing Home v. NLRB, 389 F.3d 1262, 176 LRRM 2147 (D.C. Cir. 2004) (Board's factual findings may only be set aside when the record is so compelling that no reasonable factfinder could fail to find to the contrary); Allegheny Ludlum Corp. v. NLRB, 301 F.3d 167, 170 LRRM 2923 (3d Cir. 2002); WXGI, Inc. v. NLRB, 243 F.3d 833, 166 LRRM 2797 (4th Cir. 2001); NLRB v. Gimrock Constr., Inc., 247 F.3d 1307, 167 LRRM 2153 (11th Cir. 2001). *See also* TNS, Inc. v. NLRB, 296 F.3d 384, 170 LRRM 2474 (6th Cir. 2002), *cert. denied*, 537 U.S. 1106, 171 LRRM 2768 (2003) (noting that such deference is not trivial; in addition to verifying that there is evidence to support Board's determination, courts must take into account contradictory evidence as well).

[34] Valmont Indus., Inc. v. NLRB, 244 F.3d 454, 166 LRRM 2782 (5th Cir. 2001).

2. *Questions of Law*

As discussed in the Main Edition, the courts generally defer to the Board's interpretation of the Act. However, where the Board's interpretation is contrary to the text and structure of the statute,[35] or where the Board's decision fails to apply its own precedent properly,[36] courts will not defer. Nor will the courts defer to the Board's interpretation of a decision by the Supreme Court or other judicial precedent.[37]

In *Pall Corp. v. NLRB*,[38] the D.C. Circuit noted that it reviews the classification of subjects of bargaining by the Board with "considerable deference" because of the Board's "special expertise." It found, however, that the Board's decision that an agreement to recognize the union at a new facility was a mandatory subject of bargaining failed "even this relatively lenient test." The court refused to defer to the Board's determination that a letter of agreement that extended recognition to the union of employees at the employer's third site concerned a mandatory subject of bargaining because the letter of agreement did not address the employer's incentive to transfer work out of the bargaining unit.

Further, where the Board's conclusions of law rest on interpretations of statutes other than the NLRA or judicial precedent, the courts apply de novo review to those conclusions.[39] Similarly, the Board's interpretation of a disputed collective bargaining agreement is subject to de novo review.[40]

---

[35]NLRB v. Kentucky River Cmty. Care, 532 U.S. 706, 167 LRRM 2164 (2001); BPH & Co. v. NLRB, 333 F.3d 213, 222, 172 LRRM 2865 (D.C. Cir. 2003).

[36]*See* Titanium Metals Corp. v. NLRB, 392 F.3d 439, 176 LRRM 2073 (D.C. Cir. 2004).

[37]*See* McDonald Partners v. NLRB, 331 F.3d 1002, 1005, 172 LRRM 2815 (D.C. Cir. 2003).

[38]275 F.3d 116, 169 LRRM 2065 (D.C. Cir. 2002).

[39]*See, e.g.,* Albertson's v. NLRB, 301 F.3d 441, 448, 170 LRRM 2769 (6th Cir. 2002); Sandusky Mall Co. v. NLRB, 242 F.3d 682, 166 LRRM 2641 (6th Cir. 2001).

[40]*See, e.g.,* Stanford Hosp. & Clinics v. NLRB, 370 F.3d 1210, 174 LRRM 3389 (D.C. Cir. 2004)(noting that while the courts defer to the Board's judgment regarding the scope of an appropriate unit for bargaining, they need not defer to the Board's interpretation of a provision within a collective bargaining agreement relating to the composition of the bargaining unit); Commonwealth Communications, Inc. v. NLRB, 312 F.3d 465, 468, 171 LRRM 2513 (D.C. Cir. 2002); NLRB v. Cook County Sch. Bus, Inc., 283 F.3d 888, 892, 169 LRRM 2882 (7th Cir. 2002).

3. Issues That Can Be Raised on Review

A reviewing court may not consider an issue that was not raised before the Board unless there are extraordinary circumstances.[41] To preserve an issue for review, a party must make more than just a passing reference to an issue,[42] and must raise the issue in its opening brief, not in its reply brief for the first time.[43] However, a party does not waive the right to review if it cites specific cases on review that were not cited before the Board.[44]

The courts apply this principle not just to bar new issues, but to new arguments regarding old issues, as well. In *MacMillan Publishing Co. v. NLRB*,[45] the D.C. Circuit refused to consider different grounds offered by Board counsel to support an order where those grounds were not adopted by the Board.

Where the Board rests its decision on a theory not litigated before the ALJ, the aggrieved party must raise that issue before the Board on a petition for reconsideration; otherwise, the courts have no jurisdiction to consider the issue.[46] This is the case even if the aggrieved party prevailed before the ALJ, only to have the Board make a contrary determination.[47] Similarly, to preserve an issue for review that was raised for the first time in a Board member's dissenting opinion, a party must likewise petition for reconsideration before the Board.[48]

---

[41] *See* Woelke & Romero Framing v. NLRB, 456 U.S. 645, 110 LRRM 2377 (1982); *see also* Joseph T. Ryerson & Son, Inc. v. NLRB, 216 F.3d 1146, 164 LRRM 2856 (D.C. Cir. 2000) (holding that the responsibility of Board to uphold "fundamental principles of labor law" does not qualify as an extraordinary circumstance). *See, e.g.*, Beverly Cal. Corp. v. NLRB, 227 F.3d 817, 165 LRRM 2257 (7th Cir. 2000), *cert. denied*, 533 U.S. 950, 167 LRRM 2640 (2001); Schnurmacher Nursing Home v. NLRB, 214 F.3d 260, 164 LRRM 2531 (2d Cir. 2000); Elizabethtown Gas Co. v. NLRB, 212 F.3d 257, 164 LRRM 2257 (4th Cir. 2000).

[42] *Elizabethtown*, *supra* note 41, 212 F.3d at 265; Prime Serv. v. NLRB, 266 F.3d 1233, 168 LRRM 2545 (D.C. Cir. 2001) (objection to the Board's bargaining order "in its entirety" is too generalized to preserve issue for appeal).

[43] *See* Multi-Ad Servs. v. NLRB, 255 F.3d 363, 167 LRRM 2450 (7th Cir. 2001); SCA Tissue N. Am. LLC v. NLRB, 371 F.3d 983, 174 LRRM 3377 (7th Cir. 2004) (court found agreement was waived in opening brief).

[44] *See* NLRB v. Pepsi Bottling Co., 258 F.3d 305, 167 LRRM 2786 (4th Cir. 2001).

[45] 194 F.3d 165, 162 LRRM 2769 (D.C. Cir. 1999).

[46] *See* Painters Local 970 v. NLRB, 309 F.3d 1, 4–5, 171 LRRM 2065 (D.C. Cir. 2002).

[47] *See* Des Moines Mailers Union, Teamsters Local 358 v. NLRB, 381 F.3d 767, 770 n.1, 175 LRRM 2660 (8th Cir. 2004).

[48] *See* Contractors' Labor Pool v. NLRB, 323 F.3d 1051, 1061, 172 LRRM 2065 (D.C. Cir. 2003).

In *NLRB v. Monson Trucking*,[49] the ALJ ruled for the employer, and the general counsel filed exceptions to the ruling on grounds not raised before the ALJ. The employer filed a response but did not address the general counsel's new argument. The Board agreed with the general counsel's new argument, and the employer did not file a motion for reconsideration. On the board's petition for enforcement, the Eighth Circuit held that it did not have jurisdiction to consider the employer's responsive argument because the employer failed to make that argument in its response to the general counsel's exceptions.

Even the grounds for a subject-matter jurisdiction appeal must be carefully preserved. The Seventh Circuit followed the rule set forth in *NLRB v. Konig*,[50] that although "the Board's statutory jurisdiction may be raised at any time, the facts upon which the Board determines it has jurisdiction may be challenged only upon timely exception."[51] In *Sommerville Construction Co.*,[52] the employer's answer admitted that it performed services valued in excess of $50,000 in states other than its own. The ALJ relied on this fact in determining that the Board had subject-matter jurisdiction. The court held that because the employer did not file an exception to that determination, the employer was barred from raising that issue for the first time on appeal.

A party must take special care to preserve for judicial appeal an issue raised at a representation proceeding. Board regulations prohibit a party that has litigated an issue during a representation proceeding from relitigating that same issue in an unfair labor practice proceeding.[53] However, the courts require at least some mention of that issue during the unfair labor practice proceeding in order to preserve it for review.[54] The courts are split as to the specificity of language required in order to preserve an issue. In *Schnurmacher*

[49]204 F.3d 822, 824 163 LRRM 2592 (8th Cir. 2000).

[50]79 F.3d 354, 151 LRRM 2682 (3d Cir. 1996).

[51]NLRB v. Sommerville Constr. Co., 206 F.3d 752, 756, 163 LRRM 2762 (7th Cir. 2000).

[52]*Id.*

[53]29 C.F.R. §102.67(f).

[54]Seattle Opera v. NLRB, 292 F.3d 757, 766, 170 LRRM 2161 (D.C. Cir. 2002); Nathan Katz Realty v. NLRB, 251 F.3d 981, 167 LRRM 2395 (D.C. Cir. 2001); Schnurmacher Nursing Home v. NLRB, 214 F.3d 260, 270, 164 LRRM 2531 (2d Cir. 2000).

Nursing Home v. NLRB,[55] for example, the Second Circuit found the party's statement, in a footnote, that it "disputes the . . . other findings as set forth in [its] Request for Review" insufficient to preserve the issues for review. In *Nathan Katz Realty v. NLRB*,[56] however, the Ninth Circuit found that a party's statement that it relied upon "the entire record in the related representation case, Case 29-RC-9265, including the September 21, 1999 Request for Review" to be sufficiently specific to preserve the party's right to judicial review.

4. *Judicial Review of Equal Access to Justice Determinations*

In *E.W. Grobbel Sons v. NLRB*,[57] the Sixth Circuit awarded the employer attorneys' fees and costs pursuant to the Equal Access to Justice Act, after the Board had rejected an identical request by the employer as untimely. The court of appeals rejected the Board's argument that only the Board had jurisdiction to consider the fee request, holding that the court had retained jurisdiction with regard to the issues on remand and therefore had the authority to consider the fee request arising out of the remand proceedings.

5. *Disposition of Cases by Reviewing Court*

Courts continue to remand cases where the Board has not properly articulated the reasoning behind its decision.[58] For example, the Eleventh Circuit remanded a case for further analysis where the Board failed to discuss its reasons for reversing the factual findings of an ALJ and where there was equally plausible evidence on both sides.[59] Additionally, the D.C. Circuit remanded a case where the Board failed to explain why its decision was not inconsistent with its own precedent.[60]

In *Cooper/T. Smith, Inc. v. NLRB*,[61] the Eleventh Circuit refused to review de novo the Board's determination regarding the

---

[55] *Supra* note 54.

[56] *Id.*

[57] 176 F.3d 875, 161 LRRM 2229 (6th Cir. 1999). *See also* Tim Foley Plumbing Serv., 337 NLRB 328, 169 LRRM 1401 (2001).

[58] *See* NLRB v. Gimrock Constr., Inc., 247 F.3d 1307, 167 LRRM 2153 (11th Cir. 2001).

[59] *Id.*

[60] *See* Brusco Tug & Barge Co. v. NLRB, 247 F.3d 273, 167 LRRM 2148 (D.C. Cir. 2001).

[61] 177 F.3d 1259, 161 LRRM 2526 (11th Cir. 1999).

nonsupervisory status of certain employees included in the bargaining unit, rejecting the employer's argument that de novo review was warranted because of the Board's "demonstrated inconsistency in past supervisory cases."[62]

7. *Interlocutory Relief Pending Review [New Topic]*

A court of appeals may grant interlocutory relief pending its final determination on appeal. In *Beverly Farm Foundation, Inc. v. NLRB*,[63] for example, the Seventh Circuit granted the Board's injunction pendent lite requiring the employer to recognize and bargain with the union, among other things, pending the court of appeals' decision on the Board's petition for civil contempt against the employer.

III. Direct Review and Enforcement

A. Review of Representation or Certification Action

Courts continue to hold that direct review of certification or representation decisions is generally unavailable.[64] In turn, employers who seek review of such decisions continue to do so indirectly by refusing to bargain and raising the certification issue by way of a defense in an unfair labor practice proceeding and on subsequent judicial review.[65]

---

[62] *Id.* at 1261.

[63] 1999 U.S. App. LEXIS 34979, 162 LRRM 2729 (7th Cir. 1999).

[64] NLRB v. City Wide Insulation of Madison, Inc., 370 F.3d 654, 657 n.1, 174 LRRM 3249 (7th Cir. 2004); NLRB v. Superior of Mo., Inc., 351 F.3d 805, 173 LRRM 2870 (8th Cir. 2003); Trimm Assocs., Inc. v. NLRB, 351 F.3d 99, 99 n.2, 173 LRRM 2801 (3d Cir. 2003); NLRB v. Dole Fresh Vegetables, Inc., 334 F.3d 478, 483, 172 LRRM 2935 (6th Cir. 2003); Aotop, LLC v. NLRB, 331 F.3d 100, 103, 172 LRRM 2691 (D.C. Cir. 2003); NLRB v. Regional Home Care Servs., Inc., 237 F.3d 62, 67, 166 LRRM 2326 (1st Cir. 2001); Public Serv. Co. of Colo. v. NLRB, 271 F.3d 1213, 1217, 168 LRRM 2833 (10th Cir. 2001); Adtranz ABB Daimler-Benz Transp., N.A., Inc. v. NLRB, 253 F.3d 19, 167 LRRM 2566 (D.C. Cir. 2001).

[65] *Id.*; NLRB v. Kentucky River Cmty. Care, Inc., 532 U.S. 706, 709, 167 LRRM 2164 (2001).

B. Review of Unfair Labor Practice Proceedings

In *Detroit Newspaper Agency v. Schaub*,[66] the Sixth Circuit reversed a federal district court that relied on the *Kyne*[67] exception to grant the employer's request for an injunction prohibiting the Board from prosecuting complaints based on alleged unfair labor practices occurring more than 6 months prior to the filing of a Board charge. The district court found that the contested Board action violated Section 10(b), and constituted the type of clear statutory violation that conferred upon the court the jurisdiction to act.[68] The court reasoned that a post hoc vindication by the court of appeals would not be sufficient relief to the employer, because it would still have been forced to litigate to administrative finality claims that it should never have been required to litigate under the explicit provisions of the Act.[69] The Sixth Circuit reversed the district court, finding that the employer would have a right to appellate court review of an adverse Board decision.[70]

In *Titan International v. Wells*,[71] a district court found the *Kyne* exception inapplicable, and declined to enjoin the Board from prosecuting a group of inter-related companies on a complaint, where the underlying charges had been amended to include that the related companies more than six months after the charging party had knowledge of the facts prompting the amendment. The court, noting that Section 10(b) precludes only complaints based upon any unfair labor practice occurring more than six months prior to filing of the charge, found that the Board's action in adding new respondents was not so manifestly a violation of the statute as to grant the district court jurisdiction under *Kyne*.[72] It was undisputed that the alleged unfair labor practices themselves occurred within six months prior to the filing of the original charges.[73]

In *Amerco v. NLRB*,[74] a district court similarly declined to enjoin the Board from consolidating unfair labor practice allegations against

---

[66]286 F.3d 391, 169 LRRM 2965 (6th Cir. 2002), *rev'g* 108 F. Supp. 2d 729, 165 LRRM 2113 (E.D. Mich. 2000).

[67]Leedom v. Kyne, 358 U.S. 184, 43 LRRM 2222 (1994).

[68]*Detroit Newspaper Agency*, *supra* note 66, 108 F. Supp. 2d at 732.

[69]*Id.* at 738.

[70]286 F.3d 391, 169 LRRM 2965 (6th Cir. 2002).

[71]168 LRRM 2283 (S.D. Miss. 2001).

[72]*Id.*

[73]*Id.*

[74]330 F. Supp. 2d 1083, 175 LRRM 2092 (D. Ariz. 2004).

a group of employers into an ongoing trial. The employers contended that the consolidated complaint was filed ex post facto and that requiring them to defend themselves mid-trial violated due process. The district court concluded that the availability of appellate review of a final Board order weighed against applying a jurisdictional exception because the parties would not be deprived of judicial review of their constitutional claim if the district court declined jurisdiction.[75]

Courts continue to hold that the general's counsel's decision not to issue an unfair labor practice complaint is generally not subject to review.[76]

---

[75] *Id.*

[76] Des Moines Mailers Union, Teamsters Local 358 v. NLRB, 381 F.3d 767, 769, 175 LRRM 2660 (8th Cir. 2004); Operating Eng'rs Local 150 v. NLRB, 325 F.3d 818, 830, 172 LRRM 2072 (7th Cir. 2003); Quick v. NLRB, 245 F.3d 231, 251, 166 LRRM 2897 (3d Cir. 2001).

TABLE OF CASES

References are to supplement chapters and footnote numbers (e.g., **8:** 3, 31 refers to footnotes 3 and 31 in Chapter 8). Union locals and other subdivisions are included with the parent unions, which are sorted by popular name (e.g., Teamsters not United Brotherhood of Teamsters). Alphabetization is letter-by-letter (e.g., "Bakersfield" precedes "Baker Victory").

A

C

D

E

I

J

K

L

M

N

O

Q

S

V

W